To Clare. Thank you for all your love, support, and encouragement.
—Paul Munford

Mastering
Autodesk® Inventor® 2016 and Autodesk® Inventor LT™ 2016

Mastering
Autodesk® Inventor® 2016 and Autodesk® Inventor LT™ 2016

Paul Munford

Paul Normand

Senior Acquisitions Editor: Stephanie McComb
Development Editor: David Clark
Technical Editor: Adrian Salariu
Production Editor: Christine O'Connor
Copy Editor: Kim Wimpsett
Editorial Manager: Mary Beth Wakefield
Production Manager: Kathleen Wisor
Associate Publisher: Jim Minatel
Book Designers: Maureen Forys, Happenstance Type-O-Rama, Judy Fung
Proofreader: Jen Larsen, Word One New York
Indexer: Ted Laux
Project Coordinator, Cover: Brent Savage
Cover Designer: Wiley
Cover Image: David Morgan/iStockphoto

Acknowledgments

Thank you for buying Mastering Inventor 2016. I want you to know why this book is so special to me.

I can't take all the credit for this book—it was first published in 2008, written by the legendary Dennis Jeffrey. Over the last eight years many of my CAD heroes have been involved with the book: Kevin Schnieder, Sean Dotson, Bill Bogan, Andrew Faix, Seth Hindman, Loren Jahraus, Shekar Subrahmanyam, Bob Van der Donck, and Thom Tremblay. These guys are awesome, I am standing on the shoulders of giants. Thank you for giving us *Mastering Inventor*—I hope that you are happy with my contribution.

Above all I need to thank Curtis Waguespack for trusting me with the product of his hard work of the last seven years. Thank you Curtis.

I would like to thank my wife Clare and my boys Danny and Joe for putting up with my absence while I've been working on the book. I'd also like to thank Tim Papworth for teaching me what to draw, Shaan Hurly for inspiring me to write a blog and Matt Murphy and Robert Green for inspiring me to teach others what I've learned. I'd like to thank my boss, Steve Houlder, for giving me the chance to turn CAD into a career.

This book is a collaborative effort involving many more people than those listed on the cover. I would like to thank Adrian Salariu for the outstanding work he performed as technical editor. Adrian has contributed many tips and tricks to this book and has taught me things I didn't know before! I would also like to thank Paul Normand for the chapters on dynamic simulation and routed systems. Any mistakes are my own.

Thank you to the team at Wiley—Stephanie McComb, David Clark, and Christine O'Connor for their patience, and teaching me how to write a book. Thank you for your focus and professionalism, without which there would be no book. Your hard work and support the effort of turning ideas into pages.

—Paul Munford

I would like to say thanks to all the fanatical and vocal users of Autodesk software that help us make the software even better and to Buzz Kross for envisioning the fantastic suite of manufacturing products we have today and assembling a great worldwide team to develop them. I would also like to thank my wife Lisa for her love, support, and encouragement.

—Paul Normand

About the Authors

Paul Munford is a self-confessed and unrepentant CAD geek. Paul spent eight years "on the tools" as a self-employed scenery designer and builder (all drawings done by hand!) before moving into the construction industry as a draftsman.

Paul has been using Autodesk Inventor for ten years to design high-end fitted furniture and joinery. Paul is a member of the Autodesk Expert Elite and writes a CAD blog called Cadsetterout.com. In his spare time Paul writes for AUGIworld and D3D magazine.

Paul recently joined Graitec, a UK-based Autodesk VAR where he has earned his Inventor professional certification and become an Autodesk Certified Instructor.

Paul strongly believes that your CAD software shouldn't limit your creativity or productivity, and spends much of his time helping people to get to grips with CAD so that they can move beyond the picks and clicks and spend their time designing— not CAD'ing.

For the last three years, Paul has been a speaker at Autodesk University. If you see him there, go and say "Hi." He's looking forward to meeting you, or find him on Twitter: @cadsetterout.

Paul Normand has been using CAD for so long, he remembers when AutoCAD came on a giant floppy disk and computers were big, heavy, and not very powerful. Prior to the 1999 release, Paul was one of the early alpha testers for Inventor, then code named Rubicon. As a mechanical designer, Paul honed his sheet metal and design chops creating high tech lab equipment. He then moved into the reseller channel selling, supporting, and training Autodesk products. Paul also founded the Portland Oregon area Inventor users group and taught Inventor classes at local community colleges.

For the past eight years, Paul has been part of the Autodesk Learning Experience and User Experience teams. A frequent speaker at past Autodesk Universities, these days he can be found at AU performing usability studies in his mad scientist lab coat. Feel free to stop by and share your thoughts.

Contents at a Glance

Contents

Introduction

The Autodesk® Inventor® program was introduced in 1999 as an ambitious 3D parametric modeler. It was based not on the familiar Autodesk® AutoCAD® software programming architecture but instead on a separate foundation that would provide the room needed to grow into the fully featured modeler it is now, more than a decade later.

Autodesk Inventor 2016 continues the development of Autodesk Inventor with improved modeling, drawing, assembly, and visualization tools. Autodesk has set out to improve this release of Autodesk Inventor by devoting as much time and energy to improving existing tools and features as it has to adding new ones.

With this book, the seventh edition of *Mastering Autodesk Inventor 2016 and Autodesk Inventor LT 2016*, I have set out to update the existing pages and add new content and exercises.

In these pages, you will find detailed information on the specifics of the tools and the principles of sound parametric design techniques.

Some readers will find this book works best for them as a desktop reference, whereas others will use it primarily for the step-by-step tutorials.

With this in mind, I've worked to shape the pages of this book with a mix of reference material, instructional steps, and tips and hints from the real world.

Who Should Read This Book

This book was written with a wide range of Autodesk Inventor users in mind, varying from beginner to advanced users and Autodesk Inventor instructors.

◆ Beginner Autodesk Inventor users who are making the move from traditional 2D CAD design to Autodesk Inventor 2016. These readers might have experience with AutoCAD and will possess an understanding of basic design and engineering concepts as well as a desire to improve their skill set and stay competitive in the marketplace.

◆ Intermediate Autodesk Inventor users who are self-taught or have gone through formal Autodesk Inventor training during their company's initial implementation of Autodesk Inventor, and who are looking for more information on a specific module within Autodesk Inventor. This book also targets users looking for a desktop reference to turn to when they come upon an area of Autodesk Inventor they do not encounter on a day-to-day basis.

◆ Advanced Autodesk Inventor users who have mastered the Autodesk Inventor tools used over and over daily but want to conquer the parts of the program they do not utilize during their normal design tasks. This book also targets advanced users who want to add to their skill set to move up the ranks within their current company or want to expand their knowledge in pursuit of a new position with another employer.

◆ Autodesk Inventor users of any skill and experience level who are preparing for the Autodesk Inventor Associate or Professional exam.

◆ CAD and engineering instructors looking for a text to use in instructor-led classroom training.

Attempting to learn all the tools in Autodesk Inventor can be an intimidating experience because of the wide range of task-specific modules available.

It is the goal of this book to separate these modules into easy-to-tackle chapters relating to real-world situations for which the tools were designed while also including chapters on general Autodesk Inventor tools, techniques, and design principles.

What You Will Learn

The following pages will explain the Autodesk Inventor settings while teaching you how each tool functions. Just as importantly, though, these pages are filled with the tips and techniques learned by the experts who spent years using, researching, and discussing the tools in Autodesk Inventor.

You should come away from reading this book with a solid understanding of the capabilities of Autodesk Inventor and a strong idea of how to tackle your design challenges in the future, as well as an abundance of time-saving tips and tricks.

What You Will Need

You can download the files needed to complete the tutorial projects in this book from the Sybex website at the following location:

www.sybex.com/go/masteringinventor2016

Download the collection of zip files and extract *all* the files to a folder on your computer, such as \My Documents\Mastering Inventor 2016. In this folder you will have a subdirectory for each of the chapters, plus a couple of other folders, as well as a file called Mastering Inventor 2016.ipj, as shown here:

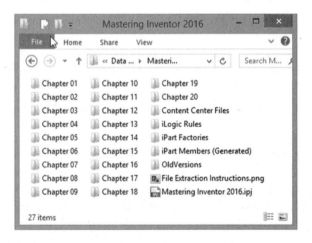

**Certification
Objective**

Once the files are in place, set the Mastering Inventor 2016 project as the active project by following these steps. Note that if you are using Autodesk Inventor LT, the use of project files does not apply, and you can skip these steps.

1. From within Autodesk Inventor, close any open files.

2. From the Get Started tab, click the Projects button.

3. From the Projects dialog box, click the Browse button.

4. From the Choose Project File dialog box, browse to the `Mastering Inventor 2016` folder, select the `Mastering Inventor 2016.ipj` file, and click Open.

5. Note that the Mastering Inventor 2016 project is denoted with a check mark as being the active project.

6. Click Done to close the Projects dialog box. Now you are ready to get started.

FREE AUTODESK SOFTWARE FOR STUDENTS AND EDUCATORS

The Autodesk Education Community is an online resource with more than five million members that enables educators and students to download—for free (see website for terms and conditions)—the same software used by professionals worldwide. You can also access additional tools and materials to help you design, visualize, and simulate ideas. Connect with other learners to stay current with the latest industry trends and get the most out of your designs. Get started today at `http://www.autodesk.com/education/`.

To install and run Autodesk Inventor, you should consult the system requirements information on the installation media and ensure that you have a system capable of running Autodesk Inventor adequately.

For basic educational purposes and dealing with small tutorial-sized assemblies, Autodesk recommends a minimum of 2GB of RAM and 16GB of available hard disk space to accommodate the installation files and temporary files created during the installation. Note that these are the minimum requirements to install and run the program, and you might see slow performance when executing operations that require heavy calculations.

I recommend a system with a minimum of 6GB of RAM for doing production work on moderate-sized assemblies and encourage you to consider an appropriate workstation for undertaking large assembly design.

The Mastering Series

The Mastering series from Sybex provides outstanding instruction for readers with intermediate and advanced skills in the form of top-notch training and development for those already working in their field, as well as clear, serious education for those aspiring to become pros. Every Mastering book includes the following:

◆ Real-world scenarios, ranging from case studies to interviews, that show how the tool, technique, or knowledge presented is applied in actual practice

◆ Skill-based instruction, with chapters organized around real tasks rather than abstract concepts or subjects

◆ Self-review test questions, so you can be certain you're equipped to do the job right

What Is Covered in This Book

This is what the book covers:

◆ Chapter 1, "Getting Started," introduces the Autodesk Inventor interface, project setup, and the concept of parametric 3D design.

◆ Chapter 2, "Taking the Workflow for a Test-Drive," explores the general workflow of modeling parts, creating detailed drawings of those parts, assembling those parts, and then detailing the assembly.

◆ Chapter 3, "Sketch Techniques," explores the principles of creating parameter-driven sketches for use in modeling features and parts.

◆ Chapter 4, "Basic Modeling Techniques," conquers creating parametric features and building 3D parts models.

◆ Chapter 5, "Advanced Modeling Techniques," explores complex feature creation, including sweeps, lofts, and more.

◆ Chapter 6, "Sheet Metal," covers how to create accurate sheet-metal models and flat patterns as well as how to create documentation and set up sheet-metal styles and templates.

◆ Chapter 7, "Reusing Parts and Features," examines the different methods for reusing parts and features for maximum consistency and design efficiency.

◆ Chapter 8, "Assembly Design Workflows," gives you a thorough understanding of this key concept of Autodesk Inventor design, including the use of Assembly constraints, subassemblies, and more.

◆ Chapter 9, "Large Assembly Strategies," explores tips and techniques to getting the best performance out of your Autodesk Inventor workstation and considers upgrade requirements for the future.

◆ Chapter 10, "Weldment Design," explores the Autodesk Inventor weldment modeling environment and the weldment documentation tools.

◆ Chapter 11, "Presentations and Exploded Views," gives you a thorough look at the presentation tools used to create exploded assembly views and animated assembly instructions.

◆ Chapter 12, "Documentation," covers how to use the Drawing Manager to create traditional 2D annotated drawings.

◆ Chapter 13, "Tools Overview," examines this collection of Autodesk Inventor utilities, including AutoLimits, the Design Assistant, the Drawing Resource Transfer Wizard, style tools, and much more.

◆ Chapter 14, "Exchanging Data with Other Systems," shows the available options for importing and working with solid models from other CAD packages.

◆ Chapter 15, "Frame Generator," covers how to get the most out of this utility when creating structural frames from the Autodesk Inventor library of common shapes.

◆ Chapter 16, "Inventor Studio," covers this powerful toolset to create photorealistic images and animations of all your Autodesk Inventor models.

- Chapter 17, "Stress Analysis and Dynamic Simulation," explores the simulation tools used to analyze load stress and mechanism motion on your models.

- Chapter 18, "Routed Systems," covers the cable and wire harness and tube and pipe environments and their uses in creating routed design layouts.

- Chapter 19, "Plastics Design Features," explores the tools used specifically for plastics design as well as the general tools used in specific ways for plastics design. Also included is the Autodesk Inventor Tooling module used to design mold tooling for plastic-part design.

- Chapter 20, "iLogic," introduces and explores the iLogic tools used to customize, configure, and automate your Autodesk Inventor design files. This chapter provides a solid foundation in the rules-based iLogic programming toolset and interface, allowing you to move forward with your advanced automation and configuration goals.

- Appendix A, "The Bottom Line," gathers together all the self-testing "Master It" problems from the chapters and provides a solution for each.

- Appendix B, "Autodesk Inventor 2016 Certification," points you to the chapters in this book that will help you master the objectives for each exam.

Autodesk Inventor LT, Autodesk Inventor, and Autodesk Inventor Professional

The Autodesk Inventor mechanical CAD software is available in three primary product configurations that offer specific levels of functionality to fit the needs of different users.

This book contains information that relates to all three of these versions of the Autodesk Inventor software. Depending on the version you have installed, you might find that parts of this book are relevant to your version.

For instance, if you have the Autodesk® Inventor LT™ program installed, you will find that Chapter 8 of this book will not apply to your version since Autodesk Inventor LT does not include tools used for assembly design. Similarly, if you have Autodesk Inventor installed, you'll find that Chapter 17 does not apply to your version since that chapter addresses tools found only in the Autodesk® Inventor Professional program.

To gain a better understanding of your version of the Autodesk Inventor software and how it relates to each subject in this book, please refer to the feature comparison matrix provided by Autodesk online. You can find this by visiting the Autodesk website.

How to Contact the Author

I welcome your feedback concerning *Mastering Autodesk Inventor 2016 and Autodesk Inventor LT 2016*. I want to hear what you liked, what you didn't, and what you think should be in the next edition. And if you catch me making a mistake, please tell me so that I can fix it on the errata page (available at www.sybex.com/go/masteringinventor2016) and in reprints. Please email me at inventormasters@gmail.com or contact Wiley customer service at http://support.wiley.com.

Thank you for purchasing *Mastering Autodesk Inventor 2016 and Autodesk Inventor LT 2016*. I hope it helps you on your way to happy and successful inventing, and I look forward to hearing your comments and questions. You can find additional tips and tricks online at my blog, http://cadsetterout.com/, and by visiting the Autodesk Discussion Groups at http://forums.autodesk.com/.

Chapter 1

Getting Started

In this chapter, you will be introduced to the concept of parametric 3D design and the general tools and interface of the Autodesk® Inventor® program. This chapter will focus on the concepts of parametric modeling and the workflow, tools, and interface elements in the Inventor software that are used to turn your ideas into a design.

In this chapter, you'll learn to

◆ Create parametric designs

◆ Get the "feel" of Inventor

◆ Use the Inventor graphical interface

◆ Work with Inventor file types

◆ Understand how project search paths work

◆ Set up library and Content Center paths

◆ Create and configure a project file

◆ Determine the best project type for you

Understanding Parametric Design

Autodesk Inventor is first and foremost 3D parametric modeling software. And although it has capabilities reaching far beyond the task of creating 3D models, it is important for you to understand the fundamentals of parametric 3D design. The term *parametric* refers to the use of design parameters to construct and control the 3D model you create. For instance, you might begin a design by creating a base sketch to define the profile of a part and then use dimensions as parameters to control the length and width of the sketch. The dimensional parameters allow you to construct the sketch with precise inputs.

Creating a Base Sketch

Well-constructed parts start with well-constructed sketches. Typically, the 3D model starts with a 2D sketch, which is assigned dimensions and *2D sketch constraints* to control the general size and shape. These dimensions and constraining geometries are the parameters, or input points, that you would then change to update or edit the sketch. For instance, Figure 1.1 shows a base sketch of a part being designed.

FIGURE 1.1
Creating a parametric
model sketch

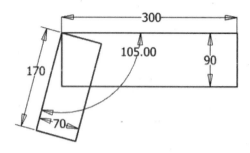

You can see four dimensions placed on the two rectangles defining the length and width of each along with a fifth dimension controlling the angle at which the two rectangles relate. These dimensions are parameters, and if you were to change one of them at any point during the design or revision of the part, the sketch would update and adjust to the change.

An important part of working with sketches is the concept of a fully constrained sketch. *Fully constrained* simply means that all the needed dimensions and sketch constraints have been applied to achieve a sketch that cannot be manipulated accidentally or as an unintentional consequence of an edit. For instance, if you were to sketch four lines to define a rectangle, you would expect two dimensions to be applied, defining the length and width. But you would also need to use 2D sketch constraints to constrain the lines so that they would stay perpendicular and equal to one another if one of the dimensions were to change. Without the sketch constraints, a dimensional edit to make the rectangle longer might result in a trapezoid or a parallelogram rather than the longer rectangle you anticipated. By fully constraining a sketch, you can anticipate the way in which it will update. Inventor helps you with this concept by automatically applying many sketch constraints and by reporting when a sketch is fully constrained. This will be covered in more detail in Chapter 3, "Exploring Sketch Techniques."

Creating a Base Feature

Not only do you add 2D sketch parameters, but you also add parameters to control the 3D properties of parts. This is done by using the sketch to create a feature such as an extrusion to give a depth value to the sketch. The depth dimension is a parameter as well, and it can be updated at any time to adjust the part model as required. Figure 1.2 shows the sketch from Figure 1.1 after it has been given a depth using the Extrude tool.

FIGURE 1.2
A basic part model
created from the
sketch

Adding More Features

Once the part is three-dimensional, more sketches can be added to any of the faces of the 3D shape, and those new sketches can be used to create some feature that further defines the form and function of the design. The model is then enhanced with more features, such as holes, fillets, and chamfers, until it is complete. Each added feature is controlled by still more parameters defined by you, the designer. If a change is required, you simply update the parameter and the model updates accordingly. This type of parametric design allows you to build robust and intelligent models quickly and update them even faster. Figure 1.3 illustrates the typical workflow of adding secondary features to a base feature to fully realize the part design, in this case a simple pivot link.

FIGURE 1.3
Adding features to complete the part model

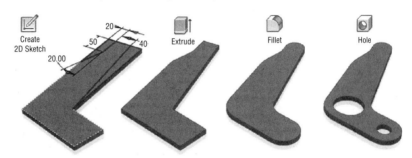

Using the Part in an Assembly

Just as well-constructed parts start with well-constructed sketches, well-constructed assemblies start with well-constructed parts. Once the part model is built up from the features you create, you can use it in an assembly of other parts created in the same manner. You can copy the part to create multiple instances of the same part, and you can copy the part file to create variations of the original part. To assemble parts, you create geometric relationships called *assembly constraints* to define how the parts go together. The constraints are parameters that can be defined and revised by you at any time in the design process as well. Part models can be arranged into small assemblies and placed into larger assemblies to create a fully realized subassembly structure that matches the way your design will be built on the shop floor. Figure 1.4 shows the part model from the previous illustrations placed multiple times in a subassembly and then that subassembly placed in a top-level assembly.

FIGURE 1.4
A subassembly and an assembly model using the part model

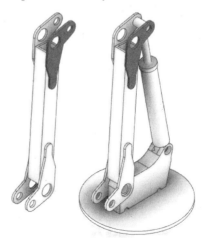

Making Changes

Once parts are created, they are then used in assemblies, which also employ parameters to define the offsets and mating relationships between assembled parts. Designing with the use of parameters allows you to make edits quickly and lends itself to creating product configurations, where parameter values are changed to create variations of a basic design.

Of course, as with building anything, there are general rules and best practices to be learned and followed to prevent your work from "falling apart." For instance, what if the pivot link used in the previous examples were to incur a design change that made one leg of the link longer? How would the holes be affected? Should they stay in the same place? Or should they stay at some defined distance from one end or the other?

Anticipating changes to the model is a large part of being successful with Inventor. Imagine, for instance, that a simple design change required that the pivot link become 50 millimeters longer on one leg. This should be a simple revision that requires you only to locate the dimension controlling that leg length and change the parameter value. Unfortunately, if you did not follow the best-practices guidelines when creating the part originally, the change in the length might displace the secondary features such as holes and material cuts and require you to stop and fix each of those as well. This is one of the most frustrating parts of learning Inventor for any new user who has not taken the time to learn or follow the known best practices of parametric modeling. Fortunately for you, within the pages of this book you will learn how to create models that are easy to update and do not "fall apart" during design changes.

Understanding History-Based Modeling and Dependencies

Inventor is often referred to as a history-based modeler, meaning that as you create sketches and turn them into features and then add more features and still more features, each addition is based on a previous feature, and so the model is said to have history. This history is recorded and tracked in the Model browser. The Model browser is a panel that displays onscreen and shows every feature you create during the design of your part. Figure 1.5 shows the Model browser for the pivot link file.

FIGURE 1.5
The Model browser showing the feature tree (history) of a part named Pivot: _Link.ipt

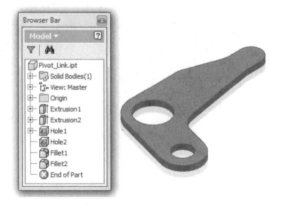

You can see that each feature is listed in the browser in the order in which it was created, forming a history tree. To create a part that handles changes predictably, you must create a solid foundation on which to build the rest of the model. In most cases, when you are designing a part model, you will start with a sketch, much like the one shown earlier in Figure 1.1. This base sketch will be your foundation, and therefore you must create it to be as stable as possible.

Each part, no matter what it is or what it looks like, has a set of origin geometry in the form of the origin planes, origin axes, and a single origin point. You can find these origin features by expanding the Origin folder in the Model browser. Figure 1.5 shows the Origin folder not expanded. If you expand the Origin folder in any part or assembly file, you will see the following items:

- ◆ YZ plane, the plane that runs infinitely in the Y and Z directions
- ◆ XZ plane, the plane that runs infinitely in the X and Z directions
- ◆ XY plane, the plane that runs infinitely in the X and Y directions
- ◆ X-axis, the axis running infinitely in the X direction
- ◆ Y-axis, the axis running infinitely in the Y direction
- ◆ Z-axis, the axis running infinitely in the Z direction
- ◆ Center point, the point found at zero in the X, Y, and Z directions

When creating the base sketch of a part file, you typically start on one of the origin planes. Because the origin plane cannot be edited, deleted, redefined, or upset in any manner, this base sketch is inherently stable, and as a result, the base feature you create from it is stable as well. If the second sketch of your part is created on a 3D face of the base feature, this sketch is dependent on the base sketch and is considered slightly less stable than the base sketch. This is because the base sketch could be edited, deleted, or redefined in a way that would upset the secondary sketch.

Understanding how dependencies are created when a sketch and features are based on one another will help you avoid creating a "house of cards" that will fall apart if the base is upset. Although you could base all your sketches and features on origin geometry to minimize dependencies, it is generally not practical to do so. It should be your goal, however, to keep the number of chained dependencies to a minimum. Assemblies work in much the same way, using the faces and edges of parts to constrain them together and as a result building dependencies between them. Just like part files, assembly files have origin planes, axes, and a center point that can be used to minimize chained dependencies, thereby creating a more stable model.

Taking a Closer Look at Sketch Dimensions

A large part of creating a stable sketch comes from understanding the way sketch dimensions work in Inventor. To do so, you might compare Inventor dimensions with standard dimensions in Autodesk® AutoCAD® software. When you create a design in AutoCAD, that design process is not much different from creating the same design on a paper drawing. But in AutoCAD, you can draw precise lines, arcs, circles, and other objects and place them precisely and with accurate dimensions reflecting your design in a way that you cannot do by hand. When a design requires modification, you erase, move, copy, stretch, and otherwise manipulate the existing geometry more quickly than you can by hand. But other than those gains in speed and accuracy, the workflow is much the same as working with pencil and paper. In short, AutoCAD automates drafting tasks but does less to speed up and enhance the design process. By comparison, Inventor's sketch dimensions allow you to add design parameters and a bit of intelligence to your sketches.

DRIVEN DIMENSIONS

Standard dimensions in AutoCAD are called driven or reference dimensions. A *driven dimension* is controlled by the geometry, and it reflects the actual value of the geometry being referenced by the dimension. If you stretch a line, for example, the dimension attached to the line will update to the new value. If you think about it, the only reason for a dimension on a traditional AutoCAD drawing is to convey the value of a feature or part to the person who is going to build it. If you import that 2D file into computer-aided manufacturing (CAM) software, no dimensions are needed because the line work contains all the information about the part.

PARAMETRIC AUTOCAD

Starting with AutoCAD 2010, you can create 2D parametric dimensions and constraints much as you can in Inventor.

DRIVING DIMENSIONS

The workflow in Inventor sketching is substantially different from that in traditional AutoCAD, even beyond dimensions. In Inventor, you create sketches in 2D and then add geometric constraints such as Horizontal, Vertical, Parallel, and so on, to further define the sketch entities. Adding the geometric constraints allows line work to adjust in a predictable and desired manner and helps control the overall shape of the sketch. Once geometric constraints are in place, you add parametric *driving dimensions* to the sketch geometry. By changing the value of these driving dimensions, you change or drive the size of the sketch object. Because of this, the Inventor dimension is far more powerful than the standard AutoCAD dimension because it not only conveys the value of a feature or part but also serves as a design parameter, allowing you to change the dimension to update the design. This is done simply by double-clicking the dimension and typing in a new value. Figure 1.6 shows a dimension being edited in a sketch on the left and the result on the right.

FIGURE 1.6
Editing Inventor
sketch dimensions

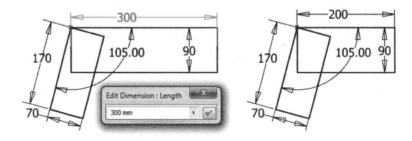

Following Part Modeling Best Practices

A solid sketch is the foundation on which stable parts are built. Many new users do not understand the importance of having fully constrained sketches, and they find it highly frustrating to have a model fail when a simple change is made, all because a sketch was not properly constructed. You can avoid this frustration by following some basic best practices.

KEEP SKETCHES SIMPLE

The most effective way to create a healthy sketch is to keep it simple. The purpose of keeping your base sketch simple is to get it fully defined, leaving no part of it up for interpretation. Underdefined sketch entities (lines without defined lengths, circles without defined diameters, and so on) will most likely not update properly and will cause your sketches to distort and break when you try to update them. And because you often base the rest of your model on the initial sketch, your entire feature tree might incur errors, requiring you to stop and spend time rebuilding it again. Examine the sketch in Figure 1.1 and compare it to the finished shape shown earlier in Figure 1.5. As you can see, the simple sketch containing two rectangles dimensioned at an angle defines the basic shape and is much easier to sketch and fully constrain than the finished shape would be.

If the idea of simple sketches seems at first not to fit the type of design you do, understand that most designs will benefit from the simple-sketch philosophy. More important, if you start out employing simple sketches, you will more quickly master the sketch tools and then be ready to create more complex sketches when a design absolutely requires it.

CREATE SIMPLE FEATURES FROM SIMPLE SKETCHES

Another aspect of creating simple sketches is that it allows you to create simple features. Parametric, feature-based modeling relies on the creation of numerous simpler features within the model to achieve a complex design in the end. By creating a number of features within the model, you are able to independently change or modify a feature without rebuilding the entire model. An example of editing a feature would be changing a hole size. If you create a simple rectangular base feature first and then create a hole feature as a secondary feature to that base feature, you can make changes to both independently. By contrast, if you were to include a circle in your base sketch and use that to create the base feature with a circular profile pocket, your hole would no longer be as easily updated.

PATTERN AND MIRROR AT THE FEATURE LEVEL

Although there are mirror and pattern (array) tools in the sketch environment, it is generally best to create a single instance of the item in the sketch, then create a feature from it, and finally create a mirror or pattern feature from that feature. The logic behind this is based on the idea of keeping sketches simple in the anticipation of future edits. Should the mirror or pattern feature need to be updated, it is much easier to update it as a separate feature.

CREATE SKETCH-BASED FEATURES AND THEN PLACED FEATURES

Part features can be separated into two categories: sketch-based and placed. *Sketch-based features*, as you might guess, are created from sketches. *Placed features* are features such as fillets and chamfers that are placed by using model edges or faces and have no underlying sketch. Issues arise when placed features are created too early in the development of the part because you may then be required to dimension to the placed feature, which creates a weak dependency. For instance, you might place rounded fillet features along the edges of a part. Then you could use the tangent fillet edges to define the placement of a hole. But then if you realize that machining capabilities require a beveled chamfer edge rather than a rounded filleted one and delete the fillet feature, the hole feature is sure to fail because the tangent fillet edges used to define the hole placement no longer exist. Keep this in mind as you create placed features such as fillets and chamfers and reserve placed features for the end stages of the part.

UNDERSTAND DEPENDENT AND INDEPENDENT FEATURES

Parametric model features are typically either dependent or independent of one another. A *dependent* feature depends on the existence or position of a previously created feature. If that previously created feature is deleted, the dependent feature will either be deleted as well or become an independent feature. As mentioned earlier, each part file contains default origin geometry defining the x-axis, y-axis, and z-axis of the part. These origin features are used to create the first sketch in every part by default. An *independent* feature is normally based on an origin feature or is referenced off the base feature.

For instance, to create the base feature for the pivot link, you would create a sketch on a default origin plane, such as the XY plane. Because the XY origin plane is included in every part file and cannot be changed, your base feature is stable and independent of any other features that may follow. To create a hole in the base feature, you would typically select the face of the base feature to sketch on. Doing so would make the hole feature dependent on the base feature. The hole feature is then inherently less stable than the base feature because it relies on the base feature to define its place in 3D space.

Although the specifics of how sketches, features, and parts are created will be covered in the chapters to come, remember these principles concerning part file best practices, and you will find Inventor (and any other parametric modeler) much more accommodating.

Following Assembly Modeling Best Practices

Once you've created part files, you will put them together to build an assembly. And when you do, you want to build it to be as stable as possible so that if you move, replace, or remove a part, the rest of the assembly will not fall apart. There are two entities to an assembly file: links to the component files (parts or subassemblies) it is made of and the geometric information about how those components fit together. Basic assemblies are not much more than that, and understanding those two concepts will go a long way toward building stable assemblies.

UNDERSTAND FILE LINKING AND RELATIONSHIPS

You can think of an assembly file as an empty container file to start. Once you place the first part in the assembly, the assembly file contains a link to the file for that part. When you place a second part and fit it to the first, the assembly then contains links to the two files and the information about how those parts go together in this particular assembly. If you decide to rename the first part file and do so using Windows Explorer, the assembly file will still look for the file by the old name. When this happens, you will be prompted with a file resolution dialog box asking you to locate the file. You can then browse and manually point the assembly to that file, and the assembly will record the new name in its internal link. If you decide to move the second part file to a folder other than its original, the assembly file might again prompt you to find it manually, depending on the folder structure. It should be your goal to never need to resolve file links manually, and understanding this part of how assemblies work is the first step in reaching that goal. In the coming chapters you will learn how to set up Inventor properly so it can find your files.

ALWAYS MAINTAIN AT LEAST ONE GROUNDED COMPONENT

To understand how grounded parts help you build stable assemblies, you should first understand a little about the assembly Model browser. Figure 1.7 shows the Model browser for an assembly model of a small hobby-type CNC router.

FIGURE 1.7
The Model browser showing the model tree of an assembly named Router.iam

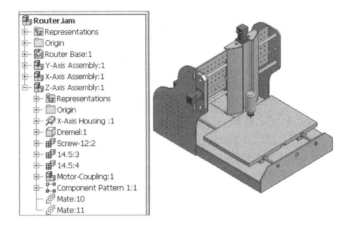

The Model browser shows an assembly named Router Base at the top and under it three other subassemblies named Y-Axis Assembly, X-Axis Assembly, and Z-Axis Assembly. The Z-Axis Assembly is expanded in the browser so you can see the parts it contains as well. You should note that the Router Base subassembly is shown in the browser with a pushpin button. This denotes that this subassembly is grounded, or pinned in place, and its coordinates cannot accidentally change. Keeping one grounded component in each assembly will allow you to fit other parts to it without it moving or rotating off the x-, y-, and z-coordinates.

Recall the old carnival game where you throw a ball at a pyramid stack of metal bottles. To win the game, you had to knock down all the bottles. However, if the bottle in the center on the bottom were nailed down, it would be impossible to win the game, and as a matter of physics, it would be difficult to knock down the bottles next to it. Having a grounded component in your assemblies, one that is "nailed down," will likewise keep your assemblies from falling over as you build onto them. By default, the first component you place into an empty assembly file will automatically be grounded. You can unground it and ground another if need be, but you should always maintain at least one grounded component. You can also have more than one grounded component.

MAKE YOUR MODELS MIMIC THE MANUFACTURING PROCESS

The simplest advice that new users can receive on the subject of assemblies is to structure them as you would in real life. For example, if in the design you plan to assemble several parts into a transmission and then drop that transmission into a housing, you should make the transmission a subassembly and insert it into the upper-level housing assembly. Alternatively, a new user might place all the parts into one big assembly, only to later realize that subassemblies are needed for the purpose of getting the bill of materials (BOM) organized. This can be accomplished by using the Demote assembly tool to create the subassemblies and then demote the parts from the top-level assembly to these new subassemblies. By making your models mimic the manufacturing process, you can also find possible flaws in your design, such as fasteners that cannot be accessed or areas where parts may interfere with each other during assembly.

In some instances, a model will be developed in the research and development (R&D) department and then handed to the manufacturing engineering (ME) department to be built. Although the people in R&D may enjoy the freedom of "dreaming up" anything they can think of, an effective R&D designer will always think about what can actually be built within the capabilities of the shop floor. Keep this in mind during the initial development cycle, and it will prevent those downstream from having to re-create much of your work. However, if restructuring the components into more or fewer subassemblies is required after the initial design, Inventor has demote and promote tools to assist with that. These tools will be covered in the chapters to come.

CONSTRAIN TO ORIGIN GEOMETRY

As mentioned earlier in this chapter, each part file has default origin geometry built in. You should build parts around the origin geometry whenever possible. For instance, a transmission has gears, bearings, seals, and so on, that are all concentric with the shaft. If you model all the parts so their x-axes will be aligned in the assembly, then you can use the x-axis of each part to constrain to in the assembly and it will be much more stable. However, if you constrain the parts by selecting model features, you run the risk of constraints failing once a revision to a part changes or removes the originally referenced geometry. To build a completely "bullet-proof" assembly, you could constrain the origin geometry of each part to the origin geometry of the assembly. In this way, no matter how the geometry of the parts changes, it will not cause issues with assembly constraints.

You will learn more about how to create assemblies, set up search paths to avoid manual file resolutions, and work with grounded components in the coming chapters, but you should remember these concepts and work to abide by them.

Understanding the "Feel" of Inventor

To the new user, the ever-changing Inventor interface may seem a bit disorienting. Taking a few minutes to understand why menus and tools change from one context to another will go a long way in getting comfortable with the "feel" of Inventor and anticipating the way the user interface works. If you've used other applications with the Microsoft ribbon-style interface, you're probably already familiar with much of this context-specific behavior.

Understanding the Intuitive Interface

The overall user interface of Inventor could be called *context intuitive*, meaning that menus change depending on the task and the environment. Inventor is organized by tools grouped onto tabs, offering only the tools needed for the appropriate task at hand. If you are sketching a base feature, the tools you see are sketch tools. In Figure 1.8, the Sketch tab is active, and the displayed tools are the ones used to create and dimension sketches.

FIGURE 1.8
The Sketch
tab and
sketch tools

Upon the completion of a sketch, click the Finish Sketch button on the far right, and you will exit the sketch. The 3D Model tab then becomes active, and the Sketch tab is hidden. This allows you to see the tools that are appropriate for the immediate task, and only those tools, without having to hunt around for them among tools that you are not able to use at the current moment. If you create a new sketch or edit an existing one, the Sketch tab is immediately brought back. Figure 1.9 shows the active 3D Model tab.

FIGURE 1.9
The 3D Model
tab and model
tools

When you work with assemblies, the active tab changes to the Assemble tab (as shown in Figure 1.10), allowing you to place components, create new components, pattern them, copy them, and so on. When in the assembly environment, there are also a number of other tabs shown that you can manually switch to (by clicking them) at any time to use the tools they contain.

FIGURE 1.10
The Assemble
tab and assembly
tools

When you create a 2D drawing of parts or assemblies, you are automatically presented with tools needed to create views and annotation. By default, the Place Views tab is displayed because you need to create a view of a model before annotating it. However, you can manually switch to the Annotate tab by clicking it. Figure 1.11 shows the active Place Views tab and the inactive Annotate tab next to it.

FIGURE 1.11
The drawing tabs
and drawing
tools

As you can see, the collection of tabs (called the ribbon menu) changes intuitively with every task or environment you switch to. With this task-based user interface, there is no need to display every possible tool at once. In the next section, you will explore more of the user interface.

Using General Tools vs. Specific Commands

In this section you'll see how Inventor tools are set up, using AutoCAD tools as a comparison. If you've never used AutoCAD, you can still gain some insight from this section, although you may have to use your imagination concerning the references to AutoCAD. A key difference between AutoCAD and Inventor is that in AutoCAD many commands are very specific. For example, there are different dimension commands for lines, angles, and circles. In contrast, Inventor has one General Dimension tool that creates the appropriate dimension based on what you select.

For instance, in AutoCAD you might select the Horizontal dimension tool to place a dimension on a horizontal line, select the Diameter dimension tool to place a dimension on a hole, select the Radius dimension tool to place a dimension on a fillet, and so on. But in Inventor you select the General Dimension tool and select a horizontal line and you get a horizontal dimension; then, without exiting the General Dimension tool, you select a circle and you automatically get a diameter dimension. And of course to dimension a fillet, you continue with the General Dimension tool and you will automatically get a radius dimension.

DRAWING IN AUTOCAD BECOMES SKETCHING IN INVENTOR

The fundamental difference between traditional AutoCAD and Inventor is that in AutoCAD you draw and in Inventor you sketch. This difference sounds subtle, but it is important. In AutoCAD, you likely construct lines precisely to specific dimensions to form the geometry required. In Inventor, you create lines and geometry that reflect the general form and function of the feature and then use constraints and dimensions to coax it into the desired shape. Expecting Inventor to work just like AutoCAD is probably the single biggest stumbling block that experienced AutoCAD users face when starting to use Inventor.

When in Doubt, Right-Click

Inventor is very right-click–driven, meaning that many of the options are context specific and can be accessed by right-clicking the object in question. For instance, if you want to edit a sketch, you right-click the sketch in the browser and choose Edit Sketch. The same is true of a feature. If you want to change a hole feature from a countersink to a counterbore, you right-click it in the browser and choose Edit Feature. You can also right-click many objects in the graphics window, with no need to locate them in the browser. Figure 1.12 shows a typical right-click context menu with the default marking menu option enabled.

FIGURE 1.12
A typical right-click
marking menu

Also worth mentioning are the options in the context menus. For instance, if you are editing a part in an assembly and want to finish the edit and return to the assembly level, you could use the Return button on the Sketch tab menu, or you could just right-click (taking care not to click any sketch object) and choose Finish Edit from the context menu. Both options do the same thing.

TRADITIONAL RIGHT-CLICK MENUS VS. THE MARKING MENUS

When enabled, marking menus replace the traditional right-click context menu. Since marking menus are customizable, this book references the traditional right-click menu, so specific references to items in the right-click menus may need to be interpreted if you choose to use the marking menus or have customized your marking menus. To enable or disable the marking menus, select Customize on the Tools tab of the ribbon and then select the Marking Menu tab. Then check or uncheck the Use Classic Context Menu check box.

Selections from the marking menu can be made in either menu mode or mark mode.

Menu Mode When you right-click in the graphics window, menu items surround the cursor. Simply click a menu item to select it.

Mark Mode When you press and hold the right mouse button and immediately move the cursor in the direction of a known menu item, a "mark" trail appears. Release the mouse button to select the menu item corresponding to the direction of cursor movement in the marking menu.

Using the Graphical Interface

The Inventor graphical interface might be different from what you are accustomed to in other general software applications and even different from other design software. In Figure 1.13, you see the entire Inventor window, which shows a part file open for editing.

FIGURE 1.13
The complete Inventor screen in part modeling mode

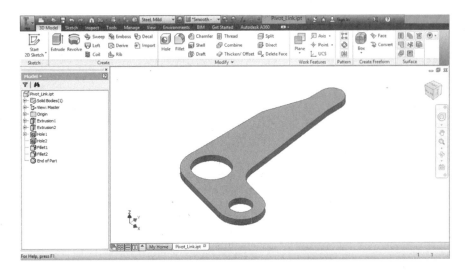

Inventor Title Bar

Starting at the upper left of the Inventor window, you'll see the Inventor button (look for the large *I* character), which has a drop-down panel similar to the File menu in previous versions. Next to the Inventor button, the title bar includes two toolbars:

◆ The Quick Access bar has frequently used tools.

◆ The Help toolbar provides access to help files and Autodesk websites.

You can customize the Quick Access bar for each file type by selecting and deselecting buttons from a list. You can access the list of available tools by clicking the drop-down arrow shown on the far right of Figure 1.14.

FIGURE 1.14
The Inventor button and Quick Access bar

Table 1.1 defines the default Quick Access bar buttons available in part modeling mode.

TABLE 1.1:   Quick Access bar buttons

BUTTON	DEFINITION
	The New button launches the New File dialog box. The drop-down list allows you to create a new part, assembly, drawing, or presentation file using the standard templates.
	The Open button launches the Open dialog box. It displays a location defined in your active project.
	The Save button saves the file.
	The Undo button undoes the last action. The Undo list tracks changes for the current Inventor session, not just the current document. If you have two part files open, this button will undo changes that are made in both files. Undo will also close files if your undo sequence takes you back past the point of a file being opened or created.
	The Redo button restores a change that was removed with Undo. It will reopen a file that was closed with Undo.
	The Update button updates the files. For example, if you edit a part in an assembly, other parts might need to be updated because of the changes. This button is grayed out unless the file needs to be refreshed.

TABLE 1.1:   Quick Access bar buttons   *(CONTINUED)*

BUTTON	DEFINITION
	The Select button allows you to choose a filter for object selection.
	The Refine button can be used to speed up large Assembly performance by providing a coarser image (Disable Automatic Refinement must be turned on in Applications Options > Display).
	The Material button and drop-down box allow you to change the component material. Clicking the button displays the material browser. Selecting a material from the drop-down changes the component's material property.
	The Appearance button and drop-down box allow you to change the component color. Clicking the button displays the appearance browser. Selecting an appearance from the drop-down changes the component's color appearance.
	The Adjust button allows you to modify the color and texture appearance.
	The Clear button allows you to remove overrides to the component's color and texture appearances.
	The Parameter button is used to access the parameters table, where you can rename, change, and create equations in dimension and design parameters.
	The Design Doctor button launches a dialog box that helps you diagnose and repair issues with a file. The button is grayed out unless there is an issue.

Graphics Window Tools

Inventor has two sets of tools for manipulating the graphics window:

◆ The ViewCube allows you to change the view orientation.

◆ The Navigation bar has tools such as Zoom and Pan.

EXPLORING THE VIEWCUBE

The ViewCube, shown in Figure 1.15, is a 3D tool that allows you to rotate the view.

FIGURE 1.15
The ViewCube

Here are some viewing options:

◆ If you click a face, edge, or corner of the ViewCube, the view rotates so the selection is perpendicular to the screen.

◆ If you click and drag an edge, the view rotates around the parallel axis.

◆ If you click and drag a corner, you can rotate the model freely.

◆ If you click a face to have an orthogonal view, additional controls will display when your mouse pointer is near the cube.

◆ The four arrowheads pointed at the cube rotate the view to the next face.

◆ The arc arrows rotate the view by 90 degrees in the current plane.

If you click the Home button (it looks like a house), the view rotates to the default isometric view. Clicking the drop-down arrow or right-clicking the Home button reveals several options to change the default isometric view behavior. For instance, you can modify the home view to any view you like, and you can reset the front view in relation to your model so the named views of the cube match what you consider the front, top, right, and so on.

USING A WHEEL MOUSE AND 3D-INPUT DEVICE

Using a wheel mouse with Inventor is recommended. Scrolling the wheel will zoom in or out, while pressing the wheel will perform the Pan function. In Inventor, the wheel zoom is reversed from AutoCAD. You can change this setting by clicking Application Options on the Tools tab, selecting the Display tab, and selecting Reverse Direction in the 3D Navigation group.

Another useful tool for navigating in Inventor is a 3D-input device. A popular brand is the Space series made by 3Dconnexion. These devices are small "joysticks" or "pucks" that sit on your desk. The user grasps the puck and, by making very slight movements with the device, moves the model on the screen. Pulling, pushing, and twisting the puck allows you to zoom, pan, and orbit the model onscreen. Although you may find using one of these devices awkward at first, most users say they could never work as efficiently without one after just a few days of use.

A LOOK AT THE NAVIGATION BAR

Continuing with the interface tour, you'll see the Navigation bar located on the right side of the graphics window. At the top of the bar is the steering wheel. Below the steering wheel are the other standard navigation tools: Pan, Zoom, Orbit, and Look At. Figure 1.16 shows the Navigation bar.

FIGURE 1.16
The Navigation bar

You can use the Navigation bar's steering wheel to zoom, pan, walk, and look around the graphics area. Also available is the ability to rewind through previous steering wheel actions. The steering wheel has more functionality than can be explored in this book. You should review the help topics for more information (click the steering wheel and then press F1).

The Ribbon Menu

The *ribbon menu* is composed of tabs and panels and is similar to the menu used in Microsoft Office products (starting with Office 2007). Each tab contains panels for a particular task, such as creating sketches, and each panel contains related buttons for the tools. As previously mentioned, the ribbon will change to the proper tab based on the current task (for example, sketching brings up the Sketch tab, which allows you to click the Line tool button), but you can select a different tab as needed.

You can customize the ribbon by right-clicking it and choosing among the following:

◆ Turning off tool button text, reducing button size, or using a compact button layout

◆ Turning off panels that you don't use

◆ Adding frequently used commands to a tab

◆ Changing the ribbon appearance

◆ Undocking the ribbon so it becomes a floating tool palette

◆ Docking the ribbon on the left, right, or top of the Inventor window

THE GET STARTED TAB

On the Get Started tab of the ribbon, the tools on the Launch panel are used to access and create files. The rest of the buttons on the Get Started tab link to help topics. You can use the What's New button to read about the new features for the current release as well as the last few releases. The Videos and Tutorials tools contain built-in tutorials and a collection of learning resources. Figure 1.17 shows the Get Started tab and its tools.

FIGURE 1.17
Tools on the Get Started tab

THE VIEW TAB

The View tab, shown in Figure 1.18, has controls for object visibility and appearance, window control, and navigation. There are some variations in the buttons, depending on the environment, but most of the buttons are used in all the modeling environments.

FIGURE 1.18
The View tab

Visibility Panel

The Visibility panel has tools for controlling which objects are visible. When you click Object Visibility, a large list is displayed so you can control the visibility of the listed objects in your graphics window.

Appearance Panel

The Appearance panel has tools for controlling the way models are displayed. You can display the model in a number of visual styles, such as Realistic, Shaded, Shaded With Edges, Illustration, and many more.

VISUAL STYLES AND PERFORMANCE

Inventor includes a number of enhanced visual styles, shadows, and reflection options that might have a negative impact on your graphics performance if your workstation is a bit older. If you notice issues with your graphics display, you can go to the Tools tab, click the Application Options button, click the Hardware tab, and then select the Performance or Compatibility option.

Another important option on the Appearance panel is the View Camera Projection setting, which allows you to choose between orthographic and perspective views. Setting the perspective options to be current displays the model with a vanishing point, as it would be in the real world. With the Orthographic option, points of the model are projected along lines parallel to the screen.

Using a perspective view may be desirable when viewing the model in a 3D view, but it can be distracting when sketching on a flat face or viewing the model from a standard 2D orthographic view because you see what appear to be tapering faces and edges. However, you can get the best of both projections by setting the ViewCube to Perspective With Ortho Faces so that the model is displayed in orthographic mode when one of the standard orthographic faces is active and in perspective mode in any other view. To do this, simply right-click the ViewCube and you will see the option. Note that this setting is set for each document rather than for the application itself, so you will typically need to do this for each model.

Windows Panel

Most of the tools in the Windows panel are standard controls, such as for switching tiling windows. If you click User Interface, a list of items such as the ViewCube and the status bar are displayed. The Clean Screen button hides most of the UI elements. Only the title bar and a minimized ribbon bar are displayed. Although the Clean Screen setting certainly maximizes your screen real estate, it turns off one critical interface object, the browser pane. To use the Clean Screen function effectively, you must turn the browser pane back on. To do so, click the View tab, use the User Interface drop-down, and select the Browser option. You can click the View tab again and then click the Clean Screen button again to disable it and display the tools panels.

Navigate Panel

Also on the View tab is a Navigate panel. The tools in the Navigate panel are the same as those on the Navigation bar, as discussed earlier in the chapter. Many of these tools, such as Pan, Zoom, and Orbit, can be accessed by using the buttons on your mouse or by using the function keys. For instance, spinning the wheel on a standard three-button mouse allows you to zoom in and out. Similarly, if you hold down the **F4** button on the keyboard, you will see that the Orbit tool is active.

The Browser Pane/Model Browser

The *browser pane* (often called the Model browser) is a listing of everything that makes up an Inventor file. The part browser shows all the features, the assembly browser shows all the components, and the drawing browser shows the sheets with the views. Because Inventor files are similar to actual parts and assemblies, the browser plays an important role in navigating the files.

TURNING ON A MISSING MODEL BROWSER

Although it isn't common to need to turn the Model browser off, you can do so. More commonly, you may accidentally turn it off by clicking the X button on the right side of the browser title bar. To display it again, from the View tab click the User Interface button on the Windows panel. You'll most likely want to have all the items in this list selected.

Dialog Boxes and the In-Canvas Mini-Toolbars

As you use Inventor, you will notice that there are often two sets of input controls: the traditional dialog box controls and the in-canvas mini-toolbars. The inputs in the dialog box are the same as those found in the mini-toolbars, and therefore you can use either one to input information or change options. Changing an option in one updates it in the other. You can use the arrow at the bottom of the dialog box to expand or collapse it. Figure 1.19 shows both sets of controls as they appear for editing a simple extrusion.

FIGURE 1.19
Dialog box and mini-toolbar controls

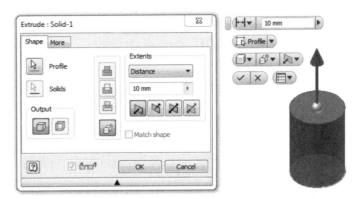

If you find the mini-toolbar controls become distracting by popping up in a position that is in the way of making selections onscreen, you can use the Mini Toolbar Options menu button (the button on the far right of the last row) to pin the mini-toolbar to a location onscreen of your choosing.

Task-Based Tools

You saw in the previous section that the tabs of the ribbon menus update based on the current environment. For instance, when in the sketch environment, the Sketch tab is active. The task-based nature of the available tools is common throughout Inventor. For example, many Inventor dialog boxes are also task-based. Instead of containing every control needed for every environment, most dialog boxes display only the controls necessary for the current task. Figure 1.20 shows two Extrude dialog boxes.

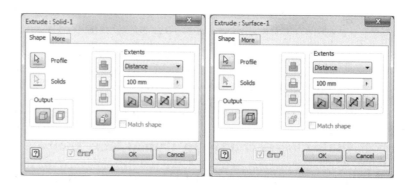

Because creating and editing a solid extrusion is different from creating and editing a surface extrusion, some options are simply grayed out and not available. You will notice this throughout Inventor because options are offered and suppressed depending on the task at hand.

Learning the File Types in Inventor

If you've used AutoCAD, you might be accustomed to having the DWG (.dwg) file format as your primary file format; in Microsoft Word you might use primarily just a DOC (.doc) file; and in Microsoft Excel, you might use the XLS (.xls) file type for most of the work you do. All three of these commonly used programs use a single primary file type throughout. Inventor, on the other hand, follows the structure common to most other 3D modelers in the engineering field today and uses different file types for different tasks.

The purpose of using multiple file types is so the data load is distributed into many different files instead of having all information in one file. For instance, you use an IPT (.ipt) file to create an Inventor part file, an IAM (.iam) file to assemble that part with other parts, and an IDW (.idw) file to make a detail drawing of the parts and the assembly.

Placing the data in multiple files permits quicker load times, promotes file integrity, and vastly improves performance across the board on large designs. For example, when you open an assembly made of 12 different part files, only the information concerning the file paths and the way the parts fit together in the assembly is loaded along with the information required to display the parts. It is only when you decide to edit a part that the information about all of that part's features is loaded. As you learned in the previous section, having different file types allows you to use environment-specific tools. So if you edit a part from within an assembly file, Inventor automatically presents the part-editing tools.

TURNING ON FILENAME EXTENSIONS

It's often helpful when working with Inventor files to be able to view the filename extensions. By default, Windows hides the extensions for known file types. To show filename extensions, follow these steps for Windows 7:

1. Open Folder Options by clicking the Start button, clicking Control Panel, and then clicking Folder Options. (If Folder Options is not available, change View By to Large Icons in the upper-right portion of the Control Panel.)

2. Select the View tab and uncheck the Hide Extensions For Known File Types option.

Another payoff of multiple file types is exemplified in the comparison between the way AutoCAD handles tasks related to model space/paper space and the way Inventor handles the same tasks. To put it simply, in Inventor the part and assembly files are the model (model space), and the drawing file is in effect paper space. Using multiple file types to handle the separate tasks required for modeling vs. detailing simplifies the interaction between both tasks, and as a result, the headaches of managing model space and paper space that exist in AutoCAD are eliminated in Inventor.

Table 1.2 describes the filename extensions for the file formats commonly used in Inventor.

TABLE 1.2:   Common filename extensions in Inventor

EXTENSION	DESCRIPTION	USE
.ipj	Inventor project file	Used to manage file linking paths
.ipt	Inventor single-part file	Used to create individual parts
.iam	Inventor assembly file	Used to assemble parts
.ipn	Inventor presentation file	Used to create exploded views of assemblies
.idw	Inventor 2D detail drawing file	Used to detail part, assembly, and presentation files
.ide	Inventor iFeature file	Used to save features to the iFeature library for reuse in future designs
.dwg (Inventor)	Inventor 2D detail drawing file	Like IDW files, used to detail part, assembly, and presentation files
.dwg (AutoCAD)	AutoCAD nonassociative drawing file	Used to convert an Inventor drawing file to a standard AutoCAD file
.xls	Excel files that drive iParts, threads, and other data	Used to manage tabulated data linked or embedded in a part, assembly, or drawing file

Although this table may seem intimidating, once you become familiar with Inventor, having many different file types will be less of a concern. The benefit of using multiple file types to have fully associative, automatically updating designs is a cornerstone of most 3D parametric modelers. Performance and stability in the use of Inventor require good data management principles, including storing the saved files in an efficient and organized manner.

DWG FILE SIZE

Although the benefits of using an Inventor DWG instead of an IDW may be favorable, you should be aware that the extra abilities of the DWG file do come at the expense of file size. Inventor DWGs are typically two to three times larger than identical IDW files. If you create large assemblies, it is advisable to use the IDW template as opposed to the DWG to keep files manageable. The extent to which the DWG in Inventor is employed will largely be determined by the amount of collaboration required between Inventor and AutoCAD users.

What Is an Inventor Project?

Whether you use Inventor as a stand-alone user or as part of a design group, you should configure and use an Inventor project file to help Inventor resolve file links and keep your designs organized. You can think of project files in Inventor simply as configuration files that tell Inventor where to look for component files when working with assemblies and drawings. For instance, an Inventor assembly file is essentially an empty "bucket" into which parts (and subassemblies) are placed and assembled. Therefore, the assembly file contains only the file path references for the components it is composed of and the information about how those components are assembled. As a result, the location of referenced files is a key issue.

If, when an assembly is opened, referenced files cannot be found at the search path recorded in the assembly file, a manual file resolution process is activated. This happens most often when component files are renamed or moved outside the search path established in the project file.

A NOTE TO AUTODESK® INVENTOR LT™ USERS

If you are using the Autodesk Inventor LT software, you should be aware that it doesn't use project files, and therefore this book's instructions concerning Inventor project files do not apply.

Project Files and Search Paths

Project files are often referred to as IPJ files because .ipj is the extension for project filenames. You can create a project file anywhere it makes sense to do so, and Inventor will look at that location and lower in the directory structure for the files in your design. Take a moment and study the file structure shown in Figure 1.21.

FIGURE 1.21
A job-based folder structure

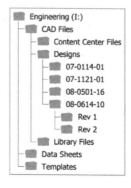

Figure 1.21 shows a typical job-based folder structure, where all files are located on the Engineering (I:) drive. Engineering contains three subfolders: CAD Files, Data Sheets, and Templates. In the CAD Files folder are three more folders: Content Center Files, Designs, and Library Files. The Designs folder contains a folder for each job (named using the job number) and subfolders containing revisions. So, where would you create an Inventor project file? There are two basic solutions: create multiple IPJ files for each new job or create a single all-encompassing IPJ file for the entire engineering drive. Which method you should use depends largely on the way your engineering department operates.

JOB-BASED IPJ SETUPS

You could create one project file for each of the four jobs. You would have a file named 07-0114-01.ipj in the 07-0114-01 folder, one named 07-1121-01.ipj in the 07-1121-01 folder, and so on. This strategy can work fine if you typically work on one project at a time and then "close" the project upon completion. In Inventor, you would simply switch to the specific project file that matches the job number for the job you are working on (for example, 07–0114–01), and because the IPJ file is stored in that folder, Inventor will search for design files only in its *workspace*. The workspace is defined as the folder containing the IPJ folder and everything below it. It may help to think of a workspace as a search cone, starting at the IPJ and spreading out from that point.

This job-based approach is fairly intuitive and is what people generally think of when they see the term *project file*: one IPJ file for each job/project. This is a common approach when a job has a long development cycle and designs are specific to that job.

But what happens if you wanted to use a part that was created for job 07–0114–01 in job 08–0614–10? You could place the part into the 08–0614–10 assembly, but the next time you opened that assembly, Inventor would not be able to find it because it exists outside the 08–0614–10 workspace. If you were to move a part file from the 07-0114-01 folder into the 08-0614-10 folder, Inventor would not find it while you were working on job 07–0114–01 because it would now be outside of its workspace. Likewise, if you moved the file up to the Designs folder, to the CAD Files folder, or to (almost) any location that is not next to or below the 07-0114-01.ipj file, Inventor would not find it as long as you are working with the 07-0114-01.ipj project file. If you copy the file to the 08-0614-10 folder, then you have two versions of it and it becomes difficult to track changes because you need to update both copies to keep everything up-to-date.

The solution would be to configure the IPJ file to include a *library*. When a folder is config-ured to be used as a library in an IPJ file, Inventor sees all the files in that folder (and its sub-folders) as read-only. This protects commonly used files from being accidentally changed and upsetting all of the many designs in which they may be used.

To solve the issue of the commonly used part in this example, you could configure each of your IPJ files to use the folder named Library Files as a library of approved, read-only parts to be used across multiple jobs. Whenever you open an assembly, Inventor first looks in the library path for the parts and then looks at the workspace. So, to convert a part created as part of the 07–0114–01 job into a library part, you would follow these steps:

1. Copy the file to the library folder.

2. If the original file has a job-specific name, rename the copy according to a defined library nomenclature.

3. Open the assembly (or assemblies) that uses the original part.

4. Use the Replace Components tool to replace the original part with the library part in the assembly.

5. Save and close the assembly.

6. Delete the original part so that no duplicate is present.

SINGLE IPJ SETUPS

The multiple project file strategy described previously is often not the best approach for many design departments, because of various contributing factors. When this is the case, you should consider using a single project file. Using the same folder structure shown in Figure 1.21 as an example, you could use a single all-encompassing IPJ file and place it in the Designs folder. By doing so, you would be setting the workspace at that level. This configures the search paths in Inventor to look for files in the Designs folder and everything below it. Essentially, you have expanded the search cone by moving it up a level compared to the job-based setup. Now if you need to use a part that resides in the 07-0114-01 folder in the 08–0614–10 assembly, you can do so and Inventor will be able to find it, without requiring it to be in a library folder.

Of course, you can still use library folders when using the single IPJ file approach, and in fact it is generally recommended that you convert common parts to library parts when they are being used in many different designs. Because folders configured as libraries in the IPJ file are handled as read-only, this protects them from accidental modifications.

One major caveat to using just a single IPJ file is that in order to prevent the possibility of the wrong part being loaded in an assembly, it is important for every part located in the search path to have a unique name. If Inventor finds two files named BasePlate01, it will either use the first one it finds or stop and make you decide which one to use. In either case, you should consider a nomenclature that references the job number, date, or other unique identifier in the name.

ITEM-BASED SETUPS

If your company uses an item-based file management setup and tracks each part you create or purchase as an item, you are probably not concerned with job numbers as much as you are about part numbers. Most likely you will want to employ a single IPJ file setup as described previously and again place the IPJ file in the Designs folder. Additionally, your file structure may be a bit flatter and look like Figure 1.22, where the Designs folder has no subfolders.

FIGURE 1.22
An item-based folder structure

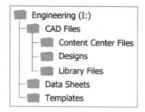

In this flatter structure, you can simplify the folder structure and drop all files into the Designs folder, as shown in Figure 1.23.

FIGURE 1.23
A simplified folder structure

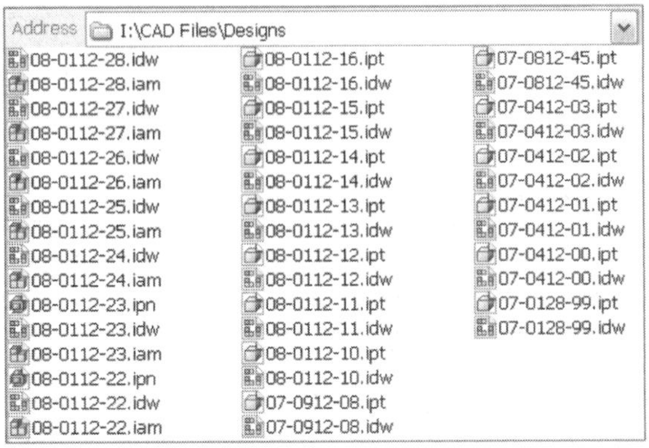

Address	I:\CAD Files\Designs	
08-0112-28.idw	08-0112-16.ipt	07-0812-45.ipt
08-0112-28.iam	08-0112-16.idw	07-0812-45.idw
08-0112-27.idw	08-0112-15.ipt	07-0412-03.ipt
08-0112-27.iam	08-0112-15.idw	07-0412-03.idw
08-0112-26.idw	08-0112-14.ipt	07-0412-02.ipt
08-0112-26.iam	08-0112-14.idw	07-0412-02.idw
08-0112-25.idw	08-0112-13.ipt	07-0412-01.ipt
08-0112-25.iam	08-0112-13.idw	07-0412-01.idw
08-0112-24.idw	08-0112-12.ipt	07-0412-00.ipt
08-0112-24.iam	08-0112-12.idw	07-0412-00.idw
08-0112-23.ipn	08-0112-11.ipt	07-0128-99.ipt
08-0112-23.idw	08-0112-11.idw	07-0128-99.idw
08-0112-23.iam	08-0112-10.ipt	
08-0112-22.ipn	08-0112-10.idw	
08-0112-22.idw	07-0912-08.ipt	
08-0112-22.iam	07-0912-08.idw	

Of course, you could also still populate the Designs folder with subfolders named by product line, by top-level item, or for each job, just as it was done in Figure 1.21. Typically, it is best to set up the IPJ file to accommodate your current file management system. However, if your current system is a mess or is simply no longer a good fit for your company, you might take the opportunity to reorganize and plan a good system and set up Inventor accordingly.

Library Folders and Library Editor IPJ Files

As described earlier, library folders contain existing, shared components. Library folders are useful repositories for purchased parts such as fasteners, clamps, motors, and connectors as well as any other common, standard components. Library folder paths are defined in the IPJ file. Once the IPJ file is configured and set active, all components stored in a folder designated as a library file are considered to be read-only by Inventor. This prevents the component from being unintentionally edited or from being revised without appropriate approvals. For example, before you modify a design that was completed as part of another job, it's important to determine where else that part was used. The goal is to ensure that the changes you plan will not render the part unusable for other designs.

Library folders should be located outside the main IPJ workspace path. In the job-based directory structure example shown in Figure 1.21, the Library Files folder is on the same directory level as the Designs folder and therefore outside the workspace search path. Library folders can be located anywhere outside the primary project data path, even on different drives or mapped servers. You should note that if you set up a library path in the IPJ file to a folder that does not exist, Inventor will create the folder as specified in the path. A good way to set up libraries is to set the path, let Inventor create the folder so that you know it's in the right place, and then populate the folder with the library files.

So if folders configured as libraries are configured as read-only in the IPJ file, how are controlled, purposeful revisions carried out on library files? The answer is to create an IPJ file configured to look at the library folder as a standard folder. For instance, you might create an IPJ file in the Library Files folder and assign it no library path. You would then switch to this IPJ file only when doing library maintenance. Because this IPJ has no library path called out, the files are not handled as read-only when Inventor is using this IPJ file. Often in a large engineering department only a couple of people have access to the library editor project file. When other team members see a need to change a library file, they would submit a change order, and the designated person (or people) would then make the change.

Content Center Files

In the previous figures you may have noticed a folder called Content Center Files. This is a special kind of library that stores component files generated by Inventor's Content Center tools. The path to this folder is specified in the IPJ file, much like a library file is.

It is important to understand what Content Center is and how it works. Content Center libraries are collections of table data containing the definitions used to create more than 800,000 standard parts and features. This database is managed by the *Desktop Content* settings or the *Autodesk Data Management Server (ADMS)*. Once you've installed the content libraries, you can use the content in your designs. To do this, choose a component from the database to place into your design, typically by using the Place From Content Center button in the assembly environment. It is at this point that the Content Center part file is created. Up to this point, the part existed only as a definition in the database table.

In your IPJ, you need to specify a Content Center file store location so that Inventor knows where to save the file and where to find it next time. The file store folder will include additional subfolders where Content Center files will be stored once they are used in your designs. These additional folders are created automatically as parts are created. The next time a part is specified from Content Center libraries, Inventor first searches Content Center file store directories and then creates the part from the database only if the part file does not already exist in the file store location. It is required that the Content Center file store location be outside the main project data path. From this discussion of libraries, you can see that high importance is placed on planning the correct part locations and workflow.

How Search Paths and Project Files Are Used

The IPJ files in Inventor are easy to create and use, provided you understand how Inventor uses them. An Inventor project file is a configuration file that lists the locations and functions of each search path. Inventor uses these definitions to resolve file links and locate the files needed for the parts and assemblies on which you want to work. Figure 1.24 shows how Inventor loads assemblies and parts inside an assembly file.

When opening an assembly file, Inventor finds files by searching for the first file to be located within the assembly file. Inventor first looks in the library folders for that file. Next, Inventor searches in the local workspace for the file. When a file is not found in any of the referenced folders, Inventor launches a manual file resolution dialog box offering you the opportunity to browse and point to the file manually.

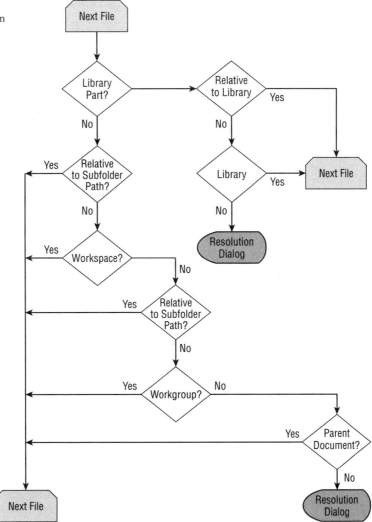

Exploring Project File Types

As mentioned previously, file management in Inventor is handled through the use of a project file (*.ipj). A *project file* is a configuration file set up and used to control how Inventor creates and resolves file links, where you edit files, how many old versions of the files to keep, and how Content Center files are stored and used. In the early days of Inventor, Autodesk offered two basic project types: single-user projects and multiuser projects. At this point, the Autodesk Vault project has replaced the earlier multiuser project types.

Unless you are planning to use Vault, the default project type is the single-user project. The term *single-user* could be considered a misnomer because this project type is widely used by one-person shops and multiseat design departments alike. Single-user does not mean that only one user can access the files in the project, as it might suggest; instead, it refers to the fact that there are no means of preventing files from being accessed for editing while another user is already editing the file. This can create a last-person-to-save-wins situation if you aren't careful.

SINGLE-USER PROJECTS AMONG MULTIPLE USERS

What happens when two users access the same file in a single-user project? Typically this is first noticed when one of the two tries to save the file. Inventor notifies the person trying to save that they are not working with the most current version and gives the other user's name (depending on the network setup) so the first user knows what is going on. Inventor instructs the user that they must save the file using a different name to prevent losing the changes made.

Typically, at this point a conversation takes place to determine how to proceed. If it is decided that the first person is the one who needs to save changes, then the file this person was working on is saved using another name, the original file is deleted (or renamed as a reserve), and the other file is renamed to replace the original. In this way, the changes that were made to the original file are preserved.

Although this may seem like a terrible hassle, there are many design departments that use single-user projects in a team setting effectively and only rarely run into this situation. More than likely you already have an idea of how often you and your colleagues handle the same files at the same time. But if you try to use single-user projects and find this situation happens fairly often, you should consider a true multiuser project.

Many design departments use single-user projects effectively in collaborative environments because of workflows that lend themselves to this type of project; others make it work by simply maintaining good communication among the design team. For collaborative environments that require some safeguard against situations in which users could potentially save over one another's work, using a *multiuser* project (Vault project) is recommended.

Autodesk Vault is a data management application that, as the name implies, locks down files for their protection. Once a file is in Vault, it must be checked out by a user to be edited. Vault typically resides on a file server where the entire design team can access it. When the file is checked out of the Vault server, it is placed on the user's local machine for editing. The next user who comes along and attempts to access that file can access only a read-only version. Once the first user has finished editing, the file is checked back into Vault and automatically versioned.

It is also important to note that Inventor installs with a *default* project setup. The default project is typically not used for production work because it is not fully configurable and will almost always lead to file resolution issues because it has no defined search path.

CREATING A GOOD DATA-MANAGEMENT PLAN

A good data management plan is the key to using Inventor projects successfully. Using Vault will not resolve a poor project file or data management strategy.

One part of a successful Inventor deployment is the hardware network on which the software will run. It is important that the engineering group has buy-in by the IT group. You will need to discuss several issues with this group, including hardware for servers and workstations, the network setup (100BaseT or Gigabit), mapped network drives, and user permissions. A good server can be the difference between success and failure in your rollout.

Although you do need to think about your file structure, don't obsess over it. Most likely you will end up changing the structure at least a few times before you settle on a final structure. Keep an open mind, and realize that if you have five people in a room discussing file structures, you'll end up with five different ideas. Again, involve IT in your discussions.

Finally, you should designate one person in engineering to be the engineering administrator. This person needs to have administrative privileges on the engineering server or network share. IT may resist, but you have to keep pushing. This is important because you will need the ability to easily create, delete, and move files and folders without having to submit a help-desk ticket. Nothing will slow down a design process faster than having to wait for IT to make a simple change. Explain this need to your IT administrator, and most likely they will understand.

Creating a Project File

Whether you choose to use a single-user or multiuser project file, it is important that you pick one. Without a project file to configure Inventor's search path, you are likely to create a file structure that will be problematic as you create more and more files in Inventor.

Certification
Objective

Creating Single-User Projects

Probably the best way to learn about projects is to create a test single-user project. With single-user projects, you can open, edit, and save files without checking the files in or out. In the following sections, you will investigate the single-user file project mode. Once you gain an understanding of single-user projects, you will be ready to investigate the other project file types. To create a test project, you will use the Inventor Project Wizard.

THE INVENTOR PROJECT WIZARD

To get the most out of this exercise, open your version of Inventor, ensure that you have closed all the open files, and then access the Inventor Project Wizard by clicking the Projects button on the Get Started tab. Then follow these steps:

1. In the Projects dialog box, click the New button at the bottom.

2. Select New Single User Project, as shown in Figure 1.25, and then click Next.

FIGURE 1.25
Creating a single-user project

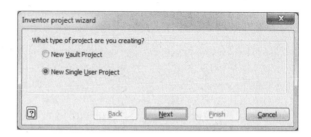

3. Enter **MI_Test_Project** in the Name field.

4. Enter **C:\ MI_Test_Project** in the Project (Workspace) Folder field.

Figure 1.26 shows a Project File page specifying the project.

FIGURE 1.26
The Project File page filled in

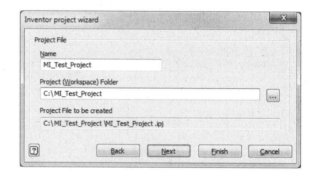

5. Click Next to advance to the next page of the wizard.

6. If you already created a folder for your library files and used those libraries in a previous project, their locations will appear on the Select Libraries page, shown in Figure 1.27. When creating a new project, you can choose to include some, all, or none of the defined library locations. Click the Finish button to include no libraries at this point.

FIGURE 1.27
Select Libraries page

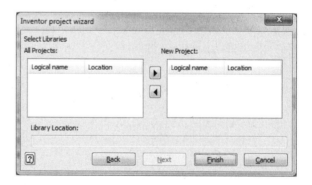

7. Click OK in the message box informing you that the project path entered does not yet exist.

SWITCHING AND EDITING PROJECTS

Only one project can be active at a time. To switch projects, you must first close all files that are open in Inventor. You cannot edit the file paths of the active project, but you can edit the file paths of items such as Content Center libraries that are included. You can edit anything in an inactive project.

Certification
Objective

THE PROJECTS DIALOG BOX

Now that you have created your sample project file, you'll explore the options and settings available for your new project. To activate and use your new project, highlight the new project and click Apply. You can also activate or select a new project link by double-clicking the project link. Notice the check mark next to the project name MI_Test_Project, indicating that the project is now active, as shown in Figure 1.28.

FIGURE 1.28
Projects dialog box

In the lower pane, you can view and access parameter settings for the following:

♦ Project type

♦ Project location

♦ Optional included project file

♦ Appearance libraries path

♦ Material libraries path

♦ Workspace path

♦ Optional workgroup paths

- Libraries you want to use

- Frequently used subfolders

- Folder options

- Other project options

Right-click a parameter group to view the settings available within that group. In the Project group, you can change the project type, view the project location, and include other project files. Project types were discussed earlier in this chapter. The project location is a read-only parameter. Included files deserve some additional discussion because the Included File parameter allows you to apply a master project to your current project; this setting, as well as the other project settings, is discussed in the coming pages.

Included Files

Although it's not required, you can include an existing project in the configuration of the current project by right-clicking Included File. The properties and settings in the project file that you attach override the settings in the current project file. This is useful for restricting and controlling a user's ability to change the project file. Also, if you frequently create new project files, you might consider creating a master project file that contains library locations and other settings you commonly use and then including the master project file in each new project file.

Appearance Libraries

An appearance library is a collection of appearances (for instance, colors) that either are installed with Autodesk Inventor or are created by the user. User-created libraries can contain appearances and materials in the same appearance library. The Autodesk Appearance Library contains only appearances. The active library is shown in bold text.

Material Libraries

A material library is a collection of material definitions (for instance, physical materials such as Stainless Steel) that either are installed with Autodesk Inventor or are created by the user. User-created libraries can contain materials and appearances in the same material library. The Autodesk Material Library contains only materials. The Inventor Material Library provides a basic set of manufacturing-related materials and appearances. The libraries that are installed with Autodesk products are read-only libraries. Custom libraries can be set to read-only or made writable using the file's read-only attribute. The active library is shown in bold text.

Workspace

For single-user projects, the workspace is defined by the location of the project file (*.ipj). For Vault projects, the workspace is defined on the workstation and is configured to match the Working Folder setting in the Vault settings. The workspace is the folder that files are copied to when they are checked out. The Workspace folder may include any number of subfolders as required for your file management needs.

Workgroup

The workgroup search path specifies a location outside the current project file paths where Inventor can search for existing files that are not included in a library. A workgroup is specified when the project is created. Each single-user project should have no more than one workgroup. Using a workgroup path is not required and is not a common configuration to make.

Style Library

Inventor uses styles to specify dimensions, text, colors, materials, and other properties. This is similar to styles used in AutoCAD. Inventor stores styles locally within the templates or in an external style library that may be used with any project file.

The Use Style Library function in projects specifies whether the project uses only read-only or read-write style libraries. The read-only style library is recommended for projects that have multiple users. With multiple users, changing or editing the style library on the fly can cause downstream problems. To change the Use Style Library parameter, right-click and select the new setting.

Remember that for your projects, you can right-click to select another option when it is appropriate. Click Read-Only (the default) if you want to access style libraries and local styles without enabling style-editing capabilities. Click Read-Write if you want to be able to coordinate style by saving them into the style library.

Library Options

Next on the list are libraries. Library folders are usually located outside the project file path. They may be located anywhere on your system or on your server. If you are sharing library files, you should place them on your server in a commonly accessed location. Inventor considers the contents of directories specified as libraries to be read-only.

In your newly created project file, you have not added any library folders. If at any time you want to add library folders, you can do so by right-clicking Libraries and choosing Add Path, Add Paths From File, or Paste Path, as shown in Figure 1.29.

FIGURE 1.29
Adding library paths by right-clicking

You can manually add a path, either by browsing or by typing a new file location. Be sure to give the library a descriptive name that identifies the contents of the file location. Add Paths From File permits you to extract library paths from another project file. Paste Path allows you to copy and paste. Once you have specified library paths, the Delete Section Paths option becomes available, and you can remove paths not needed by the project. Deleting unused library paths reduces search and resolution time.

Shortcuts to Frequently Used Files

Frequently used subfolders are similar to the bookmarks you can set in Internet Explorer. The subfolders must already be nested within the current project workspace, workgroup, or library. Adding frequently used subfolders to your project provides navigation links in your open, save, and place dialog boxes so you can quickly navigate to those locations. In the Mastering Inventor project that you will use throughout the rest of this book, the chapter folders have been added as frequently used subfolders.

Folder Options

The Folder Options setting allows your project to access other file locations that are specified on the Files tab of the Application Options dialog box. Keep in mind that you may have to close and reopen Inventor in order to reinitialize the optional project file locations. You can use this option to specify different default locations for templates, design data (styles, and so on), and Content Center files. When the locations are set to the defaults, the location/storage of the files is specified on the Files tab of the Application Options dialog box. Right-click any of the option entries to change the storage and access location. You can find more information about Content Center in Chapter 7, "Reusing Parts and Features."

Project Options

Expand the Options heading to show the global defaults for the selected project. The Options settings in a project determine file management functions; right-click an option to edit it.

Versioning and Backup

Use the Options settings to determine how many old versions or backup copies of each file to save. The Old Versions To Keep On Save option specifies the number of versions to store in the Old Versions folder for each file saved. The first time a file is saved in a project, an Old Versions folder for that file is created. When the file is saved, the prior version is moved automatically to the file's Old Versions folder. After the number of old versions reaches the maximum in the setting, the oldest version is deleted when a newer version is moved into the folder.

If you are familiar with AutoCAD, you may expect Inventor versioning to be similar to AutoCAD's backup scheme. AutoCAD creates a *.bak file saved in the same folder as the design. Inventor saves the backup files in a separate Old Versions folder. All versions located in the Old Versions folder have the same name and extension, except that a number is appended after the name. In the project options, the default setting of 1 creates one backup file in the Old Versions folder. If you are working with a complex model, you might decide to specify additional backup versions by changing this setting to a higher number; however, remember that with each additional backup version you are creating additional files (and using additional space) on your hard drive. Setting Old Versions to –1 will cause Inventor to save all backup files.

RESTORING AN OLD VERSION

Occasionally a file may become corrupt, or you may have accidentally saved a design change that you did not intend to. In these cases, you can browse to the Old Versions folder and open the versioned file. Upon doing so you will be presented with these three options:

- Open Old Version (Save Not Allowed)
- Restore Old Version To Current Version
- Open Current Version

Filenaming Conventions

The Using Unique File Names setting in the options will allow Inventor to check for unique part names for all files in the project, including subfolders. Libraries are excluded in this option. Proper design workflow demands that each unique part have a unique filename. When a part is reused, you should ensure that any revision to it is acceptable to all designs in which it is used. If the revised part cannot be used in all the designs, you should use a new part name because you have now created an additional unique part.

Setting the Using Unique File Names option to Yes will cause Inventor to search the entire project workspace to compare filenames but does not prevent users from creating duplicate filenames. Having this option set to Yes can cause issues when a large number of files are present, particularly when those files are organized with a large number of subfolders. If the Using Unique File Names option is set to No, Inventor will not search to compare filenames.

If you do not have a part-numbering scheme already, take the time to implement one to make working with your Inventor files easier. Keep in mind that the most effective numbering schemes are often the simplest. Many an engineering department has eventually run into unanticipated limitations when using a numbering scheme that is too specific or when attempting to include too much information in some built-in code.

 **Real World Scenario**

THE USING UNIQUE FILE NAMES SETTING AND SLOW SEARCH TIMES

The Using Unique File Names option for your project is set to Yes. You have an engineering directory with 8,500 folders and subfolders containing thousands of files. You have a drawing file that references a part file named 12-865.ipt, but you've renamed the part file to 22-865.ipt using Windows Explorer.

Because the internal link in the drawing file is still looking for 12-865.ipt, when you open the drawing file that references the renamed part file, Inventor will search through all 8,500 folders and subfolders looking for the missing file. When it doesn't find the file, it will finally present the File Resolution dialog box, allowing you to point the drawing file to 22-865.ipt.

continues

continued

Because of the number of folders and files, this search may take several minutes. By contrast, if you had the same scenario but your project file option Using Unique File Names was set to No, Inventor would not search for the missing file. Instead, it would immediately present you with the File Resolution dialog box and allow you to point the drawing to 22-865.ipt. For this reason, you should set this option to No when large file collections are present. However, even if it is set to No, you should employ a unique filenaming scheme for all your files.

Keep in mind that you can toggle this option to Yes if you find yourself needing to search the project for unique filenames.

Here are a few suggestions that may help you in determining a numbering scheme that will work well for you:

Sequential Project-Based: 0910–00001   Here, the first four digits correspond to the project number, and the last five are sequenced, starting at 00001. This numbering system works well when parts are not often used across different projects. Common parts might be created under a "common part project" prefix such as 7777.

Generic Date-Based: 09–0707–01   Here, the first six numbers are assigned by using the current date when the part number is created. In this example, the part number was created on July 7, 2009. The last two digits are sequenced starting with 01. This is a highly flexible numbering system that allows 100 part numbers to be created per day. If more than 100 are needed, then backdating using an unused date can be done. The date itself holds no real significance, other than helping to ensure the unique part numbers.

Sequential Product-Based: NG-00001   Here the first two letters reflect a specific product line, such as the Next Generation (NG) line, and the last five are sequenced starting at 00001. This numbering system works well when products lines are engineered and maintained separately.

Once you've decided on a part numbering scheme, you will want to come up with a central part number log file or tracking system to be used in assigning numbers to ensure that there are no duplicates. If you have a resource planning system (commonly referred to as a manufacturing resource planning [MRP] or enterprise resource planning [ERP] system), you likely have the ability to manage part numbers using that software. If not, you can use a simple XLS spreadsheet file to assist with this task.

THE PROJECTS DIALOG BOX'S TOOL PANEL

The buttons along the right side of the lower pane of the Projects dialog box provide access to tools that allow you to add, edit, and reorder project parameter settings and paths; check for duplicate filenames; and configure Content Center libraries used for the active project.

Use the magnifying glass button located on the lower-right side of the Projects dialog box to check your project paths for duplicate filenames. Figure 1.30 shows the result of searching a project where someone has not been careful to ensure that duplicate filenames are not used.

FIGURE 1.30
The Non-Unique Project File
Names dialog box

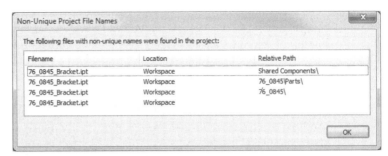

WHY RELATIVE PATHS?

An Inventor assembly file records relative paths when it links a subassembly or single parts to itself. The use of relative paths in assembly files allows the relocation of an assembly and its associated parts and subassemblies to other locations on servers or drives without requiring the resolution of a new location. Relative paths, however, introduce the danger of the assembly locating only the first of two parts that happen to have the same name. For instance, if you've saved files named Part1 in two different file folders, Inventor might resolve the link to the first one it finds and then stop searching.

To prevent the possibility of the wrong part being loaded in an assembly, ensure that every part located in the search path has a unique name.

The Projects dialog box supports the configuration of one or more Content Center libraries. Content Center provides multiple database libraries that can be used in assemblies or by the design accelerator.

If you elected to install Content Center libraries while installing Inventor, you must configure Content Center libraries in the project before you can access them. Click the Content Center button in the lower-right corner of the project editing dialog box. Then select Content Center library or libraries you want to use and click OK. Figure 1.31 shows the Configure Libraries dialog box.

FIGURE 1.31
Configuring Content Center

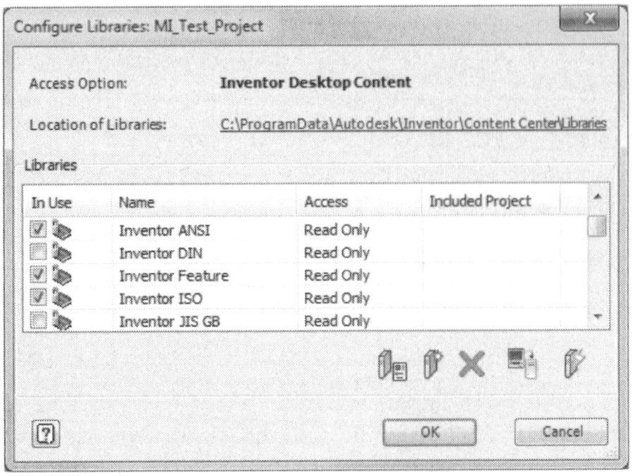

Select the Content Center libraries you think you'll use. Installing all the Content Center libraries may slow your system down significantly when you are accessing Content Center because Inventor will need to index each library upon initialization.

When you finish editing the project file, click Save and then make sure your desired project file is active before clicking Done to exit the Projects dialog box.

Creating Multiuser Projects

Working as a team can increase productivity many times over. In a collaborative design environment, several users may be working on a project at the same time. When you use Vault data management software, you are prevented from working on the original version of a file located in Vault. Each user creates a local Vault project file that specifies a personal workspace located on the local drive and includes search paths to one or more master projects.

WHAT IS AUTODESK VAULT AND WHO NEEDS IT?

Autodesk Vault is a file management tool integrated with Inventor. Essentially, Vault allows you to check in and check out files in a collaborative workgroup so users do not accidentally save over one another's work. Not every design department needs to use Vault, and in fact many find that it is not a good solution for their particular needs. However, you should investigate Vault to see what it has to offer, even if you already have a data management system in place.

To edit a "Vaulted" file, the user must check the file out of Vault. The process of checking the file out copies the file to the local workspace. When someone checks out a file for editing, the original stored in Vault is flagged as "checked out" to that particular user. Other users can view the checked-out files in read-only mode, but they can't edit it.

The user who checked out the file can edit and save the file in their local workspace without checking the file back into Vault. When they save the file, they will be prompted to choose whether they want to check the file back into Vault. If they choose to check the file into Vault, the file will be saved into Vault and is then available for editing by a different user. Optionally, they may save the file into Vault but keep it checked out to their local workspace, allowing other users to view the updated file without being able to edit it.

PROJECT SHORTCUTS

If you right-click a project in the Project dialog box, you can choose Delete to remove it from the list. But if you browse to the file location, you'll see that the IPJ file is still there. What is going on?

When you create a new project file or point Inventor to an existing project file, Inventor will create a shortcut to that file. When you choose Delete and remove the project from the list, you are not actually deleting the IPJ file but instead deleting the shortcut. When you choose Browse and locate the IPJ file to add back to the list, the shortcut is re-created.

You can set the path to the shortcuts by accessing the Tools tab of the ribbon and choosing Application Options. In the Application Options dialog box, click the Files tab and set the project's folder path.

Collaborative design project files are created using the Inventor Project Wizard in much the same manner as a single-user project file is created. The file resolution process within a collaborative project file functions in the same way.

With Vault installed on your server or your own system, verify that Vault is correctly installed and that you can open and create a new Vault file store using the ADMS console. The new Vault file store must be accessible on your local system from Vault Explorer. If Vault functions correctly, you are now ready to create a Vault project file. As with a single-user project, use the Inventor Project Wizard to name the project, specify the workspace, assign libraries for use with the project, and configure project parameters.

Again, as in other project file types, you will need to edit the default settings in your project file and optionally configure your Content Center for use.

IMPLEMENTING AUTODESK VAULT

Once the Vault software is installed on your system, you can find the Autodesk Vault Implementation Guide in PDF in the Help folder of the install directory. Or you can search the Internet for *autodesk+vault+implementation+guide*. This detailed guide provides you with information on Vault fundamentals and installation as well as information on configuring and maintaining Autodesk Vault for your data management needs.

Understanding Inventor Templates

You can create template files in Inventor by opening an Inventor file, making the desired edits to the file, clicking the Inventor button, choosing Save Copy As, and then choosing Save Copy As Template. It is typically recommended that you set the Template directory by configuring your project file using the Folder Options node and setting the Template path to a network location. Often when creating a template, you might set up the following items in the file before saving:

◆ Custom iProperties

◆ User parameters

◆ Cached styles

◆ Specific document settings such as units (by clicking the Document Settings button on the Tools tab)

When creating any template file, it is a good idea to work with a file that is as "clean" and uncluttered with extra styles as possible. The best way to do this is to hold down the **Ctrl** and **Shift** keys and click the New button; then select the type of file you want to create from the list, as shown in Figure 1.32.

FIGURE 1.32
Creating a new clean file

Working with Styles, Style Libraries, and Company Standards

Your Inventor files will use a number of *styles* to allow you to maintain consistencies and to save you from needing to define common setups over and over. In part files, the style collections include lighting styles, color styles, and material styles. Color and lighting styles allow you to change the appearance of your model, and material styles allow you to change its physical properties. In drawing files, style collections include such things as dimension styles, balloon styles, parts list styles, and much more. These drawing style collections are organized in *standards*, which are used to manage the standard company styles used within your organization. You can even set up multiple standards, allowing you to change from one set of styles to another quickly and consistently.

The Bottom Line

Create parametric designs. The power of parameter-based design comes from the quick and easy edits when changing a parameter value drives a change through the design. To make changes easily, though, you need to follow certain general rules so that the changes update predictably.

Master It You want to create a model of a base plate, a rectangular-shaped part with a series of holes and rectangular cutouts. What would your initial sketch look like in Inventor?

Get the "feel" of Inventor. The interface contains many elements that change and update to give you the tools you need to perform the task at hand. Getting comfortable with these automatic changes and learning to anticipate them will help you get the "feel" of Inventor.

Master It You create an extrude feature using the Extrude button, but you cannot seem to find an Edit Extrude button. How can you edit the extruded feature to change the height?

Use the Inventor graphical interface. Inventor 2016 uses the ribbon interface introduced in Inventor 2010. Tools are grouped, which makes finding them intuitive once you become familiar with the basic layout.

Master It You are trying to draw a line on the face of a part, but you seem to have lost the Sketch tab in the ribbon. How do you get it back?

Work with Inventor file types. Inventor supports many different file types in its native environment, separating tasks and files to improve performance and increase stability.

Master It You have trouble keeping the various file types straight because all the file icons look rather similar to you. Is there a way you can see which file is what type?

Understand how project search paths work. Knowing how Inventor resolves file paths when it opens linked files, such as assembly files and drawings, goes a long way toward helping prevent broken links and repairing links that do get broken.

Master It What type of file does Inventor use to point the assembly file to the parts that it contains?

Set up library and Content Center paths.   Library and Content Center paths are read-only library configurations set up in the project file.

> **Master It**   When you set up a library or Content Center path to a folder that does not exist, what happens?

Create and configure a project file.   Project files are a key component of working successfully in Inventor, but for many people, this is a one-time setup. Once the project is created, for the most part you just use it as is.

> **Master It**   After creating a project file initially, you want to make one or more changes to the configuration, but you can't seem to do so. What could be the problem?

Determine the best project type for you.   Although the Autodesk solution to a multiuser environment is Autodesk Vault, many people may not be able to use Vault. For instance, if you use another CAD application that links files like Inventor, Vault will likely not know how to manage the internal links for those files.

> **Master It**   Because you generally do not work concurrently on the same files as your co-workers, you think it might be best to set up a single-user project for now while you continue to investigate the Vault solution, but you are not sure if that will work. Can single-user projects be used in this manner?

Chapter 2

A Hands-on Test-Drive of the Workflow

In this chapter, you will explore the basic steps involved in creating part models, creating drawings of those parts, putting those parts together into an assembly model, and then creating a drawing of that assembly. At this point, it is assumed that you have taken the time to read Chapter 1, "Getting Started," and are familiar with the Autodesk® Inventor® software interface and navigation tools. If you have not done so, you might want to take the time to read that chapter before continuing.

Although Inventor includes a number of tools that go far beyond the simple tasks of creating parts, drawings, and assemblies, the workflow involved in creating and detailing your designs is the foundation upon which you will build as you learn Inventor. The goal of this chapter is to get you familiar with the overall workflow. In the chapters to follow, you will explore the tools and environments in more depth.

In this chapter, you'll learn to

- ◆ Create a part model
- ◆ Create and detail drawings of part models
- ◆ Put part models together in assembly files
- ◆ Create and detail drawings of assembly models

Creating a Part Model

Throughout this chapter you will be working toward creating the simple mechanism shown assembled in Figure 2.1.

To become familiar with this assembly, you can open mi_2a_180_Complete.jpg, mi_2a_180_Video.mov, or mi_2a_180_Video.mp4; all are located in the Chapter 02 directory of your Mastering Inventor 2016 folder once you've downloaded this book's companion files and created the folder structure Inventor expects for them, as described in the "Before You Start…" sidebar.

To create a model of a part, you will use an Inventor *.ipt file template. Once your new file is created, you will create basic profiles using sketching tools such as lines, arcs, and circles to define the shape of the features that make up the part. You'll also add dimensions and geometric constraints to the sketch. You'll then use the sketched profiles to create the 3D features that will define the parts. Figure 2.2 shows the basic workflow involved in creating a part from sketches and features.

FIGURE 2.1
An assembly created
with Inventor parts

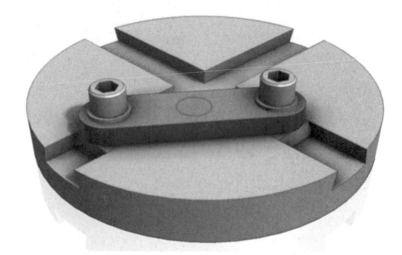

FIGURE 2.2
Creating a part model

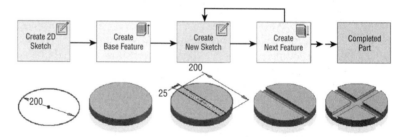

BEFORE YOU START...

Before you begin, make sure you have downloaded the tutorial files from www.sybex.com/go/masteringinventor2016. Place the files in a folder on your computer (such as \My Documents\Mastering Inventor 2016).

If you are using the Autodesk® Inventor LT™ program, the use of project files does not apply, so you can skip the steps listed here. If you are using the full version of Inventor, follow these steps to set the Mastering Inventor 2016 project to be the active project:

1. From within Inventor, close any open files.

2. On the Get Started tab, click the Projects button.

3. In the Projects dialog, click the Browse button.

4. In the Choose Project File dialog, browse to your Mastering Inventor 2016 folder, select the Mastering Inventor 2016.ipj file, and click Open.

5. Note that the Mastering Inventor 2016 project is denoted as being the active project with a check mark.

6. Click Done to close the Projects dialog box.

Now you are ready to get started with this book's exercises.

Starting with a Part Template

Inventor installs with several part templates that you can use to create your part files. In the following steps, you'll use a millimeter-based part template to start your model:

1. On the Get Started tab, click New (or press **Ctrl+N** on the keyboard). Alternately, you can use the buttons in the New area of the Home screen.

2. In the Create New File dialog box, expand the Templates folder (if required) and select the Metric folder from the list on the left.

3. Click Standard (mm).ipt from the list of part templates on the right side of the dialog box. Figure 2.3 shows the metric templates displayed in the Create New File dialog box.

FIGURE 2.3
Creating a file from a metric part template

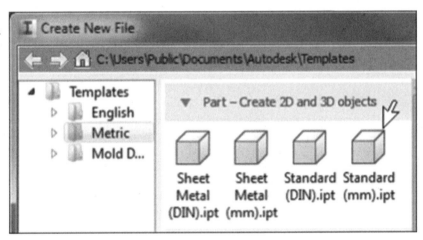

4. Click the Create button at the bottom of the dialog box to create a new file from the selected template.

Leave the file open and continue to the next section to create a base sketch in this new part file.

Understanding Origin Geometry

When you start a new file from a part template, the file contains some basic origin geometry located in the Origin folder. The Origin folder is found in the browser. Figure 2.4 shows a model of a screw with the Origin folder expanded and the origin geometry set to be visible. You can see the geometry browser nodes in the list on the left and the origin planes and axes displayed on the right as they run through the screw geometry.

To create a base sketch for your part, you will use an origin plane to sketch on. Because origin geometry cannot be changed, using an origin plane to sketch on allows you to anchor your base sketch in space and provides a stable foundation upon which to create your part.

For a new file, the origin geometry is typically set to be invisible, but you can right-click any origin geometry and choose Visibility to make it appear. Right-clicking again and deselecting Visibility will toggle the origin feature's visibility back off.

FIGURE 2.4
Origin geometry
in a part model

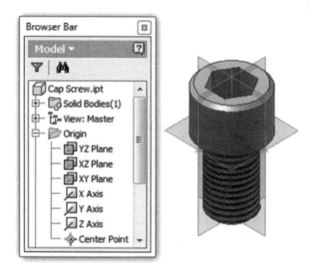

Creating a Base 2D Sketch

When you create a new part, Inventor will prompt you to select an origin plane on which to sketch, or it will create a new sketch for you on a designated origin plane. You can control this behavior by selecting the Tools tab and clicking the Application Options button. On the Part tab, you will find the Sketch On New Part Creation option.

If this option is set to No New Sketch, Inventor will prompt you to select an origin plane to create your base sketch; otherwise, the base sketch will be created on the plane designated by this option automatically. Figure 2.5 shows the option for controlling the sketch behavior for new parts.

FIGURE 2.5
Setting the Sketch On
New Part Creation
option

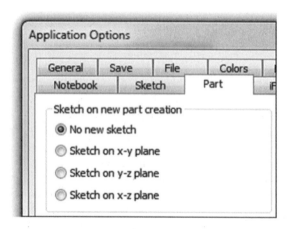

In the following steps, you will create a simple sketch to use as the base for your part. If the option for controlling the sketch behavior for new parts was set to use one of the origin planes automatically, then you can skip these steps.

1. On the 3D Model tab, click the Start 2D Sketch button.

Inventor will temporarily turn on the origin geometry and pause for you to select one of the planes to sketch on, as shown in Figure 2.6.

FIGURE 2.6
Selecting a plane to sketch on

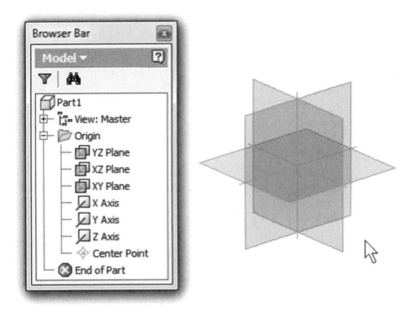

2. Expand the Origin folder in the browser and watch the selection highlight to select the XY origin plane to place your sketch on. Note that you can select an origin plane by clicking it in the browser or by selecting the edge of the plane in the graphics area.

Once you've selected a plane to sketch on, you will see a Sketch node created in the browser. The Sketch tab is now active and displays the sketch tools, as shown in Figure 2.7.

FIGURE 2.7
A new, active sketch

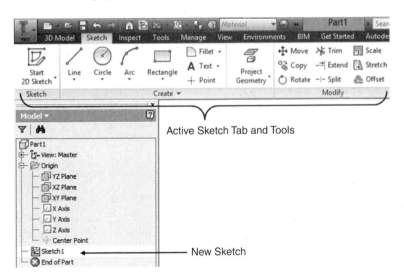

Creating a Profile in the Sketch

Now that you have a sketch created and active for editing in your new part file, you will create a profile to form the base feature of your part.

1. On the Create panel of the Sketch tab, click the Center Point Circle button.

You should see a dot in the center of your sketch; this is the projected origin center point of your part.

2. Click the dot to place your cursor on the origin center point so that the circle is centered and anchored to the origin of the part.

3. Enter **Dia = 200** for the diameter of the circle, as shown in Figure 2.8.

FIGURE 2.8
Creating a sketched circle

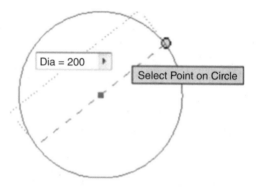

Entering Dia = 200 does two things at once. Entering 200 defines the value of this dimension parameter. Preceding it with Dia = defines the name of the parameter, making it easier to recall later.

4. Press the **Enter** key to create the circle.

5. Right-click and choose OK or Cancel to exit the Circle tool.

6. On the Sketch tab, click the Finish Sketch button to exit the sketch environment.

Creating a Base 3D Feature

Next, you'll use the circle in your sketch as the base profile for the base 3D feature for this part.

1. On the 3D Model tab, click the Extrude button.

2. Enter **25** for the extrude distance.

Note that you can enter the value in the dialog box or in the mini-toolbar controls, and each will have the same result. You might need to click the black arrow to expand the Extrude dialog box in order to see the buttons within it.

3. Click the OK button (or the green check mark button) to create the extrude feature.

Notice that an extrusion feature has been created in the browser, and if you expand it, you'll find Sketch1, as shown in Figure 2.9.

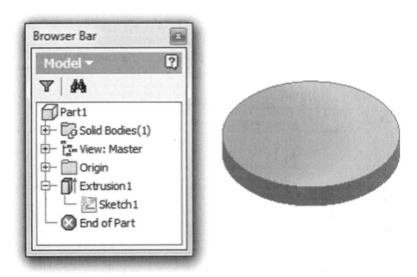

If you needed to change or add something to Sketch1, you could do so by right-clicking Extrusion1 or Sketch1 in the browser and choosing Edit Sketch. Likewise, if you wanted to modify Extrusion1, you could right-click Extrusion1 and choose Edit Feature.

Creating a Secondary 2D Sketch

Next, you'll create a new sketch on the top face of the extrusion you just created.

1. On the 3D Model tab, click the Start 2D Sketch button.

2. Click the top face of the extrusion to place the sketch.

3. On the Create panel of the Sketch tab, click the flyout arrow of the Rectangle button and then select the Two Point Center Rectangle tool, as shown in Figure 2.10.

4. Select the projected center point to place the rectangle.

5. Enter **Dia** for the first input and then press the **Tab** key on the keyboard. This will recall the value of the diameter dimension you created previously.

By reusing the diameter parameter when creating the rectangle, you are linking the diameter and the width of the rectangle. This means that if you were to change the diameter value at some point, the rectangle width would automatically adjust as well.

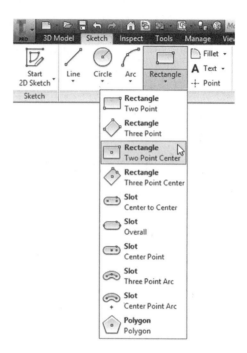

6. Enter **25** for the second input and then press the **Enter** key.

7. Right-click and choose OK or Cancel to exit the Rectangle tool.

8. Select the outer projected edge of the base feature (the circle) and then use the Construction button on the Format panel to toggle the line type to a dashed construction line.

This allows Inventor to ignore the circle as a profile boundary in the steps to come. Figure 2.11 shows the circle being set to a construction line.

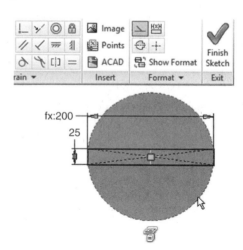

9. When your sketch looks like Figure 2.12, click the Finish Sketch button to exit the sketch environment.

FIGURE 2.12
The finished sketch

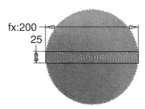

Creating a Secondary 3D Feature

Next, you'll cut a dovetailed slot from the part using the sketch created in the previous steps. If you did not complete the steps up to this point, you can open the file mi_2a_001.ipt, located in the Chapter 02 directory of your Mastering Inventor 2016 folder.

1. On the 3D Model tab, click the Extrude button.

2. If needed, click the black arrow to expand the Extrude dialog box in order to see the buttons within it. Enter **10** for the extrude distance.

Recall that you can enter the value in the dialog box or in the mini-toolbar controls, and each will have the same result.

3. In the Extrude dialog box, click the Cut button to ensure that the rectangle is cut from the base feature (or set the Solution drop-down to Cut in the mini-toolbar controls).

4. If necessary, change the extrude direction using the orange plane and black arrow icon buttons.

5. Click the More tab in the dialog box and enter **12** for the taper angle.

6. Click the OK button (or the green check mark button) to create the extrude feature.

Notice that another extrusion feature for this dovetailed cut has been created in the browser; if you expand it, you'll find Sketch2, as shown in Figure 2.13.

FIGURE 2.13
The dovetail
cut extrusion

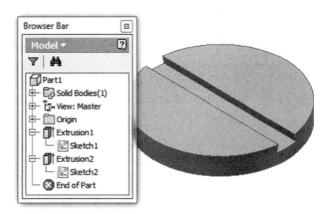

Patterning a 3D Feature

Next, you'll pattern the dovetailed slot to create a second, cross slot. If you did not complete the steps up to this point, you can open the file mi_2a_002.ipt located in the Chapter 02 directory of your Mastering Inventor 2016 folder.

1. On the 3D Model tab, find the Pattern panel and click the Circular Pattern button.

2. For the Features selection, click Extrusion2 in the browser list.

3. Right-click and choose Continue to switch from the Features selection mode to the Rotations Axis selection mode (or you can click the red arrow in the dialog box).

4. Click the outer face of the part to use the cylindrical surface as the rotation axis.

5. Enter **2** for the count.

6. Enter **90** for the angle.

Figure 2.14 shows the Circular Pattern dialog box at this point.

FIGURE 2.14
The patterned dovetail slot

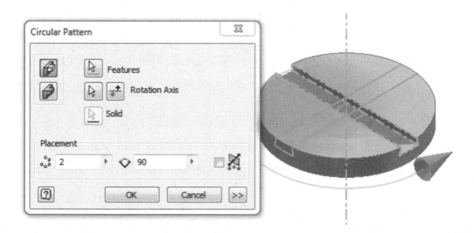

7. Click the OK button to create the pattern feature.

This concludes the creation of this basic part model. Although this model is somewhat simple, it demonstrates the workflow used to create much more complex part models. Keep in mind that for the majority of the part models you will use this workflow:

1. Create a new file using an Inventor *.ipt file template.

2. Create basic profiles using sketch tools to define the shape of the features that make up the part.

3. Use the sketched profiles to create the 3D features that will define the parts.

🌐 **Real World Scenario**

EXPLORE DESIGN ITERATIONS USING SAVE COPY AS

Often when you are designing a part file, you might come to a point in your design at which you want to explore a design idea, without altering your current design. You can do this in Inventor by using the Save Copy As option to save a reserved copy of your current work while still continuing to work on the current file.

The steps to use the Save Copy As option are described here:

1. Click the Inventor button at the top left of the screen.

2. From the drop-down menu, select Save As.

3. From the Save As flyout menu, select Save Copy As.

4. Give the file a name that represents the stage of the design, such as `mi_2a_002_ without holes.ipt`.

Creating and Detailing Drawings of Part Models

In this section, you'll open an existing drawing and create views of a part model, and then add dimensions and annotations. In the real world, often you'll use a drawing template to create a new drawing, much as you did with the part model template. Other times, you will be editing existing drawings just as you will be doing in these steps.

Creating a Base View on a Drawing

In Inventor, drawing views are created by referencing model files. In the following steps, you'll open a part model and then create a view of it on an existing drawing. (We will discuss documenting designs in detail in Chapter 12.)

1. On the Get Started tab, click the Open button.

2. Browse for the part file `mi_2a_004.ipt` in the `Chapter 02` directory of your `Mastering Inventor 2016` folder and click Open.

If you'd like, spin the part around and take a look at it using the ViewCube or the Orbit tool. Note that this is basically the same part created earlier in this chapter, with a couple of modifications. Do not close the part; you will want to have it open in the upcoming steps.

3. On the Get Started tab, click the Open button; then browse for the drawing file `mi_2a_004.idw` in the `Chapter 02` directory of your `Mastering Inventor 2016` folder and click Open.

This is a drawing file that has been created using rather poor techniques. In the following steps, you'll clean up this file and create views of the same part file but with much better results.

4. Hover your cursor over the part on the drawing sheet, and you will see a dotted outline of the view.

5. Right-click the dotted view border and choose Delete; then click the OK button to confirm that you want to delete the view.

6. On the Place Views tab, click the Base button to create a base view.

7. Inventor will place your base view in the center of the drawing area (see Figure 2.15).

FIGURE 2.15
Base view options

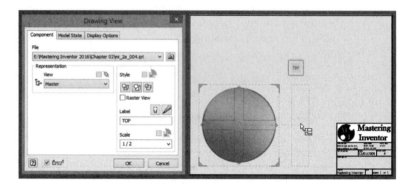

Note that all open model files are listed in the File drop-down list. You can select any open model file from the list or click the Browse button to select another file.

8. In the Scale field, enter **0.5**, or use the drop-down list to select 1/2. You can also change the view scale "in canvas" by hovering over the outer corner of the view preview. When the corner turns red and you see the scale icon, left-click and drag to change scale.

9. To change the view orientation, use the ViewCube that you can see in the view preview.

10. In the Style area, click just the middle button to create an unshaded view with no hidden lines.

11. Click OK to create the base view.

12. Hover your cursor over the view until you see a dotted outline of the view; then click and drag it to move the view to the lower left of the page so that it fits well.

Figure 2.16 shows the drawing with the base view.

FIGURE 2.16
A well-placed base view

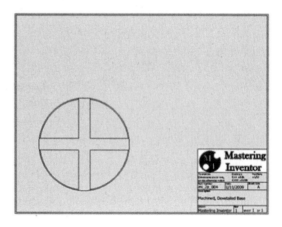

Creating Projected Views on a Drawing

Next, you'll use the base view you created to project other views onto the page. If you did not complete the previous steps, you can open the file mi_2a_005.idw located in the Chapter 02 directory of your Mastering Inventor 2016 folder.

1. On the Place Views tab, click the Projected button to create views projected from the base view.

2. Click the base view on the drawing sheet.

3. As you drag your mouse pointer around the base view, notice the view previews that are being generated.

4. Drag straight to the right and click. You will see a rectangular bounding box, indicating that a view will be placed there.

5. Drag diagonally up and to the right from the base view (toward the top-right corner of the page) and click.

6. Right-click and choose Create to generate the projected views.

7. Select the view border (dashed bounding box) of the top-right view; then right-click and choose Edit View.

8. In the Style area of the dialog box, click just the button on the right to shade the view and then click the OK button.

Figure 2.17 shows the drawing with the additional projected views.

FIGURE 2.17
Projected views

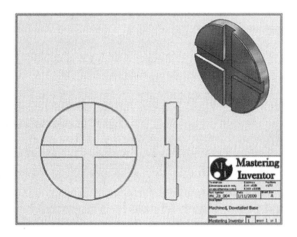

Creating Dimensions on a Drawing

Next, you'll add dimensions to the views. If you did not complete the previous steps, you can open the file mi_2a_006.idw located in the Chapter 02 directory of your Mastering Inventor 2016 folder.

1. Switch from the Place Views tab to the Annotate tab and then click the Dimension button.

2. Click any of the circular edges around the perimeter of the base view.

3. Move your cursor to the outside of the part.

Note that Inventor will give you a radius dimension if you select an arc edge, and it will default to a diameter dimension if you happen to select an edge that is a circle. Often, edges in views overlap, making it difficult to predict whether the selection will return a radius or a diameter. To deal with this, you can right-click and switch the result.

4. With the dimension still previewing at your cursor, right-click and choose Dimension Type; notice the various dimension types you can place with the current selection.

5. Choose Diameter as the type and then click on-screen to place the dimension (if the Edit Dimension dialog box appears, you can just click OK without making any edits).

6. Note that the Dimension tool is still active. Click the line on the left side of the dovetailed slot (make sure you're not clicking the green midpoint dot), and notice that the results display the length of the selected line.

7. Click the line on the right side of the dovetailed slot, and notice that the results display the distance between the two selected lines, as shown in Figure 2.18. You can click the drawing sheet to place the dimension.

FIGURE 2.18
Placing dimensions

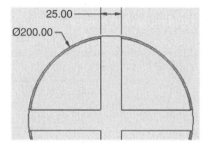

You can continue experimenting with the Dimension tool if you'd like, or you can move on to the next section and take a look at assemblies. Keep in mind that there is an entire chapter of this book devoted to the topic of creating and dimensioning drawing views, but this section ideally gave you an idea of the workflow used in Inventor to create drawings from models.

Putting Part Models Together in Assembly Files

In this section, you will explore the workflow used to create assembly models. Assembly files start out as empty container files, into which you place your part models. Once the parts are placed, you can begin to assemble them using what are known as *Assembly constraints*. Assembly constraints are simply relationships between the geometry of different parts.

In the next set of steps, you will assemble a simple mechanism composed of just a handful of parts. You can open mi_2a_180_Complete.jpg, mi_2a_180_Video.mov, or mi_2a_180_Video.mp4 in the Chapter 02 directory of your Mastering Inventor 2016 folder to take another look at the final assembly in action.

INVENTOR LT AND ASSEMBLY FILES

If you are using Inventor LT, you will not have the ability to create assembly files with your version. If you find that you need to assemble part files, you might look into upgrading to the full version of Inventor.

Placing, Rotating, and Moving Parts in an Assembly File

In the next set of steps, you will open an assembly file and place a part in it. Then you will rotate and move the free-floating or unconstrained parts around in the assembly. As you'll see, when parts are placed into an assembly, they are initially free to move and rotate in all directions.

1. On the Get Started tab, click the Open button.

2. Browse for the assembly file mi_2a_190.iam in the Chapter 02 directory of your Mastering Inventor 2016 folder and click Open.

This assembly file was created from an assembly template much like the part template you used at the beginning of this chapter. Most of the parts have been placed into the assembly. However, there is one more part that needs to be placed, and you will do this next. Once the part is added, you will take a few moments to rotate and move parts around the assembly.

3. On the Assemble tab, click the Place button (or right-click in the graphics area and choose Place Component).

4. Browse for the part file mi_2a_183.ipt in the Chapter 02 directory of your Mastering Inventor 2016 folder and click Open.

5. Click in the graphics area to place the part into the assembly.

6. Note that you have the opportunity to place another instance of the same part. In this case, though, you will right-click and choose Cancel to exit the Place Component tool.

7. Notice that the components are listed in the browser. Take a moment to click the various components, and notice that when selected in the graphics area, the component is highlighted in the browser. When selected in the browser, it is highlighted in the graphics area. To deselect components, you can just click an empty space.

TURNING ON A MISSING MODEL BROWSER

Although it isn't common to need to turn off the Model browser, you can do so. More commonly, you may accidentally turn it off by clicking the X button on the right side of the browser title bar. To display it, on the View tab click the User Interface button in the Windows panel. You'll most likely want to have all the items in this list selected except for possibly the iLogic browser.

---

8. Click the Free Rotate button on the Position panel of the Assemble tab (or press **G** on the keyboard).

9. Click any of the parts other than the large, round base part to select a part for rotating.

10. Click and drag in the center of the rotate "target" to orbit the part around.

11. Click and drag the outside of the rotate "target" to rotate the part around.

12. Click and drag one of the horizontal or vertical lines on the rotate "target" to rotate the part on that axis.

13. Click another part to set it active for rotating.

14. Click anywhere in the graphics area that is not on a part to exit the Free Rotate tool.

15. Next, click and drag any of the parts, other than the large round base part, to move the part.

Note that the large, round base part cannot be rotated or moved because it is grounded in place. If you right-click it and deselect Grounded, it will be available to rotate and move. However, it's always best to have one base part that is grounded in place to provide a stable foundation on which to build your assembly.

EDITING A COMPONENT BY ACCIDENT

If you happen to accidentally double-click a component from within an assembly file, Inventor will switch from the assembly environment to the part-editing environment. You'll be able to see that you've done this when the browser shows the other components grayed out and the 3D Model tools are displayed in the ribbon. To exit the part-editing environment and return to the assembly environment, you can right-click and choose Finish Edit, or you can click the Return button on the far right of the 3D Model tab.

As you've seen, when parts are placed into an assembly, they are initially free to move and rotate in all directions. This ability to move is referred to as the parts' *degrees of freedom*. Your goal when creating assemblies is to remove these degrees of freedom until your assembly behaves as designed. You can close this file without saving changes and continue to the next section, where you will put the parts together.

Working with Degrees of Freedom in an Assembly

As you saw in the previous section, parts are initially free to move and rotate when placed into an assembly. Next, you'll open another version of the assembly file and examine the behavior of a partially constrained part.

1. On the Get Started tab, click the Open button.

2. Browse for the assembly file mi_2a_191.iam in the Chapter 02 directory of your Mastering Inventor 2016 folder and click Open.

3. Click and drag the screw, and notice that it can move freely.

However, you'll notice that the round base part cannot move. This is because it is grounded in place. To help better visualize how under-constrained parts can move, you can turn on the degrees of freedom (DOF) icons.

4. On the View tab, click the Degrees Of Freedom button.

You'll notice that arrows and other icons are overlaid on the screw. These are the DOF indicators and are displayed to show you the remaining degrees of freedom present. Figure 2.19 shows the screw with all of its DOF icons displayed. This part can move in the x-, y-, or z-axis and can rotate around all those axes as well.

FIGURE 2.19
Six degrees of freedom

In Figure 2.20, the part has only two remaining degrees of freedom because it has been constrained to a hole. It has the ability to move in one axis and rotate around that same axis. This is because the centerline of the part and the centerline of the hole have been constrained together.

FIGURE 2.20
Two degrees of freedom

Next, you'll place an Assembly constraint to insert the unconstrained screw into the hole on the large base part.

5. On the Assemble tab, click the Constrain button (or press **C** on the keyboard).

6. In the Type area of the Place Constraint dialog box, select the Mate button (hover your cursor over the buttons to see their names).

7. Select the cylindrical face of the screw shaft for Selection 1. Notice that the highlight shows that the centerline is selected.

8. Select the cylindrical face of the hole on the large round base part for Selection 2.

9. Click the OK button in the Place Constraint dialog box to create the Mate constraint.

10. In the browser, expand the browser nodes for either of the parts, and you will see the Mate constraint you just placed listed under it.

Notice that all but two of the DOF arrow icons have been removed from the screw part in the graphics area, and the remaining icons indicate that the screw is free to rotate in the hole and slide in and out of the hole. You can click and drag the screw to confirm this.

Constraining parts to remove degrees of freedom is the way you assemble parts in an assembly file. If the goal is to create a mechanism that moves in a predictable manner, you will leave some degrees of freedom unconstrained so that those parts can still move. You can close this file and continue to explore this idea further.

Placing Assembly Constraints to Define Mechanical Movement

In this section you will place Assembly constraints between parts within an assembly file. Your goal is to constrain the parts in a way that allows the assembled mechanism to operate as it does in the video file (see mi_2a_180_Video.mov or mi_2a_180_Video.mp4).

USING MATE CONSTRAINTS TO CREATE SLIDING BEARINGS

In the following steps, you'll place Mate constraints on square bearings and the base part to create a sliding motion for the bearings:

1. On the Get Started tab, click the Open button.

2. Browse for the assembly file mi_2a_192.iam in the Chapter 02 directory of your Mastering Inventor 2016 folder and click Open.

3. Select the View tab; then click the Degrees Of Freedom button to turn on the degrees of freedom triad for each part that is not grounded or fully constrained.

4. On the Assemble tab, click the Constrain button (or press **C** on the keyboard).

5. In the Place Constraint dialog box, ensure that the Assembly tab is active and the Mate button is selected for the type. Make sure the Preview check box is selected and the Predict Offset And Orientation check box is cleared.

Here is an explanation of these two options:

Predict Offset And Orientation   This button measures the distance between the selected faces, allowing you to eyeball a part placement and then retrieve the distance. If the check box is not selected, a default of 0 is entered for the offset.

Preview   This check box, denoted by the eyeglasses icon, controls whether the selected components will adjust position or orientation so you can review the constraint before clicking Apply or OK to actually create it.

6. For Selection 1, click the blue face on one of the square bearings. Watch the onscreen highlights to be sure you select the face and not an edge. It may be helpful to zoom in.

7. For Selection 2, click anywhere on the blue *x*-shaped face of the base part, as shown in Figure 2.21.

You should see the part "snap" into place based on your selection points. This is just a preview of the constraint and is controlled by the Preview check box. To place the constraint, you need to click the Apply or OK button. Clicking the Apply button places the constraint and then leaves the dialog box open so you can place another constraint, whereas clicking the OK button places the constraint and then closes the dialog box.

FIGURE 2.21
Mate constraint selections

8. Click Apply to place the Mate constraint between the two parts.

9. Place another Mate constraint using the tapered side face of the *x*-shaped slot feature and the tapered side face of the same bearing part.

The selection order is not important, but be sure you are selecting faces, not edges, because edges will give you a different result. It might help to zoom in to select the faces. Recall that you can use the wheel button on your mouse to zoom in and out. Figure 2.22 shows the faces to be selected.

FIGURE 2.22
Tapered face selections for the second Mate constraint

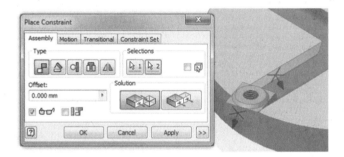

10. Once your selections are made, click the OK button to place the constraint and close the dialog box.

11. Click and drag on the bearing part to see it slide in the groove.

Notice too that the DOF icons for the bearing have changed to indicate that it can move in only one axis now.

12. Apply two more Mate constraints to the other bearing part so that it will slide in the other cross groove.

You can open the file mi_2a_193.iam to see the assembly completed at this stage and compare it to yours.

USING INSERT CONSTRAINTS TO FASTEN PARTS TOGETHER

Next, you'll constrain the remainder of the assembly using the Insert constraint. An Insert constraint places a mate between a center axis and a circular edge all at once, and it's ideal when you are constraining fasteners and other cylinder-shaped parts to holes.

You can continue using mi_2a_192.iam from the previous steps or close it and open mi_2a_193.iam in the Chapter 02 directory of your Mastering Inventor 2016 folder.

1. Select the View tab; then click the Degrees Of Freedom button to turn on the degrees of freedom triad for each part that is not grounded or fully constrained.

2. On the Assemble tab, click the Constrain button (or press **C** on the keyboard).

3. In the Place Constraint dialog box, ensure that the Assembly tab is active and then click the Insert button for the type. Make sure the Preview check box is selected and the Predict Offset And Orientation check box is cleared.

4. For Selection 1, click the circular edge of one of the bearings, as shown in Figure 2.23.

FIGURE 2.23
Selection 1 for the
Insert constraint

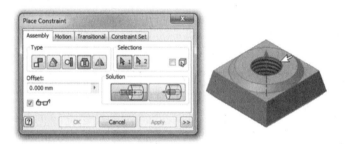

5. For Selection 2, click the circular edge of one end of the oblong link, as shown in Figure 2.24.

FIGURE 2.24
Selection 2 for the
Insert constraint

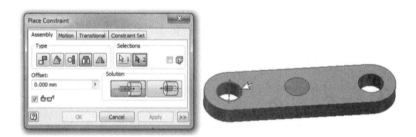

6. Click Apply to place the Insert constraint between the two parts.

7. Place another Insert constraint using the circular edge on the other bearing and the bottom edge of the oblong link.

Note that because the hole is concentric to the round end of the link, this selection is the same as the circular edge of the hole. Figure 2.25 shows the edges to be selected.

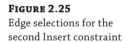

FIGURE 2.25
Edge selections for the
second Insert constraint

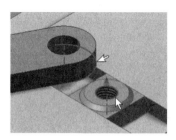

8. Once the second insert is placed, exit the Place Constraint dialog box, and test the motions of the assembly by clicking and dragging the green dot in the center of the oblong link and "tracing" the outer circular edge of the large, round base part.

To complete the assembly, place an Insert constraint between the flat washers and the holes on the top of the oblong link and then place Insert constraints between the bottom edge of the screw heads and the top of the flat washers. When you've finished, you can open the file mi_2a_194.iam in the Chapter 02 directory of your Mastering Inventor 2016 folder to compare it to your results. Then you can close all the files you have open and continue to the next section to explore the tools used to document assemblies in the 2D drawing environment.

Creating and Detailing Drawings of Assembly Models

In this section, you'll open an existing drawing and add a detail view to the sheet. Then you'll use the annotation tools to place a parts list and part number balloons in the drawing. Finally, you'll export the finished drawing as a PDF file so that it can be shared with people who do not have Inventor.

INVENTOR LT AND ASSEMBLY FILES

If you are using Inventor LT, you will not have the ability to create drawings of assembly files with your version. If you find that you need to create and detail assembly models, you might look into upgrading to the full version of Inventor.

Creating an Assembly Detail View

In the following steps, you'll open a drawing that contains a single base view of an assembly model. You'll create a detail view by referencing the existing base view.

1. On the Get Started tab, click the Open button.

2. Browse for the drawing file mi_2a_195.idw in the Chapter 02 directory of the Mastering Inventor 2016 folder and click Open.

3. On the Place Views tab, click the Detail button.

4. Click anywhere on the existing base view to use it as the basis of the new detail view. This will open the Detail View dialog box.

In the Detail View dialog box, you can adjust the View/Scale Label And Style settings as needed.

5. Set Scale to **1:1**.

6. Next, you'll create the detail boundary by clicking the existing base view. To do so, click the base view approximately in the center of the screw on the right, as shown in Figure 2.26.

7. Drag the boundary out to a size close to that shown in Figure 2.26. The goal is to encircle the screw, the washer, and the yellow bearing.

FIGURE 2.26
Placing a detail view

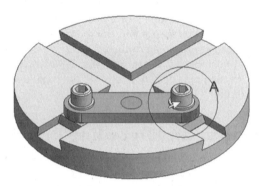

8. Click the screen to set the boundary size.

9. Move your cursor to the top left of the drawing and click the screen where you want to place the detail view.

10. Click the detail boundary on the base view, and note the six green grips. Click and drag any of the outer grips to resize the boundary, and use the center one to control the location. Make adjustments as needed to center the boundary on the area of detail.

11. Hover your cursor over the detail view on the page, and you will see a dotted outline of the view. Click and drag this border to adjust the placement of the detail view.

12. Click and drag the label text for the detail view (it will likely read "Detail A") to move it up.

Figure 2.27 shows the detail view placed on the sheet.

You can experiment with moving and resizing the detail boundary on the base view, and notice that it will automatically update the detail view. In the next section, you'll add a parts list to the drawing.

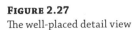

FIGURE 2.27
The well-placed detail view

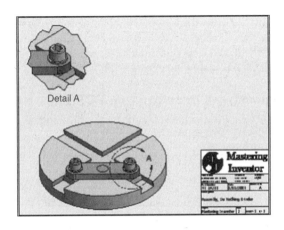

Placing a Parts List and Balloons

Next, you'll create a parts list table in the upper-right corner of the drawing and then add callout balloons. You can continue using the drawing you have open or open the file mi_2a_196.idw located in the Chapter 02 directory of your Mastering Inventor 2016 folder.

1. Switch from the Place Views tab to the Annotate tab and click the Parts List button (it's toward the right, on the Table panel).

2. The source file should already be set; if it isn't, click either the base view or the detail on the sheet to point the parts list to the assembly file.

3. Click the OK button and then snap the parts list to the top-right corner of the drawing border.

4. On the Annotate tab, click the Balloon button.

5. In the base view, select the edge of the large, round base part and move your mouse out; click once to place the balloon on the sheet, right-click, and choose Continue.

6. Repeat step 5 for each part in the detail view and then right-click again and choose Cancel to exit the Balloon tool.

You can click the balloons to adjust the placement of the balloon end or the arrowhead end if needed. Figure 2.28 shows the balloon placement.

FIGURE 2.28
Assembly part callout balloons

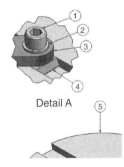

You can open the file mi_2a_197.idw in the Chapter 02 directory of your Mastering Inventor 2016 folder to compare your results. When you're satisfied with your balloon placement, you can continue to the next section to explore the steps used to export the drawing as a PDF file so that it can be emailed and viewed by others who do not have Inventor.

Exporting a Drawing to a PDF File

In the following steps, you can use the drawing file you have been working on, or you can open the file mi_2a_197.idw in the Chapter 02 directory of your Mastering Inventor 2016 folder.

1. Click the Inventor button located at the top left of the screen.

2. From the drop-down menu, select Export.

3. From the Export flyout menu, select PDF.

4. Name the file as you like and then click the Options button.

5. Select the Remove Object Line Weights option and set Vector Resolution to **600 DPI**.

Note that if the drawing happened to have multiple sheets, this is where you'd choose to include all the sheets in one PDF file.

6. Click the OK button in the PDF Drawing dialog box and then click the Save button to create the PDF in the Chapter 02 directory of your Mastering Inventor 2016 folder.

Review the PDF file, or open the file mi_2a_199.pdf located in the Chapter 02 directory of your Mastering Inventor 2016 folder to see the result of the PDF export.

The Bottom Line

Create a part model.   The process of creating a part model starts with an *.ipt template file. Once you've started a part model from a template, you create sketches to define feature profiles, and then you turn those profiles into 3D features using one of the 3D modeling feature tools.

> **Master It**   You created a base 3D feature for your parts by extruding a sketch profile at a distance of 15 mm. Then you created other sketches on the top face of the base feature. However, you now realize that the base feature should have been 25 mm thick. Can the base feature be changed after you've created other features on it?

Create and detail drawings of part models.   The process of creating a drawing file starts with an *.idw template file. Once you've started a drawing from a template, you create views of a referenced part model file. After the views are created, you can add dimensions and other annotations to the view.

> **Master It**   You've created a drawing of a part model and then realize that you need to make a change to that model. How will the change to the part model be handled by the drawing file?

Put part models together in assembly files.   The process of creating an assembly model starts with an *.iam template file. Once you've started an assembly model from a template, you place part model files into the assembly and then use Assembly constraints to arrange and assemble the part models.

Master It   You've assembled your part models in an assembly file and then need to make a change to a part-model file. How will the change to the part model be handled by the assembly file?

Create and detail drawings of assembly models.   The process of creating an assembly drawing starts with an *.idw template file, just as it did with creating part drawings. Once you've started a drawing from a template, you can create views of a referenced assembly model file. After the views are created, you can add annotations such as parts lists and callout balloons, as well as dimensions, text notes, and so on.

Master It   You've created a drawing of an assembly model and then realize that you need to make a change to one of the part files within that the assembly model. How will the change to the part model be handled by the drawing of the assembly?

Chapter 3

Sketch Techniques

This chapter will cover the principles of creating parametric sketches used in part modeling within the Autodesk® Inventor® and Autodesk® Inventor LT™ programs. All the skills discussed in this chapter are based primarily on creating a single part, whether in a single-part file or in the context of an assembly file.

Inventor utilizes two types of sketches: a 2D sketch and a 3D sketch. A 2D sketch is created on any geometry plane and is the more common of the two types. A 3D sketch is not limited to a sketch plane and can comprise geometry in any point in space. 3D sketches are often created from existing geometry. Both 2D and 3D sketches are controlled by two basic parameter types: dimensions and sketch constraints.

In Inventor, sketches are generally "roughed out" with basic geometry and sketch constraints first and then fully defined with dimensions that drive the geometry.

The dimensions dictate the length, size, and angle of the sketch geometry. For the dimensions to do this predictably, sketch objects must know how to interact with one another. This interaction is defined by the sketch constraints. This chapter will cover how to create part features using basic 2D and 3D sketches, including the tools and settings that govern their creation. Also covered is how to use Autodesk® AutoCAD® data to create sketches.

In this chapter, you'll learn to

- ◆ Set up options and settings for the sketch environment
- ◆ Create a sketch from a part file template
- ◆ Use sketch constraints to control sketch geometry
- ◆ Master general sketch tools
- ◆ Create sketches from AutoCAD geometry
- ◆ Use 3D sketch tools

Exploring the Options and Settings for Sketches

Before you jump into creating a part sketch, take a look at the options and settings Inventor provides for sketches. Options and settings in part files are located in two different areas of Inventor, depending on whether the focus of these settings affects the application (Inventor) or the document (your part file). You'll look at both application options and document options in the following sections.

If you have not already downloaded the Chapter 3 files from www.sybex.com/go/masteringinventor2016, please refer to the "What You Will Need" section of the introduction for the download and setup instructions.

Application Options

In this section you'll explore the options and settings in the application options collection. Application options change settings for your installation of Inventor. You can adjust the application settings as follows:

1. On the Tools tab, click the Application Options button.

2. Choose the Sketch tab, as shown in Figure 3.1.

FIGURE 3.1

Sketch tab of Application Options dialog box

The application options on the Sketch tab are as follows:

Constraint Settings Area   The options in this section determine the method and options involved in creating and managing 2D sketch constraints. When you click the Settings buttons, you are presented with the Constraint Settings dialog box. Note that you can also access the constraint settings by selecting the Constraint Settings button on the Constrain panel of the Sketch tab. There are three tabs in this dialog box.

   General   Use these options to set default display and behaviors for sketch constraints and dimensions. Figure 3.2 shows the General settings tab.

FIGURE 3.2
Constraint Settings dialog box

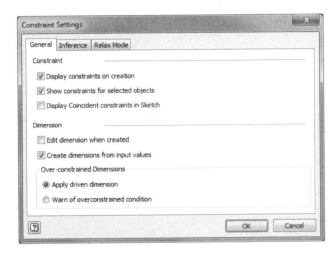

Inference Use these options to set default behaviors for inferred or automatically placed sketch constraints. Figure 3.3 shows the sketch inference settings.

FIGURE 3.3
Sketch inference settings

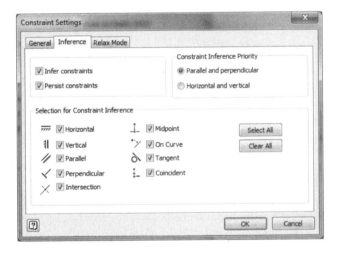

Relax Mode With the Enable Relax Mode options selected, conflicting sketch constraints are removed when you add new constraints or dimensions. Essentially this allows the last constraint placed to "win" in instances where placing a new sketch constraint conflicts with an existing sketch constraint. Figure 3.4 shows the Relax Mode tab settings.

Display Area Located in the upper-right portion of the Sketch tab, this area gives you settings for grid lines, minor grid lines, axes, and a 2D coordinate system indicator. All of these options set different visual references in the form of grid lines and coordinate indicators. You can experiment with these settings by deselecting the box next to each option and clicking the Apply button while in sketch mode.

FIGURE 3.4
Constraint relax mode

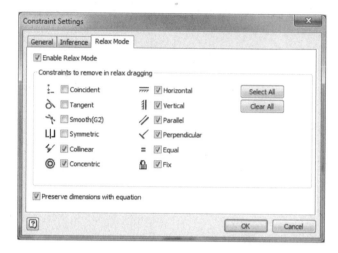

Spline Fit Method Area   This determines the initial type of transition for a spline between fit points. Figure 3.5 shows two splines drawn with the same input points. On the left, the standard spline solution is in bold with the AutoCAD solution dashed; on the right, the standard solution is dashed with the AutoCAD solution in bold.

FIGURE 3.5
Standard spline fit (left) and
AutoCAD spline fit (right)

Standard   Creates a spline with a smooth continuity (G3 minimum) between points. This spline type tends to overshoot at sharp transitions. Use this for Class A surfaces such as automotive design.

AutoCAD   Creates a spline using the AutoCAD fit method (G2 minimum). This is not used for Class A surfaces.

Minimum Energy   Sets the fit method to create a spline with smooth continuity (G3 minimum) and good curvature distribution. Multiple internal points are used between fit points, resulting in a nice, heavy curvature. This can also be used for Class A surfaces, but it takes the longest to calculate and creates the largest file size.

ABOUT CURVE CLASSIFICATION

Curves are classified by how smooth the continuity is where they connect to one another. This classification is as follows:

◆   G0 controls the position at which curves touch one another.

◆   G1 controls the tangent angle at which curves connect.

◆   G2 controls the radius at which curves connect.

◆   G3 controls the acceleration or rate of change of curves.

Snap To Grid Check Box   This allows your mouse pointer to snap to a predefined grid spacing. The grid spacing is controlled per file in the document settings, as will be discussed in the coming pages.

Autoproject Edges During Curve Creation Check Box   This allows you to reference existing geometry from your sketch plane and have that geometry automatically included in your sketch. For example, if you sketch on the top face of a part that has a hole on the bottom face, you might want to find the center of the hole to reference in your sketch, but since that hole exists on a different plane, it needs to be projected up into your current sketch before you can do so. Enabling this option allows you to "rub" your mouse over the hole and have it automatically projected into your sketch. Figure 3.6 shows a line being sketched from the middle of the cylinder to the center of a hole on the bottom face. With this option on, simply rubbing the edge of the hole will project it to the top face so that the line can be sketched to the center of the projected circle. This option can also be toggled on and off by selecting AutoProject in the context menu of most of your sketch tools, such as Line, Circle, Arc, and so on.

FIGURE 3.6
Autoprojecting a hole edge while sketching on the top face

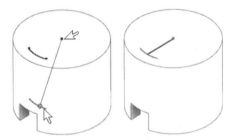

Autoproject Edges For Sketch Creation And Edit Check Box   This automatically projects the edges of the face when you create a sketch on it. Although this ability can be convenient in some cases, it can also become counterproductive because it places extra line work into your sketches. This can add a level of complexity to your sketches that is not required. Figure 3.7 shows the results of selecting this option on the left and of having this option unselected on the right.

FIGURE 3.7
Results of the Autoproject Edges For Sketch Creation And Edit check box

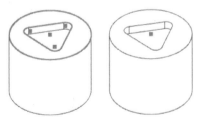

Look At Sketch Plane On Sketch Creation Check Box   This reorients the graphics window so that your view is always perpendicular to the sketch plan while you are creating or editing a sketch.

Autoproject Part Origin On Sketch Create Check Box This automatically projects the part's origin center point whenever a new sketch is created. The origin center point is point 0 in the X, Y, and Z directions. Projection of this point makes it easy to constrain and anchor your sketch. If this option is not selected, you are required to manually project this point.

Point Alignment On Check Box This allows endpoints and midpoints to be inferred by displaying temporary, dotted lines to assist in lining up sketch entities. Figure 3.8 shows an endpoint being located using the Point Alignment On option.

Certification
Objective

FIGURE 3.8
Point alignment
inferring endpoint

Enable Heads-Up Display (HUD) Check Box This allows you to input numeric and angular values directly into input boxes when creating sketch entities. For instance, if you were to sketch a circle without HUD on, you'd rough in the approximate size and then use the Dimension tool to give the circle an exact diameter. With HUD, you can specify the diameter as you create the circle. Clicking the Settings button opens the Heads-Up Display Settings dialog box, where you can adjust the HUD settings.

Auto-Bend With 3D Line Creation Check Box This allows corners to be automatically rounded when you're creating a 3D sketch. This feature can also be turned on and off via the context menu when using the Line tool in a 3D sketch. Figure 3.9 shows corners created without the auto-bend feature enabled. The default auto-bend radius size is set per file via the document settings but can be edited once the bends are created.

FIGURE 3.9
A 3D sketch line with Auto-Bend
With 3D Line Creation

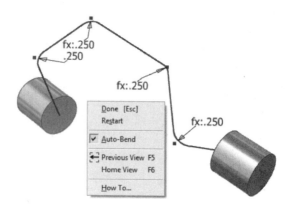

To set changes made to the application options, you can click the Apply button. You can save the changes you make to the application options for backup or distribution among other users by clicking the Export button at the bottom of the Application Options dialog box. In the resulting Save Copy As dialog box, simply specify the name of the XML file and click OK. You can import this XML file at any time to restore your custom settings by using the Import button at the bottom of the Application Options dialog box.

Document Settings

In addition to the previous settings, which are set application-wide, there are settings that control options per file. Document settings vary depending on the file type you are in. For part files, you can modify the sketch settings by clicking the Document Settings button on the Tools tab of the ribbon while you are in an open part file. Once the Document Settings dialog box is open, click the Sketch tab to access the following settings:

Snap Spacing   This sets the spacing between snap points to control the snap precision when you're sketching in the active part or drawing. This is relevant only when using the Snap To Grid option on the Sketch tab of the Application Options dialog box. The settings for the x- and y-axes can be different.

Grid Display   This sets the spacing of lines in the grid display for the active file.

Line Weight Display Options   These set the options for line weight display in the sketch environment. This setting does not affect line weights in printed model sketches, just the onscreen display.

Auto-Bend Radius   This sets the default radius for 3D sketch line corners when the auto-bend feature is used.

You may want to configure the document settings in a template file and then save those settings to that file so they are always set to your specification. To do so, click the Inventor button at the top-left corner of the screen and select Save As ➤ Save Copy As Template. This will open the template file location and allow you to save the file as a template. Note that Inventor uses the template path to designate templates rather than using the filename extension. Therefore, any IPT file saved under the template path is considered a template.

CHANGING THE UNITS OF A PART FILE

If you start a part file using the wrong template (inches instead of millimeters or millimeters instead of inches), you can change the base units of the file by clicking the Document Settings button on the Tools tab of the ribbon and selecting the Units tab. Changing the base units will automatically convert parameters but will not override parameter inputs. For instance, if you enter a value of 3 inches for a dimension and then change the units of the file to millimeters, the dimension will show 76.2 mm; however, when you edit the dimension, you will see the original value of 3 inches.

Sketching Basics

Now that you've explored the sketch options and settings, you will explore the sketching tools by placing sketches on an existing 3D part. This will give you an introduction to creating 2D sketches in 3D space. The basic workflow for creating any 2D sketch is as follows:

1. Establish the plane on which you want to sketch.

2. Project geometry from an existing feature to position new geometry.

3. Create geometry such as lines, arcs, circles, and so on.

4. Place sketch constraints on the geometry so the lines, arcs, and circles know how to relate to one another.

5. Dimension the geometry so it is fully defined and there is no part of the sketch that can be accidentally adjusted.

MARKING MENUS

Throughout this chapter, you will be instructed to right-click and select certain options as needed. If you have the marking menus enabled, some of the right-click options might vary, such as in exact placement of the option. Therefore, you should be prepared to interpret the instructions to what you see onscreen if you prefer to use the marking menus. If you prefer to have options in this chapter's exercises match exactly what you see onscreen, you can disable the marking menus and use the classic right-click context menu. This can be done by selecting the Tools tab and clicking the Customize button. On the Marking Menu tab, you will find an option called Use Classic Context Menu.

Keep this workflow in mind as you go through the following steps and explore the basics of sketch creation. To get started, you will open an existing file and sketch on the faces of the part.

Creating a Sketch on an Existing Sketch

1. On the Get Started tab, choose Open (or press **Ctrl+O** on the keyboard).

2. Browse for the file mi_3a_001.ipt in the Chapter 3 directory of your Mastering Inventor 2016 folder and click Open.

This file consists of a stepped block with one beige face, one face with two holes in it, and one face with a triangular feature on it. To start, you will create a sketch on the top, beige face. Before getting started, set your application options so you will not see any unexpected results as you follow these steps.

3. On the Tools tab, click the Application Options button.

4. In the Application Options dialog box, click the Sketch tab.

5. In the Sketch tab, ensure that all the check boxes are set as shown in Figure 3.10.

FIGURE 3.10
Setting sketch options

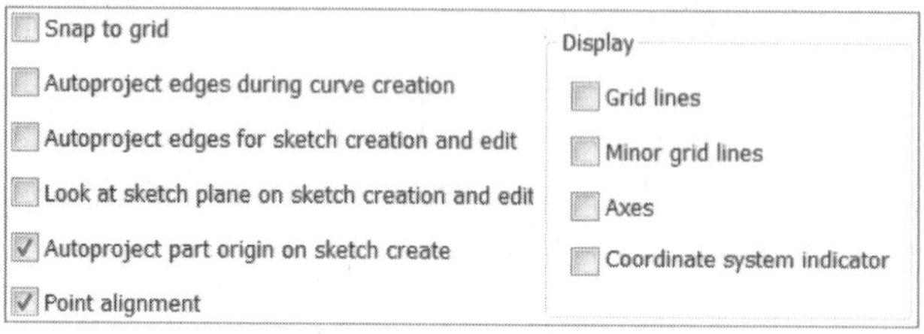

6. Click Apply, click Close to set your sketch options, and close the Application Options dialog box.

7. Hover your cursor over the ViewCube until you see the Home button (it looks like a house) and then click it to make sure you are looking at the model from the predefined home view.

8. On the 3D Model tab, click the Start 2D Sketch button.

To create a 2D sketch, you must select a plane to sketch on, as indicated by the glyph now present at your cursor (it looks like a pencil and paper). You should also note the input prompt found either at the bottom left of your screen or at your mouse pointer, depending on the Dynamic Prompting settings you have active.

9. Click the top, beige face to create the new sketch on it.

TURN ON DYNAMIC PROMPTING

As you use the various available tools, Inventor will prompt you with a short message concerning the input needed from you to complete a task. By default, the prompts are displayed at the lower left of the screen. To help you notice them better, you can set them to display onscreen at your cursor. To do so, on the Tools tab, click Application Options. Select the General tab, select the Show Command Prompting (Dynamic Prompts) check box, then click Apply, and finally click Close.

Once you've selected the face, you'll notice the change in the tools displayed on the ribbon and the activation of the Sketch tab. You should also notice that the browser has grayed out all the other features and only the new sketch (it should be named Sketch6) is active, as shown in Figure 3.11.

FIGURE 3.11
Creating a new sketch

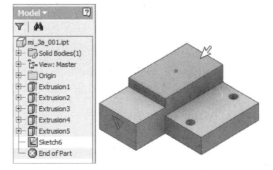

Projecting Geometry into Your Sketch

You'll also notice that a sketch point (a small dot in the center of the beige face) has been automatically created. This is the 0,0,0 origin point of the part. It has been automatically projected into your sketch because of the Autoproject Part Origin On Sketch Create setting, as shown in

Figure 3.10. Next, you'll continue with the file you've been working with and project geometry into your sketch.

1. Select the Project Geometry tool from the Sketch tab and then click somewhere in the middle of the beige face. You will now see the rectangular edges of the beige face displayed as sketch lines.

2. Right-click and choose OK or Cancel to exit the Project Geometry tool (or press the **Esc** key on the keyboard).

3. In the browser, click the plus sign next to the Sketch6 browser node. You will see a projected loop listed under the sketch, as shown in Figure 3.12.

FIGURE 3.12
A projected sketch loop

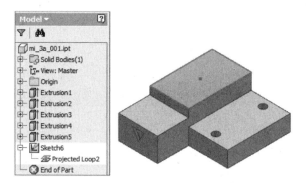

The projected loop consists of lines that trace the outer edges of the beige face. These lines were created by projecting the beige face into your sketch. These projected sketch lines are currently locked in place to always remain associative to the face from which they were created. In the next step, you will break the associative link between the projected edges and the face.

4. Right-click the projected loop in the browser and choose Break Link, as shown in Figure 3.13.

FIGURE 3.13
Break link for a projected loop

When you break the link, the projected loop node disappears in the browser, and the projected lines around the beige face change color. The color change indicates that the sketch lines are no longer associated with the face.

If you click and drag any of the projected lines, you'll notice that they can be dragged around anywhere in the sketch plane. Because the sketch plane extends past the beige face, the lines can be dragged out even beyond the extents of the face. A 2D sketch stretches out infinitely in the two directions that make up the plane. Next you'll clean up the projected lines and project more lines.

5. Hold down the Ctrl key on the keyboard and select all four of the lines. Notice the color change indicating the selection status of the lines. If you want to remove a line from the current set of selected objects, you can click it again while holding the Ctrl key. To add it back, you would click it again, still holding the Ctrl key.

6. With all four lines selected, right-click and choose Delete.

7. Select the Project Geometry tool again, and this time, select just the circular edges of the two holes found on the lower step of the part.

Watch the color-coded selection closely to ensure that you are getting just the hole edges and not the entire face the holes are on. If you choose the entire face, you will get the four rectangular edges as well as the two hole edges, and a projected loop will be created under the sketch in the browser. If you do accidentally select the face, use the Undo button on the Quick Access bar and then repeat step 7.

Since you selected just the circular edges, there is no projected loop created. However, the circles are still created so that they are associative to the holes from which they were created. This means that if the original holes change locations or diameter, the projected circles will adjust accordingly.

Another point to note is that when you project the edges of the holes into your sketch, they are projected up onto the sketch plane even though the holes are at a lower elevation. To see this clearly, you can use the ViewCube to adjust your viewing angle.

8. Click the face of the ViewCube labeled Front, and you will be able to see that the projected hole edges are in the same plane as the beige face on which you created your sketch.

9. Click the Home button on the ViewCube to set your view back to the home view.

10. Right-click and choose OK or Cancel to complete the project geometry command.

Breaking Links to Projected Geometry

Next, you'll continue working with the same file and will break the link with the projected circles and the holes from which they were created. Since no projected loop was created when you projected just the edges, there is no projected loop node listed under the Sketch node in the browser. Projected loops are created only when faces are selected. Instead, you will break the link by selecting the circles in the graphics area:

1. Right-click one of the circles and choose Break Link from the context menu. The circle will change color, indicating it is no longer associative to the hole and, therefore, no longer constrained in place.

2. Click the nonassociative circle and notice that you can resize it by clicking and dragging the circle itself, and you can move the circle by dragging the center point.

Deleting a Sketch

In the next steps, you will exit the current sketch and then delete the entire sketch. Deleting sketches from the browser is a common task, and understanding how to remove unneeded sketches is an important concept in learning how to manage sketches in the Model browser. Follow these steps, using the same file you've been using:

1. Click the Finish Sketch button on the Sketch tab (or right-click and choose Finish 2D Sketch). Notice that the Sketch node is no longer highlighted in the browser and the Sketch tab has disappeared, leaving the 3D Model tab active.

2. Right-click the Sketch6 node in the browser and choose Delete. You will notice that the Sketch node is removed from the browser, and therefore the projected circles are removed from the graphics area.

Creating Another New Sketch

Next, you'll create a new sketch on the face with the triangular cut in it. Rather than using the Start 2D Sketch button as you did before, you will create the sketch through the context menu.

1. Right-click the face with the triangular cut in it and then choose New Sketch, as shown in Figure 3.14.

FIGURE 3.14
Creating a sketch from
the context menu

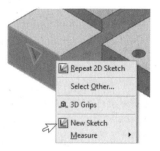

You will see the new Sketch node created in the browser, the Sketch tab appear in the ribbon, and the projected origin point appear in the sketch (the dot in the center of the triangle).

2. Click the face labeled Front on the ViewCube to set your view perpendicular to the sketch plane.

3. Select the Center Point Circle tool from the Create panel of the Sketch tab.

4. Click to the left of the model to set the center of the circle and then move the mouse out to draw the circle, as shown in Figure 3.15. Then type **100** in the Heads-Up Display input box and press the **Enter** key on the keyboard to set the diameter. (If you do not see the Heads-Up Display input, check your settings against those shown in Figure 3.10.)

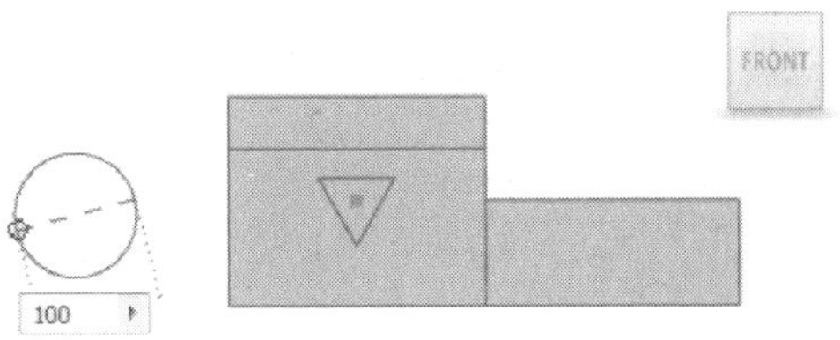

FIGURE 3.15
Placing a circle in the sketch

5. Select the Project Geometry tool from the Sketch tab and then select the face with the triangular cutout.

Creating Dimensions

You can use sketch dimensions to specify the size and position of your sketch entities. Keep in mind that Inventor's sketch dimensions are used to "drive" the sketched objects into shape and into position. Using dimensions in this way allows you to specify the intent of your design and manage it with dimensional parameters. Continue following these steps using the same file you've been working with:

1. Select the Dimension tool from the Sketch tab and then click the projected bottom point of the triangle and the center point of the circle. Move your cursor down until you see the dimension.

2. Click the screen to set the dimension and then enter **150** into the input box; click the green check mark to apply the input.

You will see that the circle is "driven" into place and repositioned to be 150 mm from the point of the triangle. This is what is meant by a driving dimension. The circle's position is driven by the dimension.

3. With the Dimension tool still active, select the center point of the circle and then the horizontal line of the triangle and move your cursor to the left until you see the dimension.

4. Click the screen to set the dimension and then enter **150** into the input box; click the green check mark to apply the input.

5. Right-click and choose Cancel to exit the Dimension tool.

At this point, your sketch should be fully constrained, as noted in the lower right of the screen, and it should resemble Figure 3.16.

FIGURE 3.16
The circle dimensioned in the sketch

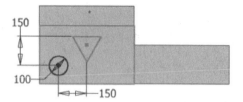

6. Use the Finish Sketch button to exit the sketch.

7. Click the Home button on the ViewCube to set your view back to the home view.

EDIT DIMENSIONS WHEN CREATED

There is an option that controls the behavior related to the creation of new dimensions and the automatic display of the dimension edit box. If you go to the Tools tab on the ribbon, click the Application Options button, and then select the Sketch tab, you will see a Settings button in the Constraint Settings area. When you click this button, you will find an Edit Dimension When Created check box in the Dimension area of the General tab. Typically this check box is selected.

This concludes the steps in this introductory exercise. You should now be familiar with the basics of creating sketches on existing part faces and projecting existing geometry, as well as deleting geometry and sketches. You can close the file without saving changes or experiment with this part and create more sketches just for fun.

As you create 2D sketches in Inventor, you will often do so by selecting a face on the existing model, as you did in this exercise. If no plane exists, you can create what is called a *work plane* and sketch on it (work planes will be covered in the next chapter). In the next section, you will create a new part from a template file and create a base sketch.

Creating a Sketch in a New Part

When you create a new part file from a template, Inventor can create the first sketch for you on one of the origin planes. You can also configure Inventor not to create the initial sketch and allow you to create it yourself. This option is set by going to the Tools tab and clicking the Applications Options button and then clicking the Part tab. In the following exercises, you will create a new part file and further explore the tools used to create sketch entities. To create a part model in Inventor, you will typically start with a 2D sketch and build a base feature from that sketch.

Creating a New Part File from a Template

You create new part files from an IPT template. Once you open the IPT template, you will automatically be in the sketch environment. In this exercise, you will use the Standard(mm).ipt file.

To explore sketch fundamentals in the next exercise, you should disable the HUD tools on the Sketch tab of the Application Options dialog box. The HUD tools allow you to place dimensions as you create sketch geometry rather than having to go back and place dimensions later. Although the HUD tools are helpful and you will most likely want to turn them back on later, for the purpose of understanding sketch constraints and degrees of freedom, it is best to leave the dimensioning as a final step.

To disable the HUD tools, click Application Options on the Tools tab. Select the Sketch tab and uncheck the box labeled Enable Heads-Up Display (HUD). You can turn this helpful feature back on later, but understand that the following steps assume it is disabled and your results may not match the exercise otherwise.

To create a new file from a template, follow these steps:

1. On the Tools tab, click the Application Options button.

2. Select the Part tab and set the Sketch On New Part Creation option to Sketch On X-Y Plane; then click the OK button to close the Application Options dialog box.

3. On the Get Started tab, click the New button. This will bring up the list of templates in the New File dialog box.

4. In the New File dialog box, select Metric from the list on the left and then select the Standard(mm).ipt button (see Figure 3.17).

5. Click Create to create a new part file based on this template.

FIGURE 3.17
Templates on the Metric tab

Creating Lines Using the Line Tool

Your screen should now show the Sketch tab set active on the ribbon, and a sketch called Sketch1 has been created and set current in the Model browser. In the following steps, you will create simple geometry using the Line tool. These steps will focus on the creation of 2D sketch constraints as well.

1. Pause your mouse pointer over the Line tool in the Sketch tab's Create panel. (See Figure 3.18 for the location of the Line tool.)

FIGURE 3.18
Locating the Line tool
on the Sketch tab

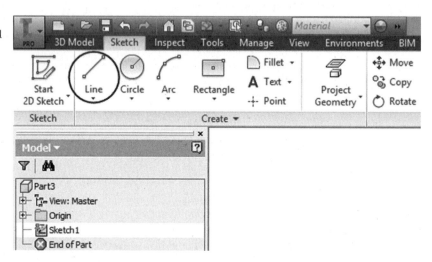

2. Note the tool tip that appears, providing the tool name, keyboard shortcut (in this case L), and a brief description of the tool. If you hover the pointer over the tool long enough, a second stage of the tool tip appears with a more detailed description.

3. Click the Line button to start the Line tool.

4. Hover your mouse pointer over the dot in the center of the drawing area. This is the 0,0,0 origin point that has been automatically projected into Sketch1.

Note that when your mouse pointer moves over the dot, the dot changes to green and shows a small glyph symbol. This green dot is a snap symbol indicating that a point, endpoint, or midpoint has been located. The glyph symbol indicates that a sketch constraint is being placed. In this case, it is a Coincident constraint, which ensures that the endpoint of the line will stay coincident to the projected origin point. See Figure 3.19 for reference.

FIGURE 3.19
Endpoint snap symbol
and coincident glyph

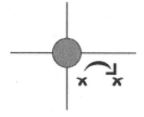

5. Start your line on this point by clicking the dot and releasing the mouse button.

6. Move your mouse pointer directly to the right, and you will see another glyph indicating that a Horizontal sketch constraint is being placed. The Horizontal constraint ensures that the line will stay positioned horizontally. Note that if you move your mouse pointer so that the line is being drawn at an angle, the glyph disappears.

TURNING ON THE PROJECTED ORIGIN POINT

If you do not see a sketch center point in your file, close the file and follow these steps to turn this option on:

1. On the Tools tab, click Application Options.

2. Choose the Sketch tab.

3. Select the Autoproject Part Origin On Sketch Create check box.

4. Click OK.

5. Start a new file using the Standard(mm).ipt template.

---

7. Notice the status bar at the bottom of the screen indicating the length and angle of the line as you move the mouse pointer. Click the graphics window while the horizontal glyph is displayed to create a line roughly 45 mm long (the length is shown at the bottom right of the screen).

Don't worry about getting an exact length. You will set the precise length later; for now, you are just "roughing in" a general shape. Note that the line continues when the first line segment is placed, and you can add more segments as required.

TEMPORARILY DISPLAYED CONSTRAINT GLYPHS

If you see a gray temporarily displayed horizontal constraint glyph above the line at this point, this is because of the setting found by going to the Tools tab, clicking the Applications Options button, clicking the Sketch tab, and then clicking the Settings button in the Constraint Settings area. On the General tab you'll see the Display Constraints On Creation option, which controls this.

---

8. Move your mouse pointer straight up to add another line segment, and note that another glyph appears at the mouse pointer. This is a perpendicular glyph indicating that a sketch constraint is being placed that will hold the first and second line segments perpendicular (see Figure 3.20 for reference).

FIGURE 3.20
Creating a vertical line with an automatic Perpendicular constraint

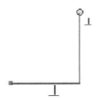

9. Click the graphics window to create the second segment at roughly 45 mm long and perpendicular to the first segment.

10. Right-click and choose Cancel to exit the Line tool. Note that the Esc key will also exit the active tool, as indicated in the context menu.

You should now have a single horizontal line and a single vertical line making a backward L shape. If you made a mistake, simply use the Undo button at the top of the screen (or press **Ctrl+Z**) to undo and try again. Leave this file open for use in the next set of steps.

Certification Objective

Understanding Sketch Constraints

The glyphs you were observing while creating the line segments were indicators that Inventor was placing sketch constraints automatically as you were sketching the lines. By default, the sketch constraints have their visibility turned off. To see the sketch constraints that are present and how they work, continue with the following steps:

1. Right-click anywhere in the graphics window other than on the lines and choose Show All Constraints (or press **F8** on the keyboard). You will now see the Sketch Constraint icons for the constraints that were inferred as you created the line segments.

2. Hover your mouse pointer over the Perpendicular constraint at the corner of the two line segments to see both lines highlighted, which indicates that these are the objects involved in this particular constraint definition.

3. Hover your mouse pointer over the yellow dot at the corner of the two line segments, and you will see two Coincident constraints appear, as shown in Figure 3.21. Hovering your mouse pointer over each will highlight the line to which it belongs. Coincident constraints are initially "rolled up" in this way because they are generally numerous and tend to clutter the sketch when all constraints are shown.

FIGURE 3.21
Showing constraints

WHEN IN DOUBT, RIGHT-CLICK

Inventor is very right-click-driven, meaning that often you can find the option you are looking for by right-clicking the object you are dealing with.

In Inventor, the right-click context menus are specific to the objects you have selected. If no objects are selected, right-clicking gives you the default context menu.

Unlike in some other applications, the Esc key does not clear selected onscreen entities in the graphics area. Instead, you can click any blank area in the graphics area to make sure you have nothing selected before right-clicking. This way you can be certain the context menu you get is not specific to an accidentally selected object.

4. Click the X on any of the constraints to hide just that particular constraint.

5. Next, right-click anywhere in the graphics area other than on the lines and choose Hide All Constraints (or press **F9** on the keyboard). You can toggle the visibility of all sketch constraints on and off as needed to determine how sketch entities are constrained together.

6. Select the corner point of the two line segments and hold down and drag around in a circle. You will notice that the horizontal line will stretch as required but will always remain horizontal; the vertical line will always remain perpendicular.

7. Select the uppermost endpoint of the vertical line and drag around in a circular motion. Note that the two lines will adjust lengths as permitted but will always honor the sketch constraints they have placed on them.

8. Let up on the end of the line and press **F8** to show the constraints again.

9. Right-click the Horizontal constraint.

10. Choose Delete to remove this constraint.

11. Press **F9** to hide the constraints again.

12. Click the corner of the lines and hold down and drag around in a circular motion. Note that the lines will stretch and adjust orientation but will maintain their perpendicular and coincident relationships.

At this point, the constraints present in your sketch were all inferred (placed automatically). Letting Inventor infer sketch constraints is the quickest and often most desirable way to place them; however, sometimes you'll need to constrain sketch elements manually. To do so, you can use the constraint tools in the Constrain panel of the ribbon.

To place the Horizontal constraint back on the line from which you removed it, follow these steps:

1. On the Constrain panel of the ribbon, click the Horizontal Constraints icon (Figure 3.22).

FIGURE 3.22
Placing a Horizontal
constraint manually

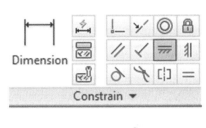

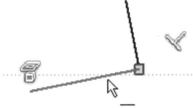

2. Click the first line segment you sketched to set it back to horizontal. Be careful to select the line itself and not the midpoint of the line (the midpoint shows as a green dot when selected).

Use the Line tool to add three more line segments to the sketch to complete the shape, as shown in Figure 3.23. Pay attention to the cursor glyphs as you sketch, and do not be concerned with the precise lengths of the lines or the angle of the diagonal line. You can keep this file open for use in the next set of steps or close it and use the file provided.

FIGURE 3.23
Completed sketch profile with all constraints shown

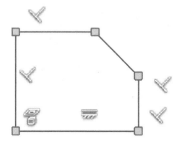

CONSTRAINT INFERENCE AND PERSISTENCE

You can suppress the automatic placement of sketch constraints (constraint inference) temporarily by holding down **Ctrl** on the keyboard as you sketch. You can disable constraint inference and persistence permanently by clicking Sketch Tab > Constrain Panel > Constraint settings Button, navigating to the Inference tab and un-checking Infer Constraints and Persist Constraints. If constraint persistence is disabled, you will still see the Constraint Glyph icon when sketching, and you will be able to place sketch entities in accordance with the displayed glyph; however, no actual constraint will be placed on the sketched object. For instance, sketching a line that is oriented perpendicular to an existing line without actually having a Perpendicular constraint placed automatically is possible by toggling off the constraint persistence. Coincident constraints at the endpoints of the lines will still be placed.

Constraint persistence is automatically disabled if constraint inference is turned off, but inference can be on with persistence turned off.

Using Degrees of Freedom to View Underconstrained Sketch Elements

Typically, your goal is to create fully constrained sketches so that no aspect of the sketch can be changed without deliberate action. To examine your sketch for underconstrained elements, you can use the Degrees of Freedom (DOF) tool. To explore DOF, you can use the file you have been working with in the previous steps or open the file mi_3a_002.ipt from the Chapter 3 directory of your Mastering Inventor 2016 folder. Make sure Sketch1 is active for edits by right-clicking it and choosing Edit Sketch. Then follow these steps:

1. To view the DOF arrows for your sketch entities, right-click anywhere in the graphics area that is not on a sketch object and choose Show All Degrees Of Freedom. Your sketch should resemble Figure 3.24.

FIGURE 3.24
Showing the degrees of
freedom in a sketch

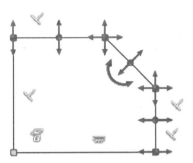

2. Notice the arrow indicators showing the DOF for each sketched line.

3. Drag a line endpoint, and you will see that the sketch lines will drag only in a direction or orientation that follows the DOF arrows. If your sketch becomes distorted in an undesirable way, use the Undo button at the top of the screen or press **Ctrl+Z** to set it back as it was.

DRAGGING TO REFINE YOUR SKETCH

Experienced Inventor users rely on the click-and-drag technique to fine-tune the general shape of a sketch rather than trying to get things precisely right from the beginning. Become familiar with this technique so you can use it to your advantage.

---

4. To toggle the DOF visibility back off, right-click again and choose Hide All Degrees Of Freedom.

5. Note that you can right-click an individual sketch object or a selection set of sketch objects and choose Display Degrees Of Freedom to show the DOF for just those selected objects.

6. Right-click and choose Show All Degrees Of Freedom again to have these displayed for reference in the next steps.

Using Dimensions to Fully Constrain a Sketch

To work toward your goal of a fully constrained sketch, you will now add dimensions to lock down lengths, angles, and so on. Adding dimensions will remove degrees of freedom from your sketch objects and help you define the intent of your design. You will use the General Dimension tool to place dimensions on your sketch. Note that although the tool is called General Dimension, the button simply reads Dimension.

You can continue with the file you are working or open the file mi_3a_002.ipt from the Chapter 3 directory of the Mastering Inventor 2016 folder. If you're opening the prepared file, ensure that Sketch1 is active for edits by right-clicking it and choosing Edit Sketch; then right-click and choose Show All Degrees Of Freedom. After that, follow these steps:

1. On the Sketch tab of the ribbon, click the Dimension button in the Constrain panel.

2. In the graphics area, click the bottom horizontal line and move down to display the dimension.

3. Click below the line to place the dimension; you should see an Edit Dimension box, as shown in Figure 3.25. If you do not see the Edit Dimension box, you can right-click anywhere in the blank space of the graphics area and click Edit Dimension to ensure that this box shows up after each dimension is placed. Then simply click the dimension to open this input box.

FIGURE 3.25

Placing a dimension on the sketch

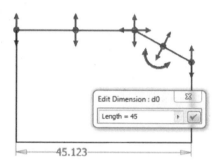

4. In the Edit Dimension dialog box, type **Length = 45**. Because you are working in a millimeter-based part file, the units are assumed to be 45 mm, and Inventor will add the mm automatically.

Notice that the Edit Dimension box caption reads something such as d0. This indicates that this dimension parameter is named d0. Initially, Inventor names the first dimension used in the file d0, the next is named d1, and so on. By entering **Length = 45**, you are renaming the dimension from d0 to Length and changing this length value from the sketched value to a precise value of 45 mm. You are not required to rename your dimensions, but it is good practice to name any that you intend to reference later.

5. Click the green check mark in the Edit Dimension box, or press the **Enter** key to set the dimension value. Take note that the dimension "drives" the sketch line to be 45 mm long. Also notice that some of the DOF arrows have been removed.

6. Click the 45 mm dimension to edit it. Notice that the Edit Dimension box caption now reads Length, and the value now reads 45 mm.

7. Change the value to **50 mm** and click the green check mark.

8. Click the bottom horizontal line again and move up, but do not click to place the dimension. You will see the same horizontal dimension displayed.

9. Click the top horizontal line and move down; you will see the dimension change from the horizontal dimension evaluating the length of the bottom line to a vertical dimension evaluating the distance between the top and bottom lines.

10. Click in the graphics area to place the dimension.

11. Enter **Width =**.

12. Click the 50 mm dimension you placed in the previous steps. Notice that clicking one dimension while editing another will create a reference between the two.

13. Complete the formula to read **Width = Length/2**, as shown in Figure 3.26.

FIGURE 3.26
Referencing one
parameter to another

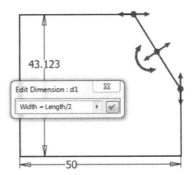

14. Click the green check mark or press the **Enter** key to set the dimension value. Observe that the Width dimension is evaluated at half the Length dimension and that it displays an *fx:* before the value to denote that there is a function used to evaluate this dimension. Also notice that more DOF arrows have been removed as you have further defined the sketch.

15. If your sketch has become a bit skewed, exit the Dimension tool by right-clicking and choosing Cancel (or by pressing the **Esc** key).

16. Click the top endpoint of the vertical line to the right and drag it so that the general shape of the profile is restored.

17. On the Sketch tab of the ribbon, click the Dimension icon in the Constrain panel, or just press **D** on the keyboard to start the Dimension tool again.

18. Click the vertical line to the right and then click the diagonal line. Take care to click the lines and not the endpoints of the lines because clicking the endpoints will result in a different dimension type.

19. Click in the graphics area to place the dimension. You will be presented with an edit box for an angle dimension. Enter **Angle1 = 108** and click the green check mark.

20. Last, on the Sketch tab of the ribbon, click the Equal button in the Constrain panel to place an Equal constraint. Select the top horizontal line and the vertical line on the right to set those two lines equal, as shown in Figure 3.27.

Your sketch is now fully constrained and should resemble Figure 3.28.

FIGURE 3.27
Applying an equal constraint

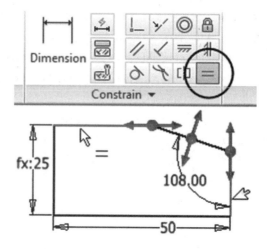

FIGURE 3.28
A fully constrained sketch

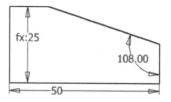

A fully constrained sketch is evident by taking note of the following:

◆ All the DOF arrows are now gone.

◆ You will see *Fully Constrained* in the status bar at the bottom right of the screen.

◆ Your sketch lines will have turned a different color than they were originally, before the sketch became constrained.

◆ A "thumb tack" appears (upper left) on the Browser Sketch icon once the sketch is fully constrained.

Understanding the Save Options

At this point, you may have seen a save reminder balloon in the top-right corner of the screen. It is always good practice to save often when working in any application. To save a part file, you must first exit the sketch and then save.

1. On the ribbon's Sketch tab, click Finish Sketch in the Exit panel. Or right-click in the graphics area and choose Finish 2D Sketch from the menu.

2. Click the Inventor button and then select Save.

3. Select your Chapter 3 folder and name the file **mi_001**.

You should be aware of all the save options you have and how they differ. They can all be accessed by clicking the Inventor button and choosing Save or Save As from the Application menu. Here's a list:

Save   Choosing this option saves the active document contents to the file specified in the window title, and the file remains open.

Save All   Choosing this option saves all open document contents to the file specified in the window title, and the files remain open.

Save As   Choosing this option saves the active document contents to the file specified in the Save As dialog box. The original document is closed, and the newly saved file is opened. The contents of the original file are unchanged.

Save Copy As   Choosing this option saves a copy of the active file as specified in the Save Copy As dialog box, and the original file remains open.

Save Copy As Template   Choosing this option saves a copy of the active file as a template to the template folder, and the original file remains open.

ADJUSTING THE SAVE OPTIONS

Inventor does not have an automatic save function but instead has a save reminder utility that allows you to save by just clicking within the bubble to launch a standard save operation. To adjust the save timer settings, click the Application Options button and then select the Save tab.

Making a Sketch Active for Edits

To save a file, you are required to exit the sketch. To continue making edits to the sketch once it's saved, you need to set the sketch active for edits. Here's how to activate the sketch:

1. Locate Sketch1 in the Model browser to the left of your screen and either right-click and choose Edit Sketch or double-click the Browser Sketch icon.

2. Notice that the Sketch node listed in the browser consists of the Sketch icon and the sketch name. Clicking the sketch name once and then again (don't double-click) allows you to rename the sketch. Therefore, you may want to develop a habit of double-clicking the Sketch icon rather than the sketch name to make a sketch active for edits.

Look at the browser and notice that the rest of the browser nodes are grayed out and Sketch1 is highlighted, letting you know that the sketch is active for editing. You'll also notice that the sketch tools are available.

Using Construction Geometry

Now that the sketch is active, you will add more geometry and dimensions to further explore the sketch tools. You'll start by sketching a line and then converting that line to a construction line. Construction geometry is often used to help locate and constrain normal sketch geometry.

The primary difference between construction geometry and standard geometry is that construction geometry is filtered out of profile calculations. In other words, if you have a part profile consisting of a rectangle and you run a construction line down the middle of it, resulting in two halves of the original profile, Inventor will ignore the construction line and see only one profile when you create a solid part from the sketch. To create a construction line in your sketch, follow these steps:

1. Click the Line tool in the Sketch tab's Create panel. (Recall that you can access the Line tool by pressing the **L** key on the keyboard as well.)

2. Start the line at the bottom-left corner of the profile, keeping an eye on your mouse pointer to ensure that you see the green dot (indicating the endpoint) and the constraint glyph (indicating that a Coincident constraint is being inferred).

3. Set the second point of the line on the midpoint of the diagonal line. Again, you should see a green dot and a coincident glyph, as shown in Figure 3.29.

FIGURE 3.29
Placing a construction line showing steps 2 and 3

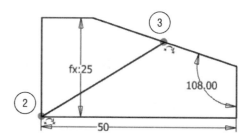

4. Right-click and choose Cancel to exit the Line tool.

5. Select the new diagonal line you just created.

6. On the Sketch tab (to the far right), click the Construction icon in the Format panel to set the diagonal line as a construction line, as shown in Figure 3.30.

FIGURE 3.30
Converting to a construction line

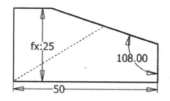

Notice that the line has changed from a solid line to a dashed line, indicating that it is now a construction line. If you were to turn this sketch into a 3D solid at this point, Inventor would not recognize the construction line as a boundary and would therefore see only one profile from which to create the solid. However, if you had not made the diagonal line a construction line, Inventor would see two profiles, one on each side of this diagonal line.

Using the Polygon Tool and Creating an Aligned Dimension

Next, you will need to add a polygon to the midpoint of the construction line and manually place a constraint to position it in place. You will then need to place a dimension to size it.

1. In the Sketch tab's Create panel, click the Polygon tool (found in the Rectangle flyout menu).

2. Select the midpoint of the diagonal construction line, keeping an eye on your mouse pointer for the green midpoint dot and the coincident glyph.

3. Leave the polygon settings at the defaults and move your cursor out until the size and orientation roughly match Figure 3.31. Click once to finish creating the polygon.

FIGURE 3.31
Creating a polygon

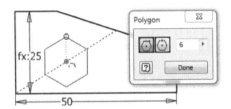

4. In the Sketch tab's Constrain panel, click the Parallel Constraint icon.

5. Choose any of the flats on the polygon and the diagonal profile line, as shown in Figure 3.32, to make the two lines parallel.

FIGURE 3.32
Setting the two edges
to be parallel

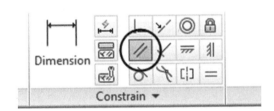

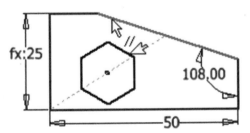

6. In the Sketch tab's Constrain panel, click the Dimension tool.

7. On the polygon, click two opposing points to create a dimension between the two points.

8. Pull your mouse pointer to the side to preview the dimension. Notice that the orientation wants to be horizontal or vertical depending on the location of your mouse pointer.

9. Right-click and choose Aligned to force the aligned solution for this particular dimension, as shown in Figure 3.33.

FIGURE 3.33
Creating a point-to-point aligned dimension

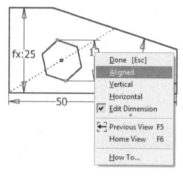

10. Click the graphics window to place the dimension.

11. Enter **Hex_Size = 0.375 in**.

12. Click the green check mark or press the **Enter** key to set the dimension value. Notice that although you entered an Imperial unit of inches, Inventor converted the value automatically to the file default of millimeters. This is a powerful function that allows you to use dimension inputs to do conversion calculations on the fly.

USING AN UNDERSCORE IN PARAMETER NAMES

When specifying parameter names, keep in mind that spaces are not allowed, but you can use underscores.

CREATING MIXED-UNIT FORMULAS

You can mix any acceptable units in the same parameter formula and allow Inventor to do the conversion. For instance, entering the following into a dimension is perfectly acceptable:

3.25 ft – 1 m + 3 cm + 0.125 in

This will return a value of 23.775 mm in a millimeter part.

Using Offset and Creating a Three-Point Rectangle

You will now use the Offset and Three Point Rectangle tools to create more sketch geometry.

1. In the Sketch tab's Modify panel, click the Offset tool.

2. Before selecting any geometry, right-click anywhere that is not on the sketch geometry.

3. Ensure that the Loop Select and Constrain Offset options are both selected.

    ◆ Selecting Loop Select means that all joined geometry will be selected as a loop. With this option toggled off, individual line or curve segments are selected.

    ◆ Selecting Constrain Offset means the new geometry is constrained to be equidistant to the original. If you turn this option off, the new geometry is created unconstrained to the original.

4. Click the polygon and move the cursor to the outside.

5. Click in the graphics window to set the offset distance.

6. Right-click and choose Cancel to exit the Offset tool.

7. In the Sketch tab's Constrain panel, click the Dimension tool (or press **D** on the keyboard).

8. To dimension the offset, select an edge of the original polygon and then select the corresponding edge on the new offset polygon.

9. Move the dimension out from the center of the polygon and place it anywhere.

10. Enter **Hex_Offset = 1/16 in** and click the green check mark. The result should appear similar to Figure 3.34.

FIGURE 3.34
The offset polygon

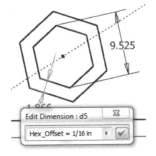

11. In the Sketch tab's Create panel, click the Rectangle flyout and choose Rectangle Three Point (Figure 3.35).

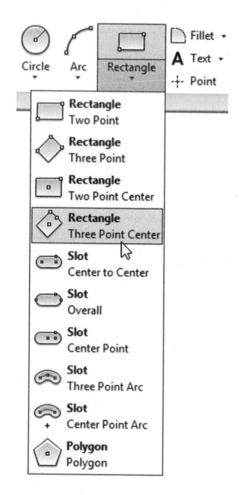

12. Create the rectangle using the three points shown in Figure 3.36. Click the top-left point first, then the top-right point, and finally the bottom-middle point. Make certain you are seeing the green snap dots and Coincident constraint glyphs at each point.

FIGURE 3.36
Placing a three-point
rectangle

13. Right-click and choose Cancel. If your rectangle is not fully constrained, click the corner and drag it away from the line and then back to the line, setting it on the line when you see the constraint glyph.

This completes the creation of most of your sketch objects in this exercise. Save your file and use it in the next set of steps. Your sketch should resemble Figure 3.37.

FIGURE 3.37
Your completed sketch

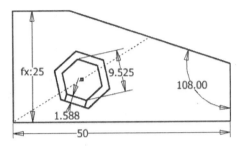

TO TRIM OR NOT TO TRIM

You can find the Trim tool in the Sketch tab's Modify panel. Although you might be tempted to use the Trim tool to tidy up the sketch, keep in mind that in Inventor you are creating solid models from these sketches, and therefore trimming "extra" lines from a sketch is not required.

More important, though, trimming these extra lines in a sketch often does more harm than good. This is because all the lines in the sketch have constraint relationships between them. When you use the Trim tool, you are inadvertently removing constraints that were holding your sketch objects together. As a rule, use the Trim tool only when necessary.

You might find the Split tool is actually what you want. Split will divide a line into separate segments without removing them. And it will also maintain sketch constraints. You can find the Split tool in the Sketch tab's Modify panel as well. Hover your mouse pointer over it for a moment, and you will get a dynamic tool tip showing you how it works.

Creating Driven Dimensions

Now you'll take a look at creating driven dimensions and editing the parameters you just created through the Parameters dialog box. Because dimensions define the parameters of your design, you can use them to control the design intent. At other times you may want to place a dimension that does not drive the design but instead is driven by other parameters. In those cases, such dimensions are called *driven* dimensions.

Unlike Inventor's standard parametric dimensions, driven dimensions do not change the geometry but instead change when the geometry changes. Driven dimensions are created either by placing a dimension on already defined geometry or by explicitly making them driven.

You can use your current file or open the file mi_3a_003.ipt from the Chapter 3 directory of your Mastering Inventor 2016 folder. If you're opening the prepared file, ensure that Sketch1 is active for edits by right-clicking it and choosing Edit Sketch. Follow these steps to explore driven dimensions:

1. Double-click the 50 mm Length dimension.

2. Replace the value of 50 with **60** and press the **Enter** key.

3. Take note that the vertical dimension retains the intent of your design and remains at half the Length value.

4. In the Sketch tab's Constrain panel, click the Dimension tool (or press **D** on the keyboard).

5. Select the vertical line on the left of the sketch and click the graphics window to place the dimension.

6. Depending on the options you have selected in the Sketch tab of the Application Options dialog box, you might be presented with a dialog box warning you that this dimension will overconstrain the sketch. If so, click Accept. In either case, you'll place the dimension as a driven dimension by clicking the screen.

Notice that the dimension is created in parentheses, denoting it is driven by other parameters and, therefore, is considered a reference parameter. Driven dimensions are useful in capturing dimensions for use in the calculations of other features.

7. Switch from the Sketch tab to the Manage tab on the ribbon.

8. Click the Parameters tool. This will open the Parameters dialog box listing all the dimensions you've created in this part as parameters, as shown in Figure 3.38.

FIGURE 3.38
Parameters dialog box

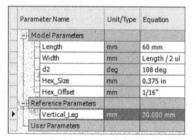

Parameter Name	Unit/Type	Equation
– Model Parameters		
Length	mm	60 mm
Width	mm	Length / 2 ul
d2	deg	108 deg
Hex_Size	mm	0.375 in
Hex_Offset	mm	1/16"
– Reference Parameters		
Vertical_Leg	mm	30.000 mm
User Parameters		

9. Enter **Vertical_Leg**, replacing d5 for the reference parameter name. Be sure to use an underscore rather than a space.

10. Still in the Parameters dialog box, change the Length value from 60 mm to **65 mm**.

If you have the Immediate Update check box selected, the dimension is automatically updated in the sketch. If not, you will need to update the dimension manually by clicking the Update button on the Quick Access bar at the top left of the screen, as shown in Figure 3.39.

FIGURE 3.39
Update button on the
Quick Access bar

11. Ensure that the Immediate Update check box is selected; then click Done to return to the sketch.

12. Right-click in the graphics area and choose Dimension Display ➢ Expression from the context menu. Observe the dimension names and expression values, as shown in Figure 3.40.

FIGURE 3.40
Displaying dimension
expressions

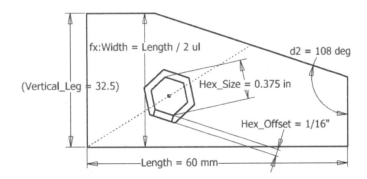

13. Right-click in the graphics area and choose Dimension Display ➤ Value from the context menu to set the dimension display back to display the calculated value.

You can leave this file open and use it in the next set of steps.

DIMENSION ARRANGEMENT

Although the arrangement of sketch dimensions is not all that important because these dimensions will ultimately be consumed by a solid model, it is still helpful to be able to read them in the sketch. You can rearrange jumbled sketch dimensions by clicking the text/numbers and dragging them as you like. Note too that this must be done once you've exited the Dimension tool because clicking a dimension with the Dimension tool active edits that dimension. You'll notice that because of the intelligence you've built into the sketch, when you modify and update the Length dimension (parameter) value, the dependent values change as well.

Next, you'll change a driving dimension to a driven dimension and a driven to a driving. By doing this, you can modify the intent of your design and change which parameter is a key input. You can use your current file or open the file `mi_3a_004.ipt` from the `Chapter 3` directory of your `Mastering Inventor 2016` folder. If you're opening the prepared file, ensure that Sketch1 is active for edits by right-clicking it and choosing Edit Sketch. Then follow these steps:

1. Click the 65 mm Length dimension.

2. In the Sketch tab's Format panel, click the Driven Dimension tool. Notice that the Length dimension is now set in parentheses, indicating that it is now driven rather than driving.

3. Click any blank area in the graphics window to deselect the previous dimension.

4. Select the vertical dimension that is in parentheses.

5. Click the Driven Dimension tool again to toggle this dimension from a driven to a driving dimension.

6. Double-click the vertical dimension to edit its value.

7. Enter **40 mm** and click the green check mark. Notice that the Vertical_Leg parameter now drives the Length parameter, which still drives the Width dimension.

You are beginning to see the power of parametric design. Next, you'll add a user parameter and use it to drive the design. A *user parameter* is a design input that is not based on the geometry in the sketch. This allows you to enter user variables to drive your design.

8. On the Manage tab on the ribbon, select the Parameters tool. This will open the Parameters dialog box.

9. Click the Add Numeric button at the bottom of the dialog box to create a new user parameter.

10. Enter **Wrench_Size** for the user parameter name.

11. Click mm in the Unit/Type column and select the inch input from the Length category.

12. Enter **0.4** for the Equation column input.

13. Edit the equation input for the Hex_Size parameter and replace 0.375 in with **Wrench_Size**.

You have now set the Hex_Size parameter to be driven by your user parameter named Wrench_Size. Your inputs should look like Figure 3.41.

FIGURE 3.41
Creating a user parameter

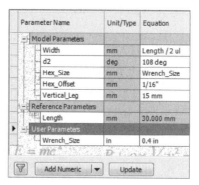

Parameter Name	Unit/Type	Equation
— Model Parameters		
Width	mm	Length / 2 ul
d2	deg	108 deg
Hex_Size	mm	Wrench_Size
Hex_Offset	mm	1/16"
Vertical_Leg	mm	15 mm
— Reference Parameters		
Length	mm	30.000 mm
User Parameters		
Wrench_Size	in	0.4 in

Add Numeric | ▼ | Update

14. Click the Done button to close the Parameter dialog box and then use the Update button to update the sketch if needed.

Now that you've been introduced to the basics of creating a parametric sketch, you'll take a more in-depth look at these tools in the next sections. You can close this file without saving the changes.

Certification
Objective

Taking a Closer Look at Sketch Constraints

In the following sections, you'll take a closer look at each of the available sketch constraints. As you proceed, it may occur to you that you could use other sketch constraints in place of the one suggested in the exercise steps. Be aware that as you create sketch constraints, there are often multiple solutions to get the same result.

In the following exercises, you will be opening a series of part files, setting the sketch as active for edits, and applying different sketch constraints. Each of these files demonstrates the function of a different type of sketch constraint. All of these files contain a sketch called

<—Double Click to Edit (Sketch 1). You will edit the sketch in each file and apply the appropriate sketch from the Constrain panel of the Sketch tab, shown in Figure 3.42.

FIGURE 3.42
Constraint tools

The Tangent Constraint

The Tangent constraint places one object or edge in a tangency to another object or edge. Objects can be tangent to each other even if they do not share a physical point. Follow these steps to explore the Tangent constraint:

1. On the Get Started tab, click the Open button (or press **Ctrl+O** on the keyboard).

2. Browse for the file mi_3h_001.ipt in the Chapter 3 directory of your Mastering Inventor 2016 folder and click Open.

3. In the Model browser, double-click Sketch1 to edit it. Or right-click it and choose Edit Sketch.

4. Press the **F8** key to show all the constraints. Note that there is no Tangent constraint between the large circle and the lines.

5. In the Sketch tab's Constrain panel, click the Tangent button. Click the line and circle, as shown in Figure 3.43.

FIGURE 3.43
Placing a Tangent constraint

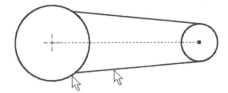

6. Repeat to set a Tangent constraint on the top line and the same circle.

7. Right-click and choose Cancel.

8. Press the **F8** key to show all the constraints and note the new Tangent constraints.

9. You can exit the file without saving once you have finished.

The Perpendicular Constraint

The Perpendicular constraint constrains objects or edges to be always perpendicular. Follow these steps to explore the Perpendicular constraint:

1. On the Get Started tab, click the Open button.

2. Browse for the file mi_3h_002.ipt in the Chapter 3 directory of your Mastering Inventor 2016 folder and click Open.

3. In the Model browser, double-click Sketch1 to edit it. Or right-click it and choose Edit Sketch.

4. In the Sketch tab's Constrain panel, click the Perpendicular button.

5. Click the vertical line, as shown in Figure 3.44, and then select either of the horizontal lines.

FIGURE 3.44
Placing a Perpendicular constraint

6. Right-click and choose Cancel.

7. Press the **F8** key to show all the constraints, noting the new Perpendicular constraint.

8. You can exit the file without saving once you have finished.

The Parallel Constraint

The Parallel constraint constrains objects or edges to be always parallel. Follow these steps to explore the Parallel constraint:

1. On the Get Started tab, click the Open button.

2. Browse for the file mi_3h_003.ipt located in the Chapter 3 directory of the Mastering Inventor 2016 folder and click Open.

3. In the Model browser, double-click Sketch1 to edit it. Or right-click it and choose Edit Sketch.

4. In the Sketch tab's Constrain panel, click the Parallel button.

5. Click the lines as shown in Figure 3.45.

FIGURE 3.45
Placing a Parallel constraint

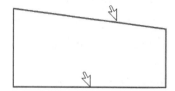

6. Right-click and choose Cancel.

7. Press the **F8** key to show all the constraints, and note the new Parallel constraint.

8. You can exit the file without saving once you have finished.

The Coincident Constraint

The Coincident constraint places objects or points in contact with another object. Follow these steps to explore the Coincident constraint:

1. On the Get Started tab, click the Open button.

2. Browse for the file named `mi_3h_004.ipt` in the `Chapter 3` directory of the `Mastering Inventor 2016` folder and click Open.

3. In the Model browser, double-click Sketch1 to edit it. Or right-click it and choose Edit Sketch.

4. In the Sketch tab's Constrain panel, click the Coincident button.

5. Click the center of the circle and then on the center point, as shown in Figure 3.46.

FIGURE 3.46
Placing a Coincident constraint

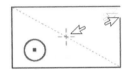

6. Right-click and choose Cancel.

7. Click the endpoint of the vertical line at the top-right corner of the rectangular shape and hold down as you drag to close the profile. Note that a Coincident constraint is placed.

8. Press the **F8** key to show all the constraints, and note the new Coincident constraints, as shown by the yellow dots.

9. Hover your mouse pointer over the dots to see Coincident constraint symbols.

10. You can exit the file without saving once you have finished.

The Concentric Constraint

The Concentric constraint places arcs and circles so that they share the same center point. Follow these steps to explore the Concentric constraint:

1. On the Get Started tab, click the Open button.

2. Browse for the file `mi_3h_005.ipt` located in the `Chapter 3` directory of your `Mastering Inventor 2016` folder and click Open.

3. In the Model browser, double-click Sketch1 to edit it. Or right-click it and choose Edit Sketch.

4. In the Sketch tab's Constrain panel, click the Concentric button.

5. Click the edge of the circle and then the arc, as shown in Figure 3.47.

FIGURE 3.47
Placing a Concentric
constraint

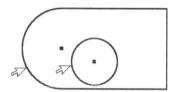

6. Right-click and choose Cancel.

7. Press the **F8** key to show all the constraints, and note the new Concentric constraint.

8. You can exit the file without saving once you have finished.

The Collinear Constraint

The Collinear constraint lines up a line object or ellipse axis on the same line as another line object or ellipse axis. Follow these steps to explore the Collinear constraint:

1. On the Get Started tab, click the Open button.

2. Browse for the file `mi_3h_006.ipt` located in the `Chapter 3` directory of your `Mastering Inventor 2016` folder and click Open.

3. In the Model browser, double-click Sketch1 to edit it. Or right-click it and choose Edit Sketch.

4. In the Sketch tab's Constrain panel, click the Collinear icon.

5. Click the lines as shown in Figure 3.48.

FIGURE 3.48
Placing a Collinear
constraint

6. Right-click and choose Cancel.

7. Press the **F8** key to show all the constraints, and note the new Collinear constraint.

8. You can exit the file without saving once you have finished.

The Horizontal Constraint

The Horizontal constraint makes an object line up parallel to the x-axis. Two points may also line up horizontally. Follow these steps to explore the Horizontal constraint:

1. On the Get Started tab, click the Open button.

2. Browse for the file `mi_3h_007.ipt` located in the `Chapter 3` directory of your `Mastering Inventor 2016` folder and click Open.

3. In the Model browser, double-click Sketch1 to edit it. Or right-click it and choose Edit Sketch.

4. In the Sketch tab's Constrain panel, click the Horizontal button.

5. Click the line as shown in Figure 3.49, noting the new horizontal alignment (make sure you don't select the middle of the line showing up with a green dot).

6. Click both of the points, as indicated in Figure 3.49, noting that they will line up horizontally.

FIGURE 3.49
Placing Horizontal constraints

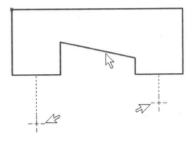

7. Right-click and choose Cancel.

8. Press the **F8** key to show all the constraints, and note the new Horizontal constraints.

9. You can exit the file without saving once you have finished.

HORIZONTAL AND VERTICAL ORIENTATION

Because the terms *horizontal* and *vertical* are dependent on your current view orientation, placing Horizontal and Vertical constraints can sometimes be confusing. To help with this, Inventor will display a light dotted line when placing a Horizontal or Vertical constraint. This line shows the orientation that Inventor is considering correct at the time of placement.

Keep in mind that no matter how you change your view orientation, Inventor maintains the definition of *horizontal* and *vertical* based on the coordinate system of the file.

Certification
Objective

The Vertical Constraint

The Vertical constraint makes an object line up parallel to the y-axis. Two points may also line up vertically. Follow these steps to explore the Vertical constraint:

1. On the Get Started tab, click the Open button.

2. Browse for the file mi_3h_008.ipt located in the Chapter 3 directory of your Mastering Inventor 2016 folder and click Open.

3. In the Model browser, double-click Sketch1 to edit it. Or right-click it and choose Edit Sketch.

4. In the Sketch tab's Constrain panel, click the Vertical button.

5. Click the line as shown in Figure 3.50, noting the new vertical alignment (make sure you don't select the middle of the line showing up with a green dot).

6. Click both of the points as indicated in Figure 3.50, noting that they will line up vertically.

FIGURE 3.50
Placing Vertical
constraints

7. Right-click and choose Cancel.

8. Press the **F8** key to show all the constraints, and note the new Vertical constraints.

9. You can exit the file without saving once you have finished.

The Equal Constraint

The Equal constraint makes two objects equal in length or radius. Follow these steps to explore the Equal constraint:

1. On the Get Started tab, click the Open button.

2. Browse for the file `mi_3h_009.ipt` located in the `Chapter 3` directory of your `Mastering Inventor 2016` folder and click Open.

3. In the Model browser, double-click Sketch1 to edit it. Or right-click it and choose Edit Sketch.

4. In the Sketch tab's Constrain panel, click the Equal button.

5. Click the two circles as shown in Figure 3.51, and notice that they become equal.

FIGURE 3.51
Placing Equal
constraints

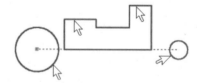

6. Click the lines, as indicated in Figure 3.51, noting that they too will become equal. You can make two of the vertical lines equal as well if you like.

7. Right-click and choose Cancel.

8. Press the **F8** key to show all the constraints, and note the new Equal constraints.

9. You can exit the file without saving once you have finished.

The Fix Constraint

The Fix constraint anchors any geometry or point in place within the part sketch. You should use this constraint sparingly. Follow these steps to explore the Fix constraint:

1. On the Get Started tab, click the Open button.

2. Browse for the file mi_3h_010.ipt located in the Chapter 3 directory of your Mastering Inventor 2016 folder and click Open.

3. In the Model browser, double-click Sketch1 to edit it. Or right-click it and choose Edit Sketch.

4. Drag the corner as indicated in Figure 3.52, and notice that it may be repositioned freely.

FIGURE 3.52
Placing Fix constraints

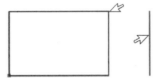

5. In the Sketch tab's Constrain panel, click the Fix button.

6. Click the same corner as before.

7. Right-click and choose Cancel.

8. Drag the corner again, and notice that it is now fixed to that position.

9. Apply another fixed constraint to the vertical line next to the rectangle, and be sure to click the line rather than the endpoint.

10. Right-click and choose Cancel to exit the constraint tool; then drag either endpoint of the line. While the line position is fixed, the endpoints are still free to change.

11. Press the **F8** key to show all the constraints, and note the new Fix constraints.

12. You can exit the file without saving once you have finished.

The Symmetric Constraint

The Symmetric constraint creates a "mirror" constraint between two similar objects. This constraint relies on a line to serve as a centerline about which objects are to be symmetrical. You need to specify the centerline only once during the command cycle. Follow these steps to explore the Symmetric constraint:

1. On the Get Started tab, click the Open button.

2. Browse for the file mi_3h_011.ipt located in the Chapter 3 directory of your Mastering Inventor 2016 folder and click Open.

3. In the Model browser, double-click Sketch1 to edit it. Or right-click it and choose Edit Sketch. You'll work with the sketch shown in Figure 3.53.

FIGURE 3.53
Placing Symmetric constraints

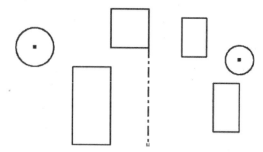

4. In the Sketch tab's Constrain panel, click the Symmetric button.

5. Click the circle on the left and then click the circle on the right.

6. Click the centerline and observe that the circles become symmetric.

7. Continue by clicking a line on the square on the left side of the sketch.

8. Click the corresponding line on the square on the right. Notice that this time you did not need to select the centerline. When using the Symmetric constraint, you need to establish the centerline only once.

9. Continue making the sketch symmetric by selecting lines on the left of the sketch and then selecting the corresponding lines on the right side.

10. Right-click and choose Cancel when the sketch is symmetric.

11. Press the **F8** key to show all the constraints; note the new Symmetric constraints.

12. You can exit the file without saving once you have finished.

Certification Objective

The Smooth Constraint

The Smooth constraint creates a continuous curvature (G2) condition between a spline and another sketch object, such as a line, arc, or spline. The G2 condition brings the curve out past the tangency point to create a smooth transition from one curve into the next. Follow these steps to explore the Smooth constraint:

1. On the Get Started tab, click the Open button.

2. Browse for the file mi_3h_012.ipt in the Chapter 3 directory of your Mastering Inventor 2016 folder and click Open.

3. In the Model browser, double-click Sketch1 to edit it. Or right-click it and choose Edit Sketch.

4. In the Sketch tab's Constrain panel, click the Smooth button.

5. Click the spline and arc as indicated in Figure 3.54.

FIGURE 3.54
Placing a Smooth constraint

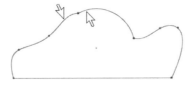

6. Right-click and choose Cancel.

7. Press the **F8** key to show all the constraints; note the new Smooth constraint.

8. You can exit the file without saving once you have finished.

Gaining More Sketch Skills

Many tools are available in the sketch environment, each used to draw different types of geometry or modify geometry in a different way. Many of these are covered in the following pages, but as a reminder, if you hover your mouse pointer over the tool and then pause, you will see a tool tip appear; hover a bit longer, and a larger, more informative tool tip will appear. These progressive tool tips are a great help when you're attempting to use tools that you don't often use and you need a helpful hint to remember what they do and how they do it.

Creating Arcs

You can create sketch arcs by using one of three arc tools available in Inventor's sketch environment. All three arc types are available in a drop-down menu in the Sketch tab's Create panel. Once placed, the three arcs behave the same; it is simply the manner in which they are created that differentiates them.

A three-point arc is an arc defined by two endpoints and a point on the arc. The first click sets the first endpoint, the second sets the other endpoint, and the third point sets the direction and radius of the arc, as shown in Figure 3.55.

FIGURE 3.55
A three-point arc

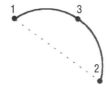

A center-point arc is an arc defined by a center point and two endpoints. The first click sets the center point, the second sets the radius and start point, and the third sets the endpoint and/or arc length, as shown in Figure 3.56.

FIGURE 3.56

A center-point arc

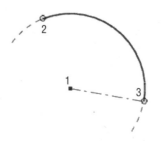

A tangent arc is an arc from the endpoint of an existing curve. The first click must be on the endpoint of an existing curve and sets a Tangent constraint on the endpoint. The second point sets the end of the tangent arc, as shown in Figure 3.57.

FIGURE 3.57

A tangent arc

Additionally, you can create arc segments while using the Line tool, as illustrated in Figure 3.58.

FIGURE 3.58

Creating an arc with the Line tool

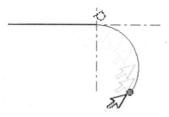

To do so, follow these steps:

1. On the Get Started tab, click the Open button.

2. Browse for the file mi_3h_013.ipt located in the Chapter 3 directory of your Mastering Inventor 2016 folder and click Open. The goal here is to re-create the oblong shape already present in the sketch.

3. In the Model browser, double-click Sketch1 to edit it. Or right-click and choose Edit Sketch.

4. In the Sketch tab's Create panel, click the Line icon.

5. Click the projected origin point as the start point of the line and then release the mouse button. This is the small dot located below the oblong shape and at 0,0 of the sketch.

6. Pull your mouse pointer to the right, making sure you see a horizontal or parallel glyph, indicating that your line is horizontal.

7. Click the screen to set the second point of the line and then release the mouse button.

8. Now to sketch an arc without exiting the Line tool, click and hold the endpoint you just created and then (still holding down on the mouse button) drag your mouse pointer out to preview the arc. If the arc previews in the wrong direction, simply return your mouse pointer to the endpoint and try again. It may be helpful to "trace" the guideline cross and exaggerate the arc size to get the direction established and then bring your mouse pointer back in to get the size you want.

9. Release the mouse button to end the arc and continue the Line tool.

10. Continue creating line/arc segments, or right-click and choose Cancel to exit the Line tool. Practice this a few times, and you'll have it mastered in a short time.

Creating Automatic Tangents with the Line Tool

When adding tangent line segments to a circle or arc, you can apply the Tangent constraints automatically. To do so, start the Line tool and click and hold on the circle or arc on which you intend to create the tangent line. You will see a tangent glyph. You can drag the line segment out to the length and orientation desired. To change the tangent direction, simply rub your cursor over the tangent point again and drag the line segment the other direction. Figure 3.59 illustrates this technique.

FIGURE 3.59
Creating an arc with the Line tool

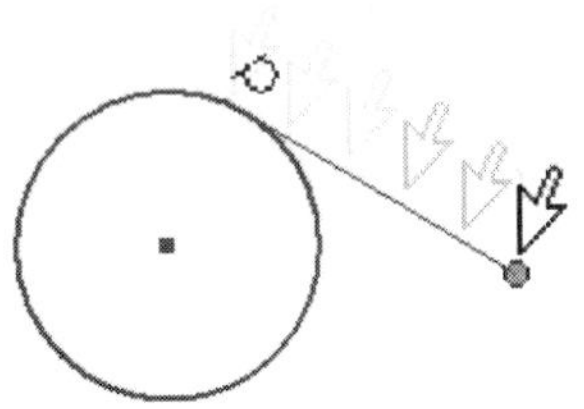

Understanding the Point/Center Point Tool

You can use the Point/Center Point tool, found in the Sketch tab's Create panel, to create center marks for locating hole centers and specific coordinate points. Center points are used by the Hole and Sheet Metal Punch tools in the modeling environment to automatically locate hole centers. Points, or sketch points as they are often called, are initially ignored by the Hole and Punch tools but can be manually selected for use. Another key difference between the two point types is that sketch points are deleted when the associated geometry is deleted. Center points are not.

You can change the center point to a sketch point, or vice versa, by selecting the point and clicking the Center Point button on the Format menu of the Sketch tab, as shown in Figure 3.60.

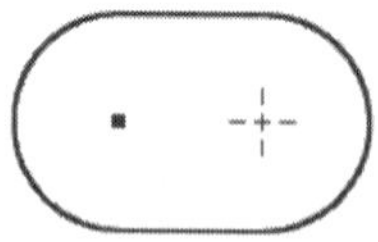

FIGURE 3.60
Using the Center Point button to switch points from simple sketch points (right) to center points (left)

CREATING SKETCHED SLOTS

In Inventor 2016 you can use the new slot sketch tools on the Sketch tab in the Rectangle flyout to create the following types of slots:

♦ Center to Center Linear Slots

♦ Overall Length Linear Slots

♦ Center Point Slot

♦ Three Point Arc Slots

♦ Center Point Arc Slots

To see how each slot type is created, you can pause your cursor over the tool and wait for the extended flyout panel to show you the "picks and clicks."

Projecting Geometry

When creating a sketch on the face of existing geometry or a work plane, you can project existing points and edges into the sketch by using the Project Geometry tool in the Sketch tab's Create panel. To take a quick look at this functionality, follow these steps:

1. From the Get Started tab, click the Open button.

2. Browse for the file mi_3h_014.ipt in the Chapter 3 directory of your Mastering Inventor 2016 folder and click Open.

3. In the Model browser, double-click Sketch3 to edit it. Or right-click and choose Edit Sketch.

4. In the Sketch tab's Create panel, click the Project Geometry icon.

5. Click the edges of the red oval-shaped profile.

6. When you have the complete profile projected into the sketch as shown in Figure 3.61, click the Finish Sketch button.

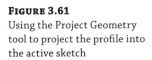

FIGURE 3.61
Using the Project Geometry tool to project the profile into the active sketch

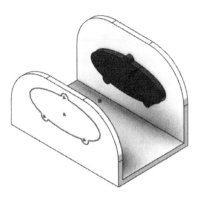

7. Next, in the Model browser, double-click Sketch4 to edit it. Or right-click and choose Edit Sketch.

8. Once the sketch is active, right-click and choose Slice Graphics (or press **F7** on the keyboard) to slice the part along the sketch plane.

9. In the Sketch tab's Create panel, click the drop-down for Project Geometry and choose Project Cut Edges.

You'll see that the sliced edges are now projected as sketch lines into the sketch. These lines can be used to dimension or constrain other sketch geometry too and will remain associative to the sliced features. Oftentimes a work plane is used to create a sketch in the middle of a part such as this. Work planes are covered in Chapter 4, "Basic Modeling Techniques." For now, you can finish the sketch and close the file without saving changes.

BREAKING THE LINK WITH PROJECTED GEOMETRY

Projected geometry is created by projecting an edge or a face. When you project faces, a browser node for a projected loop is created under the Sketch node. When you project edges, no browser node is created. You might need to break the link of the projected geometry in order to modify it.

◆ To break the link of projected faces, right-click the Projected Loop browser node and select Break Link.

◆ To break the link of projected edges, right-click the edge itself and choose Break Link.

Learning More about Dimensions

In the following sections, you'll take a look at more Dimension tools and settings to help you master this important part of sketch creation.

USING ONE GENERAL DIMENSION TOOL TO DO IT ALL

It is important to understand that you get different results from the Dimension tool depending on what geometry is selected or in what order it is selected. Here are the dimension types you can place with the General Dimension tool.

Linear dimension from one object.

Linear dimension between two objects.

Aligned dimension between two objects. Select the objects and right-click to choose the Aligned solution.

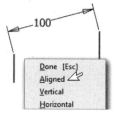

Angular dimension between two edges.

Angular dimension between three points.

Dimensions to circles or arcs. Select the object and then right-click to switch between diameter or radius solutions for either arcs or circles.

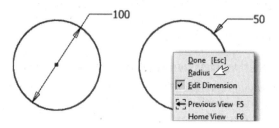

Dimension to the center of arcs and circles. Select the first element of the dimension and then click anywhere on the arc or circle. Note the linear glyph indicating the linear solution you will get.

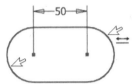

Dimension to the tangent of arcs and circles. Select the first element of the dimension and then click the tangent when you see the tangent glyph appear.

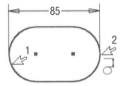

SETTING UP AUTOMATIC DIMENSIONS

In addition to the General Dimension tool, Inventor has an Automatic Dimensions And Constraints tool. It is generally poor practice to use the Automatic Dimensions And Constraints tool to apply all dimensions to your sketches because it will do so in an illogical way. However, you can benefit from this tool by placing the dimensions that define the intent of your design with the General Dimension tool and then allowing the Automatic Dimensions And Constraints tool to place the remaining dimensions to fully constrain the sketch.

To take a look at the Automatic Dimensions And Constraints tool in action, follow these steps:

1. On the Get Started tab, click the Open button.

2. Browse for the file named mi_3h_015.ipt in the Chapter 3 directory of your Mastering Inventor 2016 folder and click Open.

3. In the Model browser, locate Sketch1; double-click to edit or right-click and choose Edit Sketch.

4. In the Sketch tab's Constrain panel, click the Automatic Dimensions And Constraints icon. Notice that the Auto Dimension dialog box shows the number of dimensions required to fully constrain the sketch.

5. Accept the default settings to add both dimensions and constraints.

6. With the Curves button enabled, select all the geometry in the sketch (you can do this quickly with a selection window).

Figure 3.62 shows that two dimensions will be added to fully constrain the sketch.

FIGURE 3.62
Adding automatic dimensions

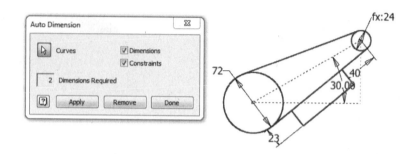

7. Click Apply to add dimensions to the selected geometry.

8. When finished, click Done.

9. You can close the file without saving changes.

Note that you can also use the Automatic Dimensions And Constraints tool to apply just sketch constraints by deselecting the Dimensions check box.

WORKING WITH SKETCH CENTERLINES

You can create centerlines in sketches either by creating a regular line and then changing it to a centerline or by changing the line type to centerline first and then creating the line. Dimensioning to a centerline gives you a diametric solution by default, but you can opt for a linear solution by right-clicking and deselecting Linear Diameter, as shown in Figure 3.63. In the following exercises, you will find the steps for both methods of centerline creation as well as how to change the solution when dimensioning to a centerline.

FIGURE 3.63
Dimensioning to a centerline

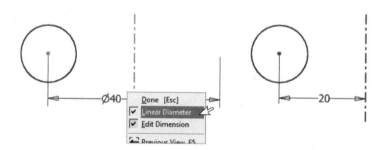

To change to centerline line type before creating sketch geometry, follow these steps:

1. Ensure that the sketch is active for editing by double-clicking it or right-clicking and choosing Edit Sketch.

2. On the Sketch tab, click the Centerline icon in the Format panel.

3. Now use the Line tool to sketch lines as you would normally. Note that the Centerline icon stays pushed in (On) until you click it again.

To change an existing line to a centerline, follow these steps:

1. Ensure that the sketch is active for editing by double-clicking it or right-clicking and choosing Edit Sketch.

2. Select the sketch lines you intend to be centerlines.

3. On the Sketch tab, click the Centerline icon in the Format panel.

To create a dimension to a centerline, follow these steps:

1. Ensure that the sketch is active for editing by double-clicking it or by right-clicking and choosing Edit Sketch.

2. On the Sketch tab, click the Dimension icon in the Constrain panel.

3. Select an object to the side of the centerline.

4. Click the centerline. Note the diametric diameter.

5. Right-click and note the Linear Diameter option.

6. Place the dimension on the screen.

Certification Objective

Measuring Geometry

You can use the Measure tools to gather measurements from your model without the need to place a dimension in your sketch. You can access these tools by using the Inspect tab, by using the Tools tab, or by right-clicking any empty place in the graphics area of the screen and choosing Measure from the context menu. When using the Tools tab, you can click the drop-down on the Measure panel to reveal the Region Measure option. The measurement tools include the following:

Measure Distance   Measures the length lines and arcs, the distance between points, and the radius or diameter of a circle.

Measure Angle   Measures the angle between two lines or points.

Measure Loops   Measures the length of closed loops.

Measure Area   Measures the area of enclosed regions.

Get Region Properties   Measures the area and perimeter and the Area Moment Of Inertia properties of sketch loop regions. This tool is available only while editing 2D sketches. Figure 3.64 shows the use of the Measure Region tool.

FIGURE 3.64
Measuring a region

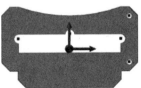

Creating Sketches from AutoCAD Geometry

Converting accurate, dimensioned 2D drawings eliminates the need to redraw all the original geometry. Inventor allows selective importing of 2D drawing geometry directly into a new part sketch. If you have an existing drawing library of 2D AutoCAD files, you may find it beneficial to use those files to create new 3D feature-based parametric parts in Inventor. Success in importing existing drawings depends on the following criteria:

♦ The AutoCAD file must contain accurate original geometry.

♦ Duplicate geometry must be deleted from the AutoCAD file.

♦ Proper AutoCAD drawing techniques must be employed in creating the AutoCAD file. For example, there must be only one line segment between any two points. Two shorter lines appearing as a single line will be imported exactly as drawn in the AutoCAD file.

♦ For dimensions to be converted to Inventor parametric dimensions, the existing AutoCAD dimensions must be associative to the geometry. Disconnected dimensions (AutoCAD Defpoints not snapped to the proper geometry location) will cause problems when converted to Inventor dimensions.

Importing Existing AutoCAD Designs

You begin the process of converting an AutoCAD drawing to Inventor parts by creating a new part file. When in active sketch mode, you can import AutoCAD sketch geometry by selecting the Insert panel on the Sketch tab and clicking the Insert AutoCAD File icon. To see this process yourself, follow these steps:

1. On the Get Started tab, select the New button.

2. In the New File dialog box, click Metric in the left pane and click the Standard(mm).ipt icon.

3. Click Create to create a new part file based on this template.

4. On the Insert panel of the Sketch tab, click the Insert AutoCAD File icon.

5. In the resulting dialog box, select the file Import1.dwg from the Chapter 3 directory of your Mastering Inventor 2016 folder.

6. Click Open to start the conversion process. Once the AutoCAD file opens, you will move into a series of Import Destination Options pages. The first page is mostly grayed out except for specifying units, constraining endpoints, and optionally applying geometric constraints upon import under most conditions. Set your selections as shown in Figure 3.65.

FIGURE 3.65
DWG import options

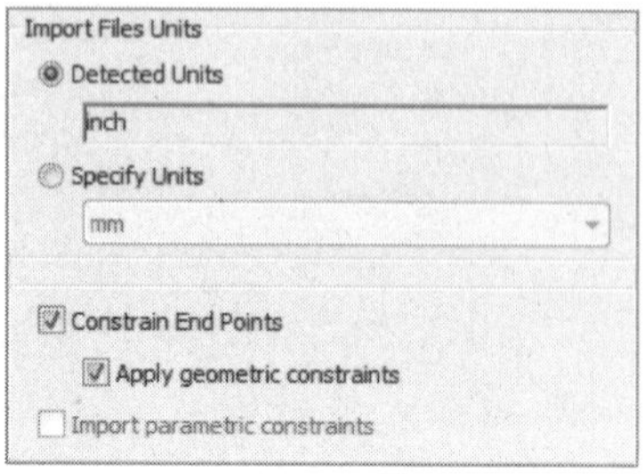

7. Click Finish to complete the import.

 Real World Scenario

CREATING SKETCHES FROM A GRAPHIC IMAGE

Occasionally you may need to create a part from a scanned image or napkin sketch. To do this, you can insert the scanned image or napkin sketch right into your sketch and sketch over the top of it. Although this is generally not a good approach for reproducing precise machined parts, it is a valid workflow when designing consumer products and the general shape and feel of parts need to be captured. If you have a need for this type of design on a regular basis, you may want to investigate Autodesk® AliasStudio™ software. Here are the general steps for creating sketches from an image:

1. Place an image into a part sketch by clicking the Insert Image icon on the Sketch tab.

2. Browse for the image you want to place into the sketch and click Open when the image is located.

3. The mouse pointer is then attached to the upper-left corner of the image. To place the image, simply click an insert point onscreen.

4. Once the image is placed, the edges of the image can be dimensioned and constrained like any other sketch entity.

Now you can sketch on top of the image, tracing the edges to create the profile and then use the Dimension tool to tweak the sketch as required.

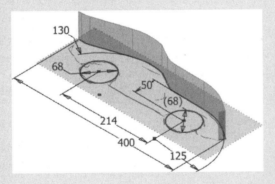

When an AutoCAD drawing is imported into a sketch, Inventor records the unit type of the AutoCAD file. By default, the unit type is displayed within the import dialog box but grayed out. If the unit type is not correct or the unit is of a different type than you require, you may input a different input-unit type.

Selecting the Constrain End Points box allows insertion of Coincident constraints between sketch objects found to have endpoints that occupy the same coordinates. When the Apply Geometric Constraints box is checked, Inventor will add minimal constraints to the imported AutoCAD geometry. Note too that although some dimensions will not be imported, those that are will be parametric Inventor dimensions. Figure 3.66 shows the result of importing the file Import1.dwg.

FIGURE 3.66
Original DWG (left)
and finished imported
sketch (right)

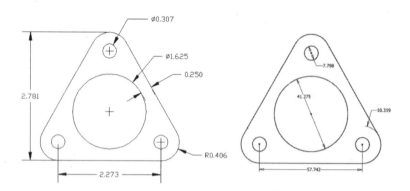

If the AutoCAD geometry was created at the 0,0 origin, then it should import into Inventor at the same location. If the AutoCAD geometry is not located at the origin of the sketch, you can use the Move command, selecting both the geometry and any dimensions, to move the entire imported sketch into the proper location. You might also prefer to redefine the geometry origin in AutoCAD and then import or reimport it into Inventor.

You should note that this imported drawing might be further broken down into separate features. For instance, each hole could be a separate feature. Note too that having the round corners modeled as features separate from the base feature allows for easier edits in Inventor.

Copying and Pasting Existing AutoCAD Designs into Inventor

Although using the import wizard as described earlier works without having AutoCAD open or even installed, you can import AutoCAD geometry in an even more efficient manner by simply copying from an open AutoCAD file straight into an Inventor sketch, as described in these steps:

1. Open the existing file in AutoCAD.

2. From an open AutoCAD file, simply select the geometry you want to import, right-click, and choose Copy, thereby copying the selected objects to the Windows clipboard.

3. In Inventor and with a 2D sketch active for editing, right-click and choose Paste. You will be presented with a bounding-box preview of the pasted entities.

4. At this point, you can right-click and choose Paste Options to ensure that the insert scale is correct or click the graphics window to place the pasted geometry.

Although importing geometry from AutoCAD can be an efficient way to reuse existing AutoCAD files, experienced Inventor users generally prefer to model parts from scratch rather than import from AutoCAD. Importing from AutoCAD almost never provides results that are in line with the design intent of the part unless you just get lucky. Although you may find this to be helpful initially, you will learn that importing AutoCAD files has a place in Inventor but should not be used as a substitute for creating robust parametric Inventor models.

Creating and Using 3D Sketches

3D sketches permit the creation of nonplanar 3D features. 3D sketches are created in single-part files only and comprise geometry located in various XYZ locations or points within the file. Although a 3D sketch may lie in a 2D plane, in most designs that will not be the case. 3D sketches should never be used for creating geometry that could be created within the 2D sketch environment. The 3D sketch tool is accessible only from within the part environment; however, you can project geometry from an assembly into the part to create the 3D sketch.

Certification Objective

Creating a 3D Path

3D sketches are often used to define paths for modeling features such as sweeps and lofts and are generally created based on existing geometry. You can use a 3D sketch to create objects such as tubes, pipes, and wires as well as negative features such as cam paths, recessed parting lines, and so on.

In this exercise, you will use the 3D Line and Spline tools to create a path along which a profile can be swept. This is a common use of 3D sketches. To start the exercise, follow these steps:

1. On the Get Started tab, click the Open button.

2. Browse for the file mi_3h_016.ipt in the Chapter 3 directory of your Mastering Inventor 2016 folder and click Open.

3. On the 3D Model tab, select the Sketch panel and click the drop-down arrow below the Start 2D Sketch button. Then click the Start 3D Sketch button. Or right-click in an empty area of the graphics window and choose New 3D Sketch.

Notice that although this is a part file, it has some reference surfaces in it already. These were included simply to emulate a situation where you might be creating a part within the context of an assembly. You will learn more about creating parts within an assembly in the chapters to come.

There is also a 2D sketch called Profile1 already in the Model browser; you'll use this sketch at the end of this exercise. Your goal is to create a 3D sketch running from the center of the connection input of the box through each of the large holes in the flange brackets.

4. On the 3D Sketch tab, click the drop-down arrow on the Spline tool button to reveal the Control Vertex and Interpolation spline options; then select the Interpolation option. You'll see the 3D coordinate triad appear.

5. With the Spline tool still active, select the Draw panel bar to reveal the flyout menu and then click the Precise Input button.

Now you will see the Inventor Precise Input toolbar appear. The Precise Input toolbar allows you to enter coordinates to move the 3D triad. The triad displays the x, y, and z planes and the corresponding axes in the form of three arrows. The red arrow indicates the x-axis, the green arrow indicates the y-axis, and the blue arrow indicates the z-axis. Notice that the triad is first positioned at 0,0,0.

6. Specify a start point for the spline by clicking the front, circular edge of the connection input.

7. Click the center of the large hole of the first triangular flange bracket. It makes no difference whether you choose the front or back edge of the hole.

8. Do the same for the other two flange brackets.

9. Right-click and choose Create to complete the spline.

10. Right-click again and choose Cancel to exit the Spline tool. Your screen should look similar to Figure 3.67.

In the next section, you will add a 3D line to your 3D spline.

FIGURE 3.67
3D sketch spline

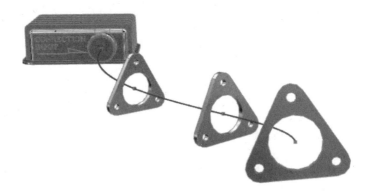

Using the 3D Coordinate Triad

Before continuing with the 3D sketch, take a moment to explore the 3D coordinate triad and its functionality. Each part of the triad is selectable for different tasks, as you'll see in the coming paragraphs. Figure 3.68 shows the anatomy of the triad.

FIGURE 3.68
Inventor's Precise
Input toolbar and the
3D coordinate triad

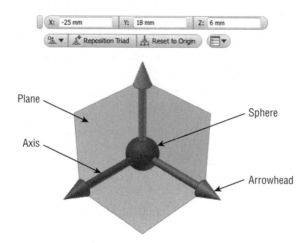

1. Still in the 3D sketch, click the Line tool button on the 3D Sketch tab.

2. Notice the return of the triad and Precise Input toolbar.

3. Click the endpoint of the spline to set the start of the line on this point.

You will see the triad move to the spline endpoint. Notice that the triad is not lined up to be truly perpendicular with the bracket flange. To remedy this, you will use the Precise Redefine button found on the Precise Input toolbar. Your goal is to set the X (red), Y (green), and Z (blue) arrows of the triad to the orientation shown in Figure 3.69.

FIGURE 3.69

Using the Reposition Triad button to realign the triad

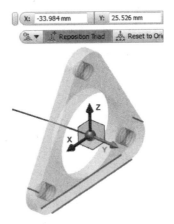

4. On the Precise Input toolbar, click the Reposition Triad button, as shown at the top of Figure 3.69.

5. Select the shaft of the red X arrow and then click one of the bottom edges of the triangular flange bracket, as shown in Figure 3.69.

Note that if your X arrow faces the opposite direction, you will repeat steps 4 and 5 and select the other edge along the bottom of the bracket.

6. Next, click the Reposition Triad button again, and this time select the shaft of the green Y arrow.

7. Click one of the small edges on the sides of the flange, as shown in Figure 3.69.

Again, if the result of your selection leaves your Y arrow facing the opposite direction, you will repeat steps 7 and 8 and select another edge along the side of the bracket.

Once the triad orientation is set so that it matches Figure 3.69, you will draw a line by entering coordinates.

8. Click the triad plane between the blue and green arrows to isolate that plane to sketch on.

The triad plane should highlight red and then stay highlighted when selected (although this highlighting can be difficult to see depending on the color scheme in use). When the plane is selected, you will see a 0 placed in the X cell of the Precise Input toolbar.

9. With 0 in the X input cell, enter **300** in the Y cell, enter **25** in the Z cell, and press **Enter**.

Note that you can press the **Tab** key to switch among the X, Y, and Z input cells. Values will be input as relative coordinates. Recall that with relative coordinates, the new input coordinate point is based on the previous point rather than the absolute 0,0,0 origin point. You will now have a line running from the end of the spline out at 300 mm in the y-axis with a 25 mm rise in the z-axis.

10. Still in the Line tool, right-click and ensure that Auto-Bend is selected in the context menu. Auto-Bend will place a radius at the corners in your line route. The default radius size can be set by selecting Document Settings from the Tools tab and then selecting the Sketch tab. Once bends are placed, they can be edited like any other dimension.

11. With the Line tool still active, click the plane between the green and red arrows on the triad to isolate the XY triad plane, and enter **200** in the X input, enter **200** in the Y input, and leave 0 in the Z input. Press **Enter** on the keyboard to set this line point. You will see a small dimensioned radius at the corner of your two line segments. This is a result of the Auto-Bend option.

12. Right-click and choose Cancel to exit the Line tool. Your 3D sketch should resemble Figure 3.70.

FIGURE 3.70
3D sketch path

13. Click the Dimension button in the 3D Sketch tab and add dimensions, as shown in Figure 3.71. Note that you can edit the bend radius dimension that was created with the Line tool.

FIGURE 3.71
3D sketch dimensions

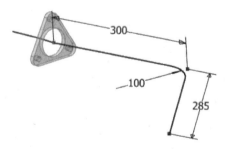

14. Right-click and choose Cancel to exit the Dimension tool.

15. Right-click and choose Finish 3D Sketch.

As a test to see whether you have successfully created your 3D sketch for its intended purpose, run a sweep along the path. Recall that there is a 2D sketch named Profile1 in the browser. This will be your sweep profile, and the 3D sketch just created will be your path.

1. In the 3D Model tab's Create panel, click the Sweep button. Profile1 will be automatically selected as the sweep profile unless you have another unconsumed, closed profile sketch in your part, in which case you will need to select Profile1 manually.

2. Once the profile has been selected, ensure that the Path button in the Sweep dialog box is enabled and then click the 3D sketch you just created. Your sweep should look like Figure 3.72.

FIGURE 3.72
Sweeping along a 3D sketch

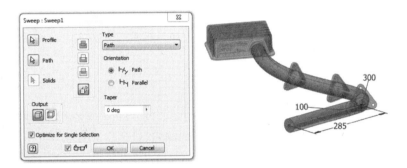

You will look at the Sweep tool in more depth in Chapter 5, "Advanced Modeling Techniques." As a final note, the connection box and triangular bracket flanges have been derived into this part file as a reference feature. In the real world, once you've finished with the part, you would locate that feature in the browser and turn off the visibility. To do this, in the browser expand the feature called `DerivedPart1.ipt`. Right-click the feature called Derived Work Body1 and uncheck the Visibility box. If you'd like, you can save and close the part.

Exploring More 3D Sketch Tools

In addition to the Line and Spline tools used for sketching 3D geometry, several tools permit you to include and combine existing geometry to create 3D sketch elements.

Certification
Objective

INCLUDING 3D GEOMETRY

You'll often need to use edges of parts as a path for another feature, in much the same way you project geometry in a 2D sketch. In a 3D sketch, however, you are not really projecting the geometry onto a sketch plane but simply including it for use in your 3D sketch. To see how this works, follow these steps:

1. On the Get Started tab, click the Open button.

2. Browse for the file `mi_3h_017.ipt` in the `Chapter 3` directory of your `Mastering Inventor 2016` folder and click Open.

This file has a 2D sketch named Lip Profile already created and ready to be used in a sweep feature. However, before you can do that, you'll define a path along which to sweep the profile.

3. On the 3D Model tab, select the Sketch panel and click the drop-down arrow below the Start 2D Sketch button. Then click the Start 3D Sketch button. Or right-click in an empty area of the graphics window and choose New 3D Sketch.

4. On the 3D Sketch tab, click the Include Geometry button. Next, click each edge along the curved edge, as shown in Figure 3.73, to define the sweep path.

FIGURE 3.73
Including geometry
in a 3D sketch

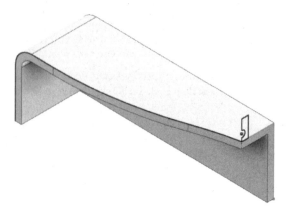

5. Once the edges are selected, right-click and choose Finish 3D Sketch.

The path created by including geometry could not have been created with a 2D sketch because it does not exist in a single plane. You can use this path to experiment with the Sweep tool to sweep the profile along the path if you'd like. The Sweep tool is covered in more depth in Chapter 5.

Certification
Objective ## USING AN INTERSECTION CURVE

You can use a 3D sketch to find the intersection of two surfaces, sketch profiles, work planes, or some combination thereof. The resulting sketch is fully associative and will update automatically should the curves change. To see it in action, follow these steps:

1. On the Get Started tab, click the Open button.

2. Browse for the file mi_3h_018.ipt in the Chapter 3 directory of the Mastering Inventor 2016 folder and click Open.

3. On the 3D Model tab, select the Sketch panel and click the drop-down arrow below the Start 2D Sketch button. Then click the Start 3D Sketch button. Or right-click in an empty area of the graphics window and choose New 3D Sketch.

4. On the 3D Sketch tab, click the Intersection Curve button.

5. Click the surface and the curved face, as shown in Figure 3.74.

FIGURE 3.74
3D intersection curve

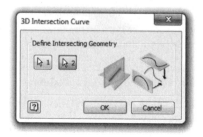

6. Click OK.

7. Right-click the surface and choose Visibility to toggle the visibility off. Note the resulting intersecting curve.

8. You can close the part without saving changes.

USING THE PROJECT CURVE TO SURFACE TOOL

You can find intersections of curves and faces using the Project Curve To Surface tool in a 3D sketch. This tool outputs three variations of projected geometry. Geometry created using these tools will adjust if the original geometry changes. Or, if you desire, the link can be broken from the parent geometry to prevent it from adjusting automatically. To see it in action, follow these steps:

1. On the Get Started tab, click the Open button.

2. Browse for the file mi_3h_019.ipt in the Chapter 3 directory of your Mastering Inventor 2016 folder and click Open.

3. On the 3D Model tab, select the Sketch panel and click the drop-down arrow below the Start 2D Sketch button. Then click the Start 3D Sketch button. Or right-click in an empty area of the graphics window and choose New 3D Sketch.

4. On the 3D Sketch tab, click the Project To Surface button.

The first output, Project Along A Vector, requires a face, a curve, and a direction. Projecting to a continuous face such as a cylinder results in a 3D sketch entity that follows the surface as if the curve were slicing straight down through the face.

5. Click the face of the cylinder.

6. Click the Curves button. Note the Direction button, which allows you to change the projection direction. In this case, the default direction will work, so you can leave this as is.

7. Click the line on the far left.

The second output is called Project To Closest Point and projects curves in the shortest possible path normal to the surface. The result of a 3-inch line to a convex surface would be a curve less than 3 inches because the endpoints of the line would take the shortest path to the curve rather than wrapping about it.

8. In the Output area of the Project Curve To Surface dialog box, click the middle button to choose the Project To Closest Point output.

9. Click the face of the cylinder.

10. Click the Curves button.

11. Click the line in the middle.

The third output is Wrap To Surface. This output creates a curve that will be the same overall dimension as the curve from which it was created. If you wrap a string around a cylinder, the string stays the same length.

12. In the Output area of the Project Curve To Surface dialog box, click the right button to choose the Wrap To Surface output.

13. Click the face of the cylinder.

14. Click the Curves button.

15. Click the line on the right.

16. Click OK.

17. You can close the part without saving changes.

Figure 3.75 shows all three outputs; note the different outputs created from three identical lines. You can break the link of the projected curves by locating the curves in a 3D sketch from the Model browser, right-clicking them, and choosing Break Link. You must have the sketch active for edits to break the link. Doing this disallows the ability for the projected curves to update if the founding geometry is updated.

FIGURE 3.75
Project Curve To
Surface tool

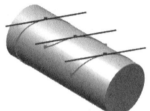

USING A HELICAL CURVE

You can create 3D helical curves such as thread paths and coils by using the Helical Curve tool within the 3D sketch tools. Helixes can be specified by pitch and revolution, pitch and height, revolution and height, or a true spiral. A helix can be combined with other 3D sketch objects to compose as complex a path as required. Follow these steps to explore using the Helical Curve tool:

1. On the Get Started tab, click the Open button.

2. Browse for the file mi_3h_020.ipt in the Chapter 3 directory of the Mastering Inventor 2016 folder and click Open.

3. Notice the existing 2D sketch consisting of a single line.

4. On the 3D Model tab, select the Sketch panel and click the drop-down arrow below the Start 2D Sketch button. Then click the Start 3D Sketch button. Or right-click in an empty area of the graphics window and choose New 3D Sketch.

5. On the 3D Sketch tab, click the Helical Curve button.

6. For the start point, select one end of the line.

7. Select the other end of the line for the endpoint of the helical curve.

8. Click in the graphics window to rough in the diameter.

9. Set the precise diameter value to **25 mm**, as shown in Figure 3.76.

FIGURE 3.76
A helical curve

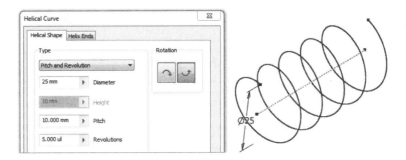

10. Enter **10 mm** for the pitch.

11. Enter **5** for the revolutions.

12. Click OK.

13. Examine the resulting helical curve, as shown in Figure 3.76.

14. Note that you can change the inputs of the curve by right-clicking it and choosing Edit Helical Curve.

15. You can close the part without saving changes.

Certification
Objective ## USING A SILHOUETTE CURVE

You can create an associative 3D curve along the outer boundary of a body as defined by a selected direction. Imagine a beam of light cast on an object from a single direction. The curve created where the shadow line begins would be the silhouette curve. You can use the Silhouette Curve tool to determine the parting line of organic shapes; just follow these steps:

1. On the Get Started tab, click the Open button.

2. Browse for the file mi_3h_021.ipt in the Chapter 3 directory of the Mastering Inventor 2016 folder and click Open.

3. On the 3D Model tab, select the Sketch panel and click the drop-down arrow below the Start 2D Sketch button. Then click the Start 3D Sketch button. Or right-click in an empty area of the graphics window and choose New 3D Sketch.

4. On the 3D Sketch tab, click the Silhouette Curve button.

5. For the Body selection, click anywhere on the part.

6. For the Direction selection, click the work axis.

7. Click OK. Note the resulting curve, as shown in Figure 3.77. You can exit the sketch and close the file when finished.

FIGURE 3.77

A silhouette curve

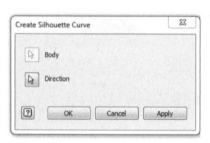

You can break the link of the projected curves by locating the curves in a 3D sketch from the Model browser, right-clicking them, and choosing Break Link. Doing this disallows the projected curves to update if the founding geometry is updated.

REFINING AND CONSTRAINING A 3D SKETCH

You can anchor and constrain a 3D sketch in much the same fashion as you do a 2D sketch using dimensions and constraints. Additionally, with 3D splines you can add vertex points and control curve fit with handles. Further refining can take place because you can adjust the fit method and spline tension to create the exact curve shape desired.

Best Practices for Working with Sketches

Here is a list of points to remember as you continue working with sketches in Inventor. Keep in mind that sketches are the foundation for good modeling, and therefore the importance of creating stable, fully constrained sketches cannot be overstated.

- ◆ Keep sketches simple.

- ◆ Your goal should always be to have a fully dimensioned and constrained sketch.

- ◆ Sketches that are not fully constrained tend to distort unpredictably when you make modifications and updates.

- ◆ Rough out size and shape before adding dimensions and constraints to avoid distorting the sketch when dimensions and constraints are added.

- ◆ Add dimensions to lock down shape and then come back to change the size.

- ◆ Endpoint, midpoint, center, and intersection snap points can be helpful when creating sketch entities, but be aware of how they affect dimensions compared to selecting the line itself rather than the snap points.

- ◆ You can use the Backspace key to clear the last-selected points. For instance, if you select a point for the end of a line and then realize you should have selected another point instead, use the Backspace key to clear the first selection and then start the line where it should have been.

♦   Use centerlines to define revolution axes and diametric dimensions.

♦   Use construction lines to further define sketches and create "helper" geometry.

♦   When you need to select multiple sketch entities, you can use a crossing selection or a window selection. A crossing selection is created from right to left and selects any object that is touched or contained by the window. A window selection is created from left to right and selects only objects that are completely contained in the window.

♦   Use the Delete key on the keyboard to quickly remove accidentally created geometry.

♦   Use the Split tool rather than the Trim tool when you can because the Split tool does not break previously defined constraints.

♦   Turn off automatic edge projection to avoid extra sketch geometry and project only the edges you need. This will make sketches easier to edit.

♦   Reserve fillets and chamfers for the feature level whenever possible. Although you can fillet and chamfer at the sketch level, it is generally best to keep your sketches simple and fillet and chamfer the solid features rather than the sketches.

♦   You can create pattern and mirrored geometry in the sketch, but it is generally best to make a simple sketch, then create a feature from it, and finally pattern or mirror the feature. The results are often the same, but the feature patterns are much easier to edit.

The Bottom Line

Set up options and settings for the sketch environment.   Understanding the settings and options that apply to the sketch environment is an essential first step in working with Inventor.

> **Master It**   You want to configure your own set of options and settings for your sketch environment and then back them up and/or distribute them to other workstations. How would you do this?

Create a sketch from a part file template.   Creating a sketch in a blank template file is the fundamental step in creating 3D parametric models. You will use this basic step to start most of your part designs.

> **Master It**   How would you capture the intent of your design when creating a base sketch for a new part?

Use sketch constraints to control sketch geometry.   Understanding what each sketch constraint does when applied will allow you to determine when to use each type. Recall that often more than one constraint will work in any given situation.

> **Master It**   How would you create a sketch that allows you to test "what if?" scenarios concerning the general shape and size of your part?

Master general sketch tools.   Learning the features and tricks of the sketch tools will allow you to master Inventor sketching.

Master It   You are given a print of mixed units to work from, and you need to enter dimensions exactly as they are on the print. You understand that you can enter any dimensions in any unit simply by adding the correct suffix. But how would you create a radius dimension on a circle or a dimension from the tangents of a slot?

Create sketches from AutoCAD geometry.   You can use existing AutoCAD files to create a base sketch for an Inventor model of the same part.

Master It   You have many existing 2D AutoCAD drawings detailing legacy parts. You want to reuse these designs as you convert to 3D modeling. How would you proceed?

Use 3D sketch tools.   Much of working with a 3D parametric modeler can be done by sketching in a two-dimensional plane and then giving depth to the sketch to create 3D features. However, sometimes you need to create paths or curves that are not planar. In those cases, you use the 3D sketch tools.

Master It   You know the profile of a complex curve as viewed from the top and side. How would you create a 3D sketch from this data?

Chapter 4

Basic Modeling Techniques

This chapter covers the principles of creating a 3D parametric part with the Autodesk® Inventor® and Autodesk® Inventor LT™ programs, which makes it one of the most important chapters in this book. You'll start by looking at the general options and settings associated with Inventor and part files and then move on to a basic exercise exploring the fundamentals of creating parametric models. Then you'll take a deeper look at the options found in the primary feature tools.

All the skills in this chapter are primarily based on creating a single part, whether in a single-part file or in the context of an assembly file. Do yourself a favor and learn or review these basics before jumping into the more complex features.

In this chapter, you'll learn to

◆ Configure options and settings for part modeling

◆ Create basic part features

◆ Use the Extrude tool

◆ Create revolved parts and thread features

◆ Create work features

◆ Use the Fillet tool

◆ Create intelligent hole features

◆ Bend parts

Exploring Application Options and Settings for Part Modeling

As in previous chapters, you should make sure your settings in the Application Options dialog box match the approach we're using in this book. This will ensure that the examples you work on will match the results you see here.

Specifying Global Settings

You maintain global settings for Inventor within the Application Options dialog box. For this section of the chapter, you will be concentrating on the Part tab, which allows you to maintain part-specific settings. You can adjust the application settings as follows:

1. On the Tools tab, click Application Options.

2. Choose the Part tab, as shown in Figure 4.1.

FIGURE 4.1
The Part tab

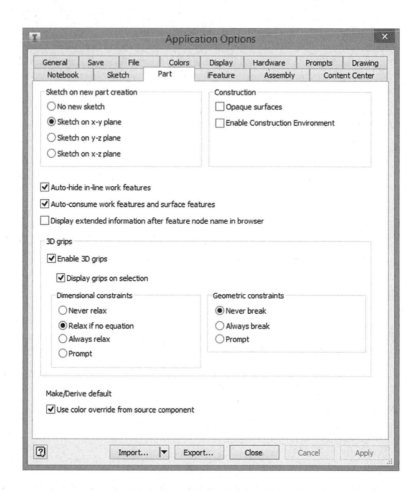

The Part tab settings have the following functions:

Sketch On New Part Creation   This section allows you to predetermine the origin plane in which to place the first sketch. If No New Sketch is selected, Inventor will create a new part file without an initial sketch. You can then determine the origin plane for the first sketch.

Construction   The Opaque Surfaces setting determines whether created surfaces will be translucent by default or as opaque as parts are. The Enable Construction Environment setting allows you to work with the construction environment tools when repairing imported surface models.

Auto-Hide In-Line Work Features   This option allows automatic hiding of a work feature when it is consumed by another work feature. For instance, if you create a work plane by clicking a work axis and a work point, the work axis and work point will be stacked under the work plane in the browser.

Auto-Consume Work Features And Surface Features   This option allows Inventor to consume surfaces when converted to a solid in addition to consuming work features.

Display Extended Information After Feature Node Name In Browser   This option allows you to see more information about each browser feature. In addition to the names of part features, the size and settings of the feature will be shown to allow better identification of the part features. This option can be toggled on and off from the Browser Filters menu as well as through the Application Options dialog box. Be aware that you cannot edit the content or format of the feature name extensions.

3D Grips   These settings affect how 3D grips can modify a part file. In normal use, you can modify part features by selecting and dragging a 3D grip. If a dimension is controlling the feature, the dimension will update to reflect the changes in the part.

If Never Relax is selected, any features controlled by the dimension will not change.

When Relax If No Equation is selected, a dimension value will update unless that dimension value is determined by an equation. Selecting Always Relax will always allow the use of 3D grips, even when controlled by an equation. The Prompt setting will prompt you to accept any changes during drag operations.

The settings in the Geometric Constraints area control how constraints will be handled during drag operations. Never Break prevents grip editing when sketch constraints are controlling a sketch. Always Break allows constraints to be broken as required during grip edits. The Prompt setting asks you to make a decision on a case-by-case basis for each grip edit.

Make/Derive Default   This check box is a global override switch for the Use Color Override From Source Component option, which is available in Derived Assembly, Derived Part, Make Part, and Make Component dialog boxes.

This option controls the pushing of Master Part appearance overrides from the derived part into the new part.

This global setting can be set to default the Use Color Override From Source Component check box to remain checked or unchecked throughout your session.

Specifying Document-Specific Settings

To change the options in a specific part file, you'll need to access the part's Document Settings dialog box by selecting the Tools tab and clicking Document Settings while that part is open. The Document Settings dialog box that opens allows specific settings for an individual file in the following areas:

◆ Lighting styles

◆ Materials

◆ Units

- ◆ Modeling dimension display values

- ◆ Individual sketch settings

- ◆ Model values

- ◆ Bill of materials (BOM)

- ◆ Default tolerances

Any changes made in the part's Document Settings dialog box will be applied only to the current document. Current document settings will not affect the settings in other parts within an assembly.

THE STANDARD TAB

Figure 4.2 shows the part's Document Settings dialog box with the Standard tab active. The Standard tab controls the active lighting style of the current graphics window. In addition, you can set the physical material properties and the display appearance of the current part here.

FIGURE 4.2
The Standard tab in a part's Document Settings dialog box

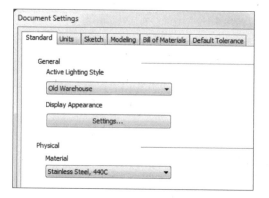

The lighting style is selected from a preset list in the drop-down menu, as is the physical material. The display appearance is configured by clicking the Settings button and adjusting the various settings in the resulting dialog box. To use the display appearance settings configured in the part file, you must first select the Display tab of the Application Options dialog box and select Use Document Settings.

THE UNITS TAB

The settings on the Units tab allow you to change the unit specification values, as shown in Figure 4.3. For example, you could open a metric (mm) part and change the input settings to inches.

FIGURE 4.3
The Units tab in
Document Settings

FIGURE 4.3
The Units tab in
Document Settings

The Units tab settings have the following functions:

Modeling Dimension Display   These settings allow you to define the model dimension's display precision by the number of decimal places and define how that dimension will be displayed. Many people prefer the Display As Expression setting because it shows the dimension name along with any expression that exists in the dimension; if no expression exists, the dimension name and dimension value are displayed.

Default Parameter Input Display   These settings allow you to see the parameter name in the input box when you're editing a dimension or feature input. Figure 4.4 shows the option set to display as the expression on the left and set to display as the value on the right. You can also access this setting from the context menu.

FIGURE 4.4
Modeling dimension
display

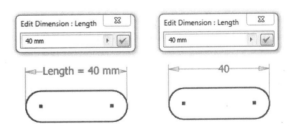

THE SKETCH TAB

On the Sketch tab, shown in Figure 4.5, you can adjust how the 2D sketch tools work and appear in an active sketch. In addition, you can change the preset value for Auto-Bend Radius in the 3D Sketch area.

FIGURE 4.5
Sketch tab in
Document Settings

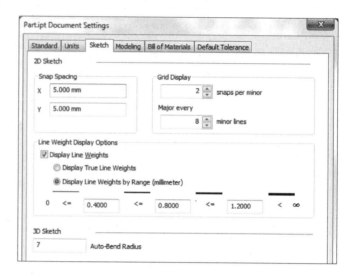

Here are the Sketch tab settings along with a description of their functions:

Snap Spacing   This option allows you to set the spacing between snap points to assist with precise layouts. For instance, if you are using Frame Generator to create a steel frame with uprights at 2000 mm on center, you might set the snap spacing to 2000 mm and, then on the Sketch tab in the Application Options dialog box, set the sketch to Snap To Grid. Then, when creating your skeletal base sketch, you can set line segments and spacing to 2000 mm with precision.

Grid Display   These settings allow you to set the major and minor grid spacing. If Snaps Per Minor were set to 2 with the 2000 mm snap spacing used in the previous example, the spacing between grid lines would be 4000 mm. If Major Every were set to 5, distance between the major grid lines would be 20,000 mm. To display grid lines, you select the Sketch tab in the Application Options dialog box.

Line Weight Display Options   These options allow the display of unique line weights in model sketches. Note that this does not influence line weights in printed model sketches. Display True Line Weights displays line weights onscreen as they would appear on paper regardless of the onscreen zoom level. Display Line Weights By Range displays line weight according to the entered values.

3D Sketch   This area contains only one setting, Auto-Bend Radius. When creating a 3D line, you can turn on the Auto-Bend Radius option and have intersecting line corners automatically rounded. This setting controls the default radius at which bends are created. Once they are made, the bends can be edited to a different value.

THE MODELING TAB

Figure 4.6 shows the Modeling tab, which allows changes to the behavior while modeling the current active part. Note that if you are using Inventor LT, some of these settings might vary or might not be present.

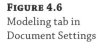

FIGURE 4.6

Modeling tab in
Document Settings

Here are the settings found on the Modeling tab of the Document Settings dialog box:

Adaptively Used In Assembly   This option is available only when a part is adaptive. When it is deselected, an adaptive part becomes static. This setting can also be controlled by right-clicking an adaptive part in the assembly browser.

Compact Model History   This option allows Inventor to purge all rollback document history when you save the current file. Compacting the model history improves performance in large assembly files. You should select this option only when performance is affected in large assembly files or when existing disk space is limited.

Advanced Feature Validation   This option permits Inventor to use a different algorithm to compute features. Using this option can produce more accurate feature results in rare cases such as Shell, Draft, Thicken, and Offset features. However, this option is slower in calculation than the default option and should be used only on rare occasions where the accuracy of the model may be in question.

Maintain Enhanced Graphics Detail   This option enables graphics information to be saved with the file on disk. This information is used in the graphics display if the display quality is set to Smoother in the Application Options dialog box.

Participate In Assembly And Drawing Sections   When this option is not selected, the part will default to None in the section participation settings of an assembly or drawing section view. However, you can adjust each instance of the part to section or not section as needed. For instance, if you created a part file for an O-ring and intended to use it in the design of several shaft assemblies, you could deselect this option in the O-ring file to ensure that the O-ring remained unsectioned in the section drawing views of the shafts you used the O-ring on. If you needed to show a particular section view of the shaft assembly with all parts sectioned, you would do so by setting the section participation settings for the O-ring to section in that one section view of the drawing.

Tapped Hole Diameter   This option determines how the size of tapped hole features are controlled. Thread representations in drawings are generated correctly only when Tapped Hole Diameter is set to Minor.

User Coordinate System   Click the Settings button to access the UCS Settings dialog box, where the UCS naming prefix can be set, the default plane defined, and the visibility of UCS and its features determined.

3D Snap Spacing   These options establish the spacing between snap points in 3D sketches. The settings also control the snap precision when the Move Bodies tool is used to free-drag a solid body.

Initial View Extents   These options set the initial visible height and width of the graphics window when you're creating a model from a template. For instance, if you create a lot of steel frames, you may find it helpful to create a template with the setting adjusted so that your initial sketch is not always zoomed in to a small area. Configure these settings in your template files to affect new files. You can set the initial height and width of the graphics window. The settings affect only the initial sketch when a template is used. When you're creating a secondary sketch or opening an existing part, the view is controlled by the size of the part.

Naming Prefixing   These options set the default file-naming convention for parts generated from multi-body part designs. These tools are covered in Chapter 5, "Advanced Modeling Techniques."

Make Components Dialog   Clicking Options in the Make Components Dialog area opens the Make Components Options dialog box. The Make Components settings shown in the options dialog box are specific to the active project. These options are employed when creating multi-body parts, as described in Chapter 5.

THE BILL OF MATERIALS TAB

The Bill Of Materials tab determines the structure of the current file and how that structure relates to the bill of materials (BOM) in an Inventor assembly. Figure 4.7 shows the settings for structure and quantity.

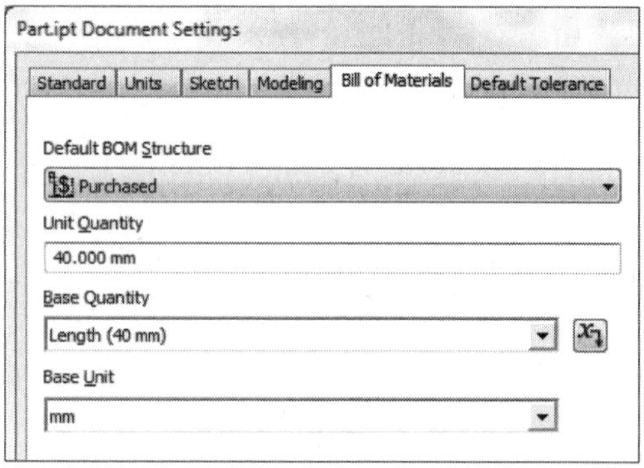

FIGURE 4.7
Bill Of Materials tab
in Document Settings

You can add BOM structure properties to individual parts in the Document Settings dialog box. Figure 4.7 shows the choices available in a model or assembly file for setting individual file properties.

Here are the details:

Normal   These components are given an item number and included in quantity calculations. The placement of normal parts in the bill of materials is determined by the parent assembly properties. A normal subassembly may be composed of any combination of inseparable, phantom, purchased, and reference parts without having any effect on how those parts are listed in the BOM. Normal is used for most components.

Inseparable   These components are assemblies that allow the inclusion of press-fit, glued, welded, or riveted components that might be damaged if taken apart. A good example is a hinge that is fully assembled but should be listed in the BOM as a single part. Although the Inseparable structure is listed in the part's Document Settings dialog box, it is intended as an assembly property.

Purchased   These components are parts that are not normally fabricated or manufactured by your company but instead purchased from vendors. Any purchased component, whether part or assembly, will be listed in a parts-only parts list. A purchased component assembly will not normally have the component parts listed in the BOM because that component will be purchased as a single unit.

Phantom   These components exist in the design but are not included as specific line items in the BOM. A construction assembly that exists as a container (subassembly) within a higher-level assembly, simply to hold a number of components together for assembly purposes, can be set to Phantom. When this assembly is set to Phantom, it will not appear in the parts list; however, the parts included within the construction assembly will be listed as individual parts. Phantom components are ignored by the BOM. No item number is assigned, and no quantity calculations are performed on the phantom assembly. However, the quantity of individual parts contained within the phantom assembly will be multiplied by the quantity of the phantom component included in the top-level assembly.

Reference   These components are used to provide reference information within an assembly design. An example of a reference part might be a product container placed in a conveyor assembly. The conveyor components are the parts and assemblies you are designing, but the container is required to ensure the clearance and function of your design. In a drawing, reference parts will be indicated in the view as hidden line geometry. Reference components are excluded from the BOM and are excluded from quantity, mass, and value calculations.

Base Quantity   Use this to change how the part's Base Quantity property is displayed in the BOM or parts list. You can change the value from Each to any parameter, such as one called Length. You will find that components generated by the Frame Generator tools are automatically set to use a length parameter for the base quantity. Once a parameter is selected, you can change the Base Unit, from mm to M for example.

THE DEFAULT TOLERANCE TAB

Figure 4.8 shows the Default Tolerance settings. Creating tolerance values affects sketches and parts only. When you add tolerance values to a part file, you can select either Use Standard Tolerancing Values or Export Standard Tolerance Values, or you can select both options.

FIGURE 4.8
Default Tolerance tab
in Document Settings

You can select the Use Standard Tolerancing Values box to use the precision and tolerance values set in this dialog box. You can select the Export Standard Tolerance Values box to export tolerance dimensions to the drawing environment.

Once you've selected an option, you can then add linear or angular tolerance values. You can add any number of tolerance values by precision to this part. When you have added your values to the part, click the Apply button to stay in the dialog box and apply the new settings to this tab, or click the OK button to apply the settings and exit the dialog box. Chapter 5 covers the use and setup of part tolerances in more detail.

Key Concepts for Creating Basic Part Features

Inventor 3D part modeling is based on the principle of creating a base feature and then adding features to the base feature to build a more complex part. Figure 4.9 illustrates the basic workflow for creating a part composed of multiple features.

FIGURE 4.9
Part-creation
workflow

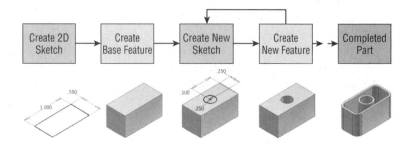

CREATE YOUR OWN TEMPLATE FILES

This may seem like a lot of settings, and it's true there are a lot, but you need to set them only once. Open a template, adjust all your settings the way you want them for a particular type of part (for instance, an inch unit part), and then use the Save Copy As Template option. Your settings will then be available in a template when you create a new part. Make another template for metric parts. Make another for sheet-metal parts, and so on, as you like. You can make as many as you think you'll use, each with its own set of document settings specific to the template.

A good idea is to make a folder in your template directory named, for example, My Templates, and store all your templates in it. This folder (and any other folder in the template directory) will show up as a tab in the New File dialog box. This way, you will still have access to Inventor's standard templates as well as your custom templates.

You can set the template file location in two places.

◆ On the Tools tab of the ribbon, click Application Options and select the File tab in the dialog box that opens.

◆ On the Get Started tab of the ribbon, click Projects and select the Folder Options entry in the dialog box that opens.

Keep in mind that if the settings in these two locations are not the same, Inventor will use the Projects setting.

As you create parts in Inventor, keep in mind the following concepts because each will go a long way toward making your modeling endeavors more productive:

◆ Anchor and orient your base sketch to the 0,0,0 origins of the part file. This will make your parts much easier to manage as you go forward. The base feature will generally be the largest feature in the part, unless you have a specific reason for not making it so.

◆ Look for areas of your design that are likely to change and create your part features to accommodate these future edits. For example, the plate thickness might change as loads are determined throughout the rest of the design. Creating the plate sketch from the end view and then extruding the length would make it easy to modify the length of the plate but not as easy to modify the thickness. Therefore, a better choice would be to create the base sketch of the top view and extrude the thickness.

◆ Identify relationships between design parameters. For instance, there may be a requirement that the distance from the edge of a part to the edge of a bolt hole always has to be two times the diameter of that hole. You can set that formula directly in the distance dimension, and then whenever you change the hole diameter, the distance from the edge adjusts automatically.

◆ Keep an eye out for patterned and symmetrical design features. It is much easier to create and modify the first instance of a pattern than it is to edit several identical features that were created separately.

◆ Build logical feature dependencies. Features are considered dependent on other part geometry when you cannot delete or modify a portion of the part or feature without affecting another feature built later in the part. For example, if you were to create a simple block and then create an additional feature on that block, you could not delete the block without upsetting the new feature.

◆ Because fillets and chamfers often change, it is best to place them at the end of the design process as much as possible. Placing them at the beginning and then having to change them is likely to upset other features you have created afterward that might depend on the filleted or chamfered edges.

◆ Create simple sketches to create simple features to create complex parts. Using numerous features within a 3D model allows simplified control over modifications of the model in the future. Separate features may be suppressed or modified to alter the design without having to make changes in a complicated sketch. Instead of attempting to create all the geometry in a single sketch, analyze the proposed part first and create a simple base sketch for the first feature.

 Real World Scenario

CONSIDER MODELING VS. MACHINING

Although the "design as you'd manufacture" paradigm is a great philosophy to follow when creating 3D parts, there are differences between modeling and machining. One major difference is that you have the ability to add material when modeling, whereas a machining operation takes only material away. Deciding which route to take depends on what resources are available in your shop and how much time you have.

Modeling and machining are important subjects to consider when designing parts. Inventor offers a lot of features that may make it easy to design a part that might be impossible or at least expensive to make with the tooling equipment your shop has available. In some cases, although a part may be easier to model as one piece, it might be less expensive to machine as multiple pieces. Also, consider the size of the equipment and tooling, such as end mills and drills, when creating parts. For example, in Inventor you can create small fillets or square corners in a design, but try to machine a 0.010-inch fillet in a cavity that is 3 inches deep, and you'll likely earn a scolding from the people on the shop floor who are required to turn your design into reality.

One example for how to make a realistic design for your shop is the fixture block, as shown here. If a CNC machine center is available, this simple part is easy to model in Inventor and not a problem to create in the shop.

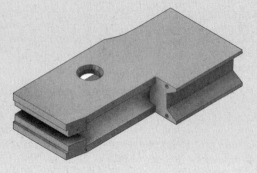

However, without a CNC approach, even this simple model might prove to be difficult or expensive to produce by more traditional machining techniques. Reconsidering the design to match the shop's abilities will be required. In this case, you might consider a sandwich block design of simple parts welded and fastened together to achieve the same end result, as shown here.

Although this might require more thought and planning on your part within Inventor, it will make the design achievable with the tools and technology at hand. Often the best resource for helping you determine what your shop's capabilities are will be the people who will be making the parts.

Simplifying Your Sketches

When learning to master creating parts in Inventor, there is probably no concept more important than the idea of creating simple sketches from which to build simple features that will add up to create complex parts. Standard 2D drafting practice requires you to place all part details or components within a single view. However, it is not good practice to use the same 2D drafting workflow within any feature-based 3D modeler. Complicated sketches can drag down sketching performance and virtually eliminate easy changes to features. Consider the part shown in Figure 4.10. This illustration shows the base sketch that is then revolved to form the shaft.

FIGURE 4.10
A complex sketch for a revolved part

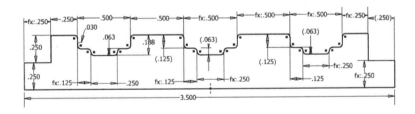

Now compare the same part modeled using the simple-sketches approach shown in Figure 4.11.

FIGURE 4.11

Simple sketches and placed features create a revolved part

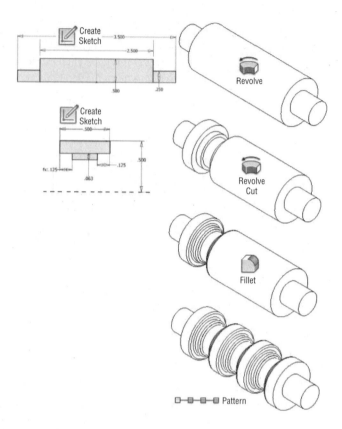

The version in Figure 4.10 would prove difficult to modify because of the number of sketch constraints and dimensions required to create it. Most likely a seemingly simple change would result in some part of the sketch breaking. By comparison, the version in Figure 4.11 would be easy to modify because each feature is broken out into its own sketch or placed feature.

Of course, sometimes creating a more complex sketch is required, but if you follow the simple-sketch rule of thumb, you will find Inventor much more accommodating, and you will quickly master part creation and be ready to tackle complex sketches when they are needed.

At the end of this chapter you will find an exercise that builds a part by first creating a simple sketch and constructing a base feature from it. The exercise continues adding simple features to build complexity into the part. But before you get to that exercise, you'll find several shorter exercises exploring many of the tools used to create part features. If you have not already downloaded the Chapter 4 files from www.sybex.com/go/masteringinventor2016, please refer to the "What You Will Need" section of the introduction for the download and setup instructions.

Exploring the Extrude Tool

The Extrude tool allows you to add volume to a closed sketch profile to create a 3D solid and allows you to add length to an open sketch profile to create a 2D or 3D surface. You can also use the Extrude tool to create cutouts in solids.

To truly master the Extrude tool, you have to understand several options. In the next several pages, you will open a series of files that have been set up to demonstrate the various options available to you. You can find all these files in the Chapter 4 directory of your Mastering Inventor 2016 folder.

Extruding Basic Features

Certification Objective

The Extrude tool is often used to create base features on which other features are created. To explore the creation of a base extrude feature, follow these steps:

1. Open the file mi_4a_008.ipt.

2. Click the Extrude button on the 3D Model tab (or press **E** on the keyboard).

Because the sketch in this part file contains five profiles from which you can choose, the Extrude tool requires you to select the profile or profiles you want to extrude. Note that the large, dashed circle in the center of the hexagon is not recognized as a profile because it is set as a construction line in the sketch.

USE SKETCH CENTER POINTS TO CREATE PROFILES

In Sketch1 of mi_4a_008.ipt, you might have noticed the presence of four sketch center points at the intersection of the hexagon and the two circles. Sketch center points placed at the intersection of overlapping profiles allow Inventor to see the profile as separate sketch profiles, without the need to split or trim the sketch geometry.

---

3. Hover your cursor over each profile to see it highlight.

4. Click in the center of the hexagon, and you will see a preview of the extrusion that will be created from this profile.

5. Click and drag the arrow at the center of the preview to change the extrusion distance and/or direction.

6. Use the Flip button to change the direction of the extrusion so that it goes down away from the sketch, as shown in Figure 4.12.

FIGURE 4.12
Creating a base extrude feature

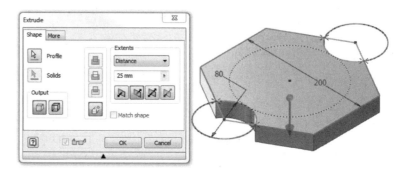

7. Set the extrude Distance to **25 mm** and then click the OK button.

Notice that a feature called Extrusion1 has been created in the Model browser tree. If you click the plus symbol next to it, you'll see that Sketch1 is listed under it, because Extrusion1 consumes Sketch1.

8. Locate Sketch2 in the Model browser and right-click it; then select Visibility to turn this sketch on.

9. Click the Extrude button on the 3D Model tab (or press **E** on the keyboard).

10. Set the extrude Distance to **60 mm** and ensure the direction is facing up and the type is set to Join, as shown in Figure 4.13; then click the OK button.

FIGURE 4.13
Creating a secondary
extrude feature

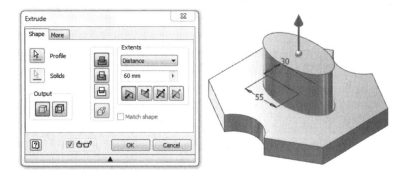

Creating basic extrusions from a sketch profile is quite a simple operation and one that you will use often in creating your designs. You can close the part without saving changes and continue to explore the Extrude option.

DIRECT MANIPULATION TOOLS

The Direct Manipulation toolset is a set of user interface tools enabling you to modify a model while viewing the changes in real time. The buttons on the in-canvas display correspond to the buttons and inputs in dialog boxes and menus. You can choose to use the Direct Manipulation tools, or you can use the traditional dialog boxes and menus to achieve the same result.

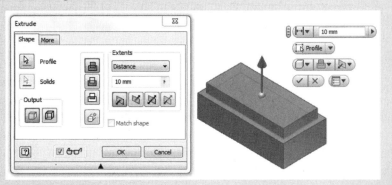

The Direct Manipulation In-Canvas Display consists of selection tags, manipulator arrows, value input boxes, and mini-toolbars.

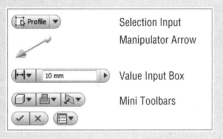

continues

continued

Once you become comfortable with the Direct Manipulation tools, you can use the arrow at the bottom of the dialog box of each tool and choose to roll it up to save screen space. Note that you cannot disable the Direct Manipulation tools.

One tip to be aware of is the ability to pin the Direct Manipulation mini-tools in place. For instance, you can drag the mini-toolbars to the upper-right corner of your graphics screen, near the ViewCube, and then use the options menu pull-down button to select the Pin Mini-Toolbar Position option. Doing so will ensure that these tools will appear in this location each time you use the tool.

Editing an Extrusion Feature

Once you create extrusions, you can quickly and easily modify them by using the same inputs used to create the original feature. In the following exercise, you'll open an existing part and edit an extrusion feature to change the length of the part:

1. Open the file `mi_4a_009.ipt`.

2. Locate the feature named Extrusion2 in the Model browser and then double-click it or right-click and choose Edit Feature.

3. Set the Distance to **100 mm** and then click the OK button.

4. Expand the Extrusion1 node in the browser to reveal Sketch1.

5. Right-click it and choose Edit Sketch, or double-click it to edit the sketch.

6. Edit the Hex_Size dimension by double-clicking it; then set it to **30 mm**.

7. Click the Finish Sketch button to exit the sketch and set the change.

Making edits to existing extrusions features is as simple as editing the extrusion feature or the sketches used to create them. You can close the part without saving changes and continue to explore the Extrude option.

Extruding with Cut and Taper

Certification Objective

You can use the Extrude tool's Cut option to remove material from your parts. Although you may think of this as a tool to create holes, keep in mind that Inventor's Hole tool is the better choice to create standard holes because of the advanced detailing functions that accompany the Hole tool. With that said, the Cut option in the Extrude tool will allow you to cut material using any sketched profile that you might come up with. To explore the Taper option in the Extrude tool, follow these steps:

1. Open the file mi_4a_010.ipt.

2. Click Extrude on the 3D Model tab (or press **E** on the keyboard).

3. Select the rectangle shape for the extrude profile (if it does not select automatically) and set the distance to **20 mm**.

4. Choose the Cut option and just drag the manipulator arrow down into the part; notice that the preview turns red and the direction automatically switches. Change the direction so the preview is going up out of the part and then click the OK button.

5. Note that an error is generated, and it states that the feature you specified did not change the number of faces. Keep this in mind as you use the Extrude tool. Inventor will generally set the correct direction for you, but occasionally you might need to set the direction manually. Click the Edit button to return to the extrude options.

6. Change the direction again so you are indeed cutting the part and adjust the distance to **20 mm** as required.

7. Click the sphere on the manipulator arrow or click the More tab, as shown in Figure 4.14.

FIGURE 4.14
A tapered cut extrusion

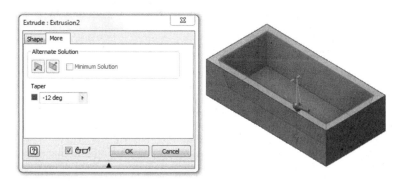

8. Enter **-12** in the Taper input box and click the OK button to create a tapered cut. When finished, you can close the part without saving changes.

Extruding with Intersect

Certification
Objective

So far you have created extrusion features using the Join option and the Cut option. Next, you will use the Intersect option of the Extrude tool to modify an existing solid. The Intersect option allows you to select a sketch profile and keep only material that intersects the existing solid and the sketch profile. You can create complex shapes by sketching an intersect profile and then using the extrude Intersect option to keep the combined volume of the existing solid and the sketch profile, as shown here:

1. Open the file mi_4a_012.ipt.

2. Click Extrude on the 3D Model tab (or press **E** on the keyboard).

Rather than cutting the small profiles out of the existing part, you'll use the Intersect option to discard all areas of the part that are not common between the existing part and the current sketch.

3. Select the large H-shaped sketch profile.

4. Change the Extents drop-down from Distance to All.

5. Click the Intersect button, make sure the extrude direction is going down through the existing part, and then click the OK button.

6. Click the end-of-part marker in the Model browser and drag it down below the sketch called Slot Locations so the Slot Locations sketch is visible and available for use.

This sketch consists of several small slots. You could select each slot and cut it from the existing part, but doing so would be time-consuming and subject to a missed selection, which will give you errant results. Instead, you'll use the Intersect option to choose the area between the slots.

7. Click Extrude on the 3D Model tab (or press **E** on the keyboard).

8. Select anywhere in the rectangular sketch profile so the selection results in a rectangle with the slots are omitted.

9. Change the Extents drop-down from Distance to All.

10. Click the Intersect button, make sure the extrude direction is going down through the existing part, and then click the OK button.

Figure 4.15 shows the progress of the part using the Intersect option to refine its shape.

FIGURE 4.15
A complex shape generated using the intersect extrusion

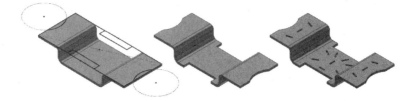

For another example of using the Intersect option, take a look at using it to create the tapered corners on a common hex head bolt, as demonstrated in the following exercise:

1. Open the file mi_4a_013.ipt.

2. Click Extrude on the 3D Model tab (or press **E** on the keyboard).

3. Select the visible sketch for the extrude profile (if it's not automatically selected).

4. Set the distance to **100 mm**.

5. Click the Intersect button, and make sure the extrude direction is correct. You want the extrusion going down though the bolt head and shaft.

6. Click the sphere on the manipulator arrow or click the More tab in the dialog box.

7. Enter **30** in the Taper input box, as shown in Figure 4.16, and click the OK button.

FIGURE 4.16
A tapered intersection extrusion

Your extrude options create a cone with a 30° taper, and the Intersect option keeps only the volume of the part shared by the existing features and the intersect cone feature, in this case the entire bolt except the tapered corners of the hex head. When finished, you can close the part without saving changes.

Extruding Surfaces from Open Profiles

Certification Objective

In addition to creating solids with the Extrude tool, you can create surfaces. If the profile is open and there is no other geometry to relate to, the surface solution is automatically selected. For closed profiles, you are required to switch the output from solid to surface manually, as shown here:

1. Open the file mi_4a_014.ipt.

2. Click the Extrude button on the 3D Model tab (or press **E** on the keyboard).

3. The visible shape will automatically be selected because it is the only available profile. Because it is found to be an open profile, the Surface output is automatically selected as well.

4. Change the distance to **25 mm**.

5. Set the direction arrow to the symmetric option so that the surface is extruded in both directions from the profile, as shown in Figure 4.17. Then click the OK button.

FIGURE 4.17
Extruding an open profile sketch to create a surface

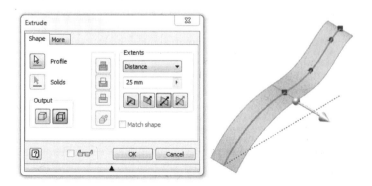

6. To explore how to create a surface extrusion from a closed profile, right-click Sketch2 in the browser and turn on the visibility.

7. Select the Extrude tool, and notice that Inventor automatically selects the profile and sets the output to Solid in the dialog box.

8. Click the Surface button to change the output to an extruded surface and then change the Extents option to To.

9. Doing so allows you to specify a point or surface to extrude to. You might notice that the surface created in the previous step was created in two halves. Select the arc-shaped half (rather than the spline-shaped half), and notice that the preview terminates as if the arc half-wrapped around.

10. Deselect the check box next to the To selection arrow (the Terminate Feature On Extended Face check box), and you will notice that the preview terminates at the farthest extent of the selected surface, matching the spline shape.

If you receive an error stating that the attempted surface did not terminate the tool body, review step 5 and ensure that your first extrusion was set to extrude symmetrically from the original sketch.

11. Click the OK button to create the extruded surface.

Figure 4.18 compares the two termination solutions when using the To option. Keep in mind that although this example used surface extrusions, the To option works the same for solids. You can close the file without saving changes.

FIGURE 4.18
Extruding a surface to terminate at the farthest extent of another surface

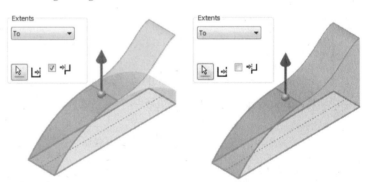

Extruding Solids from Open Profiles

In addition to extruding surfaces from open profiles, you can extrude solids, provided sufficient geometry is present to allow the open profile to solve correctly. This technique employs the Match Shape option and is the default solution when an open profile is selected in the Extrude tool while the solid output is selected. Follow these steps:

1. Open the file mi_4a_016.ipt.

2. Click the Extrude button on the 3D Model tab (or press **E** on the keyboard).

3. Click the arc profile, and notice that the Match Shape check box is automatically selected in the dialog box; in addition, the preview has extended the arc down toward the plate to provide a closed profile.

4. Click in the highlighted profile to select it.

5. Change the Extents drop-down to Distance and enter **60 mm**.

6. Set the direction to go into the base plate feature and click the OK button. Your result should look like Figure 4.19. You can close the file without saving changes.

FIGURE 4.19
Extruding an open profile

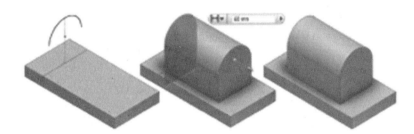

To take a look at the Match Shape option and how it can be used to change the output, you'll open a file that has two possible solutions for the final matched shape. One solution will match the shape of the existing geometry, and the other will not. Follow these steps to see how this works:

1. Open the file mi_4a_018.ipt.

2. Click the Extrude button on the 3D Model tab (or press **E** on the keyboard).

3. Click the visible profile sketch in the center of the part.

4. You'll notice that Inventor attempts to create a closed profile from this open profile by extending the profile past the extents of the existing geometry. Select the profile on the side with the grid feature.

5. Change the Extents drop-down to Distance, enter **1 mm**, and click the OK button. Notice how the extrusion fills the shape of the part.

6. Edit the extrusion you just created, and deselect the Match Shape box in the dialog box. Then click the OK button.

7. You'll notice that the extrusion runs through the grid feature, ignoring the shape.

Figure 4.20 compares the results of an open profile extrusion with and without the Match Shape option selected. You can close the file without saving changes.

FIGURE 4.20
Match Shape option for open profile extrudes

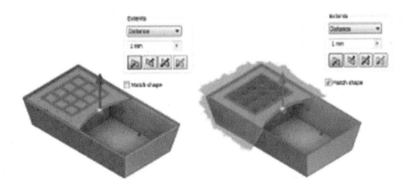

Extruding with To

It is often helpful to extrude to existing geometry rather than entering a distance value. In this way, if the existing feature changes, so too will your extrusion. When you use the Extrude To option, you can extrude to faces and vertices as well as work planes and work points. In the following exercise, you'll explore the Extrude To option:

1. Open the file mi_4a_020.ipt.

2. Click the Extrude button on the 3D Model tab (or press E on the keyboard).

3. For the profile, select one of the rectangular profiles.

4. Change the Extents drop-down from Distance to To.

5. Select the yellow face, and click the OK button.

You will receive an error stating that the termination plane does not completely terminate the profile because of the way that the yellow face would wrap around in a circle if extended.

6. Click the Edit button in the error dialog box to return to the Extrude dialog box.

7. Uncheck the Terminate Feature On Extended Face check box in the Extents area, as shown in Figure 4.21, and then click the OK button.

FIGURE 4.21
Extruding to an extended face

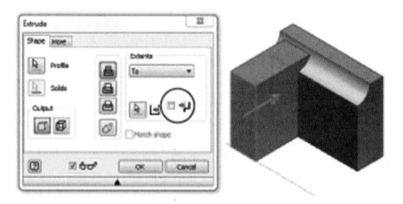

8. Use the Extrude tool and select the remaining rectangle.

9. Change the Extents drop-down from Distance to To.

10. Select the red face, and you will see that the preview terminates along the extended red face.

11. Uncheck the Terminate Feature On Extended Face check box in the Extents area, and you see the preview extend to the yellow face.

12. Click the OK button to create the extrusion. You can close the file without saving changes.

Although in this case the results of the two extrusion features are the same, you can see that the selected termination face and the termination check box can provide different results when used in combination.

Follow these steps to take a look at some other Extrude To options:

1. Open the file mi_4a_022.ipt.

2. Click the Extrude button on the 3D Model tab (or press **E** on the keyboard).

3. For the profile, select one of the ellipse-shaped profiles.

4. Change the Extents drop-down from Distance to To. Select the yellow face and ensure that the Terminate Feature On Extended Face check box is checked. In this case, you would receive an error if this check box were not selected. Figure 4.22 shows the correct selections.

FIGURE 4.22
Extruding to a face

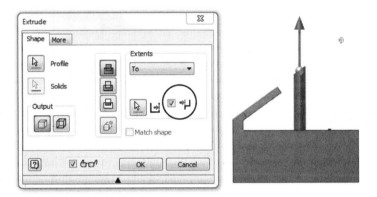

5. Click the OK button, and you'll see that the ellipse face takes on the angle of the face to which you extruded.

6. Use the Extrude tool again, select the other ellipse profile, and change the Extents drop-down from Distance to To. This time select the work point for the terminating object and click the OK button.

7. You'll see that the ellipse extrudes up to the work point height, as shown in Figure 4.23.

FIGURE 4.23
Extruding to a point

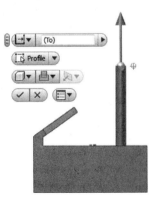

Although in this case you've used a work point to extrude to, often you can use the vertex point of an existing feature to extrude to. Feel free to experiment with this part and extrude shapes to an existing point on the yellow face. When finished, you can close the file without saving changes.

Extruding with the Minimum Solution Option

Often when extruding to a cylindrical face, you will need to set the extrusion to solve for the minimum solution since the face is continuous all the way around. To do this, follow these steps:

1. Open the file mi_4a_024.ipt.

2. Click the Extrude button on the 3D Model tab (or press **E** on the keyboard).

3. For the profile, select the hex-shaped profile.

4. Change the Extents drop-down from Distance to To, select the outside face of the cylinder, and then click the OK button.

You will notice that the hex shape stops at the closest face of the pipe. This is because the Minimum Solution option is the default. However, if the goal were to extend the profile to the farthest extent of the cylindrical face, you would need to adjust the settings to the farthest extent of the cylindrical face.

5. To fix this, edit the extrusion you just created and click the More tab (or click the sphere on the onscreen manipulator arrow).

6. On the More tab, deselect the Minimum Solution check box, as shown in Figure 4.24, and then click the OK button.

FIGURE 4.24
Extruding to the
minimum solution

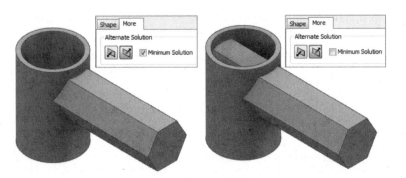

You'll see that without the Minimum Solution option selected, the extrusion extends to the far side of the selected face. You can close the file without saving changes.

Extruding with To Next

**Certification
Objective**

Similar to extruding to a selected entity, you can use the To Next option and let Inventor automatically select the next available surface or face for you. It should be noted that solutions with through voids may not work with this option. To explore the Extrude tool's To Next option, follow these steps:

1. Open the file mi_4a_026.ipt.

2. Click the Extrude button on the 3D Model tab (or press **E** on the keyboard).

3. For the profile, select the rectangular profile marked Profile1.

4. Change the Extents drop-down from Distance to To Next, and click the OK button.

5. Repeat the same steps for Profile2. When you click the OK button, you will receive an error because the extrusion cannot build to this solution.

6. In the error message dialog box, click the Edit button and then set the extrude extents to To.

7. Select the back (yellow) face for the face to extrude to and then click the OK button.

Oftentimes the geometry may require a bit of experimenting to achieve the solution you want. Just knowing the abilities and limitations of each option goes a long way toward knowing how to proceed. You can close the file without saving changes. Figure 4.25 shows the results of using the To Next option.

FIGURE 4.25
Extruding with To Next

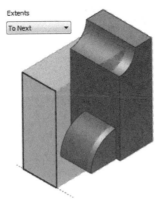

Extents

To Next

Extruding Between

Certification
Objective

You may need to define a beginning and an end of an extrusion that are not common to your sketch plane. To do this, you can use the Between option.

1. Open the file mi_4a_028.ipt.

2. Click the Extrude button on the 3D Model tab (or press **E** on the keyboard).

3. For the profile, select Circle.

4. Change the Extents drop-down from Distance to Between.

5. Select both pipe-shaped pieces to define the From and To options.

6. Because you are extruding to hollow objects, you'll need to use the Minimum Solution option. Click the More tab, and make sure the Minimum Solution check box is selected.

7. Flip the direction using a direction button next to the Minimum Solution check box. Click the OK button.

Figure 4.26 shows the results of using the Between extents option. You can close the file without saving changes.

FIGURE 4.26
Extruding with Between

Extruding Multi-body Solids

You may have noticed a couple of other buttons in the Extrude dialog box, one called Solids and the other called New Solid. Figure 4.27 shows both buttons in the dialog box. These options allow you to create separate solid bodies within the part or choose which existing solid bodies to modify.

FIGURE 4.27
Multi-body solid options

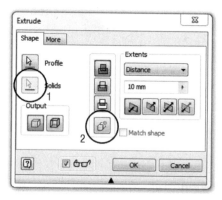

The first option allows you to select the solids you want to modify. Use this when selecting multiple solid bodies in which to create a cutout feature, for instance.

When selected, the second option allows the Extrude tool to create a separate solid body, rather than creating a feature of an existing solid. Separate solids can then be moved, rotated, colored, and modified individually.

To explore the multi-body extrude options, follow these steps:

1. Open the file mi_4a_030.ipt.

2. Click the Extrude button on the 3D Model tab (or press E on the keyboard).

3. For the profile, select the visible rectangular sketch profile (if it is not automatically selected).

4. Change the Extents drop-down from Distance to To and select the yellow face on the existing part feature.

5. Click the New Solid button, as shown in Figure 4.28, to set this extrusion as a separate solid body; then click the OK button.

FIGURE 4.28

A multi-body part

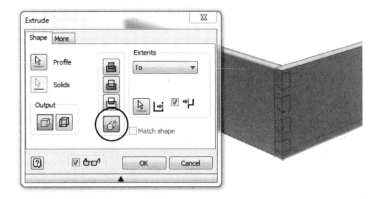

Because you used the New Solid option, you now have a part file with two separate solid bodies. You can expand the `Solid Bodies` folder in the browser to identify each one, as shown in Figure 4.29. Currently, the second solid interferes with the first and needs to be dovetailed to fit.

FIGURE 4.29

Multiple solid bodies in the `Solid Bodies` folder

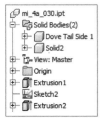

6. On the Modify panel of the 3D Model tab, click the Combine button.

7. Choose the new solid for the Base selection and choose the original solid (the one with the yellow face) as the Toolbody selection.

8. Set the operation to Cut (middle button).

9. Select the Keep Toolbody check box and then click the OK button.

You should see the original solid disappear and the new solid result in a dovetail where it intersected with the first. Expand the `Solid Bodies` folder and ensure that you have two solid bodies still. If not, use the Undo button and repeat steps 6 through 9.

10. Right-click and choose Show All to turn the visibility of the solid back on.

Next you'll use an existing sketch to cut a notched edge into both of the solid bodies at the same time.

11. Locate the sketch named Base Inset Sketch in the Model browser, right-click it, and select Visibility.

12. Using the Extrude tool, set the operation to Cut and then use the Solids button (found under the Profile button) to select both dovetailed bodies.

13. Set the distance value to **3 mm** and then click the OK button.

You can use the ViewCube to examine the resulting cut. You'll learn more about multi-body parts in Chapter 5, including how to use the Make Components tool to write out each solid body as an individual part file. You can close the file without saving changes.

Creating Revolved Parts

Creating turned and revolved parts is a regular occurrence in many engineering departments because of the types of parts designed and manufactured. The parts consist of circular features around a common axis. There are two different workflows for creating circular parts, each with its own advantages and disadvantages. Creating threads on a part presents another challenge.

You can create circular parts using a single sketch and revolving it around a centerline axis. Alternatively, you can create multiple circular extrusions to produce the same part.

There are also two different workflows for creating threaded features on a part. You can add threaded features to any circular component by means of the Thread feature, which creates cosmetic threads on the part, or through the use of the Coil feature, which creates physical threads. Typically, physical threads are created only when that geometry is required for the model. Generally, using cosmetic threads is sufficient because they are an intelligent feature that can be retrieved in the detail drawing of the part and called out as per the specifications of the feature.

Revolved Cylindrical Parts vs. Stacked Circular Extrusions

Revolved cylindrical parts utilize a sketch with a center axis. Figure 4.30 illustrates two ways to create the same sketch. The view on the left shows a sketch profile anchored at the origin and dimensioned from the origin. The view on the right illustrates the same sketch anchored at the origin but dimensioned from a created centerline, which creates diametric dimensions. The two sketches will create the same revolved feature, the difference being that the centerline allows you to dimension the sketch using diameter dimensions to maintain the design intent of the part.

FIGURE 4.30
Dimension to the sketch vs. centerline

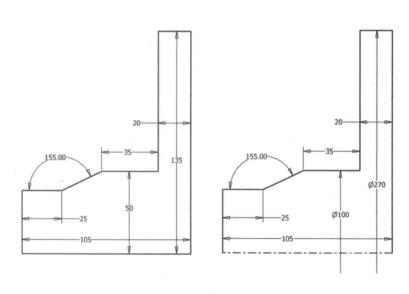

You create the centerline by using the Line tool with the Centerline tool toggled on. In this example, the centerline was created starting at the origin point and continuing to the right of the sketch, extending beyond the sketch for selection ease. When dimensions are created on the sketch and terminated at the centerline object, they will actually extend to the other side of the revolved part diameter.

You could create most revolved shapes by extruding sketched circles as well, but it's often best to use a revolve feature instead. The advantage of creating a revolved profile rather than creating stacked circular extrusions is that the relationship of every portion of the sketch can be easily visualized from the start. The disadvantage is that a contour sketch is not always easily edited to remove or change a portion of the feature. In addition, if the sketch is not fully dimensioned and constrained, it can create errors down the line with faces and edges. For this reason, you should always fully dimension and constrain your sketches. Figure 4.31 shows the same part modeled using both approaches.

FIGURE 4.31
Revolved circular feature vs. stacked circular extrusions

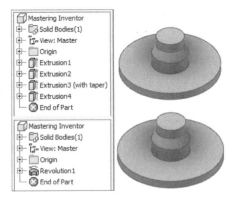

Creating Revolved Parts

Revolved features can be used to create parts or features, and they can be created as solids or surfaces. Follow these steps to see how revolves are created:

1. Open the file mi_4a_032.ipt.

2. Select the Revolve button on the 3D Model tab, or press **R** on the keyboard.

3. For the profile, select the rectangular sketch profile and the small circle.

4. Click the Axis button in the Revolve dialog box and then select the line indicated on the part for the axis.

5. Set the operation to Cut so that you are milling out the revolved profile.

6. By default the Extents drop-down is set to Full, giving you a 360-degree revolve. In this part, though, a full revolve cut would cut away a portion of the existing part. So, you will set the Extents drop-down to Angle instead. Notice the other extents options available. They should all look familiar as options from the Extrude tool.

7. Set the angle to **180** and then click the OK button. Figure 4.32 shows the revolve options.

FIGURE 4.32
Revolving a cut
feature

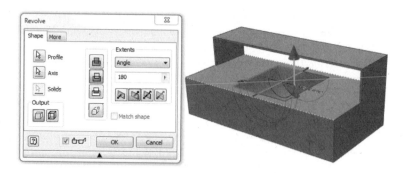

This demonstrates how to create a revolved cut at a specified angle. You can close this file and continue to explore the use of the Revolve tool to create surface features.

Next, you'll use the Revolve tool on an open profile to create a revolved surface. You'll then use a tool called Thicken to turn the surface into a solid.

1. Open the file mi_4a_034.ipt.

2. Before creating the revolve feature, you need to supply the sketch with some missing dimensions. To do so, right-click Sketch1 in the browser and choose Edit Sketch.

3. Place dimensions from the points shown in Figure 4.33 to the centerline, and you'll notice that because the line is a centerline type, the dimensions are automatically diameter dimensions. Before placing the dimension, you can right-click and choose Linear Dimension if a diameter is not the correct choice.

FIGURE 4.33
Adding dimensions
to a centerline

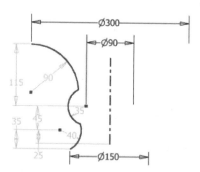

4. Once you've added the dimensions, press **R** to start the Revolve tool or click the Finish Sketch button and click Revolve on the 3D Model tab.

5. For the profile, select the sketch profile.

6. Click the Axis button and then select the centerline.

7. Because the sketch was an open profile, the Surface output is automatically selected. Click the OK button to create the revolved surface.

8. Next, you'll add some fillets. On the 3D Model tab, click the Fillet button and click the intersecting circular edges on the surface feature.

9. In the Fillet dialog box, change the radius to **12 mm** and then click the OK button.

10. In the Modify panel on the 3D Model tab, click the Thicken/Offset button.

11. Click the Quilt option in the Thicken/Offset dialog box to allow you to select all the surface faces at once and then click anywhere on the surface. Then click the OK button.

12. Rotate the part or use the ViewCube, and you'll see that the surface is still visible. Locate it in the Model browser and then right-click and turn its visibility off. Figure 4.34 shows the revolved shape.

13. You can close the file without saving.

FIGURE 4.34
A revolved surface

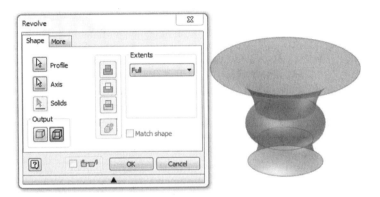

Creating Work Features

A *work feature* is construction geometry used when part geometry is not present to create new features. There are three types of work features: work planes, work axes, and work points. In addition to work features that you might create, each part contains origin planes, axes, and an origin point. You can view these by expanding the Origin folder in the Model browser (as shown in Figure 4.35), right-clicking each feature, and selecting Visibility. Note that in Figure 4.35 the 3D indicator arrows have been drawn in for clarity. If it helps you, though, you can turn the indicator on and have it display in the lower left of your screen by selecting the General Sketch tab of the Application Options dialog box.

FIGURE 4.35
Origin work features
turned on

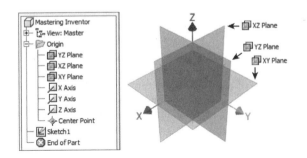

Work Planes

A *work plane* is an infinite construction plane that is parametrically attached to a feature or features, typically to help you define other geometry. Work planes are created based on the geometry you select. Every work plane type is created by defining a location and an orientation. You can use the generic Plane button to create work planes or use the buttons in the Plane drop-down menu. The following brief exercises will demonstrate the creation of each type of work plane.

MIDPLANE BETWEEN TWO PARALLEL PLANES

To create a plane running midplane between two parallel planes, follow these steps:

1. Open the file mi_4a_040.ipt.

2. Click the Plane button on the Work Features panel.

3. Select the yellow faces on each side of the part, and you will see a work plane placed halfway between them.

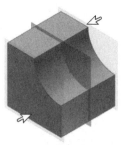

THREE POINT

To create a three-point work plane, follow these steps:

1. Open the file mi_4a_041.ipt.

2. Click the Plane button on the Work Features panel.

3. Select the corner vertices indicated by the yellow corner faces, and a work plane will be created using these three points.

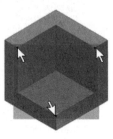

NORMAL TO AXIS THROUGH POINT

To create a plane that is normal to an axis and running through a point, follow these steps:

1. Open the file mi_4a_042.ipt.

2. Click the Plane button on the Work Features panel.

3. Select the corner vertex indicated by the yellow corner pointer face at the sharp point and the edge indicated by the other, and a work plane will be created using these two points.

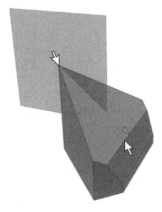

PARALLEL TO PLANE THROUGH POINT

To create a plane running parallel to another plane and running through a point, follow these steps:

1. Open the file mi_4a_043.ipt.

2. Click the Plane button on the Work Features panel.

3. Select the corner vertex indicated by the yellow corner pointer face at the sharp point and the large yellow face, and a work plane will be created using these two points.

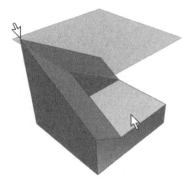

TWO COPLANAR EDGES

To create a plane using two coplanar edges, follow these steps:

1. Open the file mi_4a_044.ipt.

2. Click the Plane button on the Work Features panel.

3. Select the edges indicated by the yellow pointer faces, and a work plane will be created using these two edges.

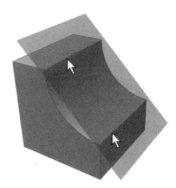

OFFSET FROM PLANE

To create a plane offset from another plane or face, follow these steps:

1. Open the file mi_4a_045.ipt.

2. Click the Plane button on the Work Features panel.

3. Click the yellow face and drag in the offset direction.

4. Enter the offset distance and click the green check mark to create the plane.

5. Double-click the work plane in the modeling area or the browser to change the offset value.

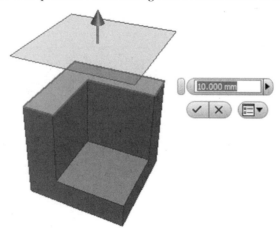

ANGLE TO FACE AROUND EDGE

To create a plane on an edge at an angle to a face, follow these steps:

1. Open the file `mi_4a_046.ipt`.

2. Click the Plane button on the Work Features panel.

3. Select the edge indicated by the yellow pointer face and the yellow face.

4. Enter an angle relative to the selected face and click the green check mark to create the plane.

5. Double-click the work plane in the modeling area or the browser to change the angle value.

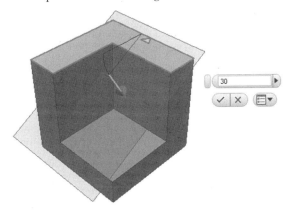

TANGENT TO SURFACE AND PARALLEL TO PLANE

To create a plane tangent to a surface and parallel to another plane, follow these steps:

1. Open the file `mi_4a_047.ipt`.

2. Click the Plane button on the Work Features panel.

3. Select the yellow curved face and then select the flat yellow face, and a work plane will be created tangent to the curved face and parallel to the flat face.

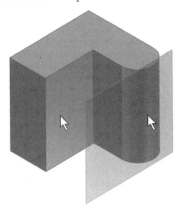

TANGENT TO SURFACE THROUGH EDGE

To create a plane tangent to a surface running through an edge, follow these steps:

1. Open the file named mi_4a_048.ipt.

2. Click the Plane button on the Work Features panel.

3. Select the yellow curved face and the edge indicated by the yellow pointer face, and a work plane will be created tangent to the curved face and running through the selected edge.

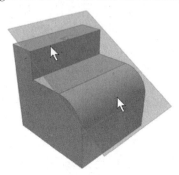

TANGENT TO SURFACE THROUGH POINT

To create a plane tangent to a surface running through a point, follow these steps:

1. Open the file mi_4a_049.ipt.

2. Click the Plane button on the Work Features panel.

3. Select the yellow, curved face and the endpoint of the sketch line, and a work plane will be created tangent to the curved face at the end of the selected line.

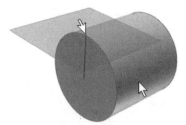

NORMAL TO CURVE AT POINT

To create a plane normal to curve at a point, follow these steps:

1. Open the file mi_4a_050.ipt.

2. Click the Plane button on the Work Features panel.

3. Select any of the sketch points and then select the arc, and a plane will be created at the intersection of the two.

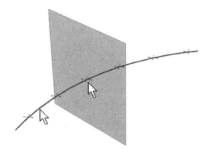

MIDPLANE OF A TORUS

To create a plane that runs midplane of a torus, follow these steps:

1. Open the file mi_4a_051.ipt.

2. Click the flyout arrow (the small black arrow below the Plane button) on the Work Features panel.

3. Click the Midplane Of Torus button.

4. Select anywhere on the torus, and the plane will be created.

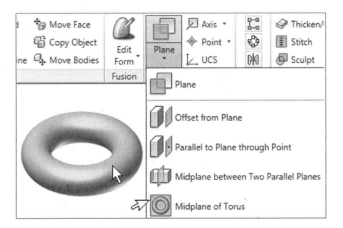

WORK PLANE TIPS

Here are some other points to remember about work planes:

◆ You can right-click a work plane in the browser or the graphics window and then select Show Inputs to see how that work plane was created.

◆ You can move a work plane by clicking an edge and dragging. This will slide the work plane in the plane of its definition only.

◆ When you place the mouse pointer on any corner of the work plane, a resize arrow appears, allowing you to drag the corner of the work plane to resize it.

- You can also right-click and set a work plane to autoresize, allowing it to resize off the extents of the part as it changes.

- Work planes have a positive side and a negative side to them. The normal (positive) side has an orange tint, and the non-normal (negative) side has a blue tint. You can right-click a work plane and choose Flip Normal if needed.

- If you do not have the geometry you need present when creating work planes, you can right-click and choose Create Axis or Create Point to create an *in-line work feature*. In-line features are stacked in the Model browser and automatically set not to display.

- When you start the Work Plane tool, you can right-click and choose Repeat Command to set the work feature tools to stay on until you right-click and choose Done. This helps when you are creating a lot of work features because you do not have to keep clicking the button each time.

Work Axes and Work Points

Certification Objective

Much like a work plane, a work axis or work point can be used to create helper geometry in your model. Work points are often created in order to define work planes or work axes. Work axes are often created to help define work planes.

WORK AXES

A *work axis* is a construction line of infinite length that is attached to a part based on the geometry used to create it. You can create a work axis on linear edges through circular faces and edges; through any combination of work points, midpoints, and vertex points; along 2D and 3D sketch lines; and at the intersection of work planes. You can locate several input-specific buttons for creating work axes by clicking the flyout button next to the Axis button, as shown in Figure 4.36.

FIGURE 4.36
Methods for creating
work axes

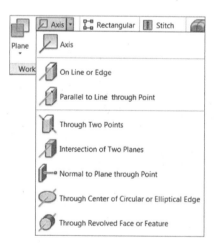

WORK POINTS

Work points can be created at the intersection of planes, surfaces, edges, work axes, 2D or 3D sketch lines, work points, and sketch points, in any combination. They can also be placed directly on sketch points, vertex corners, center points, edge midpoints, or grounded work points. You can locate several input-specific buttons for creating work points by clicking the fly-out button next to the Point button, as shown in Figure 4.37.

FIGURE 4.37
Methods for creating work points

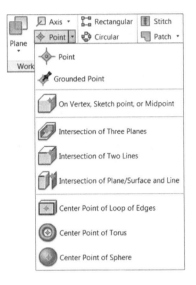

GROUNDED WORK POINTS

Grounded work points are much like regular work points, but they have all of their degrees of freedom removed and are therefore locked to a specific coordinate. To edit a grounded work point, you can right-click it, choose 3D Move/Rotate, and then use the precise input toolbar to make adjustments. You can right-click a regular work point and choose Ground to convert it to a grounded work point.

RENAMING WORK FEATURES

Taking the time to rename work features can be helpful if you find that you must create and edit a lot of them. However, if you use just one or two here and there, it may not be that helpful. Using a consistent naming scheme will help you easily determine the work feature's use.

Creating Fillets

Certification
Objective

The Fillet tool in Inventor may seem daunting at first because of the number of buttons and the combination of options, but once you understand the layout of the dialog box and the intended use of the options, you'll be able to create fillets of all types. There are three basic types of fillets:

Edge Fillets These are fillets created based on selected edges.

Face Fillets These are fillets created between two faces or face sets.

Full Round Fillets These are fillets that are tangent to three adjacent faces or face sets.

When you start the Fillet tool (on the Modify panel of the 3D Model tab), it will default to edge fillets. You can switch the fillet type by using the buttons on the left of the dialog box.

Certification
Objective

WORK FEATURE VISIBILITY VS. DISPLAY

Many Inventor users fight the control of visibility of work features (work planes, work axes, and work points) because of a lack of understanding of the tools available to control it. There are basically two methods of preventing work features from displaying onscreen.

◆ Right-click the work feature and toggle off Visibility. (Always use this at the part level.)

◆ On the View tab, click Object Visibility and then use one of the options listed. (Do not use this at the part level but only at the assembly level.)

Both methods turn off the display, but only the first toggles the visibility setting for each object. The second is a display override that suppresses the work feature display but does not change the visibility setting.

The difference between the two methods becomes important at the assembly level. If you've used the Object Visibility tool to "override" the work feature visibility setting at the part level, you will find that all the work features will display when you place the part into an assembly. This requires you to toggle them all off again at the assembly level, and you will be required to do so for each instance of the part placed. You could use the Object Visibility tool in the assembly and suppress the display of all the work features for the entire assembly, but doing so doesn't allow you to access one or two work features at a time. As a result, you end up with all or none of the work features displaying.

To properly control work feature visibility, you should develop the habit of always right-clicking the work features at the part level and explicitly toggling off the visibility setting, and you should never use the Object Visibility override in a part. If you do this, then when the part is used in an assembly, you can control the work features on an individual basis, per instance of the part. Then you can use the Object Visibility tool to toggle all the visible work features on and off effectively.

Edge Fillets

Certification
Objective

Edge fillets are the most common type and therefore naturally have the most options. When edge fillet is the active type, you'll see three tabs across the top of the dialog box, allowing you to set the following edge fillet subtypes: constant, variable, and setbacks.

CONSTANT FILLETS

Constant fillets have the same radius along the entire length of the edge. On the Constant tab, you can select a group of edges and then set the radius and type. You can create a new size group by clicking the Click To Add row in the selection pane and changing the radius size. Figure 4.38 shows two constant fillet groups being created. In this case, each group contains only one edge, but they vary in radius.

FIGURE 4.38
Creating two edge fillets of different sizes

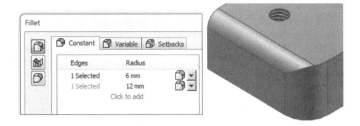

FILLET FAILURES

If you attempt to place multiple fillets at once, you might be alerted to the fact that some of the edges could not be blended successfully using the current radius size, in which case you can choose to place the successful fillets and skip the others.

One of the most common issues with edge fillets arises when you select multiple edges that converge on a single corner vertex. Unfortunately, when this happens, the error message might erroneously indicate an issue with the fillet size. However, you can generally resolve this issue by removing one or more of the competing edges from the selection, applying the fillet feature, and then applying another fillet feature using the previously removed edges. Keep this in mind as you place edge fillets, and remember that just because you can place multiple sizes of edge fillets all in one feature doesn't mean it's always the best solution.

Also on the Constant tab you can change the selection method from Edge to Loop or Feature. Figure 4.39 shows the selection method set to Feature and the results of selecting a hole. Note that all edges created by the hole feature are selected.

FIGURE 4.39
Fillet selection by feature

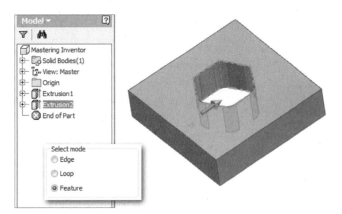

You can also select All Fillets (inside corners) or All Rounds (outside corners) to apply fillets to a part quickly, where it makes sense to do so. Figure 4.40 shows the same part with all fillets applied on the left and all rounds applied on the right. Keep in mind that you can select all rounds and fillets at once as well.

FIGURE 4.40
All fillets vs. all rounds

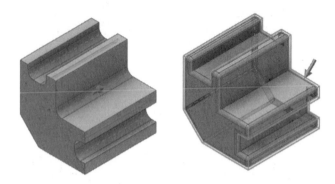

VARIABLE FILLETS

In contrast to constant-edge fillets are variable-edge fillets. Variable-edge fillets can have multiple radius sizes along the length of the edge. To create variable fillets, click the Variable tab and then select an edge to make it variable. By default, the start points and endpoints are added to the right pane. You can add points by simply clicking the edge in the place or places you want to transition to a different radius.

Once points are selected, you can change the radius and position of each point. The number listed in the Position column is a decimal percent of the edge length rather than the length. For instance, Figure 4.41 shows a point has been added at 0.5 ul or 50 percent of the edge length coming off the start end. Recall that *ul* is simply Inventor's abbreviation for unitless, which is automatically applied to parameters that do not require a unit suffix.

FIGURE 4.41
A variable-edge fillet

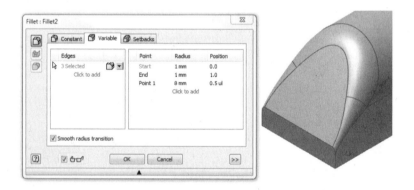

SETBACKS

Setbacks define the corner where multiple-edge fillets come together. Once you select edges in the Constant tab, you can switch to the Setbacks tab and select corners to apply setbacks to. Setbacks are typically used for cast and molded parts where the corners cannot be too sharp.

On the Setbacks tab, select a corner using the Vertex pane first. Then enter a setback distance for each edge. Setback values should be no longer than the length of the edge they are placed on. You will typically get an error if you attempt to specify a value that is larger. If you click the Minimal check box, the setbacks will automatically adjust to the smallest length that can be built. Figure 4.42 shows a setback being created, along with the result.

FIGURE 4.42
A setback fillet

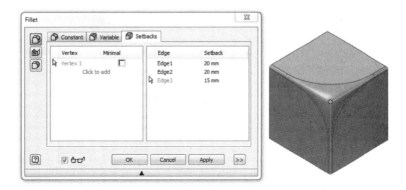

Face Fillets

Face fillets are added between two selected face sets. These faces or sets of faces do not need to share a common edge. You can adjust the radius once the fillet is previewed, but typically if you do not get a preview, it indicates an invalid selection set. You can add more faces, or you may need to use a different type of fillet solution.

Two options are selected by default:

Include Tangent Faces Use this option to allow the fillet to continue over tangent, adjacent faces. Deselect this option to ensure that the fillet is only between selected faces.

Optimize For Single Selection Deselect this option when making multiple selections per face set. When this option is selected, the selection automatically changes from selection set 1 to selection set 2.

Figure 4.43 shows a face fillet created between the two dark faces.

FIGURE 4.43
Creating a face fillet

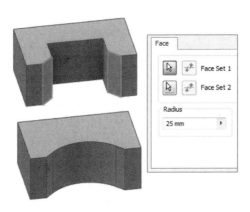

Full Round Fillets

Full round fillets can be used to quickly round over a feature without having to know the radius that would complete the full round. You can also use this option to create a full round on faces that are not parallel. To create this type of fillet, simply select the faces in the order in which they occur from side to center to other side, and the center face will be replaced with the radius face. Figure 4.44 shows a full round. The selection options are the same as described previously for the face fillet.

FIGURE 4.44
A full round fillet

Working with Fillet Features

In this section, you'll create the various types of fillets discussed in the previous pages. To begin, open the file mi_4a_053.ipt. Then follow these steps:

1. Select the Fillet tool on the Modify panel of the 3D Model tab (or press **F** on the keyboard).

2. You'll create a simple edge fillet. Select the vertical edge where the yellow and blue faces intersect.

3. Set the fillet radius to **18 mm** and click the Apply button.

4. Next, you'll create a variable fillet. Click the Variable tab in the Fillet dialog box.

5. Select the edge where the purple and red faces intersect.

6. Set the radius for the start and endpoints to **2 mm**.

7. If needed, click the word *Start* to set the dialog box from edit mode back to selection mode and then click anywhere on the edge between the purple and red faces.

8. Change the radius to **6 mm** and then set the position to **0.5** to set the new variable point to be halfway between the start and endpoints. Note that you could add additional variable points to further define the variation of the fillet. In this case, though, just click the Apply button to create the variable fillet.

9. Next you'll create a fillet setback. To do so, switch back to the Constant tab and set the radius to **2 mm**.

10. If needed, click the Pencil icon in the current row to set it from edit mode to selection mode.

11. Select the edge between the yellow and pink faces and then the edge between the yellow and green faces. It may help to zoom in on the corner.

12. In the Fillet dialog box, click the Click To Add text to add another row to the list.

13. Change the radius to **3 mm** and then click the Pencil icon to set the row back to selection mode, if needed.

14. Select the edge between the pink and green faces.

15. Select the Setbacks tab in the Fillet dialog box.

16. Choose the corner where the yellow, pink, and green faces intersect. You should see the vertex highlight as you locate it.

17. Enter **6 mm** for all of the setback values and then click the Apply button to create the fillets with setback.

18. Next, you'll create a face fillet. Click the Face Fillet button on the left of the Fillet dialog box (the one in the middle).

19. For Face Set 1, choose one of the orange faces; for Face Set 2, choose the other. Then click the Apply button.

20. And finally, you will create a full round fillet. Click the Full Round Fillet button on the left of the Fillet dialog box.

21. Select the tan faces on the protruding front feature in consecutive order (the right face for Side Face Set 1, the top face for Center Face Set, and the left face for Side Face Set 2, for example).

22. Click the OK button to create the fillet and close the Fillet dialog box.

Take a look at the fillet features in the browser tree. You can right-click any of them and choose Edit Feature to adjust the fillet as needed. To add edges to or remove edges from any given fillet feature, you can use the Ctrl key and then click the edges onscreen. Figure 4.45 shows the part before and after fillets were applied. You can close the file without saving changes.

FIGURE 4.45
Before and after fillets

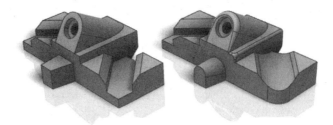

Note that if you try to place a fillet along the edges where the pink and red faces intersect, you will receive an error because of the way the resulting fillet tapers. However, if you also choose the corresponding edges on the opposite of the rounded feature, the fillet will build without problems. Keep this in mind as you work with fillets that form sharp tapers.

COLOR OVERRIDES

To change the color of any individual face on a model, you can right-click the face and choose Properties from the context menu. You can do the same for entire features by right-clicking them in the browser and choosing Properties.

To remove color overrides for entire solids, you can expand the Solid Bodies folder in the browser, right-click a solid, and choose Properties. In the Body Properties dialog box, you can set Body Appearance to As Part, select the Clear All Overrides check box, and then click the OK button. Be aware that parts translated from other file formats often come in with many color overrides and the Clear All Overrides action can take a while to process.

Creating Threaded Features

Inventor offers the option of creating cosmetic threads that represent actual threads in the part, and it creates 2D geometry information for detailing those threads. Cosmetic threads are created with a threaded hole feature. Or you can use the Thread tool on the Feature panel bar to add threads to existing part features. The thread features are added to the Model browser as separate features.

Creating Cosmetic Threads Using the Thread Tool

Creating cosmetic threads on a circular part is a relatively simple procedure. Cosmetic threads work by wrapping a scaled graphic around the feature to represent threads. This allows the model file size to stay smaller because it is not required to calculate all the extra edges and faces of the threads. However, the cosmetic Thread tool does create fully intelligent thread features based on the specifications you choose, allowing you to detail the threads quickly and accurately in the drawing environment.

In the following steps, you will use the Split tool to divide a cylindrical surface into multiple faces and then apply cosmetic threads to them:

1. Open the file mi_4a_056.ipt.

2. On the 3D Model tab, click the Split button.

3. Select Work Plane1 for the Split tool, select the face of the cylinder it runs through, and then click the OK button.

4. Right-click the edge of Work Plane1 and choose Visibility to turn the plane off. Recall that work planes are selectable only by their edges.

5. Now that the part is divided into two faces, click the Thread button from the Modify tab and select the shortest face.

6. Click the Specification tab, set Size to **17** and Designation to **M17×1** and then click the Apply button.

7. Switch back to the Location tab and click the end of the middle cylinder.

8. Uncheck the Full Length check box and enter **5 mm** for the Offset and **30 mm** for the Length. Click the direction button if you do not see the threads appear. Click the Apply button.

9. Run your mouse pointer over the third cylinder, and notice that as you get closer to one end or the other, the offset and direction switch.

10. Click the face and apply another set of threads of any type you like; when you've finished, click the OK button. Figure 4.46 shows the Thread tool options.

FIGURE 4.46
Placing cosmetic threads

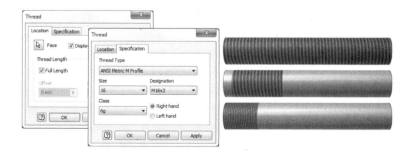

3D THREADS FROM YOUR COSMETIC THREADS

Unless you are going to actually cut threads directly from your 3D model, cosmetic threads are usually sufficient. The advantage of these threads is that they contain all the thread information in the model that can later be extracted in a drawing without carrying the burden of complex modeling features.

Inventor pulls its thread specification information from the Thread.xls file found in the Design Data folder. You can edit this file to contain custom thread specifications and include proprietary threads or industry-specific threads not commonly listed.

If you find that you do need to generate 3D threads from your cosmetic threads, maybe for a 3D printed part, for example, you can download the ThreadModeler tool from the Autodesk Exchange Apps website: http://apps.exchange.autodesk.com.

Using the Coil Tool to Create Physical Threads

In addition to using the ThreadModeler add-in tool at the http://apps.exchange.autodesk.com website, you can create physical threads using the Coil tool. Physical threads create large file sizes compared to cosmetic threads and can seriously affect performance and assemblies. As a result, physical threads should be used only where absolutely necessary, such as in the design of a bottle or jar top or other geometries such as a worm gear. You can explore the creation of a physical thread with the Coil tool in these steps:

1. Open the file mi_4a_057.ipt.

2. In the Model browser, select the sketch called Thread Cut Sketch, right-click, and select Edit Sketch.

3. Right-click and choose Slice Graphics (or press **F7** on the keyboard) to temporarily slice away the material that hinders your view of the sketch. Recall that this option is available only while creating or editing a sketch that runs through a solid.

4. Zoom in on the sketch, change the depth dimension to **2 mm**, and then click the Finish Sketch button to exit the sketch.

5. Zoom out (or double-click the mouse wheel to zoom all) and then locate and click the Coil tool on the Create panel.

6. Select the sketch profile if it does not automatically select and then select the work axis in the center of the cylinder for the axis.

7. Use a direction button to make sure the coil is running the correct way and then click the Cut button.

8. Click the Coil Size tab, change the pitch to **4 mm** and the revolution to **12**, and then click the OK button.

Figure 4.47 shows the Coil Size tab. Be aware that you can create coils by specifying pitch and revolution, revolution and height, and pitch and height, or by defining a spiral. Also note the suffix of *ul* shown in the Revolution drop-down box. This suffix just means that the value is unitless. You do not have to specify this because Inventor will do so as needed.

FIGURE 4.47
Creating a physical thread
with the Coil tool

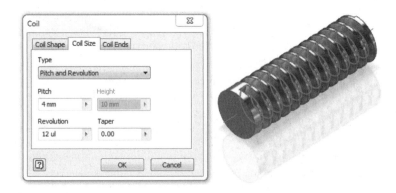

Hole Features

Using Inventor's Hole tool, you can create counterbore, countersink, spotface, and drilled holes with user-defined variables such as thread designation and drill point angle. You can also specify a simple hole, a tapped hole, a tapped tapering hole, or a clearance hole.

Using the Thread and Clearance Spreadsheets

Two external files are related to the Hole tool: Thread.xls and Clearance.xls. Both files load at the time of installation to a Design Data folder in the install directory location, such as C:\ Users\Public\Documents\Autodesk\Inventor2016\Design Data\XLS\en-US. If the Design Data folder has been relocated, you can determine its location by following these steps:

1. On the Get Started tab, click Projects.

2. In the Projects dialog box, ensure that you are looking at the correct project and locate and expand the Folder Options node in the lower pane.

3. Note the Design Data path listed.

4. If the Design Data path says = `Default`, then your project is reading the path from Inventor's options, so you should select the Tools tab, click Application Options, and select the File tab in the dialog box that opens. Note the Design Data path listed.

Once the path is determined, you can browse to the path, find the thread and clearance spreadsheets, and make customizations as follows. To edit the thread spreadsheet, follow these steps:

1. Close Inventor.

2. Make a copy of the original spreadsheet and store it in a safe location (this is just a precaution).

3. Open the `Thread.xls` file in Microsoft Excel.

4. To add or modify custom thread designations for an existing thread type, do the following:

    a. Choose the worksheet you want to customize.

    b. Edit the values in the Custom Thread Designation column to include your designations. These will then be available in the Thread and Hole tools and can be recovered in hole notes in a drawing.

    c. Edit cell B1 to change the name Inventor displays in the Hole and Thread tools.

    d. Edit cell D1 to change the order in which Inventor lists the thread types in the Hole and Thread tool dialog boxes.

5. To add a new thread type, complete these tasks:

    a. Copy an existing worksheet of the same type (parallel or taper).

    b. Rename the custom worksheet as required.

    c. Delete most or all of the rows below row 3. You may want to keep at least one row to use as a reference, at least temporarily.

    d. Add rows as required.

    e. Edit cell B1 to change the name Inventor displays in the Hole and Thread tools.

    f. Edit cell D1 to change the order in which Inventor lists the thread types in the Hole and Thread dialog boxes.

    g. Hover your mouse pointer over cell A1 to see the tool tip containing the letter designations and mark your sheet as appropriate.

6. Save the spreadsheet.

7. Restart Inventor. Changes are read when Inventor loads.

The process to modify `Clearance.xls` is similar.

Creating Holes in Parts

Certification
Objective

You have four options for placing holes with the Hole tool:

◆   From Sketch

◆   Linear

◆   Concentric

◆   On Point

To explore these placement options, open the file mi_4a_055.ipt from the Chapter 04 folder of your Mastering Inventor 2016 directory, and follow these steps:

1. Select the Hole tool on the 3D Model tab (or press **H** on the keyboard).

2. You'll notice that the Placement option is set to From Sketch. This is because Inventor has detected that there are two sketches available for use. Click Cancel to exit the Hole tool.

3. Right-click Sketch5 in the Model browser and choose Visibility to turn off the visibility of this sketch.

4. Start the Hole tool again. This time Inventor detects that there is only one sketch available and automatically selects the center point found in that sketch.

5. Click the counterbore option, set the counterbore (as shown in Figure 4.48), and then click the OK button.

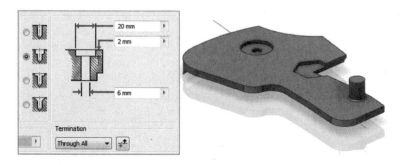

FIGURE 4.48
Counterbore settings

6. Right-click Sketch5, turn the visibility back on, and then click the Hole button again. Notice that it selects the center points automatically again. This is helpful; however, you do not want the hole in the hex-shaped cutout to be the same size as the others in this sketch. Hold down the Ctrl key and click the center point at that location to remove it from the selection.

7. Choose the spotface option, and notice that it is essentially the same as the counterbore with the exception of the depth measurement. In the spotface, the depth is measured from the bottom of the bore. Set the spotface as shown in Figure 4.49 and click the OK button.

FIGURE 4.49
Spotface settings

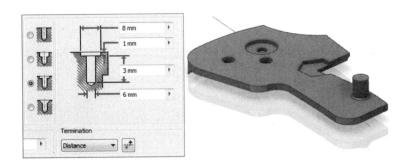

8. Since you removed the one center point before placing the spotface holes, you will reuse that sketch to place the next hole. To do so, that sketch must be visible. The Hole tool has toggled the visibility back off, so you need to locate Sketch5 again and make it visible.

9. Place a simple drilled hole using the center point in the hex-shaped cutout. Set the termination to Through All and the diameter to **9 mm**, and click the OK button. Then turn the visibility of the sketch off one last time.

10. Start the Hole tool again. You'll note that because there are no longer any visible sketches, the From Sketch option is no longer the default placement option. Set the placement to Concentric and select the top face of the part for the Plane input.

11. Next, you need to specify a concentric reference. Select one of the yellow faces (or the circular edge of the yellow face).

12. Set the hole to the countersink option and then set the inputs as shown in Figure 4.50. Click the Apply button (not the OK button just yet).

FIGURE 4.50
Countersink settings

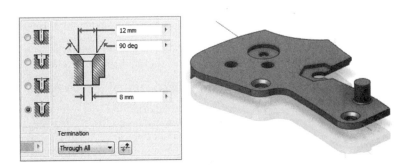

13. Set the plane, use the other yellow face to place another countersink of the same size, and then click the OK button.

14. Change your view so that you can see the work point at the work axis intersection of the green face.

15. Start the Hole tool again and set the placement option to On Point.

16. Select the work point for the point input and then the work axis for the direction. Flip the direction if needed, using the button next to the Termination drop-down.

17. Leave the hole at the simple drilled option and set the Termination drop-down to To.

18. For the To selection, click the bore face of the counterbore hole and click the Terminate Feature check box.

19. Click the clearance hole option, set the options as shown in Figure 4.51, and click the OK button.

FIGURE 4.51
Clearance hole settings

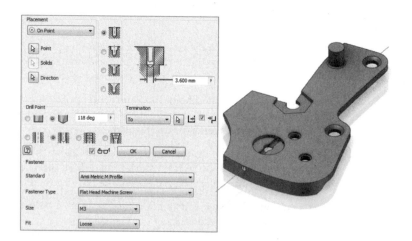

20. Rotate the part so that you can see the underside and zoom in on the feature with the red face.

21. Start the Hole tool again and select the red face for the Face input.

22. Select one of the longer straight edges for Reference1 and set the dimension to **8 mm**. Select one of the shorter edges and set the dimension to **12 mm**.

23. Set the termination to Through All and the hole type to Taper Tapped Hole.

24. Choose Din Taper from the Thread Type list, set the size to **M5**, and then click the OK button. You'll note that the hole is cut with the appropriate taper.

You can close the part without saving changes when you have created all the holes.

As you can see, the Hole tool has an abundance of options allowing you to specify holes in a variety of ways. Keep in mind that features created with the Hole tool carry more intelligence with them than a simple circular extrude cut. This is particularly true when you begin to detail a part in the drawing environment.

Setting Tolerance Values in Holes

You can set tolerances for hole dimensions in the Hole dialog box. When setting a hole dimension, right-click a dimension edit box and then select Tolerance, as shown in Figure 4.52.

FIGURE 4.52
Tolerance settings

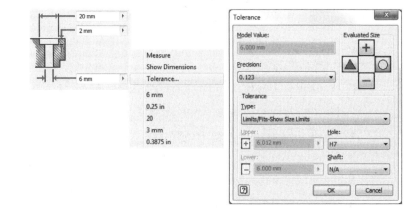

You can use these general steps to access the tolerance settings:

1. In the Tolerance dialog box, change the values as desired:

- In Precision, click the arrow to set the decimal precision of the dimension.

- In Evaluated Size, select Upper, Nominal, Median, or Lower to use when evaluating the dimension. This will set the size at which the hole is actually created.

- In Type, click the arrow and select a tolerance type for the selected dimension.

2. Depending on your selection, enter values to set the upper and lower tolerance range and the tolerance for the hole and shaft dimensions (for Limits and Fits).

3. Click the OK button.

This will return you to the Hole dialog box. Keep in mind that although the value in the hole input will not change, the hole will be drawn to the tolerance you selected in the model. For instance, if the Upper option were selected in the hole shown in Figure 4.52, the hole would measure 6.012 mm rather than 6.000 mm. You'll learn more about using tolerances in Chapter 5.

Bend Parts

You can use the Bend Part tool to bend a part based on a sketched bend line. You can specify the end of the part to bend, the direction of the bend, the angle, the radius, and the arc length. You can find the Bend Part tool on the Modify tab of the 3D Model tab. By default, it is hidden from view and must be accessed by using the flyout (the small black triangle on the Modify panel).

Here are some guidelines to be aware of when using the Bend Part tool:

- Sketches used for bend lines must be visible and unadaptive and should be located on a plane or surface that contacts the part.

- A sketched line on the top face of a part does not allow for the part to be bent down, only up, whereas a sketch that runs through the part allows the bend to be built up or down.

- Bend Part does not account for bend allowances in the way sheet-metal features do and therefore should not be used with sheet-metal parts.

- You can specify the bend by Radius & Angle, Radius & Arc Length, or Arc Length & Angle.

Follow these steps to create a simple bend part:

1. Open the file named mi_4a_058.ipt.

2. Select the Bend Part tool from the flyout of the Modify panel.

3. Select one of the sketch lines as the bend line.

4. Adjust the arrow buttons so that just the end is bent up. Notice that if you try to bend the end down, it will not work. This is because of the position of the sketch.

5. Set the radius to **100 mm** and then click the OK button.

6. The bend will consume your sketch. Expand the Bend Part1 node; then click and drag Sketch2 above Bend Part1 in the feature tree to share Sketch2 and make it visible.

7. Create another bend to your specifications, experimenting with the other solutions.

Figure 4.53 shows the Bend Part tool in action. You can close the file without saving changes when finished.

FIGURE 4.53
Bending a steel shape

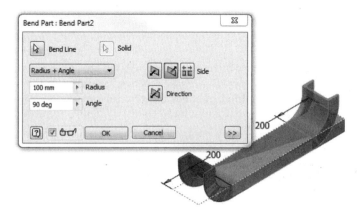

Part Modeling Exercise

In the pages that follow, you will create a part similar to the part shown in Figure 4.54. You'll employ some of the tools covered in this chapter and preview some that are covered in Chapter 5.

FIGURE 4.54
The part you'll create in this exercise

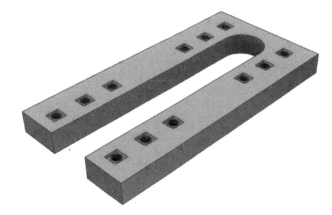

Creating a Base Feature

You'll begin by creating a new part file from the Standard(mm).ipt template.

1. On the Get Started tab, click the New button.

2. On the Metric tab of the New File dialog box, select the Standard(mm).ipt template.

3. On the Sketch tab, locate the rectangle drop-down menu (the small black arrow next to the Rectangle button) and click the Rectangle Two Point Center tool.

PROJECTING THE ORIGIN POINT

If you do not see an origin point in your sketch, you may want to take this opportunity to turn on the option that will automatically project it into every new sketch. To do so, just follow these steps:

1. On the Tools tab, click Application Options.

2. Choose the Sketch tab.

3. Ensure that the Autoproject Part Origin On Sketch Create option is selected and click the OK button.

4. Start a new file from a template, and you will see that the origin point is now present.

---

4. Place the rectangle on the projected origin point.

5. Use the Dimension tool on the Sketch tab to dimension the sketch at 150 mm by 300 mm, as shown in Figure 4.55.

6. Press E to start the Extrude command or right-click and choose Finish 2D Sketch; then click the Extrude button on the 3D Model tab.

7. If needed, click the corner of the ViewCube to find an isometric view of the sketch so you can see the preview (if it's not displayed, select the View tab, select the Windows panel, click the User Interface button, and click the drop-down arrow).

FIGURE 4.55
Initial sketch

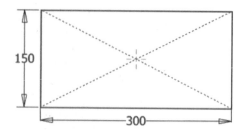

8. Generally, Inventor will select the profile for you if you have just one closed profile present to extrude. If the profile is not selected, click anywhere in the rectangle to select it.

9. Enter **25 mm** in the Distance input box. Click the arrow buttons to change the extrude direction just to see how the preview updates. Then click the left arrow button and click the OK button.

Creating a Second Feature

Now that you've created your base feature, you will continue by adding features to it. Before doing so, it is a good idea to save your part. Click the Save icon from the Quick Access bar at the top of the screen, or click the Inventor button and then select Save. You can save the file in the Chapter 04 folder and name it anything you like.

Now that the part is saved, it's time to create a second feature.

1. Press **S** to start a new sketch or, on the 3D Model tab, click the Start 2D Sketch button and then click the large front face of the part. Sketch2 is now created and active.

2. Use the ViewCube to orient your view of the part so that you have a flat 2D view of your sketch plane with the rectangle running horizontally on your screen.

3. If you see sketch lines outlining the base feature, then you have the Autoproject Edges For Sketch Creation And Edit option turned on. If you do not see those sketch lines, select the Project Geometry tool on the Sketch tab and select the face again to project the edges.

ENABLING PROJECT EDGES ON SKETCH CREATION

If you see the outline of the faces automatically projected into your new sketches, you may want to consider turning it off. In general, I do not recommend you use this. It may be helpful in the beginning, but be aware that your sketches can become cluttered with unneeded geometry. When all edges are projected, it is more difficult to determine the design intent and edit sketches. Instead, consider disabling this option and developing a practice of projecting only necessary edges.

To do so, follow these steps:

1. On the Tools tab, click Application Options.

2. Choose the Sketch tab.

3. Ensure that the Autoproject Edges For Sketch Creation And Edit option is selected to enable it or deselected to disable it and click the OK button.

4. Sketch a rectangle on the face selected for the sketch. Place this rectangle in the middle of the face, being careful not to accidentally constrain it to the origin point or the edge of the base feature (you will relocate it using a sketch constraint later).

5. Select the Circle tool on the Sketch tab; then sketch a circle at the end of the rectangle starting with the midpoint of the vertical line on the right and snapping to the endpoint of the top or bottom line. You don't need to trim the circle before converting this sketch into a feature, and in fact, unneeded trimming of sketch entities often works against you because it may remove sketch constraints.

6. Use the Dimension tool on the Sketch tab and add a dimension to the circle. Rather than just entering a value, enter **Diameter = 40 mm**, thereby assigning the dimension a name and a value (be sure you have named this dimension because you will be using it in the steps to come).

7. You'll next create an equation for the length of the rectangle based on the length of the diameter value. With the Dimension tool, select the long edge of the rectangle and enter **Slot_Length =**.

8. Click the 40 mm diameter dimension you just created. This will link the two dimensions. Finish the equation with ***5** so that your end equation reads Slot_Length = Diameter*5. Note that you must use an underscore here because spaces are not allowed in parameter names. Your sketch should look similar to Figure 4.56.

FIGURE 4.56
Creating and dimensioning geometry in Sketch2

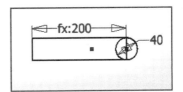

9. Create a Coincident constraint between the midpoint of the left vertical line of the rectangle and the midpoint of the left, projected, vertical line of the base feature.

10. Select one (or all) of the projected lines of the base feature and convert it to a construction line (this ensures that Inventor will not attempt to extrude the large projected profile in the next step).

USE WORK FEATURES TO ANCHOR YOUR SKETCHES

Another way to anchor this sketch to the midplane of the rectangle is by using work features. Before starting a sketch, click the Plane icon on the Work Features panel. Select one side of the rectangular feature and then the other. This will create a parametrically centered work plane.

Then you can create a sketch and in that sketch use the Project Geometry tool to project the edge of the work plane. This will project the work plane as a line onto the sketch plane. You can then use this line as a centerline in your sketch-creation sequence. If you were to ever change the size of the base feature and then the work plane and the projected line, this sketch would all update and remain centered.

11. Press **E** to start the Extrude tool or finish the sketch and choose Extrude on the 3D Model tab.

12. If needed, use the ViewCube to view the part from an isometric view.

13. Select the rectangle and the circle you just created for the profile.

14. Click the Cut button (the second button down in the list of operation buttons) so that the profiles will be cut out of the base feature. Your preview should be red when the Cut operation is selected. Check the direction arrow to ensure that the cut is going in the correct direction.

15. In the Extents drop-down, select All. The All option extrudes the profile through all the current features of the entire part in the specified direction or in both directions if you chose the Midplane option. If the size of the base part features change, the cut extrusion feature will update accordingly. Click the OK button when your options look like Figure 4.57 and then save your file.

FIGURE 4.57
Extruding (cutting) the second feature

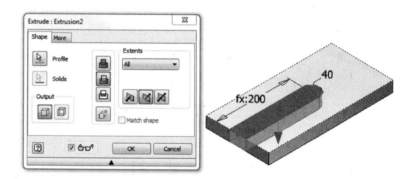

Creating a Sketch-Based Hole Feature

Hole features are powerful components of Inventor. Many methods are available for creating holes. You can create holes in the following ways:

◆ By utilizing existing sketches containing sketch center points

◆ By distance from two planar edges

◆ On a face by referencing a concentric edge or concentric face

◆ By using a work point feature

You can continue with the file you are working on or open the file mi_4a_060.ipt. Follow these steps to create another sketch and then use that sketch to place a hole:

1. Press the S key or, on the 3D Model tab, click the Start 2D Sketch button and then click the large front face of the part (or right-click the face and select New Sketch). Sketch3 is now created and active.

2. If needed, use the ViewCube to orient your view of the part so that you have a flat 2D view of your sketch plane with the rectangle running horizontally on your screen.

3. You might see the outline of the sketch plane face automatically projected into your sketch (if not, click the Project Geometry button and select the sketch plane).

4. On the Sketch tab, select the Offset button on the Modify panel.

5. Before selecting anything to offset, right-click and ensure that both the Loop-Select and Constrain Offset options are selected.

Loop-Select   This option selects lines/curves joined at their endpoints. Deselect to select one or more lines/curves individually.

Constrain Offset   This option constrains the distance between the new geometry and the original to be equidistant.

6. Click the radius and then move the offset profile so that it is created to the inside of the part. Then right-click and click Cancel.

7. Place a dimension between the offset profile and the outside edge of the part and enter **Offset = 20 mm** in the input box (again, be sure to name this because you will be using it in the steps that follow).

8. Window-select the entire part/sketch so that all of the lines are selected; then click the Construction button and convert the lines to construction lines.

SELECT OBJECTS WITH A WINDOW SELECTION

You can create multiple entity selections using what is referred to as a *window selection*. Window selection sets include objects differently depending on whether the window is created from left to right or right to left:

◆   Position the pointer slightly above and to the left of the leftmost entity to select and then click and drag the pointer slightly below and to the right of the rightmost entity you want to select. All objects that are fully enclosed within the rectangle are selected and highlighted.

◆   Position the pointer slightly below and to the right of the rightmost entity to select; then click and drag the pointer slightly above and to the left of the leftmost entity you want to select. All objects that are enclosed by or intersected by the rectangle are selected and highlighted.

You can use the Ctrl and Shift keys to add entities to and remove entities from the selection sets.

---

9. Select the Point tool on the Create panel of the Sketch tab and place a point on the corner of the offset loop, as shown in Figure 4.58.

10. Press **H** to start the Hole tool or finish the sketch and choose the Hole tool on the 3D Model tab.

11. If needed, use the ViewCube to view the part from an isometric view.

FIGURE 4.58
Placing a sketch point for hole placement

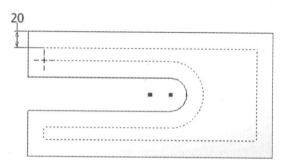

12. The Hole tool should have automatically selected your sketch point; if not, make sure the Placement drop-down is set to From Sketch and the Centers button is selected and then select the sketch point onscreen.

13. In the Termination drop-down, select Through All to ensure that the hole depth always cuts through the part. Then set Type to Tapped, set the Threads options to ISO Metric Profile, set Size to **10,** and set Designation to **M10×1.5** (as shown in Figure 4.59). Click the OK button and save your part.

FIGURE 4.59
Hole options

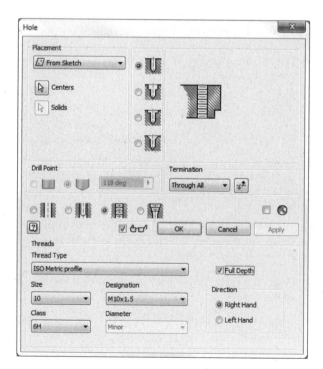

SELECTING SKETCHED HOLE CENTERS

The Hole tool will automatically select sketched center points as long as only one visible unconsumed sketch is available. If you find that the Hole tool is not picking up your center point automatically, check to see that you haven't accidentally created an extra sketch in the model tree. You can hover your mouse pointer over the Sketch node in the browser to see the sketched entities highlight on the screen. If you determine that you have accidentally created an extra sketch, you can right-click it and click Delete.

Note, too, that only center points (small cross marks) are automatically selected by the Hole tool and simple points are not. However, you can manually select simple points for hole placement. You can also convert center points to simple points, or vice versa, by using the Center Point button on the Sketch tab (you'll find it next to the Construction tool).

Creating a Rectangular Hole Pattern

So far, the features you've created have been based on a sketch. These types of features are, therefore, referred to as *sketched* features. Features not based on sketches are referred to as *placed* features. Placed features are solely dependent on existing part geometry. In the pages to come, you will explore the steps necessary to create a placed feature in the form of a rectangular pattern.

When creating patterns, you have the choice of creating them at the feature level or at the sketch level. For instance, you could have patterned the sketch point using a sketch pattern and then placed multiple holes at once using the Hole tool. It is generally best, though, to create patterns as features rather than sketch patterns. Here are some reasons to consider feature patterns:

◆ A feature pattern saves time when creating spaced, multiple instances of a feature, and it makes editing the spacing easily accessible.

◆ Using a feature pattern in a part allows you to later use that pattern to create a component pattern in an assembly and follow the original part pattern. For instance, if you placed this part into an assembly, you could pattern a bolt to occupy every hole within the pattern by simply constraining one bolt into the original hole feature and then use the Component Pattern tool to automatically pick up the hole pattern count and spacing. The Component Pattern tool is available only within the assembly environment.

◆ The number of holes will not update when changing the sketched pattern of points. If you decide to change the number of patterned points in the sketch, you will need to manually edit the hole feature and add the new points to be used in hole operation.

First you'll need to determine the pattern spacing. From the creation of the second feature, you know the round end of the slot has a width of 40 mm. From the creation of the placed hole, you know the offset from the slot edge is 20 mm. From this information, you can determine that the spacing of the two rows of holes is (2 × offset value) + 40 mm, which is therefore 80 mm. Assume the design specification requires eight holes in each row and they need to be spaced at a distance of 25 mm apart. With this information, you are now ready to proceed with creating the hole pattern. You can continue with the file from the previous section or open the file mi_4a_061.ipt. Then follow these steps:

1. On the 3D Model tab, click the Rectangular Pattern button on the Pattern panel.

2. In the Rectangular Pattern dialog box, you are being asked to select the features to pattern. You can select the hole from the graphics area, but you may find it easier to do so from the Model browser. No matter what method you use, check the Model browser to ensure that only Hole1 is highlighted (you can use Ctrl+click to deselect any accidentally selected features).

3. Click the arrow button under Direction 1 and select the edge of the slot cutout. Use a direction button to change the direction, if required, and set the count and spacing to **8** and **25 mm**, respectively. You can confirm that your settings look similar to Figure 4.60.

FIGURE 4.60

List parameters in the Rectangular Pattern dialog box

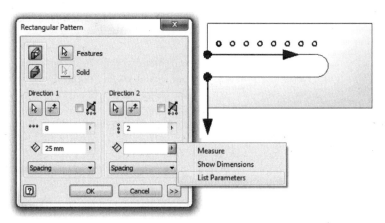

4. Click the arrow button under Direction 2 and select one of the short ends of the part. Use a direction button to change the direction, if required, and set the count to **2**.

Although you could just change the spacing value to 80 mm and complete the pattern, you might want to consider what would happen if the width of the slot feature were to change. If that were to happen, the hole pattern spacing would stay at 80 mm and no longer remain symmetric to the slot width. To avoid this, you will make the pattern spacing parametric by calling the dimensions of earlier features into your pattern spacing. In this way, you are building a formula right into the pattern so that if those dimensions change, the spacing setting will follow.

5. To do this, first clear the Direction 2 length input box.

6. Click the arrow at the right of the length input box and click List Parameters from the flyout shown in Figure 4.60.

7. Choose Diameter from the list, then choose List Parameters again, and, finally, choose Offset.

8. Edit the input to read **Diameter + 2* Offset**.

9. If the text shows in red, there is an error. When you have a valid formula, it will display in black. Check the preview, ensure that the pattern looks correct, and then click the OK button. Confirm that your part looks like Figure 4.61 and then you can save your file.

FIGURE 4.61
A rectangular hole pattern

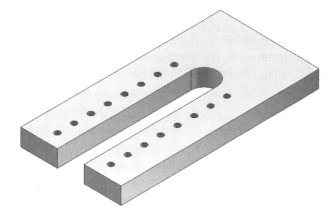

Editing Sketches and Features

You will often need to modify a sketch and/or feature after you have created it. Oftentimes you may find that because designs are similar, it is most efficient to copy an existing part and then make changes to the copy.

In the next steps, you'll edit some of the features you've just created, but before doing so, it will be helpful to understand the behaviors associated with the model tree and browser nodes. When a feature is sketch-based, you can expand the plus sign next to it to reveal the sketch. Likewise, when a feature has multiple elements such as a pattern, you can expand it to view and control each element. If a feature is placed rather than sketch-based, it may not have any elements and, therefore, will lack a plus sign. Figure 4.62 shows the anatomy of the three browser nodes.

FIGURE 4.62
Editing features and sketches

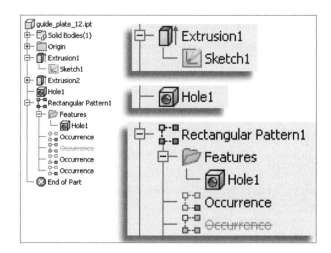

The extrusion is based on Sketch1, as you can see. However, the hole in Figure 4.62 is a placed feature based solely on the edges of other features and, therefore, contains no sketch (you'll place a hole of this type in the pages to come). The pattern, when expanded, shows the features that it contains and each occurrence of those features.

EDITING A SKETCH

To edit a feature or a sketch, you can right-click it and choose Edit Feature or Edit Sketch, or you can double-click the Browser Node icon for that feature/sketch. Be sure to double-click the node icon rather than the node text; otherwise, you set the text active for renaming. Follow these steps to explore the edit procedures of features and sketches:

1. On the Get Started tab, choose Open (or press **Ctrl+O** on the keyboard).

2. Browse for the file mi_4a_062.ipt located in the Chapter 04 directory of your Mastering Inventor 2016 folder and click Open.

3. In the Model browser, right-click Extrusion2 and choose Edit Sketch. You'll notice that the sketch becomes active for edits, and the part displays in a rolled-back stage as it existed when the sketch was originally created.

4. You want to edit the diameter dimension and change it to an inch-based value. To do so, double-click the dimension, type **2 in** into the input box, and then press **Enter**.

You'll notice that Inventor converts the value to a millimeter equivalent for you. You can mix units as required, but know that any value that does not have a unit is assumed to be the part's base unit. This means if you were to enter **2** without the abbreviation for inch (in), the diameter would be set to 2 mm because this part is mm-based.

5. Click the Finish Sketch button on the Sketch tab (or right-click and click Finish 2D Sketch) to return to the feature level of the part.

You'll also notice that as a result of the sketch edit of the diameter, the length of the slot cutout adjusts automatically as well because it contains a formula to ensure that it is always five times the diameter of the circle.

EDITING A FEATURE

Note that the spacing for the rectangular pattern adjusted automatically on each side of the slot cutout but did not adjust for the length of the pattern. This is because the pattern contains a parametric formula that controls the width spacing but not the length. To fix this, you'll edit the rectangular pattern, as shown in these steps:

1. Double-click Rectangular Pattern1 in the browser to open the edit dialog box.

2. On the left side, clear the value of 25 mm, click the arrow button, choose List Parameters from the flyout, and select Slot_Length from the list.

3. The spacing is now adjusted so that the holes are patterned at the Slot_Length value. Looking at the preview, obviously this is not correct. To fix this, click the drop-down at the bottom left and change it from Spacing to Distance. Click the OK button to accept these changes.

You might decide that the rectangular pattern needs to include features that were not origi-nally present when the pattern was created, such as Extrusion3 and Chamfer1 found in this part. If you edit the pattern, you'll notice that the part rolls back to the state that it existed in at the time the pattern was created; therefore, you cannot add the new features to the pattern. To resolve this, you will reorder the features and then edit the pattern.

4. In the Model browser, select Extrusion3 and Chamfer1 and drag them above the rectan-gular pattern.

You can reorder features in this way so long as they are not dependent on one another. For instance, if you attempt to drag Chamfer1 above Extrusion3, you'll find that it can't be done. This is because the chamfer is based on the geometry of the extrusion.

5. Once the features have been reordered, double-click the rectangular pattern to edit it or right-click and choose Edit Feature.

6. Ensure that the Features button is selected and select Extrusion3 and Chamfer1 from the Model browser so that they are added to the pattern. Your preview should update as well. Click the OK button to accept these changes.

You may decide that although the pattern provides the correct spacing of the elements, you need to exclude some of the middle instances to accommodate other features. You can do this easily by suppressing the instances you do not need and still maintaining the constant pattern spacing.

7. Expand the rectangular pattern feature in the browser, and note that all the instances of the patterned features are listed as occurrences.

8. Roll your mouse pointer down over the list, and you will see the instances highlight onscreen, each indicating which occurrence it is.

9. Identify the fourth and fifth instances on each side of the pattern, right-click them, and choose Suppress. You can do this one at a time or hold Ctrl as you select them and sup-press them all at once. Notice that these occurrences are no longer present on the part and are marked with strikethrough in the browser. Figure 4.63 shows the results of these edits. You can close the part without saving changes.

FIGURE 4.63
The edited part

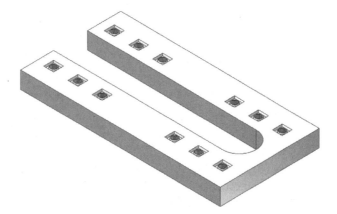

Repairing Features and Sketches

Ordinarily, you want to create chamfer and fillet features at the end of the overall part-creation process. Creating chamfers and fillets at the end of the process reduces errors caused by feature dependencies associated with these features. In the following exercise, however, you will create a chamfer before creating a hole and then make a change to illustrate both the folly of creating placed features too early in the design and the method of repairing a feature error:

1. On the Get Started tab, choose Open (or press **Ctrl+O** on the keyboard).

2. Browse for the file mi_4a_063.ipt located in the Chapter 04 directory of your Mastering Inventor 2016 folder and click Open.

3. Select the Chamfer tool on the 3D Model tab and select the corner indicated with the red arrow.

4. Set the distance to **30 mm** and click the OK button.

5. Click the Start 2D Sketch button and create a sketch on the yellow face.

6. Use the Point tool to place a point near the chamfered corner, dimension it as shown in Figure 4.64, and then click Finish Sketch.

FIGURE 4.64
Pacing the counterbored hole on the sketched point

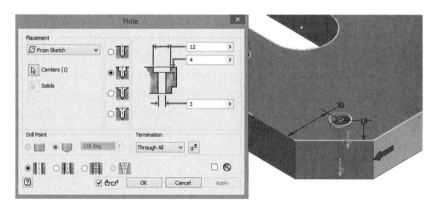

7. Select the Hole tool on the 3D Model tab and place a counterbore hole, as shown in Figure 4.64.

8. At this point you decide that the chamfered corner will not work with this design and should have been a rounded corner. To make this change, right-click the chamfer feature in the Model browser and choose Delete from the menu.

9. Because the counterbore hole is dependent on the chamfer, you are prompted with the option to keep it or let it be deleted also. You will choose to keep it by deselecting the Dependent Sketches And Features box and clicking OK.

10. Notice the hole feature in the browser now has a marker symbol next to it indicating it is "sick" and is in need of some repair. Expand the Hole2 feature node, and you will see that the sketch is also marked as "sick." Right-click the sketch and choose Recover, as shown in Figure 4.65.

FIGURE 4.65
Selecting Recover to examine sketches with errors in them

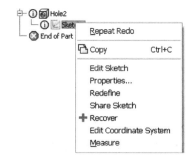

11. In the Sketch Doctor dialog box, you will see a list of the issues present in the problematic sketch. Click Next to see the recommendations for resolving this problem. The recommendation is to edit the sketch.

12. Click Next again, and you will see that there is only one treatment option in this case.

13. Click Finish and then click the OK button in the message box informing you that you are being taken to the sketch environment.

Depending on the extent of the error, the Sketch Doctor may offer you the ability to delete objects, close open loops, and so on. Of course, you could have just edited the sketch originally and ended up with the same result in this case. But in cases where you do not know the extent of the problems, the Recover option is often helpful in determining the issue.

14. In the sketch, you will see the unresolved sketch entities highlighted in magenta. Right-click the magenta line and choose Break Link. This breaks the link with the missing chamfer edge but does not fully fix the problem.

15. Select the magenta endpoints and use the context menu's Break Link option on them as well. This results in the diagonal line being underconstrained. You have two choices to resolve this.

    ◆ Use the Coincident constraint along with the General Dimension tool to lock down the diagonal line.

    ◆ Delete the diagonal line and its referencing dimensions and redimension the hole center point off the edges of the base part.

16. Once you have reconstrained the hole center by one of these methods, click Finish Sketch and return to the feature level of the part. Notice that the hole and sketch are no longer "sick."

17. Choose Fillet on the 3D Model tab and select the same edge previously used by the chamfer to place a 30 mm fillet. Once you have finished, you can close the file without saving changes.

Although there is probably no way you will ever completely avoid having to repair features and sketches, using placed features such as chamfers and fillets as late in the design as possible will go a long way toward reducing these issues. You should also strive to avoid referencing these features with dimensions when they are present.

The Bottom Line

Configure options and settings for part modeling.   Understanding the settings and options that apply to the modeling environment is essential for getting the results you want from Inventor.

> **Master It**   You want to configure your options and settings for your sketch environment and then back them up and distribute them to other workstations. How would you go about doing this?

Create basic part features.   In this chapter, you learned how to plan a workflow that allows you to create stable, editable parts that preserve the design intent.

> **Master It**   You need to create a fairly complex part consisting of many extrusions, revolves, sweeps, and lofts. In addition, you will need to create holes, fillets, chamfers, and other part modifiers. This part may need significant modification in the future by you or by other designers. What considerations will guide your part creation?

Use the Extrude tool.   The Extrude tool is one of the most commonly used feature tools in the Inventor modeling toolset. Understanding the options and solutions available in this tool will prove useful throughout your designs.

> **Master It**   Imagine that you need to create an extruded feature but don't know the exact length; instead, you know the extrude will always terminate based on another feature. However, the location of that feature has not been fully determined just yet. How do you get started on the feature?

Create revolved parts and thread features.   Creating revolved features and parts in Inventor can often resemble the creation of turned parts and features in the real world. Applying thread features to a cylindrical face allows you to specify threads without having to actually model them.

> **Master It**   Let's say you have a part that you intend to fabricate on a lathe. Although you could create the part with a series of stepped circular extrusions, it occurs to you that the Revolve tool might work also. How do you decide which method to use?

Create work features.   Using work features, work planes, work axes, and work points enable you to create virtually any part or feature. Work features are the building blocks for sketch creation and use.

> **Master It**   Your design will require creating features on spherical and cylindrical faces. You need to precisely control the location and angle of these features. How do you do that?

Use the Fillet tool.   The Fillet tool has a great deal of functionality packed into it. Taking the time to explore all the options on a simple test model may be the best way to understand them all.

> **Master It**   You are trying to create a series of fillets on a part. You create four sets of edge selections to have four different fillet sizes, but when you attempt to apply them, you receive an error stating that the feature cannot be built. What went wrong?

Create intelligent hole features.   Although you can create a hole in a part by sketching a circle and extrude-cutting it, this is typically not the recommended approach.

Master It   You need to create a part with a series of various-sized holes on a plate. You would like to lay out the hole pattern in a single sketch and then use the Hole tool to cut the holes to the sizes required. However, when you select the From Sketch option in the Hole tool, it selects all the holes, so you think you must need to sketch out the hole pattern as circles and then use the Extrude tool to cut them out. Is this really the way to proceed?

Bend parts.   You can bend a portion of a part after you define a bend line using a 2D sketch line. You can specify the side of the part to bend; the direction of the bend; and its angle, radius, or arc length.

Master It   You need to create a model of a piece of rolled tube and would like to specify the bend direction, but when you use the direction arrow, you get a preview in only one direction. How can you get a preview in either direction?

Chapter 5

Advanced Modeling Techniques

Chapter 4, "Basic Modeling Techniques," introduced some of the primary modeling tools you need when creating a 3D parametric part. Parametric modeling utilizes numerous tools to create stable, editable parts. The basic workflow of creating a part is to create a base feature and then build upon that base. The tools used to build the additional features can vary depending on your need and may range from simple extruded features to complex combinations of different feature types. In this chapter, you will explore some of the more complex and curvy modeling techniques used to create models with the Autodesk® Inventor® and Autodesk® Inventor LT™ programs. Some of these features involve creating a base profile sketch along with support sketches used for defining paths and shape contours. Such features are based on the same rules used to create simpler features, such as extrudes and revolves, but they take it to the next level by using multiple sketches to define the feature. Other advanced features covered in this chapter depart from these concepts and move into the new territory of feature creation. In either case, having a strong understanding of sketch-creation and editing principles is assumed and recommended. All the skills in this chapter are primarily based on creating a single part, whether in a part file or in the context of an assembly file.

In this chapter, you'll learn to

- ◆   Create complex sweeps and lofts

- ◆   Work with multi-body and derived parts

- ◆   Utilize part tolerances

- ◆   Understand and use parameters and iProperties

- ◆   Troubleshoot modeling failures

Creating Complex Sweeps and Lofts

Now that you have moved on from creating simple features, you can explore the use of sweeps and lofts to create features with a bit more complexity. Both sweeps and lofts require one or more profiles to create a flowing shape. Sweeps require one sketch profile and a second sketched sweep path to create 3D geometry. Lofts typically require two or more sketch profiles and optional rails or points that assist in controlling the final geometry.

Creating and Using Sweeps

You can think of a sweep feature as an extrusion that follows a path defined by another sketch. 2D or 3D sketch paths can be used to create the sweep feature. Like most Inventor geometry, a sweep can be created as either a solid or a surface. Sweeps can add or remove material from a part, or you can use the Intersect option like you can with the Extrusion tool. If your intent is to create multi-body parts, you can choose the New Solids option also.

CREATING 2D PATHS

When creating a sweep feature, you will typically want to first create the path sketch and then create a profile sketch that will contain the geometry to be swept along the path. To create the profile sketch, you will need to create a work plane at the end of your path. This plane will be referenced to create a new sketch. It's not mandatory that you create the path and then the profile, but it is easier to define the profile sketch plane (that is, a work plane) by doing it this way. Normally, this geometry will be perpendicular to one end of the sweep path.

A basic rule of sweep features is that the volume occupied by the sweep profile may not intersect itself within the feature. Some self-intersecting features are currently supported, but many will fail. An example of a self-intersecting feature is a sweep path composed of straight-line segments with tight radius arcs between the segments. Assuming that the sweep profile is circular with a radius value larger than the smallest arc within the sweep path, the feature will self-intersect and the operation will fail. For a sweep to work, the minimum path radius must be larger than the profile radius. In the 2D sketch path example shown in Figure 5.1, the path radius is set at 12 mm. Knowing that the minimum path radius value is 12 mm, you can determine that the sketch profile radius must be less than or equal to this value.

FIGURE 5.1
2D sketch path

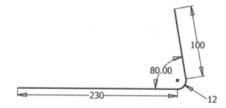

CREATING THE SWEEP PROFILE

Once a sketch path has been created, you can create a work plane on the path and then sketch the profile on that plane. To see this process in action, follow these steps, starting with the creation of the path:

1. On the Get Started tab, click the New button.

2. On the Metric node of the New File dialog box, select the Standard(mm).ipt template.

3. Create a 2D sketch, as shown in Figure 5.1.

4. Once you've created the sketch path, right-click and choose Finish 2D Sketch; then click the Plane button on the 3D Model tab to create a work plane.

5. Select the endpoint of the 2D sketch path and then the path itself to create the plane. This creates a plane on the point normal to the selected line. Figure 5.2 shows the created work plane.

FIGURE 5.2
Creating a work plane
on which to sketch

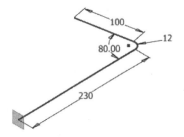

6. Once you've created the work plane, right-click the edge of it and select New Sketch.

7. In the new sketch, use the Project Geometry tool to project the 230 mm line into this new sketch. It should come in as a projected point.

8. Create a circle anchored to the projected point, give it a value of **20 mm** in diameter, and then click the Finish Sketch button.

9. Select the Sweep tool. If you have a single sweep profile, it should automatically select the profile and pause for you to select a path.

10. Select a line in the path sketch to set it as the path.

Note that you can select either Solid or Surface for the feature. The sweep type will default to Path, and the orientation will default to Path as well. The Sweep tool also has options to taper and twist the sweep feature, as shown in Figure 5.3.

FIGURE 5.3
Sweep dialog box
options

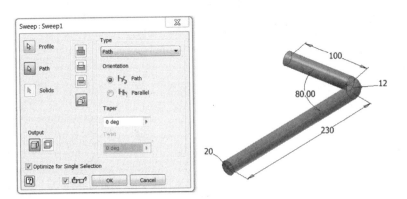

A number less than zero for the taper will diminish the cross section as the profile follows the path. A positive number will increase the cross section. If the taper increases the cross section at the radius of the path to a value that exceeds the radius value, the feature will fail because this will create a self-intersecting path.

11. Adjust the taper to a negative value to see the preview update. Note that if you enter a positive value that's 0.5 or more, the preview will fail, indicating a self-intersecting path. Set the taper back to **0**, and click the OK button to create the sweep.

You'll notice that this sweep feature includes both sketches in the browser, just as an extruded feature consumes the sketch it is created from. To edit the sweep, you can expand the browser node by clicking the plus sign and access both the profile and path sketches to make edits. You can also right-click the sweep feature node and choose Edit Feature to change the options in the Sweep dialog. Explore the ways to edit the sweep you just created, and then you can close the file without saving changes. In the next section, you will look at more sweep options.

Exploring Sweep Options

Although sweeping along a path is the default option, you can also utilize the Path & Guide Rail or Path & Guide Surface option to control the output of the Sweep tool. These options provide additional control for more complex results. Often these options are utilized on sweeps based on a 3D sketch path, but this is not required. You can create a 3D sketch path by using the Include Geometry tool, or you can just use the existing geometry edges where valid selections exist.

PATH & GUIDE RAIL OPTION

Certification
Objective

The Path & Guide Rail option provides a means to control the orientation of a profile as it is swept along a path. In Figure 5.4, the rectangular sweep profile will be swept along the straight path but controlled by the 3D helical rail. This approach is useful for creating twisted or helical parts.

FIGURE 5.4
Sweep profile, Path & Guide Rail option

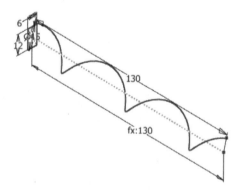

The 3D helical rail is guiding the rotation of the profile even though the sweep profile is fully constrained with horizontal and vertical constraints. Creating this part starts with creating the sweep path as the first sketch followed by creating a second sketch perpendicular to the start point of the sweep path. The 3D helical rail is created using the Helical Curve tool in a 3D sketch. Follow these steps:

1. Open the file `mi_5a_004.ipt` from the `Chapter 05` directory of your `Mastering Inventor 2016` folder. If you have not already downloaded the Chapter 5 files from www.sybex.com/go/masteringinventor2016, please refer to the "What You Will Need" section of the introduction for the download and setup instructions.

2. Click the Sweep button on the 3D Model tab.

3. Change the Type drop-down to Path & Guide Rail, choose the straight line as the path and the helix as the guide rail, and then click the OK button. Your result should resemble Figure 5.5.

FIGURE 5.5
Sweep feature with Path & Guide Rail option

Using guide rails to control the path and further define the shape of the sweep greatly expands the range of shapes you can create with the Sweep tool. You can close the current file without saving changes and take a look at the use of the Twist option in the next section.

PATH & TWIST OPTION

In this exercise, you'll use the Twist option to provide the helical twisting of the sweep feature:

1. Open the file mi_5a_005.ipt from the Chapter 05 directory of your Mastering Inventor 2016 folder.

2. Click the Sweep button on the 3D Model tab. Note that because there is only one profile and one path, the Sweep tool automatically selects them for the Profile and Path selections.

3. Enter **90** in the Twist input box and note the preview.

4. Change the Twist input to **360** in the Twist input box and note the new preview.

5. Next, change the Twist input to **-360** and again note how the preview changes.

6. Lastly, change the Twist input to **-360*3** and again take note of the change to the preview.

7. Click the OK button to create the twisted sweep.

Using the Twist option, you're able to quickly create twisted, swept features without the use of a guide rail sketch. Feel free to experiment with the Twist option using this file, and then you can close it without saving changes and take a look at the use of a guide surface in the next section.

PATH & GUIDE SURFACE OPTION

At times you will need to sweep a profile that will conform to a specific shape and contour. This is often necessary when working with complex surfaces, particularly when cutting a path along such a surface. In the following exercise, you will use some surface tools to manipulate a solid shape while exploring the sweep guide's Surface option:

1. On the Get Started tab, click Open; open the file mi_5a_006.ipt from your Chapter 05 folder.

2. Click the Replace Face tool on the Surface panel of the 3D Model tab. Figure 5.6 shows the Surface panel.

FIGURE 5.6
Surface tools

3. Click the Replace Face tool, select the red face as the existing face, select the wavy surface for the new face, and click the OK button.

4. Right-click ExtrusionSrf1 in the browser and select Visibility to turn it off.

5. Click the Plane button on the 3D Model tab, click and hold down on the yellow surface, and then drag up to create an offset work plane at 85 mm.

6. Right-click the edge of the work plane and choose New Sketch.

7. Using the Project Geometry tool, select the wavy face. This will result in a projected rectangle in your sketch.

8. Create a circle with the center point at the midpoint of the projected rectangle and the tangent point on the corner of the rectangle so that your results look like the image on the left of Figure 5.7. Click the Finish Sketch button to exit the sketch.

FIGURE 5.7
Creating a sweep path

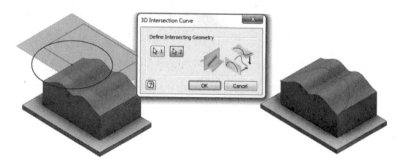

9. Click the Start 3D Sketch button on the Sketch panel, or right-click in the empty space of the graphics window and choose New 3D Sketch from the context menu.

10. Click the Intersection Curve tool on the 3D Sketch tab and choose the circle and the wavy face. Finish the 3D sketch and turn off the visibility of the 2D sketch and the work plane. The result will be a curve, as shown on the right of Figure 5.7.

11. Create a 2D sketch on the front face, as shown in Figure 5.8. Be sure to select the projected edges and make them construction lines so that Inventor won't pick up the entire front face as a sweep profile. The top two corners will be coincident to the curved construction line along the top. When the sketch is fully constrained and completed, as shown in Figure 5.8, click Finish Sketch.

FIGURE 5.8
Creating a sweep profile

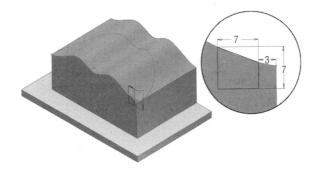

12. Select the Sweep tool and choose the profile you just sketched for the profile input.

13. Select the 3D intersection curve for the path.

14. Click the Cut button to ensure that this sweep removes material from the part and click the OK button.

15. The resulting cut sweep will be too shallow in some places, as shown on the left of Figure 5.9.

16. Edit the sweep, and set the Type drop-down to Path & Guide Surface. Select the wavy surface as the guide surface and then click the OK button. The result will look like the image on the right of Figure 5.9.

FIGURE 5.9
Path vs. Path & Guide
Surface

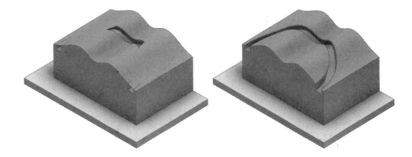

Using a guide surface to match the exact curvature of a complex shape is often the only way to achieve the type of features found on plastic parts and other consumer products of stylized form. You can close this file without saving changes and move on to the next section to explore lofted features.

SWEEP ALONG AN EDGE

It's often useful to sweep a profile along an existing edge or edges in order to create a complex sweep shape. In the past you might have been required to create a 3D sketch beforehand and use the Include Geometry option. But you can now just use the edges for the sweep path, and Inventor will create the 3D sketch and included geometry for you, as demonstrated in the following steps:

1. On the Get Started tab, click Open; open the file mi_5a_007.ipt from your Chapter 05 folder.

2. Click the Sweep button on the 3D Model tab.

3. The profile should be selected automatically since there is just one sketch to use. Select the outer edge of the part for the sweep path.

4. Click the OK button to create the sketch.

5. Expand the sweep feature in the browser, and notice the presence of the automatically created 3D sketch.

As you can see, setting up a part file to use the edges for a sweep path can provide a quick and powerful way to create otherwise difficult features. You can close this file without saving changes and continue on to explore loft features.

Creating Loft Features

Whereas a sweep allows the creation of single profile extruded along a path, loft features allow the creation of multiple cross-sectional profiles that are used to create a lofted shape. The Loft tool requires two or more profile sections to function. Rails and control points are additional options that help control the shape of a loft feature. A good example of a lofted shape is a boat hull.

LOFT WITH RAILS

You could create a boat hull by defining just the section profiles, but you can gain more control over the end result by creating a loft with rails. Figure 5.10 shows the completed wireframe geometry to create a section of a boat hull. The geometry includes four section sketches, each composed of a 2D spline sketched onto a work plane. There are two rails: the top and bottom composed of 3D sketch splines.

Follow these steps to explore the creation of a loft feature with the use of rails:

1. On the Get Started tab, click Open; open the file mi_5a_008.ipt in your Chapter 05 folder.

2. Select the Loft tool on the 3D Model tab.

FIGURE 5.10
Loft with rails
geometry

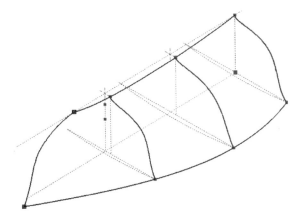

3. Since the four section sketches are open profiles, the Loft tool will automatically set the output to Surface. Select the four cross-section sketches in consecutive order, front to back or back to front.

4. Click the Click To Add button in the Rails section of the dialog box and select 3D sketches named Rail1 and Rail2.

5. If you have the Preview option selected at the bottom of the dialog box, you should see a preview of the surface indicating the general shape, as shown in Figure 5.11. Click the OK button, and the surface will be created.

FIGURE 5.11
A surface loft with rails

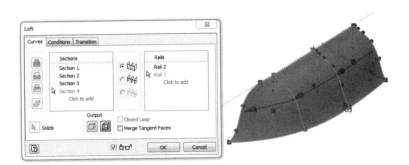

PATCH AND STITCH SURFACES

That concludes the lofting part of the boat hull, but if you'd like, you can continue with the following steps to learn a bit more about working with surfaces:

1. To finish the hull, select the Mirror tool on the Pattern panel of the 3D Model tab.

2. Select the hull surface for the Features selection and then click the Mirror Plane button.

3. Expand the Origin folder in the browser, click YZ to use it as the mirror plane, and click the OK button.

4. Next, you will create a 3D sketch to create a line for the top edge of the transom (back of the boat); right-click in the graphics window and choose New 3D Sketch.

5. On the 3D Sketch tab, click the Line tool and draw a line across the back of the boat to form the top of the transom. Draw another line across the bottom of the transom where the two sides do not quite meet. Figure 5.12 shows the back of the boat with the 3D sketch lines.

FIGURE 5.12
3D sketch lines for the transom

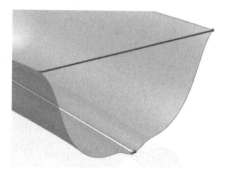

6. Click Finish Sketch when the lines are drawn.

TURNING OFF THE TRANSLUCENCY OF SURFACES AND SHADOWS TO SEE BETTER

If you have difficulty seeing the endpoints when attempting to draw the 3D Sketch line, you can expand the mirror feature in the browser, locate the loft surfaces, and then right-click and deselect Translucent. Alternately, you can expand the Surface Bodies folder in the browser and then right-click the surfaces to deselect Translucent.

It might also help to go to the View tab and deselect all the shadows options.

---

7. Select the Patch button on the Surface panel of the 3D Model tab to bring up the Boundary Patch tool and ensure the Automatic Edge Chain option is not selected. Then select your 3D sketch lines and the back curved edges to create a surface for the transom. When creating boundaries, you need to select the lines in the order in which they occur in the boundary. Click the Apply button and then create another boundary patch across the top by selecting the two edges of the sides and the top edge of the transom. Figure 5.13 shows the selections.

FIGURE 5.13
Boundary patch selections

8. You'll notice the gap in the base of the hull. Use the Boundary Patch tool to create a surface by clicking both edges of the gap and the small edge at the bottom of the transom.

9. Select the Stitch tool on the Surface panel and select all five of the surfaces you created. It's easiest to window-select them all at once.

10. Click the Apply button and then the Done button.

USING THE SHELL TOOL

You should now have a solid boat. If you didn't complete the previous exercise, you can open the file mi_5a_009.ipt to explore the Shell tool. If you're continuing with the boat you created from the loft exercise, be sure to save your file. This is just good practice before running calculation-intensive operations like the Shell tool, particularly on free-form shapes like this boat hull. Once you've saved your file or opened the one provided, follow these steps to explore the Shell tool:

1. Once your file has been saved, select the Shell tool on the Modify panel of the 3D Model tab.

2. Click the top face for the Remove Faces selection and set Thickness to **10 mm**.

If your system is a bit undersized, you might want to skip the next two steps and click the OK button now to let the shell solve for just one thickness. Otherwise, you'll specify a unique thickness for the transom.

3. Click the >> button to reveal the Unique Face Thickness settings, click the Click To Add row, and then click the transom face.

4. Set the unique face thickness value to **30 mm** and click the OK button to build the shell. Figure 5.14 shows the completed boat.

FIGURE 5.14
The completed boat

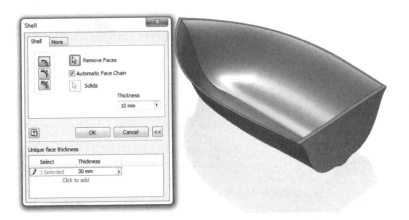

Although at this point you have gone far past the initial lofted surface to finish the boat model, you started by creating a loft from the 2D sketch profiles and then used the 3D sketches as rails to further define the shape. Of course, if you are a boat designer, you might see a few areas of the design that need improvement. But, for now, you can close the file without saving changes and move on to explore the area loft options in the next section.

AREA LOFT

Area loft is used in the design of components where the flow of a gas or liquid must be precisely controlled. Area loft is a different way of controlling the finer points of creating a loft shape. Figure 5.15 illustrates what might be considered a fairly typical loft setup, consisting of three section profiles and a centerline. The goal here is to create a loft from these profiles and to create a fourth profile to control the airflow through the resulting part cavity so that it can be choked down or opened up as needed.

FIGURE 5.15
Area loft profiles

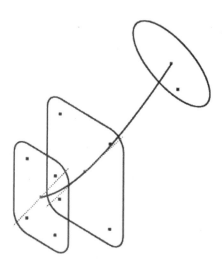

Follow these steps to explore the creation of an area loft:

1. On the Get Started tab, click Open; open the file mi_5a_010.ipt from your Chapter 05 folder.

2. Start the Loft tool and select the three sections in order, starting with the small rectangular shape.

3. Right-click, choose Select Center Line, and then click the centerline sketch line running down the middle of the profile sketches.

4. Right-click again and choose Placed Sections; notice as you choose an option from the context menu that the dialog box updates to reflect your selections. You could have just as easily used the dialog box controls to do this, but oftentimes it is easier not to create the extra mouse travel.

5. Slide your mouse pointer over the centerline and then click roughly halfway between the circular section and the middle section.

Once you click a location, the Section Dimensions dialog box appears, as shown in Figure 5.16, giving you control over the position and section area of the placed section. You can switch the position input from Proportional Distance, where you enter a percentage of the centerline length, to Absolute, which allows you to enter an actual distance if you know it.

FIGURE 5.16

Section Dimensions
dialog box

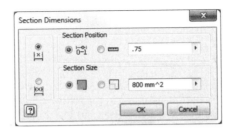

In the Section Size area, you specify the actual area or set a scale factor based on the area of the loft as calculated from the sections before and after the one you are creating. On the far left, you can switch the section from driving to driven, letting the area be calculated from the position. Any number of placed sections can be used to create precise control of the feature.

6. Leave Section Position set to Proportional Distance, change the position to **0.75**, set the area to **800** (as shown in Figure 5.16), and click the OK button. You can access the section again by double-clicking the leader information.

7. Double-click the End section leader text and change it from Driven to Driving using the radio buttons on the left. Notice that you can set the area but not the position.

8. Change the area to **800** and then click the OK button in the Section Dimensions dialog box. Then click the OK button in the Loft dialog box to create the lofted solid.

Figure 5.17 illustrates the placed loft section and the modified end section.

FIGURE 5.17

Creating an area loft

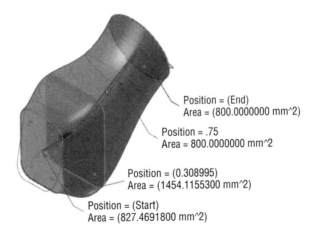

Position = (End)
Area = (800.0000000 mm^2)

Position = .75
Area = 800.0000000 mm^2

Position = (0.308995)
Area = (1454.1155300 mm^2)

Position = (Start)
Area = (827.4691800 mm^2)

You may have noticed that by changing the end section to an area of 800 square millimeters, you altered the size of the end profile from the original shape, in this case slightly reducing the diameter of the circle. Keep this in mind as you create area lofts, and you can use the original sketch to just rough in the shape and not worry as much about getting the size exactly right until you refine the area loft profile. Of course, as always, you should still fully constrain the sketch profile. You can close this file without saving changes and take a look at the centerline loft options in the next section.

CENTERLINE LOFT FEATURE

The centerline loft feature allows you to determine a centerline for the loft profile to follow, just as you did with the area loft. In the following steps, you'll create a wing feature using the center-line loft and look at some of the condition options available in lofted features as well:

1. On the Get Started tab, click Open; open the file mi_5a_012.ipt in your Chapter 05 folder.

2. Click the Loft button and select the edge of the yellow face of the wing stub feature and the sketch point at the end of the arc as sections.

3. Right-click, choose Select Center Line, and then click the arc. Notice how the lofted shape now holds the centerline, as shown in Figure 5.18.

FIGURE 5.18
A loft with and without centerline

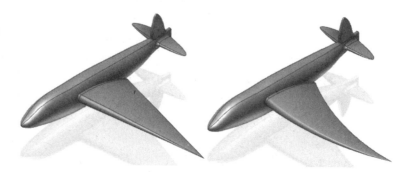

4. Click the Conditions tab in the Loft dialog box so you can control the curve weight and transition type at the work point and wing stub profile.

5. Click the drop-down next to the Edges1 (Section) and set it to Tangent. Change the weight to **0.5** to adjust the blend from the wing stub feature.

6. Click the small drop-down to set Point Sketch2 to Tangent and then set the weight to **1.5**.

7. Currently, the loft is extending out past the work plane. Often, this can be a problem because the work plane may have been established for the overall length of the part. To resolve this, set the drop-down to Tangent To Plane and select the work plane on the screen. Notice the adjustment. Figure 5.19 shows the preview of the adjustments before and after the tangent plane is selected.

8. Click the OK button and examine your lofted shape.

9. You can use the Mirror tool to mirror the loft you just created and the wing stub feature using the work plane in the tail area.

Feel free to edit the loft to adjust the shape of the wing to something a bit more to your liking. Here is the full list of conditions available, depending on the geometry type:

FIGURE 5.19
Adjusting the curve
weight and condition of
the loft

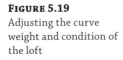

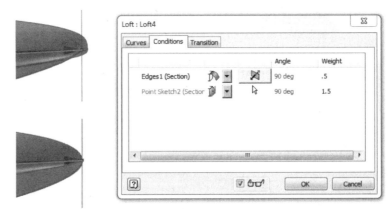

Free Condition   No boundary conditions exist for the object.

Tangent Condition   This condition is available when the section or rail is selected and is adjacent to a lateral surface, body, or face loop.

Smooth (G2) Condition   This option is available when the section or rail is adjacent to a lateral surface or body or when a face loop is selected. G2 continuity allows for curve continuity with an adjacent previously created surface.

Direction Condition   This option is available only when the curve is a 2D sketch. The angle direction is relative to the selected section plane.

Sharp Point   This option is available when the beginning or end section is a work point.

Tangent   This option is available when the beginning or end section is a work point. Tangency is applied to create a rounded or dome-shaped end on the loft.

Tangent To Plane   This option is available when the beginning or end section is a work point. The planar face must be selected. This option allows the transition to a rounded dome shape.

The angle and weight options on the Conditions tab allow for changes to the angle of lofting and the weight value for an end condition transition. Click the weight, and change it to **3** to see how the end condition will change in the preview. Experiment with the weight to see the changed conditions. If a value is grayed out, the condition at that point will not allow a change. Keep in mind that adding more intermediate profiles to the loft is often the best way to control and define a specific loft shape.

Creating a Part Using Loft and Sculpt

It is often useful to create lofted surfaces when curved corners of differing radii are present. In the next exercise, you'll use the Loft tool to create the gently sloping edges of a tablet device housing. Then you'll use the Mirror tool to duplicate the surface, and finally you'll use the Sculpt tool to convert the enclosed surface into a solid.

1. On the Get Started tab, click Open and open the file mi_5a_015.ipt from your Chapter 05 folder.

2. Click the Loft button and set the output to be a surface using the Output button.

3. Select sections End Profile1 and End Profile2 from the browser.

4. Right-click and choose Select Rails; then select the 3D sketches named Top Rail and Bottom Rail from the browser.

Figure 5.20 shows the Loft dialog box and model preview with the selections made.

FIGURE 5.20
Creating a surface loft

Selecting the sketches from the browser isn't required, but it does eliminate the chance you might accidentally select an edge rather than the sketch if you try to select them onscreen.

5. Click the OK button to create the lofted surface.

6. Use the Stitch tool (on the Surface panel of the 3D Model tab) to stitch the lofted surface you just created and Boundary Patch1 together.

7. Use the Mirror tool (on the Pattern panel of the 3D Model tab) to mirror the stitched surface, Extrusion1, Split1, and Fillet1. Use the YZ plane in the Origin folder as the mirror plane selection.

8. Use the Mirror tool again, and this time select the mirror feature you just created as the feature to mirror and use the XZ plane in the Origin folder as the mirror plane selection.

9. On the Surface panel, click the Sculpt button. Select all four quadrants of the surfaces as the surfaces selection and then click OK. Your result should look like Figure 5.21. You can close the file without saving.

FIGURE 5.21
A solid model created
from surface lofts and
the Sculpt tool

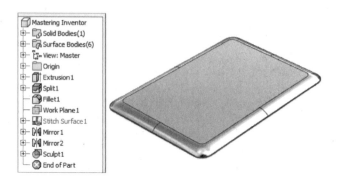

Creating Multi-body Parts

It is possible to create a multi-body part file with separate solids representing each part of an assembly and then save the solids as individual parts, even having them automatically placed into an assembly. Creating multiple solid bodies in a single-part file offers some unique advantages compared to the traditional methods of creating parts in the context of an assembly file. For starters, you have one file location where all your design data is located. Second, it is often easier to fit parts together using this method by simply sketching one part right on top of the other, and so on.

These two advantages are also the main two disadvantages. Placing large amounts of data (and time and effort) into a single file can be risky should that file be lost. And creating a part with an overabundance of interrelated sketches, features, and solid bodies can create a "house of cards" situation that makes changing an early sketch, feature, or solid a risky endeavor. Used wisely, though, multi-body parts are a powerful way to create tooling sets, molds, dies, and other interrelated parts.

If you do large-machine design, you would be wise to create many smaller, multi-body part files rather than attempting to build one large one. Or you might find that using multi-body parts will work well for certain interrelated components, whereas using traditional part/assembly techniques works for the rest of the design.

Creating Multiple Solids

In the following steps, you'll explore the creation of multi-body parts by building a simple trigger mechanism. The challenge here is to define the pawl feature on the trigger lever as it relates to the hammer bar. Figure 5.22 shows the trigger mechanism in its set position on the left and at rest on the right.

FIGURE 5.22
A simple trigger
assembly

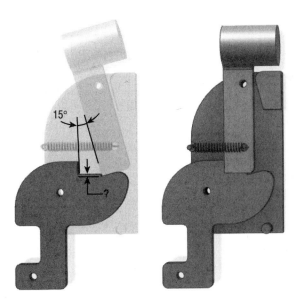

As the trigger lever is engaged, the hammer bar overcomes the pawl (lip), and the spring is allowed to force the hammer bar to swing. In the following steps, you'll explore the multi-body solid options as you use one solid to determine the precise fit with the other:

1. On the Get Started tab, click Open; open the part named mi_5a_016.ipt in your Chapter 05 folder.

2. Create a sketch on the front face of the plate.

3. Create a rectangle, as shown in Figure 5.23, using the top hole as a reference to anchor the rectangle.

FIGURE 5.23

The hammer-bar sketch

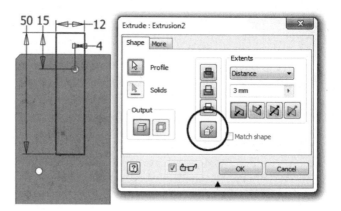

4. Extrude the rectangle 3 mm away from the plate and use the New Solid option in the Extrude dialog box (leave the circle unselected from your extrude profile so that you end up with a hole).

5. When you click the OK button, you'll see that the Solid Bodies folder in the model tree now shows two bodies present, one representing the base plate and another representing the hammer bar.

6. Create another sketch on the front of the plate and create another rectangle toward the bottom, referencing the end of the hammer bar, as shown in Figure 5.24. Project the lower left circle.

FIGURE 5.24

The trigger-lever sketch

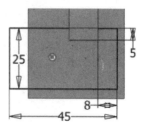

7. Leave the circle unselected from the profile and extrude the rectangle **3 mm** away from the plate. Use the New Solid option in the Extrude dialog box and then click the OK button. This completes the base feature for the trigger lever.

8. Expand the Solid Bodies folder in the browser and notice that there are three solids listed (if you see fewer than three, edit your extrusions and make sure you used the New Solid option).

9. Double-click the text that is your hammer bar and rename it **Hammer Bar**, for reference later.

10. Right-click the solid that is your trigger lever and choose Properties. In the resulting dialog box, set the name to **Trigger Lever** and change the solid to a blue color; then click the OK button.

Here are several things to note at this point:

◆ If you expand the browser node for each solid listed in the Solid Bodies folder, you can see the features involved in each.

◆ You can right-click a solid or solids, choose Hide Others to isolate just the selected ones and then use Show All to bring back any hidden solids.

◆ You can select the solid and then choose a color style from the Color Override drop-down on the Quick Access bar (at the top of your screen).

◆ You can right-click each solid and choose Properties to set the name and color, view the mass properties, and strip previously overridden values. For instance, if you set just the front face of one of the solids to be red and then decided you wanted the entire solid to be blue, you could use the Strip Overrides option to remove the red face and set the solid to blue. If you did not use the Strip Overrides option, the red face would remain red, and the other faces would become blue.

Using One Solid to Shape Another

Certification Objective

Next, you'll create the pawl notch in the trigger lever. To do so, however, you will first make a copy of the hammer bar and then turn that solid into a combined solid that represents the hammer bar in both the set and resting positions. After that, you'll cut that solid away from the trigger lever. You can continue with the file from the previous steps or open the part named mi_5a_017.ipt from your Chapter 05 folder. Then follow these steps:

1. Use the ViewCube to change the view so that you can see the cylindrical face of the hole in the hammer bar and then choose the Circular Pattern tool on the Patterns panel.

2. Select the Pattern Solids button and click the hammer bar for the Solid selection.

3. Click the cylindrical face of the top hole for the rotation axis and set the placement count and angle to **2** and **15** degrees, respectively.

4. Use the button at the top-right corner of the dialog box to set the output to Create New Solid Bodies (the rightmost button), as shown in Figure 5.25.

5. Ensure that the rotation direction is counterclockwise; use the Flip button if it is not and then click the OK button.

FIGURE 5.25
A circular pattern
to create a new solid

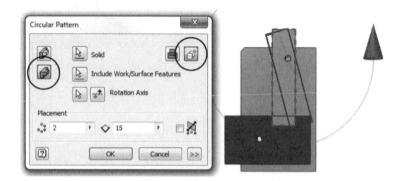

If you expand the Solid Bodies folder in the browser, you will see that there are now four solids, the last being the patterned copy of the hammer bar. You will now turn the visibility of the original hammer bar off and use the copy to cut a pawl notch in the trigger plate.

6. Right-click the solid named Hammer Bar in the Solid Bodies folder and choose Visibility to hide that solid.

7. Select the Circular Pattern tool again and choose the Pattern Solids option, as you did previously.

8. Click the cylindrical face of the top hole for the rotation axis and set the placement count and angle to **2** and **15** degrees, respectively.

9. Set the rotation direction to go clockwise using the flip button. This should place the patterned copy in place of the original hammer bar.

10. This time use the buttons at the top-right corner of the dialog box to set the output to Join and then click the OK button. This will merge the selected solid with the new patterned one. Figure 5.26 shows the selections.

FIGURE 5.26
Using a circular pat-
tern to join a copy to
another solid

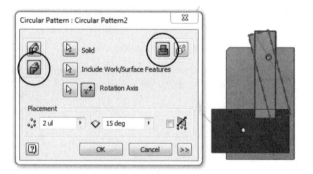

11. Select the Combine tool on the Modify panel and select the blue trigger lever for the Base selection.

12. Select the fused, rotated body for the Toolbody selection and then set the operation type to Cut so that you are subtracting it from the trigger lever. Then click the OK button.

13. Select any solid in the `Solid Bodies` folder and choose Show All to turn the visibility of all solids back on.

Now that you've solved the trigger-pawl shape and size by using a multi-body part, you could finish the parts by adding features to each body. You'll note that if you create an extrusion, for instance, you can select which solid to add that extrusion to. If it is a cut extrusion, you can select multiple bodies and cut them all at once. The same is true of fillets, holes, and so on.

MOVE AND ROTATE SOLID BODIES

**Certification
Objective**

Use the Direct Edit command in the Modify panel and then select the Solids option to Move, Scale, and Rotate solid bodies. This is the preferred method to manipulate bodies. You can also use the Move Bodies tool to reposition solids. Try both commands on your trigger-mechanism parts. Note that to free-drag a solid with the Move Bodies tool, you have to click the edges or outlines of the preview object rather than on the original object as you might suppose. You can also create a rotation using the Move Bodies tools, or you can move and rotate a body at the same time by creating a two-line action in the Move Bodies dialog box. To locate the Move Bodies tool, click the Modify panel flyout arrow. Figure 5.27 shows the Move Bodies options.

FIGURE 5.27
Moving a solid body
within a part file

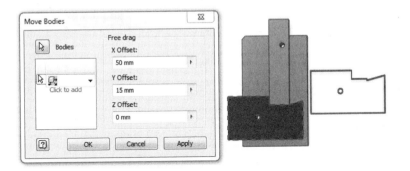

When you click the cube icon above the words Click to add, a drop list appears. The options are as follows:

Free Drag   Move via X, Y, and Z offsets or, better yet, just click the preview and drag it.

Move Along Ray   Select an edge or axis to define the move direction and then specify an offset value or just click and drag it in that direction.

Rotate About Line   Select an edge or axis to define the rotational pivot and then specify an angle or click and drag it.

Click To Add   Create as many move actions as you want and do them all at once.

SPLIT SOLIDS

Another tool that you may find useful when working with multi-body parts is the Split tool. For instance, if you create a simple solid block by sketching a rectangle on the XY plane and then extruding it 40 mm in both directions, you could then use the XY plane as a parting line to split the solid into two separate solids. You could also create a sketched curve, extrude it as a surface, and use it to split or trim the solid.

MAKE PART AND MAKE COMPONENTS

Once you have created your multi-body part, you can write out each solid as an individual part file. The resulting part files are known as *derived* parts. You can think of these derived parts as just linked copies of the solid bodies. If you make a change in the multi-body part, it will update the derived part. You can break the link or suppress the link in the derived part as well. Using the Make Part and Make Components tools allows you to detail each solid body individually in separate drawings. If you attempt to detail the multi-body part in the drawing, you will see all the solids at once. Create View representations in the part file to turn off individual bodies and then specify the representation in a drawing view.

Additionally, you can choose to take your multi-body part and write the whole thing to an assembly. The assembly will consist of all the derived parts placed just as they exist in the multi-body part. These files will be grounded in place automatically so that no Assembly constraints are required to hold them in place. If you decide you would like to apply constraints to all or some of the parts, you can unground them and do so, as well as organize them into subassemblies, and so on.

You should be aware, too, that any additional modeling that you do in the derived part or assembly will not push back to the multi-body part file. Although this may seem like a limitation, it can also be viewed as a good thing, allowing for the separation of design tasks that some design departments require. Here are the general steps for creating components from a multi-body part file:

1. Click the Make Components button on the Manage tab and then select the solid bodies from which you want to create parts.

2. Select additional solids to add to the list or select from the list and click Remove From Selection to exclude any solids that you decide you do not want to create parts from.

3. Select Insert Components In Target Assembly; then set the assembly name, the template from which to create it, and the save path, or clear this option to create the parts only. If the assembly already exits, use the Target Assembly Location's Browse button to select it.

4. Click Next to accept your selections, shown in Figure 5.28.

5. The next dialog box allows you to name and set paths for the derived parts. Click the cells in the table to make changes for the parts as required:

   ◆ Click or right-click a cell to choose from the options for that cell type, if any.

   ◆ You can Shift+select multiple components and use the buttons above the Template and File Location columns to set those values for multiple parts at once.

6. Click the Use Color Override From Source Component option to preserve the colors. Click the Link Sheet Metal Styles option to include sheet metal styles. Click Include Parameters to choose which layout model parameters to have present in the derived parts.

FIGURE 5.28
The Make
Components:
Selection dialog box

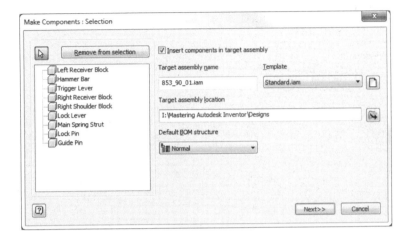

7. Click the Apply button or the OK button to make the components (Figure 5.29). If the component files are created in an assembly, the assembly file is created with the parts placed and left open in Inventor, but the assembly and parts are not saved until you choose to do so. If you choose to create the parts without an assembly, you are prompted to save the new files.

FIGURE 5.29
The Make
Components:
Bodies dialog box

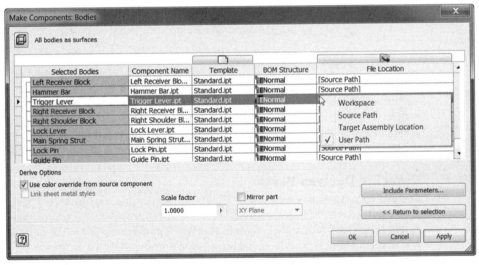

You can set default behaviors of the Make Components dialog box in a multi-body part file (or a template file) by selecting the Tools tab, clicking Document Settings, selecting the Modeling tab in the dialog box that opens, and clicking the Options button. Figure 5.30 shows these options.

FIGURE 5.30
Setting the Make
Components Options
defaults

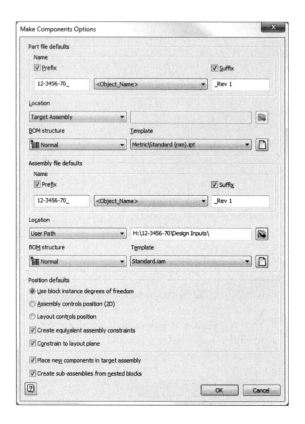

Creating Derived Parts and Assemblies

You can create parts derived from other components using the Derive tool. Common uses of the Derive tool are to create scaled and mirrored versions of existing parts, to cut one part from another part, and to consolidate an assembly into a single-part file. Nonlinear scaling is accomplished using an add-in available in the Inventor installation directory or the Direct Edit tool.

Creating Derived Parts

Derived parts are base solids that are linked to the original feature-based part. Modifications to the derived part in the form of additional features are allowed. Original features are modified in the parent part, and changes to the parent part are moved to the derived part upon save and update. There is no reasonable limit to the number of times the parent part or succeeding derived parts can be derived again into more variations.

Deriving a Part File

Certification Objective

To derive a single-part file, follow these steps:

1. From a new part file, select Derive on the 3D Model tab or click the Manage tab and then click the Derive button.

2. In the Open dialog box, browse to the part file and then click the Open button.

3. Select from one of these derived styles:

   ◆ A single solid body with no seams between faces that exist in the same plane

   ◆ A single solid body with seams

   ◆ One or more solid bodies (if the source part contains multiple bodies)

   ◆ A single surface body

4. Use the status buttons at the top to change the status of all the selected objects at once or click the status icon next to each individual object to set the include/exclude status.

5. Optionally, click the Select From Base button to open the base component in a window to select the components.

6. Specify the scale factor and mirror plane if desired.

7. Click the OK button.

If the part being derived contains just one body, it is displayed onscreen. If the part being derived is a multi-body part, the visible bodies are marked include and the invisible bodies are marked Exclude. Select the bodies to include by expanding the Solid Bodies folder and toggling the status. To include all bodies, change the status button next to the Solid Bodies folder to Include. Figure 5.31 shows the Derived Part dialog box.

FIGURE 5.31
Derived Part options

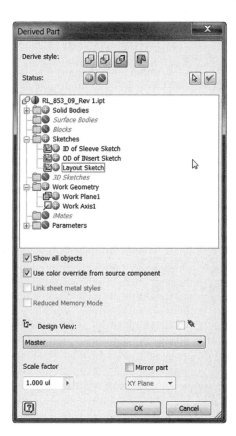

Deriving an Assembly File

To derive an assembly file, follow these steps:

1. From a new part file, select Derive on the 3D Model tab or click the Manage tab and then click the Derive button.

2. In the Open dialog box, browse to the assembly file and then click the Open button.

3. Select from one of these derived styles:

    ◆ A single solid body with no seams between faces that exist in the same plane

    ◆ A single solid body with seams

    ◆ One or more solid bodies (if the source part contains multiple bodies)

    ◆ A single surface body

4. Use the status buttons at the top to change the status of all the selected objects at once, or click the status icon next to each individual object to set the include, exclude, subtract, bounding box, or intersect status.

5. Optionally, click the Select From Base button to open the base component in a window to select the components.

6. Click the Other tab to select which component sketches, work features, parameters, iMates, and part surfaces to include in the derived assembly.

7. Click the Representations tab to use a design-view representation, positional representation, or level-of-detail representation as the base for your derived part.

8. Click the Options tab to remove geometry, remove parts, fill holes, scale, or mirror the assembly.

9. Click the OK button. Figure 5.32 shows the Derived Assembly dialog box.

FIGURE 5.32
Derived Assembly dialog box options

Modifying Derived Parts

Often, you will need to modify a derived part source file after having derived it into a new part. To do so, you can access the source part or assembly from the Model browser of the derived part by double-clicking it in the browser or by right-clicking it in the browser and choosing Open Base Component. The original file is opened in a new window where you can make changes as needed. To update the derived part to reflect changes to the source file, use the Update button on the Quick Access bar (the top of the screen).

You can edit a derived part or assembly by right-clicking it in the browser and choosing Edit Derived Part or Edit Derived Assembly. This will open the same dialog box used to create the derived part so that you can change the options and selections you set when the derived part was created. Updates will be reflected in the file when you click the OK button. The Edit Derived Part and Edit Derived Assembly options are unavailable if the derived part needs to be updated.

You can also break or suppress the link with the source file by right-clicking the derived component in the browser and choosing the appropriate option. Updates made to the source file will not be made to the derived part when the link is suppressed or broken. Suppressed links can be unsuppressed by right-clicking and choosing Unsuppressed Link From Base Component. Breaking the link is permanent; it cannot be restored.

Using the Component Derive Tool

Another way to derive components is to use the Component Derive tool on the Assemble tab ➤ Productivity panel while in an assembly file. This tool allows you to select a part onscreen (or select a subassembly from the browser) and then specify a name for the new derived part file. You'll then be taken into the new derived part file. The resulting derived part or assembly uses the default derive options and the active assembly representations as they are saved in the source file. You can use the edit option in the derived part to change the settings if needed.

Working with Patterns

Certification
Objective

Inventor includes two tools to create patterns:

- ◆ Circular Pattern tool

- ◆ Rectangular Pattern tool

The Circular Pattern tool does just what you'd expect it to; it patterns a feature or set of features around an axis. The Rectangular Pattern tool also does what you'd expect, plus more. Using the Rectangular Pattern tool, you can create a pattern along any curve. If you select two perpendicular straight lines, edges, or axes, the result will be a rectangular pattern. However, if you select an entity that is not straight, the pattern will follow the curvature of the selected entity.

Rectangular Patterns

Certification
Objective

Rectangular patterns use edges to establish the pattern directions. You can select a single feature or several features for use in the pattern. Be sure to check the Model browser to see that you have only the features that you intend to pattern-select because it is easy to accidentally select base features when attempting select negative cut features. Start your exploration of patterns by creating a simple rectangular pattern, as shown here:

1. On the Get Started tab, click Open.

2. Open the file mi_5a_018.ipt in your Chapter 05 directory.

3. Click the Rectangular Pattern button on the Pattern panel of the 3D Model tab.

4. With the Features button enabled, select the three features whose names start with the word *switch* in the browser.

5. Right-click, choose Continue to set the selection focus from Features to Direction 1, and then click the straight edge, indicated in Figure 5.33. Use the Flip Direction button to ensure that the direction arrow is pointing toward the round end of the part.

FIGURE 5.33
Creating a rectangular pattern

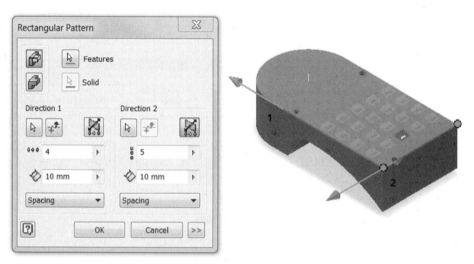

6. Set the count to 4 and the spacing length to **10 mm**.

7. Click the red arrow button under Direction 2 to set it active and then click the straight edge along the bottom, indicated in Figure 5.33.

8. Set the count to 5 and the spacing length to **10 mm**.

9. Click the Midplane check box in the Direction 2 settings to ensure that you get two instances of the pattern to each side of the original.

10. Click the OK button, and you will see the resulting pattern.

Circular Patterns

Certification Objective

You can pattern features around an axis using the Circular Pattern tool. Angular spacing between patterned features can be set in two ways.

Incremental   Positioning specifies the angular spacing between occurrences. Example: four holes at 90-degree increments.

Fitted   Positioning specifies the total area the pattern occupies. Example: four holes fit into 90 degrees.

You can enter a negative value to create a pattern in the opposite direction, and you can use the Midplane check box to pattern in both directions from the original.

Continue from the previous exercise with the open file, or open mi_5a_020.ipt to start where that exercise ended.

1. In the Model browser, select the end-of-part marker, and drag it down below the feature named Indicator Cut. Or right-click the feature named Indicator Cut and choose Move EOP Marker.

2. Click the Circular Pattern button on the Pattern panel of the 3D Model tab.

3. With the Features button enabled, select the feature named Indicator Cut.

4. Right-click and choose Continue to set the selection focus from features to axis.

5. Select the center face of the feature named Indicator Stud Hole.

6. Set the count to **4** and the angle to **90**; then click the >> button.

7. In the Positioning Method area, click the Incremental option so that the four occurrences of the pattern are set 90 degrees apart rather than being fit into a 90-degree span. Alternatively, you could set the angle to 360 and leave the positioning method to Fitted and get the same result.

8. Click the OK button. Figure 5.34 shows the resulting circular pattern.

FIGURE 5.34
Creating a circular pattern

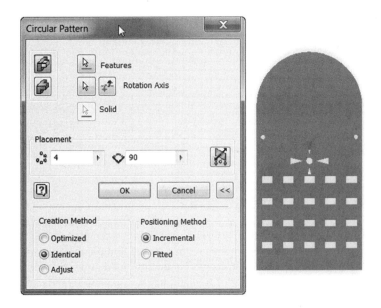

You'll note that your patterned objects require some adjustments. One of the occurrences of the Indicator Cut interferes with the switch feature, and the one opposite of that does not cut through the part correctly (use the ViewCube to look underneath the part to see this clearly). To resolve this, you will first edit the circular pattern and change the way the occurrences solve, and then you'll suppress the occurrence of the switch feature in the rectangular pattern.

9. Right-click the circular pattern in the browser and choose Edit Feature, or double-click it in the browser.

10. Click the >> button to reveal the Creation Method area and then select the Adjust option. This allows each instance of the pattern to solve uniquely based on the geometry of the model when the feature is using a Through or Through All termination solution.

11. Click the OK button and examine the pattern again, and you'll notice that the top instance of the indicator cut that was not cutting all the way through the part now is.

12. Expand the rectangular pattern in the browser to reveal the listing of each pattern occurrence.

13. Roll your mouse pointer over each occurrence node in the browser until you highlight the one that interferes with the circular pattern.

14. Right-click that occurrence and choose Suppress.

Any occurrence other than the first can be suppressed to allow for pattern exceptions or to create unequal pattern spacing. Figure 5.35 shows the adjusted patterns.

FIGURE 5.35
The adjusted patterns

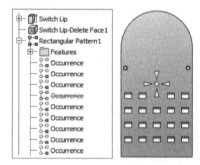

Patterns Along Curves

Certification
Objective

Although the Circular Pattern tool allows you to pattern objects around a center axis, it does not provide a way to keep the patterned objects in the same orientation as the original. To do so, you can use the rectangular pattern. Keep in mind that the term *rectangular pattern* is a bit of a misnomer; this tool might more accurately be described as a Curve Pattern tool because it allows you to select any curve, straight or not, and use it to determine the pattern directions. Continue from the previous exercise with the open file, or open mi_5a_022.ipt to start where that exercise ended; then follow these steps:

1. In the Model browser, select the end-of-part marker and drag it down below the feature named Pin Insert Path Sketch. Or right-click the sketch named Pin Insert Path Sketch and choose Move EOP Marker.

2. Click the Rectangular Pattern button on the Pattern panel of the 3D Model tab.

3. With the Features button enabled, select the feature named Pin Insert Cut.

4. Right-click and choose Continue to set the selection focus from Features to Direction 1.

5. Click the sketched curve (line or arc).

6. Set the count to **10**, and notice that the preview extends out into space.

7. Click the >> button to reveal more options.

8. Click the Start button in the Direction 1 area and then click the center of the Pin Insert Cut feature onscreen to set that center point as the start point of the pattern.

9. Change the solution drop-down from Spacing to Curve Length, and note that the length of the sketch curve is reported in the length box.

10. Change the solution drop-down from Curve Length to Distance and then type **-14** at the end of the curve length value to compensate for the start point and endpoint adjustments.

11. Toggle the Orientation option from Identical to Direction 1 to see the difference in the two and then set it back to Identical.

12. Click the OK button to set the pattern. Figure 5.36 shows the resulting pattern and the dialog box settings.

FIGURE 5.36

A pattern along a curve

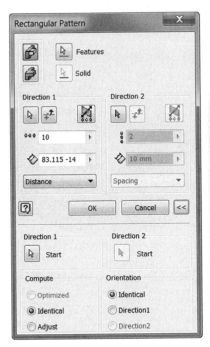

The Coil Tool and Spiral Patterns

In addition to creating patterns based on edges and sketches, you can use surfaces to define the pattern direction. In this exercise, you'll use the Coil tool to create a surface coil to use as a pattern direction. You can continue on from the previous exercise with the open file, or you can open mi_5a_024.ipt to start where that exercise ended. Then follow these steps:

1. In the Model browser, select the end-of-part marker and drag it down below the feature named Coil Pattern Sketch. Or right-click the sketch named Coil Pattern Sketch and choose Move EOP Marker.

2. Click the Coil button on the 3D Model tab.

3. In the Coil dialog box, set the output to Surface.

4. In the graphics area onscreen, choose the line segment in the Coil Pattern Sketch feature at the base of the part for the Profile selection.

5. Select the visible work axis in the center of the part for the Axis selection.

6. Click the Coil Size tab and set the type to Revolution and Height.

7. Set Height to **25 mm** and Revolutions to **4**.

8. Click the OK button to create the coiled surface.

You'll now create two work points based on the coil location for use in placing holes. Once the holes are placed, you can pattern them using the surface coil.

9. Click the Point button on the Work Features panel of the 3D Model tab and select the vertical tangent edge and the surface coil to create work points at the intersections, as shown in Figure 5.37.

FIGURE 5.37
Work points at the coils and tangent edge intersections

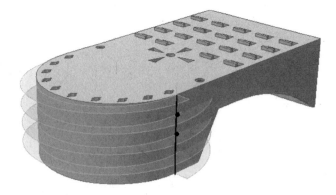

10. Click the Hole tool on the 3D Model tab and set the Placement drop-down to On Point.

TURN ON EDGES TO SEE TANGENT LINES

If you cannot see the tangent edges on your model, you can go to the View tab and set the Visual Style tool to Shaded With Edges.

11. Select one of the work points for the Point selection and then select the flat side face of the part to establish the direction.

12. Set the Termination drop-down to To and then select the inside circular face of the part.

13. Set the diameter to **3 mm** and then click the Apply button.

14. Repeat the previous three steps to place the second hole and then click the OK button.

15. Click the Rectangular Pattern button on the 3D Model tab.

16. Click the two holes for the features (it might be easiest to select them from the browser) and then right-click and choose Continue.

17. Select the surface coil for Direction 1 and use the Flip button to change the direction so that you see the previewed pattern.

18. Set the count to **10** and the length to **10 mm**.

19. Click the >> button and choose Direction 1 for the orientation.

20. Set the Compute option to Adjust and then click the OK button to create the pattern.

21. Right-click the coil and work points and turn off the visibility of these features to see the finished part clearly. Figure 5.38 shows the pattern.

FIGURE 5.38
A spiral pattern

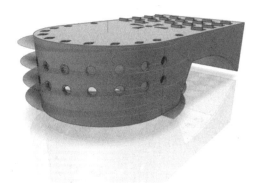

Pattern Solids

Certification Objective

Oftentimes a part can be modeled as a base feature and then patterned as a whole to create the completed part. Once the part is patterned, nonsymmetrical features can be added or patterned occurrences can be suppressed. You can also use the Pattern Entire Solid option to create separate solid bodies when creating multi-body part files is the goal. To take a look at patterning these options, open the part named mi_5a_028.ipt and follow these steps:

1. Select the Rectangular Pattern tool on the Pattern panel of the 3D Model tab.

2. Click the Pattern Solids button so that the entire part is selected to be patterned. Notice the two buttons that appear in the top-right corner of the dialog box:

   Join   This option is used to pattern the solid as a single solid body.

   Create New Bodies   This option is used to pattern the solid as separate solid bodies for multi-body part creation.

3. Leave this option set to Join and set Direction 1 to pattern the solid in the direction of the part width four times at a spacing of **10 mm**.

4. Set Direction 2 to pattern the solid in the direction of the part thickness two times at a spacing of **3 mm**, as shown in Figure 5.39. Click OK to finish.

FIGURE 5.39

Patterning a solid

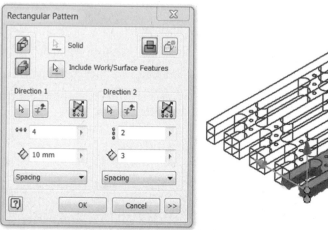
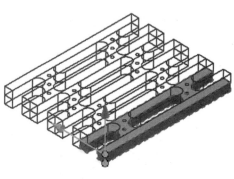

5. Expand the pattern in the Model browser and right-click to suppress the two middle occurrences on the top level. Roll your mouse pointer over each occurrence to see it highlight onscreen to identify which occurrences are the correct ones. Figure 5.40 shows the results of suppressing the correct occurrences.

6. Now you'll pattern the entire solid again. Select the Rectangular Pattern tool again and click the Pattern Solids button.

7. Set Direction 1 to pattern the solid in the direction of the part length two times at a spacing of **50 mm**.

FIGURE 5.40
Suppressed
occurrences

FIGURE 5.40
Suppressed
occurrences

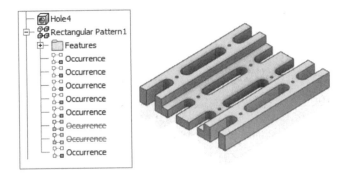

8. Set Direction 2 to pattern the solid in the direction of the part width two times at a spacing of **40 mm**, as shown in Figure 5.41. Click OK to finish.

FIGURE 5.41
Patterning the solid
again

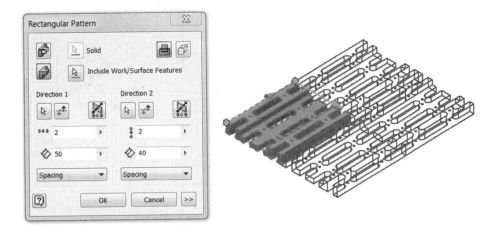

9. Create a new 2D sketch on one of the long narrow faces and project the tangent edge of the slot cuts or sketch a rectangle on the face. Do this for both ends of the face. Then use the Extrude tool, set the extents to To, and select the vertex, as shown in Figure 5.42. The result will be the removal of all the partial slot features.

FIGURE 5.42
Filling the end slots

10. Create another sketch on the same face, sketch an arc from corner to corner of the top long edge, and set the radius to **400 mm**. Then use the Extrude tool to extrude just the arc as a surface (click the Surface Output button in the Extrude dialog box). Set the extents to To again and select the same vertex you previously selected.

11. Select the Replace Face tool from the Surface panel of the 3D Model tab.

12. Select the two recessed faces for the Existing Faces selection and then select the extruded surface for the New Faces selection, as shown in Figure 5.43. Click OK and then turn off the visibility of ExtrusionSrf1 in the browser.

FIGURE 5.43
Replacing faces

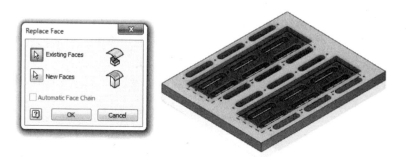

13. Create a sketch on the top face and create two rectangular profiles to use for creating an extrude cut, as shown in Figure 5.44. This cut removes the middle slots and holes, resulting in two long slots down the middle.

FIGURE 5.44
Cutting the slots

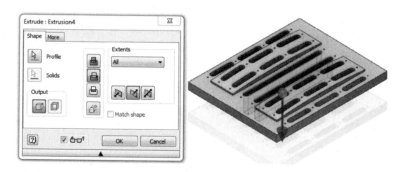

14. Select the Shell tool from the Modify panel. Choose the bottom face as the Remove Faces selection and set Thickness to **1 mm**. Figure 5.45 shows the finished part from the top and bottom views.

FIGURE 5.45
The finished part

Dynamic Patterns

It is often desirable to have features such as holes set up in a standard spacing that will dynamically update based on changes to the overall length. You can do this by setting up your patterns with parameter formulas to calculate the spacing from the length parameter. Parts set up in this way can then be saved as template parts, allowing you to select them for new part creation and simply edit the length parameter. To set up a dynamic pattern, open the file mi_5a_032.ipt and follow these steps:

1. Click the Manage tab and select the Parameters tool.

2. Notice that many of the dimensions in this part have been named. This is good practice when creating formulas. To create a formula to determine the spacing, click the Add Numeric button in the lower-left corner of the dialog box. This will create a new user-defined parameter. Enter **Adjust_Len** for the parameter name (recall that spaces are not allowed in parameter names).

3. Click the unit cell and set the Units to **ul**, meaning unitless.

4. Type **isolate(Length - End_Offset;ul;mm)** into the Equation column. There are two parts to this equation.

   Length - End_Offset   Subtracts the distance from the end of the part from the overall length of the part

   Isolate (*expression; unit; unit*)   Neutralizes the distance unit mm so that the Adjust_Len parameter can read it as unitless

5. Click the cell for the Count equation and enter **isolate(ceil(Adjust_Len / Spacing);ul;mm)** in the cell. There are three parts to this equation.

   Adjust_Len / Spacing   Divides the adjusted length distance by the value specified in the pattern spacing

   Ceil (*expression*)   Bumps the value up to the next highest whole number

   Isolate (*expression; unit; unit*)   Neutralizes the distance unit mm so that the Count parameter can read it as unitless

6. Make sure Immediate Update is selected in the dialog and then click Done. If Immediate Update is not selected, you can use the Update button on the Quick Access bar at the top of the screen. Figure 5.46 shows the Parameters dialog box.

FIGURE 5.46

Formulas to adjust the
hole spacing

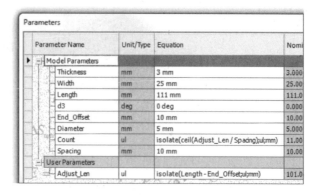

Parameters			
Parameter Name	Unit/Type	Equation	Nomi
— Model Parameters			
Thickness	mm	3 mm	3.000
Width	mm	25 mm	25.00
Length	mm	111 mm	111.0
d3	deg	0 deg	0.000
End_Offset	mm	10 mm	10.00
Diameter	mm	5 mm	5.000
Count	ul	isolate(ceil(Adjust_Len / Spacing);ul;mm)	11.00
Spacing	mm	10 mm	10.00
— User Parameters			
Adjust_Len	ul	isolate(Length - End_Offset;ul;mm)	101.0

You might notice that because the length value is currently set to 111 mm, the last hole
is running off the part. Because the equation used the Ceil function to bump the calculated
value to the next whole number, the count will always be on the high end. Depending on the
part length, this may leave you with an extra hole. You can suppress the occurrence of this
hole in the Model browser quite easily. Another approach is to remove the Ceil function and
allow Inventor to round the calculated value up or down automatically. Depending on the
length and spacing values, this might leave you with a missing hole at the end of the pattern
where a value gets rounded down. Both are valid options, and you can decide which works
best for your situation.

Edit Extrusion1 to adjust the part length, and try different values to see how the hole count
drops out. You can also open the files mi_5a_033.ipt and mi_5a_034.ipt to examine similar
hole patterns. In mi_5a_033.ipt, the Distance option is used in the pattern feature to evaluate the length of the part. It holds an end offset value and then spaces the holes evenly along
that distance. In mi_5a_034.ipt, the pattern is calculated from the center of the part rather
than coming off one end. These are just a few examples of how to use user parameters to create
dynamic patterns. There are other variations as well. In the next sections, you'll take a more in-
depth look at parameters.

Setting iProperties and Parameters

Parameters in part and assembly files can provide powerful control over individual parts and
assemblies while also improving efficiency within designs. Part parameters enable the use of
iParts, which are a form of table-driven parts. Assembly parameters enable the use of table-
driven assemblies and configurations. You access parameters through the Quick Access bar and
the Assemble and Manage ribbon tabs. In addition to parameters, you can use iProperties to add
information to your files.

iProperties

Certification
Objective

iProperties, generically known as *file properties*, allow the input of information specific to the
active file. Right-click the top node of a component in the browser or click the file drop-down to
access the iProperties dialog box. You can also modify the iProperties of multiple components
in the assembly Bill of Materials. iProperties are a powerful way to pass information from the

model files to the drawing file, allowing you to fill out information in title blocks, standard notes, and parts list automatically. The dialog box contains several tabs for input of information:

General Contains read-only information on the file type, size, and location. The creation date, last modified date, and last accessed date are preserved on this tab.

Summary Includes part information such as title, subject, author, manager, and company. Add information to the Keywords field to let Inventor search for related files.

Project Stores file-specific information that, along with information from the Summary, Status, Custom, and Physical tabs, can be exported to external files and used in link information within the 2D drawing file.

Status Allows the input of information and the control of the design state and dates of each design step.

Custom Allows the creation of custom parameters for use within the design. Parameters exported from the Parameters dialog box will also appear in the list. Formulas can be used within a custom parameter to populate values in preexisting fields within the Project and Status tabs.

Save Determines the behavior of the current file upon save.

Physical Allows for changing the material type used in the current file and displays the calculated physical properties of the current part, such as mass and moment of inertia, as determined by the material type.

Active use of iProperties will help the designer in improving overall productivity as well as provide the ability to link part and assembly information into 2D drawings. Adding search properties in the Summary tab will assist Inventor in locating similar files.

Custom iProperties are either created manually in the Custom tab of iProperties or created automatically by exporting individual parameters from the Parameter dialog. Custom iProperties may be linked to drawings and assemblies for additional functionality.

ACCESSING IPROPERTIES THROUGH WINDOWS EXPLORER

When you right-click an Inventor file in Windows Explorer and choose Properties, you can select the iProperties tab from the file properties dialog box. Clicking the iProperties button on the iProperties tab opens an Inventor iProperties dialog box similar to what you would see in Inventor.

This can offer people in the office who do not have access to Inventor the ability to view and change iProperties when needed. For instance, someone in the manufacturing department can use this to set the Mfg. Approved Date iProperty once a part has been successfully built on the shop floor based on a given drawing or part file. To change iProperties without having Inventor installed, you can install Inventor View. Inventor View can be downloaded for free from the Autodesk website.

You can also use the Details tab in this way to quickly confirm the Inventor version the file was created in and last saved under.

Part Parameters

Part parameters are composed of model parameters, user parameters, reference parameters, and parameters created by linking a file. Model parameters are automatically embedded as a part is dimensioned and features are created. Most are a mirror image of the sketch-creation process. As each dimension is created on a sketch, a corresponding model parameter is created, starting with a parameter called d0 and incrementing each time a new parameter is created. When you name a dimension, you are changing the automatically assigned parameter name. To access the list of parameters, select the Manage tab and click the Parameters button. Figure 5.47 represents a typical parameter list.

FIGURE 5.47
Part parameter list

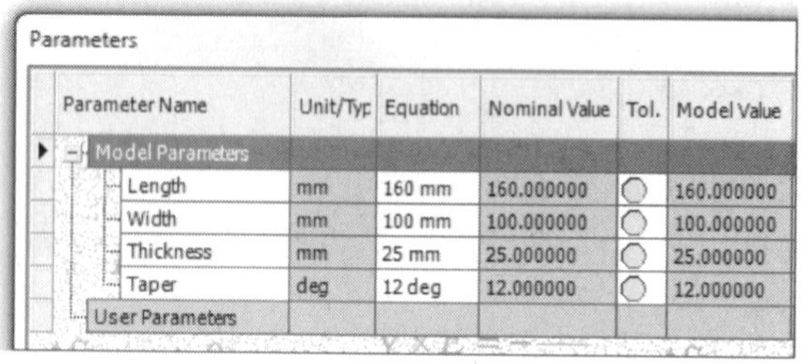

Parameter Name	Unit/Typ	Equation	Nominal Value	Tol.	Model Value
⊟ Model Parameters					
Length	mm	160 mm	160.000000	○	160.000000
Width	mm	100 mm	100.000000	○	100.000000
Thickness	mm	25 mm	25.000000	○	25.000000
Taper	deg	12 deg	12.000000	○	12.000000
└ User Parameters					

Looking across the top of the dialog box, you will see columns for the parameter name, unit type, equation, nominal value, tolerance type, model value, key status, parameter export, and descriptive comments.

Parameter Name The values in this column correspond to the name of the parameters assigned as the part is built. Each parameter name starts with a lowercase *d* followed by a numeric value. The parameters can be renamed to something that is more familiar, such as Length, Height, Base_Dia, or any other descriptive single word. Spaces are not allowed in the parameter name. Hovering your mouse pointer over a name will initiate a tool tip that will tell you where that variable is used or consumed. Parameters can be of three types:

◆ Model parameters are created from dimensions or dialog box inputs that drive the geometry.

◆ Reference parameters are created from dimensions that are driven by other geometry entities.

◆ User parameters are created by you, the user, and are used in formulas and iLogic rules or referenced by model parameters.

◆ Linked parameters are created by linking to Inventor parts or assemblies and Excel files.

Unit/Type The unit type defines the unit used in the calculation. Normally, the unit type will be set by the process that created it. When a user parameter is created, you will be presented with a Unit Type dialog box when you click in the Unit column. This will allow you to select a particular unit type for the user parameter.

Equation This column either specifies a static value or allows you to create algebraic-style equations using other variables or constants to modify numeric values.

Nominal Value This column displays the result of the equation.

Tolerance This column shows the current evaluated size setting for the parameter. Click the cell to select Upper, Lower, Median, or Nominal tolerance values. This will change the size of tolerance features in the model.

Model Value   This column shows the actual calculated value of the parameter based on the tolerance type.

Key   Select the Key parameter to designate a row as important. Key values are also useful if you create iParts and iAssemblies.

Export Parameter   These check boxes are activated to add specific parameters to the custom properties for the model. Downstream, custom properties can be added to parts lists and bills of materials by adding columns. Clearing the check box will remove that parameter as a custom property. After a parameter is added, other files will be able to link to or derive the exported parameter. Text and True/False parameters cannot be exported.

Comment   This column is used to help describe the use of a parameter. Linked parameters will include the description within the link.

USER PARAMETERS

User parameters are simply parameters that a user creates by clicking the Add button in the lower-left portion of the Parameters dialog box. A user parameter can also be created by right-clicking a linked or embedded row and selecting Add to User Parameters. You can add numeric, text, and True/False parameters; however, only numeric parameters may be exported or contain expressions. Text and True/False parameters can be created for use in iLogic rules. User parameters can be used to store equations that drive features and dimensions in the model. The user-created parameter can utilize algebraic operators written in the proper syntax that will create an expression in a numerical value.

REFERENCE PARAMETERS

Reference parameters are driven parameters that are created through the use of reference dimensions in sketches and the use of derived parts, attached via a linked spreadsheet, created by table-driven iFeatures, or created through the use of the application programming interface (API). For instance, Inventor sheet-metal parts create flat pattern extents, which are stored as reference parameters.

FORMATTING PARAMETERS

If needed, you can format the parameter to display differently than the default display. To do so, you must first select the Export Parameter check box in the Parameters dialog box for the parameter you intend to customize. Once the parameter is selected for export, you can right-click that parameter and choose Custom Property Format to access the Custom Property Format settings. In the Custom Property Format dialog box you can change property type, units, format, and precision as well as control the display of unit strings, leading zeros, and trailing zeros. When you've configured the parameter formatting, it is reflected in the custom iProperty for that parameter.

For instance, if you have a part dimension length of 100.00 mm and you want to call that length into the part description but do not want to see the units string (mm) or the zeros after the decimal point, you would go to the Manage tab, click the Parameters button, and then select the Export Parameter check box for the length parameter. Then, you'd right-click the length parameter and choose the Custom Property Format option. Finally, you'd uncheck the Unit

String and Leading Zeros options. To see the results, you'd exit the Parameters dialog box and then right-click the top-level node in the browser (typically the filename), choose iProperties, and then click the Custom tab to find the custom iProperty that corresponds to the exported parameter.

PARAMETER FUNCTIONS

One of the most important aspects of working with parameters is the ability to create expressions using the available parameter functions. The functions in Table 5.1 can be used in user parameters or placed directly into edit boxes when you are creating dimensions and features.

TABLE 5.1: Functions and their syntax for edit boxes

SYNTAX	UNIT TYPE	DESCRIPTION
cos (*expression*)	Unitless	Calculates the cosine of an angle.
sin (*expression*)	Unitless	Calculates the sine of an angle.
tan (*expression*)	Unitless	Calculates the tangent of an angle.
acos (*expression*)	Angularity	Calculates the inverse cosine of a value.
asin (*expression*)	Angularity	Calculates the inverse sine of a value.
atan (*expression*)	Angularity	Calculates the inverse tangent of a value.
cosh (*expression*)	Unitless	Calculates the hyperbolic cosine of an angle.
sinh (*expression*)	Unitless	Calculates the hyperbolic sine of an angle.
tanh (*expression*)	Unitless	Calculates the hyperbolic tangent of an angle.
acosh (*expression*)	Angularity	Calculates the inverse hyperbolic cosine of a value.
asinh (*expression*)	Angularity	Calculates the inverse hyperbolic sine of a value.
atanh (*expression*)	Angularity	Calculates the inverse hyperbolic tangent of a value.
sqrt (*expression*)	Unit^0.5	Calculates the square root of a value. The units within the sqrt function have to be square mm in order to return mm. For example, sqrt(144 mm^2) returns 12.
sign (*expression*)	Unitless	Returns 0 for a negative value, 1 if positive.
Exp	Unitless	Returns an exponential power of a value. For example, exp(100) returns 2.688E43.

SYNTAX	UNIT TYPE	DESCRIPTION
floor (*expression*)	Unitless	Returns the next-lowest whole number. For example, `floor(3.33)` returns 3.
ceil (*expression*)	Unitless	Returns the next-highest whole number. For example, `ceil(3.33)` returns 4.
round (*expression*)	Unitless	Returns the closest whole number. For example, `round(3.33)` returns 3.
abs (*expression*)	Any	Returns the absolute value of an expression. For example, `abs(3*-4)` returns 12.
max (*expression1*; *expression2*)	Any	Returns the larger of two expressions. For example, `max(3;4)` returns 4.
min (*expression1*; *expression2*)	Any	Returns the smaller of two expressions. For example, `min(3;4)` returns 3.
ln (*expression*)	Unitless	Returns the natural logarithm of an expression.
log (*expression*)	Unitless	Returns the logarithm of an expression.
pow (*expression1*; *expression2*)	Unit^expr2	Raises the power of *expression1* by *expression2*. For example, `pow(3 ul;2 ul)` returns 9.
random ()	Unitless	Returns a random number.
isolate (*expression*; *unit;unit*)	Any	Used to convert the units of an expression. For example, `isolate(Length;mm;ul)`, where `Length=100mm`, returns 100 ul.
PI	Internal Parameter	Returns the constant equal to a circle's circumference divided by its diameter, 3.14159265359 (depending on precision). For example, `PI*50 mm` returns 157.079633.
E	Internal Parameter	Returns the base of the natural logarithm 2.718281828459 (depending on precision).
*1 *unit* or / 1 *unit*	Any	Used to convert unit types of an expression, much like `isolate`. For example, `100 mm *10 ul` returns an errant value for a unitless parameter. `100 mm / 1 mm * 10 ul` returns 1000 ul. `100 mm * 10 ul / 1 mm` also works.

 **Real World Scenario**

SETTING UP USER PARAMETERS IN YOUR TEMPLATES

Although many times parameters are used to control design input on a per-design basis, you can often use preestablished parameters in template files, so only a couple of key parameters need to be changed in the part file to create a new variant of a standard part. User parameters are especially powerful when these types of template parts are created.

Consider, for example, a standard-type mounting bracket. The general shape is carried through in all iterations, but you can identify several key dimensions that are driven by the particulars of each new design situation. Dimensions such as length, width, height, and thickness are good examples of parameters that can be identified and set up in a template part.

Other things to consider for use as parameters would be critical dimensions such as the locations of holes from the edge of the part, hole sizes, hole counts, and hole spacing. If the hole offset is determined by the material thickness and hole size, then a formula can be established in the part template to calculate the minimum offset value.

Once the part parameters are created and tested for accuracy, the part can be turned into a template by using the Save Copy As Template option in the Save As menu. This will save the part file in the Template directory. Template parts can be as simple or complex as you need, but generally this works best for simple parts. For more complex parts, consider creating iParts, covered in Chapter 7, "Reusing Parts and Features."

When creating parameter-based template parts, you might want to consider creating user parameters with descriptive names for all the key parameters so they are all grouped together. This way, you (or another user) can quickly identify key parameters used to drive the design later when creating parts in your real-world designs.

Assembly Parameters

Assembly parameters function in much the same way as part parameters except they will generally control constraint values such as offset and angle. When you're authoring an iAssembly, other parameters will be exposed for usage, such as assembly features, work features, iMates, and component patterns, as well as other parameters that may exist within an assembly.

Adding Part Tolerances

Inventor allows you to analyze parts in a manner that ensures valid fit and function at dimensional extremes. When parts are assembled within an Inventor assembly file, you can check to ensure that the parts can be assembled without interference, by setting each part to evaluate at the upper or lower tolerance value. By specifying dimensional tolerances within parts, you are capturing valuable design data that will assist in manufacturing and assembly. In addition to creating the parts separately and then assembling them, you can use multi-body parts to create mated parts in one file, making it easy to design tolerances across multiple parts.

LESS IS OFTEN MORE WITH TOLERANCES

When considering part designs for manufacturing, be careful not to apply precise tolerance values where they are not necessary for the design and assembly. Excessive and unneeded tolerances during the design phase can substantially increase the cost to manufacture each part. The secret to good design is to know where to place tolerances and where to allow shop tolerances to occur.

Tolerances are an important tool for communicating design intent to manufacturing. Large tolerances indicate that the dimensions aren't critical to the part's function, whereas tight tolerances indicate that manufacturing needs to pay extra attention to that machining operation. Loosening up tolerances can help manufacturing reduce the reject rate, while tightening up certain tolerances can reduce rework during the assembly process or in the field.

Tolerances in Sketches

You can add tolerances to any individual sketch dimension by right-clicking and choosing Dimension Properties to set precision and tolerance values. You can also access the tolerance setting from within the dimension edit box to set the tolerance as you set the value. Altering the dimension to adjust for tolerance and precision using either method will not affect any other dimension within the part. However, a global file tolerance can be specified within a part using the Document Settings dialog box and will affect every dimension within the model.

In addition to the Dimension Properties menu option and the dimension edit box option, you can access and modify tolerances in the Parameters dialog box. Using the Parameters controls, you can set parameter values for multiple dimensions to include the tolerance as needed. No matter how you access the tolerance setting, you can use four options to evaluate the dimension/parameter.

+ Upper   The upper tolerance value in a stacked display. This value should be Maximum Material Condition (MMC). For a hole, the smallest diameter is MMC, whereas for a shaft the largest diameter is MMC.

① Median   The midway point between the upper and lower tolerances. This is commonly used when Computer Numerical Control (CNC) machines are programmed from the solid model.

– Lower   The lower tolerance in a stacked display. This value should be Least Material Condition (LMC). For a hole, the largest diameter is LMC, while for a shaft the smallest diameter is LMC.

· Nominal   This is the actual value of the dimension.

Figure 5.48 shows the access to the tolerance settings through the sketch dimension edit box as well as the settings in the Tolerance dialog box. In this case, a deviation tolerance is placed on the 36 mm diameter, and the model is set to evaluate at the upper value (note that the plus sign is selected). Since this document's settings are defaulted to three places, all sketch dimensions are in three places to start. In the illustration, the precision has been set to just two decimal places, for just this dimension.

FIGURE 5.48
Sketch showing
tolerances

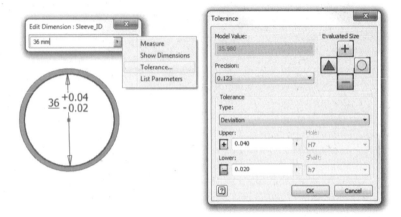

TOLERANCE VS. ALLOWANCE

Tolerance is the acceptable (but undesired) deviation from the intended (nominal) dimension.
Allowance is the intended (desired) difference of dimensions between two mating parts, depending on the type of fit specified.

Setting Global File Tolerances

Adding tolerances during the design phase pays dividends down the road. There will be fewer errors creating drawings, and tolerances provide clues to design decisions that are useful when updating an existing part. You might find using standard tolerances makes the design process more efficient because the designer needs to focus only on the general tolerance for a dimension (two-place vs. three-place tolerance) and apply special tolerances where needed. You can create custom templates to store tolerance types and other settings for each standard. When the part is created using such a template, standard tolerance values can be overridden for specific dimensional values, or you can override all tolerances within a file or just a specific dimension.

An example of this type of tolerance would be a tolerance rule that states that all decimal dimensions held to two places shall be +/− 0.05 and all decimal dimensions held to three places shall be +/− 0.001, meaning a dimension of 0.50 would be held to an upper limit of 0.55 and a lower limit of 0.45, whereas a dimension of 0.500 would be held to an upper limit of 0.501 and a lower limit of 0.499.

You can create and modify global tolerance values within a single part by selecting the Tools tab, clicking Document Settings, and then clicking the Default Tolerance tab within an active part file or template. By default, a file will not be using any tolerance standards. In Figure 5.49, the Use Standard Tolerancing Values box has been selected to enable the addition of new standards for the file. To export the tolerance values to the drawing files, the Export Standard Tolerance Values would need to be selected as well.

FIGURE 5.49

Document settings for tolerance

Once the tolerance values are set, the dimension in the part will evaluate at the nominal value, meaning that if you entered a value of 36 for a part length, that is what the length would be. To evaluate the model at its upper limit at +/− 0.001, you would edit the dimension for the length and set the precision to three places and the evaluated size to Upper (using the + button). The length would then change to 36.05, if you are using the earlier example. The default tolerances are set to +/− tolerances. To select another tolerance standard, simply override the existing tolerance values in the tolerance setting and choose another tolerance type, such as deviation. You can see all of this in action in the following steps:

1. On the Get Started tab, click Open; then open the part named mi_5a_035.ipt in the Chapter 05 folder.

2. Select the Tools tab and then click the Document Settings tab.

3. Select the Default Tolerance tab and notice that there are two linear tolerance standards and one angular tolerance standard already set up. Note that there is a linear precision for one decimal and another for two decimals, but there is not one for three decimals. Keep this in mind as you proceed.

4. Click the check box to use the standard tolerancing values, click the Apply button, and then click the Close button.

Now that the part is set to use a global part tolerance, you will edit a dimension and change the precision setting to two decimals so it will use one of the global linear tolerance settings. It is important to note that the dimension precision for all the dimensions in the part is currently set to three decimal places (the default setting).

5. Edit the 15 mm dimension by double-clicking the text of the dimension.

6. Click the flyout arrow in the dimension input box and select Tolerance.

7. Set the precision to just one decimal place and then click the blue plus sign to evaluate the dimension at its upper value.

8. Click the OK button to exit the Tolerance dialog box and then click the green check mark in the dimension edit box.

9. Although the sketch automatically updates to evaluate the dimension at its upper value, you'll need to update the model to see the solid update. Click the Update button on the Quick Access bar (at the top of the screen; it looks like a lightning bolt).

10. To evaluate the entire part at the lower value, select the Manage tab and click the Parameters button.

11. In the Parameters dialog box, click the red minus sign in the Reset Tolerance area and then ensure the Immediate Update check box is selected to see the Model Values column update.

Compare the nominal and model values in the parameter table to see that some of the dimensions are now reevaluated. Since the dimension default precision for the part is set to three places, the 25 mm and 3 mm dimensions are using that precision (for which no tolerance was set) and therefore have no lower value. Don't be confused by the precision being displayed in the Parameters table because that precision is display only. You can click the Equation cell for each dimension and then right-click and choose Tolerance to access the tolerance and precision settings for each dimension to see or change them.

12. Click Done to exit the Parameters dialog.

13. To change the global dimension precision, select the Tools tab and click the Document Settings button.

14. Select the Units tab and set Modeling Dimension Display for Linear Dim Display Precision to two places; then click the OK button.

Now the 25 mm dimension is using the file default precision of two places, and since it is still set to evaluate at the lower value, it changes to 24.99. You can begin to see the power of using tolerances in your models to evaluate tolerance ranges as you design. You can close this file without saving changes. In the next section, you'll look at using limits and fits tolerances.

PART TOLERANCES IN DRAWINGS

Keep in mind that when a part is used in the drawing environment, it will reflect the current evaluated model dimensions and will show the tolerance callout only for retrieved dimensions.

Typically, it is best to create multiple dimension styles with various precision and/or tolerance options in the drawing environment and handle tolerance dimensioning for the print using those tools. You must keep in mind that the tolerance settings in the part are designed to function with the assembly environment and allow calculating tolerances and stack-ups within the assembly. They are not meant to provide tolerancing in the drawing environment.

Working with Limits and Fits

A fit tolerance defines the way two components mate together. There are three basic categories of fits.

Clearance   This allows the mating components to slide together freely so they can be assembled and disassembled easily.

Transition   This provides a fit close enough to securely hold the two components together but still allow them to be disassembled.

Interference   Often called a press fit or friction fit, Interference provides a means to hold two components together by slightly oversizing one component that fits into the other. Some force is required to achieve the fitting of the two components together, and disassembly is not intended.

You can create parts according to fits by adding tolerance values to sketch dimensions and setting the tolerance type to one of the Limits/Fits options. Using a fits table as a reference, you can then set the tolerance according to the desired fit type.

In the following exercise, you will edit a part and set tolerances for the two mating solid bodies, using Table 5.2 as guide for the fits. To start, you will set the inside and outside diameters to use tolerances based on a common diameter of 36 mm. The goal is have a loose fit that allows the insert to slip freely into the sleeve. Follow these steps:

1. On the Get Started tab, click Open; then open the part named `mi_5a_036.ipt` from your `Chapter 05` folder.

2. Select the dimension called Sleeve_ID and double-click to bring up the dimension edit box.

3. Click the flyout arrow and choose Tolerance from the list.

4. Set the Type drop-down to Limit/Fits-Show Size Limits.

5. Set the Hole drop-down to H11 to create a loose running fit, as listed in Table 5.2.

TABLE 5.2:   Example of limits and fits using a hole basis system

TYPE	FIT	USE	HOLE	SHAFT
Clearance	Loose running	General fits with smaller clearances.	H11	c11
Clearance	Sliding	Very small clearances for accurate guiding of shafts, with no noticeable clearance once assembled.	H7	g6
Transition	Locational	Snug fit with small clearance. Parts can be assembled and disassembled manually.	H7	h6
Transition	Keying	Small clearances or slight interferences. Parts can be assembled with little force, such as with a rubber mallet.	H7	k6
Interference	Press	Guaranteed interference, using cold pressing.	H7	p6
Interference	Shrink	Medium interference, using hot pressing or large-force cold pressing.	H7	s6

6. Click the red minus sign to evaluate the inside diameter at its lower limit.

7. Click the OK button to exit the Tolerance dialog box and then click the green check mark in the dimension edit box.

8. Select the dimension called Insert_OD and double-click it to bring up the dimension edit box.

9. Click the flyout arrow and choose Tolerance from the list.

10. Set the Type drop-down to Limit/Fits-Show Size Limits.

11. Set the Shaft drop-down to c11 to create the other half of the loose running fit.

12. Click the blue plus sign to evaluate the outside diameter at its upper limit.

13. Click the OK button to exit the Tolerance dialog box and then click the green check mark in the dimension edit box.

14. Zoom in on the cutout in the sleeve, and you'll see a green arrow on one corner. Zoom in closer on the green arrow, and you will see the gap between the diameter sketches of the sleeve and the insert reflecting your tolerance edits. However, the model itself currently displays no tolerance and needs to be updated to match the sketch.

15. Click the Update button on the Quick Access bar (it looks like a lightning bolt at the top of the screen).

You should see a gap between the solids, providing a loose running fit. Because the current model is being evaluated at the extremes (the upper tolerance for the inside diameter and the lower for the outside diameter), you can determine whether the current design will provide the correct fit. In the real world, you might determine that the outside diameter of the insert needs to be less than 36 mm for the nominal value so that you can ensure a better fit.

Continue with the following steps to explore more options when working with part tolerances.

16. Zoom back out and then click once on any blank area of the graphics screen (to clear any currently selected entities). Then right-click, choose Dimension Display, and choose Tolerance from the flyout menu. This will show you the evaluated dimension values, as shown in Figure 5.50.

FIGURE 5.50
Dimensions showing
limit/fits

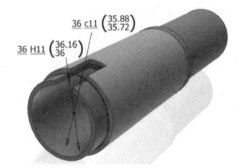

17. Right-click either of the dimensions and choose Dimension Properties.

You'll notice that you can set and adjust the tolerance options in this menu as well. You can use the Document Settings tab to set up standard tolerances for the entire file and change the precision and dimension display. These are the same settings you accessed by editing the dimensions and parameters in the previous steps.

This concludes the formal steps of this exercise, but you can continue experimenting with the tolerances using Table 5.2 as a reference. For instance, you might set up a press fit and evaluate the inside diameter at the upper value and the outside at the lower to check to see whether there is indeed enough interference to provide a solid press fit when both dimensions are evaluated at their extremes. (Note that Table 5.2 is not a complete fits list and is provided as reference for this exercise only.)

Working with Free-Form Modeling and Direct Editing Tools

Traditionally 3D parametric modelers such as Inventor have operated on the concepts of sketch and feature dependencies and a model history tree; this approach allows you to step back into the design and change parameters in order to edit the model. With the free-form modeling tools, you create features by moving, rotating, and scaling surface model points, edges, and faces. The Direct Editing tool allows you to add edits to the model tree without stepping back into the model design tree.

Free-Form Modeling

The typical free-form workflow starts with creating a free-form shape such as a box, sphere, cylinder, torus, or quad-ball. Once the shape is created, you use the free-form edit tools to refine and define the shape by selecting points, faces, or edges of the shape and then moving, rotating, or scaling those selections.

Once the shape has been created and edited to the desired shape, you exit the free-form editing mode and are returned to the standard modeling mode where you can sketch and add features to further refine the model as needed.

CREATING A FREE-FORM SHAPE

To explore the free-form modeling tools, you'll open a file that has been derived from another file. This file contains a motorcycle frame, upon which you will create a fuel tank using the free-form tools.

1. On the Get Started tab, click Open; then open the part named mi_5a_037.ipt in the Chapter 05 folder.

2. On the 3D Model tab, locate the Create Freeform panel and click the Box button.

3. Choose the XY Plane for the first selection.

4. Choose visible work point in the graphics area (or select Work Point1 from the browser) for the second selection.

5. Set the Length input to **560 mm**, set the Width input to **210 mm**, and set the Height input to **260 mm**.

6. Set the Faces input for the Length to **4** and leave the others at the default.

7. Click the Both Direction button in the Direction control to have the box form created equally on each side of the XY work plane.

8. Click the OK button to create the box form.

Figure 5.51 shows the box form inputs.

FIGURE 5.51
Creating a box form

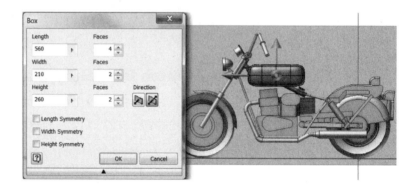

Once your box is created, you'll notice the form feature node created in the model browser as Form1 or something similar. Notice, too, that once you create a form, you are still in the free-form editing mode, as indicated by the available selections in the ribbon menu. You can close this file without saving changes.

ADDING SYMMETRY TO A FREE-FORM SHAPE

When you create a free-form shape, it is often helpful to allow the edits to the form to be made symmetrically in one or more planar directions. In Figure 5.51 you can see three check box controls that allow you to specify that the form you create will automatically edit symmetrically in the selected directions. This can be useful if you know that the form will be symmetric in advance, but you can also turn symmetry on or off at any point in the free-form editing process, as illustrated in the following steps:

1. On the Get Started tab, click Open; then open the part named mi_5a_038.ipt in the Chapter 05 folder.

2. In the browser, locate the feature named Form1 and double-click it (or right-click and choose Edit Freeform).

3. On the Freeform tab, locate the Symmetry panel and click the Symmetry button.

4. Click two opposing faces in order to establish symmetry down the center of the motorcycle, as shown in Figure 5.52.

FIGURE 5.52

Adding symmetry to
a form

5. Next click the OK button to set the symmetry.

6. Observe the dashed line running through the center of the form that signifies a symmetry condition exists on the form.

7. Click the Edit Form button on the Edit panel of the Freeform tab to bring up the Edit Form dialog box.

8. Click any face on the form shape and notice that the opposing, symmetric face is automatically selected also.

9. Click and drag one of the arrow controls in the graphics area to see the symmetric edit in action.

10. Click and drag a different arrow control to see the symmetric edit in action again.

11. Experiment with the controls as you like (these will be explained in more detail in the steps to come) and then click the OK button to create the edits.

12. Click the drop-down arrow below the Symmetry button to expose the list of editing tools. Click the Clear Symmetry button in the list and then select the freeform shape. Notice that the dashed symmetry line running through the center of the form has been removed.

Adding symmetry to a free-form shape allows you to more quickly and accurately create shape modifications when a symmetric relationship is desired. You can close this file and continue to the next section to further explore the free-form editing tools.

EDITING A FREE-FORM SHAPE

The Edit Freeform tool contains several controls that can be used in combination or individually to manipulate a free-form shape precisely or visually. For instance, if you wanted to select a face and move it up based on your current view, you could change the Selection button from All to Face, change the Transform Mode button from All to Translation, and change the Transform Space button to View. Figure 5.53 shows the Edit Form dialog box controls followed by a short description of most of the buttons.

FIGURE 5.53
Edit Form tool
controls

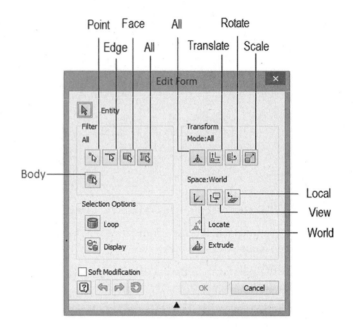

Soft Modification

Soft Modification controls are shown enabled in Figure 5.53. Enable Soft Modification to control how the vertices near the selection are influenced, the amount of change, and the falloff shape of the edit.

Selection Buttons

The Selection buttons set a filter status allowing you to select only points, edges, faces, or bodies, or to select any of them. The controls provided are as follows:

Point Filters the selection for only vertex points.

Edge Filters the selection for only the edges between faces.

Face Filters the selection for only faces.

All Allows the selection of any entity. This is the default.

Body Filters the selection for entire solid bodies.

Transform Buttons

You can use the Transform buttons to isolate the edit actions. The controls provided are as follows:

All (Mode)   Allows translation, scaling, and rotation edits. This is the default.

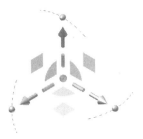

Translation (Mode)   Allows selections to be moved in one of the three selected axis directions.

Rotation (Mode)   Allows selections to be rotated around one of the three selected axis directions.

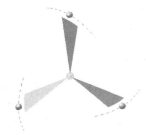

Scale (Mode)   Allows selections to be scaled in one of the three selected axis directions.

World (Space)   Sets the x-, y-, and z-axes based on the world coordinate.

View (Space)   Isolates two axes based on the current view.

Local (Space)   Sets the x-, y-, and z-axes based on the local coordinate.

In the following steps, you will use the free-form editing tools to change the free-form box shape into a fuel tank for the motorcycle:

1. On the Get Started tab, click Open; then open the part named mi_5a_039.ipt in the Chapter 05 folder.

2. In the browser, locate the feature named Form1 and double-click it (or right-click and choose Edit Freeform).

3. Click the Edit Form button on the Edit panel of the Freeform tab to bring up the Edit Form dialog box.

4. In the Selection area of the Edit Form dialog box, click the Body button.

5. In the Transform area of the Edit Form dialog box, click the Rotation button.

6. Click the box form shape in the graphics area to select it for the rotation.

7. Click the front view of the View Cube; then click (but do not drag) the rotation control. Enter **-20** for the rotation input and then click OK.

Figure 5.54 shows the rotated box form.

FIGURE 5.54
Rotating the box form

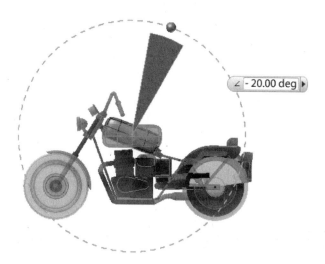

8. Click the Home button on the View Cube (looks like a house).

9. In the Selection area of the Edit Form dialog box, click the Face button.

10. In the Transform area of the Edit Form dialog box, click the Translation button.

11. Click once in empty space of the graphic area to clear your selection; then hold the **Ctrl** key on the keyboard and click the two faces, as indicated in Figure 5.55.

FIGURE 5.55
Editing the free-form shape

FIGURE 5.55
Editing the free-form shape

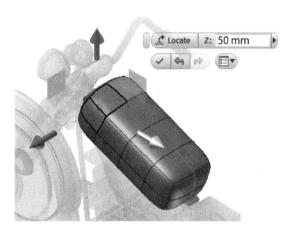

12. Click the control arrow pointing to the left of the motorcycle (in the Z direction) and then enter **50** into the input box.

13. Click OK to finish the edit.

Figure 5.56 shows the finished fuel tank created with the free-form tools.

FIGURE 5.56
Finished fuel tank

Here are a few tips to know about when working with the free-form editing tools:

◆ Select points in order to add more roundness or less roundness to an area of the free-form shape.

◆ You can use the ViewCube in combination with the View (Transform Space) button to set custom directions quickly.

◆ You can click and drag a control in order to visually edit, or you can click the control and then enter an input.

◆ You can click, drag, and hold a control and then enter an input.

◆ By default the controls center on the selections you've made; however, you can use the Locate button to select an edge or point to change the center of the controls in order to get a different result.

◆ You can use the Toggle Smooth button to toggle between smooth and blocky model display.

◆ Explore more editing tools in the Modify pane, such as Insert Edge, Subdivide, Bridge, Match Edge, and so on. If you pause your cursor over each button, Inventor will display a description of the functionality for each tool.

When you're finished experimenting with this file, you can close it without saving changes. You can refer to the file named mi_5a_039_done.ipt for a reference if you'd like.

Using the Direct Edit Tool

The Direct Edit tool lets you make quick edits to existing features. You can make adjustments to the location, shape, and size of features by directly editing the geometry, rather than editing the sketch or feature that originally created the feature. Specifically, you can use the Direct Edit tool to do the following:

◆ Quickly explore "what if" design alternatives

◆ Modify imported parts

◆ Scale the model

◆ Limit modifications to only the feature you choose, without risking the accidental modification of dependent features

◆ Quickly update a complex model created by another user without needing to diagnose the feature structure

Figure 5.57 shows the Direct Edit tools.

FIGURE 5.57
The Direct Edit controls

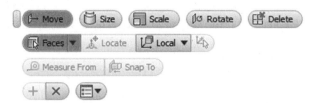

Troubleshooting Failures with the End-of-Part Marker

Once in a while, even the most skilled design engineer experiences a modeling or design failure. The part may have been supplied by a customer or co-worker who did not practice sound modeling techniques, or you may have to drastically modify a base feature in a part you designed. These kinds of edits change a base feature to the point that dependent features cannot solve, and a cascade of errors can occur. Knowing how to fix these errors can save you hours of work.

One of the best ways to troubleshoot a part and determine exactly how the part was originally modeled is to use the end-of-part (EOP) marker to step through the creation process. In the Model browser, drag the end-of-part marker to a location immediately below the first feature. This will effectively eliminate all other features below the marker from the part calculation.

Often when making modifications to a part, you might change a feature that causes errors to cascade down through the part. Moving the end-of-part marker up to isolate the first troubled feature allows you to resolve errors one at a time. Many times, resolving the topmost error will fix those that exist after it. Figure 5.58 shows a model tree with a series of errors. On the right, the end-of-part marker has been moved up.

FIGURE 5.58
Using the end-of-part marker to troubleshoot feature errors

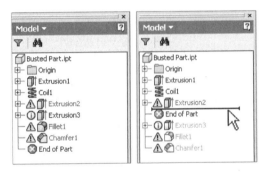

Step 1: Editing the First Feature

Normally, the first feature will start with a sketch. Right-click the first feature and select Edit Sketch. Examine the sketch for a location relative to the part origin point. Generally, the first sketch should be located and anchored at the origin and fully dimensioned and constrained. If the sketch is not fully constrained, then add dimensions and constraints to correct it.

If you see sketch entities highlighted in magenta, you probably have projected geometry that has lost its parent feature. To resolve errors of this type, it is often required to break the link between the missing geometry and allow the projected entities to stand on their own. To do so, right-click the objects in the graphics area or expand the sketch in the browser and right-click any projected or reference geometry that is showing errors; then choose Break Link. This frees up the geometry so that it can be constrained and dimensioned on its own or simply deleted. Figure 5.59 shows the Break Link option listed in the context menu for a projected loop.

FIGURE 5.59
Breaking projected object links

Once the sketch is free of errors, you can return to the feature level. Often, you'll be greeted by an error message informing you that the feature is not healthy. Click Edit or Accept. Then edit the feature. Most often you will simply be required to reselect the profile or reference geometry. Once the feature is fixed, drag the end-of-part marker below the next feature and repeat the step. Continue through the part until all sketches are properly constrained.

Occasionally, a base sketch may become "lost" and may need to be reassociated to a sketch plane. To do so, you can right-click and choose Redefine, as shown in Figure 5.60. Depending on how drastic the change in the sketch plane is, this may be all that is required. Often, though, you will need to edit the sketch, clean up some stray geometry using the Break Link option, and then dimension and constrain it so that it is stable.

FIGURE 5.60

Redefining a sketch

Step 2: Moving the EOP Marker Down One Feature at a Time

Step 2 might be called "learn from your mistakes" (or other people's mistakes). When you have part/feature failures, you should take advantage of them and analyze how the part was created to determine why the sketch or features became unstable. It's always good practice to create the major features first and then add secondary features such as holes, fillets, and chamfers at the end of the part. On occasion, loft and sweep features may fail or produce incorrect results because fillets and chamfers were created before the failed feature. To determine whether this is the case in your model, suppress any holes, fillets, chamfers, or any other feature that you think might be causing the failure.

Once the failed feature is corrected, introduce one suppressed feature at a time until you encounter a failure. This will identify the cause. You may then attempt to move the offending feature below the failed feature and examine the result. If you are unable to move the offending feature, instead reproduce the same feature below the failed feature and leave the original suppressed. When the problems are corrected in a part, you can go back and delete the suppressed offending features.

Although it's not always a silver bullet, you might want to try the Rebuild All tool right after fixing the first broken sketch or feature. Often if the fix was fairly minor, Rebuild All will save you from having to manually edit dependent features one at a time. You can access this tool by selecting the Manage tab and selecting Rebuild All.

USING THE END-OF-PART MARKER TO TIME-TRAVEL

The end-of-part marker is a powerful yet often-neglected tool. With this tool, you can go "back to the future" and edit or add features to your model. A good example of using the EOP marker is to preserve design intent. Let's say you created a base feature, placed some holes down the center of the part (based on dimensions), and then altered the side faces of the part. The holes are linked to the unaltered edges of this part. You now want to tie the holes to the midplane of this part regardless of the feature size.

continues

continued

You could do this by placing a centered work plane down the part. However, you cannot do this now because when you go back to edit the hole sketch, the work plane would not be available for projection onto the sketch plane. You also cannot drag the work plane above the holes because it was created on the new, altered base feature faces. In this case, you'll want to drag the EOP marker above the hole feature. Now you can place the work plane centered on the two faces. Drag the EOP marker back down to the bottom of the tree. Now edit the hole feature and project the work plane so that the hole centers can be constrained to it.

You can also use the EOP marker to reduce file size when you email a model. If you drag the EOP marker to the top of the browser, only the feature tree (commonly called the *part DNA* or *part recipe*) is saved to disk. When the EOP marker is dragged down to the bottom again, all the feature data is recalculated.

The Bottom Line

Create complex sweeps and lofts.   Complex geometry is created by using multiple work planes, sketches, and 3D sketch geometry. Honing your experience in creating work planes and 3D sketches is paramount to success in creating complex models.

> **Master It**   How would you create a piece of twisted, flat bar in Inventor?

Work with multi-body and derived parts.   Multi-body parts can be used to create part files with features that require precise matching between two or more parts. Once the solid bodies are created, you can create a separate part file for each component.

> **Master It**   What would be the best way to create an assembly of four parts that require features to mate together in different positions?

Utilize part tolerances.   Dimensional tolerancing of sketches allows you to check stackup variations within assemblies. When you add tolerances to critical dimensions within sketches, you can adjust parts to maximum, minimum, and nominal conditions.

> **Master It**   You want to create a model feature with a deviation so you can test the assembly fit at the extreme ends of the tolerances. How would this be done?

Understand and use parameters and iProperties.   Using parameters within files assists in the creation of title blocks, parts lists, and annotation within 2D drawings. Using parameters in an assembly file allows the control of constraints and objects within the assembly. Exporting parameters allows the creation of custom properties. Proper use of iProperties facilitates the creation of accurate 2D drawings that always reflect the current state of included parts and assemblies.

> **Master It**   You want to create a formula to determine the spacing of a hole pattern based on the length of the part. What tools would you use?

Troubleshoot modeling failures.   Modeling failures are often caused by poor design practices. Poor sketching techniques, bad design workflow, and other factors can lead to the elimination of design intent within a model.

> **Master It**   You want to modify a rather complex existing part file, but when you change the feature, errors cascade down through the entire part. How can you change the feature without this happening?

Chapter 6

Sheet Metal

The sheet-metal functionality in the Autodesk® Inventor® program is an extremely powerful toolset, centered on productivity and capturing your manufacturing intent. When you first begin working in the sheet-metal environment, you may feel overwhelmed because the tools and methods you have become familiar with to create other parts in Inventor do not yield good results in the sheet-metal file. However, a mastery of some basic fundamentals in sheet-metal tools can make Inventor sheet metal straightforward and highly integrated with your manufacturing environment. The Autodesk® Inventor LT™ program does not include the sheet-metal tools discussed in this chapter.

In this chapter, you'll learn to

- ◆ Take advantage of the specific sheet-metal features available in Inventor
- ◆ Understand sheet-metal templates and rules
- ◆ Author and insert punch tooling
- ◆ Utilize the flat pattern information and options
- ◆ Understand the nuances of sheet-metal iPart factories
- ◆ Model sheet-metal components with non-sheet-metal features
- ◆ Work with imported sheet-metal parts
- ◆ Understand the tools available to annotate your sheet-metal design

Understanding Sheet-Metal Parts

The sheet-metal environment was introduced in Inventor 2. Since sheet-metal parts have so many unique requirements, such as flat patterns and manufacturing-specific features, a modified part file is used. The same .ipt filename extension is used for sheet-metal parts, but extra sheet-metal capabilities and data are added. To create a sheet-metal part, you can use the Sheet Metal.ipt template or simply click the Convert To Sheet Metal button on the Environments tab of a standard part file.

To understand how sheet-metal parts work, it is important to keep in mind that sheet-metal design is driven by manufacturing considerations. A basic sheet-metal part consists of flat faces joined by bends. For cost-effective manufacturing, all the bends and corner reliefs are generally the same radius. The sheet-metal template style contains the sheet thickness, bend, and relief information in a rule, and the style is then used during modeling. This saves you considerable time during design because the features automatically use the settings in the predefined style. If you have to make a change, such as a different material thickness or bend radius, you can select a different style and the part automatically updates. These sheet-metal-specific styles are referred to as a *sheet-metal rule*.

Many sheet-metal parts are brackets or enclosures designed to fit a particular assembly. The sheet-metal tools simplify the process of creating and updating models. For example, you can change a bend to a corner seam simply by right-clicking the bend in the browser and selecting Change To Corner from the context menu.

Getting to Know the Features

The Inventor sheet-metal environment contains numerous specialized tools to help you design components that follow your sheet-metal-manufacturing guidelines and process restrictions. The following sections describe general feature classifications and capabilities that will provide you with a quick road map to the features. Once you understand how the features work, you will be able to build models that capture your design intent.

Starting with a Base Feature

Out of all the sheet-metal tools provided, only four create what are referred to as *base features*. Base features are simply the first features that appear in the feature history. The following tools can create base features:

- Face
- Contour Flange
- Contour Roll
- Lofted Flange

FACE TOOL

The Face tool is the simplest base feature; it utilizes a closed profile to produce a simple extrusion with the height automatically set to the Thickness parameter value. The profile can be constructed out of any shape and can even contain interior profiles, as shown in Figure 6.1. Profiles for face features are often generated from the edge projections of planar faces or surfaces found in other part files, and this capability enables numerous assembly-based and derived workflows.

FIGURE 6.1
Face base feature containing an internal profile

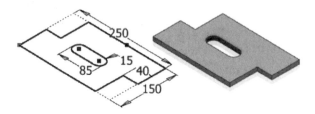

CONTOUR FLANGE TOOL

The Contour Flange tool is a sketch-based feature (using an open profile) that has the ability to create multiple planar faces and bends as the result of a single feature, as shown in Figure 6.2. Profile sketches should contain only arcs and lines; if sketch intersections are not separated by an arc, a bend equal to the BendRadius parameter will automatically be added at the intersection, as determined by the sheet-metal rule. To create base features with a profile sketch, contour flanges have a width extent option called Distance, which allows a simple open profile to be utilized to create a sheet-metal condition extrusion of the thickened, filleted profile.

FIGURE 6.2
Contour Flange
base feature

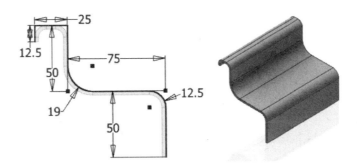

You can use the Contour Flange tool to create sheet-metal base features; in fact, it is often the fastest way to create them. Although you could create the part shown in Figure 6.2 by using the Face tool and then adding flanges, it would be more time-consuming. Using the Contour Flange tool has one drawback, however. Since you are combining many features, you lose some flexibility for revising the shape.

Follow these steps to explore the basics of creating a base feature with the Contour Flange tool:

1. Click the Get Started tab and click Open.

2. Open the file named mi_6a_001.ipt from the Chapter 6 directory of your Mastering Inventor 2016 folder. If you have not already downloaded the Chapter 6 files from www .sybex.com/go/masteringinventor2016, please refer to the "What You Will Need" section of the introduction for the download and setup instructions.

3. Select the Contour Flange tool from the Create panel of the Sheet Metal tab.

4. For the Profile selection, click anywhere along the sketch profile.

Depending on where you clicked on the sketch, the preview will show either the outside or inside of the sketch. Also notice that the corners at each end of the 25 mm leg are automatically rounded even though no radius was specified in the sketch. This is because of the predefined BendRadius parameter.

5. Use the Flip Side In The Offset Direction area buttons (three arrow buttons) to change the preview so you can see how each changes the result. Then set the side so that the preview is to the inside of the sketch profile (as in Figure 6.2) and therefore holding the overall dimensions of the sketch.

6. Enter **6 mm** in the Bend Radius input box, and notice that the corners at each end of the 25 mm leg are updated.

Entering a value in the Bend Radius input box overrides the predefined BendRadius parameter and sets this contour flange feature to always use 6 mm. If the part were set to use another predefined style, bends in this feature would not update to follow the style but would instead stay at 6 mm.

7. Click the >> button to expand the Contour Flange dialog box (if it isn't already expanded) and then set the Distance input box to **150 mm**.

8. Use the ViewCube to change the view so you can see the direction of the contour.

9. Click the Distance Mid-Plane button so the part is created equally to both sides of the sketch.

10. Click the OK button to create the feature.

In the preceding steps you created a base feature using an open profile sketch and the Contour Flange tool. From this point, you could begin adding secondary features as required. For now, though, you can close this file without saving changes and continue looking at other tools used to create base features.

CONTOUR ROLL TOOL

The Contour Roll tool is a variation of the Contour Flange tool. To create a contour roll, you sketch an open profile, but you revolve it instead of extruding it. Sketch geometry is limited to lines and arcs, and the Contour Roll tool will automatically add a bend at line intersections. The rolled hat flange in Figure 6.3 was created using the simple sketch geometry shown.

FIGURE 6.3
Contour Roll base feature

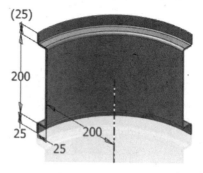

Follow these steps to explore the basics of creating a base feature with the Contour Roll tool:

1. Click the Get Started tab and click Open.

2. Open the file mi_6a_002.ipt from the Chapter 6 directory of your Mastering Inventor 2016 folder.

3. Select the Contour Roll tool from the Create panel of the Sheet Metal tab.

4. Set the Unroll Method drop-down box to Centroid Cylinder if it is not already. For the Profile selection, click anywhere along the sketch profile.

5. Select the centerline for the Axis selection.

   Note the options in the Unroll Method drop-down box.

   Centroid Cylinder The neutral cylindrical surface is derived by the centroid location of the profile, based on the selected axis. The neutral radius and unrolled length are displayed.

   Custom Cylinder This allows you to select a sketched line to define the cylindrical neutral surface. The unrolled length is displayed.

   Developed Length This allows you to enter the developed length and displays the adjusted neutral radius.

   Neutral Radius This allows you to enter the neutral radius and displays the adjusted unrolled length.

These options all derive the developed length by multiplying the rolled angle by a neutral radius but differ from one another by the type of input specified.

6. Set the unroll method to Custom Cylinder and select the sketch line denoted as Custom Neutral Axis for the Neutral Axis selection. Note the displayed unrolled length.

7. Set the unroll method to Neutral Radius and enter **60 mm** in the input box. You'll notice that the displayed unrolled length adjusts based on the change.

8. Set the unroll method to Developed Length and enter **100 mm** in the input box. You'll notice that the displayed neutral radius adjusts based on the change.

9. Click the OK button to create the feature.

10. Click the Create Flat Pattern button on the Sheet Metal tab.

11. Right-click the Flat Pattern node in the browser and choose Extents. You'll see that the width of the flat pattern has been held to 100 mm, honoring your final input value.

12. Click the Close button in the Flat Pattern Extents dialog box and then deselect the Flat Pattern node in the browser (you can do so by clicking onscreen anywhere in the graphics area).

13. Click the Go To Folded Part button on the Sheet Metal tab to return to the folded model.

In the preceding steps, you created a base feature using an open profile sketch and the Contour Roll tool. You can close this file without saving changes and continue looking at other tools used to create base features. Before continuing, though, you can open the file mi_6a_003 .ipt and try creating a secondary contour roll feature based on the first.

LOFTED FLANGE TOOL

The Lofted Flange tool creates sheet-metal shapes typically seen in HVAC transitions and material-handling hoppers. Figure 6.4 shows a square-to-round transition. Basically, you create sketches of the beginning and end of the transition and then use the Lofted Flange tool to transition between the two. The Lofted Flange tool gives you the option of a die form or a press brake transition. For press brake transitions, you can define the bends by chord tolerance, facet angle, or facet distance. The chord tolerance is the distance between the angled face and the theoretical curved surface. As the chord tolerance is decreased, more facets are added.

FIGURE 6.4
Square-to-round
lofted flange

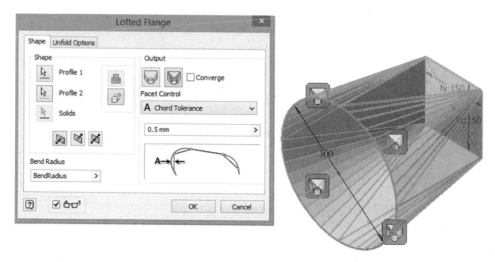

To create a lofted flange, follow these steps:

1. Click the Get Started tab and click Open.

2. Open the file mi_6a_004.ipt from the Chapter 6 directory of your Mastering Inventor 2016 folder.

3. Click the Lofted Flange button in the Create panel.

4. Select the square and the circle for the profile selections.

5. In the output area of the dialog box, click the Die Formed button, and note that the preview changes to remove the press brake facets and that the facet controls in the dialog box are hidden.

6. Click the Press Brake button and use the Facet Control drop-down to experiment with the Chord Tolerance, Facet Angle, and Facet Distance options to familiarize yourself with their behavior.

   Chord Tolerance   This value sets the maximum separation distance from the arc segment to the chord segment.

   Facet Angle   This value sets the maximum angle to the chord segment at the facet face vertex.

   Facet Distance   This value sets the maximum width of the length of the chord.

   Converge   This check box sets the bends of the flattened faceted sections to converge near a singular point.

Deciding which of these options to use depends largely on the design inputs you know and the equipment to be used to create the part on the shop floor.

7. Ensure that the Converge check box is not selected, set the Facet Control drop-down to Facet Distance, and change the distance to **50 mm**.

Note that there is a glyph icon at each of the transition corners on the model preview. If you hover your cursor over them, you can see them better. Clicking one of these *Bend Zone Edit glyphs* displays a dialog box to change the facet control and also displays individual glyphs for each bend. The Bend Zone Edit dialog box enables you to change the facet control for the corner corresponding to the glyph you clicked, as shown in Figure 6.5. Clicking one of the bend glyphs displays a Bend Edit dialog box that enables you to override the bend radius and unfold rule for an individual bend.

FIGURE 6.5
Bend Zone Edit dialog box

Continuing with the previous steps, investigate the use of Bend Zone Edit glyphs for yourself with these steps:

8. Click one of the Bend Zone Edit glyphs.

9. Click the check box in the Bend Zone Edit dialog box and select Number Of Facets.

10. Enter **2** in the edit field and note that the preview updates.

11. Click one of the Bend Edit glyphs and then click the Bend Radius check box in the resulting Bend Edit dialog box.

12. Change the bend radius to **BendRadius*10** and note the preview.

13. Click the OK button and note that the Bend Edit glyph has changed. A pencil is added to indicate that it has been overridden.

14. Click the OK button in the Bend Zone Edit dialog box. Hover your cursor over the glyph and note that a pencil has been added to it as well.

15. Click the OK button in the Lofted Flange dialog box to create the feature.

16. Click the Create Flat Pattern button on the Sheet Metal tab. Note that the part isn't flattened because it is a continuous piece.

17. Click the Go To Folded Part button on the Sheet Metal tab to return to the folded model.

To get the lofted flange transition to flatten, you'll need to create a rip feature in one of the faces. The Rip tool will be discussed in the section "Adding, Removing, or Deforming Material" later in this chapter. For now, you can close the file without saving changes and continue to the next section to explore the creation of flanges.

Creating Secondary Flange Features

Once a base feature is created, you can add secondary features in the form of flanges. Flanges are planar faces connected by a bend and can be created using a number of tools. The Flange tool automatically creates bends between the flanges and the selected faces. You can also use the Contour Flange tool to create several flanges at once. The Hem tool allows you to create specialized flanges to hem sharp edges or to create rolled flange features. Another tool commonly used along with these tools is the Face tool. Depending on the selected tool, you can either control flange options or allow Inventor to apply predefined relationships and values.

FLANGE TOOL

The Flange tool creates a single planar face and bend for each edge selected, with controls for defining the flange height, bend position, and relief options at the edge intersections. For flanges referencing a single edge, width extent options are also available by clicking the >> button in the Flange dialog box. If multiple edges have been selected for flange locations, corner seams are automatically added, as shown in Figure 6.6. The bend and corner seam dimensions follow the sheet-metal rule unless a value is entered to override them per that particular feature. The preview displays glyphs at each bend and corner seam. If you click a glyph, a dialog box appears so you can override the values.

FIGURE 6.6
A multi-edge flange feature preview with bend and corner edit glyphs

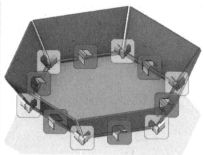

Certification
Objective

Creating Basic Flanges

To explore the Flange tool, follow these steps:

1. Click the Get Started tab and click Open.

2. Open the file mi_6a_005.ipt from the Chapter 6 directory of your Mastering Inventor 2016 folder.

3. Select the Flange tool from the Create panel of the Sheet Metal tab.

4. Currently the Edge Select Mode button (on the left side of the Edges selection box) is selected, allowing you to select only one edge at a time. Click the Loop Select Mode button so you can select multiple edges at once.

5. Place your cursor over the top face of the hexagonal-shaped base feature. Click the edge when you see all six edges highlight. Note that if you chose the bottom edge rather than the top, you can use the Flip Direction button to change the direction.

6. Click the Edge Select Mode button and then hold the **Ctrl** key and click one of the currently selected edges to deselect it. The Edges selection box will indicate that you now have only five selected.

7. Set the flange height to **100 mm**.

8. Set the flange angle to **60**.

9. Click the Corner tab, uncheck the Apply Auto-Mitering check box to observe the preview change, and then reselect the check box to allow the flanges to flare out into the mitered corners.

10. In the Miter Gap input box, enter **1 mm** to reduce the gap size from the current default value (the GapSize parameter is currently set at 3 mm in the sheet-metal rule).

11. Click the Apply button to create the five flanges and leave the Flange dialog box open (recall that clicking the OK button creates the feature and closes the dialog box, and clicking Apply creates the feature but does not close the dialog box).

12. Click the Shape tab and ensure that the Edge Select Mode button is selected.

13. Click the edge that you removed from the previous selection set. Note that if you chose the bottom edge rather than the top, you can use the Flip Direction button to change the direction.

14. Set Flange Angle to **90**.

15. Set the Height Extents drop-down box to To and then click the topmost corner vertex of any of the existing flanges. Figure 6.7 shows the To point being selected.

FIGURE 6.7
Setting a flange height using the To option

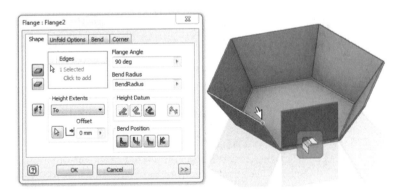

16. Click the OK button to create the flange.

If you click the front plane on the ViewCube, you can see that all the flanges terminate in the same plane. Keep this in mind as you create flanges of varying angles. You will explore the tools used to close the remaining gaps in this flange combination later in this chapter, when looking at the Corner Seam tool, but for now you can close the file without saving changes and continue to explore the Flange tool.

Control Flange Widths

In this next set of steps, you'll create flanges of varying widths by adjusting the extents options.

1. Click the Get Started tab and click Open.

2. Open the file mi_6a_006.ipt from the Chapter 6 directory of your Mastering Inventor 2016 folder.

3. Select the Flange tool from the Create panel of the Sheet Metal tab.

4. Select the top edge of the yellow face to place a flange along the edge.

5. Set the flange height extents to **50 mm** and leave the angle at 90 degrees.

   Note that currently the flange runs along the extents of the edge. If you imagine the flat pattern that would result from adding this flange, you'll understand that creating this flange would create a conflict at the inside corner. Although Inventor will not prevent you from creating the flange as is, it will issue an error to the flat pattern. To resolve this, you will set the flange width and an offset to hold it back from the corner. There are four possible Width Extents settings.

   Edge Runs the flange the length of the selected edge

   Width Allows you to specify the width of the flange and position it centered on the selected edge or offset from a selected reference point

   Offset Allows you to specify offsets from both ends of the selected edge or from selected references.

   From To Allows you to specify a start and end reference to establish the flange width

In the real world, the option you use will depend on the result you are trying to achieve and the available existing geometry. Here, you'll use the Width option.

6. Click the >> button to expand the Flange dialog box.

7. Change Width Extents Type to Width.

8. Enter **96 mm** in the Width input box.

9. Switch the option from Centered to Offset.

10. Enter **0 mm** for the offset value.

11. Click the Offset1 button on the left of the offset value and then click the end of the selected edge farthest from the green face to establish the offset point. Use the Offset Flip button to redirect the flange if needed.

12. Click the OK button to create the flange.

13. Click the Go To Flat Pattern button on the Sheet Metal tab to take a look at the resulting flat pattern.

You can close the file without saving.

Although the flange width options are easy to overlook because they are initially hidden in the More Options area of the dialog box, you should keep them in mind as you create flanges. For now, you can close this file without saving changes. Here are more options to be aware of when creating flanges:

Flange Height Datum   Three Height Datum solutions are available. These options control which faces are used to determine the height measurement. In Figure 6.8, each of the options is shown using a 40 mm flange.

FIGURE 6.8
Flange height datum solutions

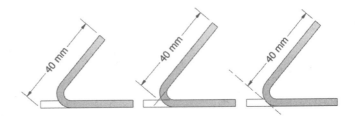

Bend From The Intersection Of The Two Outer Faces   Measures the flange height from the intersection of the outer faces, as shown on the left in Figure 6.8

Bend From The Intersection Of The Two Inner Faces   Measures the flange height from the intersection of the inner faces, as shown in the center in Figure 6.8

Parallel To The Flange Termination Detail Face   Measures the flange height parallel to the flange face and tangent to the bend, as shown on the right in Figure 6.8

Orthogonal and Aligned Flanges   You can use the Aligned VS Orthogonal toggle button to determine whether the height measurement is aligned with the flange face or orthogonal to the base face. In Figure 6.9, the flange on the left is orthogonal, and the measurement on the right is aligned.

FIGURE 6.9
Orthogonal and aligned flanges

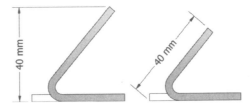

Bend Position   There are four options to select from to determine the bend position relative to the face of the selected edge. Figure 6.10 compares the four options, with the dashed line representing the selected edge of the base feature.

FIGURE 6.10
Bend positions compared

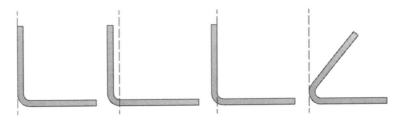

Inside Of Base Face Extents Positions the flange so that it honors the overall dimension of the selected base part, as shown on the far left of Figure 6.10

Bend From Adjacent Face Holds the face of the selected edge as the start of the bend, as shown on the center left of Figure 6.10

Outside Of Base Face Extents Positions the inside face of the flange so that it remains outside of the face of the selected edge, as shown on the center right of Figure 6.10

Bend Tangent To Side Face Holds the bend tangent to the face of the selected edge, as shown on the far right of Figure 6.10

Old Method When checked, this option disables the functionality introduced in the Autodesk® Inventor® 2008 program. If you open a file created in an older version, the features will likely have this option selected. You can uncheck the box to update the file to use all the available options. There is no reason to check this box on parts that you create with the current version of Inventor.

Bend and Corner Edit Glyphs Although you will often create flanges along multiple edges as a single flange feature, you can still control the bend and corner options individually by using the edit glyphs displayed on the features in the graphics area. You can access the edit glyphs by expanding the Flange node in the browser and then right-clicking the bend or corner and choosing Edit Bend or Edit Corner. Once they are displayed, you can click the edit glyph for the bend or corner you want to edit and make changes on an individual basis. You can click the edit glyphs during the creation of flanges as well. Once bends or corners are edited, they can be reset to the defaults by expanding the Flange node in the browser, right-clicking the bend or corner, and choosing Reset All Bends/Corners.

Certification Objective

CONTOUR FLANGE TOOL

In addition to creating base features as explored previously, the Contour Flange tool can be used to add flanges to an existing feature. Since the Contour Flange tool uses open profile sketches, it is ideal for quickly creating complex shapes and enclosure designs. As discussed earlier, the Contour Flange tool can either automatically bend line intersections or use sketched arcs for bends. A contour flange automatically creates a bend between itself and a selected edge on an existing face. The sketch profile for the Contour Flange tool does not need to be coincident with the edge; it simply needs to be sketched on a plane that is perpendicular to it. If the sketch profile is coincident with an edge, a bend will automatically be positioned to connect the sketch profile to the face. If the sketch is not coincident with a reference edge and the width extent option is changed to Distance, the result will be a contour flange that isn't attached to the part.

Just as with the Flange feature, automatic mitering of adjacent flanges and the placement of corner reliefs occur when multiple edges are selected, as shown in Figure 6.11.

FIGURE 6.11
A multi-edge Contour Flange feature with automatic mitering and large radius bends

To explore the Contour Flange tool a bit more, follow these steps:

1. Click the Get Started tab and click Open.

2. Open the file mi_6a_007.ipt from the Chapter 6 directory of your Mastering Inventor 2016 folder.

3. Select the Contour Flange tool from the Create panel of the Sheet Metal tab.

4. Select the visible sketch profile as the Profile selection.

5. Select one of the edges (top or bottom) that have the two work planes running through it.

   You'll note that you cannot add any more edges to the selection. This is because the sketch is disconnected from the base feature and therefore can be used only to create a flange along the one edge. Next, you'll use the work planes to define the width of the flange.

6. Click the >> button to expand the dialog box and reveal the Width Extents options.

7. Set the Type drop-down box to From To.

8. Select the two visible work planes as the From and To selections.

9. In the Bend area, click the left button (Extend Bend Aligned To Side Faces).

10. Click the OK button to create the contour flange.

    You should notice that the flange width starts and stops at the work planes selected for the width extents. You'll also notice that the edge of the base feature extends to meet the flange. This is because of the Bend Extension option. The Bend Extension options are as follows:

    Extend Bend Aligned To Side Faces   Extends the base feature to meet the flange.

    Extend Bend Perpendicular To Side Faces   Extends the flange to meet the base feature. This is the default.

    You'll explore these options a bit more in the upcoming pages, but for now you'll edit the flange and toggle this option to compare the results.

11. Right-click the Contour Flange feature in the browser and choose Edit Feature.

12. In the Bend area, click the right button (Extend Bend Perpendicular To Side Faces).

13. Click the OK button, and note that the flange has now extended to the base feature, as shown on the right of Figure 6.12.

FIGURE 6.12
Bend Extension options

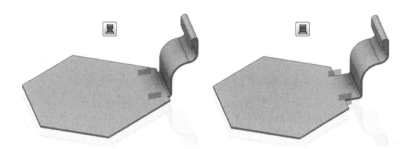

14. Right-click Sketch3 in the browser and turn on the visibility.

15. Select the Contour Flange tool from the Create panel of the Sheet Metal tab.

16. Select the sketch profile in Sketch3 as the Profile selection.

17. Select the five edges of the hex-shaped face that were not used in the previous contour flange.

18. Notice the automatic mitering of the corners; if this was not the desired result, you could disable the Apply Auto-Mitering check box option on the Corner tab.

19. Click the OK button to create the flanges.

As you can see, the Contour Flange tool can be used to quickly create multiple bend flanges from a basic open profile sketch. This is often the quickest way to create even simple flanges when they are the same on all edges of a base feature, particularly when the flanges require a miter fit. You can close this file without saving changes and continue to the next section to explore hems.

Certification
Objective

HEM TOOL

The Hem tool is like a contour flange because it has the ability to create multiple planar faces and bends for a selected edge, but it is restricted to predefined common hem profiles and geometric relationships.

To explore the different hem flange types and options, follow these steps:

1. Click the Get Started tab and click Open.

2. Open the file mi_6a_008.ipt from the Chapter 6 directory of your Mastering Inventor 2016 folder.

   In this file, each of the four hem types has been created on one side of the part. You can use the cutouts on the other side to create a hem matching each of the ones on the left. Once you have experimented with the hem types using the cutouts, proceed to create a hem on the edge of the yellow face.

3. Use the ViewCube to find a view of the yellow interior face.

4. Select the Hem tool from the Create panel of the Sheet Metal tab.

5. Set Type to Single.

6. Select the edge along the outside of the yellow face.

7. Set Gap to **2 mm**.

8. Set Length to **12 mm**.

9. Click the >> button to expand the dialog box.

10. Change Width Extents Type to Offset.

11. Use the appropriate offset input box to set the end that will interfere with the existing hem to **5 mm**.

12. Set the other offset to **0 mm** so that no offset is created.

13. Click the OK button to create the Hem flange.

Although the Hem tools are fairly straightforward, it is often the use of offsets that allows you to place hems as needed. You can close this file without saving changes and continue to the next section.

Certification Objective

FACE TOOL

The last feature capable of creating flanges is the Face tool. The Face tool uses a closed profile sketch, and it can automatically create an attaching bend on a selected edge. This automatic edge creation is powerful because it allows you to create a skeletal surface model of your design, project the planar surfaces into sketches, and create face features with attached bends. The manual controls can be utilized to connect face features to preexisting geometry, create double bends (*joggles*), or even deselect edges that have been automatically inferred because they share a common edge.

You can also use the Face tool to create models from 2D flat patterns that were created in another application, such as the Autodesk® AutoCAD® program. When the 2D flat pattern is imported, the Face tool can be used to thicken it to the desired value. A flat pattern can be produced for a planar face (no unfolding needs to actually occur), which enables a variety of uses.

In the following steps, you'll derive a frame into your sheet-metal part and use it as a reference to create a face. You'll then create another face and use the built-in Bend tools to connect them.

1. Click the Get Started tab and click Open.

2. Open the file mi_6a_009.ipt from the Chapter 6 directory of your Mastering Inventor 2016 folder.

3. Select the Manage tab and click the Derive button on the Insert panel.

4. Open the file mi_6a_888.ipt from the Chapter 6 directory of your Mastering Inventor 2016 folder.

5. In the Derived Part dialog box, select the Body As Work Surface button at the top. This brings the frame in as a surface that can be turned off later.

6. Click the OK button to create the frame surface.

7. Expand the mi_6a_888.ipt node in the browser and right-click the Frame:mi_6a_888.ipt node.

8. From the context menu, deselect the Translucent option. This will make the frame edges easier to see.

9. Right-click the face of the frame side with the triangular corner gussets and choose New Sketch to create a 2D sketch on the side of the frame.

Certification Objective

10. Click the Project Geometry drop-down menu and select Project Cut Edges. This will project the face of the frame into the sketch. Alternatively, you can use the Project Geometry tool and select the four outer edges and the eight holes.

11. Once the projected edges are created, click the Finish Sketch button to return to the Sheet Metal tab.

12. From the Sheet Metal tab, select the Face button.

13. Choose the sketch boundary (or boundaries) so that the entire side of the frame, minus the holes, is selected.

14. Ensure that the face is not going into the frame, use the Offset button if the direction needs to be adjusted, and then click the OK button to create the face feature with holes. Figure 6.13 shows the frame and face.

FIGURE 6.13
Face from a
derived frame

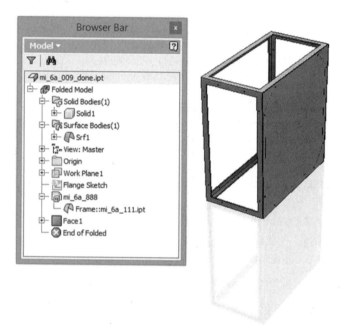

15. Locate the sketch called Flange Sketch in the browser and then right-click it and choose Visibility from the context menu. This sketch was prepared in the sheet-metal file ahead of time for this tutorial, but in the real world you would create it by referencing the frame as you did for the first face feature.

16. On the Sheet Metal tab, select the Face tool again and choose the rectangular profile minus the slots as the Profile selection.

17. Use the Offset button to ensure that the face is coming out away from the frame.

18. Click the Edges button in the Bend area of the dialog box and then select the left vertical edge of the first face feature. This will create a bend connecting to two faces.

19. Click the OK button to create the new face with the bend feature.

If you examine the slotted flange face, you might notice that it does not rest on the face of the frame. This is because the premade sketch that you made visible was created on a work plane at 302 mm from the center of the 600 mm–wide frame. Using the offset work plane, a 2 mm gap was created, allowing space for the bend radius, insert studs, and spacer hardware that might be required.

Be aware that when you have finished with a derived work surface (the frame in this case), you can right-click it in the browser and toggle off the visibility. This leaves only the sheet-metal part showing.

To create the next sheet-metal part of the frame, such as the front or back covering, you could create your next component as a new body. Once all the parts are complete, you can derive them into an assembly file knowing that they will all fit around the frame they were based on. For now, though, you can close this file without saving changes and continue to the next section.

Adding, Removing, or Deforming Material

Once the general shape of a sheet-metal component is roughed in, in most cases material will need to be removed, deformed, or added. Several sheet-metal-specific features have been created to optimize the process of adding, removing, and deforming sheet-metal parts because most sheet-metal-manufacturing operations (punch presses, for example) create features perpendicular to the surface. The current capabilities of Inventor assume that these manufacturing operations are done in the flat prior to folding and therefore should not interfere with unfolding (Inventor does not support post-folding manufacturing operations such as gussets, for example).

CUT TOOL

The Cut tool is a special sheet-metal extrude. It creates a hole based on a sketched profile. The Cut tool helps simplify the options of the regular Extrude tool because the distance parameter defaults to Thickness, and therefore cut features automatically update if the sheet-metal part is changed to use a different material thickness. If a cut is not intended to be the full depth of the material thickness, you can enter an equation based on the thickness value, such as **Thickness/2** to create half-thickness cuts.

Creating Cuts Across Sheet Metal Bends

The Cut tool can also wrap the sketch profile across planar faces and bends, as shown in Figure 6.14. This option is particularly helpful because it allows you to force a uniform cut across multiple planar faces and bends with a value greater than zero and equal to or less than Thickness.

FIGURE 6.14
The cut feature using the Cut Across Bend option

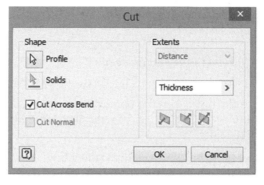
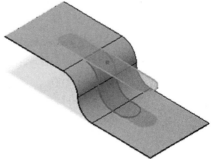

USING CUTS

With sheet-metal parts, it is often best to create your base features and flanges and then apply the cuts as required. You will find that this provides a more stable model when creating a flat pattern and allows you to edit features individually. It's generally best practice to use the Cut tool whenever possible rather than creating voids in the base sketch.

To explore the options of the Cut tool, follow these steps:

1. Click the Get Started tab and click Open.

2. Open the file mi_6a_010.ipt from the Chapter 6 directory of your Mastering Inventor 2016 folder.

3. In the browser ensure that the view representation named Top Slot View is active. If it is not, simply expand the View browser node and double-click the Top Slot View node.

4. Select the Cut tool from the Modify panel of the Sheet Metal tab.

5. Click the OK button to create the cut feature. Note how the cut remains only in the top plane and is not accurate for a slot that would be cut in the flat pattern.

6. Right-click the cut feature in the browser and choose Edit Feature.

7. Select the Cut Across Bend check box, note the preview, and then click the OK button to create the cut feature. You'll notice that it cuts through the part and across the existing bends.

8. Click the Go To Flat Pattern button on the Sheet Metal tab to examine the slot cut in the flat pattern. You'll notice that the cut edges are normal to the flat sheet as expected.

9. Click the Go To Folded Part button on the Sheet Metal tab to return to the folded model.

10. Edit the cut feature again, enter **Thickness/2** in the Distance input box under Extents, and then click the OK button.

As you can see, the Cut tool allows you to create partial depth cutouts across bends as well. Using the Cut Across Bend option allows cut features to be created in the formed part model that are accurate to the way the cutout is created in the flat pattern and then bent in the finished folded part, just as would be done in the real world.

You can leave this file open and continue to the next exercise to explore the creation of angled cuts held normal to the sheet-metal flat pattern.

Creating Angled Features Cut Normal to the Flat Pattern

To create angled cuts held normal to the sheet-metal flat pattern, follow these steps:

1. If you do not already have file mi_6a_010.ipt open, then click the Get Started tab and click Open; then select the file mi_6a_010.ipt from the Chapter 6 directory of your Mastering Inventor 2016 folder.

2. In the browser, ensure that the view representation named Rod View is active. If it is not, simply expand the View browser node and double-click the Rod View node.

You'll see a yellow surface representing a keyed rod that runs through the sheet-metal bracket. Your goal is to create a cut feature in the bracket that allows the rod to fit through.

3. Select the Cut tool from the Modify panel of the Sheet Metal tab. The Profile shape should be automatically selected for you since there is only one visible sketch available (the Rod CutOut sketch).

4. Set the Extents drop-down box from Distance to All.

5. Set the Direction button to go in both directions.

6. Click the OK button to create the cut feature.

7. Click the Go To Flat Pattern button on the Sheet Metal tab to examine the cuts in the flat pattern. You'll notice that the cut edges have bevels and are not normal to the flat sheet as you would want them to be if the cutouts were to be punched or laser cut.

8. Click the Go To Folded Part button on the Flat Pattern tab to return to the folded model.

9. Right-click the cut feature in the browser and choose Edit Feature.

10. Select the Cut Normal check box and then click the OK button.

11. Click the Go To Flat Pattern button on the Sheet Metal tab again and notice the cuts in the flat pattern no longer have the beveled edges.

These exercises demonstrate the use of the Cut Across Bend and Cut Normal options in the Cut tool. As a general rule, you should use the Cut tool to create cutouts in a sheet-metal part file, rather than the Extrude tool as you would in a standard part file. When you've finished exploring the Cut tool, you can close this file without saving and continue to the next section.

PUNCH TOOL

You can use the Punch tool to either remove material or deform it by placing predefined Punch tool geometry, as shown in Figure 6.15. Punches are special versions of iFeatures; they can be predefined with additional manufacturing information and can be built using a variety of standard and sheet-metal features.

FIGURE 6.15
Multiple-instance punch feature placing a footing dimple

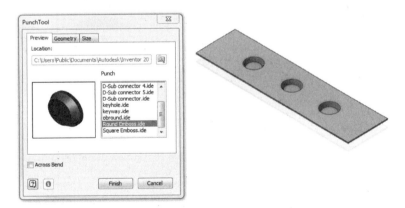

To explore the methods and options used to place punch features, follow these steps:

1. Click the Get Started tab and click Open.

2. Open the file `mi_6a_011.ipt` from the `Chapter 6` directory of your `Mastering Inventor 2016` folder.

3. Click the Punch Tool button on the Modify panel of the Sheet Metal tab.

4. In the Punch Tool dialog box, navigate to the `Chapter 6` folder.

5. Locate and select the file `Knockout_73x.ide` and then click the Open button.

SETTING THE SHEET-METAL PUNCH TOOL DEFAULT LOCATION

By default, Inventor is set to look for the punch library in the install directory on your local drive. If you're working on a network share drive, you will most likely want to point the Punch tool to automatically go to a path on the network. To do so, click the Application Options button on the Tools tab, select the iFeature tab, and set Sheet Metal Punches Root to the path of your choosing.

---

6. Because this part has two visible sketches, no centers are automatically selected. Select any one of the center sketch points on the part.

7. Continue selecting center points, and note that you can select only points that share the same sketch. Sketch2 contains three sketch points, toward one end of the part, and Sketch3 contains five sketch points grouped together at the other end.

8. When you have added all the center points you can (it will be either three or five, depending on which sketch the points are in), select the Size tab.

WINDOW-SELECT MULTIPLE PUNCH CENTER POINTS

With the Geometry tab active, you can use a crossing window selection to select multiple punch center points at once. A window selection from left to right will select only items contained in the window. A window selection from right to left will select all items that touch the window or are contained in the window. If you window-select an item already selected, it will be removed from the selection set. Note, too, that you can hold the **Ctrl** key and select in empty space to clear the selection set.

---

9. Enter **35 mm** for the diameter value and then press Enter or click in the space below the Diameter row in the dialog box to commit your changes.

10. Click the Refresh button to see the diameter update onscreen. Note that if the diameter does not update, you probably did not click out of the Diameter row to set the edit. The Refresh option is a bit picky in this way. Keep in mind, however, that the punch preview does not need to be refreshed to build correctly.

11. Click the Finish button to create the punches.

12. Right-click and choose Repeat Punch Tool; then, in the Punch Tool dialog box, locate the `Chapter 6` folder.

13. Once again, locate and select the file called `Knockout_73x.ide`; then click the Open button.

14. You'll notice that because you have only one visible sketch now, all of the center points in the sketch are automatically selected.

15. Click the Geometry tab and then click the Centers button.

16. Press and hold the **Ctrl** key on the keyboard and then deselect any one of the selected center points by clicking it in the sketch. Note that it is often easier to do this when viewing the sketch from straight on.

17. With all but one of the available center points selected, change Angle to **45** degrees. Note that all the current punches are rotated.

18. Click Finish to create the punches.

19. Locate the sketch with the unused sketch point in the browser; then right-click it and choose Visibility to turn it back on.

20. Right-click and choose Repeat PunchTool; then in the Punch Tool dialog box, navigate to the `Chapter 6` folder.

21. Locate and select the file `Knockout_73x.ide` and then click the Open button.

22. The final center point should be automatically selected. If not, select it and then click Finish to create it at the default size and orientation.

You can close this file without saving changes, but before moving on to the next topic, take a moment to understand how punch placement sketches and punch features work. In the preceding steps, you explored the options and methods used to place sheet-metal punches on an existing sketch. The process of applying a published Punch tool to your sheet-metal design is fairly straightforward. When you're authoring a Punch tool, the first sketch-based feature referenced to create the Punch tool must contain a single sketched center mark. To place a Punch tool, at least one sketched center mark is required in the placement sketch. Creating punch features (and regular iFeatures) is covered in Chapter 7, "Reusing Parts and Features."

Corner Round and Corner Chamfer

Corner Round and Corner Chamfer are special sheet-metal tools that allow you to remove or break sharp edges, similar to filleting and chamfering. Edge selection has been optimized within the two tools, filtering out edges that are not normal to the sheet top and bottom faces for easy application. To explore the methods and options used to place round and chamfer features, follow these steps:

1. Click the Get Started tab and click Open.

2. Open the file `mi_6a_012.ipt` from the `Chapter 6` directory of your `Mastering Inventor 2016` folder.

3. Select the Corner Round tool on the Modify panel of the Sheet Metal tab.

4. Set the radius to **8 mm** and then click the Pencil icon in the Corner Round dialog box to change the focus from edit to select.

5. Select the two sharp corner edges on the green flange and then click the OK button.

6. Right-click and choose Repeat Corner Round and then set the Select Mode radio button to Feature.

7. Select any of the yellow flanges, and you will see that the two outside sharp corners for the feature called Flange1 are automatically selected.

8. Change the radius to **15 mm** and then click the OK button to create the rounds.

9. Select the Corner Chamfer tool from the Modify panel of the Sheet Metal tab.

10. Select the remaining four sharp corners and set the distance to **18 mm**. Click the OK button to create the corners.

As a final step you might want to right-click Flange1 in the browser, choose Properties, and set Feature Color Style to As Part. You can do the same to Flange2. When finished, you can close the file without saving the changes and continue to the next section.

CORNER SEAM TOOL

The Corner Seam tool allows you to extend (as shown in Figure 6.16) or trim flange faces to manage the seam between them and select corner relief options. The Corner Seam dialog box contains numerous options for specifying the seam and contains two fundamentally different distance definition methods: Maximum Gap and Face/Edge. In older versions of Inventor, only the Face/Edge method was available for the Corner Seam tool. The Face/Edge method works for many situations but also tends to suffer from an inability to maintain a constant seam gap between planar faces that do not have an identical input angle. The Maximum Gap method was developed from the perspective of a physical inspection gauge, where the nominal value of the seam is exactly the value entered at every point, but you just might need to twist the tool as you draw it through the seam.

FIGURE 6.16
The Corner Seam feature, applying the No Overlap seam type

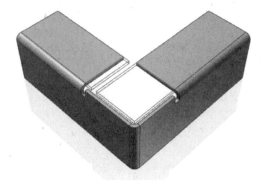

Creating a Basic Corner Seam

To explore the Corner Seam tool and its options, follow these steps:

1. Click the Get Started tab and click Open.

2. Open the file `mi_6a_013.ipt` from the `Chapter 6` directory of your `Mastering Inventor 2016` folder.

3. Select the Corner Seam tool on the Modify panel of the Sheet Metal tab.

4. Select the left edge of the yellow face and either edge of the blue face next to it. In the preview, the red edges represent the material to be removed and the green edges represent the material to be added.

5. In the Seam area of the Corner Seam dialog box, select the Symmetric Gap option if it's not already selected.

6. Set the gap to **1 mm** and notice the change to the preview.

7. Click the Apply button to create the seam feature.

8. Select the right edge of the orange face and either edge of the blue face next to it and then click the OK button to create this seam and close the dialog box.

As you can see, corner seams are useful when you need to close up a corner between two seams. You can close this file without saving changes and continue with the next set of steps to explore more of the settings in the Corner Seam tool.

Understanding Corner Seam Gap and Overlap Settings

In these steps, you'll explore the gap and overlap settings found in the Corner Seam tool:

1. Click the Get Started tab and click Open.

2. Open the file `mi_6a_014.ipt` from the `Chapter 6` directory of your `Mastering Inventor 2016` folder.

3. Select the Corner Seam tool on the Modify panel of the Sheet Metal tab.

4. Select the short edge of the orange flange nearest the yellow flange and the short edge of the yellow flange nearest the orange flange.

5. You'll note that the preview shows that the two flanges come together in a 45-degree miter. Click the Overlap button to see the preview change to extend one of the flanges so it overlaps the other.

6. Click the Reverse Overlap button to see the opposite overlap in the preview.

7. Click the Apply button to create the seam.

8. Click a short edge of the yellow flange nearest the blue flange and a short edge of the blue flange nearest the yellow flange.

9. Set the Seam option to Maximum Gap Distance (if it is not already) and click the Symmetric Gap button.

10. Click the OK button to create the corner seam and then click the top face on the ViewCube to observe the corner of the yellow and blue flanges. Note that it may be helpful to zoom up on the corner.

If you measure the gap distance at the inside vertices between the two flanges, it will be 3 mm, which is what the Gap parameter is set to, as shown on the left of Figure 6.17.

FIGURE 6.17

Maximum Gap Distance compared to Face/Edge Distance

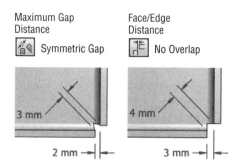

11. Edit the corner feature you just created, switch the radio button to Face/Edge Distance, and then click the OK button.

Now the Gap parameter holds the distance between the face and edge of the two flanges, as shown on the right of Figure 6.17.

12. Edit the corner feature again, and this time click the Overlap button.

13. Enter **0.5** in the Percent Overlap input box and then click the OK button.

You will see that the yellow flange overlaps the edge of the blue flange exactly halfway, or 50 percent. You can specify the overlap as a percentage of the flange thickness using a decimal value ranging from 0.0 to 1.0. For instance, 1.0 equals 100 percent, 0.5 equals 50 percent, and so on.

14. Edit the corner feature once again and click the Reverse Overlap button.

15. Enter **1.0** in the Percent Overlap input box and then click the OK button.

You will see that the blue flange now overlaps the yellow flange completely, or the full 100 percent. Figure 6.18 shows a comparison of overlap values with the same gap setting of 3 mm. On the left the overlap is set to 1.0, or 100 percent of the 3 mm gap. In the middle the overlap is set to 0.5, or 50 percent of the 3 mm gap. And on the right the overlap is set to 0.0, or 0 percent of the 3 mm gap.

FIGURE 6.18

Overlap comparisons

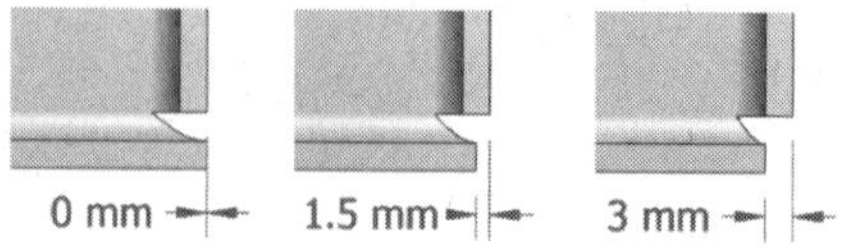

In the previous steps you explored the gap and overlap settings of the Corner Seam tool. You can close this file without saving changes and continue with the next set of steps to explore one more set of options in the Corner Seam tool.

Understanding Corner Seam Extend Options

In the following steps, you will look at the options for controlling the way flanges are extended when their edges are not perpendicular:

1. Click the Get Started tab and click Open.

2. Open the file mi_6a_015.ipt from the Chapter 6 directory of your Mastering Inventor 2016 folder.

3. Select the Corner Seam tool on the Modify panel of the Sheet Metal tab.

4. Select the shorter edge of the blue flange and the closest edge of the yellow flange.

5. Click the >> button in the Corner Seam dialog box and set the Extend Corner option to Perpendicular; then click the Apply button.

6. Select the taller edge of the blue flange and the closest edge of the orange flange.

7. Click the >> button in the Corner Seam dialog box again (if needed) and toggle the Extend Corner option between Perpendicular and Aligned to see the difference.

8. Set the Extend Corner option to Perpendicular and click the OK button.

Figure 6.19 shows a comparison of the Perpendicular and Aligned extend options. In the image on the right, the frontmost flange uses the Aligned solution and the other uses the Perpendicular solution.

FIGURE 6.19
Perpendicular and Aligned extend corner options

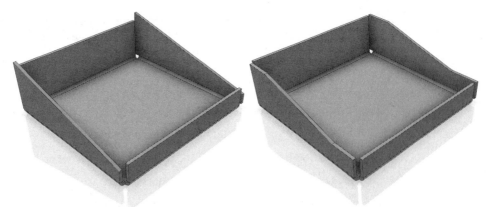

As you can see, becoming familiar with all the settings in the Corner Seam tool can make you aware of a great number of combinations and in the end provide the exact corner you are trying to achieve. You can close this file without saving changes and continue on to explore the Fold tool.

FOLD TOOL

The Fold tool enables you to design a flange with a unique profile by allowing you to sketch the position of the bend centerline on a planar face and then fold the part using the sketch line, as shown in Figure 6.20.

FIGURE 6.20
The Fold tool being applied to a face with a spline contour

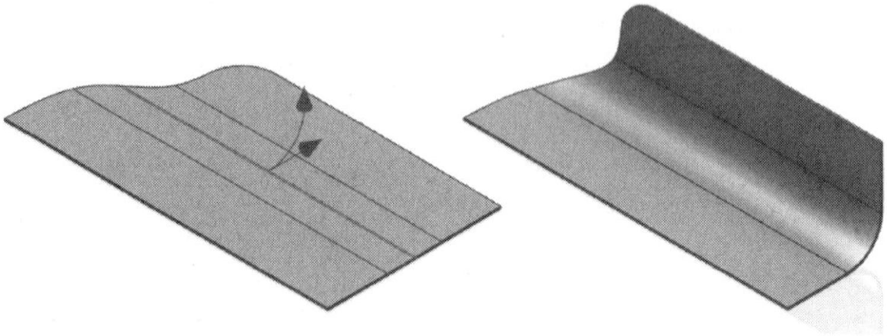

This tool is a sketch consumption feature and contains numerous controls for specifying exactly how a planar face should be manipulated into two planar faces connected by a bend. The sketch bend centerline must be coincident with the face extents, requiring you to project edges and constrain the sketch. When utilizing the Fold tool, remember that the feature works from the opposite design perspective of other sheet-metal features, where bend allowance is actually consumed, not added to the resulting folded feature. The Fold tool can be combined with the Face tool to help import preexisting 2D flat patterns and then deform them into their final shape.

To explore the Fold tool, follow these steps:

1. Click the Get Started tab and click Open.

2. Open the file mi_6a_016.ipt from the Chapter 6 directory of your Mastering Inventor 2016 folder.

3. Select the Fold tool on the Create panel of the Sheet Metal tab. (Be aware that there is an Unfold button and a Refold button as well. You will explore those in the coming pages, but for now ensure that you select the Fold tool.)

4. Select the visible sketch line on the circular feature for the Bend Line selection.

5. Use the Flip Side and Flip Direction buttons to set the preview arrows so that they are going up and out from the center of the part.

6. Set Fold Angle to **45** (degrees) and Bend Radius to **16 mm**.

7. Use the Fold Location buttons to set the fold so that it does not include the cutout.

8. Click the OK button to create the folded feature.

9. To reuse the sketch containing the bend lines, you'll need to make it visible again. To do so, expand the Fold feature in the browser and then click and drag the sketch above the feature.

10. Create a fold for each of the remaining lines, setting Fold Angle to **90**, Bend Radius to **2 mm**, and Fold Location to Centerline Of Bend. Use the flip controls to set the folds so they are all going up and out from the center of the part.

Although not the most commonly used of the sheet-metal tools, the Fold tool can be useful in some circumstances. If you happen to have a lot of flat pattern drawings done in AutoCAD, for instance, you can use the Fold tool to convert them to folded models. You can close this file without saving changes and continue on to explore the Bend tool in the next section.

BEND TOOL

The Bend tool allows you to connect two planar faces by selecting a pair of parallel edges. Since Inventor allows the modeling of multiple disconnected faces, the Bend tool can add either a single bend or a double bend, depending on the number of selections you make. For design situations in which multiple disconnected faces have been produced, the Bend tool is often used to combine the faces into a single body.

There are four possible double-bend results, depending on the orientation of the edges and selected option. If the sheet-metal edges face the same direction, the tool creates either a full round bend or two bends connected with a face. If the sheet-metal edges face in opposite directions, a joggle is created with either two 45-degree bends and one edge fixed or both edges fixed and the angle calculated. In both cases, the faces will be extended or trimmed as necessary to create the bends.

Exploring Bend Options

The following example demonstrates the various ways in which double bends can be created:

1. Click the Get Started tab and click Open.

2. Open the file mi_6a_017.ipt from the Chapter 6 directory of your Mastering Inventor 2016 folder.

3. Select the Bend tool from the Create panel of the Sheet Metal tab.

4. Select an edge along each of the yellow faces for the Edges selection. Note that the Full Radius and 90 Degree Double Bend controls are enabled.

5. Set the Double Bend option to Full Radius.

6. Toggle the Flip Fixed Edge button, and note how the preview updates. Then set it so that the upper face is the fixed edge (the preview will display partially into the lower face).

7. Click the Apply button to create the Bend feature.

8. Select an edge along each of the orange faces for the Edges selection.

9. Set the Double Bend option to 90 Degree.

10. Set the Flip Fixed Edge button so that the lower face is the fixed edge and the bend previews on the outermost edge.

11. Click the OK button to create the Bend feature, and note how the lower face width is carried through to the upper face.

12. Right-click the Bend feature you just created in the browser and choose Edit Feature.

13. Click the Extend Bend Aligned To Side Faces button in the Bend Extension area and then click the OK button. Notice how the upper face width is now carried through to the bend.

14. Select the Bend tool again. Select an edge along each of the blue faces for the Edges selection. Use the Flip Fixed Edge to set the upper face as fixed.

15. Set the bend radius to **18 mm** and then click the OK button.

16. Right-click the Bend feature you just created in the browser and choose Edit Feature.

17. Change the Double Bend option to Fix Edges and then click the OK button.

Although this file showcases the available options of the Bend tool, you would not typically create faces that just float in space above or below one another. Instead, these tools are often used to create bends on faces that are modeled to fit around other existing parts, most often by projecting edges in from an assembly file. You can close this file without saving changes and take a look at the next steps to see the Bend tool used in a more realistic manner.

Using the Bend Tool to Create an Enclosure

In the following steps, you will mirror an existing side of an enclosure around the centerline of a derived frame and then use the Bend tool to join the two halves:

1. Click the Get Started tab and click Open.

2. Open the file mi_6a_018.ipt from the Chapter 6 directory of the Mastering Inventor 2016 folder.

3. Click the Mirror button on the Pattern panel of the Sheet Metal tab.

4. Select the features called Right_Side_Face, Front_Flange, and Back_Flange from the browser for the Features selection.

5. Click the Mirror Plane button in the Mirror dialog box and then choose the visible YZ plane. Recall that you must select work planes by clicking their edges in the graphics area or by selecting them from the browser.

6. Click the OK button to create the mirror feature.

7. Select the Bend tool on the Create panel of the Sheet Metal tab.

8. Select the top edges of the original and the mirrored faces, leave the Double Bend option set to 90 Degree, and note the preview of the bend connecting the two faces.

9. Click the OK button to create the bend feature. Figure 6.21 shows the two sides being connected with the Bend tool.

FIGURE 6.21
Creating a bend to connect the sides of an enclosure

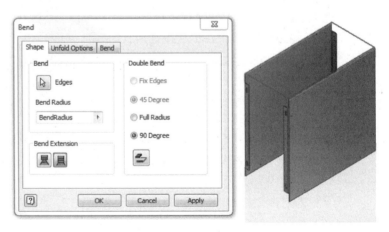

In the previous steps, not only have you created bends, but you have essentially defined the entire top face of the enclosure with the Bend tool. Using the Bend tool to connect faces in this manner can be a quick way to use geometry projected in from an assembly or a derived work surface. You can close this file without saving changes and continue on to the next section to explore the Rip tool.

Rip Tool

The Rip tool creates a gap in a sheet-metal part. A common workflow is to create a transition with the Lofted Flange tool and then add a Rip feature so it can be flattened. The Rip tool creates a gap that is cut normal to the selected face. The Rip tool interface is optimized to create a simple gap with minimal inputs.

Inventor has three options for creating a rip, as follows:

Single Point   If the corner of a face is selected as the single point, the rip will follow the edge. If a sketch point located on an edge is selected, the rip will be perpendicular to the edge.

Point To Point   For Point To Point, a linear rip is created between the two points.

Face Extents   For face selection, all edges of the face are ripped.

Follow these steps to create a simple Rip feature on a square-to-round transition:

1. Click the Get Started tab and click Open.

2. Open the file mi_6a_019.ipt from the Chapter 6 directory of your Mastering Inventor 2016 folder.

3. Click the Rip button in the Modify panel on the Sheet Metal tab.

4. Set the Rip Type drop-down box to Point To Point.

5. Select the yellow face for the Rip Face selection.

6. Select the midpoint of the arc along the top of the yellow face and the midpoint of the arc along the bottom of the yellow face for the Start Point and End Point selections.

7. Click the OK button to create the Rip feature. Figure 6.22 shows the Rip tool selections.

FIGURE 6.22
Ripping a crease on a square-to-round transition

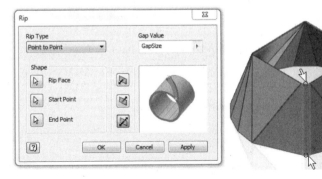

Creating Rip features allows you to open a part for unfolding in a quick and easy manner. Keep in mind that, while you could use an extruded cut to do this, in most cases the Rip tool will be the best tool to use. You can close this file without saving changes and continue on to the next section to explore the Unfold and Refold tools.

Unfold and Refold Tool

The Unfold and Refold tools are a powerful tool combination that allows you to unfold and then refold the model. There are several reasons to do this:

♦ To add features in the unfolded state

♦ To refold the model in bend order to see the manufacturing stages of the part

♦ To change the orientation of the folded model in space

One of the limitations in early versions of Inventor was that you couldn't fold a deformation. Using Unfold or Refold, you can add a deformation that crosses the bend zone and then refold it. Since the deformation is simply calculated around the bend, there can be distortion issues when the deformation is large with respect to the bend radius. For best results, limit the deformation to the material thickness. For larger deformations, make sure the final results match what would be created in the shop.

Another aspect of the Unfold and Refold tools involves bend order. Many sheet-metal parts are complex, with several bend-order possibilities. Using Unfold or Refold allows you to experiment with bend order so you can determine the best way to manufacture the part.

Changing the orientation of the folded model allows for some interesting workflows. When you unfold a model, you select a face that remains stationary. When you refold the model, you also have to select the stationary face. If you select a different stationary face for the refold than you did for the unfold, the model will have a different orientation when you have finished.

Unfolded vs. Flat Pattern

The flat pattern is a separate model object that shows the completely flattened part for documentation. The flat pattern also contains manufacturing information such as bend direction. Unfold and Refold features can't be directly accessed in the drawing, so you can't have views showing different states of the same model. To show intermediate fold states in a drawing, use derived parts or an iPart to create models with refold features suppressed and then create views of those models.

Unfolding and Refolding Sheet-Metal Parts

The Unfold/Refold process is straightforward. The selections have filters for the correct geometry, so you are not required to focus on a small target. Follow these steps:

1. Click the Get Started tab and click Open.

2. Open the file mi_6a_020.ipt from the Chapter 6 directory of your Mastering Inventor 2016 folder.

3. Click the Unfold button in the Modify panel.

4. Select the blue face on the part for the Stationary Reference selection.

5. Select each of the bends on the folded model. Each bend will highlight when you hover your mouse pointer over it, so you know when you have a valid selection. The unfolded preview updates as you select each bend. Alternatively, you can use the Add All Bends button.

6. Click the Sketches button and select the visible sketch in the graphics window so that it is unfolded to match the face it resides on.

7. Click the OK button. The model should look like Figure 6.23. Note that a copy of the sketch was placed on the unfolded model and that the original (Sketch12) is still displayed as a reference.

FIGURE 6.23
Unfolded model with sketch

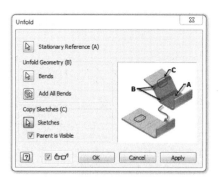
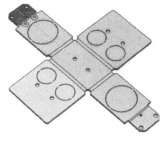

8. Right-click Sketch12 in the browser and choose Visibility to toggle off its visibility so that the copied sketch can be more easily viewed.

You may have noticed that there was an option to turn off the visibility of the parent sketch in the Unfold tool as well. Most likely that is the way you would handle copied sketches, but in this case you've been instructed to do this manually to observe the way the sketches are copied. In the next steps you will create formed slots using the copied sketch.

9. Click the Cut button in the Modify panel.

10. Select the two oblong profiles in the copied sketch and click the OK button.

11. Select the 3DModel tab and click Extrude.

12. Select the two oblong profiles in the copied sketch.

13. Click the flyout arrow in the Distance input box and choose List Parameters; then select Thickness from the list (or just type **Thickness** in the input box).

14. Click the Symmetric button so that the extrusion will extend equally in both directions from the sketch plane and then click the OK button.

15. Expand the Unfold1 feature in the browser, right-click Sketch12:Copy and choose Visibility to turn off the sketch.

16. Select the Sheet Metal tab and click Refold in the Modify panel.

17. Select the yellow face on the part to use as the new stationary reference.

18. Click the Add All Bends button to automatically select all the bends. Then click the OK button.

Note that the model is in a different position than it was before the unfold action since the yellow face was kept stationary during the refold. If you drag the End-of-Folded marker above the Unfold feature, the model will be in its original position. As you can see, using the Unfold and Refold tools offers a lot of possibilities for placing features in a flattened version of the model. You can close this file without saving changes.

Unfolding and Refolding Contour Rolls Features

You can also unfold or refold a contour roll. If the tools detect that the part is a contour roll, work planes are displayed on each end face. Since a flat reference face is required, you can select one of the work planes and then unfold the contour roll, as shown in Figure 6.24.

FIGURE 6.24
Unfolding a contour roll

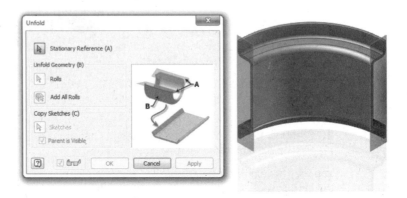

You can open the file mi_6a_030.ipt located in the Chapter 6 directory of your Mastering Inventor 2016 folder and experiment with unfolding and refolding the part. Can you unfold the part until you end up with a flat sheet?

Certification Objective

PROJECT FLAT PATTERN TOOL

A well-hidden segment of sheet-metal-specific functionality is a special version of sketch projection called Project Flat Pattern (nested at the end of the sketch projection flyout). Project Flat Pattern is available from the folded model environment and is utilized to include the projected edges of the flattened sheet-metal component, oriented to the sketch plane that is active.

This option is powerful when combined with the Cut Across Bend option because it allows you to create parametric dimensions and constrained relationships from the perspective of the flattened sheet. When utilizing the Project Flat Pattern option, it isn't necessary to select every face; just pick the ones at the extremities (ensuring that they're on the same flattened side of the part as your sketch), and all the connecting planar faces and bends will automatically be included.

In the following steps, you'll use the Project Flat Pattern tool to place sketch entities as they would be on the flat pattern. You'll then use the Cut Across Bends option of the Cut tool to create the features in place on this rather extreme example of a bent sheet-metal part.

1. Click the Get Started tab and click Open.

2. Open the file mi_6a_021.ipt from the Chapter 6 directory of the Mastering Inventor 2016 folder.

3. Select the orange face and create a new 2D sketch on it.

4. Click the drop-down arrow next to the Project Geometry button and select Project Flat Pattern from the drop-down menu.

5. Select one of the yellow faces to project the chain of faces between it and the orange face into the sketch; then select the other yellow face to complete both sides.

6. Try to select the blue faces to project into the sketch, and you'll note that nothing happens.

Nothing happens because the blue faces are actually opposite the original orange face when this part is flattened out. You could select the underside of the blue faces to include them in the sketch, but in this case you can just use the green faces.

7. Select the green faces to project the remainder of the flat pattern into the sketch. Keep in mind that you really only need to project the faces you plan to use in the sketch, but for this example you've been instructed to select them all.

8. Next, add three circles to the sketch. Two of the circles are to be placed at the center points of the projected yellow faces and will be **50 mm** in diameter, and the third circle will be **25 mm** in diameter and is to be placed in line with the center of the part and **375 mm** off the tip of the orange face. Figure 6.25 shows the completed sketch.

FIGURE 6.25
Adding geometry to a projected flat pattern sketch

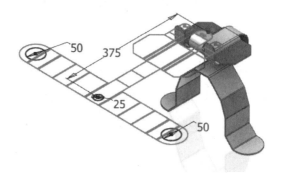

9. Click the Finish Sketch button when the sketch is complete and then select the Cut tool from the Modify panel.

10. Select all three of the circles for the Profile selection.

11. Select the Cut Across Bend check box and then click the OK button.

The result is that the circular cuts are placed on the folded model in accordance with their position in the flat pattern. This ability to lay out features in the flat pattern and then cut them across existing bends is a subtle but powerful tool. Keep in mind, too, that the projected flat pattern is fully associative and will update along with changes made to the features from which it was created. You can close this file without saving changes and continue on to the next section.

Using Sheet-Metal Templates and Rules

Inventor offers the ability to create sheet-metal rules that can be stored in the Inventor style library. The style library makes sheet-metal definition information more manageable, more reusable, and ultimately more powerful than simply using a template file to manage sheet-metal styles; however, using sheet-metal styles and templates to manage material and unfolding setups is supported.

What Are Sheet-Metal Rules?

Sheet-metal parts of a certain material and thickness often share bend, corner, and gap parameters. The unfold, bend, and corner settings as well as representation of punch features in the flat pattern and the bending angle or open angle option when the part is shown in the flat pattern all make up a sheet-metal rule. For instance, you might have a sheet-metal rule called 3 mm Galvanized Steel. In this rule, the material would be set to galvanized steel and the thickness to 3 mm. The bend, corner, punch representation, and flat pattern bend angle settings would be configured to output those features consistently.

When a new part is created, you can select the predefined sheet-metal rule, and the part will follow the settings outlined within it. When a new feature such as a flange is added, the bend and corner options defined in the rule are automatically used to define it. If a setting such as a corner relief needs to deviate from the rule, it can be modified in the feature as needed. If the part is changed to use a different sheet-metal rule, the overridden settings honor the overrides, and all others update to match the rule settings.

CREATING A SHEET-METAL RULE

Sheet-metal rules are created and accessed in one of two ways. You can click the Styles Editor button on the Manage tab, or you can click the Sheet Metal Defaults button found on the Sheet Metal tab. The Sheet Metal Defaults dialog, shown in Figure 6.26, allows you to specify the sheet-metal rule and whether to use the thickness, material style, and unfold rules defined in the sheet-metal rule or to override them.

FIGURE 6.26
The Sheet Metal
Defaults dialog box

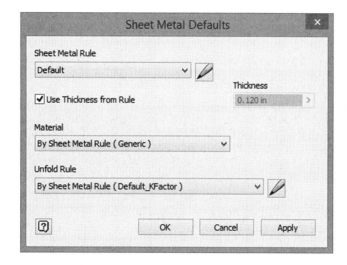

To create or edit a sheet-metal rule, from the Sheet Metal Defaults window click the Edit Sheet Metal Rule button (it looks like a pencil), and the Style And Standard Editor appears. Figure 6.27 shows the sheet-metal rule options in the Style And Standard Editor.

FIGURE 6.27
The Sheet Metal
Rule page in
the Style And
Standard Editor
dialog box display-
ing an active rule

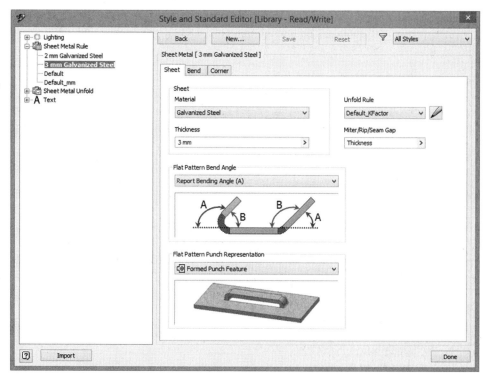

Follow these general steps to create a new rule:

1. Select an existing rule and click the New button at the top of the screen.

2. Enter a name for the new rule.

3. Set the sheet material and thickness.

4. Set an unfold rule to use.

5. Set the gap thickness to use. You can set this to Thickness so that it will update to match the sheet thickness, or you can set it to a fixed value.

6. Set the bend angle to either Bending Angle or Opening Angle.

7. Set the Flat Pattern Punch Representation style.

8. Click the Bend tab and set the bend options.

9. Click the Corner tab and set the corner options.

10. Click the Save button along the top of the Style And Standard Editor dialog box. The rule is now saved in the current part file.

11. Optionally, right-click the new unfold rule name in the left list and choose Save To Style Library to write the new unfold rule to the external style library XML file.

    Note: For this you need to have the Library option as Read/Write in the project editor window. Refer to "The Projects Dialog Box" in Chapter 1.

12. Click Done to exit the Style And Standard Editor dialog box.

SHEET-METAL RULES VS. SHEET-METAL STYLES

Sheet-metal rules are set up using the Style And Standard Editor. Initially, the rules are created in a part file as a local style, meaning they exist in that part file only. If you save the part file as a template file, all of your new parts will contain the sheet-metal rule. In addition to using templates to manage sheet-metal rules, you can add the rules to the style library. Style libraries are XML files that are stored externally to the part files and therefore can be used by newly created parts or existing parts. You save a rule to a library by right-clicking the rule in the Style And Standard Editor and selecting Save To Style Library.

UNFOLD RULES

Whenever you fold a sheet-metal part on the shop floor, some material deformation occurs at the bend location. To the outside of the bend the material stretches, and to the inside of the bend the material is compressed. To calculate this deformation for each bend, Inventor uses *sheet-metal unfold rules*. Sheet-metal unfold rules control the method of unfolding used to calculate the flat pattern for a folded sheet-metal part. You can create unfold rules using a *K-factor* or a *bend table*.

K-Factors

K-factors define the theoretical percentage of the material thickness where a folded part is neutral and neither expands nor contracts. The reason this surface is referred to as the *neutral* surface is that it defines a measurable position within the bend that has the same value in the folded and unfolded states. For instance, if your material is 10 mm thick and you use a K-factor of 0.44, bends and folds are calculated so that deformation of the bend takes place at 4.4 mm (or 44 percent of the material thickness). Unfolding with a K-factor is accomplished by determining the bend allowance (the amount of material required to produce a bend) for a given bend using the sheet thickness, the bend angle, the inner bend radius, and a K-factor value. The K-factor you use will depend on numerous factors, including material, thickness, and tooling. Most likely, you will need to perform a number of test bends on a specific press brake to determine the ideal K-factor for you.

The following equation is used to determine the developed flat pattern length using a K-factor:

$$\text{Total Length} = \text{Leg 1} + \text{Leg 2} + \text{Bend Allowance}$$

The bend allowance is calculated using this equation:

$$BA = \pi \times (A/180) \times (R + K \times T)$$

In this equation, the abbreviations have the following meanings:

- BA = Bend allowance

- A = Bend angle in degrees

- R = Inside bend radius

- K = K-factor

- T = Material thickness

Figure 6.28 shows a basic bend.

FIGURE 6.28
Basic bend references

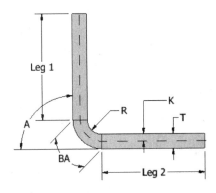

CUSTOM UNFOLD EQUATIONS

In addition to K-factors and bend tables, you can create custom unfold equations to use as an unfold method. You can find more information concerning custom unfold equations searching for *Unfolding* in the Inventor help.

To create an unfold rule to use a K-factor, follow these general steps:

1. Select the Manage tab and click the Styles Editor button to open the Style And Standard Editor dialog box.

2. Click the plus sign to the left of the Sheet Metal Unfold Rule node in the left pane of the Style And Standard Editor dialog box to display the existing unfold rules.

3. Click an existing rule to serve as the template for the new rule.

4. Click the New button along the top of the Style And Standard Editor dialog box.

5. Enter the name of the new sheet-metal unfold rule and click the OK button.

6. Ensure that the unfold method is set to Linear.

7. Enter a new K-factor value.

8. Click the Save button at the top of the Style And Standard Editor dialog box. The rule is now saved in the current part file.

9. Optionally, right-click the new unfold rule name in the left list and choose Save To Style Library to write the new unfold rule to a Read/Write external style library XML file.

10. Click Done to exit the Style And Standard Editor dialog box.

Bend Tables

An alternative to using K-factors is to create a bend table. Using bend tables is the most accurate method of unfolding because bend tables are created by taking measurements of actual bent test parts of the exact material and thickness made on the shop floor. To create a bend table in Inventor, you must first gather accurate bend information by creating bend tests. The granularity of the experimental values is up to you. It could be based on 15-degree increments or perhaps 0.5-degree increments; it depends on how much experimental data you have.

Typically, a number of test blanks are cut from a given material and thickness and then bent to the most common angles and radii used. If you measure the folded sample using virtual sharp locations, the values obtained will inherently be too large. The overmeasurement of the test fold sample needs to be compensated for by deducting an amount of length. By subtracting your combined measurements from the initial measurement of the sample taken prior to folding, you will be able to determine the value of excessive length (overmeasurement); this is what gets entered into the bend table and is where the method name *bend deduction* comes from. Bends are then calculated as follows:

$$\text{Total Length} = \text{Leg } 1 + \text{Leg } 2 - \text{Bend Deduction}$$

You can set up a test bend table as described in the following steps:

1. Click the Get Started tab, and click Open.

2. Open the file `mi_6a_022.ipt` from the `Chapter 6` directory of your `Mastering Inventor 2016` folder.

3. On the Sheet Metal tab, select Sheet Metal Defaults.

4. Click the Edit button for Unfold Rule (it looks like a pencil).

5. In the Style And Standard Editor, expand the Sheet Metal Unfold node from the list on the left (if it's not already expanded), select Default_KFactor and then click the New button at the top. This creates a new unfold rule based on the existing one.

6. Enter **Mastering Bend Table** for the name and click the OK button.

7. Change the Unfold Method drop-down box to Bend Table.

8. Set Linear Unit to millimeter (mm) to match the units of this part file.

9. Click the Click Here To Add row in the Thickness box and enter **2.00** for 2 millimeters.

10. Enter **30** into the leftmost cell of the table to define the angle at 30 degrees.

11. Enter **1.0** in the topmost cell to define the bend radius at 1 mm.

12. Enter **0.5** in the cell to the right of the angle cell and just under the bend radius cell. This is the bend deduction (in this case, 0.5 is a hypothetical value).

13. Add another bend angle row by right-clicking the cell containing 30 and choosing Insert Row.

14. Enter **45** for the angle and **0.6** for the bend deduction.

15. Add another bend radius column by right-clicking the cell containing 1.000000 and choosing Insert Column.

16. Enter **2.0** in the column header for the bend radius and then enter **0.55** for the 30-degree row and **0.65** for the 45-degree row.

17. Add a third row of **60** degrees with **0.70** and **0.75** bend deductions in the 1.000000-degree and 2.000000-degree columns, respectively.

18. Add a third column of **3.0** mm with **0.60**, **0.70**, and **0.80** for the 30-, 45-, and 60-degree rows, respectively.

19. Bends greater than 90 degrees and bends less than 90 degrees are handled differently, so in this case you want to set the Angle Reference radio button to use the Bending Angle Reference (A) option. This allows the table to match the existing part. If you wanted to use the Open Angle Reference (B) option, your table angles would need to be 150, 135, and 120. You can check your table against the one in Figure 6.29.

FIGURE 6.29
The sample bend table

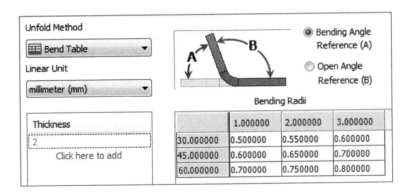

20. Click Save and then Done to finish the bend table.

21. In the Sheet Metal Defaults dialog box, choose Mastering Bend Table from the Unfold Rule drop-down box to make it the active unfold rule for this part and then click the OK button.

BENDING ANGLE AND OPEN ANGLE REFERENCES

Originally, the Inventor bend table was designed to reference an *open angle* datum structure (which is still the default) for measuring bends. However, the sheet-metal features all use a *bending angle* datum structure to create bent features. As a means to bridge this disparity in measurement convention, the Bend Angle option at the top of the bend table interface allows you to declare the structure in which your values were measured; Inventor will use this option to convert the values internally if necessary. Keep in mind that the angular values are not altered within the table when this option is changed.

As you can see, the process of creating a bend table in Inventor is a straightforward endeavor. Typically, the real work is in creating the test blanks and bends to gather the information to put into the table.

Here are a few more things to know about creating bend tables:

◆ Note that you can reorder columns by clicking the header cell and dragging them into place.

◆ You can also right-click the top, leftmost cell and choose Paste Table to paste in a table copied from an Excel spreadsheet. Likewise, you can choose Copy Table to copy the table into Excel.

◆ You can add a bend table for each thickness required by clicking the Click To Add row in the Thickness box.

◆ If the bend deduction is outside of the values defined in the table, Inventor uses the Backup K-factor. You can think of this as an insurance plan that allows you to obtain a flat pattern even if your bend table doesn't define what deduction to use for smaller or larger combinations of bend angle and radius.

◆ For combinations that fall within the table boundaries but not exactly at angle/radius coordinate values, Inventor uses linear approximation to derive a value; depending on the change in bend compensation between steps in the table, you can achieve better results with smaller angle increments.

◆ You can specify a table tolerance to allow Inventor to include thicknesses, radii, and angles that are within the specified tolerance. For example, if the angle tolerance is 0.004 and a bend angle measures 30.002, Inventor would use the 45-degree row in your table to calculate the deduction.

To test the bend table, you can examine the flat pattern in mi_6a_022.ipt, where a sketch has already been placed to display the flat pattern length. Because the part file has a current thickness of 2 mm, a bend angle of 60 degrees, and a bend radius of 2 mm, the bend deduction indexed from the bend table will be 0.75 mm, as shown in Figure 6.29.

In this case, then, the bend deduction is calculated as follows:

Leg 1 + Leg 2 − Bend Deduction = Total Flat Pattern Length
25 mm + 25 mm − 0.75 mm = 49.25 mm

If you were to change the angle to 45 degrees (and click the Update button) and check the flat pattern again, you would expect to see this:

25 mm + 25 mm − 0.65 mm = 49.35 mm

What would happen if you were to set the angle to 37.5 degrees, which is halfway between 30 and 45 degrees? Because the bend table has no entry for 37.5 degrees, Inventor uses a linear extrapolation of the bend deductions of 0.55 mm for 30 degrees and 0.65 mm for 45 degrees and arrives at the halfway point of 0.60 mm for 37.5 degrees. If you check the flat pattern, you will expect to see this:

25 mm + 25 mm − 0.60 mm = 49.4 mm

 Real World Scenario

K-FACTORS AND BEND TABLES: WHICH SHOULD I USE?

The most common question asked about flat patterns concerns the use of K-factors and bend tables. Which to use depends on your manufacturing processes and the capabilities of your machines. These are the main questions to ask when determining which is right for you:

◆ Do you outsource your sheet-metal manufacturing?

◆ How accurate do your parts need to be?

Whether you build the parts in-house or you outsource them, you should be able to get the data from the shop. If your sheet-metal shop is unsophisticated, they may use rules of thumb to determine the bend allowance. In that case, you need to work with them to determine whether a K-factor or a bend table is the best solution. One of the advantages of using sheet-metal rules is that you can create rules for each shop. For example, if you generally use your shop but you outsource when you are busy, you can select the rule for the other shop, and the flat pattern will automatically update.

In general, K-factors are used for parts with large tolerances. Since the K-factor is an approximation, the actual value will vary depending on the machine. For parts with very tight tolerances, you need to know specific compensation values for the bend radius and angle for the machine, material type, and thickness. Depending on the material, you might need different values based on the grain direction. For extremely tight tolerances with certain material types, you might even need different values for each shipment of material.

Bend Compensation

In addition to using K-factors and bend tables, you have the ability to enter an expression for a *bend compensation*. Instead of entering values for specific bend angles and using linear interpolation between the values, you can enter ranges of bend angles that use an expression to determine the proper compensation within that range. To access the Bend Compensation settings, click the Style Editor button on the Manage tab and then expand the Sheet Metal Unfold node in the left pane. Finally, select BendCompensation. Figure 6.30 shows the BendCompensation settings.

FIGURE 6.30

BendCompensation settings

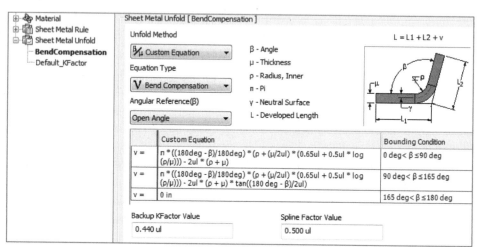

Working with Styles and Templates

It is important to understand what has been defined within your template and what has been stored within the style library. For example, suppose you have a sheet-metal rule named MyRule1 with the Thickness value equal to 2 mm stored only locally in your template file, and another sheet-metal rule also named MyRule1 but with the Thickness value equal to 5 mm, also stored in your style library. Each time you start a new design from the template referencing MyRule1, you will see a Thickness value of 5 mm being applied. The reason for this is that the style library is the "published" source of your standards; its definition will always win. After saving your design, if you want to make changes to the Thickness value of MyRule1, you can apply the changes without fear that they might be automatically overwritten because this occurs only when creating a new document using the template. (As a side note, if you did want to overwrite the local/document definition with the style library's definition, right-clicking an existing rule will present a context menu from which you can select Update Style, which will manually refresh the rule's definition in the document.)

It is a good practice when using the style library to have only a single generic sheet-metal rule embedded in your template file (at least one is required). Once you know what sheet-metal rule you want to apply to your model, selecting it either in the Style And Standard Editor dialog box or in the Sheet Metal Defaults dialog box will automatically draw the information into the active document. This process keeps extraneous information out of your document, providing a smaller footprint, and helps reduce the chance of style information mismatch. If you have a template file that has numerous sheet-metal rules stored within it, after publishing them to the style library, you can use the purge functionality with the Style Management Wizard to remove them.

Certification
Objective

Working with the Flat Pattern

The flat pattern derived from the folded model ties the design to the manufacturing environment. Within Inventor, the flat pattern model is an actual flattened version of the folded model vs. a sheet that has been pieced together and thickened. Numerous tools, utilities, and data sources have been provided to enable the flat pattern to suit your individual manufacturing and documentation needs.

The flat pattern contains a wealth of manufacturing information that is stored progressively during the design process. Punch and bend information is stored within the flat pattern model specifically so that customers working with drawings, customers working with the application programming interface (API), or those who want to translate the flat pattern to a different file version can control all their options in a common location; the flat pattern is commonly referred to as the *jumping-off point* for all downstream consumers.

The following sections detail these capabilities and tools.

Exploring the Flat Pattern Edit Features

The flat pattern environment has its own panel bar containing a customized set of modeling tools drawn from the Part Features panel bar and the Sheet Metal Features panel bar. The flat pattern tools are referred to as *flat pattern edit features* because they are intended to apply small alterations to the flat pattern model instead of doing large-scale modeling. Flat pattern edit features are applied only to the flat pattern, whereas folded model features are first applied to the folded model and then carried over to the flat pattern. The flat pattern can be imagined as a derivative of the folded model, establishing a parent-child relationship (flat pattern edit features are not reflected in the folded model). There are many situations in which the generated flat pattern is not exactly what you need for manufacturing; flat pattern edit features are ideal for making small associative tweaks that previously required exporting the flat pattern to an external (disassociated) file.

Adding Manufacturing Information to the Flat Pattern

There are two features specifically designed to allow you to add manufacturing information to the flat pattern. The Bend Order Annotation tool enables you to specify the order in which bends are created. The Cosmetic Centerlines tool marks bend locations, such as cross brakes, where there is mild deformation.

Bend Order Annotation When you click the Bend Order Annotation icon in the Manage panel, the bends are automatically numbered. You can renumber individual bends by double-clicking the number glyph or right-clicking and choosing one of two options for overriding the numbering: Directed Reorder and Sequential Reorder. Figure 6.31 shows the bend order being edited.

FIGURE 6.31
Editing the bend
order annotation

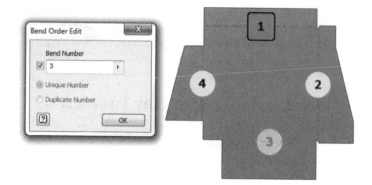

Directed Reorder With this option you are prompted for the selection of a start glyph and an end glyph. An algorithm is used to renumber bend centerlines that lie between the selected start and end glyphs.

Sequential Reorder With this option you select each bend centerline glyph in the reorder sequence.

You can follow these general steps to adjust bend order:

1. Click the Go To Flat Pattern button on the Sheet Metal tab.

2. Click the Bend Order Annotation button on the Flat Pattern tab ➤ Manage panel.

3. You can select a specific bend centerline glyph (or glyphs) and enter the new order number or right-click and choose one of the reorder methods.

4. Right-click and choose Finish Bend Order.

Cross Breaks, Creases, and Cosmetic Centerlines When working with large parts made with thin sheet materials (such as in HVAC designs), you may have a need to show cross-break information. Adding these features in the folded model is a challenge and is generally not required. Instead, you can add cross-break information to the flat pattern in the form of cosmetic centerlines. Cosmetic centerlines capture bend information in the flat pattern without changing the model. Figure 6.32 shows the Cosmetic Centerlines tool in use.

FIGURE 6.32
Creating cross breaks
with the Cosmetic
Centerlines tool

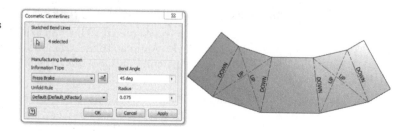

To create cross-break lines, follow these general steps:

1. Click the Create Flat Pattern button (or the Go To Flat Pattern button if it's already created) on the Sheet Metal tab.

2. Create a new 2D sketch on the appropriate face of the flat pattern (click the OK button if warned about the sketches on the flat pattern not carrying over to the folded model).

3. Use the Line tool to create the cross-break lines as needed.

4. Click the Finish Sketch button on the Sketch tab.

5. Click the Cosmetic Centerline button (on the Create panel in the Flat Pattern tab) and select any previously sketched lines.

6. Adjust the manufacturing information using the controls in the Cosmetic Centerline dialog box and then click the OK button.

A Cosmetic Centerline feature will be created in the browser, and it will consume the sketch you created. You can edit it as you would any other feature if needed.

Using the Flat Pattern Definition Dialog Box

You can manipulate the flat pattern model by using a tool called Edit Flat Pattern Definition, which is available by right-clicking anywhere in the graphics area and selecting Edit Flat Pattern Definition. The Flat Pattern Definition dialog box allows you to control a number of aspects pertaining to the flat pattern's orientation and the information stored within it, as shown in Figure 6.33.

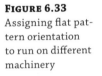

FIGURE 6.33
Assigning flat pattern orientation to run on different machinery

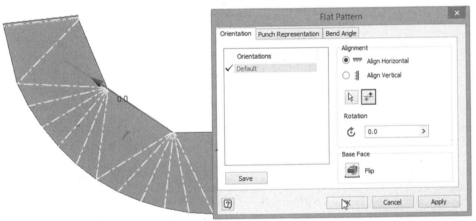

The first tab of the Flat Pattern Definition dialog box relates to the flat pattern orientation. The selection control allows you to select either an edge or two points to define the horizontal or vertical orientation. The orientation of the flat pattern is important because the implied x-axis is used to calculate Flat Pattern Extents and the rotational angle of Punch tools that have been applied to the model. When you orient the flat pattern to your specific punch equipment, the required tool rotation angle should be directly available from your flat pattern.

Since the flat pattern base face is going to be either the face already selected or the backside, the control of the base face has been simplified to a "flip" option. Base face definition is critical because it establishes a directional reference for bends and punch tooling as well as an association with the front navigation tool view and the default Drawing Manager view.

The second tab is the Punch Representation tab, which allows you to override the representation setting in the sheet-metal document without having to edit the active sheet-metal rule.

The third tab is the Bend Angle tab, which allows you to declare how bend angles should be reported to the API and Drawing Manager. For example, this means that by changing the Bend Angle option to an open angle, Drawing Manager annotations of your flattened bends will recover the complementary angle of the bending angle.

CONTROLLING THE FINISHED FACE OF THE FLAT PATTERN

If you work with prefinished surface materials, having the finish side up when laser cutting, punching, or breaking is often an important consideration.

You can set the top face of the unfolded part using the Define A Side tool in the Sheet Metal tab ➤ Flat Pattern panel.

You can also control the upward-facing surface when creating the flat pattern. You can select any face of the folded part on the finished side and then click the Create Flat Pattern button. Inventor will hold the selected face as the base face.

If you need to change the base face, you can redefine the top face using the A-Side tools in folded part mode or use the Flip button in the Pattern Definition dialog box during unfolded mode.

Do this by clicking the Go To Flat Pattern button, right-clicking the Flat Pattern node in the browser, and selecting Edit Flat Pattern Definition.

Manufacturing Your Flat Pattern

There is a close association between sheet-metal design and manufacturing, and the flat pattern solution within Inventor embraces this relationship. Inventor generically supports the ability to translate models to a variety of file formats, but Inventor sheet metal actually has its own utility to support the translation to SAT (.sat), DWG (.dwg), and DXF (.dxf) formats.

SAVING FLAT PATTERNS

After selecting the Flat Pattern browser node, you can right-click and select Save Copy As. After choosing a file type and clicking Save, the Flat Pattern Translation dialog box will be launched. For SAT files, a simple option defining the file version will be presented. For DWG and DXF file formats, an extensive list of options and file-processing capabilities is made available to you.

Within the Flat Pattern Translation dialog box, you will find standard options for file type, but there is also a Layer tab that supports layer naming and visibility control. The last tab is the Geometry tab, which allows you to decide whether you want to apply a variety of manufacturing-specific options to the translation. The first of these options is for spline simplification because many Computer Numerical Control (CNC)–profile manufacturing centers cannot leverage splines and are restricted to arcs and lines.

TRANSLATING SPLINES

The translation utility allows you to apply faceting rules to break the outer contour of flat patterns into linear segments. The second options group relates to the post-processing of the translated file, allowing you to force the 2D result into positive coordinate space and to merge interior and exterior contours into polylines, which may be critical for a path-based tool. Figure 6.34 shows these settings.

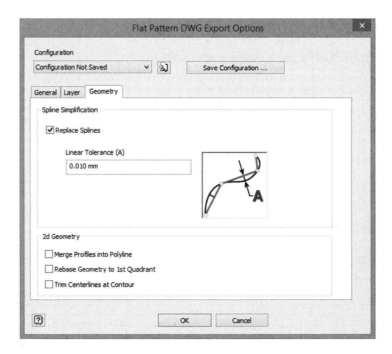

SKETCHING ON FLAT PATTERNS

Sometimes you'll need additional tool path manufacturing information such as etch lines in your DXF/DWG output. For this, the flat pattern has the ability to export unconsumed sketches created on the flat pattern. With these you can create a sketch containing the lines you need on the flat pattern. Once you save the DXF or DWG file, any visible sketches located on the flat pattern are exported, and a layer called IV_UNCONSUMED_SKETCHES is added to contain these sketches. Note that sketch text will not export using this method. If you need to add single-line text paths to your flat pattern for laser engraving, the best method is to do so in the DWG or DXF after it has been exported from Inventor.

Using Sheet-Metal iPart Factories

iParts are part configurations or part families that allow you to create a base part and then add a table to it. Once the table is added, the part features can be suppressed or configured to create a family of parts based on the original. The configured part is referred to as an iPart factory, and the individual configurations are called *members*. Sheet-metal iParts have a number of uses, from creating variations of basic parts to creating progressive die parts.

MORE iPART INFORMATION

You can find more information, including step-by-step instructions for creating iParts and sheet-metal iParts, in Chapter 7.

---

iParts for Configurations

Using iParts for sheet-metal configurations is common for parts that are basically the same but vary in the size, material, or inclusion of certain features. For example, a bracket could be designed and configured in basic mild steel, or optionally in an upgraded stainless steel version. Or you could create an iPart to handle variable hole locations on a standard-shaped bracket. Another common use would be a series of brackets that are identical in material and fold information but vary in length. Sheet-metal configurations via iParts could be beneficial and profitable to a company that deals in varieties of components that need to fit into the same space but utilize different materials or manufacturing processes or contain different features. Once different members of the iPart factory are configured, you can use the Generate Files option shown in Figure 6.35.

FIGURE 6.35
Sheet-metal iPart factory example, displaying Generate Files for selected member files

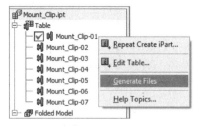

This tool is intended to support the batch creation of member files on disk; it can also be used to force updates, such as the flat pattern, out to the member files already in existence. In addition, you can use a pull method vs. a push method. If you open the iPart factory, execute the Rebuild All operation, and then save the rebuilt and migrated data, the member files when individually opened will "see" that they are out-of-date with the factory. Selecting the now-enabled Update button within the individual member file will then draw in the flat pattern information automatically.

iParts for Fold Progression

If you have the need to show the order in which a part is created, such as detailing progressive dies, you might want to explore the use of iParts and the Unfold tool. Once a folded part is complete, you can convert it to an iPart and use the Unfold tool to detail each step of the progression. In the iPart, the unfold features can then be suppressed to show the part folding back up. Because each iPart member (in this case representing the same part in different stages) can be detailed on a drawing, you can quickly illustrate the progression of the blank, flat piece to the finished part.

Modeling with Non-Sheet-Metal Features

Although the sheet-metal feature set is extensive, sometimes using non-sheet-metal features can be helpful or possibly even required to accomplish your design. The challenge when using non-sheet-metal features is to honor the guiding principles of sheet-metal design so that the resulting component can be unfolded; in addition, you want to incorporate sheet-metal conditions so that the features are manufacturable and therefore cost-effective.

Selecting Problematic Features

Although it's possible to design sheet-metal components using lofts, solid sweeps, and shells, these features can produce unpredictable and hard-to-control results. The Loft tool, unless highly restricted, produces doubly curved surfaces that cannot be unfolded properly. It's possible to utilize rails to control loft curvature, but it's time-consuming and invariably frustrating. Solid sweeps are a measure better than lofts, but these too can create unintended doubly curved surfaces. The Shell tool can be used nine times out of ten to successfully create a legitimate sheet-metal feature, but the tenth time, if it doesn't work and it's not clear why, will be confounding. If you use the parameter Thickness to shell your component, you'll probably be in fairly good shape, but there are certain situations in which the Shell tool cannot assure uniform thickness after the shell. These situations are not always simple to predict.

Certification Objective

Using Surface-Based Workflows

In addition to the sheet-metal-specific tools, you might sometimes need to use standard non-sheet-metal tools to create complex parts or features. The most successful non-sheet-metal feature workflows typically use a surface that is later thickened. The reason these workflows are so successful is that it's often easier to ensure that the resulting model embodies sheet-metal conditions (the side faces are perpendicular to the top and bottom faces and the part maintains a constant thickness) since the part can be thickened normal to the surface using the Thicken/Offset tool. When you're constructing surfaces that will be thickened, the Extrude and Revolve tools are excellent choices because they have restricted directions in which features are created, which can help ensure that only cones, cylinders, and planes are created (these can be unfolded).

The Sweep tool is possibly another good choice, but care needs to be taken to ensure that the profile and the sweep path do not contain any splines or ellipses that might prevent unfolding. For thickened, extruded, revolved, or swept features, the sketch profile geometry should ideally be limited to arcs and lines to help ensure the creation of unfoldable geometry. When you're using the Sweep tool, the Guide Surface option (see Chapter 5, "Advanced Modeling Techniques") is ideal because the swept profile is rotated along the path to ensure that it remains normal to the guide surface. Sometimes a thickened sheet-metal component needs to be trimmed with a complicated profile. For these situations, a swept surface combined with the sculpt feature can result in a model that still has sheet-metal conditions.

Another common surface-generating workflow is to use a derived component, where you select the Body As Work Surface option when placing the derived component into the sheet-metal file. This workflow can be combined well with either a thicken feature or a sheet-metal face feature after creating projected sketches for each planar surface. This was the method used earlier in this chapter when you used the Bend tool to create an enclosure from the derived frame.

One of the biggest benefits of working with surfaces is that you can apply complicated alterations to the surface prior to thickening. Some of the most common features utilized to create cutting surfaces are Extrude, Revolve, and Sweep. Additionally, the Split tool (and perhaps Delete Face) can be utilized to remove faces from the thickened surface selection.

Working with Imported Parts

The Inventor sheet-metal environment has been designed to work with imported geometry because its solid unfold engine is concerned with topology, not with features. This means that files imported directly from other 3D modelers such as SolidWorks, CATIA, and Pro/ENGINEER, as well as neutral file types such as STEP, SAT, and IGES files (`.step`, `.sat`, and `.iges`) can be brought into Inventor. Once imported, they can be modified with additional features and unfolded, provided they maintain a constant thickness that matches the thickness set in the part.

MORE ON IMPORTING PART FILES

You can find more information about importing part files and exchanging data with other CAD systems in Chapter 14, "Exchanging Data with Other Systems."

Setting Yourself Up for Success

There are two main methods for importing parts into Inventor: the Open dialog box and the Import tool that's on the Insert panel of the Manage tab. A standard part template is used by default to embed initial styles and document options, so the first step will be to use the Convert To Sheet Metal tool to draw the sheet-metal subtype options and rules into the document. Opening a Sheet Metal template and choosing Import does not require this step.

The next step you need to accomplish is the measurement of the sheet thickness of your imported model; Inventor will pick this value up automatically if the part is of a constant thickness. Once you have this value, you can match it with an appropriate sheet-metal rule (or create a new one). Matching the thickness can be as simple as taking a measurement from the sheet and overriding the Thickness value within the Sheet Metal Defaults dialog box with a simple copy and paste. Since the solid unfolder works with evaluated topology to facilitate the unfolding, the thickness of the actual part must match the thickness of the active sheet-metal rule exactly.

If the imported part contains portions that are not of uniform thickness, proper unfolding may not be possible; spend some time evaluating your imported model to ensure that it conforms to sheet-metal conditions. If your imported model contains faces defined by splines or ellipses, you are not going to be able to unfold your part. In these cases, removing these faces and replacing them with faces defined by tangent arcs may be an acceptable modification.

Converting Components

On the Environments tab is the Convert To Sheet Metal tool. The purpose of this tool is to take a component that has been designed with a regular part template and convert that document to a sheet-metal subtyped document. This means all the sheet-metal reference parameters and the default sheet-metal rule and unfold rule are automatically added to the document.

You can also convert a sheet-metal part back to a part document. Basically, this deletes the flat pattern and disables the sheet-metal functionality, but the sheet-metal parameters are not deleted.

BE CAREFUL WHEN CONVERTING BACK TO A STANDARD PART

You should convert a sheet-metal part back to a standard part file only if the manufacturing process for a part has changed. Some people have gotten into the habit of using the convert tools to access the part-modeling tools. Using the convert tools to navigate back and forth can have undesirable effects. Most notably, it can delete your flat pattern and break associations with downstream documentation; therefore, use the convert tools sparingly.

Certification
Objective

Annotating Your Sheet-Metal Design

The Drawing Manager environment contains several tools and functions specifically focused on helping you document your sheet-metal design. A quick overview of sheet-metal annotation tools might help you understand them a bit better.

Creating a View of Your Sheet-Metal Design

The first step in creating your documentation will be to choose which model file to reference, but with sheet metal comes the added requirement of deciding between a folded model and a flat pattern view, as shown in Figure 6.36. Once a sheet-metal model file is selected on the Component tab, a Sheet Metal View options group will appear immediately below the Representations drop-down. The displayed options allow you to choose between creating a folded or flat pattern view. In the case of a flat pattern, you can choose whether you want the bend extents for folds and center marks for punches to be recovered.

FIGURE 6.36
The Drawing Manager: the Drawing View dialog box's Component tab with options displayed for sheet-metal view creation

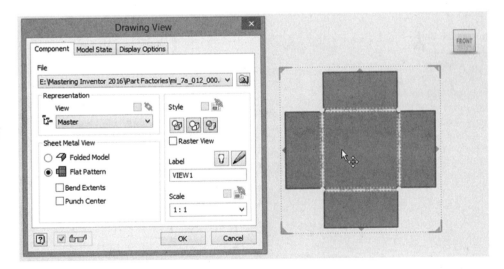

The default view options will change based on your selection because the flat pattern has a clear distinction between its top (default) face and its bottom (backside) face. The actual orientation of the 3D flat pattern defines what is a top face and what is a bottom face. This also impacts bend orientation with respect to what is reported as up and what is reported as down. All punch angular information is based on the virtual x-axis previewed during flat pattern orientation.

The Model State tab may also be of interest because sheet-metal iPart members can be individually selected when a factory file is referenced, as shown in Figure 6.37. Choosing between a folded model and a flat pattern is also necessary when creating a drawing view of the sheet-metal iPart member. If the member has not already been placed, selecting the member from the Drawing View dialog box will automatically create the file.

FIGURE 6.37
The Drawing Manager: the Drawing View dialog box's Model State tab with options displayed for sheet-metal iPart member view creation

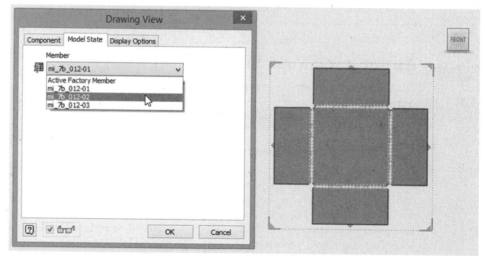

The last tab is the Display Options tab, which controls other annotations such as work features and tangent edges, as shown in Figure 6.38.

FIGURE 6.38
The Drawing Manager: the Drawing View dialog box's Display Options tab with options displayed for sheet-metal bend extents

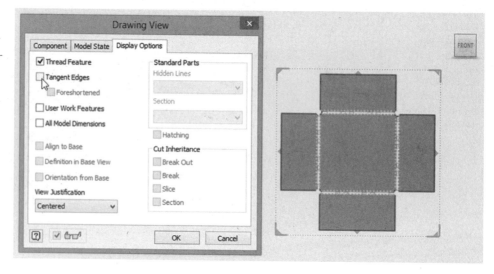

Adding Bend, Punch, and Flat Pattern Annotations

Once you've created the view of your sheet-metal component, you can switch to the Annotate tab to complete the documentation of your design. The sheet-metal annotation tools within the Drawing Manager are specific to flat pattern views. You can add bend notes and punch notes, as shown in Figure 6.39.

FIGURE 6.39

The Drawing Annotate tab with Punch and Bend tools displayed

BEND ANNOTATION TABLES

Bend notes allow you to recover bend angle, bend direction, bend radius, and K-factor (which is not on by default) for any bend centerline. You can utilize the General Table tool to create a Drawing Manager bend table (not to be confused with bend tables utilized for unfolding) that documents all the bends in a selected view. To create a Drawing Manager bend table, follow these steps:

1. Select General from the Table panel of the Drawing Annotation tab.

2. Select an existing flat pattern view.

3. Decide whether the chosen columns are acceptable (bend direction, angle, and so on); if not, alter the selected columns.

4. Choose the Bend ID format and enter a prefix if desired.

5. Click the OK button to create the bend table.

PUNCH ANNOTATION TABLES

The punch note allows you to select a formed punch, center mark, or 2D alternate punch representation in order to recover the punch angle, punch direction, punch ID, and punch depth (punch ID and depth need to be added to the Punch tool description when the punch feature is authored). When editing the punch note, you will also see a Quantity option that allows you to recover the number of instances of the same Punch tool in the view.

Punch table creation is a little different from bend table creation because it has been incorporated within the preexisting hole table annotation tools. The reason punch support was combined with hole tables is that you most likely used the Hole tool out of convenience, not necessarily to convey a manufacturing process. To make sure all of this tool-based information is consolidated, an enhancement to hole tables was made. After invoking the Hole Table – View tool and selecting a flat pattern view, you will see that the standards in the toolbar have changed to reflect predefined hole table standards. Within this list (as shown in Figure 6.40) is an example standard for punch tables, which prevents you from having to first create a standard hole table and then edit it to add all the punch information columns.

FIGURE 6.40
Drawing Manager
active-style toolbar
showing punch table
style preset

FIGURE 6.40
Drawing Manager
active-style toolbar
showing punch table
style preset

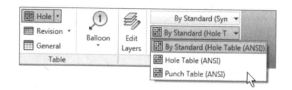

From within the Text tool, you can reference the sheet-metal flat pattern extent values by selecting a new Sheet Metal Properties option from the Type list, as shown in Figure 6.41. Once you've selected the Sheet Metal Properties type, the Property list will provide options for entering the flat pattern extents area, length, or width in the text box.

FIGURE 6.41
The Drawing Manager:
the Format Text dialog
box displaying the
Sheet Metal Properties
option for flat pattern
extents

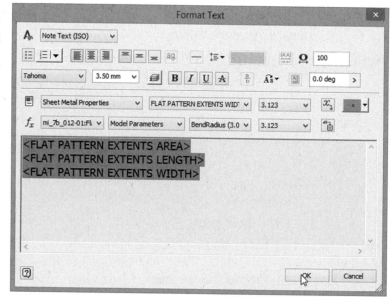

USE SHEET-METAL MANUFACTURING ANNOTATION EFFECTIVELY

You may have noticed that different toolmakers and machinists like to see different annotations. Although there are some definite right and wrong ways to annotate a part, a lot of gray area exists concerning this because there is no specific way to annotate the part "correctly." It is in these areas where you must talk to your fabricators and outside vendors to determine what information they'd like to see on the prints and to explain what type of annotation you plan to provide. Don't be afraid to ask the fabricators what information would make their job easier. As long as it does not impact your workflow dramatically, it might just save you some time and money on your parts.

The last annotation tool that can interact with sheet-metal properties is the Parts List tool. To recover flat pattern length and width extents within the parts list, follow these steps:

1. From within your sheet-metal model, right-click the filename node in the Model browser and choose iProperties.

2. Select the Custom tab and create a new custom iProperty named **Length**.

3. Ensure that the type is set to Text.

4. Enter a value of = <FLAT PATTERN LENGTH> cm.

5. Repeat steps 2 through 4 for a custom iProperty named **Width**, entering a value of = <FLAT PATTERN WIDTH> cm.

6. Save the sheet-metal model file.

7. From within the Drawing Manager, launch the Parts List tool.

8. Using the Select View tool, select a flat pattern view of the sheet-metal model containing the custom iProperties, click the OK button, and place the parts list on your drawing.

9. Right-click your parts list and select the Edit Parts List tool.

10. Right-click the table heading and select Column Chooser.

11. Select the New Property tool and enter **Length** and then click the OK button.

12. Repeat step 11, creating an additional property named **Width**.

13. Click the OK button.

14. Select the new column named Length, right-click, and select the Format Column tool.

15. Change the formatting and precision of the length to match your needs.

16. Repeat step 15 for the Width column, clicking the OK button when complete.

SAVING TIME WITH CUSTOM iPROPERTIES

If custom property information is something you might routinely want to access, create the custom iProperty values in your sheet-metal template file so that they are always available.

The Bottom Line

Take advantage of the specific sheet-metal features available in Inventor. Knowing what features are available to help realize your design can make more efficient and productive use of your time.

Master It Of the sheet-metal features discussed, how many require a sketch to produce their result?

Understand sheet-metal templates and rules. Templates can help get your design started on the right path, and sheet-metal rules and associated styles allow you to drive powerful and intelligent manufacturing variations into your design; combining the two can be productive as long as you understand some basic principles.

Master It Name two methods that can be used to publish a sheet-metal rule from a sheet-metal part file to the style library.

Author and insert punch tooling. Creating and managing Punch tools can streamline your design process and standardize tooling in your manufacturing environment.

Master It Name two methods that can be utilized to produce irregular (nonsymmetric) patterns of punch features.

Utilize the flat pattern information and options. The sheet-metal folded model captures your manufacturing intent during the design process; understanding how to leverage this information and customize it for your needs can make you extremely productive.

Master It How can you change the reported angle of all your Punch features by 90 degrees?

Understand the nuances of sheet-metal iPart factories. Sheet-metal iPart factories enable you to create true manufacturing configurations with the inclusion of folded and flat pattern models in each member file.

Master It If you created sheet-metal iPart factories prior to Inventor 2009, any instantiated files contain only a folded model. Name two methods that you could use to drive the flat pattern model into the instantiated file.

Model sheet-metal components with non-sheet-metal features. Inventor doesn't always allow you to restrict yourself to sheet metal–specific design tools; understanding how to utilize non-sheet-metal features will ensure that your creativity is limitless.

Master It Name two non-sheet-metal features that can lead to unfolding problems if used to create your design.

Work with imported sheet-metal parts. Understanding the way in which Inventor accomplishes unfolding as well as how to associate an appropriate sheet-metal rule are keys to successfully working with imported parts.

Master It Name the one measured value that is critical if you want to unfold an imported part.

Understand the tools available to annotate your sheet-metal design. Designing your component is essential, but it's equally important to understand the tools that are available to efficiently document your design and extract your embedded manufacturing intent.

Master It What process is required to recover flat pattern width and height extents within your Drawing Manager parts list?

Chapter 7

Reusing Parts and Features

The ability to reuse parts and features in other designs is an important step in increasing productivity. The Autodesk® Inventor® software provides this ability through different workflows. This chapter introduces you to several methods that will assist you in achieving your goal.

Developing the proper workflow for your company will depend on several criteria. Depending on your involvement with the functional-design aspect of Inventor, you may be converting some iParts to Content Center components. Additionally, you may decide to utilize iParts and iFeatures for design development if your design needs require them.

In this chapter, you'll learn to

◆ Create and modify iParts

◆ Create and use iFeatures and punches

◆ Copy and clone features

◆ Link parameters between two files

◆ Configure, create, and access Content Center parts

Certification Objective

Working with iParts

iParts differ from standard parts in that they are essentially table-driven part factories, allowing for many different variations to be generated from the same basic design. When an iPart is inserted into an assembly, a dialog box appears that allows you to specify a variation of the original part from the table. Figure 7.1 shows an example of three variations of the same base iPart.

FIGURE 7.1
Three variations of the same part

Within the iPart factory, you can configure feature sizes by specifying different values for the same parametric dimension, you can choose to include or suppress entire features, and you can configure the iProperties of a part. In addition to these general configuration controls, you can configure thread features and work features such as work planes, axes, and points. There are two basic forms of iParts: table-driven and custom. Both types can be combined to create a table-driven part that allows custom input.

Each original iPart, often called a *factory part*, generates individually derived, noneditable *member parts*. Member parts placed within an assembly can be replaced with a different member of the factory. When a member part is replaced, generally all existing Assembly constraints will be retained.

iParts bring several advantages within assemblies. They essentially function as completely different parts, allowing dimensional changes, feature suppression, and transfer of iProperties and other values.

Creating and Modifying iParts

iParts are created from an existing part. Existing parts already contain features and parameters. Although you can modify a standard part by changing the parameter values, this will affect the part wherever it is used. To create configurations of a standard part, you must first convert the part into an iPart.

You can publish iParts to a custom content folder for use as Content Center components or as additional content for functional design, such as Bolted Connections. Published iParts can also be used in other aspects of functional design such as Frame Generator.

MODIFYING THE PARAMETER LIST

Before converting a standard part into an iPart, you should modify the parameter list and rename the parameters to something more meaningful than the default names, such as renaming d1 to Length. To explore these tools, follow these steps:

1. On the Get Started tab, click the Open button.

2. Browse for the file mi_7a_001.ipt located in the Chapter 7 directory of your Mastering Inventor 2016 folder and click the Open button.

WHERE TO GET THE FILES

If you have not already downloaded the Chapter 7 files from www.sybex.com/go/mastering inventor2016, please refer to the "What You Will Need" section of the introduction for the download and setup instructions.

---

3. Click the Parameters button on the Manage tab.

4. The Parameters dialog box opens, and you'll note that many of the parameters have been named already. Change the names of the unnamed parameters d0, d1, and d2 to **Length**, **Width**, and **Height**, as shown in Figure 7.2, and then click Done to exit the Parameters dialog box.

FIGURE 7.2
The Parameters dialog box

Parameters		
Parameter Name	Unit/Type	Equation
▸ ⊟ Model Parameters		
Length	mm	100 mm
Width	mm	50 mm
Height	mm	20 mm
d3	deg	0 deg
RevDia	mm	20 mm

 Real World Scenario

TIPS FOR WORKING WITH PARAMETERS

Recall that you cannot use spaces in parameter names; however, you can use an underscore or capital letters to help separate words in the parameter names, such as Base_length or BaseLength.

Be aware that modifying the parameter name after creating an iPart table will not automatically update the parameter name in the table; therefore, parameters should always be named before being included in the iPart table to maintain consistency.

Parameter names will be used as column header names in the iPart table. Parameters that have been renamed will automatically be pulled into the iPart table. You can manually add unnamed parameters to the iPart table; however, it is a best practice to give all parameters to be used in the iPart meaningful names.

Selecting the Export Parameter column permits creation of custom iProperties within the part file. By exporting parameters as iProperties, you can easily access them in parts lists and bills of materials (BOMs).

 Certification Objective

CREATING THE IPART

Continuing from the previous steps where you modified the parameter list, you'll next create the iPart table, configure it to include columns of features you want to modify, and add rows for each new configuration of the part you want to create.

1. On the Author panel of the Manage tab, click the Create iPart button. All the named parameters will automatically show up in the iPart table.

2. To remove columns that you do not want to include in the table, click the parameter in the right pane and use the << button. You can also select column headers in the table and then right-click and choose Delete Column. Remove all the columns except Length, Width, and Height. (Tip: you can **Shift**-select all columns and then right-click delete them.) Note that the Member and Part Number columns are default columns and cannot be removed.

3. Add a row to the table so that you can create a variation of this part. Right-click anywhere in row 1 and choose Insert Row.

4. Set Height to **40 mm** and leave the other values as they are.

5. Create additional rows until you have eight rows with the Length, Width, and Height values, as shown in Table 7.1.

TABLE 7.1 iPart table information

LENGTH	WIDTH	HEIGHT
100 mm	50 mm	20 mm
100 mm	50 mm	40 mm
100 mm	75 mm	20 mm
100 mm	75 mm	40 mm
200 mm	50 mm	20 mm
200 mm	50 mm	40 mm
200 mm	75 mm	20 mm
200 mm	75 mm	40 mm

6. Once your table is complete, click the OK button.

7. Find the Table node in the browser and click the + sign to expand the node. You will see each member (variation) of the iPart table listed, as shown in Figure 7.3.

FIGURE 7.3
iPart browser list

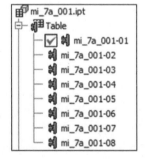

You can switch between members of the iPart by double-clicking a member in the list or by right-clicking it and choosing Activate. Making changes to the features or sketches will change the active member but will not automatically update the table. If you make a change and then go to set another member as active, you will be prompted to save the changes to the table or discard them. This is because the default edit mode is set to edit the entire iPart factory rather than the members individually. Changes made in the table will be carried through to the members either way. You'll learn more about adjusting the edit scope in the sections "Working with Sheet-Metal iParts" and "Changing Color in iParts" later in this chapter.

You can close this file without saving changes and continue on to the next section to explore the tools used to edit iParts.

Certification
Objective

EDITING THE IPART TABLE

To edit an iPart, you can double-click the Table node in the Model browser, or you can right-click and choose Edit Table. You can also right-click and choose Edit Via Spreadsheet to edit the table with Microsoft Excel. Although some iPart table-editing tasks can be done in both Inventor and Excel, others should be done only in Inventor. Follow these steps to explore the process of editing an iPart table:

1. On the Get Started tab, click the Open button.

2. Open the file mi_7a_003.ipt from the Chapter 7 directory of your Mastering Inventor 2016 folder.

3. Right-click the table in the browser and choose Edit Table.

4. In the iPart Author dialog box, right-click the Length column header and choose Key. Then click the arrow and select 1 to designate that this is the first parameter by which this part should be specified.

5. Set the width to be key 2 and the height to be key 3; then click the OK button to close the iPart Author dialog box.

6. Right-click the table in the browser and choose List By Keys. This sets the members to be listed by parameter keys in descending order, creating a drill-down tree so you can select the length, then the width, and then the height, as shown in Figure 7.4. Note that the active member is designated by a check mark next to the appropriate key.

FIGURE 7.4
iPart browser
listed by keys

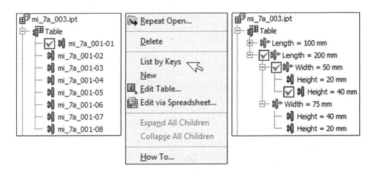

KEY SELECTION IS IMPORTANT WHEN CREATING IPARTS

You should take time to consider how your users will utilize the parts. For example, consider a socket head cap screw iPart. In the iPart, you might have diameter (1/4", 5/16", 3/16"), pitch (UNC or UNF), length (2", 3", 4", 5"), and material (stainless steel, alloy steel). Each of these columns could be key 1, but you should consider what makes it easiest to navigate to the correct part. In many cases, you might want to make the material the primary key, with the diameter, pitch, and length as the second, third, and fourth keys. This means that the user will first select the material and only then be presented with the remaining diameters, pitches, and lengths for that given material. It would be a poor choice (in most cases) to have the pitch as the primary key because this is usually not the first descriptive factor when choosing a fastener.

7. Right-click the table in the browser and choose Edit Table again.

8. Click the Properties tab to see the list of iProperties that are available for this part.

9. Locate the Project category in the left pane and expand it to reveal the Description property.

10. Select Description and use the >> button to include it in the iPart table.

11. Confirm that the Description column shows as a column in the table and then click the OK button.

12. Right-click the table in the browser and choose Edit Table Via Spreadsheet to open the table in Excel.

13. Select cells F2 through F9 and then right-click and choose Format Cells.

14. Set the cells to General and click the OK button. This is necessary to allow Excel to evaluate the expression you will build in the next step.

15. In cell F2, enter = C2 & "X" & D2 & "X" & E2.

16. Right-click cell F2 and choose Copy.

17. Then select cells F3 through F9, right-click, and select Paste. Figure 7.5 shows the Excel table complete.

FIGURE 7.5
Excel table used to add descriptions

	A	B	C	D	E	F
1	Member<defaultRow><	Part Number [Project]	Length<ke	Width<ke	Height<ke	Description [Project]
2	mi_7a_001-01	mi_7a_001-01-01	100 mm	50 mm	20 mm	100 mm X 50 mm X 20 mm
3	mi_7a_001-02	mi_7a_001-01-02	100 mm	50 mm	40 mm	100 mm X 50 mm X 40 mm
4	mi_7a_001-03	mi_7a_001-01-03	100 mm	75 mm	20 mm	100 mm X 75 mm X 20 mm
5	mi_7a_001-04	mi_7a_001-01-04	100 mm	75 mm	40 mm	100 mm X 75 mm X 40 mm
6	mi_7a_001-05	mi_7a_001-01-05	200 mm	50 mm	20 mm	200 mm X 50 mm X 20 mm
7	mi_7a_001-06	mi_7a_001-01-06	200 mm	50 mm	40 mm	200 mm X 50 mm X 40 mm
8	mi_7a_001-07	mi_7a_001-01-07	200 mm	75 mm	20 mm	200 mm X 75 mm X 20 mm
9	mi_7a_001-08	mi_7a_001-01-08	200 mm	75 mm	40 mm	200 mm X 75 mm X 40 mm

F2 = C2 & "X" & D2 & "X" & E2

18. Save the spreadsheet and close Excel.

19. Because your table now contains data that is not in the part file, you will be prompted to update the file. Click Yes in the message dialog box.

20. Right-click the table in the browser and choose Edit Table.

21. In the iPart Author dialog box, notice that the cells in the Description column are highlighted to inform you that there is a formula in those cells.

22. Click the OK button (or Cancel if no changes were made) to exit the iPart Author dialog box.

You can examine the iProperties of the part file by clicking the part name in the Model browser and choosing iProperties from the context menu. If you check the Description field on the Project tab, you'll see the value from the iPart table/Excel spreadsheet. When you switch members of the iPart, the description is now automatically updated. You can then close the file without saving changes and continue to the next section.

CONVERTING AN IPART TO A STANDARD PART

You can convert an iPart to a standard part file by right-clicking the table in the Model browser and choosing Delete. The part will assume the active members' feature values and states.

INCLUDING AND EXCLUDING FEATURES

A common use of iParts is to create a configuration of a part family that might include features in some cases and not include them in others. You can add a column to the table to control feature suppression. To do this, follow these steps:

1. On the Get Started tab, click the Open button.

2. Open the file named mi_7a_005.ipt located in the Chapter 7 directory of your Mastering Inventor 2016 folder.

3. Right-click the table in the browser and choose Edit Table.

4. In the iPart Author dialog box, click the Suppression tab.

5. Select the feature called Round_Boss1 and click the >> button to add it as a column in the table.

6. Enter **Suppress** for the all the 100 mm length rows.

SUPPRESSING VS. COMPUTING

You can enter **Suppress** or **Compute**, **S** or **C**, and **0** or **1** for the suppress/compute cells. You can mix these options as well, meaning you can change only some values from **Compute** to **S**, for instance.

---

7. Click the Verify button to ensure that you haven't entered a value that will not work, such as a spelling error. Errant cells will highlight in yellow, and you should fix them.

8. Click the OK button to return to the model.

9. Use the browser tree to activate different members, and notice that the boss features will be suppressed for all the 100 mm members. Figure 7.6 shows the iPart Author dialog box.

FIGURE 7.6
Suppressing features

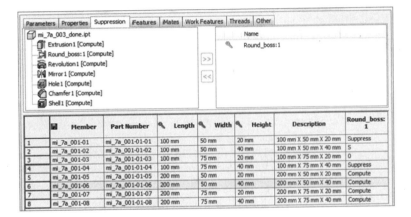

You'll notice that by suppressing the boss feature, you have suppressed both instances of the boss. This is because the boss was mirrored. To suppress just one boss, you could suppress the mirror feature; however, doing so would suppress one of the revolved features as well because it was included in the mirror. Keep this in mind when creating left and right configurations of the same part. Often, you will need to create separate features so that they can be controlled independently.

CREATING STACKED, TOGGLED FEATURES

Often when creating part configurations, you might need to create two features at the same location so you can toggle between the two features depending on the configuration. For instance, you might have an existing rectangular cut but then want to add an oblong cut in the same location so you can set the iPart to toggle between the two. When you attempt to place the oblong cut, Inventor warns that the feature did not change the number of unique faces and then results in an error. To correct this problem, simply accept the error and then right-click the oblong cut and choose Suppress Features. Then you can set up the iPart table to toggle between the two features.

INCLUDING OR EXCLUDING WORK FEATURES IN iPARTS

You can use the Work Features tab to indicate whether each work feature is included or excluded individually. A common use for this would be to create several work features in an iPart and then include only the one that is to be used for mating the specific iPart member in the assembly environment to control a specific offset value.

WORKING WITH THREADED iPART FEATURES

You can change the thread parameters of a tapped hole or external thread feature for each member of the iPart table independently. Just use the Thread tab to include any thread parameters, which will vary. You should include all parameters that will vary between any of the table members; otherwise, the hole/thread feature may generate errors when you're switching between members. Often these errors may not become apparent until you attempt to publish your iPart to Content Center.

An example of this would be if you neglected to add the Class parameter to the table, even though not all the members in the table have the same thread class. The thread class would then be set to the original thread class and would not be changed when the iPart is switched to a thread that does not include the original thread class. The same would be true, of course, if the Class column were included but not changed.

WORKING WITH SHEET-METAL iPARTS

You can configure a family of sheet-metal parts in the same way you would with a standard iPart—by adjusting lengths, widths, and so on—but sheet-metal parts have some additional controls that can be configured in an iPart. For instance, you can specify the sheet-metal rule, the sheet-metal unfold, and a named flat pattern orientation for individual members in an iPart. To edit the bend order, you must edit the member scope as opposed to making the edits per the iPart factory. Once the iPart is set to Member Scope, bend-order changes in the flat pattern are set to the active member. You can follow these general steps to set the scope of the edits:

1. On the Manage tab, locate the Author panel.

2. Click the Edit Factory/Member Scope drop-down and set it to Edit Member Scope. Figure 7.7 shows the drop-down.

FIGURE 7.7
Setting the iPart edits
to Member Scope

MEMBER SCOPE VS. FACTORY SCOPE

When you set the edit scope to Edit Member Scope, changes to the model such as suppressing a feature are automatically added to the iPart table.

Once the scope is set to edit just members, you follow these steps to adjust the bend order per iPart member:

1. Activate the iPart member using the iPart table in the browser.

2. Click the Go To Flat Pattern button on the Sheet Metal tab.

3. Click the Bend Order Annotation button on the Sheet Metal tab.

4. You can select a specific bend centerline glyph (or glyphs) and enter the new order number, or you can right-click and choose one of these reorder methods:

   Directed Reorder   You are prompted for the selection of a start glyph and an end glyph. An algorithm is used to renumber bend centerlines that lie between the selected start and end glyphs.

   Sequential Reorder   You select each bend centerline glyph in the reorder sequence.

5. Right-click and choose Finish Bend Order.

When you edit the iPart table, you will see that the FlatPatternBendOrder column is automatically added (because you are working under the member scope edit mode). The cell for the edited iPart member will show that it is using something other than the Default bend order.

CHANGING COLOR IN IPARTS

To set iPart members to be different colors, you can create a custom iPart parameter on the Other tab. Right-click the column header and choose Appearance Column to get it to the Appearance Column option. Then you can edit each member row of the iPart to be a different color/appearance. It is important that the name matches exactly, however, so be careful to match case. This means that entering **red** for **Red** will cause a mismatch. To avoid this, it is recommended that you use the member scope edit mode, as described in the previous section, to make color style edits to the part. This way, you can just set the member as active, change its appearance, and have the appearance change recorded in the iPart table automatically. To set up an Appearance column, follow these steps:

1. On the Get Started tab, click the Open button.

2. Open the file mi_7a_012.ipt from the Chapter 7 directory of your Mastering Inventor 2016 folder.

3. Right-click the table in the browser and choose Edit Table.

4. In the iPart Author dialog box, click the Other tab.

5. On the Other tab, click the Click Here To Add Value line.

6. Type **Color** for the value name.

7. Right-click the column header and choose Appearance Column, as shown in Figure 7.8.

FIGURE 7.8
Creating an
Appearance column

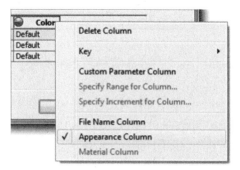

8. Type **Default** into the Appearance column for each of the three rows. Then click the OK button to exit the iPart Author dialog box.

SETTING COLORS

Note that if you do not enter Default or a valid Appearance style, you will receive a warning that states "Errors occurred while setting factory to specified member." You can click Accept and then edit the table again.

---

9. Ensure that Edit Member Scope is set (on the Manage tab, locate the Author panel and then set the drop-down to Edit Member Scope).

10. From the Quick Access bar (located at the top of the screen), select the Appearance Style drop-down and choose Cyan.

11. Expand the iPart table, use the keys to set the 25 mm × 50 mm member active, and then set its color to Red.

12. Change the edit scope to Edit Factory Scope using the iParts/iAssembly toolbar.

13. Use the keys to set the 50 mm × 50 mm member active and then set its color to Gold.

14. Right-click the table in the browser and choose Edit Table. You will receive a message asking whether you would like to set the table to match the document (that is, the part).

This demonstrates that when you are making edits to the model with the edit scope set to Factory, the changes to members do not get written back to the table automatically. Using the Edit Member Scope option is therefore recommended. You also get this message if you change the active member because the table is verified every time you switch members.

15. Click Yes; then take a look at the Appearance column to ensure that the colors match what you have set them to.

As mentioned earlier, you could also just edit the table and type in the color name. Experiment with this as you like, and then you can close the file without saving changes and continue to the next section.

EXPLORING THE AUTHORING OPTIONS

The Options button, located in the lower-left corner of the authoring dialog box, allows you to create and edit part numbers and member names for iParts. You will typically want to set these naming options before you begin adding rows to the iPart table so that as rows are added, they are automatically named according to these options.

Notice the disk symbol located in the Member column header in Figure 7.9. This indicates that the Member column will be used as the filename for each iPart member. If you prefer to have the Part Number column used for the filenames, you can right-click that column header and select File Name Column.

FIGURE 7.9
Member column used for filename

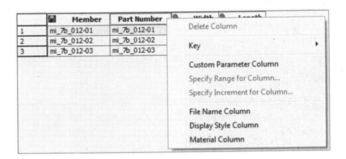

A Member Name value is automatically created for each member as rows are added based on the settings for the part number and member name options. You can override these by editing the table in Excel, and you can even use a formula to create the names based on a concatenation of other column values in the table.

GENERATING MEMBER FILES

Once your iPart table is complete, you may want to generate the parts from the table. You can do this so the parts are established ahead of time, or you can allow the files to be generated automatically as they are used. If you have an iPart table with two dozen rows, it might make sense to generate them ahead of time. However, if you have an iPart table of 200 member rows, then it might make sense to allow parts to be generated only when, for example, a particular size is used. To generate member part files, right-click the table and choose List By Member Name. Use **Shift**+select to select all the members and then right-click to generate files. Each member in the row will be created as a derived part based on the table values.

iPart Member File Save Locations

Because these parts are often used over and over in many assemblies, I recommend that you store them in a library folder. Recall that folders designated as libraries in your project file are handled as read-only by Inventor. The library directory where you want to save the iPart members is set up by you, and it is required that you use the same name as the factory library but preceded with an underscore. As an example, if you place the iPart factory file in a library folder named `Fasteners`, Inventor will automatically place all iPart members generated from that factory part in a second library folder named `_Fasteners`.

However, you are not required to store iParts in libraries. If you do not use libraries and you place an iPart member into an assembly or use the Generate Members option, Inventor will create a folder of the same name, and at the same level, as the iPart factory and store the iPart members there. For example, if you have an iPart factory file named `ClipBracket.ipt` saved at `C:\Mastering Inventor\`, then when `ClipBracket.ipt` is used in an assembly, a subdirectory called `ClipBracket` is created (`C:\Mastering Inventor\ClipBracket`), and the iPart member file is created there. Custom iPart members are always stored in a location specified by the user.

Creating Custom iParts

A custom iPart is an iPart factory that has one or more columns designated as a custom parameter column. A custom parameter column allows input of any value and, in turn, generates a custom iPart with infinite variations. Custom iParts are valuable for creating tube and pipe lengths, structural steel members, and other parts that require unique size input at the time of insertion. To designate a column as a custom parameter column, simply right-click the column and select Custom Parameter Column. Columns that are set as keys are not permitted to be custom columns.

Rather than setting an entire column to be custom, you may want to set only the column entry for a single member to be custom. To do this, you can right-click any cell in a nonkey column and choose Custom Parameter Cell. Once cells or columns are designated as custom, you can right-click and set both columns and cells to restrict input to a specified range and increment.

Here is a common example of setting a range for a custom part:

1. Right-click the column to set the Length column to be custom (it cannot be a key column).

2. Right-click the column to set the range so the part can be placed only in lengths from 25 mm to 150 mm.

3. Right-click the column to set the increment to 5 mm so the lengths are limited to standard sizes within that range.

4. When the custom iPart is placed into an assembly, the size is then specified.

5. Unlike standard iParts, custom iParts are saved to a location of your choice at the time of placement.

Figure 7.10 shows the options for creating a custom column.

FIGURE 7.10

Custom column settings

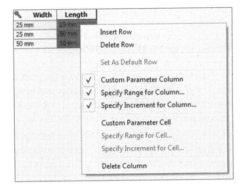

TESTING THE IPART

Before placing a completed iPart into production for others to use, test the accuracy and interface of your part by inserting the iPart using Place Component within a blank assembly file. Using Place Component, insert every member in the table and inspect or measure the placed component.

Moving the test forward, create an IDW file with a base view of your assembly. You will also need to generate a parts list with the desired columns and verify the accuracy of each cell. Once you are assured of having accurate member components, you can place this iPart into a project library folder or other location to be used in production. If using this iPart in conjunction with the functional-design features of Inventor, you will need to publish the factory iPart to a custom Content Center library. Publishing to Content Center is covered in more depth later in this chapter.

NO ZERO-VALUE DIMENSIONS

You should not attempt to create a zero-value dimension as a method of suppressing features. Zero-value dimensions can create unpredictable results when the zero value is set back to some value greater than zero. Often the dimension will solve in the wrong direction, causing feature profiles to become invalid and create errors within your iPart. It is better to create a column to suppress individual features, rather than attempt to do so through dimensions.

EDITING THE IPART FACTORY

Editing an original iPart factory follows the same workflow as creating an iPart. If you've placed the original iPart factory into a project library folder, you will not be able to edit it within that same project. Instead, you should create a new project file for the purpose of editing library parts. When creating a new project file, you can either define the workspace for the project file by placing the project file in the library subfolder or just duplicate your original project file and remove the library paths using the Project Editor dialog box. Any files within the library path will now be editable with this specific project file.

With the new Library Edit project file active, open the iPart you want to edit. Locate the table in the Model browser and either double-click or right-click to activate the iPart Author dialog box. At this point, you can edit any part of the table. When you have completed your editing, you can save the part to its original location.

CAN'T GENERATE IPART MEMBERS?

When changes are made to an iPart factory and they impact existing iPart members, you should be able to use the Generate Files option to replace the iPart members (provided the folder or files are not set as read-only by Windows). However, sometimes you'll find that Inventor won't generate new versions of existing iPart members once edits are made, even when you right-click them in the table and choose Generate Files and have checked the read-only status. Although the reason for this behavior is often unclear, you can generally get around it by browsing to the location of the iPart members and deleting them. Then you can return to the iPart Factory and choose Generate Files.

You can convert an iPart factory component into a standard parametric part by deleting the table attached to the iPart. Simply right-click the table in the Model browser and select Delete. The part will revert to a parametric part with no history of the iPart functionality.

Using iParts in Designs

Using an iPart in an assembly design is a bit different from creating parts within an assembly. To place an iPart member of a particular size into an assembly, you will use the Place Component tool to browse and place the iPart factory. Upon placing the iPart factory into the assembly, you'll be presented with the Place iPart dialog box, from which you can specify the member or choose from the keys you set previously. Keep in mind that if you didn't set any keys in the iPart table, all of the columns will be listed in the Keys tab of the Place Standard iPart dialog box. Figure 7.11 shows the placement of an iPart that has three keys set.

FIGURE 7.11
Placing an iPart into an assembly

In Figure 7.11, Length is Key 1, Width is Key 2, and Height is Key 3. Keep in mind that for the best results, keys should be set from top to bottom in the Place iPart dialog box because the values are filtered in that order. However, Inventor does not prevent you from setting Key 3 first and then Key 1. But working out of order with keys can create some confusion and unexpected results in the values you see listed in the drop-downs.

Once an iPart is placed, you might find that you need to change to another size, color, or configuration. To change between iPart members, follow these steps:

1. Locate and expand the iPart in the assembly browser tree.

2. Right-click the table.

3. Choose Change Component.

This opens the iPart placement dialog box, which allows you to specify a new member to be used in place of the existing one. Figure 7.12 shows the specific selection path for changing the component. This replacement procedure will replace only the selected component instance.

FIGURE 7.12
Changing the component

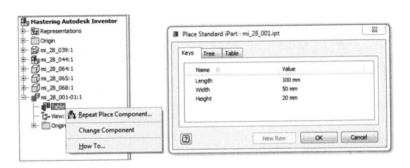

If you want to replace all exact duplicate members of the iPart within this assembly, follow these steps:

1. Right-click the part within the graphics window or the Model browser.

2. Select Component.

3. Choose Replace All. A dialog box appears, allowing you to select the original iPart factory.

4. Once the original iPart factory is selected, you will be prompted with the iPart placement dialog box to allow you to select the specific member to be used as the replacement.

When a component is replaced with a different member of the same family, as with iParts, normally all Assembly constraints will be retained. If the replaced component is of a different family, the Assembly constraints might be broken. The same is true of parts in the same family if the original part used a certain feature to constrain to and the replacement part has that feature suppressed.

Certification
Objective

> ### iPart Factories in Assemblies
>
> You should be aware that Inventor does not allow an iPart factory file to be placed into an assembly. If you attempt to do so, only a member of the factory will be placed instead. However, keep in mind that if you create a regular part file, place it into an assembly, and then turn it into an iPart factory, changing the factory table does not place a member file but simply updates the factory. Using factory files in assemblies in this manner is not the intended workflow for iParts.
>
> iFeatures are features that have been extracted from an existing part file and configured for reuse in other parts. If you are familiar with Autodesk® AutoCAD® software, you might relate iFeatures to blocks, in that you can write out blocks for reuse in other drawings. Any feature based on a sketch can be used as an iFeature, but there are some best practices to follow when creating sketches and features to be extracted for iFeatures. Once extracted, the iFeature is stored in an external location and can be placed into any other part file. Inventor is supplied with a number of standard iFeature files as well. iFeatures cannot currently be published to Content Center.

Working with iFeatures

Using iFeatures in your designs can greatly simplify your workflow and accelerate productivity, especially if your designs contain repetitive features. Figure 7.13 shows an example of a sheet-metal part that could be created quickly using iFeatures.

FIGURE 7.13
Sheet-metal part with
iFeatures

iFeatures used in sheet-metal parts are authored with center points that allow them to be placed as sheet-metal punches. iFeatures are stored in a Catalog folder defined in the Inventor application options. By default, the catalog is located in the Inventor install directory, but you can customize the location by selecting the Tools tab, clicking Application Options, and then choosing the iFeatures tab. On the iFeatures tab, you can set the catalog path to a directory of your choosing, most often located on a network server. You can create additional subfolders in the Catalog folder as required to better organize your iFeatures. Extracted iFeatures are saved with .ide filename extensions. iFeatures are also available online from such locations as http://cbliss.com/inventor/iFeatures/index.htm. Often these online files contain the extracted iFeature and the original file it was created from. These can serve as good examples of how to set up complex geometry for iFeature extraction.

The following are some tips for working with iFeatures:

◆ Keep your iFeatures clean, and do not include projected geometry or reference geometry unless required.

◆ If dependent geometry is required, have it dependent only on geometry within the iFeature.

◆ You should avoid the use of origin work planes, axes, and the origin center point for work features.

◆ Use parallel and perpendicular constraints to other geometry in the iFeature rather than horizontal and vertical constraints.

◆ Know that updating table-driven iFeatures does not update existing instances of the iFeature.

◆ Save iFeatures before placing them in other parts.

Creating iFeatures

Once you have a part that consists of a feature or features that you want to reuse in the design of other parts, you can easily extract those features and place them into the catalog. The chief advantage of using iFeatures is that the original part does not need to be open in order to copy the feature. In addition, you can alter any of the parameters at will when inserting the feature into a new part.

To extract a part feature or features, go to the Manage tab and click the Extract iFeature button on the Author panel. Select the feature to be extracted, from either the Model browser or the graphics window. If additional features exist that are dependent on the selected feature, they will be included in the feature selection as well but can then be removed during the iFeature creation process if not needed.

Recall that a feature is dependent on another feature if it uses the other feature as a reference in the sketch or feature creation. For instance, if you created a sketch on the face of an Extrude feature, that sketch (and any feature created from that sketch) is inherently dependent on the base Extrude feature because it uses the face as a reference plane. Therefore, if you extracted the base Extrude feature, the dependent feature is automatically included, but it can be removed if not needed. Figure 7.14 illustrates how to remove a dependent feature (Fillet1) while creating an iFeature.

FIGURE 7.14
Removing a dependent feature

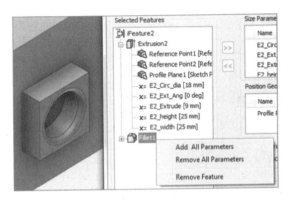

A standard iFeature will typically require a profile plane in order to position the geometry onto a new part. Named parameters and values involved in the selected feature are transferred from the existing part into the new iFeature. In Figure 7.15, notice that prompts will be added for each of the named parameters. You can edit the prompts as needed. You'll also notice that range and list limits have been set for some of the parameters. This allows you to control the input for iFeatures by limiting them to a predefined list of sizes or a specified range between sizes. When inserting this iFeature into a different part in the future, you will be prompted to enter new values for these parameters.

FIGURE 7.15

Parameters and prompts

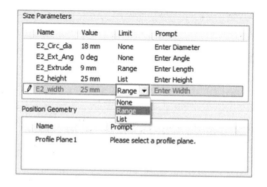

PLACING AN IFEATURE

To place an iFeature in a standard part (not a sheet-metal part), browse to the stored iFeature and select the face you want to use for placement. During the placement, you can adjust the rotation angle and size parameters. To see a simple example of how iFeatures are extracted and placed, follow these steps:

1. On the Get Started tab, click the Open button.

2. Open the file mi_7a_017.ipt from the Chapter 7 directory of the Mastering Inventor 2016 folder.

3. On the Manage tab, click the Extract iFeature button.

4. In the Model browser, click Extrusion2 as the selected feature. The dialog box will be populated with the parameter information found in that feature.

5. Click the parameter named E2_Ext_Ang and use the << button to remove it from the parameter list. This parameter is the taper angle of the extrusion, and by removing it from the list, you are ensuring that users of iFeatures in the future cannot specify a taper.

ADJUSTING EXTRACTED FEATURES

In this case, the parameters have been renamed previously using the Parameters dialog box. However, you can adjust parameter names and the corresponding prompts at this point if needed.

You can also adjust the default values for the parameters without adjusting the current model, as well as add lists and ranges to each parameter using the Limits column.

6. For this example, accept the default for the rest of the parameters and click Save.

7. Notice that Inventor takes you straight to the Catalog folder. This location is specified in the Application Options dialog box on the iFeature tab and can be changed if needed. Use the list of Frequently Used Subfolders on the left of the Save As dialog box to go to the Chapter 7 folder and name this iFeature **SquareSocket.ide**. Click the Save button to save the file.

8. Next, you'll place the iFeature back into the model as a test. On the Manage tab, select the Insert iFeature tool.

9. Navigate to the Chapter 7 folder.

10. Locate and select the SquareSocket feature you just created (or use the file called mi_7a_025.ide) and click the Open button.

11. Select the top face of Extrusion1 to use as the profile plane.

12. Once the plane is selected, set the angle to 45 degrees, use the flip arrow to ensure that the feature is placed in the correct direction, and then click Next.

13. Enter **20 mm** for the E2_Circ_Dia parameter and then click the edit icon (it looks like a pencil), or click in the space below the Diameter row or on another row in the dialog box to set the row out of edit mode.

14. Click the Refresh button to see the diameter update onscreen. Note that if the diameter does not update, you probably did not click out of the Diameter row to set the edit as active. The refresh option is a bit picky in this way. Keep in mind, however, that the preview does not need to be refreshed to build to the specified value correctly.

15. Once the size parameter has been adjusted, as shown in Figure 7.16, click Next.

FIGURE 7.16
Inserting a simple iFeature

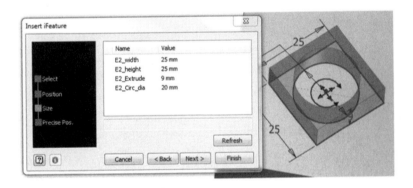

16. You will be presented with two options for placing the iFeature; choose Activate Sketch Edit Immediately and then click Finish.

17. You will see that the iFeature sketch is set and ready to be edited and constrained into place so that it can't be moved accidentally.

You'll notice that there is some extra geometry included in the sketch. This geometry came from the original feature from which you extracted the iFeature.

It would have been the best practice to prep the sketch and remove this geometry from the sketch before extracting. However, in this case you were not instructed to do so in order to illustrate the presence of relic geometry at this point. It's often a good idea to save a copy of your original part file and use it to clean up unwanted geometry before extracting iFeatures.

You can click the Finish Sketch button and close the file without saving changes.

TAKING THE TIME TO CONSTRAIN THE SKETCH

You should also notice that the sketch is currently underconstrained. In particular, it has no dimensions or constraints holding it in position. You can place general dimensions into the sketch to anchor it in place. Also present is some relic geometry that originated from the sketch from which the iFeature was extracted. It is poor practice to extract iFeatures without cleaning them up first, so eliminate this stray geometry beforehand.

It is also good practice to create a separate part file from which to generate an iFeature rather than attempting to use a part file designed for production. You can copy the part features from a production part into your iFeature test part using one of the copy or cloning methods discussed in the upcoming pages.

EDITING AN IFEATURE FILE

Once iFeature (IDE) files have been extracted and tested, you can open them in Inventor and edit them much as you do iParts. Follow these steps to explore the options involved in editing an iFeature:

1. Select the Get Started tab, click the Open button, and then browse for the Chapter 7 directory in your Mastering Inventor 2016 folder.

2. Locate and open the file SquareSocket.ide you created in the previous exercise. If you did not complete that exercise, you can use the file mi_7a_025.ide in the Chapter 7 directory.

Continue exploring the iFeature edit tools by following these general instructions:

◆ Use the Edit iFeature icon to refine parameter names, sizes, and instructional prompts for the placement of iFeatures.

◆ If the iFeature has dependent features, you can edit them as well.

◆ You can rename the iFeature if you want by clicking twice on the current name in the Edit iFeature dialog, and you can also configure it in a more in-depth manner by using the iFeature Author Table dialog box.

◆ The iFeature Author Table dialog box allows a table to be added to the iFeature so that rows and columns can be added to configure the iFeature in the same way you configured a part file using the iPart Author dialog box.

◆ Once you've added the table to the iFeature, you can further edit it by clicking the Edit Using Spread Sheet icon to open the table in Microsoft Excel.

When creating iFeatures, you'll find it a good idea to keep the original IPT file that you used to create the IDE file. This file is often useful in case you want to totally redesign the iFeature or make a similar iFeature.

Creating Punch Features

Punch features are really just iFeatures with extended functions that are slightly different in behavior from standard iFeatures. Punch features must have a single sketch center point in the base sketch to be extracted. The sketch center point will be used to locate the punch feature upon insertion into sheet-metal parts. The destination parts will require an active sketch containing sketch center points for the location of the punch feature. It is the center point in the iFeature punch and the center point in the placement sketch that allow punch features to be precisely placed and constrained beyond the capabilities of the standard iFeature.

INCLUDING PLACEMENT INSTRUCTIONS

You can embed an instructional document detailing the placement selection requirements for more complex shapes that require faces to be selected in a certain order or need more information about size and settings. Here are the steps for including placement instructions:

1. On the Tools tab, click Insert Object.

2. Select Create From File, browse for the precreated instruction file and then click the OK button.

3. The file will show in the 3rd Party browser node, as shown here:

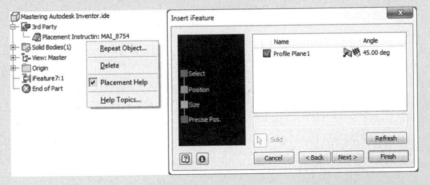

4. Right-click the embedded object and select Placement Help to allow this file to be accessed from the feature's dialog box during placement.

PUNCH FEATURES IN STANDARD NON-SHEET-METAL PARTS?

Although the Punch tool is not available for use in the standard part-modeling environment, you may have a need to quickly and precisely place a feature multiple times in a way that lends itself to the Punch tool.

To do this, you can use the Convert To Sheet Metal Part button (on the Model tab) to temporarily convert the part to a sheet-metal part. Once this is done, you can use the Punch tool as required.

continues

continued

> After you've placed the punches, you can use the Convert To Standard Part button (found in the Setup drop-down of the Sheet Metal tab) to convert the part back. This will leave some relic sheet-metal parameters in your part file, but that shouldn't cause an issue.

CREATING PUNCH FEATURES

When creating a punch feature, consider that in normal use most features extend through the thickness of the sheet metal. Therefore, it is important to use the Thickness parameter when creating the iFeature. Constructed properly, the punch feature will adjust to the thickness of any sheet-metal part to which it is applied.

The part used in the following steps is a simple sheet-metal part with one cut feature. Figure 7.17 shows the sketch underlying the cut feature. The sketch was created utilizing a single center point, which will be used for placement when inserting the punch feature. There was no need to anchor the sketch since it was created for the sole purpose of extracting a punch iFeature.

FIGURE 7.17

A sheet-metal sketch

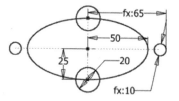

Follow these steps:

1. On the Get Started tab, click the Open button.

2. Open the file `mi_7a_027.ipt` from the `Chapter 7` directory of your `Mastering Inventor 2016` folder.

3. On the Manage tab, select the Extract iFeature tool (you'll find it on the Author panel).

4. Select Cut1 in the Model browser.

5. Click the radio button at the top of the dialog box to toggle the iFeature type from Standard iFeature to Sheet-Metal Punch iFeature.

> ### PUNCHES AND CENTER POINTS
>
> If you have created multiple center-point locations within your sketch, you will receive an error message when trying to create the punch feature. Recall that by using the Center Point icon next to the Construction icon, you can switch extra center points in your sketch to standard points so that they will not interfere. In this example, you have only one center point within the sketch, even though there are other points locating two of the circles on the ellipse. The others have been made standard points as described ahead of time.

6. Under the Manufacturing area, specify the punch ID as **K775**. Although not required, if it's included, this punch ID can be retrieved and placed onto a drawing in the form of a punch note or punch table so the shop floor will know which punch to use.

7. Click the Select Sketch button for Simplified Representation and then click Sketch3 in the Model browser. Simplified sketches are optional but may help represent complex sketches more cleanly in the detail drawing.

8. When your dialog box resembles Figure 7.18, click Save and then select the Punches folder in the Chapter 7 folder of your Mastering Inventor 2016 directory.

FIGURE 7.18

Extracting a sheet-metal iFeature

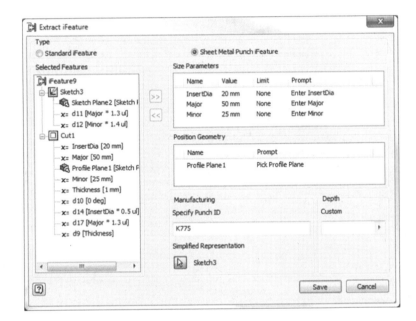

9. Name the punch feature **K775.ide** and then save the file.

IFEATURES ARE POWERFUL TOOLS

These tools allow you to quickly create standard features in your models. Examples include o-ring grooves, louvers, bosses, ribs, electrical connector punches, patterns of holes, and an infinite number of other features. Another major advantage of iFeatures is that they enforce standards. Since the iFeature can be designed to allow the user to select predefined sizes only, the possibility of error is greatly reduced. Take a few moments to examine your designs, and you'll likely see many opportunities for iFeatures.

PLACING A SHEET-METAL PUNCH FEATURE

When working on a sheet-metal part, you can access iFeatures through the Punch tool or the Insert iFeature button on the Manage tab. The Punch tool is optimized for sheet-metal parts, so unless you are placing a regular iFeature, you should always use the Punch tool. Prior to placing a feature, you must have an unconsumed, visible sketch containing one or more center points from which the punch will position itself. Follow these steps to place a sheet-metal punch:

1. On the Get Started tab, click the Open button.

2. Open the file `mi_7a_029.ipt` from the `Chapter 7` directory of your `Mastering Inventor 2016` folder.

3. Inspect the Model browser to see that Sketch2 is visible. This sketch has been prepared for you to use in placing your new punch feature on the three center points.

4. Locate and select the Punch Tool button on the Sheet Metal tab.

5. Select the `K775.ide` file you created in the previous exercise from the Punches folder and click the Open button. (If you did not complete the previous exercise, you can browse to the Punches folder of the `Chapter 7` directory and choose file `K777.ide`.) You will notice that every unconsumed center point within the sketch will be populated with the selected punch.

CENTER POINTS

If you want to reserve a sketch center point for some other feature, click the Geometry tab in the Punch Tool dialog box and hold down the **Ctrl** key while selecting the center point to be removed. If you want to place only one center point, hold down the **Ctrl** key, click the sketch away from a center point and then click the center point where you want the punch. If you have more than one visible, unconsumed sketch, the center points will not be automatically selected because you will need to tell Inventor which sketch to use.

6. Click the Geometry tab and set the angle to **90**.

7. Click the Size tab and set InsertDia to **20 mm**, Major to **50 mm**, and Minor to **25 mm**.

8. Click the Edit icon (it looks like a pencil) or click in the space below the Diameter row or on another row in the dialog box to set the row out of edit mode.

9. Click the Refresh button to see the diameter update onscreen. Note that if the diameter does not update, you probably did not click out of the Diameter row to set the edit as active. The refresh option is a bit picky in this way. Keep in mind, however, that the preview does not need to be refreshed to build to the specified value correctly. Figure 7.19 shows the punch parameters.

10. Click the Finish button to complete the punch action.

11. Click the Go To Flat Pattern button to view the flat pattern.

12. Right-click the Flat Pattern node in the Model browser and choose Edit Flat Pattern Definition.

13. Click the Punch Representation tab, set the drop-down to 2D Sketch Rep And Center Mark, and then click the OK button. Note the simplified version of the punches. This can be useful for placing grouped punches or helping to simplify drawings that have many punches on them.

FIGURE 7.19
Placing a punch

Note that you could use the Insert iFeature option to place the punches, but you would not be offered the same placement options. Instead, its behavior would be similar to that of a standard iFeature, requiring constraint of the placed punch by anchoring it to the base feature. In general, it is best to use the Punch tool for sheet-metal parts rather than placing punches as a standard iFeature.

Note that whereas the iFeature tool is available in the standard and sheet-metal environments, the Punch tool is available only in the sheet-metal environment. You can close this file without saving changes when you have finished.

Reusing Existing Geometry

Geometry reuse is a productive technique in Inventor. You can reuse existing features and sketch geometry to create additional features within the same part or even on other open parts. You don't need to create additional new sketches to utilize this technique. The following sections show how to copy sketches and features and develop dependent and independent relationships between the features.

Certification
Objective

Copying Features

Copying features in Inventor is a relatively simple procedure using the Model browser. In an existing model, simply right-click a feature within the browser and select Copy. Next, select a different face within the model, right-click, and select Paste. Figure 7.20 shows a preview of the placement and the Paste Features dialog box.

FIGURE 7.20
Copied features

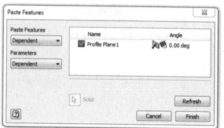

BEWARE OF PROJECTED LOOPS

When you select a face with the Project Geometry tool rather than selecting individual edges, a projected loop is created. If you select an edge, a projected edge is created. It is important to understand that when you right-click a feature that is based on projected loops, you will not get an option to copy it.

To resolve this, you can locate the projected loop by expanding the Sketch node in the browser and then right-clicking it and choosing Break Link. Once you break the link of the projected loop, you can copy the sketch. When you select just an edge to project, rather than a face, the result is a projected edge. Projected edges can be copied without breaking the link. But if you have the need to break the link of a projected edge, you can do so by right-clicking it in the graphics area and choosing Break Link.

There are two questions to consider when copying a feature:

◆ What should Inventor do with features that are built based on the feature you are copying?

◆ What should Inventor do with the dimensions for your new feature?

You'll explore the features first.

1. On the Get Started tab, click the Open button.

2. Open the file `mi_7a_031.ipt` from the `Chapter 7` directory of your `Mastering Inventor 2016` folder.

3. Right-click Extrusion2 in the Model browser, and notice that there is no Copy option. This is because there is a projected loop present in the sketch.

4. Choose Edit Sketch from the context menu.

5. Expand the Sketch2 node in the browser and notice the projected loop. This was created when the face the sketch is on was projected into the sketch.

6. Right-click the Projected Loop node and choose Break Link.

Now that the link from the loop to the face is broken, the sketch is underconstrained. In real life, you'd take the time to re-constrain the sketch so that future changes to the base feature would not upset Sketch2 or Feature2. Most likely you'd do this by deleting the projected outer lines and reapplying the 20 mm dimensions to the projected edges of the base feature. For this exercise, though, you can leave the sketch underconstrained.

7. Click the Finish Sketch button to exit the sketch.

8. Right-click Extrusion2 in the Model browser and choose Copy.

9. Right-click anywhere in the blank space of the graphics area and choose Paste.

10. Drag your cursor over any face of the part, and you will see a preview of the copied feature.

11. In the Paste Features dialog box, set the Paste Features drop-down to Dependent, and you will notice that the fillets are now in the preview as well because they are dependents of Extrusion2.

12. Click the front face of the part to position the new feature, as shown in Figure 7.20.

13. Use the plus sign–shaped arrows in the center of the copied feature to move the feature around the selected face.

14. Use the C-shaped arrow to rotate the new feature, and notice that the rotation angle is reflected in the dialog box and can be adjusted there as well.

By default, the dimensions of the new feature will be independent, meaning that because the original feature has a width of 25 mm, the new feature will have the same value, but the two will not be linked. However, if you set the Parameter drop-down to Dependent, the dimensions of the new feature will reference the original feature so that if the original width changes from 25 mm to 35 mm, the new feature follows.

15. Set the Parameter drop-down to Dependent also and then click Finish.

16. Locate and edit Sketch2 in Extrusion2 and set the diameter dimension to **6 mm**.

17. Finish the sketch, and notice that the new feature follows the edits of the original.

Once you've copied the feature, you should edit the copied feature sketch to properly anchor the sketch on the destination face. When editing a dependent sketch, notice that the dimensions indicate that they are being driven by a parameter from the original feature. If you change the dimensions from a parameter value to a numeric value, you will break the dependency with the original sketch. You can close this file without saving changes, or you can leave it open to experiment with cloning a feature from one part to another part in the next section.

Cloning

Cloning is the process of copying feature geometry from one open part to another. The cloning process creates independent features, meaning that the new feature in the new part will have no relationship to the original feature in the original part unless set up manually.

To clone a feature from one part to another, you must first have both parts open in Inventor. Here are the general steps:

1. From the source part, right-click the feature to be copied in the Model browser and choose Copy.

2. Switch to the destination part, right-click anywhere and choose Paste.

3. Drag your cursor over the face of the part you want to paste onto, and you will see a preview of the copied feature.

4. Click the face and then click Finish when the part is positioned to your liking.

The primary difference between copying features within the same part and cloning features between two parts is that parameters can be set to be independent only during the cloning process.

It will be necessary to fully constrain and anchor the feature sketch to the new part once the feature has been copied. To accomplish this, simply edit the new feature sketch and project construction geometry from the new part base feature to serve as anchor points.

Certification
Objective ## Linking Parameters Between Two Files

You can establish a relationship between two parts, between two assemblies, or between a part and an assembly by linking the files' parameters. This can allow you to place all the design information in one file and link other files to it so the intent of the design is maintained. Here are the steps to do this:

1. On the Get Started tab, click the Open button.

2. Open the file mi_7a_033.iam from the Chapter 7 directory of your Mastering Inventor 2016 folder.

This is a simple pin and plate assembly. Your goal is to link the shaft diameter of the pin to the hole diameter in the plate. To do this, you will first edit the pin part called mi_7a_034.ipt.

3. Select mi_7a_034.ipt from the browser, right-click, and choose Edit (or just double-click the pin in the graphics area).

4. Once the part is active for edits, click the Parameters button on the Manage tab.

5. At the bottom of the Parameters dialog box, click the Link button, as shown on the left of Figure 7.21.

FIGURE 7.21
Linking parameters

6. Adjust the Files Of Type drop-down to show Inventor Files; then open the file `mi_7a_035.ipt` from the `Chapter 7` directory of your `Mastering Inventor 2016` folder and click the Open button.

7. This opens the Link Parameter dialog box, allowing you to choose which parameters to link to this part. Click the button next to the parameter named Diameter and then click the OK button.

This will add the selected parameter to the user parameters in the pin part, making it available for you to reference in another parameter.

8. Locate Shaft_Diameter in the list, activate the cell in the Equation column, and clear the existing value.

9. Click the flyout arrow, as shown in Figure 7.22, and choose List Parameters from the flyout menu.

FIGURE 7.22
Setting a parameter to reference a linked parameter

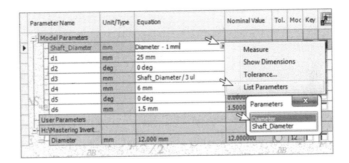

10. Select Diameter from the Parameters lists and then add **- 1 mm** so that your final shaft diameter equation is **Diameter - 1 mm**. Subtracting 1 mm from the shaft diameter creates a loose hole.

11. Click Done at the bottom of the dialog box to return to the model.

12. Click the Update button from the Quick Access bar (at the top of the graphics area) to see the model update if needed. If you have the Immediate Update check box selected in the Parameters dialog box, the part updates right away, but the updates may need to be pushed up to the assembly.

13. Finally, right-click and choose Finish Edit to return to the assembly level.

Now the shaft diameter is linked to the hole diameter in the part called `mi_7a_035.ipt`. You can open or edit `mi_7a_035.ipt` and change the hole diameter value to see the change carry through to the shaft of the pin. Linking parameters in this way allows you to place design information in one location and pull it into many other parts for automatic updates.

Copying Sketches

Quite often it is desirable to copy existing part sketches to another location within the same part or a different part. A good example of this would be creating a loft feature where each profile sketch may simply change size.

In the example shown in Figure 7.23, the part contains one unconsumed sketch and multiple work planes parallel to the XY origin plane. To copy an existing sketch, simply right-click the target sketch and select Copy. Then select the destination work plane, right-click, and select Paste. Pasted sketches are always independent of the original sketch and will create additional parameters for each copy.

FIGURE 7.23

Copying a sketch

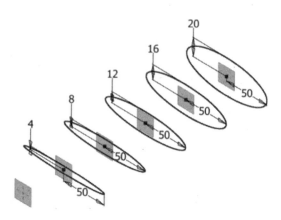

The following exercise will explore copying sketches:

1. On the Get Started tab, click the Open button.

2. Open the file mi_7a_039.ipt from the Chapter 7 directory of the Mastering Inventor 2016 folder.

3. Right-click Sketch1 in the Model browser and choose Copy.

4. Click any edge of the work plane closest to the sketch and then right-click and choose Paste.

5. Repeat this for each of the remaining work planes.

6. Select the 20 mm dimension in each of the copied sketches and adjust the minor axis on each of the sketches, decreasing the dimension value by 4 mm on each subsequent sketch, as shown in Figure 7.23.

7. Edit Rectangular Pattern1 and change the pattern count to 6.

8. Right-click any edge of the new work plane and choose New Sketch.

9. If it's not done automatically, project the origin center point to the sketch. You can use the Project Geometry tool on the Sketch tab and select the center point of the ellipse in any of the other sketches.

As you can see, copying sketches can be a quick way to duplicate repetitive geometry. To carry this thought through, you can create a loft utilizing all the sketches, including the sketch consisting of just the projected origin point. Apply a tangent condition to the projected point to achieve a result that holds the work plane as the extent of the loft.

In this example, you copied a sketch within the same part. The procedure to copy an existing sketch to another part requires that both parts be open at the same time. Right-click the original sketch and then select Copy. Then, after selecting the destination part work plane or part face in the second file, right-click and select Paste.

Once the sketches are pasted, they can be edited at any time by adding additional geometry, changing dimensions, or simply using the pasted geometry for reference.

USING FLIP NORMAL

At times you may find that your sketch "flips" when you're pasting it onto a work plane. In many cases, you can easily fix this by right-clicking the work plane and selecting Flip Normal. This flips the positive axis of the work plane. Then when you paste the sketch onto the work plane, it will no longer be flipped.

Introducing Content Center

Content Center is available in two forms: Desktop Content and the traditional Autodesk Data Management Server (ADMS)–based Content Center. The ADMS-based Content Center is a set of database libraries contained in Microsoft SQL and is generally used when sharing a central customized Content Center over a network. The other is a stand-alone install of Content Center that typically resides on your local machine. The stand-alone install is the default form of Content Center. No matter how you choose to install Content Center, you can select which libraries to use. These libraries provide standard content in several common international standards, such as ANSI, ISO, and DIN, just to name a few. Figure 7.24 shows the complete list. Once properly configured and populated, Content Center provides an organized method for part and feature reuse.

FIGURE 7.24
Content Center libraries

You can think of these libraries simply as recipes for creating parts because no actual part files exist in the Content Center file store. Instead, Content Center is a table of part parameters stored in the Content Center database. Once these library databases are installed, you can access them from Inventor and place common parts into your designs.

Understand that it is at this point the Content Center part file is created. Up until this point, the part existed only as a definition in the database table. If you work in a shared environment, the Content Center part files might typically be stored on a network server so that as users collaborate on designs, they have access to the same part files used within the assemblies. Because the Content Center library database files are just definitions of the files, they can be installed on the users' local machines or on a network server, or both.

Content Center provides support for functional design using the design accelerator, Frame Generator, and other features within Inventor. When you're using these tools, the parts generated are pulled from the Content Center libraries. You can use Content Center in conjunction with standard iParts and iFeatures organized within libraries in the project.

Configuring Content Center

Content Center, loaded with all the standard libraries, provides in excess of 800,000 variations in parts. To optimize loading, you will want to configure only the appropriate standards for your use. Installing all libraries will cause Inventor to take more time to search and index the data. There are two installation strategies for Content Center. Depending on how you work, you may want to install the desktop Content Center or the ADMS version.

INSTALLING CONTENT CENTER FOR A STAND-ALONE USER

If you work as a stand-alone user, I recommend you use the Desktop Content method. No server setup or login is required because the Content Center libraries are installed in the Libraries folder, at a path similar to C:\ProgramData\Autodesk\Inventor 2016\Content Center\Libraries\. You can insert the install media and install or reinstall the Content Center libraries at any point by following the installation steps. Once the libraries are installed, you use the Place From Content Center tool or the Open From Content Center tool to access the Content Center libraries.

INSTALLING CONTENT CENTER FOR A COLLABORATIVE ENVIRONMENT

If working in a shared group, you will likely want to install Content Center on a server location instead of, or in addition to, the Desktop Content libraries. When installing on a server, you will install the libraries on the Autodesk Data Management Server. The ADMS is essentially just the interface with which you interact with the SQL database program. Once the ADMS is installed and the required Content Center libraries are loaded, users log into the ADMS through Inventor.

When deciding whether to install Content Center libraries on a network server or install them locally, consider whether you plan to create and use a custom library. If not, you may not need to install Content Center on a server, and you can choose to install the libraries on all the local machines only. Because the standard Content Center libraries are all read-only databases, they cannot become out of sync; therefore, two users can access two different instances of the standard libraries and work without issue. If you plan to create custom Content Center libraries, however, I recommend you install on a network server so that as the library is updated over time, all users are pulling from the same source. You can consult the installation media for more information on installing the ADMS and the Content Center libraries.

DESKTOP CONTENT VS. ADMS CONTENT CENTER LIBRARIES

If both the Desktop Content and the ADMS Content Center libraries are installed, you can control which one is used by going to the Tools tab, clicking the Application Options button, selecting the Content Center tab, and selecting a radio button in the Access options. By default this is set to Inventor Desktop Content and will need to be changed to Autodesk Vault Server if the ADMS Content Center libraries are installed and are intended to be used.

MANAGING YOUR MEMORY FOOTPRINT

Installing all libraries into the ADMS will increase your overall memory usage substantially. As mentioned earlier, installing only the libraries you use will keep Content Center efficient. As you will see in the coming pages, you can create a custom Content Center library based on the standard libraries and include only what you require. Once the custom library is created, standard libraries can be removed from the ADMS. You can add them back at any time by reinstalling them from the Inventor installation disks.

CONFIGURING CONTENT CENTER LIBRARIES IN THE PROJECT FILES

Once you've installed the ADMS and the required libraries, you will need to configure the project file to ensure that all required libraries are included in the project. To do this, you will want to close all files in Inventor so that the project file can be edited. Then follow these steps:

1. In Inventor, select the Get Started tab and click the Projects button.

2. In the Project Editor dialog box, ensure that your project is set as active and click the Configure Content Center Libraries button at the lower right of the Projects dialog box to open the Configure Libraries dialog box, as shown in Figure 7.25.

FIGURE 7.25
Configuring Content Center libraries

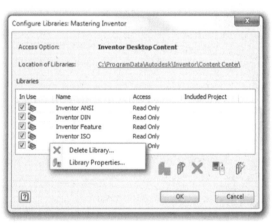

3. The buttons at the bottom of the dialog box are used to update, import, add, or remove libraries for the project. The check boxes to the left of each library will load or unload a library from your project. You can speed up Inventor's use of libraries by unchecking any libraries that you don't need to use on your current project. Unloading libraries from a project will speed up the interaction between Inventor and Content Center because fewer libraries will need to be indexed and searched.

If you only occasionally access a certain library because you typically do not work with that standard, you might install it but uncheck the In Use setting for your Inventor project. When you do need to access this library, open the Configure Libraries dialog box, check the In Use setting to load it for use, and then unload it once you have finished. Although the suggestion to add and remove libraries may seem like a hassle, it will pay off in time savings because you will not find yourself waiting for the libraries to load every time you access Content Center.

Using Content Center

Content Center is used in many areas of Inventor. Components from Content Center are used in functional-design tools, such as the Shaft Generator or Frame Generator, as well as in individual, reusable components in general assembly design. Content Center is also available for use within the part environment using the Place Feature tool.

Placing Components into an Assembly

Let's take a closer look at placing components into an assembly from Content Center.

1. Make sure you have either Desktop Content or the ADMS installed and the ANSI content library loaded to continue with this example.

2. If you are running Content Center through the ADMS, ensure that you are logged in to the ADMS by clicking the Inventor icon and selecting Vault Server ➤ Content Center Log In.

If you are already logged in or logged into Vault, Log In will be grayed out and will not be an option in your menu.

3. Enter your login information, if known. By default, the ADMS installs with a user account called Administrator with no password set. You can also select the Content Center library's Read-Only check box to access content without logging in.

4. Specify the name of the server on which you installed the ADMS. If you have installed the ADMS on your local machine, enter **localhost**. In the Database text box, enter the name of the ADMS database; the default is Vault.

Placing Parts from Content Center

Once logged in to the ADMS or if you have installed Desktop Content (there is no login required), you are ready to place parts from Content Center. To do so, follow these steps:

1. From the Get Started tab, click the Open button.

2. Open the file mi_7a_044.iam from the Chapter 7 directory of your Mastering Inventor 2016 folder.

3. On the Assemble tab, click the Place From Content Center icon. Check to see that the three buttons indicated in Figure 7.26 are selected. From left to right these buttons are Filters, AutoDrop, and Tree View.

FIGURE 7.26
Place From Content
Center settings

Filters Button   Select ANSI to filter out all other standards. To turn the filter off after this exercise, click the Filters button again and deselect ANSI. If you do not have the ANSI library installed, you can select another library, but the size and bolt names will differ from the following steps.

AutoDrop Button   This button turns on the ability to automatically size components based on geometry in the model.

Tree View Button   This button splits the screen so that the Category View pane is accessible on the left of the dialog box.

4. Select the Fasteners category in the left pane, browse to Bolts and then Round Head, select Cross Recessed Binding Head Machine Screw – Type I, and click the OK button.

5. In the model, zoom in to one of the caster wheel assemblies and take note of the empty holes.

6. Pause your mouse pointer over one of the holes on the castor plate.

You will see the AutoDrop icon activate and flicker as Inventor indexes the database for an appropriate size. If no matching size can be found in the database, a cursor note will appear saying so. If an appropriate size is found, a cursor note will display it, and a preview of the part will be shown.

7. Once the size appears, click the edge of the hole to set the screw in place. The AutoDrop toolbar will appear along with the red grip arrow.

8. Drag the grip arrow up or down to specify the length of the screw. Note that only lengths found in the database are available.

9. Click the Apply button and continue placing screws as you see fit. Experiment with placing the mouse pointer over one of the large diameters in the caster assembly to watch AutoDrop attempt to find an appropriate size. Figure 7.27 shows the AutoDrop toolbar.

FIGURE 7.27
Placing a screw
with AutoDrop

Once you've experimented with placing bolts from Content Center, you can close this file without saving changes or continue exploring the other options discussed. Here is a brief description of each of the tool icons shown in the AutoDrop toolbar in Figure 7.27:

Insert Multiple The first icon is available when Inventor identifies multiple targets that are like the selected target. In this case, the other holes in the plate are picked up and previewed. If you apply the screw now, four screws will be placed at once. If you do not want the multiples to be placed, you can click the Insert Multiple icon to turn it off.

Change Size The second icon is grayed out while Insert Multiple is on. It inserts the part and opens the Part Family dialog box, which allows you to edit the component.

Bolted Connection The next icon opens the Bolted Connection Component Generator and allows you to place bolt, nut, and washer sets as a group.

Apply The fourth icon sets the previewed components and allows you to continue placing more components of the same family.

Place The last icon sets the components and exits the AutoDrop mode.

The AutoDrop toolbar is context-sensitive, so the icons may vary depending on the component to be placed and the selected geometry. If you press **F1** on the keyboard while the AutoDrop toolbar is displayed, Inventor will open the help file and list all the icons and their descriptions.

Now that you've placed Content Center components, let's examine where Inventor is storing the newly generated Content Center files. Select the Tools tab, click Application Options, and then click the File tab. Look for the file path indicating the default Content Center files, as shown at the top of Figure 7.28.

FIGURE 7.28
Content Center
files storage path

This is where Inventor will place all standard parts placed from Content Center by default. Typically you should change this path to a path that is on the network server, particularly if you're working in a multiuser environment. If you work only on your local hard drive, you will still likely want to change the path to be similar to the path where you save your Inventor designs.

If this path is left at the default, Content Center part files will be saved on your local machine. This causes a problem when a co-worker opens an assembly you created. There is one more place where you can set this path, and that is in the project file under Folder Options, as shown at the bottom of Figure 7.28. It is important to note that a path set in the project file takes precedence over a path set in the application options. If the project file is set as Content Center Files = [Default], then the files are stored at the application options path.

Only standard Content Center files are stored at this location. Custom-sized Content Center part files, such as standard steel shapes, pipes, and so on, are stored at a path chosen by you at the time of their creation.

CUSTOMIZING CONTENT CENTER LIBRARIES

You should be aware of a few options customizing Content Center Libraries. You can find these settings on the Content Center tab of the Application Options dialog box.

Refresh Out-Of-Date Standard Parts During Placement When this option is selected, existing standard part files are automatically replaced with newer versions. For instance, if you update a standard part with your part number in the Content Center library tables but that part has already been placed in other assemblies and therefore already exists in the Content Center parts file folder, having this option selected will update the Content Center file folder and place the new version in the assemblies.

Custom Family Default Set this option to place a custom Content Center part as a standard part. When you place a custom part as standard, the part file is saved in the Content Center files folder and is considered a standard part.

Access Options This sets the source of the Content Center libraries. You can choose between Desktop Content and the ADMS/Vault server.

Standard Content Center libraries supplied with Inventor are designated as read-only and cannot be modified. If you need to create custom part libraries or modify standard content such as adding part numbers or material types, you can do so by creating a custom Content Center library. Custom libraries are initially set as read/write libraries so that you can add and modify content.

DO YOU NEED TO USE CONTENT CENTER?

Many people find the file structure of Content Center–generated files to be at odds with the way they store purchased and standard parts. If you find this is the case with your setup, you might want to use Content Center to generate parts but then save copies of them under your own file structure as needed. Often, commonly used components are generated from Content Center in this manner and then placed in a company's purchase part directory after the Part Number and Description iProperties are adjusted.

CREATING CUSTOM LIBRARIES FOR ADMS INSTALLS

You add libraries from the Autodesk Data Management Server console when using Content Center with the ADMS. You can access the ADMS by selecting Start ➤ All Programs ➤ Autodesk ➤ Autodesk Data Management ➤ Autodesk Data Management Server Console. Typically this would be done on the server machine. Figure 7.29 shows how to create a custom library.

FIGURE 7.29
Creating a custom
library in the ADMS

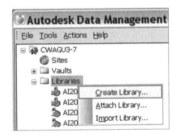

Once you're logged into the ADMS console, expand the folder in the top of the left pane, right-click the Libraries subfolder, and select Create Library. Create a new library called **Mastering Inventor**.

Once the library is created, follow these steps:

1. Select the Get Started tab.

2. Click the Projects button.

3. Click the Configure Content Center Libraries button at the bottom-right corner of the Project Editor dialog box.

4. Ensure that the In Use check box for this new library is selected so that the project is configured to include it.

CREATING CUSTOM LIBRARIES FOR DESKTOP CONTENT

You can create a custom Content Center library for Desktop Content through the Content Center configuration of the Project Editor. To do so, follow these steps:

1. Select the Get Started tab.

2. Click the Projects button.

3. Click the Configure Content Center Libraries button at the bottom-right corner of the Project Editor dialog box.

4. Click the Create Library button and enter **Mastering Inventor** into the input box, as shown in Figure 7.30.

FIGURE 7.30
Creating a custom library with Desktop Content

5. Click the OK button.

6. Ensure that the In Use check box for this new library is selected so that the project is configured to include it. Click OK to close the Configure Libraries window and then click Save on the project editor window.

COPYING EXISTING LIBRARIES INTO CUSTOM LIBRARIES

After creating a custom library, you can copy entire or partial contents of existing standard libraries into your custom library. You might use this process when you want to simplify one of the standard libraries, remove portions of the library that are not needed in your work environment, or edit component properties such as part numbers. Here are the steps to copy families to a custom library:

1. Access the Content Center Editor from within Inventor by selecting the Manage tab and clicking the Editor button on the Content Center panel. (If you don't have a file open, you will find the Content Center Editor under Tools ➤ Content Center.) This editor looks similar to the Content Center dialog box.

2. Locate the library or the part family within a library that you want to copy, right-click, and choose Copy To ➤ Mastering Inventor, as shown in Figure 7.31.

FIGURE 7.31
Copying a Content
Center family

The library must be included in the project file configuration list in order to be visible within the editor. If you copy an entire library to your custom library, then the entire folder structure and contents will be replicated in your custom library. If you copy an individual part to your custom library, then only the affected category structure will be replicated in the custom library along with the copied part.

To copy only a portion of the category structure, browse to the last hierarchical portion of the structure that you want to replicate. Otherwise, starting from the top and copying the structure will replicate the entire structure.

SETTING CATEGORY PROPERTIES

Each category within Content Center contains category properties. Within the category properties is general information regarding the category itself. The General tab contains the category name, category image, and source library.

CREATING MULTIPLE MATERIAL TYPES FOR CONTENT CENTER FAMILIES

It's pretty easy for your design department to have the Content Center parts reflect their own internal part numbers so that bills of materials and parts lists will extract this information automatically. Doing this is as simple as copying the appropriate standard Content Center categories to a custom read/write library and editing the tables to include the new part numbers.

However, if multiple material types are used for the same component type, then multiple copies of the family can be made to accommodate this. For instance, if you use stainless steel fasteners of a given type for certain design instances and also use galvanized fasteners of the same type in other design instances, you would most likely need these to have separate part numbers.

You can use the Material Guide to add materials in one of three ways.

◆   You can edit a family table and select the members to add new materials to. Then click the Material Guide button or right-click and choose Material Guide to copy the selected members, add them to the family table, and assign the new materials to them.

◆   You can use the Material Guide for an entire family, copying all members with a new material and adding them to the existing family. Select the family in the Content Center Editor and click the Material Guide button, or right-click and choose Material Guide. Then choose the option called Add Materials As New Family Members, thereby copying all members into the same family table and setting a new material at the same time.

◆   You can create new families of a different material as well. Select the family in the Content Center Editor and click the Material Guide button, or right-click and choose Material Guide. Then choose the option Create New Family For Each Material, thereby copying the entire existing family and setting a new material for this new family at the same time.

The Parameters tab contains parameters used within the category to assist in the description of parts located within that category. Figure 7.32 illustrates the parameter list in the ANSI Socket Head category.

FIGURE 7.32

Socket head parameters

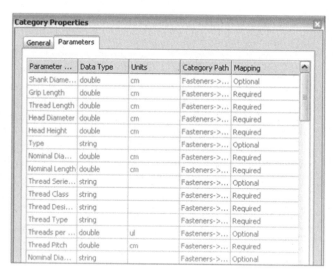

Within these parameters, some are optional and some are required. If you are placing a part within this category, you must map your part properties to all required fields for proper operation. Optional fields do not require mapping.

What this means is that if you are planning on publishing a large number of your own parts to Content Center, your part parameters must match the category parameters. If you are unable to match the parameters, consider creating a new category.

EXPECT SOME INCONSISTENCY

The mapping required for Content Center is not consistent for all types of parts because of the evolution of these tools over time. Some of the categories require authoring before you can publish a part. Other categories are open for publishing without authoring. The requirements for restricted categories are driven by tools such as the design accelerator, Bolted Connection, and AutoDrop, which require certain parameters so they can intelligently place components. One inconsistency is Frame Generator. Since Content Center steel shapes predate Frame Generator, which originally had its own shape library, there weren't any authoring requirements. Just be aware of the inconsistencies.

Right-clicking an individual Content Center part will allow you to view the family properties and mapping of that part. Compare the category parameters of the part with the parameters of the intended category. Matching the two parameter lists ensures that the part will map easily into that category.

EDITING A CUSTOM CONTENT CENTER FAMILY

A Content Center family is an individual part, similar to an iPart. The part consists of a standard factory part with a family table attached that generates any of the optional table values.

You can edit any individual part by first switching the library view to your custom library designation, as shown in Figure 7.33.

FIGURE 7.33
Editing a Content
Center part

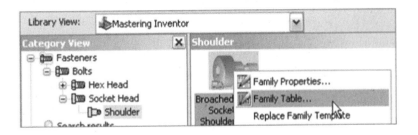

In the previous example, you switched the library view to the Mastering Inventor custom library. Right-click a part located within the custom library and select Family Table. This launches a dialog box that allows the user to modify values, copy/paste, add/delete rows, or suppress existing rows within the table. The dialog box also allows the addition, deletion, and modification of columns and properties, and you have the option to edit tables in Excel.

Publishing Parts to Content Center

Developing a process for reusing parts within your company's design environment is essential for standardization and improved productivity. Part of this process may include publishing existing Inventor parts stored in project libraries. Both normal parts and iParts can be published to a custom Content Center library.

The act of publishing a standard part into the custom library adds a family table to the published part. Exported part parameters will be converted to table parameters when published to the custom Content Center. iPart tables are converted to family tables when published.

PREPARING THE PART FOR PUBLISHING

If the part you intend to publish will be included in an existing Content Center family category (that is, fasteners, shaft parts, and so on), you can use the Component Authoring tool to prepare components with the necessary properties for use as "smart" content in the Content Center library. You can do this by following these steps:

1. On the Get Started tab, click the Open button.

2. Open the file mi_7a_064.ipt from the Chapter 7 directory of your Mastering Inventor 2016 folder.

3. Select the Manage tab and click the Component Authoring button on the Author panel (you may need to use the drop-down to find it).

4. From the drop-down list, select Fasteners ➤ Bolts and select Other. Note that the graphics and selection prompts change depending on the category of component selected.

5. Select the geometry for each row in the dialog box that corresponds to the dialog box graphic to map iMate placement to this part (iMates are preprogrammed Assembly constraints).

6. Click the Parameter Mapping tab. Note that the parameters listed in the light yellow/orange rows are required, whereas the others are optional. Click the … button for the Grip Length row.

7. In the Part Template Parameters dialog box, expand the browser to find Parameters ➤ User and select GripLength. This maps the part parameter to the corresponding family table parameter. Click the OK button.

8. Map the Nominal Diameter and the Nominal Length parameters to the NomDiameter and NomLength model parameters, respectively (you can find these at Parameters ➤ Model rather than Parameters ➤ User).

9. Click the OK button to write the mapped parameters and iMates to the part file. You could also click the Publish Now button to start the publishing process.

You can author parts ahead of time and use the Batch Publish tool to publish one or more unopened parts at once. Or you can publish one part at a time, as covered in the next section. Figure 7.34 shows the Component Authoring dialog box tabs. You can close this part without saving changes and move on to the next section, which is about publishing parts.

FIGURE 7.34
Component
Authoring tabs

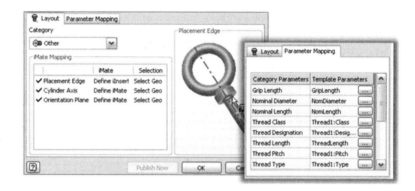

PUBLISHING THE PART

To publish a part to Content Center, you must have a custom library with read/write capability created, and your current project file must be configured to include this custom library. In this example, you will publish a simple part that has already been authored to the custom read/write Content Center library called Mastering Inventor. If you haven't already created this library, review the steps in the section "Creating Custom Libraries for Desktop Content" or "Creating Custom Libraries for ADMS Installs," depending on which method applies to your setup. Follow these steps to publish a part:

1. On the Get Started tab, click the Open button.

2. Browse for the file `mi_7a_068.ipt` located in the `Chapter 7` directory of the `Mastering Inventor 2016` folder and click the Open button.

3. Select the Manage tab and click the Publish Part button on the Content Center panel.

4. Select the Mastering Inventor library, and set the language as required; then click Next.

5. Ensure that Category To Publish To is set to Fasteners ➤ Bolts ➤ Other; then click Next.

6. Notice that most of the parameters are already mapped; this is because this part has previously been authored following the steps in the section "Preparing the Part for Publishing." Recall that all parameters in the light yellow/orange rows are required. Click the ... button for the Thread Type row.

7. In the Part Template Parameters dialog box, expand the browser to find Threads ➤ Thread1, select Type, and then click the OK button.

8. Click Next in the Publish Guide dialog box.

9. Select Nominal Diameter, Nominal Length, and Part Number in the left pane and use the arrow button to include them in the right pane. This defines keys that are available for selection upon placement of the Content Center part once published. At least one Key column must be defined. Click Next to continue.

10. Enter **EyeBolt** for the family name and set the Standard Organization option to ANSI. Only the family name is required; however, designating the Standard Organization option allows the part to be listed when filtering per standard. You can also type a custom standard into the field, such as your company name. This allows you to create a filter for the parts you published.

11. Click Next, and notice the preview thumbnail. You can use the Browse icon to select a different graphic file for use as a thumbnail, if one exists.

12. Click Publish to complete the task and add this part to your custom Content Center library. Click the OK button in the successful publish confirmation box.

This creates the part family table in the Content Center library, but at this point there is only one row in the table. Typically you will want to add a row for each size or different type of the component. You can do this by using the Content Center Editor (on the Manage tab). Figure 7.35 shows the family key and properties steps of the Publish Guide. You can close this part without saving changes.

FIGURE 7.35
Publishing a part to Content Center

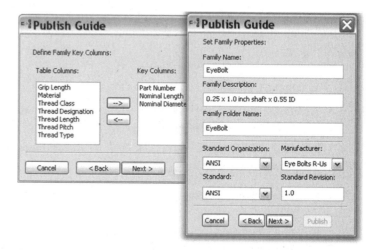

You can also convert a part to a table-driven iPart before publishing and include the rows for each size and type of the part configuration in the iPart table. Once you have a workable iPart that behaves correctly, you can open the original factory iPart and publish the part. The iPart may be a custom iPart or a fully table-driven factory. iParts containing multiple row definitions in the table will convert to a fully table-driven Content Center part. You can find more information on iParts in the section "Working with iParts" at the beginning of this chapter.

Before using a newly published Content Center component in production, test the part in a blank assembly for proper function.

ADDING A NEW CATEGORY TO CONTENT CENTER

If you need a unique category for your own specific parts, you can simply add a new family of parts instead of using an existing category. You can do this from the Content Center Editor (accessed from the Manage tab). Make sure the library view is set to view only the read/write library in which you intend to create the new category and that the tree view is enabled. Then right-click in the blank space in the Category View pane and choose Create Category. You can also create a subcategory by right-clicking an existing category and selecting Create Category.

The Bottom Line

Create and modify iParts. iParts are the solution to creating parts that allow for an infinite number of variations without affecting other members of the same part family already used within your designs.

> **Master It** You use a purchased specialty part in your designs and would like to create the many size configurations that this part comes in ahead of time for use within assembly design. How would this be done?

Create and use iFeatures and punches. Creating a library of often-used features is essential to standardization and improved productivity within your design workflow.

> **Master It** You want to be able to place common punches, slots, and milled features quickly rather than having to generate the feature every time. What is the best way to approach this?

Copy and clone features. You do not have to create iFeatures to reuse various part features in your designs. If a part feature will have limited use in other designs, it is often better to simply copy it from part to part or from face to face on the same part.

> **Master It** You need to reuse features within a part or among parts. You consider iFeatures but realize that this feature is not used often enough to justify setting up an iFeature. How would you proceed?

Link parameters between two files. Linking design parameters between two or more files allows you to control design changes from a single source, making it easy to update an entire design from one file.

Master It You want to specify the overall length and width of a layout design in a base part and then have other components update as changes are made to this part. What are the methods to do this?

Configure, create, and access Content Center parts. Content Center provides a great opportunity to reuse database-created geometry within assemblies and within functional-design modules. The Content Center Editor provides the means to add custom content into Content Center. You can create and add custom libraries to your current project file.

Master It You would like to change the part numbers in some Content Center components to match the part numbers your company uses. You would also like to add proprietary components to Content Center. How do you customize Content Center?

Chapter 8

Assembly Design Workflows

A typical assembly file is composed of links to the included *components* and *assembly relationships* *(constraints)*. The components are parts or subassemblies that exist as separate files. When components are placed into an assembly file, links to those individual files are created in the assembly file. Initially a component is free-floating and can be moved and rotated in any direction unless it's grounded in place or constrained to other components.

For example, if you were to create an assembly of a simple drilled base plate and a bolt to be inserted in the hole, you would have three files.

◆ The assembly file (with a filename extension of .iam)

◆ The base plate part file (with a filename extension of .ipt)

◆ The bolt part file (with a filename extension of .ipt)

When the part files are placed into the assembly file, links are created to the locations of those files. If the hole in the base plate part is moved, the assembly is automatically updated to reflect that change since it is linked to the part file. To assemble the plate and bolt, at least one assembly relationship would be created by selecting the shaft of the bolt and the hole in the plate. Assembly relationships can be created using the Constraint tool or the Joint tool. Assembly relationships have two functions:

◆ They define how two or more components relate to one another.

◆ They limit the degrees of freedom any one component has in the assembly.

Developing a good assembly design workflow is paramount to achieving performance, flexibility, and stability in your designs. In this chapter, you'll explore several types of workflows to achieve that goal. Included in this chapter is a discussion on how to use subassemblies to enhance performance. Using subassemblies within your design can substantially improve performance. Component count can be in the hundreds of thousands of parts, as long as you have sufficient memory on your system.

In this chapter, you'll learn to

◆ Create assembly relationships using the Constraint and Joint tools

◆ Organize designs using structured subassemblies

◆ Work with adaptive components

◆ Create assembly-level features

- Manage bills of materials

- Use positional reps and flexible assemblies together

- Copy assembly designs for reuse and configuration

- Substitute a single part for entire subassemblies

- Work with assembly design accelerators and generators

- Use design calculators

Assembly Relationships

Mastering the use of the Constraint and Joint tools to create functional assembly relationships is an important part of learning to create assemblies in the Autodesk® Inventor® program. Assembly relationships are the glue and nails of construction when it comes to building your assemblies. Properly using assembly relationships will permit the construction of stable assemblies, assist in developing stack-up tolerances, and allow parts to be driven to show the animation of a process.

If you use assembly relationships improperly, you can create a nightmare of broken and redundant relationships, preventing assemblies from functioning properly, destroying assembly performance, and causing rework. Understanding how assembly relationships function in an assembly will help assure success in building and editing your design.

Another important concept for assembly relationships is the idea of removing or defining a component's degrees of freedom. When you create relationships between assembly components, you are also changing the way those components are allowed to move in the assembly, just as you do when you assemble parts in the real world.

Degrees of Freedom

Initially each component within an assembly file possesses six degrees of freedom. The degrees of freedom (DOF) are bidirectional and consist of three axial degrees of freedom along the origin x-, y-, and z- axes, as well as full rotational freedom around the same axes. You might think of degrees of freedom like the roll, pitch, and yaw of an aircraft. For a pilot to maintain control of the aircraft, the side-to-side roll, the up-and-down pitch, and the clockwise or counterclockwise yaw of the aircraft must be controlled. Likewise, you will create assembly relationships between your components to prevent them from moving freely or at least to control the way in which they are allowed to move.

For ease of use when learning to create assembly relationships between components, it might help to make the degrees of freedom visible through the View tab by clicking the Degrees Of Freedom button. As constraints are applied to your component, the DOF triad will change to show only the remaining DOF. When the component is fully constrained, the triad will disappear. Figure 8.1 shows the Degrees Of Freedom button and the resulting triad.

You can also analyze the degrees of freedom for the complete assembly. The Degree Of Freedom Analysis button is located in the Productivity panel drop-down list on the Assemble tab. A dialog box displays each component (part or subassembly) at the active level of the assembly. The number of translation and rotation DOF are listed.

FIGURE 8.1

Activating the Degrees
Of Freedom view

If you select Animate Freedom at the bottom of the dialog box and then select a component in the list, it will move to show the DOF, assuming it is not already fully constrained. Figure 8.2 shows the Degree Of Freedom Analysis dialog box.

FIGURE 8.2

Animating an under-
constrained compo-
nent from the Degree
Of Freedom Analysis
dialog box

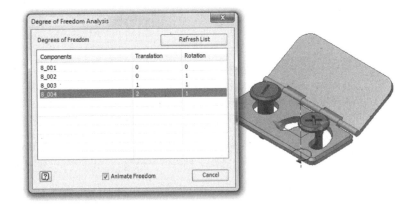

Follow these steps to animate the underconstrained component:

1. Click the Get Started tab and choose Open.

2. Browse for the file `mi_8a_001.iam` located in the `Chapter 08` directory of your `Mastering Inventor 2016` folder and click the Open button.

3. Click the View tab and then click the Degrees Of Freedom button to turn on the degrees-of-freedom triad for each part.

You'll notice that each part has an icon denoting the axes it is able to translate along or rotate around. There are only three triads shown because the part called 8–001 is grounded and cannot move at all. You can see this by looking at the browser and noting the push pin icon shown on that part.

ENABLE THE PRODUCTIVITY PANEL

If you don't see the Productivity panel, you might need to enable it. To do so, first make sure the Assemble tab is active; then right-click anywhere on the ribbon menu and choose Show Panels. Select Productivity from the list.

4. Click the Assemble tab, click the drop-down on the Productivity panel, and select Degree Of Freedom Analysis.

5. Select Animate Freedom at the bottom of the dialog box.

6. Click 8_002 in the list. Watch it rotate in the free axis, demonstrating its DOF.

7. Click 8_003 in the list. Watch it rotate and move up and down, demonstrating its DOF.

8. Click 8_004 in the list. Watch it rotate and slide along the face of the plate in two directions, demonstrating its DOF.

These tools can be helpful when you are trying to determine the assembly relationships applied to components in an existing assembly. In addition to animating DOF, you can also just click and drag a part to see how it can move. In either case, you might find that leaving the DOF triads turned on will help you as you learn how assembly relationships work and are created. You can close the current file without saving changes and continue on to the next section.

Grounded Components

A component can be grounded in place so that it cannot move or rotate unintentionally. A grounded component is fully constrained and has 0 degrees of freedom. Every assembly should have at least one grounded component so that it will be stable. If components are not grounded, the assembly can become misaligned from the x-, y-, and z-axes and will cause problems when you try to detail the assembly in the drawing environment. You can ground or unground any component in an assembly by right-clicking it and selecting Grounded from the context menu.

PLACING COMPONENTS IN AN ASSEMBLY

To place components in an assembly, you can use the Place button on the Assemble tab and then browse to locate the component. To ground a component while you place it, you can right-click during the placement preview and choose Place Grounded At Origin.

Additionally, you can drag part and assembly files from Windows Explorer and drop them into the assembly. To place additional instances of components already in the assembly, you can copy and paste components from the graphic window or simply click and drag them from the browser.

In certain workflows where parts are placed into the assembly in the correct position and orientation to begin with, all components can be grounded. This is done automatically when an assembly is created from a multi-body part using the Make Components tool. If a particular component needs to be adjusted, it can be ungrounded and then constrained using Assembly constraints or assembly connections.

The ground-all strategy can also be used to rebuild assemblies that have a great many errant Assembly constraints resulting from major uncontrolled changes. For instance, if you opened an assembly that has 50 constraints and of those 42 have errors, you might be better off to select all the components and ground them in place. Next, you would expand the Relationships folder in the browser and then select all the relationships with errors and delete them. You could then leave everything grounded, or unground and reconstrain them one at a time in order to fix the assembly.

How the Constrain Tool Works

In Inventor, Assembly constraints are used to attach parts or subassemblies together, creating assembly relationships between the components and therefore defining the way they fit together based on the selection of faces, edges, or vertices and user-defined parameters. In general practice, the function of constraints follows real-world assembly techniques where fasteners, adhesives, and welds attach one component to another.

There are eight basic types of constraints in Inventor. Most of the constraint types have multiple solution types that can be used to achieve the result you are looking for. Here is a list of the constraint types and their solutions:

Mate constraints position components face to face or adjacent to one another.

◆ *The Mate solution* positions selected faces normal to one another, with faces coincident; imagine two plates butted together.

◆ *The Flush solution* aligns components adjacent to one another with faces flush; imagine two plates flushed along an outside corner.

Angle constraints position two components at a specified angle to define a pivot point.

◆ The *Directed Angle solution* always applies the right-hand rule to selected faces or edges.

◆ The *Undirected Angle solution* allows either orientation and is used in situations where component orientation flips.

◆ The *Explicit Reference Vector solution* defines the direction-of-rotation axis.

Tangent constraints position two components to contact at a point of tangency.

◆ The *Inside solution* positions the first selected component inside the second selected component at the tangent point.

◆ The *Outside solution* positions the first selected component outside the second selected component at the tangent point.

Insert constraints are a combination of a face-to-face Mate constraint between planar faces and a Mate constraint between the axes of the two components.

◆ The *Opposed solution* aligns the mates for the second selected component.

◆ The *Aligned solution* reverses the mate direction of the second selected component.

Symmetry constraints position two components symmetrically to both sides of a selected plane or planar face. The Symmetry constraint is typically used in conjunction with other assembly relationships.

Rotation constraints allow one component to rotate based on the selection of a second component.

◆ *The Rotation solution* allows the first selected component to rotate in relation to another component using a specified ratio; imagine two gears.

◆ *The Rotation-Translation solution* allows the first selected component to rotate as it translates the face of another component; imagine a rack and pinion.

Transitional constraints specify the relationship between a cylindrical component and a contiguous set of faces on another component, such as a cam in a slot.

UCS constraints can align components using a custom user coordinate system (UCS) from each component.

When using constraints, a minimum of two constraints are required to fully constrain two components together so that their relationship is fully defined. Underconstrained components allow motion in the unconstrained axis or plane. Components that are fully contained within a subassembly will not figure into the constraint analysis when the top-level assembly is opened or modified, so it is typically best for the performance of your assembly files to fully constrain all components that are not meant to be moveable. See "Working with Constraints" later in the chapter for more information.

How the Joint Tool Works

The Joint tool allows you to define the working relationship between a pair of components with a single joint relationship. With the Constraint tool you might create multiple constraint relationships to remove degrees of freedom; by contrast, you might achieve the same results with just one joint relationship by defining the degrees of freedom you intended to remain. Although you can achieve the same result using the Constraint tool that you can with the Joint tool, the Joint tool results in fewer assembly relationships, which can be much easier to manage later.

Inventor offers six basic types of joints, as well as an Automatic option that will choose a type based on the selected inputs. Here are the joint types and options:

Automatic joints create either a Rigid, Rotational, Cylindrical, or Ball joint, depending on the geometry of the selections.

Rigid joints position a component in place and remove all degrees of freedom. This joint type is used for glued, welded, or bolted joints that do not move.

Rotational joints position a component in place and create one rotational degree of freedom. This joint type is used for hinged joints and levers, and it can be created with a specified limit value.

Cylindrical joints position a component in place and create one translational and one rotational degree of freedom. This joint type is used for creating a joint between a shaft and a hole, for example, and can be created with a specified limit value.

Ball joints position a component in place and create three rotational degrees of freedom. This joint type is used for socket and ball joint type joints and can be created with a specified limit value.

Slider joints position a component in place and create one translational degree of freedom. This joint type is used for hinged joints, levers, and so on, and it can be created with a specified limit value.

Planar joints position a component in place and create two translational and one rotational degree of freedom perpendicular to the planar face. This joint type is used when one object will move along a planar surface such as a conveyor, and it can be created with a specified limit value.

See "Working with Joint Relationships" later in the chapter for more information.

Working with Constraints

As mentioned, several types of constraints are available for use in an assembly. To know which one to use and when, you should be familiar with each. Keep in mind, however, that certain constraint types are used more often than others. In the following pages, you will explore the creation of the various constraint types.

THE MATE CONSTRAINT

The Mate constraint type consists of two solutions: Mate and Flush. Figure 8.3 compares the two solutions. On the far left the selections are shown, in the middle the Mate solution is shown, and on the right the Flush solution is shown.

FIGURE 8.3
Mate and Flush
solutions

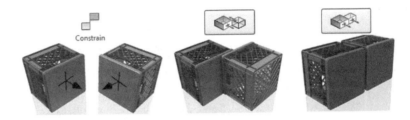

To explore the Mate constraint options, you will open a simple fixture assembly and assemble two plates to match the completed assembly next to it:

1. Click the Get Started tab and choose Open.

2. Browse for the file `mi_8a_002.iam` located in the `Chapter 8` directory of your `Mastering Inventor 2016` folder and click the Open button.

3. Select the View tab and click the Degrees Of Freedom button to turn on the DOF triad for each underconstrained part.

4. On the Assemble tab, click the Constrain button (or press **C** on the keyboard).

5. In the Place Constraint dialog box, ensure that the Assembly tab is active and the Mate button is selected for the type. Make sure the Preview check box is selected and the Predict Offset And Orientation check box is cleared.

Within the Place Constraint dialog box, you have three check boxes.

Pick Part First   This check box, indicated by the small red cube, is useful when parts are partially obscured or are positioned in such a way that clicking a face or edge is difficult. This option requires you to first select the component and then filters the selectable geometry to that single component.

Predict Offset And Orientation   This button measures the distance between the selected faces, allowing you to eyeball a part placement and then retrieve the distance. If the check box is not selected, a default of 0 is entered for the offset.

Show Preview   This check box, denoted by the eyeglasses icon, controls whether the selected components will adjust position or orientation so you can review the constraint before clicking the Apply button or the OK button to actually create it.

6. For Selection 1, click the orange face on the part with the triangular feature. Watch the onscreen highlights to be sure you select the face and not an edge. It may be helpful to zoom in.

7. For Selection 2, click the circular face on the base part.

You should see the part "snap" into place based on your selection points. This is just a preview of the constraint and is controlled by the Preview check box. Notice that the first and second geometry-selection buttons are color-coded in the Place Constraint dialog box. Also notice that as you select faces, they are shaded to match the first and second geometry selections.

8. To adjust the constraint selection, click the Selection 2 button in the Place Constraint dialog box. This removes the previous selection (the circular face) and allows you to reselect the mating face.

9. For the reselection, click the orange face on the base plate.

10. Click Apply to place the Mate constraint on the two parts.

11. Select the yellow face of the base plate and the yellow face of the side plate for Selection 1 and Selection 2 (again, ensure that you are selecting faces and not edges).

12. You should see the two yellow faces mate together in a way that is not what you want. Click the Flush button in the Solutions area of the dialog box, and you should see the preview update to give a more desirable result.

13. Click the OK button to place the Flush constraint and close the dialog box.

At this point, the DOF triad should have only one remaining arrow, indicating that all of the other DOF triads have been removed as the constraints were added.

14. Click and drag the part with the triangular feature and note that it will slide in the direction indicated by the DOF symbol, and only in that direction.

You can click and drag the part and see that it slides back and forth in the unconstrained direction indicated by the arrow. Leave this file open and continue to the next section, which discusses the Free Rotate and Free Move tools.

Using Free Rotate and Free Move

Next, you will place the final constraint required to fully assemble the two parts. But before placing the remaining constraint, it may be helpful to rotate the part so that you can easily select the required faces. To do so, you will use the Free Rotate tool. The Free Rotate tool allows you to rotate a selected component and rotate just it in the assembly. The Free Rotate tool suspends any assembly relationships currently involving the selected component to allow it to be rotated. The assembly relationships are reactivated when the Update button is clicked or when some other action, such as placing another constraint, forces an update. The Free Move tool works the same as the Free Rotate tool regarding assembly relationships. Continue from the previous step to see how this works:

1. On the Assemble tab, click the Free Rotate button.

2. Select the part with the triangular feature, and you will see the rotate "globe" appear.

◆ For free rotation, click inside the rotate globe and drag in short strokes.

◆ To rotate about the horizontal axis, click the top or bottom handle of the rotate globe and drag vertically.

◆ To rotate about the vertical axis, click the left or right handle of the 3D rotate symbol and drag horizontally.

◆ To rotate flat to the screen, place your cursor over the edge of the globe until the symbol changes to a circle and then click and drag around the globe.

3. Spin the part so you can see the purple face.

4. Right-click and choose Done to exit the Free Rotate tool.

5. On the Assemble tab, click the Constrain button.

6. Select the purple face on each part and then click the OK button.

This will fully constrain the part and remove the final DOF arrow from the display. You can continue to experiment with Assembly constraints on your own by copying and pasting multiple instances of the parts and then constraining them together, or you can close this file without saving changes and continue to the next section to explore more constraint options.

Editing and Deleting Constraints

Each of the constraints you placed in the previous steps was added to the browser under the parts involved. You can access these constraints to make changes or delete them by expanding the browser node for one of the components. In the following steps, you will edit and delete a constraint:

1. Click the Get Started tab and choose Open.

2. Browse for the file mi_8a_003.iam located in the Chapter 08 directory of your Mastering Inventor 2016 folder and click the Open button.

3. Expand the plus icon next to both of the parts in the browser to reveal the constraints listed below them. There are two Mates and one Flush constraining these two parts.

4. Right-click the Flush constraint and select Edit.

   You'll notice that the options are much like those used to create the constraint. You can reselect selection inputs 1 and 2, modify the solution from Flush to Mate, or even change the type. In this case, you will add an offset value.

5. Enter –10 mm in the Offset input box. If the preview button is selected, you should see the part adjust to preview the flush offset.

6. Click the OK button to accept the edit.

7. Click the Flush constraint in the browser again. Notice that it now displays the offset value.

8. At the bottom of the browser is an input box where you can adjust the offset without needing to bring up the edit dialog box. Type **12 mm** and press the **Enter** key on the keyboard. The part will adjust to the new offset.

9. Double-click the icon next to the Flush constraint in the browser.

10. An Edit Dimension box appears, offering another way to edit the offset parameter for this Flush constraint.

THE SHOW AND HIDE RELATIONSHIPS TOOLS

In addition to locating constraints in the browser, you can use the Show Relationships tool to select a component and locate all the assembly relationships that involve it. Once the relationship glyphs are shown, you can right-click any of them and choose from a number of options, such as Edit, Delete, Suppress, and so on. You can then use the Hide All Relationships tool to turn off the display of the relationship glyphs in the graphics area.

If any assembly relationships contain errors, you can use the Show Sick Relationships tool to find them quickly.

---

11. It is often helpful to name constraint offset parameters for use later. Type **Block_Offset = 40 mm** into the box and then click the green check mark button (or press the **Enter** key).

12. On the Manage tab, click the Parameters button.

13. In the resulting dialog box, you'll see the Block_Offset parameter in the list. Note that the other two parameters are for the Mate constraints. Click the Done button to exit the Parameters dialog box.

14. Select the View tab and click the Degrees Of Freedom button to turn on the DOF triad for each underconstrained part. In this case, no triads appear because the assembly is currently fully constrained.

15. Right-click the Flush constraint in the browser and choose Delete. You'll now see a DOF arrow showing you that the part is free to slide along one axis.

16. Click and drag the part to see it move in its free axis.

17. On the Assemble tab, click the Constrain button.

18. In the Place Constraint dialog box, click the Predict Offset And Orientation check box (find it next to the Preview check box).

19. Set the solution to Flush and then select the yellow faces of the two parts.

20. Note the offset value reports the current distance between the two yellow faces. Enter **Block_Offset = 20 mm** and then click the OK button.

Mate and Flush constraints will likely make up a majority of the constraint types you edit and create. Take the time to master these constraints, and you will find the other constraint types much easier to learn. You can close this file without saving changes. If you'd like more practice with Mate and Flush constraints, you can open the files `mi_8a_104.iam`, `mi_8a_105.iam`, `mi_8a_106.iam`, and `mi_8a_107.iam` (located in the `Chapter 08` directory of your `Mastering Inventor 2016` folder) and assemble them using the concepts you just learned. Use the assembled parts as an example to put together the unassembled parts in each of these files.

Mate to Edges, Centerlines, and Vertices

In addition to selecting faces for creating Mate constraints, you can use edges, centerlines, and vertices as selections. When using edges or centerlines, keep in mind that you are defining a different number of degrees of freedom than when using faces; therefore, the results can be quite different. It is also important to understand that edges and centerlines have no negative or positive value, and therefore edge-to-edge type constraints are not a good choice for creating mate offsets. Instead, use a face-to-edge mate in those cases.

Depending on the available geometry, you will often need to use the Select Other drop-down menu tool to cycle through the available selections to select an edge or vertex. To use the Select Other tool, hover over a selection and wait for the Select Other drop-down menu to appear. Then select the available geometry from the list. Figure 8.4 shows the Select Other tool being used to select a center point on the left, an axis in the center, and a cylindrical face on the right.

FIGURE 8.4
Using the Select Other tool

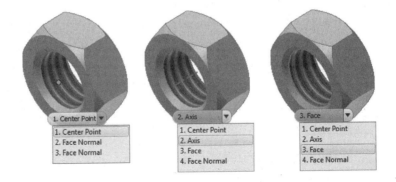

THE ANGLE CONSTRAINT

The Angle constraint permits three solutions within this constraint type. The solutions are Directed Angle, Undirected Angle, and Explicit Reference Vector. The Directed Angle solution always applies the right-hand rule, meaning the angle rotation will function in a counterclockwise direction.

The Undirected Angle allows either counterclockwise or clockwise direction, resolving situations where a component orientation will flip during a constraint drive or drag operation.

The Explicit Reference Vector solution allows for the definition of a z-axis vector by adding a third click to the selection. This option will reduce the tendency of an Angle constraint to flip to an alternate solution during a constraint drive or drag. Figure 8.5 illustrates the selections required for this solution.

FIGURE 8.5

Explicit reference vector

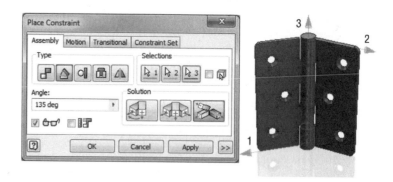

Follow these steps to explore the Angle constraint:

1. Click the Get Started tab and click the Open button.

2. Browse for the file mi_8a_007.iam located in the Chapter 08 directory of your Mastering Inventor 2016 folder and click the Open button.

3. On the Assemble tab, click the Constrain button (or type **C** on the keyboard).

4. In the Type area of the Place Constraint dialog box, select the Angle button.

5. In the Solution area, click the Directed Angle button.

6. For Selection 1, click the large face of the painted board that the hinges are mounted on.

7. For Selection 2, click the large face of the unpainted board that the hinges are mounted on.

8. Enter **90** into the Angle input box, and note that the preview displays as expected.

9. Click the Selection 1 and Selection 2 buttons to clear them and then select the unpainted board for Selection 1 and the painted board for Selection 2. Pay attention to which selection button is pushed in as you select to ensure that you get this right.

PLACE ASSEMBLY CONSTRAINTS USING ALT+DRAG

Rather than using the Place Constraint dialog box, you can press and hold the **Alt** key and then drag a component into position. Constraints are inferred based on the type of geometry selected. The constraint is previewed in the graphics area as you drag over the components involved. To set a specific constraint, release the Alt key and enter one of the following shortcut keys. You can press the **spacebar** to flip the constraint solution, from Mate to Flush, for example.

◆ **M** or **1** changes to a Mate constraint.

◆ **A** or **2** changes to an Angle constraint.

◆ **T** or **3** changes to a Tangent constraint.

◆ **I** or **4** changes to an Insert constraint.

◆ **R** or **5** changes to a Rotation motion constraint.

◆ **S** or **6** changes to a Translation motion (slide) constraint.

◆ **X** or **8** changes to a Transitional constraint.

You will see from the result that the 90-degree angle is dependent on the selection order. In this case, you could enter **–90** to flip the angles also, but had you selected edges rather than faces, entering **–90** would not work. Next, you will explore the Undirected Angle solution.

10. To clear your selections and input before continuing, click the Cancel button to exit the Place Constraint dialog and then click the Constrain button to bring it back up.

11. In the Type area of the Place Constraint dialog box, click the Angle button; then in the Solution area, click the Undirected Angle button.

12. Select the two faces and enter **90** (for 90 degrees) again. You'll note the preview updates as expected.

13. Click the Selection 1 and Selection 2 buttons to clear them and then select the unpainted board for Selection 1 and the painted board for Selection 2. Pay attention to which selection button is pushed in as you select to ensure that you get this right.

You will notice that the angle is not dependent on the selection order. And if you try entering **–90** for the angle input, you'll see that the negative value does not change the angle. This option can be more stable for use in setting up angles that will be changed in configurations, animations, and so on, but it is still largely dependent on the other constraints in the assembly. If the constraints holding the hinge to the boards were modified, the Undirected Angle constraint may need to be adjusted. Next, you will explore the Explicit Reference Vector solution to see that it allows you to more fully define the angle.

14. Click the Cancel button to exit the Place Constraint dialog and then click the Constrain button to bring it back up.

15. In the Type area of the Place Constraint dialog box, click the Angle button; then in the Solution area, ensure that the Explicit Reference Vector button is selected.

16. For Selection 1, click the large face of the painted board that the hinges are mounted on.

17. For Selection 2, click the large face of the unpainted board that the hinges are mounted on.

18. Run your cursor over the cylindrical faces in the center of either hinge. You should see the direction arrow flip back and forth depending on which face is highlighted.

19. When you find a face that points the arrow out away from the center of the assembly, click it. This selects the center axis of the hinge pivot and therefore defines the entire Angle constraint without relying on other existing constraints to establish the vector reference.

20. Enter **90** degrees.

You'll note that the preview updates incorrectly, flipping the assembly down and causing an interference situation. To correct this, you can enter a negative angle, or you can simply reselect Selection 3 so that it points the other way.

21. Click the Selection 3 button again to clear it and then find a face that makes the arrow point in toward the center of the assembly and select it. You'll notice that the preview updates to flip the assembly up, as desired.

You may be wondering why there are so many angle options. Originally Inventor did not include all three of these angle solutions, and options were added to improve the predictability of Angle constraint updates. At this point, though, if you use the default Explicit Reference Vector solution, your Angle constraints will update predictably.

As a final note on Angle constraints, you will probably find that using edges rather than faces for Angle constraints will provide more predictable results, particularly when setting up constraints to be used in creating positional variations for animation or documentation purposes. You can close this file without saving changes and continue to the next section.

USING THE RIGHT-HAND RULE

A good way to visualize the Explicit Reference Vector command is to use the right-hand rule. Take your right hand and make a "gun" shape with your index finger pointing out and your thumb pointing up. Now point your middle finger to the left, 90 degrees to the index finger. Your hand will then be making the three major axes. You can then use your thumb to determine the positive axes of the cross product of the x- and y-axes (the index and middle fingers).

THE TANGENT CONSTRAINT

Certification
Objective

A Tangent constraint results in faces, planes, cylinders, spheres, and cones coming in contact at a point of tangency. Tangency can exist inside or outside a curve, depending on the direction of the selected surface normal. The number of degrees of freedom a Tangent constraint removes depends on the geometry. When a Tangent constraint is applied between a cylinder and a planar face, the constraint will remove one degree of linear freedom as well as one degree of rotational freedom from the set.

1. Click the Get Started tab and click the Open button.

2. Browse for the file mi_8a_008.iam located in the Chapter 08 directory of your Mastering Inventor 2016 folder and click the Open button.

3. On the Assemble tab, click the Constrain button (or type **C** on the keyboard).

4. In the Type area of the Place Constraint dialog box, click the Tangent button.

5. For Selection 1, click the face of one of the sphere-shaped ball bearings.

6. For Selection 2, click the face of one of the half-sphere cutouts in the block.

7. Note that the preview sets the bearing to the outside. To fix this, click the Inside button in the Solution area of the Place Constraint dialog box.

8. Click the Apply button and then create an identical Tangent constraint for the second ball bearing.

9. Create another Tangent constraint, but this time use the Outside solution and select the cylinder of the shaft and the spherical face of one of the ball bearings. Click the OK button to create the constraint and exit the Place Constraint dialog box.

10. Before creating the last Tangent constraint, click the shaft and pull it up toward the top of the ball bearing it is tangential with. This is just so that the next Tangent constraint will not solve to the lower hemisphere and run the shaft into the block.

11. Create another Tangent constraint, again using the Outside solution, and select the cylinder of the shaft and the spherical face of one of the ball bearings.

Tangent constraints are fairly straightforward, and although they are not the most common constraint type to use, they are often the only one that will allow you to get the result you need when working with cylinders, spheres, and curved faces. You can test the function of the shaft and bearing constraint set by clicking and dragging the shaft to see it rotate, and then you can close the file without saving changes. Figure 8.6 shows the placement of a Tangent constraint.

FIGURE 8.6
Tangent constraints

THE INSERT CONSTRAINT

Certification
Objective

The Insert constraint is probably the best choice for inserting fasteners and other cylindrical objects into holes or for constraining any parts where circular or cylindrical geometries are to be constrained to one another. A single Insert constraint will replace two Mate constraints (one along the edge and one through the centerline), retaining one rotational degree of freedom. Options for the Insert constraint are Opposed and Aligned. The Insert constraint also allows for specifying offset values between components. Figure 8.7 shows common uses of Insert constraints.

FIGURE 8.7
Insert constraints

Follow these steps to explore the Insert constraint:

1. Click the Get Started tab and click the Open button.

2. Browse for the file mi_8a_009.iam located in the Chapter 08 directory of your Mastering Inventor 2016 folder and click the Open button.

3. On the Assemble tab, click the Constrain button (or type **C** on the keyboard).

4. In the Type area of the Place Constraint dialog box, select the Insert button.

5. Select the bottom edge of one of the screw heads for Selection 1. Notice that the highlight shows that the edge and the centerline are selected.

6. Select the top edge of one of the eight holes on the plate for Selection 2.

7. Toggle the solution button to see the difference in the two solutions and then set the solution to Opposed.

8. Enter **2 mm** in the Offset input box and then click the Apply button.

9. Select the edge of one of the washers and then the bottom edge of the screw head you just inserted to place and apply another Insert constraint.

10. Set another Insert constraint using the edge of the yellow face of one of the boss features on the end flange and one of the nuts. Use the Aligned solution to flip the nut so it is set down inside the boss feature.

11. Use Insert constraints to place the blue cover on the base part by selecting the rounded corners.

You can continue to practice with the remaining hardware. Use Copy and Paste to add more instances if you'd like. When you've finished, you can close the file without saving changes. For further practice with Insert constraints, take a look at mi_8a_109.iam and mi_8a_110.iam. You can investigate the constraints used in the assembled versions of these models to help if needed.

MINIMUM DISTANCE USING THE MEASURE TOOL

You can find the minimum distance between two assembly components by using the Measure tool. To access the Measure tool, select the Inspect tab and select Measure Distance from the Measure panel. Click the Priority drop-down box in the Measure Distance tool and set it to Part Priority. Next, select the first part and then select the second part. The returned value is the minimum distance between the two parts.

THE SYMMETRY CONSTRAINT

Certification
Objective

The Symmetry constraint, shown in Figure 8.8, positions two components symmetrically to each side of a plane or planar face. When one of the components is moved or its orientation is changed, the other component maintains its symmetrical relationship based on the existing degrees of freedom of each component.

FIGURE 8.8

Symmetry constraint

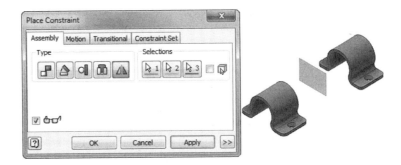

Follow these steps to explore the Symmetry constraint:

1. Click the Get Started tab and click the Open button.

2. Browse for the file mi_8a_130.iam located in the Chapter 08 directory of your Mastering Inventor 2016 folder and click the Open button.

The goal for this assembly is to create a symmetry relationship in order to maintain the same distance for the number 1 and number 2 bolts as they are threaded into the yellow receiver part. Currently the assembly has a number of constraints in place to help define the mechanism; however, there is still something missing. If you click and drag on the number 1 screw, you'll see that the behavior is not quite correct. If you click and drag on the yellow receiver part, you'll see something closer to the correct behavior, but the bolts do not maintain a symmetrical distance. You'll add the missing constraint to resolve this.

3. On the Assemble tab, click the Constrain button (or type **C** on the keyboard).

4. In the Type area of the Place Constraint dialog box, select the Symmetry button.

5. Select the blue face of one of the bolt heads for the first selection.

6. Select the blue face of the other bolt head for the second selection.

7. For the third selection, choose the visible work plane in the center of the yellow receiver part.

8. Click the OK button to create the constraint.

9. Now you can click and drag bolt number 1 to see that the two bolts maintain a symmetrical relationship on each side of the selected work plane.

Symmetry constraints are a quick and easy way to set up your assembly to hold components equidistant to a planar face or work plane or maintain a symmetric orientation. In this particular assembly, there are two motion constraints in place that allow the assembly to perform the threading action. In the next sections, you'll explore these constraints. You can close this file without saving changes in order to continue.

Within the Place Constraint dialog box are the Motion tab and the Translational tab. On the Motion tab, you can add Rotation constraints and Rotation-Translation constraints. A Rotation constraint is typically placed between two components, such as gears, simulating a ratio-based rotation. Rotation-Translation constraints allow a linear distance and revolution ratio to be applied for component pairs such as rack and pinion sets. On the Translational tab, you create constraints between a rotating and nonlinear translating face, such as cams and followers.

THE ROTATION CONSTRAINT

To create a simple Rotation constraint, first place two components constrained around their axes. Neither component should be grounded; instead, they should be constrained to allow rotation around the axes. The Rotation constraint applies a Forward or Reverse solution to the two components, along with a ratio that will determine rotation speeds, as shown in Figure 8.9.

FIGURE 8.9
Rotation constraint
options

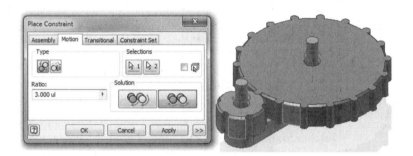

In the following steps, you will create a reverse Rotation constraint on a small cog set:

1. Click the Get Started tab and click the Open button.

2. Browse for the file mi_8a_010.iam located in the Chapter 08 directory of your Mastering Inventor 2016 folder and click the Open button.

3. On the Assemble tab, click the Constrain button (or type **C** on the keyboard).

4. Click the Motion tab in the Place Constraint dialog box.

5. In the Type area of the Place Constraint dialog box, select the Rotation button.

6. For Selection 1 click the yellow face on the large cog, and for Selection 2 click the yellow face on the small cog.

7. In the Solution area, click the Reverse button.

8. Note that the ratio is automatically set to 3 ul (*ul* means unitless). You could enter any value you want, but in this case you'll leave it at 3 based on the selected geometry. You should be aware had you selected the cogs in the opposite order, the ratio would be 0.333, the reciprocal of its current value. Click the OK button to create the Rotation constraint.

Currently, the assembly is fully constrained and will not rotate. This is because of the Mate constraint named Alignment Mate, which has been placed on the XZ origin planes of each cog. The purpose of this Mate constraint is simply to line up the cogs in their start position. To let the Rotation constraint work, the mate must be suppressed or deleted.

9. Locate the Alignment Mate constraint in the browser. You can do so by expanding either of the cogs in the browser.

10. Right-click the Alignment Mate constraint and choose Suppress. The constraint will now be grayed out and will not calculate against the assembly.

11. Click and drag either of the cogs to rotate them.

If you start the rotation with both yellow faces showing and count the number of times the small cog rotates before the yellow face on the large cog comes back around, you will see it make three revolutions for every one of the large cogs, as specified by the ratio in the constraint input. You can close the file without saving changes and continue to the next set of steps, where you will create a Rotation-Translation constraint.

THE ROTATION-TRANSLATION CONSTRAINT

Certification Objective

In the following steps, you will create a Rotation-Translation constraint as would be used to constrain a rack and pinion gear set:

1. Click the Get Started tab and click the Open button.

2. Browse for the file mi_8a_011.iam located in the Chapter 08 directory of your Mastering Inventor 2016 folder and click the Open button.

3. On the Assemble tab, click the Constrain button (or type **C** on the keyboard).

4. Click the Motion tab in the Place Constraint dialog box.

5. In the Type area of the Place Constraint dialog box, select the Rotation-Translation button.

6. Hover over any of the component geometry and notice that the selection glyph displays a rotation arrow, indicating it is looking for the rotational selection. Selection order is important in this case. For Selection 1, click the yellow face on the cog.

7. For Selection 2, click along the bottom edge of the rack. Be certain to select the edge, not the face. Although there is nothing preventing you from selecting the face or anything indicating that it is not the correct selection, the constraint will simply not work if the face is selected.

8. Note the value added to the Distance input box. This is the total travel of the rack for one revolution of the cog. This value is initially calculated from the selections, but you can enter your own value as required. In this case, the number is not a whole number because of the mix of Imperial and metric dimensions used in this model. Click the OK button to create the constraint.

Figure 8.10 shows the constraint selections.

Currently, the assembly is fully constrained and will not rotate. This is because of the Mate constraint named Start Point Mate, which has been placed on the rack and cog. To let the Rotation-Translation constraint work, the mate must be suppressed or deleted.

9. Locate the Start Point Mate constraint in the browser. You can do so by expanding the rack in the browser.

FIGURE 8.10
Rotation-Translation
constraint options

FIGURE 8.10
Rotation-Translation
constraint options

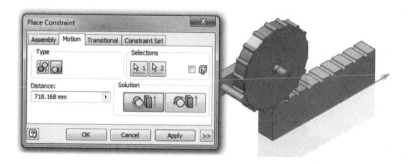

10. Right-click the Start Point Mate and choose Suppress. The constraint will now be grayed out and will not calculate against the assembly.

11. Click and drag the rack to see the rotation and translation take place.

Although motion constraints are easy to place, be aware that often the real work is in the calculations to create components with the correct geometry beforehand. If you have a need to create a lot of gears, you'll want to explore the gear generator found in the design accelerator tools. For now, you can close the file without saving changes and continue to the next section.

TRANSITIONAL CONSTRAINTS

Certification
Objective

Transitional constraints allow the movement of an underconstrained component along a path in a separate part. To create a Transitional constraint, you first select a moving face on the underconstrained component. Then you select a transitional face or edge on a fully constrained or grounded part. Figure 8.11 illustrates a cam and follower with a Transitional constraint applied.

FIGURE 8.11
A Transitional constraint

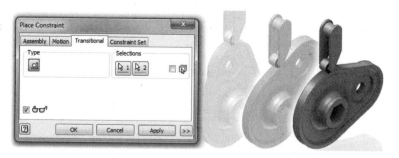

Follow these steps to explore the Transitional constraint:

1. Click the Get Started tab and click the Open button.

2. Browse for the file mi_8a_012.iam located in the Chapter 08 directory of your Mastering Inventor 2016 folder and click the Open button.

3. On the Assemble tab, click the Constrain button (or type **C** on the keyboard).

4. Click the Transitional tab in the Place Constraint dialog box.

5. For Selection 1, click the yellow face on the follower wheel. Note that the first selection must be the moving face.

6. For Selection 2, click the orange face on the cam. Note that this selection must be the translational face.

7. Click the OK button to create the constraint.

8. Click and drag the cam and rotate it around the axis to see the assembly in action.

Components used in Transitional constraints must always be in contact for them to work; therefore, no offsets are permitted. The translational face (in this case the cam) can be any combination of flat, arced, or spline-defined faces, but it is generally best to avoid sharp corners. When finished examining the Translational constraint functionality, you can close the file without saving changes.

Additional Constrain Tools and Options

In addition to knowing the basic constraint types and options, you should be aware of a number of other tools and options. These tools and options are covered in the following pages.

USING THE ASSEMBLE TOOL TO PLACE CONSTRAINTS

The Assemble tool allows you to move a component into place and place a constraint based on the selected geometry. This tool is designed to select a component and then fully constrain it. When using the Assemble tool, you select the component you want to move into place first, and then you select the component you want to constrain to. Because of this, you can constrain only one component at a time with this tool. To constrain a second component, you must click the OK button to exit the Assemble tool and then select the Assemble button again, or you can right-click and select Repeat Assemble.

As constraints are placed, the geometry involved is left highlighted onscreen. These new constraints are not created until you exit the Assemble tool by clicking the OK button. If any conflicts with existing constraints are created, you are presented with the Assemble Constraint Management dialog box. You can find options in this dialog box to resolve the conflicts.

You can open the file mi_8a_013.iam to explore the Assemble tool, following these general steps:

1. On the Assemble tab, click the Assemble button, using the Relationships panel drop-down.

2. Select some geometry on the component to be moved into place.

3. Select some geometry on the component that is intended to stay in place.

4. Enter values such as offsets or angle values if needed.

5. If necessary, change the solution type (from Mate to Flush, for example).

6. From this point, you can do any of the following:

- ◆ Click the Apply button and continue to define other constraints for the selected component.

- ◆ Click the OK button to create the constraints based on the previous selections and exit the Assemble tool.

- ◆ Click the Undo button to delete the current selections and then continue defining constraints.

RELATIONSHIP AUDIO NOTIFICATION

When you place a relationship in an assembly, Inventor makes a sound at the time of the preview or at the time of the constraint creation, depending on the preview option at the time. You can disable this sound by selecting the Tools tab, clicking Application Options, and then selecting the Assembly tab. Uncheck the Relationship Audio Notification check box to disable the sound.

You can change the sound by replacing the default sound file with one of your choice. The sound file is `Connect.wav` and is in the `C:\Program Files\Autodesk\Inventor 2016\Bin` folder (assuming that is the install path).

CONSTRAINT SETS

Constraint sets allow you to constrain two components together using their user coordinate systems. You define the UCS in the part or subassembly file first and then place constraints on the coordinate system planes and axes rather than the component geometry.

You can open the file `mi_8a_014.iam` to explore constraint sets, following these general steps:

1. On the Assemble tab, click the Constrain button.

2. In the Place Constraint dialog box, click the Constraint Set tab.

3. Expand the browser nodes for both components so you can see the UCS features listed.

4. Select UCS1 in each part for Selections 1 and 2.

5. Click the OK button to create a set of constraints between the two UCS triads.

Constraint sets can often be helpful when components are modeled referencing a common datum set in each component. When finished creating the constraints, you can close the file without saving changes.

CONSTRAINT LIMITS

Constraint limits allow you to define minimum and maximum constraint values so components can move freely within the limits but not beyond them. You can imagine a model of a door hinge. You might want the hinge to swing from 0 to 270 degrees, but not outside of that range or the hinge might interfere with itself.

You can open the file `mi_8a_015.iam` to explore constraint limits. In this assembly, there are four parts. These would be four subassemblies in reality, but for the sake of simplicity, they have been condensed into part files. The router base is grounded in place, and the y- and z-axis assemblies have been fully constrained with constraint limits, so they are free to slide within the bounds of the bearing rods and gantry uprights. You can click and drag the z-axis assembly to see how it behaves in a realistic manner thanks to the existing constraint limits. But if you click the x-axis assembly, you will see that it does travel along the bearing rods realistically, but it can continue sliding through the router base and beyond. To fix this, you will add a constraint set to the x-axis assembly, limiting its travel to a more realistic result.

1. On the Assemble tab, click the Constrain button (or type **C** on the keyboard).

2. Leave the constraint Type set to Mate and set the solution to Flush.

3. Select the two yellow faces for Selection 1 and Selection 2, making sure to select the large yellow face on the router base for Selection 1 and the smaller yellow face on the x-axis assembly for Selection 2.

4. Click the >> button to expand the dialog box.

5. Click the Maximum and Minimum check boxes.

6. Enter **-10 mm** for the maximum value.

7. Enter **-395 mm** for the minimum value.

8. Click the Use Offset As Resting Position check box.

9. Enter **-150** for the offset value (located back toward the top of the dialog box).

10. Enter **X Travel** in the Name input box and then click the OK button to create the constraint.

11. Click the x-axis assembly, and you will see that it now stops before running through the other components.

Figure 8.12 shows the constraint limit being created.

FIGURE 8.12
Placing constraint limits

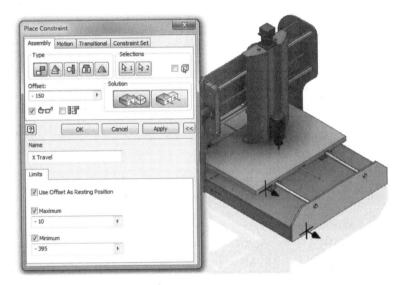

You can drag the x-axis assembly to its minimum and maximum limits, but when you let go, it returns to the resting value you set in the dialog box. Keep in mind you are not required to use the resting position option. If no resting value is used, the assembly will stay where it was last placed, which is the behavior exhibited by the z-axis assembly.

Constraint limits are a great tool to use in the set up of free-moving components to get them to behave predictably. However, you should be aware that there may be a small performance hit when using too many of these at once. So, keep that in mind as you use them. You can close the assembly without saving changes.

DRIVING RELATIONSHIPS

It is often desirable to simulate motion by driving a relationship through a beginning position and an ending position to confirm the intent of the design. In general, Offset and Angle constraints may be selected to drive components within an assembly. To accomplish this, simply right-click the desired constraint and select Drive (as shown in Figure 8.13).

FIGURE 8.13

Driving a constraint

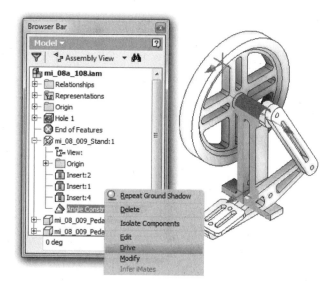

You can open the file mi_8a_016.iam to explore the drive constraint options. If you expand the Z-Axis Assembly node, you will find two constraints labeled Drive Me. When you right-click a constraint and choose Drive, the Drive Constraint dialog box appears, allowing you to alter the constraint by specifying steps between the start position and the end position. When a constraint is driven, any components constrained to the driven component will move in accordance to their particular shared constraints. The motion may be set to forward or reverse, stopped at any time, and even recorded (click the Record button prior to activating the move). If any of the affected components are constrained to a grounded component or if the movement will violate any existing constraint, then the drive constraint will fail.

Expanding the dialog box as shown in Figure 8.14 by clicking the >> button will reveal additional controls over the drive constraint.

The increment of movement can be controlled by a value or by a total number of steps from beginning to end. The length of a particular driven constraint can be controlled by the number of allowable repetitions from Start to End or can be reversed by using the Start/End/Start option. The constraints in mi_8a_016.iam are set up in this manner.

FIGURE 8.14
Drive constraint
dialog box options

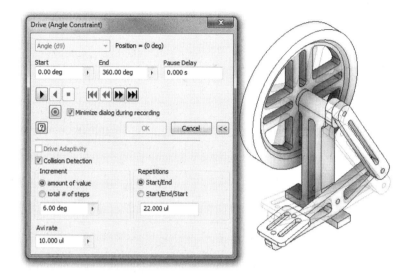

For a continuous revolution by degrees, you may exceed 360 degrees by specifying the total number of degrees of revolution or by including an equation such as 360 deg * 3. Another approach is to set the End rotation to 360 degrees and then simply increment the Repetitions value for the number of revolutions. You can open the file mi_8a_108.iam to further explore constraint limits.

Other adaptive parts properly constrained within the driven assembly will adjust to changes if the Drive Adaptivity option is selected. This particular option allows determination of a maximum or minimum condition for the adaptive part.

Checking the Collision Detection option allows for determination of an exact collision distance or angle between the driven parts. Using the Collision Detection option will help you determine interferences between moving parts so that those parts can be modified before manufacturing. In mi_8a_108.iam there is a small red link that can be swiveled out of the way to avoid a collision of parts. If you leave it sticking out and drive the Drive Me constraint and enable the Collision Detection option, you can determine where the parts come into contact with one another. Inventor reports the angle of collision in the Drive Constraint dialog box. You can change the Increment value to a fraction of a degree to see a more exact value.

CONTACT SOLVER

Another method for driving components within an assembly involves the Contact Solver option. With this option, only minimal constraints are required to drive a number of components. Components are not required to be constrained to one another for the Contact Solver to work.

The Contact Solver works in much the same way as parts interact in the real world. Without the Contact Solver applied, moving parts can be run through one another, creating interference. With the Contact Solver applied, parts will stop when they contact one another. A simple example of this is the slide arm in Figure 8.15. On the left, you can see that the arm segments have been extended past the point that they could be in reality, allowing the slide stops to run through the slide slot. On the right, the parts have been added to a contact set, and the Contact Solver has been turned on, preventing the slide stops from running through the slots.

FIGURE 8.15
With and without Contact Solver

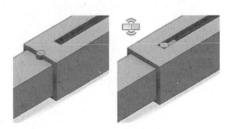

To add parts to a contact set, right-click the part and choose Contact Set from the context menu. An icon appears before each component showing when it has been added to the contact set. In addition to adding parts to a contact set, you must ensure that the Contact Solver is turned on; do this by choosing Activate Contact Solver from the Inspect menu. Once all active participants within the contact set are selected and the Contact Solver is activated, then a single driven constraint can provide a real-life simulation. Note that it is best practice to turn the Contact Solver off when performance is a consideration.

To explore the contact sets, open the file mi_8a_017.iam and follow these basic steps:

1. Select any components you want to be added to the contact analysis.

2. Right-click the selected components and choose Contact Set from the context menu.

3. Select the Inspect tab and click the Activate Contact Solver button.

4. Drag the part with the black end cap in and out to see the assembly extend and contract based on the contact points.

USING THE CONTACT SOLVER FOR COLLISION DETECTION

If you have parts that interfere (such as a dowel pin in a hole) and have the Collision Detection option selected, the Drive Constraint command will stop immediately because it will have detected this interference. If you need to test the collision of parts, look into using the Contact Solver.

REDUNDANT RELATIONSHIP AND CONSTRAINT FAILURES

Excessive relationships are considered redundant when you have overconstrained components. Redundant relationships will interfere with the proper operation of your assemblies and can cause relationship errors and performance issues.

Two toggles will assist in flagging bad constraints; you can find them by selecting Tools ➤ Application Options and selecting the Assembly tab. Enabling Relationship Redundancy Analysis allows Inventor to perform a secondary analysis of Assembly constraints and notifies you when redundant constraints exist.

Enabling Related Relationship Failure Analysis allows Inventor to perform an analysis to identify all affected constraints and components if a particular constraint fails. Once analysis is performed, you will be able to isolate the components that use the broken constraint (or constraints) and select a form of treatment for individual components.

Because analysis requires a separate process, performance can be affected if these two check boxes are active. Because of this, it is advisable to activate the analysis only when problems exist.

Working with Joint Relationships

The Joint tool allows you to define the working relationship between a pair of components with a single joint relationship. This is done by pairing joint points found on faces and edges of components. Several types of joints are available for use in an assembly, so in order to know which joint type to use and when, you should be familiar with each. Although you can achieve the same result using the Constraint tool that you can with the Joint tool, the Joint tool results in fewer assembly relationships, which can make managing them later much easier. You can also use the Joint and Constraint tools together to fully define the assembly relationship of your design as you see fit.

JOINT SELECTION INPUTS

All of the joint types are created by defining two origin selections and two alignment selections. Keep in mind that the alignment selections are created automatically based on your origin set selections. However, the inferred selections are often not the correct solution for particular joint, resulting in a preview that is incorrect. In these cases, you can simply click the Alignment selection buttons again to reselect edges or faces for alignment.

CONSTRAINTS OR JOINTS: WHICH SHOULD YOU USE?

Because the Constraint and Joint tools provide two methods of doing the same thing, when you are creating assembly relationships, you might wonder which you should use. The answer will likely depend on your experience and familiarity with both tools. If you are comfortable with the Constraint tool, you might find that it fits your approach to creating assembly relationships best, in which case you might find that you seldom end up using the Joint tool. Conversely, if the Constraint tool seems less intuitive to you, you might find that you prefer the Joint tool.

The preference for one or the other of these tools might depend on the type of designs you create. For instance, if you create frame structures or weldments with mostly static components, you might find that you lean toward creating Rigid joints, rather than Mate and Flush constraints. Of course, you might also use a mix of constraints and joints, choosing the relationship type that works best for you.

RIGID JOINTS

The Rigid joint type creates a joint between points on a pair of faces, a pair of edges, or an edge and a face. Rigid joints remove all degrees of freedom creating a "fixed" joint. You can use the Flip Component and Invert Alignment buttons to adjust the orientation of the component if the preview shows the component incorrectly. Figure 8.16 shows connection points being selected for a Rigid joint.

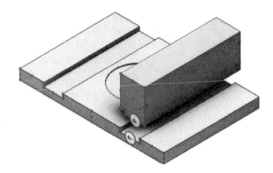

To explore the Rigid joint options, you will open a simple fixture assembly and assemble two components using a Rigid joint.

1. Click the Get Started tab and click the Open button.

2. Browse for the file mi_8a_120.iam located in the Chapter 08 directory of your Mastering Inventor 2016 folder and click the Open button.

3. On the Assemble tab, click the Joint button.

4. Use the Type menu to select Rigid from the list.

5. For the first origin selection, hover over the yellow face of the component named Side_302.

6. Move your cursor down to select the center-bottom connection point, as shown in Figure 8.16.

7. For the second origin selection, hover over the yellow face of the base component and choose the center-top connection point, as shown in Figure 8.16.

8. Use the Flip Component and Invert Alignment buttons to correct the alignment of the Side_302 component.

9. Enter **-5 mm** in the Gap input box to set the far faces flush.

10. Click the OK button to create the Rigid joint. Figure 8.17 shows the result.

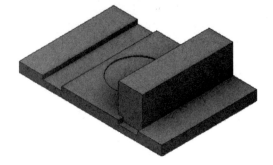

Next, you'll edit the Rigid joint you just created and adjust the selections. You can continue with the file you have open or close it and open the file `mi_8a_121.iam`.

1. Locate and expand the `Relationships` folder in the Model browser and then right-click the Rigid joint and choose Edit.

2. Click the second origin button in the Connect area of the dialog box in order to clear the selection.

3. Click the first origin button in the Connect area of the dialog box in order to clear that selection as well.

4. Next, with the first origin button active still, select the center connect point of the bottom edge of the Side_302 component, as shown in Figure 8.18.

FIGURE 8.18
Selecting an edge connection point

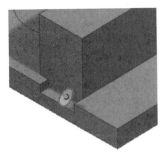

5. For the second origin selection, select the center connect point of the top edge of the base component, as shown in Figure 8.19.

FIGURE 8.19
Selecting the other edge connection point

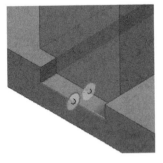

6. Note that the -5 mm gap distance results in a different offset when the two edges are selected compared to when the two faces were selected.

7. Set the Gap value to **0 mm**.

8. Enter **Yellow Edges** in the Name input box, then click the OK button to apply the changes.

You'll note that the name in the browser is now changed to read Yellow Edges. Naming joints in this manner allows you to organize and quickly locate joints for editing. You can close this file when finished and continue to the next section to explore Rotational joints.

ROTATIONAL JOINTS

The Rotational joint type creates a joint between points on a pair of faces, a pair of edges, or an edge and a face. Rotational joints specify one degree of freedom, creating a rotating joint based on the connection points you select. You can use the Flip Component and Invert Alignment buttons to adjust the orientation of the component if the preview shows the component incorrectly. Additionally, you can create a rotational limit so that the rotational joint will rotate only through a specified set of angles.

To explore the Rotational joint options, you will open a simple assembly and create one Rotational and one Rigid joint to define the rotation of a handle crank.

1. Click the Get Started tab and click the Open button.

2. Browse for the file `mi_8a_122.iam` located in the `Chapter 08` directory of your `Mastering Inventor 2016` folder and click the Open button.

   Take a moment to examine the parts listed in the model tree. If you drag your cursor over each part name, you will see that part highlight in the browser. You'll refer to these part names in the following steps.

3. On the Assemble tab, click the Joint button.

4. Use the Type menu to select Rotational from the list.

5. For the first origin selection, hover over the yellow face of the component named 8_105.

6. Move your cursor down to select the connection point at the center of the hole.

7. For the second origin selection, choose the connection point at the center of the yellow face of the component named 8_104 (the gray base component).

8. Click the Limits tab in the Place Joint dialog box.

9. Click the check box for the Angular Start option and enter **360 deg** in the input box.

10. Enter **180 deg** in the End input box.

11. Click the OK button to create the rotational joint. Figure 8.20 shows the result.

FIGURE 8.20
The Rotational joint results

You can click and drag the 8_105 component to see it rotate through the range of motion specified in the Limits tab. This allows the joint to work realistically so that it stops without running through the other component. Next, you'll add a Rigid joint to complete the assembly. You can continue with the file you have open or close it and open the file mi_8a_123.iam.

1. On the Assemble tab, click the Joint button.

2. Use the Type menu to select Rigid from the list.

3. For the first origin selection, hover over the red face of the component named 8_106 and then click to select the center connection point of the hole.

4. For the second origin selection, hover over the red face of the component named 8_105 and then click to select the center connection point.

5. Click the first alignment button and choose the blue face on the inside of the keyway; you might need to zoom in closely to select it.

6. Then click the blue face on the key feature on the 8_105 component and click the Invert Alignment button to set the proper alignment.

7. Click the OK button to create the rigid joint and then click and drag the components to see the behavior you've achieved. Figure 8.21 shows the completed assembly.

FIGURE 8.21
The completed assembly

Here you've used a rigid joint in combination with a rotational joint to define the rotational limits and assembly alignment of a simple mechanism. Keep in mind that you could have achieved the same results using the Constraint tool instead of the Joint tool, or you could have used the two in combination. You can close this file and continue to the next section to explore the Slider joint type.

JOINT SELECTION OPTIONS

You can find three right-click context menu options to help you when creating joints.

◆ **Infer Origin:** This is the default option, where the origin is inferred based on the selections.

◆ **Offset Origin:** You can drag the manipulator arrows or input an offset value to change the location of the origin.

◆ **Between Faces:** You can specify a virtual midpoint between two selected faces by selecting the two faces and a point.

To use these options, click the Joint tool and then right-click and choose one of the options from the context menu.

SLIDER JOINTS

Much like the Rigid and Rotational joints, the Slider joint type creates a joint between points on a pair of faces, a pair of edges, or an edge and a face. Slider joints specify one translational degree of freedom, defining a sliding action. As with other joint types, you can use the Flip Component and Invert Alignment buttons to adjust the orientation of the component if the preview shows the component incorrectly. Additionally, you can create a linear travel limit so that the joint will only slide through a specified linear distance.

To explore the Slider joint options, you will open a simple assembly and create a couple of Slider joints.

1. Click the Get Started tab and click the Open button.

2. Browse for the file mi_8a_124.iam located in the Chapter 08 directory of your Mastering Inventor 2016 folder and click the Open button.

In this file there are three bearing pads. One of the bearing pads has been set up to slide in the first rail channel already. This was done using the Constraint tool. If you expand the Relationships folder in the browser, you'll find two Mate constraints and one flush constraint. The three of these together create the relationship that allows the bearing pad to slide through a specific linear distance in the first rail channel. You'll use the Joint tool to create the same relationship for the remaining two bearing pads with just a single slider joint for each pad.

3. On the Assemble tab, click the Joint button.

4. Use the Type menu to select Slider from the list.

5. For the first origin selection, hover over the yellow face on either of the unconstrained bearing pads.

6. Move your cursor to select the connection point at the center of the edge near the red face, as shown in Figure 8.22.

7. For the second origin selection, hover over the yellow face of the center channel on the rail.

FIGURE 8.22
Connection point on the bearing pad

8. Move your cursor to select the connection point at the center of the edge near the red face, as shown in Figure 8.23.

FIGURE 8.23
Connection point on the channel

9. Click the Align buttons to see which faces are being used as the alignment selections. If the red faces on each part are not selected, select them so that both red faces are aligned, as shown in Figure 8.24.

FIGURE 8.24
The correct alignment of the bearing pad

10. Click the Limits tab in the Place Joint dialog box.

11. Select the Linear Start check box and then enter **0 mm** in the input box.

12. Select the Linear End check box and then enter **-250 mm** in the input box. The rail is 300 mm long and the bearing pad is 50 mm long, so the linear limit is 300 − 50, or 250, and you use a negative value to control the direction.

13. Click the OK button to create the slider joint.

You can click and drag the bearing pad to see it slide through the range of linear motion specified in the Limits tab. This allows the pad to work as if the rail had end stops in place. And note that you've created this relationship with just a single joint, whereas the existing relationship required three constraints.

Next, you'll add another slider joint to the remaining bearing pad. You can continue with the file you have open or close it and open the file mi_8a_125.iam.

1. On the Assemble tab, click the Joint button.

2. Use the Type menu to select Slider from the list.

3. For the first origin selection, hover over the yellow face on the unconstrained bearing pad.

4. Move your cursor to select the connection point at the center of the yellow face, as shown in Figure 8.25.

FIGURE 8.25
The center connection point of the bearing pad

5. For the second origin selection, hover over the yellow face of the remaining free rail slot and then click to select the center connection point, as shown in Figure 8.26.

FIGURE 8.26
The center connection point of the rail slot

6. Click the Align buttons to see which faces are being used as the alignment selections. If the red faces on each part are not selected, select them so that both red faces are aligned.

7. Click the Limits tab in the Place Joint dialog box.

8. Select the Linear Start check box and then enter **125 mm** in the input box.

9. Select the Linear End check box and then enter **-125 mm** in the input box. The rail is 300 mm long, and the bearing pad is 50 mm long. But since the connection points are in the center of each, you'll use half of these values to come up with the offsets: 150 – 25 = 125. You use the negative of this number to specify the other direction.

10. Click the OK button to create the slider joint.

You can click and drag the bearing pad to see it slide through the range of linear motion specified in the Limits tab. If the bearing pad does not stop at the ends of the rail slot, edit the Slider joint and check your inputs and alignment selections.

Creating a slider joint is a straightforward process; however, some thought is required to select the correct connection points and specify the correct limit values to achieve the correct relationship for each situation. Once you're satisfied with the slider joints you've created, you can close this file without saving changes and continue to the next section.

CYLINDRICAL JOINTS

The Cylindrical joint type creates a joint between points on a pair of faces, a pair of edges, or an edge and a face. Cylindrical joints specify one rotational degree of freedom and one translational degree of freedom, defining a sliding and rotating action. As with other joint types, you can use the Flip Component and Invert Alignment buttons to adjust the orientation of the component if the preview shows the component incorrectly. For Cylindrical joints you can create both angular and linear limits.

To explore the Cylindrical joint options, you will open a simple slip latch assembly and create a Cylindrical joint.

1. Click the Get Started tab and click the Open button.

2. Browse for the file mi_8a_126.iam located in the Chapter 08 directory of your Mastering Inventor 2016 folder and click the Open button.

3. On the Assemble tab, click the Joint button.

4. In the Type menu, select Cylindrical from the list.

5. For the first origin selection, select the circular yellow face of the tan-colored part.

6. For the second origin selection, select the yellow face of the small latch catch part.

7. Click the Align buttons to see which faces are being used as the alignment selections. If the red faces on each part are not selected, then select them so that both red faces are aligned.

8. Click the Limits tab in the Place Joint dialog box.

9. Select the Angular Start check box and then enter **-80 deg** in the input box.

10. Select the Angular End check box and then enter **-20 deg** in the input box.

11. Select the Linear Start check box and leave the input box value at 0 mm.

12. Select the Linear End check box and then enter **200 mm** in the input box.

13. Click the OK button to create the cylindrical joint. Figure 8.27 shows the result.

You can click and drag the slide bolt to see it slip through the range of angular and linear motion specified in the Limits tab. You'll note that the catch on the slide bolt can pass through the rise in the latch body that defines the slot. To prevent this, you could create a contact set and turn on the Contact Solver as mentioned earlier in this chapter. When you've finished exploring the results of the cylindrical joint, you can close the file without saving changes and continue to the next section.

FIGURE 8.27
A slip latch with a cylindrical joint

PLANAR JOINTS

The Planar joint type is pretty basic and creates a joint between points on a pair of faces, a pair of edges, or an edge and a face. Planar joints specify two translational degrees of freedom and one rotational. As with other joint types, you can use the Flip Component and Invert Alignment buttons to adjust the orientation of the component if the preview shows the component incorrectly. However, unlike many other joint types, Planar joints have no Limit options.

To explore the Planar joint options, you will open a simple assembly and create a Planar joint between game pieces and a game board.

1. Click the Get Started tab and click the Open button.

2. Browse for the file mi_8a_127.iam located in the Chapter 08 directory of your Mastering Inventor 2016 folder and click the Open button.

3. On the Assemble tab, click the Joint button.

4. Use the Type menu to select Planar from the list.

5. For the first origin selection, select the circular yellow face on the bottom of either of the tipped-over game pieces.

6. For the second origin selection, select the center connection point of any of the squares on the game board.

7. You can click the Align buttons to see which faces are being used as the alignment selections, although in this case the alignment is not important.

8. Click the Limits tab in the Place Joint dialog box.

9. Notice that both the Angular and Linear limits options are grayed out and cannot be selected, indicating that they are not available for planar joints.

10. Click the OK button to create the planar joint.

11. Click and drag on the game piece you placed, and you'll note that it can slide along in any direction but will stay fixed to the top plane of the game board. Figure 8.28 shows the game pieces in place.

Although the planar joint might seem too basic to be of much use, it is often used in combination with one of the other joint or constraint types to further define a mechanism or movement that translates in any direction along a planar surface. When finished, you can close the file without saving changes and continue to the next section.

FIGURE 8.28
Planar joints placing game pieces

BALL JOINTS

The Ball joint type is most often used to create a joint between center points of a pair of spherical faces; however, it can use a connection point found on any pair of faces, a pair of edges, or an edge and a face. Ball joints specify three rotational degrees of freedom. As with other joint types, you can use the Flip Component and Invert Alignment buttons to adjust the orientation of the component if the preview shows the component incorrectly. However, there are no Limit options for Ball joints.

To explore the Ball joint options, you will open a simple assembly and create a joint between two parts.

1. Click the Get Started tab and click the Open button.

2. Browse for the file mi_8a_128.iam located in the Chapter 08 directory of your Mastering Inventor 2016 folder and click the Open button.

3. On the Assemble tab, click the Joint button.

4. Use the Type menu to select Ball from the list.

5. For the first origin selection, select the center connection point on the spherical yellow face on the blue arm part.

6. For the second origin selection, select the center connection point of the yellow face on the gray socket part.

7. Click the Limits tab in the Place Joint dialog box.

8. Notice that both the Angular and Linear limits options are grayed out and cannot be selected, indicating that they are not available for planar joints.

9. Click the OK button to create the planar joint.

10. Click and drag the blue arm part to see that it rotates in the socket. You'll notice that it can currently pass though the other part.

11. Select both parts and then right-click and choose Contact Set.

12. Go to the Inspect tab and click the Activate Contact Solver button to turn the solver on.

13. Now you can click and drag the blue arm part and see that it will not pass through the socket part. Figure 8.29 shows the resulting assembly.

Although the Ball joint has a fairly specific use, it can often be the only choice for creating certain types of relationships between parts. When you've finished exploring the Ball joint tools, you can close the file without saving changes and continue to the next section.

Understanding Subassemblies

You create assemblies by placing assembly relationships between parts to position and hold those parts together. When working with small assemblies, you can often assemble all the parts together at one level. Working with larger assemblies, however, often requires the use of multiple levels of assemblies for the sake of organization and performance. An assembly inside an assembly is referred to as a *subassembly*.

Imagine a common caster-wheel assembly. Although it may seem like a simple component, it is, of course, made up of many small parts. If you needed to use this caster in an assembly multiple times, you wouldn't place all the small parts into an assembly individually over and over. Instead, you would package them as a subassembly and place multiple instances of the subassembly throughout the top-level assembly. Figure 8.30 shows a caster-wheel assembly ready to be placed as a subassembly.

Most things you design and build are typically made from subassemblies of some sort. In manufacturing it makes sense to create subassemblies of common parts to make the assembly process easier. It makes sense to design in the same fashion. In the caster example, it saves you from having to duplicate the work of assembling the caster parts repeatedly for each instance of the caster that exists in the top-level assembly.

FIGURE 8.30
A caster-wheel assembly

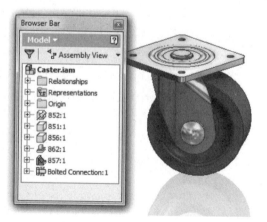

A second benefit to using subassemblies is the flexibility they add to the bill of materials. Using the caster as a subassembly rather than as loose parts provides the ability to count the caster as a single item, to count the total of all the caster parts, or to do both.

KNOWING WHEN TO USE ASSEMBLIES

Although it is often necessary to create parts as assemblies (to have a correct bill of materials or to provide the correct motion), it is not always the best choice. For example, in the caster example, unless you need the casters to swivel in your assembly, consider modeling the caster as a single part or deriving the assembly into a single part. This will lower the overhead of your models as well as reduce the number of parts to track throughout your design.

There is a third and important concept to consider when working with subassemblies: model performance. Imagine that you decided to place four instances of the caster into an assembly as loose parts rather than as a subassembly. For the sake of simplicity, say it takes 28 relationships among the caster parts and two relationships between the caster and the top-level assembly, for a total of 30 relationships. You do this for all four casters, for a total of 120 relationships in the top-level assembly. Had you assembled the caster as a subassembly and then placed that subassembly into the top-level assembly, you would have used just 28 in the caster subassembly and two per caster, as shown in Figure 8.31, for a total of only 36 relationships.

FIGURE 8.31
Reduced assembly relationships

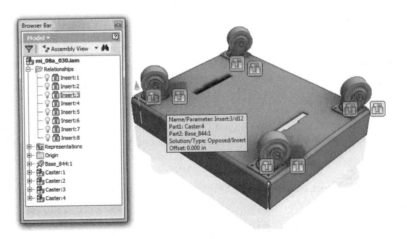

If you consider assembly relationships to be nothing more than calculations that Inventor must make to hold the assemblies together, then by using subassemblies, you have required Inventor to create and maintain 86 fewer calculations overall. This reduction in constraints can have a significant impact on the assembly's performance and make the task of editing the assembly much easier.

Top-Down Design

Inventor allows you to approach the creation of parts and assemblies in three basic ways. Figure 8.32 shows these three distinctive workflows for assembly design.

FIGURE 8.32

Design workflows

Top Down	**Middle Out**	**Bottom Up**
Design Within Assembly	Design Within Assembly	Create Single Parts
Utilize Subassemblies	Utilize Subassemblies	Create iParts & Features
Share Part Geometry	Share Part Geometry	Develop Library Items
Most Efficient Workflow	Insert Parts and Assemblies	Repair Imported Parts
Facilitates Middle-Out Design	Most Commonly Used	Least Efficient

The first of these methods is called *top-down* design. In the purest sense, top-down design is performed completely within the top-level assembly of a machine or device. Parts and subassemblies are created from within the uppermost assembly, as opposed to creating components outside the top-level assembly and then placing these components later. Using this approach, you can reference and project geometry from other parts within the assembly into new parts, thereby ensuring the fit of the new parts. Another benefit to top-down design is that the designer can better visualize how each part relates to others within the assembly. When it's properly utilized, you minimize the number of overall Assembly constraints required and allow for a stable design.

The second method works by creating parts independently and then placing and constraining them into the assembly. This method is called *bottom-up* design. Bottom-up design is common when creating parts from existing drawings and new pencil sketches. This workflow is ideal for repairing imported geometry, creating standard parts for your library, and converting standard parts into iParts and iFeatures. Working in the single-part environment does not easily allow you to create or reference other parts that will be utilized within your assembly design. As a result, this is probably the least efficient workflow for 3D design but is often the one employed by new users.

The third method is some combination of top-down and bottom-up design and is the most common. This approach might be called *middle-out*. This is top-down design with the ability to add existing subassemblies and parts as needed. Utilizing various functions such as parts libraries, Frame Generator, Bolted Connections, and Content Center components within an assembly file is an example of middle-out design.

Developing an Efficient Assembly Workflow

Certification Objective

Consider an example of a top-down workflow to better understand the benefits and efficiency of this type of design. Within this workflow, you will first create the top-level assembly file and then create the part files:

1. On the Get Started tab, click the New button and select the Standard.iam template.

2. Click Create on the Assemble tab, or right-click in the browser or graphics area and select Create Component. The default option in the Create In-Place Component dialog box is to create a new component as a standard single-part file. Instead, click the drop-down arrow in the Template area and select Standard.iam.

3. Name this assembly **2nd Level Assembly** and then set New File Location to the Chapter 8 folder.

If it is known at the time of creating the subassembly file, determine the BOM structure for this subassembly. Note that you can change this later using the BOM Editor as needed. Figure 8.33 illustrates the selection choices for the BOM structure.

FIGURE 8.33
BOM structure options

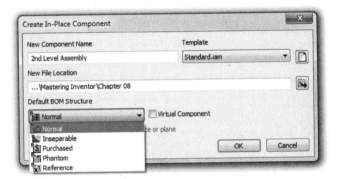

The choices for BOM structure are listed here with a brief description. You'll take a more in-depth look at BOM structure settings later in this chapter in the "BOM Structure Designations" section.

Virtual Components These components require no geometry, such as paint, grease, and so on.

Normal This is the default structure for all parts that are intended to be fabricated.

Purchased These are parts or assemblies that are not fabricated in-house.

Inseparable Generally, these are assemblies that cannot be disassembled without damage, such as weldments, riveted assemblies, and so on.

Phantom Typically, this is a subassembly created to simplify the design process by reducing Assembly constraints and to roll parts up into the next-highest assembly level.

Reference This is used for construction geometry or to add detail and references to the top-level assembly.

4. In this top-down design example, you will be using Normal components. Confirm that Default BOM Structure is set to Normal and click the OK button.

5. You will then be prompted to select a sketch plane for the base component of this assembly. In the Model browser, expand the assembly origin folder and select the XY Plane option.

This will place and anchor the new assembly to the top-level assembly origin. The origin planes of the new assembly will be anchored to the selected top-level assembly origin plane upon creation and will be grounded to the top-level origin plane. This new, second-level assembly will be activated within the Model browser, ready for editing, as shown in Figure 8.34.

FIGURE 8.34

Second-level assembly active

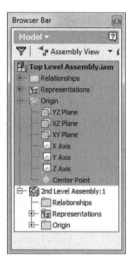

6. With the second-level assembly active, select Create Component once again, and this time use the Standard.ipt template to create a new part. Name this component **Rotary Hub** and set it to be saved in a subdirectory called Parts within your workspace, as shown in Figure 8.35. If the subdirectory does not exist, you will be prompted to create it. Leave the BOM structure setting as Normal and then click the OK button.

FIGURE 8.35

Creating Rotary Hub.ipt in the Parts subdirectory

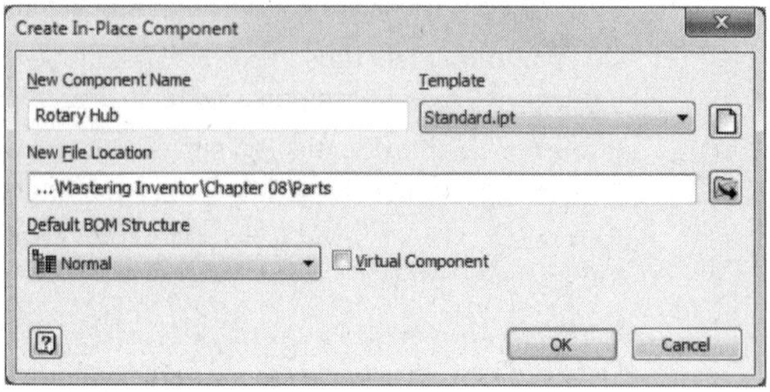

7. To place the part, select the XZ plane from the `Origin` folder in `2nd Level Assembly.iam`.

8. Now you are in the Rotary Hub part file. Use the Start 2D Sketch button and select the XZ plane. You might need to expand the `Origin` folder to determine which plane is the XZ plane.

9. Create and dimension the sketch, as shown in Figure 8.36.

FIGURE 8.36
Rotary Hub sketch

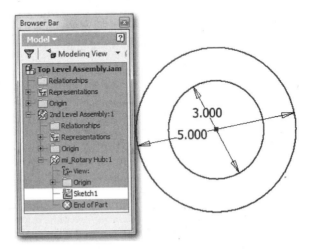

10. Press **E** to display the Extrude dialog box and extrude the outer ring to a length of 1 inch.

11. Create a sketch on the top face of the ring. Sketch a concentric circle offset 0.5 inch to the inside of the overall diameter. Place a center point on the offset circle.

12. Start the Hole tool. The center point will be automatically selected. Set the diameter to **0.375 inch**, and set Termination to Through All.

13. Create a circular pattern of the hole feature with six instances, as shown in Figure 8.37.

FIGURE 8.37
A circular pattern of
the hole feature

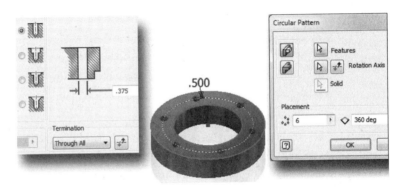

14. Click the Save icon. Since the part is active, it is saved, but the top- and second-level assemblies are not. Click the Return button twice to return to the top-level assembly.

15. Click Save again, and you will be prompted to name the top-level assembly file. Name the file **Top Level Assembly** and click the Save button.

16. The Save dialog displays the state of all the assembly files. Both of the assembly files are marked Initial Save. This means they exist only in memory and haven't been saved to the hard drive (or network drive) yet. If you were to click in the Save column to change it to No, the files would be closed without saving, and you would just have the part file on the disc drive. Confirm that the both files are marked Yes, and click the OK button.

These steps illustrate the method of creating a true top-down design, starting with the assembly, then defining the subassembly, and finally creating a part to reside in the assembly structure. If this seems like a purely academic exercise because it is not the way you typically work, you might find that the concepts can still be useful to you every now and again. Often, the top-down, middle-out, or bottom-up approach is dictated by the need to assign part numbers and create assembly structure to match. Keep these things in mind as you work with Inventor assemblies, and you will more than likely find an opportunity to use them somewhere along the way.

Layout Sketches

Certification Objective

Another top-down (or middle-out) design workflow is the use of *layout sketches*, or sketch blocks. Layout sketches are created in a part file, using sketch blocks to represent individual parts as basic 2D symbols. The 2D blocks are "assembled" in the part sketch and can be dimensioned and constrained to simulate simple assembly mechanisms to test function and to some extent fit. The first step in creating a layout sketch is to create a part file and a sketch. Next, 2D sketch geometry is created and turned into sketch blocks, with a single block representing each component within the mechanism. Nested blocks (blocks made of other blocks) can be used to represent subassemblies and can even be set as flexible to allow them to pivot around or translate motion along an axis. Once the basic 2D layout design is complete, you can use the Make Part and Make Component tools to write out the blocks as individual part models from the sketch blocks. From there, a 3D assembly can be created based on, and linked to, the sketch blocks. In this way, if you update the sketch layout, the parts and assemblies will automatically update.

The following example will introduce layout and sketch-block functionality:

1. Click the Get Started tab and click Open.

2. Browse for the file mi_8a_019.ipt located in the Chapter 08 directory of the Mastering Inventor 2016 folder and click Open.

3. Locate the sketch called Layout Assembly in the browser and click the plus sign to expand it.

4. Notice that the sketch contains a block called Base Mount. Right-click the sketch and choose Edit Sketch.

5. Select the Create Block button from the Create panel (note that you might need to use the small black arrow to expose the flyout menu).

6. Select all the geometry on the left of the sketch with the visible dimensions.

7. Click the Insert Point button in the Create Block dialog box and then select the lower-left corner of the rectangle as the insert point.

8. Enter **Base Plate** for the block name and then click the OK button to create the block.

9. Expand the Blocks folder in the browser and notice that the Base Plate block has been added to the block definitions. The geometry you selected has been converted to a block as well and now behaves as a single entity.

10. Place a Concentric constraint on each of the half-circle shapes on the base plate and the corresponding half-circle shape on the base mount. Exit the Constraint tool by right-clicking and clicking the OK or Cancel button.

11. Select the Arm Assembly block from the Blocks folder and drag it into the graphics area to place an instance of it.

12. Place a Concentric constraint on the right circle of the Base Mount block and the large dashed circle on the bottom link of the Arm Assembly block. Exit the Constraint tool by right-clicking and clicking the OK or Cancel button.

13. Select the Cylinder Assembly block from the Blocks folder and drag it into the graphics area to place an instance of it.

14. Place a Concentric constraint on the left circle of the Base Mount block and the larger circle on the Cylinder Assembly block. Exit the Constraint tool by right-clicking and clicking the OK or Cancel button.

15. Right-click the Cylinder Assembly block and choose Flexible. This allows the underconstrained geometry to solve independently at the top-level block.

16. Click and drag the free end of the Cylinder Assembly block to see the plunger slide in the cylinder.

17. Place a Concentric constraint on the free end of the Arm Assembly block and the free end of the Cylinder Assembly block.

18. Click Finish Sketch to return to the feature level. Figure 8.38 shows the layout sketch.

FIGURE 8.38
Blocks folder and blocks in the sketch

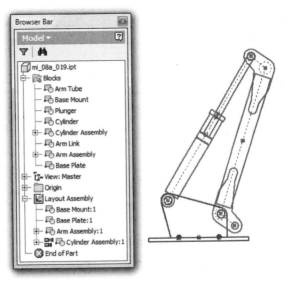

Notice that you can continue to drag the sketch assembly to see the adjustment of the cylinder and the angle for the arm assembly. As you can see, creating layout sketches in this fashion allows you to solve linear and pivot motion layouts in 2D. Once the sketch layout has been completed, you can use the Make Components tool to write each block out to an individual part or assembly file. You can close the current file without saving changes or use it to explore the Make Components workflow using these general steps:

1. Click the Make Components button on the Manage tab and then select the sketch blocks you want to create components for.

2. Select additional blocks to add to the list, or select from the list and click Remove From Selection to exclude any blocks you decide you do not want to create components for.

3. Select Insert Components In Target Assembly and then set the assembly name, the template from which to create it, and the save path (or clear this option to create the parts only). If the assembly already exists, use the target assembly location's Browse button to select it.

4. Click Next to accept your selections.

5. The next dialog box allows you to name and set paths for the files to be created. Click the cells in the table to make changes for the components as required:

   ◆ Click or right-click a cell to choose from the options for that cell type, if any.

   ◆ You can **Shift**+click multiple components and use the buttons above the Template and File Location columns to set those values for multiple components at once.

6. Click Include Parameters to choose which layout model parameters to have present in the created parts.

7. Click the Apply or OK button to make the components. If the component files are created in an assembly, the assembly file is created with the parts (and subassemblies) placed and left open in Inventor, but the assembly and parts are not saved until you choose to do so. If you choose to create the components without an assembly, you are prompted to save the new files as they are created.

8. You can then open each part file and create 3D geometry based on the sketch block. Changes to the original layout sketch push through to the 3D part and assembly.

Layout sketches can boost your productivity. During the initial stage of design, there are frequent changes as you nail down the details. When you initially create the layout sketch, you can easily investigate "what if?" scenarios. You can add as much or as little detail as you need to define the function and form. If you do need to make a change in the relationship of components, you can do that in the layout sketch, and then the update will get pushed to all the components. Once components are generated from the blocks, you can edit them and build the model parts based on the basic blocks. You can open the assembly called mi_8a_020.iam to examine a simple assembly created from the layout sketch used in the completed version of the previous exercise.

Flexibility

When multiple instances of the same subassembly are used within a design, each instance can be made flexible, allowing underconstrained components in the subassembly to be solved at the top-level assembly. The caster assemblies in Figure 8.39 have been made flexible so they can be swiveled and positioned independently as they would in the real world.

FIGURE 8.39

Flexible subassemblies

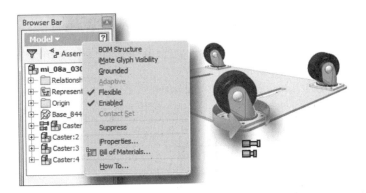

A subassembly instance is made flexible by right-clicking the instance within the browser and selecting Flexible. Flexible subassemblies are displayed with an icon next to the instance name in the browser so that you can easily determine which instances are flexible.

Flexible assemblies can be nested into flexible subassemblies and will still update whenever the original assembly is changed. One common use of flexible assemblies would be in the creation of hydraulic cylinders that require extensions of different lengths when used in multiple locations within a top-level assembly. When each instance of the assembly is made flexible, each cylinder can move accordingly within the top-level assembly.

If a subassembly with nested flexible subassemblies is to be placed into a top-level assembly, you simply right-click that subassembly to bring forward the flexibility of the nested flexible assemblies. Consider the example of the hydraulic cylinder. Multiple instances of the cylinder might be placed into an extension arm assembly, and each instance can be made flexible so that they can be allowed to adjust as they are constrained to the extension-arm parts.

If two instances of the extension arm are then placed into a top-level assembly, those instances need to be made flexible as well to allow the cylinders to demonstrate flexibility. You can use the file mi_08a_030.iam to explore flexible subassemblies.

Adaptivity

Cross-part adaptivity is a powerful feature of Autodesk Inventor, and it can be turned on or off at will. Adaptivity is an option that allows a sketch or feature in one part to update based on a sketch or feature in another part. Although adaptivity is a powerful tool when properly used, it can also cause performance problems when used indiscriminately in large assemblies or when an adaptive part is utilized in another assembly without its related part. But you can fix both situations with simple methods.

Because active adaptive parts can cause performance issues in large assemblies, you should turn off adaptivity after use. If a related part is edited, adaptivity on the associated part should be turned on, and the assembly should be updated to reflect the changes on the related part. Once this is done, that adaptivity should be turned off once again.

TRACKING ADAPTIVITY

It is a good idea to turn off adaptivity when it's not in use; however, Inventor does not have a good method to tell you what parts *were* adaptive. One way is to rename the browser nodes so that you can tell what parts were adaptive. A simple way to do this is to append -A on the browser node. Now you'll know which parts were adaptive even where they are not currently adaptive.

If an adaptive part is to be used in other designs, save the part with a different filename and remove the adaptivity from the new part. Otherwise, the adaptive relationships will carry over into the other design, and you won't be able to edit shared parts.

Creating Adaptivity

This example creates an adaptive relationship between two parts and demonstrates how they are linked together:

1. On the Get Started tab, click Open.

2. Browse to Chapter 08 in the Mastering Inventor 2016 directory and open mi_08a_021.iam.

3. Click the Create button on the Assemble tab, or right-click in the browser or graphics area and select Create Component.

4. Name the new part file **Gasket**. For New File Location, browse to the Chapter 08 folder, confirm that Constrain Sketch Plane To Selected Face Or Plane is selected, and click the OK button.

5. Select the top face of the rotary hub part for the new part sketch. Depending on the Application Options Sketch settings, Inventor might create Sketch1 for you, or you might need to do this manually. If no sketch is created, use the Start 2D Sketch button and select the top face of the rotary hub part again.

6. Click Project Geometry on the Sketch tab and select the top face of the existing part. The geometry is projected into the sketch. Note that adaptive glyphs have been added to the browser to indicate that the part and sketch are adaptive. Also, there is a Reference1 node nested under the sketch. This node contains the information linking the two parts, as shown in Figure 8.40.

FIGURE 8.40
Part marked with the
adaptive icon in the
browser

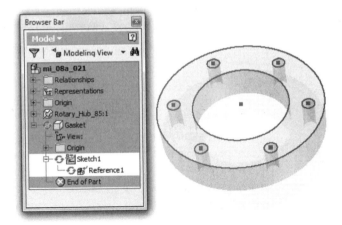

The adaptive glyph is displayed when adaptivity is turned on. You can turn adaptivity on and off by right-clicking the node in the browser. You can toggle the feature or sketch adaptivity while editing the part, but you have to return to the assembly level to toggle adaptivity on the part. Additionally, you can disable the creation of adaptive loops when projecting geometry altogether; to do so, select the Tools tab, click Application Options, select the Assembly tab, and then uncheck the Cross Part Geometry Projection option.

7. Finish the sketch by right-clicking and selecting Finish 2D Sketch from the context menu, as shown in Figure 8.41. Do not click Finish Edit or Inventor will not only finish the sketch but will also exit the part and return you to the assembly.

FIGURE 8.41
Selecting Finish 2D
Sketch, not Finish Edit

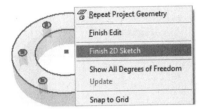

8. Extrude the Gasket part to a thickness of 2 mm, click the Return button to return to the assembly, and then click Save.

9. To see how adaptivity works, double-click the rotary hub component to activate that part for editing. You can double-click the part in the graphics area or the icon next to the part name in the Model browser to activate any part for editing.

10. In the Model browser, right-click Extrusion1 and select Edit Sketch. Change the overall diameter from 130 mm to **160 mm** and click the OK button.

You will notice that the overall diameter and the diameter of the hole pattern of the rotary hub component have changed, but the corresponding gasket part remains unchanged.

11. Click Return to move up to the second-level assembly design state once again. Both parts are active at the subassembly level, so the gasket part updates to match the rotary hub component.

As you can see, the ability to adapt one part to another can make updates across parts easy. You can close this assembly without saving the changes and continue.

Removing Adaptivity from Parts

Once a design has been approved and released for production, you should completely remove adaptivity from all parts within your assembly. Removing the adaptivity ensures that the part can be reused within other designs without conflict and will not be updated accidentally.

If you decide to retain adaptivity within your original assembly but plan on using the adaptive part in other assemblies, the adaptive icon will not display on those instances of the part. This is because only one occurrence of a part can define its adaptive features. However, all occurrences reflect changes and adaptive updates, including occurrence in other assemblies. It is for this reason that you must use adaptivity carefully.

To completely remove adaptivity from a part, either activate or open the adaptive part and activate the adaptive sketch. Expand the sketch and right-click Reference to select Break Link, as shown in Figure 8.42.

FIGURE 8.42
Breaking the adaptive link

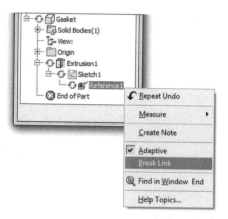

When the adaptive link is broken, the reference geometry is converted to normal sketch geometry. This geometry will need to be fully dimensioned and constrained. Once the geometry has been converted to normal sketch geometry, the part will no longer be able to be adaptive.

MAKING TEMPORARY USE OF ADAPTIVITY

Use adaptivity to find mounting holes for positioning hardware components on a base part. For example, consider a mounting clip and a base plate.

Constrain the clip to the base plate; then make the base plate active for editing and create a sketch on the plate surface. With the sketch active, project the mounting holes, locating holes, and other needed geometry from the mounting clip to the base plate. This creates adaptive relationships in the base plate to the mounting clip.

Once the design is finalized and all the mounting clips are properly located, simply turn adaptivity off on the base plate. When the design is released for production, or at any other desired time, convert the reference geometry created when you projected the geometry to normal sketch geometry. Then dimension and constrain the mounting holes as you would any other feature.

Assembly Features

An *assembly feature* is a feature created and utilized purely within the active assembly file and environment. Because this feature was created within the assembly file, it does not exist at the single part or subassembly level. A good example of an assembly feature in use is the technique of creating drilled holes through a standard tabletop within an assembly. Common practice is to place brackets on the tabletop to find the mounting-hole locations. This allows the holes to be drilled at the same time, ensuring an exact match and placement. Assembly features in Inventor mimic this approach.

Examining the individual tabletop file reveals that the part file does not contain the drilled holes, simply because the drill operation was performed at the assembly level rather than the part level. To understand the reasoning behind this, you might consider that the tabletop is a common part stocked in the shop and then machined as required for each assembly in which it is used. Although the stock part might exist as a cataloged item with no holes, it may exist in many different assemblies with holes of various sizes and locations. Using assembly features allows you to work in this manner.

Other examples of assembly features are contained within the weldment environment, where preparations used to facilitate welding components together are at the assembly level. Preparation features allow trimming of soon-to-be-welded components to eliminate interferences between welds and other parts of the weldment.

Care must be taken when creating geometry within the context of the assembly because it is easy to create an assembly feature when intending to create a part feature. Although this is a common mistake that new users will make, it is one that anyone can experience. In a multilevel top-down design, always make sure you are working in the proper assembly or component by double-clicking the assembly or component in the Model browser for the purpose of opening that component for editing.

To explore the creation of assembly features, follow these steps:

1. On the Get Started tab, click Open.

2. Browse to Chapter 08 in the Mastering Inventor 2016 directory and open mi_08a_022.iam.

This assembly consists of three parts, two of which are instances of the same part, Part_100_8. The other component, Part_200_8, currently interferes with the other two parts. Your goal is to cut a keyhole in both instances of Part_100_8 so that the keyed bar will fit into them. Part_100_8 is a stock bracket used in many assemblies; therefore, you must take care not to create a feature in it that will have a negative impact on its use in all of the assemblies that consume it. To start, you will explore a keyway created by another user at the part level.

3. Double-click the front instance of Part_100_8 to set it active for edits.

4. Locate the feature called Keyway Cut in the browser, right-click it, and choose Unsuppress Features.

5. Right-click and choose Finish Edit to return to the assembly level.

Notice how the keyway cuts the part in the same location on each instance of the part, missing the location on the second instance because of the orientation of the two instances of Part_100_8. Another important aspect of the keyway is that it impacts every instance of the part, in every assembly it was used in. To fix this, continue.

6. Double-click the front instance of Part_100_8 to set it active for edits again.

7. Locate the feature called Keyway Cut in the browser, right-click it, and choose Delete. Click the OK button in the delete confirmation dialog box.

8. Right-click and choose Finish Edit to return to the assembly level.

9. On the 3D Model tab, click the Start 2D Sketch button and choose the large front face of the front instance of Part_100_8 to create the sketch on.

10. On the Sketch tab, click the Project Geometry button.

11. Select the circular edge and the three flat edges of the keyed bar's end profile, projecting the complete key profile into the sketch.

12. Click the Finish Sketch button. Notice the sketch location in the browser.

13. On the 3D Model tab, click the Extrude button. Notice that the only operation available in the Extrude dialog box is Cut. You cannot add material at the assembly level.

14. Set the Extents drop-down box to All, ensure that the cut is going in the right direction, and then click the OK button.

15. You should see the keyhole cut through both instances of Part_100_8 and the keyed bar (Part_200_8) disappear.

16. Expand the Extrusion1 feature in the browser, and you will see the listing of all components involved in the extrusion cut.

17. Right-click Part_200_8 and choose Remove Participant so the keyway cut does not cut the keyed bar.

18. Finally, right-click either instance of Part_100_8 and choose Open. Notice that the keyhole is not present in the part file because it exists only as an assembly-level feature.

You can close this file without saving changes. You should know that in addition to removing participating components from an assembly-level feature, you can add components to an assembly feature by right-clicking the feature, choosing Add Participant from the menu, and then choosing the component from the browser. On the right of Figure 8.43, a component named Top-103:2 is being removed from the feature named Extrusion 1 so that the extrusion cut does not go through that part. On the left, another component is being added to the extrusion feature.

FIGURE 8.43
Adding/removing participants from assembly features

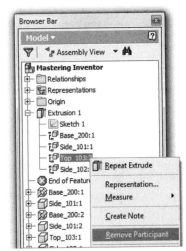

Assembly features can be made with the Extrude, Revolve, Hole, Sweep, Fillet, Chamfer, and Move Face tools. Keep in mind that all assembly features are allowed only to cut or remove material and cannot add material to a part. Other commonly used assembly feature commands within the Assembly panel environment are the Mirror and Patterns commands.

ISOLATE COMPONENTS BEFORE CREATING ASSEMBLY FEATURES

If you select the components to be involved in an assembly feature first, right-click and choose Isolate, and then create the feature, you will not need to remove participants that you didn't intend to cut in the first place. You will need to right-click again after creating the feature to choose Undo Isolate.

Managing the Bill of Materials

Certification
Objective

In Inventor, the bill of materials (BOM) is the internal, real-time database that exists within every assembly. Real-time means that as components are added to the assembly, they are automatically added and counted in the BOM. Although you might be accustomed to referring to the tabled list of parts on the 2D drawing as a bill of materials, in Inventor such a table is called a *parts list*. Parts lists pull directly from the assembly BOM.

The BOM is controlled at two levels: the part level and the assembly level. Both levels factor in certain aspects of how the bill of materials is generated, how components are represented, and ultimately how the parts list is generated within the drawing environment.

Parts-Level BOM Control

In the part environment, the designer has the ability to define the BOM structure of just a part. At this level, the structure can be defined as Normal, Inseparable, Purchased, Phantom, or Reference. Determining the default setting at the part level allows control of how the component is identified within the overall BOM for any assembly the component is used in. By setting the structure at the part level, you can control the assembly BOM display according to the part settings. Any structure settings at the part level can be overridden and changed to Reference at the assembly level.

Another important structure setting at the part level is the Base Quantity property. This setting controls how the part is listed in the BOM. If Base Quantity is set to Each, the part is tallied by count. This is the default for most standard parts. The Base Quantity can also be set to reflect the value of any given model parameter. This is most often set to a length parameter so that the Base Quantity property will tally the total length of a part used in an assembly. Parts pulled from Content Center and Frame Generator have their Base Quantity property set to pull a length parameter by default. The Base Quantity property is set by choosing Tools ➢ Document Settings and selecting the Bill Of Materials tab.

Assembly-Level BOM Control

BOM control accelerates at the assembly level. You can access the Bill Of Materials dialog box by clicking the Bill Of Materials icon on the Manage panel of the Assemble tab. In the drawing environment, the BOM Editor dialog box is accessible by right-clicking the parts list and selecting Bill Of Materials.

The Bill Of Materials dialog box allows you to edit iProperties, BOM properties, and the BOM structure; override quantities for components; and sort and create a consistent item order for generating parts lists. Figure 8.44 shows the Bill Of Materials dialog box.

FIGURE 8.44
Bill Of Materials dialog box

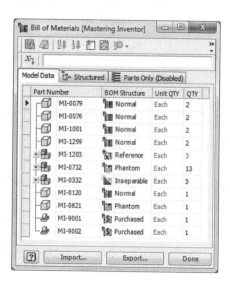

Exporting a bill of materials is a straightforward process, with icons across the top of the dialog box allowing the export of the BOM data in a structured or parts-only view in formats such as MDB, dBase, or various Excel formats. The Engineer's Notebook icon permits the export of database information as a note.

ADDING AND REMOVING COLUMNS

Certification Objective

You can add columns to the model in any of the three tabs in the Bill Of Materials dialog box by clicking the Choose Columns icon, which will display a dialog box list in which you can drag a desired column to a specified location, as shown in Figure 8.45. To remove a desired column, simply drag the column to be removed back to the dialog box list.

FIGURE 8.45
Choose Column dialog box

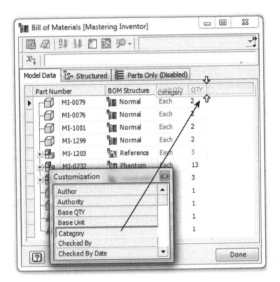

The next icon at the top of the Bill Of Materials dialog box allows you to add custom iProperty columns. The drop-down list shown in Figure 8.46 within the Add Custom iProperty Columns dialog box will display a combined list of all the available custom iProperties contained within the assembly.

FIGURE 8.46
Custom iProperty list

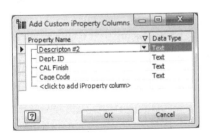

If a desired custom iProperty does not exist within the list of components, you can add it manually by selecting the <Click To Add iProperty Column> option displayed in the list box. Be sure to set the data type to the correct format when manually adding a custom iProperty to the assembly file. Manually added iProperties will be stored in the assembly file. Figure 8.47 shows the addition of a custom iProperty column called Assembly Station.

FIGURE 8.47
Creating a new custom iProperty

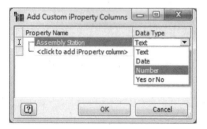

Once custom iProperty columns have been added to the assembly bill of materials, individual parts can be populated with custom iProperties as needed. Individual parts that already contain those iProperties will show the values within the respective row and column. iProperties that are edited or added to a respective part row will be pushed down to the part level; therefore, filling out iProperties at the assembly level is often the most efficient way to populate part iProperties.

The Create Expression icon located at the beginning of the Formula toolbar launches the Property Expression dialog box so you can create an iProperty expression. The newly created expression can contain a combination of custom text and iProperty names in brackets. The iProperty expression will be substituted for the field in which the expression was created once the expression is evaluated. In Figure 8.48, the expression is created in the Description field.

FIGURE 8.48
Creating property expressions

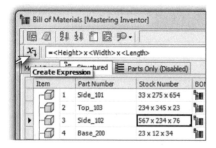

Looking across the top of the Bill Of Materials dialog box, the two icons to the far right are Part Number Merge Settings and Update Mass Properties Of All Rows. Clicking the Update Mass Properties Of All Rows icon recalculates the total mass for all components within the assembly.

Clicking the Part Number Merge Settings icon allows different components possessing the same part number to be treated as the same component. For instance, say six base plates of the same size are used in an assembly. Four of these plates have holes drilled upon installation, and two have holes placed during fabrication. As far as the shop is concerned, all six are the same part, but in the design both plate types exist as separate part files.

To have the BOM count the total number of plates, you set the Part Number property to match on both items and then use Part Number Merge Settings to have these files counted as a single item.

BOM STRUCTURE DESIGNATIONS

You can choose from five designations when assigning BOM structure to components: Normal, Inseparable, Purchased, Phantom, and Reference. Any part or assembly file can be assigned one of these designations within the BOM. The designation is then stored in the file, meaning that if a part is marked as Purchased in one assembly, it will be designated as Purchased in all assemblies. The structure designations are as follows:

Normal This is the default structure for most components. The placement and participation in the assembly bill of materials are determined by the parent assembly. In the previous example, you created an assembly file rather than a single part. As a result, you will be determining the characteristics of how this assembly file will behave in the top-level assembly bill of materials. With a Normal BOM structure, this assembly will be numbered and included in quantity calculations within the top-level assembly.

Inseparable These are generally assemblies that cannot be disassembled without damage. Examples of Inseparable assemblies might include weldments, glued constructions, and riveted assemblies. In a parts-only parts list, these assemblies will be treated as a single part. Another example is a Purchased part such as a motor.

Purchased This designation is typically for parts or assemblies that are not fabricated in-house. Examples of Purchased components are motors, brake calipers, programmable controllers, hinges, and the like. A Purchased component is considered as a single BOM item regardless of whether it is a part or a subassembly. Within a Purchased assembly, all child parts are excluded from the BOM and quantity calculations.

Phantom Use Phantom components to simplify the design process. A Phantom component exists within the design but is not shown as a line item in the BOM. A common use for a Phantom component would be a subassembly of parts that are grouped for ease of design. Setting the subassembly to be a Phantom component allows the parts to be listed in the BOM individually. Other examples of Phantom components could include hardware sets, screws, nuts, bolts, washers, pins, and various fastener-type components. A good example of a Phantom assembly would be a collection of parts that are normally assembled onto the machine one at a time. However, in the interest of reducing the overall number of Assembly constraints within the design, the engineer might choose to preassemble the various components within a Phantom assembly. That assembly could then be constrained as one component instead of multiple parts.

Reference Mark components as Reference when they are used for construction geometry or to add detail and references to the top-level assembly. A good example of a Reference component is a car body and frame that represents the outer shell for placement of a power train. In the 2D documentation, the car body and frame would be shown as hidden lines illustrating the overall design while highlighting the power train as the principal component within a view. Reference geometry is excluded from quantity, mass, or volume calculations regardless of their own internal BOM structure. As a result, they are not included within the parts list. They are placed only within the overall assembly to show design intent and position.

In addition to using these five BOM structure designations for component files, you have the ability to create a virtual component, which has no geometry and does not exist as an external file. A virtual component can have a complete set of properties that are similar to real components but are primarily used to represent bulk items such as fasteners, assembly kits, paint, grease, adhesive, plating, or other items that do not require creating an actual model. A virtual component can be designated as any of the previous BOM structure types and can contain custom properties, descriptions, and other aspects of the BOM data like any other component.

A virtual component will be shown in the Model browser as if it were a real part. Virtual components can be created by selecting the check box next to the Default BOM Structure dropdown in the Create In-Place Component dialog box, as shown in Figure 8.49.

FIGURE 8.49
Creating a virtual component

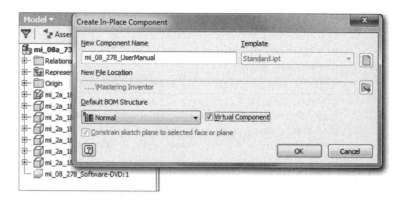

VIRTUAL COMPONENTS IN TEMPLATES

If you use the same virtual components in most of your assemblies, you might want to create them in a blank assembly, fill out their BOM properties using the BOM Editor, and then save the assembly as a template file. Then when you create a new assembly, the virtual components will already be present. Any of them not required can simply be deleted.

BOM VIEW TABS

Certification
Objective

Each tab in the Bill Of Materials dialog box represents a different BOM view. All tabs permit ascending or descending sorting of the rows in the BOM by clicking the respective column header. You can also reorder rows by simply clicking and dragging a component's icon.

With the Model Data tab active, you see the components listed just as they exist in the Model browser. You can add or remove columns to populate the Model Data tab independently of the other BOM view tabs. On this tab all components are listed in the BOM regardless of BOM structure designation. Item numbers are not assigned on the Model Data tab. The model data is not exportable or available for placement as a parts list. Instead, this tab is typically used for organizing the BOM and assigning the BOM structure designation.

Figure 8.50 shows a bill of materials on the Model Data tab. Notice that there are no item numbers listed and that all component structure types are displayed, including Reference and Phantom components. Notice too that the last two parts listed are virtual parts and have been given different BOM structure designations.

FIGURE 8.50
BOM Model Data tab

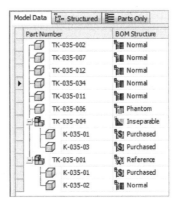

In addition to the Model Data tab are the Structured and Parts Only tabs. These tabs are disabled by default. To enable them, right-click the tab and choose Enable BOM View; alternatively, click the View Options button along the top of the Bill Of Materials dialog box.

The Structured tab can display all components of the assembly, including subassemblies and the parts of the subassemblies. In Structured view, additional icons will be active on the toolbar, allowing you to sort by item and renumber items within the assembly BOM. The order of the BOM item numbers is stored in the assembly file.

The View Options icon allows you to enable or disable the BOM view and set the view properties from the drop-down. Choose View Properties to modify the Structured view. The resulting Structured Properties dialog box contains two drop-down lists defining the level, the minimum number of digits, and the assembly part delimiter value. If the level is set to First Level, subassemblies are listed without the components contained within. If set to All Levels, each part is listed in an indented manner under the subassembly, as shown in Figure 8.51.

FIGURE 8.51
Structured Properties dialog box

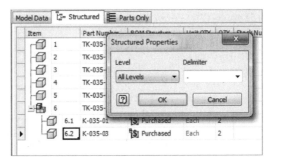

The Parts Only tab lists all components in a flat list. In this BOM view, subassemblies designated as Normal are not listed as an item, but all their child components are displayed. By contrast, Inseparable and Purchased subassemblies are displayed as items, but their child components are not displayed.

Bill of materials settings that are modified by the Bill Of Materials dialog box will carry forward into the drawing parts lists contained in the assembly. Note that if both the Structured and Parts Only views of the BOM are enabled, the same part may have a different item number in each view.

Figure 8.52 shows a bill of materials in the Structured view compared to the same assembly in the Model Data view. The first thing to note is that all the components have been assigned item numbers in the Structured view. You might also notice that the Reference and Phantom components that are listed in the Model Data view are filtered out of the Structured view. Closer inspection reveals that although the Phantom subassembly named TK-035-001 is not included in the Structured view, its child parts are listed, each with an arrow next to the icon to denote that they are promoted from a subassembly. Recall that Phantom subassemblies are used to group parts for design organization and to reduce Assembly constraints while allowing the parts to be listed individually.

FIGURE 8.52
BOM structured view

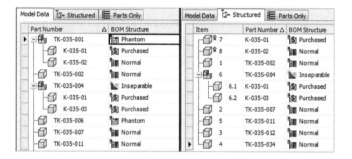

Figure 8.53 shows a bill of materials in the Parts Only view. This Parts Only view filters out Reference and Phantom components just like the Structured view does. Notice too that although the subassemblies are not listed as items, their child parts are. The exceptions to this are Purchased and Inseparable assemblies. In the figure, the Purchased subassembly is listed as a single item, since it is a Purchased component comprising two Purchased parts and is assumed to be purchased as one item. Note that if you had the need to list the parts as items rather than the subassembly, you would designate the subassembly as Phantom rather than Purchased.

Take a look also at the Inseparable subassembly named TK-035-004. It is listed as an item along with one of its child parts named K-035-01. This child part is listed because it is a Purchased item and needs to be ordered. Had both children of the Inseparable subassembly been Normal parts, neither would be listed in the Parts Only view.

FIGURE 8.53
BOM Parts Only tab

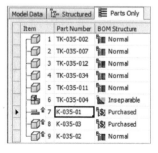

ADDING TWO PARTS WITH THE SAME PART NUMBER

You may occasionally need to add two separate part files to an assembly but have them listed as the same part number. For instance, when you're using Frame Generator, each member is created as a separate part even though those parts might be identical in profile and length. This is done so you can modify each part individually as needed. However, if the parts remain identical once the design is complete, you can use the BOM Editor and set each identical part file to use the same part number even though the part files have different names. This allows the BOM to count the parts as a single item.

Assembly Reuse and Configurations

Frequently existing assemblies are used in other designs or are used in multiple locations within the top-level assembly. There are three basic workflows for reusing and configuring assemblies in a design.

◆ Copying designs

◆ Using view, positional, and level-of-detail representations

◆ Using iAssemblies (table-driven assemblies)

Copying Designs

Often you'll need to copy a previous design to create a similar design based on the original. Part of the challenge of doing this with Inventor is creating copies of only the parts that will be modified in the new design while reusing parts that do not incur changes, all while maintaining healthy file links. To do this effectively, you can employ the Copy Components tool from within the assembly to be copied.

---

iCopy

Depending on the design, you might be called on to create subassemblies containing similar geometry but having different sizes or positions in the top-level assembly. Rather than manually creating each of these subassemblies, you can use the iCopy tool. iCopy combines skeletal modeling (using a part file as the "skeleton" on which to arrange other components) and adaptivity. If you design curtain walls, trusses, bridge-type frames, or any design where subassemblies are basically the same but vary in size and position, you may want to explore the iCopy tool. There are four general steps to using iCopy.

1. Create a target assembly using the skeletal target layout part.

2. Create the subassembly to be patterned using the template layout part.

3. Use the iCopy Author tool in the subassembly to make it usable as an iCopy template.

4. Use the iCopy tool to copy/pattern the subassembly.

To begin this process, first select the top-level assembly from the browser tree and then click the Copy button from the Pattern panel (note that you might need to click the small black arrow to find the Copy button). You will be presented with the Copy Components: Status dialog box, which lists the top-level assembly and the components within, as shown in Figure 8.54. Use the Status buttons next to each component to set the component to be copied, reused, or excluded from the copy operation.

FIGURE 8.54

Copy Components: Status dialog box

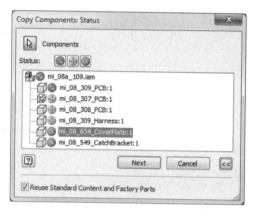

In the example in Figure 8.54, the component named mi_08_309_PCB is the only part that needs to be redesigned for the new assembly; therefore, it is the only part set to be copied. In the original design, there are two that have been excluded in this copy operation because they will be swapped out for other parts that are already created, after the copy has been made. You will notice that the other components except the top-level assembly are set to be reused. Once the copy status of each part is set, click the Next button to move to the Copy Components: File Names dialog box, shown in Figure 8.55.

FIGURE 8.55

Copy Components: File Names dialog box

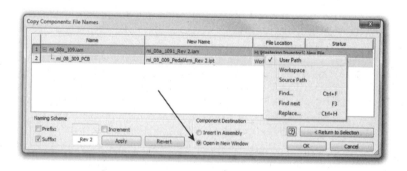

In the Copy Components: File Names dialog box, you want to set the destination button to Open In New Window in order to create a new, separate assembly file. You can then use the Prefix and Suffix controls to modify the existing filenames, or you can type in new names as required. By default, File Location is set to Source Path, meaning that the new files will land right next to the existing ones. If that is not desirable, you can right-click each File Location cell and choose User Path or Workspace. Care should be taken to ensure that file location paths are not set outside the project search path. When the filename and paths are set, click the OK button.

 **Real World Scenario**

ROLLING REVISIONS

A large part of any engineering department's time and energy is focused on revision control. You can think of a revision roll as just a copy of an existing design with improvements. Here is a general procedure for rolling the revision of an approved design, where Rev1 is complete and Rev2 is being created:

1. Open the Rev1 assembly and start the Copy Components tool.

2. Configure the Copy Components list to include, exclude, and reuse components as required for Rev2.

3. Set the destination button to Open In New Window and click the OK button to create the Rev2 assembly.

4. Rename and set the file location for all copied components as well as for the Rev2 assembly file.

5. Add additional components to the Rev2 assembly as needed and make any other modifications required.

6. Open the Rev1 drawing file and use Save As to create a Rev2 copy.

7. In the Rev2 drawing, click the Manage tab and use the Replace Model Reference button to exchange all the Rev1 views, parts lists, and other references with Rev2.

The new assembly file will open in a separate window. Interrogation of the Model browser should reveal that the components set to be reused are listed just as they were in the original assembly, the components set to be copied are listed as specified, and the components set to be excluded are not present at all.

Using Representations

Inventor provides the ability to create and store three basic types of representations within an assembly file. *Representations* allow you to manage assemblies by setting up varying views, positions, and levels of detail for your models. Each of these allows for the creation of user-defined representations, and each has a master representation. Note that although user-defined representations can be renamed and deleted as required, master representations cannot. Using representations enhances productivity and improves performance in large assembly design.

Once representations are created in an assembly, you can open that assembly file in any combination of those representation states by clicking the Options button in the Open dialog box, as shown in Figure 8.56. Keep in mind that although you can open or place a file by typing the filename rather than scrolling and clicking the icon, you cannot access the Options button without explicitly scrolling and selecting the file in the dialog box.

FIGURE 8.56
Opening a file in a representation

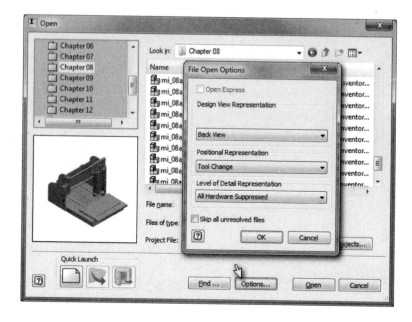

VIEW REPRESENTATIONS

Certification
Objective

View representations, also known as design views and ViewReps, are used to configure the display of an assembly and save that display for later use. View representations control the following settings:

- The visibility state of components, sketch features, and work features
- Component color and styles applied at the assembly level
- The enabled/not enabled status of components
- The "camera view," meaning the onscreen zoom magnification and orientation
- The browser tree state

In effect, view representations allow "snapshot views" of portions of an assembly file. Each view representation is saved within the assembly file and has no effect on individual parts or subassemblies. View representations are relatively simple to create and use. To create a view representation, follow these general steps:

1. While in the assembly, simply zoom and rotate your model until you have the desired view showing in the current graphics window.

2. Expand the Representations folder and right-click View to select New, as shown in Figure 8.57.

FIGURE 8.57

Creating a new view
representation

3. Turn off the visibility of a few parts; these visibility changes will take place only within this view representation.

4. After creating the new view representation, click Save to preserve the newly created representation.

You can protect the view representation you create from accidental edits by right-clicking it and choosing Lock. View representations can be accessed either by double-clicking the desired representation or by right-clicking the desired representation and selecting Activate. Private view representations are views created in early releases of Inventor and are not associative.

ACTIVATING A NEW VIEW REPRESENTATION TO PREVENT ERRORS

Probably one of the most misunderstood "errors" in Inventor is the "The current Design View Representation is locked" message. This tells you that changes will not be saved, and it alarms a lot of new users. What this means is that you have turned off the visibility (or enabled status or any number of other things) while in the master view representation. Since the master is locked, these changes will not be saved, and the next time you open the file, the model will be at the previous state. To circumvent this issue, be sure to activate a new ViewRep or use the one called Default, make your changes, and then save. This way, your visibility, color overrides, and other settings will be saved in the ViewRep.

POSITIONAL REPRESENTATIONS

Certification
Objective

Positional representations, often referred to as PosReps for short, can be employed to set up and store components in various arrangements and are used to help test and analyze assembly motion. Positional representations work by overriding Assembly constraints, assembly patterns, or component properties.

To create a new positional representation, expand the Representations heading in the browser, right-click the Position heading, and then choose New. Continue by right-clicking the component, pattern, or constraint in the Model browser that you want to change. Choose Override from the context menu. The Object Override dialog box will open to the Relationship, Pattern, or Component tab, depending on the entity type that you right-clicked. You can rename the new representation from the default name to something more meaningful; however, you cannot rename the master representation.

In the following exercise, you will create positional representations to control the movement for the components of a hobby-type CNC router. Note that there are four components in this assembly. In the real world, these four components would be modeled as subassemblies; however, they have been created as simple part files in order to simplify the model. Follow these steps to explore the options involved in creating simple positional representations:

1. On the Get Started tab, click Open and then select the file mi_08a_023.iam from the Chapter 08 folder of the Mastering Inventor 2016 folder.

2. Click and drag the component named Z-Axis Assembly_08, and notice how it can be dragged to cause interference and into an unrealistic location.

Currently this assembly has two sets of constraints defined. One set defines the X, Y, and Z travel limits, and the other set defines the home position for each of the assembly components. In the current state, all of these constraints have been suppressed. In the next steps, you will create a positional representation and unsuppress the home position constraints.

3. Click the plus sign to expand each component in the browser and notice the suppressed constraints.

4. Locate the Representations folder in the browser and then click the plus sign next to the icon to expand it.

5. Right-click Position and choose New to create a new positional representation, as shown in Figure 8.58.

FIGURE 8.58
Creating a new positional representation

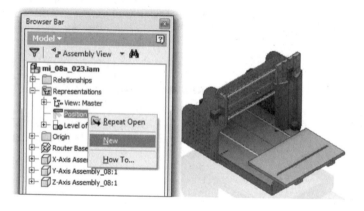

6. Expand the Position node, if needed, and notice that a positional representation called Position1 has been created and is currently active, as denoted by the check mark.

7. Select Position1; then click it and rename it **Home Position**.

8. Right-click the Z Home constraint listed under the Z-Axis Assembly component and choose Override, as shown on the left of Figure 8.59.

FIGURE 8.59

Overriding a constraint value

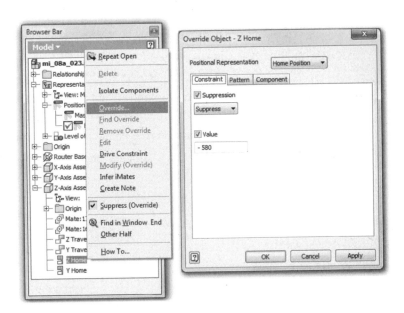

9. In the Override Object dialog box, click the Suppression check box and set the drop-down box to Enable.

10. Click the Value check box and set the value to **-580 mm**; then click the OK button. This sets the z-axis assembly to a static up and down position. You can click and drag the component to see this.

11. Right-click the Y Home constraint and choose Override.

12. In the Override Object dialog box, click the Suppression check box and set the drop-down box to Enable.

13. Click the Value check box and set the value to **-28 mm**; then click the OK button. This sets the y-axis assembly to a static left and right position. If you click and drag the z-axis assembly, you will see that it is now locked in place.

14. Right-click the X Home constraint listed under the X-Axis Assembly component and choose Override.

15. In the Override Object dialog box, click the Suppression check box and set the drop-down box to Enable.

16. Click the Value check box and set the value to **395 mm**; then click the OK button. This sets the x-axis assembly to a static forward and backward position.

17. Right-click the Master positional representation and choose Activate. Click and drag the z-axis assembly and notice that it is free to drag again.

18. Right-click the Home Position representation and choose Activate to set the assembly back to its defined home position; notice that it is constrained in place.

In the next set of steps you will create another positional representation and unsuppress the set of constraints that will control the X, Y, and Z travel limits.

19. Right-click Position at the top level of the Positional representation node and choose New to create a new positional representation.

20. Expand the Position node, if needed, and notice that a new positional representation has been created and is currently active, as denoted by the check mark.

21. Rename the new positional representation to **Set to Range**.

22. Right-click the Z Travel constraint and choose Suppress (Override), as shown in Figure 8.60.

FIGURE 8.60
Enabling a suppressed constraint

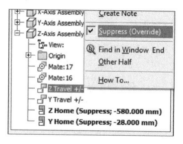

This toggles the suppression value of the Z Travel constraint and enables it so the travel is limited in the z-axis to hold it to a realistic range of motion. Next, you will do the same for the Y and X Travel constraints.

23. Right-click the Y Travel constraint and choose Suppress (Override).

24. Right-click the X Travel constraint and choose Suppress (Override). Note that you may need to expand the x-axis assembly component in the browser to find this constraint.

25. Right-click the Home Position representation and choose Activate. Click and drag the z-axis assembly to set the assembly back to its home position.

26. Right-click the Set to Range representation and choose Activate to set the assembly so it can be dragged within its defined range of travel.

As you can see from the previous steps, positional representations are a powerful way to show components in multiple positions as required during the operation of a mechanism. You can close the current file without saving changes and continue to explore the use of positional representations in subassemblies. Follow these steps to discover the tools used for handling positional representations in subassemblies:

1. On the Get Started tab, click Open and then select the file mi_08a_024.iam from the Chapter 08 folder of the Mastering Inventor 2016 directory.

2. Expand the Representations folder for the top-level assembly (located at the top of the browser tree).

3. Right-click Position and choose New to create a new positional representation.

4. Expand the Position node, if needed, and notice that a positional representation called Position1 has been created and is currently active, as denoted by the check mark.

5. Select Position1; then click it and rename it **Range of Travel**.

6. Expand the component called CNC Hobby Router and then expand the Representations folder for this subassembly.

7. Expand the Position node to reveal the positional representations already created in this subassembly.

8. Right-click the Set To Range positional representation and choose Activate.

At this point, you have created a positional representation for the top-level assembly and then set that positional representation to use the Set To Range positional representation in the subassembly.

9. Click and drag the router assembly and notice that the parts will not move. To fix this, you need to set the subassembly to be flexible within the positional representation.

10. Right-click the CNC Hobby Router (either in the browser or in the graphics area) and choose Override from the context menu. In the Override Object dialog box, you will notice that Set To Range is the active positional representation as defined previously.

11. Click the Flexible Status check box and set the drop-down box to Flexible, then click the OK button.

12. Click and drag the router assembly and notice that the parts will now move according to the Set To Range positional representation that is defined in the subassembly.

Once you've explored the nested positional representations, you can close this file without saving changes. Positional representations also allow the reuse of identical subassemblies within a top-level assembly file. By using positional representations in conjunction with flexible assemblies, you can demonstrate a subassembly in different positions. Figure 8.61 shows an assembly containing multiple instances of a cylinder subassembly, each at a different extension length. This model could be created by setting up positional representations in the cylinder subassembly defining each extension value or by leaving the cylinder subassembly unconstrained and then setting each subassembly to be flexible.

To help manage positional representations, you can set up the browser to display only the overrides present in each positional representation, as shown in Figure 8.62. The buttons along the top of the Representations browser allow you to create a new positional representation, validate the overrides to ensure that no errors are created in the representations, and manage the overrides via Microsoft Excel.

FIGURE 8.61
Multiple instances of a
cylinder subassembly

FIGURE 8.62
The Representations
browser

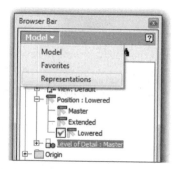

Because the positional representation properties of an assembly are stored separately, multiple views can be created in the drawing environment, representing different positions of the same assembly. Figure 8.63 shows an example of an overlay view showing both available positions of a bucket assembly on a front loader.

FIGURE 8.63
Overlay view
of a positional
representation

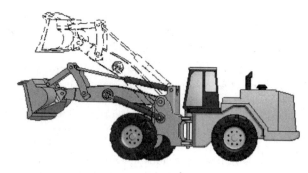

LEVEL OF DETAIL REPRESENTATIONS

**Certification
Objective**

Proper use of level of detail (LOD) improves speed and reduces the memory required to load and navigate large assemblies. When working with a large assembly, you suppress components that are not required for a certain aspect of working with the design and then save that suppression state as a level-of-detail representation. For instance, if you are designing a large material-handling unit, you might open the unit in the LOD representation with everything suppressed except the frame while you work on the frame skins, thereby significantly reducing the number of parts loaded into memory.

SUPPRESSION VS. VISIBILITY

It is a common misconception that making components invisible reduces the overhead of your assemblies. When a component's visibility is toggled off, it is still loaded into memory. To unload it from memory, you must utilize LOD reps. If you work with large assemblies, you can set All Components Suppressed as the default LOD. The assembly will open more quickly, and then you can select a previously defined LOD or unsuppress just the parts you want to work with. This method consumes less RAM than opening the complete assembly and then suppressing components.

Another common example of LOD representations might be to suppress external components while working on internal components simply for convenience. In addition to this standard method of suppressing components to create LOD, you can employ substitute LOD representations to trade out a large multipart assembly with a single part derived from that assembly.

Just as view and positional representations have master representations, so does the LOD. However, there are three additional default LOD representations: All Components Suppressed, All Parts Suppressed, and All Content Center Suppressed. These system-defined LODs cannot be removed or modified.

All Components Suppressed   Suppresses everything within the assembly, allowing you to quickly open the assembly and then unsuppress components as required.

All Parts Suppressed   Suppresses all parts at all levels of the assembly; however, subassemblies are loaded, allowing you to examine the assembly structure without loading all the part files.

All Content Center Suppressed   Suppresses any component in the assembly that is stored in the Content Center Files directory as designated by the IPJ (project) file.

Although Chapter 9, "Large Assembly Strategies," covers the specific steps to create LODs, here are the general procedures.

To create a user-defined LOD, follow these steps:

1. Expand the Representations heading in the browser, right-click the Level Of Detail heading, and then choose New Level Of Detail.

2. Continue by right-clicking the component or components you want to suppress and choosing Suppress from the menu.

3. Once this is done, you must save the assembly while still in the LOD.

4. After saving the assembly, you can create more LOD representations or flip from one to another to compare the results.

To create a substitute LOD, you start by expanding the Representations heading in the browser, right-click the Level Of Detail heading, and then choose New Substitute. There are two methods for creating substitutes. The first method simply prompts you to select any existing part file to swap out for the assembly file in the LOD, and the second creates a derived part from the source assembly. When using the Derive Assembly method, you are asked to specify a part template to use and then are brought right into the derive assembly process. The derived part is automatically marked as a substitute during the derive process and placed into the LOD.

On the left, Figure 8.64 shows an assembly in its master LOD with 302 component occurrences in the assembly and 77 unique files open in the Inventor session, denoted by the numbers at the bottom of the image. On the right, the same assembly is set to a substitute LOD and reduced to a single component in the assembly, and only two unique files open in the Inventor session. As you can imagine, you can achieve a significant savings in memory by placing an assembly with a substitute LOD active into a top-level assembly.

FIGURE 8.64
Substitute LOD
representation

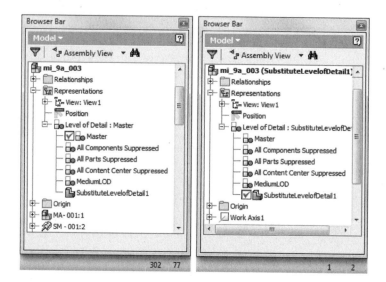

It is important to understand that substitute LODs are intended to be used either by excluding components during the derive process or in combination with user-defined LODs to exclude components. Simply making a substitute LOD of an assembly with all components included may not give you the performance gain you anticipated unless you have made the substitute from another LOD that has parts suppressed or you have excluded parts while creating the substitute LOD.

LOD states are created automatically when you suppress components while in the master LOD. To save suppressions to a new LOD representation, click Save, and you will be prompted to click Yes or No to save the LOD. If you choose Yes, you can specify a name for the LOD. If you choose No, the suppression states of the component are discarded, and the assembly is saved in the master LOD.

Temporary LOD representations are created in subassemblies when a subassembly component is suppressed from a top-level assembly. A tilde and index number are listed after the subassembly name to denote a temporary LOD state. Note that the subassembly is not modified. You can open the subassembly on its own and save the suppression states as a named LOD if desired.

It is important to understand the difference between LOD representations and iAssembly configurations with respect to how they affect the bill of materials. Although you can suppress features at will and substitute part files for assemblies with the use of LOD representations, Inventor still understands that all the parts in the master LOD will be included in the bill of materials. When you suppress a component in an LOD representation used in a drawing view, the view updates, and any balloons attached to that component are deleted. However, the parts list will still list the component because it always refers to the master bill of materials.

If your intent is to create an assembly configuration where some parts are to be listed in the bill of materials and others excluded, an iAssembly is the correct tool.

LODs and Parts Lists

New Inventor users often attempt to use LODs to create a parts list in the drawing environment that shows only the unsuppressed components. However, this is not allowed outright. To use an existing LOD for parts-list purposes, you should right-click it in the browser and choose Copy To View Rep. Once the View Rep is created, it can be used in the parts list by editing the parts list, clicking the Filter Settings button in the Parts List edit dialog box, and then selecting Assembly View Representation from the list.

Using iAssemblies

Certification Objective
An iAssembly is a table-driven assembly file that allows the use of component part configurations to build variations of a design. Some of the strengths of assembly configurations of this type are the abilities to swap out one component for another, to include or exclude components altogether, and to adjust assembly constraint offset values to create various configurations of the original assembly.

It is important to understand that when you create an iAssembly, you create what is called an iAssembly *factory*. The configurations that will be output from this factory are called the iAssembly members. It may help to think of the factory as the parent file and the members as children.

To create an iAssembly, most often you start with an assembly composed of iParts. First, the iParts are created for all parts that will vary in size or configuration of features. Next, create the assembly using iPart members where required. Once the basic assembly is created, you add the configuration table, turning the assembly into an iAssembly.

The assembly used in the next exercise represents a simplified push-button panel. Your goal is to create an assembly configuration with variations in the number and type of buttons used, as shown in Figure 8.65.

FIGURE 8.65
Configurations of a push-button panel

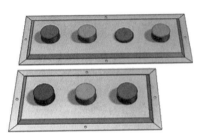

Follow these steps:

1. On the Get Started tab, click Open.

2. Browse to Chapter 08 in the Mastering Inventor 2016 directory and open mi_08a_025.iam.

3. Switch to the Manage tab and click Create iAssembly on the Author panel. This will open the iAssembly Author dialog box, shown in Figure 8.66.

FIGURE 8.66

The iAssembly Author dialog box

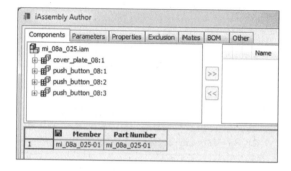

4. The first thing you should do is consider the naming conventions for the iAssembly members. Click the Options button at the bottom of the dialog box to bring up the naming options. Here, you would typically configure the name for the member part number and the member names so that as you add rows to the iAssembly table, the naming drops out automatically. In this case, you will simply click the OK button to choose the defaults.

Either column can be set to be the filename column from which member part numbers are generated. You can do so by right-clicking the Member or Part Number column headers and choosing File Name Column from the menu. The filename column is indicated by the save or disk symbol.

5. Examine the Components tab and expand the tree next to the part called cover_plate_08:1. In the tree of each part are four different nodes that you can use to add a column to the table. Select Table Replace from the tree and use the >> button to add it as a column in the table.

6. Now that you have added a column to the table, you will add a row. Right-click anywhere on row 1 in the lower pane of the dialog box and choose Insert Row. Your table should now resemble Figure 8.67.

The Table Replace column allows you to replace an iPart member for another iPart member within the assembly. In this case, the part named CP_001-03 is the sheet-metal cover plate. This plate is an iPart that has four different sizes within the iPart table.

7. Click the cell in row 2 in the cover_plate_08:1 Table Replace column to activate a drop-down menu.

FIGURE 8.67
Configuring an iAssembly table

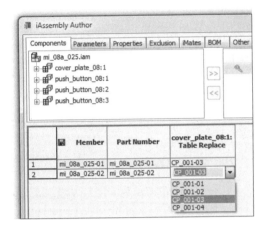

8. Click the arrow for the drop-down menu, as shown in Figure 8.67. Then select CP_001-04 and click the OK button to exit the dialog box.

9. Examine the Model browser, and you will notice that a table has been added to the browser. Expand the table, and you will find a listing of the iAssembly members, mi_08a_025-01 and mi_08a_025-02.

10. mi_08a_025-01 will have a check mark next to it, informing you that this is the active member of the iAssembly. To set mi_08a_025-02 as active, right-click it and choose Activate, or simply double-click it.

WORKING WITH IASSEMBLIES

Many iAssemblies require only a few size variables and a few components that can be interchanged. Although in the exercise using iAssemblies both the plate and buttons are iParts, often an iAssembly requires only a few components to be iParts for configuration.

It is typically best to tackle iAssemblies in a structured manner, configuring only one part of the table at a time and then returning to the model to test that change. Making many changes in the table at once may make it difficult to determine how changes affect the model.

Once a couple of rows are added using the iAssembly Author interface, you can edit the table with Microsoft Excel to add many rows at once and quickly make changes to the column entries. Also in Excel, you can create formulas to concatenate column entries, calculate entries, or use an if/then statement to determine entries.

---

11. Now that you have used a different-sized plate, you will need to add another button to the assembly. To do so, select the existing black button and use Copy and Paste to add a new instance to the assembly.

12. Place an Insert constraint between the new instance of the button and the empty hole on the plate, as shown in Figure 8.68.

FIGURE 8.68

Adding an Insert constraint

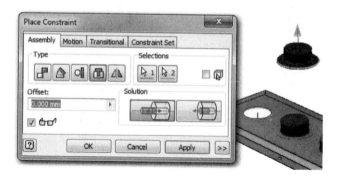

FIGURE 8.68

Adding an Insert constraint

13. Once the new button is constrained, set mi_08a_025-01 to be active again in the table tree, and notice that you are presented with an error message warning you that the new constraint is looking at geometry that is no longer present. Click Accept in the error dialog box.

Notice that the new button remains even though the hole it was constrained to is gone. To address this, you need to edit the table further and configure the iAssembly to suppress the extra button when not needed.

14. Right-click the Table icon in the Model browser and choose Edit Table.

15. Locate part push_button_08:4 in the tree and use the >> button to place Include/Exclude in the table as a column.

16. Set the value for this column to be Exclude for row 1, as shown in Figure 8.69. Click the OK button to return to the model, and activate both members to see that no constraint errors occur.

FIGURE 8.69

Exclude/include components in an iAssembly

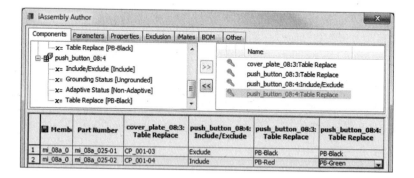

17. Next, you will change out the black buttons in member mi_08a_025-02 to use a second green and a second red button. Edit the table, and choose the last two instances of part push_button_08 from the tree in the top-left pane. Locate the Table Replace parameter for each and use the >> button to include them in the table.

18. Set the Table Replace values in row 2 to Red and Green, as shown in Figure 8.70.

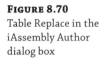

FIGURE 8.70
Table Replace in the
iAssembly Author
dialog box

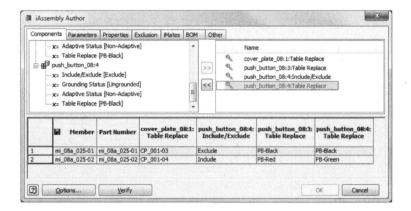

You do not need to change the values in row 1 because one of the buttons is already set to Black as required, and the other, as you recall, you excluded so that it does not show in the row 1 configuration.

19. Click the OK button to exit the table-authoring dialog box and then activate mi_08a_025-02 from the table. Note the changes to the four-button configuration. You should now have two red and two green buttons in an alternating pattern.

20. Last, you will set one of the buttons to be in a different position. Edit the table to return to the iAssembly Author dialog box again and activate the Parameters tab.

21. Expand the Relationships folder, select Insert:1, and use the >> button to add it as a column in the table.

22. Set the value of this column to **7 mm** for row 2 of the configurations.

23. Click the OK button to exit the dialog box, and notice that one of the buttons is now pushed in because you have modified the constraint offset value.

You can close this assembly file without saving changes. iAssemblies allow you to create configurations of your assemblies by including and excluding components, configuring constraints values, setting iProperties, and much more. When creating drawing files for iAssemblies, you often need a drawing for each member. The members have the same annotations and tables, with only some values differing.

Use Assembly Design Accelerators

The functional-design tools enable you to create complex geometry by entering size data. Before any geometry is created, you can verify whether the design meets the requirements by performing calculations. The formulas used for the calculations are based on international standards, and they are fully documented in the *Engineer's Handbook* (the *Engineer's Handbook* is an online resource; to open it, go to Design > Power Transmission > handbook). This allows you to override or ignore certain calculations when experience dictates.

Functional Design vs. Geometric Modeling

Rather than modeling geometry first and then hoping that the form satisfies all the design criteria, in the functional-design method, you use the tools to make sure the design operates correctly given the design criteria prior to finalizing the product's shape. If functional design is done well, the geometry will be the result of the design process rather than the input to it.

FUNCTIONAL DESIGN IN THE REAL WORLD

You might already use functional design every day but might not identify it by that name. Consider the following scenario: You're called on to specify a V-belt for a current pulley system design. You could space the pulleys and then hope to find a belt that fits well, but that wouldn't be typical. Instead, you'd most likely narrow down the general size of the belt needed and determine the load and speed required and then use this information to look up a proper belt size from a supplier catalog, thereby letting the function drive the design and assist you in specifying the belt. You can use design accelerators in Inventor to do the same thing.

Working with Design Accelerators

Design accelerators can be overwhelming at first because of the sheer number of accelerators and because the user interface is slightly different from the rest of Inventor. Therefore, you'll look at the dialog boxes, the browser structure, and the user interface for these tools.

DESIGN ACCELERATORS INPUT

Design accelerators are available only in the assembly environment. Design accelerator dialog boxes are tabbed dialog boxes, as shown in Figure 8.71. The Design and Calculation tabs appear in most of the dialog boxes. Two particular areas in these dialog boxes are worth pointing out.

FIGURE 8.71
A typical design accelerator dialog box

The Results pane displays the calculated values for a particular design. The Summary pane indicates whether a design is acceptable with the given parameters. These panes are hidden by default and can be displayed by double-clicking the double line on the right and bottom edges of the dialog box or by clicking the >> button along the borders. The border of the design accelerator window turns red to indicate a design failure or to flag a more general error.

The calculation is not an automatic operation; for example, if a calculation fails and the values turn red, you typically change the parameters to correct the problem. You will not see the result of your change unless you click the Calculate button. Many calculators offer different types of calculations. Choosing a particular calculation method will disable certain fields (driven values) and enable some other fields (input values).

REMEMBER TO CALCULATE (OR NOT TO CALCULATE)

One common mistake is not clicking the Calculate button. The design accelerators will not update when you simply change values. You *must* click the Calculate button.

Also keep in mind that you can deselect the Calculate button in order to not calculate the design and just place design accelerator components that might not comply with design inputs. This can often be helpful in the early stages of a design when you just need a form to start with.

DESIGN ACCELERATORS OUTPUT

There are two sorts of functional design tools: generators and calculators. It is important to understand the difference between these two categories. The output generated by design *generators* consists of subassemblies with actual geometry in them. For example, the V-belt generator will generate a belt part. But it can create pulleys as well.

Design *calculators* don't generate any geometry, but the result of the calculation places a subassembly node in the browser and can be edited and repeated with different values. The dialog box for calculators is also restricted to one tab: the Calculation tab.

Most (but not all) design generators use parts generated from Content Center. Table 8.1 lists the various design accelerators and their dependency on the Content Center library databases.

TABLE 8.1:   Design accelerators' use of Content Center database

GENERATOR/ACCELERATOR	NEEDS CONTENT CENTER
Bolted Connections	Yes
Weld Calc	No
Tolerance Stack Up Calc	No
Limits and Fits Calc	No
Column Calc	No (but recognizes section properties of Content Center and Frame Generator parts; see Chapter 15, "Frame Generator").
Plate Calc	No

continues

TABLE 8.1: Design accelerators' use of Content Center database *(CONTINUED)*

GENERATOR/ACCELERATOR	NEEDS CONTENT CENTER
Shaft Generator	No
Cam Generator	No
Gear Generator	No
Bearing Generator	Yes
Key Connection Generator	Yes
Spline Generator	No
Belt Generator	No
Sprocket and Chain Generator	Yes
Spring Generator	Yes (but only for Belleville springs)
Pins Generator	Yes
Seals and O-rings Generator	Yes
Engineer's Handbook	No

DESIGN ACCELERATOR SOLVE STATES

Many design accelerators use solve states to control when and how they solve for and update the geometry contained within them. The solve state of the generator subassemblies is indicated by an icon in the browser. Manual Solve is the default mode, but you can change it to Automatic Solve by right-clicking the design accelerator component, selecting Component, and then selecting the solve mode you want to use. Figure 8.72 shows the Automatic Solve icon next to the synchronous belt component.

FIGURE 8.72
Synchronous belt in
Automatic Solve mode

There are three solve states that can be changed in the Component context menu, as described in Table 8.2.

TABLE 8.2:   Solve states of design accelerator components

STATE	EXPLANATION
Solve Off	Changes to design accelerator input conditions have no effect on the design accelerator component.
Manual Solve	Changes to design accelerator input conditions have an effect only after editing the design accelerator component.
Automatic Solve	Changes to design accelerator input conditions immediately affect the design accelerator component.

The Solve Off, Manual Solve, and Automatic Solve options are mutually exclusive, meaning that when you select one option, it turns the current one off. The Solve Off menu does what its name suggests: it turns off the solver completely so that the design accelerator component is frozen until the next edit.

The difference between Manual Solve and Automatic Solve is simple. Using the example of a V-belt, when the distance between the axes changes, a V-belt will automatically readjust the pulley positions if Automatic Solve is on. If Manual Solve is on, the user will have to update the pulley positions by clicking the Manual Solve menu. A red lightning bolt will appear in the browser. Manual Solve is used as the default for performance reasons and to prevent interactions with the assembly solver.

The Calculate option on the context menu is a toggle between two states; clicking it once turns it on, and clicking it again turns it off. You can toggle this option by using the Calculate button at the top right of each design accelerator dialog box as well. When calculation is turned off, the performance of the generator is faster.

Because design accelerator assemblies typically consist of multiple parts that are constrained together, Inventor offers specific edit, delete, promote, and demote tools for design accelerator entities.

USING DEFAULT VALUES

The values used in the last calculation of a design accelerator component will be reused when you create a new design accelerator component with the same generator. If you want to use the default values of a design accelerator, hold down the **Ctrl** key when starting the design accelerator tool.

BOLTED CONNECTION GENERATOR

Certification
Objective

This generator is the most popular design accelerator tool because it is able to make an entire set of bolts, washers, nuts, and the necessary holes in the supporting geometry as an all-in-one operation. Figure 8.73 shows placement options for the Bolted Connections tool; you might notice the similarity between these options and the Hole tool placement options.

FIGURE 8.73

Placement options in a
bolted connection

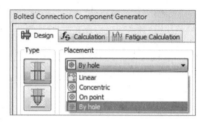

There are four placement options.

Linear   Allows the creation of a bolted connection without any preexisting sketch by selecting a distance to two different linear edges

Concentric   Uses any circular edge (the edge does not have to be part of a hole feature; the edge can be part of a cylindrical extrusion) to make a bolted connection with a larger or smaller hole size

On Point   Requires an existing work point or vertex as input

By Hole   Requires an existing hole, and the bolted connection will incorporate the existing hole

Although the Bolted Connections tool will create holes for you, it is often best to create the holes first with the regular Hole tool and then use the By Hole option rather than using the Linear or Concentric option. The disadvantage of the latter two options is that they create only a point in a sketch, but the point is not dimensioned and could easily move. When the sketch point moves, the bolted connection will *not* follow the new position of the hole.

When you use By Hole, the bolted connection will automatically follow any *positional change* of the preexisting holes but will not follow *diameter changes* automatically. Keeping the diameter of the holes generated by the bolted connection in sync with the diameter changes in the preexisting hole requires manually selecting a different diameter in the Diameter field of the bolted connection. The reason this was done is to give you a choice because you don't necessarily want all your bolts to increase in diameter when the underlying hole diameter increases.

Placing a Bolted Connection Pattern

In the following example, you will connect the cap with the plate using bolted connections. The cap has three holes drilled in it, and they form a circular pattern.

1. On the Get Started tab, click Open and browse to mi_08a_027.iam in the Chapter 08 folder of the Mastering Inventor 2016 folder.

2. Select the Design tab and then click the Bolted Connection button.

3. In the Placement area, confirm that By Hole is selected in the drop-down list.

4. Select the top face of the cap as the start plane.

5. Select one of the holes. Since there is a hole pattern, the preview will display at the original instance of the hole no matter which hole you select. Note too that the Follow Pattern option is displayed in the Bolted Connection dialog box. Check the box so that all the holes will get fasteners.

6. Click the Termination button and select the back side of the plate. The Bolted Connections generator is smart enough to know which side of the plate is valid for termination. When you hover over the plate, the back side highlights, and you can click to accept.

7. In the Thread area, set the diameter to **8 mm** to match the holes in the cap. In Figure 8.74, you can see that holes have been added to the dialog browser pane.

FIGURE 8.74
Following the holes of an existing pattern

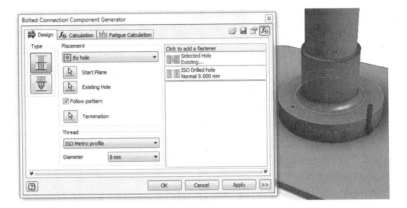

Note that there are three drilled holes automatically added to the plate. You could click the Drilled Hole bar in the right pane and then click the down arrow to select a different hole type (for example, counter bore). The Bolted Connections generator is clever enough to filter out countersink hole types for holes on faces that are not exposed.

At this point, you can add all necessary hardware to finish the connection. It is important to note that the order of the icons in the pane on the right represents the stacking order of the bolted connection beginning from the start plane and moving down. If you want to place a bolt on the start plane, you just click the area marked with Click To Add A Fastener.

8. Click the area marked Click To Add A Fastener above the holes.

9. In the resulting selection window, set Standard to DIN and Category to Socket Head Bolts.

10. Select DIN 404 (or something comparable).

The bolt is automatically sized to be long enough to go through the selected components, if the bolt type library selected has a length that is long enough. If you want to change the bolt length, you can drag the preview arrow at the end. Only valid lengths from Content Center can be selected.

11. To finish the bolted connection by adding a nut and washer, click the area marked Click To Add A Fastener below the holes and select a washer.

12. Click the lower Click To Add A Fastener bar again and select a nut.

At this point, you might realize that you want to add a washer between the bolt head and the top face of the cap part.

13. Click the Click To Add A Fastener bar below the bolt and choose a washer.

14. Click Apply to create the patterned bolted connection.

You can continue experimenting with the bolted connection tool or close the file and continue to the next section.

CREATING A THREADED HOLE IN THE PLATE

If you wanted to thread the plate to avoid adding a nut and washer, you could do so by clicking ISO Drilled Hole section of the pane and then clicking the button with the three small dots. Doing so would bring up the Hole options, allowing you to change the hole type to threaded.

Calculating the Bolt Strength

Next, you'll edit a bolted connection and calculate its strength. The design problem you are trying to solve is as follows: considering an axial force of 750 N and a tangential force of 300 N, will three bolts be sufficient to hold the cap on the plate?

1. On the Get Started tab, click Open and browse to mi_08a_028.iam in the Chapter 08 folder of the Mastering Inventor 2016 folder.

2. Locate the existing Bolted Connection in the Model browser and then right-click it and choose Edit Using Design Accelerator. Note you may need to expand Component Pattern 2 and then expand Element:1 to find the Bolted Connection node.

3. In the Bolted Connection Component Generator dialog box, click the Calculation tab.

The Calculation tab provides four strength calculation options:

- ◆ Bolt Diameter Design
- ◆ Number Of Bolts Design
- ◆ Bolt Material Design
- ◆ Check Calculation

Do you meet the design criteria with just three bolts? It all depends on the material you choose for the bolts.

4. Set the Type Of Strength Calculation drop-down to Number Of Bolts Design.

5. In the Loads area, enter **750 N** for Maximal Axial Force and **300 N** for Maximal Tangent Force.

6. Assume that this application requires fasteners with high thermal conductivity. In the Bolt Material area, check the box next to the material field and select Copper-Nickel C96200. To narrow down the material choices, type **Copper** in the text field below the Material column header. Note that the text filter name is case-sensitive.

7. Click Calculate to analyze the fasteners.

In the Bolts section, you will see that the Number Of Bolts (z) is now calculated at 4 (recall that *ul* means unitless in Inventor).

8. Click the OK button to close the Bolted Connection Component Generator dialog box.

To comply with the calculation, you need to edit the cap and update the hole pattern from three to four. Once you've done so, the bolted connection pattern will follow accordingly if the Automatic Solve option is enabled.

9. Right-click the existing Bolted Connection in the Model browser and then select Automatic Solve from the list.

10. Right-click the component named mi_08a_028_Cap in the browser and choose Edit. This will set the cap active for edits.

11. Locate the feature called Circular Pattern 1 in the browser; right-click it and choose Edit Feature. This pattern controls the number of holes.

12. Change the Placement value from 3 to **4**; then click the OK button.

13. To return to the assembly, click the Return button on the ribbon menu or right-click and choose Finish Edit.

As a result of the changes you've made to the number of bolt holes, the bolted connection pattern has updated as well. Although all the design accelerators are slightly different, they all share a common way of solving problems and creating components. Autodesk provides tutorials covering each of the design accelerators on the Autodesk Inventor wiki, under "Mechanical Design" tutorials:

```
http://help.autodesk.com/view/INVNTOR/2014/ENU/?guid=GUID-FAB20788-37A4-4A49-
BBFF-4231DEEFA8B3
```

The Bottom Line

Create assembly relationships using the Constraint and Joint tools. Assembly relationships are an important part of working with Inventor assembly files. Assembly constraints determine how assembly components fit together. As relationships are applied between components, degrees of freedom are removed.

Master It You are new to 3D and find the concept of assembly relationships a bit challenging. Where can you find a simple overview of constraints?

Organize designs using structured subassemblies. Subassemblies add organization, facilitate the bill of materials, and reduce assembly relationships; all this results in better performance and easier edits. One of the habits of all Inventor experts is their effective use and understanding of subassemblies.

Master It You need to hand off an accurate BOM for finished designs to the purchasing department at the end of each design project. How can the BOM be extracted from Inventor?

Work with adaptive components. Geometry can be set to be adaptive so that it can be sized and positioned in the context of where it is used in the assembly. You can set underconstrained geometry to be adaptive by specifying the elements allowed to adapt.

> **Master It**   You want to set a feature of a part to be adaptive so that it can adapt to another part in an assembly. However, the feature is based on a fully constrained sketch. How would this be done?

Create assembly-level features.   An assembly feature is a feature created and utilized within the active assembly file. Because the feature is created within the assembly file, it does not exist at the single-part or subassembly level.

> **Master It**   You want to make a notch in a standard part that will not affect its use in every other assembly it is used in. Can this be done?

Manage bills of materials.   Managing a bill of materials can be a large part of any assembly design task. Understanding the BOM structure goes a long way toward successfully configuring your bill of materials.

> **Master It**   You need to mark a component as a reference component in just one assembly file. However, when you attempt to do so using the BOM Editor, it is designated as a reference in every assembly. How can you set just a single instance of a component to be a reference component?

Use positional reps and flexible assemblies together.   Often, you may need to show a design in various stages of motion to test interference or proof of concept. Copying assemblies so that you can change the assembly relationships to show different assembly positions can become a file management nightmare. Instead, use flexible subassemblies and positional representations.

> **Master It**   You need to show your assembly in variations dependent on the position of the moving parts and the task the machine is accomplishing at given stages of its operation. How do you do this?

Copy assembly designs for reuse and configuration.   Because of the live linked data that exists in Inventor assemblies, using Windows Explorer to copy designs and rename parts is difficult and often delivers poor results. Using the tool provided in Inventor will allow you to copy designs and maintain the links between files.

> **Master It**   How do you duplicate an existing design to create a similar design?

Substitute a single part for entire subassemblies.   Working with large assemblies, particularly where large, complex assemblies are used over and over as subassemblies within a top-level design, can tax almost any workstation if not approached in the correct manner.

> **Master It**   You would like to swap out a complex assembly for a simplified version for use in layout designs or to use in large assemblies in an attempt to improve performance. What is the best way to do that?

Work with assembly design accelerators and generators.   Design accelerators and generators allow you to rapidly create complex geometry and the associated calculations that verify the viability of your design.

> **Master It**   Your design needs a bolted connection, but you are not certain about the number of bolts to use to ensure a proper connection. How do you determine this?

Use design calculators.   Design calculators do not create any geometry, but they permit you to store the calculations in the assembly and repeat the calculation with different input values at a later time.

> **Master It**   You need to calculate the size of a weld between two plates to withstand a certain lateral force. What tool do you use?

Chapter 9

Large Assembly Strategies

Working with large assemblies is more manageable than ever before with the Autodesk®
Inventor® software's Express mode tools. Using Express mode allows you to open a large assembly four to six times more quickly than opening the same file using Full mode. Combining Express mode with the use of tools such as shrinkwrap and substitute level of detail (LOD) representations improves performance and minimizes the time spent waiting. Substitute LODs allow you to swap out complex subassemblies with single substitute parts of less detail, all the while maintaining model properties and an accurate bill of materials (BOM).

Although each design department may have a different view on what a large assembly is, everyone can benefit from the large assembly tools and strategies discussed in this chapter. You can create fully functional digital prototypes ranging from 10 to 100,000 components if you approach the task with an eye to the topics covered here.

In this chapter, you'll learn to

- ◆ Select a workstation

- ◆ Adjust your performance settings

- ◆ Use best practices for large assemblies

- ◆ Manage assembly detail

- ◆ Simplify parts

Selecting a Workstation

Ensuring that you have an adequate system to accomplish the type of design work you intend to do is an important, but often overlooked, step in achieving successful large assembly design with any parametric modeler. Understanding the capabilities and limitations of your computer and then budgeting for upgrades is a crucial part of working in today's design world.

If you consider the time you spend waiting and the loss of work experienced when working on an undersized computer, you will likely determine that a workstation upgrade will pay for itself within a year. If you budget for upgrades every two years, you could argue that the upgrade is paying for itself in the second year of use. Although this scenario might not fit your situation exactly, it demonstrates the idea that operating costs (hardware and software alike) should be budgeted and planned for and always measured against lost work and downtime.

Physical Memory vs. Virtual Memory

When your system runs low on physical memory (RAM) and requires more to complete an operation, Windows begins writing to a portion of the system hard drive known as virtual memory to continue. Virtual memory is often called a *pagefile*.

When considering a workstation for doing large assembly design, it should be your goal to work in RAM as much as possible because when Windows begins to write to virtual memory, you will notice a considerable drop in performance. One of the weakest links in terms of speed on even the most adequate workstation is the hard drive. Accessing data from RAM can be thousands of times faster than accessing data from the hard drive. Therefore, one of the best ways to beef up a workstation is to simply add more RAM.

If you are running an older computer or you skimped on RAM when you upgraded, you will notice that as you attempt to load large assemblies or drawing files of large assemblies in Inventor, you quickly use up available RAM. You will find yourself waiting for Windows to write data to the hard drive and then read that data. Although the unknowing user might think that Inventor has suddenly become slow, you should understand that no application can overcome the hardware and operating system limitations upon which it is installed.

Autodesk recommends a minimum of 12 GB of RAM for working with large or complex assemblies, with 24 GB or more being ideal.

Hardware

Hardware upgrades are an important part of any design department. Budgeting properly and knowing what components to allocate more money to can make these upgrades more manageable. Dollar for dollar, you should give priority to the components described in the following sections, in the order listed.

RAM

When it comes to RAM, the more your system has, the better it will handle large and complex assemblies in Inventor. You can use the number of unique parts in your assemblies (unique parts as opposed to multiple instances of the same part) as a general rule of thumb when determining how much RAM to consider. Here is a list of recommendations based on unique part count:

- More than 5,000 unique parts: 6 GB of RAM

- More than 10,000 unique parts: 12 GB of RAM

- More than 15,000 unique parts: 18 GB of RAM

- More than 20,000 unique parts: 24 GB of RAM

 **Real World Scenario**

CALCULATING THE ROI OF NEW HARDWARE

It's often hard to convince management (especially nontechnical managers) that you really do need that new computer to get your job done. After all, you're currently getting your work done, right? So why do you need the faster computer? This is where a return on investment (ROI) calculation will come in handy.

Let's say you routinely have to open, modify, and print large assembly drawings. To calculate the ROI, follow these steps:

1. Measure how long it takes to complete this process on your old machine.

2. Look at some benchmarks or talk to others who have faster machines, and make a conservative estimate of how long it would take you to do the same operations on the faster machine.

3. Subtract the second number from the first. You now have your time savings per operation.

4. Multiply this by the number of times in a day or week you perform these tasks.

5. Multiply it by an hourly rate for your industry (you can always use your hourly salary) to get the dollar savings per time period (per week, month, and so on).

6. Now you can take the cost of the new system and divide it by this cost savings per unit of time. This gives you the amount of time it will take to pay off that new computer.

Furthermore, once this time period has passed, you are actually making money because you are saving the company money once the investment has been paid off. When you can show that the hardware will pay for itself relatively quickly, you should have fewer problems convincing management to upgrade your equipment.

Another consideration for the ROI is who will inherit your old system. Generally, some person in the office will also benefit from a faster system, even if they run general office applications. For instance, if the receptionist is required to access many documents quickly across a network while assisting customers and other office staff, there is a good chance that your old CAD station will improve the ability to do so. Because this key person is the first point of information for so many people, the ROI is exponential. Passing old workstations to the shop floor to allow shop staff to access digitally stored files quickly is another way to achieve ROI and justify workstation upgrades.

You can check the specifications of your motherboard to determine how much RAM your system can accept. Many RAM manufactures, such as Crucial (`www.crucial.com`), have utilities on their websites that will look at your system and tell you the RAM configurations that your system can accommodate.

GRAPHICS CARDS

In the past it was generally recommended that you consider an OpenGL (developed by Silicon Graphics) graphics card that was tailored for CAD stations via a custom driver. Graphics card manufacturers and CAD developers worked together to produce and certify cards and drivers to offer the best results. With the introduction of Windows Vista, Autodesk began developing Inventor to work with Direct3D (part of Microsoft's DirectX application programming interface). Inventor 2015 was developed to work with versions of DirectX not available on earlier operating systems; therefore, Windows 7 with a graphics card compatible with DirectX 10 or newer is recommended.

With the move to Direct3D, using OpenGL and custom drivers is no longer necessary. I recommend that to find the best card for your workstation, you buy the card with the best performance within your budget. You can research cards by using a DirectX graphics processing unit benchmark website such as PassMark (`www.cpubenchmark.net`).

> **GAMING CARDS FOR CAD?**
>
> In the past, high-performing gaming cards were not recommended for CAD applications because the drivers were developed for different purposes, and they often performed poorly when running CAD software. Now, though, with Direct3D not relying on custom drivers, gaming cards may very well offer the best performance for the dollar.

To ensure that Inventor has the optimal settings, select the Tools tab, click Application Options, and select the Hardware tab in the dialog box that opens. Inventor will automatically detect the appropriate level for your card, but you can set it manually to influence system performance if needed. You can choose from the following settings:

Quality   This setting sacrifices system performance for better graphics presentation. If you're running Windows 7 or Vista, anti-aliasing is turned on to improve the visual quality of the graphics display. For machines running Windows XP, there is no difference between Quality and Performance.

Performance   This setting favors system performance over graphic presentation. If you're running Windows 7 or Vista, anti-aliasing is turned off. This is the default setting.

Conservative   This setting favors reliability over system performance. Inventor won't push your graphics card to the max, which should lead to a more reliable performance. You may notice a lower display performance than when using the Quality or Performance setting.

Software Graphics   This setting uses software-based graphics processing instead of hardware-based processing. The setting is often used to troubleshoot issues with a graphics card.

For more information and recommendations on graphics cards and other hardware, refer to the following website:
www.inventor-certified.com/graphics/

HARD DRIVES

Inventor files are segmented, meaning that the graphics are separate from the feature information. When an assembly is first opened, only the graphics segments are loaded. When you edit a file, the additional data is loaded at that time. This makes a fast hard drive important for performance.

Another aspect of hard drive performance stems from file storage and workspace setup. In Inventor, working from your local drive is the preferred method, and Autodesk has often recommended that you avoid working on Inventor files across a network (although many or even most Inventor users do work across a network without issue). The reason for this is simply the number of files that you might be editing at one time. For instance, a change to a large assembly could potentially modify hundreds of part files, requiring all those files to be saved at once. Doing this across a network, particularly one with latency issues, may result in file corruption if the files are not saved correctly. Autodesk Vault is set up to store files on a server and copy those files locally when checked out for editing. When working in this manner, Inventor has a higher performance requirement than standard office applications, and the hard drive workload is heavy. Therefore, it may be worth it to consider upgrading your hard drive to a faster drive.

PROCESSORS

When considering processors for an Inventor 2016 workstation, the chief question should concern multicore processors. As a minimum, you should consider a dual-core processor even though Inventor is not truly a multithreaded application. (*Multithreaded* means that the operating system or the application will spread the processing load across the processor.) If you opt for a dual-core processor, you can still take advantage of it because Inventor will run on one core and other applications will run on the other. There are parts of Inventor—such as InventorViewCompute.exe, which computes drawing views, and Inventor Studio's rendering engine—that are multithreaded, so if you work with large or complex drawings or plan to do a lot of image, animation rendering, or FEA calculations in Inventor, you will likely benefit from more cores.

Working with Performance Settings

Whether or not upgrading workstations is an option, you should ensure that your system is set up for optimal performance for working with large assemblies. A number of options in Inventor will facilitate this.

Express Mode

Express mode accelerates file opening for large assembly files by not loading all the assembly tools that Inventor offers in Full mode. Once an assembly file is opened in Express mode, you can click the Full mode button to enable the additional tools when necessary. This simple but effective mode switching can allow you to access your large assembly files an average of four to six times more quickly.

Tools that are not available in Express mode include the design accelerators and the assembly-level features tools found on the Sketch, Design, and 3D Model tabs.

To open an assembly in Express mode, you first need to enable the Express mode option and then save the assembly file so that the additional Express mode information will be included in the file. You can enable Express mode by selecting the Tools tab, clicking the Application Options button, and then selecting the Assembly tab in the dialog box that opens. Select the Enable Express Mode Workflows option and then set the File Open Options to a unique file threshold that fits your typically large assembly and workstation. For instance, if your workstation typically struggles when you open an assembly that references roughly 400 unique files, you'd set this number to **400**.

You can also bypass the unique file threshold and use Express mode to open an assembly file with fewer unique files by browsing to the file, selecting it, and then clicking the Options button in the Open dialog box. Here you'll see the Open Express check box, which will force the file to open using Express mode regardless of the unique file number. If the Express mode check box is grayed out, the file needs to be saved with the Enable Express Mode Workflows option enabled first to include the Express mode information in that file.

Working with Drawing Settings

Generating and hiding lines when creating and editing drawing views in Inventor can be some of the most processor-intensive tasks in Inventor. To help ease the demand on the system when you're working with large assembly drawings, you should be aware of several settings. You can find these settings by selecting the Tools tab, clicking Application Options, and selecting the Drawing tab in the dialog box that opens, as shown in Figure 9.1.

FIGURE 9.1

Drawing application options

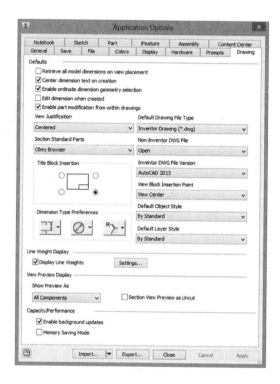

DISPLAY LINE WEIGHTS

The Display Line Weights check box enables or disables the display of unique line weights in drawings. Deselect the box to show lines without weight differences. Line weights will still print correctly, even with this box selected. Deselecting this box will speed up the performance of your drawing during edits and annotation work.

VIEW PREVIEW DISPLAY

The options in the Show Preview As drop-down box set the type of preview you get when creating a view. All Components is the default, but you will find that selecting the Partial or Bounding Box option will improve performance because Inventor will not be required to create and update the preview as you drag your mouse pointer around the screen.

The preview setting does not affect the drawing view result. Bounding Box previews a simple rectangle during the view creation, and Partial previews a simplified representation of the view. Bounding Box is the most efficient. Using the Bounding Box option is suggested if you find yourself waiting for the preview to generate during drawing view creation.

The Section View Preview As Uncut check box will also provide some performance improvements when selected. This option will allow Inventor to display the section view preview as unsectioned in order to be more efficient. The section view will still be generated as normal.

ENABLE BACKGROUND UPDATES

When background updates are enabled, *raster views* are created temporarily until the computation is complete. This is indicated by green border corners on the views and an oblique red line in the browser. Raster views are simplified placeholder pictures of the view, used to create and place the view quickly so as not to slow you down when creating views of large or complex models. Precise drawing views are calculated in the background while you work with raster views.

Heavy view computation is spread over multicore processors using `InventorViewCompute.exe`, as is evident in the Windows Task Manager.

While a view of a large assembly or complex model is computing, you can continue to create other views or annotations. However, some tools are disabled during view computation. These tools are listed here:

- ◆ Automated Centerlines

- ◆ Auto Balloon

- ◆ Project Geometry

- ◆ Hidden Annotations

- ◆ Model Features

- ◆ Retrieve Dimensions

Drawings containing raster views can be saved and closed while background computations are still working. If the drawing is closed during background updates, the updates will stop and be restarted the next time the drawing is opened.

BOM VIEWS AND PERFORMANCE

In an assembly file you can enable a Structured BOM view or a Parts Only BOM view using the BOM editor. However, if you have both views enabled, you will likely notice that your large assembly drawings take longer to open. Therefore, you should generally choose not to have both views enabled.

MEMORY SAVING MODE

The Memory Saving Mode option sets the way Inventor loads components into memory during view creation. When this option is selected, Inventor loads components into memory before and during view creation and then unloads them from memory once the view is created.

Although memory is conserved using this mode, view creation and editing operations cannot be undone while this option is enabled. You'll notice that the Undo/Redo buttons will be grayed out after a view creation or edit. This option will also have a negative impact on performance when you're editing and creating views because the components must be loaded into memory each time. Because of this, you should consider setting this option as an application setting only if you always work with large assemblies.

It is generally preferred to set this option per document by selecting the Tools tab, clicking Documents Settings, selecting the Drawing tab in the dialog box that opens, and then setting the Memory Saving Mode drop-down list to Always. Figure 9.2 shows the default setting of Use Application Options.

FIGURE 9.2
Drawing Document Settings

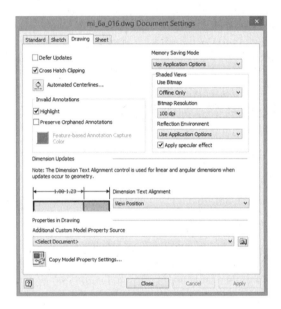

SHADED VIEWS

Also in the document settings, you can adjust the way that shaded views are displayed. Setting the Use Bitmap drop-down list to Always, as shown in Figure 9.2, improves performance by applying raster shading as opposed to a vector style. The difference impacts the display but typically does not affect printing.

You can also adjust the bitmap resolution; setting it lower conserves memory and speeds up performance. The default is 100 dpi. Setting the dpi to 200 or higher will invoke a prompt, warning you that increasing this setting for large assemblies may not be possible.

TROUBLESHOOTING GRAPHICS ISSUES AND CRASHES

It's often difficult to determine the source of graphics issues and graphics-related crashes without knowing how to isolate and illuminate some of the variables. One of the best ways to do this is to go to the Hardware tab of the Application Options dialog box and set the Graphics Setting radio button to Software Graphics.

This setting uses Inventor, rather than your graphics card, to render the onscreen graphics. Therefore, any graphics anomalies that exist while using this setting can be attributed to something other than the graphics card. If you set this option to Software Graphics and your graphics issues go away, your video card (or video card driver) is mostly likely the cause. If the issue returns when you set the option back to the recommended setting, then you should look into updating or rolling back your graphics card driver or getting a different graphics card that handles Inventor graphics better.

Keep in mind that this is a just a test, and I don't recommend running Inventor using the Software Graphics setting all of the time since it will cause Inventor to run slowly.

Working with Model Display Settings

When working within the modeling environment, you can adjust several settings to have a positive impact on performance. You can access these settings by selecting the Tools tab, clicking Application Options, and selecting the Display tab in the dialog box that opens, as shown in Figure 9.3.

FIGURE 9.3
The Display tab in the Application Options dialog box

APPEARANCE

All the various display options can be controlled as application settings or as document settings. Using the application settings allows consistency across all the documents that you work with. Document settings will adopt the settings that were used when the document was saved.

Not all settings are controlled by the Appearance option, but you can define useful settings such as displaying the model in orthographic or perspective view and what visual style you want active.

DISPLAY QUALITY

Setting the Display Quality drop-down shown in Figure 9.3 to Rough will speed up performance by simplifying details. Navigation commands such as zooming, panning, and orbiting are particularly affected by this setting. If you find that the rough display is not to your liking, you can toggle back and forth according to the size of the assembly model you are working with.

VIEW TRANSITION TIME (SECONDS)

The View Transition Time (Seconds) setting controls the time required to transition smoothly between views when using zooming and viewing commands. A zero transition time takes you from the beginning view to the end view instantaneously. For instance, if you were zoomed in on a small component and wanted to zoom to show all components while this slider was set to zero, you would not see the gradual zooming out. While this might provide a gain in performance, understand that it can make display changes concerning position and orientation less clear, with the result that your adjustments would appear somewhat erratic.

MINIMUM FRAME RATE (Hz)

You can use the Minimum Frame Rate (Hz) setting to specify how slowly the display updates during zooming and orbiting commands. It may be hard to see the effects of this option on a normal-sized part or assembly because the views will typically update more quickly than the rate of this setting, but with large assemblies the results become obvious as components are dropped from the display during zoom and orbit updates. Here is a quick description of how the slider setting corresponds to the frame rate:

- 0 always draws everything in the view, no matter the time required.

- 1 tries to draw the view at least one frame per second. (Inventor will simplify or discard parts of the view if needed but will restore them when movement ends.)

- 5 draws at least five frames per second, 10 draws at least ten frames per second, and so on, up to a maximum of 20. Using the maximum frame rate of 20 will speed up zoom and orbit operations and give you the best results for large assemblies.

The settings in the Display tab can affect the performance of the system as well as the user's comfort when working in Inventor.

Working with General Settings

The following sections describe a few general settings that you can adjust to help the performance of large assemblies. You can access these settings by selecting the Tools tab, clicking Application Options, and selecting the General tab in the dialog box that opens. Figure 9.4 shows that tab.

FIGURE 9.4
Default application options

UPDATE PHYSICAL PROPERTIES ON SAVE

When checked, the Update Physical Properties On Save setting, located in the Physical Properties area on the right side of the dialog box, recalculates the mass properties of the model when you save the file. This ensures that mass properties are up-to-date. Setting this to Parts Only will ensure that the parts are all up-to-date without requiring you to wait on the recalculation for large assemblies. Note that this setting is disabled altogether by default but is recommended to be set to Parts Only if you find it helpful. Note too that the same function can be performed manually from the Bill Of Materials Editor and the Manage tab.

UNDO FILE SIZE

The Undo File Size option, on the lower-right side of the dialog box, sets the maximum size of the temporary file that records changes to a file so that actions can be undone. It's typically required to increase the size of this setting when working with large models and drawings because each undo action is typically a larger calculation. Autodesk recommends adjusting this in 4 MB increments to a maximum of 4095 MB.

Enable Optimized Selection

The Enable Optimized Selection setting, located on the lower-right corner of the dialog box, improves the performance of graphics during pre-highlighting in large assemblies. When the Enable Optimized Selection setting is activated, the algorithm for the Select Other function filters for only the group of objects closest to the screen. If you click through this first group of objects, the next group is considered for highlighting.

Status Bar

The status bar displays information concerning the number of files being accessed by Inventor, at the bottom-right corner of the Inventor screen, as shown in Figure 9.5. The number to the left is the total number of occurrences of all components in the active document. The next number is the total number of files open in the Inventor session.

FIGURE 9.5
The status bar

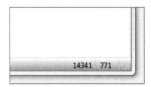

Using the Memory Probe

Included in your install of Inventor is a utility designed to monitor memory use for your system. The MemProbe utility, shown in Figure 9.6, looks at the Inventor process and displays its use of physical and virtual memory. It can often be useful in troubleshooting issues of capacity and slow performance. You can find this tool at the following location: C:\Program Files\Autodesk\ Inventor 2016\Bin\memprobe.exe. You might find it useful to create a desktop shortcut to it, if you find yourself using it often.

FIGURE 9.6
The MemProbe utility

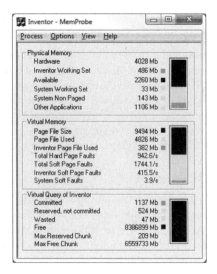

Working with System Settings

You can adjust several settings in the operating system to help with performance. Inventor users commonly set the page file size to twice the amount of RAM to gain performance. There are also many visual effects that you may have grown accustomed to that actually cost you resources. If you are serious about turning your workstation into a large-assembly workhorse, it is advisable to disable these features.

ADJUSTING THE VIRTUAL MEMORY PAGING FILE SIZE

To change the size of the virtual memory paging file in Windows 7, right-click the Computer icon and choose Properties. On the System Properties tab, click the Advanced System Settings tab, click Performance Options, and, finally, under Virtual Memory, deselect Automatically Manage Paging File Size For All Drives. Then click Change.

Windows 7 is set to an Automatic or System Managed paging file size. If you choose to set a Custom paging file size, you should refer to the recommended size that the dialog box offers and set the minimum and maximum to the same value to minimize fragmentation of the paging file if it needs to expand. Figure 9.7 shows the Virtual Memory dialog box.

FIGURE 9.7
Setting the pagefile size

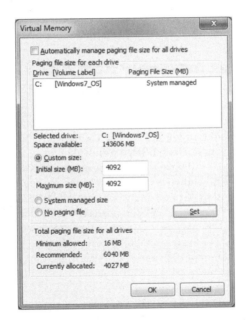

SETTING VIRTUAL MEMORY

Search the Internet and you will find hundreds of incorrect theories as to how to set the values for your virtual memory. One of the major myths is that you should set the initial and maximum to different values. If you are dedicating a portion of your hard drive for a pagefile, why start it small and then let it grow? Just provide the maximum amount of space you can and let it be.

DISABLING COMMON VISUAL EFFECTS

Windows provides many options to set the visual effects of your computer. Many of them have a surprisingly high impact on performance when memory is scarce. Here are a few you might consider disabling in order to conserve resources:

Screen Saver   To disable the screen saver, you can right-click your desktop and choose Personalize; then set the Screen Saver option to None. While you are working, screen savers are just another running process. You may want to set the Power Saving Mode option to turn off the monitor after a certain amount of time. If you use an LCD monitor, understand that screen savers do nothing to save an LCD screen.

Visual Settings   Many of the fade and shadow settings used in Windows look nice but come with a performance price if your system is on the slow side. To adjust these settings, you can right-click your desktop and choose Personalize; then select the Windows Classic theme.

Screen Resolution   If you're fortunate enough to have a nice, large-screen monitor, you probably have set up the screen resolution to maximize your space. However, this may be working against your large assembly pursuits. Experiment with setting the screen resolution to a lower setting such as 1024×768 to see whether you gain any performance when working with large assemblies.

Large Assembly Best Practices

Oftentimes, Inventor users don't think about large assembly performance until it has already become an issue with the model on which they are working. It is possible for two Inventor users working on two identical workstations to create two seemingly identical models, and yet those two models might perform in dramatically different ways.

If the first user has been mindful of large assembly management all along, his model and drawings will be much easier to open and work with. If the second user concentrated only on her design and gave no thought to the memory demands of the files she was creating, her model will be slow to open and work with and ultimately more likely to cause application crashes and data corruption. When the next job comes along, user 1 can reuse his model to create a similar design, whereas user 2 will likely re-create the assembly model because she does not trust the integrity of the first model she created.

Understanding where performance savings can be gained as you create the model will pay off once the large assembly is created and will make it much more manageable to work with along the way. And of course, a large assembly model can be revisited and cleaned up according to best practices to make it more manageable as well. Either way, having a model that is manageable and can be reused for similar work in the future should always be your goal.

You should be considering assembly performance when creating and editing a model, when opening the model, and also when detailing and annotating the model.

Working with the Model

You can use several methods to ensure that your large assembly will not become unmanageable. It is important to remember that the term *large assembly* is subjective. To you a large assembly may be 200 components, whereas it may be 20,000 to someone else. Either way, following best practices ensures that you are developing good procedural habits and are prepared for the day when you are asked to design a much larger assembly than you typically do today.

As was discussed earlier in this chapter, hardware limitations might be an obstacle that you cannot overcome even if you follow every best practice, but you'll need to follow these practices to know that for certain. Conversely, even if you have a workstation that is extremely capable, you will still benefit by developing good work habits and making your models easier to handle on less-capable workstations of others you collaborate with.

Improving File Open Time

It is a good practice to shut down Inventor and other Windows applications if you will be leaving them for an extended period of time. Closing these applications can allow the system to free up memory "leaked" by drivers and subroutines that take up memory when executed but do not release it when finished, even if you don't use those functions again.

When working with large datasets, shutting down the application and reloading the model can be time-consuming. There is a default setting on the File tab of the Application Options dialog box that saves the last-opened assembly and its component files in cache. You can also define a specific file to be kept so that you can work with others and maintain the benefits of the Quick File Open setting for a specific assembly.

Reducing Assembly Constraints

Using subassemblies within upper-level assemblies can reduce assembly constraints. The importance of this concept cannot be overstated. Reducing assembly constraints can eliminate the number of redundant calculations Inventor must make to solve your model, and therefore it pays off immediately in that respect. The improved organization and ability to reuse components already organized into subassemblies is a benefit that may be realized in the future.

To reorganize an assembly that has not been created using subassemblies, you can use the Demote option. To explore this concept, let's make some changes to an assembly:

1. Open the file mi_9a_001.iam located in the Chapter 9 directory of your Mastering Inventor 2016 folder. If you have not already downloaded the Chapter 9 files from www.sybex.com/go/masteringinventor2016, please refer to the "What You Will Need" section of the introduction for the download and setup instructions.

Although not a large assembly by anyone's standard, this assembly has been created without using subassemblies to demonstrate the ability to demote components into subassemblies from the top down. Currently, this assembly has a total of 31 constraints being used at the top-level assembly. Your goal is to restructure this assembly into three subassemblies so that you can reduce constraints and create subassemblies that can be used in other stapler designs.

2. At the top of the Model browser, you'll see the words Assembly View with a drop-down arrow next to them. Use the drop-down arrow to change the browser view to modeling view.

Assembly View Displays assembly constraints and connections nested below the assembly components, as well as in the Relationships folder. Part modeling features are hidden.

Modeling View Displays all assembly constraints and connections in a folder named Relationships at the top of the browser tree. Each part's modeling features are displayed below the part.

3. Click the plus sign next to the Relationships folder found at the top of the browser tree to display the list of all the constraints in the assembly.

4. In the Model browser, select all the components with a prefix of 100.

5. Once you've selected those components, right-click and choose Component ➤ Demote, as shown in Figure 9.8.

FIGURE 9.8
Demoting components to a subassembly

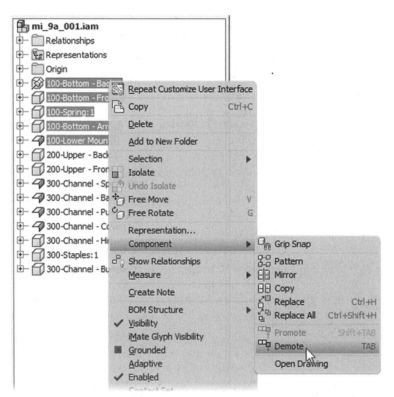

6. You are presented with a Create In-Place Component dialog box, where you can specify the name of the new subassembly, the template file, the file location, and the default

BOM structure. Enter **100** for the name, set the BOM structure to Phantom, and then click OK.

PHANTOM SUBASSEMBLIES

Setting a subassembly as Phantom prevents it from being listed in the bill of materials while still allowing the parts contained within the subassembly to be listed.

---

7. Click Yes in the warning stating that assembly constraints will be moved with the demoted components, shown in Figure 9.9.

FIGURE 9.9
Restructuring components warning

This warning simply states that any constraints between the 100-series parts and the 200- and 300-series parts will now be redefined to be between subassembly 100 and the 200- and 300-series parts. The constraints between the 100-series parts and other 100-series parts are maintained in subassembly 100.

This is important in large assemblies because it can significantly reduce the number of constraints used. Consider the five components you selected to demote in the stapler. If these components all had just one assembly constraint, each relating it to some part that will not be in the new subassembly, those five constraints will be discarded.

Continuing with the example, you should now see the subassembly named 100.iam in the Model browser. Because of the restructure, you will need to ground the assembly so that it cannot be accidentally moved. Then you can continue to demote components into another subassembly.

8. Right-click 100.iam and click Grounded to set it in place.

9. In the Model browser, select all the components with a prefix of 200.

10. Right-click and choose Component ➢ Demote.

11. Enter **200** for the name, set the BOM structure to Phantom, and then click OK. Click Yes in the warning dialog box.

12. Repeat the steps for demoting for all the components with a prefix of 300 until your browser looks similar to Figure 9.10.

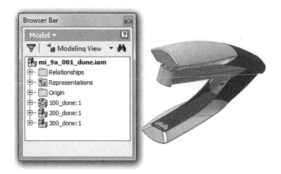

If you look in the Relationships folder at the top of the browser tree, you'll see that the number of constraints that exist at the top level of the assembly has been reduced considerably.

You can also restructure components by dragging a component listed in the assembly browser, either in or out of a subassembly browser node. Moving components up out of a subassembly is called *promoting* rather than *demoting*. Because you can promote or demote unconstrained and underconstrained components, you may need to edit the subassembly and ensure that components are constrained properly within that subassembly.

ASSEMBLY CONSTRAINT AND ADAPTIVITY OPTIONS

There are three Application Options settings to be aware of that can impact assembly performance. When working with large assemblies, you might want to have all three of these options deselected. You can find them by selecting the Tools tab, clicking the Application Options button, and then selecting the Assembly tab. The options are as follows:

◆ Enable Relationship Redundancy Analysis

◆ Enable Related Relationship Failure Analysis

◆ Features Are Initially Adaptive

Adaptivity

Too many cross-part adaptive features can cripple the performance of even a modest-sized assembly if used without discretion. As discussed in Chapter 8, "Assembly Design Workflows," adaptivity should generally be turned off once the adaptive feature or part is created.

Often features and parts are made adaptive during the early design stages of a model, when changes are made quickly and you want many parts to follow these changes. Turning off the adaptive status on the part ensures that your assembly performance will not be affected. If the adaptive part needs to be edited, you can turn on its adaptive status so that you can make adjustments.

Many times parts become adaptive by default when a new part or feature is created in an assembly, because a reference sketch is projected from one part to another. You can disable this by clicking Application Options on the Tools tab, selecting the Assembly tab in the dialog box that opens, and then deselecting the Enable Associative Edge/Loop Geometry Projection During In-Place Modeling option under Cross Part Geometry Projection.

You can also hold the **Ctrl** key while selecting individual edges for projection into your sketch. This works only when you're selecting individual edges. Selecting a face will build an adaptive relationship. Either technique will create fewer accidental adaptive parts but may require more manual effort in projecting geometry across parts.

Selection Tools

When working with a large assembly, combing through all the many parts within that assembly that you want to select for a given task can be time-consuming and difficult if you attempt to locate them using the standard Pan, Zoom, and Orbit methods. Instead, make yourself familiar with the options in the assembly selection tools.

You can use selection tools to suppress sets of components based on such factors as size, internal components that are not visible because of the presence of external housings, and so on. For instance, to maintain performance, you may not want to load all the internal components into memory when they are not important to your current design task. Once you've selected the internal components, you can suppress them and create an external-part-only level of detail representation. If you haven't created level of detail (LOD) representations before, you can find information on how to do so in Chapter 8.

Another use of assembly selection tools is to create view representations in the assembly to aid in the creation of views in the drawing file. As an example, when you place a view in the drawing using a design view that was created with the All In Camera tool, only the components in the screen view plane are calculated. This increases performance and memory capacity. Figure 9.11 shows the available selection tools.

FIGURE 9.11
Available selection tools

The following selection tools are available:

Select Component Priority   Sets the selection to pick up the topmost structure level of components. If set, this will pick up subassemblies and not their children.

Select Part Priority   Sets the tool to select parts, no matter what their subassembly structure.

Select Body Priority   Sets the tool to select solid bodies within their parent part file, no matter what their subassembly structure. This option works best when using the Modeling view. When using the Assembly view, the Find In Browser option does not work.

Select Feature Priority   Selects individual features rather than the parts that contain them.

Select Faces And Edges   Allows you to highlight and select faces or the curves that define those faces.

Select Sketch Features   Allows you to highlight and select sketches or the curves that define those sketches.

Select Visible Only   Selects only visible components in a selection set.

Enable Prehighlight   Displays prehighlighting when your cursor moves over an object. This does not affect the Select Other tool, which always shows prehighlighting.

Invert Selection   Deselects all components previously selected, and selects all components previously unselected.

Previous Selection   Reselects all components in the previous selection set.

Select All Occurrences   Selects all instances in the current file of the selected component.

Select Constrained To   Selects all components constrained to a preselected component or components.

Select Component Size   Selects components by the percent set in the Select By Size box. Size is determined by the diagonal of the bounding box of the components. Click the arrow to select a component and measure its size to use as a scale. Figure 9.12 shows the Select By Size dialog box.

FIGURE 9.12
Select By Size dialog box

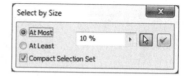

Select Component Offset   Selects components fully or partially contained within the bounding box of a selected component plus a specified offset distance.

Select Sphere Offset   Selects components fully or partially contained within the bounding sphere of a selected component plus a specified offset distance.

Select By Plane   Selects components on a specified side of a face/plane. You can choose which side of the plane to consider and include partially or fully contained components.

Select External Components   Selects external components based on a percentage of the component's viewable surface.

Select Internal Components   Selects internal components based on a percentage of the component's viewable surface.

Select All In Camera   Selects all components in the current view screen based on a percentage of the component's viewable surface.

USING THE FEATURE SELECTION FILTER TO SELECT WORK PLANES

It can be a major pain to try to select a work plane while in a busy assembly file. To make it easier, use the Select Feature Priority filter or the Select Faces And Edges filter. Your cursor will no longer select parts but only features, making it easy to select even the most obscured work planes.

View Representations

View representations are often used in large assemblies to navigate to a predefined viewing angle so that you do not have to tax your system with heavy graphics regeneration. For instance, if you have an assembly that contains an entire production line of material-handling equipment, you may find it difficult to orbit around to the backside of the assembly to complete a simple task such as selecting a face or just looking at the assembly. If you set a design view before orbiting and then set another once you have orbited to the desired view, you can then easily toggle between the two views of this assembly, thereby increasing performance during navigation between these predefined views.

View representations have other large-assembly benefits as well. When creating a drawing view of a large assembly, you can specify a preset view representation and reduce the time it takes to create the drawing view. If you have turned off the visibility of some components in the assembly view representation, the drawing view can generate even faster and provide you with a clearer and more concise view. Of course, if you already have the assembly open when creating the drawing view, the components are likely already loaded into memory.

Another way that the experienced Inventor user may use view representations is to navigate the Model browser. For instance, if you set up a view representation to zoom in on a particular subassembly so that you can navigate to that component quickly, you can save that view representation while the entire model tree is rolled up and only the subassembly of interest is expanded. This browser state will be saved within the view representation.

Once a view representation is created, you can right-click it and choose Copy To Level Of Detail to copy the view representation to an LOD representation. This allows you to transfer the visibility settings from the view representation to the LOD where they will be suppressed. In this way, you do not have to duplicate the process of turning parts off.

Find

Navigating a large-assembly Model browser can be a chore. To help with this, you can employ the Find tool to define search criteria for constraints, components, features, sketches, and welds.

Searches can be saved for future use and recalled as needed using the Open Search button, shown in Figure 9.13.

FIGURE 9.13
The Find tool in an
assembly file

You can access the Find tool in the following ways:

◆ From within a file, click the binoculars icon in the Model browser.

◆ In the Inventor Open dialog box, click the Find button.

Opening the Model

One of the most important aspects of working on a large assembly file is being able to open the file. Although this seems obvious, many Inventor users seem to approach opening a model as an afterthought. Consider it in this way—if you were tasked with carrying a pile of stones up a flight of stairs, you would probably be unlikely to attempt to carry them all up the stairs at once. But this is exactly the kind of heavy lifting you are asking your workstation to do when opening a large assembly.

To allow your workstation to make multiple trips when opening an assembly file, you will use LOD representations. You create LOD representations by suppressing components in an assembly. Once the LOD is created, you can access it the next time you begin to open the file by using the Options button, shown in Figure 9.14. Once the assembly file is open, you can remove the suppression of components as required, and those components will then be loaded into memory. You can also specify a default LOD so that the assembly opens to it without your having to use the Options dialog box every time. This is done from Application Options on the Assembly tab. You'll learn more about creating LODs later, in the "Managing Assembly Detail" section of this chapter.

FIGURE 9.14
Opening LODs

If you need to open a large assembly that has not been properly managed, you may find yourself having to locate or skip a number of parts and subassemblies. This can be a tedious task, but the Skip All Unresolved Files option in the File Open dialog will bypass locating missing components and load the members of the assembly that can be located automatically.

LOD IN SUBASSEMBLIES

Often, you might create a complex assembly model as a stand-alone design because you need to insert that model into an upper-level assembly as part of a larger system. Because the original design was required to generate production drawings and an accurate BOM, it includes all the components in the design.

However, because you will be placing multiple instances of this subassembly, you want to avoid placing it at the full level of detail. You might create an LOD in the subassembly where all internal components, all external hardware, and all internal and external fasteners are suppressed, leaving only the external housing and frame components.

LOD representations of subassemblies can be accessed from the Options button in the Place Component dialog box when you are placing them into upper-level assemblies. By placing a subassembly at a reduced level of detail, you have created a much smaller, top-level assembly file and yet still have the ability to pull an accurate BOM even from the top-level assembly.

Working with Large Assembly Drawings

Although large assembly files require some forethought and management, so do the drawing files of these large assemblies. Because Inventor generates the line work from the models that you create views from automatically, it is easy to take for granted the large number of calculations required to do this. Stop for a moment and consider all the hidden lines, sectioned parts, and so on, that Inventor has to consider in order to render your drawing views accurately.

It is for this reason that you will want to adopt slightly different techniques than those you use to make part or small assembly drawings. If you have not yet worked with Inventor's drawing environment much at this point, you can find more information specific to Inventor drawings in Chapter 12, "Documentation." Keep in mind that many of the options mentioned in this section are covered in more depth in Chapter 12.

WORKING WITH HIGH-SPEED RASTER VIEWS

You can enable an option to create raster views for large or complex models. When enabled, a draft preview of a drawing view will be displayed while the precise drawing view is calculated in the background. Raster drawing views enable you to continue to work and annotate the drawing while the precise calculation of a drawing view is completed.

To enable a raster view, you can use either of two methods. One creates a raster view until the view calculation is complete, at which time it converts to a precise view. The other option maintains the view as a raster view until you choose to make it a precise view.

To enable temporary raster view creation, select the Drawing tab of the Application Options dialog box and then select the Enable Background Updates option (toward the bottom) to use raster views. By default this option is not selected. This setting will create the view as a raster view but will allow the raster view to convert to a precise view when the calculations are complete.

To create views that persist as raster views, you can select the Raster View check box at the middle of the Drawing View creation dialog box, as shown in Figure 9.15. To convert a raster view to a precise view once it has been created, you can right-click the view and choose Make View Precise. You can convert it back to a raster view by right-clicking again and choosing Make View Raster.

FIGURE 9.15
Creating a raster drawing view from an LOD

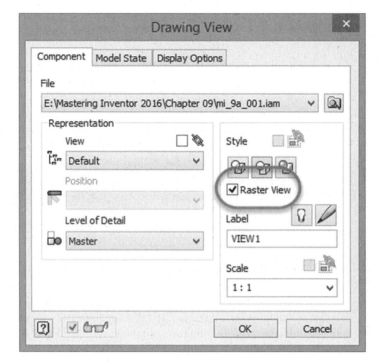

Raster views are indicated by green corner glyphs in the graphic window and by either the green circular arrows icon in the browser if the view is calculating toward becoming precise or the red slash across the view icon in the browser for a static raster view. If you place your cursor on a calculating raster view icon, you'll see a tool tip showing the progress of precise calculation.

Several features are not available or will work differently while the precise views are being calculated and the raster view is displayed. This alternative functionality is intended to handle the situations where the less-detailed raster views might cause confusion or problems.

These features are not available for raster views:

◆ Automated Centerlines cannot be created for raster views.

◆ Auto Balloons cannot be used for raster views.

◆ Model Features cannot be selected as edges in raster views.

These features work differently for raster views:

◆ Tangent model edges are always shown in raster views, and their properties or visibility cannot be edited.

◆ Interference edges are not shown in raster views.

◆ Reference Parts might have incomplete geometry in raster views.

◆ Hole Tables are not available to use the View and Feature options for raster views.

◆ Thread Annotations are not displayed in raster views. New or existing thread notes are attached to thread features after views turn precise.

◆ Printing when a drawing includes raster views provides three options: You can print the current precise views, wait until all views are precise, or cancel the print. However, I do not recommend you print raster views because geometry on printed raster views can be different from the final precise views.

◆ Export to AutoCAD DWG, DWF, DXF, or PDF cannot be completed for a drawing with raster views. If a precise view calculation is in progress, a progress bar is displayed. You can wait until the calculation finishes or cancel the export.

◆ Save and Close for drawings containing raster views can be executed as expected. If the file is closed and reopened, the raster views are automatically recalculated as precise.

CREATING LARGE ASSEMBLY DRAWING VIEWS

When creating drawings of large assemblies, it is advised that you do so from an LOD representation already created in the model. Doing so reduces the number of files Inventor is required to access to create and update the line work in the view. To create views from assembly representations, you specify the representations you want to use in the Drawing View dialog box, as shown in Figure 9.15 earlier. Keep in mind that when browsing for the file to create a view of, if you use the Options button in the Open dialog box to specify the representation, you will reduce the time it takes to create the view.

Although using LODs will help with drawing views, be aware that because Inventor employs a global bill of materials, as soon as you place a parts list, balloon, or other annotation referencing the bill of materials, the number of files loaded into memory increases to include all the parts in the bill of materials. This situation somewhat defeats the purpose of the LOD tools, but currently no solution is available.

VIEW PREVIEW DISPLAY

If you find yourself waiting for the preview of your assembly to generate before being able to proceed with view creation options, you will want to change the preview display to use bounding boxes and then enable the preview on files as required on a case-by-case basis by clicking the preview icon shown at the bottom left of Figure 9.15. Note that enabling/disabling the preview is an option only when using the Bounding Box or Partial option. To find this setting, select the Tools tab, click Application Options, select the Drawing tab in the dialog box that opens, and look in the View Preview Display section.

REDUCING HIDDEN LINES

Hidden-line generation can be one of the most memory-intensive aspects of creating a drawing view. Generally, with large assemblies it is not desirable to show the hidden lines of all components. Instead, you typically will want to enable hidden lines for just those components where hidden lines add clarity.

Rather than selecting the Hidden Line style in the Drawing View dialog box, first create the view with no hidden lines. Next, locate and expand the view you just created in the browser, and select the components you intend to be shown with hidden lines. Right-click the components, and choose Hidden Lines.

You will be prompted with a message box informing you that you are changing the view style to show hidden lines and that any children of this view will be granted an independent view style based on their current setting, as shown in Figure 9.16. The result will be that only the components you chose will be displayed with hidden lines.

FIGURE 9.16
Managing hidden lines

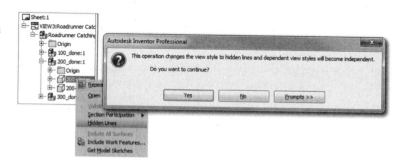

CREATING TITLE BLOCK LOGOS

A sure way to slow down your drawing's performance is to create an unnecessarily complex title block. If you have included a bitmap of your company logo in your title block, ensure that the bitmap file is reduced in resolution and file size as much as possible. You can use any photo editor to do this.

Once you've reduced the bitmap file as much as possible, consider embedding the file into the title block rather than linking it. Although linking the bitmap does give you greater flexibility in updating the logo independent of the title block, Inventor will be required to locate the bitmap each time the drawing is loaded. To embed rather than link the logo bitmap, simply deselect the Link check box when inserting the bitmap.

If you have pasted the logo in from Autodesk® AutoCAD® software, ensure that the logo is as clean as possible. You may be better off removing the hatches from the logo in AutoCAD and then adding them using the Fill/Hatch Sketch Region tool in Inventor.

REDUCING THE NUMBER OF SHEETS AND VIEWS PER DRAWING FILE

Although it is possible to create a large number of sheets in a single drawing file, it is generally accepted that this is not good practice. Instead, you should consider making a new file for each drawing sheet when possible. Or at the least, keep the number of sheets per file as low as possible. There are two primary reasons for doing so.

The first reason is simply to keep the file size down. If you have a drawing of a large assembly file that includes four sheets and has a file size of 80 MB, you could split this into two files, each with two sheets and a file size of approximately 40 MB. In this way, you do not need to load the extra 40 MB in sheets 3 and 4 just to make an edit to sheet 1.

The second reason to minimize drawing sheets is so you are not guilty of placing all your eggs in one basket. Creating multiple tab or sheet files in any application can be risky. Imagine you created a load calculation spreadsheet and you developed the habit of adding a tab for each new calculation you do rather than creating a new file for each calculation. If the file becomes corrupt, you've lost all your calculations rather than just one set of calculations. The same thing could happen with your Inventor drawing if you habitually create new sheets instead of new files.

Managing Assembly Detail

In Chapter 8, you learned about creating LOD representations within your assemblies to reduce the memory requirements of working with large assemblies. Here you will consider how you can use these LOD representations to handle large assemblies more efficiently.

LOD Strategies

Certification Objective

All Inventor assemblies have four default LODs predefined and ready for you to use. Learning to use them and creating your own LODs is an important part of working with large assemblies. The default LODs are as follows:

Master   This LOD shows your assembly with no parts suppressed. You can think of it as the highest level of detail for any assembly.

All Components Suppressed   This LOD suppresses everything within the assembly. You can think of it as the lowest level of detail for any assembly.

All Parts Suppressed   This LOD suppresses all parts at all levels of the assembly, but subassemblies are loaded.

All Content Center Suppressed   This LOD suppresses any component in the assembly that is stored in the Content Center Files directory as designated by the IPJ (project) file or the Application Options settings.

When opening a large assembly, you can use the All Components Suppressed LOD to quickly open the file and then manually unsuppress components as required. However, it is more practical to create your own LODs and use them to efficiently open your assemblies. Consider creating intermediate LODs based on your design process.

For a closer look at LODs in action, follow these steps:

1. From the Get Started tab, choose Open.

2. Open the file mi_9a_002.iam from the Chapter 9 directory of your Mastering Inventor 2016 folder.

3. Expand the Representations folder and the Level Of Detail node in the Model browser if they are not already expanded.

4. Right-click the Level Of Detail header and choose New Level Of Detail. Change the name from LevelofDetail1 to **MediumLOD**.

5. In the Quick Access toolbar (along the top of the screen), click the selection tool drop-down list (see Figure 9.17) and set your selection focus to Select Component Priority if it is not already.

FIGURE 9.17
Selecting internal components

6. Using the same drop-down list, now choose Internal Components, shown in Figure 9.17.

7. Set the slider to 85 percent and click the green check mark.

8. Right-click anywhere on the screen, and choose Isolate to get a better view of the components you selected. Your screen should look similar to Figure 9.18.

FIGURE 9.18
Isolated internal components

9. Now you'll bring back one component to add to your selection set. Select the component called MA-001:1 in the browser, right-click, and choose Visibility. You should see the motor subassembly become visible.

10. Select all the components on the screen. You can use a crossing window to do this quickly.

11. Right-click and choose Suppress.

12. Right-click anywhere and choose Undo Isolate to bring back the visibility of the remaining unsuppressed components.

13. Save the assembly to ensure that the changes to your newly created level of detail are recorded.

14. Switch back and forth between the master LOD and your MediumLOD to observe the differences.

15. To modify MediumLOD, activate it and suppress any component you'd like; then save the assembly.

In the preceding steps you used selection filters to quickly select the internal parts and then used the Isolate tool to toggle the visibility setting of the unselected components. Then you suppressed the visible components. Understand that it is the Suppress option that creates and modifies LOD representations. Changing visibility affects only view representations and has no impact on the LOD. When you've finished experimenting with this file, you can close it and continue to the next section.

Substitute LODs

**Certification
Objective**

You can use substitute LOD representations to trade out a large multipart assembly with a single part derived from that assembly. Substitute LODs improve efficiency by reducing the number of files Inventor is referencing and, if created from other LODs, can also reduce the amount of geometry required.

For example, in the blower assembly, you could create a substitute LOD from the entire assembly and then place that substitute into a top-level assembly as needed. You would certainly gain some efficiency by doing this because the top-level assembly is referencing only one file. However, if you created a substitute from MediumLOD, you would be maintaining an even higher level of performance in the top-level assembly because all the internal geometry that was suppressed in the creation of that LOD would be omitted.

To create a substitute LOD, follow these steps:

1. From the Get Started tab, choose Open.

2. Browse for the file mi_9a_003.iam located in the Chapter 9 directory of the Mastering Inventor 2016 folder and click Open.

3. Expand the Representations folder and the Level Of Detail node in the Model browser if they are not already expanded.

4. Double-click MediumLOD to set it as the active LOD if not already done.

5. Right-click the Level Of Detail header in the browser and choose New Substitute and then Shrinkwrap. Notice that Inventor is asking you to specify a filename, a file template, and a location to create this file.

6. Enter **mi 9a 003 Substitute 100** for the name in the New Derived Substitute Part dialog box and leave the template and file location at the defaults.

7. Click OK. Inventor opens a new part file and takes you directly into the shrinkwrap process, bringing up the Assembly Shrinkwrap Options dialog box.

8. In the Style area at the top, ensure that the Single Composite Feature option is selected. The following are the descriptions of each of the four available options:

Single Solid Body Merging Out Seams Between Planar Faces   Produces a single solid body without seams. Merged faces become a single color, where required.

Solid Body Keep Seams Between Planar Faces   Produces a single solid body with seams. Colors are retained.

Maintain Each Solid As A Solid Body   Produces a single part file with multiple bodies. This is the closest approximation to an assembly.

Single Composite Feature   Produces a single surface composite feature and the smallest file. Colors and seams of the original components are maintained. The mass properties of the original assembly are stored in the file for reference.

9. Ensure that the Remove Geometry By Visibility check box is selected.

10. Select Whole Parts Only.

11. Play around with the slider, clicking the Preview button to see what is removed.

12. Set the slider to 78 percent.

13. Under Hole Patching, select All.

14. Ensure that Reduced Memory Mode is selected at the bottom of the dialog box. When selected, this option allows the derived part to be created using less memory by not including the source bodies of the assembly parts.

15. Refer to Figure 9.19 to check the settings and then click OK.

FIGURE 9.19
Deriving a shrinkwrap
LOD

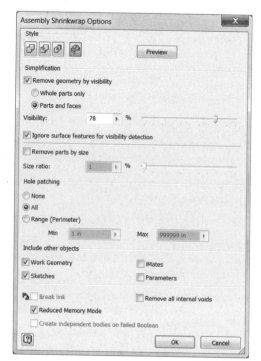

16. Click Yes when asked about the mass properties. Note that Inventor closes the derived part file and returns to the assembly and that an LOD named SubstituteLevelofDetail1 has been created. You can rename it if you like by clicking it once and then a second time.

17. Save the assembly.

18. Double-click MediumLOD to set it as active and compare the substitute LOD by clicking back and forth between the two.

19. To see that the substitute shrinkwrap is a surface model, click the View tab and choose the Half Section View icon from the drop-down list on the Appearance panel.

20. Click Workplane2 in the Model browser.

21. Right-click and choose OK.

22. Choose End Section View from the drop-down list on the Appearance panel to turn off the section view.

Figure 9.20 shows the substitute LOD as it appears in the browser.

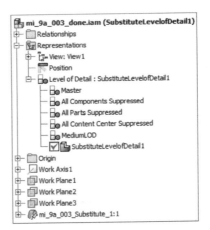

FIGURE 9.20
Substitute LOD

Recall that all LODs maintain an accurate BOM listing. To confirm this, select the Assemble tab, click Bill Of Materials, and interrogate the BOM to see that even though the substitute LOD consists of a single part, Inventor still maintains the BOM information for the entire assembly. You can close this file without saving changes and move on to the next section.

Subassembly LODs

Certification Objective

Subassembly use is where LOD representations really begin to pay off in terms of performance. Once LOD representations have been created in your assembly, you can switch the LOD in the subassemblies to match in three ways:

◆ Place the subassemblies into a top-level assembly with the matching LOD by using the Options button.

◆ Switch the LOD manually in the subassembly in the Model browser.

◆ Use the Link Levels Of Detail tool at the top-level assembly to automatically set the subassemblies to the matching LOD.

In Figure 9.21, all of the subassemblies contain LODs named Frame Layout, Exhaust Connection, and Harness Layout set up within them. These LODs were linked using the Link Levels of Detail tool, as indicated in the browser by the LOD name shown in parentheses next to the assembly name.

FIGURE 9.21
Nested LODs with a consistent naming scheme

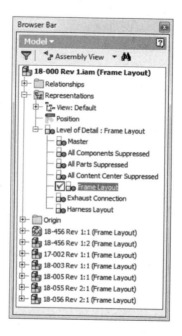

You might take this concept one step further and edit your assembly templates to automatically include standard LOD names already in them. This way you do not have to create the LODs, but instead you can simply activate them and then suppress parts as required to "fill them out."

Recall that Inventor specifies your template location on the File tab of the Application Options dialog box. Note that this can be overridden in your project file. Check this by selecting the Get Started tab and then clicking the Projects button, and look in the Folder Options section of the Project File Editor that opens. If a path is specified there, that is where your templates are located. If it shows = Default, the path found in Application Options is where your templates are located.

In the following exercise, the subassemblies all have LODs created in them. These are called Bolts, Washers, Nuts, and Galvanized. Each subassembly was configured with these LODs set up as described in the previous exercise. The top-level assembly has three LODs created, called Bolts, Washers, and Nuts. Although these LODs have been created, they have not been configured and currently do not differ from the master LOD. The following steps take you through the linking of the Bolt LOD at the top-level assembly to the Bolt LODs in the subassemblies:

1. From the Get Started tab, choose Open.

2. Open the file `mi_9a_004.iam` from the `Chapter 9` directory of your `Mastering Inventor 2016` folder.

3. Expand the `Representations` folder and the Level Of Detail node in the Model browser.

4. Double-click the LOD named Bolts to set it active, or right-click it and choose Activate.

5. Click the Assemble tab, expand the drop-down list for the Productivity panel, and choose Link Levels Of Detail.

6. Click Bolts in the Link Levels Of Detail dialog box.

7. Click OK in the Link Levels Of Detail dialog box and click OK to accept the warning that the assembly will be saved.

Note that the subassemblies have all been set so that the Bolts LOD is active in them. If one of the subassemblies did not have an LOD called Bolts, it would be left at its current LOD. You can continue this exercise by repeating these steps for the Washers and Nuts LODs if you'd like. Note too that each of the subassemblies has an LOD called Galvanized in which all parts that are not galvanized steel have been suppressed. You can create an LOD called Galvanized in the top-level assembly and then use the Link LODs tool to suppress all the parts not made of galvanized steel. You can also set different instances of a subassembly to display differing LOD representations. You can close the file without saving.

Using LOD Naming Conventions

There is an infinite number of naming conventions for LODs, including the one suggested here (High, Moderate, and Low). Making LODs that have certain parts of the design turned on can be useful as well—for example, Frame Only, Frame & Transmission, Transmission Only, Conveyors Off, No Robots, and so on. If you give them descriptive names, other users can select the appropriate LOD for the work they need to complete.

Simplifying Parts

It's often suggested that things be made as simple as possible but not simpler. This is a good concept to keep in mind when creating models in Inventor. Adding extraneous details to common parts can have a negative impact on large assembly performance. Of course, if the part file is to be used for fabrication, then a certain level of detail is required. Oftentimes, though, you'll create models of common parts to be used in an assembly for the end goal of getting an accurate bill of materials. Assembly performance could most likely be improved by reducing the amount of detail in those types of parts.

Removing or Suppressing Unneeded Features

Reducing the number of edges and faces in a part is a sure way to minimize the size of the part file. Removing fillets and chamfers for purchased parts is a good way to eliminate extra faces. If you have common parts that are used in large numbers throughout your assemblies, you might consider creating two versions of these parts: one version for use in large assemblies and another for use in creating production drawings and Inventor Studio renderings. In Figure 9.22, you can see two versions of the same part. The file for the part on the left is approximately 600 KB, whereas the one on the right is less than 175 KB.

FIGURE 9.22
A simplified part

In the following steps, you will derive a simplified version of a part and set the part numbers to match so the two files report the same in the BOM and parts lists. To create a simplified part, follow these steps:

1. From the Get Started tab, choose Open.

2. Open the file mi_9a_010.ipt from the Chapter 9 directory of the Mastering Inventor 2016 folder.

3. Click the end-of-part (EOP) marker in the Model browser and drag it to just below the feature named Revolution1 (or right-click Revolution1 and choose Move EOP Marker).

4. Change the appearance to Generic (at the top of the screen in the Quick Access toolbar, click the Appearance drop-down arrow and scroll for Generic).

5. Do not save the part.

Figure 9.23 shows the end-of-part marker being placed above the existing features.

FIGURE 9.23
Using the EOP marker to simplify the original part

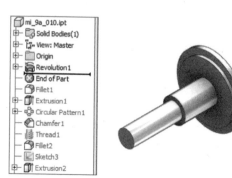

6. From the Get Started tab, choose New.

7. Choose the `Standard.ipt` template to create the new file and click the OK button.

8. In the new part, right-click and choose Finish Sketch if required. This might not be needed if you have your Application Options setting set up so that a new sketch is not created automatically when a new part is created.

9. On the Manage tab, click the Derive button on the Insert panel.

10. In the resulting Open dialog box, browse for the file `mi_9a_010.ipt` located in the `Chapter 9` directory of your `Mastering Inventor 2016` folder and click the Open button.

11. In the resulting Derived Part dialog box, choose the Derive Style option called Single Solid Body Merging Out Seams Between Planar Faces as the derive style.

12. Click the OK button to create the derived body.

13. In the Model browser, right-click the part name `mi_9a_010.ipt` and choose Suppress Link With Base Component. This ensures that the derived part will remain in the simplified state when you set the original part back to its fully detailed state.

14. Right-click the filename at the top of the Model browser and choose iProperties.

15. Choose the Project tab of the iProperties dialog box and enter **mi_9a_010** as the part number. This ensures that as you use the simplified part in an assembly, it will have the same part number as the original part and report an accurate BOM.

16. Click OK to accept changes and save the file as **mi_9a_010_simple.ipt**.

17. Return to the original part (`mi_9a_010.ipt`).

18. Either close the file and click No when asked to save changes or drag the EOP marker back to the bottom of the Model browser, reset the part color, and then save the file.

As a result you will have two files representing the same part. Both will be listed as the same component in the BOM, but the derived component will add far less overhead when used over and over in an assembly. Note that if the original part were to require a revision to the overall length, you would want to edit the simplified part file and unsuppress the link so that the changes are carried through. You can place both files in an assembly file to test this workflow if you'd like, or you can close these files.

The Bottom Line

Select a workstation. Having the right tool for the job is the key to success in anything you do. This is true of selecting a large assembly workstation. You have learned that for optimal performance you should strive to keep your system working in physical memory (RAM).

> **Master It** You notice that your computer runs slowly when working with large assemblies, and you want to know whether you should consider a 64-bit system. How do you determine whether your system is adequate or whether it's time to upgrade?

Adjust your performance settings.   You have learned that there are many settings in Inventor and in Windows that you can use to configure the application to work more efficiently with large assemblies.

> **Master It**   You want to make your current workstation run as efficiently as possible for large assembly design. What are some ways to do that?

Use best practices for large assemblies.   Knowing the tools for general assembly design is only half of the battle when it comes to conquering large assemblies. Understanding the methods of large assembly design and how they differ from those for general assembly design is a key to success.

> **Master It**   You want to create adaptive parts so that you can make changes during the initial design stage and have several parts update automatically as you work through the details. But you are concerned about how this will adversely affect your assembly performance. How do you keep your performance level high in this situation?

Manage assembly detail.   Inventor includes several tools to help manage assembly detail so that you can accomplish your large assembly design goals.

> **Master It**   You want to reduce the number of files your large assembly is required to reference while you are working on it and yet maintain an accurate bill of materials. How do you do that?

Simplify parts.   Creating highly detailed parts may be required for generating production drawings or Inventor Studio renderings, but using those high-detail parts in large assemblies may have an adverse effect on performance.

> **Master It**   You want to create a lower-level-of-detail part file for common parts to be reused many times over in your large assemblies but are concerned about managing two versions of a part. How do you avoid versioning problems?

Chapter 10

Weldment Design

For this chapter, you must have a good understanding of parts, assemblies, and drawings. You will explore the various aspects of weldment design. Starting from weldment workflows and design methodologies, you'll look at preparations, weld beads, machining features, and weld symbols, as well as how to document the weldment design. You will also learn some tips and tricks along the way.

Weldments are available in the assembly environment as a subtype of the assembly document. Most of the topics in this chapter involve working with assembly files. Therefore, this chapter is not applicable if you have only the Autodesk® Inventor LT™ program installed.

In this chapter, you'll learn to

- ◆ Select and use the right weldment design methodology
- ◆ Create and edit weld preparations and machining features
- ◆ Create and edit different kinds of weld beads, such as cosmetic, fillet, and groove
- ◆ Document weldment stages in drawings
- ◆ Generate and maintain a consistent BOM across welded assemblies, drawings, and presentations

Exploring Weldment Design Methodologies

One of the basic questions in weldment design is what design methodology should be used to create weldments. Unfortunately, there is no "one-size-fits-all" strategy. The design methodology you use depends on your individual needs and requirements. You will start by defining the different design methodologies.

As-assembled   A view of the assembly with no weld preparations, beads, or machining features.

As-welded   A view of the assembly with weld preparations and weld beads but no machining features.

As-machined   A view of the final welded assembly with the machining features created after the welding had been done. This view includes features that might penetrate or cut through weld beads.

All these represent the various stages in weldment design. Once the weldment design is done, it helps to document the various stages of weldment design in the drawing.

Depending on the need for documentation, interference analysis, mass properties, and other design criteria, you can group the weldment design methodologies into the following four broad categories, which are defined in more detail in this section:

◆ Part files and part features

◆ Weldment assembly and derived technology

◆ Weldment assembly

◆ Multi-body part files

Part Files and Part Features

You can create a weldment design using part features in part files. With this approach, you use the rich modeling features of the part (sweeps, chamfers, fillets, and lofts) to create a wide variety of weld bead shapes. However, this will be one big mess of a design that has no logical partitions. The main difficulty is creating drawings with different stages—for example, as-assembled, as-welded, and so on—from a single design. You will not be able to see certain edges separating weld beads and components in drawings because they will not even exist (they will be merged out) in the part design. In addition, the bill of materials (BOM) will not list all the individual components needed to assemble the welded structures. Still, this might be an acceptable strategy for small weldment designs that have minor design changes over a period of time. Besides, the assumption is that the designer does not need to create the different stages in design documentation from a single weldment assembly. You could place the part weldment into an assembly and then create presentations and drawings of that assembly. (However, in drawings, you will not be able to create the different stages of weldment design.) Figure 10.1 shows this methodology.

Figure 10.1
Part files and part features

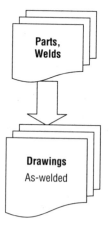

Weldment Assembly and Derived Technology

With this approach, you can derive the weldment assembly (.iam) into a single-part file (.ipt) and model the welds in the derived assembly file using part features. Optionally, you can derive the part file into another part file to show machining on welded assemblies. Disadvantages similar to the ones mentioned in the first method exist; however, you can modify assembly constraints to create variants of weldment assemblies with this approach. The preparations, welds, and machining features will all exist in the derived component files. This might be a good strategy for weldments where a BOM listing is required and there is no need to document different stages of weldment design from a single weldment assembly. Figure 10.2 shows the document layout of this methodology.

Figure 10.2
Weldment assembly and
derived technology

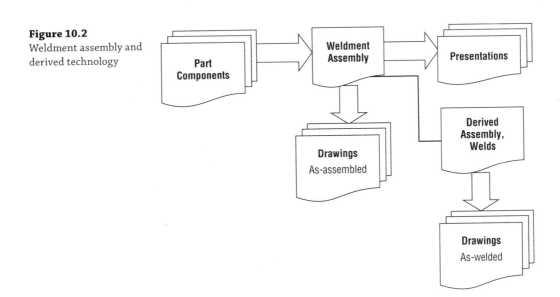

Weldment Assembly

With this approach, you use a mixture of cosmetic, fillet, and groove welds with preparations, machining features, and weld symbols at the assembly level. The main advantage is that the weldment can be documented as-assembled, as-welded, and so on. The BOM outlines the different part components. It does not preclude finite element analysis (FEA) since the weldment assembly can be derived into a part. You might find this approach difficult initially, but you can see large gains in productivity later while documenting the weldment. This is the recommended approach for large weldments that need mass properties, interference analysis, and complete documentation. (Examples are structural frames, piping, industrial gates, fences, and steel furniture.) You can use a combined approach of all four methods if that's what works best for your needs. However, when new enhancements are made to weldments, this approach lends itself to easily leveraging the new functionality. Figure 10.3 shows the document layout of this design methodology. (The figure doesn't show the various subassemblies that the weldment assembly might contain by breaking it into logical pieces.) Good planning helps in generating a well-built design that can be understood and easily maintained by designers. All in all, you should use this design methodology if you cannot decide on one of the other three methods.

Figure 10.3

Weldment assembly
design methodology

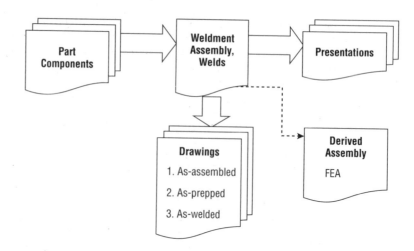

Multi-body Part Files

Since a completed weldment exists in a larger assembly as a single component, an interesting way of defining the weldment can be by using multi-body parts. To use this approach, you create separate bodies within the single part file by using the New Solid option in the Extrude, Revolve, and other sketched feature dialogs. This creates a virtual assembly made up of multiple features in a single file. Once the component is defined, it can be divided into an assembly using the Make Components tool, as described in Chapter 5, "Advanced Modeling Techniques." From that point on, you can treat your weldment assembly as though you created it from separate part files from the beginning, with one notable exception: You can then update the assembly and the weldment by editing the multi-body part you created initially. Figure 10.4 shows the layout of the multi-body method.

Figure 10.4

Using multi-body part files

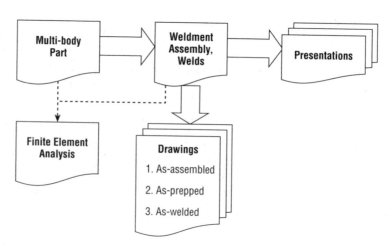

You can create a weldment assembly in two ways. For the first method, you create a new weldment assembly by selecting any of the weldment templates provided by the Autodesk® Inventor® software. To do this, just select the Get Started tab, click the New button, and then select an assembly template designated as a weldment template. Or you can convert an existing assembly document into a weldment assembly by selecting the Environments tab and clicking Convert To Weldment.

Once you convert an assembly into a weldment, it is not possible to convert it into a regular assembly. Also note that in a weldment document, you cannot create new positional representations or use flexible assembly functionality because a weldment is meant to be an assembly of parts fixed in place. Once you've created a weldment assembly, you can go to the next logical step of modeling preparations.

COMMUNICATION IS THE KEY TO DEALING WITH WELDMENTS

Depending on your needs, weldments can be as simple as a single part or as complex as assembly weldments with preparations, welds, and machining. Talk to the group that is going to be manufacturing your parts (whether the job is farmed out or in-house) and find out what level of detail the group requires when making the parts to your prints. Often, you will find that what is important to the designer is not as important to the welder (and vice versa). By speaking with these groups, you'll get a better understanding of what path you should take for your weldment models and drawings.

Modeling Preparations

Imagine that you've created the weldment assembly for a boxed container and want to add weld beads. Before adding the weld beads, the assembly needs weld preparations to create space for the weld bead to be placed. You can model a variety of preparation features to mill or remove material. Note that preparations are assembly features only, meaning that these features exist only in the assembly and not at the part level. Here are the most common preparation features:

- Extrude
- Revolve
- Hole
- Sweep
- Chamfer
- Fillet
- Move Face

Figure 10.5 shows the preparation environment and the relevant tools. To create the features in the previous list, you use the same set of steps that you used in part (Chapter 4, "Basic Modeling Techniques") or assembly modeling (Chapter 8, "Assembly Design Workflows"). The Move Face functionality is primarily intended for weld preparation in the assembly environment and is available in both the part and assembly environments.

Figure 10.5
Weldment features

Groove welds are classified by the different kinds of weld preparations. Figure 10.6 shows some commonly used weld preparations. In the left column, from top to bottom, you can see the Square Groove, Bevel Groove, and U-Groove types. In the right column, from top to bottom, you can see the Double Bevel Groove, V-Groove, and Double-U Groove types. Observe that these preparations might be referred to by slightly different names in the welding industry. Although most groove welds require nothing more than a simple chamfer, in most cases groove welds require some sort of material-removal preparation.

Figure 10.6
Types of weld preparations

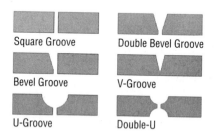

The alternative to weld preparation is to build the shape of the preparation using the sketch and then a swept volume (Extrude, Revolve, and Sweep) cut using that sketch to create the feature shape in the part file. However, it is recommended that you use the weld preparation feature, which helps show the manufacturing process. In addition, it aids in documenting the weldment in a drawing with just the components and preparations. Another advantage is that the designer, weld fabricator, or manufacturing instruction–generating program can easily find these features in one place—in other words, in the Preparations folder. This might be useful for generating the desired manufacturing information.

Certification
Objective

To create a preparation feature, follow these steps:

1. On the Get Started tab, click the Open button.

2. Open the file mi_10a_045.iam from the Chapter 10 directory of your Mastering Inventor 2016 folder.

If you have not already downloaded the Chapter 10 files from www.sybex.com/go/masteringinventor2016, please refer to the "What You Will Need" section of the book's introduction for the download and setup instructions.

3. You have three choices for this step: double-click the Preparations folder in the Model browser to activate the weld bead features, right-click the Preparations folder and select Edit, or click the Preparation button on the Process panel of the Weld tab.

4. Click the Chamfer button on the Preparation And Machining panel and select the bottom edge of the yellow face.

5. Set the chamfer size to **7 mm** and click OK.

6. Exit the preparation environment either by clicking the Return button or by right-clicking and choosing Finish Edit.

You can double-click the Preparations folder and edit the individual preparation features as needed. Think of the Preparations folder as a separate environment with its own set of tools. The End Of Features (EOF) node in the browser works differently than the End Of Part (EOP) node in the part modeling browser. In the part modeling browser, when the EOP node is moved around, it sticks at that location even after an update.

In the preparation environment, the EOF node can be moved to above or below any feature location in the Preparations folder, just as in part modeling. However, when you leave the preparation environment—either by double-clicking the top-level assembly node in the weldment assembly or by right-clicking and selecting Finish Edit in the graphics window—the EOF node is rolled all the way to the end in the Preparations folder. It might be thought of as a browser node that does not stick in its dragged browser location, unlike parts. The EOF node has similar behavior whether you are in the preparation, welds, or machining environment.

Once you've placed the weld preparations, you are ready to place welds. Keep in mind that you do not have to create preparations. Also, you can return to the preparation environment even after having placed welds.

Exploring Cosmetic Welds

To create or edit a weld feature, click the Welds button on the Process panel, or right-click the Welds folder in the Model browser and select Edit. You can also double-click the Welds folder and edit the individual features. Figure 10.7 shows the available features in the welds environment.

The Cosmetic Weld feature is available by clicking the Cosmetic button in the Weld panel. Figure 10.8 shows the Cosmetic Weld dialog box. When using the Cosmetic Weld feature, you simply select edges of the model. These edges can belong to part components or other weld beads.

Figure 10.7
Weld features panel

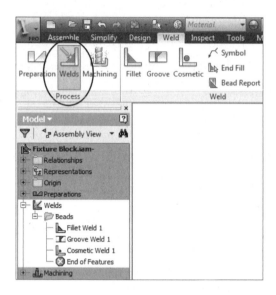

Figure 10.8
Cosmetic Weld dialog box

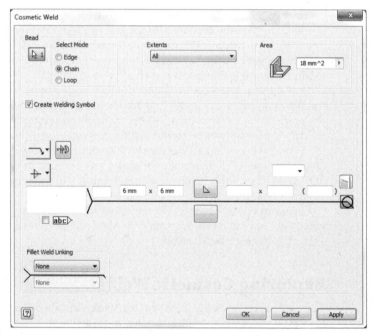

Cosmetic welds are recommended for use when you have the following conditions:

◆ A need for lightweight representation.

◆ No requirement for interference analysis.

◆ No need for the estimated total mass of the assembly with solid weld beads. However, you could optionally have the cosmetic weld participate in mass property calculations.

Note that the bead (which you define in the upper portion of the weld dialog boxes) and the weld symbol (defined in the lower portion of the weld dialog boxes) are decoupled; in other words, optionally you can create a weld symbol. This applies to all types of weld beads. In addition, you can use a single weld symbol to denote multiple welds involving cosmetic, fillet, and groove welds. Cosmetic welds can represent a wide variety of welds. You can create them using edges (the Edge option), tangent continuous sets of edges (the Chain option), or loops (the Loop option).

Selecting the option of applying a weld symbol will place a symbol on the screen without being prompted for its placement. You can move the symbol after the weld has been added. Close the file without saving.

Certification Objective

Creating a Simple Cosmetic Weld

In this exercise, you'll create a basic cosmetic weld and a weld symbol by selecting model's edges and entering the specification of the desired weld:

1. On the Get Started tab, click the Open button.

2. Browse for the file `mi_10a_001.iam` located in the `Chapter 10` directory of your `Mastering Inventor 2016` folder and click the Open button.

3. You have three options for this step:

    ◆ Double-click the `Welds` folder in the Model browser to activate the weld bead features.

    ◆ Right-click the `Welds` folder and select Edit.

    ◆ Click the Welds button in the Process panel of the Weld tab.

4. Once the weld environment is set active by using one of the three methods listed, click the Cosmetic button on the Weld panel.

5. In the Cosmetic Weld dialog box, select the Create Welding Symbol check box (if it is not already selected).

6. Select the Chain option and select the edges as shown in Figure 10.9. The Chain option is similar to the Automatic Edge Chain option in the Fillet dialog box in part modeling. It collects all the tangent continuous edges in a loop on a single face. Note that you may need to use the Select Other tool to toggle through the available loops.

Figure 10.9
Creating a cosmetic weld

7. Enter **6 mm** for both legs in the weld symbol, as shown in Figure 10.8.

8. In the Area input box, enter **18 mm** ^2 for the bead cross section based on the leg lengths.

The bead cross section can be calculated using the following equation:

$$\text{Bead cross section} = (1/2 \times \text{Leg Length 1} \times \text{Length 2})$$

9. Click the OK button to create the weld and close the dialog box.

The bead cross section area value is critical in determining the mass of cosmetic welds. Later, in the section "Understanding Bead Property Report and Mass Properties," you'll see how to use this for mass-properties calculations. For now, though, you can close this file without saving changes and continue on to explore more options for the cosmetic weld.

Using Split Faces to Place Cosmetic Welds

In certain cases when there is no edge to click as input, you can split the faces of the components in the part file (.ipt) at the location where it is welded and use the split edges as input to the cosmetic weld feature. On the left of Figure 10.10, for example, there are no explicit edges to click at the intersection of the planar face on the hollow tube and the cylindrical face on the cylinder. Therefore, you could edit the cylindrical part and create a work plane that is offset from the end of the cylinder and then use the Split tool to split the cylindrical face of the cylindrical part with the work plane so that you can use those split edges to create the cosmetic weld feature. The center of Figure 10.10 shows the split edge. Work points cannot be clicked as part of the cosmetic weld feature. The edges need to have finite length in order to be clickable for the cosmetic weld feature.

Figure 10.10
Cosmetic welds using split edges

Certification
Objective
Placing Cosmetic Welds with Extents

You can specify extents with parallel planes or planar faces. The extent trims the cosmetic weld bead between the From and To termination planes or planar faces.

To generate the From-To cosmetic weld in Figure 10.11, follow these steps:

1. On the Get Started tab, click the Open button.

2. Open the file mi_10a_002.iam from the Chapter 10 directory of your Mastering Inventor 2016 folder.

3. You have three options for this step:

   ◆ Double-click the `Welds` folder in the Model browser to activate the weld bead features.

   ◆ Right-click the `Welds` folder and select Edit.

   ◆ Click the Welds button in the Process panel of the Weld tab.

4. Click the Cosmetic weld tool on the Weld panel. Select the edge shown in Figure 10.11.

Figure 10.11
Cosmetic welds with extents

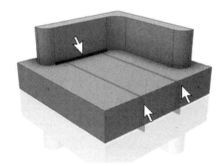

5. In the Extents drop-down menu in the Cosmetic Weld dialog box, select From-To.

6. Click the From button and select one of the assembly work planes.

7. Click the To button and select the other assembly work plane.

8. Click OK in the Cosmetic Weld dialog box to create the weld and see the result. Close the file without saving.

Creating Weld Beads

A weld bead feature is a parametric, solid representation of the real-world weld bead. It can be generated from input faces of a single component or from input faces of multiple components, including the faces of existing weld beads in the weldment assembly. You can also create a weld on a single part that is placed in a weldment assembly. Here are some examples:

Example 1 Place a single sheet-metal part in a weldment assembly and create fillet welds at flange corners to create a container.

Example 2 Create a fillet or groove weld between two plates (two parts or one part that has two extrusion features for the plates).

Example 3 Create a fillet or groove weld between two plates and another weld bead.

Weld beads automatically contribute to mass property calculations and can take part in interference analyses. All weld bead features create an independent body that does not take part in Boolean operations with the assembly components. Other machining features can cut into weld beads. There are two major weld features to create physical 3D welds.

Fillet Weld Feature   A fillet weld builds up corners by adding weld material between faces. Fillet welds are the most commonly used type of weld in industrial machinery. You should use this feature when there is no gap between the components. A specialized kind of fillet weld with a gap is supported.

Groove Weld Feature   A groove weld feature predominantly fills gaps between components. However, you can also use it when the components are touching each other. There are many opportunities to combine fillet and groove welds to generate the desired weld beads.

WELD CALCULATORS

The weldment environment also has several weld calculators (only if the design accelerator add-in is loaded). Weld calculators assist you in the design of weld joints. You can check typical welds with different types of loading. You can use these calculators to check static weld loading and to check butt and fillet weld joints for both static and fatigue loading.

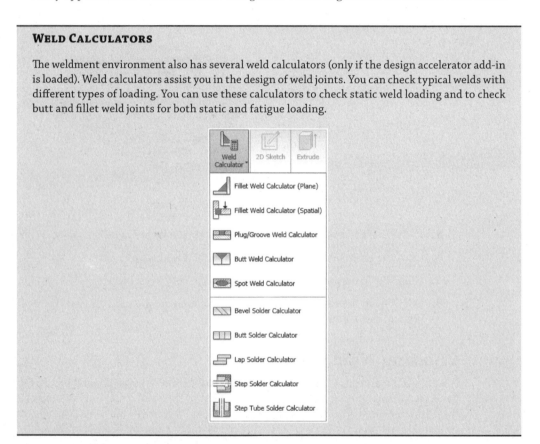

Creating Fillet Welds

The basic idea behind a fillet weld is that you are joining two sets of faces. You can control the weld bead definition parametrically by using the parameters shown in Figure 10.12. This is known as *leg-length measurement*. You can enter the two leg lengths used to generate the bead and also specify the throat measurement. Throat measurement is the distance from the root of the fillet weld to the center of its face. You just enter the throat length, and Inventor calculates the rest of the size of the weld bead. The offset value has relevance only when you declare the weld to be concave or convex. Figure 10.12 shows the two leg lengths and the two types of measurement.

Figure 10.12
Fillet weld definition

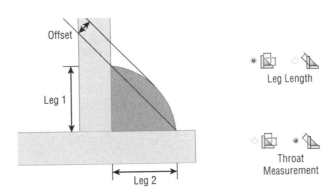

The top shape of a fillet weld can be flat, convex, or concave, as shown in Figure 10.13 (from left to right). For flat, the offset is 0.0. For concave or convex based on the offset, Inventor calculates the necessary bump or depression shape.

Figure 10.13
Flat, convex, and concave shapes for fillet welds

Certification Objective

Modeling a Fillet Weld

Fillet welds are likely the most common weld type you will use in your weldment designs. To create a simple fillet weld, follow these steps:

1. On the Get Started tab, click the Open button.

2. Open the file mi_10a_003.iam from the Chapter 10 directory of your Mastering Inventor 2016 folder.

3. You have three choices here: double-click the Welds folder in the Model browser to activate the weld bead features, right-click the Welds folder and select Edit, or click the Welds button in the Process panel of the Weld tab.

4. Click the Fillet weld tool on the Weld panel. You will see the dialog box shown in Figure 10.14.

5. Enter the leg length value for the Leg1 in the input box as **15 mm**. Leg2 is assumed to be the same as Leg1 if the input box is left blank.

6. Ensure that the first Select Faces button (the red arrow) is selected and then click the yellow face.

Figure 10.14
Fillet Weld dialog box with start and end offsets

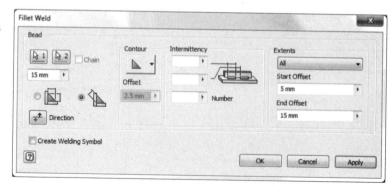

7. Click the second Select Faces button (or right-click and select Continue) and then click the red face. Note the lightweight weld bead preview, as shown in Figure 10.15.

Figure 10.15
Fillet weld preview and fillet weld

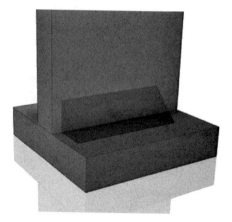

8. In the Extents area of the dialog, enter **5 mm** in the Start Offset box.

9. Click the Direction button on the left of the dialog box to change the start position of the weld bead.

10. Enter **15 mm** in the End Offset box and click OK.

11. Locate the Welds folder in the Model browser and expand it to find the Beads folder.

12. Expand the Beads folder, right-click the weld bead found within, and then click Edit Feature.

13. In the Extents area of the Fillet Weld dialog box, click the top drop-down list and change the extents solution from All to Start-Length.

14. Notice that Start Offset remains the same but End Offset is replaced with a length input. You can use this option to specify a known weld length when required.

15. Set the length to **50 mm** and click OK.

This exercise has illustrated a basic fillet weld and some of the extents options available. You can close this file without saving changes and continue reading about other options for placing fillet welds.

Fillet Welds and Gaps

You can place a fillet weld between two parts even if they do not contact, using the fillet weld to bridge the gap. If the goal is to fill the gap, you would likely use a groove weld. Figure 10.16 shows a hole gap through which a cylinder is passing. You can use a fillet weld to bridge the gap, but it will not fill the gap. The fillet weld will work even if the two components are separated by a gap at some places and touch at other places.

Figure 10.16
Shaft through plate

To create these fillet welds, you still click the two faces, as shown in Figure 10.16. Inventor infers the gap and generates the fillet weld bead. To fill the gap between the two mating faces of components, you should use groove welds.

Figure 10.17 shows another variant of two components that are separated by a gap. Here, the solution is dependent on the size of the weld and the amount of face available. On the left, a 10 mm weld comes up short on the corners. On the right, an 18 mm weld runs past the flat edges of the tube and therefore will not build as selected. The weld adjusts to fit as required. If the weld size is too small to bridge the gap at all or is too large for the selected face, the weld will not be built.

Figure 10.17
Shaft through hollow tube

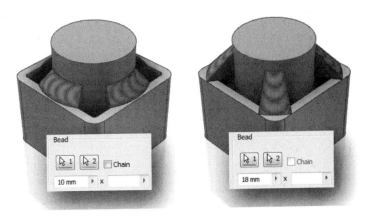

Figure 10.18 shows a simple gap being bridged with two fillet welds.

Figure 10.18
Fillet welds across a gap

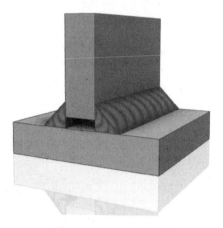

Don't Forget to Speak with Those Manufacturing the Parts

Inventor provides just about every possible option that you could want as a designer with regard to weld sizes, shapes, and contours. However, you should always speak with those who will be manufacturing the parts to determine whether what you have designed can be built efficiently. It would be unfortunate to spend a lot of time with specific contours, sizes, and finishes if the weld shop is just going to give you a standard fillet weld regardless of the details you call out. You'll need to decide whether it's time to find a new welder or whether you are putting too much information into the part. More than one designer has found this out the hard way when that $10 bracket suddenly ends up costing $100 because of the demanding weld callouts placed on the print.

Creating Intermittent Fillet Welds

Intermittent fillet welds essentially produce patterns of the weld bead along a set of edges. Figure 10.19 shows an example of an intermittent fillet weld using the Start-Length extents solution to adjust the orientation to avoid interference with the existing holes.

Figure 10.19
Intermittent ISO fillet weld

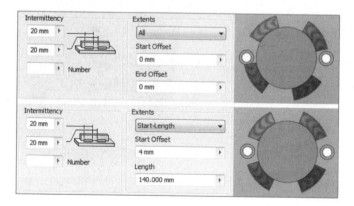

There are three ways that intermittent welds can be specified, depending on which standard you are using. To change the standard, select the Tools tab and click the Document Settings button. From there you will see the Default Standard setting on the Standard tab. Here is a list describing the differences, as shown in Figure 10.20:

Figure 10.20
Intermittent fillet weld parameters

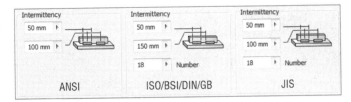

ANSI Standard   Specify bead length and the distance between bead centers.

ISO, BSI, DIN, and GB Standards   Specify the bead length, the spacing between beads, and the number of beads.

JIS Standard   Specify the bead length, the distance between bead centers, and the number of beads.

The Extents control allows you to select the beginning and ending planar faces or planes between which the weld bead will be created. The steps to produce a From-To fillet weld bead are similar to the steps outlined for extents and cosmetic welds earlier in this chapter. When you're welding a long piece of metal, often intermittent welds are cost effective and reduce warping in the part.

Creating Groove Welds

A groove weld is primarily used to fill gaps between two sets of faces. Once such gaps are filled, you might top the groove weld with a fillet weld. Figure 10.21 shows some examples.

Figure 10.21
Groove weld examples

Like a fillet weld, a groove weld needs two sets of facesets. The Full Face Weld option, when selected, tells Inventor to use the full face to generate the weld. When this option is not selected, only a portion of the face will be used to generate the weld. Inventor calculates the specific portion of the face by projecting the smaller faceset to the larger faceset (if the two facesets are the same size, Inventor picks one of them to project). Figure 10.22 shows the resulting weld beads with Full Face Weld off (left) and on (right).

Figure 10.22
Full Face Weld option

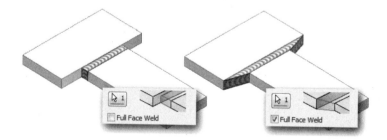

The Ignore Internal Loops option controls whether to ignore or consider the internal loop to generate the weld bead. When selected, it results in a "solid" weld bead (Figure 10.23, left); when it's not selected, the result is a "hollow" groove weld (Figure 10.23, right).

Figure 10.23
Ignore Internal Loops option

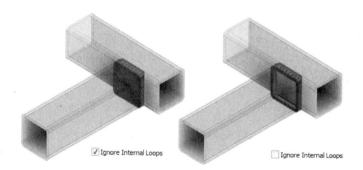

The fill direction is used to project one set of faces to another to generate the groove weld bead. In Figure 10.24, you can see the difference between the resulting weld bead shapes.

Figure 10.24
Fill direction

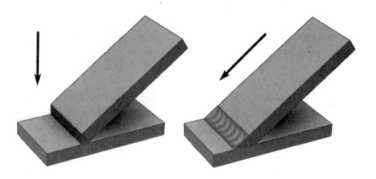

Be aware that the Fill Direction option is not available when you use the Full Face Weld option for both faceset 1 and faceset 2 or when using the Radial Fill option. When you are using the Fill Direction option, you might observe that Inventor can create welds that are not manufacturable, depending on the direction you choose.

You can select the following for the fill direction:

◆ Planar faces and work planes (specifies the direction normal to chosen face/plane)

◆ Cylindrical, conical, or toroidal faces (specifies the direction of the surface's axis)

◆ Work axes

◆ Linear part edges

One question that comes up frequently is, what direction should be selected for the fill? One guideline you can use is to imagine the average geometric center of faceset 1 and the average geometric center of faceset 2. The line connecting the two geometric centers will be the fill direction to generate the groove weld bead. You are not required to calculate the geometric centers of the facesets. It is advisable to try different fill directions to get the desired weld bead shape.

You can use the Radial Fill option to project the weld bead around a curve. When you're using the Radial Fill option, the Fill Direction option is not available. Figure 10.25 shows a radial-filled groove weld.

Figure 10.25
The Radial Fill option

Certification Objective

To create a simple groove weld, follow these steps:

1. On the Get Started tab, click the Open button.

2. Open the file mi_10a_004.iam from the Chapter 10 directory of your Mastering Inventor 2016 folder.

3. You have three options for this step: double-click the Welds folder in the Model browser to activate the weld bead features, right-click the Welds folder and select Edit, or click the Welds button in the Process panel of the Weld tab.

4. Click the Groove weld tool on the Weld panel.

5. Select the yellow face for faceset 1 and the red face for faceset 2. Note that you may need to rotate the view to see the red face.

6. Click the Fill Direction button and click the visible work axis or any edge or face that establishes the direction to be the same as the work axis.

7. Select the Full Face Weld option for faceset 1 to extend the weld to cover the entire yellow face. Note that selecting Full Face Weld for faceset 2 does not change the weld since the weld bead already covers the entire face.

8. Click OK; your result should resemble Figure 10.26. Close the file without saving.

As a general rule, if the preview comes up, it is almost certain that the bead will succeed.

Figure 10.26
Groove weld results

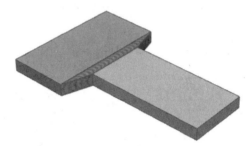

Performing Machining Operations

Once you've created the preparations and welds, you can create machine features. The features available for machining are similar to the features in the preparation environment. In terms of operations, they are performed after the generation of weld beads. One of the main advantages of providing the machining operations in a separate environment is that in drawings you can document them in the as-machined state. Holes and extrude cuts are typical post-weld machining features.

Figure 10.27 shows a welded assembly with machining operations performed on it.

Figure 10.27
Machining features on a weldment assembly

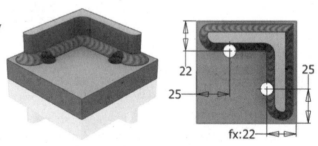

Certification
Objective

To create the machining features, follow these steps:

1. On the Get Started tab, click the Open button.

2. Open the file mi_10a_005.iam from the Chapter 10 directory of your Mastering Inventor 2016 folder.

3. Double-click the Machining folder in the Model browser to activate it for editing, right-click the Machining folder and select Edit, or click the Machining button in the Process panel of the Weld tab.

4. From the Weld tab, click the 2D Sketch button to create a new sketch.

5. Choose the yellow face to place the sketch and place two hole centers corresponding to the two holes shown in Figure 10.27.

6. Right-click and choose Finish 2D Sketch; then select the Hole feature from the Preparation And Machining panel.

7. Set the hole size to **10 mm** and the termination to Through All, and click OK.

8. Right-click and choose Finish Edit (or double-click the top-level assembly in the browser) to exit the machining environment.

Holes that are important to the location of welds should be placed into the parts that are being welded together. Because the machined view of the weldment is a subset of the welded view, you cannot refer to "machined" holes when detailing an as-welded model.

Machining features include, but are not limited to, the following:

◆ Extrude

◆ Revolve

◆ Hole

◆ Sweep

◆ Chamfer

◆ Fillet

◆ Move Face

Exploring Weld Properties and Combinations

The following sections cover the additional aspects of weldments: setting weld properties, replicating welds, combining fillet and groove weld beads to produce the desired weld bead shape, and using the split technique.

Weld Properties

To turn off the visibility of all weld beads in an open assembly, select the View tab and select Object Visibility ➢ Welds. You can also expand the Welds folder in the Model browser, right-click the Beads folder, and then deselect Visibility to turn off the weld beads of a particular assembly or subassembly. You can suppress individual weld bead features in the Model browser; the suppress feature is similar to part feature suppression.

Certification Objective

You can choose the weld material during the initial conversion of an assembly to a weldment or change it after the fact. Welded Aluminium-6061 is the default material in the Weld Bead Material drop-down list in the Convert To Weldment dialog box, as shown in Figure 10.28. To change it after the fact, you can right-click the Welds node in the browser and choose iProperties. Then select the Weld Bead tab of the iProperties dialog box to change appearance of the weld bead or select the Physical tab to change material.

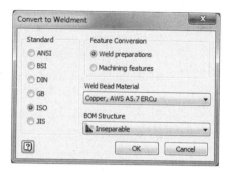

In existing weldments, you can change the weld color styles using the weld properties. In the Model browser, right-click the Welds node, select iProperties, select the Weld Bead tab, and choose the weld bead color style or the end fill color style. You can use the weld bead color style to assign different color styles to the weld bead. Similarly, the end caps (faces) that you selected in the weldment assembly can be assigned an end fill color style.

Replication

Welds (cosmetic, fillet, and groove beads) can be copied or mirrored in assemblies through the Copy Components and Mirror Components tools. Both sets of components that support the weld need to be copied or mirrored for the welds to be copied or mirrored. For example, if a cosmetic weld exists only on component Plate1, and if Plate1 is copied or mirrored, the cosmetic weld is also copied or mirrored. You cannot copy or mirror the weld without its components being copied or mirrored. Weld beads can be derived from the assembly into another part document using the Derived Component tool in parts.

Groove and Fillet Weld Combinations

Most welds can be generated using a combination of groove and fillet welds. Figure 10.29 shows an example of welding two hollow tubes with a groove weld. The horizontal tube is welded with a vertical tube. Faceset 1 comprises the two fillet faces on the horizontal member, and Faceset 2 consists of the single mating face on the bottom of the vertical member. The fill direction is established by selecting a vertical edge or a horizontal face.

Figure 10.29
Generating the groove weld bead

In Figure 10.30, a fillet weld is applied. Faceset 1 is composed of three faces, the top horizontal face and the two corresponding fillet faces, as indicated by the light arrows. Faceset 2 is composed of the three corresponding component faces on the vertical tube, as shown by the dark arrows in Figure 10.30. A second fillet weld would then be generated in the same way on the other side.

Figure 10.30
Generating the fillet weld bead

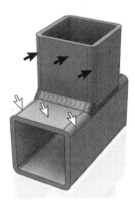

Split Technique

Since welds work on input faces (the two facesets that you select to do the weld), it is sometimes required and at other times desirable to split the input faces in order to have the weld bead only on a certain portion of the face or to have better control of the resulting weld. Essentially, you are helping Inventor use the partial face that is generated from the split.

In certain situations, using fillet welds that involve multiple possibilities might make it difficult to control the placement of welds. One instance of this is when controlling the offset of welds around a cylindrical face. Figure 10.31 shows the difference between using a cylinder with a split face and one without. If the cylindrical face is split, you can place the weld in two parts and control the start and end offsets so that holes are given proper clearance. If the face is not split, Inventor automatically breaks the weld where it encounters the holes, but you can adjust the offsets for the first hole only.

Figure 10.31
Using a split to create multiple fillet welds

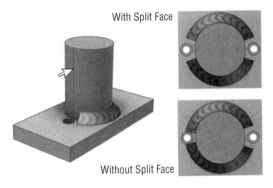

Certification
Objective

In the following steps, you will use the Split tool to control the start and stop positions of the weld bead:

1. On the Get Started tab, click the Open button.

2. Open the file mi_10a_006.iam from the Chapter 10 directory of your Mastering Inventor 2016 folder.

Take a look at the existing fillet weld around the blue cylinder. Notice that the offset on the one hole is not adequate. You will create a similar weld on the yellow cylinder but use the Split tool to ensure that you have full control of the offsets.

3. Locate the part called mi_10a_014 in the Model browser and double-click it to set it active for edits (or right-click and choose Edit).

4. Click the Split button on the Modify panel of the 3D Model tab.

5. Select WorkPlane1 from the Model browser for the Split tool.

6. Select the cylindrical face for the Faces selection.

7. Click OK. Note that the cylindrical face is now split into two halves. Figure 10.32 shows the Split selections.

Figure 10.32
Creating a split face in the part

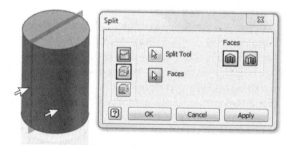

8. Return to the weldment assembly by right-clicking in the graphics screen and choosing Finish Edit.

9. You have three options for this step: double-click the Welds folder in the Model browser to activate the weld bead features, right-click the Welds folder and select Edit, or click the Welds button in the Process panel of the Weld tab.

10. Click the Fillet Weld button to bring up the input dialog.

11. Click one of the cylindrical halves for faceset 1.

12. Click the top (red) face of the mating plate for faceset 2.

13. Enter **10 mm** for the Leg 1size.

14. Enter **4 mm** in the Start Offset and Stop Offset boxes, as shown in Figure 10.33.

Figure 10.33
Creating a fillet weld with
start and end offsets

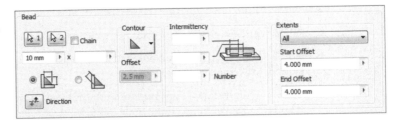

15. Click Apply, repeat steps 11 through 14 to create the other half of the weld, and click OK.

16. Right-click and choose Finish Edit (or double-click the top-level assembly in the browser) to exit the weld environment.

17. Compare the welds you created to the existing weld.

If you do not want to see the split edges in the weldment drawing, you can turn those edges off individually by right-clicking them in the drawing view and deselecting Visibility, as shown in Figure 10.34.

Figure 10.34
Turning off split edges in a drawing

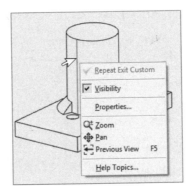

Using the Weld Symbol

You can create a weld symbol in assemblies by clicking the Welds folder and using the Weld Symbol tool. In drawings, you can find this tool on the Annotate tab. You have to decide to create them in the right place (assemblies or assemblies and drawings) based on your communication with the welding department and other departments that are involved in producing the weldment. The weld symbol, which is optional in the assembly environment, has certain key characteristics.

♦ It cannot be created without a weld bead consuming it.

♦ The primary bead is the weld bead to which the welding symbol is attached.

♦ You're allowed to activate the weld symbol grips and reattach the weld symbol to any other visible bead edge from that symbol's group.

♦ Multiple weld beads (including cosmetic weld beads) can be grouped under a single weld symbol.

- The weld symbols are listed in a separate folder below the Weld Beads folder.

- A bead can be consumed by only one welding symbol object at any given time.

- A linked bead that is moved out of its welding symbol group causes the parent welding symbol to become unassociated.

- Cross-highlighting is supported for both the bead objects and the welding symbol object. If you select a welding symbol node in the Model browser, the welding symbol and all the beads consumed by that welding symbol will be cross-highlighted in the graphics window. Alternatively, if you select a bead node from either the welding symbols portion of the browser or the Beads folder portion of the browser, the bead will be cross-highlighted in the graphics window.

- A new welding symbol can be created for an already created weld feature.

- Welding symbols have visibility control.

- If a weld symbol references a weld feature, then it is consumed. Otherwise, the bead is unconsumed by any weld symbols. Therefore, three browser filtering options are available from the Beads folder context menu: Show All, Show Consumed Only, and Show Unconsumed Only.

Figure 10.35 shows a single weld symbol for the multiple weld beads.

Figure 10.35

Single weld symbol for multiple welds

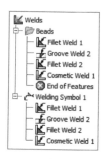

To add multiple weld beads to the same existing symbol, follow these steps:

1. Right-click the desired weld symbol.

2. Choose Edit Welding Symbol and activate the Bead button.

3. Add weld beads by selecting them in either the model window or the Model browser.

Only unconsumed weld beads should appear highlighted in the model window. Right-clicking the browser or model window lets you select weld beads and quickly see which weld beads have been unconsumed. To disassociate a weld bead from its corresponding symbol, right-click the bead in the Model browser and choose the Unconsumed Bead tool from the context menu.

Understanding Bead Property Report and Mass Properties

To estimate accurate weld rod usage, fabrication time, and bead weights, the weld property reporting tool is available in assemblies. This can be used to help estimate costs. This tool allows you to query the mass, volume, length, type, and name of individual beads in the assembly. Through an option (available after you select Bead Report from the Weld panel of the Weld tab), you can retrieve this data for the current assembly and all of its child weldment assemblies. This information will be exported to a standard Microsoft Excel spreadsheet, as shown in Figure 10.36. In the weldment workflow, you can generate a weld bead report for the core packaging unit that contains the three subassemblies.

Figure 10.36
Weld bead property reporting in assemblies

Document	ID	Type	Length	UoM	Mass	UoM	Area	UoM	Volume	UoM
c:\bead_report1.xls										
	Fillet Weld 3	Fillet	59	mm	0.001	kg	1.32E+03	mm^2	390.921	mm^3
	Groove Weld 2	Groove	N/A		0.008	kg	2.30E+03	mm^2	2.79E+03	mm^3
	Groove Weld 3	Groove	N/A		0.008	kg	2.30E+03	mm^2	2.79E+03	mm^3
	Groove Weld 4	Groove	N/A		1.597	kg	4.76E+04	mm^2	5.89E+05	mm^3
	Groove Weld 5	Groove	N/A		0.029	kg	6.07E+03	mm^2	1.07E+04	mm^3
	Fillet Weld 4	Fillet	150	mm	0.02	kg	794.955	mm^2	7.50E+03	mm^3

To calculate the total length of weld beads, you can sum up the total length using the Excel Sum functions. Length and area values are not reported for groove welds. The default "save to" location is the parent assembly's directory, but you can change this location. Weld properties are, at best, estimates. Many factors can change the weight of a weld bead. If the weight of a part is critical, consider machining the part to meet the criteria after welding.

The cross section entered in the Cosmetic Weld dialog box is multiplied by the length of the cosmetic weld bead and is optionally considered in the mass properties to calculate volume. When the Include Cosmetic Welds option is checked in the Physical tab of the iProperties dialog box, this volume is included in the calculations. The mass is determined by the selected weld material. This option is useful where you need only lightweight representation but at the same time need the welds to participate in mass properties.

Creating Drawing Documentation

The Welding Symbol dialog box, being the same in assemblies and drawings, is specific to the engineering standard you're using. Figure 10.37 shows an example of the Welding Symbol (ISO) dialog box in drawings, and when you hover your mouse pointer over each input control, a tool tip will show its title. Table 10.1 describes what the various controls do.

Figure 10.37
Welding Symbol dialog box in an ISO drawing; see the definitions of the controls in Table 10.1.

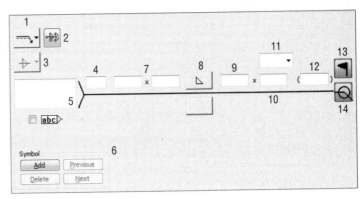

TABLE 10.1: Welding Symbol dialog box controls

Control*	Definition
1	Select this option to have the identification line above or below the symbol or to omit it.
2	Toggle this to switch the values and options from above the reference line to below the reference line, and vice versa.
3	Select this option for fillet weld symbols when they are set on both sides of the reference line. This option includes the following settings: No Stagger Weld Stagger – Move (ANSI) Weld Stagger – Move (ISO) Weld Stagger – Mirror
4	Enter a prefix for the symbol, such as depth of bevel, size, and strength, depending on the weld.
5	Select this option to specify text to be associated to the welding symbol, such as specification, process, or reference text. The Enclose Text option will enclose the note in a box at the tail of the symbol.
6	Use these controls to specify multiple welding symbols attached to a single leader: Add: Adds a symbol to the current symbol Delete: Removes the current symbol Previous: Cycles to the last symbol Next: Cycles to the next symbol
7	Enter the leg lengths for fillet weld. Other weld types may specify size, depth diameter, and so on, in this area, depending on the type of weld.
8	The Symbol drop-down menu lets you select different types of welds, such as V-Groove Weld, Flare-Bevel Weld, Seam Weld, Spot Weld, and so on. If you're using a drafting standard based on ANSI, a secondary fillet-type button can be used.
9	Specifies the number of welds, if applicable to the standard.
10	Specifies the length of the weld.
11	Specifies the contour finish of the weld. Choose from Flush or Flat finish, Convex finish, or Concave finish, or if using the DIN standard, you can choose Toes Blended Smooth.
12	Specifies the space between welds.
13	Use this option to add the field weld flag to the welding symbol.
14	The All Around Symbol toggle allows you to add an all-around symbol to the welding symbol. Note that the GB standard includes a third symbol; all other standards will present a dual-state toggle.

* Referenced by number in Figure 10.37.

BE EXPLICIT WITH SYMBOLS

Although you can refer to any textbook on welding for the correct use of the symbols in Table 10.1, keep in mind that many shops have their own "shorthand" versions of weld symbols. It is imperative that you communicate with the welders to make sure you agree on the symbols. Many weld shops do not know the "standard" yet still produce excellent parts.

A perfect example is the "all-around" symbol. Some shops take this to mean only opposite sides of the indicated line, whereas others interpret this symbol to mean you want all contiguous surfaces welded. When in doubt, you should be explicit with your symbols.

Weldment Design Stages

Now that you've explored the tools available in the weldment environment, you'll explore how to document the four major stages of weldment design in the drawing. You can create a weldment drawing in the following stages:

Assembly   As-assembled with no assembly features

Preparation   As-prepped

Welds   As-welded

Machining   As-machined

Figure 10.38 shows a weldment in the four stages during its creation.

Figure 10.38
Four stages of the weldment assembly

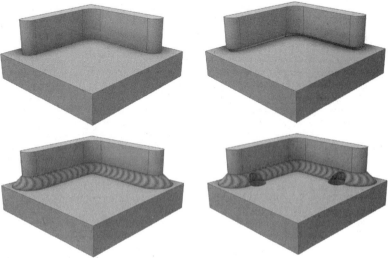

Figure 10.39 shows drawing views of the same weldment detailed at the various stages.

Figure 10.39
Four stages of the weldment
assembly as drawing views

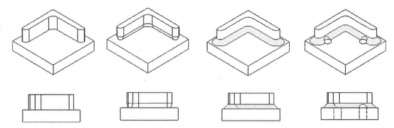

To create a model state view as shown in Figure 10.39, follow these steps:

1. Create a new drawing from an IDW or DWG template of your choosing.

2. Right-click and select Base View, browse for the file mi_10a_007.iam located in the Chapter 10 directory of your Mastering Inventor 2016 folder, and click the Open button.

3. In the base view preview on your drawing sheet, use the ViewCube to set Orientation to the Home view.

4. Click the Model State tab and select Assembly, Machining, Welds, and Preparation while watching your view preview. Notice that the view changes for each weldment stage as you select it.

5. Select Preparation and click the drop-down list to explore the options. Note that you can detail each part file individually, showing its preparations clearly without having to perform any extra steps to hide other parts in the assembly.

6. Once you've explored the different model states, set the Weldment option to Machining.

7. Check the options for Weld Annotations and Model Welding Symbols, and click OK to create the view.

8. Check to see that your view resembles Figure 10.40.

Figure 10.40
A weldment view created with weld annotations
and welding symbols turned on

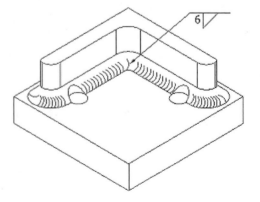

MORE ON WELDMENT DRAWINGS

You can find more about working with weldment drawings in the section "Working with Weldment Views" in Chapter 12, "Documentation."

You can retrieve the associative weld symbols from the model by right-clicking the drawing view and selecting Get Model Annotations ➤ Get Welding Symbols. You can retrieve associative weld end fills in the model by right-clicking the view and selecting Get Model Annotations ➤ Get Weld Annotations. You can also add nonassociative weld annotations to your drawing. You can create cosmetic weld symbols or weld beads using the Annotate tab by clicking the Welding or Caterpillar tool on the Symbols panel. Figure 10.41 shows the annotation retrieval tools in drawings.

Figure 10.41
Retrieving weld symbols

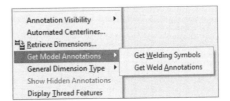

End Fill

In the Symbols panel, you will see the End Fill tool, which is used to represent seam weld end fills and the gap/groove process shape (concave and convex). Clicking the End Fill tool brings up the End Fill dialog box, shown in Figure 10.42. Note that you can create any weld process shape that is desired in drawings without generating the specified weld in the model.

Figure 10.42
The End Fill dialog box

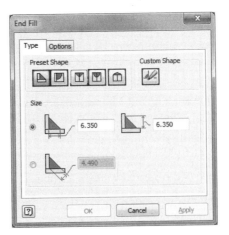

To create a seam weld process shape, follow these steps:

1. Click the End Fill button on the Symbols panel of the Annotate tab (you might need to use the flyout menu to find it).

2. Select the preset shape—for example, Seam Weld.

3. Select two points that represent the shape's arc chord length to create an arc. Move the cursor above or below the chord line to have the arc above or below. Click once more to set the direction.

4. Select the Options tab and select Check Solid Fill.

5. Select a color, such as orange. Select OK to complete the command.

In the End Fill dialog box, the fillet process shape has Leg1 and Leg2 as parameters. J-Type, V-Type, and U-Type Preset Shape have controls for the width and depth.

Drawing Weld Symbols

If your assembly has weld beads modeled and weld symbols created in the model, using the Get Welding Symbols option shown in Figure 10.41 is the best way to add weld symbols to the drawing.

If your assembly has weld beads modeled but does not have weld symbols created in the model, you can use the Welding symbol tool and then select a weld bead to retrieve the bead information automatically, based on the information found in the weldment model. However, you should be aware that the symbol won't update if the weld bead is updated in the model.

Many times you may need to just create the weld symbol in the drawing without having to create any weld beads in the assembly. Although this may suffice for your needs much of the time, remember that you cannot perform any interference analysis or mass-properties calculations the way you can with modeled welds.

To create a welding symbol in the drawing, follow these steps:

1. Select the Welding symbol button on the Symbols panel of the Annotate tab (you might need to use the flyout menu to find it).

2. This activates the selection. The command message string displays the text "Click On A Location."

3. Select a weld bead (if present) or any entity or location in the graphics area to define the location of the welding symbol.

When placing a symbol in the drawing, you can create a complex leader by selecting more than one point as you are placing the symbol. If you would like to add more later, you can do so by right-clicking the existing leader and selecting Add Vertex/Leader in the context menu.

4. Right-click within the graphics area and select Continue from the context menu. The Welding Symbol dialog box appears.

5. Specify the desired welding symbol.

6. The welding symbol preview dynamically updates.

7. Click OK, and the specified welding symbol appears at the specified location.

Caterpillar

You can create and use caterpillars (2D weld representations) in drawings when you want to use a lightweight representation for solid weld beads. As long as the welder is comfortable with this representation, you can use caterpillars. Figure 10.43 shows the dialog box for the Weld Caterpillars tool in drawings. You can create weld caterpillars using the boundary (extent) edges of the welds. This drawing annotation is not associated with weldments in the assembly model. In other words, you can create the caterpillar on any edge without the presence of any corresponding weld bead in the assembly. This is useful when you want to quickly document weld beads in drawings. The caterpillar could be used in addition to the weld symbol to make the documentation better.

Figure 10.43
Weld Caterpillars dialog box

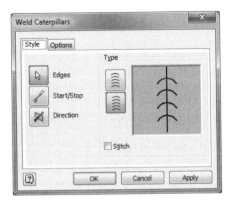

Certification
Objective

To create a caterpillar, follow these steps:

1. Select the Caterpillar tool from the Symbols panel on the Annotate tab.

2. Click Edges and select one of the long edges (the lateral edge) of the groove weld.

3. Click Options and enter the Width parameter. Adjust other parameters such as Angle, Arc %, and Spacing.

4. Click the direction to change the shape to concave or convex.

5. The Start/Stop options in the dialog box, which are specified by points, are useful to terminate the caterpillar between the From and To locations. The caterpillar preview shows the effect of changing options.

Figure 10.44 shows the resulting caterpillar for a groove weld.

Caterpillars can be useful when you want to represent a weldment using a single-part file and create a drawing from it. You can then indicate the position and detail of the welds along the edge. Use the Split tool, which will allow you to create edges where none may exist.

Figure 10.44
Weld caterpillar

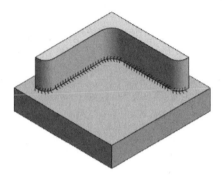

Generating a Bill of Materials and Parts List

Once a weldment design is done, you typically need to generate a bill of materials (BOM) and a parts list. Also, you'll want to customize the BOM to represent a weldment.

You can automatically generate and maintain a consistent bill of materials across welded assemblies, drawings, and presentations. Components that are deemed "inseparable" are assemblies that cannot be taken apart without doing damage to one or more of their components, typically weldments. Manufacturing processes treat inseparable assemblies like purchased components, and they are represented as a single line item.

When documented in its own context, an inseparable assembly is treated as a standard one in that all of the parts are listed. Figure 10.45 shows the BOM for an assembly that consists of a weldment assembly and single-piece part. On the left, the weldment is shown in a structured BOM view, listing the weldment and the parts within. On the right, the BOM is shown as Parts Only; note that the weldments are listed as a single component.

Figure 10.45

Inseparable components as handled by the BOM

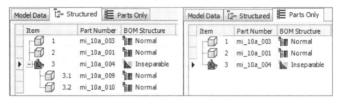

To modify the BOM structure, follow these steps:

1. Open the weldment assembly.

2. Click the Bill Of Materials button on the Manage panel of the Manage tab.

3. While in the Model Data tab, double-click in the BOM Structure cell, select the drop-down for each component, and select Inseparable.

4. Click Done in the Bill Of Materials dialog box.

To change the BOM structure of several components at once, you can click and drag the small black square in the bottom-right corner of the cell or right-click the cell. Choose Copy, Shift, or Ctrl, clicking multiple components, and then right-click and choose Paste.

The Bottom Line

Select and use the right weldment design methodology. You've been shown three weldment design methodologies. Before you start on any weldment design, it is imperative to keep the documentation, interference analysis, mass properties, and other design criteria in perspective and select the right design methodology.

Master It How do you choose the right weldment strategy for you?

Create and edit weld preparations and machining features. Following the weldment methodology, you need to plan on creating the gaps needed (weld preparations) to deposit the weld beads. You need to create post-weldment machining features that go through the weld beads.

Master It Weld preparations and machining features are similar to part modeling features. Based on the weld-bead shape needed, you should plan on creating the preparations in advance. Once the welds are done, you must create the features for the machining processes. Where can you find preparation and machining features, and when do you use them?

Create and edit different kinds of weld beads, such as cosmetic, fillet, and groove.   Weldment design involves the optimal mix of cosmetic and solid weld beads based on the requirements of your design goals and model verification needs.

Master It   You should create the weld annotations only in drawings, without any need to create them in the model. You have weld subassemblies that need only lightweight representation in both the model and drawings. In situations involving accurate interference and mass properties, you require accurate weld beads. The question is, what type of weld beads should you use?

Document weldment stages in drawings.   Welds need to be documented in assemblies or drawings. It is important to show the different stages of weldment design in drawings to get a good idea of how to manufacture the weldment. You can use the drawing tools effectively to annotate the welds in drawings. This will help the welder understand the design intent better.

Master It   Several tools are used for weld documentation. You can annotate the welds in assemblies. If you prefer to document the welds in drawings, you could document the four stages of weldment design: the as-assembled, as-prepped, as-welded, and as-machined stages in drawings. Name two other drawing tools that customize weld documentation.

Generate and maintain a consistent BOM across welded assemblies, drawings, and presentations.   You have been shown how to generate and maintain a consistent bill of materials for weldment assemblies and a parts list in drawings. Mark parts or assemblies as inseparable to designate them as weldments.

Master It   How do you generate the BOM and parts list for your weldment?

Chapter 11

Presentations and Exploded Views

Standard 2D drawings don't always communicate your 3D design information as clearly as you intend. A different way to present your design is an *exploded* view. You can see an example of this in Figure 11.1.

An exploded view describes an assembly by moving components out of their assembled position. Exploded views are not available in the Autodesk® Inventor LT™ program.

Exploded views can use *trails* to show how the components have been moved from their assembled position to their exploded position. These moves are called *tweaks*.

Exploded views are particularly helpful to document the installation sequence of an assembly. In this chapter, you'll learn to

◆ Create an exploded assembly presentation

◆ Create linear tweaks

◆ Create rotational tweaks

◆ Create an exploded view on a drawing from a presentation file

◆ Group, reorder, and animate tweaks

◆ Publish presentation files to DWF

FIGURE 11.1
An exploded view in a 2D drawing

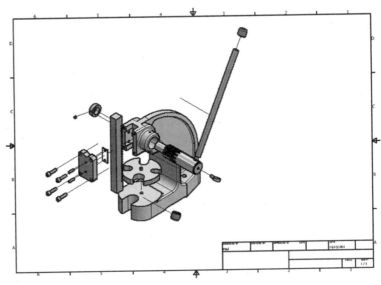

Getting Started

If you have not already downloaded the Chapter 11 files from www.sybex.com/go/masteringinventor2016, please refer to the "What You Will Need" section of the introduction for the download and setup instructions.

Before you start, preview the final goal for this chapter by opening Windows Explorer and navigating to the Chapter 11 directory of your Mastering Inventor 2016 folder. Use Internet Explorer to open mi_11_001.dwfx by right-clicking the file and choosing Open With ➤ Internet Explorer, as shown in Figure 11.2.

FIGURE 11.2

A presentation file opened with Internet Explorer

CHOOSING THE DEFAULT PROGRAM FOR DWFX

If Internet Explorer is not available in the Open With option, click Choose Default Program and then expand Other Programs to find Internet Explorer. You can click Allow Blocked Content In Internet Explorer if you receive a message window about blocked scripts and ActiveX controls.

Working in the Presentation Environment

In Inventor, a presentation is used to create an exploded view of your 3D model, which can be referenced in your drawings or recorded as an animation, as shown in Figure 11.3. Exploded views are created in a *presentation* file, which has the .ipn file extension.

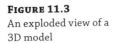

FIGURE 11.3
An exploded view of a
3D model

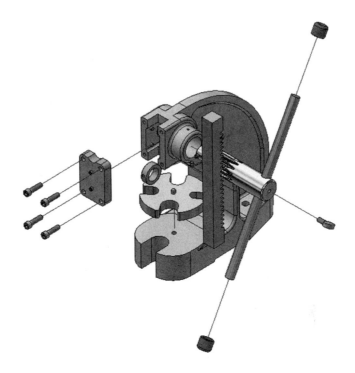

Joints and constraints contained in your assembly files are ignored in the presentation file environment; however, the assembly structure is preserved. Edits to the assembly structure and edits to individual parts will update in the presentation file.

An assembly file can be exploded automatically, or components can be moved individually and in groups. These moves are called *tweaks*. Tweaks can be ordered into tasks and sequences to demonstrate the proper order of assembly to the end user of your documentation.

You can create multiple explosions within an assembly file. Each explosion can be linked to an assembly view. For example, you could use this ability to show a subassembly being assembled, before showing how it gets assembled into the top-level assembly.

◆ Multiple *exploded views* can be created in a presentation file.

◆ Each exploded view contains multiple *tasks*.

◆ Each task can contain multiple *sequences*.

◆ Each sequence can contain multiple *tweaks*.

◆ Each tweak can reference multiple components (parts and assemblies).

You could use your exploded presentation to create a 2D exploded view in a drawing file (DWG or IDW).

You could also use your exploded presentation to record an animation of the assembly, moving from the assembled view to the exploded view (and back!). You can record this animation as an MWV or AVI file.

You could publish your presentation to Autodesk Design Review format (`.DWF` or `.DWFx`) with the animations, task, and sequences enact. The DWF can combine the presentation with the 2D drawings and BOM to create a complete package of information—a complete *technical product specification*.

Creating an Automatically Exploded Presentation

Let's jump right in by creating an automatically exploded presentation and using it to create a drawing view. Start from the Inventor home page, as shown in Figure 11.4.

FIGURE 11.4
The Inventor My Home Page ➤ New Panel

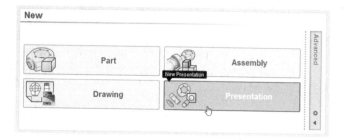

CREATING AN AUTOMATICALLY EXPLODED PRESENTATION

To create an automatically exploded presentation, follow these steps:

1. Create a new presentation from your standard IPN template. From the My Home page, select New Panel ➤ Choose Presentation.

2. Pick an assembly to create the presentation view from; on the Presentation tab, click the Create View button (as shown in Figure 11.5).

FIGURE 11.5
The Autodesk Inventor 2016 Presentation tab

3. Click the Open An Existing File button (it looks like a folder with a magnifying glass).

4. From the Chapter 11 directory of your Mastering Inventor 2016 folder, select the file mi_11_001.iam and click the Open button.

5. Check the Explosion Method ➤ Auto Explode box. Choose All Trails. Choose Default Trails ➤ All Components. Set Distance to **100**. See Figure 11.6 for reference.

FIGURE 11.6
The Select Assembly dialog box, set up to automatically explode

6. Click the OK button to create the exploded view in the new presentation file.

7. Save the file in the Chapter 11 folder, naming it `mi_11_100.ipn`.

Inventor will create your exploded view. The lines between parts are *tweak trails,* which show you how the parts have moved from their original position to their new position.

ANIMATING AN EXPLODED PRESENTATION

Now that you've told Inventor where your parts are at the start of your explosion and you've told Inventor where you want the parts to end up, you can ask Inventor to show you an animation of the parts moving from one position to the other.

1. Click the Presentation tab and then click the Animate button.

2. Choose Parameters ➤ Interval and change the value to **10**. (This speeds up the animation.)

3. Click the Apply button.

4. Click the Play Forward button.

5. Click the Cancel button to close the dialog.

Inventor will animate each part moving along its tweak trail from its exploded position to its assembled position.

You can see how this should look by browsing to the Chapter 11 directory of your Mastering Inventor 2016 folder and opening mi_11_001.avi.

You'll take a longer look at animations later in the "Preparing the Exploded Presentation to Be Used in an Animation" section. Right now, you'll learn how to use your exploded model in a drawing.

CREATING AN EXPLODED DRAWING VIEW

Now it's time to find out how to capture your presentation's exploded view on a 2D drawing.

1. In the browser, select the Explosion1 node.

2. Right-click and choose Create Drawing View.

3. Choose your drawing template file, and click OK.

4. A drawing file will open, and Inventor will open the Drawing view dialog with your exploded view active.

5. Click OK to place your view.

Inventor will create a drawing view of your exploded assembly that you can use to communicate how your design should be assembled.

You can use exploded views on drawings with a parts list and balloon callouts to create a really powerful, clear, and complete set of design information.

YOU'VE DONE IT!

This was a quick introduction to presentations and exploded views. You might want to add a few tweaks to your presentation or edit the existing tweaks slightly. You'll learn how to do this in the next section.

You can close your presentation and drawing files now. You don't need to save them; you can use the files provided for the next exercise.

EXPLOSIONS AND ASSEMBLY VIEWS

You can associate an explosion with a view that is saved in your assembly (see Figure 11.7). This can be helpful if you want to create an explosion of a subassembly but want the part numbers to read correctly from the main assembly's BOM.

FIGURE 11.7
The File Open Options
dialog box (Select
Assembly ➤ Options)

1. To create an explosion that is associated with an assembly view, click the Create View button on the Presentation tab.

2. In the Select Assembly dialog, click Open An Existing File and choose your assembly.

3. Next, click the Options button in the File drop-down.

4. Check the Associative box to make sure that edits saved in the assembly file propagate through to the presentation.

Notice that you can choose from assembly views, positional representations, and level of detail representations (or a combination of all three!).

5. Click OK to return to the Select Assembly dialog and continue creating your explosion.

Note that you can change the view representation of an existing view by right-clicking the browser node and choosing Representations.

Creating Tweaks Individually

The Auto Explode feature is great for small, logically constrained subassemblies. In the real world, you will want more control. In this section, you will learn how to add individual tweaks to your sequence.

Open `mi_11_002.ipn` from the `Chapter 11` directory of your `Mastering Inventor 2016` folder.

THE TWEAK MINI-TOOLBAR

The Tweak mini-toolbar contains all the tools you will need to "tweak" (move and rotate) your components to create your exploded view, as shown in Figure 11.8.

FIGURE 11.8
The Tweak mini-toolbar

TYPE OF TWEAK

First choose what kind of tweak you want to create. Use the Move button for translation tweaks and the Rotate button for rotational tweaks. The Continuous Move button retains the selection set at the end of each tweak, allowing you to build a sequence of tweaks.

DIRECTION OF TWEAK

Next, place the triad on the feature you want to use to set the orientation of the tweak. Make sure you have the Locate button highlighted.

Local will orientate the triad to the part you are mousing over.

World will maintain the triad to your IPN file's coordinate system.

continues

continued

> **Tip:** Hold down the **Shift** key while selecting the triad location to prevent the component from being added to the selection set.
>
> **Tip:** Hold down the **Ctrl** key while moving over a feature to limit the point selection for the move triad to that individual face.
>
> ### COMPONENTS TO TWEAK
>
> Now choose the components to include in your tweak. You can set the filter to Part or Component and select components in the graphics window or browser.
>
> Hold down the **Ctrl** key and select components to add or remove them from your selection set.
>
> ### TWEAK TRAILS
>
> Select the drop-down arrow next to Default Trails to choose whether to create no trails, a single trail, trails per part, or trails per component.
>
> You can use the Add button to manually add a trail from a feature of your choice on the component or use Delete to remove trail segments.
>
> ### COMMIT THE TWEAK
>
> The Undo (blue arrow) button will undo the last tweak you created and keep the command running for you to create another tweak.
>
> The + (Apply) button will save your current tweak and wait for you to create another tweak.
>
> The red X (Cancel) button will cancel your current tweak and quit the command.
>
> The OK button will save your current tweak and quit the Tweak command.

Creating a Liner Tweak

In this example you'll add a linear tweak to the hex socket bolt cap screws that attach the face plate to the arbor frame.

To create a linear tweak, you will first tell Inventor in which direction you want to move the components. Then you will tell Inventor which components you want to move. Finally, you will tell Inventor how far you want to move the components.

Begin by zooming in on the yellow face of the face plate until you can see the cap screws clearly.

1. Click the Tweak Components button on the Presentation tab.

2. First you will place the direction triad. Hover your cursor over the yellow front face of the face plate. Hold down the **Shift** key to prevent this component from being added to the selection set. Select the center node on the yellow face as the placement for the triad (see Figure 11.9 for an example).

3. In the browser, expand MI_11_001.1 and select CAP SCREWS:1,2,3 and 4 to add them to your tweak.

4. Note that the orange arrow is showing you which direction the parts will move. Click and drag the orange arrow to see the components move "by eye." Now type **100mm** in the pop-up box and press the **Enter** key on your keyboard to move the components precisely.

5. Although the parts have moved, the tweak hasn't been created yet.

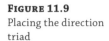

FIGURE 11.9
Placing the direction triad

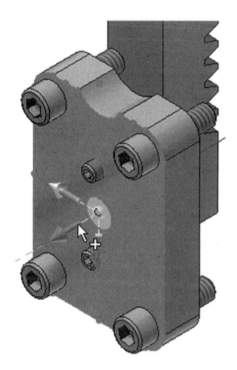

You could change the distance you've moved the parts by continuing to type values or by dragging the orange arrow. In this case, click the green check mark on the Tweak mini-toolbar to commit this tweak.

The four cap screws will be moved 100 mm from the base plate, and a tweak trail will be created to show the move graphically. In the browser, a tweak has been added under each bolt.

Note that you can add tweaks to parts and assemblies. You don't have to follow the assembly structure with your tweaks. If you tweak an assembly, all parts within the assembly will move. Alternatively, you can move multiple parts with one tweak.

Keep the file open for the next exercise, or open mi_11_003.ipn from the Chapter 11 directory of your Mastering Inventor 2016 folder.

Creating a Rotational Tweak

In this section, you will add a rotation tweak to simulate the bolts being tightened as the face plate is attached to the arbor frame.

Expand the browser tree before you start so that you can see the four cap screws that are contained in subassembly mi_11_001.1.

1. Click the Tweak Components button on the Presentation tab.

2. In the mini-toolbar, click the drop-down arrow next to the Component button and change the selection to Part.

3. Click the Rotate button to change the tweak type.

4. Click the Locate button and hover over the circular end of CAP SCREW: 3 (at the top right of the face plate) until you pick up the center of the circular face as a reference, as shown in Figure 11.10. (You can hold down the **Ctrl** key to limit the selection to the features on that one face.)

FIGURE 11.10
Placing the rotation triad

5. You can use the orange ball to drag the part to a new position, but instead type **-1080deg** (rotate counterclockwise three times) into the box and press **Enter** on your keyboard.

6. Click the green check mark on the floating toolbar to commit the move. A circular tweak trail is added in the graphics window to show the move, and a tweak is added under CAP SCREW: 3 in the browser.

Follow the previous instructions to animate your presentation. You'll notice that the cap screw rotates *before* it is used to connect the face plate to the arbor frame. You can see this happen by opening mi_11_003.avi in the Chapter 11 directory of your Mastering Inventor 2016 folder.

In the next section, you will learn how to edit tweaks and change the order in which they happen.

Take a few minutes to experiment with using different features (faces and edges) as data for linear and rotation moves, and try toggling between the local and world orientations. Then close the file without saving.

Preparing the Exploded Presentation to Be Used in an Animation

In this section, you will learn how to edit, reorder, and group your tweaks to make sure that the components move in the right order as you animate them.

Before you start the exercise, take a look at the browser. At the top of the browser is a filter, which is currently set to *Assembly View* (Figure 11.11). An assembly view shows you the explosions you have created with the components below it. Below each component you can see the tweaks that have been applied to the component.

For this exercise you will switch to tweak view. Open mi_11_004.ipn from the Chapter 11 directory of your Mastering Inventor 2016 folder.

Click Assembly View, and choose Tweak View from the drop-down list. You will now see the tweaks that have been applied with the components they are tweaking below them.

FIGURE 11.11

The presentation browser view filter—assembly view, tweak view, and sequence view

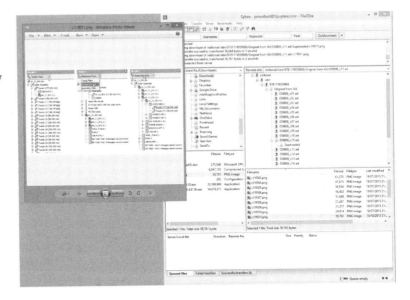

EDITING TWEAKS

To delete a tweak from the graphic window, follow these steps (see Figure 11.12 for reference):

1. Select the lower tweak between Lever Arm and Handle Cap: 1 (Tweak:8).

2. Right-click and choose Delete.

To delete a tweak from the browser, follow these steps:

1. Select Tweak: 6 in the browser.

2. Right-click and choose Delete.

FIGURE 11.12

Deleting a tweak from the graphics window or browser

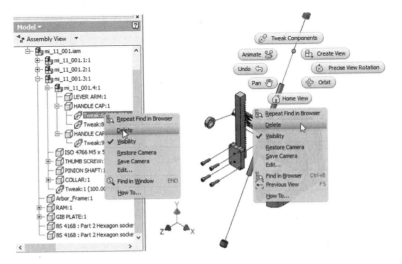

To edit a tweak in the graphic window, follow these steps:

1. Double-click the trail that shows the movement of `mi_11_001.2:1` in the graphics window.

2. Change the tweak value to 50 mm by typing **50mm** in the pop-up window.

3. Press the **Enter** key on your keyboard.

4. Click the green check mark to commit the edit.

To edit a tweak from the browser, follow these steps:

1. Select Tweak: 1 in the browser.

2. Notice the input window that appears at the bottom of the browser. Type **-100mm** into the input window.

3. Press the **Enter** key on your keyboard to commit the edit.

4. Deselect the tweak by clicking any empty space in the graphic window.

To add components to tweaks, follow these steps:

1. In the browser, click the + symbol next to Tweak: 2 to expand the node.

2. Expand `mi_11_001.iam` in the same way.

3. Drag RAM: 1 from the assembly to the tweak (see Figure 11.13 for reference).

FIGURE 11.13
Dragging a component
in the browser to add it
to a tweak

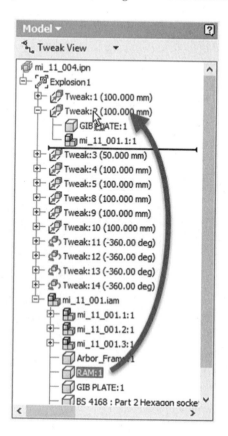

4. Note that the graphics window updates and a trail is added.

To remove components from tweaks, follow these steps:

1. In the browser, right-click Tweak: 1 ➤ RAM: 1 and choose Delete.

2. In the graphic window, right-click a component in the graphic window and choose Delete Tweaks ➤ Last Or All.

In this section, you learned how to sort the browser by tweak view and add or edit tweaks to suit your assembly sequence. In the next section, you will learn how to change the order that your tweaks happen. You can close your presentation file now without saving.

Changing the Order of Tweaks

The order the tweaks will animate in depends on the *sequence* they belong to. You can see the sequences in your design by changing to sequence view.

Open mi_11_005.ipn from the Chapter 11 directory of your Mastering Inventor 2016 folder. Click at the top of the browser in tweak view and choose Sequence View from the drop-down (see Figure 11.11 for reference).

You will now see the browser sorted into *explosions*, *tasks*, and *sequences*. Under each sequence you will find the tweaks you created previously.

Notice that there are multiple tasks in the explosion (see Figure 11.11). You can create multiple tasks by right-clicking the Explosion node and selecting Create Task.

Tasks are published to DWF and can be used in your documentation to help clarify what needs to be done at each stage of assembly.

You will begin by playing your animated sequence again. Click the Animate button on the Presentation tab. Click Play Forward.

You'll notice that the cap screws are added to the face plate before the face plate is attached to the arbor. You may also notice that Inventor is moving and rotating the cap screws as separate actions.

You can change this sequence to better reflect how the design will be assembled.

To add tweaks to a sequence, follow these steps:

1. With the browser in Sequence View, click the + symbol to expand the Fix Face Plate task node and the Gib Plate Screws, Cap Screws, and Cap Screw Rotate sequence nodes.

2. Drag and drop CAP SCREW:1,2,3 and 4 (-360deg). Rotate tweaks from the Cap Screw Rotate sequence to the Cap Screws sequence (Figure 11.14).

Notice the Cap Screw Rotate tweak is empty and disappears from the browser. You have just created one sequence from a number of tweaks. In this case, the Cap Screws tweak will now move *and* rotate at the same time!

You can also combine sequences by selecting multiple sequences, right-clicking, and choosing Group Sequences.

To reorder the tweak sequence, drag and drop the Fix Face Plate Task ➤ Face Plate sequence to above the Cap Screws sequence (Figure 11.15).

The face plate will now correctly seat itself on the arbor, before the cap screws are inserted and tightened up. Play the animation one more time to see the changes.

FIGURE 11.14
Dragging a tweak in the browser to add it to a sequence

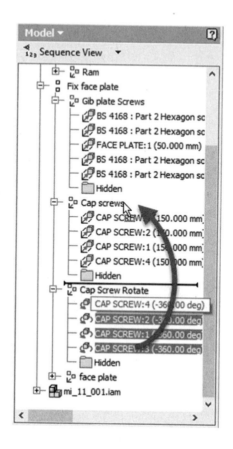

FIGURE 11.15
Dragging a sequence in the browser to change the order of animation

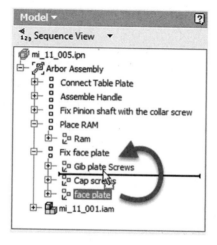

EDITING TASKS AND SEQUENCES

Would you like to know how to animate individual tasks and sequences and save camera-associated camera views?

Before you start the next section, right-click the Fix Faceplate task node and choose Edit. This will bring up the Edit Task & Sequences dialog box shown in Figure 11.16.

FIGURE 11.16
The Edit Task & Sequences dialog box

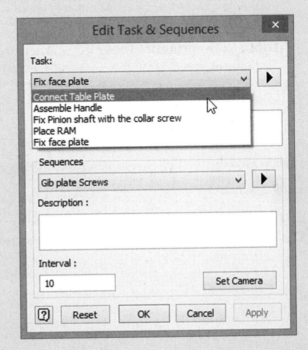

The dialog is divided into three sections. In the top section, you can pick a task from the drop-down. You can edit the description of what needs to happen during this task. You can also animate this individual task by clicking the Play Forward button.

Try it now.

(You will need to click the Reset button after you play each animation.)

The second section of the dialog allows you to pick a sequence within a task. Once again you can edit the sequence description and play its animation.

Take a moment to play each sequence in turn.

(You will need to click the Reset button after you play each animation.)

Task and sequence descriptions are published to DWF and can help illustrate what needs to happen at each stage of assembly. You could use them to highlight actions that are not shown in your assembly such as Add Grease.

You can slow down or speed up each task or sequence animation by editing the interval.

continues

continued

> Finally, you can save the camera view for this task or sequence. Use Inventor's zoom and pan controls to get the view you want to show in the graphics window and then click Set Camera to save the view.
>
> When you play back your animation, the camera will pan and zoom around your model to highlight each tweak.
>
> Close your presentation file now, ready for the next exercise.

Hiding Components from View During Animations

You might want to hide components that are not part of the current task or sequence. This is a great way to focus attention on the instruction in your current sequence. To do this, you can drag components from the assembly node to the Hidden folder in the sequence you are working on, as shown in Figure 11.17.

FIGURE 11.17
Dragging components to the Hidden folder

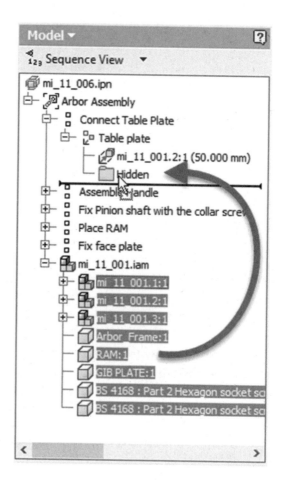

In the following exercise, you will hide all the parts in your presentation, for the first move of your animation, except for the arbor and the table plate.

Open `mi_11_006.ipn` from the `Chapter 11` directory of your `Mastering Inventor 2016` folder.

To add items to the Hidden folder, follow these steps:

1. Expand the Arbor Assembly node.

2. Expand the Connect Table Plate node.

3. Expand the Table Plate Sequence node.

4. Expand the `mi_11_001.iam` assembly node.

5. **Shift**-select to highlight all the components in the feature tree.

6. Drop them into the Table Plate Sequence ➤ Hidden folder.

To show items that have been hidden, follow these steps:

1. Expand the Table Plate Sequence ➤ Hidden node.

2. Select the Arbor Frame part, right-click, and choose Delete.

3. Select the mi_11_001.2:1 assembly. Right-click and choose Delete.

Click the Animate button on the Presentation tab and play your animation. You should see each group of parts appear as each sequence runs.

You can see this happen by opening `mi_11_006.avi` from the `Chapter 11` directory of your `Mastering Inventor 2016` folder.

ALL ABOUT TRAILS

Trails are lines that show the relationship between the component that has been moved and its original position in the assembly. Trails can be shown in the presentation file and in the drawing. By default, trails will start at the center of gravity of the tweaked component.

In an IDW or DWG file that contains a view of a presentation file, double-click the view to edit it and check the Show Trails box in the Presentation area of the Component tab to toggle the visibility of trails on and off.

Back in the presentation file, you can edit a tweak in the graphics window by selecting the trail and then selecting the green circular grip that shows up. Click and drag your cursor to edit the tweak "by eye."

You can create trails manually from any point on a component (see the section on the Tweak minitoolbar for details). To hide individual trails, select the trail in the graphics window, right-click, and choose Visibility. You can show and hide trails by finding the tweak in the browser, right-clicking, and choosing Visibility.

You can hide all trails by right-clicking in the graphic area with nothing selected and choosing Hide All Trails, as shown in Figure 11.18.

continues

continued

FIGURE 11.18
Hide All Trails menu
option

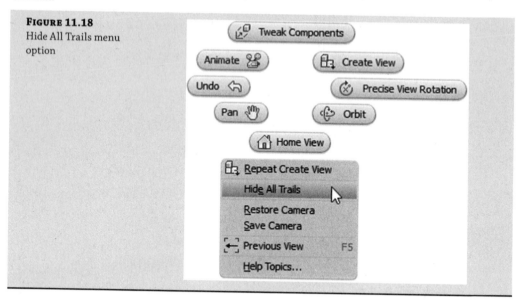

Rounding Up Presentation Preparation

Creating a presentation with the Auto Explode feature can be quick and easy. Inserting a view of an exploded presentation into your drawing can instantly provide extra clarity of your design.

Recording an animation of your explosion can provide significant additional value to go along with your 2D documentation.

Finally, you can create and publish a complete set of 2D drawings, with BOM and animated assembly instructions to DWF, which can include your commentary.

Creating and Publishing Animations

Still images are no fun! In this section, you will learn how to create an animation of your presentation. You will learn how to group sequences so that they animate at the same time, reorder the animation of sequences in the Animation dialog box, and record your animation as a WMV or AVI file.

You should still have mi_11_006.ipn open from the Chapter 11 directory in your Mastering Inventor 2016 folder.

1. Click the Animate button on the Presentation tab.

2. Make sure that Interval is set to **10**.

3. Make sure that Repetitions is set to **1**.

4. Make sure that the Minimize Dialog During Recording box is checked.

5. Click the Record button.

6. Set the file type to AVI. Chose a file location and name for your recording.

7. Click the Save button.

8. When the Video Compression box pops up, choose OK.

9. Press Play.

When the animation finishes, your recording will be ready.

Animation File Types and Compression Codecs

This section describes the various types of files and compression codecs.

AVI vs. WMV

Both AVI and WMV files are video format files developed by Microsoft. AVI files are more likely to be recognized by Linux or Apple players and are better if you intend to edit the video later. WMV is a more compressed format that is designed for web streaming.

WMV Export Properties

When recording via WMV, you will be presented with the WMV Export Properties dialog. You can control the file size of your exported WMV by choosing from the Network Bandwidth and Image Size options, as shown in Figure 11.19.

FIGURE 11.19
The WMV Export Properties dialog box

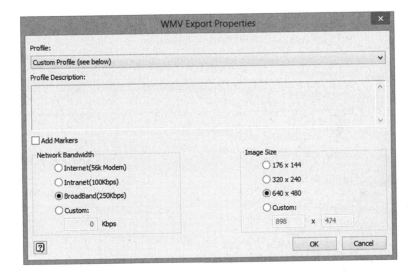

AVI Codecs

When recording to AVI, you will be offered a choice of codecs, as shown in Figure 11.20. The best-quality codec that comes with Inventor is the Full Frames codec, which is totally uncompressed but has a *huge* file size!

FIGURE 11.20
Inventor codecs available out of the box

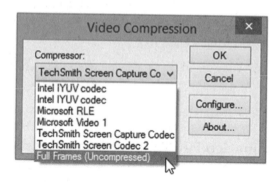

For good quality and a smaller file size, you can download a choice of many free codecs. I have had great success with the TechSmith codec, which you can download and install from here:

```
https://www.techsmith.com/download.html
```

AUTO EXPLODE

You can use the Auto Explode command when you initially create your presentation view, or you can use it on individual subassemblies after you have created a presentation view.

The Auto Explode command will try to use your assembly constraints to work out how it should move your components. If you don't have any Assembly constraints, you will get the message "No Applicable assembly Constraints exist."

Table 11.1 shows how Inventor's Auto Explode command will map your assembly constraints to tweaks.

TABLE 11.1:   Auto Explode Command and Assembly Constraints

GEOMETRY FOR MATE	RESULT OF AUTO EXPLODE COMMAND
Face to face	Explodes normal to face
Face to plane	Explodes normal to face
Face to edge	Explodes normal to face
Face to point	Explodes normal to face
Face to axis	Explodes normal to face
Plane to plane	Explodes normal to plane
Plane to edge	Explodes normal to plane

GEOMETRY FOR MATE	RESULT OF AUTO EXPLODE COMMAND
Plane to point	Explodes normal to plane
Plane to axis	Explodes normal to plane
Point to point	No action
Point to axis	No action
Axis to axis	No action
Edge to edge	No action
Edge to point	No action
Edge to axis	No action
Insert (axis and face mate)	Explodes normal to face along axis
iMate – insert	Explodes normal to face along axis
Tangent	Explodes normal to planar face
iMate – tangent	Explodes normal to planar face
Angle	No action
iMate – angle	No action
iMate to face	Explodes normal to face
iMate – plane	No action

The Bottom Line

Create an exploded assembly presentation.   You can show the inner workings of your design or provide some instruction on how your design should be assembled using an Exploded view.

You can use presentation files to virtually dissemble your design. Presentation exploded views can be referenced in 2D drawings or recorded as an animation.

Master It   What is the simplest way of creating an exploded view in a presentation file?

How would you create an exploded view at the part level?

How would you create an exploded view at the component level?

How would you create an exploded view from an assembly view rep?

Create linear tweaks.   Linear tweaks are used to move (translate) components along a specified axis. This allows you to pull your assembly apart to show how it goes together.

Master It How would you apply a tweak to multiple components at the same time?

Can you add components to a tweak after you have created the tweak?

Create rotational tweaks. Rotational tweaks allow you to move components around an axis. You could show a fixing being turned into a threaded hole or show a hinged component opening or closing.

Master It How would you rotate a component through multiple turns?

Can you choose a rotational axis that is not part of the component you are rotating?

Create an exploded view on a drawing from a presentation file. An exploded view on a drawing is a traditional, and still useful, way of showing how a design fits together. Exploded views work really well with item number balloons and a parts list that both add data to the graphic image.

Master It What is the quickest way to add an exploded view to a drawing?

How would you create a drawing view of an exploded subassembly or view rep, while retaining item numbers and BOM data that match your original assembly file?

Can you change the view angle of your exploded view in your drawing view?

Group, reorder, and animate tweaks. Once you have created your tweaks, you can re-order them or group several of them together to control the sequence in which they trigger.

Master It You created a presentation explosion to use in a 2D drawing. Your boss now wants you to record this as an animation to aid the installation team in visualizing the correct sequence of fit.

Can you fix it? How?

Publish presentation files to DWF. DWF files can be used to provide a full technical specification, such as drawings, model files, and BOM, including your saved model views and animated explosions.

Master It Publishing a presentation file publishes only the data held in the IPN to DWF. How would you add the 2D drawings to the DWF to create the full package?

Chapter 12

Documentation

One of the disadvantages of old-fashioned 2D CAD is its single-document workflow. If one of your team members is struggling to complete a set of drawings on time, there is little you can do to help.

As a CAD manager, Inventor gives a huge advantage when you are up against a time crunch. You can break the work up among the team with modeling, assembling, and drawing running (almost!) concurrently.

In this chapter, you will learn how to document your design with 2D annotated drawings. You will learn how to output your documentation in a variety of file formats, including DWF and PDF.

In this chapter, you'll learn to:

◆ Create templates and styles

◆ Utilize drawing resources

◆ Edit styles and standards

◆ Create drawing views

◆ Annotate part drawings

◆ Annotate assembly drawings

◆ Work with sheet-metal drawings

◆ Work with weldment views

◆ Work with iParts and iAssembly drawings

◆ Share your drawings outside your workgroup

Creating Drawing Views

I love drawings (see Figure 12.1). I always strive to make my drawings efficient and easy to read—but I like them to look nice as well!

For many years I've heard that drawings will no longer be required, but I haven't seen it happen yet. A 3D model may contain *all* the information required to define your design, but the people who procure, manufacture, install, and commission your design won't want *all* the information; they just want the information that relates to their part of the work.

FIGURE 12.1
A 2D drawing
created with
Autodesk Inventor

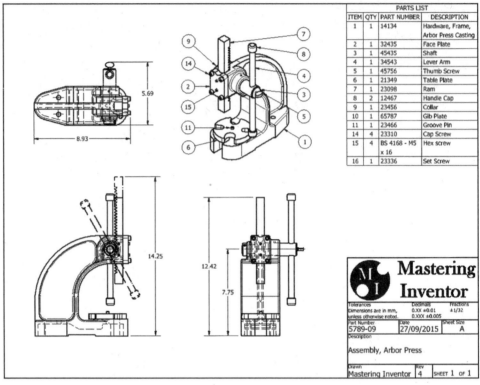

PARTS LIST			
ITEM	QTY	PART NUMBER	DESCRIPTION
1	1	14134	Hardware, Frame, Arbor Press Casting
2	1	32435	Face Plate
3	1	45435	Shaft
4	1	34543	Lever Arm
5	1	45756	Thumb Screw
6	1	21349	Table Plate
7	1	23098	Ram
8	2	12467	Handle Cap
9	1	23456	Collar
10	1	65787	Gib Plate
11	1	23466	Groove Pin
14	4	23310	Cap Screw
15	4	BS 4168 - M5 x 16	Hex screw
16	1	23336	Set Screw

Mastering Inventor

Tolerances	Decimals	Fractions
Dimensions are in mm, unless otherwise noted.	0.XX ±0.01 0.XXX ±0.005	±1/32

Part Number	Date	Sheet Size
5789-09	27/09/2015	A

Description

Assembly, Arbor Press

Drawn	Rev	
Mastering Inventor	4	SHEET 1 OF 1

This is where drawings come in. A drawing is simply one view of your 3D model/database with specific information on it for your internal or external customer.

In this section, you will explore the various view-creation and editing tools in Inventor and see how to document different types of 3D models, including part, assembly, sheet metal, weldment, and iPart/iAssembly models.

Creating a Base View

Creating views in an Inventor drawing is an intuitive process. You'll start by creating some basic views of a part file while exploring the procedure and options along the way.

If you have not already downloaded the Chapter 12 files from www.sybex.com/go/ masteringinventor2016, please refer to the "What You Will Need" section of the introduction for the download and setup instructions.

Before you create any views, first open the part to become familiar with it.

1. On the Get Started tab, click the Open button.

2. Browse for mi_12a_048.ipt in the Chapter 12 directory of your Mastering Inventor 2016 folder and click the Open button.

3. Spin the part around and take a look at it using the ViewCube or the Orbit tool. Do not close the part.

4. On the Get Started tab, click the New button.

5. Select the Metric folder from the list on the left, choose the ANSI (mm) . idw template from the Drawings section on the right, and click the Create button.

6. On the Place Views tab ➤ Create panel, click the Base button to create a base view.

7. The Drawing View dialog box will open, and you will see a preview of your part on the screen.

8. Notice that the view orientation is taken from the ViewCube.

9. In the Scale input box, enter **2** or use the drop-down to select 2:1. You can specify scales in fractional or decimal formats (1/2 or 0.5 both work for half-scale).

10. Click the lightbulb button to turn on the View/Scale label.

11. In the View Label input box, type **Front**.

12. Use the In Canvas ViewCube to re-orientate your base view. I would like you to use the TOP view as your first view.

13. Notice the style area. The Shaded button can be toggled on and off independently of the other two, but the Hidden Lines and No Hidden Lines buttons are mutually exclusive to one another.

14. Click the drawing once above the base view, once to the right of the base view, and once above and to the right of the base view; previews of the views will be created, according to the First/Third Angle projection setting in your drawing styles (more on this later in the chapter).

15. Go back to the ViewCube and re-orientate the view. Notice that the other views will re-orientate themselves based first view placed.

16. Finish with the RIGHT view selected, and click OK to create the views. Compare your results to Figure 12.2.

FIGURE 12.2
Creating a
base view with
Autodesk Inventor

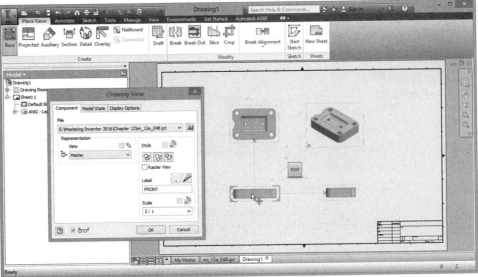

At this point, take a look at the Browser window. Notice that VIEW1 and VIEW2 are children of view FRONT. Notice that VIEW3 is independent. This will be important in the next section.

GREEN BRACKETS AND RASTER VIEWS

The Raster View option in the Drawing View dialog box creates a static raster-based view that approximates some view features. If this check box is selected, the computation of the view is quicker, but the view is less precise. Raster views (Figure 12.3) can be used to speed up the drawings of large and complex general assemblies.

Green corner brackets around the drawing view are used to denote that a view is a raster view. Additionally, raster view browser nodes are marked with a red diagonal line through the browser node icon.

You can right-click a view in the graphics area or on a view's browser node to toggle it between precise and raster view methods. You can also right-click in the graphics area and select Make All Views Precise or select Make All Views Raster to toggle all the views from one method to the other.

FIGURE 12.3
Raster views

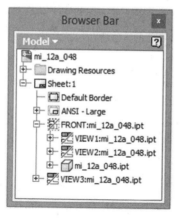
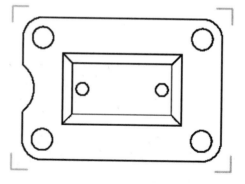

The base view is also known as the *parent* view. Here are some tips for working with base views:

- Hover over a view until you see a red dotted border. Right-click the border and choose Open to open the model.

- Double-click the view border to edit the view. Notice that only the base view has the option to re-orientate it with the ViewCube. The child views will automatically re-orientate themselves to suit the base view.

- To delete a view, select its border and click the Delete button on your keyboard.

- Toggle display of tangent edges and thread features by editing the view, selecting the Display Options tab, and checking the boxes.

- Views can be moved by selecting the border and dragging.

◆   Clicking a line or lines in a view gives you control options for just those lines.

◆   Right-click lines, arcs, or circles and uncheck Visibility to hide those entities.

◆   Right-click the view border and choose Show Hidden Edges to bring back lines that were hidden.

◆   Each base view created is listed in the browser, with the part or assembly it is referencing listed below.

◆   Expanding the view node in the browser shows the model tree for that view. You can select all the edges of features at once and then right-click the selected objects on the page and toggle off the visibility, change the layer, and so on.

◆   To rotate a child view, right-click it and choose Rotate; then select an edge to make it horizontal or vertical or use the drop-down to specify the angle.

◆   You can have as many base views as you need on a drawing, but the iProperties used by the title block will be pulled from the first view placed.

◆   Views can be renamed in the browser or by editing the view.

◆   You can suppress a view by right-clicking it and choosing Suppress.

SET VIEW PREFERENCES IN THE STANDARD

You can set up view preferences for your company standard by accessing the Styles Editor, selecting Standard, and then selecting the View Preferences tab. This allows you to choose which properties to display or not display in the view label, set the First or Third Angle projection, and much more.

The projected views that are based on your base view are also known as *child* or *dependent* views. Here are some tips for working with projected views. See Figure 12.4 for an example:

FIGURE 12.4
Drawing views in the browser

◆   Orthographic projected views are linked to the parent view in style and alignment and stacked below it in the browser tree.

◆   To break the style link between a projected view and its parent view, double-click to edit the projected view and deselect the Style From Base check box.

- Isometric views are not linked to the parent view in style and alignment and are listed separately in the browser tree.

- To break the alignment between a projected view and its parent view, right-click the projected view and choose Alignment ➤ Break. A view arrow will be placed next to the parent view, and the projected view will be labeled to match.

- To turn off the view arrow—edit the view and uncheck Display Options ➤ Definition in base view.

- To reset the alignment, right-click the projected view and choose Alignment and then Horizontal or Vertical as appropriate. The projected view will move back into place. Choose In Position to link the projected view to the parent in its current position.

- By default, deleting a parent view or a base view will remove all projected views as well.

- To delete a parent view without removing the projected views, click the >> button in the Delete View dialog box; then click Yes next to the views you want to keep and set them to No.

- Projected views can be created from views other than base views, such as detail views, section views, and even other projected views.

- You can select the parent view first and then issue the projected view tool, or you can issue the tool and then select the view. If you have a view selected and click the projected view button, that will be the view you are projecting. Use the Escape key to deselect views.

- You can suppress a view by right-clicking it and choosing Suppress.

You can close the current file without saving changes and continue.

Moving and Copying Views

You can move drawing views between sheets by dragging and dropping the browser nodes. When a projected view is moved to a different sheet than its parent, a view arrow is generated automatically on the parent view.

To move a view, follow these steps:

1. On the Get Started tab, click the Open button.

2. Browse for mi_12a_050.idw in the Chapter 12 directory of your Mastering Inventor 2016 folder and click the Open button.

3. Expand the Front view node in the browser to show projected views 2 and 3.

4. Click the browser node of View2 and drag it down to the Sheet2 browser node.

5. Rest your mouse pointer over the top of the Sheet2 browser node icon and release the mouse button.

6. Sheet2 becomes active to show you where View2 has been moved. Notice that there is a browser icon for the Front view with an arrow and the sheet name in parentheses. This indicates it is linked to the parent view on Sheet1. Notice too that the moved view has been renamed.

7. Right-click the Front view icon in the Sheet2 browser and choose Go To to be returned to Sheet1.

8. Notice that a view arrow has been created next to the Front view.

To copy a view, follow these steps:

1. With mi_12a_050.idw still open, make sure you are on Sheet1 (double-click the Sheet:1 node to activate it).

2. Right-click View3 and choose Copy.

3. Right-click the browser node for Sheet2 and choose Paste.

4. Sheet2 becomes active to show you where the view has been copied to. Notice that the new view has been named with the next available view number.

Copying and moving views is often useful when you've detailed a complex view on one sheet and then have run out of space and need to expand the drawing to another sheet.

Note that when you copy or move a view with dimensions or other annotations applied, the annotations are moved or copied as well. You can close the current file without saving changes and continue.

Creating Section Views

Certification Objective

Section views are created by "sketching" a line across an existing view to define the section cut. The sketch is created automatically for you as you define the section line.

To create a section view, follow these steps:

1. On the Get Started tab, click the Open button.

2. Browse for mi_12a_051.idw in the Chapter 12 directory of your Mastering Inventor 2016 folder and click the Open button.

3. On the Place Views tab ➢ Create panel, click the Section button.

4. Click the Front view to choose it as the view to be sectioned.

5. Hold down the Ctrl key and click to the left of the view. (This ensures that you do not accidentally constrain the start point of your section line to any midpoints, center points, or endpoints.)

6. Release the Ctrl key, move your cursor across the part, and click to the right of the part, ensuring that you are getting a straight line.

7. Right-click and choose Continue.

8. In the Section View dialog box, note that you can change the section identifier, scale, style, and section depth. You can also create a zero-depth section called a *slice*. Leave all these options at the defaults.

9. Drag your cursor above the original view, and notice how the placement is constrained perpendicularly to the section line. (Holding down the Ctrl key will allow you to place the section view anywhere you like.)

10. Click to place the view.

11. The sketched line is converted to a section line indicator. Click and drag the section line up or down to see the section update automatically.

Look at the browser to see how the section view was added as a child view of the base.

FINDING A DRAWING VIEW IN THE BROWSER

Right click on the view boundary on the drawing and choose Find in Browser.

Notice the sketch that was created on the base view listed just above the section view node. This sketch is the section line itself and can be edited like any other sketch by right-clicking it and choosing Edit.

To precisely position your section line, edit the sketch and the use the Project Geometry tool to project a feature from the component into the view (see Figure 12.5). You can now apply constraints to the sketch line to position it, using your projected geometry as a reference.

FIGURE 12.5

A part section view

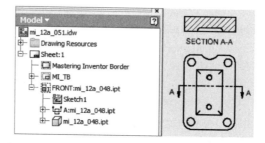

Here are some tips for working with section views:

♦ Section line appearance is controlled by your drawing styles just like most other annotation objects.

♦ Create a projected view of a section view to create an isometric section.

♦ Edit or hide a hatch by right-clicking it.

♦ Display a hidden hatch or turn a hatch on for isometric section views by editing the view (right-click and select Edit View), selecting the Display Options tab, and selecting Hatching.

♦ You can hatch by material if you have mapped the materials and hatch patterns in your standard.

♦ Flip the section arrow direction by right-clicking the section line and choosing Reverse Direction.

♦ Show just the arrows of the section line by right-clicking the section line and choosing Show Entire Line.

◆ Edit the section depth by right-clicking the section line and choosing Edit Section Properties.

◆ You can constrain a section line to a feature when as you create your section by running your cursor over the feature while you are creating the sketch line.

◆ If you need to put views on different sheets, you can indicate where a view has come from by editing its view label. Edit the view, click the Edit View Label button (looks like a pencil), click into the text box, and choose View Label Properties ➤ PARENT SHEET NAME from the drop-downs, before clicking the Add Text Parameter button.

You can close the current file without saving changes and continue.

You defined the section line on the fly during the previous exercise. Now you will bring in a sketch created in the part model and use it to create a section view. Figure 12.6 shows the sketched line in the model.

FIGURE 12.6
Section line sketch on model

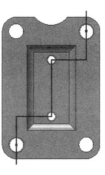

MAPPING MATERIALS TO HATCH PATTERNS

You can set up your template to use a predefined hatch pattern per the material of the sectioned part so that copper parts are hatched with one hatch pattern, mild steel parts are hatched with another, and so on.

1. With your template drawing open, select Manage tab ➤ Styles And Standards ➤ Styles Editor.

2. In the left pane, expand Standard and then click your standard.

3. In the right pane, click the Material Hatch Pattern Defaults tab.

4. Set the Default Hatch Style option for new materials added in the mapping.

5. Click the From File button to select a part file that contains all the material styles you want to import or use the From Style Library button.

6. For each imported material, click the Hatch Pattern field and select a new hatch pattern from the list. Use Ctrl or Shift to change several materials at the same time.

7. Click Save to save the changes to the current document; then click Done to close the dialog box.

8. Remember to use the Styles And Standards ➤ Save button to save this to your style library; save this drawing file as your new template.

To create a section from a model sketch, follow these steps:

1. On the Get Started tab, click the Open button.

2. Browse for mi_12a_052.idw in the Chapter 12 directory of your Mastering Inventor 2016 folder and click the Open button.

3. Locate the sheet node in the browser and then click the plus symbol to expand it.

4. Expand the view node called Front to reveal the model.

5. Finally, expand the model node to reveal the part features.

6. On the part node (mi_12a_048.ipt), right-click and choose Get Model Sketches.

7. You will now see that a model sketch called Section Sketch:Model is present; right-click it and choose Include.

8. This will reveal a zigzag line on the part view.

9. On the Place Views tab, click the Section button.

10. Click any part of the included sketch, or click the sketch in the browser to use it as the section line.

11. In the Section View dialog box, click the Include Slice check box and then select the Slice The Whole Part check box to create a zero-depth section. Leave the other options at the defaults.

12. Click to the right of the original view to create the section.

13. To change the section properties, right-click the section line and choose Edit Section Properties.

14. Deselect the Slice The Whole Part check box and the Include Slice check box to change the section to a full-depth section; then click the OK button.

15. Right-click the hatch and choose Edit; then click the Double check box.

16. Click the OK button to close the Edit Hatch Pattern dialog box.

Your section should look similar to Figure 12.7.

FIGURE 12.7
Section using model sketch

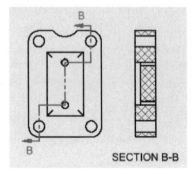

SECTION B-B

> **IMPORT HATCH PATTERNS**
>
> You can load hatch patterns from an external PAT file to add custom hatch patterns to your drawings. To do this, edit a hatch, select Other from the Pattern list, and then click Load. You can also do this in the Style And Standard Editor to add custom hatches to your company standard.

You can close the current file without saving changes and continue.

Slice Views

You can use the Place Views ➤ Modify ➤ Slice tool to create multiple sliced sections at once.

To create a slice view, you will need a target view (the view that will be sliced), a source view (the view where you will define the slices), and a sketch associated with the source view that defines the slices.

To create a slice operation defined by two existing views and the associated sketch geometry, follow these steps:

1. Create a source view and a target view.

2. Hover over the border of the source view. When the red dotted outline appears, click it to select the view. (This associates the sketch with the view. If you don't have a view selected when you start the sketch tool, the sketch will not be linked to the view.)

3. From the Place Views tab ➤ Sketch panel, click the Start Sketch button.

4. Create sketch geometry to define an open profile to use for the slice (one single line that crosses back and forth over the component).

5. Click the Finish Sketch button to exit the sketch.

6. From the Place Views tab ➤ Modify panel, click the Slice button.

7. Select your target view; the Slice dialog box displays.

8. Select the previously defined sketch profile to use as the Slice Line Geometry selection.

9. You can choose to select the Slice All Parts check box in order to override the browser component section settings and slice all parts in the view (assuming the slice sketch runs through them).

10. Click the OK button to create the slice operation (see Figure 12.8).

FIGURE 12.8
A sliced view and the sketch used to slice

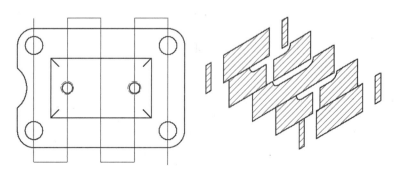

When working with assemblies and the slice tool, you can control which components are sliced by expanding the node for the target view in the browser and then right-clicking each component in the view model tree and choosing the Slice option from the Section Participation flyout menu.

USING SLICE PARTICIPATION WITH ASSEMBLY VIEWS

You can use the Slice tool to fine-tune your assembly views. However, there is a trick to getting it to work correctly.

1. Start the Slice tool.

2. Select your cutting line, but do not select the Slice All Parts check box.

3. You will be prompted with a warning: "The slice operation did not result in any sliced components...." Click the OK button in the warning dialog box.

4. In the browser, find the node for the assembly model of the sliced target view and right-click it; then choose Section Participation and select Slice. This will slice all the parts in the assembly.

5. Then you can select individual components and change the Section Participation back to none as you see fit.

The trick here is that if you had selected the Slice All Parts option when creating the slice, you would not be allowed to control the individual section participation in the target view components.

Using Breakout Views

The Breakout tool is used to create cutaway views of your design, which can help show internal features or components. Unlike the Section View tool that creates a new view, a breakout is an operation you perform on an existing view. To create a breakout view, you'll need to prepare a closed-loop profile associated with the view that you want to cut away.

It is important to note that to use a sketch for a breakout, it must be associated with the drawing view. To create an associated sketch, first select the view and then click the Create Sketch button.

Clicking the Create Sketch button without selecting the view first will result in a sketch that is not associated with any view.

To create a breakout view, follow these steps:

1. On the Get Started tab, click the Open button.

2. Browse for mi_12a_067.idw in the Chapter 12 directory of your Mastering Inventor 2016 folder and click the Open button.

3. Select the view named Front View. (Look at the browser—if the view is selected, the browser node will be highlighted.)

4. On the keyboard, click the S key to start a new sketch.

5. Sketch a shape similar to Figure 12.9. The results don't need to be exact, but you do need to ensure that the sketch is a closed loop.

FIGURE 12.9

Creating a breakout sketch

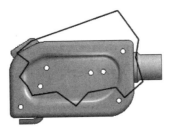

6. Click the Finish Sketch button on the Sketch tab when your sketch is complete.

7. To ensure that the sketch has been created correctly, you can select the view on the sheet and move it. If the sketch travels with the view, then it is associated with the view. If it stays put, it is not. You can also look at the browser and ensure that the Sketch node is stacked under Front View. If you see it above Front View, it is not associated and will not work for the breakout.

8. On the Place Views tab ➤ Modify button, click the Break Out button.

9. Select Front View.

10. Your sketch should automatically be selected as the profile, provided you have only one unconsumed sketch. Otherwise, you will select the sketch for the profile. If you cannot select the sketch, review step 3.

11. Make sure the Depth area is set to From Point and then click the upper-rightmost hole.

12. Enter a depth value of **25 mm** and click the OK button.

Your result should look similar to Figure 12.10.

FIGURE 12.10

The Break Out view node and the resulting sketch

 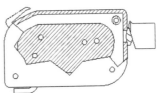

Note the Break Out view node in the browser. You may be able to see some portions of the internal parts because they have been cut away as well. You'll explore how to control this in the coming pages; for now, you can close the file without saving changes.

Next, you'll open a file and modify a breakout view to explore the other depth options.

1. On the Get Started tab, click the Open button.

2. Browse for `mi_12a_072.idw` in the Chapter 12 directory of your `Mastering Inventor 2016` folder and click the Open button.

3. In the browser, right-click the Break Out node and choose Edit Break Out. You may have to expand the sheet node and the Front View node to locate it.

4. In the Depth area, set the drop-down to To Sketch.

5. Select the zigzag sketch line in the top view. Note that this sketch was associated with the top view by selecting the view first and then creating the sketch. This is required to use it as a To Sketch.

6. Click the OK button.

Examine the isometric view, and you will see that the breakout used the zigzag line as the depth extents and cut the internal and external parts. You can adjust this by going to the model tree and removing the file from section participation, as explained in the following steps.

7. Select the model node for Front View. Hover your mouse pointer over model nodes in the browser and watch the views on the sheet to make sure you are selecting the one for Front View.

8. Expand the model node to reveal all the part files and select the parts ending in 04 through 07, as shown in Figure 12.11.

9. Right-click the selected parts, choose Section Participation, and then select None.

10. The views will update on the sheet to show these parts unsectioned.

11. In the browser, right-click the Break Out node and choose Edit Break Out. Click the Section All Parts check box. This will override the Section Participation settings.

12. Change the Depth option to To Hole and click the hole/circular edge in the view named Top View.

FIGURE 12.11

Removing parts from the breakout

13. Click the OK button.

14. Notice that the zigzag sketch line reappears because it is no longer used by the breakout. Also notice that the breakout depth has adjusted to stop at the center of the hole.

15. Edit the breakout once again and set the Depth drop-down to Through Part.

16. In the browser, select the parts ending in 02, 03, 08, and 09 (use the Ctrl key to select multiple parts at the same time) to ensure that they are sectioned through.

17. Click the OK button; your results should be similar to Figure 12.12.

FIGURE 12.12
A breakout using the Through Part option

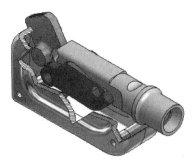

You can turn on the hatching of the sectioned parts in this view by editing the view (double-click the view or right-click and choose Edit View and then select the Display Options tab and click the Hatching check box).

SECTION PARTICIPATION

Section participation can be controlled per the part file or per the part instance. If the part is a standard part such as a fastener, you might want to set section participation per file so the part is never sectioned. If you just want to exclude a part from a particular section or breakout view for clarity, you can do so per instance.

To control section participation per file, open the part file you want to change the section participation for, select the Tools tab, select Document Settings, and then choose the Modeling tab. Uncheck the Participate In Assembly And Drawing Sections check box. The part will now default to None in Section Participation for new section and breakout views, but it can be set to participate on a per-instance basis.

To control section participation per instance, place the section or breakout view of the assembly, expand the view node in the browser, and then locate the browser node for the parts for which you want to adjust section participation. Right-click, choose Section Participation, and set it to None as needed.

If the part was set to be sectioned in the document settings before a view was created and you change the document settings so it is not to be sectioned, the drawing view will stay sectioned and will need to be changed per instance.

You will have noticed that as you modified the breakout, the isometric view was linked to those changes. This is because isometric projected views created for views that already have a breakout inherit the breakout by default. Orthographic projected views, such as the top view, do not inherit the breakout.

To switch the inheritance setting of the isometric view, select the view boundary, right-click, and select Edit View. In the Display Options tab in the Drawing View dialog box, deselect the Break Out check box in the Cut Inheritance area, as shown in Figure 12.13.

FIGURE 12.13
Cut Inheritance settings for isometric views

You can also turn on hatching from this tab. You can use the current file to explore these hatch settings, and then you can close the file without saving changes.

Using Detail Views

You can use the detail view to enlarge and segregate a particular portion of a drawing view as a new view. Follow these steps to explore the options of detail views:

1. On the Get Started tab, click the Open button.

2. Browse for mi_12a_077.idw in the Chapter 12 directory of your Mastering Inventor 2016 folder and click the Open button.

3. On the Place Views tab, click the Detail button.

4. Click the boundary of the Front view to use it as the basis of the new detail view.

5. In the Detail View dialog box, you can modify the View/Scale Label And Style settings just as you can in other view-creation dialog boxes. You can also set a fence and cutout shape. The Full Boundary and Connection Line options are available only if you're using the Smooth Cutout option. Figure 12.14 shows examples of the Smooth Cutout options.

6. Leave the dialog options set at the defaults and then click the Front view, approximately in the center of the crescent-shaped feature, as shown in Figure 12.14.

7. Drag the boundary out to a size close to that shown in Figure 12.14.

8. Click the screen where you would like to place the detail view, and the detail is created.

9. Click the detail boundary on Front View, and note the six green grips. Click and drag the three quadrant grips to resize the boundary and use the center one to control the location.

10. Click and drag the View letter to move it, and double-click the two grips near the arrow-head and change the head style.

FIGURE 12.14

Detail view options

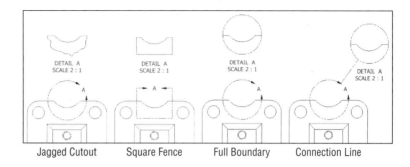

Here are more options for detail views:

◆ Right-click the detail boundary and choose Attach to anchor the detail to a specific point on the base view.

◆ Right-click the detail boundary and choose Options to change the detail from rough to smooth, then to add a full detail, and then to add a connection line.

◆ To move the detail label character out away from the boundary, right-click the detail boundary, click Leader, and then click the detail label character and drag it; it will be attached with a leader.

◆ Right-click or double-click the detail view to edit the view and change scale, style, detail name, and so on, as you would any other view.

◆ When editing a detail view, you click the Edit View Label button (it looks like a pencil). You can also use the Type drop-down and select View Label Properties. Then you can use the Property drop-down to add the parent sheet name or index to your view label. This will place the parent view information in the view label for detail views. This is often useful when the view resides on a different sheet.

Use the current file to explore these detail options and then close the file without saving changes.

USING DETAIL VIEW ANNOTATION

Although detail views are created at a scale larger than the base view, Inventor takes this into account when creating dimensions for the detail view. All your dimensions will be to the correct scale.

Tip: Right-click a detail view callout and choose Attach to relate the detail view to the geometry it is relevant to. Now, when you update your design, the detail view will follow the changes made to the model.

Creating Break Views

Often when detailing components that are much longer proportionally than they are tall, such as frame components, it is a good idea to use the Break tool to remove portions of the model. This allows the detail of the end treatments to be the focus of the drawing.

Follow these steps to explore the Break tool:

1. On the Get Started tab, click the Open button.

2. Browse for mi_12a_078.idw in the Chapter 12 directory of your Mastering Inventor 2016 folder and click the Open button.

3. Click the Place Views tab ➤ Modify panel ➤ Break button.

4. Click anywhere on the Front view.

5. In the Break dialog box, set the gap to **10 mm**.

6. Click the view just to the left of where it extends past the drawing border on the left side.

7. Move your mouse to position the break symbol. Move your cursor just to the right of where the view extends past the drawing border on the right side and then click onscreen.

8. Notice that the break is carried through to both views.

9. Zoom in on the break symbol and then click it.

10. Click and drag the green grip point to the left to reposition it.

11. Select the right half of the break symbol and drag it to the right and then let up. This will remove more material from the view.

12. Select the right half of the break symbol and drag it to the left and then let up. This will add more material to the view.

13. Adjust the view until it fits on the drawing sheet.

14. Click the view named Top View, right-click, and choose Edit View.

15. Click the Display Options tab and uncheck the Break check box in the Cut Inheritance area. Then click the OK button. You'll notice that the view no longer inherits the break from the parent view (in this case, Front View).

16. Click the break symbol on Front View and press the Delete key.

17. Right-click Sheet 2 in the browser and choose Activate.

18. Click the Break button and select the view named Top View.

19. With the Break dialog box open, notice the Propagate To Parent View check box. Uncheck this option to break only the view named Top View and leave the parent view from which it was created without a break.

20. Click the start point and endpoint on the view to create the break, and you'll see that the parent view is left as is.

You can continue to experiment with the Break tool and then close this file without saving changes. Here are some more points to know about break views:

♦ To edit an existing break, right-click the break symbol and choose Edit Break.

♦ The distance value entered in the Break dialog box refers to the space on the paper between the break symbols.

◆ You can break views vertically and horizontally using the options in the dialog box, but there is not a way to break a view at an angle when a component is not vertical or horizontal.

◆ There is no "pipe break" symbol for round components.

◆ By default, a dimension placed on the view will show the broken dimension symbol as well, to indicate that it should not be scaled from.

◆ You can slide the broken dimension symbol under the dimension text to hide it on a per-instance basis.

◆ You can edit the dimension style and turn off the dimension break symbol option if you like. The setting is on the Display tab of the dimension style settings in the Style And Standard Editor.

Figure 12.15 shows a broken view.

FIGURE 12.15
A broken view

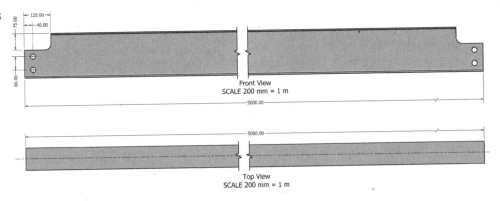

BREAK SYMBOLS FOR STRUCTURAL DETAILING

If you detail plate girders and build up members with vertical stiffeners, gussets, clip plates, and so on, you might find that the break symbol on the drawing view causes confusion.

To break a view without showing the break symbol, you can configure it so that it does not show, as described here:

1. Use the slider bar in the Break dialog box to set the break symbol to the smallest scale (slide it to the far left).

2. Set the break gap to **0.0001** or some number nearing zero (Inventor will not allow a zero value).

3. Select the break symbol (it will now display as a vertical line) and then switch to the Annotate tab. Use the Layer drop-down box to place the break symbol on a nonplotting layer (you will need to create this layer in your drawings).

You can try this with the file named mi_12a_078.idw; there is a layer called No Plot already created in this drawing.

Cropping Views

You can use the Crop tool on the Modify panel of the Place Views panel to crop unneeded areas of a drawing view, in much the same way a photograph is cropped.

You can specify the crop boundary as part of the crop operation or create a sketch on the view first and then use it as the crop boundary.

When you create a sketch to be used as a crop boundary, you must first select the view and then create the sketch to associate the sketch to the view. Unassociated sketches cannot be used as a crop boundary.

The following view types *cannot* be cropped:

♦ Views containing a view break

♦ Views with overlays

♦ Views that have been suppressed

♦ Views that have already been cropped

Using Draft Views

Draft views are essentially just 2D sketches created in a drawing and packaged in a view "container," allowing them to be scaled and handled like other drawing views. For instance, if you have standard details drawn in AutoCAD, you might copy them into a draft view and then place and scale them as needed.

To create standard details from Inventor views, you can use Save Copy As to create an AutoCAD DWG file and then paste the detail back into Inventor as a draft view.

Draft views have limited capabilities for sharing between drawings; they cannot be copied or moved between different sheets or between different drawings. If you copy the whole sheet into a new drawing, it will bring in the Draft view as well. You might consider using sketched symbols for standard details you plan to use over and over.

To create a draft view, follow these general steps:

1. From the Place Views tab, click the Draft button on the Create panel.

2. In the Draft View dialog box, set the label and scale and then click the Label Visibility button (it looks like a lightbulb) to display the view name and scale on the drawing.

3. Click the OK button to close the Draft View dialog box.

4. An empty view and sketch are created. Use the sketch tools to add geometry, text, and dimensions as needed, or paste in copied geometry from AutoCAD.

5. Click the Finish Sketch button to create the sketch and draft views.

Creating Overlay Views

Overlay views help to show the change in position of a moving component. Overlay views work with positional representations to capture the move at significant points on its journey.

To create an overlay view, the assembly must first have positional representations set up to be used. Follow these steps to explore overlay views:

1. On the Get Started tab, click the Open button.

2. Browse for mi_12a_080.idw in the Chapter 12 directory of your Mastering Inventor 2016 folder and click the Open button.

3. On the Place Views tab ➤ Create panel, click the Overlay button and select the existing view on the sheet.

4. In the Overlay View dialog box, choose Closed from the Positional Representation drop-down and then click the OK button.

The result is a view of the alternative position shown in a phantom linetype overlaid on the original.

You can dimension to the overlay lines as you would any others to capture a mechanism's extension length, rotation angle, and so on. The key to overlay views is in setting up the positional representations in the assembly beforehand.

When you create the overlay, you are also given the opportunity to specify a view representation for the overlay view. It's recommended that before you create an overlay view, you create a view representation that isolates only the components that move as a result of the positional representation. Otherwise (as is the case in this example), all the nonmoving components are redrawn over the same components in the base view.

To change positional representations used in an overlay view, edit the existing overlay view and specify a different positional representation. Also, be aware that because weldments are not allowed to use positional representations, overlays are not allowed for weldment drawing and will be removed if they exist when an assembly is converted to a weldment.

You can close the file without saving changes.

VIEW REPRESENTATIONS AND POSITIONAL REPRESENTATIONS

It's helpful to create a view representation in your assembly and turn off the visibility for all the parts that are not moving. Then you can use this view representation in your overlay view for added clarity.

Annotating Part Drawings

Once you've created the appropriate views to document the model, you can add annotations. You can find the annotation tools on the Annotate tab. The Annotate tab is divided into several groups of tools, including Dimension, Feature Notes, Text, Symbols, Sketch, Table, and Format tools. The following sections explore the annotation tools.

Using Centerline and Center Marks

There are four standard centerline and center mark tools as well as an automated centerline tool. These tools are called Centerline, Centerline Bisector, Center Mark, and Centered Pattern, and you can access them from the Symbols panel of the Annotate tab (look for the four buttons next to the Start Sketch button).

TAKE ADVANTAGE OF TOOL TIPS

Remember that hovering your mouse pointer over a tool button provides a tool tip with the button name and that hovering a moment longer displays a dynamic tool tip showing an illustrated example of the tool.

The automated centerline tool is accessed differently than the other centerline and center mark tools, as explained in the coming pages.

CENTERLINE

Use Centerline to draw a centerline-style line, arc, or circle by specifying points. When centerline arcs are created using circles or arcs as the selection points, a center mark is drawn on the arc along with the centerline.

1. On the Get Started tab, click the Open button.

2. Browse for mi_12a_082.idw in the Chapter 12 directory of your Mastering Inventor 2016 folder and click the Open button.

3. From the Annotate tab ➤ Symbols panel, select the Centerline tool.

4. On VIEW 1, click the hole at the 12 o'clock position and then the hole at 2 o'clock. Notice that the tool is drawing a straight line at this point.

5. Click the hole at 4 o'clock and notice that the centerline becomes an arc.

6. Continue around, clicking each hole, and then close the centerline by clicking 12 o'clock once again; then right-click and choose Create. Your centerline should resemble the one on the left of Figure 12.16.

7. You should still be in the Centerline tool at this point. On VIEW 4, click the hole A1, then B1, then B2, and finally A4.

8. Right-click and choose Create; then right-click and choose Cancel. Your centerline should resemble the one on the right of Figure 12.16.

FIGURE 12.16
Centerlines

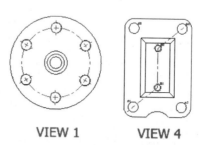

VIEW 1   VIEW 4

As you can see, the Centerline tool will triangulate the first three points and attempt to establish a centered pattern. In this way, you can use it to draw centerline arcs, circles, and lines. However, if you just need to draw a series of lines, this functionality can get in the way.

To draw just centerlines, click the first two points and then click any blank space on the sheet; then click the next two points and click a blank area again, and so on. The blank clicks are the same as right-clicking and choosing Create.

Try this on VIEW 5 to draw centerlines between each of the corner holes.

WATCH YOUR MOUSE CLICKS DURING CENTERLINE CREATION

The Centerline tool is a bit specific in the order it wants to see mouse clicks. After you have selected the final features on which to place the center mark, right-click and select Create. If you do not select Create and continue to select the next hole, you might end up with undesirable results. It takes a little getting used to, but you'll figure it out.

CENTERLINE BISECTOR

Use Centerline Bisector to create a centerline halfway between two edges or two points. Note that the edges do not have to be parallel or the same length. You can even select two circles, and you will get a centerline halfway between them.

1. Still in mi_12a_082.idw, select the Centerline Bisector tool on the Annotate tab ➤ Symbols panel.

2. Zoom in on the center shaft area of view Section A-A.

3. Click the top and bottom lines on the shaft to create a centerline running down the middle of the section view. Notice that the distance between the two lines is bisected with a centerline.

4. Place bisector centerlines in two holes in Section A-A by clicking the opposing lines for each.

5. Right-click and choose Cancel.

6. Click the centerline you placed in the center shaft and drag out the left end so it extends past the shaft. Bisector centerlines are created based on the size of the lines you choose and may need to be adjusted. Your section view should resemble Figure 12.17.

FIGURE 12.17
Bisecting centerlines

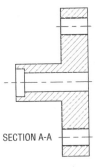

SECTION A-A

CENTER MARK

Use the Center Mark tool to annotate hole centers, circular edges, cylindrical geometry, and arcs such as filleted corners.

Center marks, as well as centerlines, are primarily formatted by the Center Mark style, but there is a distinct difference between how ANSI and non-ANSI center marks are drawn, so be sure your active standard is set properly for your needs. Follow these steps to explore the Center Mark tool:

1. Continuing with `mi_12a_082.idw`, select the Center Mark tool on the Annotate tab ➤ Symbols panel.

2. Zoom in to VIEW 2.

3. Click the edge or the centers of each hole.

4. Click the outermost circle as well.

5. Right-click and choose the OK button (or Cancel).

6. Select the large center mark you just created and then click the Style drop-down box (on the Format panel of the Annotate tab).

7. Select the style called Center Mark (ISO) from the list to set the existing center mark to the ISO style. You'll notice the change in style.

Here are some Center Mark tool options to be aware of:

◆ For large center marks that are mostly solid lines, you can right-click them, choose Edit ➤ Add/Remove Dashes, and then click the lines to place the dashes. Do the same to remove extra dashes once they are placed.

◆ Once extra dashes have been added, click them to slide them into place.

◆ To lock down extra dashes, right-click and choose Edit ➤ Uniform Dashing.

◆ You can align center marks with an angled edge by right-clicking them, choosing Edit ➤ Align To Edge, and then selecting a diagonal edge in the view.

◆ You can adjust center mark overshoots by clicking the ends and dragging in or out as required.

◆ To reset overshoots, right-click the center mark and choose Edit ➤ Fit Center Mark.

◆ To simplify center marks to just a center cross, right-click them and choose Edit ➤ Extension Lines.

◆ You can right-click a center mark and choose Edit Center Mark Style to adjust the way center marks are drawn by default.

CENTERED PATTERN

Use Centered Pattern to create a centerline on parts or features that have a consistent pattern. If the pattern is circular, a center mark is automatically placed.

1. Continuing with `mi_12a_082.idw`, select the Centered Pattern tool on the Annotate tab ➤ Symbols panel.

2. Zoom in to VIEW 3.

3. Click the center hole first to establish the pattern axis.

4. Click all the holes in the pattern and click the starting hole again to close the pattern.

5. Right-click and choose Create and then right-click and choose Cancel.

There are many options for creating centerlines and center marks manually, but in the next section you'll create them in a more automatic fashion. You can close the current file without saving changes and continue.

Automated Centerlines

Rather than placing centerlines and center marks manually, you can use the Automated Centerlines tool.

This tool is in the context menu of each view, and you can run it on multiple views on the same sheet at one time (multiselect views while holding your Ctrl key down before executing the tool). Follow these steps to explore the Automated Centerlines tool:

1. On the Get Started tab, click the Open button.

2. Browse for `mi_12a_084.idw` in the `Chapter 12` directory of your `Mastering Inventor 2016` folder and click the Open button.

3. Hold the Ctrl key and select all four views.

4. Right-click and choose Automated Centerlines. If you do not see this option in the context menu, you have most likely selected something other than a view (such as a line or hatch pattern).

5. In the Automated Centerlines dialog box, use the Apply To buttons to select the type of objects to which you want to apply center marks and centerlines. In this case, choose all of the following:

- Hole features

- Cylindrical features

- Revolved features

- Circular patterned features

6. In the Projection area, ensure that both the Axis Normal and Axis Parallel projection buttons are selected; otherwise, the sections' views will be ignored.

7. In the Radius Threshold area, enter **3** in the Maximum box for Circular Edges. This will ensure that no center mark is placed for the outer edge of the revolved part or for the 3.94 radius circle in the hub.

8. Click the OK button and notice the centerlines and marks that have been created.

You can set the defaults for automated centerlines by selecting the Tools ➤ Document Settings ➤ Drawing ➤ Automated Center Lines.

Do this in your template, and you will not have to go through the process of selecting the Apply To buttons or specifying minimum and maximum threshold values each time.

Use the Undo button to reset the drawing and then experiment with the options to gain more understanding of the different features. When you have finished, you can close the file without saving changes.

Creating Dimensions

Certification
Objective

A significant portion of any detailing job is placing and modifying dimensions; therefore, it is important to become familiar with the various dimension tools and formatting options available in the Drawing Manager.

Here is a quick reference of the dimension types available:

♦ Linear dimension from one element. For instance, select a line, and drag and drop the dimension.

♦ Linear dimension between two elements. Select two endpoints, and drag and drop the dimension.

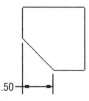

♦ Aligned dimension between two elements. For instance, select two endpoints of an angled line, right-click, and select Aligned to force an aligned solution.

♦ Angular dimension between three points. Select three points; they can be endpoints, mid-points, center points, and so on.

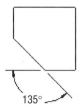

♦ Angular dimension of an interior angle. Select two angular lines and drag to the minor angle.

◆ Angular dimension of an exterior angle. Select two angular lines and drag to the major angle.

◆ Angular dimension from a reference line, such as a line from an object line and a centerline or a projected work axis.

◆ Radius dimension. Select any circle or arc and right-click to choose either a radius or a dimension. Radius is the default for arcs.

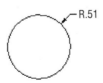

◆ Diameter dimension. Select any circle or arc and right-click to choose either a radius or a dimension. Diameter is the default for circles.

◆ Baseline dimensions. Select objects and then set the direction and base dimensions.

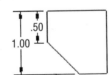

◆ Ordinate dimensions. Select objects and then set the direction and origin dimensions.

◆ Chain dimensions. Select objects and then set the direction and chain dimensions.

◆ Implied intersection dimension. Select the first intersecting object, then right-click and choose Intersection, and finally select the second intersecting object. Next, select an object to dimension the intersection point to.

◆ Apply General, Ordinate, and Baseline dimensions to spline endpoints.

◆ Apply General and Ordinate dimensions to the X and Y Min/Max points of a spline.

Most of these dimensions can be created with just one tool, the General Dimension tool.

GENERAL DIMENSIONS

Certification
Objective

You can find the General Dimension tool by clicking the Dimension button on the Annotate tab. This will be your primary dimensioning tool. It works like the Sketch Dimension tool in that this single tool can generate several different types of dimensions depending on the geometry you select.

Once geometry is selected, you can right-click to choose the applicable options for placing the type of geometry you've selected. You can also control snap options, arrowhead options, and leader options specific to each dimension type from the context menu.

For instance, once an arc is selected (not a full circle), a radius dimension is created by default, but prior to placement, you can right-click and choose Diameter, Angular, Angular Foreshortened Arc Length, Arc Length Foreshortened, or Chord Length from the Dimension Type flyout, as shown in Figure 12.18.

FIGURE 12.18
Arc dimension options

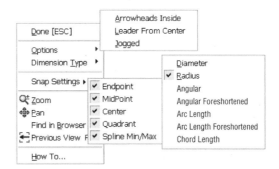

Prior to placing a linear dimension between two points or two parallel lines, you can create Linear Diameter, Linear Symmetric, or Linear Foreshortened dimensions by choosing from the dimension's context Dimension Type flyout.

These types of dimensions are used commonly with symmetrical parts, especially turned cylindrical parts. Figure 12.19 shows the Linear dimension options available when two points or two parallel lines have been selected.

FIGURE 12.19
Linear dimension options

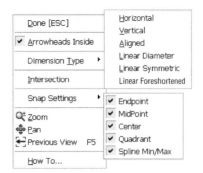

Prior to placing diameter dimensions, you can right-click and switch to a radius or change the leader options, as shown in Figure 12.20.

FIGURE 12.20

Diameter dimension options

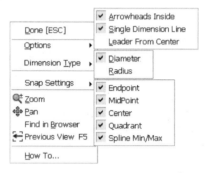

DIMENSION FILTERS

You can create and access selection filters by holding your Shift key down and right-clicking or by clicking the selection drop-down from the Quick Access bar at the top of the screen.

Selection filters specify the elements that can be selected when working in a drawing. For instance, if you choose the Detail selection filter, only objects common to detailing tasks are selectable, and items such as view boundaries, view labels, section view lines, and so on, are filtered out and cannot be selected.

If you choose Select All Inventor Dimensions, you can quickly select all the drawing dimensions and then use the Style drop-down menu to change them all to a different dimension style.

You can create a custom filter also by Shift+right-clicking and choosing Edit Select Filters.

RECOVERING MODEL DIMENSIONS

Another way to quickly add dimensions to your model views is to use the Retrieve Dimensions tool.

You can access this tool from the view's context menu or from the Annotate tab. This tool allows you to recover sketch and feature dimensions that were used to model your part and bring them into the drawing view. To recover model dimensions, follow these steps:

1. On the Annotate tab, click the Retrieve button.

2. Select the view you want to retrieve dimensions for.

3. You can choose to retrieve dimensions per feature or per part, depending on what makes sense. You might choose per part when working with an assembly view, for instance.

4. Select the features or parts in the graphics window. You can select multiple objects by holding down the Shift or Ctrl key as you select them. Or you can window-select the whole view.

5. When selected, the part or feature will display all the dimensions normal to the view. Click the Select Dimensions button to choose which dimensions to keep. Again, you can use a window selection to select them all.

6. Click the Apply button and then select another view to retrieve or click the OK button.

BE WARNED ABOUT MODEL DIMENSIONS

You should be aware that there are often dimensions required to model features that are not necessarily required or desired for use on a drawing. For example, if you were to recover model dimensions for View 7 in the file mi_12a_084.idw, you would see that the pocket is dimensioned from one end of the part and the holes are dimensioned from the other end. Not only is this poor practice since it requires the machinist to rezero the mill, but it can cause a tolerance stack-up.

Recovered model dimensions behave similarly to regular, placed dimensions with respect to editing and formatting. Recovered model dimensions cannot be detached or reattached from the geometry they're referencing.

Model dimension values can be directly edited from the drawing view, thus changing the model parameter value and affecting the size and shape of your model feature. Access the dimension value by selecting Edit Model Dimension from the dimension's context menu.

The ability to edit the model by changing model dimension values is turned on by default. To turn this feature off, go to Tools ➤ Application Options ➤ Drawing tab and uncheck Enable Part Modification From Within Drawings.

EXERCISE CAUTION WHEN EDITING MODEL DIMENSIONS

The option to enable edits of model dimension values from the drawing can be powerful and dangerous. Editing a model dimension from a drawing is a quick way to edit the size and shape of a model, but it is often blind to other issues it may create. For example, if a part is used in an assembly and another part references holes adaptively in that assembly, changing the model dimension may affect this second part without your knowledge. It is suggested that you always open the assembly to see what else your changes will affect.

Once a particular model dimension is recovered in one view, it cannot be recovered again in any other view in the same file. You can move recovered model dimensions between views, however, provided appropriate attachment points exist in the target view. To do this, right-click the dimension and choose Move Dimension.

BASELINE DIMENSIONS AND BASELINE DIMENSION SETS

Certification Objective

Baseline dimensions are a series of linear dimensions that terminate at a common point (or baseline). The Baseline Dimension and Baseline Dimension Set tools offer a mechanism to quickly add dimensions to a drawing view.

When you execute the Baseline Dimension tool, you're left with a series of conventional linear dimensions. This tool simply automates what you could do on your own with the General Dimension tool.

The Baseline Dimension Set tool, however, generates a collected group of linear dimensions that are edited and moved (through dragging and editing) as a single group.

To understand this more fully, open the file mi_12a_085.idw in the Chapter 12 directory of your Mastering Inventor 2016 folder and compare the two dimensioned views. The one on the left was done with the Baseline Dimension tool, and the one on the right was done with the Baseline Dimension Set tool.

Use the views on the bottom to create baseline dimensions. Start either tool, click the left vertical part edge (this will be the baseline), and then manually select or multiselect additional features (these can be model edges or hole centers).

When you've selected all the geometry you want to dimension, right-click, choose Continue, and click to place the dimensions (shown in Figure 12.21).

After you place the dimensions, you can continue to select points on the view (points on geometry rather than explicit geometry), or you can right-click and select Create.

FIGURE 12.21

Baseline dimensions

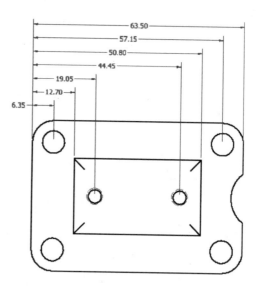

Once a baseline set is created, you can right-click any of the dimensions and choose from the options to add a member, delete a member, detach a member, and arrange the entire set.

You can also choose Make Origin to reset the base of the set. You can find the Baseline Dimension Set tool by clicking the small arrow next to the Baseline Dimension tool to reveal the drop-down list. You can close the file without saving.

CHAIN DIMENSIONS AND CHAIN DIMENSION SETS

Certification
Objective

Chain dimensions and chain dimension sets enable you to quickly select objects and then place a chain of dimensions from point to point along the selected direction.

To understand chain dimensions more fully, open the file mi_12a_092.idw in the Chapter 12 directory of your Mastering Inventor 2016 folder and compare the two dimensioned views.

The one on the top left was done with the Chain Dimension tool, and the one on the top right was done with the Chain Dimension Set tool.

Use the view on the bottom left to create chain dimensions.

1. From the Dimension panel of the Annotate tab, select Chain.

2. On the drawing, select the geometry to be dimensioned by clicking to select individual edges or by clicking and dragging a window from right to left to select multiple edges.

3. Right-click and select Continue.

4. Move your cursor to preview the placement and then click to set the direction.

5. When finished, right-click and select Create.

Use the Chain Dimension tool to select the baseline dimensions in the bottom-center view to convert them to chain dimensions.

1. From the Dimension panel of the Annotate tab, select Chain.

2. On the drawing, select all the baseline dimensions by clicking and dragging a window from right to left.

3. Right-click and select Continue.

4. Select the center marks for the two smaller holes to add additional dimensions.

5. Right-click and select Continue; then right-click and select Create.

Note that there appears to be a bit of a bug in the way the dimensions are arranged. To remedy this, use the Arrange button, as described here.

6. From the Dimension panel of the Annotate tab, select Arrange.

7. On the drawing, select all the chain dimensions you just created by clicking and dragging a window from right to left.

8. Right-click and choose Contour Entity.

9. Select the edge of the part (or optionally click anywhere to the right of the part).

Use the view on the bottom right to create a chain dimension set.

1. From the Dimension panel of the Annotate tab, select Chain Set from the Chain drop-down list.

2. On the drawing, select just the top and bottom edges of the part and any one of the holes.

3. Right-click and select Continue.

4. Move your cursor to preview the placement and then click to set the direction.

5. Select an additional hole to add to the set.

6. Right-click and select Create.

7. Add more members to the set by right-clicking the set and choosing Add Member.

8. Select all the geometry needed to complete the set so that it matches the top-right view and then right-click and choose Done.

9. Right-click any of the dimensions in the set and choose Delete Member.

Once you've experimented with the chain dimension options, you can close the file without saving changes.

ORDINATE DIMENSIONS AND ORDINATE DIMENSION SETS

Certification
Objective
Ordinate dimensions and ordinate dimension sets are created much the same way as baseline and chain dimensions and dimension sets. Again, a dimension set is managed and formatted as a single, selectable object (with some exceptions), whereas the Ordinate Dimension tool results in independently controlled dimensions.

Another key difference between ordinate dimensions and an ordinate dimension set is that you can have multiple ordinate sets on a single view with different origin points.

However, once you specify an origin for ordinate dimensions on a view, all ordinate dimensions placed on that view will reference that origin as well as any hole tables referencing that view. The reverse is true as well: once an origin is specified for a hole table, ordinate dimensions on that view share the origin.

CHANGING ORIGINS

You can set the origin for an ordinate dimension set after you have selected the geometry.

The default origin is the first selected geometry, but you can change it. This is powerful for updating a drawing.

For ordinate dimensions, you can click the origin indicator and drag it to a different endpoint, midpoint, or center point to change the geometry reference.

You can also hide the origin indicator by right-clicking it and then show it again by right-clicking any of the origin dimensions.

To understand this more fully, open the file mi_12a_099.idw in the Chapter 12 directory of your Mastering Inventor 2016 folder and compare the two dimensioned views.

The one on the left was done with the Ordinate Dimension tool, and the one on the right was done with the Ordinate Dimension Set tool.

Use the views on the bottom to create ordinate dimensions and ordinate dimensions sets matching the views at the top. Once they are created, explore the context menu options for the dimensions and the dimension set.

You can find the Ordinate Dimension Set tool by clicking the small arrow next to the Ordinate Dimension tool to reveal the drop-down list.

DIMENSIONS IN ISOMETRIC VIEWS

You may have been taught that dimensions should never be placed on isometric views. This is possibly because traditional detailing techniques do not allow an accurate dimension to be pulled from an isometric view.

Inventor can overcome this by pulling the intelligence from the physical model. When you use the General Dimension tool to add dimensions to an isometric view, the resulting dimensions are fundamentally different from those you place in orthographic views.

This is immediately noticeable when you see how the resulting dimensions are drawn on the sheet. All the dimension geometries (text, arrowheads, extension lines, and dimension lines) are drawn in 3D space and not in sheet space.

Dimensions generated on isometric views are called *true* (meaning they reflect the true model-space dimensional value).

Dimensions added to orthographic views are known as *projected* because the dimension value represents the calculated distance or angle between endpoints or geometry projected onto the sheet.

When placing an isometric dimension, Inventor tries to determine an appropriate annotation plane based on your geometry selection. In many cases, particularly with linear dimensions, multiple inferred annotation planes are available. Prior to placing the dimension, you can toggle through these inferred annotation planes by pressing the spacebar.

If none of the inferred work planes meets your needs, you can project the dimension either onto the sheet plane or onto a model work plane. For instance, oftentimes you will find that hole notes and leader dimensions such as radii and diameters look better placed on the sheet plane rather than in the isometric plane; therefore, you can right-click and choose Use Sheet Plane when placing them.

The change in dimension behavior (true vs. projected) happens automatically depending on the view orientation. Any projected isometric or base isometric view results in true dimensions. As a rule, newly added dimensions to a view are treated as true if none of the model's origin planes is parallel to the sheet (with the exception of auxiliary views). You can override this rule on a view-by-view basis by right-clicking a view and changing the dimension type (true or projected).

RETRIEVE DIMENSIONS FROM ISOMETRIC VIEWS

A quick way to place dimensions on an isometric view is to right-click the view and choose Retrieve Dimensions.

Isometric dimensions are functionally identical to orthographic dimensions; however, they cannot be "moved." That is, they cannot be detached and reattached to different geometry, and they can't be moved using the dimension Move option on the dimension's context menu. All formatting options and behavior are otherwise identical.

Although placing isometric dimensions may seem unconventional, you can, in fact, often eliminate the number of views required to concisely communicate the design by placing dimensions on an isometric view. Try adding dimensions to the isometric view in `mi_12a_105.idw`, as shown in Figure 12.22.

FIGURE 12.22

Isometric view dimensions

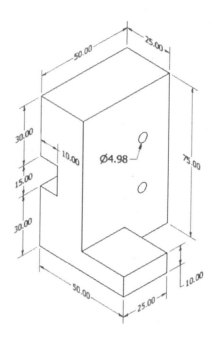

FORMATTING AND EDITING DIMENSIONS

All the different types of dimensions discussed in this section are initially formatted by an associative dimension style. Indeed, each different type of dimension can be set to use a different dimension style if needed.

Almost every formatting option available for dimensions is set through the dimension style. There are dozens of individual style settings—too many to list here. To learn how to change dimension formatting through styles, in the following steps, you'll walk through setting up a new dimension style to apply a symmetrical tolerance:

1. On the Get Started tab, click the Open button.

2. Browse for mi_12a_107.idw in the Chapter 12 directory of your Mastering Inventor 2016 folder and click the Open button.

3. On the Manage tab ➤ Styles And Standards panel, click the Styles Editor button.

4. In the Style And Standard Editor, expand the Dimension node on the left side and click the Default–mm (ANSI) dimension style.

5. Click the New button along the top, thus creating a new style based on the Default–mm (ANSI) style. You can also right-click the dimension style you want to start from and choose New Style.

6. Enter **PM1** for the dimension name and click the OK button.

7. Click the Tolerance tab and set the Method drop-down to Symmetric.

8. Enter **0.100** for the Upper value field and then set Linear Precision to three places, as shown in Figure 12.23.

FIGURE 12.23
Dimension style tolerance settings

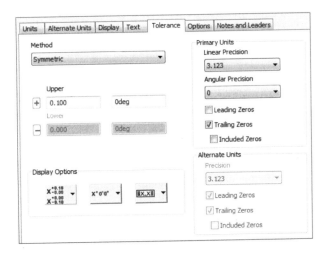

9. Select the Units tab and change the Linear Precision setting to three places (3.123).

10. Click the Save button along the top and click Done to close the Style And Standard Editor dialog box.

11. Apply this dimension style to the existing dimensions on the sheet by first selecting them and then selecting the Annotate tab and choosing PM1 from the Style drop-down (found just under the Layer drop-down to the top right of the screen). The selected dimensions will immediately update to reflect the new style assignment.

CREATING DIMENSION STYLES

It is a good idea to create all your standard dimension styles before rolling out your style library. By creating standards for all users to use, you eliminate any discrepancy that comes from multiple users all trying to create drawings that look the same.

You can create all your decimal-place dimensions (one place, two place, three place, and so on), toleranced dimensions, and even dowel-pinhole-toleranced dimension styles that users need only select.

---

12. Double-click the 25 mm dimension to edit it and click the Precision And Tolerance tab. The ±0.100 tolerance setting is reflected here in the Edit dialog box. Change the tolerance value to **±0.200** and then click the OK button.

You've now created two formatting overrides for the 25 mm dimension. You have overridden the standard dimension style assignment by setting it to a dimension style other than the By Standard style, and you then set a tolerance override. In addition to making style-level formatting changes to dimensions, you can copy and paste dimension formatting between dimension objects on your sheet.

13. Right-click the 25 mm dimension you just edited and select Copy Properties.

14. Click the 30 mm dimension. It will adopt both the style formatting and the local tolerance value override from your source dimension.

You can configure which properties are copied before selecting the target dimension by right-clicking and selecting Settings after invoking the Copy Properties tool.

To edit a dimension's style, right-click the object and choose Edit Dimension Style, which will take you right into the Style and Standard Editor and highlight the dimension style. You can do this with just about any annotation object. You can close the file without saving.

Hole and Thread Notes

A hole note differs from a traditional diameter dimension by calling out feature information beyond just the hole diameter. The Hole/Thread Notes command (in the Feature Notes panel) generates a leadered note that displays all pertinent hole feature information derived from the hole edge that is selected.

For example, a hole note pointing to a simple blind hole might appear as 10 × 20. A hole note pointing to a through partial-tapped hole might appear as 10–32 UNF-2B × 20.00. Inventor provides you with the ability to tailor the exact contents of the hole note through your dimension style.

You can use the hole note in mi_12a_109.idw to explore the following options.

Use the Hole/Thread Notes tool to add a single note for the mounting hole and tapped hole in the faceplate front view. You can configure hole notes to display whatever string of description text you prefer, as well as set the various hole parameter values' Precision and Tolerance settings. These preferences are set and stored in the dimension style.

You can configure more than 50 types of holes in this interface; they generally correspond to the different kinds of holes you can create using the Hole feature tool in part and assembly modeling ("holes" as a result of circular-extruded cuts, voids, or circular sheet-metal cut features are also recognized by hole notes).

You can configure hole notes to display the hole quantity as part of the note. You can add a quantity note either directly on an individual note through the Edit Hole Note dialog box (right-click a hole note and choose Edit Hole Note) or at the style level (right-click a hole note and choose Edit Dimension style) so they appear for all holes of the same type.

To add a quantity note at the style level, make sure you're editing the dimension style associated with the hole notes on your drawing (the best way to ensure this is to right-click the hole note and choose Edit Dimension Style).

Select Blind – Depth Thread in the Note Format drop-down and then click in the text field so that the cursor is in front of the note text; finally, click the button with the # sign on it. This inserts the <QTYNOTE> variable token in front of the note, as shown in Figure 12.24.

You can customize the quantity note by clicking the Edit Quantity Note button on the dimension style's Notes And Leaders tab, as shown at the bottom left of Figure 12.24. By default, the quantity note is set up as a prefix to the full hole note (2 ×).

This dialog box also lets you set how the hole quantity is determined (either the number of holes in a feature or pattern or a complete evaluation of identical holes in a view where all the hole axes are normal to the view).

As soon as you save the changes to your dimension style, you should see the hole note for the tapped holes update to include the quantity of holes (2 ×).

FIGURE 12.24

Hole note settings in dimension style

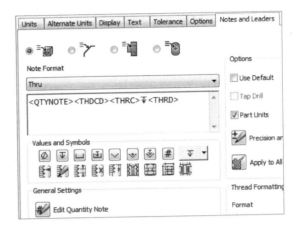

The dimension style's Notes And Leaders tab also enables you to preconfigure other kinds of feature notes, including chamfer notes (which are actually calculated notes and not feature-dependent), punch notes, and bend notes (the latter two of which are available only for views of sheet-metal parts).

Leadered Symbols

Many of the annotations you can apply to a drawing belong to a common class of annotations often referred to as *leadered symbols*.

These are all grouped together in the Drawing Annotation panel: Surface Texture Symbol, Welding Symbol, Feature Control Frame, Feature ID Symbol, Datum ID Symbol, and five different Datum Target tools. Each of these is created the same way, and each is formatted with its own dedicated style.

In the following steps, you will walk through an exercise that involves adding geometric dimensioning and tolerancing symbols to a drawing of a faceplate:

1. On the Get Started tab, click the Open button.

2. Browse for `mi_12a_109.idw` in the `Chapter 12` directory of your `Mastering Inventor 2016` folder and click the Open button.

3. On the Annotate tab, use the drop-down on the Symbols panel and click the Datum Identifier Symbol button.

4. Click the far-right edge of the part and drag the leader to the desired length.

5. Click the screen to set the leader and then right-click and choose Continue.

6. Accept the default A value in the text editor and click the OK button.

7. Click the bottom edge to add a second datum ID (B), but rather than placing a leader, right-click and choose Continue immediately after clicking the initial part edge point. You can do this with most Inventor leader features.

8. On the Annotate tab, use the drop-down on the Symbols panel and choose the Feature Control Frame button.

9. Rather than attaching the frame to the part, attach the frame to the hole note. Hover over the hole note text until you see the bottom green dot appear and then click.

10. A leader will appear between the frame and the hole note text. Right-click and choose Continue to place the frame without a leader. This will attach the frame to the dimension text.

11. Fill out the appropriate fields for a positional tolerance relative to the A datum and the B datum, as shown in Figure 12.25; then click the OK button.

FIGURE 12.25

Feature control frame attached to hole note

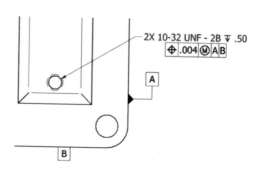

Drawing Text

You can add text to your drawing in multiple ways. The Text tool (on the Annotate tab) is used to create general drawing notes. This kind of text is limited because it can't be associated (constrained) to a drawing view and because it offers no control over which component iProperties and parameters are being accessed when you have multiple components detailed on the same sheet.

In addition to using the Text tool, you can use the Leader Text tool (also on the Annotate tab), which can be associated to a view or a component, allowing you to extract and display iProperty and model parameter values from the component to which the leader is attached.

If view associativity is required but you don't want a leader, you can right-click the leader text and choose Delete Leader.

Each of these tools utilizes the generic Format Text dialog box. This dialog box is used to edit any text-specific annotations as well as annotations such as hole tags and datum and feature IDs.

The general text formatting for any drawing annotation containing text ultimately comes from a text style. Text style formatting (size, font, color, and so on) can be overwritten in the Format Text dialog box.

General Tables

You can create a table on a drawing sheet by using the General Table tool on the Annotate tab (the button is located on the Table panel and is called General).

When you click the General button, you are presented with the Table dialog. You can create an empty table and then add information, or you can choose a data source from which to populate the table.

iParts and iAssemblies   These can be used to create tabulated configuration tables. For instance, you might have an iPart bracket in six different lengths. You could select the iPart file to use as the table data source and then place a table with a row for each of the six lengths listed by their part numbers. You would choose the Length parameter to use as the column, and each row would be populated with the appropriate length value, as defined in the iPart. You can then place a view of one of the brackets and edit the dimension to read Length rather than the numeric value.

Sheet-Metal Parts   These parts can be used to create bend tables. Selecting an existing flat pattern view as the data source allows you to choose the parameters you want to use in the bend table and then place a table indexing the bends on the flat pattern. Bend ID numbers are automatically placed on the flat pattern view. Editing the bend ID in the table updates the ID number on the flat pattern. Editing the table overrides the bend order annotation of the part file; therefore, it is typically best to use the Bend Order Annotation tool in the sheet-metal part to set the order.

XLS Files   You can link an Excel spreadsheet file to a general table. Use the General Table tool and select the XLS file to place the table on the drawing sheet and link to the original file.

- To update the table, right-click it in the browser and choose Edit to open the XLS file. If the XLS file is linked, you can edit it outside of Inventor and right-click to choose Update to bring in the changes.

- To point the table to a different XLS file, expand the 3rd Party folder, right-click the table link, and choose Change Source. Be aware that there are limitations to the number of rows you can have using this method. Also note that blank rows in the XLS file will be read as the end of the table.

SPLITTING TABLES

If your table has a large number of rows, it might be too long to fit on the drawing sheet. In these cases you can split the table.

To do so, click text in the row where you want to split the table and then right-click and choose Table ➤ Split Table. You can split a table into multiple sections by using the Split Table option on a previously split table. Be sure to select text in the table row and not the table line before you right-click; otherwise, the Split Table option will be grayed out.

Once the table is split, you can drag the sections into place on the sheet as needed. In the browser you'll see the split section nested under the original table node.

You can move the split table to another sheet by clicking and dragging on it in the browser and dropping it on the browser node of another sheet.

To rejoin the table, you can right-click the browser node or the actual table and choose Table ➤ Un-split Table. Changes to the original table section are applied to all split sections; however, changes applied to a split section are applied to it alone.

You can use the Split Table option on general tables, parts list tables, revision tables, and hole tables.

Hole Tables

You can document hole descriptions, quantities, and locations on a view by using a hole table rather than using hole notes. Indeed, you can use the hole table to document not only hole features but sheet-metal punches as well.

You can even use a hole table to call out locations of recovered work points in your model. This technique can be used to detail specialized features such as slots and bosses.

Hole tables, like most types of annotation in Inventor, are initially formatted by an associative style—a Hole Table style in this case.

The Hole Table style enables you to select which columns you want displayed in your table, format precision and units for the X and Y location columns, change line formatting, filter on different hole types, and configure various grouping mechanisms depending on your needs.

Everything about the hole table is formatted by the Hole Table style except for the description string for the hole. The description string uses the same configuration as your hole notes and receives this particular formatting by the hole tag's dimension style (hole tags are created with the hole table and are formatted by a dimension style).

In the following steps, you'll walk through setting up a Hole Table style and creating a hole table for the faceplate:

1. On the Get Started tab, click the Open button.

2. Browse for `mi_12a_111.idw` in the Chapter 12 directory of your Mastering Inventor 2016 folder and click the Open button.

3. On the Manage tab, click the Styles Editor button.

4. In the left pane of the Styles Editor, expand the hole table node, and click the style named Hole Table–mm (ANSI). The right pane will update to show the settings for this style, as shown in Figure 12.26.

FIGURE 12.26
Hole Table Style dialog box

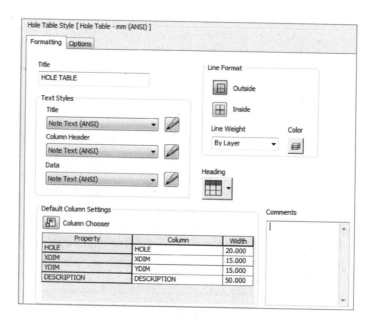

5. At the top of the right pane, click the New button and set the name of the new hole table style to **HT_02**; then click OK.

6. Click the Column Chooser button and select the Quantity property on the left of the resulting property list.

7. Click the Add button to add it to the included list of columns on the right.

8. Use the Move Up button to move the Quantity column up in the list as you like; then click the OK button.

9. Right-click the XDIM property in the Default Column Settings frame and select Format Column.

10. In the Format Column dialog box, change the precision to three places and change the column heading to X LOCATION. Note that you can format columns in this manner in almost all the annotation tables, such as parts lists, and so on.

11. Click the OK button and repeat for the YDIM column.

12. Click the Save button to save the changes and exit the Style And Standard Editor dialog box by clicking the Done button.

You will now need to place a hole table on the drawing. Three hole table variations are available on the Table panel of the Annotate tab.

Selection   This option allows you to select the holes you want to include in the table, and then only those holes are included.

View   This option documents all holes in a view, although you can use filters to exclude certain hole types. As holes are added to the part, the hole table updates to include them.

Features   This option allows you to select an instance of the types of holes you want to include in the table, and then all holes of that type are included.

To continue this exercise, you'll choose to place a hole table using the View method.

1. On the Annotate tab, select the Hole drop-down on the Table panel and choose Hole View.

2. Select the view on the sheet.

3. Next, you need to place the origin on the view. You can click any edge or vertex of the part, or you can project the edges to find the apparent intersection of the lower-left corner.

4. To place a table using the table style you created, choose HT_02 from the Style drop-down at the top right of the screen.

5. Click the screen to set the hole table on the sheet.

FINDING A CORNER INTERSECTION

To find an apparent intersection for placement of an origin marker, zoom into the lower-left corner of the part. Then scrub your mouse pointer over the vertical and horizontal edges of the part and bring it to the apparent intersection; you should see the edge projected down and over and see a yellow dot at the intersection. When you do, click the dot to set the origin at that point. Be sure you run over the edges (lines) and not just the endpoints of the edges.

For each hole in the view, a hole tag is placed next to the hole edge, and a corresponding row is generated in the hole table.

Notice that because each hole is called out individually in this table, each row has a quantity of 1 (shown in Figure 12.27).

FIGURE 12.27

The hole table generated for the face plate

HOLE TABLE				
HOLE	QUANTITY	X LOCATION	Y LOCATION	DESCRIPTION
A1	1	6.35	6.35	⌀.27 ▽ .75
A2	1	38.10	6.35	⌀.27 ▽ .75
A3	1	6.35	57.15	⌀.27 ▽ .75
A4	1	38.10	57.15	⌀.27 ▽ .75
B1	1	22.23	19.05	10-32 UNF - 2B ▽ .50
B2	1	22.23	44.45	10-32 UNF - 2B ▽ .50

Edit the hole table by right-clicking it and choosing Edit Hole Table. From there, you can set the table to roll up all A-type holes and all B-type holes from the Options tab by selecting the Rollup radio button. Click OK when you are finished.

You can also edit the Tag, Note, or Description text by right-clicking the text in the table. You can make direct overrides to hole descriptions by double-clicking the description text, and you can override X and Y location precision by right-clicking an individual cell.

You can access several other options by right-clicking the text in the table as well, so be certain to explore them all. When finished, you can close the file without saving changes.

HOLE TABLES SAVE TIME ON LARGE PARTS

For large plates with many different holes, hole tables are wonderful. A large plate could take a half hour or more to fully dimension. Furthermore, it's often difficult for a machinist to tell where all five of the same holes are located if they are not all called out individually. The hole table gives the machinist X and Y locations of the holes that they can use to program their CNC milling machine extraordinarily quickly. Don't be surprised if the machinist asks you to dimension all your parts using hole tables.

Annotating Assembly Drawings

Creating/annotating drawing views of assemblies is similar to doing so for parts.

All the same views and annotation tools discussed in the previous sections can be executed when working with assembly and presentation models.

When creating views of assemblies, you will typically create parts lists and balloons and may need to control reference parts, interference edges, and assembly representations.

These subjects and others dealing specifically with assembly files are covered in the following sections.

Assembly Representations

The view options available for assembly views are among the most significant differences between part and assembly model views. When an assembly file is referenced in the base view, representation options become available on the Component tab of the Drawing View dialog box. These controls allow you to specify which assembly view, positional, or level-of-detail (LOD) representation is displayed in the resulting drawing view.

View representations can optionally be made associative to the view (using the check box at the top of the View Representation control). Specifically, an associative view representation means that as a component's visibility is changed in the assembly, the change is witnessed in the drawing view as well.

If the associative option is deselected, you can toggle component visibility from the drawing itself by expanding the view node in the browser, expanding the model tree on the view node, and then right-clicking a component and choosing Visibility.

If the Visibility option is grayed out, the view is associative, and the component visibility is being controlled in the assembly.

MAKING YOUR VIEWS ASSOCIATIVE

Most of the time you will want to make your views associative. If you do not, you'll be scratching your head trying to figure out why the drawing view is not matching your view representation.

Recall the general definitions of each assembly representation type.

View Representations   These control component visibility, color overrides, and parts list filters.

Positional Representations   These show an assembly in different physical positions.

Level-of-Detail Representations   These control visibility and manage memory consumption by suppressing components.

In the next several steps, you will edit a view of an assembly to see how to use assembly representations in drawing views:

1. On the Get Started tab, click the Open button.

2. Browse for mi_12a_115.idw in the Chapter 12 directory of your Mastering Inventor 2016 folder and click the Open button.

3. In the browser, expand the Sheet1 node to reveal the node for each existing view.

4. Expand the Main View node to reveal the assembly node and then expand the assembly node to reveal the parts tree.

5. Right-click the view called Main View and choose Edit View to examine the view options dealing with representations. Notice the different representations, as shown in Figure 12.28.

FIGURE 12.28
Assembly base
view creation

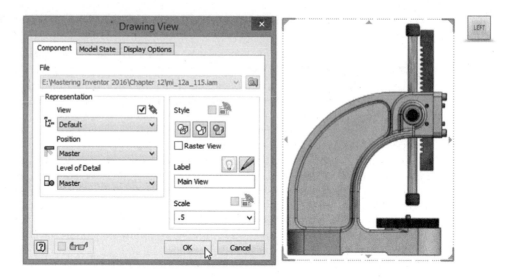

6. In the View area, choose the view representation named Frame And Ram and then click the OK button.

You'll notice that all the parts are gone now except the frame and ram. This was set up in the assembly by toggling the visibility state off for all the other parts and then saving the view configuration as a view representation. Examining the browser, you'll see that the parts set to not be visible are grayed out.

7. Right-click the view called Main View and choose Edit View again.

8. In the Level Of Detail area, choose the representation named Handle And Ram and then click the OK button.

You'll note that only the ram remains onscreen. This is because you have the view set to use two different representations at once. In the view representation, the visibility is turned off for everything but the frame and ram, but the frame was suppressed in the level of detail. Examining the browser, you'll see that suppressed parts are not listed.

Typically, it's best not to use these two representations together because it can be confusing as to what is being controlled where. However, there are times when this is the best way to achieve the desired results.

9. Right-click the view called Main View and choose Edit View once again.

10. Set the view representation to Master and set the positional representation to Closed (leave the LOD as is); then click the OK button.

You'll see that now just the handle, shaft, and ram parts are shown (because of the LOD representation), and the positional representation is controlling the positions of these parts.

11. Right-click the view called Main View and choose Edit View once more.

12. Set the view representation to Default and click the Associative check box button (it looks like a chain link).

13. Set the LOD representation to Master and then click the OK button.

14. In the browser, right-click the Arbor Frame node and notice that the Visibility option is grayed out.

15. Right-click the Main View node and choose Edit View one more time.

16. Uncheck the Associative check box button and then click the OK button.

17. In the browser, right-click the Arbor Frame node and notice that the Visibility option is now available.

18. Click Visibility to toggle it off and notice that the frame is removed from the view.

You are now controlling component visibility at the drawing level rather than using the assembly view representation's visibility controls.

You can continue experimenting with the representation options and then close the file without saving changes.

OPEN ASSEMBLY DRAWINGS WITH THE FAST OPEN OPTION

When you select a drawing file to open in the Open dialog box, you can then click the Options button and select the Fast Open option to open the drawing quickly.

When the Fast Open option is selected, Inventor skips all the model file references, making no attempt to find the referenced files. Once the drawing is open, the drawing behavior is that of a drawing that had been opened with no file references found. You can make changes to the drawing such as text notes, and so on, and then save the changes.

If you'd like to make the file references live once it is open, you can click the top-level node in the browser and choose Resolve File.

Reference Data in Drawing Views

Part and assemblies can have their BOM value set to Reference. You can apply this attribute as a document setting on the part or assembly file itself or on a per-instance basis when it's placed in a higher-level assembly.

In addition to being omitted from the assembly mass property calculations, BOM, and subsequent drawing-parts lists, reference components are drawn and calculated differently in assembly drawing views.

By default, all reference component edges are mapped to a unique layer with a broken line style (double-dash chain). Hidden-line calculation, by default, is run separately for reference components and non-reference components.

Finally, reference components do not affect the calculation of the drawing boundary. This means that if you have a reference component well apart from nonreference parts in an assembly, it may not be visible in a drawing view until you increase the reference margin.

To explore these settings, you can open the file mi_12a_117.idw in the Chapter 12 directory of your Mastering Inventor 2016 folder and compare the two views.

The view on the left shows the reference part at the default settings.

The view on the right has been adjusted to show the reference part as a standard part.

Right-click the view and choose Edit to adjust all the reference data view behaviors on the Model State tab of the Drawing View dialog box. Figure 12.29 shows the default settings.

Close without saving when you are finished exploring.

FIGURE 12.29
Reference data settings

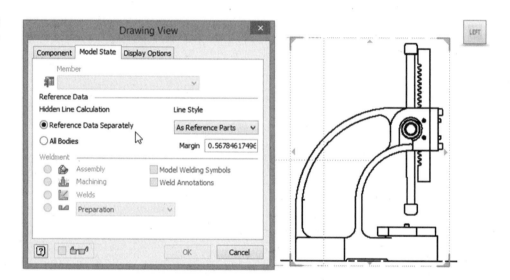

Interference and Tangent Edge Display

As you place and constrain components in an assembly file, it may be necessary to create an interference condition between parts.

This is common for press-fit conditions such as pins in undersized holes. This condition is common in Inventor even when you have a threaded fastener being inserted into an equal-diameter threaded hole. These edges are designated as interference edges and can be turned on or off as needed.

You can also control the display of tangent edges for cylindrical faces, fillet edges, and so on, in your drawing views. Both tangent and interference edges can be enabled by editing the view and selecting the Interference Edge check box on the Display Options tab.

Figure 12.30 shows the difference between two views with these edges turned off and turned on. The interference edge in this case is the small set screw in the middle of the plate. All other differences are tangent edges.

FIGURE 12.30
Tangent and
Interference edges

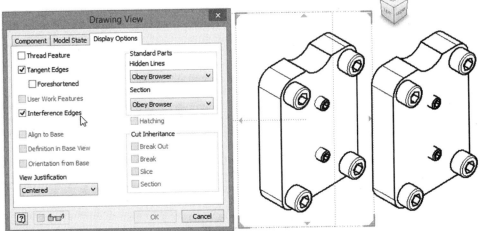

Parts Lists

A parts list is a formatted report of the assembly bill of materials placed on the drawing in a table.

Most of the data you see in a parts list comes ultimately from the assembly BOM, but the BOM and the parts list are managed separately inside Inventor, providing control and flexibility for managing both.

Parts lists have a dedicated formatting style that provides dozens of formatting variations. In the following steps, you'll walk through a typical parts-list editing and creation workflow to see what kind of capabilities can be leveraged in the parts lists:

1. On the Get Started tab, click the Open button.

2. Browse for `mi_12a_119.idw` in the `Chapter 12` directory of your `Mastering Inventor 2016` folder and click the Open button.

3. On the Manage tab, click the Styles Editor button, expand the Parts List node, and click the style named MI_PL_02.

4. Click the Column Chooser button and add the Material property from the list on the left. Then click the OK button.

5. Click the Heading button and change the placement to Bottom.

6. Save your changes and exit the Style And Standard Editor dialog box using the Done button.

7. On the Annotate tab, click the Parts List button.

The Parts List dialog box allows you to either click an assembly or presentation drawing view or browse directly to an assembly or presentation file (you can create a parts list on a drawing with no drawing views). You can choose either a structured (first or all levels) or parts-only parts list. If the parts list is too long for the sheet size you're placing it on, you can also enable the option to wrap the parts list based on a specified number of rows.

8. Click the view on the sheet, and ensure that Structured is selected for the BOM view type and the Direction To Wrap Table option is set to Right. Click the OK button and then snap the parts lists to the lower-left corner of the drawing border.

Although you can specify the default column width at the style level, you may need to adjust the width based on the length of the text strings read in from the component iProperties. You can adjust column width by clicking and dragging the vertical column lines on the parts list on your sheet.

9. Resize the Material column on the parts list to better accommodate the long description text.

The initial item numbering for the components and the row order come from the last saved state of the assembly BOM but can be changed by editing the parts list.

10. Double-click the parts list to launch the Parts List dialog box (or right-click and choose Edit).

11. Click the Sort button, sort by part number in descending order, and then click the OK button.

12. Click the Renumber Items button and notice how new item numbers are assigned based on the sort order.The new item numbers appear blue and bold in the Parts List dialog box to indicate that they do not match the BOM. Changes you make to any of the cells in the Parts List dialog box (except for custom rows or custom columns) are treated as overrides to the BOM data. However, only item number overrides can be written back to the BOM. All other overrides are preserved at the parts-list level, allowing for greater flexibility of parts-list edits at the drawing level without worries that they will be discarded if updated in the BOM. Item number changes can be saved to the assembly BOM cell by cell from the context menu or for the entire parts list in one of three ways.

 ◆ While editing the parts list, click the Save Item Overrides To BOM button along the top.

 ◆ Right-click the parts list itself on the sheet and choose Save Item Overrides To BOM.

 ◆ Right-click the Parts List browser node and choose Save Item Overrides To BOM.

If you intend for the overrides of properties other than the item numbers to match in both the BOM and the parts list, you should make those edits in the BOM, where they will push through to the parts list. You can access the BOM quickly by right-clicking the parts list and choosing Bill Of Materials. Edits made in the BOM editor are written back to component iProperties and, therefore, push through to the parts list, provided no parts list overrides have already been made.

13. Click the OK button to apply the changes and exit the Parts List dialog box.

14. Right-click the drawing view and choose Edit View.

15. Set the view representation to Frame And Ram and then click the OK button.

Notice that the parts list still displays the full assembly even though the view now shows only the frame and ram parts. To set the two to coincide, you will apply a parts list filter.

16. Edit the parts list and click the Filter Settings button, found along the top of the Parts List dialog box.

17. From the Define Filter Item drop-down box, select Assembly View Representation.

18. Choose Frame And Ram from the drop-down box and then click the green check mark. Then click the OK button to apply the filter.

19. Click the OK button in the Parts List dialog box.

You'll see the parts list update to show only the parts corresponding to the view representation.

The parts list is not directly associated with any drawing view (if you choose a view when you create the parts list, it acts only as a pointer to the assembly file itself).

You can close the file without saving changes. In the next section, you'll explore balloons.

AUTOSORT AND UPDATE PARTS LISTS

When sorting a parts list, you can use the Auto Sort On Update option to maintain the sort order even when future parts are added to the assembly file.

Balloons

Certification
Objective

Assembly drawing views are related to parts lists by ballooning the components in the assembly drawing view.

Balloons are perhaps the only type of annotation relevant for assembly views. By default, balloons are set to display just a component's assigned item number, but through changes to the balloon style, a balloon can be configured to display any component iProperty or BOM property.

You'll learn how to create and edit balloon styles in "Editing Styles and Standards" later in this chapter.

You should know that only items visible in a view can be selected for placing a balloon; however, you can string multiple balloons together on a single leader, including parts that are not visible, virtual parts, and even line items added to the parts list that do not exist in the assembly BOM. This is also a common technique when ballooning a collection of hardware such as a screw, lock washer, and split washer.

Follow these steps to explore methods and options for balloon placement:

1. On the Get Started tab, click the Open button.

2. Browse for `mi_12a_120.idw` in the `Chapter 12` directory of your `Mastering Inventor 2016` folder and click the Open button.

3. On the Annotate tab, click the Balloon button. Select the cap on the end of the handle, drag out and click to place the balloon on the sheet, right-click and choose Continue, and then right-click again and choose Cancel.

4. Right-click the balloon and select Attach Balloon.

5. Click the lever arm. The balloon for the lever arm is shown attached to the handle cap's balloon (Figure 12.31). Move your mouse pointer around the balloon to set the position of the attached balloon (above, below, or next to the original balloon) and then click to place it.

FIGURE 12.31
Attached balloons

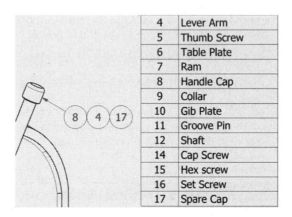

4	Lever Arm
5	Thumb Screw
6	Table Plate
7	Ram
8	Handle Cap
9	Collar
10	Gib Plate
11	Groove Pin
12	Shaft
14	Cap Screw
15	Hex screw
16	Set Screw
17	Spare Cap

6. Right-click the balloon and select Attach Balloon From List.

7. Select the box next to Spare Cap and click the OK button. The spare cap is a custom part that has been added only to the parts list in the drawing and doesn't appear in the assembly BOM.

Balloons can be added one at a time, or you can use the Auto Balloon tool (under the Balloon flyout) to quickly add multiple balloons to a drawing view.

8. Click the drop-down on the Balloon button and select Auto Balloon.

9. Select the view on the sheet and then window-select all the components in the view.

10. Click the Select Placement button and change the placement options to Around. Move your mouse pointer around the sheet to see how the preview graphics update.

11. Set the placement option to Horizontal, click to place the balloons above the assembly, and then click the OK button.

Here are some tips for working with balloons:

◆ Click a balloon center to reposition it onscreen.

◆ Click the leader end point and drag it off the part edge and onto a part face if using the edge does not make clear what part is being specified.

◆ Be aware that items are not updated in balloon contents when they're not attached to an edge, so if you pull a balloon from the edge of item 1 and place it on the face of item 2, the balloon will still read *item 1*.

◆ Unattached balloons will be floating and will not move with the view.

◆ You can re-associate balloons from one part to another part by dragging the arrowhead from one part edge to the edge of a different part.

◆ Balloons not attached to an edge use an alternative leader style (most often a dot). You can specify a different default alternative leader style in the balloon style.

◆ If you right-click a balloon and choose Edit Balloon or double-click anywhere on the balloon, you can change the item number and have it update the part list. Or, you can type in an override, and it will not update the parts list.

◆ If you right-click a balloon leader, you can choose Attach Text To Leader and add text along the leader line.

◆ You can window-select multiple balloons, and on the right-click Align menu you can choose Vertical, Horizontal, Vertical Offset, Horizontal Offset, or To Edge to align them to a selected view edge.

◆ If you right-click a balloon leader, you can choose Add Vertex/Leader to and connect more parts to it.

◆ In the parts list filer you can specify Ballooned Items Only, and as soon as you start adding balloons, the referenced parts will be added to the table.

Explore the balloon options and then close the file without saving changes.

Center of Gravity Display

You can display the center of gravity (COG) of a part or assembly in a drawing view as a center mark. Only one COG can be shown per view, with the exception of overlay views. Using a drawing containing an overlay view, you will take a look at displaying the COG marker in a drawing to show the change in the COG between the two overlaid positional representations.

1. On the Get Started tab, click the Open button.

2. Browse for mi_12a_123.idw in the Chapter 12 directory of your Mastering Inventor 2016 folder and click the Open button.

3. Expand the sheet node in the browser and locate the Base View node and expand it.

4. Right-click the mi_12a_115 assembly icon and select Center Of Gravity.

Doing so recalculates the model's center of gravity (it does not read the value in from the model's physical properties) and draws a center mark at the calculated location.

5. Locate the overlay node in the browser and expand it.

6. Right-click the mi_12a_115 assembly icon listed in the overlay tree and select Center Of Gravity.

7. Finally, dimension the location of these center marks relative to the bottom-right corner of the Arbor Press frame.

8. Double-click to edit one of these dimensions and add **(COG)** as a suffix to the dimension value on the Text tab of the Edit Dimension dialog box.

9. Right-click the dimension and use the Copy Properties option to copy this appended text to the other COG dimensions, as shown in Figure 12.32.

FIGURE 12.32
Overlay view with
recovered COG

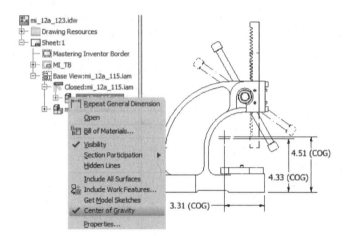

Close the file without saving when you are finished.

Working with Sheet-Metal Drawings

Drawing views of sheet-metal parts offer some unique options beyond those normally available for conventional part files.

Among these are the inclusion of bend notes, bend lines, punch notes, and bend tables, as well as the creation of flat pattern views.

Flat Pattern Views

Certification
Objective

When a sheet-metal part file has a flat pattern definition, you can create a drawing view of the folded model or the flat pattern.

You can include both views, but you need a separate base view in the drawing for each model view to do so.

To take a look at these options, follow these steps to create a flat pattern drawing view to start off:

1. On the Get Started tab, click the Open button.

2. Browse for mi_12a_130.idw in the Chapter 12 directory of your Mastering Inventor 2016 folder and click the Open button.

3. Right-click the existing isometric view and choose Open to open the model file.

4. Take a look at the model and note that this file has been created using the sheet-metal tools discussed in Chapter 6, "Sheet Metal," and that a flat pattern has been generated in the model.

5. Use the file tabs at the bottom of the screen to switch back to the drawing file (or press Ctrl+Tab).

6. On the Place Views tab, click the Base View button.

7. Ensure that the component listed in the File drop-down is `mi_12a_130.ipt`.

8. On the Component tab in the Drawing View dialog box, select the Flat Pattern option as well as the recover Punch Center option, set the scale to fit that sheet, and then place the view of the flat pattern on the sheet.

Leave this file open because you will use it in the following pages.

Bend Centerlines and Extents

**Certification
Objective**

Bend centerlines are drawn on sheet-metal flat pattern views where the center of the bend is located on the material face.

Inventor tracks negative and positive bend centerlines independently of one another to enable users to apply different line formatting for these two conditions.

This has already been done in `mi_12a_130.idw`, but it should be noted that the default behavior is to have both positive and negative bend lines placed on the same layer.

If you want to separate them, simply create a new layer called Bend Centerline (negative); then under Object Defaults in the Style And Standards Editor, assign Sheet Metal Bend Centerline (+) and (-) to the appropriate layers.

Lines representing bend extents can be enabled by right-clicking the flat pattern view, choosing Edit View, selecting the Component tab, and selecting the Bend Extents option.

Bend and Punch Notes

**Certification
Objective**

You'll find two sheet-metal-specific annotation tools on the Annotate tab: Bend Notes and Punch Notes.

Bend notes are placed on bend centerlines in sheet-metal flat pattern views and can convey information about the bending operation, including the bend radius, direction, angle, and K-factor.

To place bend and punch notes, continue working with the `mi_12a_130.idw` file or open this file and activate Sheet2 to pick up from this point.

1. Click the Bend button on the Feature Notes panel of the Annotate tab.

2. Click one of the bend centerlines in the drawing view to place a single note.

3. To place the rest of the bend notes, window-select the entire view. This tool looks only for bend centerlines, so you needn't be concerned about unintentionally selecting regular model edges.

By default, the bend notes are drawn adjacent to the bend centerlines, but where the note may be obscured in the view, you can drag individual bend notes to flip them to the opposite side of the bend centerline, or you can drag away from the bend centerline, and a leader will be generated back to the bend centerline.

Try this with the two outermost bend notes on the electrical-box flat pattern view (shown in Figure 12.33).

The style formatting and direct editing of bend notes is identical to formatting and editing hole notes. You can preconfigure the contents of the note with the note's dimension style by adding one or more variable tokens for the bend note attributes.

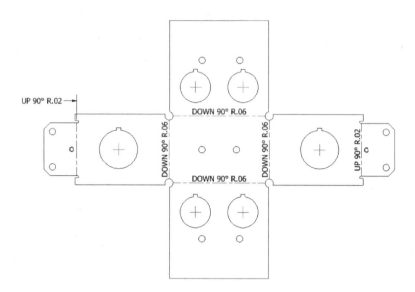

FIGURE 12.33
Bend notes in flat
pattern view

Punch notes are used to convey information about sheet-metal punch features (a special kind of iFeature). Punch notes can be applied only to flat pattern views of sheet-metal parts. They can be attached to recovered punch centers (shown as center marks in the flat pattern drawing) or on any model edge generated by the punch.

Punch notes can be configured to display the punch identifier (defined as part of the iFeature definition), the punch angle, the depth, and the direction. Punch notes are likewise formatted through dimension styles and have a similar editing interface to hole notes.

Bend Tables

Bend information can alternatively be displayed in a table rather than a note. A bend table is generated using the General button on the Table panel on the Annotate tab.

The Table tool basically morphs into several different kinds of tables depending on what you specify as a data source. If a flat pattern view is selected, a bend table will be generated.

To create a bend table for mi_12a_130.idw, activate Sheet3 and then follow these steps:

GENERAL TABLES

If no data source is selected in the Table dialog box, you'll end up with an empty table that you can populate manually. You can also browse and import data from a CSV or XLS file into the table.

---

1. Click the General button on the Table panel of the Annotate tab.

2. Select the flat pattern view.

3. Click the Column Chooser button and select Bend Radius from the list on the right.

4. Click the Remove button and then click the OK button.

5. For Bend ID, select the Alpha option and then click the OK button.

6. Place the table on the sheet and adjust the bend ID tags as required by clicking them and dragging.

A bend table is edited and maintained like a parts list. The Table dialog box is essentially identical, and any changes to the cell data are treated as overrides to the data source (in this case, the bend data stored in the sheet-metal file).

You can close the file without saving changes. Figure 12.34 shows a simple bend table and bend ID tags.

FIGURE 12.34
Bend table

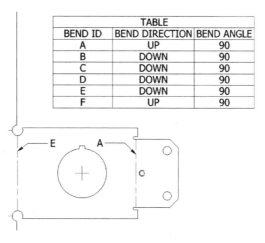

TABLE		
BEND ID	BEND DIRECTION	BEND ANGLE
A	UP	90
B	DOWN	90
C	DOWN	90
D	DOWN	90
E	DOWN	90
F	UP	90

Punch Tables

Punch information can likewise be displayed in a table, but because punches closely resemble holes with respect to the kind of information required to be displayed, a hole table is used to generate tabulated punch data.

The only difference between creating a hole table and creating a punch table is that you use a predefined hole table style that is set to pick up only sheet-metal punch features. Here are the general steps used to create a punch table:

1. Ensure that your flat pattern view has been set to collect punch centers. (Right-click and select Edit View ➤ Punch Center.)

2. Start the Hole Table–View tool (using the Hole View button found on the Table panel of the Annotate tab).

3. Select the flat pattern view.

4. Select an origin point.

5. Prior to placing the table, change the table's style to a punch table style. If you forget this step, you can always select the existing hole table and change it to the punch table style using the Style drop-down (top right of the screen).

Figure 12.35 shows a simple punch table.

Figure 12.35

Punch table

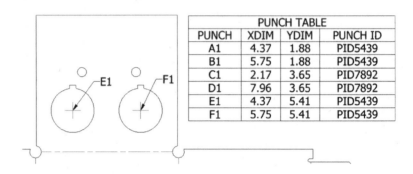

PUNCH TABLE			
PUNCH	XDIM	YDIM	PUNCH ID
A1	4.37	1.88	PID5439
B1	5.75	1.88	PID5439
C1	2.17	3.65	PID7892
D1	7.96	3.65	PID7892
E1	4.37	5.41	PID5439
F1	5.75	5.41	PID5439

Working with Weldment Views

Weldments are a special kind of assembly model and offer unique drawing view and annotation options in the Drawing Manager.

In this section, you'll take a quick look at the way drawing views handle weldment stages for detailing.

For more information on working with weldments and weldment annotation, refer to Chapter 10, "Weldment Design." A drawing view of a weldment assembly can display any of the weldment states, which are as follows:

Assembly Displays the base assembly prior to the preparation, welding, and machining stages.

Machining Displays assembly features that represent the post-weld machining and finishing.

Welds Displays the assembly as it exists during the weld stage, before machining but after preparations have been made. Weld beads are also shown.

Preparations Displays assembly features such as chamfers, extrude cuts, and holes used to remove material to prepare the assembly for welding. You can set the view to display the entire assembly during the preparation stage or set the view to look at a single component as it exists at the preparation stage.

Follow these steps to explore the way weldments are handled in drawings and drawing views:

1. On the Get Started tab, click the Open button.

2. Browse for mi_12a_139.idw in the Chapter 12 directory of your Mastering Inventor 2016 folder and click the Open button.

3. Notice the following about the views on this drawing sheet:

   ◆ View-1 through View-4 show the assembly with no preparations, welds, or machining.

   ◆ View-P1 through View-P3 show each part at the preparation stage.

   ◆ View-W1 shows the weldment with welds but no machining done after the weld stage.

4. Right-click View-1 and choose Edit View; then click the Model State tab in the Drawing View dialog box.

5. Currently, this view and the views projected from it are set to the assembly state. Select the Machining option, as shown in Figure 12.36, so the view displays the completed weldment. Click the OK button.

FIGURE 12.36
Weldment state settings

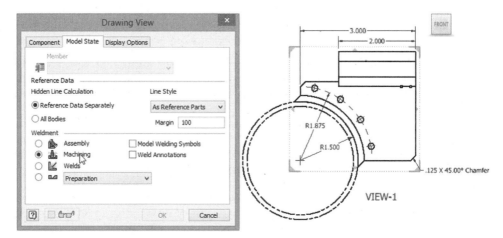

6. Notice that View-1 through View-4 now show the weldment at its completion, including the machined holes that run through the weld on one side (see Detail A).

7. Edit View-W1 and check the Model State tab to see that it is set to the Welds option.

8. Select the options to recover weld annotations and model weld symbols. Then click the OK button.

9. Because the weldment included the weld symbols, they can be pulled into the drawing. Click each symbol and use the grip snaps to arrange them as you like.

You'll also notice a series of arcs indicating the weld bead brought in via the Weld Annotations option. You can right-click those and choose Edit Caterpillar to adjust the appearance of each, or you can turn the visibility off as required. Figure 12.37 shows the view with recovered weld annotation and symbols.

FIGURE 12.37
Weldment drawing with
recovered annotation
and weld symbols

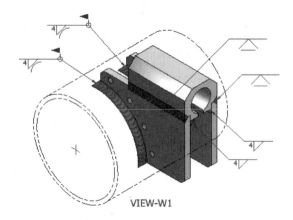

VIEW-W1

10. Edit View-P1 through View-P3 to check the Model State tab settings for these views. Notice that each of these views is actually created from the assembly file but is set to look at the individual parts at their preparations stage.

You might also note that the balloons on View-P1 through View-P3 are calling out the file-names and that both of the side plates are the same file but have opposing chamfers. This is because a common plate was used for both sides and then prepared as required in the weldment assembly.

If you were to make views of the parts themselves instead of each part at the weldment prep-aration stage, the chamfers would not be present. You can close this file without saving changes.

If you don't need to use the weldment tools in assembly modeling but still need to convey welding information in a drawing, you can create weld symbols and weld annotations (end fills and caterpillars) manually on the drawing view.

Each is available in the Symbols panel of the Annotate tab (as shown in Figure 12.38) and is formatted by a dedicated style (the Weld Symbol style and Weld Bead style, respectively).

FIGURE 12.38
Weldment annotation
and weld symbols
can be created in the
drawing.

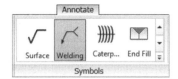

Working with iParts and iAssembly Drawings

When your drawing view references an iPart or iAssembly, you can choose, from the drawing view Model State tab, which member file you want to document.

Annotations (particularly dimensions) attached to drawing views of iParts and iAssemblies generally remain attached if you edit the base view and change the iPart member on the Model State tab.

This means you can fully annotate just one iPart or iAssembly member and select Save Copy As for each unique member after changing the member referenced in the base view.

Or you can create a tabulated drawing detailing all the iPart/iAssembly members on a single sheet. To look at this workflow, follow these steps:

1. On the Get Started tab, click the Open button.

2. Browse for `mi_12a_148.idw` in the `Chapter 12` directory of your `Mastering Inventor 2016` folder and click the Open button.

3. On the Annotate tab, click the General button on the Table panel.

4. Select the flat pattern view on the sheet to set the focus of the table.

5. Because this part file is both a sheet-metal part and an iPart, you are given the choice to create either a bend table or an iPart table (you can create both but need to do so in successive steps). Set the table data source to iPart/iAssembly Table.

6. Click the Column Chooser button and use the Add button to include the Length parameter; then click the OK button.

7. Click the OK button in the Table dialog box and place the table on the sheet.

8. Right-click the 100 mm dimension at the top of the flat patter, and choose Edit. Select the Hide Dimension Value box and then type **Length** in the text box below. Then click the OK button.

9. Right-click the table and choose Edit; then right-click the Member header in the table and select Format Column.

10. Deselect the Name From Data Source box, enter **Mark #**, click the OK button, and then click the OK button again to return to the sheet. Your table should resemble Figure 12.39.

FIGURE 12.39

A tabulated iPart drawing

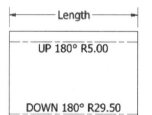

TABLE	
Mark #	Length
001	200 mm
002	100 mm
003	80 mm
004	75 mm
005	70 mm
006	50 mm

If you create a tabulated drawing in this manner and then add rows to the iPart/iAssembly table, your drawing table will automatically add the new rows as well.

Rows can then be hidden in the table if needed simply by editing the table on the sheet and then right-clicking the row in the table editor and unselecting Visibility. You can close the file without saving changes.

Drawing Standards

Now that you know how to use the Inventor drawing tools to document your design, I'll bet you're itching to tweak the drawing styles and standards so that they look how you want them to look.

These Drawing Manager tasks are discussed in the following sections:

◆ Creating templates and styles

◆ Utilizing drawing resources

◆ Editing styles and standards

Creating Templates and Styles

Inventor ships with multiple drawing templates. Which ones you see in the templates file will depend on which style libraries you chose when you installed Inventor.

◆ ANSI (both Imperial and metric units)

◆ BSI

◆ DIN

◆ GB

◆ GOST

◆ ISO

◆ JIS

Before you begin to document your own designs and models, you will want create your own custom template or templates to best meet your needs.

Most users have to adhere to a specific set of drafting standards dictated by their company, customer, or vendor specifications. These standards are typically derivatives of one of several international drafting standards such as ANSI, ISO, or DIN.

If your requirement is pretty close to an existing standard, you can start with a standard template and tweak it.

If your standard is completely unique (or you have CAD Manager's OCD), you can start with a completely blank template and build from scratch.

Creating templates in the Drawing Manager is not unlike creating templates in other applications. The primary difference is that many applications use a special file format for template files, whereas Inventor uses the same file format but uses a folder location to designate all files within the template location as templates.

As a result, you can use any IDW or DWG file as a drawing template; you just need to save it in the template location.

To create a drawing template from an existing, Autodesk-provided template, follow these steps:

1. Click the New File button from the Get Started tab.

2. Choose an IDW or DWG template that is close to your needs (for instance, you might select the DIN.idw file if your company uses the DIN standard).

3. Click the Inventor button (the large *I* in the upper-left corner) and choose Save As ➢ Save Copy As Template.

4. Create a subfolder for your custom template in the template files location.

5. Rename your custom template to a name of your choice.

6. Make changes to the styles and standards as needed and then use the Save Copy As Template option to update the template file.

To create a drawing template from a "clean" template file that contains no styles, follow these general steps:

1. Hold down the Ctrl and Shift keys and click the New File button from the Get Started tab, as shown in Figure 12.40.

FIGURE 12.40
Creating a new file with no styles

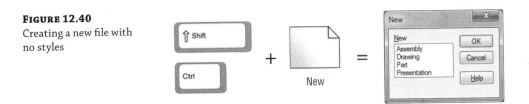

2. Select Drawing from the New dialog box and then click the OK button.

3. Click the Inventor button and choose Save As ➤ Save Copy As Template.

4. Create a subfolder for your custom template in the template file's location.

5. Rename your custom template to a name of your choice.

6. Make changes to the styles and standards as needed and then use the Save Copy As Template option to update the template file.

Understanding Template Locations

By default, Inventor templates are stored in and accessed from `C:\Users\Public\Documents\Autodesk\Inventor 2016\Templates`.

You set the default location initially from the Tools tab by clicking the Application Options button and then selecting the File tab and entering a folder location in the Default Templates box.

For stand-alone users working on a local drive, consider using the same location where you store your design projects for your template file location. If you're part of a networked design group, you should create a template folder on a shared network drive and change the default template path accordingly.

The default template location can be overridden on a per-project basis by setting the template location in the project file configuration.

Keep in mind that if you have a template location set in Application Options and another set in the project file, the project file always takes precedence.

Setting the template path in the project and having everyone use the same project file can often be the best way to ensure that all members of the design group are using the same templates.

STANDARD TEMPLATES

If you use the New File drop-down menus to access templates, you should know that these templates are hard-coded to use files named Standard.ipt, Standard.iam, Standard.ipn, and Standard.idw (or .dwg) located at the route of your template location. If you remove or rename the files named Standard, the drop-down menus will not work. Unfortunately, there is no way to point the drop-downs to use a template of a different name. However, if you create a copy of your template files, place them at the root of your template directory, and name them **Standard**, you can then access your customized templates using the standard drop-down menus.

Choosing a File Format

Prior to Inventor 2008, the IDW file format was the only native 2D file type recognized by Inventor. DWG TrueConnect, introduced with Inventor 2008, enables you to use both DWG and IDW as valid file formats in the Drawing Manager.

Using DWG as your file format enables you to open Inventor DWG files in the AutoCAD® program (or an AutoCAD vertical product such as AutoCAD® Mechanical) without going through a translation process.

Although the data you create natively in Inventor cannot be manipulated directly in AutoCAD, all the Inventor data can be viewed, measured, and printed using conventional AutoCAD commands.

By choosing DWG as your default file format, you allow downstream users of your designs to view the 2D drawing documents in AutoCAD without having to purchase or install Inventor or download the Inventor file viewer.

Vendors, customers, or other internal personnel can open the native Inventor DWG file and view, measure, and print the Inventor data, or they can even add AutoCAD data to the file to create a hybrid document that can be viewed quickly and efficiently in either application.

AutoCAD users with older versions of AutoCAD might need to download the Autodesk DWG TrueConnect Object Enablers to view the Inventor proxy objects. Use the search phrase *TrueConnect Object Enabler* to locate the downloads online.

BE AWARE OF FILE SIZE

Although many design departments find the convenience of having their Inventor drawings in DWG format well worth it, you should understand that Inventor DWG files will be larger than Inventor IDW files.

The difference in size may vary depending on the content; Inventor views are turned into AutoCAD blocks, and Inventor hatches are rendered in AutoCAD as individual lines.

Differences of up to three times as large can be common. Save a dozen typical drawing files as both Inventor DWG and IDW and compare the sizes yourself to determine which is right for you.

For Inventor users, there is essentially no difference between using DWG and using the traditional IDW file format.

The native DWG file includes a Layer 0 in the layer list and an AutoCAD Blocks folder in Drawing Resources. These are the only noticeable differences between the two file formats.

An IDW file can always be saved as an Inventor DWG, and vice versa, without any loss of fidelity or data. If there's a good chance of someone wanting to see a DWG version of your Inventor file, you might consider choosing DWG as your default file format.

The Task Scheduler in Inventor enables you to batch-convert a set of IDW files into DWG files.

Utilizing Drawing Resources

There are three areas of the template for you to customize to conform to your chosen drafting standards and personal preferences: Drawing Resources, Document Settings, and Styles And Standards.

Drawing resources are reusable sketches and formats that are stored in a drawing file. There are four types of drawing resources: sheet formats, borders, title blocks, and sketched symbols. If you've decided to use DWG as your template format, you'll notice that AutoCAD blocks are also managed as Inventor drawing resources.

Drawing resources are accessed from your drawing browser in the Drawing Resources folder, as shown in Figure 12.41.

FIGURE 12.41
The Drawing Resources node in the drawing browser

If you expand the Drawing Resources node, you'll see a folder for each of the drawing resource types listed, and contained in each of the subfolders are drawing-resource definitions. Double-click any drawing resource to place an instance in your drawing.

You can employ several document-management techniques with respect to templates, sheet sizes, borders, and title blocks.

Although you could create and maintain separate drawing templates for each sheet size and title block you might need, it's generally recommended that a single drawing template be used to maintain each of these different configurations.

In the following sections, you will take a look at the various drawing resources.

Sheet Size

When you start a new drawing from one of the templates installed with Inventor, a border and title block are already present on the sheet, and the sheet is set to a default size.

You can change the default sheet size by right-clicking the sheet in the browser and choosing Edit Sheet from the context menu.

For example, if you are using the ANSI (in) template, the default sheet size is C. If you change the sheet size to D, the border on the sheet updates automatically to accommodate the change in sheet size.

To have your templates default to a different sheet size, follow these steps:

1. On the Get Started tab, click the Open button.

2. Browse to your template location and open a drawing file, such as Standard.idw (see the section "Understanding Template Locations" earlier in this chapter).

3. Right-click the sheet in the browser and choose Edit Sheet.

4. Click the arrow in the drop-down box and choose the size or sheet format from the list.

5. Click the Inventor button and choose Save (or press Ctrl+S on the keyboard).

Now when you start a new file from the template, this new sheet size will be active.

Multiple Sheets

If needed, you can add sheets to your template, which is recommended if most of your design documents require more than one sheet. To insert a new sheet into your document, follow these steps:

1. Right-click any blank area on the page and choose New Sheet (or click the New Sheet button on the Place Views tab).

2. Note that this adds the border and title block and the same size sheet as the active sheet.

3. To switch between sheets, double-click the sheet node in the browser.

MULTIPLE SHEET DRAWING FILES

Use caution when creating multiple sheet sets of a sizable number because performance will likely suffer, depending on the size and complexity of the models you are detailing. Be aware too of "putting all of your eggs in one basket" should a file become corrupted or lost. It is generally considered best practice to create a single drawing for each part number in an assembly, rather than attempting to manage an entire drawing set for an assembly in a single drawing file. However, certain industries approach this aspect of drawing sets differently.

Creating a Border

The default border used on the Inventor templates may not meet your needs. To create a new border, you'll first follow these steps to remove the instance of the old border:

1. Expand the sheet node in the browser.

2. Right-click the border instance and choose Delete.

Doing so removes the instance of the border from the sheet. The border definition is still stored in the Borders folder of the Drawing Resources node. To create a new, custom border in your template, follow these steps:

1. In your template file, expand the Drawing Resources node in the browser.

2. Right-click the Borders folder and choose Define New Border. You might have the option to choose Define New Zone Border, but you'll use a simple border here to explore the steps required. Here is a brief description of both border types:

   Define New Zone Border   Brings up an input dialog box where you can specify the number of horizontal and vertical zones, alpha or numeric zone labels, font and font size, and margin spacing. A sketch is created from your input automatically.

   Define New Border   Creates a sketch with the four corners of the sheet projected in. You can sketch a rectangle to create a simple custom border and use dimensions to specify the margins from the sheet corners. Dimensioning to the sheet corners allows your border to automatically resize to any sheet size, holding the specified margins. Borders can be as simple or complex as required, but the sketch should always be fully constrained.

3. On the Sketch tab, select the Two Point Rectangle tool.

4. Sketch a small rectangle on the screen; ensure that you do not sketch it on the sheet corners because this will constrain the rectangle to the corners.

5. On the Sketch tab, select the Dimension tool.

6. Place dimensions from the corners of your rectangle to the projected corner points of the sheet so that the edges of the rectangle will be 10 mm from the edge of the sheet.

FORMATTING COLOR AND LINE WEIGHT IN A BORDER SKETCH

By default, all geometry created in a border is set on a layer named Border. You can change the color and line weight of that layer to modify all the entities of your border, or you can override the properties of individual entities as required. To do the latter, right-click the object you want to modify and select Properties.

---

7. When your border sketch is complete, right-click and choose Save Border (or click the Finish Sketch button on the Sketch tab).

8. Enter the name of your border definition.

9. Click Save.

10. Look in the Borders folder of the Drawing Resources node in the browser for your new border definition.

11. Right-click your border and choose Insert to place an instance of it on the current sheet.

12. If you need to modify the border definition, right-click your border instance or the definition in Drawing Resources and choose Edit Definition or Edit.

Because the border is dimensioned to the edge/corners of the sheet, if you edit the sheet size, the border will automatically resize as needed, holding the margin distance, 10 mm in this example.

Creating a Title Block

Title blocks are customized in much the same way borders are customized. Title blocks typically contain more text-based information than borders, so the focus will be on creating sketch text in this section. There are three common ways of creating a custom title block.

◆ You can use an existing title block originally drawn in AutoCAD.

◆ You can modify a default Inventor title block.

◆ You can create one completely from scratch in Inventor, drawing the line work and inserting the text fields.

In this section, you will bring in an existing AutoCAD title block and make it intelligent to Inventor. In doing so, you will explore the tools used to create a title block employed in the other tile block creation methods mentioned.

You should probably first delete the default title block from your current sheet before creating a new title block, just to reduce confusion.

Once you're sure you have the Chapter 12 files in place, follow these steps to explore the creation of a title block:

1. From your template file (or any standard Inventor drawing file), expand the sheet node in the browser.

2. Right-click the title block instance and choose Delete.

3. On the Get Started tab, click the Open button.

4. Browse for mi_12a_033.dwg in the Chapter 12 directory of your Mastering Inventor 2016 folder. You may need to change the Files Of Type drop-down to All Files or AutoCAD Drawings (*.dwg) to locate the file.

5. Click the Options button in the Open dialog box.

6. Ensure that Open is selected; otherwise, Inventor will take you to the DWG/DXF File Wizard.

7. Click the OK button.

8. Click the Open button.

Notice that when you open an AutoCAD drawing in Inventor, you can view and measure the file. You should see a black background, and if you check the browser, you will see that you are viewing the model space environment of the file.

9. Right-click the title block and choose Copy.

10. Use the Open Documents tabs at the bottom of the screen to switch back to your template file (or press Ctrl+Tab on the keyboard).

11. In the Drawing Resources folder in the browser, right-click the Title Blocks folder and choose Define New Title Block. This will place you in the Sketch environment.

12. Right-click in the graphics area and choose Paste.

13. Click in the middle of the sheet to place the title block.

You'll notice that the line work is under-constrained and not dimensioned at all. You can take the time to dimension it if you'd like, but because this will become a block and therefore a static entity, you most likely will not need to do so. Don't worry about the position of the title block on the drawing sheet. Inventor will help you with this later.

Continue adding intelligence to the text now.

14. Right-click the text field containing CDW and choose Edit Text.

15. In the Format Text dialog box, select the text and press Delete on the keyboard.

16. Locate the Type drop-down and set it to Properties–Drawing, as shown in Figure 12.42.

FIGURE 12.42
Customizing the title block

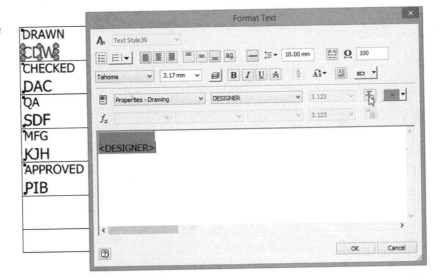

17. Set the Property drop-down to Designer.

18. Click the Add Text Parameter button to set the Designer property to the text field.

19. Click the OK button.

20. Repeat steps 14 through 19 for the date field directly to the right of the field you just edited. Use the Creation Date property instead of Designer.

21. Right-click and choose Save Title Block (or click the Finish Sketch button on the Sketch tab).

22. Enter a name for the new title block definition, such as **My Title Block**.

23. Look in the Title Block folder of the Drawing Resources node in the browser for your new title-block definition.

24. Right-click your title block and choose Insert to place an instance of it on the current sheet. Inventor will automatically place the title block in the lower-right corner of your drawing border.

25. If you need to modify the title block definition, right-click your title block instance or the definition in Drawing Resources and choose Edit Definition or Edit.

Obviously, you have not configured the entire title block at this point, but before going any further, it is important to understand where the properties you linked to the title block text fields are coming from.

You can find these properties in the file iProperties. Follow these steps to change an iProperty in the drawing file and see that change show up in the title block:

1. Click the Inventor button and choose iProperties.

2. On the iProperties Project tab, change the Designer input to **Test Designer**.

3. Change the Creation Date input field to **1/1/2015**.

4. Click the OK button to apply the changes and close the iProperties dialog box.

Your title block will have updated the two fields automatically based on the iProperty changes you made, demonstrating that you have linked those fields to the iProperties of this particular drawing file.

If you intend to use this title block for your drawing template, you should continue to configure your title block to retrieve the iProperties needed, until all the fields are automatically filled out by updating the iProperties.

For now, you can close the file you have open without saving changes and continue to the next section to learn more about iProperties.

IPROPERTIES AND TITLE BLOCKS

Each Inventor file has its own set of iProperties, allowing you to pull information from that file into your title block. There are two distinct methods you can use to retrieve iProperties into your title block:

♦ You can retrieve iProperties from the drawing file.

♦ You can retrieve iProperties from the model file that is referenced in the drawing file.

The following is a list of the standard iProperties available. Each of these can be accessed from the Type drop-down in the Text Format dialog box as described in the previous steps. You'll learn more about iProperties in Chapter 13, "Tools Overview."

Appearance	Design Date	
Author	Designer	Mfg Approved Date
Authority	Eng Approval Date	Part Number
Category	Eng Approved By	Project
Checked By	Engineer	Revision Number
Checked Date	Estimated Cost	Status

Comments	Filename	Stock Number
Company	Filename And Path	Subject
Cost Center	Keywords	Title
Creation Date	Manager	Vendor
Description	Mfg Approved By	Weblink

LINKING YOUR MODEL AND DRAWING IPROPERTIES

Often, you will want the iProperties for the model file and drawing file to match. You can use the Copy Model iProperty Settings option to have this happen automatically.

To do so, open your drawing template, select the Tools tab, click Document Settings, select the Drawing tab in the dialog box that opens, and click the Copy Model iProperty Settings button at the bottom. You can have some or all the model properties copied to the drawing.

Note that once copied, the properties do not update automatically when they are changed in the model. To update them, select the Manage tab and click Update Copied Model iProperties.

Follow these steps to modify a title block so it is pulling information from the model iProperties. You'll note that this title block is calling the model filename iProperty for the drawing title. Most of the other fields are being pulled from the drawing file's iProperties. The field you will be modifying is static and needs to be set to pull from the model file's iProperties. Here are the steps:

1. On the Get Started tab, click the Open button.

2. Browse for `mi_12a_024.idw` in the `Chapter 12` directory of your `Mastering Inventor 2016` folder.

3. Expand the sheet node in the browser (if it is not already expanded).

4. Right-click the title block instance (named MI_TB_04) in the browser and choose Edit Definition.

5. Zoom up on the title block and locate the Part Number area toward the bottom.

6. Right-click the text field showing ### and choose Edit Text.

7. In the Format Text dialog box, select the text (###) and press Delete on the keyboard.

8. Locate the Type drop-down and choose Properties–Model.

9. Set the Property drop-down to Part Number.

10. Click the Add Text Parameter button to set the property to the text field.

11. Click the OK button.

12. Right-click and choose Save Title Block (or click the Finish Sketch button on the Sketch tab).

13. Click Yes at the Save Edits prompt.

To ensure that the part number in the title block is coming from the part model and not the drawing file, you will open the model file and change its iProperties.

14. Locate the View2:Arbor_Frame.ipt node in the browser and then right-click it and choose Open.

15. Once the part model is open, right-click the top-level node (Arbor_Frame.ipt) in the browser and choose iProperties.

16. Select the Project tab and then edit the Part Number field to read **98765**.

17. Click the Apply button and then the Close button.

18. Use the Open Documents tabs at the bottom of the screen to switch back to the drawing file (or use Ctrl+Tab to switch between all open documents).

You will see that the title block has read the model part number and displays the change in the Part Number field.

Experiment with the title block to understand the way it works with iProperties from the model, and then you can close the file without saving changes.

You might notice that this title block does not contain dimensions. Instead, the objects within it were anchored in place using sketch constraints.

GENERAL FILE PROPERTIES AND TITLE BLOCKS

In addition to iProperties, you can use some other standard file properties to fill out your title block automatically.

You can access them from the Type drop-down in the Text Format dialog box just as you did the iProperties. Table 12.1 lists several general properties that can be called into a text field.

TABLE 12.1: Available properties

PHYSICAL PROPERTIES OF THE MODEL	GENERAL DRAWING PROPERTIES	DRAWING SHEET PROPERTIES	SHEET-METAL FLAT PATTERN PROPERTIES
Area	Number Of Sheets	Sheet Number	Flat Pattern Extents Area
Density		Sheet Revision	Flat Pattern Extents Length
Mass		Sheet Size	Flat Pattern Extents Width
Volume		Initial View Scale	

Follow these steps to set up the sheet number area of the title block to call on general file properties of the drawing file to automatically fill out the title block:

1. On the Get Started tab, click the Open button.

2. Browse for `mi_12a_025.idw` in the `Chapter 12` directory of your `Mastering Inventor 2016` folder.

3. Expand the sheet node in the browser.

4. Right-click the title block instance (named MI_TB_05) and choose Edit Definition.

5. Zoom up on the title block and locate the SHEET ?? OF ??? area at the bottom right.

6. Right-click the text field showing SHEET ?? OF ??? and choose Edit Text.

7. In the Format Text dialog box, select the two question marks between the word *SHEET* and the word *OF* and press Delete on the keyboard.

8. Locate the Type drop-down and choose Sheet Properties.

9. Set the Property drop-down to Sheet Number.

10. Click the Add Text Parameter button to set the Number Of Sheets property to the text field.

11. Still in the Format Text dialog box, select the three question marks after the word *OF* and press Delete on the keyboard.

12. Locate the Type drop-down and choose Drawing Properties. (Note that there is one called Properties–Drawing also, so ensure that you have the correct one.)

13. Set the Property drop-down to Number Of Sheets.

14. Click the Add Text Parameter button to set the Sheet Number property to the text field.

15. Ensure that the text in the text displays as SHEET <Sheet Number> OF <Number of sheets>. Then click the OK button.

16. Right-click and choose Save Title Block (or click the Finish Sketch button on the Sketch tab).

17. Click Yes at the Save Edits prompt.

Experiment with adding new sheets and reordering the sheets (just drag and drop the sheets in the browser) to see how the title block updates, and then you can close the file without saving changes.

Prompted Entry

You can create fields in your title block to enter information manually. This is known as a *prompted entry*.

Prompted entry text is keyed in by the user and not retrieved from the file properties in the way that iProperties are. Because of this, experienced Inventor users will tell you that iProperties are favored over prompted entries for two reasons.

First, information entered into a prompted entry field is stored in that one title-block instance and nowhere else.

If you need to update the title block for your entire drawing library at some point in the future, you can do so easily with the Drawing Resource Transfer Wizard, which can swap out old title-block definitions with a new one, en masse. (See Chapter 13 for more on this Inventor tool.)

This works well when title blocks have been populated with iProperties because the information resides in the file, not the title block. However, if a prompted entry was used, that information will not be carried over because it exists only in the old title-block instance.

Second, since iProperties are stored in the file, there are a couple of important tasks that can be performed on them.

◆ iProperties can be viewed, searched, and copied easily using a number of tools such as Find, Design Assistant, and Vault.

◆ Non-Inventor users can use iProperties to sign off on drawings without opening the file in Inventor.

Getting in the habit of using iProperties will pay large dividends in the future, once you have created many Inventor files. With these things in mind, you should use prompted entries in title blocks rarely.

Here are the steps for creating a prompted entry in a title block if you determine that it is required:

1. On the Get Started tab, click the Open button.

2. Browse for mi_12a_026.idw in the Chapter 12 directory of your Mastering Inventor 2016 folder.

3. Expand the sheet node in the browser.

4. Right-click the title block instance (named MI_TB_06) and choose Edit Definition.

5. Zoom up on the title block and locate the Tracking Code area at the bottom left.

6. Right-click the text field showing ##### and choose Edit Text.

7. Locate the Type drop-down and choose Prompted Entry.

8. Replace ##### with **Enter Tracking Code**.

9. Click the OK button.

10. Right-click any empty space in the graphics area and choose Save Title Block.

11. Click Yes at the Save Edits prompt.

12. Enter **12345** for the tracking code, when prompted.

13. Click the OK button.

You can edit a prompted entry in a title block by expanding the block instance in the browser and double-clicking the Field Text node.

If no prompted entry is established, you will be able to only view the fields.

If you edit Sheet 2 and add the MI_TB_06 title block to it, you will immediately be prompted for the tracking-code entry.

When you've finished exploring prompted entries, you can close the file without saving changes.

Sketched Symbols

Sketched symbols are created, edited, placed, and managed much like other drawing resources, but unlike borders and title blocks, there is no limit to the number of sketch symbol instances you can place on a sheet.

Like other drawing resource definitions, sketched symbols are placed by double-clicking the definition node in the browser or using the Insert Sketched Symbols button on the Symbols panel of the Annotate tab.

Sketched symbols can optionally include a leader. Using a leader, you can associate a sketch symbol with a model so that model-specific properties can be displayed in the symbol. For example, you could create a sketch symbol that calls out a component's mass.

1. On the Get Started tab, click the Open button.

2. Browse for `mi_12a_030.idw` in the `Chapter 12` directory of your `Mastering Inventor 2016` folder.

3. Expand the `Drawing Resources` browser folder.

4. Right-click the `Sketch Symbol` folder and select Define New Symbol.

5. In the Draw panel of the Sketch tab, click the Text button (or press **T** on the keyboard).

6. Click anywhere on the page to set the text location.

7. In the Format Text dialog box, type in a static text string that reads **Mass:** (be sure to include a space after the colon).

8. Locate the Type drop-down and choose Physical Properties–Model.

9. Set the Property drop-down to MASS.

10. Click the Add Text Parameter button to set the MASS property to the text field.

11. Click the OK button.

12. Right-click anywhere in the graphics area and choose the OK button.

13. Right-click and choose Save Sketched Symbol from the context menu.

14. Enter **Mass** for the name and click Save.

15. To insert the symbol into the drawing, click Annotate tab ➤ Symbols panel ➤ Insert Sketch Symbol.

16. Ensure that the Mass symbol is chosen from the list on the left side of the Sketch Symbols dialog box and select the Leader option.

17. Click the OK button.

18. Click any model edge in the drawing view.

19. Click again for each leader vertex you'd like and then choose Continue from the context menu. (Alternatively, double-click to place your symbol.)

20. Continue to place additional symbol instances, but be sure to point to a different Arbor Press component each time.

You'll notice that the symbol in Figure 12.43 has a bit more geometry than the simple symbol you just created.

FIGURE 12.43
Applying sketched symbols to a drawing view

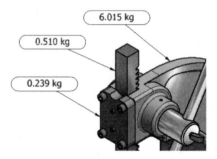

You can make a sketch symbol as elaborate as you like, but for the purposes of this exercise, the Mass property reference is all that is required. A finished symbol named Mass_2 has been created for you in this drawing file.

If the mass shows up as N/A, it indicates that the model needs to be updated. You can open the assembly model, select the Manage tab, and click the Update Mass button to do this. Then return to the drawing to see the update.

FORMATTING YOUR TEXT TO CENTER YOUR SYMBOLS

Generally, text objects are created with a justification setting other than middle center. However, a middle-center justification will allow you to center your text in the symbol geometry by using sketch constraints.

Here are some more sketch symbol points to remember:

◆ Sketched symbols are often used to create standard blocks of text notes.

◆ Sketched symbols can be placed as needed on new documents or placed on the template itself, which can be useful for standard drawing notes that will be placed in every drawing.

◆ If there is field text in the sketch symbol, it becomes populated just like title block field text when you create a new drawing.

◆ If you need to establish a symbol reference to a model but do not want to see the leader, you can edit the symbol and then double-click or select Edit Symbol from the symbol's context menu and uncheck the leader Visibility option.

◆ You cannot graphically rotate or scale static sketched symbols as you can symbols that are not static.

◆ Sketched symbols placed by double-clicking the definition are set to Static by default; you can set this option prior to placement if you click the User button on the Symbols panel of the Annotate tab.

♦ Sketched symbols placed by clicking the User button on the Symbols panel of the Annotate tab are set to have more controls than static symbols initially.

♦ You can switch a static symbol to be not static by right-clicking it and choosing Edit Symbol.

♦ When you mouse over a sketch symbol that is not static, a single blue hot point is shown on the center top of the symbol and four yellow hot points are displayed at the four corners of the symbol.

♦ Clicking and dragging the blue hot point causes the symbol to rotate, whereas clicking and dragging any of the yellow hot points enables dynamic scaling.

♦ You can change the insert point of a sketched symbol by adding a point to the sketch and then using the Set Insertion Point Grip button to mark it as the insertion point. This button can be found next to the Driven Dimension button on the Format panel of the Sketch tab.

♦ Sketched symbols can be patterned by right-clicking an instance of a symbol and choosing Pattern Symbol.

♦ Sketched symbols are a good place to use prompted entry text.

AutoCAD Blocks

Blocks created in AutoCAD can be used in Inventor in the same way sketched symbols are used. However, differences exist between the way they are created and used.

AutoCAD blocks are available for use only when you are using an Inventor DWG file, and they cannot be used in an Inventor IDW file. Also, you cannot create or edit AutoCAD blocks in Inventor. There are two ways to bring blocks into an Inventor DWG file.

♦ Copy and paste from AutoCAD.

♦ Right-click the `AutoCAD Blocks` folder in the `Drawing Resources` folder and choose Import AutoCAD.

Here are some other points to remember about blocks:

♦ Once blocks are imported, you can scale, rotate, and pattern them by right-clicking the block instance.

♦ Blocks containing attributes can be modified by right-clicking the block instance and choosing Edit Attributes.

♦ Color and layer properties can be modified by right-clicking the block instance and choosing Properties.

♦ You can create a block from your drawing views by right-clicking the browser node for the view and selecting Insert In Model Space from the context menu.

Sketched Symbol Libraries

Sketched symbols can be saved in your drawings files, or they can be saved out to a common library.

This is the standard path for your Sketch Symbol library:

`C:\Users\Public\Documents\Autodesk\Inventor 2016\Design Data\Symbol Library`

CHANGING THE LOCATION

You can customize and change the location in Application Options ➤ File tab.

To organize your sketched symbols in your template file, right-click the Sketch Symbol node in the browser and choose New Folder. You can now drag and drop sketched symbol definitions into folders to keep them tidy.

To save individual sketched symbols to your library, right-click the symbol definition in the browser and choose Save To Symbol Library.

To save *all* your sketched symbols to your library, including your folder structure, right-click the Sketch Symbols node in the browser and choose Save All To Symbol Library. In the Save to Symbol Library dialog box that pops up, remember to check the Retain Resource Folder Structure box.

Notice the Create New Library button at the bottom of the Save To Symbol Library dialog box. Clicking this button will create a new IDW file in the default location in which to keep your sketched symbols.

Notice that you can't delete an IDW file from here, but you can navigate to the Symbol Library folder in Windows Explorer and add or delete IDW files to your symbol library.

Sheet Formats

Sheet formats are preset collections of drawing sheets, borders, title blocks, sketched symbols, and/or base and projected views.

They essentially give you the ability to quickly generate multiview drawings just by referencing a single model file.

To create a multiview drawing, follow these steps:

1. On the Get Started tab, click the Open button.

2. Browse for mi_12a_037.idw in the Chapter 12 directory of your Mastering Inventor 2016 folder.

3. Expand the Drawing Resources browser folder.

4. Expand the Sheet Formats folder.

5. Right-click the A Size, 4 Views, 1/2 Scale format, and choose New Sheet.

6. Browse for mi_12a_038.ipt in the Chapter 12 directory of your Mastering Inventor 2016 folder and click the Open button.

7. Click the OK button in the Select Component dialog box.

You will note that a new sheet has been created to the specifications of the sheet format and set active. This technique is ideal if you find yourself detailing similar designs of common size and complexity. You can close the file without saving changes.

To save your own sheet format, set up your sheet the way you like it, right-click the active sheet node in the browser, select Create Sheet Format, and then name the sheet format as you'd like.

Here are some more sheet format points to remember:

◆ Only base and projected views are saved in a sheet format. Section, detail, and other such views will not be included.

◆ Placed drawing resources such as standard notes (in the form of sketched symbols) can be included in a sheet format.

◆ You can preload your drawing template as a sheet format as well. Simply open a template, create base and projected views of any model, and then save and close them. When you next use your template for a new drawing, you'll be immediately prompted to reference a model file, and the drawing views will be automatically created.

◆ You can copy Sheet Formats node or individual configurations and paste them in other drawings.

Transferring Drawing Resources

You can copy drawing resource definitions from drawing to drawing by following these steps:

1. Right-click the definition of the title block, sketched symbol, or other drawing resource you want to copy and select Copy from the context menu.

2. Right-click the appropriate drawing resource node (or the Drawing Resources folder itself in the target document).

3. Select Paste.

You can use this technique to add new drawing resources and update existing resources.

You can also select the entire Drawing Resources folder in one drawing and paste it into the Drawing Resources folder of another drawing.

You will be prompted to replace or make a new instance of any duplicate resources.

The copy-and-paste technique is efficient for single changes or transfers between two drawings, but to push one or more new or updated design resource definitions to multiple drawings, use the Drawing Resource Transfer Wizard discussed in Chapter 13.

AREA CODE CHANGES

In 2002, the phone number area code for Rochester, New York, and the surrounding areas changed from 716 to 585.

This meant that every manufacturing, engineering, and architectural group in the area suddenly had hundreds and thousands of working drawings with the wrong phone number in the title block.

Many companies that wanted or needed to update their title blocks had to manually copy and paste title blocks on each drawing in their archives (the savvier groups wrote custom application scripts to perform this task).

Unfortunately, the Drawing Resource Transfer Wizard was not released until some years later. It would have likely saved thousands of hours of work.

Editing Styles and Standards

As it does with color, material, lighting, and sheet-metal styles in the modeling environment, the Drawing Manager makes heavy use of XML-based styles.

The basic framework of drawing styles is no different from those in the modeling environment. Drawing style settings are viewed and edited using the Style And Standard Editor dialog box. They can be shared among a workgroup via the library that contains the modeling styles, and they can be imported and exported as stand-alone XML files.

Drawing styles differ from modeling styles more in concept than in practice, however, and the drawing styles themselves are a collection of drafting rules that include the following and many more:

♦   Dimension styles

♦   Text styles

♦   Balloon styles

To explore the use of styles, study the scenario described in the Real World Scenario entitled, "Styles in Use, a Case Study," and refer to it in the example to come.

 Real World Scenario

STYLES IN USE, A CASE STUDY

A standard is a collection of styles. A company called Mastering Inventor, Inc., has created a basic company standard using dimension styles, text styles, and balloon styles. The various styles' names are listed here, followed by the style category:

Dim_Shop: Dimension style

Dim_Client: Dimension style

Dim_Marketing: Dimension style

Text_125: Text style

Text_250: Text style

Text_Script: Text style

Text_Partslist: Text style

Balloon_Item_Count: Balloon style

Balloon_Partnumber: Balloon style

Balloon_Partname: Balloon style

Having these styles set up allows Mastering Inventor, Inc., to create three types of standard drawings.

♦   The majority of the drawings are created for use by the shop floor to make parts. These drawings are required to be clear, concise, and detailed with tolerances.

- ◆ Also required are client approval drawings, showing some design specifics but also purposely limited in detail so that a competitor cannot manufacture from them.

- ◆ Occasionally, stylized drawings for use on the company web page or at trade shows are created.

To facilitate this, Mastering Inventor, Inc., has created a separate dimension style for each of these three drawing types.

The company has also created several different text styles, which are called into the dimension styles and used independently as notes, and so on.

Also created were balloon styles, each set up to call different iProperties from the models.

This works well because Inventor users can quickly switch to the style needed without having to stop and define a style, override another style, or worry about not maintaining consistency or corrupting the company standard.

The question then becomes this: If this company has three sets of styles in the company standard, how does Inventor know which one to use by default? The answer is *object defaults*.

Object Defaults

Certification
Objective

The true key to understanding how styles are used to determine the formatting of everything you can create on a drawing sheet is the notion of object defaults.

In the case study example, it is clear that the majority of a designer's day-to-day drawing work is focused on creating prints for manufacturing. Therefore, the styles used for that type of drawing would be the styles set up as the object defaults.

Object defaults are automatically set as the current styles in the template drawings. For this scenario, the object defaults would likely be configured as shown in Table 12.2.

TABLE 12.2:   Object-default styles

STYLE TYPE	OBJECT DEFAULT
Dimension style	Dim_Shop
Text style	Text_125
Balloon style	Balloon_Item_Count

Now that you understand the overall concept of object defaults, follow these steps to see how they are managed:

1. On the Get Started tab, click the Open button.

2. Browse for mi_12a_041.idw in the Chapter 12 directory of your Mastering Inventor 2016 folder.

3. Zoom to the top of the drawing, and note the three balloons.

Each balloon on the sheet is using a different balloon style. Each balloon style is calling a different set of iProperties, as you will see by comparing the balloons to the parts list.

To see how object defaults work, you'll now create more balloons on the ram part, which is the square-shaped bar with teeth cut into it.

4. Select the Annotate tab and then click the Balloon button (on the right side).

5. Note the two style drop-downs all the way to the right of the Annotate tab. The top one controls layers, and the second controls styles.

6. Click the Style drop-down to show the available balloon styles. You should see one style denoted as By Standard and three listed below that, one of which is the one called out in the By Standard line.

7. Select the Balloon_Partname style from the list and then select any edge of the ram.

8. Place the balloon on the page by double-clicking.

9. Repeat steps 6 through 9 for the other two balloon styles, until you have three balloons on the ram part, each using a different balloon style.

10. Right-click and choose Cancel when complete.

This demonstrates the use of different styles and shows that one of these styles is set as the company standard default style. You'll now go into the Style And Standard Editor and change the object default for the balloon style.

11. Select the Manage tab and then click the Styles Editor button. You will be presented with the Style And Standard Editor. (It may take a few seconds to index the styles initially.)

12. Ensure that the filter at the top right is set to Active Standard and then use the plus sign to expand the Balloon, Dimension, Object Defaults, and Text style categories, as shown in Figure 12.44. Note the style names listed under each style category.

FIGURE 12.44
Standards, styles, and object defaults

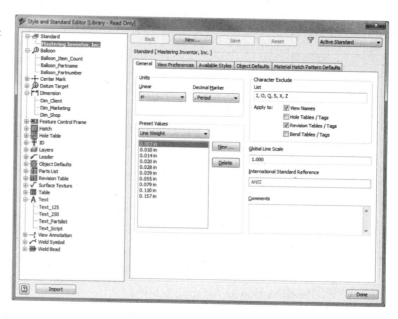

Look at the following items:

- ◆ Company Standard (Mastering Inventor, Inc.)
- ◆ Balloon styles
- ◆ Dimension styles
- ◆ Object Defaults (Mastering Inventor, Inc.)
- ◆ Text styles

13. Click Object Defaults (MI, Inc.).

14. Locate the Balloon row in the Object Type column.

15. Click the Object Style cell for the Balloon row and set the drop-down to Balloon_Item_Count.

16. Click the Layer cell for the Balloon row and set the drop-down to Balloons.

17. Click the Save button at the top of the editor.

18. Click Done to exit the editor.

19. Select the Balloon button from the right of the Annotate tab.

20. Select any edge of the ram and place another balloon just as you did before.

21. Note that the Balloon tool now defaults to the Balloon_Item_Count style and is placed on the Balloon layer.

When setting object defaults, you typically want to use the most common style. Of course, you can always use another style by manually selecting the style from the Style drop-down as you place the object.

You can also select an existing object, and the Style and Layer drop-downs will display that object's style and layer, allowing you to change layer and style assignment as needed.

Objects that have been set to a specific style, rather than following the By Standard option, will not update if you make any modifications to the object defaults. However, the objects will update if the specific style is updated.

A quick way to get a set of objects (like your balloons, for example) to return to their object default is to window-select or Ctrl+click the objects on the screen and then select By Standard from the style drop-down.

All the objects will update to use the newly selected standard. You can close the file without saving.

SET THE STYLE DROP-DOWN TO LAST USED

You can set the Style drop-down to remember the last-used object style by selecting the Tools tab, clicking the Application Options tab, and then selecting the Drawing tab.

On the right side of the Drawing tab, you will find a Default Object Style setting. If you set the drop-down to Last Used, the last-used object and dimension style is the default.

> For example, if you are placing dimensions on a drawing using a fractional style but the decimal style is the default, you can set the application option to Last Used so you do not need to keep changing the style back to fractional every time you access the dimension style.
>
> The Last Used setting is for the current editing session for the drawing, so if you close the file and reopen it, the Object Default will list again, until it's changed.

Creating Styles

As evident in the balloon example, you can have multiple styles for the same object type. Or you can have a single style that you always use. It's up to you to choose how many styles you have for each type, and this will be dictated largely by need. Although this section will not go through all the settings for all the styles, you will explore how to create and configure a new style as a foundation to creating all style types.

Here are the steps:

1. On the Get Started tab, click the Open button.

2. Browse for mi_12a_046.idw in the Chapter 12 directory of your Mastering Inventor 2016 folder.

3. Select the Manage tab and click the Styles Editor button.

4. Ensure that the filter drop-down at the top right is set to Active Standard and then in the left pane expand the Text node to see the list of text styles.

5. Expand the Balloon node to see the list of balloon styles.

6. Click the balloon style named Balloon_Partnumber to display the style settings in the right pane.

7. Click the New button at the top of the editor dialog box and enter **Balloon_Item_Qty** for the style name.

8. Ensure that the Add To Standard check box is selected and click the OK button.

9. In the Balloon Style settings, under the Sub-Styles section, use the drop-down to set the text style to use the style called Text_Script.

10. Click the Shape button and select the second shape (Circular–2 Entries) from the list.

11. Below that, in the Property Display area, click the Property Chooser button.

12. Click the Part Number property in the right pane and click the Remove button to take it out of the property list for this balloon style.

13. In the Left pane, locate the ITEM and ITEM QTY properties and use the Add button to pull them into the right pane. Do this one at a time.

14. Use the Move Down and Move Up buttons to set ITEM as the top property.

15. Click the OK button.

16. Click the Save button.

17. Click the Help button in the lower-left corner of the Style And Standard Editor, and notice that this takes you to the online help listing and description of each setting in the balloon style. This is true of all the style types.

18. Close your browser and click Done in the Style Editor.

19. Select the Annotate tab and click the Balloon button.

20. From the Styles drop-down on the far right of the Annotate tab, choose your new Balloon style, Balloon_Item_Qty, from the list.

21. Click the edges of parts to place on the drawing balloons that will list the item number and quantity using a script font for the text.

Although the settings for each style type vary, the steps for creating them remain consistent throughout all styles. The steps are as follows:

1. Create a new style based on an existing style.

2. Specify substyles (if applicable).

3. Configure the style settings as desired.

4. Save the new style.

USING A SKETCH SYMBOL AS A BALLOON SHAPE

You can use a sketch symbol as balloon shape if the available list is not sufficient for you. In the Style And Standard Editor's Balloon section, you can click User Define Symbol under Balloon Shape and then choose from the drop-down list of existing symbols in the drawing. The button will become active only if you have symbols in the Drawing Resources section of the browser.

Working with Substyles

A basic example of a substyle in the modeling environment is the color style, which is a substyle of the material style.

Once you apply a new material to a part, not only are you changing its physical parameters, but you're also potentially changing its color so that it shows the material's color substyle.

In the previous balloon style exercise, you used a text substyle called Text_Script when creating the balloon style.

The use of substyles in the Drawing Manager is extensive. Almost every kind of annotation you create in a drawing contains some kind of text (dimensions, weld symbols, and parts lists), and many make use of leaders.

The text style and leader style, therefore, are frequently used as substyles of other styles.

This basically provides one-stop shopping if you want to quickly change all the text on your document. If you wanted to change the font for all text, for example, you wouldn't have to go to the parts-list style and change the font and then to the dimension style and change the font, and so on; instead, you would simply change just one or two text styles that are being called into those other styles.

Substyles are coupled with their parent styles, which means a substyle cannot be purged if it's in use by another style. If you cache a high-level style into your document from the library or if you save a high-level style into the library from your file, all substyles participate in those operations.

Styles are extremely powerful formatting tools that enable you to quickly change the entire face of a document. This also serves as a warning that modifying styles without understanding how they work can quickly generate unexpected results.

TAKE THE TIME TO UNDERSTAND STYLES

Although there's probably never been a single person who decided to use Inventor just for the "exciting" styles and standards tools, these tools are extremely powerful, and you'll be doing yourself a disservice if you don't spend some time getting to know them.

They may seem complex at first, but once you understand them, they will become powerful tools. Play around with changing styles in a scratch drawing to see how the annotations change.

Once you have a good understanding of styles, sit down with your design group and come up with a set of standards with which everyone is happy.

Apply these styles to your documents and use them for a while. One of the great aspects of the style library is that if you want to make a change, you can make it to the library, and everyone will have access to this new/changed style each time they open a file.

Drawing Style Administration

Each drawing template that comes with Inventor has a full set of styles saved (cached) in the drawing document. Although you can use the style library as a sharing and update tool, there is no direct link between objects on your sheet and styles in your library. Any in-use style is loaded into your document either automatically or manually.

If your project is set to use the style library (the Use Style Library setting is Yes or Read Only), then it's important to keep your style definitions in sync between your template file and the library.

If your project is using the style library, you have a style in the library that has the same name as a style in your template, and those styles have different settings, then the definition in the library automatically overwrites the definition in the template each time it's used to start a new drawing (a warning dialog box is shown when this condition is detected).

The best way to ensure synchronization is to open your template file and run either the Update Styles tool (which pulls updates from the library) or the Save Styles To Style Library tool (which pushes updates back to the library), depending on which way you want to transfer the styles.

You can find both of these options and the Purge tool on the Manage tab.

Sharing Your Drawings Outside Your Workgroup

Once your design is fully annotated, you can share the design documents with others in numerous ways.

Of course, the traditional hard-copy route is available from the Print tool, but there are electronic means to share your Inventor drawings with people who do not have Inventor.

The native file formats offer several possibilities. Inventor IPT, IAM, IPN, and IDW files can be viewed using the freely distributed Inventor View application. A version of this is already installed with Inventor but can be downloaded for free from the Autodesk website.

As mentioned earlier, if you use DWG as your drawing-file format, anyone with a copy of AutoCAD or AutoCAD LT® 2007 software or newer can view, plot, and measure the Inventor drawing.

Using the Publish tool you can generate a DWF or DWFx file. The DWF or DWFx file can store both your 2D drawing and the 3D models referenced in the drawing.

DWF files are viewed using Autodesk Design Review, which is available for download from the Autodesk website. To publish a DWF file, first click the Inventor button (the large *I* in the upper-left corner) and then select Export ➤ Export To DWF.

You can find any of the products mentioned earlier by going to www.autodesk.com or www.google.com and searching for one of these terms:

◆   *Autodesk Inventor View*

◆   *Autodesk Design Review*

PDF is a popular publishing format that can be read by Adobe Acrobat Reader. You can save a PDF from Inventor using the Save Copy As option and changing the file type to PDF or by using Export ➤ Export To PDF. You can also download a number of PDF printer drivers that will allow you to print to PDF. Acrobat Reader is available for download from Adobe's website: www.adobe.com.

There are some options for creating PDFs found by clicking the Options button in the Save Copy As dialog box when the file type is set to PDF. For instance, you might want to include all sheets in the PDF and create it in black and white. You can do so using the Options button. Unfortunately, you cannot configure these options to be the defaults.

You should note that the option to have the PDF viewer automatically open the PDF when it is created is a bit hidden and is set with the Publish options used when creating a DWF.

To disable the automatic view of PDFs, click the Inventor button (the large *I* in the upper-left corner) and select Export ➤ Export To DWF. Then uncheck the Display Published File In Viewer option.

The Bottom Line

Create templates and styles.   Inventor provides numerous methods to create, store, and use drawing templates and styles. Careful planning as to how and where to manage these resources is important. Consideration must be given to how templates are deployed on your network and whether to use the style library.

> **Master It**   Rather than using one of the out-of-the-box drawing settings, you need to set up a drawing template, a drafting standard, and annotation styles to conform to a particular international, industry, or company drafting standard. How do you get started?

Utilize drawing resources.   Each Inventor drawing file contains a number of commonly used drawing-resource definitions, such as title blocks, borders, symbols, and so on. These resource definitions allow you to store preconfigured items for quick and easy reuse.

Master It You have blocks of general notes that you place on every drawing file. However, some drawings get one set of notes and others get another, so making these notes part of the title block seems to be the wrong approach. Is there a way to handle this in Inventor?

Edit styles and standards. Inventor's drawing styles and standards allow you to set up your dimension styles, layer styles, and so on, in advance so that you can maintain consistency across all your drawings.

Master It You have set up your object defaults to use an inch-based dimension style, but occasionally you want to place a millimeter-based dimension. Can this be done easily, or do you have to override the dimension style?

Create drawing views. Drawing views allow you to make 2D views of your 3D models. The hidden line generation and alignment of your projected views are automatic, as are updates to the 2D views when your 3D models change.

Master It When placing a drawing view, the lines on curved edges don't show up. Is there an option to turn these on?

Annotate part drawings. Adding annotation to your part drawings is accomplished primarily using the tools on the Annotate tab. Many of these tools automate traditional drafting annotation, but you might still find the need to add annotation in a more manual way.

Master It You need to create sheet-metal flat patterns for your parts with laser etching on them. Often this is text, but you've noticed that if you attempt to create text as an extrusion on the part, you end up with a stencil effect, rather than single-line characters used for etching. Is there a way to do this?

Annotate assembly drawings. Often, much of the annotation created for assembly drawings concerns bill of materials information, but you can use most of the same annotation tools used for part drawings in an assembly drawing.

Master It You created a section view of your assembly model and then noticed that you could hide the hatch pattern by right-clicking it and choosing Hide. But now when you right-click the drawing view, you can't find an option to bring back the hatch pattern. Is it gone for good?

Work with sheet-metal drawings. Inventor sheet-metal drawings give you access to the folded model and the flat pattern, provided that a flat pattern has been created in the 3D model.

Master It When you place a bend note on a flat pattern drawing, it places the direction, angle, and bend radius. Your shop is accustomed to seeing only the direction and angle. Is there a way to remove the bend radius?

Work with weldment views. Weldment views offer some extra functionality over standard assembly views in that they allow you to document your assembly in each weldment stage.

Master It You want to create a drawing package that shows all the weldment pieces in the prepped stage and then show the weldment assembly in the completed form. What's the best way to do this?

Work with iParts and iAssembly drawings.   One of the benefits of creating part and assembly families as iParts and iAssemblies is the ability to create tabulated drawings that show each member and its key dimensions in a table.

> **Master It**   You've created an iPart table and want to set the dimension on the sheet to match the table heading. Is this possible?

Share your drawings outside your workgroup.   You can save your drawings in DWF, DWFx, and PDF formats in order to share them with people who do not have Inventor. You can use Autodesk Design Review to access DWF files and Adobe Acrobat Reader to access PDF files; both are free viewer applications.

> **Master It**   You have a multipage Inventor drawing, but when you export it as a PDF file, you get only the first page. Is this a bug, or is it just the way it is?

Chapter 13

Tools Overview

Using the various Autodesk® Inventor® software tools effectively helps you improve your productivity and get the most out of the program. In this chapter you will explore many of the tools that are included with your Inventor installation. Some of these are located within Inventor, and others are external applications. Initially, a certain amount of familiarity is required to be productive with these tools; however, spending the time to become familiar with them pays off in the long run.

Most of the topics in this chapter do not apply to the Autodesk® Inventor LT™ program.

This chapter assumes you have a good understanding of parts, assemblies, and drawings. You will learn about the various aspects of Inventor tools and about some of the add-ins. You'll look at the key aspects of the tools and add-ins that come with Inventor as well as relevant workflows. Many other tools can be built using the application programming interface (API). Although the API is not covered in this book, you can find a great deal of information online about using it to develop your own tools.

This chapter covers a number of tools, including the BIM Exchange, AutoLimits, Design Assistant, Drawing Resource Transfer Wizard, style tools, Supplier Content Center, the Task Scheduler, the iProperties tool, the Measure tool, the Customer Involvement Program (CIP), customer error reporting (CER), and more.

In this chapter, you'll learn to

- ◆ Take your models from Inventor to the Autodesk® Building Systems program
- ◆ Create AutoLimits (design sensors)
- ◆ Manage design data efficiently using Inventor tools
- ◆ Manage styles
- ◆ Create expressions with iProperties
- ◆ Give feedback to Autodesk

Exploring the BIM Exchange

The Building Information Modeling (BIM) Exchange is an add-in environment for parts and assemblies. Using the BIM Exchange, you can import Inventor models into the AutoCAD® MEP and Autodesk® Revit® MEP products, which are used for building design and construction systems. The MEP products are used to document the mechanical, electrical, and plumbing information of the designs. To access the BIM Exchange environment, you must first have a part file or an assembly file open and then select the Environments tab and click BIM Exchange.

Assembly Model Simplification

Typically, when you author an Inventor model for use with a building systems application (such as Revit, for example), you will want to reduce the amount of detail in that model so the file size is smaller and so you are not giving away too much intellectual property. You can start with an assembly file and use the Simplify tools to prepare your model for exporting and sharing with BIM applications. To access these tools, you can click the Simplify tab in the assembly environment, where you will find the following tools:

Include Components   Use this tool to create a view representation using only the selected components. You can then choose this view representation to create the exported BIM model. For instance, you might use this tool to select only the externally visible components of a condensing unit assembly to prepare it for use in Autodesk Revit MEP. The result would be a new view representation created in the Representations folder of the browser and named something like Simple View1. To edit the resulting view representation, you simply right-click it in the browser and choose Edit Include Components.

Define Envelopes   Use this tool to replace an assembly component with a rectangular or cylindrical bounding box. For instance, you might use this to remove extra detail for components such as fasteners. Defining the envelope of a bolt allows a model to be used for fit checks and sizing where, for example, a protruding bolt head might be important, while at the same time it greatly reduces the number of model faces and edges the component consists of.

Create Simplified Parts   Use this tool to create a simplified part file from an assembly view by referencing the current view representation. For instance, if you used the Include Components tool to create a view representation of just the externally visible components of a condensing unit assembly, you could then use the Create Simplified Part tool to combine the remaining visible components into a single part model.

Exploring the Include Components Tool

If you have not already downloaded the Chapter 13 files from www.sybex.com/go/masteringinventor2016, please refer to the "What You Will Need" section of the introduction for the download and setup instructions.

Once you're sure you have the Chapter 13 files in place, follow these steps to see the Include Components tool in action:

1. On the Get Started tab, click the Open button.

2. Browse for mi_13a_014.iam in the Chapter 13 directory of your Mastering Inventor 2016 folder and click the Open button.

3. From the Simplify tab, click the Include Components button.

4. In the tool controls, locate the Select All Occurrences button and click it. When it's selected, you'll see a check mark next to the button, as shown in Figure 13.1.

FIGURE 13.1

The Select All Occurrences button in the tool controls

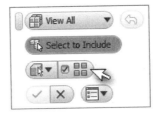

5. Next, use the browser to locate and select all the components *except* the ones named as follows:

   ◆ mi_13a_Clip

   ◆ mi_13a_Washer

6. Once your selection is complete, use the tool controls to toggle the view control to View Excluded. The result should turn off all of the components, except the ones listed in step 5.

7. Use the tool controls to toggle the view control to View All and then click the OK button (the green check mark button) to create the simplified view representation. Figure 13.2 shows the results.

FIGURE 13.2

The resulting simplified view representation

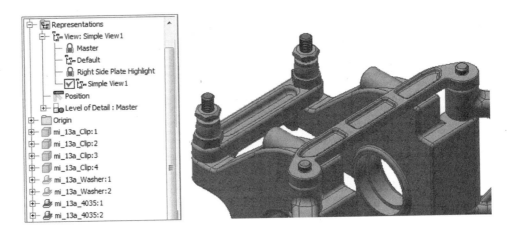

8. Expand the Representations folder in the browser, if required, and locate the node for the active, simple view representation. It will have a check mark next to it.

9. Right-click the simple view representation and choose Edit Include Components to bring back the Include Components tools.

10. Hold the **Ctrl** key on the keyboard, click the components named mi_13a_4035 to exclude them from the simplified view representation, and then click the OK button in the tool controls to update the simplified view representation. Figure 13.3 shows the results.

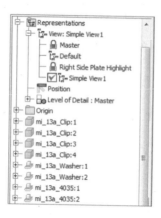

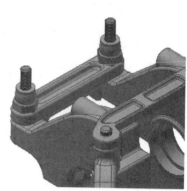

In this example, the resulting simple view representation is not really that much simpler, but you've explored the methods used to create and update a simplified view representation using the Include Components tool. You can close the current file without saving changes and continue to the next section.

EXPLORING THE DEFINE ENVELOPES TOOL

The Define Envelopes tool can be used to reduce the number of faces and edges present in an assembly model, which will help reduce the file size of the BIM export version. You can follow these steps to see the Define Envelopes tool in action:

1. On the Get Started tab, click the Open button.

2. Browse for `mi_13a_016.iam` in the `Chapter 13` directory of your `Mastering Inventor 2016` folder and click the Open button.

3. From the Simplify tab, click the Define Envelopes button.

4. In the tool controls, locate the Select All Occurrences button and ensure that the check box is selected.

5. Find an instance of the cap screw named mi_13a_4762 and select it.

6. In the tool controls, locate the Bounding Box/Bounding Cylinder control and change it to Bounding Cylinder, as shown in Figure 13.4.

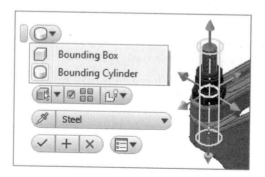

7. Use the grip arrows to adjust the size of the bounding cylinder, click a radial arrow, then click the Align button, and then select the circular face of the bolt to set the envelope size.

8. Click the Apply button (it looks like a green plus sign) found in the tool controls to define the bounding envelopes for the screws.

9. Notice that the browser nodes for both of the mi_13a_4762 components are gray, indicating that they have been hidden. And notice, too, that a browser node named Envelope1 has been created to represent the screws.

10. Select one of the mi_13a_Bushing components, set it to use a bounding cylinder, and then click the OK button to create the bounding cylinder for both bushings, as shown in Figure 13.5.

FIGURE 13.5
The resulting envelopes

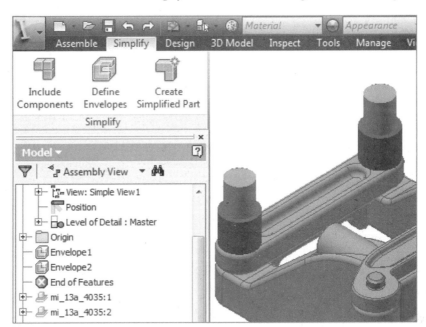

You'll notice that a new envelope is created in the browser for the bushing components. If you need to modify the envelope, you can right-click it and choose Edit Envelope, Delete, or Show Original. Feel free to experiment with the Define Envelope tool to see how you can use it to reduce the details of other components in the assembly. When you have finished, you can close the current file without saving changes and continue to the next section.

EXPLORING THE CREATE SIMPLIFIED PART TOOL

The Create Simplified Part tool can be used to derive the active assembly file into a new part file, using the current view representation and any component envelopes that might be present. You can follow these steps to create a derived part using the Create Simplified Part tool:

1. On the Get Started tab, click the Open button.

2. Browse for mi_13a_018.iam in the Chapter 13 directory of your Mastering Inventor 2016 folder and click the Open button.

3. From the Simplify tab, click the Create Simplified Part button.

4. Use the Combine Style buttons to select a Solid Body style. This option handles how the components of the assembly will be combined as solid bodies in the resulting derived part file. If your goal is to reduce the amount of intellectual property in the file you provide others, you'd want to use the leftmost button to merge the seams between solid bodies and make it more difficult for the file you create to be used to reverse-engineer the design.

5. Enter **Simple_mi_13a_018** in the New Component Name input.

6. Accept the default value for the template file or use the Browse Templates button (it looks like a blank sheet of paper) to select a different part file template.

7. Set the New File Location path to the Chapter 13 directory of your Mastering Inventor 2016 folder and then click the OK button. Figure 13.6 shows the Create Simplified Part dialog entries and selections.

FIGURE 13.6
Creating a simplified part

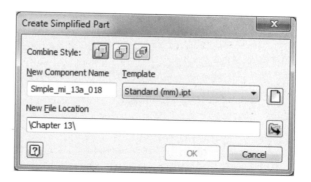

8. Examine the browser in the resulting new part file to find the derived assembly node and extrusion features for each assembly-level envelope, as shown in Figure 13.7.

FIGURE 13.7
The simplified derived part

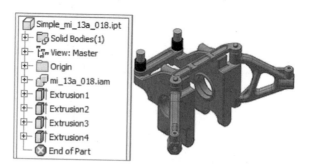

The simplified derived part behaves the same as any other derived part, which means that edits to the original assembly file are carried through to the simplified part version unless you right-click the derived assembly browser node and choose to suppress or break the link to the base component. Keep in mind that, at this point, your new simplified derived part exists only in the current Inventor session and has not yet been saved to disk. If you'd like to explore the link between the original file and the simplified file, you can save both files now. Otherwise, you can close the current simplified part file and the original assembly file without saving changes and continue to the next section.

Part Model Simplification

In addition to the tools available to simplify assembly models, you can also use the BIM Feature Recognition and Simplify tools in the parts environment to reduce details that are not needed for BIM models, and you can use the Recognize Revit Features tools to make your models friendlier to Autodesk Revit.

SIMPLIFY PART MODELS

One of the issues with handing part models created in Inventor to the BIM user is that the models often contain cosmetic or manufacturing features that are important in the mechanical design but are not required for the BIM layout and planning application. For example, if you create a model of a machined part in Inventor, you will likely need to include and specify rounded edges, holes, and other features as part of the mechanical design. However, these features are not important to the BIM user and can slow down the BIM application. So to help with this, Inventor includes part simplification tools to remove detail and voids, as well as reduce the number of faces and edges in a part model.

You can find the Simplify tools by going to the Environments tab and clicking the Recognize Revit Features button or by right-clicking anywhere on the 3D Model tab and choosing Show Panels and then Simplify. The Simplify tools include the following:

Remove Details   Use this tool to reduce the number of faces and edges by removing small cosmetic fillets and chamfers as well as any other face selections you decide to remove.

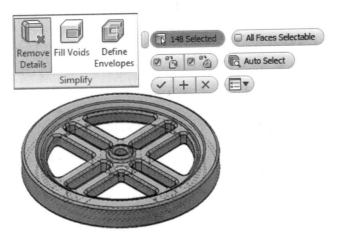

Fill Voids   Often a part contains holes and pockets that are meaningful in the mechanical design but are not important in BIM layout. You can use this tool to select and fill these voids in order to reduce the number of edges and faces and therefore simplify the model's geometry.

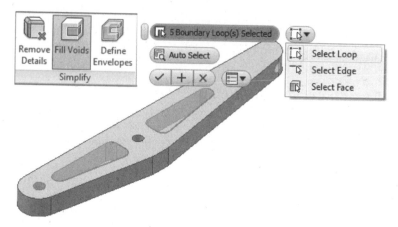

Define Envelopes   Use this tool to reduce the number of faces and edges of complex features in order to make part models easier to work with. For instance, you might represent a highly intricate machined feature with a simple bounding box.

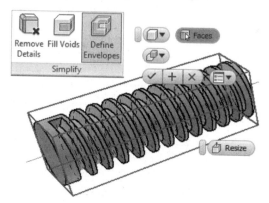

RECOGNIZE REVIT FEATURES

Many Inventor users create models to be used in Autodesk Revit libraries. To assist with this, it can helpful to set up the model so that it imports into Revit smoothly and predictably. You can make your models more "Revit ready" by using the Recognize Revit Features tools. Once features are recognized, you can enter the BIM Exchange environment to author the model for Revit export.

Recognize Extrude   Recognizes Inventor extruded features and converts them to extrusions recognized by Revit

Recognize Revolve   Recognizes Inventor revolved features and converts them to revolutions recognized by Revit

Recognize Sweep   Recognizes Inventor swept features and converts them to sweeps recognized by Revit

Auto Recognize   Automatically recognizes Inventor extruded and revolved features and removes fillets and chamfers

Model Authoring

The BIM Exchange environment allows you to author Autodesk Revit family data in your Inventor model and create connector objects such as cables, conduits, ducts, and pipes on the simplified model. These connector objects define the interfaces, which are the connection points between Inventor and the BIM. Inventor allows you to create, edit, and delete connector objects. Here are the steps to create a conduit connector:

1. On the Get Started tab, click the Open button.

2. Browse for mi_13a_444.ipt in the Chapter 13 directory of your Mastering Inventor 2016 folder and click the Open button.

3. Select the Environments tab and click the BIM Exchange button.

4. From the MEP Author panel, click the Conduit Connector button.

5. In the Conduit Connector dialog box, select Circular as the shape for the connector (using Undefined allows you to select any oval, circular, or rectangular face).

6. Select the yellow circular face to place the connector. The location of the connector appears as a cylindrical arrow. Click the direction button to reverse the connector direction so that it points out away from the box.

7. Click the check box in the Size field and enter a value. Or you can leave the check box deselected to have the value linked to the model.

8. In the Connection Type drop-down menu, select Threaded.

9. Click the OK button to create the connector. Figure 13.8 shows the Conduit Connector dialog box.

FIGURE 13.8
Adding a conduit connection

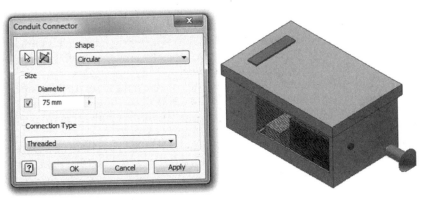

10. Use the Pipe Connector button on the MEP Author panel to add a supply pipe connection to the blue circular face. Take a moment to explore the System Type options and author this connection with a type and property values of your choice.

11. Use the Duct Connector button on the MEP Author panel to add an exhaust duct connector to the rectangular face on the top of the unit. Again, set the properties to values of your choice and explore the options available.

12. Expand the MEP System Connections folder in the browser, as shown in Figure 13.9, and you'll find all your connections categorized in subfolders. You can edit, delete, and suppress connectors as needed.

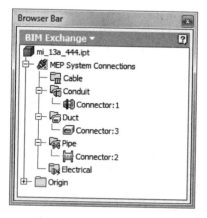

Feel free to create new connections to explore these tools further. When finished, you can close the file without saving changes.

Model Publishing

A *part* in the BIM Exchange is the basic unit; that is, a specific size of the component placed within a part family. The part has instance-specific properties associated with it, such as a name and geometric representation. You can use the Export Building Components tool to save model geometry, properties, and connectors to an Autodesk exchange file (*.adsk) or a Revit family file (*.rfa). An ADSK file can be read by programs such as Revit MEP and AutoCAD MEP. However, Revit family files are typically preferred by Revit users because they provide a more direct handoff of the library data.

When publishing a model, it's often useful to set up the user coordinate system (USC) to match the destination coordinate orientation so that the models do not import upside down or flipped over. You can do this in the BIM Exchange environment by creating a UCS and then specifying its use when exporting the data.

 Certification Objective

In the following exercise, you will set up a model to be exported from Inventor and imported into Autodesk software. Follow these steps to publish a model in the BIM Exchange tools:

1. On the Get Started tab, click the Open button.

2. Browse for mi_13a_445.ipt located in the Chapter 13 directory of your Mastering Inventor 2015 folder and then click the Open button.

3. Choose the Environments tab and then click the BIM Exchange button. Note that the connectors have been authored already. Do not be too concerned that this exercise model is not realistic in its configuration; its purpose is merely to demonstrate the available tools.

4. Click the UCS button in the BIM Exchange tab to define a new user coordinate system.

5. Specify the origin by choosing the vertex at the bottom corner indicated with the black arrow, as shown in Figure 13.10.

FIGURE 13.10

Creating a new user coordinate system

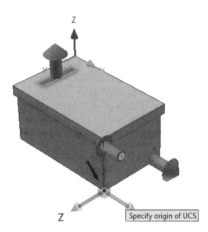

6. Specify the x-axis by choosing the corner near the black X, and specify the y-axis by choosing the corner near the black Y.

7. Notice the new UCS node in the browser. You can rename it by clicking it twice slowly.

8. Click the Check Design button and notice the listing of information. The green check marks indicate that the information required is present. Yellow check marks warn you if some information is missing. Click the OK button.

9. Click the Check Revit Features button and wait for the *.html report to open in your web browser.

In the Feature Check Report you'll see that there is an error with the feature called Base2. To resolve this, you could exit the BIM Exchange environment and use the BIM Feature Recognize tool to convert Base2 into extrude features that Revit will recognize. For now, though, you can ignore the error, close the report, and continue.

10. On the BIM Exchange tab, click the Export Building Components button.

11. To set the component type, click the Browse button.

12. Choose the following selections from the drop-down menu using the plus buttons to expand the selections:

◆ 23.75.00.00 Climate Control (HVAC)

◆ 23.75.70.00 HVAC Distribution Devices

◆ 23.75.70.17 Water Heated And Cooled

◆ 23.75.70.17.34 Unit Heaters

13. Click the OK button.

14. Enter the following information in the Component Properties area. All iProperty fields pulled from the model have a cyan background. When the Model Property option is selected, model properties are exported with the component. You can clear this if you do not want to include this information.

Description   Enter **Climate Control Unit Heater.**

Manufacturer   Enter **MI, Inc.**

Model   Enter **12345–6T.**

15. Choose a user UCS from the Orientation drop-down.

16. Change the File Type drop-down at the top of the dialog box so that it is set to Autodesk Exchange Files (`*.adsk`).

17. Set the Thumbnail option to Import From File and then click the Import button to browse for the file called `Unit Heater 1200 Series.png`, found in the `Chapter 13` folder.

18. When the thumbnail is set, click the Apply Changes button.

19. Click the OK button in the Export Building Components dialog box to save an ADSK file (you can click Cancel and choose not to save this file if you'd like).

🌐 Real World Scenario

A TYPICAL SCENARIO FOR THE BIM EXCHANGE

Say your company uses Inventor and specializes in electrical and mechanical designs and that you supply the air conditioner for a building being designed by an architectural firm. To minimize the risk of losing information and future rework, you meet with the architectural and construction firms to ensure that the interfaces between your product and the building are all agreed on. The architects and contractors do not care about any internal details of the air conditioner unit and actually prefer having a lightweight model that will not add extra overhead to the Revit model, but they are extremely sensitive to any changes in the interfaces between your product and their work.

The plan is to author your model and interfaces in Inventor and send the design to the architectural firm so that they can use your model to know exactly the dimensions and locations to tie into. Although you can output the files from the BIM Exchange tools to Revit users as is, it becomes apparent that having your products authored in Revit format will allow Revit designers to specify your products in their designs more quickly and accurately.

Depending on the relationship you have with the architectural firm, you may be able to trade the simplified models that you output from the BIM Exchange tools in return for the fully functional and tested Revit family files to be placed on your company's website for download by other firms that would like to specify your product line in their designs. If the architectural firm does not have the time to do this for you, it may be determined that hiring outside help to test and verify Revit files is the way to go.

Using AutoLimits

The AutoLimits tool allows you to monitor model changes so that you can reduce errors and engineering changes. You can think of it as a sensor. For example, say you are a plastics manufacturer and want to analyze the situation when the wall thickness of the components becomes too thin, or perhaps you are a machinist and want to know when two holes come too close to one another. You want to define this "check" and ensure that such a situation is caught early in the design. With AutoLimits, you can set up these limits and let the system warn you.

The AutoLimits that you create with the tool are passive and do not drive geometry or stop a feature from violating a limit. They simply notify you when it does. Another way to look at the AutoLimits tool is as a persistent Measure tool. With the standard Measure tool, the result of a measurement is not saved, whereas with the AutoLimits tool the measurement persists. When you open a file, the AutoLimits you have created are not shown unless you activate the AutoLimits panel bar.

The AutoLimits tool monitors the following limits:

Dimensional Length, Distance, Angle, Diameter, Minimum Distance

Area-Perimeter Area, Perimeter

Physical Property Volume, Mass

Figure 13.11 shows the AutoLimits tool icons as accessed from the AutoLimits panel of the Inspect tab.

FIGURE 13.11
AutoLimits access

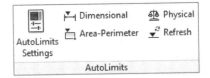

TURN ON AUTOLIMITS

If you do not see the AutoLimits tools on the Inspect tab, navigate to the Tools tab and click the Add-Ins button. Click AutoLimits in the Add-Ins list and then select the Loaded/Unloaded check box at the bottom of the dialog to load the AutoLimits tools. You can select the Load Automatically check box to have Inventor load them for you on startup.

Feedback is given to the user in terms of shape and color, as in the following examples:

◆ A green circle means it is within the boundary limit.

◆ A yellow inverted triangle means it is near the boundary limit.

◆ A red square means it is beyond the limit.

Figure 13.12 shows the different types of AutoLimits and their settings. (Click the AutoLimits Settings button shown in Figure 13.11 to access this dialog box.) You can control the visibility of each AutoLimits type by using the On and Off radio buttons. In an assembly, only the edited document's AutoLimits are visible in the browser; in other words, AutoLimits at subassembly levels are not visible or available unless that subassembly is edited.

FIGURE 13.12

The AutoLimits Settings dialog box

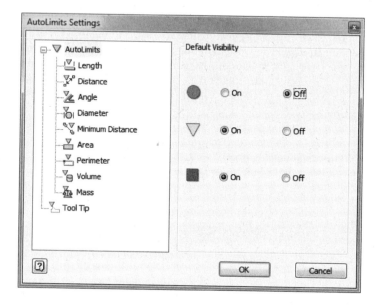

To see AutoLimits in action, follow these steps:

1. On the Get Started tab, click the Open button.

2. Browse for `mi_13a_002.ipt` located in the `Chapter 13` directory of your `Mastering Inventor 2015` folder and click the Open button.

3. On the Inspect tab, click the AutoLimits Settings button, ensure that all three Default Visibility options are enabled, and then click the OK button. This part has a layout sketch on which the solid was based. The length has been left undefined by creating the visible driven dimension. Two AutoLimits have been added. The first alerts you if the distance from the front edge to the rectangular cut becomes too thin, and the second alerts you if the mass of the part becomes too heavy. To adjust the model, follow these steps:

   A. Click the sketched point or construction line and drag in or out.

   B. Use the Update button (select it from the Quick Access bar) to see the edit take place.

4. Drag the sketch point out so that the visible dimension is around 470 and click the Update button. Note the red square in the middle of the part. This is the Mass AutoLimit, indicating that the current length causes the part to be too heavy.

5. Drag the sketch point in so that the visible dimension is less than 300 and click the Update button. Note the red square on the edge of the part; this is a lower limit, Length AutoLimit, indicating that the current overall length causes the width between the rectangular cut and the edge of the part to become too thin.

To see these AutoLimits in the browser, you can click the white arrow on the browser bar and change from the Model browser to the AutoLimits browser (you might need to use the Refresh button on the AutoLimits panel first). Once you've explored these existing AutoLimits, you can close this file without saving the changes and continue to create AutoLimits.

LOADING AUTOLIMIT TOOLS

When you load a file that contains existing AutoLimits, the AutoLimits tools are not loaded or displayed in that file until you use an AutoLimits tool. A quick way of doing this is to use the Refresh button on the AutoLimits panel.

Creating AutoLimits

AutoLimits come in three types: Dimensional, Area-Perimeter, and Physical Properties. In the following steps, you'll create a Minimum Distance limit and then define the limit boundaries:

1. On the Get Started tab, click the Open button.

2. Browse for `mi_13a_003.ipt` located in the `Chapter 13` directory of your `Mastering Inventor 2016` folder and click the Open button.

3. On the Inspect tab, click the AutoLimits Settings button.

4. Check that all three settings are On and click the OK button.

5. Click the Dimensional button in the AutoLimits panel.

6. On the left of the dialog box, click the Minimum Distance AutoLimits button (the last one on the bottom).

7. For the selections, you can click the edges with work axes running through them, or you can click the axes (the axes are not required and have been placed just to help identify the correct edges).

8. Click the Boundary tab.

9. Click the Click To Add bar to place the green target AutoLimit.

10. Set the Lower value to **50 mm**.

11. Rather than setting an Upper value, you will change the USign column so that the Upper limit is open-ended. Click the < under USign and choose the blank or empty entry from the drop-down.

12. You want to add another row to define the lower limits. To do so, hold down the **Ctrl** key and click the Click To Add bar. The new row should appear above the previous row in the table.

13. Click the yellow triangle twice slowly in the Level column and change it to the red square in the drop-down.

SETTING AUTOLIMITS BOUNDARIES

Hold down **Alt** and click the Click To Add bar before you add any boundaries. This will place all five boundary levels at once, allowing you to define the green "target" boundary as well as a yellow "warning" and a red "danger" boundary on each side of the target.

Clicking the Click To Add bar always adds an upper boundary unless the green target boundary has been set to have no upper value. Clicking the Click To Add bar while holding down the **Ctrl** key always adds a lower boundary unless the green target boundary has been set to have no lower value.

You can add as many ranges as required when using the standard Click To Add or **Ctrl+click** methods; however, you can have only one range (five boundaries) when using the **Alt+click** method.

14. Set the Upper value to **49.999 mm**.

15. Change the LSign column so that the lower limit is open-ended. Click the < under LSign and choose the blank or empty entry from the drop-down. Your boundary definition should resemble Figure 13.13.

FIGURE 13.13
The Dimensional AutoLimits dialog box

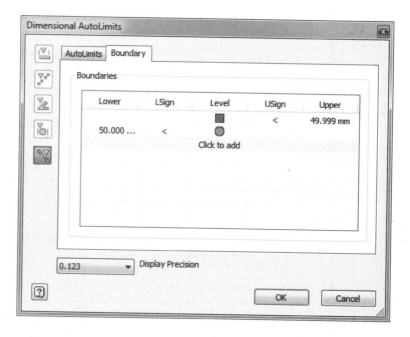

16. Click the OK button and then click the OK button in the message dialog box.

17. You should see a green dot appear on your model; this is your AutoLimit.

18. Double-click the Length dimension and change the value to **299 mm**.

19. Click the Update button (select it from the Quick Access bar) to see the edit take place. Note that the AutoLimit displays the red square, indicating that the distance is now below the value set as acceptable.

20. Change Length Dimension to **300 mm** and click Update. Note that the AutoLimit displays a gray X. This indicates that there is a gap in the AutoLimit.

21. Hover your mouse pointer over the gray X until it changes color; then right-click and choose Edit AutoLimits.

22. Click the Boundary tab.

23. Select the Lower limit for the green row, change 50 mm to **49.9999 mm**, and then click any other cell. Note that it sets the value back to 50.000 mm.

24. Click the OK button to return to the model and note that the AutoLimit is now green, as shown in Figure 13.14.

FIGURE 13.14
Length AutoLimits

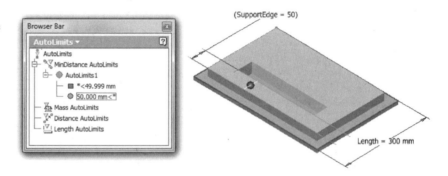

AutoLimits are quite simple to set up and use. You can continue experimenting with this file and create other types of AutoLimits. Then you can close the file and continue.

Editing AutoLimits

You can view all the existing AutoLimits in your model by clicking the white arrow on the browser bar and changing from the Model browser to the AutoLimits browser. You can edit AutoLimits in the AutoLimits browser by selecting an AutoLimits entry and right-clicking it. I recommend you set the selection filter to Feature Priority because doing so makes it easier to select the AutoLimits glyphs. You can copy or delete AutoLimits by right-clicking them in the browser and choosing the appropriate command.

You can also create a group of AutoLimits to control the visibility of related AutoLimits. To do so, follow these steps:

1. Right-click the top node in the AutoLimits browser and select Create Group.

2. Right-click any AutoLimit and choose Copy AutoLimit.

3. Right-click the group and choose Paste AutoLimit.

4. Right-click the group to toggle visibility.

> **DON'T GO CRAZY WITH AUTOLIMITS**
>
> In an assembly, use only the minimum number of AutoLimits required to monitor just the critical design information of interest. Using more than 10 AutoLimits can begin to impact the processing speed of your model. You can use AutoLimits in all environments except the Inventor Studio environment, the BIM Exchange, Dynamic Simulation, the construction environment, Solid Edit, the Flat pattern environment, and Engineer's Notebook.

Using the Design Assistant

The Design Assistant helps you find, manage, and maintain Inventor files and related documents, spreadsheets, and text files. Imagine your company is evaluating a new design that involves making minor changes to an existing design. You would like to reuse the parts, assemblies, drawings, and presentations as much as possible. Once you make the required changes and finish the new design work, you need to send the existing and modified designs to another department for their input on the overall design. The Design Assistant and Pack And Go tools can help in this scenario. You can perform searches, create file reports, and work with links across Inventor files. In addition, you can preview and view the iProperties.

You can launch the Design Assistant in any of these three ways:

◆ Within Inventor, while a file is open, click the Inventor button and choose Manage ➤ Design Assistant.

◆ Right-click a file in Windows Explorer and select the Design Assistant tool.

◆ Select Start ➤ All Programs ➤ Autodesk ➤ Autodesk Inventor 2016 ➤ Design Assistant 2016.

> **MANAGING FILES IN THE DESIGN ASSISTANT**
>
> Note that the Manage button will not be visible if you open the Design Assistant from an actively open file in Inventor. To manage the links, you must open the file from the Design Assistant directly or via Windows Explorer, and they cannot be open in Inventor while you do this.

The Design Assistant dialog box, shown in Figure 13.15, contains three buttons in the left column: Properties, Preview, and Manage. You can open files using File ➤ Open. Figure 13.15 shows the result of selecting File ➤ Open in an assembly named Demote_Stapler.iam. The assembly is listed in the left pane, and all parts related to the assembly are listed in the right pane.

FIGURE 13.15
The Design Assistant
dialog box

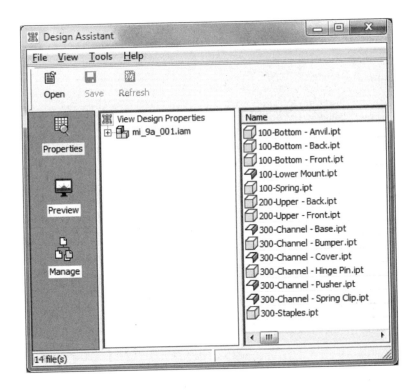

You can right-click any file in the Design Assistant and select View With Inventor View 1.0, which launches the Inventor View dialog box, shown in Figure 13.16. In this dialog box, you can use view functions such as Zoom, Pan, and Rotate.

FIGURE 13.16
The Inventor View
dialog box

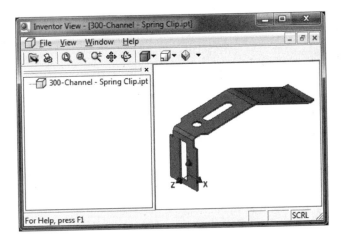

To view the preview in the Design Assistant, you can click the Preview button in the Design Assistant dialog box, shown in Figure 13.17. The Design Assistant shows the preview for all the files. The figure shows the preview of the top-level assembly and one of the parts contained in the assembly. You can choose any listed file to display its preview.

FIGURE 13.17
The Preview button in the Design Assistant dialog box

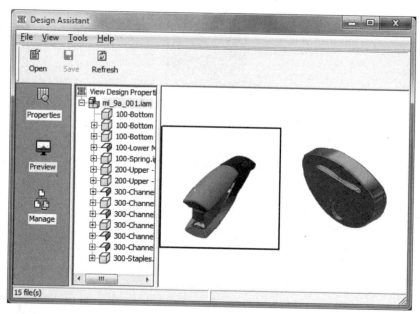

Using the Find Files Tool

You can use the Find Files tool to locate all references to a specified file. This can be useful when you are trying to determine how an edit, revision, or change order will affect existing designs. To use the Find Files tool, follow these steps:

1. Click the Manage button in the left column, as shown in Figure 13.18.

2. Click the Drawings, Assemblies, and Parts check boxes. These check boxes are located next to the text Include Files Of Type in the Design Assistant dialog box (only two are shown in Figure 13.18).

FIGURE 13.18
Using the Find Files
function

3. You can check Search Subfolders, shown next to the Parts check box in the Design Assistant dialog box, to include subfolders.

4. Find Files will find the files that use the selected file. In Figure 13.18, 300-Channel– Spring Clip.ipt has been selected, as is shown in the top pane (the .ipt file extension is not shown), and the referencing files found are listed in the bottom pane.

Right-clicking a file and selecting iProperties gives you the properties for the selected part or assembly without opening the part or assembly in Inventor, as shown in Figure 13.19. Note that you do this after clicking the Properties or Preview button; the iProperty option is not available from the Manage view.

FIGURE 13.19
iProperties in the
Design Assistant

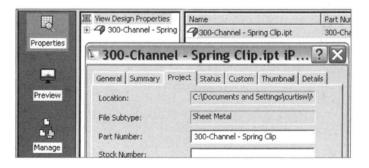

Using the Where Used Tool

Selecting Tools ➤ Find ➤ Where Used shows all the files that use the current file. For example, to find out which files use Assembly1.iam, you can do the following:

1. Select Tools ➤ Find ➤ Where Used (in the Design Assistant dialog box). You will see the dialog box shown in Figure 13.20.

FIGURE 13.20
The Where Used
dialog box

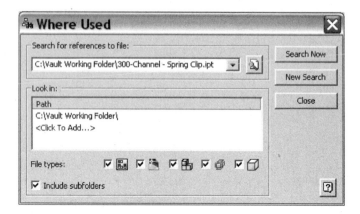

2. Select options in the Where Used dialog box, such as Parts, Drawings, Include Subfolders, and so on.

3. Click Search Now.

In the Path area under Look In, you can add paths that you want to search. The Where Used tool will list all the files where the specified file is used in some way. File relationships can include but are not limited to derived components and using a part file or assembly file in an assembly, drawing, presentation, and so on. Figure 13.21 shows a Where Used search that has been run using the Design Assistant on a file in the local Autodesk® Vault data management software workspace. However, the Design Assistant is often used without Vault.

FIGURE 13.21
Results of clicking
Search Now in the
Where Used dialog box

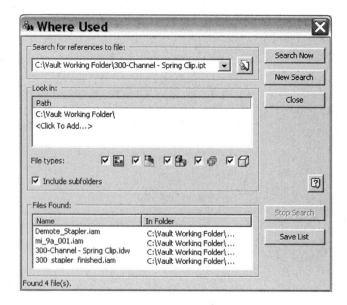

Renaming, Copying, and Replacing Files

You can use the Design Assistant to perform management tasks such as renaming, copying, and replacing Inventor files without breaking the links to the files that reference them. This is because the Design Assistant not only performs the management task on the files but also "cracks" the referencing files and updates the link to the file at the same time. This is the fundamental difference between doing these operations in Windows Explorer (generally not recommended) and doing them in the Design Assistant.

RENAMING FILES WITH THE DESIGN ASSISTANT

To rename a file that is in an assembly, drawing, or presentation, follow these steps:

1. Close Inventor.

2. Open the assembly, drawing, or presentation file in the Design Assistant.

3. Click the Manage button. In the Manage browser, click to select the component to be renamed. Right-click in the Action column and select Rename. All occurrences of the component are highlighted.

4. Right-click the Name column and select Change Name. In the Open dialog box, change the name and select Open (you're not really opening anything; you are just setting the name).

5. Click Save to apply the changes.

COPYING FILES WITH THE DESIGN ASSISTANT

To copy a file that is in an assembly, drawing, or presentation, follow these steps:

1. Close Inventor.

2. Open the file in the Design Assistant.

3. Click the Manage button. In the Manage browser, click to select the component to be renamed. Right-click the Action column and select Copy. All occurrences of the component are highlighted.

4. Right-click the Name column and select Change Name. In the Open dialog box, enter the name of the new copy and select Open (you're not really opening anything; you are just setting the name).

5. Repeat steps 3 and 4 for all the files you want to copy. For instance, if you are copying a drawing and the part that this drawing details, you would complete steps 3 and 4 for both the drawing and the part.

6. Click Save to create the copies. Your copies will be created right next to the original files.

This technique can be incredibly useful when you want to create a copy of an existing detailed design so that you can make changes to the copy. Create the copy of the drawings and the components and then make the changes.

REPLACING FILES WITH THE DESIGN ASSISTANT

If you want to replace a part or assembly file with an assembly, you can right-click the Action cell and then select Replace. Right-click the Name cell for the component and then click Change Name. In the dialog box, select the replacement file. After a file is replaced, renamed, or copied, other files that reference the original file need an update. The Update option will be useful, as shown here:

1. Open the assembly file in the Design Assistant.

2. Click Manage and select files that are being modified from the upper browser.

3. In the lower browser, select the file types you want to include in the update.

4. Click Find Files. The referencing files are displayed in the lower browser.

5. Click the Save button to apply the changes.

The Design Assistant cannot make changes in certain circumstances. For example, it can't make changes when the design state of a file is set to Released, when read-only permissions are set, or when the files need migrating to the latest release.

THE DESIGN ASSISTANT VS. AUTODESK VAULT

The Design Assistant can make many of the changes discussed here, but if you find yourself copying designs, changing filenames, and relinking projects often, you owe it to yourself to investigate Autodesk Vault. Vault can do all of these operations and much, much more.

Using Pack And Go

You can use the Pack And Go tool to package an Inventor file, such as a top-level drawing or assembly, and collect all of its referenced Inventor files in a single location. This is a useful feature for archiving a design and all the files related to the design into a single ZIP file. For example, suppose you had the following assembly:

◆   Assembly1.iam

◆   Part1.ipt

◆   Part2.ipt

◆   Part3.ipt

The problem is that you are not sure what directories the part files are in. Pack And Go can find all the parts for Assembly1.iam and copy them into a new directory. You can then zip the files in that new directory to be archived or sent to other users. You can access the Pack And Go tool by right-clicking an Inventor file in Microsoft Windows Explorer or from a Design Assistant session started outside Inventor. Click the Properties or Preview tab and right-click the assembly to access the Pack And Go tool.

To use Pack And Go on an assembly, follow these steps:

1. Click the Inventor button and choose Save As ≻ Save As Pack And Go. This will open the Pack And Go dialog box.

2. Set the destination directory to the folder in which you want to copy the files.

3. If you have multiple project files, use the Browse button to ensure that you are looking at the proper one.

4. Click the More button to display more Pack And Go options, as shown in Figure 13.22 (once clicked, the More button toggles to the Less button).

FIGURE 13.22

The Pack And Go dialog box

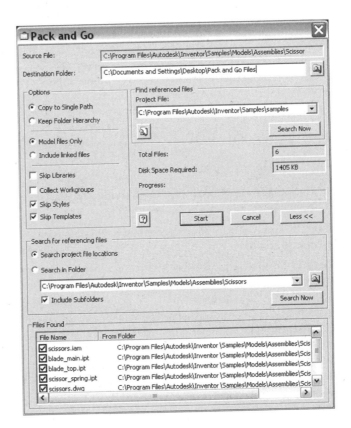

5. Click Search Now to find the IPT and IAM files that are referenced by the assembly file. They will appear in the Files Found section at the bottom of the dialog box.

6. This finds all the files referenced by the assembly file, but what if you know that the assembly and part files have drawings detailing them? To search for referencing files, click the Search Now button in the Search For Referencing Files area.

7. If files are found, you can select which ones to add and then click the Add button. Note that there is no progress bar in this dialog box, so you have to watch the top of the dialog box and wait for "Found # file(s)" to appear to know that it is done, as shown in Figure 13.23.

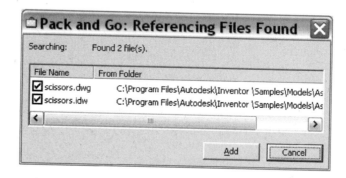

8. Click the Start button to start the copying process. Once the files are copied, the Cancel button turns into a Done button to let you know.

Typically you will want to configure some of the options because these will yield different Pack And Go results.

Copy To Single Path   This copies the referenced files to a single folder, reducing folder hierarchies. If any files have the same filename, only one of the files can be placed at the destination folder.

Keep Folder Hierarchy   This preserves the folder hierarchy under the destination folder. Use this option for round-trip file transfers such as sending files to a contract worker or customer or when you are packing files to work on a laptop while offsite. Maintaining the folder hierarchy will allow you to move the files back to the original destination smoothly when they return.

Model Files Only   This copies only Inventor files (with filename extensions .iam, .ipt, .idw, .dwg, and .ipn) to the destination folder. Referenced files such as spreadsheets, embedded pictures, and text files are not copied.

Include Linked Files   This includes referenced files such as spreadsheets, embedded pictures, and text files.

Skip Libraries   When this is selected, all files found in a library path, such as Content Center files and user-defined library files, are excluded from the Pack And Go tool.

Collect Workgroups   If this is selected, workgroups and the workspace are collected into a single folder. This is typically relevant only when working with a legacy project type.

Skip Styles   If this is selected, style XML files are not copied with the packaged file.

Skip Templates   Templates are not copied with the Pack And Go files when this option is selected. You can generally use this option and deselect it only for special circumstances.

It is important to note that Pack And Go does not modify the source files. When you package Inventor files, they are copied to the new destination. A log file and a copy of the original project file with a `.txt` suffix are also copied to the destination folder. Changes made to the packaged files do not affect source files.

Here are some common uses for Pack And Go:

◆ Archiving so that you can package files on a CD or DVD.

◆ Sending files to another user.

◆ Separating the referenced files from other files in the same source folders.

◆ Copying an assembly to a new location and then creating a design variant by making changes to the copy. The original is unaffected.

USING PACK AND GO AS A CLEANUP TOOL

Pack And Go can be useful as a project cleanup tool. Often a project folder will become cluttered with numerous unused files. Use Pack And Go on the top-level drawing or assembly and copy all the files to a secondary location. Then delete the contents of the original folder and replace them with the cleaned-up copies.

Pack And Go uses the active project file. You can change the active project file. If you have files in multiple locations, the project file must specify all those locations.

Using the Drawing Resource Transfer Wizard

The Drawing Resource Transfer Wizard helps copy drawing resources such as borders, title blocks, and sketched symbols from one source drawing to one or more destination drawings. To use the tool, you have to close Inventor just to avoid a situation where you are in the middle of modifying a drawing and you want to use that drawing as part of the process for transferring resources.

For example, imagine your company has hundreds of drawings in Inventor. However, there has been a change in the standard note that is on every drawing. If the standard note was created as a sketched symbol, this update can be batched. The transfer wizard is an ideal solution to solve this kind of problem.

Follow these steps to use the wizard:

1. Select Start ➢ All Programs ➢ Autodesk ➢ Autodesk Inventor 2016 ➢ Tools ➢ Drawing Resource Transfer Wizard.

2. On the welcome screen, click Next.

3. On the Select Source Drawing And Resources screen, select the drawing template and then click the OK button.

4. This loads the preview (if available) under Preview and shows the available drawing resources hierarchy in the source under Source Resources. You can deselect the resources you don't want to transfer to the destination. Figure 13.24 shows the source drawing resources.

FIGURE 13.24
Selecting source drawing resources

5. Click Next to go to the Select Target Drawings screen. On this page, select one or more drawings (by **Shift**+clicking) and click Open. You can click the file or path column name to sort files.

6. Click Next and select Yes or No for replacing resources in the target file with the same name as in the source. If you select Yes, the same name is used as the source for the target file. Selecting No gives a unique name to target drawing resources that have the same name as those in the source file. For instance, instead of writing over a title block definition named TB_100, you would end up with TB_100 and Copy Of TB_100 in your files.

7. Click Start, which shows the progress bar and a Pause button to temporarily halt the process.

8. When the progress bar finishes, click Exit to complete the process.

If you have a number of old drawings that you need to bring up-to-date with a new standard, this tool is useful.

USING THE WIZARD FOR NEW TITLE BLOCKS

A problem that pops up quite often in manufacturing is changing title blocks. Companies change addresses, change logos, and get bought or merged; any number of things can happen to require you to have to change your title block. This is where the Drawing Resource Transfer Wizard can come in handy. Simply edit the title block as required in your template file and then transfer it to all your old drawings.

Using the Style Library Manager

A helpful style tool that is external to Inventor is the Style Library Manager. This tool can be used to manage style libraries in your template files and set up style libraries. You should consider using this tool when attempting to remove unwanted styles from templates. You can access it by selecting Start ➤ All Programs ➤ Autodesk ➤ Autodesk Inventor 2016 ➤ Tools ➤ Style Library Manager.

You can use this tool to migrate, copy, rename, and delete style libraries. For example, imagine you are a CAD administrator who rolls out all the standards for your company, and you want to ensure that a good library of styles exists for others to use. The Style Library Manager comes to the rescue in this situation. You can create a new style library using the Create New Style Library button, shown in Figure 13.25 under the Style Library 2 column. Any changes in the style library are not available in other documents until Inventor closes and a new session is reopened.

FIGURE 13.25
The Style Library Manager

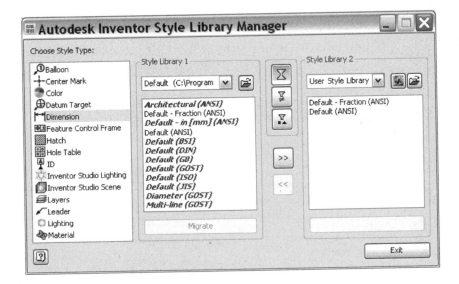

You can reuse your styles by copying them from one style library to another. Follow these steps:

1. Click the Style Library Manager tool.

2. In Style Library 1, click the drop-down arrow to select the source library styles you want to copy or use the Browse button.

3. In Style Library 2, you have three options.

    ◆ Choose an existing library.

    ◆ Copy an existing style library.

    ◆ Create an empty style library.

    ◆ Use the Create New Style Library button to select the last two options or use the Browse button to use the first. Figure 13.26 shows a new empty library being created.

FIGURE 13.26
Creating a new style
library

4. Click one or more styles in Style Library 1 and then click the >> button to add them to Style Library 2. Click the arrow buttons to add styles to or remove styles from the destination as desired.

Creating a new empty library and then bringing in approved styles one at a time is the best way to ensure that you a get a clean style library with only the styles you want and nothing else.

5. In Style Library 1 or 2, you can right-click a style name and select Rename or Delete. A warning will appear that all document links to that style will be broken or the style will be permanently deleted from the style library. Click Yes to continue and enter a new name. Click No to cancel the Rename or Delete operation. Note that you cannot undo or reverse a deletion.

6. Changes are saved as you make them. Once all changes have been made, click the Exit button.

Using the Task Scheduler

A large design repository needs to have a way to manage tasks for efficiency and repeatability. Nonproductive and mundane tasks tend to be expensive and tedious. The purpose of the Task Scheduler is to precisely automate such tasks. To access the Task Scheduler, select Start ➤ All Programs ➤ Autodesk ➤ Autodesk Inventor 2016 ➤ Tools ➤ Task Scheduler.

Imagine you are working for a service company that handles outsourcing work for auto suppliers. The supplier works with hundreds of files and is trying to decide whether to move to Inventor 2016. You have been asked to evaluate this for the supplier. You want to do testing and present quantitative data on the results of migration or some other custom tasks the supplier normally performs on legacy files. The main purpose of the Task Scheduler is to automate the tasks and quickly give you results. The Task Scheduler has the ability to create tasks such as the following:

- ◆ Migrating a set of files from Autodesk AutoCAD, Autodesk Mechanical Desktop, and Autodesk Inventor software

- ◆ Converting Inventor IDWs to Inventor DWGs

- Publishing DWF files

- Importing files and exporting files

- Updating parts, assemblies, and drawings

- Checking out and checking in from Vault

- Retrieving files from Vault

- Printing sheet sets

- Refreshing Content Center components used in assemblies

- Running a custom macro (such as a Visual Basic routine)

- Creating a single part from an assembly using the Shrinkwrap tool

Creating a Task for Migrating Files

To create a task to migrate files in Task Scheduler, follow these steps:

1. Open Task Scheduler by selecting Start ➤ All Programs ➤ Autodesk ➤ Autodesk Inventor 2016 ➤ Tools ➤ Task Scheduler.

2. Select Create Task ➤ Migrate Files, as shown in Figure 13.27.

FIGURE 13.27

The Create Task menu

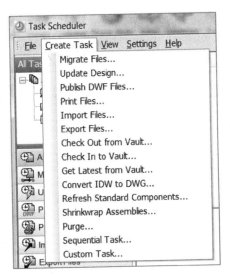

3. In the Migrate Files dialog box (see Figure 13.28), enter the task name, frequency, start time, and start date. If Immediately is checked, the task will start immediately after you click the OK button. The log file helps you to see the output of the task.

FIGURE 13.28
Migrating files

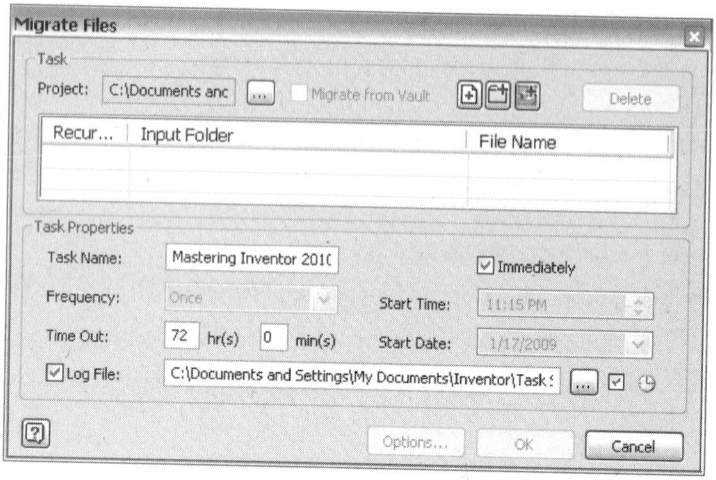

4. Use one of the three buttons along the top to add files in one of the following ways:

   Add Files   Select files from the active project to add to the task.

   Add Folder   Browse to a folder or folders to add to the task. Use the File Name drop-down to select which file type to process. Ensure that the Recursive check box is selected to include subfolders.

   Add Project   Select a project to include all files in that project's search paths.

5. Click the Options button to open the Migration Options dialog box, shown in Figure 13.29. The options are also listed here:

   Total Rebuild   This rebuilds all the parts and assemblies.

   Skip Migrated Files   This ignores files created in the current version or files already migrated.

   Skip Files With Unresolved References   This ignores files with broken links and references.

   Include Assembly Graphics For Express Mode   This setting allows you to save Express mode graphics in the assembly when migrating assembly files. With Express mode graphics included, your migrated assemblies can then be opened in Inventor's Express mode. Without these graphics, assembly files can be opened only in Full mode.

   Set Defer Updates (Drawings Only)   This toggles on the setting that allows drawings to be made static so that they do not update as the part or assembly they detail updates. This can be toggled off manually from the drawing later.

   Make All Raster Drawing Views Precise   This updates drawing views from the draft preview of the drawing view (Raster View) to a fully calculated (Precise) drawing view.

   Update Local Materials and Appearances   This updates the material and appearance styles found in the file to match the material and appearance library styles.

   Purge Old Versions   This deletes former versions after the migration task finishes, keeping file size to a minimum.

Compact Model History   This purges file history used for fast feature editing. This is intended for working with large assemblies when you experience capacity limitations. Do not select this option when migrating files to a new release.

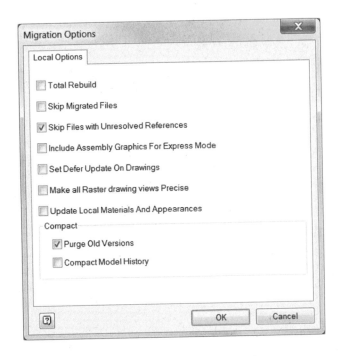

6. Click the OK button to run the task. When the task is done, you will see the status shown as completed.

   Users can run, edit, delete, or disable tasks once they are created, as shown in Figure 13.30. Tasks are also saved so they can be run again. You can click the Task ID or Name column to sort the data by task ID or name.

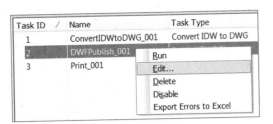

Performing Sequential Tasks

You can create several subtasks to set up multiple tasks and schedule them to run in a specified sequence at a specified time. Custom subtasks can be used also in a sequential task. One subtask can depend on the output of the previous subtask. Here are some examples of multiple subtasks:

- Importing files
- Updating designs
- Publishing DWF files
- Printing files
- Generating a cost report (custom task)

Performing Custom Tasks

A form of a COM object that implements the COM interface could be a custom task. For instance, you can use a custom task to open a batch of text files. A type library file called ServiceModuleInterfaceDef.tlb is shipped with the Task Scheduler. To access the COM interface, reference this file within your project. You can create custom tasks in any programming language that supports COM.

Tweaking Multi-Process Settings

In the Multi-Process Settings dialog box, shown in Figure 13.31, you can tweak parameters to complete batch jobs in less time by leveraging the multiprocess support in the Inventor Task Scheduler. Up to 16 processes can be run at the same time. You can set the number of processes and the amount of memory to be used. You can find this setting in Task Scheduler by selecting Settings ➤ Multiple Process.

FIGURE 13.31
The Multi-Process Settings dialog box

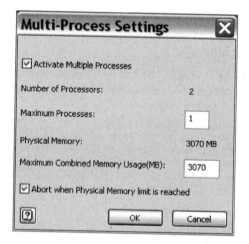

BATCH PLOTTING WITH THE TASK SCHEDULER

One of the most powerful uses of the Task Scheduler is to batch-plot a number of drawings. Simply select Print Files from the Create Task menu and then select the files to be printed. Click Options to set the paper size and other print parameters.

Publishing DWF Files and Filenames

If you were to use the Task Scheduler to publish a DWF file named `MI777.ipt`, then that would become the destination file `MI777.ipt.dwf`. Some users find this file naming scheme difficult to accept. The motivation to rename it not as *filename*.dwf is as follows: If Inventor were to produce `MI777.dwf` from `MI777.ipt`, it might be overwritten if you have two files with the same name but different file extensions, that is, `MI777.ipt` and `MI777.idw`. Therefore, the Task Scheduler takes the current filename with the extension (such as `.ipt` or `.idw`) and appends `.dwf` at the end. There are programs available on the Internet or Windows scripting commands to rename files from `MI777.ipt.dwf` to `MI777.ipt` to fix the filenames.

Using iProperties

Inventor files have file-specific properties known as iProperties. The iProperties dialog box helps you specify and view them. You can enter custom data into iProperties, search by those fields, and update your title blocks and parts lists in drawings and BOMs. You can launch this dialog box by clicking the Inventor button and then iProperties or by right-clicking the filename in the browser and selecting iProperties. Figure 13.32 shows the iProperties dialog box for a part. The iProperties dialog box in the parts and assemblies environments contains seven tabs, whereas the iProperties dialog box in the drawing environment contains only six tabs (the latter is missing the Physical properties tab).

FIGURE 13.32
Physical properties with aluminum as the material

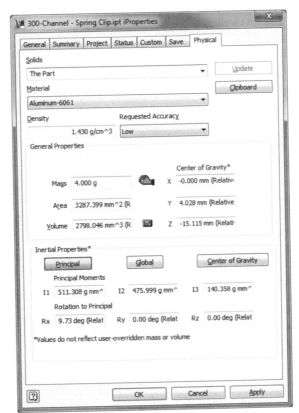

You can also right-click a file in Windows Explorer and choose Properties ➤ iProperties to add or edit iProperties outside of Inventor. Or from Windows Explorer, right-click a file and choose Design Assistant to work with files outside of Inventor. In the iProperties dialog box, you can modify data on the Summary, Project, Status, and Custom tabs. On unsaved files, changing the iProperties using the Design Assistant could lose unsaved changes. You can save any open Inventor files before using the Design Assistant to change iProperties.

The various tabs in the iProperties dialog box are as follows:

General   Contains fields that cannot be modified by the user.

Summary   Contains fields that can be modified by the user, such as Title, Subject, and Author.

Project   Contains important fields such as Part Number, Revision Number, and Project.

Status   Contains drop-down controls for Part Number, Status, Checked Date, and so on.

Custom   Helps define your attributes. These attributes follow the Name, Type, and Value format. For example, you can have Name=Department, Type=Text, and Value=Design123.

Save   Helps you specify whether to save the preview picture of the file so that it can be used in most "browse for file" dialog boxes. You can also specify an image file to use for this preview picture.

Physical   Lets you calculate and display the physical properties (area, volume, inertia, and so on) for a part or an assembly. The material selected is used to calculate the mass properties. The Update button on the Physical tab is useful to update the physical properties based on changes to your models.

The Summary, Project, Status, and Custom tabs are used to search files to update the BOM and parts lists.

Figure 13.32 shows an example of iProperties on a simple part. If this were a multi-body part, the mass properties of an individual property could be evaluated by setting the Solid drop-down to look at just the specified solid.

Also notice the hand icon next to the Mass input box. This indicates that the mass has been overridden or manually entered rather than being calculated from the part. The calculator icon shown next to the Volume input box indicates that the volume is being calculated from the part and will update as changes are made. The Density field cannot be changed in this dialog box. To change the density for this example, select Tools ➤ Materials, and find Aluminum-6061 under Material. Then change the density in the Physical tab ➤ Density field.

OVERRIDING MASS AND VOLUME FOR A SIMPLIFIED REPRESENTATION

Sometimes you'll want to model a simplified representation of a part but still need to have an accurate measure of its mass or volume. In these cases, type over the mass or volume in the iProperties dialog box. The calculator icon will then change to the hand icon, signifying that the mass and/or volume has been overridden. To allow Inventor to recalculate the mass or volume, delete all the text from the box and click the Update button. Inventor will then compute the mass and volume based on the size and density of the model.

Copying iProperties to Drawings

You can copy the model iProperties to the drawing iProperties so that they are the same. Copied model iProperties can be used in part lists, title block standard notes, or any annotation that accesses the iProperties. If the iProperties are set up in your drawing template, when you place views of the model on a new drawing, the selected iProperties are copied to the drawing from the source file.

Be aware that, once copied, the properties do not update automatically when changed in the model. To update the copied model iProperties in the drawing, select the Manage tab (from the drawing file) and click Update Copied Model iProperties. Note also that a drawing will pull properties from only one source. So if you have views of two different models on a single drawing, the properties are pulled from the first model from which a view was created. If you remove all the views of the first model, the drawing will pull from the second model, but you will need to use the Update button to make this happen.

You can copy iProperties from a model file to a drawing file by following these steps:

1. In the Drawing file, select the Tools tab and click Document Settings; then select the Drawing tab.

2. Click the Copy Model iProperty Settings button, which opens the dialog box shown in Figure 13.33.

3. Select the boxes for the properties you want to copy. You can select the All Properties check box at the bottom to copy all the properties.

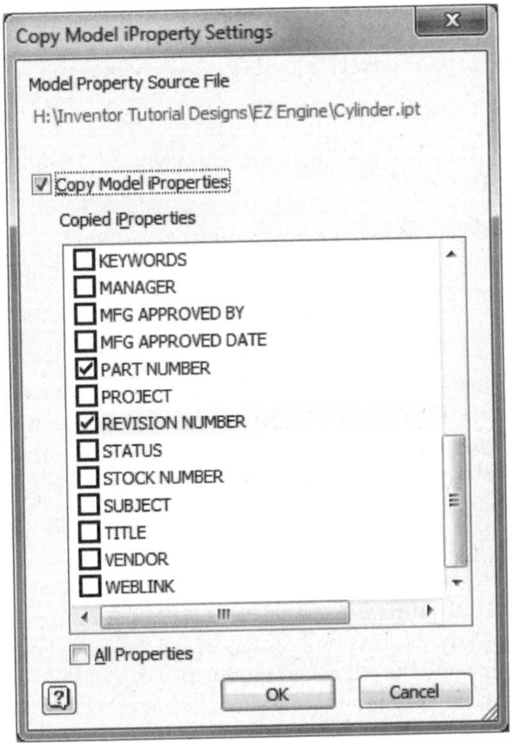

FIGURE 13.33
The Copy Model iProperty Settings dialog box

Creating Expressions with iProperties

If you have a need to create a "stock size" of your parts to be used in your BOM with associativity to model parameters, you can create and manage expressions for iProperties by using the following steps:

1. Click the Inventor button and then iProperties, and select the Summary, Project, Status, or Custom tab. Then click a field where an expression needs to be created.

2. Start with the = sign and type the text. If you want to include parameters or iProperty names, simply include them in brackets. A detected expression is denoted by *fx*. Figure 13.34 shows an expression that concatenates the thickness, width, and length parameters. This is the expression used:

   = <Thickness> × <Width> × <Length>

FIGURE 13.34
Concatenating text and parameters in iProperties

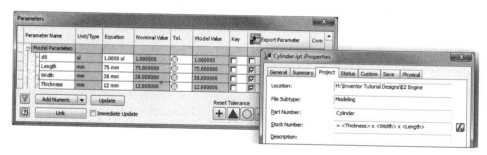

The resulting Stock Number property is as follows:

   12.000 mm × 38.000 mm × 75.000 mm

3. To edit an existing expression, you can right-click the expression and choose Edit Expression.

Before creating the expression from parameters, you should visit the Parameters dialog box (select the Manage tab and click the Parameters button) and do the following:

♦ In the Export Parameter column, click the check box next to all parameters you want to use in expressions. If you forget this step, the expressions will not build.

♦ In the Equation column, right-click the parameter and choose Custom Property Format. The Export parameter must be selected to get this option. Figure 13.35 shows the Custom Property Format options. Notice that you can click the option to apply the formatting to all comparable parameters. In other words, if it's a length parameter, set this format for all length parameters; if it's a volume parameter, set this format for all volume parameters; and so on.

To promote reuse, create a template file with predefined expressions for iProperties that lets you unify your parts list and other documentation. The Bill Of Materials dialog box provides the Property Expression Builder, which helps you create expressions for iProperties as well. You can then copy the expression to the parameter field of multiple parts in the Bill Of Materials Editor. Using the Bill Of Materials Editor allows you to "reach into" several parts at once and set an expression en masse. Figure 13.36 shows an iProperty expression being created in the Bill Of Materials Editor.

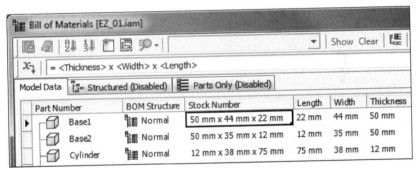

Working with the Design Assistant and iProperties

You can use the Design Assistant to copy design properties from one Inventor file to another. To do so, use the following procedure:

1. In Inventor, click the Inventor button and choose Manage ➢ Design Assistant.

2. In the Design Assistant, select Tools ➢ Copy Design Properties to access the Copy Design Properties dialog box.

3. Set the source file in the Copy From box.

4. Select the properties to copy.

5. Select the destination files to receive the properties.

6. Click the Copy button.

7. If the properties exist in the destination file, you are prompted to overwrite them one by one; you can choose Yes To All or No To All as well.

8. Once the properties are copied, click Done.

9. You can then step into the files (from Inventor or the Design Assistant) and change the values of the copied iProperties as required.

Figure 13.37 shows the custom iProperties of one file being copied to another file. You can refer to the section "Using the Design Assistant" earlier in the chapter to learn more about the Design Assistant and iProperties. You cannot copy properties to a file that is read only or checked out to someone else.

FIGURE 13.37
Copying custom iProperties from one file to another

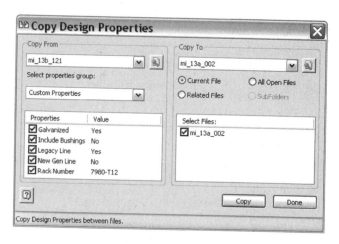

Creating Design Property Reports

You can use the Design Assistant to create a design property report that shows the iProperties you've selected. The report is written out to a TXT file. In the properties view browser in the Design Assistant, you can select the design properties to display for files:

1. While in the properties view, select View ➤ Customize in the Design Assistant and select the required property group.

2. Select the properties to display. Clicking the Add or Remove button helps you move a property from the Available Properties list to the Selected Properties list. You could also double-click it. The Name property is a default property that is mandatory in all displays.

3. To include custom properties that you've created yourself, follow these steps:

   A. Set the Property Group drop-down to Custom Properties.

   B. Click the New button.

   C. Expand the Add New Property column using the >> button.

   D. Use **Ctrl** or **Shift** to select multiple properties.

   E. Click Apply. Note that only nine properties may be listed.

4. Click Done. Notice that the properties you selected are now listed as columns.

5. Select Tools ➢ Reports and choose the report type you want:

   Hierarchy Report   Shows the hierarchy within the selected folder or assembly. If a folder is selected, the report shows the subfolders it contains. If an assembly file is selected, the report shows the paths for the files in the assembly.

   Design Property Report   Shows values of the specified properties for the files in the selected file or group of files.

6. Choose the number of levels to display and click Next.

7. Specify the report name and save location.

Using the Measure Tools

The Measure tools let you measure distances, angles, loops, and areas. These tools, shown in Figure 13.38, are available by selecting the Inspect tab and then looking on the Measure panel. They are available in the assemblies, parts, sheet-metal, flat pattern, construction, and 2D and 3D sketch environments. You can select sketches, edges, faces, bodies, and work geometry to take measurements. In addition to the measurement tools mentioned, you can use Measure Regions while in a 2D sketch.

FIGURE 13.38
Measure tools

Distance   Lets you measure the length of a line, an arc, or the distance between points and so on.

Angle   Lets you measure the angle between points, edges, or two lines. To measure between points, click two points to define a line and then a third point to measure the angle.

Loop   Gives you the length of open and closed loops.

Area   Gives you the area of closed regions.

Region Properties   Calculates the area, perimeter, and the area moment of inertia properties of 2D sketch loops. Measurements are taken from the sketch coordinate system.

Using Measurement Helpers

Measurements can be accumulated, cleared, and displayed in different ways. Figure 13.39 shows some of the options that are useful while using the Measure tools.

Add To Accumulate   Adds the current measurement to the total sum

Clear Accumulate   Resets the sum to zero

Display Accumulate   Displays the current sum

Dual Unit   Lets you see the measurement in the desired units

Precision   Displays eight formatting values and the option to display all decimals

FIGURE 13.39
Measurement helpers

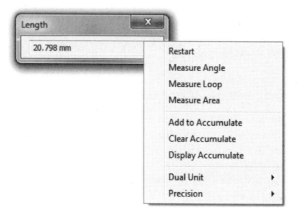

One of the advantages of using the Measure tools is the ability to enter feature parameters by measuring instead of by directly entering them. For example, in Figure 13.40, extrusion depth can be entered as a known value. Alternatively, you can select the Measure tool from the Depth flyout and then select a model edge. The length of the edge will appear in the Depth control of the Extrude dialog box. This is a convenient way to input dimensions by measuring instead of directly entering the values into the dialog box. In the graphics window, click the geometry to measure. The measurement is transferred to the dialog box automatically. Note that this tool can be used with sketch dimensions as well.

FIGURE 13.40
Measure tool and
feature parameters

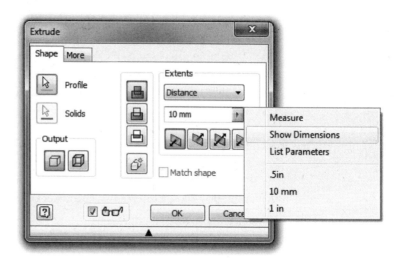

Also shown in Figure 13.40 is the Show Dimensions option. Choosing this option allows you to select an existing feature to temporarily see the consumed dimensions within that feature. You can then select a dimension onscreen to link the value of that dimension to the dimension you are currently entering. This differs from the Measure method in that the value will update if the object changes, whereas the measured value will stay static.

Measuring in Assemblies

Since you have faces and components in assemblies, there is a need to differentiate measuring between them. In the context menu, you can change the selection priority.

When Component Priority is selected, the minimum distance is measured between subassemblies. Part priority signifies measurement between parts only. Faces And Edges Select Priority lets you select only faces and edges, which is the default when nothing is preselected. Changing the selection priority resets any existing selections. Figure 13.41 shows the priority type pull-down with the selection filters for Component, Part, and Faces/Edges.

FIGURE 13.41
Selection priority for measurements

You can measure preselected entities by selecting the object first and then clicking the Measure button. If a selection set is valid for a measurement, the select filter in the Measure dialog box is updated, and the measurement is displayed. For example, if you select two points and then start the Measure Distance tool, you will get the distance between the points. However, if you select three points and start the Measure Angle tool, the selection set is cleared because the tool doesn't know which point is the vertex of the angle.

Participating in the CIP and CER

The Customer Involvement Program (CIP) aids in collecting information about your use of the Inventor software. Customer error reporting (CER) aids in sending information to Autodesk when the software program closes unexpectedly.

Participating in the CIP

To guide the direction of the Autodesk design software in the future, your use of the Inventor software is forwarded to Autodesk if you participate in the CIP. You can access this feature by selecting Help ➤ Customer Involvement Program. In the Customer Involvement Program dialog box, you can select a level of participation and then click the OK button. The following information might be collected:

- Autodesk product version and name

- Inventor commands and time spent

- Error conditions (catastrophic and nonfatal)

- Information such as system configuration, IP address, and so on

The CIP is committed to privacy protection. It can collect neither drawing or design data nor personal information such as names, addresses, and phone numbers. It will not contact users by email or any other way. The Customer Involvement Program aids in letting Autodesk know about the most commonly used tools and features, the most common problem areas, and so on. You can stop participation at any time by accessing the controls from the Autodesk Help menu. Your system administrator can also choose to block the CIP.

Participating in CER

Customer error reporting is a process by which Inventor users can report crashes to Autodesk. A software crash happens when the software program closes unexpectedly. When you have an unexpected error, Inventor shows a dialog box, and you can choose to send the error to Autodesk. CER records the subset of the code that was in use before the crash. The CER report collects a variety of information, such as the following:

♦ Operating system and graphics driver name, version, and configuration

♦ Autodesk software name and version

♦ List of recently used Autodesk commands

♦ Lines in the code where the crash happened

You can enter the step-by-step process that led to the crash. In addition, you can include your email and contact information. The error data is sent to Autodesk using a secure Internet connection in an encrypted form. If you have concerns about security and personal confidential information being sent to Autodesk, please do not send the customer error report.

At Autodesk, an automated system sorts the reports based on the code call stack so that the Autodesk development teams can analyze them. Each set of reports is prioritized based on the number of users having the same issue and how often the problem happens. If there is no current update, Autodesk will use that information for a future update or major release. When the issue is fixed, it is included in either a future maintenance update or a future release of the product. Customers who reported the error are notified. If there is a current update (immediate update notification), it is immediately sent to the customer. If not (delayed update notification), customers are notified when their error is addressed in a future software update.

Using Miscellaneous Tools

In the following sections, I will cover some miscellaneous tools: the Inventor Multi-Sheet Plot, the Add-In Manager, and the Project Editor. The tools are available by choosing either Start ➢ All Programs ➢ Autodesk ➢ Autodesk Inventor 2016 or Start ➢ All Programs ➢ Autodesk ➢ Autodesk Inventor 2016 ➢ Tools. If you find that you are using these tools often, it may be helpful to create a desktop shortcut to them.

Using the Autodesk Multi-Sheet Plot Tool

The Autodesk Multi-Sheet Plot tool opens the dialog box shown in Figure 13.42. It allows you to print one or more drawing sheets of various sizes. Clicking Next takes you to another dialog box that allows you to select drawings. Once the drawings are selected, you can schedule to print the multisheet. This tool helps you reduce paper usage and reduce plot setup time. Besides, it optimizes sheet layout on a selected paper size that you can print directly or save as a batch file. You can access the Multi-Sheet Plot tool by choosing Start ➤ All Programs ➤ Autodesk ➤ Autodesk Inventor 2016.

FIGURE 13.42

The Autodesk Multi-Sheet Plot dialog box

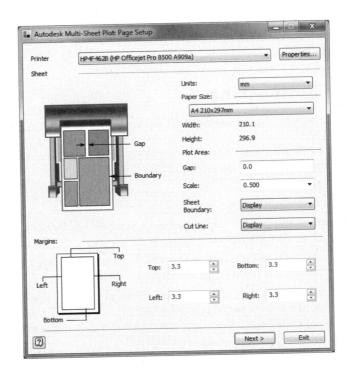

Using the Add-In Manager

The Add-Ins button opens an Add-In Manager dialog box that lets you select the add-ins you want to load or unload when Inventor starts. You can access this tool by choosing Start ➤ All Programs ➤ Autodesk ➤ Autodesk Inventor 2016 ➤ Tools or, when in Inventor, by selecting the Tools tab and clicking the Add-Ins button on the Options panel. Once the Add-In Manager dialog box is open, click the add-in in the Available Add-Ins area, and at the bottom of the dialog box under Load Behavior, deselect the Loaded/Unloaded option to unload it.

USING THE ADD-IN MANAGER TO SPEED INVENTOR LOAD TIME

If there are add-ins you know you do not use, you can use the Add-In Manager to prevent them from loading when Inventor loads. This will slightly speed up the load time (and reduce the amount of RAM Inventor uses). Be sure you understand what specific add-ins do because some are required for the proper operation of the software.

Using the Project Editor

Selecting the Project Editor tool opens a dialog box for the Inventor Project Editor. This is similar to the dialog box that opens after you select the Get Started tab and click Projects in Inventor. You can select each project, make changes to it, and save it without having to open Inventor. You can access this tool by choosing Start ➤ All Programs ➤ Autodesk ➤ Autodesk Inventor 2016 ➤ Tools or by right-clicking any IPJ file from Windows Explorer and choosing Edit. Project files can also be edited from within Inventor by selecting the Get Started tab and clicking the Projects button.

The Bottom Line

Take your models from Inventor to the Autodesk Building Systems program.   If you frequently need to take your Inventor models to ABS, BIM Exchange can help you in this process with three simple steps. Inventor provides a variety of ways to simplify the model and author it. Such models can be published in ABS.

Master It   Describe the basic steps involved in moving Inventor models to Autodesk Building Systems.

Create AutoLimits (design sensors).   You use AutoLimits to monitor design parameters in which you are interested.

Master It   You want to use AutoLimits for every dimension in your model. How many AutoLimits can you use at once?

Manage design data efficiently using Inventor tools.   There are different tools for managing design data, which is typically distributed across part, assembly, and drawing files. You can associate Excel spreadsheets, text files, Word documents, and so on, with these tools.

Master It   Name some of the Inventor tools for managing design data. Describe what each one does and how to initiate it.

Manage styles.   You can use the Style Library Manager to organize your styles to keep them simple and clean.

Master It   Styles normally need to be copied, edited, and deleted. How do you manage your styles? How can you create a central repository of styles?

Create expressions with iProperties.   Property fields can be concatenated to produce desired customized information in BOM and parts lists. For example, you can break down your parts by stock size to be used in your BOM with associativity to model parameters.

Master It   How do you create and manage expressions for iProperties?

Give feedback to Autodesk.   You can participate in the Customer Involvement Program (CIP). Customer error reporting (CER) helps Autodesk know about any issue you might experience.

Master It   You have a repeatable crash that you suspect is related to a specific file or a specific machine and want to know whether Autodesk can help you determine this.

Chapter 14

Exchanging Data with Other Systems

Many Autodesk® Inventor® software users need to bring files created by other CAD applications into Inventor or need to export files from Inventor to other formats.

For instance, if you design components that others use in their designs, you might need to output files to a standard format so that others can use them with a different software package. Or, if you are a manufacturing "job shop," you may receive many different file formats from customers that you need to bring into Inventor.

In this chapter, you'll learn to

◆ Import and export geometry

◆ Use Inventor file translators

◆ Work with imported data

◆ Work with Design Review markups

Importing and Exporting Geometry

Three data types make up a 3D model.

◆ Curves (or wires)

◆ Surfaces

◆ Solids

Wireframe models are composed of only wires that define the size and shape but lack volume. A surface model, on the other hand, is composed of wires and faces that define the surfaces but still lacks a solid filled volume. A solid model is composed of wires and faces that define surfaces that in turn define the solid filled volume.

Understanding the hierarchy of geometry data will help you understand the issues that can occur when translating from one of these data types to another.

There are different ways in which wires and curves are defined. If you are translating files that represent wires and curves as Non-Uniform Rational B-Splines (NURBS) to a format that represents wires and curves as simpler basis splines (B-splines), there might be something lost in translation.

Likewise, when you translate a surface model, if the surface normal direction were to get reversed (think positive vs. negative), you will have translation issues. And so it is with translating solids; if a solid model is translated so that a gap is formed where two surfaces meet, then translation may not be complete.

Translation of curves, surfaces, and solids occurs between different software packages because these packages use different modeling kernels—different mathematical engines that create the geometry that lead to different methods of geometric accuracy.

Accuracy controls such things as how close two points in space are before being considered a single point or how close two edges can be before they are considered connected, and so on.

If you have not already downloaded the Chapter 14 files from `www.sybex.com/go/masteringinventor2016`, please refer to the "What You Will Need" section of the introduction for the download and setup instructions.

Importing vs. Referencing Geometry

Inventor has the option to attach some of the most common CAD file formats as a reference model, where updates created to the original geometry are reflected in Inventor. Inventor can also import geometry, which automatically converts the file into Inventor geometry.

It is assumed that referenced files are stored in Inventor's project file path and worked on with the native application without moving the files. Referenced files can be Stored in Vault, Vault plug-ins for SolidWorks, Rhino, and ProE/Creo; these programs are available from the Autodesk app store:

`https://apps.autodesk.com`

Referenced Models can be used when you are not required to edit the geometry—when you are expecting the files to be edited in the native software that created them and you want to be able to use the updated model in Inventor.

Converting the model is usually to be used when you need to modify the geometry and you don't want to maintain a link to original files.

Importing as a reference model has several benefits, and while associativity is by far the most important, there are others as well.

Maintaining the link with the referenced file will in fact increase speed because the model is not translated but rather read directly with multithread CPU support. There are no translation errors and no need to use the repair environment to fix and patch missing or discontinued faces. You don't need to import the model every time a change occurs, and you can use several CAD packages to complete a project if you feel there are better tools elsewhere.

When you import a file, Inventor will detect whether it is a part or assembly and will create a new file accordingly, but you can also import an assembly inside a part by opening an existing or new part and using the Import command.

Imported parts can be edited using Inventor 3D modeling commands.

Importing into an assembly file will allow you to add assembly-level features, move or constrain the model, create design view representations, and access the bill of materials structure. In an assembly, you can link visibility with the imported model, and the visible/hidden status of parts is set as per the original files.

On the negative side, you cannot edit referenced geometry because no additional files are created on disk, and data is read directly from original files. Also, you cannot edit the BOM structure, and you cannot mirror the imported components.

When importing the model, you have the option to specify which parts to import into an assembly file or which bodies to import into a part file. You should keep in mind that any excluded components during the import process will also be excluded from the BOM structure and parts list, but at any time you can edit the imported model and include/exclude components as needed in your project.

Inventor attempts to maintain the assembly and subassembly structure and will create features based on geometry and topology (surfaces, wires, bodies) of the source files.

To create accurate BOM and part lists, Inventor will carry over any metadata and properties from the original model into iProperties. The mapping process can be configured by editing the XML files located in your `Design Data` folder's `Import Properties` subfolder.

Each metadata file can be imported into multiple iProperties, and to each iProperty file the metadata can be assigned multiple properties from the source file. By default the Design Data folder in Windows 7 is located in `C:\Users\Public\Documents\Autodesk\Inventor 2016`.

Navigate to the `Import Properties` folder in your `Design Data` folder and open the `PropertyMap_Creo.xml` file using a free editing program such as Notepad or a viewer such as Internet Explorer. Notice the way `Designer` iProperty is mapped from the ProE/Creo `Modeled_By` field.

```
<Property Name="Designer">
    <Source Name="Modeled_By" />
```

In the `Property Name` part, you should specify the Inventor iProperty field you want the data translated to, and in the `Source Name` you should enter the exact name of the metadata you would like to be mapped.

Ask your collaborators and foreign data suppliers to provide a list of properties, and with proper planning and care, you can have a fully detailed bill of materials and parts list just as you would if the files were created in Inventor.

Similar to derived files, you have the options to suppress or break the link to the original geometry, and by using the latter, Inventor will create the files on disk, and you will be prompted to specify a name and location for the files. However, be warned that once a link is broken, it cannot be linked back, and you will need to restart the import process.

If you are using Vault, you need to have the original models located in the Vault workspace scope because they will be included in the check-in operations. If the files are renamed or moved or they are falling outside the workspace scope, the check-in will be interrupted, and you will need to resolve the links first.

When using Pack And Go to send data to other people, Inventor will include any referenced models imported as well.

The workflow for importing foreign data is the same in all cases except for files created in PTC ProE/Creo and for DWG files.

Each time you save a file in ProE/Creo, the program will create a new file on disk, and it will increment the numerical value in the file extension, so additional steps are required. You will learn how to handle this later in the chapter.

DWG files are also a special case because of the DWG Underlay technology, which allows associative import of AutoCAD files to create 3D models from 2D layouts. You can also use DWG files as a sketch symbol library to be used in Inventor drawings; you'll learn more about this later in the chapter.

To import with automatic detection of the file type (assembly or part), use one of the following options:

◆ Choose the Inventor menu ➢ Open ➢ Import CAD Files.

◆ Choose Get Started ➢ Launch ➢ Import CAD Formats (might be hidden under the New button flyout).

◆ Drag and drop single or multiple files at once from Windows Explorer:

1. Drag to the Inventor title bar.

2. Drag into the Inventor graphical window. (This will work only if you don't have any opened files in Inventor.)

To import files into an assembly, use one of the following:

♦ Choose Assemble ➤ Component ➤ Place Imported CAD Files (might be hidden under the Place button flyout).

♦ With a new or existing assembly open, drag and drop files from Windows Explorer in the graphics window.

To Import into a part file, use one of the following:

♦ 3D Model ➤ Create ➤ Import

♦ 3D Model ➤ Insert (you might need to make it visible first) ➤ Import

♦ Manage ➤ Insert ➤ Import

EXPLAINING THE IMPORT OPTIONS

The Import window dialog has two tabs to further help you filter and customize your files. In the Import Type section of the Options tab (Figure 14.1), you can specify how you want to import the model. If you select Reference Model, then no additional files are created on disk, the model is read directly, and the files will update as changes occur on the original model.

FIGURE 14.1
Import dialog's
Options tab

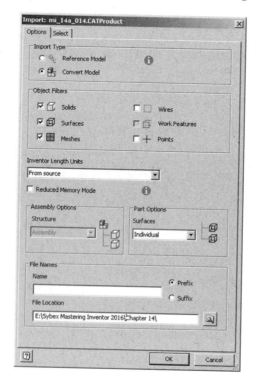

The Object Filter section allows you to specify what to read from the original file. Visualization is the only operation permitted on imported meshes.

In the Inventor Length Units section of the Options tab, you can specify the units to use for imported geometry and parameter values. Remember that you can also change them later with the Document Options command on the Tools tab.

If you choose Convert Model in the Import Type section, then further options are revealed. Reduced memory mode will convert and save each file on disk during the import process to increase performance and minimize memory consumption.

The Assembly Options section allows you to specify how to import solids. This is available when you try to place the files inside a new or existing assembly.

◆ Assembly will preserve the source structure.

◆ Multi-body Part will import assemblies as solid bodies in a single part.

◆ Composite Part will import assemblies as composite features in a single part.

If you choose an assembly structure or you used the Import CAD Files option instead, then each part can be converted as follows:

◆ Composite imports the model as a single composite feature in the part environment.

◆ Individual brings the geometry as multiple surfaces in part environment.

◆ Stitch attempts to connect multiple surfaces or faces with matching edges in part environment

In the File Names section, you can specify a name for the model, and you can tell Inventor to add a numerical incremented value as a prefix or suffix to the filename to avoid duplicate names. File Location allows you to browse and select the save folder location.

On the Select tab, you can visualize the model and specify what to include from the original model (Figure 14.2).

FIGURE 14.2
Import dialog's
Select tab

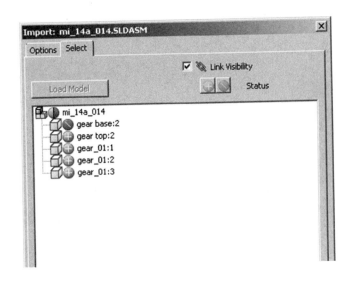

The Load Model button will read the file in memory and will display it on the graphics window. You can spin, pan, and change the visual style to better investigate the model.

You can click the round status icons to change the import status for the selected object. The round yellow button will include them, while the gray button will exclude them. Alias (*.wire) File also has a round white button that will import the object as individual surfaces (Figure 14.3).

FIGURE 14.3
Importing Alias files

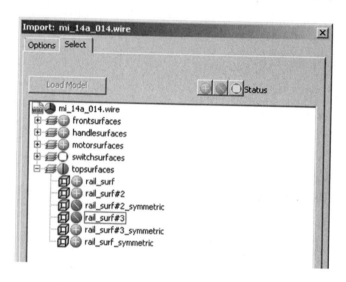

To import a model and edit its geometry, follow these steps:

1. Click Import CAD Files on the Get Started tab (you might need to expand the New button flyout).

2. Set the Files Of Type drop-down to All Models to view all files that can be imported.

3. Browse for and select the file `pulley.prt.1` located in the `Chapter 14` directory of your `Mastering Inventor 2016` folder and click the Open button.

4. On the Import dialog's Options tab, check the Reference Model And Solids box in the Objects Filter section.

5. Switch to the Select tab, click the Load Model button to preview the model, and then click OK in the Import dialog.

6. In the 3D Model tab ➤ Modify panel, click the Delete Face button.

7. Thick the Heal box, select the three faces of the keyway, and click OK (Figure 14.4).

8. Click the Direct Edit button on the 3D Model tab ➤ Modify panel.

9. On the Modify mini-toolbar, activate the Size command, and underneath Size on the flyout menu, choose Diameter.

10. Click the inside face of the mounting hole and, in the Diameter, change the value from 10 in to 8 (Figure 14.5).

FIGURE 14.4
Deleting faces

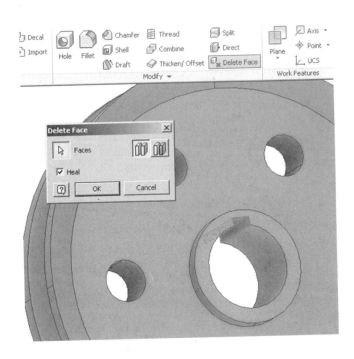

FIGURE 14.4
Deleting faces

FIGURE 14.5
Modifying the diameter

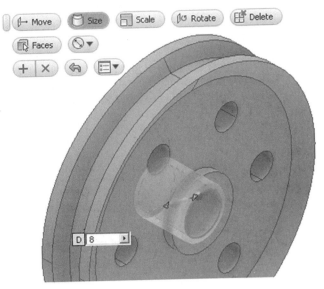

11. Press **Enter** or click Apply on the mini-toolbar (the green plus button).

Should the imported file be modified in the native program, you will see the Update Required icon on the component in the browser, and the Update button on the Quick Access bar will become active.

You can close the file without saving.

To insert a model in an assembly, follow these steps:

1. Click Open on the Get Started tab.

2. Browse for and select the file mi_14a_010.iam located in the Chapter 14 directory of your Mastering Inventor 2016 folder and click the Open button.

3. Click the Place Imported CAD Files button on the Assemble tab ➤ Component panel (you might need to expand the Place flyout menu).

4. Browse for and select the file mi_14a_014.SLDASM located in the Chapter 14 directory of your Mastering Inventor 2016 folder and click the Open button.

5. On the Options tab, make sure you marked the import of Solids and of type Referenced Model.

6. On the Select tab, click the Load Model button.

7. Click the status icon in front gear base:2 and change it from Include (yellow circle) to Exclude (gray circle).

8. Click OK in the Import dialog and then click anywhere in the graphics window to place the component or right-click and choose Place Grounded At Origin.

9. To finish the Place command, hit the **Escape** key, or right-click and choose OK or Cancel.

10. Right-click the mi_14a_004 file in the graphics window or browser bar and choose Edit Import.

11. Switch to the Select tab (optional), right-click gear_top in the import window or the graphics window, or choose Exclude; then click OK in the import dialog.

    If the mode is imported as a reference, then you can edit it at any time to include exclude geometry. On the right-click contextual menu, you have the option to select Suppress/Unsuppressed Link as well as Break Link.

12. Right-click the mi_14a_004 file in the graphics window or browser bar and choose Break Link. Click Yes in the prompt window to save the assembly and continue.

    You are presented with a Save External dialog similar to the Import window ➤ Options tab. Breaking the link will convert the model and create files on disk.

13. Click Cancel in the Save External dialog (Figure 14.6).

FIGURE 14.6

Save External dialog

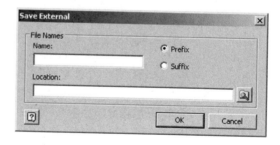

So far you have seen how to import non-native files to Inventor, converting them to Inventor files as you go, and how to import non-native Inventor files as a reference, preserving the link to the original file.

There is one caveat to working with reference files that you should know about, and that is when the reference file is created with a software version newer than Inventor can read. In this situation, you will need to use a neutral data file format.

To help with translating from one software package to another, you can create an intermediate, or neutral, file.

Some common neutral file formats are Initial Graphic Exchange Specification (IGES), Standard for the Exchange of Product (STEP), and Standard ACIS Text (SAT), among others.

Other common translations include importing files from the Autodesk® AutoCAD® and Autodesk® Mechanical Desktop® software into Inventor. In these cases, you will be working with the DWG file type.

Working with Neutral File Formats

Although using neutral formats will help avoid problems, keep these things in mind when translating files:

◆ You should use the neutral file format only if the files were created in CAD software newer than the translator used by Inventor. (Check the Autodesk Inventor Help for a complete list of file formats and the latest software version that can be translated.)

◆ Generally speaking, you should strive to keep the number of file translations between the source software and the destination software as low as possible.

◆ Not all neutral file formats are created equal.

Translating DWG and DXF Files

DXF files can be converted only, and associativity is not maintained to the original files. When a DWG file is imported into Inventor, you have the option to maintain associativity or to translate it into an Autodesk Inventor part, assembly, or drawing file, based on the import settings and the geometry present in the original file.

When exported from Inventor to a DWG or DXF, a file is translated into AutoCAD objects and a new file is created.

The new translated document is not linked to the Inventor file from which it was created. Instead, the DWG or DXF data is fully editable within AutoCAD.

The process of importing a DWG file will give different results depending on where and how you access it. You will use the file mi_14a_014.dwg in the Chapter 14 directory of your Mastering Inventor 2016 folder to explore the import options for DWG files.

Importing as DWG Underlay

Referencing a 2D AutoCAD model space drawing to an Inventor part file is a great way to build a 3D Inventor model using a native 2D AutoCAD underlay.

The referenced DWG geometry can be projected into Inventor sketches to use a reference while modeling or can participate in assembly constraint operations to help with the creation of layouts. The 2D geometry can be updated by editing a DWG file outside Inventor. Only one DWG file can be imported at a time, but the same 2D DWG can be imported a number of times.

To explore importing as a DWG underlay, follow these steps:

1. Click Open on the Get Started tab.

2. Browse for and select the file mi_14a_011.ipt located in the Chapter 14 directory of your Mastering Inventor 2016 folder and click the Open button.

3. The Import command is located in the 3D Model tab ➤ Create panel or in the Mange tab ➤ Insert panel.

4. Click the Import button and then browse for and select the file mi_14a_014.dwg located in the Chapter 14 directory of your Mastering Inventor 2016 folder and click the Open button.

5. Click the XY plane in the graphics window or in the browser and then click the Origin Center Point in the graphics window or browser pane.

6. Click OK in the information window and then right-click the new browser node created for this drawing. It has a DWG icon, and it's called mi_14a_014.dwg just like the filename of the drawing you imported.

Notice that you can right-click to suppress/unsuppress or break the link. You can also translate (move) the geometry and toggle the visibility of the drawing or individual layers.

7. On the right-click contextual menu of the browser node, choose Translate, and in the mini-toolbar, click Locate button. The triad will snap to end or middle points, helping you choose a new reference. Click the cyan circle representing the side view of the main shaft.

8. In the Translate mini-toolbar, click Snap To and then select the Origin Center Point in the graphical window or browser panel. Now click OK on the right-click mini-toolbar green check mark.

9. Start a new 2D sketch from the 3D Model tab and choose XY Plane.

10. Click Project DWG Geometry on the Sketch tab ➤ Create panel (you might need to expand the Project Geometry flyout menu).

11. Make sure that Project Single is selected in the new mini-toolbar, and then select the cyan geometry representing the circle and the end lines defining the main shaft.

You can project single geometry, open or closed loops, or block geometry. The geometry can be projected in other parts if they are placed in an assembly. Both parts will update in form and position when the original DWG file will be changed.

12. From the 3D Model tab, choose Extrude on the Create panel, and notice that the circle is selected, being the only closed region in the sketch.

13. Delete the value in the extrude distance, and on the right-side flyout arrow choose Measure.

14. Click the middle of the cyan edge and then click the middle of the other cyan edge to get a value of 62 inches.

While you can measure on the fly and create features, they will not be adaptive and will not change with the 2D DWG file. Also, you can click the existing 62-inch dimension that came during import to use it as a reference dimension as you would a regular sketch. You can also create driven dimensions and reference those.

15. Click Cancel in the Extrude dialog to go back in the sketch and then click Dimension in the Sketch tab ➤ Constrain panel.

16. Click one of the projected shaft end lines and then the other. (Depending on your Inventor settings, you might get a warning message that a driven dimension will be created.) Click anywhere in the graphics window to place the dimension.

17. From the 3D Model tab, choose Extrude again and change the direction to Symmetric.

18. Delete the extrude distance value and then click the driven dimension you created earlier. You should see d0 in the distance value, meaning that the extrusion distance will now update when the shaft length is changed in the 2D DWG file. Compare your results with Figure 14.7.

FIGURE 14.7

Extrusion of DWG underlay geometry

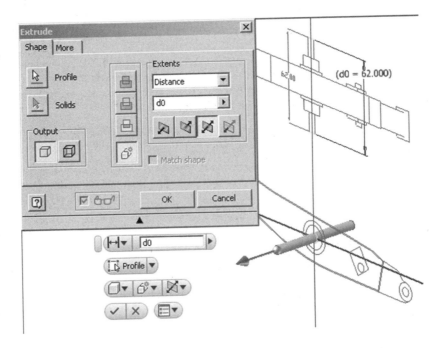

19. To improve visibility and de-clutter the screen, right-click the DWG browser node and choose Layer Visibility. The three buttons at the top will help you to select all, clear all, and invert the selection.

20. Click the Clear All button and then select Construction; then click OK to close and accept the changes in the Layer Visibility dialog, as in Figure 14.8.

FIGURE 14.8

Layer Visibility dialog

If you have AutoCAD installed, continue with the exercise. If not, read along to understand how the update will work.

21. Open the file mi_14a_014.dwg with AutoCAD. Double-click the cyan circle and, in the Properties window, change Diameter from **6** to **8**. (You can also select the circle and then click and drag one of the quadrant nodes to change the diameter.) Save the file and switch back to the Inventor window.

22. Notice the Update Required icon on the DWG browser node and on the Quick Access bar. Click Update on the Quick Access bar to update the diameter of the shaft.

Although a DWG underlay is a part-only functionality, the geometry can participate in assembly constraint operations, and the Project DWG Geometry command will be available in assembly sketches as long as the DWG is left visible inside parts. When you are finished with this file, you can close it without saving.

OPENING DXF AND DWG FILES

To view and interrogate a DWG file with tools such as Print, Measure, and so on, in Inventor, you can use the Open command.

You can access the Open command on the Quick Access bar, on the Get Started tab, on the Inventor menu (the big orange *I* on the top left), on the Open submenu, or by pressing **Ctrl+O**.

1. Click Open on the Get Started tab.

2. Set the Files Of Type drop-down to AutoCAD DWG Files (*.dwg).

3. Browse for and select the file mi_14a_014.dwg located in the Chapter 14 directory of your Mastering Inventor 2016 folder.

4. Click the Options button and choose Open. Click OK in the File Open Options dialog and then click Open.

5. With the model space active in the browser, use the Orbit tool to spin the model and try the Measure tool.

When you are finished investigating the file, you can close the file without saving.

TRANSLATING DXF AND DWG FILES

In this section, you will translate DXF and DWG files. To import a DWG file, follow these steps:

1. Click Open on the Get Started tab.

2. Set the Files Of Type drop-down to AutoCAD DWG Files or DXF (*.dwg or *.dxf).

3. Select the file you are going to import.

4. Click the Options button and choose Import. (If you are translating a number of files, you can set Import to be the default by clicking the Tools tab, selecting the Application Options button, choosing the Drawing tab, and setting Non-Inventor DWG File to Import.)

5. Once you've selected Import, as shown in Figure 14.9, click the OK button.

FIGURE 14.9
Importing a DWG file

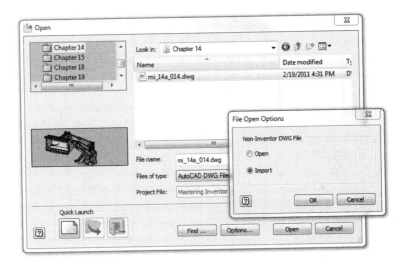

6. This returns you to the Open dialog box, where you will click the Open button to start the DWG/DXF File Wizard. Note the Configuration drop-down box.

7. If you have an import configuration already saved, you can specify it now and click Finish. If you have not yet created a configuration template, click Next to go to the Layers and Objects Import Options, where you can chose which layers to import (see the explanation in the next section), and then click Next again to go to Import Destination Options dialog.

You need to consider a number of options when importing DWG files, depending on the DWG data input and the intended translation output. The following sections discuss these considerations in relation to the import options.

LAYERS AND OBJECTS IMPORT OPTIONS

Once you click Next in the DWG/DXF File Wizard dialog, you will be presented with the Layers And Objects Import Options dialog.

In this dialog, you can select which layers or objects to include or exclude for importing. These two methods of selection are available:

Select By Layer   Use the check boxes to control which layers will be imported. Unchecking a layer will exclude all objects located on that layer.

Select By Object   Uncheck the All check box and then select objects in the Import Preview dialog.

You can combine layer and object selections to create a specific selection set. Once the layers and objects are selected, you can click the Next button to continue to the Import Destination Options dialog.

IMPORTING 3D SOLIDS

Once you've selected the layers and objects to be imported, you will be presented with the Import Destination Options dialog. If the AutoCAD DWG has 3D solids, you can check the 3D Solids check box to translate them into Inventor part files.

Use the Solids To Single Part File check box if you want multi-body solids to be translated into an Inventor part file. Leave this option unchecked if you want each solid body in the DWG to be created as an individual Inventor part file and automatically placed in an Inventor assembly.

Figure 14.10 shows the import options for 3D solids.

FIGURE 14.10
3D data options

Set the destination folder to a path in which you want to have the part files created and choose Use Default File Names to allow Inventor to name the resulting part files automatically. If you choose this option, the new Inventor parts will be given a name based on the DWG name and be incremented by a value of 1.

For instance, if the DWG is named Engine.dwg, then the solids in the DWG will be named Engine1.ipt, Engine2.ipt, Engine3.ipt, and so on. If Use Default File Names is left unchecked, each solid in the DWG will be named Part1.ipt, Part2.ipt, Part3.ipt, and so on.

IMPORTING 2D DATA

If the DWG contains a combination of 3D and 2D data that you want to import, you can set the options in the Destination For 2D Data area to handle the 2D data.

If the DWG has only 2D data or has both but you want to import only the 2D data, then you can leave the 3D Solids check box deselected and set only the Destination For 2D Data area of the Import Destination Options dialog box, as shown in Figure 14.11.

Selecting the New Drawing radio button translates the DWG data to a new Inventor DWG or IDW. If you check Promote Dimensions To Sketch, the 2D data is placed in a draft view that is created in the Inventor drawing.

FIGURE 14.11
2D data options

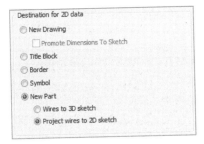

IMPORTING TITLE BLOCKS AND BORDERS

You can use the Title Block and Border radio buttons to convert an AutoCAD title block DWG into an Inventor title block or border. When you do this, be sure to click the Mapping Options button (located in the lower-left corner of the dialog box) to set the layer and font mapping options shown in Figure 14.12.

You can click the Symbol radio button to translate the 2D data into a sketched symbol for use in an Inventor DWG or IDW file.

FIGURE 14.12
Mapping Options

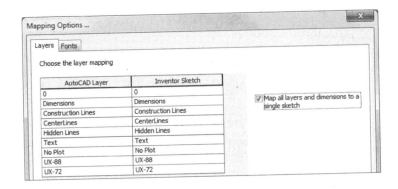

Importing AutoCAD Blocks as Sketched Symbols

One way to import AutoCAD blocks as Inventor sketched symbol definitions is to use the Symbol radio button. This can provide a quick way to convert common drawing symbols for use in your Inventor drawing templates.

Importing AutoCAD Part Drawings as New Inventor Parts

Click the New Part radio button to translate AutoCAD 2D data into a new IPT sketch to be used for creating a new part model. Choose to create either a 3D or 2D sketch within the file, depending on the type of geometry needed.

Inventor has both a decimal unit style and a fractional unit style for dimensions. When dimensions are translated, if Inventor detects that the AutoCAD file employs a scientific, decimal, engineering, or Windows desktop style, those styles are converted to decimal style. AutoCAD fraction and architectural styles are mapped to Inventor fractional style.

THINK BEFORE IMPORTING AUTOCAD GEOMETRY

You might be tempted to import or copy and paste 2D AutoCAD geometry as a basis for a 3D Inventor part—but *wait*.

If this is a simple part model that will never change, you may get away with this time-saving shortcut, but if you want to use this part in an assembly or you want the part to be able to change parametrically, it is worth taking the time to re-model it in Inventor from scratch.

Creating the model again in Inventor will allow you to build in your "design intent," creating all the features in the proper order, with the proper constraints that will allow others to easily modify your part in the future.

It is worth noticing that part geometry is assessed by Inventor's Assembly constraint solver, and parts with under-constrained sketches can affect assembly performance.

Referencing AutoCAD DWGs in Inventor assemblies for the creation of a layout that you will use for aligning Inventor models is a fantastically useful tool—but it is probably overkill to reference a DWG file into a part model, just for the purpose of building a part.

UNITS, TEMPLATES, CONSTRAINTS, AND CONFIGURATIONS

Whether importing to 2D or 3D, you will use the Templates area to specify which template to use for each of the file types to translate to. In the Import Files Units area, you can specify the units if they do not match the units that Inventor detects from the AutoCAD file. The detected unit is based on the INSUNITS system variable in the DWG file.

You can use the Constrain End Points and Apply Geometric Constraints check boxes to allow Inventor to place constraints on sketch entities when it can. Endpoints found to be coincident will be given Coincident constraints, lines found to be parallel will be given parallel constraints, and so on.

Once all these options are configured, you can click the Save Configurations button, shown in Figure 14.13, to write out a file to use the next time you convert a DWG file. Doing this allows you to convert files more accurately and more quickly.

FIGURE 14.13
More import destination
options

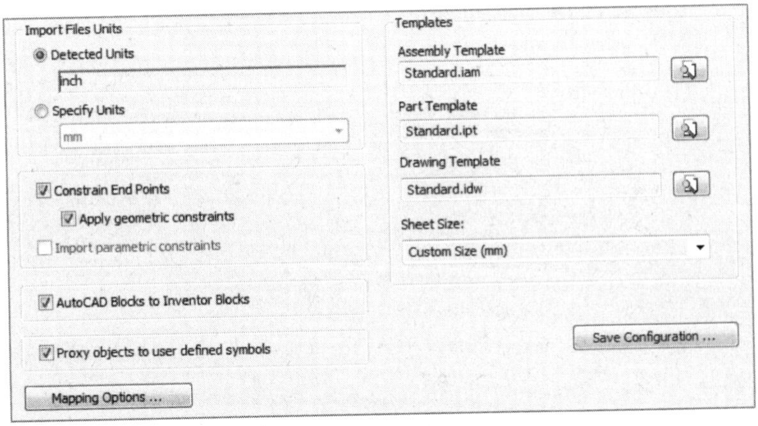

When all the configuration settings have been made and saved, click Finish to start the import process. Inventor will create the new files based on your configurations and leave the files open in the current Inventor session.

Mechanical Desktop DWG

Autodesk Mechanical Desktop (MDT) was a 3D parametric modeler similar to Inventor that was developed on top of the existing AutoCAD platform.

Once Inventor was created, Autodesk stopped developing MDT and has since discontinued support for it. If you have files that were created using MDT, they can be translated to Inventor part and assembly files, but unlike other CAD formats will not maintain associativity when referenced.

If the source files contain geometry or features that are not recognized in Inventor, they are omitted, and the missing data is noted in the browser or the translation log file.

No links are maintained to the existing MDT files. You must have MDT on your computer to import files into Inventor.

MDT's native file format was the DWG file, and you can import MDT DWG files using the Options button in the Open dialog box just as you would a regular DWG. However, if Inventor detects that it is an MDT file, you are given the option to read the data as an MDT file or as an AutoCAD or AutoCAD Mechanical file, as shown in Figure 14.14.

FIGURE 14.14
Reading MDT file
contents

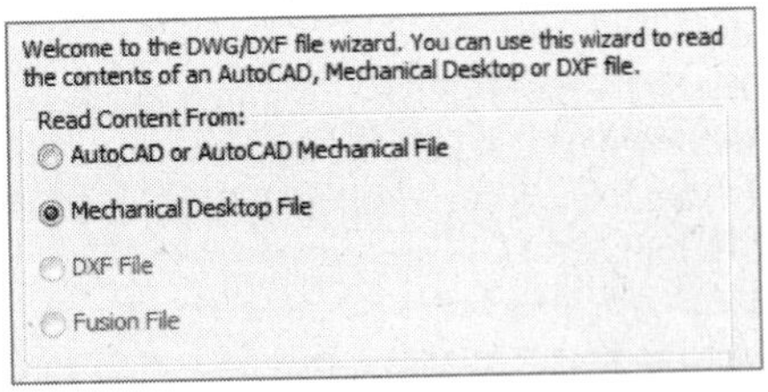

Although many of the options for templates, units, and configuration settings are the same as previously described for regular DWG files, the assembly and part options are specific to MDT files, as shown in Figure 14.15.

FIGURE 14.15
MDT assembly and
part options

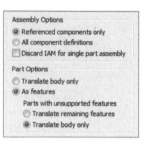

Consider the following items when migrating MDT files to Inventor:

◆ Broken views, base section views, and breakout section views from MDT will be turned into base views.

◆ Exploded views will become unexploded views (no tweaks applied).

◆ Importing discards (AMPARDIMS) from MDT automatically creates associative model dimensions in Inventor.

◆ If Move With Parent is selected in an MDT file, Inventor aligns all views according to the view type.

◆ If a parent view is missing in an MDT file, a child view is not created in Inventor.

◆ Inventor centerlines and center marks are automatically generated during translation; therefore, they might not be the same as in the MDT file.

◆ Radial section views have broken alignment in Inventor.

In addition to importing MDT files one at a time, you can use the Inventor Task Scheduler to batch the translation from MDT to Inventor. It is important to ensure that the MDT files are migrated to the latest version of MDT before attempting to translate them into Inventor files.

STEP and IGES

Standard for the Exchange of Product (STEP) and Initial Graphic Exchange Specification (IGES) are nonproprietary file formats you can write data to in order to exchange data among proprietary software.

When a STEP or IGES file is opened in Inventor, one part file will be created if the file contains only one part body; otherwise, you can create multiple Inventor part files placed within an assembly file. Importing STEP and IGES will convert the models and will not maintain associativity with native files.

Although no links are maintained between the original STEP or IGES file and the Inventor files created from them, when importing an updated STEP or IGES file, Inventor updates the geometry and maintains all modeling constraints and features applied to that STEP or IGES file.

You can use the files called mi_14a_014.stp and mi_14a_014.igs located in the Chapter 14 directory of your Mastering Inventor 2016 folder to explore the import options for STEP and IGES files.

To import a STEP or IGES file, follow these steps:

1. Click Open on the Get Started tab and set the Files Of Type drop-down to STEP Files (*.stp, *.ste, *.step) or IGES Files (*.igs, *.ige, *.iges).

2. Select the file you intend to import.

3. Click the Open button.

In the Import Options dialog, you need to specify a name and location for the file. The rest of the options are as presented in the "Explaining the Import Options" section earlier in this chapter.

The new Inventor parts will be given a name based on the filename, and the prefix or suffix will be incremented by a value of 1. For instance, if the specified name is 4278_T and Suffix is marked, then the Inventor parts will be named 4278_T 1.ipt, 4278_T 2.ipt, 4278_T 3.ipt, and so on.

Many Inventor users prefer to send and receive STEP files to and from vendors or clients because they find that STEP files import better than other file formats such as IGES. Here is a list of attributes that make STEP a popular choice:

◆ STEP files can retain the original part names when importing to an assembly.

◆ STEP creates instances for duplicated parts. If you are sent a STEP of an assembly created in another software package and that assembly has 12 instances of a certain screw size, Inventor will typically create just one file for the screw and instance it 12 times instead of creating 12 different files.

◆ STEP files can maintain assembly hierarchy, meaning that subassembly structure can be translated. In other formats, assemblies may be translated with all parts at the top-level assembly.

◆ STEP translates part colors, whereas other formats generally do not contain the information needed to carry part colors across different platforms.

◆ The STEP format is governed independently and is not tied to a particular modeling kernel; as a result, it is often considered a more standard format.

CHANGING THE DEFAULT BROWSER NODE DISPLAY NAME

The STEP part numbers will be translated to the Part Number field in the properties of the Inventor document; however, the browser name for IGES and STEP will be the filename.

You can use the Assemble tab ➤ Productivity panel ➤ Rename Browser Nodes command to change the default browser node display name from File Name to Part Number.

To export a file as a STEP, click the Inventor button and then select Save Copy As. In the resulting dialog box, set Save As Type to STEP Files (*.stp, *.ste, *.step). Click the Options button to set the STEP version. You can also choose to include sketches. Included sketches are translated to the STEP file in named groups.

To export a file as an IGES, click the Inventor button, select Save Copy As, and set Save As Type to IGES Files (*.igs, *.ige, *.iges). Click the Options button to set the IGES output to surfaces, solids, or wireframe. You can choose to include sketches. Included sketches are translated to the IGES file in named layers.

SAT

Standard ACIS Text (SAT) files are written in the standard file exchange format for the ACIS solid modeling kernel. You can use the file mi_14a_014.sat located in the Chapter 14 directory of your Mastering Inventor 2016 folder to explore the import options for SAT files. To import a SAT file, follow these steps:

1. Click Open on the Get Started tab.

2. Set the Files Of Type drop-down to SAT Files (*.sat).

3. Select the file you want to import.

4. Click Open.

You will be prompted how to import the data. You can create it as an assembly, multi-body part, or composite feature part, as in Figure 14.16.

FIGURE 14.16
SAT import prompt

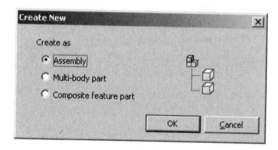

Once you select the data import type, you will be shown the Import Options dialog where you need to specify a name and location for the file. The rest of the options are as presented in the "Explaining the Import Options" section earlier in this chapter.

To export a file as SAT, click the Inventor button, choose Save Copy As, and set Save As Type to SAT Files (*.sat). Click the Options button to set the SAT version. The default is version 7.0. You can also choose to include sketches. Included sketches are translated to the SAT ungrouped.

WATCH FOR SAT FILE VERSIONS

As of Inventor release 5.3, Autodesk broke away from the ACIS SAT standard when it created its ShapeManager kernel. This means that Inventor cannot read in any SAT file that is newer than version 7.0. Keep this in mind when requesting models from third parties or when downloading them from a vendor's website.

CATIA Import Options

When importing Computer-Aided Three-Dimensional Interactive Application (CATIA) V4 or V5 files, you can choose between solids, surfaces, meshes, wires, and points.

You can use the file `mi_14a_014.CATProduct` in the `Chapter 14` directory of your `Mastering Inventor 2016` folder to explore the import options for these files. To open CATIA files, follow these steps:

1. Click Open on the Get Started tab.

2. Set the Files Of Type drop-down to CATIA V5 Files (`*.CATPart; *.CATProduct`).

3. Select the CATIA file you want to open and click the Open button.

The Import Options dialog will show up as presented in the "Explaining the Import Options" section earlier in this chapter.

Pro/ENGINEER Import Options

Files created with PTC ProE/Creo need special considerations and better planning before importing.

Proe/Creo creates a new file on disk every time you save the file, and the extension, a numerical value starting at 1, will be incremented by 1 with every save.

Because of this, the updated model will not be seen by Inventor unless it has the same filename. For this you can either rename the new file and specify the name it had when you first imported the model or ask the collaborator handing over the file to do a bit of cleanup beforehand.

Ask the collaborator to use the Delete Old Versions button in the File menu or use some free utilities that can automate this such as ProPurge or SPurge. This will delete old versions and rename the latest version to extension 1 so that Inventor will see the updates in the file.

You can use the file `mi_14a_014.asm` located in the `Chapter 14` directory of your `Mastering Inventor 2016` folder to explore the import options for Pro/ENGINEER files. To open models created in Pro/ENGINEER, follow these steps:

1. Select Open from the Get Started tab.

2. Set the Files Of Type drop-down to Pro/ENGINEER and Creo Parametric Files (`*.prt*; *.asm*`), Pro/ENGINEER Granite Files (`*.g`), or Pro/ENGINEER Neutral Files (`*.neu*`).

3. Select the Pro/ENGINEER file you want to open and click the Open button.

The Import Options dialog will show up as presented in the "Explaining the Import Options" section earlier in this chapter.

If you want to import a part or assembly that contains family table instances, you need to ask your collaborator to save the accelerator files (`.xpr` or `.xas`) along with the part.

Unigraphics and Parasolids Import Options

You can access Unigraphics and Parasolids files in the same way you would Pro/ENGINEER files.

You can use the file `mi_14a_014.prt` located in the `Chapter 14` directory of your `Mastering Inventor 2016` folder to explore the import options for Pro/ENGINEER files. To do so, follow these steps:

1. Click Open on the Get Started tab.

2. Set the Files Of Type drop-down to Parasolid Text Files (`*.x_t`), Parasolid Binary Files (`*.x_b`), or NX Files (`*.prt`).

3. Browse for the file you want to open and click the Open button.

The Import Options dialog will show up as presented in the "Explaining the Import Options" section earlier in this chapter.

SolidWorks Import Options

You can use the file mi_14a_014.SLDASM located in the Chapter 14 directory of your Mastering Inventor 2016 folder to explore the import options for SolidWorks files.

To open models created in SolidWorks, follow these steps:

1. Click Open on the Get Started tab and set the Files Of Type drop-down to SolidWorks Files (*.prt, *.sldpart, *.asm, and *.sldasm).

2. Select the SolidWorks file you want to open and click the Open button.

The Import Options dialog will show up as presented in the "Explaining the Import Options" section earlier in this chapter.

Rhino Import Options

You can use the file mi_14a_014.3dm located in the Chapter 14 directory of your Mastering Inventor 2016 folder to explore the import options for Rhino files. To open models created in Rhino, follow these steps:

1. Click Open on the Get Started tab and set the Files Of Type drop-down to Rhino (*.3dm).

2. Select the Rhino file you want to open and click the Open button.

The Import Options dialog will show up as presented in the "Explaining the Import Options" section earlier in this chapter.

SMT Import Options

You can open SMT file type created with Autodesk Shape Manager. To open models created in Autodesk Shape Manager, follow these steps:

1. Click Open on the Get Started tab and set the Files Of Type drop-down to SMT files (*.smt).

2. Select the file you want to open and click the Open button.

The Import Options dialog will show up as presented in the "Explaining the Import Options" section earlier in this chapter.

JT Import Options

To open JT files, follow these steps:

1. Click Open on the Get Started tab and set the Files Of Type drop-down to JT files (*.jt).

2. Select the file you want to open and click the Open button.

The Import Options dialog will show up as presented in the "Explaining the Import Options" section earlier in this chapter.

STL Import Options

To open STL files, follow these steps:

1. Click Open on the Get Started tab and set the Files Of Type drop-down to STL files (`*.stl`).

2. Select the file mi_14a_017.stl and click the Options button.

The Import Options dialog will show up (Figure 14.17) where you can select where and how to save the file, set the translation report, specify import units, and set the STL color format.

FIGURE 14.17
STL options

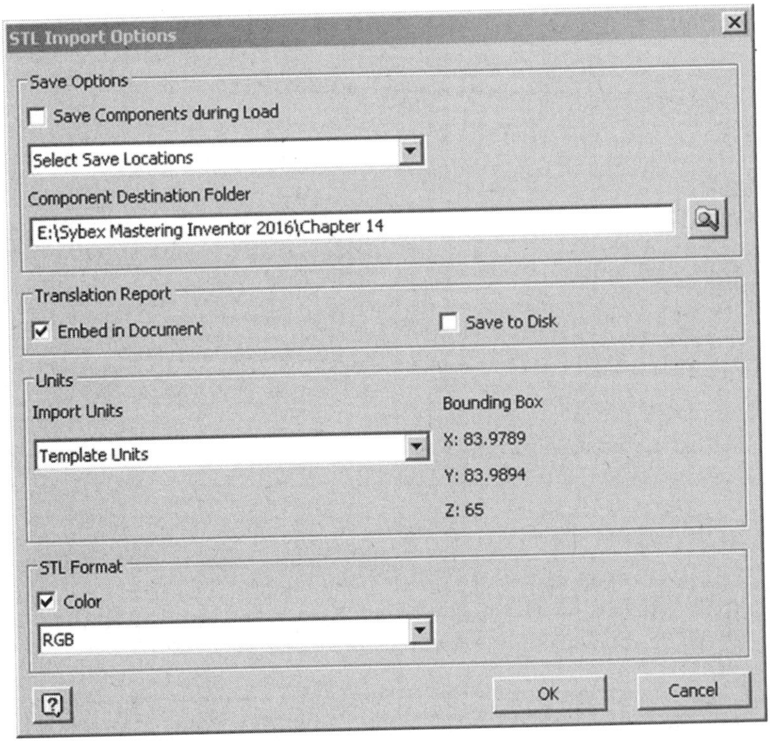

IDF Board Files

Intermediate Data Format (IDF) is the standard data exchange format for transferring printed circuit assembly (PCA) files between printed circuit board (PCB) layouts and mechanical design programs.

You can access IDF board files by clicking Open on the Get Started tab and setting the Files Of Type drop-down to IDF Board Files (`*.brd`, `*.emn`, `*.bdf`, and `*.idb`).

IDF board files can be imported into Inventor as assembly or part files. When brought in as an assembly, board components are translated into individual parts contained in the new assembly. When imported as a part, the board components are translated into sketches and features. Inventor will translate IDF outlines, keepouts, group areas, drilled holes, and components.

Part files are automatically named based on the information in the existing board file. Once imported, the files can be placed into Inventor assemblies and detailed in Inventor drawings just as you would any other Inventor model. Figure 14.18 shows the IDF import options. You are presented with this dialog box automatically when you open an IDF board file.

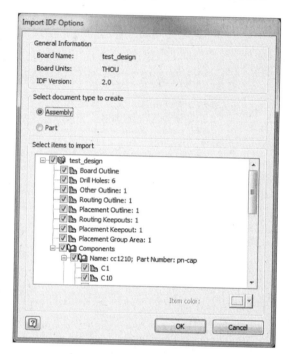

You can use the file mi_14a_014.brd located in the Chapter 14 directory of your Mastering Inventor 2016 folder to explore the import options for IDF files.

CONFIGURING YOUR SYSTEM TO TRANSLATE AUTOMATICALLY

Depending on how you work with translated files, you might want to configure your system to automatically translate other CAD formats to Inventor files when they are accessed.

For instance, if you use a lot of supplier content from a website that downloads in the form of STEP files, you could set up Inventor to be the default application to open STEP files.

To do so, right-click a STEP file in Windows Explorer, choose Open With, and then choose Default Program. In the resulting dialog, choose Inventor or click the Browse button and browse for Inventor.

Now when you double-click a STEP file, it will automatically be translated and opened as an Inventor file with the last set of options you used.

Working with Imported Data

In a perfect world, you would not need to import or export data at all. Instead, all files would exist in one perfect, universal file format.

Of course, this perfect world does not exist, and you are probably required to import files created in another program from time to time.

In a near-perfect world, imported data would always come in healthy and without any problems.

Repair Tools

When importing data becomes a struggle, you can often (but not always) use tools in Inventor to fix the imported geometry.

Typically, the biggest struggles come with importing surface models that did not convert well from the original CAD software.

Inventor provides a Repair environment for repairing poorly converted surfaces. Once repaired, imported surfaces must be promoted to the part environment for use in parametric modeling or so they can be seen in an assembly.

To access the Repair environment, you simply select the converted geometry from the browser and choose Repair Bodies.

In the Repair environment, you can use the tools covered in the following sections to fix the following types of imported surface geometry issues:

- Self-intersecting surfaces or curves
- Intersecting faces
- Modeling uncertainty (miscellaneous topology and geometry errors)
- Irregular surfaces
- Face normal direction pointing the wrong way
- Gaps between surfaces
- Holes in surfaces
- Overlapping faces

You can find further information about the Repair environment in the Inventor Help files, including helpful Show Me Video instructions.

Edit Solid Tools

You might find that a model imports well but you need to make some modifications to the single solid body.

In this case, you can add features to the base solid by sketching on any of the desired faces and using the standard Inventor part modeling tools. To edit the body itself, you can use Inventor's direct editing tools.

AN ALTERNATIVE METHOD FOR EDITING BASE SOLIDS

There is a slightly hidden alternative method of editing base solids that you might not be aware of. To find it, right-click a solid body in the feature browser. You'll see how it works in the following exercise.

To explore the basics of editing an imported solid body, follow these steps:

1. On the Get Started tab, click the Open button.

2. Browse for and select the file mi_14a_003.ipt located in the Chapter 14 directory of your Mastering Inventor 2016 folder and click the Open button.

3. Once the file is open, right-click the Base1 feature in the browser and choose Edit Solid.

This will activate the Edit Base Solid tab and display the base solid editing tools, as shown in Figure 14.19.

FIGURE 14.19

Editing a base solid

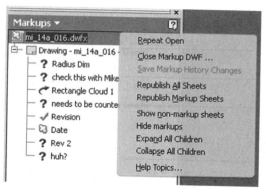

4. Next use the ViewCube to rotate the model so that you can see the circular face shown in Figure 14.19.

5. Select the Move Face tool from the Modify tab and then click the circular face.

6. Click and drag on the blue Z arrow in the triad and lengthen the shaft of the part by **25 mm**, as shown in Figure 14.20; then right-click and choose OK.

FIGURE 14.20

Using the Move Face tool to lengthen the part

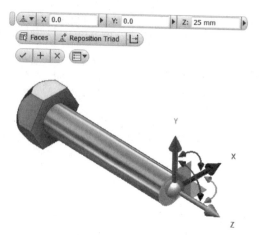

7. Select the Offset tool from the Modify tab and then click the cylindrical face of the shaft.

8. Click and drag the manipulation arrow up and down to see the diameter of the shaft shrink and grow, as shown in Figure 14.21.

FIGURE 14.21
Using the Offset tool to change shaft diameter

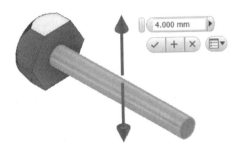

9. Settle on an offset value that reduces the diameter shaft by **4 mm**; then right-click and choose OK.

10. Select the Extend/Contract Body tool from the Modify tab and then select YZ Plane from the Origin folder (in the browser).

11. Ensure the Expand button is selected in the Extend or Contract Body dialog box; then enter a distance of **15 mm** and click the OK button.

Figure 14.22 shows the Extend Or Contract Body dialog box.

FIGURE 14.22
Using the Extend/Contract Body tool

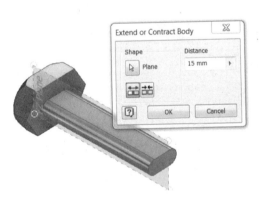

In these steps, you used the Edit Solid tools to modify a base solid that was originally imported from another file format.

These tools can be quite useful for making small modifications to models obtained from supplier websites, particularly if you don't need to track the change (if you *do* need to track the change in the Feature tree, use direct edits).

You can close this file without saving changes and continue to the next section.

USE EDIT SOLID TO MODIFY PURCHASED PARTS

Oftentimes you're able to locate a STEP file of a purchased component from a supplier website but then find that you need to make modifications to it for use in your assembly design.

For instance, you might find an accurate model of an air cylinder of the correct size from a designated supplier's website. Then you realize that you need a similar model but one that is longer.

You could use the Edit Solid tools to create a new longer version from the existing model.

Viewing DWF Markup

The Autodesk® Design Review (ADR) software offers Inventor users and anyone they work with a simple and effective way to view and mark up both 2D and 3D DWF files.

Design Web Format (DWF) files are lightweight versions of your Inventor files that you can publish from Inventor and email to a collaborator to be viewed and redlined with ADR. Non-Inventor users can download and install ADR free from the Autodesk website.

The DWF markup process begins from within Inventor where you will publish a DWF from your Inventor files. Once the DWF is published, it is sent to the reviewer and marked up with ADR.

You can then bring those markups into your Inventor file and change the status of a markup, add comments, or accept the markup. You have the additional choice of publishing to DWFx format, allowing reviewers to access the file directly through Internet Explorer.

A typical DWF markup process is as follows:

Publish   You write out the DWF file from Inventor 2D and/or 3D files.

Receive   The reviewer receives the DWF file from you and opens it with ADR to check for errors and omissions.

Review   The reviewer can comment on and mark up the DWF file using callouts, text blocks, shapes, dimensions, stamps, and custom symbols. Then they save those markups to the DWF file.

Return   The reviewer then sends the markups back to you for your review.

Revise   You load the marked-up DWF into Inventor and revise the Inventor files as required.

Republish   After revising, you write out the DWF file from Inventor 2D and/or 3D files again.

Publishing a DWF or DWFx File

With the file that you intend to publish open in Inventor, click the Inventor button and select Export ➤ Export To DWF, which opens the Publish dialog box. There are three options for publishing the DWF or DWFx.

Express Publishes only the active sheet without the 3D model.

Complete Publishes all sheets and all 3D models except sheets excluded from printing.

Custom Chooses sheets and 3D models to publish, depending on the type of file you are publishing. Extra tabs appear in the Publish dialog box for each file type as required. Here's what's included for each file type when you are using the Custom option:

Drawing Files The DWF or DWFx file includes all sheets and tables as well as the complete referenced 3D models.

Assembly Files The following assembly options are available:

- The DWF or DWFx file includes the assembly with view and positional representations as well as enabled BOM views.

- The DWF or DWFx file includes all members and the iAssembly table with view and positional representations.

- The DWF or DWFx file includes the assembly with view and positional representations as well as enabled BOM views, weld beads, and weld symbols.

- When an assembly is at any LOD other than the master, only that LOD is published to the DWF or DWFx. All view and positional representations, as well as enabled BOM views, are also published.

Part Files The following part options are available:

- The DWF or DWFx file includes only the part model.

- The DWF or DWFx file includes the folded model and flat pattern (if one exists).

- The DWF or DWFx file includes all iPart members and the iPart table.

- The DWF or DWFx file includes only the iPart model.

- The DWF or DWFx file includes the model with stress/constraint indicators as well as a stress scale.

Presentation Files The DWF or DWFx file includes the presentation views, animations, and assembly instructions as well as the complete assembly.

DWF or DWFx files can be published with the ability to measure, print, and enable and disable markups. They can be password protected for security also. Figure 14.23 shows the publish options for an iAssembly factory.

Once you choose the appropriate options, click Publish to specify either the DWF or DWFx format and specify a location to create the file. The resulting file can be opened in Design Review to create markups.

FIGURE 14.23
DWF or DWFx
publish options

FIGURE 14.23
DWF or DWFx
publish options

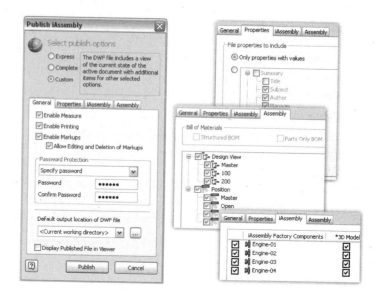

Reviewing and Marking Up DWF and DWFx Files

Once a DWF or DWFx file is open in Design Review or Internet Explorer (DWFx only), you can create markups in the form of callouts, text blocks, shapes, stamps, custom symbols, and measurements. Figure 14.24 shows the Markup & Measure tab.

FIGURE 14.24
Markup & Measure
tools

When markups are created, they are listed in the Markups palettes and organized by the sheet on which they reside.

Most markups contain the following collection of properties: Status, Notes, History, Created, Creator, Label, Modified, and Sheet. Drawn markups such as lines do not have properties.

Each markup can have its own status. The status can be <None>, For Review, Question, or Done. When you click a markup in the Markups palettes, the screen will zoom to the markup at the same zoom scale at which it was created. Once markups are complete, the DWF or DWFx file can be saved. Figure 14.25 shows a view marked up in Design Review.

FIGURE 14.25

Marked-up view in
Design Review

Accessing DWF or DWFx Markups in Inventor

To open a markup set in Inventor, select the Get Started tab and click Open; then choose DWF
Markup File from the Files Of Type drop-down and select the DWF file to bring in.

The DWF markups will be overlaid onto the Inventor drawing, and the Markups browser
will display the markup set in the tree view. You can then edit the status and properties of each
markup by right-clicking the markup in the browser, as shown in Figure 14.26.

FIGURE 14.26

Markups loaded into
Inventor

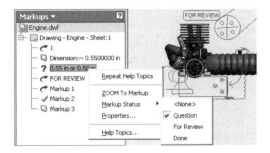

To experiment with markups, you can open the file mi_14a_016.idw from the Chapter 14 directory
of your Mastering Inventor 2016 folder and use the file mi_14a_016.dwfx to import the markups.

DWF in the Real World

When communicating with vendors and clients who have never used Design Review and are accustomed to receiving PDF files, I recommend you do not force DWF on them.

Generally, you will have much better luck getting the uninitiated to use and eventually request
DWF files if you send them both PDF and DWF files initially.

Include a link to the Design Review download on the Autodesk website in your email and mention
that the download is free and that the files can be viewed in 3D. This approach allows the person
on the other end to make the choice at their convenience. Typically, once they have used Design
Review, this is the format they will request.

Once you've reviewed all markups, you can save the markups back to the DWF or DWFx file. You can choose to republish only the sheets that are marked up or republish all sheets. You can access these commands by right-clicking the DWF or DWFx filename in the Markups browser, as shown in Figure 14.27.

FIGURE 14.27

Saving and republishing markups

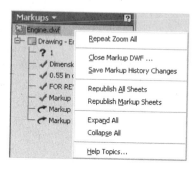

The Bottom Line

Import and export geometry. In the design world today, you most likely need to transfer files to or from a customer or vendor from time to time. Chances are, the files will need to be translated to or from a neutral file format to be read by different CAD packages.

Master It You are collaborating with another design office that does not use Inventor. You are asked which you would prefer, IGES or STEP files. Which one should you request?

Use Inventor file translators. Inventor offers native file translators for CATIA, Pro/ENGINEER, SolidWorks, Unigraphics, and other CAD file types. This allows you to access these file formats with Inventor and read the files into Inventor files directly.

Master It You are a "job shop" and in the past have been required to maintain a copy of SolidWorks in addition to your copy of Inventor to work with customers who send you SolidWorks files. You would like to eliminate the cost of maintaining two software packages. What is a good strategy for doing that?

Work with imported data. Using the construction environment in Inventor, you can repair poorly translated surface files. Often, a file fails to translate into a solid because of just a few translation errors in the part. Repairing or patching the surfaces and promoting the file to a solid allows you to use the file more effectively.

Master It You download an IGES file from a vendor website, but when you attempt to use the component in your design, the surface data is found to have issues. How should you proceed?

Work with Design Review markups. Design Review offers you and the people who collaborate with you an easy-to-use electronic markup tool that can be round-tripped from Inventor. Design Review markups can be made on both 2D and 3D files.

Master It You want to use Design Review to communicate with vendors and clients to save time and resources, but you have found that others are unsure of what Design Review is and how to get it. What are some good ways to help others begin to use this handy application?

Chapter 15

Frame Generator

Frame Generator consists of several tools to automate frame modeling. You can select lines, edges, and points to specify the location of members. Frame Generator derives the selections into a part. This part is called a *skeleton* because it provides the framework for the members. The skeleton part automatically updates when a change is made to the original geometry, which updates the frame member size or position.

Frame Generator gets structural profiles from Content Center. In addition to the structural profiles included in the Autodesk® Inventor® software libraries, you can author and publish your own profiles. This capacity is useful for adding profiles of extruded aluminum, plastic, and other materials because the structural profiles in the Inventor libraries are standard steel shapes.

In this chapter, you'll learn to

◆ Work with frame files

◆ Insert frame members onto a skeleton model

◆ Add end treatments to frame members

◆ Make changes to frames

◆ Author and publish structural profiles

◆ Create BOMs for Frame Generator assemblies

Accessing Frame Generator Tools

The Frame panel, shown in Figure 15.1, is on the Design tab in the Assembly Environment. It has tools specific to Frame Generator plus the Beam/Column Calculator from the design accelerators.

FIGURE 15.1
Frame Generator tools on the Design tab in the Assembly Environment

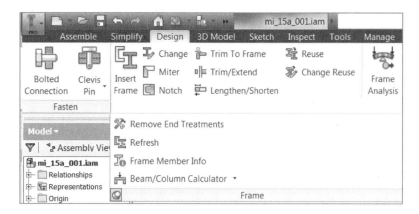

The tools fall into four categories.

Creating Frame Members   Frame members can be created using the Insert Frame and Change tools.

Creating End Treatments   End treatments can be created with these tools:

- Miter

- Trim To Frame

- Trim/Extend

- Notch

- Lengthen/Shorten

- Remove End Treatments

Performing Maintenance   Maintenance can be performed with the Frame Member Info and Refresh tools.

Performing Calculations and Analysis   Calculations and analysis can be performed with the Beam/Column Calculator, Plate Calculator, and Frame Analysis module.

ABOUT FRAME GENERATOR

The Frame Generator application is an add-in that uses the Inventor application programming interface (API). Since the API does not provide access to all the Inventor functionalities, there are some user interface differences between add-ins and core Inventor tools. For example, the edit fields in the core Inventor tools have an extensive flyout menu. The add-ins do not have access to this functionality, so their edit fields are more limited.

Exploring the Frame Generator File Structure

When you create the first members in a frame assembly, a dialog box prompts you for filenames. Frame Generator creates a subassembly and a skeleton file in the parent assembly. The subassembly does several things. It acts as a container for the skeleton and frame members, isolating them from the assembly solver, and it acts as a filter so Frame Generator tools, such as Frame Member Info, ignore other assembly components. The skeleton file is created in the subassembly and consists of all the edges and points you select when placing frame members. Each frame member is created as a separate file and saved into a subdirectory named after the frame assembly.

As an example, imagine you create a cube to use as the basis on which to model a frame. You name the cube file Cube_Frame and then place this cube into an assembly called Cube_Frame_Assembly. Both files are saved in a folder called My_Frames. You could then use the cube to create a basic frame, using each of its edges as a placement reference for the frame members. When you create the frame, you will be prompted to supply the following items:

- A new frame filename and location; these are the name and location of the frame subassembly.

- A new skeleton filename and location; these are the name and location of the frame skeleton reference.

If you just accept the defaults, you will end up with a folder such as \My_Frames\Cube_Frame_Assembly\Frame\. In this folder (once you have saved the top-level assembly), you will find an assembly file named Frame0001.iam and a part file named Skeleton0001.ipt. Special attributes in the frame subassembly contain references to the parent assembly. This enables the frame skeleton to maintain references to the other assembly components. Figure 15.2 shows the default frame subassembly and skeleton file naming.

FIGURE 15.2
Creating a new frame

MAKE SURE YOU SAVE

When you click the OK button to create the Frame Generator assembly and place the first members, a folder is created in the directory. However, like all Inventor files created in the context of an assembly, the parts are not written to disk until you save the assembly. This is true when you create frame members as well, and since it is so easy to create members, it may not be obvious that you need to save them after the initial creation. Pay attention to the Save reminders and limit the amount of data you risk losing between saves.

COPYING FRAMES

If you have a completed frame design that you would like to copy, you can use the iLogic Design Copy tool (see Chapter 20, "iLogic") to do so. Keep in mind that you needn't have used iLogic to use the iLogic Design Copy tool for copying frames. You can find the iLogic Design Copy tool by closing all your Inventor files and then going to the Tools tab and looking on the iLogic panel.

Use the Assemblies list panel in the iLogic Design Copy dialog box to select the frame assembly you want to copy. All files referenced by the frame assembly will be selected in the other lists. You can then specify a target folder to copy to and specify a naming prefix or suffix as needed.

Once you start the copy process, the frame files will be copied, and the internal references will be updated.

Note that there are a couple of limitations to be aware of. First, you cannot create more than one frame subassembly in the same assembly. Another limitation is that you can't use copies of the frame generated with the assembly Copy tool in other assemblies and maintain Frame Generator functionality.

Exploring the Anatomy of a Frame Member

Frame Generator initially creates frame members the same length as the selected geometry. When you add end treatments, the length is adjusted to make the member longer or shorter. To accomplish this, the structural profiles are created with a From-To extrusion between two work planes, as shown in Figure 15.3.

FIGURE 15.3

A typical frame member

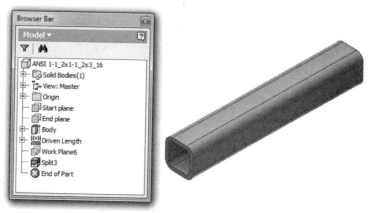

When the part is first created, the start plane is coincident with the XY plane, and the end plane is set to the initial length. When an end treatment is added, the start or end plane is moved to shorten or lengthen the member.

The parameter relationships that control the length are complex. Three parameters drive the length, two parameters are driven by those parameters to determine the length, a reference parameter reports the overall length, and a parameter is used in the BOM, as indicated in Figure 15.4.

FIGURE 15.4

Frame member parameters

Parameter Name	Unit/Type	Equation	Nominal Value	Tol	Model Value	Key		Comment
Model Parameters								
d4	deg	0 deg	0.000000		0.000000			
d7	mm	G_JR	10.000000		10.000000			
d9	mm	G_W	50.000000		50.000000			
d11	mm	G_H	50.000000		50.000000			
d12	mm	G_T	5.000000		5.000000			
d13	mm	-G_OFFSET_START	-0.000000		-0.000000			
d14	mm	G_OFFSET_END + B_L	300.000000		300.000000			
d15	mm	d9 / 2 ul	25.000000		25.000000			
d16	mm	d11 / 2 ul	25.000000		25.000000			
d17	deg	90 deg	90.000000		90.000000			
Reference Parameters								
d18	mm	300.000 mm	300.000000		300.000000			
User Parameters								
G_W	mm	50 mm	50.000000		50.000000			Width
G_H	mm	50 mm	50.000000		50.000000			Depth
G_T	mm	5 mm	5.000000		5.000000			Thickness
G_JR	mm	10 mm	10.000000		10.000000			Radius r1
G_L	mm	d18	300.000000		300.000000			Length
G_OFFSET_START	mm	0.00000000 mm	0.000000		0.000000		✓	
G_OFFSET_END	mm	0.00000000 mm	0.000000		0.000000			
B_L	mm	300.00000000 mm	300.000000		300.000000			
MAS	kg/m	6.56 kg/m	6.560000		6.560000			

Table 15.1 lists the length parameters.

TABLE 15.1:   Frame member parameters

PARAMETER	DESCRIPTION
B_L	The initial length of the member.
G_OFFSET_START	The offset value of the start work plane.
G_OFFSET_END	The offset value of the end work plane.
d13	The parameter for the start work plane. It is driven by G_OFFSET_START.
d14	The parameter for the end work plane. It is driven by G_OFFSET_END.
d19	A reference dimension that measures the overall length of the part.
G_L	The length parameter that is used in the BOM. It is equal to the reference dimension.

Inserting Frame Members

The process for inserting frame members can be broken down into three basic steps. You select the frame member profile (this comes from Content Center), select the placement geometry for placing the frame members, and then adjust the orientation of the frame members.

Specifying a Structural Shape

The left side of the Insert dialog box, shown in Figure 15.5, has a series of drop-down fields for specifying the structural shape.

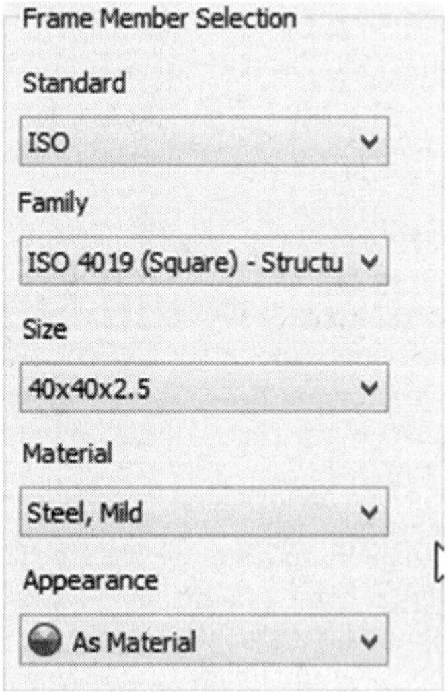

FIGURE 15.5
Frame Member
Selection group

Frame Member Selection

Standard

ISO

Family

ISO 4019 (Square) - Structu

Size

40x40x2.5

Material

Steel, Mild

Appearance

As Material

You use the Standard, Family, and Size fields to select the member from Content Center. These fields are progressive from top to bottom, with one updating when changes are made to the one above it. However, the update behavior varies depending on the field selected. If you select a new standard, the first family is automatically selected. If you select a new family, the size is not automatically selected.

Changing the Orientation

After you have selected the placement geometry, you can change the position and orientation of the member. A thumbnail of the profile is displayed in a grid of radio buttons that control the position of the member, as shown in Figure 15.6. These positions are based on the rectangular bounds of the profile. As a result, the corner positions of a pipe that's 1 inch in diameter are the same as they are in a 1-inch-by-1-inch square tube.

FIGURE 15.6

Orientation group

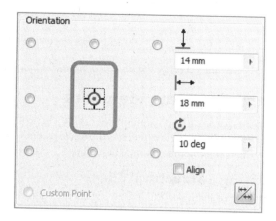

You can fine-tune the placement position by entering values in the horizontal and vertical offset fields. You can also rotate the member. For example, food processing equipment frequently has horizontal members rotated 45 degrees so spilled food doesn't build up on top of square tubing.

You can see the Mirror Frame Member button in the lower-right corner of Figure 15.6. This button is used for profiles that don't have rotational symmetry, such as C-channel and angle iron. The orientation changes affect all the members of a select set. Depending on the geometry, it might be more efficient to use a batch select tool and change the orientation of a few members afterward, or you might want to select only those members that have a similar orientation.

Since structural shapes are extruded, Frame Generator needs a method for determining the extrude direction. When an edge is selected, Frame Generator uses the closest endpoint as the start of the extrusion. Depending on where you select an edge, the same radio button can cause the member to be in a different position. The thumbnail is the view of the profile looking at the XY plane. It takes some practice to get a good feel for the relationship between how an edge is selected and the behavior of the radio buttons. Once you understand this relationship, you will be able to predict the behavior and use it to increase your productivity.

"Do I Need to Use 3D Sketches with Frame Generator?"

Although you can use 3D sketches to base a frame on, you don't need to do this. You can create 3D solids or surfaces to create a frame base. Once you have a 3D shape, you can then add 2D sketches to the various faces and use those sketches as selection edges as well. So, you don't need to be well versed in the 3D sketch tools to create 3D frames.

When you're using a custom profile with an alternate insertion point defined, the Custom Point control is enabled. This adds another insertion point to the nine standard ones. The custom point is not displayed in the thumbnail image, so you should confirm that the preview is in the expected position relative to the selected edge. Figure 15.7 shows a profile with an alternate insertion point.

Figure 15.7
Profile with an alternate insertion point

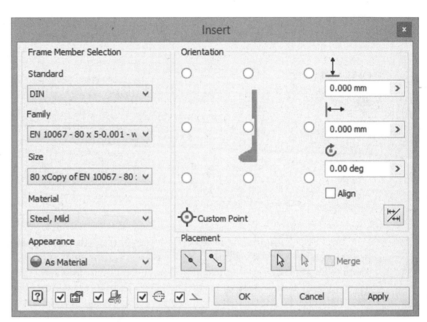

Selecting Placement Geometry

When selecting placement geometry, you can select edges of 3D models and visible sketch lines, or you can select two endpoints. For instance, if you had a cube-shaped base solid, you would use the edges to place vertical and horizontal frame members. To place diagonal cross bracing, you would use the corner endpoints.

Insert Selection Methods

When you use the default Insert Members On Edges option, you can select edges and lines for placement references. Using edges for placement allows you to insert multiple members at once. When you use the Insert Members Between Points option, you select two vertices or endpoints. This method allows you to place only one member at a time. The most common placement method is by selecting lines and edges. This allows the most flexibility in geometry selection and the use of batch select tools.

There are two philosophies for placing frame members. Some people like to place frame members individually, making sure each one is in the correct position and orientation. Others like to place as many members as possible and then edit them as necessary. The method you choose will depend on the type of models you work with, how much effort you put into setting up the skeleton models, and, most importantly, the way you like to work.

BATCH SELECT TOOLS

Frame Generator has several tools for selecting geometry. Multi Select is the default selection mode. The standard methods for creating a Multi Select selection allow you to select individual edges, use selection windows, and use the **Shift** and **Ctrl** keys to add and remove objects to or from the selection. In addition to Multi Select, two other select modes are available in the context menu shown in Figure 15.8; they are Chain Select and Sketch Select.

FIGURE 15.8
Select mode context menu

Chain Select automatically selects all lines and edges that are tangentially connected to the selection. Chain Select will not follow past a point that has multiple lines or edges, even if one of them is tangential. For instance, if you have a rectangular sketch profile with rounded corners, you can use Chain Select and select just one of the lines or arcs, and all the others will be added automatically. By contrast, if you have the same profile in a 3D shape, Chain Select will not automatically select the edges because each edge of the 3D shape has multiple edge intersections.

Sketch Select selects all the lines in a sketch. You can select the sketch in the browser or click a line in the graphics window. For instance, if you have a ladder-shaped sketch, you can use Sketch Select and automatically select the rungs and rails all at once.

The Merge option is enabled when there are connected lines or edges. Merge combines the selections into one member. Although Merge is useful when you want to have one continuous member, you cannot add end treatments to merged members.

Creating a Basic Frame

To create an elementary frame, you'll use a prepared file that has been set up for you. If you have not already downloaded the Chapter 15 files from www.sybex.com/go/masteringinventor2016, please refer to the "What You Will Need" section of the introduction for the download and setup instructions.

The prepared file you'll be using is an assembly file consisting of just two parts and the frame subassembly. One of the parts contains an unconsumed sketch that you will use to place frame members. The frame members will be automatically placed in the predefined frame subassembly. When creating your own frame designs from scratch, you'll be asked to supply the name and locations for the frame subassembly and skeleton files. In this design, you'll add frame members to be embedded in a monument base to support a sign plate.

1. On the Get Started tab, click the Open button.

2. Browse for `mi_15a_001.iam` located in the `Chapter 15` directory of your `Mastering Inventor 2016` folder and click the Open button.

3. From the Design tab, click the Insert Frame button.

4. Set the Standard drop-down box to use the standard of your choice.

5. Set the Family drop-down box to use a square tube or square hollow section profile.

6. Set the Size drop-down box to use an 80 mm×80 mm (or 3"×3") section, using a wall thickness of your choice.

7. Select the middle vertical sketch line on the back of the sign plate in the model.

8. Use the radio buttons in the Orientation area of the Insert dialog box to orient the frame member so it matches up with the square cutout in the base.

9. Select the other four vertical sketch lines as well. Note that the two end members are not centered in the cutouts.

10. Holding the **Ctrl** key, select the two end members to remove them from the selection.

11. Click the OK button to generate the frame members; then click the OK button in the Frame Member Naming dialog box to accept the defaults.

12. Click the Insert Frame button again and click the bottom half of one of the outside vertical sketch lines.

13. Use the radio buttons in the Orientation area to orient the frame member so it matches up with the square cutout.

14. Select the bottom half of the other outside vertical sketch line and notice that the frame member preview does not match the cutout.

15. Using the Orientation radio buttons, you'll notice that none of the solutions allows both members to match the cutouts.

16. Holding the **Ctrl** key, click one of the frame members to remove it from the selection.

17. Select the sketch line again, this time toward the top, and you'll see that this flips the orientation to provide the correct solution.

18. Uncheck the Prompt For File Name check box (found along the bottom of the dialog box). This suppresses the filenaming dialog prompt and automatically accepts the default naming for the frame members.

19. Click the OK button. Your assembly should resemble Figure 15.9.

FIGURE 15.9
Frame members placed
using Frame Generator

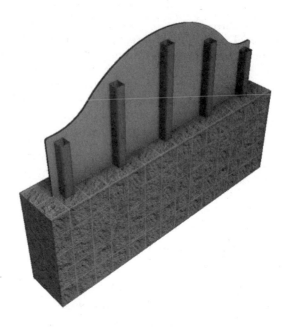

   In this simple example you explored the basics of placing frame members, noting the use of the Ctrl key on the keyboard to remove selections. You also noticed that orientation of frame members is sometimes influenced by the location of your lines or edge selections. You can close this file without saving changes and continue to the next section. In the next example, you'll explore more selection and orientation options.

WHERE ARE THE OTHER COMMON SIZES?

You might note that there are several common sizes you use daily that are not listed in the Size drop-down. This is because Inventor includes only the sizes that are ratified to the various structural shape standards. Of course, most mills produce other sizes commonly used in general design. You can add those sizes using the Structural Shape authoring tools.

   In the following steps, you will explore the offset, rotation, and merge options, as well as the context menu selection options:

1.   On the Get Started tab, click the Open button.

2.   Browse for mi_15a_002.iam in the Chapter 15 directory of your Mastering Inventor 2016 folder and click the Open button.

3.   From the Design tab, click the Insert Frame button.

4.   Set the Standard drop-down box to use the standard of your choice.

5.   Set the Family drop-down box to use a flat bar section profile.

6.   Set the Size drop-down box to use a 50 mm (or 2-inch) bar, using a thickness of your choice.

7.   Right-click in the graphics area and set the selection method to Chain Select.

8. Click any part of the C-shaped sketch and notice that the entire sketch loop is selected; you don't need to click each sketch segment.

9. Set Horizontal Offset to **-100** mm.

10. Set Rotation to **90** degrees.

11. Click the Merge check box to ensure that the result is a continuous piece of rolled flat bar rather than a piece for each segment of the loop.

12. Click Apply to create the frame member.

13. Right-click in the graphics area and set the selection method to Sketch Select.

14. Select any of the segments in the ladder sketch and notice that the entire sketch is selected.

15. Set the horizontal offset to **0** mm and the rotation to **0** degrees.

16. Click Apply to create the frame members.

17. Right-click in the graphics area and set the selection method back to the default Multi Select option.

18. In the Placement area of the Insert dialog box, click the Insert Members Between Points button and then select endpoints of the gap in the C-shaped sketch.

19. Set the rotation to **90** degrees.

20. Click the OK button to create the short length of flat bar and close the dialog box. Figure 15.10 shows the final result.

FIGURE 15.10
Flat bar frame members

As you can see, the selection options along with the offset, rotation, and merge options allow you to create frame members using just a simple sketch and still get a varied result. You can close this file without saving changes and continue to the next section.

Aligning Frame Members

Frame Generator follows two rules to give a frame member its initial orientation. If you are creating the first member in a selection set, the member is aligned to adjacent geometry or the coordinate system. For the rest of the selection set, Frame Generator tries to align the members to the first selection. These rules work well for most rectangular machine frames. However, if part of the frame is at an angle and there isn't a good reference, Frame Generator might select an orientation that doesn't match your design intent.

The frame in Figure 15.11 has two sketch lines running down from the center point to be used for supports. The members for the base and back have already been inserted, and the two angled supports need to be inserted. When a member is inserted on angled lines, the orientation is skewed, as shown in the inset in Figure 15.11.

FIGURE 15.11
Skewed orientation

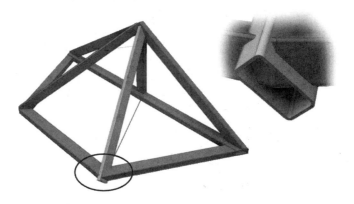

To resolve this, a reference line can be selected first to establish the orientation, and then the angled line can be selected to add the support member and have it follow this orientation. Once the angled line is selected, the reference line can be deselected, and the angled line will hold the proper orientation, as shown in Figure 15.12.

FIGURE 15.12
Using a helper line to establish orientation

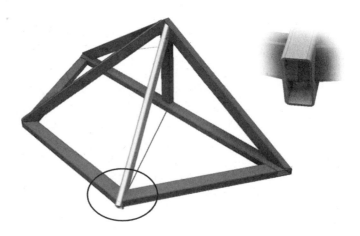

Using reference geometry for angled frame members is a bit of an art. If you regularly create these types of frames, you will develop a feeling for the ways that Frame Generator aligns members, and you will learn when and how you need to add references. To better understand the use of reference geometry for alignment, follow these steps:

1. On the Get Started tab, click the Open button.

2. Browse for `mi_15a_003.iam` located in the `Chapter 15` directory of your `Mastering Inventor 2016` folder and click the Open button.

3. From the Design tab, click the Insert Frame button.

4. Set the Standard drop-down box to use the standard of your choice.

5. Set the Family drop-down box to use a rectangular tube or rectangular hollow section profile.

6. Set the Size drop-down box to use a 100 mm×50 mm (or 4"×2") tube, using a thickness of your choice.

7. Ensure that the placement option is set to Insert Members On Edges and that the offsets and rotation fields are set to zero. Set the orientation to be centered and then click the diagonal line that runs into the frame peak.

8. Click the OK button to create the member.

Notice how the frame member is coming in at a skewed orientation. To resolve this, you will first delete this member and then place another, but this time you'll use a helper edge to establish the orientation.

9. In the browser, expand `Frame_MI_1503` so you can see the frame members.

10. Hover over each member until you see the one you just created highlighted in the graphics area (it should be at the bottom of the list).

11. Right-click it and choose Delete With Frame Generator.

Using this option not only deletes the part but also cleans up any end treatments involving other members related to the deleted one.

12. Click the Insert Frame button again. Click the diagonal line that runs into the frame peak first and then select the Align check box.

13. Click the sketch line located in the base of the frame to use as the alignment selection.

14. Adjust the rotation angle by 90 degrees.

15. Click the OK button to create the frame member in the correct orientation.

Keep this alignment trick in mind as you create frames, and you will likely find it to be very helpful. You can close the file without saving changes.

Using the Change Tool

You can use the Change tool to change the standard, family, size, material, color, and orientation of an existing frame member. You can use the check boxes to set the various options to allow or prevent changes. To see the Change tool in action, follow these steps:

1. On the Get Started tab, click the Open button.

2. Browse for `mi_15a_004.iam` located in the `Chapter 15` directory of your `Mastering Inventor 2016` folder and click the Open button.

3. From the Design tab, click the Frame panel drop-down arrow.

4. Select the Frame Member Info button from the list.

5. Click one of the shorter uprights in the frame. The Frame Member Info dialog box displays the information about this part. Click Done to close the dialog box.

6. From the Design tab, click the Change button.

7. Click one of the shorter uprights in the frame again and then select the other one. Notice that the selection allows only one frame member to be selected at a time.

8. Click the Multi Select check box in the Change dialog box and then select the other short upright member.

9. Set the rotation to **45** degrees.

10. Change the Appearance setting to Cadet Blue or something similar and then click the OK button.

This simple exercise demonstrates the use of the Change tool to modify frame members. Keep in mind that if you make a change that requires a new file to be generated, such as changing the size, the old part will be replaced with a new one, but the old file will remain in the folder in which it is saved. You can close this file without saving changes.

Adding End Treatments

The end treatments are among the most powerful Frame Generator tools. As you add end treatments, the frame member length automatically updates. The end treatments also carry over if you change the frame member to a different profile. End treatments are listed under the frame member node in the browser and can be accessed by expanding the browser node, as shown in Figure 15.13.

FIGURE 15.13
End treatments in the browser

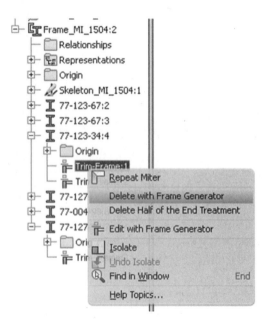

You can delete end treatments from the browser, or you can use the Remove End Treatments tool on the Frame drop-down list of the Design tab. When you use the Remove End Treatments tool, all end treatments are stripped from the selected frame member and its counterpart. Additionally, you can right-click the end treatment node and select Delete Half Of The End Treatment.

If a member has end treatments on it already and you attempt to add another, you will need to select the Delete Existing End Treatment(s) check box in the dialog box; otherwise, an error such as the one shown in Figure 15.14 may be created.

FIGURE 15.14
Conflicting end treatment error

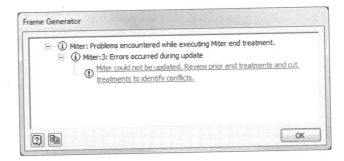

If you do encounter an error, simply undo the change and reapply the end treatment, this time using the Delete Existing End Treatment(s) option.

Miter

The Miter end treatment makes angle cuts on two members. Figure 15.15 shows the Miter dialog box. You can miter multiple members by applying the end treatment to each pair of members. You can add a gap between the members by entering a value in the gap input box. The default gap is split between the two members. If you want the gap to be taken from just one member, you can use the Miter Cut At One Side button, and the gap will be taken from the first member you selected. Figure 15.15 shows the gap option buttons and input box.

FIGURE 15.15
Miter dialog box

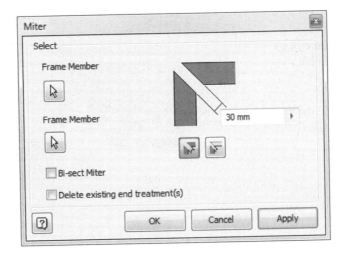

The default selections cut along an angle, resulting in full-face contact between the members, as shown in Figure 15.16. Bi-sect Miter splits the angle between the members. Figure 15.17 shows that the cut is located where the centers of the two members intersect.

FIGURE 15.16
The standard miter joint has full-face contact

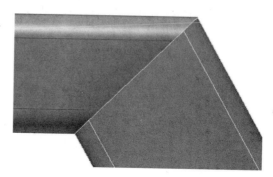

FIGURE 15.17
The optional bi-sect miter cuts both members at the same angle

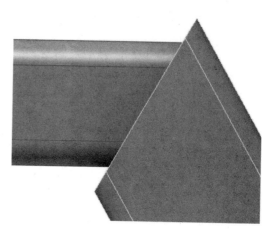

Figure 15.18 shows a one-sided gap where the horizontal member was selected first.

FIGURE 15.18
Miter gap on one member

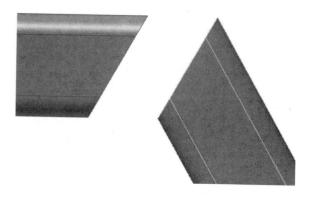

Figure 15.19 has a miter end treatment between the two angled members and a vertical member running through them. The vertical member needs to be mitered to fit. Figure 15.19 shows the left member and the vertical member being selected for the first step to create the miter.

FIGURE 15.19
First miter cut

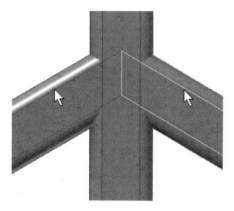

The vertical member still needs a miter to trim the other side, so the miter is repeated with the same settings, this time choosing the member on the right and the vertical member, as shown in Figure 15.20.

FIGURE 15.20
Second miter cut

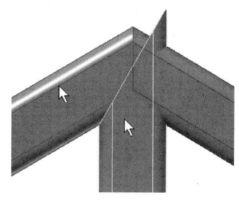

The resulting miter, shown in Figure 15.21, requires two cuts on each member. An alternate method that produces a more cost-effective joint can be made using the Trim/Extend To Face tool.

FIGURE 15.21
Resulting miter joint
between the three
members

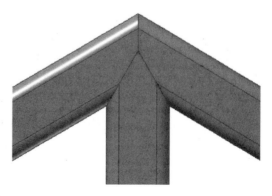

You can open the file mi_15a_006.iam to explore the Miter tool. Practice creating miter gaps and two- and three-member miters to understand the process.

Trim/Extend to Face

This end treatment is the only one that can trim multiple members at once. When trimming or extending to a face, you select the members you want to trim and then select the cutting face. A separate end treatment feature is created for each frame member. If you edit or delete the end treatment for a particular member, it does not affect the other members. Figure 15.22 shows a typical trim-to-face situation. You would select the vertical member for the member to trim and the top face of the horizontal member as the face to trim to.

FIGURE 15.22
A trim-to-face scenario

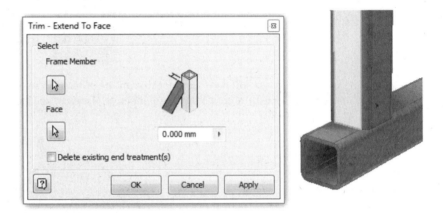

This end treatment can also be used to create miters. Applying miter end treatments to already mitered frame members results in a costly complex joint cut for all three members. Trimming the third member to fit the first two angled members using the Trim/Extend To Face tool results in the less-expensive detail shown in Figure 15.23.

FIGURE 15.23
Creating a miter using Trim

You can open the file mi_15a_007.iam to explore the Trim/Extend tool. Remember, you can select multiple frame members to trim to the same face. Experiment with this file as you like—there is no set solution to the final frame outcome.

WHICH SIDE IS TRIMMED?

Be aware that when using the Trim tools in Frame Generator, the short end is always the one to be discarded.

Trim to Frame Member

This end treatment trims or extends both members so they are flush. The first selection is made flush to the second selection, and the second selection butts up to the first. Figure 15.24 shows the selections, and Figure 15.25 shows the results.

FIGURE 15.24
Trim To Frame selections

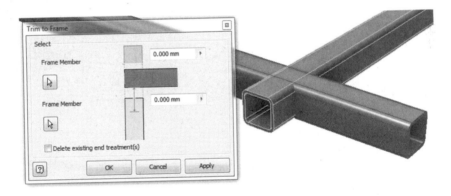

FIGURE 15.25
Trim To Frame results

You can open the file mi_15a_008.iam to explore the Trim To Frame tool. Experiment with this file as you like—there is no set solution to the final frame outcome. If you cannot get the result you want from the Trim To Frame tool alone, consider the Trim/Extend To Face tool as well. These tools are often used together to achieve a specific result.

Notch Frame Members

The Notch tool cuts one frame member to match the other. It uses the profile to create a cutting surface. By default you can't create an offset, so the cut is an exact match. This is simply a cut operation, so the frame member is not shortened or extended before the cut. If you have authored a notch profile into a custom frame member library file, you can select the Apply Notch Profile check box; however, if the member does not contain a notch profile definition, the check box is grayed out.

If you were to notch the shorter I-beam shown in Figure 15.26, which extends past the taller I-beam, the extra lump would remain on the left, as shown in Figure 15.27. If the members don't intersect, the notch will have no effect.

FIGURE 15.26
Frame members
before notch

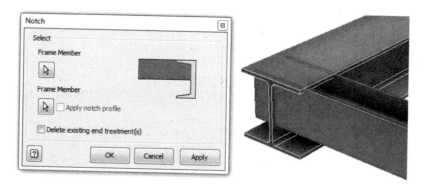

FIGURE 15.27
The result of removing the intersecting
material

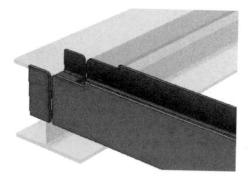

Because of this, it's often best to create a notch as a secondary end treatment. For example, if you had two intersecting frame members as shown in Figure 15.26, it might be best to add a Trim/Extend To Face end treatment first and then use a notch to remove any intersecting material. To explore the Notch tool, open the file mi_15a_009.iam. Use the flanged beams to create notches in the T-shaped members.

> **CREATING ACCURATE NOTCHES**
>
> Notch shapes are driven by manufacturing requirements. Typically, the shape is simplified to reduce cost, and there may be a gap between the members to allow for tolerances. The easiest way to create these shapes is to add a Trim/Extend To Face treatment to make the member the correct length and then add an iFeature to trim the end of the member to the correct shape. You can also define notch profiles in custom frame member definitions.

Lengthen/Shorten Frame Member

You can use the Lengthen/Shorten tool to change the length of a frame member. By default, frame members are initially assigned the length of the reference edge or the distance between selected points. However, you will often need to change the length. Much of the time you will simply use another frame member and one of the Extend or Trim tools. Sometimes, though, there isn't another frame member you can use as a reference, so in those cases you would use the Lengthen/Shorten tool.

When you use the Lengthen/Shorten At One End option, the Extension value is applied to the end closest to the pick point, meaning that if you select a vertical frame member toward the top end and specify an extension length of 100 mm, that value will be applied to the top end. When using the Lengthen/Shorten At Both Ends option, the Extension value is applied to both ends. So if you applied a 100 mm extension value, the frame member would grow 100 mm on both ends for a total of 200 mm. If you enter a negative value, the frame member will be shortened.

> **FRAME END TREATMENTS ARE NOT EXEMPT FROM DESIGN INTENT**
>
> You should spend time planning your frame design to minimize the number of end treatments required because each end treatment is an opportunity for the model to fail if a change is made. For example, if you create a skeleton to the inside dimensions of a frame, you can offset members during placement so the members butt against one another without adding end treatments.

Reuse Frame Members

When you use the Insert Frame tool, Inventor creates a new part file for each new frame member you insert. This allows you to create separate part files that allow separate end treatments. For instance, you might initially insert two identical frame members but then choose to miter both ends of one but only one end of the other. Having two separate part files allows this.

However, there are often times when you might want to reuse the same frame member over and over. In these cases you would prefer not to have separate part files and could use the Reuse tool to ensure that the same part file is being reused as needed. To see the Reuse tool in action, follow these steps:

1. On the Get Started tab, click the Open button.

2. Browse for `mi_15a_005.iam` located in the `Chapter 15` directory of your `Mastering Inventor 2016` folder and click the Open button.

3. From the Design tab, click the Reuse button.

4. For the Source Member selection, click the longer existing member from the graphics area.

5. Click the longer sketch line to use as the Placement selection, but be sure to select it at the end of the line furthest from the existing short member (near the sketched arc).

6. Click the OK button to create the new frame member and notice the direction of the holes.

7. Next click the Change Reuse button.

8. Choose the member you just created and then click the Reverse Member Direction button; then click the OK button to see the change. Notice the direction of the holes again.

9. Click the Miter tool and select the ends of the two original frame members when they come to an intersection and then click Apply.

10. Still in the Miter tool, click the remaining end of the short member and the corresponding end of the new long frame member (even though it is already mitered) and then click the OK button.

11. Click the Reuse button and choose the shorter member for the Source Member selection.

12. Choose the remaining straight sketch line for the Placement selection and then click the OK button to create the new frame member.

13. Click the Change Reuse button, select the new short frame member, set Orientation Angle to 180 degrees, and then click the OK button.

14. Click the Miter tool and select the unmitered end of the original longer member and the corresponding end of the shorter member; then click the OK button to create the miter.

The Reuse and Change Reuse tools offer powerful options for working with repetitive frame members in your frame designs. Keep these tools in mind when working with frame design, and you can likely simplify your frame bill of materials and save yourself some work along the way.

Here are a few things to know about the Reuse and Change Reuse tools:

- The Reuse tool is available only to straight frame members and will not work for curved members.

- To convert a frame member created with the Reuse tool to a separate frame member file, you can locate it in the browser and then right-click it and choose Break Reuse Member.

- When you use Break Reuse Member, you will lose any existing end treatments found on that member.

- Frame members created using the Reuse tool might not be selectable for some end treatment and other frame modifications tools.

◆ If you modify the frame base inputs on which a Reuse frame member relies, such as the base sketch, an error message will display, and you will likely need to delete the Reuse member.

◆ You can delete a Reuse member by locating it in the browser and then right-clicking it and choosing Delete with Frame Generator.

◆ In addition to the Orientation Angle options, you might need to use the Align check box in the Reuse and Change Reuse dialog boxes to reuse members so that they are placed in the correct orientation.

When you've finished exploring the Reuse and Change Reuse tools, you can close this file without saving changes and continue to the next section.

Maintaining Frames

Maintaining existing assemblies can be time-consuming. Frame Generator provides several tools that help streamline the process of modifying end treatments and determining how frames were originally designed.

Remove End Treatments

The Remove End Treatments tool removes all end treatments from a selected frame member. You can also select multiple members for the batch removal of end treatments. This is handy if you need to change the end treatments on a few members or if you have to rebuild a frame. You can find the Remove End Treatments tool in the Frame drop-down list indicated by the small black arrow on the Frame panel of the Design tab. (See Figure 15.1 earlier in the chapter.)

Frame Member Information

The Frame Member Information tool is used to query frame members. It displays the family and size information, mass properties, and material. This is a useful tool because it quickly gives you information about a member. For example, it can help you quickly determine the difference in the wall thickness of two similarly sized hollow tubes. Since the tool filters for only frame members, you can use it at any level of the assembly. You can find the Frame Member Information tool in the Frame drop-down list indicated by the small black arrow on the Frame panel of the Design tab.

Refresh

The Refresh tool is a Content Center tool. It checks Content Center for the latest revision of the members in the frame. If a newer version is available, it will prompt you to replace it. End treatments are retained during refresh, but other features may not carry over to the new member. You can find the Refresh tool in the Frame drop-down list indicated by the small black arrow on the Frame panel of the Design tab.

MANAGING FRAME GENERATOR FILES

Frame Generator uses an algorithm to create default filenames. You can rename the files as you create them, when prompted by the Frame Member Naming dialog. But often this slows the design process and requires you to enter information you may not currently know.

Another approach is to let Inventor apply the filenames automatically. To do so, you can uncheck the filenaming prompt check box in the Insert Frame dialog box, and Inventor will create the filenames and save the files to the location specified when the frame subassembly and skeleton files were initially created. It is a good idea to set the frame subassembly and skeleton filenames and locations to use a well-planned naming scheme, whether you specify the frame member names or let Inventor do so.

If you decide to accept the default filenames, it is a good idea to use the BOM Editor to set the part number iProperty for each file to match your standard. In this way, you have a unique identifier for each part member. You can set two identical frame members to have the same part number so they are rolled up together in the BOM. Using part numbers (you can think of them as mark numbers), rather than the filenames, to manage the frame members provides a more flexible and real-world workflow for the typical frame design.

Once part numbers have been defined, you can also set the assembly browser to use the part number rather than the filenames. This allows you to quickly index individual frame parts more easily. Do this by selecting the Assemble tab, clicking the drop-down list on the Productivity panel, and choosing the Rename Browser Nodes tool.

Although Frame Generator can create frames (and therefore a lot of part files) quickly, once the frame is modeled, you should slow down and take the time to manage part numbers. This allows your design to be managed properly in the detailing and revision stages.

Performing Calculations and Analysis

Included in the standard Frame Generator tools are two calculator tools: the Beam And Column Calculator and the Plate Calculator. These calculators are design accelerator tools that can do a simple stress analysis. The Beam And Column Calculator, for instance, can analyze a single beam or column, but it assumes a uniform cross section, so it does not take into account holes or end treatments.

If you have Inventor Professional or Inventor Simulation, you can use the Frame Analysis tools that are part of those packages. You can learn more about the Frame Analysis tools in Chapter 17, "Stress Analysis and Dynamic Simulation."

The Beam and Column Calculator

You can find the Beam And Column Calculator tool in the Frame drop-down list indicated by the small black arrow found on the Frame panel of the Design tab. As with other design accelerator dialog boxes, the message pane at the bottom and the calculation results pane on the right side can be opened and closed by clicking the small >> symbols. You can drag the splitter bar (double gray lines) to resize the panes, or you can double-click the splitter bar to open or close the panes.

CALCULATING SECTION PROPERTIES

As you explore the subjects in the following pages, you can refer to the conveyor assembly in the file mi_15a_014.iam. Take a moment to open this file from the Chapter 15 directory to become familiar with it. You will use this file to complete the exercise steps presented later.

Select an Object

In this assembly, the Beam And Column Calculator might be used to calculate the loading on the power roller supports. When one of the gold tubes is selected, the calculator automatically loads the section properties from Content Center, as shown in Figure 15.28. Although Content Center has most of the section properties, be aware that some data is missing. You can use several methods for determining the properties.

FIGURE 15.28
The section properties for a selected object are loaded from Content Center.

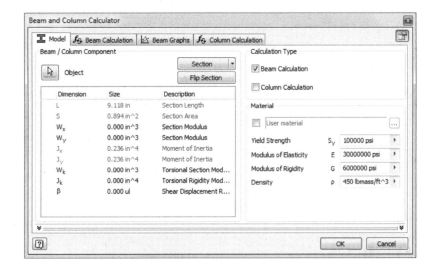

Use the Region Properties Tool

Inventor has a tool to calculate the properties of a closed sketch profile. If you want to use this tool for the section properties of a frame member, you can open the frame member, place a sketch on one end, and project the face. Once you have the profile, select the Inspect tab and click the Region Properties tool on the Measure panel. Select the profile you want to analyze and click Calculate. The basic region properties for any closed loop are calculated. You can then calculate the rest of the properties based on those results.

The region properties are calculated with respect to the sketch origin. Depending on the profile, you may have to edit the sketch coordinate system to locate the sketch origin at the center of the profile.

Use the Section Button

Another option for calculating section properties is to use the Section button in the Beam And Column Calculator. When you click the button, a list of geometric shapes appears. When you select a shape, a dialog box like Figure 15.29 appears and allows you to enter dimensions. The calculated properties assume sharp corners and constant thickness, so the results won't be accurate for profiles with tapered flanges but may be good enough for many applications.

FIGURE 15.29
Calculating section properties for a rectangle

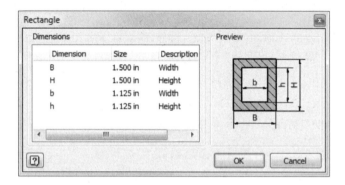

The Flip Section button is used to change the orientation of the x- and y-axes. The z-axis is always in the direction of the extrusion. Gravity is always in the negative y-axis direction, so it is important to make sure the calculation coordinates match the assembly coordinates. If the beam is at an angle, you have a couple of options for handling gravity. You can place a copy of the beam horizontally in the assembly. If you want to ignore the effect of gravity, there is an option on the Beam Calculation tab to turn the gravity load off.

Both Beam and Column calculations are available. The Beam calculations focus on deflection based on loads and supports. The Column calculation checks for buckling. You can select Beam, Column, or both calculation types. The Calculation tabs are turned on and off based on the selections.

The default material properties do not correspond to a material style and are not linked to the style library in any way. Instead, these materials provide you with a starting point and an example of the required properties. You can enter properties for a particular material, or you can select one of the generic materials listed. When you check the box, a dialog box appears with materials such as gray cast iron, steel, and aluminum. These properties can be used for initial calculations, but for more accurate results, you should enter the properties for the particular alloy you are using.

The following steps use the power roller supports found in the conveyor assembly mi_15a_014.iam. Follow these steps to enter the member data into the dialog box:

1. Click the Beam/Column Calculator button to start the calculator. Recall that this button can be found in the drop-down list indicated by the small black arrow on the Frame panel of the Design tab.

2. Select the lower, gold-colored support for the power roller.

3. If necessary, click the padlock icon for the Section Length row in the table, thereby unlocking it for editing. Change the value to **12 inch**.

4. Click the Section button and select Rectangle from the drop-down list.

5. In the Rectangle dialog box, enter the tubing dimensions. Enter **1.5 inch** for the outside dimensions (B and H) and **1.125 inch** for the inside dimensions (b and h). Then click the OK button.

6. Select both the Beam and Column calculation check boxes in the Calculation Type area.

7. Click the check box next to the Material field to launch the Material Types dialog box. Select Steel and click the OK button.

8. Note the Yield Strength of 44000 psi.

9. Leave this dialog open because you will use it in the next set of steps, where you'll work with loads and supports.

The coordinate system alignment is correct for this example. So in this case, gravity could be ignored, but having the correct orientation simplifies adding the loads and interpreting the results.

The dialog box should look like Figure 15.30. Note that all the section properties except Shear Displacement Ratio are calculated. This property is optional for the calculations. Comparing the calculated values with the original ones, Section Area and Moments Of Inertia are close but higher.

FIGURE 15.30
Model data entered into the Beam And Column Calculator

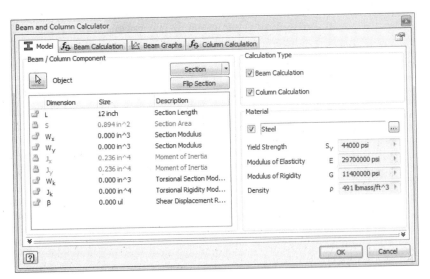

THE BEAM CALCULATION TAB

The Beam Calculation tab, shown in Figure 15.31, has controls for defining the loads and supports for beams and columns as well as the calculation options. The *Engineer's Handbook* (hidden away in the Power Transmission panel drop-down list; it's called *Handbook*) contains the equations used in the calculations. You might want to review those equations before using the calculator.

FIGURE 15.31
The Beam
Calculation tab

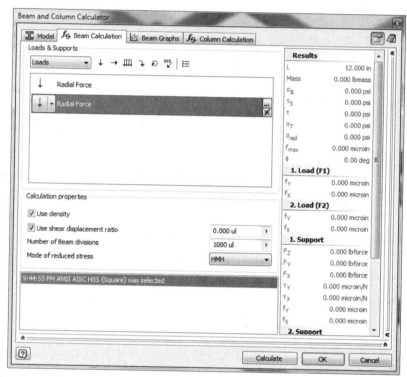

Loads & Supports

The Loads & Supports area contains controls along the top and a browser pane for adding and removing loads and supports for the frame member. All of the controls can be accessed by using the buttons at the top or by right-clicking and choosing them from the context menu in the browser pane area.

The drop-down menu switches the browser between Loads view and Supports view. The controls, shown in Table 15.2 and Table 15.3, change depending on whether Loads or Supports is set to current.

TABLE 15.2:   Loads buttons

BUTTON	DESCRIPTION
↓	Adds a force.
→	Adds an axial force.

BUTTON	DESCRIPTION
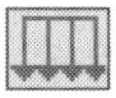	Adds a distributed force.
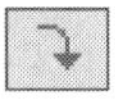	Adds a bending moment—a single twisting force perpendicular to the z-axis.
	Adds a torque load—a twisting force around the z-axis. Two equal and opposite torque loads are required.
	Adds a combined load—any of the forces added at the same point on the beam.

TABLE 15.3: Supports buttons

BUTTON	DESCRIPTION
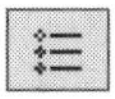	Displays the Options dialog box
	Adds a fixed support
	Adds a free support
	Fixes one end of the beam

The Options dialog box, shown in Figure 15.32, gives access to visibility controls for the 2D and 3D previews. By default, the loads and supports dynamically update to maintain the same size as the view scale changes. You can turn off the automatic update and set a static scale value. The Options dialog box is the same whether it is launched from the Loads control or Supports control.

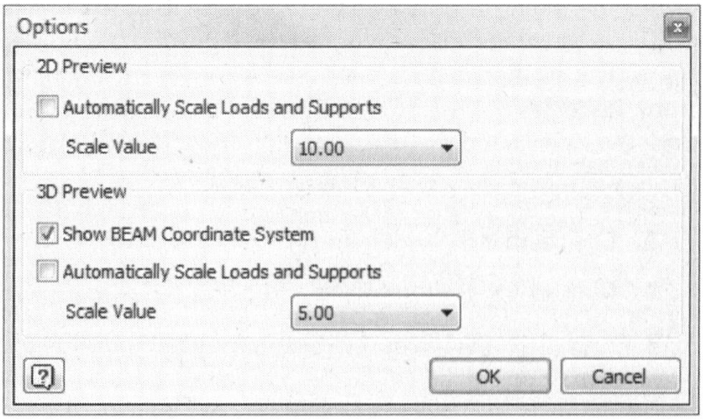

FIGURE 15.32
Loads & Supports
Options dialog box

Each load or support can be edited in the browser by double-clicking or by clicking the browse (…) button. A Properties dialog box displays controls for specifying the location, size, and direction of the force.

Calculation Properties

The Calculation Properties group, as shown in Figure 15.33, has four controls that adjust how the calculations are made.

FIGURE 15.33
The Calculation
Properties group

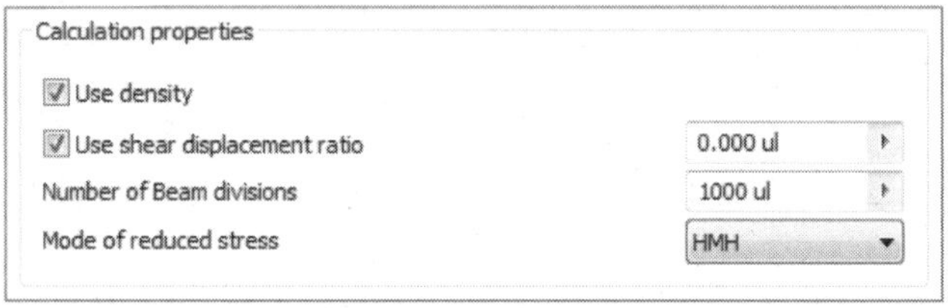

The Use Density check box adds gravity as a load. This is selected by default. The Use Shear Displacement Ratio check box is used when calculating the twist angle caused by torsional loads. The value is determined by the profile shape. It is also called the *form factor of shear*. This check box is selected by default.

The default setting for Number Of Beam Divisions is 1000. Increasing the number of divisions can result in improved accuracy for longer beams. You should experiment with different values to see whether the number of divisions causes a significant change in the results.

Mode Of Reduced Stress has two options for modeling the stress distribution. The Huber-Mises-Hencky (HMH) method is based on the maximum-energy-distortion criterion, and the Tresca-Guest method is based on the maximum-shearing-stress criterion. The HMH method is the default selection.

Results

The Results pane on the right side of the Beam Calculation tab updates when you click the Calculate button. Warnings will appear in the lower pane if the calculation indicates that stresses are too high.

For the conveyor example, the support will be welded to the frame at one end and unsupported at the other. The power roller weighs 150 pounds, and the torque is 40 pound-feet. The torque causes the power roller to twist between the supports. The edge of the flat is 1.5 inches from the center of the power roller. This means the reaction force at that point is 320 pounds. Both the weight and the reaction force are split between the two sides. Follow these steps to explore the results and calculation workflow:

1. Ensure that the first load type is set to Radial Force.

2. Click the … button to add a force for the power roller weight.

3. Enter **10** (inches) for the distance and **75** (pounds-force) for the force. This is the maximum distance for the power roller. Click the OK button to close the Radial Force dialog box.

4. Click the Add Bending Moment button to add a torque reaction force.

5. Enter **11.12** (inches) for the distance and **160** (pounds-force) for the force and then click the OK button.

6. Click the drop-down list to switch from Loads to the Supports browser.

7. Delete the Free support by selecting it and then clicking the red X button.

8. Click the drop-down arrow for the Fixed support and select Restraint.

9. Leave the Use Density option checked.

10. Deselect Use Shear Displacement Ratio since you don't have a value for that property.

11. Click the Calculate button and compare the reduced stress to the yield strength of the specified material.

12. Leave this dialog open and use it to explore the next topics.

The dialog box should look like Figure 15.34. Note that the forces and supports are displayed in the graphics window. If you hover over a force arrow or support icon in the model, a tool tip displays the information. You can drag the force to a different position, or you can double-click the force to display the properties dialog box.

FIGURE 15.34
Loads & Supports
data entered into
the calculator

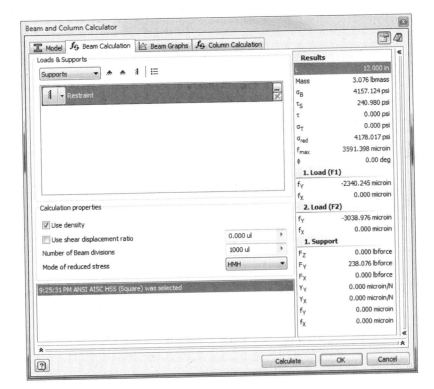

THE BEAM GRAPHS TAB

On the Beam Graphs tab, the Graph Selection pane allows you to select the results you want to display. The selected graph displays in the bottom of the Graph area. At the top of the Graph area is a schematic of the beam, supports, and loads. You can drag the supports and loads to different positions to update them. If you double-click a support or load, the properties dialog box displays so you can directly edit the data. The Calculate button is not available on the Beam Graphs tab, but the values calculate and update automatically when you change support or loads parameters.

The Beam Graphs tab is primarily intended for reviewing results. Twenty-two graphs are available on the tab. This example is a pretty simple analysis. You should experiment with other loads (torques and bending moments) and support types and then view the results on the graphs.

THE COLUMN CALCULATION TAB

The Column Calculation tab checks for column buckling. In the Loads area, you enter the axial load and the safety factor and select a coefficient for the end loading conditions. When you click the ... button, a dialog box appears with four end conditions. If you have different end conditions, you should enter the proper coefficient from a reference book.

You shouldn't need to enter any data in the Column area. The length, section area, and least moment of inertia are carried over from the Model tab. The reduced length value is calculated by multiplying the length by the end coefficient.

For example, imagine that during transport, the frame shifts and the power roller supports slam into the trailer wall. The power roller was removed during shipping, so the supports take all the force from the impact, estimated at 4,000 pounds evenly distributed across the four supports. Set the axial load to 1,000-pound force, and click Calculate to determine whether the supports will buckle. Figure 15.35 shows the results.

FIGURE 15.35
Column calculator results

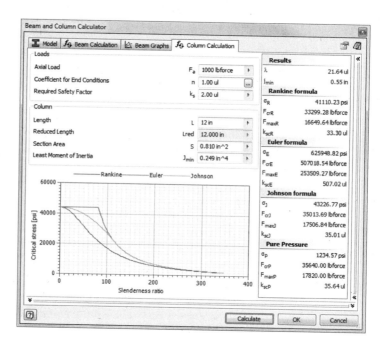

HTML RESULTS

When you click the Results button in the upper-right corner of the dialog box, an HTML page appears with all the data, calculation results, and graphs. You can save or print this file for your records.

FILE NAMING

The File Naming button, found next to the Results button in the upper-right corner of the dialog box, allows you to specify the calculation's filename. When you click the OK button to exit the Beam And Column Calculator dialog box, a subassembly file is created in the assembly file. This subassembly file is just a container for the calculations, allowing you to access them again at any point. A browser node is created for the calculations. To edit the results, simply right-click the browser node and choose Edit Using Design Accelerator.

Publishing Frame Members

Frame Generator's frame member library is integrated with Content Center. The authoring and publishing process is similar to that used to create any custom Content Center files. Since Frame Generator requires specific modeling techniques, the authoring process will make some changes to the model and the parameters to ensure that all the required parameters are included.

Authoring a Part

The authoring process for a frame member is similar to component authoring. The Structural Shape Authoring tool, located in the Author panel on the Manage tab in the Part environment, is used to prepare the part for publishing. The tool identifies the geometry used for placement, sets the parameters, and modifies the part so Frame Generator can use it.

This example uses a rubber bumper iPart file, the kind of thing that might be attached to frames to guard against impact. In the iPart table there are parameters to control the dimensions and three sizes defined. If this were a true frame member profile, the engineering properties (moments of inertia and so on) might need to be calculated, and therefore that information would be set up as well. Since this isn't a load-bearing part, those properties aren't required. To explore the authoring process, follow these steps:

1. On the Get Started tab, click the Open button.

2. Browse for `mi_15a_020.ipt` located in the `Chapter 15` directory of your `Mastering Inventor 2016` folder and click the Open button.

3. From the Manage tab, locate the drop-down list on the Author panel and then click the Structural Shape button.

4. When the authoring tool starts, everything is blank. Once a category is selected, the dialog box will update with the appropriate controls. Because this is an unusual part, select the Other category, as shown in Figure 15.36.

Frame Generator looks in the Structural Shapes category only, so you have to select one of the standard categories or create a new one in the Content Center Editor. You can't add a category through the authoring tool, so you have to add the category to Content Center before authoring. See Chapter 7, "Reusing Parts and Features," for more information on Content Center.

FIGURE 15.36

Selecting the category

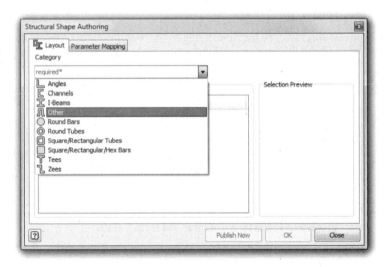

Since there is only one extrusion in the part, the base feature is automatically selected. The default base point is indicated at the center of the profile. For this part, the inside corner of the flanges is the natural insertion point.

5. Click the drop-down list, choose Select Geometry, and then select that point in the model, as shown in Figure 15.37. Note that you may need to use the ViewCube to look at the end view of the part to see the insert point selection.

FIGURE 15.37

Selecting the default base point

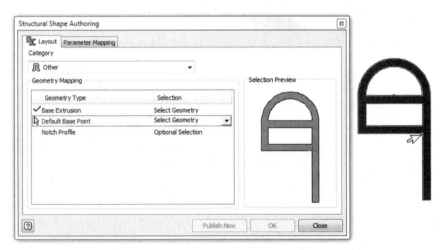

The Notch Profile option is used when you are authoring frame members and you want to include a predefined notch profile to be used with the Notch tool. In this case, there is no notch profile.

6. Click the Parameter Mapping tab.

7. Set the Base Length row to use the Length parameter by clicking the Please Select cell in the table and then choosing Length from the list.

The Parameter Mapping tab has one required field: Base Length. This is the parameter for the extrusion distance. Since this is an iPart, when you click in the field, the iPart properties are listed, as shown in Figure 15.38. If this were a regular part, the Part Template Parameters dialog box would display a browser tree, as shown in Figure 15.39. The rest of the parameters are optional. They are mechanical properties of the profile necessary for calculating loads with the Beam And Column Calculator.

FIGURE 15.38
Specifying the length parameter for an iPart

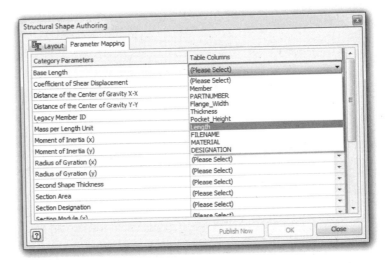

FIGURE 15.39
Specifying parameters for a regular part

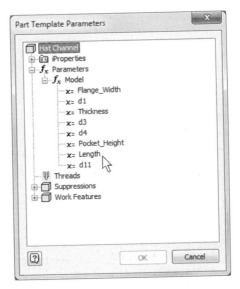

When the frame profile and Base Length parameter have been mapped, the Publish Now and OK buttons are enabled.

8. Click the OK button to update the part with the authoring changes.

Clicking either the Publish Now or OK button will update the part and close the dialog box. Publish Now will also launch Content Center publishing wizard. Once the part is updated, a dialog box displays with information about the changes. A log file that lists the changes to the part, as shown in Figure 15.40, is created in the project directory.

FIGURE 15.40

Log file for an authored part

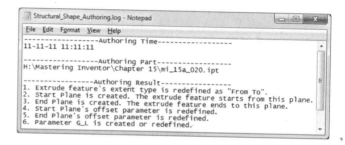

9. Click the OK button in the Structural Shape Authoring notice dialog box.

10. You can close the file without saving changes or use this file to explore the publishing options.

If you inspect the part after authoring, you will see that the browser and parameters have been updated. The details of the model and parameters are discussed in the section "Exploring the Anatomy of a Frame Member" earlier in this chapter.

TEST BEFORE YOU PUBLISH

Before you publish the member for your team to use, be sure to test it in every conceivable situation. Even a seemingly well-constructed frame member can cause issues after end treatments are applied.

Publishing a Part

The publishing process uses the Publish Guide Wizard. Since the part was authored, most of the publishing information has already been added to the file. If you aren't familiar with publishing to Content Center, review Chapter 7.

These publishing steps are important for Frame Generator:

◆ When you define the family key columns, the Length parameter must be set as a key column.

◆ In the Family Properties pane, the standard organization is used to categorize the member during insertion. If you leave this field blank, the category selection will be Unknown.

♦ In the thumbnail image pane, a special thumbnail is displayed. Since the thumbnail is used as the orientation image in the dialog boxes, it is important to use the thumbnail that Frame Generator creates.

Frame Assemblies and BOMs

By default, Frame Generator parts are set to calculate their base quantity from the length of the part. This differs from standard parts that calculate their base quantity from the number of parts in the assembly. When parts are authored for use in Frame Generator, the Base Quantity setting is automatically set to the length. To get a part count in the parts list for your assemblies, you will want to configure them to read the item quantity rather than the base quantity. You can use both columns if that fits your needs, or you can have the BOM display one quantity and the parts list display the other.

You can also use the BOM expression builder to create a description built off the Stock Number property and GL parameter (Length). You can use the CUTDETAIL parameters in expressions to show the end treatment information for each member. Note that you can copy the expression in one cell of the BOM, multiselect the rest of the column, and then right-click and choose Paste to set the expression to all the parts in the BOM. Figure 15.41 shows the BOM Editor listing the base quantity and the item quantity along with an expression being built to fill out the description.

FIGURE 15.41
Using the BOM expression builder

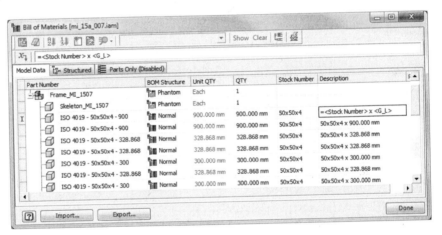

It is a good idea to let Frame Generator name the frame members for you and use the Part Number property rather than the part name to manage the parts. Once you've set an expression as just described, you can sort the BOM by that column to group the like items, set one of the part numbers, multiselect the items, and choose Paste from the context menu to set them all the same. If you want the items to be merged, leave the Part Number Merge Settings options selected. The Part Number Merge Settings button is in the top right of the BOM Editor dialog box.

In the drawing environment, use a Parts List style similar to the default Material List style found in the standard templates. This parts list is already configured to group by stock number and material, as well as sum the values of each unique stock number type. Figure 15.42 shows a parts list placed using the Material List style to roll up the lengths.

FIGURE 15.42

A parts list using the
Material List style

MATERIAL LIST		
TOTAL QTY	STOCK NUMBER	MATERIAL
548.64 cm	3x3x1/4	Steel, Mild
2194.34 cm	2x2x1/4	Steel, Mild
121.92 cm	1-1/2x1-1/2x3/16	Steel, Mild

The Bottom Line

Work with frame files.   Frame Generator puts all the members at the same level in the assembly.

Master It   You have a frame that is built up in sections that are welded together. How do you document the manufacturing process?

Insert frame members onto a skeleton model.   Frame Generator builds a skeleton model for the frame from the selected lines and edges.

Master It   Since Frame Generator builds its own skeleton model, you don't have to build a master model before you start creating the frame. What would you reference in your assembly to use as a frame skeleton?

Add end treatments to frame members.   Frame Generator does not support end treatments on merged members.

Master It   Let's assume you are building a stairway and the handrail has curved sections. How would you approach the curved handrail so that its ends can be treated?

Make changes to frames.   Inventor provides detailed frame-member information.

Master It   You need to determine the size and wall thickness of the tubing and make it either thicker or larger. How do you do that?

Author and publish structural profiles.   Frame Generator uses structural shapes from Content Center.

Master It   How would you add custom aluminum extrusions to Content Center so Frame Generator can access them?

Create BOMs for Frame Generator assemblies.   Frame Generator has special parameters for frame members.

Master It   How do you add the profile dimensions and the length of your frame members to the Description field?

Chapter 16

Inventor Studio

I'm sure that you have looked into 3D rendering as a method of creating sales material, particularly if you want to start selling your products before you've manufactured them. However, renderings don't need to be solely for the sales and marketing department.

In this chapter, you'll see how you how easy it is to create stunning images with Autodesk® Inventor® software (see Figure 16.1). Rendering with Autodesk Inventor is so easy, you could create renders just to liven up a design meeting, to add interest to a weekly report, or simply to show off.

FIGURE 16.1
A still image rendered in Autodesk Inventor Studio

In this chapter, you'll learn to

- ◆ Create and edit appearances
- ◆ Create and edit visual styles
- ◆ Create and animate cameras
- ◆ Animate components, constraints, and parameters
- ◆ Use multiple cameras to create a video production of your animation
- ◆ Use props to enhance your scene
- ◆ Render animations and video productions

How to Make Your Models Look Great, Live Onscreen

Autodesk has worked hard over the last few releases of Autodesk Inventor to improve on the way your models look onscreen.

To improve Inventor's performance, I usually do my modeling work with most of these features turned off. However, I have found that presentations to a client or internal team can really be livened up just by using these onscreen visualization tools, without having to spend lots of time on renderings.

Renderings are static or prerecorded views of your design. The tools covered in this section work "live" onscreen, allowing you to continue to manipulate your models while presenting the design.

If you have not already downloaded the Chapter 16 files from www.sybex.com/go/masteringinventor2016, please refer to the "What You Will Need" section of the introduction for the download and setup instructions.

To follow along with this section, open Inventor, go to the Get Started tab, and click the Open button. Browse for the file mi_16a_001.ipt located in the Chapter 16 directory of your Mastering Inventor folder and click the Open button.

In this workflow, you will first adjust the appearance (how your model looks), and then you'll adjust the visual styles (light, shadow, and background).

Materials and Appearances

A simple way to help your model look better is to change its appearance from Inventor's default dingy gray color. You can do this by adjusting the material, or *appearance*, of your model.

The tools you will be learning about in this section can be found in the Quick Access toolbar (QAT) and on the Tools tab ➢ Material And Appearance panel, as shown in Figure 16.2.

FIGURE 16.2
Autodesk Inventor's materials and appearances tools shown in the ribbon and QAT

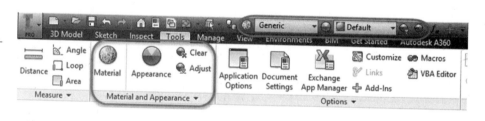

Materials in your Autodesk Inventor model have real-world values allocated to them, which allow you to make assessments of your design such as weight and strength. *Appearances* in your Autodesk Inventor model affect only the color and visual texture to improve the way the model looks onscreen.

All materials have a default appearance mapped to them. Changing the material of the part will also change its appearance.

Default appearances can be overridden; for example, if you would like your steel frame to look like it has been painted blue, you can change its appearance to Blue - wall paint - Glossy. To change the appearance for a part, use the Appearance drop-down in the QAT.

Once appearance overrides have been added, the link between the material and the part is broken, and the appearance override takes precedence. You can change the material of the part, but the appearance will no longer change, unless you change the appearance override manually or clear it completely. The appearance of a component can be overridden at the face, feature, body, or part level. You can add face, feature, or body appearance overrides to an individual part file. You can add body or part appearance overrides in an assembly file; this information will be contained in the assembly and doesn't transfer down to the part.

Appearance overrides are saved with model view representations, allowing you to create different color options to review with your customer.

APPLYING APPEARANCE OVERRIDES

Before you apply an appearance override, use the selection priority filter in the QAT to select only the faces, features, bodies, or parts you want to operate on. If you don't have anything selected, the override will be applied to the whole part that you have open. Alternatively, you can select features, bodies, and parts in the feature browser.

You can apply appearance overrides to multiple selections at the same time. Make your selection, right-click, and choose Properties to bring up a dialog box that will allow you to pick a new appearance from the standard list of appearances in your document, as shown in Figure 16.3 and Figure 16.4.

FIGURE 16.3
Applying appearance overrides by body

FIGURE 16.4

Applying appearance
overrides by feature

You can also make a selection and then use the Appearance drop-down in the QAT to apply an override from the standard list.

The most intuitive way to apply overrides is to use the Adjust tool, which is also in the QAT and the Tools tab ➤ Material And Appearance panel.

Adjusting Colors

The Adjust tool allows you to tweak the color and texture of a surface, rather than picking from the standard list. Click the Adjust tool and then select the surface whose appearance you want to adjust. You will see two new in-canvas controls. The first is the color picker, which allows you to create new colors mixed from an RGB or HSL palette.

If you don't know the values you want to type in, click and drag your cursor around the color wheel to find the color you want and then click and drag in the diamond to adjust the shade (added black) and tint (added white), as shown in Figure 16.5.

FIGURE 16.5

The in-canvas appearance Adjust tool

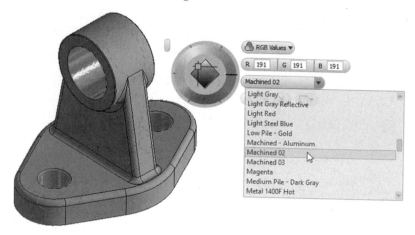

COLOR ADJUSTMENTS ARE AVAILABLE WHEN THERE IS NO TEXTURE MAP

You will be able to see adjustments in color only if there is no texture map applied to the current appearance style.

You can change appearance styles from the drop-down in the color picker. If the appearance style contains a texture map, you will be able to use the second in-canvas control, which adjusts the texture map.

Adjusting Textures

You can use the second in-canvas control to rotate, move, and scale the texture map (an image) on a face (see Figure 16.6). This can be handy when trying to get textures to match up across faces.

FIGURE 16.6
The in-canvas texture Adjust tool

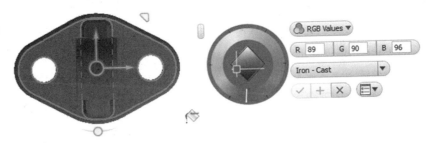

HOW TO SEE TEXTURES

If you can't see textures on your model, go to View ➤ Appearance and toggle the Textures control to ON.

Applying the Results

You can add or remove selections from the Adjust Tools selection set by holding down the **Ctrl** key and selecting more faces.

When you are happy with your adjustments, click on the Green (+) plus sign to apply them and keep working with the Adjust tool. Click the green tick (✔) to apply changes and close the Adjust tools. Click the Red (x) to close the Adjust tools without saving changes.

Clearing Overrides

To remove appearance overrides, use the Clear tool, found in the QAT and the Tools tab ➤ Material And Appearance panel.

Click the Clear button and then use the floating tools to select items that have appearance overrides you want to remove. You can use the Select All button to reset all the faces on your component back to their default appearances.

Switching Libraries

The Autodesk Inventor Material Library is a legacy tool from past releases of Inventor. It is included for consistency with models that have been created in older versions of Inventor.

Inventor now ships with the Autodesk Material Library, which provides common materials and appearances across many Autodesk products such as Showcase, 3Ds Max, and Revit (see Figure 16.7). The materials in the Autodesk Material Library generally have more realistic texture maps than the standard Inventor ones.

To switch between libraries, use the toggles at the end of the Materials and Appearances drop-downs.

FIGURE 16.7

Switching libraries from the QAT

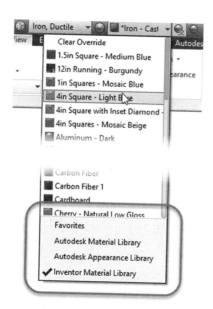

The Appearance Browser

The Materials and Appearance drop-down lists in the QAT can be tricky to navigate because they're so long. As an alternative, you can use the Appearance Browser to search for new appearances and create a list of favorites to limit the amount of scrolling you need to do to find the appearance you want.

To open the Appearance Browser, click the color wheel icon in the QAT. The first thing you'll notice is the search box. Type a search term such as *red, plastic,* or *flooring* to bring up a list of available appearances.

Right-click an appearance to add it to your current document or make it a favorite. Once the appearance is saved into your local document, you can apply it to your model (see Figure 16.8).

FIGURE 16.8

The Appearance
Browser dialog

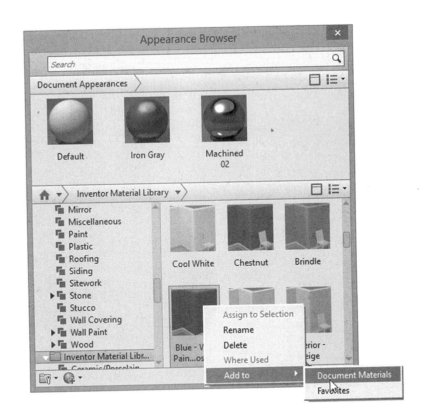

Clear the text in the search field and click the Home icon to browse the Inventor Material
Library, Autodesk Material Library, or Favorites Library. Whichever library you are looking at
when you close the dialog box will be applied to the filter on the Appearances drop-down in the
QAT when you exit the Library dialogue .

The filter will also be applied to appearance drop-down in the Adjust tool, which will limit
your choice to your current favorites.

You can close the file without saving.

MATERIALS AND APPEARANCES ROUND-UP

When you are doing some serious modeling with Autodesk Inventor, the appearance of your
model is secondary to the data and geometry in your design. But when it comes to presenting
your design to others, it doesn't hurt to add a little pizzazz (see Figure 16.9).

FIGURE 16.9
Your design with
realistic appearances
applied

FIGURE 16.9

Now that you have your model looking great, let's turn to its environment. You can use visual styles to add lighting and backgrounds to your scene to further enhance your presentation.

Visual Styles Settings

The tools you will learn about in this section are on the Appearance panel of the View tab, shown in Figure 16.10.

FIGURE 16.10
Appearance panel
of the View tab

To follow along with this section, open Inventor, go to the Get Started tab, and click the Open button. Browse for the file mi_16a_002.ipt located in the Chapter 16 directory of your Mastering Inventor folder and click the Open button.

Go to View ➤ Appearance and set the following options:

◆ Visual Style = Realistic

◆ Shadows = All on

◆ Reflections = On

◆ Lighting style = Plain Room

◆ Projection = Perspective

Your final view should look something like Figure 16.11. Awesome, right?

FIGURE 16.11
Your design with
realistic view styles
applied

> **CREATING AN ONSCREEN PRESENTATION**
>
> You can combine visual style settings with a saved view representation to create an onscreen presentation to help explain your design. Set the Inventor user interface to Clean Screen mode to reduce clutter and show off your design by using the hotkey combination **Ctrl+0.**

In the following section, you will learn what these settings are actually doing and how you can tweak them to improve your image.

VISUAL STYLE

Visual styles in Inventor are practical to use when building parts and assemblies. For example, visual styles allow you to switch between a shaded view of your design and a wireframe view, allowing you to identify hidden parts or features.

You can also use visual styles to create stylized views of your model. Try Water Color, Sketch Illustration, and Technical Illustration styles on your sample model to see how these styles look, as shown in Figure 16.12.

FIGURE 16.12
Technical, Sketch,
and Water Color
Illustration styles

You will notice that only the Realistic and Monochrome visual styles allow you to use the Ray Tracing option.

SHADOWS

Shadows add realism to your view by helping to define the edges of your model. *Ground shadows* control the shadow that your design makes as it hits the ground plane. *Object shadows* control the shadows formed on the surfaces of your design as the light hits them. *Ambient shadows* control the shadows that are caused by ambient light bouncing around your model.

Click the Settings option to tweak the lighting in your scene. You'll learn about the options available to you in this dialog box in the section "Lighting Style."

REFLECTIONS

Reflections can make your composition more interesting by adding a reflection of your design in your model's ground plane.

Click the Settings option to tweak the ground plane location. You will learn about the options available to you in this dialog box in the section "Ground Plane."

HACKING THE REFLECTION IMAGE

Who is that guy on a motorbike? This tip shows you how to change the default reflection image that Inventor uses with its standard lighting styles (the image-based lighting styles use the HDR image that they are based on).

You will find the setting by navigating to Tools ➤ Options ➤ Applications Options.

On the Colors tab of Application Options, look for Reflection Environment ➤ File Name and click the spyglass-and-folder icon. You can now choose from the .dds files in this location. I recommend Chrome.dds as a nice neutral image (see Figure 16.13). (DDS stands for Direct Draw Surface, a form of compressed texture map.)

FIGURE 16.13
Setting background image and reflection map in Application Options

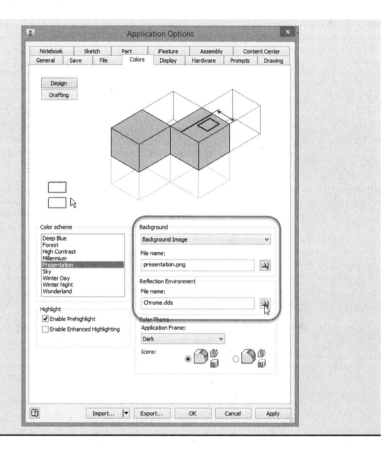

LIGHTING STYLE

Lighting styles are saved in your local document. You can switch between the standard lighting styles that are saved in your document by navigating to View ➤ Appearance ➤ Lighting Style.

SELECT A LIGHTING STYLE

Try the Empty Lab lighting style for small models such as product designs. Try the Country Road lighting style for large models such as vehicles.

You can export and import styles and save styles to your style library to make them available globally.

You can edit the lighting styles that are available in your current document by going to View ➤ Appearance ➤ Shadows ➤ Settings, by going to View Appearance ➤ Lighting Style ➤ Settings, or by going to Manage Tab ➤ Styles Editor.

Two types of lighting style are available to you in Autodesk Inventor. Standard lighting styles allow you to configure individual light sources. *IBL* styles use an image-based lighting map to add lights to your scene based on a 3D image.

Standard Lighting Style Options

An example of a standard lighting style is the Two Lights style. Open the lighting Style And Standard Editor, right-click Two Lights, and choose Active to activate it as an example to reference while looking through the options, as shown in Figure 16.14.

FIGURE 16.14
The Style And Standard Editor

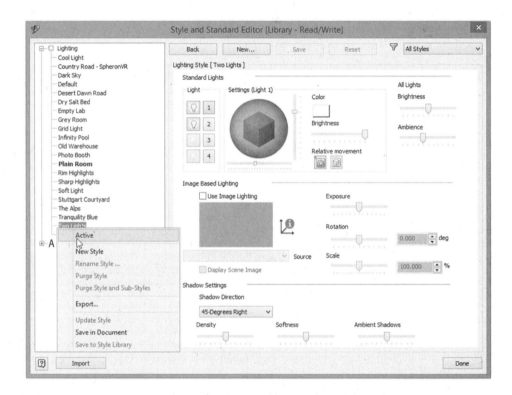

Standard lighting style contains up to four lights, which can be turned on or off by clicking the lightbulb buttons. Note: You can't add lights at specific locations or change the type of light source here; you'll need Inventor Studio for that.

To edit the position of the lights, click the number button of the light you want to edit and then use the horizontal and vertical sliders to move the light.

The position of the light can be moved relative to the camera (current view) or the ViewCube using the two buttons under Relative Movement.

ADJUST ONE LIGHT AT A TIME

I find it easier to turn all the lights off except the one I'm working on.

You can change the color and intensity of the lights individually using the Color and Brightness controls. If you find that your finished scene lighting is too bright, you can adjust the lighting brightness globally using All Lights ➤ Brightness and Ambience.

Brightness is the amount of light falling on the scene.

Ambience is the contrast between lit and unlit areas of the scene.

Notice that the image-based lighting controls are grayed out for this lighting style and the Use Image Lighting check box is unselected.

At the bottom of the dialog box, you will find the Shadow settings. You can change the direction of the shadows using the Shadow Direction drop-down.

The Density, Softness, and Ambient controls affect the quality of the shadows.

Density is the darkness of the shadow.

Softness is the amount of blur around the edges of the shadow.

Ambient Shadows is the contrast between light and shadows.

Backgrounds for Standard Lighting Styles

The background for a standard lighting style is set using in the Application Options settings. To change the background color, go to Tools ➤ Options ➤ Application Options. In the Application Options dialog box, click the Colors tab and choose a new color scheme. You can also choose between a flat background and a gradient background here.

If you are interested in adding your own background image, see "Quick-and-Dirty Backgrounds" later in this chapter.

Image-Based Lighting Style Options

An example of an image-based lighting style is the Old Warehouse style. Open the Lighting Style And Standard Editor and right-click Old Warehouse Style to activate it as an example to reference while running through the options.

Image-based lighting is based on a 3D 360-degree image that has been taken with a high dynamic range (HDR) camera. Inventor can use the lighting source location and luminance values from the image to provide realistic lighting for your scene.

In the Style And Standard Editor, you will notice that the four standard lights are turned off by default (you can add them back in if you want). The shadow options are also still available.

The Image Based Lighting check box is now ticked, and you will see a preview of the HDR map in the window. The position of the HDR map relative to your model is set using the ViewCube. You can tweak the exposure, rotation, and scale of the HDR map relative to your scene using the sliders.

You can use the Display Scene Image check box to receive lighting styles from the HDR map, while turning off the actual image in your graphics window. This is a great way to quickly get a lighting style you like into your scene, without having imagery that is unrelated to your design in the background.

FIXING DOME-LIKE APPEARANCE

If the scene appears like a dome in your graphic window, either you are zoomed out too far or the scale of the HDR map is too small compared to your model (see Figure 16.15). You can use the Scale control to correct the size of the HDR image in relation to your model.

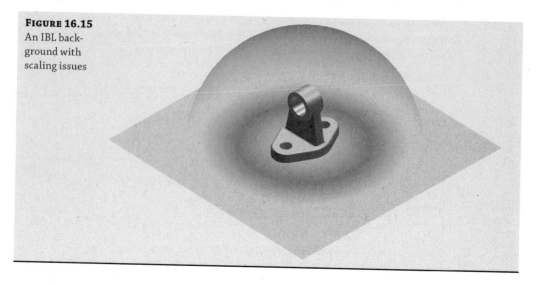

PROJECTION

The Projection setting is used to toggle between Orthographic and Perspective projections, as shown in Figure 16.16. Orthographic is easy to work in while modeling, and Perspective looks more realistic.

FIGURE 16.16
Orthographic vs.
Perspective projection

Orthographic means edges are drawn parallel onscreen.

Perspective means edges converge to a point.

GROUND PLANE

The ground plane allows you to add a floor in your design for your model to interact with, without you having to add more items to your model.

The size and orientation of the ground plane are set using the ViewCube. If the ground plane isn't orientated correctly with your model, orientate your view of your model until you are facing your front view. Now right-click the ViewCube and choose Set Current View As ➤ Front.

Ground Plane Settings

You can further tweak the location of your ground plane by using the Ground Plane Settings dialog box, opened by choosing View ➤ Appearance ➤ Reflections And View ➤ Appearance ➤ Ground Plane, as shown in Figure 16.17.

FIGURE 16.17
Ground Plane Settings dialog box

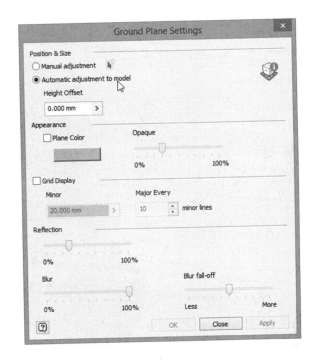

To change the position of your ground plane in relation to the height of your model, go to Position & Size ➤ Height Offset and add a value (negative values will move the floor plane down).

If your ground plane is way off, you can select Manual Adjustment to bring up a Triad control in your model window. Click the arrows to move the ground plane in the direction of the arrow, or click the black ball at the center of the arrows to move freely.

The Appearance section allows you to add a color to your ground plane and adjust its opacity (the amount you can see through it).

The Grid Display section allows you to add a grid of major and minor axes to your ground plane.

The Reflection settings allow you to tweak the amount of reflection you see of your design in the ground plane. Set the reflection high and the blur low to see more of your design. Set the reflection low and the blur high for a more subtle effect.

RAY TRACING

The Ray Tracing option is available only when the visual style is set to Realistic or Monochrome.

Ray tracing mimics the way light photons bounce around a room and can produce realistic images when used with materials and an environment that are set up to use ray tracing. For example, ray tracing will produce reflections of an object in its own surface, which looks awesome with shiny surfaces, as you can see in Figure 16.18.

FIGURE 16.18
An image using ray tracing to create reflections in the model's own surfaces

When you click the Ray Tracing button, Inventor will notify you with some text onscreen that says "Enabling ray tracing."

You can choose to render your image with Low, Draft, or High quality ray tracing. Your computer will take some time to render the view, depending on how fast your computer is and how powerful your graphics card is.

You can click the Save button in the Ray Tracing dialog box to save the rendered image as a BMP, GIF, TIFF, JPEG, or PNG file.

TEXTURES

The Textures option allows you to use Inventor's advanced texture maps to improve you image.

Texture maps combine images with *bump maps* to add texture to your model without you having to model it. Texture maps are great for adding details such as expanded meshes, threads, or knurling to a design, without adding to the model's complexity.

All appearance styles have a color associated with them that is seen only when textures are turned off. Many of the standard Autodesk Inventor appearances don't include textures.

You can switch to the Autodesk Material Library for a greater choice of realistic surface finishes. You saw how to do this in the section "Material and Appearance Styles" earlier in this chapter.

Saving an Image

You can save a still image from your screen by going to the big *I* and selecting Export ➤ Image. You can choose from BMP, GIF, TIFF, JPG, and PNG file formats.

The images saved in this way are limited in their quality. For a higher-quality image, use the Render tool to create higher-quality still images. See "How to Create a Still Image (Render)."

Rounding Up

In Figure 16.19, I have tweaked the model appearances and made some adjustments to the lighting styles. I have also prepared some saved views to make it easy to navigate the model.

FIGURE 16.19
Image using appearances, visual styles, and ray tracing

Go to the Chapter 16 directory of your Mastering Inventor folder and open mi_16a_003 .ipt to explore the final result. You can close the file without saving.

QUICK-AND-DIRTY BACKGROUNDS

This tip shows you how to quickly drop your own background into a scene. You could use this to show how your design might look in its final environment such as a farm, factory, or home.

1. Take a photograph of your background and then save it to your Backgrounds folder. The default location is as follows:

   `C:\Users\Public\Documents\Autodesk\Inventor 2016\Backgrounds\`

2. Go to Tools ➤ Application Options ➤ Colors, and from the Background section, choose Background Image from the drop-down.

3. Click the spyglass-and-folder icon to open the Backgrounds folder and pick your custom background image.

4. Set your projection to Perspective and navigate your Inventor model until it lines up with your image.

Tip: Hold down the **Ctrl+Shift** keys on your keyboard while scrolling your mouse wheel to adjust the projection of the perspective.

Looking for something better quality? Read on.

An Introduction to Inventor Studio

So far you've looked at Inventor's built-in tools for making your models look good, live onscreen. These tools create great visuals onscreen, but Autodesk® Inventor® Studio tool allows you to take your images to another level. Inventor Studio is a rendering and animation tool that is reached from the part or assembly environment.

Inventor Studio allows you to have far more control of your lighting and camera setups and allows you to animate lights and cameras, as well as your model, to demonstrate how your design might look as it is working.

In this section, you will learn the following:

◆   How to create a still image

◆   How to add lights

◆   How to add cameras

◆   How to create an animated render

To follow along with this section, open Inventor, go to the Get Started tab, and click the Open button. Browse for the file mi_16a_004.ipt located in the Chapter 16 directory of your Mastering Inventor folder and click the Open button.

Open the Inventor Studio environment by going to Environments ➤ Begin Panel ➤ Inventor Studio (see Figure 16.20).

FIGURE 16.20
Autodesk Inventor
Studio button

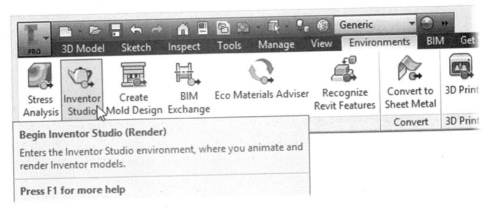

FIGURE 16.20
Autodesk Inventor
Studio button

Take notice of the new Render tab, shown in Figure 16.21, and the new nodes in the feature browser, shown in Figure 16.22. At the end of the Render tab is the big green check mark that you will click when you are finished in Inventor Studio.

FIGURE 16.21
Autodesk Inventor
Studio tools

FIGURE 16.22
Autodesk Inventor
Studio browser

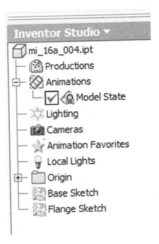

BUILDING A VIRTUAL STUDIO

The success of any rendering is in the setup of materials, lights, and the environment. You can save the time it takes to get set up for a new rendering by building a "virtual studio."

This could be a "wrapper" assembly file that contains a part file to act as a background—along with preset lights and cameras. To render your image, you just drop your part in and go!

Browse for the file `mi_16a_000.iam` located in the Chapter 16 directory of your `Mastering Inventor` folder for an example.

How to Create a Still Image (Render)

You will begin by creating a really simple still image render from your current model.

1. Click Render ➤ Render panel ➤ Render Image (looks like a teapot).

2. On the Render tab, set Render By Iteration to 1.

3. Click Render.

A new window, Render Output, will pop up, in which your image will be rendered using your current view and background settings, as shown in Figure 16.23.

FIGURE 16.23
The Render Output window

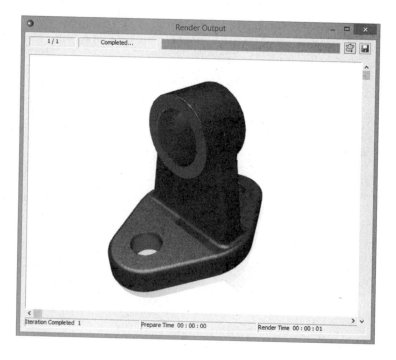

The image may look a little grainy right now, but don't worry—you'll improve on this in a minute. Note that the IBL background doesn't need to be rendered; Inventor can use this image directly.

At the top left of the new window, you will see a box containing the number 1/1. This indicates that Inventor has rendered one image in a sequence of one. When rendering animations, this number will be higher, depending on the length (time) of your animation.

The green tracker bar gives you an indication of how long your render will take to complete. The "teapot" button tells Inventor to continue rendering for a better result. You can also save your render here by clicking the diskette icon.

Saving a render as a still image from the Render Output window gives you more control over the quality of your still image. Clicking the diskette icon allows you to save your image in the BMP, JPEG, PNG, TIFF, and GIF formats. By clicking Save Window ➢ Options, you can vary the quality of the output from 72 to 300 dpi (the default is 96 dpi).

At the base of the Render Output window, you can see feedback on the number of iterations Inventor Studio took to render this image and the amount of time it took to run those iterations. This is crucial information that you can use to judge how long future renders will take to run.

Note that the size of the window is 640×480 pixels; this was set in the Render Image dialog box, which you will look at next.

Before you close this window, click the teapot button again and watch as Inventor Studio improves the quality of your rendered image by running another iteration. You'll find out what is happening here later in the chapter.

NOTES ON IMAGE QUALITY AND FILE TYPES FOR STILL IMAGES

The image that you see in the Render Output window may not look as great as you expected compared to when you save it to an image file or print it on paper.

As an Inventor user, you will probably be working on a Windows computer with a screen resolution of 96 pixels per inch (ppi). Typically, print resolution is much higher at 300 dots per inch (dpi). The more pixels your image has, the higher the quality of the final image file, but the bigger the file size is on disk.

Before you create your image, think about the purpose you need it for. For web graphics, it's best to produce the image at exactly the size you want it to display on the web page and save it at a maximum of 96 dpi. After all, this image will need to be downloaded by everyone who views the web page—so keep it small!

For print images, it may be better to produce your renders bigger than they will be printed, save them at 300 dpi, and then scale them down in your publishing software to produce a great-quality result.

For larger printed images such as posters that aren't meant to be seen close-up, it may be acceptable to reduce the print resolution to 150 dpi to keep the image file size down.

Remember that you can remove pixels when scaling images down, but you can't add them when scaling images up!

The settings controlling the image quality/size of the final output are as follows:

◆ Size of the image rendered: in pixels

◆ Resolution of the image on saving: in dpi

continues

continued

Inventor saves in the following file types:

FILE TYPE	USE FOR	DON'T USE FOR
PNG	Web graphics	Photos
JPEG	Web photos	Image editing
TIFF	Editing and storage	Online images
GIF	Logos and simple graphics	Photos
BMP	Editing	Any of the above

RENDER IMAGE SETTINGS

Now that you've seen how easy it is to create a rendered image, let's take a step back and look at the settings available in the Render Image dialog box.

Close the Render Output window by clicking the "x" at the top right. The Render Image dialog box should still be available. Figure 16.24 shows the tabs of the Render Image dialog box.

FIGURE 16.24

The Render Image dialog box

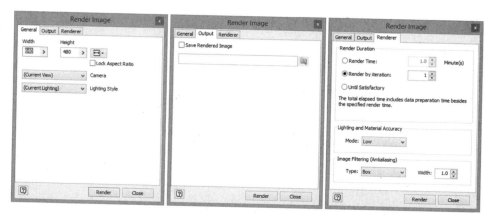

General

The General tab allows you to change the size of your image. You can override the width and height of your image here or click the drop-down to select from a list of standard sizes.

A smaller-sized image will render quicker than a large one, so it's a good idea to run a few test renders at a small size, before committing to your final image.

Active View will render exactly what you see in Inventor's graphics window.

If you like the proportions of your image but not the size, click in the Lock Aspect Ratio check box to link the current width/height ratio, before typing in a new image size to either the Width or Height input box.

On the General tab, you also have the option to pick saved camera and lighting styles. Inventor Studio cameras have a lot more fine control than the standard Inventor perspective view, and I will cover them later in this chapter.

Output

On this tab you can check the box Save As Rendered Image to save a copy of your render as soon as it is done. When the box is checked, a dialog box will open asking for a filename and folder location.

Notice that the same BMP, JPEG, PNG, TIFF, and GIF file formats are available. Clicking the Options button in the Save window allows you to set the quality of the output in dpi.

CREATING TRANSPARENT BACKGROUNDS WITH THE ALPHA CHANNEL

The Alpha Channel option is available in PNG options. This will output PNG format images with a transparent background. Note that this option is available only if you request it *before* you render the image, not afterward. You won't find this setting anywhere else.

Renderer

The Renderer tab is the most important tab of the three. This tab is where you will tell Inventor Studio what quality you want to get from your render. The quality of image you ask for directly affects how long it will take for the render to be created. Typically there will be a balance between quality and time, depending on how much time you have to run your renders.

To prevent running a render that takes a long time and being disappointed with the results, it is a good idea to run a few test renders first. The test renders will be at a smaller size or lower quality to judge whether you are happy with the camera view, appearances, and lights before you go ahead and run the full-size, high-quality render.

In the Render Duration area of the dialog box, you can choose whether to run a specific number of iterations, whether to run it for a specific time (in minutes), or whether to run the render until it is complete (Until Satisfactory). This is a great feature for producing test renders. You can set Inventor to run a small number of iterations to test your scene (5–10, for example) or set Inventor Studio to render for the entirety of your coffee break!

Coupled with the feedback from the Render Output window, you can use the number of iterations and the time it took to render them to judge how long your final render will take. Can you run your render in your lunch break, or should you leave it to run overnight?

The Lighting And Material Accuracy section of the dialog box controls the duration of the rendering.

◆ Low is recommended for quick previews of outdoor scenes.

◆ Draft is recommended for quick previews of indoor scenes.

◆ High is for the best results but is the slowest to render.

The Image Filtering (Anti-Aliasing) section of the dialog box controls how smooth the final output will be.

Like all computer software, images from Autodesk Inventor are created using pixels (tiny squares). When diagonal lines are drawn using squares, they can appear jagged. Anti-aliasing could be thought of as resolution. The higher the resolution, the sharper lines will appear to be.

- Box is the fastest, with a good result.

- Triangle is more processer intensive but better than Box.

- Gaussian is for the best results but is the slowest to render.

- Lanczos and Mitchell are alternative methods of anti-aliasing that are similar to Gaussian. Try them on more detailed renders.

The Width setting determines how many pixels are being inspected along each polygon edge during the anti-aliasing part of the render process.

Analyzing more pixels should equal a smoother result. I recommend you leave this setting at its default unless you are unhappy with the anti-aliasing in your final render.

STILL IMAGE CONCLUSION

In this section, you learned that you can create a rendered image from Inventor Studio in only two clicks! You also learned how to run test renders at a lower quality to save time and then increase the quality when it comes to your final render.

In the next section, you will learn how to add more realism to your image by adding lights and cameras.

WHAT IS RAPIDRT?

In the 2016 release, Inventor Studio uses Autodesk's RapidRT renderer. This rendering engine uses a slightly different technique to produce your images than you saw in previous versions of Inventor Studio.

In the past, each square of the image was rendered, and you would see them slowly build up in the Render Image window (this process was multithreaded, so more cores meant more little squares chasing around the screen).

In practice, this meant that your render had to be 80–90 percent done before you could judge whether it was looking good.

RapidRT renders individual pixels across the whole of your image. Each set of seemingly random pixels that are rendered are called an *iteration*. The more iterations you allow Inventor Studio to run, the more complete your image will be.

With a little practice, you can begin to judge how your image is looking after only a few iterations and decide whether to run more iterations with the same settings or whether to adjust your camera or styles before trying again.

Inventor Studio Lighting Styles

Before bringing your scene into Inventor Studio, you can set it up to use the Plain Room lighting style. You will notice this setting is retained when you start Inventor Studio.

You can change the IBL style you are using inside Inventor Studio *independently* from the scene you had in the Inventor modeling environment by clicking Render ➤ Scene Panel ➤ Studio Lighting Styles, as shown in Figure 16.25.

FIGURE 16.25

The Studio Lighting Styles dialog box

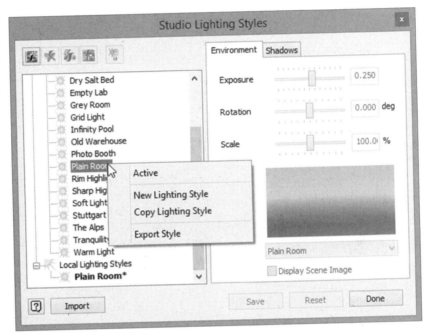

To make a Studio lighting style active in the current document, look under Global Lighting Styles, right-click your choice, and choose Activate. You will notice that the scene is copied from Global Lighting Styles to Local Lighting Styles and becomes editable. This means it has been copied from the style library to the local document.

You now have options to adjust the exposure, scale, and rotation of the HDR background image, along with the shadow softness (on the Shadows tab).

This behaves just like the image-based lighting (IBL) styles you found under View ➤ Appearance discussed earlier in this chapter.

Don't forget that the position of the HDR image that the IBL style is based on is set using the ground plane tools.

Unlike the Standard lighting style discussed earlier in this chapter, there are no additional lights shown in this dialog box. In Inventor Studio, you add lights on an individual basis.

How to Add Local Lights

Adding local lights to your scene is a great way to emphasize a specific area of your design. You could also use lights to add realism to your scene by adding light sources to lights that you have modeled in your design.

In this exercise, you will add a local light to your scene to add a highlight. Open Inventor, go to the Get Started tab, and click the Open button. Browse for the file mi_16a_005.ipt located in the Chapter 16 directory of your Mastering Inventor folder and click the Open button.

To add a light in the studio environment, follow these steps:

1. Click Environments ➤ Begin Panel ➤ Inventor Studio.

2. Click Render ➤ Scene Panel ➤ Local Lights.

3. The Local Lights dialog box will open, as shown in Figure 16.26.

FIGURE 16.26
Adding a local light

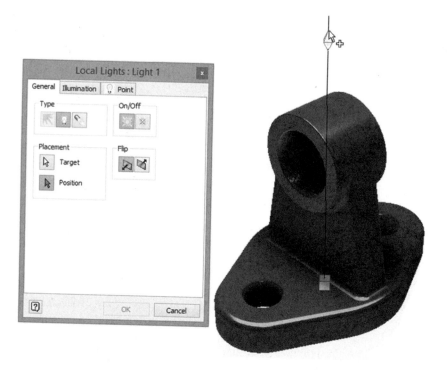

4. Click the XZ plane—the light will be created perpendicular to the surface you choose and will point at the center of the surface by default.

5. Click the line that indicates the light path, slightly above your model.

Your light is created; you will see it in the graphics window. The box indicates the focus of the light. The diamond indicates the position of the light source.

EDITING LOCAL LIGHTS

The Local Lights dialog box gives you options to tweak your new light to enhance your scene, as shown in Figure 16.27.

FIGURE 16.27

Local Lights
dialog box

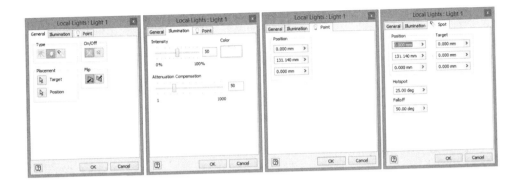

General Tab

The General tab allows you to reposition your light by reusing the same placement tools you used to add your light in the previous exercise.

The Flip tool replaces the light source with the focus and replaces the focus with the light source.

The On/Off tool allows you to turn this light source off.

The Type selection allows you to choose what kind of light to create. By default your light will be a point light. A point light casts light in all directions (think of a lightbulb).

Point Tab

The Point tab is available only for the point light type. The Point tab allows you to enter precise coordinates for your light source.

Click back to the General tab, and click the Spot button to change your light source into a spotlight. The light indicator in the graphics window will update, the diamond light source indicator is replaced by a cone, and you can see the extents of your spotlight.

Spot Tab

Click back to the Spot tab to see what new options you have for this lighting type.

A spotlight casts directional light and has additional options of Hotspot (the brightest area of light) and Fall Off (how large an area it takes for the light to dim to nothing).

You can see the Hotspot and Fall Off options in the graphics window; the hotspot is indicated by the inner circle, and the falloff is indicated by the outer circle.

The Spot tab allows you to set the precise position of the light source and target, as well as adding precise values for the hotspot and falloff angles.

Illumination Tab

Finally, switch to the Illumination tab. The controls on this tab allow you to set the intensity (brightness) of the light, as well as the attenuation (contrast with the IBL environment).

Moving the Light

Before you close the dialog box, notice that you can move your light by clicking it in the graphics window (see Figure 16.28). Where you click will tell Inventor what you want to move.

- ◆ Click and drag on the inner circle to dynamically resize the hotspot.
- ◆ Click and drag on the outer circle to dynamically resize the fall off.
- ◆ Click the box to move the focus of the light.
- ◆ Click the cone to move the light source.
- ◆ Click the line between the light source (cone) and the focus (box) to move the whole thing.

FIGURE 16.28
Moving a light

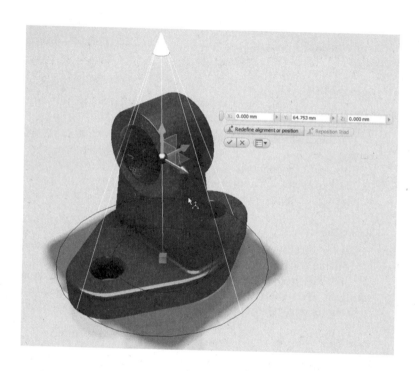

Clicking an element of the local light will reveal a Triad control. Click and dragging an arrow will move the light source in the direction of the arrow, and clicking the ball in the middle allows for a free move.

- ◆ Click the red X to cancel the move.
- ◆ Click the green ✓ to commit the move.

Clicking either control will return you to the Local Light dialog box. You can close the file without saving.

How to Add Cameras

Cameras in Inventor Studio give you a great many more options than standard Inventor views, such as depth of field. In addition, cameras can be animated to give movement to a scene.

Open Inventor, go to the Get Started tab, and click the Open button. Browse for the file mi_16a_006.ipt located in the Chapter 16 directory of your Mastering Inventor folder and click the Open button.

To add a camera, follow these steps:

1. In the feature browser, expand the Views node, right-click ISO View, and choose Activate.

2. From Environments tab ➤ Begin, choose Inventor Studio.

3. In the feature browser, right-click the Camera icon and choose Create Camera From View (see Figure 16.29).

FIGURE 16.29

Creating a camera from a view

4. Use the ViewCube to navigate to the front view. You will see your new camera in the graphics window.

CREATING A CAMERA VIEW

The workflow described here is the quickest and most intuitive way of creating a camera of the view that you want to work with. Note that by clicking in the Inventor Studio browser on your new camera, you can choose the following:

◆ Set Camera To View (moves the camera to see what you see in the graphics window)

◆ Set View To Camera (shows what the camera sees in the graphics window)

EDITING CAMERAS

Before you play with your camera, use the ViewCube to set your view to Front and zoom all (see Figure 16.30).

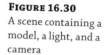

FIGURE 16.30

A scene containing a model, a light, and a camera

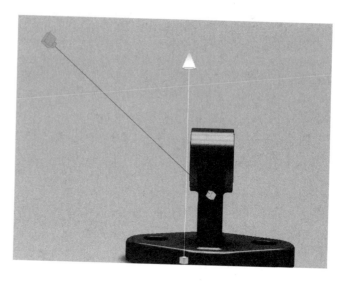

To edit your camera, right-click the camera in the browser or graphics window and choose Edit. You now have the Camera Edit dialog box open, and you will see the camera in the graphics window. The first two choices are the placement options: Target and Position. You didn't need to use these options because you created your camera from your view.

Projection works in the same way as the Projection tool you looked at in the View panel earlier in this chapter.

- ◆ Orthographic lines are drawn parallel to each other.

- ◆ Perspective lines converge to a point in the distance (choose perspective view while you explore the remaining options).

ADJUSTING THE PERSPECTIVE ANGLE

Hold down **Ctrl+Shift+F3** and then click and drag the cursor in the graphics window to adjust the perspective angle. This works really well with Link To View.

Roll Angle controls the angle of the camera; you could type **90 deg** here to "Dutch" the camera. Notice that you can also click and drag the line at the top of the wireframe of the camera view in the graphics window.

Zoom changes the view angle of the camera. Try the slider now and watch the view angle change in the graphics window. Notice that you can also click and drag the wireframe of the camera view in the graphics window.

Next, check the Link To View box. You are now seeing the view that the camera sees. Change the zoom angle again and watch the view in the graphics window change. Finish with it set to about 30 degrees, and uncheck the Link To View box before you move on.

The Depth of Field controls add realism to your render by mimicking how a real camera focuses on objects. Only objects that are in the focal field are sharp. Objects in front of the field (shallower) and objects that are beyond the field (deeper) will progressively become out of focus (blurred) the farther away from the focus they are.

Check the Enable box to turn Depth Of Field on. You will see two new indicators appear in the graphics window, as shown in Figure 16.31.

FIGURE 16.31
The Edit Camera dialog box with Depth Of Field active

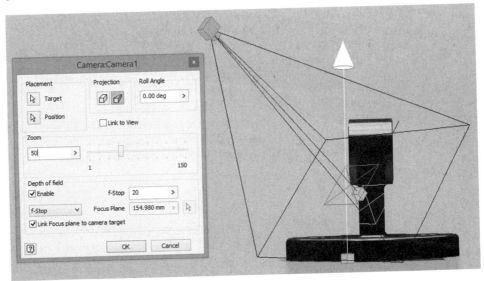

The blue indicator is controlled by the Near number box, which represents the near side of the focal plane (the start of objects that will be in focus). The green plane is controlled by the Far number box, which represents the end of the focal plane; everything beyond this will be out of focus.

Before you move on, let's test this. Set Near to **287** and Far to **295**. Click OK to close the Edit Camera box and then click the Render Image button. Create a test render using 32 iterations (make sure that you render choosing Camera1 on the Render Image window's General tab). You should see that the back of your bracket is in soft focus, as shown in Figure 16.32. Nice!

FIGURE 16.32
Test render showing depth of field

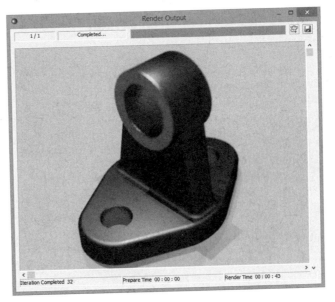

Close the Render Output Window and return to the Edit Camera dialog box to complete learning about the focal depth controls.

For those of you familiar with photography in the real world, you can change the focus type from Focus Limits to F-Stop. F-Stop represents the size of the aperture that a camera uses to let light in. The bigger the value, the more light is let in and the more of the image will be in focus (the greater the depth of field).

Try putting some values in from the range box and watch the blue and green depth of field planes move. An f-stop of 1.4 would be roughly equivalent to the 287/295 values you used previously.

The final control in this dialog box is the Link Focus Plane To Camera Target check box. This keeps the focus plane linked to the target, allowing you to move the camera or change the zoom/roll without your image going out of focus. This is particularly handy to use when animating a camera along a path. You can close this document without saving.

F-STOPS

The measurement *f-stop* is the ratio between the diameter of the lens aperture and the focal length of the lens in mm.

Common values for f-stop are listed here. Each f-stop represents double or half the value of its neighbor, by area of the aperture (the hole that lets light in).

1.4, 2.0, 2.8, 4, 5.6, 8, 11, 16, 22

How to Create an Animated Render

So far you have learned how to make your model look realistic by changing its color and texture. You also learned how to create realistic environments to place your model in. You learned how to add lights to highlight your model's features and finally add a camera to give you greater control over the lens angle and focal depth.

All of this work has allowed you to create some really nice still images, but to really bring an image to life, you need to add *movement*!

In this exercise, you will create a simple turntable animation of your design. Open Inventor, go to the Get Started tab, and click the Open button. Browse for the file mi_16a_007.ipt located in the Chapter 16 directory of your Mastering Inventor folder and click the Open button.

To create a turntable animation, follow these steps:

1. Click Render ➢ Animate Panel ➢ Camera (click OK in the warning window).

2. From the Animate tab, check that Camera1 is selected.

3. From the Turntable tab, check the Turntable box (see Figure 16.33).

FIGURE 16.33

Creating a turntable
camera animation

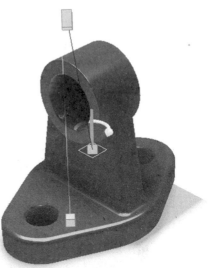

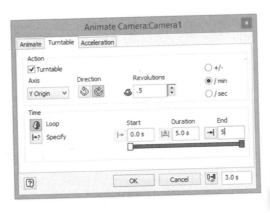

4. Set Axis to Y Origin.

5. Set Revolutions to 0.5.

6. Set Duration ➤ End to 5.0 s.

7. Click OK.

8. In the animation timeline, click Animation Options (looks like a keyboard, with two blue arrows and a pencil). Set Length to **5.0** seconds and click Constant Speed and then OK.

9. On the animation timeline, Cameras drop-down select Camera1.

10. Click the Go To Start arrow in the animation timeline.

11. Click the Play button in the animation timeline to watch a preview.

To create a turntable render, follow these steps:

1. Click the Go To Start arrow in the animation timeline.

2. Click Record Animation in the animation timeline (looks like a red button).

3. On the Output tab, check that Launch Player is selected.

4. On the Render tab, set the following:

- Render By Iteration = 5

- Lighting And Material Accuracy = Low

- Antialiasing = Box

5. Choose a file path and name and choose AVI as a file type from the Save As Type drop-down.

6. Click Render.

7. In the Compression dialog box, click OK.

The Render Output window will open, just like earlier. On my test machine, this render took about five minutes before the video player popped up and I could see the result.

You can see an example render produced by opening the file `Turntable.avi`.

I hope that you will notice how easy it is to introduce movement into your scene. I am certain that you will also notice that rendering animations can take a long time, particularly if you want to produce high-quality results. Close the file without saving.

NOTES ON IMAGE QUALITY AND FILE TYPES FOR VIDEOS

There are two choices of file types for recording animations from Inventor Studio.

◆ WMV (Windows Media Video), a compressed file format. Use this if you don't want to edit your video and intend to upload it directly to a website.

When choosing WMV, you will be prompted to define the quality, which is measured by network bandwidth. Start with 700 kps and increase from there.

◆ AVI systems format, which is uncompressed and will create larger files. This is great for editing before producing a movie in post-production.

When choosing AVI, you will be prompted to choose a video codec, which will be used to translate the still rendered images into a video.

If you aren't happy with the video codecs available with Inventor Studio, you can download codecs from TechSmith (`www.techsmith.com`) or DivX (`www.divx.com`).

Animating with Inventor Studio

Animation in Inventor Studio isn't limited to cameras. You can also animate the following:

◆ The position and orientation of cameras, components, and lights

◆ The visibility of components (fade)

◆ Parameter values

◆ Constraint values

◆ Predefined positional reps

Note that fading components and animating constraints can be applied only when animating inside an assembly.

Animating each element follows a similar workflow.

1. Choose an element to animate.

2. Define a start condition and an end condition (transformation).

3. Define a duration in which the transformation will happen.

4. Define a time during the sequence when your transformation should happen.

5. Define a start acceleration and an end acceleration.

6. Use the timeline to edit the position and duration of the transformation in your sequence.

To follow along with this section, open Inventor, go to the Get Started tab, and click the Open button. Browse for the file mi_16a_008.iam located in the Chapter 16 directory of your Mastering Inventor folder and click the Open button.

ANIMATING PARAMETERS

You can animate parameter values in Inventor Studio, allowing you to deform models—imagine a spring flexing, for example.

To animate parameters, first you have to add them to your animation favorites. To do this, activate Inventor Studio on the Environments tab and then click Render ➤ Manage ➤ Parameter Favorites.

Click the component whose parameters you want to use, and then click in the favorites check box for each parameter you want to use in Inventor Studio.

You will be able to select your new favorite parameter for animation in the Inventor Studio feature browser under the Animation Favorites node. Click Cancel to return to Studio Environment.

APPLYING ANIMATION TRANSFORMATIONS

In this section you will see how to apply animations to elements using a fade animation.
Select Render ➤ Animate ➤ Fade. The Animate Fade dialog box will open, as shown in Figure 16.34. Select your component to animate.

FIGURE 16.34
The Animate Fade dialog box

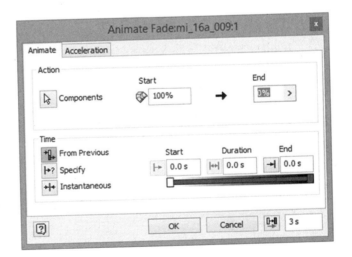

Next, define start and end conditions. In this case, choose 100% opacity for the start condition and 0% for the end condition.

The Time section of the dialog box allows you to specify when you want your condition to appear in your sequence and how long you want the transition to take.

The first three buttons allow you to choose *when* you want the transition to happen. From Previous will start your animation as soon as the previous transition has finished—or at the beginning of the timeline if this is your first transition. You will notice that you cannot adjust the figure in the Start or Duration box, only the End box. How long do you want this transition to take?

The Specify option allows you to choose a start time and an end time for your animation. You will notice that you can't edit the duration.

The Instantaneous option applies an instant transformation. You will notice that you can choose an end position for this transformation, but you can't edit Start or Duration.

In the bottom right of the dialog box next to the OK and Cancel buttons is another important control: the Complete Action And Begin New Action button. Next to it is the New Action Increment box. By clicking this button you can complete your current transformation, move the timeline by the indicated amount, and start a new action of the same type.

Let's see how this might work in sequence. Close the Fade dialog box by clicking Cancel, check the timeline is at the beginning using the Go To Start arrow, and open the Fade dialog box again.

Transformation 1

Follow these steps:

1. Select your component.

2. Set Action ➤ End to **0%**.

3. Click Time ➤ Instantaneous.

4. Set New Action Increment to **3**.

5. Click Complete Action and start a new action.

Transformation 2

Follow these steps:

1. Your component is selected.

2. Set Action ➤ End to **100%**.

3. Click Time ➤ From Previous.

4. Set Time ➤ End to **3**.

5. Click Complete Action and start a new action.

Transformation 3

Follow these steps:

1. Your component is selected.

2. Set Action ➤ End to **0%**.

3. Click Time ➤ From Previous.

4. Set Time ➤ End to **9**.

5. Click OK.

Select Camera1 in the timeline, click the Go To Start arrow, and then play the animation. You should see your component fade into existence and then fade out again. Click Stop when you've seen enough.

Applying Transformation Acceleration

To demonstrate acceleration, you will add a constraint move to your animation.

1. Set the timeline back to the beginning using the Go To Start button.

2. Click Render ➤ Animate ➤ Constraints.

3. Select the Flush:1 constraint from the browser underneath `mi_16a008`.

4. Set the End value to **-50.**

5. Set Time to Specify.

6. Set Time ➤ End to **9.**

7. Click OK.

Select Camera1 in the animation timeline, click the Go To Start arrow, and then play the animation. You should see your component fly up into the air as it appears. Click Stop when you've seen enough.

You'll notice that your component moves pretty steadily. Let's tweak the acceleration settings next.

To see the constraint animation in the timeline, click the Expand Action Editor button at the right end of the timeline dialog (looks like a mini-timeline with blue bars on it). In the timeline, right-click the Flush:1 action bar and choose Edit. Next, click the Acceleration tab.

The Acceleration tab allows you to vary the speed of the transformation over its beginning, middle, and end. The default is a smooth 20/60/20 velocity profile, as shown in Figure 16.35.

FIGURE 16.35
The Animate Fade
acceleration options

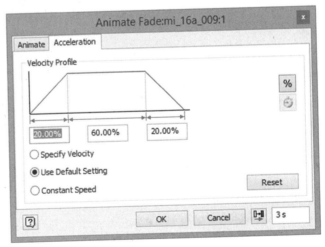

The item starts with 0 percent velocity, reaches 100 percent velocity in the first 20 percent of the sequence, continues at 100 percent for 60 percent of the sequence, and then decelerates back to 0 percent velocity in the last 20 percent of the sequence.

Click Specify Velocity and then set the values to **5%, 5%,** and **90%.** Click OK, click the Go To Start arrow, and then play the animation. You should see your component accelerate rapidly before slowing down. The longer the transformation takes to run, the more obvious the change in acceleration will be.

ANIMATING A CAMERA ALONG A PATH

Previously you learned how to move the camera around a part (turntable). To mimic how a camera would track and dolly in the real world, you can ask Inventor Studio to animate a camera along a path. The path is 2D or 3D sketch geometry that is added to a part file in your design.

To animate a camera along a path, right-click an existing camera in the Inventor Studio feature tree and choose Animate Camera.

In the Animate Camera dialog box, click the Definition button. Choose the Target Path option to animate where the camera is looking, or click the Position Path option to animate the position of the camera.

When a 2D or 3D geometry is selected as a path, you will notice two new glyphs appear on the selection, as shown in Figure 16.36. The green triangle selects the beginning of the move. The red box represents the end of the move.

FIGURE 16.36
Animating a camera along a path

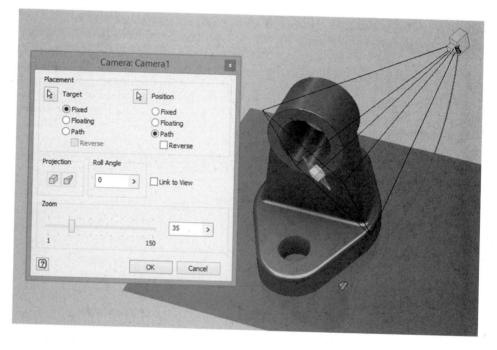

You can click and drag on these in the graphics window to edit the start and stop positions of the camera.

ANIMATING A LIGHT

While lights in the wrapper assembly can be animated, lights in subcomponents cannot. Lights cannot be animated along a path.

One common technique for animating lights is to include them in a part file and then use the Animate Components command instead.

THE ANIMATION TIMELINE

The animation timeline is the tool you use to bring your various transformations together into one complete sequence (see Figure 16.37).

FIGURE 16.37
The animation timeline

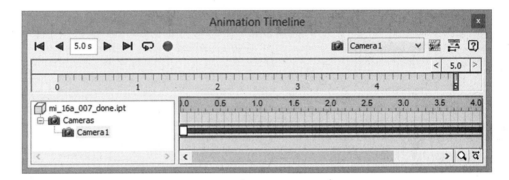

The Animation Timeline dialog will open automatically whenever you start an animation command. You can open the Animation Timeline dialog directly by clicking Render ➤ Animate ➤ Animation Timeline button. You can expand the Animation Timeline dialog to see the individual actions by clicking the Expand Action Editor button.

Actions

Every time you use an animate tool, an animation action is added to the timeline. You can use the animation timeline to edit your sequence by clicking and dragging the start and end handles of each action or by clicking and dragging the action itself to move it along the sequence.

Right-clicking an action allows you to delete it from the timeline, copy it (ready to paste a copy in elsewhere on the timeline), or mirror it (create a reverse copy on the timeline directly after the current action).

Playback

The playback tools at the top left of the window allow you to move to the start or end of the sequence, play the sequence in forward or reverse, toggle Repeat Play on, and record (render) your animation out to a file. When the animation is playing, the Play arrow will be swapped with the Stop arrow.

You will notice a vertical bar that runs across the sequence as it is played. This is called the *playhead*. You can use the playhead to manually move back and forth in your animation by clicking it and dragging left or right.

Animation Timeline Options

Click the button on the far right of the animation timeline that looks like a timeline with blue arrows on it to expand the Animation Timeline dialog box.

Click the Expand Animation Timeline button on the far right of the Animation Timeline dialog (The button looks like a timeline with blue arrow.) to expand the Animation Timeline dialoge box. Next, click the Animation Options button also on the far right of the Animation Timeline dialog (The button looks like a timeline with blue arrows and a pencil on it.), to set the duration, velocity, and default playback interval of the entire animation.

Click the Camera drop-down to play back the animation from the point of view of a different camera. You can close the file without saving.

Inventor Studio Video Producer

So far I've talked about how to animate the various items that can appear in Inventor Studio. One thing I haven't discussed is how to change cameras during a sequence—the Inventor Studio Video Producer allows you to do that.

To follow along with this section, open Inventor, go to the Get Started tab, and click the Open button. Browse for the file mi_16a_009.iam located in the Chapter 16 directory of your Mastering Inventor folder and click the Open button.

To start a new production, click Environments ➢ Inventor Studio ➢ Render ➢ Animate ➢ Video Producer (click OK in the pop-up).

The Video Producer dialog will open (see Figure 16.38). You'll notice that the controls are similar to the animation timeline.

FIGURE 16.38
The Video Producer dialog

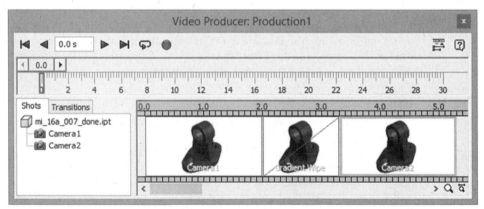

CREATING SHOTS

To create a new shot for your production, click and drag Camera1 from the Shots tab into the timeline. Now click and drag Camera2 from the Shots tab into the timeline.

Now, make sure that the playhead is back to the start of the timeline and click Play. You should see your animation play twice, once from the point of view of Camera1 and once from the point of view of Camera2.

To edit a camera shot, double-click it in the Video Producer timeline to bring up the Shot dialog box. You can see from the drop-down that this camera shot will play Animation1. You can also add precise values for the start, duration, and end of each shot here. Click Cancel to close the Shot window.

CREATING TRANSITIONS

Jumping straight from one camera angle to another can look a little jerky in your final movie. Transitions help to move you from one camera shot to another.

To add a transition, click the Video Producer Transitions tab, select Gradient Wipe, right-click, and choose Add To Timeline.

Just like in the animation timeline, you can click and drag any shot or transition in the Video Producer timeline to reorder them or click and drag on the edges to change the duration. Drag the Gradient Wipe transition until it sits between the two camera shots.

Double-clicking the Gradient Wipe Transition that you just added allows you to edit the color of the gradient wipe as well adding precise values for its start, end, and duration.

Click the red Record button on the Video Producer timeline to render a video of your final composition.

Rendering Animations

To render an animation or production, you can click Render ➤ Render ➤ Render Animation or click the red Record button, which can be found in the animation timeline or the Video Producer timeline.

The Render Animation dialog box, shown in Figure 16.39, has General and Render tabs that will be familiar to you from rendering 2D images.

FIGURE 16.39
The Render Animation dialog box

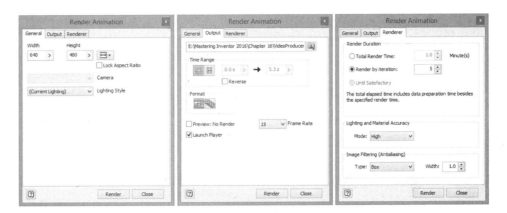

The Output tab is unique to rendering animations. Use the Time Range control to render your entire animation or choose a specified time range.

The Format controls allow you to choose between Image Sequence format and Video format.

The Image Sequence format means every frame is rendered to a still image file, such as BMP, JPEG, PNG, GIF, or TIFF. Note that rendering to PNG is the only way to include an alpha channel in your animation.

The Video format will produce a WMV or AVI file. See "Notes on Image Quality and File Types for Videos" in this chapter.

The Frame Rate drop-down is used to decide how many frames (images) to render for each second of footage. As a guide, animations for TV render at 24–30 fps. Start with 15 fps and increase from there.

The Preview: No Render check box is great for producing test animations without lighting or styles. This is really helpful to check camera positions and the movement of items before committing to a render.

Finally, you can use the Launch Player to launch your PC's default media player as soon as the animation has rendered so that you can see your results straightaway.

HOW CAN I PRODUCE MY RENDERS FASTER?

With the best will in the world, you will be sitting around for a long time waiting for Inventor to create your renders unless you have a powerful machine!

The following factors apply:

◆ The faster the CPU, the better.

◆ The more cores, the better.

◆ The more RAM, the better.

◆ The GPU (video card) has no effect on rendering.

◆ More lights will take longer to render.

◆ Soft shadows will take longer to render.

◆ Transparent components will take longer.

◆ Textures take longer.

◆ Video effects (fades and wipes) take longer.

◆ Depth of field will take longer.

As a rule of thumb, Inventor Studio requires the same hardware specification as Inventor, plus 50–100 percent more RAM and multiple CPUs and/or cores.

Rendering an animation takes the same amount of memory and power as rendering a still image—it just takes longer, because multiple images are being rendered.

Animated renderings can create large files on disk, and you may need to have a lot of drive space available to store all your hard work.

Inventor Studio Roundup

Inventor Studio is a creative, visual environment that takes a lot longer to describe than it does to use. I hope that you've been inspired by this chapter to liven up your models by adding color and texture, as well as by adding background images and lights.

Rendering still images can be quick and simple. Rendering animations can take a little longer to set up but will give an amazing wow factor to your work. Rendering animations can be a time sink, so I recommend you take some time to storyboard your animation before you start. This simply means sketching a thumbnail image for each shot you want to create. This will really help you to plan your time and stay on track while producing great work.

Here are some more tips to help you create renders and animations.

◆ Make sure your custom images and texture maps are saved in your Projects workspace or the file path specified in Application Options.

◆ Save your custom materials and appearances to your own library and save a copy of this for backup.

◆ Think about the use of constraints in your assembly and make sure that you have the ones you need to create your animation.

◆ Create views and positional reps in your parts and assemblies before bringing them into Inventor Studio.

◆ "Favorite "parameters in Inventor Studio to animate them.

◆ Build yourself a virtual studio, which is a wrapper assembly file containing preset local lights and cameras to allow you to drop a part in and start rendering straightaway.

◆ Do quick renders at a smaller size/lower quality to test before committing time to your final render.

◆ Render animations using the Preview: No Render option to render animations without lighting or styles to check your cameras and transitions before committing to your final render.

DYNAMIC SIMULATION TO STUDIO

If you use Autodesk Inventor Professionals' Dynamic Simulation tools, you may have noticed the Publish To Studio tool.

This tool allows you to render your simulation in Inventor Studio after you have run a simulation but before you leave Run mode. You *must* run the simulation before using the tool!

The tool will take you into the Inventor Studio environment where you can create a new animation called Dynamic_Simulation and add a new parameter called Simulation_Timeline. The parameter appears in your animation favorites and represents the time steps used in your simulation.

I recommend you use the same number for the parameter as time steps used in the simulation to help relate the final animation with the original simulation.

You can animate the simulation using this parameter and add lighting and scene styles to enhance the result. When you are ready, you can render this as an animation.

The Bottom Line

Create and edit appearances   Help your models to look more lifelike by editing your model's appearance (color and texture).

  Master It   How would you make your own library of appearances to reuse in future projects?

  How would you define color options in a model so that you can review them with your internal or external customers?

Create and edit visual styles.   Help your models to look more lifelike by placing them in a realistic setting.

  Master It   How would you save your favorite lighting styles for reuse on future projects?

There are three ways of adjusting the background image, including using the application options to change the background color and picking a visual style that includes an IBL environment. What's the third way?

Create and animate cameras.   Adding a camera with lifelike focus and depth of field helps to make your rendering believable. Animating cameras positions adds power to your rendering. It becomes much more dynamic.

> **Master It**   Real movie cameras track (move side to side), Dolly (move up and down), tilt (angle up and down), pan (angle side to side), and Dutch (rotate). How would you mimic this in Inventor Studio?

Animate components, constraint, and parameters.   Animating your assemblies so that the function of the mechanism is showcased is often the purpose of an assembly animation.

> **Master It**   You have an existing animation but want to do a variation on it. How do you copy and edit an existing animation?

Use multiple cameras to create a video production of your animation.   Video Producer provides the means to combine camera shots into a single video output.

> **Master It**   You have created several cameras, animated and static, and want to make a composite animation. What are the general steps you will follow?

Use props to enhance your scene.   Inventor assemblies can be combined with other components to create a more realistic scene for rendering.

> **Master It**   You have completed a design and want to render a realistic image of it in its working environment. How do you do this?

Render animations and video productions.   Inventor provides the means to render animations and video productions.

> **Master It**   You've created a wrapper assembly and set up the scene with cameras, lighting, and a scene style. Now you want to render an animation for design review and render a video production for a multidisciplinary review or marketing. What are the basic steps in each process?

Chapter 17

Stress Analysis and Dynamic Simulation

This chapter will cover the tools of the Stress Analysis and Dynamic Simulation environments in the Autodesk® Inventor® Professional software. The Stress Analysis environment allows you to perform static and modal analysis on parts and assemblies by defining component materials, loads, constraints, and contact conditions. A second type of stress analysis (referred to as *frame analysis* in this chapter) uses beam elements represented with a line segment that is centered in a Frame Generator member and interpolates the effects of loads on the geometry of the frame. This greatly improves the speed of the analysis.

The Dynamic Simulation environment allows you to analyze an assembly in motion by specifying loads, constraints, motion joints, velocities, acceleration, and environmental factors such as gravity and friction. These environments can be used together to determine motion loads enacted upon one component by another component at a given point in time.

In this chapter, you'll learn to

- Set up and run Stress Analysis simulations

- Set up and run Dynamic Simulations

- Export results from the Dynamic Simulation environment to the Stress Analysis environment

Introducing Analysis

Although the terms *stress analysis* and *finite element analysis* (FEA) are often used interchangeably in conversation, it may be helpful to understand them as they relate to the tools available to you in the Inventor Stress Analysis environment. FEA is an analysis of a complex object solved by dividing that object into a mesh of smaller elements upon which manageable calculations can be run. The stress analysis done by Inventor uses this method to allow you to analyze your design, under a given set of conditions specified by you, in order to determine basic trends in regard to the specifics of your design.

Deriving an exact answer from the analysis of a model is generally reserved for an analyst with specific training, often for a more powerful set of analysis tools. With that said, you can use the Inventor simulation tools to run basic analyses to confirm design validity. This can be useful to determine design basics before going down a wrong path. Or you can use these tools to help find out, for example, whether a component or assembly is being over- or underdesigned for a given set of loads and/or vibrations. The stress analysis tools in Inventor are also useful when determining how feature size and locations will affect the integrity of the part. For instance, how close to the edge of a bracket can you move a hole? Is another brace required to prevent a sheet-metal face from "pillow casing" because of a pressure load? These tools are ideal for questions of this nature and can significantly reduce the number of physical prototypes required to prove a final design.

Dynamic Simulation allows you to set the components of your model in motion to verify how those parts interact with one another and to determine the force enacted on one component (or group of components) by another component (or group of components). The Dynamic Simulation environment allows you to define the way parts relate to one another and how the forces present create motion in the context of a timeline. From the simulation, you can determine how and when parts interact as well as the amount of force present for any point in time. For example, you might use these tools to simulate a force applied to a shaft used to turn a lever, which in turn contacts a catch stop, where the goal is to determine the maximum force present throughout the entire sequence. Once this maximum force is determined, it can be applied to the shaft as loads in a stress analysis study.

Conducting Stress Analysis Simulations

You can simulate a stress situation on your design to determine the effects of various load and constraint scenarios to determine areas of weakness, better design alternatives, how much a part is over- or underbuilt, to what extent a design change will impact a design, and so on. Using parametric studies, you can determine a combination of these elements to see how multiple changes impact a design at the same time. For more information on this topic, refer to the section "Conducting Parameter Studies" later in this chapter. This is an important task because understanding the basic tools and workflow is the first step to setting up effective simulations.

The basic stress analysis workflow is as follows:

1. Enter the Stress Analysis environment (on the Environments tab, select Stress Analysis).

2. Create a simulation.

3. Specify the type of simulation you want to conduct (for instance, when working with assemblies, you may want to use an alternate view, positional, or level of detail representation).

4. Specify the materials for the components.

5. Specify the load types, locations, and amounts.

6. Specify the support types and locations.

7. For assemblies, gather and refine contact between components.

8. Generate a mesh.

9. Run the simulation.

10. Interpret the results.

To aid you in the process of learning how to conduct a stress analysis study, Autodesk has built in the Simulation Guide.

Simulation Guide

You can find the Simulation Guide in the Guide pane of the Stress Analysis tab once you have started to construct a simulation. To access the Simulation Guide, click the Guide button, and the Simulation Guide panel will appear.

This tool was built with two types of users in mind: the novice who is looking for an understanding of the process of conducting a simulation, and the intermediate user who has been using an FEA tool in the past and is looking for additional advice on using the Inventor toolset or seeking to improve their knowledge.

You can launch the tool before you begin a simulation, or if you've already started setting up a simulation, it will open to the next appropriate step to offer guidance. To help in selecting load and constraint types, the guide contains a series of hyperlinks that will step you through various options on how the component or assembly is constructed and how it moves or is supported. It will even check with you to see whether there are features that may not influence the result of the analysis but may add unnecessary time to the process.

Static Stress vs. Modal Analysis

You can perform static and modal stress analysis on parts and assemblies in the Stress Analysis environment. To enter this environment, click the Stress Analysis button on the Environments tab. Once in the Stress Analysis environment, you use the Create Simulation button and specify either Static Analysis or Modal Analysis. It's important to understand the difference between static and modal analysis.

Static Analysis   Attempts to determine the stress placed on a component by a particular set of loads and constraints. The stress is considered static because it does not vary due to time or temperature. You can import motion loads determined from the Dynamic Simulation environment to analyze the stress at any given time step for moving parts.

Modal Analysis   Attempts to determine the dynamic behavior of a model in terms of its modes of vibration. An example would be trying to determine whether the vibration generated by a running motor would create significant disturbance to a sensitive mechanism within the design.

Simplifying Your Model

When working with assemblies, you should exclude parts that are not affected by the simulation or do not add to its results in order to simplify the simulation and reduce the time required to run it. Excluding small parts such as fasteners, whose functionality is replicated by simulation constraints or forces, is also recommended. You can do this by expanding the assembly browser node, right-clicking the part to be excluded, and then selecting Exclude From Simulation.

When working with a part file in the simulation environment, you can suppress small features that are irrelevant to stress concentrations, such as outer fillets and chamfers. These "finish" features typically only complicate the mesh needed for the simulation and add overhead to the analysis. Other features that are typically excluded from simulations are small holes with diameters of less than 1/100th the length of the part, embossed or engraved text, and other aesthetic features. Excluding features of these types can have a significant impact on the meshing process and the simulation's run time. Figure 17.1 shows the exclusion of features from a part file on the left and the exclusion of parts from an assembly on the right. Using the appropriate selection filter, you can select features and parts to exclude in the design window using typical right-click context menu behavior while in the assembly.

FIGURE 17.1
The Exclude features for a simulation

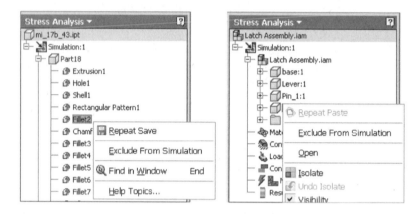

Specifying Materials

To specify the material of each part in a simulation, use the Assign button on the Material panel of the Stress Analysis tab. Material properties must be fully defined in order for the material to be used for the simulation. Materials with incomplete information are marked with an icon. Figure 17.2 shows the Assign button used to access the Assign Materials dialog box as well as the icon indicating that incomplete materials have been specified.

FIGURE 17.2
Assigning materials

Assign

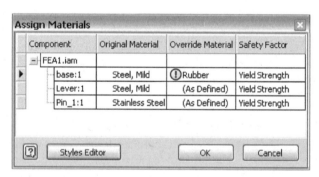

Component	Original Material	Override Material	Safety Factor
⊟ FEA1.iam			
base:1	Steel, Mild	ⓘ Rubber	Yield Strength
Lever:1	Steel, Mild	(As Defined)	Yield Strength
Pin_1:1	Stainless Steel	(As Defined)	Yield Strength

You can specify the original material for each component or specify an override (per simulation) from the Material Library. To change the original material of the part file while in the Stress Analysis environment, click the Inventor button, select iProperties, and then select the Physical tab. You can use the Styles Editor button in the Assign Materials dialog box to step into the Style And Standard Editor to edit, add, or just review the properties of any material style. You can find the physical characteristics of a given material from a number of resources on the Internet, such as www.matweb.com.

It is assumed that materials are constant, meaning there is no change because of time or temperature to the structural properties of the material. All materials are assumed to be homogenous, with no change in properties throughout the volume of the part. And it is also assumed that stress is directly proportional to strain for all materials.

By default, the browser will display the names of components with overridden materials under the material name. You can also display all materials assigned to components by right-clicking the Material category in the browser and then selecting All Materials from the context menu.

Applying Simulation Constraints

Constraints added in the simulation limit the movement or displacement of the model for the purposes of the simulation. To constrain a model for static simulations, you should remove all free translational and rotational movements. You should also strive to neither over- nor under-constrain your model because both can impact the simulation results.

You can create all the constraint types by clicking the constraint tool buttons on the Constraints panel of the Stress Analysis tab, shown in Figure 17.3.

FIGURE 17.3
The simulation
constraint tools

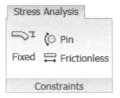

These are the types of simulation constraints available:

Fixed Constraints   These remove all translational degrees of freedom and can be applied to faces, edges, or vertices, typically to simulate a part that is bonded or welded to another component. You can click the >> button to specify the Use Vector Components option and free the component in a given vector plane. Fixed constraints can also be used to specify a known displacement of a component to determine the force required to create the displacement.

Frictionless Constraints   Use these constraints to prevent the selected surface from deforming or moving in a direction normal to it. You can also use frictionless constraints to simulate linear bearings and slides. Because most surface-to-surface situations are not entirely frictionless, you can expect the simulation to return more moderate results. If friction is considerable, it can be compensated for in the Dynamic Simulation environment, and the results can be imported into the Stress Analysis environment.

Tip: Frictionless constraints can also be used to mimic the behavior of symmetry-bonded conditions.

Pin Constraints   These are used to apply rotational constraints on a selected cylindrical face (or faces), such as where holes are or where parts are supported by pins or bearings. Use the >> button to set the direction options. A pin that rotates in a hole would have only the tangential direction free, one that slides in a hole but does not rotate would have only the axial direction free, one that slides and rotates would have both the axial and tangential directions free, and so on.

Figure 17.4 shows the simulation constraint dialog boxes.

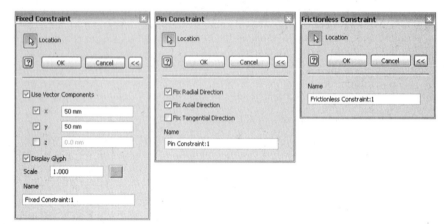

Applying Loads

Loads are forces applied to a part or assembly resulting in stress, deformation, and displacement in components. A key to applying loads is being able to predict or visualize how parts will respond to loads. For simple static simulations, this is generally fairly straightforward, but for more complex designs where one component exerts a force on another, which exerts a force on yet another, loads will likely need to be determined through the use of the Dynamic Simulation tools, as discussed later in this chapter.

You can access all the load types from the Loads panel of the Stress Analysis tab, as shown in Figure 17.5.

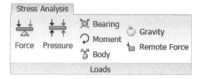

These are the types of load available:

Force   This is specified in newtons (N) or pounds-force (lbf or lbforce). Forces can be applied by selecting a single face, edge, or vertex (or a set of faces, edges, or vertices) for the location. Selection sets must be of the same type, meaning that once you select a face, you can add faces to the selection set but not edges or vertices. The force direction can be specified by selecting an edge or face and then changed using the Flip Direction button. Direction is automatically set to the normal of the face (with the force directed at that face) when a face is selected for either location or a direction. You can avoid stress singularities by selecting faces or the location rather than edges or vertices.

Pressure   This is specified in megapascals (MPa) or pounds per square inch (psi). Pressure can be applied only to a face or to a set of faces. Pressure is uniform and is applied in a direction normal to the surface at all locations. When applying loads to faces that are involved in contacts, you should use pressure instead of force.

Bearing   These are specified in newtons (N) or pounds-force (lbf or lbforce). Bearing loads are applied only to cylindrical faces. By default, the load is along the axis of the cylinder, and the direction is radial. You can specify the direction by selecting a face or edge. These are generally used to simulate a radial load such as a roller bearing.

LOADS AND CONSTRAINTS

Loads and constraints can be applied to the same entity as long as they are compatible. When incompatible loads and constraints exist on the same entity, such as a face fixed in the X direction while a load is applied in the same direction to the same face, the constraints will override the forces.

Moment   These are specified in units of torque such as newton meters (N m or N*m) or pounds-force inch (lbforce in or lbf*in). Moment locations can be applied to faces only. Direction can be defined by selecting faces, straight edges, axes, and two vertices.

Remote Force   These can be used as an alternative to applying a force load directly to a part by specifying the location in space from which the force originates. Apply Remote Force by selecting faces and specifying in N or lb.

Gravity   These are specified in units of acceleration such as millimeter per second squared (mm/s^2) or inch per second squared (in/s^2). Apply gravity to a face or parallel to a selected edge. The default gravity value is set to 386.220 in/s^2 or 9810.000 mm/s^2.

Motion   Unlike with the other forces, there is no tool to apply motion loads in the Stress Analysis environment; instead, these are created from reaction forces determined from the Dynamic Simulation environment using the Export To FEA tool for a component per specified time step. Once they are created, you can use motion loads by one of the following methods: For a new simulation, click the Create Simulation button on the Stress Analysis tab. For an existing simulation, right-click the existing simulation in the browser node and select Edit Simulation Properties.

In either case, once the Simulation Properties dialog box is open, you follow these steps:

1. In the Simulation Properties dialog box, select the Motion Loads Analysis check box.

2. Select the part from the enabled list.

3. Select the time step from the list.

4. Click the OK button.

Body   These are specified in units of acceleration such as millimeter per second squared (mm/s^2) or inch per second squared (in/s^2). Body loads are the forces acting on the entire volume or mass of a component, such as gravity, linear acceleration, centripetal force, and centrifugal force. Select a planar face for linear acceleration or a cylindrical face for an axial direction. Use a body force to simulate the effect of outside forces. Only one body force per simulation is allowed.

Use the Linear tab to specify linear acceleration and the Angular tab to specify angular velocity or angular acceleration. The Angular tab has three possible results depending on what is specified and how.

◆ Velocity and acceleration have the same rotation axis, with an unspecified location. The solver determines the location along the axis.

◆ Velocity and acceleration have different rotation axes, with an unspecified location. The solver determines the location along the axis. A point is selected along the velocity rotation axis for the acceleration location.

◆ Velocity and acceleration have different rotation axes, with a specified location. The solver determines the location the same as when you define the point with the vector components.

USING SPLIT TO APPLY LOADS ACCURATELY

When you assign bearing loads to components, you may need to split the face first in order to select just a portion of a continuous face. For instance, consider applying a load to a shaft. If you select the cylindrical face, the load might be distributed along the entire face rather than concentrated on just the area intended to be loaded. You can use a work plane to split the face. This can be useful when placing loads on flat surfaces as well. Use a sketch to divide the surface into a face appropriate to the load. You can access the Split tool in the modeling environment from the Modify panel of the 3D Model tab.

Specifying Contact Conditions

Contacts between components are detected when the simulation is run and automatically listed in the browser under the contact node. However, you can run the Automatic Contact tool to see them before running the simulation and then modify any of the automatic contacts listed or manually add other contacts. To add contacts, click either the Automatic or Manual button on the Contacts tab, shown in Figure 17.6.

FIGURE 17.6
Contact tools

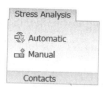

For contacts to be added, the faces must meet the following criteria:

◆ The selected faces must be within 15 degrees of parallel. This 15-degree limit is a system setting and cannot be changed.

◆ The distance between the selected faces cannot exceed the Tolerance setting specified in the simulation's properties. You can access the simulation's properties by right-clicking the simulation node in the browser for existing simulations, or you can specify them when you create the simulation.

Contacts are listed in the contact node in the browser and categorized per contact type. The type and components involved are set in the contact node name. Contacts are also listed under the browser node of each involved component. Modal analysis lists only the Bonded and Spring contact types, whereas all types are available for static analysis. You can change the contact type of automatic contacts by right-clicking a contact and choosing Edit Contact or by using the **Ctrl** or **Shift** key in the browser to multiselect contacts and then right-clicking and choosing Edit Contact. You can suppress contacts as well. Figure 17.7 shows the edit options.

FIGURE 17.7
Contact edit options

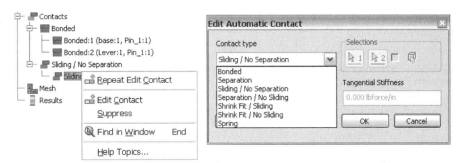

These are the available contact types:

Bonded   This creates a rigid bond between selected faces.

Separation   This partially or fully separates selected faces while sliding.

Sliding/No Separation   This creates a normal-to-face direction bond between selected faces while sliding under deformation.

Separation/No Sliding   This partially or fully separates selected faces without them sliding against one another.

Shrink Fit/Sliding   This creates conditions similar to Separation but with a negative distance between contact faces, resulting in overlapping parts at the start.

Shrink Fit/No Sliding   This creates conditions of Separation/No Sliding but with a negative distance between contact faces, resulting in overlapping parts at the start.

Spring   This creates equivalent springs between the two faces. You define total Normal Stiffness and/or Tangential Stiffness. The Normal Stiffness and Tangential Stiffness options are available for the Spring contact only.

You can change the contacts between two components to see how the simulation results change. Figure 17.8 shows the same simple assembly simulation with a different contact applied between the two plates. On the left, a bonded contact is used, and the results show that the vertical plate is deformed by the load and that stress is concentrated at, and distributed out from, the contact joint. On the right, a Sliding/No Separation joint is used, and the results show that the vertical plate is essentially pushed along the horizontal plate, with the stress being spread over the vertical plate and little or no concentration and no stress being distributed to the horizontal plate.

FIGURE 17.8

Contact comparison

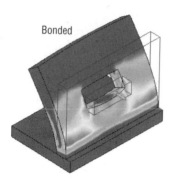

Bonded

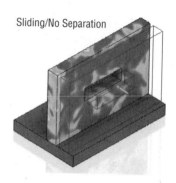

Sliding/No Separation

Preparing Thin Bodies

Your models sometimes contain components that have thin walls compared to the overall size of the model, such as sheet metal or plastic parts. As a result of this variation, standard analysis can cause long meshing times and instabilities in the computation. To deal with this, you can use the tools on the Prepare panel to simplify thin wall bodies to be seen as surface shells.

When you use the Find Thin Bodies tool, the model is scanned; any bodies found to have a high Length/Thickness ratio are identified as potential thin bodies, and you are given the option to generate midsurfaces for the body. Alternatively, you can use the MidSurface tool to generate midsurfaces for bodies you know to be considered thin bodies in advance. You can also use the Offset tool to create a shell from selected faces.

Once midsurfaces or offset shells are created, you can convert them back to solids by selecting them in the browser, right-clicking, and choosing Delete. Keep in mind that loads and constraints applied to solid bodies before preparing them as thin bodies become sick when converted to shell elements and might need to be deleted. Figure 17.9 shows the Prepare tools on the left.

FIGURE 17.9

Prepare and Mesh tools

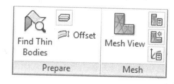

Generating a Mesh

Although you can accept the default mesh settings and run the simulation, often you will want to adjust the mesh settings to compensate for areas where a finer mesh is required. You can adjust the global mesh settings or use a local mesh control when needed. Figure 17.9 shows the Mesh tools on the right.

MESH SETTINGS

Use the Mesh Settings tool to change these mesh properties:

Average Element Size Controls the mean distance between mesh nodes. Setting Average Size to a smaller value results in a finer mesh. This setting is relative to the overall size of the model. A value from 0.100 to 0.050 is generally recommended.

Minimum Element Size   Controls the minimum distance between mesh nodes as a fraction of the Average Size value. Increasing this will decrease the mesh element density. Decreasing this value will increase the mesh element density. This setting is sensitive, and changes typically result in dramatic changes to the mesh quality. A value from 0.100 to 0.200 is generally recommended.

Grading Factor   Controls the ratio of adjacent mesh edges where fine and coarse mesh areas come together. The smaller the factor used, the more uniform the mesh will be. A value of 1 to 10 can be used, but a value from 1.5 to 3.0 is typically recommended.

Maximum Turn Angle   Controls the maximum angle for meshes applied to arcs. Specifying a smaller angle results in a finer mesh on curved areas. A value between 30 and 60 degrees is typically recommended.

Create Curved Mesh Elements   Controls the creation of meshes with curved edges and faces. If this is unselected, a less-accurate mesh is created, but performance may be better.

Use Part-Based Measure For Assembly Mesh   This sets part mesh sizes relative to the overall dimensions of the part models. Deselecting this option sets the mesh size relative to the overall assembly dimensions. Use this option for assemblies composed of several parts of varying sizes. This setting is available only in an assembly.

Once the mesh settings have been adjusted, you can click the Mesh View button to generate the mesh initially and then toggle on the visibility of the mesh afterward. It is not required that you generate the mesh manually because it will be done during the simulation, but doing so may allow you to identify areas of importance on the model that are not meshed to your liking and then apply a local mesh.

LOCAL MESH CONTROL

You can use the Local Mesh Control button to select faces and edges that require a finer meshing than what is required for the rest of the model. This allows you to manually improve the mesh quality for small or complex faces. A browser node is created in the Mesh node for each local mesh you create. You can right-click the local mesh and select Edit Local Mesh Control to change the mesh size or change the faces or edges selected.

When mesh settings or local mesh controls have been updated, a lightning bolt icon will display in the browser to indicate that the mesh is out-of-date. You can right-click the Mesh browser node and choose Update Mesh, as shown in Figure 17.10. This figure shows a simple cube with a local mesh applied to the top face; the other faces are meshed according to the mesh settings.

FIGURE 17.10
Updating a mesh

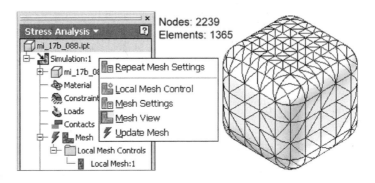

UNDERSTANDING MESH SETTINGS

To understand the way these settings affect the mesh generated, you can use the file `mi_17b_88.ipt` in the `Chapter 17` directory of the `Mastering Inventor 2016` folder and apply a mesh to it. This file is a simple cube with rounded edges. Experiment with the options using the Mesh Settings tools. Then apply a local mesh. Exit the Stress Analysis environment, edit the model, and change the value for Extrusion1 to **30** mm (all the dimensions of the cube are set to be the same and will update to match).

Return to the Stress Analysis environment, and update the mesh. Note that the mesh adjusts as the cube size increases, whereas the local mesh holds an absolute size. Use the Mesh Settings tool to take a look at the other settings as well. Understanding the impact of each setting on a simple part model will allow you to determine the effect of each setting on your more complex models.

MESH ERRORS

When model errors prevent a mesh from being created, a mesh failure warning is displayed. Errors are reported in the Mesh progress dialog box, in the Mesh browser node, and with an error label and leader on the model in the graphics area.

AN INTERFACE OPTION WORTH NOTING

The previous sections discuss the selection of materials, application of loads, and generation of meshes. These things are categorized in the browser.

An alternative to accessing the tools from the Stress Analysis tab is to right-click these categories in the browser and select the same tools from the context menu presented.

Running the Simulation

Once you have set the material, loads, constraints, and contacts, you are ready to run the simulation. To run a simulation, click the Simulate button on the Solve panel, or right-click the Simulation node in the browser and select Simulate. The Simulate dialog box displays information about the simulation to be run and will display warning and stop errors when not all criteria are available to run. For instance, if you have forgotten to set a material type, the Simulate dialog box will stop you and tell you this. If you need to cancel a simulation in process, click the Cancel button or press the Esc key.

When a simulation becomes out-of-date because of changes to mesh settings, loads, constraints, or other design parameters, you will see a red lightning bolt next to the Results browser node. To update the simulation, simply right-click the browser node and click Simulate, or just click the Simulate button on the Solve panel again.

When working with parametric studies, it is possible to run simulations for more than one configuration at a time. You can run an Exhaustive Set or Smart Set of configurations or just run the current configuration. You can find more information on simulating configurations in the section "Conducting Parameter Studies" later in this chapter.

EXTERNAL LINKED FILES CREATED BY SIMULATION RESULTS

Be aware that by default the Results files are created and linked to your file when you run a simulation. These externally linked files can cause file-resolution problems when you move or copy simulation files or if you use Autodesk Vault. You can avoid the linked files by clicking the Stress Analysis Settings button and then activating the Solver tab. Then locate the Create OLE Link To Result Files option and uncheck the check box.

To remove links created when this check box was selected, you can go to the Tools tab and click the Links button on the Options panel. In the Document Links And Embeddings dialog box, select a link path and use the Break Link button to remove the link.

Interpreting the Results

Once a simulation is run, the Results node of the browser is populated, and the graphics area updates to show the shaded distribution of stresses. You can switch between available results types by double-clicking each type in the Results browser folder. Figure 17.11 shows a typical simulation result. Note the Results folder in the browser.

FIGURE 17.11
Simulation results

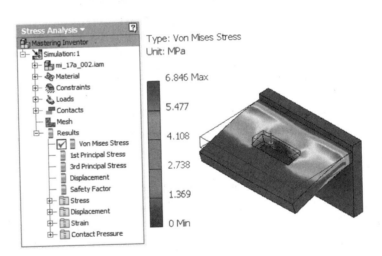

The Results node of the browser will display the subcategories of results, each displayed on the model by the use of color contours. The colors displayed on the model correspond to the value ranges shown in the color bar legend. Typically, areas of interest are displayed in warm colors such as red, orange, and yellow. These colors represent areas of high stress, high deformation, or a low safety factor. You can adjust the number of colors used in the color bar as well as the position and size of it by clicking the Color Bar button on the Display panel. Listed here are the result subcategories:

Von Mises Stress Maximum stress theory states that failure will occur when the maximum principal stress in a component reaches the value of the maximum stress at the elastic limit. This theory works to predict failure for brittle materials. However, in elastic bodies subject to three-dimensional loads, complex stresses are developed, meaning that at any point within the body there are stresses acting in various directions. The Von Mises criterion calculates whether the combining stress at a given point will cause failure. This is represented in the Results node as the Von Mises Stress, also commonly known as *equivalent stress*.

1st Principal Stress   Principal stresses are calculated by converting the model coordinates so that no shear stresses exist. The 1st principal stress is the maximum principal stress and is the value of stress that is normal to the plane in which shear stress is zero. This allows you to interpret maximum tensile stress present because of the specified load conditions.

3rd Principal Stress   The 3rd principal stress is the minimum principal stress, and it acts normal to the plane in which shear stress is zero. It helps you to interpret the maximum compressive stress present in the part because of the specified load conditions.

Displacement   The displacement results show you the deformed shape of your model in a scaled representation, based on the specified load conditions. Use the displacement results to determine the location and extent to which a part will bend and how much force is needed for it to bend a given distance.

Safety Factor   The safety factor is calculated as the yield strength of the material divided by principal stress. This shows you the areas of the model that are likely to fail under the specified load conditions. The calculated safety factor is shown on the color bar legend as the value followed by *min*. A safety factor of less than 1 indicates a permanent yield or failure.

Frequency Modes   Modal results appear under the Results node in the browser as frequency modes only when a modal analysis is running. You can view the mode plots for the number of specified natural frequencies. In an unconstrained simulation, the first six modes will occur at 0 Hz, corresponding to the six standard rigid body movements.

Using the Result, Scaling, Display, and Report Tools

You can use several display tools to adjust the Results display to clearly interpret the calculated results. You can access these tools on the Result, Display, and Report panels, as shown in Figure 17.12.

FIGURE 17.12
Result, Scaling, Display, and Report tools

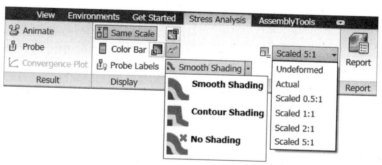

The following list describes the Result, Scaling, Display, and Report tools available on the Display panel:

Same Scale   Maintains the same scale while different results are viewed. This might be grayed out if no parametric table has been created.

Color Bar   Opens the Color Bar dialog box so you can adjust the color bar display settings.

Probe   Allows you to select the model and display results information for the selection. Right-click a label to edit or delete it.

Probe Labels Display   Toggles the visibility of probe labels.

Shading   Displays color changes using a blended transition when set to Smooth Shading, striated shading when using Contour Shading, and no color shading when set to No Shading.

Maximum   Turns on and off the display of the point of maximum result, which allows you to quickly identify the maximum result on the model.

Minimum   Turns on and off the display of the point of minimum result, which allows you to quickly identify the minimum result on the model.

Boundary Condition   Turns on and off the display of load symbols on the part.

Adjust Displacement Scale   Allows you to select from a preset list of displacement exaggeration scales.

Element Visibility   Displays the mesh over the top of the result contours.

Animate Results   Animates the displacement for the current result type and displacement scale.

Report   Generates reports of analysis simulations in HTML format with PNG graphics.

Conducting Parameter Studies

Often the purpose of a stress analysis simulation is to determine how a change to a design feature will impact the part or assembly's strength. The parametric study tools allow you to make comparative evaluations based on different parameter values at the feature, part, and assembly levels. To create a parametric study, you nominate certain parameters for evaluation in the study, define the range for each parameter, specify the design constraints that you are interested in seeing for those parameters, and, finally, analyze the results of each variation.

To create a parametric study, use these steps as a guideline:

1. Set the simulation's design objective to Parametric Dimension. How you do this depends on whether you are creating a new simulation or editing an existing one. You can set the design objective to Parametric Dimension by using the Create Simulation button when creating a new simulation or by right-clicking an existing simulation in the browser and choosing Edit Simulation Properties, as shown in Figure 17.13.

FIGURE 17.13
Setting a
simulation to
the Parametric
Dimension
design objective

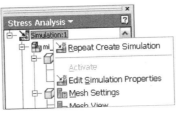
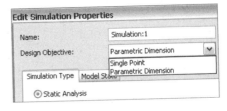

2. Nominate selected parameters for use in the study by expanding the browser node for the model and then right-clicking the assembly, part, or feature node you want to use in the study and selecting Show Parameters. Figure 17.14 shows a parameter called Side_ Offset being nominated.

FIGURE 17.14
Nominating a
parameter

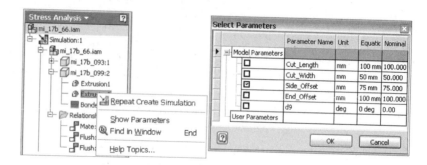

3. Define the range for the selected parameters by following these steps:

   A. Click the Parametric Table button on the Manage panel of the Stress Analysis tab.

   B. Enter a parameter range in the Values column; values must be in ascending order.

   C. Create a simple range by separating the minimum and maximum values with a hyphen; for instance, you can enter **70-85**.

   D. Specify specific values in a range by separating each value with a comma, colon, hyphen, or slash; for instance, you can enter **70, 75, 80, 85**.

   E. Add a colon to a range to specify the number of points included; for instance, you can enter **70-85: 4**.

   F. Use the slider to set the current value.

   G. Right-click the parameter row and choose from the options to generate the geometry configurations. For instance, if you were to set the range of a hole position to 70, 75, 80, 85, four model configurations would be created with the hole positioned at each of those values. Figure 17.15 shows a Parametric Table configuration for the Side_Offset parameter.

FIGURE 17.15
Defining a parameter
range

Parametric Table							
Design Constraints							
Constraint Nar	Constraint Typ	Limit		Safety Factor	Result Value	Unit	
▶							
Parameters							
Component	Feature Nar	Parameter Name	Values			Current Value	Unit
▶ mi_17b_099	Extrusion2	Side_Offset	70,75,80,85	—ⅉ—		75	mm

Promote configuration to model
Remove Parameter
Show Base Configuration
Generate Single Configuration
Generate Range Configurations
Generate All Configurations
Simulate this configuration

4. Add design constraints to the Parametric Table by following these steps:

    A. In the Design Constraints area of the Parametric Table, right-click a row and select Add Design Constraint.

    B. In the Select Design Constraint dialog box, specify a results component, such as Von Mises Stress, Displacement, Safety Factor, and so on.

    C. Specify the value of interest, such as Minimum or Maximum (this applies to all geometry).

    D. You can modify the selection set by selecting Include or Exclude and then selecting bodies, faces, or edges onscreen. Doing so focuses the results to a specific area of interest. Figure 17.16 shows the Safety Factor design constraint being added.

FIGURE 17.16
Adding a design constraint

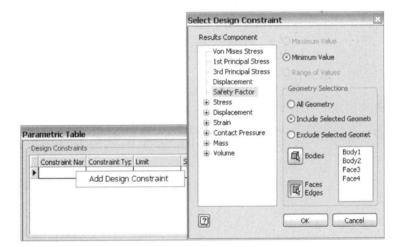

5. Specify the constraint type, set limits, enter a safety factor, and review the results using the following steps:

    A. In the Parametric Table dialog box, click the Constraint Type drop-down, and select from the list.

    B. Enter a value in the Limit column to filter the results to the set that meets the bounding limit when you're optimizing other design constraints.

    C. Enter a safety factor to specify at what extent a variable can be exceeded before causing the design constraint to fail. A comparison to the limit factored by the Safety Factor setting determines whether it meets the limit or range.

    D. The Result Value column displays the value of the design constraint for the simulation. When the value is within the limit, it displays green. When the limit is exceeded, it displays red. When out of range, it displays gray, and the closest value is displayed. Figure 17.17 shows the Mass design constraint being configured.

FIGURE 17.17
Configuring a design
constraint

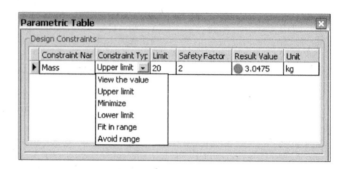

6. When multiple parameters are added to the table, configurations can be created. These configurations can then be generated and simulated by following a few simple steps:

   A. In the Parametric Table dialog box, set the parameter values to the combination you want to simulate, right-click any parameter row, and choose Simulate This Configuration.

   B. To simulate all configurations, exit the Parametric Table dialog box and click the Simulate button on the Solve panel. You can choose to run an exhaustive set, a smart set, or the current configuration.

   C. Once the simulations have been run, you can use the slider bar in the Parametric Table dialog box for each parameter to set the combinations and observe the results.

   D. The Exhaustive Set Of Configurations setting runs all possible combinations of parameter settings, whereas the Smart Set Of Configurations setting runs only those combinations of parameter settings that Inventor determines have not yet been run. Figure 17.18 shows the choices for running simulation configurations.

FIGURE 17.18
Simulation
configurations

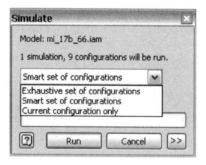

Once you determine that a given configuration satisfies your design needs using the Parametric Table dialog box, you can right-click any of the parameter rows in the table and choose Promote Configuration To Model. This will write the parameter values of the configuration to the source files.

Conducting a Frame Analysis

As you learned in Chapter 15, "Frame Generator," having a library of predefined metal shapes can save a tremendous amount of work because you won't have to re-create standardized geometry. Frame Analysis allows you to further leverage those predefined shapes by using the known behavior of the shape under load and calculating what the loads would be along the center of a length of material rather than the surface.

The process of conducting a frame analysis is similar to performing an assembly analysis, but frames add some additional tools that allow for an even more efficient solving process. Here is the process, including some optional steps:

1. Enter the Frame Analysis environment by using the Environments tab or by using the icon on the Design tab.

2. Create a simulation.

3. Specify the support types and locations.

4. Specify the load types, locations, and amounts.

5. Specify connections between beams, additional nodes, or releases (optional).

6. Run the simulation.

7. Interpret the results.

Frame Analysis Settings

You can adjust Frame Analysis settings by clicking the Frame Analysis Settings button on the Frame Analysis tab. On the General tab, you can adjust the colors, scales, and interface display. If you deselect the Use HUD In Application check box, you can use the traditional dialog box interface. By default, the Heads Up Display (HUD) interface is selected.

On the Beam Model tab, you can choose to automatically create rigid links, which allows you to adjust the model during automatic conversion. When the check box is cleared, rigid links are not created automatically during model conversion, but you can create rigid links manually later. You can also use the Trim Mitered Beam Ends option to trim overlapping ends during automatic model conversion, which simplifies the model and improves the accuracy of the simulation results.

The Solver and Diagrams tabs can be used to tweak the style of the simulation outputs and graphs ahead of time.

Frame Constraints

The concept of the constraint is the same for Frame Analysis, but the realities of how a frame is constructed can be different. Portions of the frame may be built with the ability to have one end move freely or slide along another member. This opens up the need to be able to approach things differently to assure accuracy.

You can access all the constraint types on the Constraints panel of the Frame Analysis tab, as shown in Figure 17.19.

FIGURE 17.19
The frame constraints

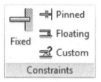

These are the types of constraints available:

Fixed Constraint   Like the Fixed constraint in FEA, it restricts all movement of the beam or node to which it is applied.

Pinned Constraint   Applying the Pinned constraint to a beam or node will allow rotation about the selected element, but it cannot move in space.

Floating Constraint   This constraint allows free rotation of the beam or node, but it also allows movement in one plane.

Custom Constraint   If you need a node or beam to be able to move or rotate within a boundary or with an amount of elasticity, the Custom constraint can establish those conditions in any or all directions, including the ability for that movement to be unidirectional for one value and free in another direction.

Frame Loads

When the need to apply a mesh to a frame model is removed, it may become necessary to define the loads in a different manner. This means that there are more options for loads in frame analysis.

The three primary loads are shown on the Loads panel of the Frame Analysis tab, as shown in Figure 17.20:

FIGURE 17.20
The frame loads

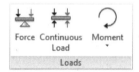

Force   This is specified in newtons (N) or pounds-force (lbf or lbforce). The value of the force can be applied to a node along the length of a beam. Once an approximate position has been selected, a dialog will appear and prompt you for the position along the beam element. The icon that appears has a series of handles that allow you to change the angle of the plane in which the force is applied and the angle to the plane of the force; if you click the arrow that represents the direction of the force, the dialog will prompt you for the magnitude of force.

Continuous Load   This is specified in newtons (N) or pounds-force (lbf or lbforce). This force applies evenly to the entire beam segment. The settings allow you to specify End Magnitude, Direction, Offset, and Length values.

Moment   This is specified in units of torque such as newton meters (N m or N*m) or pounds-force per inch (lbforce in or lbf*in). A moment can be applied to a point at the end or along the beam segment with a graphical input similar to the onscreen feedback for applying a force.

There are also two types of load you can choose under Moment in a drop-down menu.

Axial Moment   This is specified in units of torque such as newton meters (N m or N*m) or pounds-force per inch (lbforce in or lbf*in). This is a moment that can be applied along the axis of the selected beam. You can control the position of the moment along the axis, but it is automatically normal to the axis.

Bending Moment   This is specified in units of torque such as newton meters (N m or N*m) or pounds-force per inch (lbforce in or lbf*in). A bending moment can be applied to a point at the end or along the beam segment. It is applied in the plane of the axis. You can change the angle about the axis to which it is applied.

Connections

Working with Frame Generator by its nature involves situations where additional information may need to be added to the model for a proper simulation: conditions where there are gaps or flexibility in the model or you want to add additional nodes.

The tools for adding additional information are located in the Connections panel of the Frame Analysis tab, as shown in Figure 17.21.

FIGURE 17.21
The Frame constraints

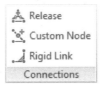

Release   This connection can be applied to a beam adjacent to another loaded beam. You can control the flexibility between the beams. The resistance to the movement can be controlled in the primary planes and around the axes using either a specific force or a partial stiffness coefficient.

Custom Node   You can add nodes along the beam to represent where contact will be made or to shortcut the loading process.

Rigid Link   If you have a machined or cast part built into your design, the Frame Analysis tool may not properly account for a rigid element between two points that appears to be free in the Frame Generator model. The Rigid Link tool allows you to select a parent node and have a child node maintain its position to it through the simulation.

Results

People doing Frame Analysis need to understand what is happening to the model along the length of a beam. In an FEA model, this is easy to visualize, and the coloration of the beam element also helps. Over time, methods for diagramming a beam have been developed, and to offer a familiar way to understand the results of the simulation, diagramming tools have been added to the Frame Analysis environment.

These tools are located in the Result panel of the Frame Analysis tab, as shown in Figure 17.22.

FIGURE 17.22
Diagramming tools

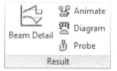

Beam Detail   This tool launches a dialog that allows you to see the basic results on the right and diagrams of the specific results for the selected beam on the left.

Animate   Results can be animated and recorded in order to observe the displacement or stress build up over a sequence of images.

Probe   Once a simulation is run, result values for specific points on the model can be visualized using the Probe tool. The Probe Labels button controls the visibility of probe results.

Diagram   Selecting this tool opens a dialog where you can request various results to be displayed on the model.

Additional tools in the Display panel will place beam and node labels in the design window (rather than highlighting them in the browser) so you can more easily understand where these elements are.

For static stress analysis, the tools offered for parts, assemblies, and frames will offer you a great opportunity to better know the effects of changes to your designs.

 Real World Scenario

CONSIDERING EVERY LOAD SCENARIO

An engineer was involved in a redesign of an equipment accessory that had unfortunately failed in the field. The problem originated from two sources. One was the use of an incorrect material that offered too much flexibility under a particular load condition.

However, the second dynamic of this failure stemmed from the way the design was actually used in the field. During the design process, the considerations were mostly focused on how the mechanism would be operated during installation and how it would hold up under its highest load during use. Both were valid design considerations, but neither predicted the ultimate failure of the design.

As it turned out, it was the way these accessories were uninstalled that led to their high rate of failure. Not having anticipated this part of the way the product was used, the design team had no means to understand the unique torque loads that would ultimately make a good design fail. In the end, a slight modification to the design and the use of a different material type resolved the issue, but not before many dollars were wasted purchasing components that ultimately could not be used.

Keep this in mind as you create simulations, and remember that the results you generate can be only as good as the assumptions you make. Simulating every loading situation your design might encounter will expose these things before the first part is made or purchased.

Conducting Dynamic Simulations

Dynamic simulation is useful during the prototyping stages of design to test the function of interacting parts and for use in failure analysis where interacting parts enact stresses upon one another. When creating a dynamic simulation, you should follow the basic workflow listed here:

1. Define joints to establish component relationships.

2. Define environmental constraints such as gravity, forces, imposed motions, joint friction, and joint torque.

3. Run the simulation.

4. Analyze the output graph to determine maximum or minimum stress at a given time step, maximum or minimum velocities, and so on.

5. Export the results to the Stress Analysis environment for motion stress analysis simulation.

To access the Dynamic Simulation tools, first open the assembly in which you want to create the simulation and then click the Dynamic Simulation button on the Environments tab.

Working with Joints

In the Dynamic Simulation environment, joints are used to define the way that components can move relative to one another. Although you might at first associate joints with assembly relationships such as constraints, joints and constraints are actually two separate concepts. In the assembly environment, all components are assumed to have six degrees of free motion until grounded or constrained in such a way that some or all of these degrees of freedom (DOF) are removed. Standard joints approach the issue of DOF from the opposite end. In the Dynamic Simulation environment, all components are assumed to have zero DOF until joints are applied to add free motion. You can then add special joint types manually to restrict degrees of freedom.

Understanding the difference between assembly relationships and joints is important when working with joints. However, if you have a properly constrained model, much of the joint creation can be automated by setting the Simulation Settings option to Automatically Convert Constraints To Standard Joints. You can do this by clicking the Simulation Settings button on the Dynamic Simulation tab. Figure 17.23 shows the Automatically Convert Constraints To Standard Joints option.

FIGURE 17.23
Automatic constraint-to-joint conversion

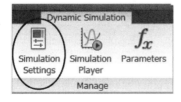

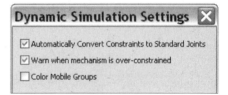

When the Convert Constraints option is on, any assembly relationships that are changed will automatically update and be converted to a standard joint when possible. You can apply relationships while in the Dynamic Simulation environment by switching to the Assemble tab.

When joints are built automatically from assembly relationships, you can retain them in the model when the translator is turned off. This allows you to customize the standard joints built from relationships and author new standard joints, without starting from scratch.

When the Convert Constraints option is off, you can use the Convert Constraints button to manually convert assembly relationships. To convert constraints manually, you must have the automatic Convert Constraints option turned off and the Convert Assembly Constraint button enabled. Using the Convert Assembly Constraint tool, you simply select the parts to which you want to apply a joint, and the Assembly constraints that exist between the two will appear in the dialog box. You can deselect one or more of the constraints to apply a less-restrictive joint solution. Figure 17.24 shows the different results achieved by selecting or deselecting the relationships that exist on a shaft and handle.

FIGURE 17.24
Manual constraint-to-joint conversion

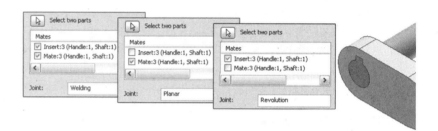

In addition to the automatic joint creation, you can (and most often need to) apply joints to your model manually. You can access the joint tool by clicking the Insert Joint button. When you do so, the Insert Joint dialog box offers a drop-down with all the joint types listed. Alternatively, you can click the Display Joints Table button next to the drop-down to display the five joint categories as buttons in the top of the table. Clicking a category button shows the available joint types for that category. Figure 17.25 shows the joint categories.

FIGURE 17.25
Joint categories

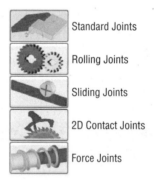

Standard Joints

Rolling Joints

Sliding Joints

2D Contact Joints

Force Joints

STANDARD JOINTS

Standard joints are created by converting assembly relationships to joints, either automatically or manually. Only one type of standard joint, called Spatial, is listed in the Display Joints table when the option to automatically create constraints is on. Here is a list of all the standard joints:

Revolution Joints   Used to create a rotational relationship between cylindrical faces and axes of two components.

Prismatic Joints   Used to constrain the edge of one component to the edge of another.

Cylindrical Joints   Used to constrain the axis of one cylindrical component to the axis of another, thereby allowing the second component to slide along the axis of the first.

Spherical Joints   Used to create ball-and-socket joints between two components.

Planar Joints   Used to constrain the planar face of one component to the planar face of another. The first component is the motionless component, and the second is allowed to move along the face of the first.

Point-Line Joints   Used to constrain the center point of a sphere to the axis of a cylinder or a point on another component.

Line-Plane Joints   Used to constrain a planar face of one component to a point on another.

Point-Plane Joints   Used to constrain the point of one component to the planar face of another.

Spatial Joints   Used to create a relationship between two components where all six degrees of freedom are allowed without causing errors of redundancy in the simulation.

Welding Joints   Used to create a relationship between two components so there are no degrees of freedom between them and they are considered a single body in the simulation.

ROLLING JOINTS

Ten types of rolling joints are available. Rolling joints are used to restrict degrees of freedom. Here is a list of the rolling joint types:

Rolling Cylinder On Plane Joints   Used to constrain a rotating cylindrical face to a 2D planar face. The relative motion between the two selected components is required to be 2D. A basic, continuous cylindrical face is required for this joint type.

Rolling Cylinder On Cylinder Joints   Used to constrain one rotating cylindrical face to another rotating cylindrical face. The relative motion between the two selected components is required to be 2D. A basic, continuous, cylindrical face is required for this joint type.

Rolling Cylinder In Cylinder Joints   Used to constrain one rotating cylindrical face to the inside of another rotating cylindrical face. The relative motion between the two selected components is required to be 2D. A basic, continuous, cylindrical face is required for this joint type.

GEARS AND ROLLING JOINTS

If you have created a gear using the design accelerator, you will find a basic surface cylinder present in the part model. To make the surface available for use in the creation of rolling joints, you can edit the part and set the surface to be visible.

Rolling Cylinder Curve Joints   Used to constrain a rotating cylindrical face to maintain contact with a curved face such as a cam. The relative motion between the two selected components is required to be 2D.

Belt Joints   Used to constrain a belt component to two cylindrical components that rotate. Faces, edges, and sketches can be selected.

Rolling Cone On Plane Joints   Used to constrain a rotating conical face to a 2D planar face. Faces, edges, and sketches can be selected.

Rolling Cone On Cone Joints   Used to constrain a rotating conical face to another rotating conical face. Faces, edges, and sketches can be selected.

Rolling Cone In Cone Joints   Used to constrain a rotating conical face to the inside face of a component that is not rotating. Faces, edges, and sketches can be selected.

Screw Joints   Used to constrain components that screw together by specifying a thread pitch to define the travel per rotation. Faces, edges, and sketches can be selected.

Worm Gear Joints   Used to constrain a component to a helical gear by specifying a thread pitch to define the travel per rotation. Faces, edges, and sketches can be selected.

Sliding Joints

The five joint types in the sliding category are used to restrict degrees of freedom between the two components selected. In all five, the relative motion between the two selected components is required to be 2D. Here are the five types of sliding joints:

Sliding Cylinder On Plane Joints   Used to constrain a cylindrical face to a 2D planar face so that it will slide along the plane without rotating

Sliding Cylinder On Cylinder Joints   Used to constrain a cylindrical face to slide on another cylindrical face

Sliding Cylinder In Cylinder Joints   Used to constrain a cylindrical face to slide inside another cylindrical face

Sliding Cylinder Curve Joints   Used to constrain a cylindrical face to slide on a curved face such as a cam

Sliding Point Curve Joints   Used to constrain a point on the second component to slide along a curve defined by the selected face, edge, or sketch on the first component

2D Contact Joints

There is only one joint type in this category, and it is used to restrict degrees of freedom.

2D Contact Joints   Creates contact between curves on two selected components. Curves can be faces, edges, or sketches, but the relative motion between the selections must be planar. The contact is not required to be permanent for this joint type.

3D Contact Joints

3D contact joints create an action or reaction force when applied. This category consists of just two joint types.

Spring/Damper/Jack Joints   These create joints for resisting forces, shock absorption, and lift jacking forces.

3D Contact Joints   These detect the contact and interference between all the surfaces of two selected parts. Subassemblies are not considered in this joint type.

More on Working with Joints

When components are assigned joints, either manually or automatically, they are grouped according to the results of the joints in the browser. For instance, if components are fully constrained to one another in the assembly, they will be assigned a weld joint and listed in the browser as a welded group. If one of those components is grounded, the welded group will be listed in the Grounded folder in the browser. If one of them is used in a motion joint, it will be listed in the Mobile Groups folder. Figure 17.26 shows an assembly with two welded groups present. One is listed under Grounded, and the other is listed under Mobile Groups. You'll notice that both are used in the joint called Revolution:2.

FIGURE 17.26

Browser grouping

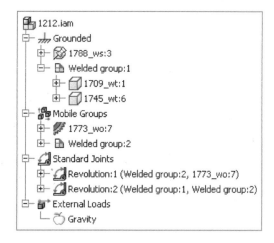

Here are some points to remember when creating joints:

◆ The Joint Table displays a pictorial representation for each joint type to assist you with determining which to use.

◆ Assembly relationships are not converted to joints in a one-to-one fashion; instead, joints are often created by combining assembly relationships. For instance, a Mate and two Flush constraints between two parts might be converted to a weld joint.

◆ Dynamic simulation performance is affected by the number of joints present. If you are simulating a particular set of components in a large assembly, it might be beneficial to manually weld most of the components and consider motion only for the set you need.

◆ When placing a joint, you are often required to align the z-axis of the joint on both components. Failing to do so will prompt a warning.

◆ If you have the option to automatically convert the assembly relationships selected, any assembly relationship you place in the Dynamic Simulation environment will automatically be converted to a standard joint.

When placing joints, you should keep an eye on the coordinate triad and ensure that the arrows align when required. Figure 17.27 shows the use of the flip arrow to align the z-axis.

FIGURE 17.27
Aligning component
axes

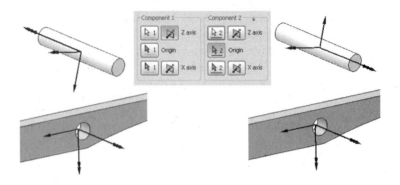

To more easily review the joints that you've placed, you can select components in the browser or the design window and joints associated with them will be highlighted in the browser.

Working with Redundancy

In the Dynamic Simulation environment, joints are said to contain redundancy when they are overconstrained or have too many unknowns to solve. When redundancy occurs in a joint, Inventor prompts you to use the Repair Redundancy tool to repair the joint. In most cases, this tool suggests one or more solutions. Figure 17.28 shows a link assembly that has a redundancy in joint 4, the cylindrical joint. To resolve this, the Mechanism Status tool is selected.

FIGURE 17.28
Using the Mechanism
Status tool to resolve
redundant joints

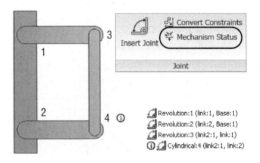

In the Mechanism Status And Redundancies dialog box, you can use the >> button to expand the options for resolving a redundancy. Typically, a new joint type is suggested for the redundant joint. Often you can expand the drop-down and select from a list of possible alternatives, as shown in Figure 17.29. This dialog can also be shown while the simulation is running.

FIGURE 17.29
Resolving a redundant
joint

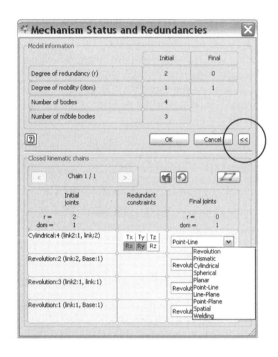

Also listed in the Mechanism Status and Redundancies dialog box are the redundant constraints. Tx, Ty, and Tz are the translational (linear) constraints, and Rx, Ry, and Rz are the rotational constraints. In Figure 17.29, the cylindrical joint shows that the Rotational X (Rx) and Rotational Y (Ry) are redundant.

Working with Environmental Constraints

Once joints are applied to the model, it is often necessary to apply environmental constraints to make the joints perform more realistically or to set the simulation up more efficiently. For example, if you apply a prismatic joint between a rail and a linear bearing pad, a certain amount of friction would be anticipated, so you would modify the joint and apply a dry friction coefficient value. You might also want to create an imposed spring to emulate a spring cushion in the slide channel or set the start position of the slide for the simulation. And then you might want to apply an imposed motion on the joint so that it moves during the simulation as expected. All of this can be done by right-clicking the joint and choosing Properties. When an environmental constraint for a particular joint is added, the constraint is marked with a green number sign next to it in the browser, as shown in Figure 17.30.

FIGURE 17.30
A joint with an
environmental
constraint set

Modifying the Initial Position

Often you will want to change the initial position of a component involved in a joint so that the simulation will run differently from the way it is constrained. For instance, the rail and bearing pad example might be constrained so that the bearing is in the start position, but for the purposes of reducing the time of the simulation, it needs to run only from the middle of the cycle to the end. Setting the initial position allows this. To adjust the initial position of a joint, follow these steps:

1. Right-click the joint in the browser and select Properties.

2. Select the appropriate DOF tab. Depending on the joint, there may be multiple DOFs.

3. Click the Edit Initial Conditions button.

4. Enter a new position value in the input box.

Here are some additional options that may apply, depending on the simulation and results you are trying to achieve:

◆ Select Locked so that the joint cannot be modified in the simulation.

◆ Deselect the Velocity check box to manually set the initial velocity of this degree of freedom or leave it selected to allow the software to automatically compute the initial velocity. I recommend you leave this set at Computed and impose a velocity using the Impose motion option (covered in the coming pages).

◆ Set the initial minimum or maximum bounds values for the degree of freedom, if desired. Value sets the boundary for the force or torque of this DOF, Stiffness sets the stiffness of this DOF, and Damping sets the damping boundary for this DOF.

Joint Torques

Joint torques can be set to control damping and friction and also to impose a spring cushion. Depending on the simulation, you can often apply these things to a few key joints and have other dependent joints react off them. Of course, this depends on the mechanism and the simulation. To adjust a joint for these things, follow these steps:

1. Right-click the joint in the browser and select Properties.

2. Select the appropriate DOF tab (depending on the joint, there may be several).

3. Click the Edit Joint Torque button (the appearance of this button varies between rotational and translational joints).

4. Select the Enable Joint Torque check box.

5. Right-click an input box and choose the input type required. Use Constant Value if the value does not change over time, or use the Input Grapher to enter a graduated input.

Figure 17.31 shows the Joint Torque properties for a prismatic joint.

FIGURE 17.31
Adding friction
and damping to
a joint

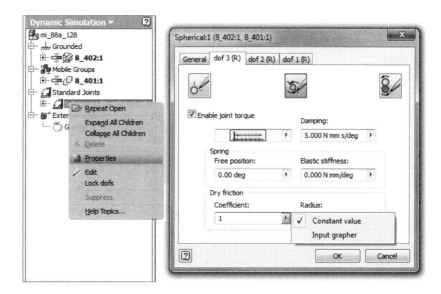

The range of inputs for Damping, Elastic Stiffness, and Friction are listed here:

◆ Damping is proportional to the velocity of the DOF.

◆ Free Position sets the position at which an imposed spring exerts no force.

◆ Elastic Stiffness sets the imposed spring stiffness.

◆ Friction is added as a coefficient between 0 and 2.

IMPOSED MOTION

Although motion can be created by applying external forces where it is important, often an imposed motion on a joint is desired to allow control of the timing and position of components not involved in an external force. For instance, in the rail and bearing pad example, the bearing might need to slide out of the way of another component that is being driven by an external force. Setting the imposed motion in the joint properties allows this to happen without the need to apply an external force on the bearing pad. To adjust a joint to include an imposed motion, follow these steps:

1. Right-click the joint in the browser and select Properties.

2. Select the appropriate DOF tab (depending on the joint, there may be multiples).

3. Click the Edit Imposed Motion button.

4. Select the Enable Imposed Motion check box.

5. Select a Driving motion parameter type and enter a value. The parameter types are as follows:

Position   Imposes a motion to a specified position, typically specified using the Input Grapher to set the position relative to a time step (for example, move 100 cm over 10 seconds).

Velocity   Imposes a motion at a specified velocity. Use constant input or use the Input Grapher to enter a variable velocity to account for startup times and so on.

Acceleration   Imposes a motion as a specified acceleration. Use constant input or use the Input Grapher to enter a variable acceleration.

Using the Input Grapher

The Input Grapher is available in a number of input boxes used throughout the Dynamic Simulation environment. When an input is set to use the Input Grapher, a Graph button is present in the input box. If no Graph button is present, you can right-click in the input box and select Input Grapher from the context menu. To open the Input Grapher, simply click the Graph button.

Typically, the Input Grapher is used to specify a value that varies over time. In Figure 17.32, a velocity is being imposed on a joint starting at 0 in/s and coming up to 100 in/s in the first 10 seconds, at which time it levels off for the next 10 seconds before returning to 0 in/s at 30 seconds. The user has right-clicked in the graph to add a control point.

FIGURE 17.32
Adding a velocity curve with the Input Grapher

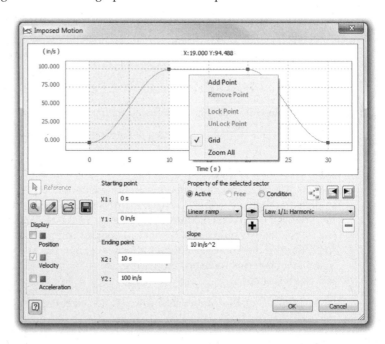

Each portion of the graph between points is selectable as a sector by clicking the graph. In Figure 17.32, the first sector is selected and is shaded. When a sector is selected, the inputs in the bottom half of the Input Grapher dialog box are specific to that sector. You can edit the sector's start point and endpoint as well as the law applied to that specific sector.

You can modify the input graph by changing the x-axis variable, the laws applied, the freeing sector condition, and more. The following sections briefly describe these graph input variables.

Input References

By default, Time is the x-axis variable for the curve graph in the Input Grapher. In many inputs, you can specify a different x-axis reference. Clicking the Reference button displays all variables available to be used as x-axis variables in the curve graph. Imposed motions cannot use x-axis references other than Time. Figure 17.33 shows a curve graph being set to call Velocity as the x-axis of the curve.

FIGURE 17.33

Setting the Input Grapher to use Velocity rather than Time

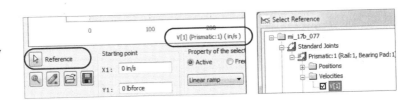

Laws

To define each sector of a curve, you can assign mathematical functions, or *laws*. These laws can be applied individually or in combination as needed to fully define the sector curve. To assign a sector a specific law, select the law from the list in the drop-down and then use the arrow button to apply the law. Use the plus button to add laws to the sector, and use the minus button to remove laws from the sector. Here is a list of the available laws:

◆ Linear Ramp

◆ Cubic Ramp

◆ Cycloid

◆ Sine

◆ Polynomial

◆ Harmonic

◆ Modified Sine

◆ Modified Trapezoid

◆ Spline

◆ Formula

Freeing and Application Conditions

Each sector can be set to Active, Free, or Condition. Active indicates that the sector has no conditions. Free indicates that the sector has no values defined. Condition indicates that one or more conditions have been assigned to the sector.

To create a condition, click the Condition radio button. By default, the Freeing Conditions dialog box appears. To edit or add a condition, click the Define Conditions button and then click the Variable, Equal, or Value link to set those options. Use the plus an minus signs to add or remove conditions. Figure 17.34 shows a condition being added.

FIGURE 17.34
Adding conditions

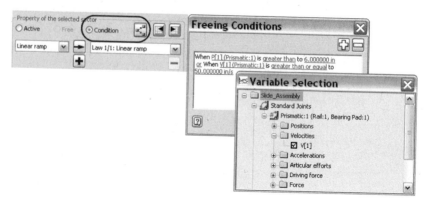

More Functions

The Input Grapher has a few functions that might not be apparent but are useful to know about when you're setting up and using it:

◆ The bottom display is dependent on what is selected in the graph. Selecting a point gives inputs for just that point, selecting a sector gives sector options, and clicking in the graph outside all sectors gives Out Of Definition options that are used to describe the part of the curve on the left or right of the first and last points.

◆ Using the wheel button on your mouse, you can pan and zoom in the graph. This can be helpful when dealing with sectors that are dramatically different in scale. You can also use the Zoom button in the Input Grapher dialog box.

◆ Curve definitions can be saved and loaded using the Save Curve and Load Curve buttons.

EXTERNAL FORCES

To set a component in motion, you can apply an imposed motion on the joint or apply an external force on the component itself. External forces consist of loads and gravity. External forces can be used to initiate, complement, or resist movement. For instance, in the rail and bearing pad example, if the bearing traveled past a catch stop mechanism designed to prevent back travel, you might apply an external force on the bearing pad at that position to ensure that it can overcome a maximum resistance. External forces are often used just to set the simulation in motion as well. Loads and gravity are further defined here.

Loads

You can apply as many force and torque loads as required and manage them from the External Loads browser node, where all force and torque loads are listed once created. To apply external load forces, click the Force or Torque button on the Load panel, and set the location, direction, magnitude, and so on, as described here:

Location For the Location setting, a vertex must be selected. You can select a vertex, circular edge, sketch point, work point, and so on.

Direction   For the Direction setting, select an edge or face and then use the Flip button to change it if needed.

Magnitude   Enter the Magnitude setting as a constant, or select Input Grapher.

Fixed and Associative Load Buttons   Use the Fixed and Associative load buttons to designate the load direction method. Fixed sets the load to be constant to the direction in which it is defined. Associative sets the direction to follow the component as it moves during the simulation. For instance, if an Associative direction is established using the edge of a hinge, the direction will stay aligned to that edge as the hinge swings.

The >> Button   Use the >> button to set the vector components as required.

Display Check Box   Set the Display check box to see the Force or Torque arrow and then set the scale and color of the arrow.

Gravity

You can define the gravity for the entire simulation by expanding the External Load node in the browser, right-clicking the Gravity button, and choosing Define Gravity. A default value of 386.220 in/s^2 or 9810.000 mm/s^2 is supplied, but you can edit this to any value required. To define gravity, you simply select an object face or edge and then use the Flip button to set the direction. You should choose static components to define gravity.

Running a Simulation

Once the model is defined with joints, loads, and environmental constraints, you are ready to run the simulation. Running the simulation involves two primary controls: the Simulation Player and the Output Grapher. The tools are generally used together.

SIMULATION PLAYER

You use the Simulation Player to run and stop the simulation. The Simulation Player is displayed by default but can be toggled on and off using the Simulation Player button on the Manage panel of the Dynamic Simulation tab. Figure 17.35 shows the Simulation Player options, and Table 17.1 provides a description of each.

FIGURE 17.35
The Simulation Player

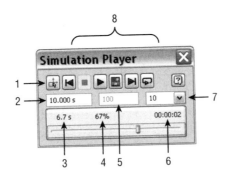

TABLE 17.1:   Simulation Player options

ITEM NUMBER	TITLE	DEFINITION
1	Construction Mode	Once the simulation is run, use this button to return to the construction mode to make changes.
2	Final Time	Enter the simulation's running time.
3	Simulation Time	This displays the current time step in the running simulation.
4	Percentage Of Completed Simulation	This displays the percent complete value for the running simulation.
5	Images	This value is set in construction mode to control the number of image frames displayed during the simulation. A higher number results in a higher-quality simulation display (smoother motion) but comes at the expense of performance.
6	Real Time Of Computation	This displays the amount of time it has taken to run the simulation.
7	Filter	This sets the number of images displayed during the simulation playback. If this is set to 10, for instance, image 1 is displayed and then image 10, skipping 2 through 9. This can be used to gain performance for large or complex simulations.
8	Player Controls	These include the standard play, stop, rewind to the beginning, fast-forward to the end, and continuous loop controls as well as a Deactivate Screen Refresh During Simulation control. Deactivating the screen refresh speeds up the simulation.

THE OUTPUT GRAPHER

You can access the Output Grapher during or after running a simulation to view and use the data collected during the simulation. Data can be exported to Microsoft Excel or marked for use in the Stress Analysis environment. You can also export the results as an IAA (*.iaa) file and import the file into another simulation for comparison of the graph results.

Once the curve type is selected, you can examine the time steps to see the value for each step. Figure 17.36 shows an acceleration curve displayed in the Output Grapher. The time step for six seconds is selected (1) and is marked in the graph area with a vertical line (2). You can click in the graph area to select a time stamp or select it from the top pane. You can also use the arrow keys on the keyboard to advance through each step.

FIGURE 17.36
An acceleration curve
in the Output Grapher

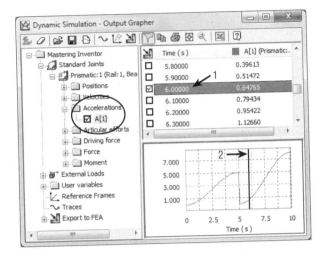

You can use the Save Simulation button to save a simulation result before making changes and then use the Import Simulation button to bring it back in once the modified simulation has been run. This allows both simulation curves to be overlaid for comparison. Figure 17.37 shows the location of the Save and Import Simulation buttons in the Output Grapher dialog box. In this illustration, the original acceleration curve has been imported and overlaid onto a modified simulation. You can see that the changes made just after six seconds have slowed the extended lag time and have reduced the end acceleration from 8 in/s in the original to just over 6 in/s in the modified version. Both simulations are marked in the browser.

FIGURE 17.37
An imported
acceleration curve

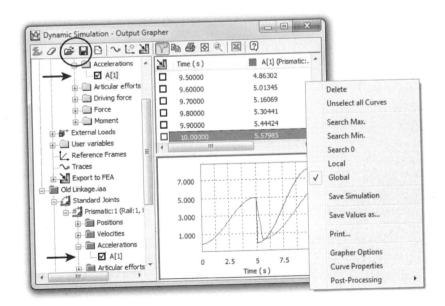

Also shown in Figure 17.37, the context menu is obtained by right-clicking either of the curve columns. From this menu you can search for the minimum and maximum values as well as zero values. You can also select Curve Properties and change the curve colors as well as analyze the average, minimum, maximum, median, standard deviation, and amplitude of the curve.

Exporting to FEA

You can use the Output Grapher to identify maximum forces and then export those forces for use in the Stress Analysis environment. Although the maximum stress is likely the most common value to be exported, you can export the force for any time step in the simulation. This can be useful when trying to focus on a particular event in the simulation. Here are the steps for exporting a maximum force:

1. Select that force in the left pane of the Output Grapher.

2. Right-click and choose Search Max.

3. Select the check box for the time step identified as the maximum value.

4. Click the Export To FEA button in the Output Grapher or on the Dynamic Simulation tab.

5. Select the part or parts to export the load information to.

6. Select the load-bearing faces on the part or parts.

Figure 17.38 shows the steps involved in exporting the time step to FEA. Notice that once the time step is exported, it is listed in the Export To FEA node in the Output Grapher browser. You should also note that you can export multiple time steps at once by selecting them all before clicking the Export To FEA button.

FIGURE 17.38
Exporting a maximum load time step to FEA

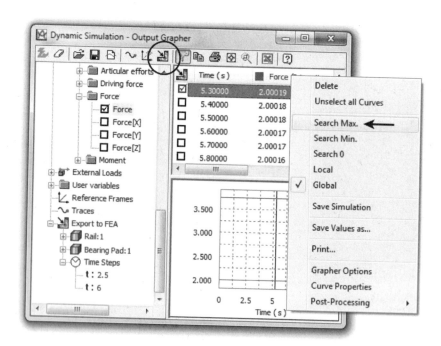

Using the Dynamic Simulation Information in Stress Analysis

Once you've exported the information from the Dynamic Simulation environment, you can select the Environments tab and click the Stress Analysis button to enter that environment. Follow these steps:

1. Click the Create Simulation button, or right-click an existing simulation and choose Edit Simulation Properties.

2. In the Simulation Properties dialog box, select the Motion Loads Analysis check box and then select the part and time step on which you intend to run the simulation analysis. Then click the OK button.

3. Make modifications to the simulation parameters if needed and then run the simulation.

You should note that a motion-loads analysis is limited to a single part occurrence and a single time step, per simulation. You can create multiple simulations to consider other time stamps or parts. All other components are automatically excluded from the simulation for motion loads. Figure 17.39 shows the Motion Loads Analysis option in the Simulation Properties dialog box.

FIGURE 17.39
Enabling motion loads from dynamic simulation

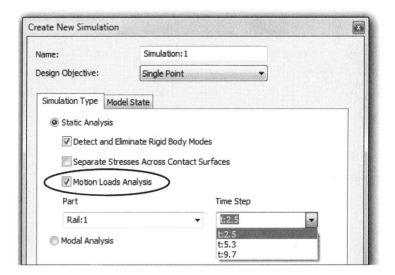

The Bottom Line

Set up and run Stress Analysis simulations. Oftentimes you may find yourself guessing at what impact a change to your design might have on the strength and overall integrity of your part. Questions such as "Can I make this part a bit lighter?" or "Can I move this cutout closer to the edge?" become important to the success of your design.

Master It Set up a parameter study in your model to explore the consequences of editing features and their locations. Nominate all the crucial parameters to the table and then create the configuration simulations for all of the combinations.

Set up and run Dynamic Simulations.   When you find yourself working out the details of a design with many moving parts, consider using the Dynamic Simulation tools early in the process to prove what will or will not work before going forward.

Master It   Even before the assembly is complete, switch to the Dynamic Simulation environment and create assembly relationships in the simulation. Test the motion as you build the parts, and attempt to understand how contact will occur from the beginning.

Export results from the Dynamic Simulation environment to the Stress Analysis environment.   Often when setting up a stress analysis simulation, you are guessing at what the loads might be, based on rough calculations. As you make changes to the design, those calculations become out-of-date and therefore invalid.

Master It   How do you use the Dynamic Simulation tools to determine the force exerted on one part by another?

Chapter 18

Routed Systems

This chapter will cover the tools of the routed systems environments in the Autodesk® Inventor® Professional suite and the Inventor Routed Systems Suite. Inventor routed systems comprise two primary toolsets: tube and pipe, and cable and harness. The tube and pipe tools are used in routing pipe and hosing through mechanical assembly designs. The cable and harness tools are used for electrical design where routing wires and cables around obstacles and checking for fit are important.

In this chapter, you'll learn to

♦ Create routes and runs

♦ Author a tube and pipe component

♦ Author an electrical component

♦ Create and document cable and harness assemblies

Tube and Pipe

The tube and pipe tools are based on fundamental Inventor concepts such as sweeps, 3D sketch paths, adaptive parts, subassembly structure, and more. The tube and pipe tools automate many of these fundamentals, making the design of tube and pipe routes faster, more intuitive, and less tedious. However, it is best to have an understanding of these fundamental concepts before jumping into the tube and pipe tools so you can understand how Inventor does things and, therefore, how to proceed when required to manually adjust or repair your designs. A lack of understanding of these fundamentals can often bring inexperienced Inventor users to a screeching halt in their tube and pipe endeavors and may leave them with a perception that the tools just don't work. Therefore, in the following sections, you will explore how to create routes, runs, and general tube and pipe assembly structure and learn how to work with tube and pipe styles.

Understanding Routes, Runs, and Assembly Structure

Understanding the way that tube and pipe assembly structure is created is an important part of successfully creating and managing your tube and pipe designs. There are three primary levels to any tube and pipe assembly:

♦ A top-level assembly

♦ A tube and pipe run assembly

♦ A run assembly

All tube and pipe designs are made up of runs. A *run* is a subassembly that contains one or more route paths, pipe or hose segments, and fittings. For instance, a standard hot-water supply line is a run.

When you begin a tube and pipe design, you start with a new assembly template and click the Tube And Pipe button on the Environments tab. Doing so opens the Create Tube & Pipe Run dialog box, prompting you to set a name and location for the tube and pipe runs assembly file and the first run assembly file. Figure 18.1 shows the Create Tube & Pipe Run dialog box for a top-level assembly, named mi_18a_100, being created. You can also add a new tube and pipe assembly to an existing assembly.

FIGURE 18.1

The Create Tube
& Pipe Run dialog box

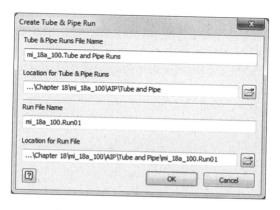

Notice that the default paths are created based on where the top-level assembly is stored. In this case, mi_18a_100.iam is stored in a subfolder of the Chapter 18 folder called mi_18a_100. The tube and pipe runs assembly is simply a container assembly created to contain the multiple runs you might create in the design. It is prefixed with the top-level assembly name, to which .Tube and Pipe Runs is added. The default save folder for the pipe runs is located under the top assembly and is named top assembly name, then AIP\Tube and Pipe.

The run assembly is prefixed with the top-level assembly name, to which .Run is added. Each run receives an incremental suffix (in this case 01) and saved to a folder with the same incremental name located under the top assembly, AIP\Tube and Pipe. Although you can change this file structure per tube and pipe assembly, accepting the default maintains a certain standardization of structure. Figure 18.2 shows the assembly browser structure and file structure of a tube and pipe design set to the default paths.

Once a run is created, you can create a route within it. *Routes* are 3D paths created to define the path for pipes, tubes, or hoses to follow. In Figure 18.2, there are two elbow fittings (DIN 2605 90 Deg Elbow) that were placed outside the run and in the tube and pipe runs assembly. Route01 was then created as a component of Run01, starting from one of the DIN elbows and running to the other. Run01 consists of Route01, three pipe segments, and two 90-degree elbows.

Although the pipe segments and the route path files were saved under the Run01 folder, you'll notice that the elbow files were saved to the Content Center Files path. Because fittings such as elbows, tees, and couplings are generated from Content Center, these part files are automatically saved to the Content Center Files path defined in either your project file or your application options (unless you have the Prompt For Fitting option selected in the settings, in which case they are saved in the Run folder).

FIGURE 18.2
Assembly and file
structure of tube and
pipe design

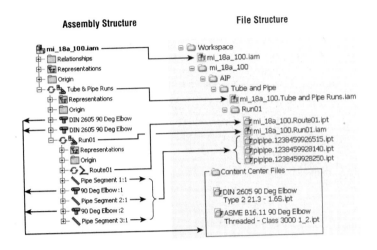

Here are a few things to note when working with tube and pipe runs.

◆ A unique part file is created for each pipe, tube, and hose segment in the run, even if more than one segment is the same length. Although this approach may seem like a departure from what you'd expect, it is key to allowing runs to be edited downstream.

◆ Enter meaningful names for the runs and routes as you create them. As you create more complex designs, having multiple Route01s scattered throughout the assembly may create confusion during edits.

Tube and Pipe Settings

You can control tube and pipe document and application settings in the Tube & Pipe Settings dialog box, shown in Figure 18.3. To access the dialog box, create the first tube and pipe run, activate the top assembly or master runs assembly, right-click in the browser, and select Tube & Pipe Settings.

FIGURE 18.3
Tube & Pipe Settings
dialog box

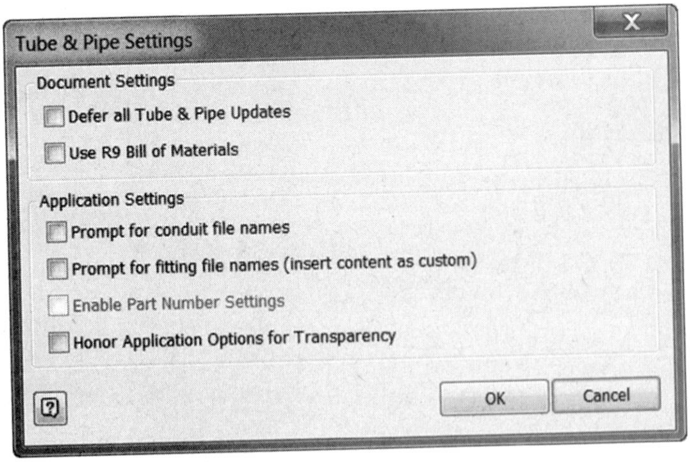

Exploring the Tube and Pipe Styles

Runs and routes are determined by tube and pipe styles. Properties such as material, diameter, and fitting types are set in the tube and pipe style. Rules such as minimum and maximum segment length can also be set in the style. The Inventor tube and pipe tools load with several default styles based on the ANSI, DIN, ISO, and JIS tube and pipe standards and the Parker hose and fittings. Styles fall into three primary categories.

Flexible Hose   These are single hose segments connected by a start point and endpoint selection. The hose style can include, but is not required to have, fittings for the start and stop points.

Tubing with Bends   This does not contain elbows and follows a default bend radius. The radius can be set per bend as needed. Minimum and maximum segment lengths are set in the style, and couplings are placed where segments connect. Couplings are optional for this style, just like start and end fittings of the hose.

Rigid Pipe with Fittings   These styles are required to include 90-degree elbow fittings and can include 45-degree elbows, flanges, and couplings. There are three subcategories for rigid piping styles.

Self Draining   These styles require a pipe, a coupling, a 45-degree elbow, a 90-degree elbow, and a custom elbow or tee to match the desired slope angle. Coupling and 45-degree elbow are optional for this style.

Butt Welded   These styles require a pipe and a 90-degree elbow. Butt welded styles require a weld gap size. A 45-degree elbow can be specified as well but is optional for this style.

Flanged   These styles require a pipe, an elbow, a flange, and optionally a gasket.

Mixed Units   If a flanged style is selected for rigid pipe, the Mixed Units option is enabled as a style choice for the end treatment. This option indicates that the style contains flanged fittings that use Imperial units and metric units.

Figure 18.4 shows a flexible hose run, a rigid tubing run, and a rigid piping run, from top to bottom.

FIGURE 18.4
Hose, tube, and
pipe runs

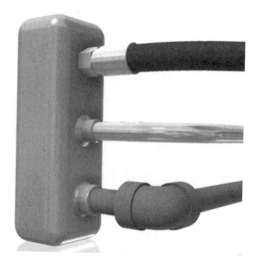

USING THE TUBE & PIPE STYLES DIALOG BOX

You can access the Tube & Pipe Styles dialog box by using the master tube and pipe runs assembly, by using the run assembly, by clicking the Tube And Pipe Styles button on the ribbon, or by using the default right-click context menu. The dialog box is divided into a pane on the left listing the styles and two tabs on the right controlling the general settings and the style rules. Figure 18.5 shows the Tube & Pipe Styles dialog box with a Hydraulic Hose style set active, denoted in bold. A second style is selected and has been right-clicked, showing the options that correspond to the buttons along the top of the dialog box.

FIGURE 18.5

The Tube & Pipe Styles dialog box

When you're editing, copying, or creating a new style, some components may be either required or optional, depending on the style type. If the component is not specified and it is required, it will be marked with a red arrow next to it on the General tab. If it is empty and shows a gray arrow, it is optional. When the component is selected, the arrow will be green. Figure 18.6 shows a pipe style being created from scratch.

This new style is a Butt Welded style and requires a pipe and a 90-degree elbow. The pipe has been selected, but the elbow is still required, as indicated by the red (dark) arrow. The 45-degree elbow is not required, and its optional status is indicated by the gray (light) arrow. In Figure 18.6 the user has right-clicked in the Elbow 90 row and selected Browse in order to specify the required elbow type. You can also double-click a row to open the style library browser.

In the style library browser, you can select from the list of available styles based on the size, schedule, and material settings made on the General tab and the availability from the Content

Center library. You can set additional filtering in the style library browser. When you set the filter to a particular standard, the materials available for that particular standard are listed. If an asterisk is displayed, all the content for that setting is displayed.

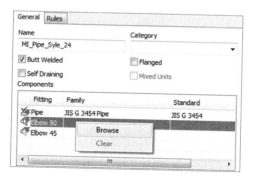

Back in the Tube & Pipe Styles dialog box, you can specify a minimum and maximum size range for creating route segments on the Rules tab. We recommend you set the minimum segment length to at least 1.5 times the nominal diameter value to avoid minimum segment length violations that occur when pipe segments are too small in relation to the nominal diameter.

Each style type has different rule criteria.

- For Rigid tubes, you can set the default bend radius for the bends. You can specify the minimum, maximum, and increment as well.

- For Flexible hoses, you can set a minimum bend radius and hose length round-up value.

- For Butt Welded pipe styles, you can set the gap size for the groove welds and control the display of the gaps in the graphics display and in drawings.

- For Butt Welded Flanged pipes, you can specify the coupling style. You can specify minimum, maximum, gap size, and control of the display of the gap as well.

- Fitting connections are determined by the end treatment set for the particular fitting.

Generally, it is best practice to set the style before creating routes and placing fittings. However, you can create and apply styles at any time. Styles can be set in a number of ways. You can change the active style for the tube and pipe assembly so that all new runs follow the style; you do this by selecting a style from the Style drop-down. Or you can change the style for the active route by setting that route as active and using the Style drop-down to select a different style. You cannot change a rigid pipe route to a flexible hose style, or vice versa. To make such a change, you must delete the route and re-create it.

AUTHORING TUBE AND PIPE COMPONENTS

Tube and pipe components, like components for other applications, require authoring before they can be published into Content Center. Only fittings that are needed to set up the tube and pipe style need to be published to Content Center; the rest can be anywhere on disk but not necessary a library folder. The tube and pipe authoring process is more complex because the router uses the component geometry. For example, the router needs to know the difference between a tee and an elbow, and it needs to know how much the connector overlaps the pipe.

If you have not already downloaded the Chapter 18 files from www.sybex.com/go/ masteringinventor2016, please refer to the "What You Will Need" section of the introduction for the download and setup instructions. Once you have the files downloaded, you can follow this example to author a PVC pipe to an NPT adapter:

1. On the Get Started tab, click the Open button and browse to the Chapter 18 directory in your Mastering Inventor 2016 folder.

2. Open the file mi_18a_010.ipt.

3. Switch to the Manage tab and select the Tube And Pipe Authoring button from the drop-down list on the Author panel (it might be displaying Component by default). The Tube & Pipe Authoring dialog box displays, and the part changes to shaded wireframe display.

4. Select Adapters from the Type drop-down, as shown in Figure 18.7.

FIGURE 18.7
Setting the fitting type

5. Change the number of connections, and observe that the connection buttons update to match. Confirm that Connections is set to **2**.

6. Confirm that End Treatment is set to Threaded and enter **1/2 in** for the Nominal Size setting.

7. By default, the button for connection 1 is active. Select one of the circular edges to define the connection point. Click the Axis button and select the z-axis from the Origin folder in the browser. You could select the circular edge again (any circular edge, for that matter). An arrow appears, showing the connection direction, as shown in Figure 18.8. The default connection type is Female, but you can set it to Male or Neutral (for flanged or butt-welded fittings).

8. The Engagement settings define the maximum and minimum overlap between the connector and pipe. The router needs a range because the pipe usually has a minimum length increment. The engagement range allows the router to adjust the position of the pipe in the fittings.

FIGURE 18.8
Defining the connection
and engagement

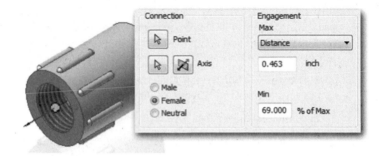

9. To determine the engagement, navigate to the Design Data folder (the default location is C:\Users\Public\Documents\Autodesk\Inventor 2016\Design Data\XLS\en-US\) and open threads.xls. Select the NPT For PVC Pipe And Fitting tab. For tapered threads, the engagement value depends on how tightly the fitting is screwed onto the pipe. You need the maximum engagement value, so add the Handtight Engagement value, which is 0.32, and the Wrench Makeup, Internal value, which is 0.1429. Set Max to Distance, and enter **0.4629** for the total value. For Min, divide the Handtight Engagement value, 0.32, by the total engagement value, 0.4629, which comes to 69 percent.

10. Click the 2 button to define the other connection.

11. In this example, we chose Socket Welded as the End Treatment setting since that seemed to be the best description. You should choose an end treatment that is consistent with your other parts.

12. Select a circle at the opposite end of the part for the connection point and select the z-axis again or the same point again for the axis. You will see that the arrow points into the adapter and the orange line representing the engagement is outside the part. Using the flip/arrow button next to the Axis button, change the direction so that the arrow is to the outside and the engagement is to the inside, as shown in Figure 18.9.

FIGURE 18.9
Connection direction
and engagement

13. The depth of the socket is 0.84 inch. You don't want to design to full-depth engagement because of tolerances, so set Max to Distance and specify **0.75** as the depth. For Min, accept the default value of 50 percent.

14. The ISOGEN data is optional. For this exercise, this information will be left blank. Click the OK button to complete authoring the adapter.

Now that the part has been authored as a tube and pipe adapter, it is ready to be published to a read/write Content Center library. This is optional; it can be stored anywhere on disk, ideally in a library folder. You can find more information on publishing parts to Content Center in Chapter 7, "Reusing Parts and Features."

Placing Fittings

Fittings can be placed from Content Center or from a user-created directory of authored fittings typically located within the project `file path.fittings`. As a rule, you should use the place tools on the Tube and Pipe tab rather than placing fittings as you would normal assembly parts. The place options on the Tube and Pipe tab ensure that the authored connections are used as intended. Figure 18.10 shows the place options available on the Pipe Run tab.

FIGURE 18.10
Place options available
on the Pipe Run tab

When fittings are placed, either from Content Center or from a user-defined library of authored fittings or any user folder, you can drag the fitting over the route segments or nodes, and you will see the placement point appear. Use the spacebar to toggle through available orientations if more than one exists. When you click to place the fitting, the Select Orientation tool appears, allowing you to rotate the orientation to the desired position.

You can edit connections by right-clicking the fitting while the route is active for edits and choosing Edit Fitting Connections. In the Edit Connections dialog box, you can select a segment and then use the X button to remove the connection. You can also select Change Fitting Diameter, as shown in Figure 18.11. Change Size will work on the current fitting only, while Change Fitting Diameter will work on multiple selections.

FIGURE 18.11
Editing fitting options

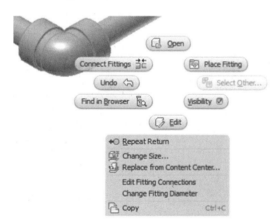

QUICKLY PLACE FITTINGS

If you need additional fittings that are identical to previously placed or populated fittings, you can select the fitting and then select the Place Fitting button from the Route panel. This will place a new fitting that matches the existing fitting. Note that you can do the same thing by selecting the fitting, right-clicking, and choosing Place Fitting.

If your model contains a fitting of a certain size and you want to place the same family of fitting but in a different size, you can select the existing fitting and then select the Place button from the Content panel. This will open Content Center with that fitting family active, allowing you to double-click the family and select the new size.

Creating Routes

Routes define the path for pipe and hose segments and the corresponding fittings. Route paths can have a simple start point and endpoint or can include as many intermediate points as are required. Several tools and options are used to start and create route paths.

Authored Connection Points You can use any of the predefined connection points for any library fitting or custom-authored part. When you move your mouse pointer over the library fitting, the connection points will highlight.

Circular Edges You can use any circular edge in the assembly to set the route point at the center of it with the exception of authored parts such as fittings. For those parts, only the authored connection points can be used.

Precise and Offset Start Points You can hover your mouse pointer over an edge to display a direction arrow. Hold the mouse over the tail of the arrow and either click to place at a visual distance or start typing a number, which will bring up the dimension dialog, or you can right-click and choose Enter Distance. If the arrow points in the wrong direction, you can use the spacebar to toggle it or right-click and choose Select Other Direction. Figure 18.12 shows the offset start point options.

FIGURE 18.12
Offsetting a start point

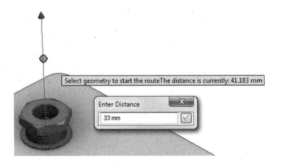

Select geometry to start the routeThe distance is currently: 41.183 mm

Enter Distance
33 mm

TURNING ON DYNAMIC PROMPTS

You can watch the lower left of your screen to see the help prompts Inventor gives you as you select tools and hover over objects on the screen, or you can turn on Dynamic Prompts to place these tips at your cursor so they are more noticeable.

To turn on Dynamic Prompts, go to the Tools tab and click the Application Options button; then click the General tab, locate the Prompting Interaction area in the dialog box, and select the Show Command Prompting (Dynamic Prompts) option.

3D Orthogonal Route Tool   Once a start point is selected, run your mouse pointer along the projected axis and click for visual node creation or just start typing a distance or use the context menu's Enter Distance option to set a value for the second point. You will then be presented with the 3D Orthogonal Route tool. You can use the control handles to change the angle or rotate the control. The cross arrow toggles between 90-degree and 45-degree solutions, and the arc arrows allow you to rotate the route tool. Just like with the axis, you can hold your pointer over an arc arrow and start typing the angle value. You can also right-click and choose Custom Bend to enter an angle other than 90 or 45. When you enter a Custom Bend angle that cannot be accommodated with an elbow fitting, Inventor will place a bend in the tube or pipe segment. Custom bends can also be added with the Bends command in the Create tab; the default radius is controlled with a B parameter, but manual values are allowed by editing each radius. When the 3D Orthogonal Route tool is displayed, you can use the + and – keys to change the size of it onscreen. Figure 18.13 shows the 3D Orthogonal Route tool in use.

FIGURE 18.13
Using the 3D
Orthogonal Route tool

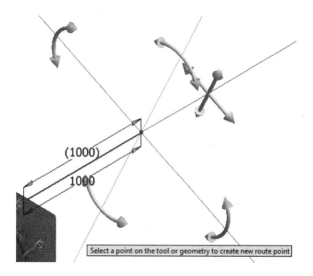

Select a point on the tool or geometry to create new route point

Route Nodes When placing a point along a route or setting an offset start point, you will see a colored dot tracking along the Route tool. If it is a yellow X, the offset is not enough to create a minimum segment as set in the style rules, and the point cannot be selected. If it is a blue dot, the segment might be too short to accommodate an elbow, but you are allowed to select it. If it is a green dot, the location is satisfactory to all the style rules. You can right-click and choose Enter Distance to display an input box. In Figure 18.14, the node (which looks like a dot) at the left of the image shows the placement with a distance of **2200 mm** entered.

FIGURE 18.14
Route nodes

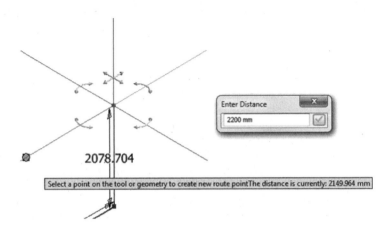

Autoroute Options You can select the start point and endpoint of a route and use the Autoroute tool to flip through the available Autoroute solutions. You can also use this to close two parts of an already created route. Use the Select Other tool to toggle through all the Autoroute variations. Once an Autoroute is created, use the Move Segment button to adjust the segments and create new solutions. Figure 18.15 shows an Autoroute with a suggested variation.

FIGURE 18.15
Autoroute and move
segment options

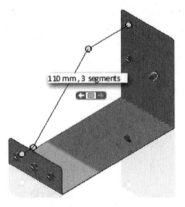

Sketched Routes Route paths can also be based on an existing 3D sketch. These 3D sketches are used as the route by deriving the geometry into the route. Changes to the 3D sketch update the route automatically. You can use the Include Geometry tool to include any existing part edges in the route. You can also select faces and planes that will create adaptive planes in your route. You can also switch to the 3D Sketch tab while creating a route and use the standard 3D sketch tools to create route geometry as required. Whether routing in the tool or using a derived route, watch the visual cues offered by the sketch.

CREATING A ROUTE FROM AN EXISTING SKETCH

Now you will use a combination of tools to create a pipe and tubing route based on an existing sketch.

1. On the Get Started tab, click the Open button and browse to the Chapter 18 directory in your Mastering Inventor 2016 folder.

2. Open the file mi_18a_015.iam.

3. From the Environments tab, click the Tube And Pipe button on the Begin panel.

4. Accept the defaults offered in the Create Tube And Pipe Run dialog by clicking the OK button.

In the browser you will see that a run has been created and it is active. There is also a specialized tab added to the ribbon named Pipe Run.

5. On the Manage panel of the Pipe Run tab, use the pull-down to select the B36.10M-ASME B16.11 – Steel Threaded Pipe style.

6. Click the New Route button on the Route panel.

7. Make note of the route part file location and then click the OK button to approve the default values for the Create Route dialog.

8. Another new tab will appear named Route. Select the Derived Route button from the Create panel.

9. Select the path that is already present in the assembly, as shown in Figure 18.16.

FIGURE 18.16
Selecting an existing 3D sketch as a piping route

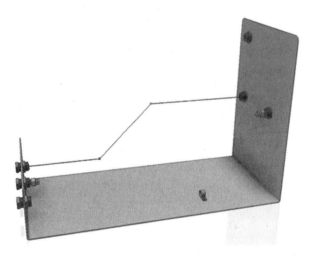

10. Right-click and select Done from the context menu to use the selected sketch as part of your pipe route.

This will add four route points to the route in the browser. Rather than focusing on all the geometry, you'll use just the points, which improves the assembly performance for the initial calculations and updates.

11. Select the Finish Route tool from the Route tab to return to the Pipe Run tools.

12. On the Route panel, click the Populate Route button to create the pipe and fittings for this route.

13. Once the route is populated, you can select the Finish Tube And Pipe Run button. Your pipe run should look like Figure 18.17.

FIGURE 18.17
The piping run created from the 3D sketch

14. Select the Finish Tube And Pipe button on the Tube And Pipe tab to exit the tube and pipe environment and return to the top level of the assembly.

15. In the browser, expand the mi_18a_012 part in the browser and double-click the 3D sketch to edit it.

16. Change the 9-inch dimension in the sketch to **11**.

17. Change the 135-degree dimension that does not have parentheses around it to **90**, as shown in Figure 18.18.

FIGURE 18.18
The updated 3D sketch

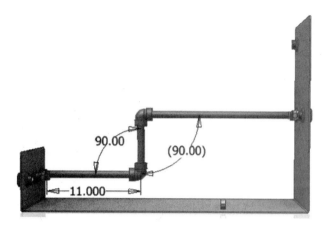

FIGURE 18.18
The updated 3D sketch

18. Click the Finish Sketch button and then click the Return button to update the assembly and the pipe route that you created based on it.

19. Turn off the visibility of the 3D sketch by right-clicking the sketch in the browser.

The use of a 3D sketch is not necessary to place a run like this, but it can be easier for some users to visualize the route before starting the routing tools. It is also a great tool for people who've used 3D sketches and sweep features to replicate piping runs in the past. You can save your work if you want to investigate the folders and file paths created, or you can close the file without saving changes and continue to the next set of steps.

CREATING A ROUTE USING THE 3D ORTHOGONAL ROUTE TOOL

Now you'll look at using the 3D Orthogonal Route tool to create a tubing section when no 3D sketch tool exists. To do so, open the file mi_18a_016.iam from the Chapter 18 directory. Then follow these steps:

1. On the Environments tab, select the Tube And Pipe button and click the OK button in the dialog to create a new run, noting that the run name has been incremented from the previous run.

2. In the Manage panel, set the style to ASTM B 88-ASME B16.22 – Soldered Copper Tubing.

3. Select the New Route button and click the OK button to accept the default naming.

4. Click the Route button on the Create panel.

5. Rotate the assembly so you can see the inside of the short flange of the base part. You will be working with the light blue center fitting.

6. As you near the fitting's point of engagement, arrows indicating the initial direction of a run will appear. If you hover your cursor over the various circular edges of the fitting,

you'll see the arrows flip directions. Select the option that will set the direction toward the fittings on the other flange of the base part, as shown in Figure 18.19, and click the mouse button when it is highlighted.

FIGURE 18.19

Setting the direction toward the other fittings

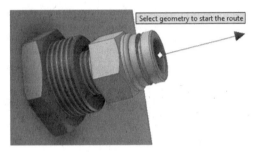

After the selection is made, a centerline will be displayed. Move your cursor along the line, and a dimension will display the distance from the selected point, as shown in Figure 18.20. You can increase the length of the line by pressing the + key on the keyboard, or you can use the keyboard to enter an explicit value. If you move your cursor to the 2.000 location or a location with a lower value, you'll see the selection indicator change to a yellow X. For anything above 2.000, the selection indicator will change to a green dot. This behavior is because of the bend radius default listed on the Rules tab of the Tube & Pipe Styles dialog box.

FIGURE 18.20

The preview allows you to visually place the end of the first segment.

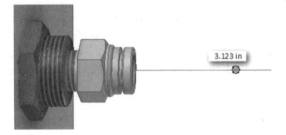

7. Click the 7 number key to set the length and then press Enter.

8. After the first segment appears and the route nodes appear, right-click in an open area of the design window and ensure that Rotation Snap is selected in the context menu.

9. Click and drag the curved arrow on the green axis, move your mouse to the opposite fitting (as shown in Figure 18.21), and select that fitting.

FIGURE 18.21
Rotation and point snaps aid in building between fittings.

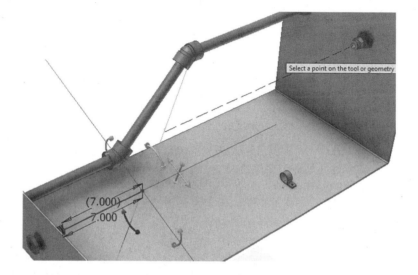

Select a point on the tool or geometry

(7.000)
7.000

This method will align the route nodes to the second fitting and allows a great deal of flexibility in building a complex route.

10. Click the end of the second fitting to set an endpoint for the route.

11. This will present a preview of a route. The preview will include the number of segments and the Select Other tool so you can cycle between options.

12. Click the green arrows of the Select Other tool until you see the option that will create three segments and then click the green icon in the center of the Select Other tool to set the route.

13. Finish the route and then click the Populate Route button from the Pipe Run tab to populate the route with parts.

14. Select Finish Tube And Pipe Run.

Using the 3D Orthogonal Route tool allows you to create a route based on existing geometry without the need to use an existing sketch. This can speed up the layout process and simplify your design. You can save your work if you want to investigate the folders and file paths created, or you can close the file without saving changes and continue to the next set of steps.

CREATING A FLEXIBLE HOSE ROUTE

Flexible hose routes are similar to rigid pipe routes with just a few exceptions. Whereas a rigid pipe path is a series of line segments connected with arcs or points, a flexible hose path consists of a single spline segment. Flexible routes offer a couple of tools and options specific to this type of route, such as the ability to right-click a surface, select Enter Offset, and then adjust the hose length. You can open the file mi_18a_017.iam from the Chapter 18 directory and use the options in these steps to create a flexible hose route.

1. Locate and right-click the Tube & Pipe Runs 01 node in the browser and choose Edit.

2. Select the Create Pipe Run button and accept the defaults.

3. Set the style to Hydraulic Hose–Male Taper Thread.

4. Select the New Route button and click the OK button to accept the default naming.

5. Click the Route button.

With this style of hose, rather than selecting an existing fitting on which the hose will begin, you'll be asked to select the location for two fittings that will be placed before any routing options are offered.

6. Place the first fitting on the remaining unused anchor fitting on the small flange of the sheet-metal base part.

7. Place the second fitting on the last remaining fitting on the opposite side.

Placing the second fitting will generate the spline centerline of the hose. At this point, you can create additional points offset from faces on the part or even use natural centers on curved faces to pass the hose through.

8. Select the curved edge of the hose retainer, as shown in Figure 18.22, to route the hose through the retainer.

FIGURE 18.22
Routing the hose
through a retainer

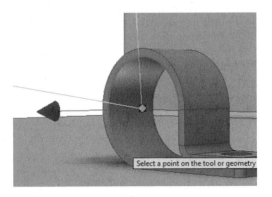

Select a point on the tool or geometry

9. Once the hose center is displayed, use the Hose Length tool in the Manage panel and use the slide bar to set the hose length to 44 inches.

10. Click the OK button to complete the path for the hose.

11. Finish and populate the route and then finish the tube and pipe run. Compare it to Figure 18.23.

FIGURE 18.23
The completed routes

There are a number of options for creating these routes that you should explore. You also have the ability to add fittings inline. These added fittings will break the segments of pipes and tubes to create room for the fittings and set their engagement with the fittings automatically. If you later remove the fitting, the pipe will be "healed" and restored to a single segment.

Exporting ISOGEN Files

Often isometric centerline drawings are required for the documentation of tube and pipe designs. The ISOGEN Output tool is available on both the Tube And Pipe tab and the Pipe Run tab. You can save all your tube and pipe runs as ISOGEN (*.pcf) files directly from the master run assembly; just click the ISOGEN Output button on the Tube And Pipe tab. Or you can use the ISOGEN Output button while at an individual run level to save just that run. When flanged routes are created, gaskets are required for flanged connections if ISOGEN files are to be created from them.

Cable and Harness

The cable and harness tools in Inventor are based on the fundamental tools of part and assembly creation; however, the parts and assemblies created with the cable and harness tools are structured differently than standard part and assembly models. Understanding these differences requires a solid understanding of the way standard parts and assemblies are created and structured. In the following sections, you will explore the creation and placement of electrical parts, harnesses, wires, cables, and segments, as well as how to copy and document cable and harness designs.

Creating and Placing Electrical Parts

You can use any Inventor model as an electrical connector by adding pin features specific to cables and harnesses to it. Parts can be created from scratch using standard modeling techniques or downloaded from supplier websites as well as a number of 3D content websites, such as http://mfgcommunity.autodesk.com/content/.

When downloading content from the Internet, you will often find models in other formats, such as STEP, IGES, SolidWorks, and so on. These files can be translated into Inventor files using the methods described in Chapter 14, "Exchanging Data with Other Systems."

AUTHORING ELECTRICAL COMPONENTS

The basic steps to turn a standard Inventor part into an electrical component are as follows:

1. Open the part file in Inventor.

2. Click the Place Pin button in the Harness panel of the 3D Model tab.

3. Select one of the following to place the pin:

   ◆ Center point of any circular edge, face, or hole

   ◆ Visible sketch points

   ◆ Work points

   ◆ Model vertex points

   ◆ Any model face

4. Enter a unique pin name/number.

5. Click the Harness Properties button in the pin-naming input box to enter additional pin properties if required.

6. Repeat steps 3 and 5 for each pin.

7. Click the Harness Properties tool in the Harness panel of the 3D Model tab.

8. Enter a reference designator (RefDes) placeholder. The RefDes property is intended to be used at the assembly level, where each instance of the connector will have a unique RefDes.

9. Select a Gender option (Male, Female, or None).

10. Set a wire offset point if required.

CREATING A CONNECTOR

In the following steps, you will open an existing Inventor part file and create pins as just described. Figure 18.24 shows the Harness tools available in the parts environment.

FIGURE 18.24
Harness part tools

Follow these steps to explore the steps used in creating a connector:

1. On the Get Started tab, click the Open button.

2. Browse for the file mi_18a_007.ipt in the Chapter 18 directory of the Mastering Inventor 2016 folder and open it.

3. Click the Place Pin button in the Harness panel of the 3D Model tab.

4. Select the visible sketch point.

5. Enter **A1** in the Place Pin input box and click the Harness Properties button.

6. Select the Custom tab, click the Name drop-down, and select Embedded Length.

7. Enter **5 mm** in the Value input box, click Add, and then click the OK button. Then click the green check mark or press **Enter** on the keyboard to set the pin.

8. To place the next pin, click the rounded edge on one of the top cutouts, enter **A2** for the pin name, and then set the pin without entering any harness properties. Click the green check mark to set the pin.

9. Click roughly in the center of the blue square face to set the third pin and enter **B1** for the name. Click the green check mark to set the pin.

10. Right-click and choose Done to exit the Place Pin tool.

11. In the Work Features panel of the 3D Model tab, click the Point button to create a work point.

12. Right-click and select Loop Select and then click the square profile edge for the remaining cutout. Be certain you are selecting the outer edge loop and not the inner loop.

13. Select the Place Pin tool again and select the work point you just created. Set the name to **B2**, click the green check marker, right-click, and choose Done.

14. Edit Extrusion1 and change the Distance from 10 mm to **15 mm**.

Notice which work points hold their positions relative to the geometry and which ones remain at the position in which they were created. You can right-click the pins that didn't update as expected and choose Redefine Feature or 3D Move/Rotate to adjust them. Understanding how pin locations will update is important when defining a connector part intended for use in iPart creation, where you will want the pin location to update as different pin sizes are created. For static pins not likely to change, nonassociative pins work just fine.

In addition to redefining the pin location, you can right-click any pin in the browser and choose Harness Properties to change the name or add/edit properties. Keep in mind that pin names must be unique.

PLACE PIN GROUPS

Although the Place Pin tool works well for defining pins not arranged in a pattern or for small numbers of patterned pins, you can use the Place Pin Group tool to place larger numbers of patterned pins. The following steps explore the Place Pin Group tool:

1. On the Get Started tab, click the Open button.

2. Browse for mi_18a_009.ipt in the Chapter 18 directory of your Mastering Inventor 2016 folder and open it.

3. Click the Place Pin Group button in the Harness panel of the 3D Model tab.

4. For Start Location, select WorkPoint1.

5. Enter **8** for the number of pins per row.

6. Enter **4.5 mm** for the pin pitch (spacing) and then select an edge to establish the pin direction. Use the flip arrow if required.

7. Enter **2** for the number of rows.

8. Enter **4.5 mm** for the row pitch and then select an edge to establish the pin direction. Use the flip arrow if required.

9. Enter **A** for the prefix letter and **101** for the start number.

10. Switch the radio button for the numbering scheme options to Sequential Column, then to Circumventing, and then back to Sequential Row to see the differences in each.

11. Click the OK button to set the pins. Figure 18.25 shows the Place Pin Group dialog box settings and pin group.

FIGURE 18.25

Creating a pin group

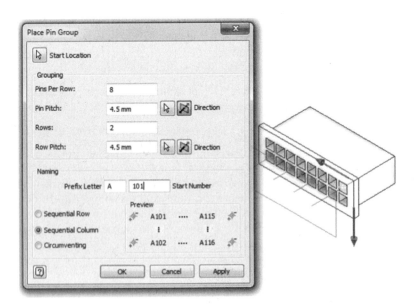

Notice the 16 pins created and listed in the Model browser. You can right-click any of the pins and choose Edit Pin Group to change the start point, spacing, and direction if required. You can also right-click and select Delete Pin Group to start over, or you can select Delete to remove an individual pin. Note too that you can right-click any of the pins and choose Redefine Feature to set an individual pin to a nonpatterned location.

As a final step, you will create four work points in front of the connector for use later as a stop point for the wire or cable segment.

12. Click the Point button on the Work Features panel of the 3D Model tab.

13. Right-click and ensure that Loop Select is not selected.

14. Click the edge of the visible work plane and then one of the work axes. You'll see a work point created at the intersection. Do the same for the remaining three axes and then right-click each axis and the plane and turn off their visibility.

The work points allow you to place the end-of-wire segments appropriately off the connector. Figure 18.26 shows a connector utilizing a segment-end work point.

FIGURE 18.26
Work points for
segment ends

Creating a Harness

Electrical components, including connectors, wires, and cables, are assembled and constructed within a harness subassembly. Although you can place connectors at any structure level within the assembly and route wires to them, as a rule you typically place connectors within the harness assembly when the harness and connectors are purchased together so that your BOM will reflect the harness as an item. The steps for creating and routing a wire harness are as follows:

1. In an assembly file, place and constrain connector parts that will not be part of the harness assembly into the assembly either at the top level or within a subassembly.

2. Click the Cable And Harness button on the Begin panel of the Environments tab.

3. Enter a name and location for the harness subassembly file to be created.

4. Place and constrain connectors to be part of the harness.

5. Use the Create Wire, Create Cable, or Create Ribbon Cable tool to connect the pins of the connectors.

6. Use the Create Segment tool to create wire bundles, routing them around geometry obstacles of other parts in the assembly.

7. Use the Route or Automatic Route tool to route the wires or cables through the segments (wire bundles).

8. Use the Create Splice tool to create wire or segment splices as required.

When a harness is created, it is composed of a harness assembly file and a harness part file of the same name. The part file is the container in which the wires, cables, and segments will be built as they are added. Both files make up the overall harness and are required for the harness to work. Inventor will warn you if you try to edit these files directly rather than through a top-level assembly using the wire harness tools.

In the following steps, you will open an existing Inventor assembly file, create a simple harness assembly, and then place connectors:

1. On the Get Started tab, click the Open button.

2. Browse for mi_18a_018.iam in the Chapter 18 directory of your Mastering Inventor 2016 folder and open it.

3. On the Environments tab, click the Cable And Harness button in the Begin panel.

4. Accept the default name and location for the new harness assembly, and click the OK button. Note the harness subassembly and part nodes listed in the browser.

5. Click the Assemble tab and then click the Place Component button.

6. Browse for and locate the connector file mi_18a_004.ipt and click the Open button.

7. Click twice in the graphics area to place two instances of the connector; then right-click and select Cancel.

To assemble the connectors (residing in the subassembly) to the base part (residing in the top-level assembly), you'll need to return to the top-level assembly and place the constraints. Parts within the harness can constrain to the parts in the top-level assembly because the harness subassembly is adaptive.

8. Click the Finish Cable And Harness button to return to the top-level assembly.

9. Place an Insert constraint on the connectors and the holes on the outside flanges. Ensure that the connector pins face the inside of the base part.

10. You can close this file when finished.

This simple exercise illustrates the steps required to create a harness subassembly and place connectors within it. You can also place connectors in the top-level assembly before creating the harness assembly and then demote components from the top-level assembly into the harness subassembly. To do so, follow these general steps:

1. Place the connectors in the top-level assembly.

2. Create the harness assembly.

3. While the harness subassembly is active, expand it in the browser.

4. Click the connector components in the browser and drag them down into the harness assembly.

> **SETTING GLOBAL HARNESS SETTINGS**
>
> You can access the settings for the entire harness by right-clicking the top-level node of the harness in the browser while it is active for edits.

Placing Wires

Once the harness assembly is created and the electrical connector parts are added and constrained, you can add wires or cables. When wires are created, you enter a unique wire ID name, select a wire category, and set the wire name (type). Then you select the two pins from which and to which you want to run a wire. To see how the Create Wire tool works, open mi_18a_020 .iam in the Chapter 18 directory of your Mastering Inventor 2016 folder and follow these steps:

1. Double-click the harness subassembly to set it active for edits (or right-click it and choose Edit).

2. On the Cable And Harness tab, click the Create Wire button.

3. Set Wire ID to **Wire101**.

4. Select Generic from the Category drop-down.

5. Set the Name drop-down to 14AWG-BLK.

6. Select Pin 1 (work point) on one of the red connectors for the Pin 1 selection. You'll see the pin number when you pause your mouse pointer over the pin. Figure 18.27 shows the pin selection and wire settings.

FIGURE 18.27
Placing a wire on
pin 1

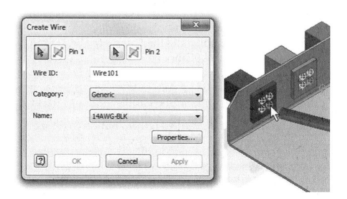

7. Select pin 1 (work point) on the other red connector for the pin 2 selection.

8. Click Apply to set the wire. It should run in a straight line between the two connectors.

9. Set the remaining three pins for the red connectors as listed here:

   ♦ Pin 2 = **Wire102**, Generic 14AWG-RED

   ♦ Pin 3 = **Wire103**, Generic 14AWG-WHT

   ♦ Pin 4 = **Wire104**, Generic 14AWG-GRN

10. Click Cancel to exit the Create Wire dialog box.

11. In this assembly, a segment (blue wire bundle) has already been created. Click the Route button to route a wire through the segment.

12. Click just one of the wires for the Wires selection and then click the segment for the First Segment selection.

13. Select the Single Segment check box and then click Apply. Note that the segment will shrink to size based on the wire.

14. Click Cancel to exit the Route dialog box and then click the Automatic Route button.

15. In the Auto Route dialog box, select the All Unrouted Wires check box, and click the OK button.

16. Expand the Harness1 part node in the browser, and you'll notice a Wires folder containing all the wires you created. Right-click Wire101 and choose Harness Properties. Browse the tab to examine the read/write and read-only properties available for this wire. When finished, return to the Occurrence tab, set Bend Radius to 2 × Diameter, and then click the OK button.

17. Right-click the Wires folder in the browser and select Bend Radius ➤ Check All Bend Radii.

18. Note that you will receive a warning stating that one or more objects contain an empty bend radius. Click the OK button, and note that wires 102 through 104 are marked with a warning icon in the browser.

In this case, the warning indicates the bend radius has not been set. You can edit the wire property, set the bend radius, and then repeat the bend radii check. If the bend radius for each wire in the model is in compliance with the setting for that wire, then the check will clear. Editing segments will be covered later, in the section "Placing and Editing Segments." Now that the problem area is identified, you could make the decision to either change the general layout of the assembly or edit the segment route to change the fit so that the bend isn't so sharp.

19. Click the Finish Cable & Harness button to return to the top-level assembly. You can close this file when finished.

This simple exercise demonstrated how to create wires in a harness and the routing of these wires in an existing segment. The wire categories and names listed in the Create Wires dialog box are drawn from the Cable & Harness library.

Using the Cable & Harness Library

The Cable & Harness library is located in the Design Data folder but can be set per harness. In most cases, you will want to configure it per the Inventor Design Data folder. You can set this option by right-clicking a harness assembly while it is active for edits, selecting Harness Settings, and then selecting the File Locations tab.

The library file that installs by default is Cable&HarnessDefaultLibrary.iwl. You can locate this file by checking the Design Data path in your Inventor project file (*.ipj) or by selecting the File tab of the Application Options dialog box. Recall that the project Design Data path trumps the application's Options path if set.

To add objects to the Cable & Harness library, click the Library button on the Manage panel of the Cable And Harness tab. You can add new wire, cable, and segment objects, just to name a few, and you can create your own custom object type. Figure 18.28 shows the library being edited.

FIGURE 18.28
The Cable & Harness library

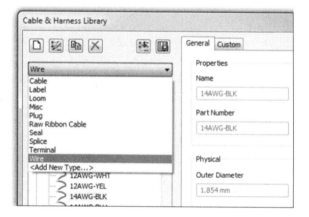

Placing Cables

Adding cables is much like adding wires. To explore the cable tools, open the file mi_18a_022 .iam in the Chapter 18 directory of your Mastering Inventor 2016 folder. Then follow these steps:

1. Double-click the harness subassembly to set it active for edits, or right-click it and select Edit.

2. Click the Create Cable button on the Cable And Harness tab.

3. Set Cable ID to **C201**, and set Category to Alpha.

4. Select 2254/4 from the Name drop-down.

5. Note that Conductor ID 1 is set active. Select pin 1 (work point) on one of the gray connectors for the pin 1 selection. You'll see the pin number when you pause your mouse pointer over the pin.

6. Select pin 1 (work point) on the other gray connector for the pin 2 selection. Note that the conductor ID advances automatically to the next line.

7. Set the remaining three pins for the gray connectors as listed here:

   ◆ Pin 2 = C201:2, Red

   ◆ Pin 3 = C201:3, White

   ◆ Pin 4 = C201:4, Green

8. Click the OK button to set the cable.

9. Click the Automatic Route button, select the All Unrouted Wires check box, and click the OK button.

10. Expand the Cables folder in the browser and then right-click the listed cable and choose Harness Properties. Note that the bend radius is set to 10 × Diameter. If you click in the input box, you will see that the value is being pulled from the Cable & Harness library. Click the OK button to exit the dialog box.

11. Right-click the cable and choose Bend Radius ➤ Check. Click the OK button in the warning dialog box.

12. Note that the cable browser node has turned red and displays a warning sign next to it to indicate a problem. Right-click it in the browser and select Bend Radius ➤ Show Violations. You will see a red marker on the segment in the graphics area along with a dialog box. Click the OK button.

13. Click the Finish Cable And Harness button to return to the top-level assembly. You can close this file when finished.

The Check Bend Radius function allows you to locate problem areas with a design. You could remedy the violation here either by adjusting the segment points in an attempt to modify the fit of the cable route or by moving components or features in the assembly. Often a design might require adjusting both the assembly arrangement and the cable routing. But it's important to be able to check for bend radius violations so that you can determine what needs adjustment. In the next section, you will explore segment creation and editing.

Placing and Editing Segments

Segments are used to define the route path in which wires and cables will be run though a design to avoid interference and identify possible problem areas where bend radii may be too tight. A segment is created by selecting geometry onscreen, either outright or as an offset base. For each selection or offset point, a work point is created.

Once segments are created, you can refine them by adding points or redefining existing points. To explore the cable tools, open the file mi_18a_024.iam in the Chapter 18 directory of your Mastering Inventor 2016 folder. Then follow these steps:

1. Double-click the harness subassembly to set it active for edits, or right-click it and select Edit.

2. Click the Create Segment button on the Cable And Harness tab.

3. You will first run a route segment from the red to green connectors. Select the work point in front of the red connector for the start point of the segment.

4. Click any circular edge on the black grommet hole; this will select the center. Repeat this for the green grommet hole.

5. For the third point, you will specify an offset value and then select the flange with the two square-shaped notches along the top.

   a. Right-click and choose Edit Offset.

   b. Enter **10 mm** in the Edit Offset box and then click the OK button.

   c. Rub your mouse pointer around on different faces to observe the way the offset behaves. Then select roughly in the center of the face of the notched flange in front of the green connector.

6. Select the work point in front of the green connector.

7. Right-click and choose Continue.

8. Create another short segment from the orange connector and tie it into the first segment. Select the work point in front of the orange connector.

9. Click the work point at the center of the green grommet hole, right-click, and select Finish. Figure 18.29 shows the segments.

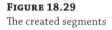
FIGURE 18.29
The created segments

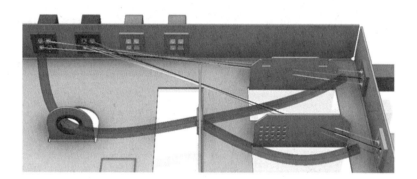

Use the Automatic Route tool and select the All Unrouted Wires option to route the wires through the segments. Upon doing so, you'll notice two things.

◆ The segments adjust to compensate for the wire diameters.

◆ The cable coming off the blue connector has routed in an undesirable way.

Use the Unroute tool and select any of the wires at the blue connector. Because they all belong to a cable, you need to select only one, and then they all highlight. Once they are unrouted, you can use the Create Segment tool to create a new segment from the blue connector to the black grommet hole and then use Route or Automatic Route to reroute the cable.

IMPORTING WIRE DATA FROM AUTOCAD ELECTRICAL

Depending on the size and structure of your design department, you might want to import schematic data created by AutoCAD® Electrical software users. You can use the Import Harness Data tool in Inventor Professional or routed systems to connect multiple wires and cables in the harness assembly based on a schematic created in AutoCAD Electrical. A key to doing this successfully is making sure the wire and connector numbering is unique throughout the schematic. To do this, you must first export the harness data from AutoCAD Electrical as described in these steps:

1. On the Import/Export Data tab, click the Inventor button.

2. In the Export dialog box, specify the scope of the export (export the project or just the current drawing) and then click the OK button.

3. In the XML File Export dialog box, define the location and filename for the export file.

Once the data is exported from AutoCAD Electrical, you can import it into Inventor as described in these steps:

1. Double-click the harness assembly in which you want to import the harness data.

2. Check or assign reference designators on the connector and splice occurrences used in the harness data file to ensure that the names match the schematic.

3. Click the Import Harness Data button on the Cable And Harness tab. Then browse for the harness data file (.xml or .csv) exported from AutoCAD Electrical. If you're importing a CSV file, click Browse to locate the configuration file (.cfg).

4. Click the OK button to add the harness data to the active harness assembly.

The properties imported from AutoCAD Electrical are as follows:

◆ Component tags imported as RefDes

◆ Wire numbers imported as the wire ID

◆ The cable conductor wire layer imported as the cable ID

You'll notice that the middle section of the segment needs to be adjusted. To do so, follow these steps:

1. Run your mouse pointer over the centerline of the segment, right-click, and choose Add Points.

2. Select roughly in the middle of the segment and then right-click and select Finish.

3. Right-click the new work point and select Redefine Point.

4. Right-click, select Edit Offset, enter **10 mm** for the offset value, and click the OK button.

5. Click roughly in the center of the square emboss on the base part.

6. Make an adjustment using the 3D triad. Right-click the same work point and select 3D Move/Rotate.

7. Click the blue cone (z-axis) of the triad, enter **4 mm**, and then click Apply.

8. Select the small plane between the blue arrow and the green arrow (YZ plane), enter **-6 mm** in both the Y and Z inputs, and then click the OK button.

9. Edit the segment type. Select Assign Virtual Parts on the Cable And Harness tab and select the centerline of all the segments. From the Type drop-down, select Loom. Set the Category drop-down to Sample, set the Name drop-down to Wire Sleeve, click the Add button, and then click the OK button. Note that the selections in this dialog box are interdependent. For instance, you might need to set the category first to get the option selections for the name.

SEGMENT DEFAULTS

You set the default Edit Offset, Color Style, and Diameter settings per harness by right-clicking the harness browser node on the assembly, selecting Harness Settings, and then selecting the Segments tab.

Because the middle segment routes all the wires and the cable, it is larger in diameter. This is based on a setting in the harness properties. To determine its evaluated size, right-click the segment centerline and choose Harness Properties. You can determine the diameter at the bottom of the Occurrence tab. Because the grommet holes have an inside diameter of 10 mm, you can make a judgment as to whether a larger hole size is required.

On the Wire/Cables tab of the Segment Properties dialog box, you can review the wire and cable information. Double-clicking a line item will open the properties of that wire or cable. Figure 18.30 shows the properties of a wire contained in a segment.

FIGURE 18.30
Wire properties

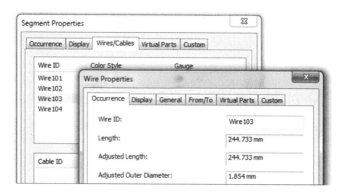

Copying Cable and Harness Designs

Because of the adaptive relationships between assemblies and the harness assemblies and their containing harness part file, copying existing harness and assembly designs must be done in a particular way so as not to break the adaptive relationship between the original files when working on the new files. Before looking at the steps to copy a harness, take a look at Figure 18.31 to understand the files involved. Each harness comprises an assembly file, where you can place connectors and other components, and a part file, where the wires, cables, segments, and other harness components are created.

FIGURE 18.31
Harness assembly structure

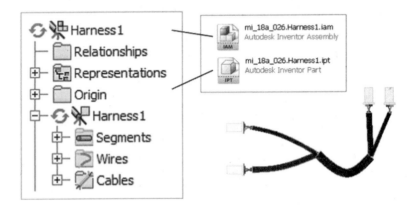

To copy a harness design, open the file `mi_18a_028.iam` in the `Chapter 18` directory of your `Mastering Inventor 2016` folder. Then follow these steps:

1. Expand the assembly browser so that you can identify the harness assembly and part nodes.

Notice that the harness used in the assembly is called mi_18a_26.Harness2 and the part within is named the same. This is because this top-level assembly file was created by using the Save Copy As tool and, therefore, still references the original harness. Although it may seem logical to use the assembly Replace tool or some other method to swap out the harness, such methods can't be used because the adaptive relationships must be updated throughout the file references.

2. Right-click the `mi_18a_26.Harness2.iam` file in the browser and choose Delete.

3. Click the No button in the prompt box so that adaptivity is not cleared in the original assembly.

4. On the Assemble tab, click the Place button.

5. Browse for the `Harness_Files` folder in the `Chapter 18` directory, select `mi_18a_26 .Harness1.iam`, and click the Open button.

6. Click anywhere in the graphics screen to place the harness; then right-click and select OK or Cancel.

7. Typically, you would constrain the harness using assembly constraints at this point. For the purpose of this exercise, though, you don't have to do so. Instead, right-click the harness assembly in the browser and choose Make Adaptive. If prompted to save, click Yes.

8. In the Make Adaptive dialog box, you can set the new names for harness files or accept the default names.

9. In the Location area at the bottom of the dialog box, click the Browse button, browse for the `Harness_Files` folder in the `Chapter 18` directory, and then click the OK button. Either change the filename of the new harness and part or specify a new folder in the Browse For location. Note that by default, a subdirectory of the same name as the top assembly is created along with subfolders for the component organization. You can accept this path and just make that part of your standard file management if you like.

10. Click the OK button and the new files are created, are made adaptive, and are ready for your design edits.

To make copies of a harness within the same assembly, you can simply copy and paste an existing harness, or you click an existing harness node and drag and drop it into the graphics area. Then right-click, choose Make Adaptive, and follow the renaming and location options detailed in the earlier steps.

Creating Nailboard Drawings

Documenting harnesses is a pretty straightforward process with purpose-built tools for detailing harnesses as traditional nailboard drawings. To explore these options, open the file `mi_18a_026.iam` in the `Chapter 18` directory of your `Mastering Inventor 2016` folder and follow these steps:

1. Double-click the harness subassembly to set it active for edits or right-click it and select Edit.

2. Click the Nailboard button on the Cable And Harness tab.

3. Select a drawing template of your choice from the Open Template dialog box and click the OK button.

4. You will be taken into an active sketch within the drawing. Click the Nailboard tab to switch to the nailboard sketch tools.

SWITCHING TO THE NAILBOARD TAB

To use detailing tools specific to nailboard drawings, you must manually switch from the Sketch tab to the Nailboard tab once the nailboard view is created or edited. Using the Dimension tool on the Sketch tab will not give you the same results as using the Harness Dimension tool on the Nailboard tab.

---

5. Use the Harness Dimension tool to place dimensions from the points on the harness. These will display as driven sketch dimensions for now but will show as drawing style dimensions once out of sketch mode.

6. Click the Pivot button on the Nailboard tab and then select the sketch point at one of the 90-degree intersections. Then click a sketch endpoint of the harness leg and drag to pivot the angle. Right-click and choose Finish.

7. Zoom to any end on the harness and select all the wires (you can use a selection window to do this quickly).

8. Once the wires are selected, the Fan In and Fan Out buttons are available on the Nailboard tab. Click the Fan Out button, enter **180**, and then click the OK button. Note the change in the wire fan angle. You can window the entire harness and use the Fan In/Out tools to set all the fans to the same angle as well. You can also manually click and drag each wire if needed.

9. Click the Finish Sketch button when you are satisfied with the dimensions, leg pivots, and fan angles.

10. Click the Place Connector Views button on the Nailboard tab.

11. Accept the defaults and click the OK button.

12. Note that a drawing view of each connector is placed near each wire fan. Right-click one of these views and select Edit View Orientation. Notice that you can change the styling, scale, and other properties, as you would with any Inventor view, but you can also change the view orientation.

13. Feel free to experiment with view settings and then click the OK button.

14. Click the Edit button on the Nailboard tab. If the Sketch tab becomes active, switch to the Nailboard tab.

15. On the Nailboard tab, click the Property Display button.

16. Set Selection Filter to All Wires.

17. Choose Wire ID from the Property Name list and then click Apply.

18. Click onscreen to establish the position of the ID label to the wire, and you will see all the wire ID labels placed. Click the OK button. Click and drag labels to adjust them.

19. Expand the Segment browser node, select all the listed segments, and then right-click and deselect the Display As Actual Diameter option.

20. Expand the Wires node, right-click one of the wires, and choose View Path. Notice how the wire path is highlighted.

21. Click the Finish Sketch button.

Here are a few more settings and options to use when working with nailboard drawings:

♦ Right-click the top-level harness node in the browser and choose Nailboard Settings to adjust the global settings of the nailboard view.

♦ You can open a drawing template first and use the Nailboard button on the Place Views tab to create a nailboard view and set the display settings, rotation, and other view options as you place the view.

♦ You can use the Table tool to place wire/pin tables from existing XLS files.

♦ You can use the Broken Sketch Entity tool in the drawing view sketch environment to break long harness runs so they will fit on the drawing sheet.

The Bottom Line

Create routes and runs.   Using routed systems tools allows you to quickly define many different route types in order to check for clearance and fits within a design, all while creating a bill of materials that can be used downstream in the manufacturing process.

> **Master It**   You have a model containing equipment and structural components defining the space requirements for a new route. Can you create a route using this geometry, or are you required to create a sketch first?

Author a tube and pipe component.   To create your own fittings, couplings, and so on, to be used within tube and pipe design, you need to first author them for use with the tube and pipe tools.

> **Master It**   How can you set the depth at which pipe, tube, or hose segments are inserted into a fitting?

Author an electrical component.   To create your own electrical connector components to be used within cable and harness designs, you need to first define pins within the parts.

> **Master It**   How can you create a family of electrical connectors with varying numbers of pins?

Create and document cable and harness assemblies.   Cable and harness assemblies are created using a specific subassembly and part structure. Each harness is contained in a harness subassembly, and the parts such as wires, cables, and segments are created within a harness part file.

> **Master It**   You have a complex design that includes many harness assemblies and would like to turn some of them off while you work on others and/or create new ones. What is the best way to do this?

Chapter 19

Plastics Design Features

When creating thin wall plastic parts, you can choose either of two popular approaches to get started. One approach is to start with a solid and shell it out; the other is to start with a surface and thicken it. Although these methods approach thin wall features from different starting points, the end result can be the same. You can also mix and match the two methods as required to achieve your design.

Typically, once you've established the base feature, you will add other plastic part features. The Autodesk® Inventor® software has several specialized tools for creating plastic part features when you are working in the parts modeling environment. You'll find these tools on the Plastic Part panel of the 3D Model tab. You might need to right-click the ribbon and choose Plastic Part In Show Panels. Although many of the other tools covered in this chapter, such as Shell and Thicken/Offset, are used to design all types of parts, they are commonly used along with the plastic-specific tools and, therefore, are covered in this chapter as well.

In this chapter, you'll learn to

- ◆ Create thicken/offset features
- ◆ Create shell features
- ◆ Create split features
- ◆ Create grill features
- ◆ Create rule fillet features
- ◆ Create rest features
- ◆ Create boss features
- ◆ Create lip and groove features
- ◆ Create snap-fit features
- ◆ Create rib and web features
- ◆ Create draft features
- ◆ Create an injection mold

Creating Thicken/Offset Features

You can use the Thicken/Offset Feature to add thickness to a surface feature to create a thin wall solid. Although you can use this tool to create surfaces and remove solid material, typically when using Thicken/Offset to create plastic thin wall features, you'll select an existing surface feature to thicken and then set the output type to produce a solid.

To create a thin wall part using the thicken method, follow these steps:

1. Click Open on the Get Started tab, browse for `mi_19a_022.ipt` in the `Chapter 19` directory of your `Mastering Inventor 2016` folder, and open it.

   If you have not already downloaded the Chapter 19 files from `www.sybex.com/go/masteringinventor2016`, please refer to the "What You Will Need" section of the introduction for the download and setup instructions.

2. On the 3D Model tab, select the Revolve tool, and notice that Output defaults to Surface because the sketch is an open profile.

3. For the profile selection, click any solid line in the sketch.

4. For the axis, select the dashed centerline.

5. Leave the extents solution set to Full and click the OK button.

6. On the 3D Model tab, locate and start the Thicken/Offset tool.

7. Switch the select mode from Face to Quilt and then select any face on the revolved surface.

8. Set Distance to **2 mm** and change the direction arrow so that the thickened material is placed to the inside of the part.

9. Ensure that the output is set to Solid and then click the OK button.

   Notice the sharp edges. Although you could use the Fillet tool to select all the outside edges of the solid and then attempt to set fillets to all the inside edges of the solid, there is an easier way. If you place the fillets on the surface, the thickened solid feature will follow the shape and include the fillets. To do this, continue with these steps.

10. From the browser, select the end-of-part (EOP) marker and drag it above the thicken feature or right-click Revolution1 and choose Move EOP Marker.

11. Select the Fillet tool on the Modify panel and set the radius to **8 mm**.

12. Set Select Mode to Feature and then select the revolved surface.

13. When you see a preview of three fillet edges, click the OK button.

14. Drag the EOP marker down below the thicken feature in the browser or right-click Thicken1 and choose Move EOP Marker, and you'll note that the thickened solid now includes the filleted edges.

15. Right-click the revolution feature in the browser and toggle the visibility off.

Figure 19.1 shows the revolved and thickened part. You can close this file without saving the changes and continue to the next section, where you'll create the same basic part but using a different method.

FIGURE 19.1

A revolved and
thickened part

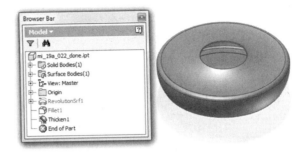

Using Plastic Part Templates

When working with plastic thin wall parts, it is helpful to follow certain design parameters
throughout the features of the part to avoid issues with shrinkage and voids caused by uneven
cooling once the part comes out of the mold. To help with this, you may want to create a plastic
part template with your design parameters already set up. Here is an example of the parameters
in such a template with the design rules already set up and ready for use:

Parameter Name	Unit/Type	Equation	Nominal Value	Tol.	Model Value	Key	Export Param	Comment
▶ Model Parameters								
User Parameters								
WL	mm	2 mm	2.000000	○	2.000000	☐	☑	Wall Thickness
OR	mm	WL + IR	2.500000	○	2.500000	☐	☑	Radius - Outside
IR	mm	WL * 0.25 ul	0.500000	○	0.500000	☐	☑	Radius - Inside
DA_MIN	deg	0.5 deg	0.500000	○	0.500000	☐	☑	Draft Angle - Minimum
DA_MAX	deg	2 deg	2.000000	○	2.000000	☐	☑	Draft Angle - Maximum
BST_A	mm	WL * 0.6 ul	1.200000	○	1.200000	☐	☑	Boss_Thickness under 3mm
BST_B	mm	WL * 0.4 ul	0.800000	○	0.800000	☐	☑	Boss_Thickness over 3mm
RIB	mm	0.7 ul * WL	1.400000	○	1.400000	☐	☑	Rib Thickness

$\Delta S_{\cdots} > 0$ $F = G \times M \times n \div d^2$ $F = G \times M \times n \div d^2$ $\Delta S_{\cdots} > 0$ $F = G \times M \times n \div d^2$

Creating Shell Features

Another approach to creating thin wall features and parts is to create a solid and then use
the Shell tool to hollow it out. When creating a shell feature, you set the wall thickness and
select the faces you want to remove. Material from the interior of the part is removed, resulting in a cavity. To create a thin wall part using the shell method, open mi_19a_024.ipt in the
Chapter 19 directory of your Mastering Inventor 2016 folder and then follow these steps:

1. On the 3D Model tab, select the Revolve tool, and notice that Output defaults to Solid because
   the sketch is closed. The profile and axis selections will automatically select because there is
   only one possible solution for each.

2. Leave the extents solution set to Full and click the OK button.

3. Click the Shell button on the Modify panel of the 3D Model tab.

4. Select the circular face on the top of the revolution feature as the Remove Faces selection.

5. Ensure that the direction is set to Inside, set the thickness to **2 mm**, and then click the OK
   button.

Notice the odd result at the opening of the part. You will fix this by creating a boundary patch surface and then using the Thicken/Offset tool to recut the hole. You'll also place some fillets on the sharp outside edges.

6. On the 3D Model tab, select the Boundary Patch tool on the Surface panel.

7. Click the larger-diameter edge of the center hole for the BoundaryLoop selection and click the OK button. This creates a surface feature you'll use to recut the hole.

8. On the 3D Model tab, locate the Modify panel and look for the Thicken/Offset tool (note you might need to look in the flyout menu). Select the Thicken/Offset tool and click the boundary patch's surface.

9. Set Solution to Cut, set Distance to **2 mm**, and set the direction to go down into the part.

10. Make sure the output is set to Solid and then click the OK button.

11. Select the Fillet tool on the Modify panel and set the radius to **8 mm**.

12. Select the three outside edges—two along the bottom and one along the top. Be certain these are the outside edges and not the inside edges; then click the OK button.

13. Drag the fillet feature above the shell feature in the browser. This will allow the shell to follow the outside fillets and translate them to the inside edges. If you cannot drag the fillet above the shell feature, mostly likely you have inadvertently selected an inside edge. If so, the fillet cannot exist before the shell because it is dependent on the edge created by the shell.

14. Right-click the boundary patch feature in the browser and toggle the visibility off. Figure 19.2 shows the revolved and shelled part.

FIGURE 19.2
A revolved and
shelled part

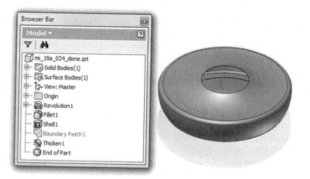

If you were to compare the parts created by the Thicken/Offset method and the Shell method, you would find that the two are not quite identical. The difference is in the opening cutout. In the shelled version, a boundary patch was used to recut the opening down into the part (along the y-axis). In the thickened version, the opening was left in its natural condition. You could use the Boundary Patch tool to clean up the opening in that case as well.

Using either method, it is also important to consider a draft angle for the walls that are in the direction in which a mold would be separated. Not including drafts early on can lead to a lot of difficult cleanup work in the long run, before a mold can be created. You can close this file without saving the changes and continue to the next section, where you'll explore the Split tool.

REORDERING SHELL FEATURES

You may find that you've added a previous feature that gives an incorrect result when creating shell features later in the design. Often, you can just click the shell feature and drag it above the other features to let it rebuild. To explore this, you can open the file `mi_19a_064.ipt` in the `Chapter 19` folder, click Shell1 in the browser, and drag it above Extrusion2. When you do so, you'll see that the resulting part is quite different from when the shell was created after the extrusion and fillet features.

Creating Split Features

Often when designing plastic parts, it is useful to create mating parts within the same file. To do this, you can use the Split tool to divide a single body into two mating bodies. You can also use the Split tool to split the surfaces on a solid so that they can be manipulated individually. To see how the Split tool is used, open the file `mi_19a_026.ipt` in the `Chapter 19` directory of your `Mastering Inventor 2016` folder and then follow these steps:

1. Expand the `Solid Bodies` folder in the browser, and notice that there is currently only a single solid listed in the folder. You will use the Split tool to divide this into two separate solids.

2. On the 3D Model tab's Modify panel, select the Split tool (look in the flyout menu under the Thicken/Offset or Combine tool).

3. For the Split tool selection, click the sketch profile running through the part.

4. For the method, click the Split Solid button (third from the top), which will split the existing part into two separate solids.

5. Click the OK button and notice that Solid1 has been replaced with two new solids in the `Solid Bodies` folder.

6. To work with just the top solid, select it in the `Solid Bodies` folder of the browser, right-click, and choose Hide Others.

7. Next, you'll create a 3D sketch to split the surface of the solid. Use the Sketch drop-down on the 3D Model tab and select Start 3D Sketch.

8. On the 3D Sketch tab, select the Silhouette Curve tool, choose the solid as the Body selection and the visible y-axis as the Direction selection, and then click the OK button.

9. This creates a sketch curve along the face where a beam of light shining down from above would create a shadow. Click Finish Sketch to exit the 3D sketch.

10. Select the Split tool again and choose the 3D Sketch curve for the Split tool selection.

11. For the Face selection, choose the face that the 3D Sketch curve is encircling. Ensure that the Faces option is set to Select and not All. This will split just the outside face of the part, whereas All would split both the outside and inside faces. Click the OK button.

12. Now select the Thicken/Offset tool, choose the bottom half of the face you just split, and set Distance to **1 mm**.

13. Ensure that Output is set to Solid, the Automatic Blending option is off, Solution is set to Join, and Direction is thickening out from the part; then click the OK button.

14. Right-click the thickened part you just created in the browser and choose Properties.

15. Set Feature Appearance to Blue – Glazing or something similar and click the OK button.

16. Right-click the solid in the Solid Bodies folder and choose Properties. Enter **Cover** for the name. Click the Update button to set the general properties of this solid. You'll notice also that you can set the color for the entire solid body here. Selecting the Clear All Overrides check box would reset the blue thicken feature to abide by the color of the entire solid. Feel free to choose a color of your liking and then click the OK button.

17. Right-click the solid in the Solid Bodies folder and choose Show All to turn the visibility of the other solid back on.

There are a number of uses for a multi-body part, but for this type of product they are invaluable. You can close this file without saving the changes and continue to the next section, where you'll learn to create grill features.

TURN ON THE PLASTIC PARTS TOOL PANEL

If you do not see the Plastic Part tool panel on your 3D Model tab, you might need to enable it by right-clicking anywhere on the tab and then choosing Show Panels and then Plastic Part. Once this is done, you will see the Plastic Part panel on the 3D Model tab.

Certification
Objective

Creating Grill Features

You can use the Grill tool to create vents and openings on thin wall parts to provide access and airflow to parts housed within an exterior part. To create grill features, use the Grill tool to project 2D sketches onto the surface of the part to create various raised or recessed features. Although the boundary sketch is the only required grill element, you can create islands, ribs, and spars and then give them all a draft angle. You can also check the flow area of the opening to ensure that it meets the required area. Open the file mi_19a_028.ipt in the Chapter 19 directory of your Mastering Inventor 2016 folder and then follow these steps to create a grill feature:

1. Select the Grill tool from the Plastic Part panel of the 3D Model tab. You'll see a sketch with all the various elements of what will become the grill within it. Figure 19.3 shows the sketch elements separated out into the grill elements.

FIGURE 19.3
Grill elements

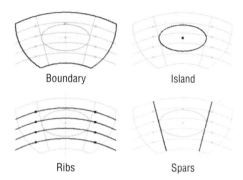

2. For the Boundary profile, select the outer profile of the sketch, as identified in Figure 19.3. Set Thickness to **2 mm**, Height to **6 mm**, and Outside Height to **2 mm**, as shown in Figure 19.4.

FIGURE 19.4
Grill boundary settings

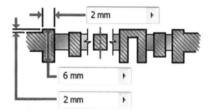

3. Click the Island tab and select the elliptical profile of the sketch, as identified in Figure 19.3. Leave Thickness set to 0 mm so that the island is a solid fill.

4. Click the Rib tab and select the four arcs identified as the ribs in Figure 19.3. Set Thickness to **2 mm**, Height to **4 mm**, and Top Offset to **2 mm**, as shown in Figure 19.5.

FIGURE 19.5
Grill rib settings

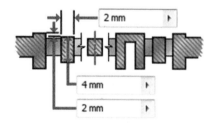

5. Click the Spar tab, and select the two lines identified as the spars in Figure 19.3. Set Top Offset to **2 mm**, Thickness to **6 mm**, and Bottom Offset to **0 mm**, as shown in Figure 19.6.

FIGURE 19.6
Spar rib settings

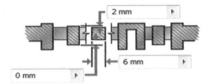

6. Click the >> button at the bottom of the dialog box and note the Flow Area setting; then click the OK button to create the grill feature.

7. Next, you'll pattern the grill feature around the parts. Click the Circular Pattern tool (located next to the Work Features tools).

8. Select the grill feature for the Features selection and then click the visible y-axis for the Rotation Axis selection.

9. Enter 3 for Occurrence Count and **90 deg** for Occurrence Angle.

10. Click the Midplane button to set an occurrence on each side of the original grill feature and then click the >> button.

11. In the Positioning Method area, select Incremental to set the spacing of the grills at 90 degrees each and then click the OK button. Figure 19.7 shows the patterned grill features.

FIGURE 19.7
Grill features
patterned

Feel free to edit the grill feature and experiment with the options, adding a draft angle and so on. You might want to drag the EOP marker above the pattern feature before doing so to allow the edits to take place more quickly. Then just drag it back down once the edits are complete. When you've finished, you can close this file without saving the changes and move on to the next section, where you'll learn about rule fillet features.

**Certification
Objective**

Creating Rule Fillet Features

With rule fillets, you can create fillets based on a list of rules you've set up to determine which edges to fillet. This approach can be a powerful time-saver when you're working with plastic parts because it allows you to create many fillets all at once without having to select each and every edge. When a part feature is changed with significance to the rule-based fillets, the rule is evaluated to determine whether it still applies. If so, the fillets are regenerated for new edges that fit the rule and discarded for edges that do not. Although the Rule Fillet tool is categorized as a plastic feature tool, you can use rule-based fillets for any part you design.

Open the file mi_19a_030.ipt in the Chapter 19 directory of your Mastering Inventor 2016 folder and then follow these steps to create a rule fillet feature:

1. Expand the Solid Bodies folder in the browser, right-click the solid named Cover, and choose Hide Others.

2. Select the Rule Fillet tool on the Plastic Part panel.

3. Click the drop-down under the Source column and select Face.

4. Rotate the part around and select the underside face of the grill features (they've each been colored yellow for easy identification).

5. Set the Radius to **2 mm** and then set the drop-down in the Rule column to Incident Edges.

6. In the Options area, deselect the All Rounds check box, leaving All Fillets selected.

7. In the Incident Edges area, select the visible y-axis as the Direction selection and then click the OK button to create all the previewed fillets. Figure 19.8 shows the results of the rule fillet on one of the grill faces.

FIGURE 19.8
An example of rule fillets

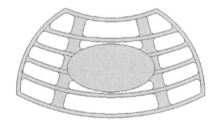

You'll notice that the edges, where one of the spars meets the grill boundary along the top, did not receive fillets. This is because those edges do not qualify according to the rule of incident edges. Although it might seem as if the rule fillet has malfunctioned, close inspection of the grill feature will show there is a small gap between the spar and the boundary face. To resolve this, the lines in the grill sketch used for the spars would need to be extended past the boundary edge. If you edit Sketch3, you can see where the issue is.

Here are brief descriptions of the results of the Rule Fillet tool when Faces is selected:

Incident Edges   Only edges contacting the source faces that are parallel to a selected axis (within a specified tolerance) are filleted.

All Edges   Edges generated by the selected faces and other faces of the part body are filleted.

Against Features   Two selection sets are created: a "source" selection and a "scope" selection. Only edges formed by the intersection of the faces in the source with features in the scope selections are filleted.

Here are brief descriptions of the results of the Rule Fillet tool when Features is selected:

All Edges   Edges generated by the selected features and the part body are filleted.

Against Part   Only edges formed by the intersection of the faces of the features and the faces of the part body are filleted.

Against Features   Two selection sets are created: a "source" selection and a "scope" selection. Only edges formed by the intersection of the features in the source with features in the scope selections are filleted.

Free Edges   Only edges formed by faces of the selected feature are filleted.

When you have finished with this part, you can close the file without saving changes and move on to the next topic: rest features.

 Certification Objective

Creating Rest Features

A rest feature is a shelf or landing area applied to a curved or slanted face of a plastic part, often used as a surface on which to mount other components. The results of the rest feature are largely dependent on the orientation of the rest sketch in relation to the target body and the combination of settings and selections you choose. The Through All option will extend the rest profile through the extents of the target body, and the direction arrow will change the results, as you can see by comparing Figure 19.9 and Figure 19.10.

FIGURE 19.9
Through All termination with the direction set downward

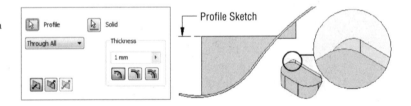

FIGURE 19.10
Through All termination with the direction set upward

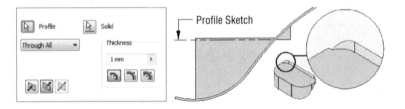

Additionally, you can set a Distance extent. Figure 19.11 shows a rest created 25 mm off the profile sketch in both directions.

FIGURE 19.11
Using Distance extents for a rest

You can also set the rest to terminate using a selected surface. Figure 19.12 shows a rest set to use the target body surface as a termination, with the direction set to go up from the sketch. The result adds material but does not create a pocket.

FIGURE 19.12
A rest using a surface termination

You can use the More tab in the Rest dialog box to set Landing options such as taper angles and termination settings. Open the file `mi_19a_032.ipt` in the `Chapter 19` directory of your `Mastering Inventor 2016` folder and then follow these steps to create a rest feature:

1. Expand the `Solid Bodies` folder in the browser, right-click the solid named Cover, and choose Hide Others.

2. On the Plastic Part panel, select the Rest tool. Because only one profile is available in the visible sketch, it is selected automatically.

3. Set the direction arrow to point up (use the flip arrow on the left).

4. Set the thickness to **2 mm** and set the thickness direction to Outside.

5. Click the More tab, set the Landing Options drop-down to To Surface, and then select the visible surface. Set the landing taper to **12 deg** and then click the OK button.

6. Turn off the visibility of the landing surface and inspect the results. You'll notice that the surface contours are translated to the tapered faces. If this is not the result you want, you can use the Delete Face option to clean up the contours.

7. On the Modify panel, use the Delete Face tool on the Modify panel of 3D Model tab to expose the flyout menu and then select the Delete Face tool.

8. Select the Heal check box. Then select the four contoured faces, as shown in Figure 19.13, and click the OK button.

FIGURE 19.13
Deleting and healing
faces

The Delete Face tool is a good way to clean up geometry when needed, but it should not be used indiscriminately because it may create unpredictable results during feature edits. If you have the option to edit an existing sketch or feature to get the same result as using the Delete Face tool, then that is typically the best option.

There are also times when cleaning up geometry can be bypassed by using a different technique. Rather than cleaning up an interior corner to apply an edge fillet, you may be able to apply a two-face fillet and have the fillet feature "absorb" the inconsistent faces that would be patched over. Also, it is a good idea to create small selection sets to delete multiple faces rather than trying to delete them all at once. For example, in this design you would need to delete the contours on the sides of the rest feature on all the inside and outside faces to remove the contours completely. This would be best to do as several different features, each created with the Delete Face tool. Once you've experimented with the Delete Face tool, you can close this file without saving changes and continue to the next section, where you'll learn about boss features.

Certification
Objective # Creating Boss Features

To hold plastic parts together without risking damage to the thin wall features, boss features are often used to provide a more rigid connection point than just a simple hole. You can use the Boss tool in Inventor to create matched pairs of bosses on mating parts. The half accepting the fastener is the *head*, and the other half is the *thread*. You can create both types of bosses using the Boss tool. When required, you can add strength ribs so that the boss features will not be snapped off under load. As a rule, you should consider adding ribs when the length of the boss exceeds the diameter by more than three times.

Open the file mi_19a_034.ipt in the Chapter 19 directory of your Mastering Inventor 2016 folder and then follow these steps to create boss features:

1. Expand the Solid Bodies folder in the browser, right-click the solid named Base, and choose Hide Others.

2. Because the Base part has an uneven edge, the boss features to be created will be different heights. To locate the bosses, you will first create work points. Select the Point tool on the Work Features panel.

3. To create a work point, select the edge of Work Plane4 and then select the inside edge of the base near the intersection of the work plane and the edge.

REPEAT COMMAND FOR WORK FEATURES

When you start any of the work feature tools (Work Planes, Work Axis, and Work Point), you can right-click and choose Repeat Command to set the work feature tools to stay on until you right-click and choose Done. This helps when you are creating a lot of work features because you do not have to click the button each time.

---

4. Repeat this for Work Plane5 and the inside edge of the part. You'll note that the work points are placed at different heights from the bottom of the base part. Figure 19.14 shows the resulting work points.

FIGURE 19.14
Work point locations

5. Next, you will create grounded work points to establish the inset location for the boss features. Use the drop-down on the Work Features panel to select the Point tool.

6. Select the first work point you created at the intersection of the part edge and Work Plane4. You will see the 3D Move/Rotate dialog box, and the triad will appear at the work point location.

7. Click the Redefine Alignment Or Position button in the dialog box.

8. Next, select the small plane on the triad running between the green y-axis and the red x-axis (you might need to rotate your view). Then select the edge of Work Plane4. The triad will realign to the work plane.

9. Now you are ready to place the grounded work point. To do so, first click the red cone shape (arrowhead) of the triad for the x-axis. This will isolate x-axis input in the dialog box. Enter **15 mm** (if the red arrow is pointing on the outside of the part enter **-15** to bring it back in) and click Apply. This will create a grounded work point.

10. Next, click the Redefine Alignment or Position button to redefine the triad location. Click the black/purple ball at the center of the triad first and then select the work point at the intersection of the Work Plane5 and the inside edge of the part.

11. Click the blue cone shape (arrowhead) of the triad for the z-axis. This will isolate the z-axis input in the dialog box. Enter **-15 mm** (or just click and drag the blue arrowhead into position). If the blue arrow is pointing on the outside of the part enter **15** to bring it back in. Then click the OK button. This will create a second grounded work point and exit the Grounded WorkPoint tool.

12. Now you are ready to create the boss features. Select the Boss tool on the Plastic Part panel.

13. Make sure the Placement drop-down is set to On Point and then select the two grounded work points for the Centers selection. Click the visible y-axis for the Direction selection, and ensure that the preview shows the bosses extending down toward the part base. If they do not, use the Flip arrow to change the direction.

14. Click the Head tab. Note the buttons on the left of the dialog box. If you click the lower one, the Head tab becomes the Thread tab, allowing you to place a different boss type. In the Head tab, click the (+) plus button next to the Draft Options area to view the draft inputs available. You can leave the inputs at the defaults.

15. Click the Ribs tab and select the Stiffening Ribs check box to set these options active. Enter **4** in the Number Of Stiffening Ribs input box.

16. Enter **6 mm** for the Shoulder Radius input and then click the (+) plus button next to the Fillet Options area to view the fillet inputs available. Leave the inputs at the defaults.

17. Click the Start Direction button at the bottom of the dialog box and then select either Work Plane4 or Work Plane5 to establish the direction. (You can also just enter **45 degrees** as the angle, in this particular case.)

18. Click the OK button to create the boss features. You'll notice that each is created at a different height.

19. Use the Mirror tool to mirror the boss feature, using the YZ origin plane as the mirror plane. Figure 19.15 shows the completed bosses. Use >> on the Mirror tool and set the Creation Method to Adjust.

FIGURE 19.15
Plastic boss features

Now that the Base half of this design has the head-boss features completed, you can create the sketch or work points at the centers of each boss, toggle the visibility of the cover and base so that the cover is visible, and then use those points to create the thread bosses in the cover in the same manner you just created the head bosses in the base. To explore the placement of boss features using a sketch, you can open the file `mi_19a_035.ipt` from the `Chapter 19` directory of your `Mastering Inventor 2016` folder. Once you've finished exploring the Boss tool, you can close the file without saving changes and continue to the next section.

> **TURNING OFF WORK FEATURE VISIBILITY**
>
> Recall that it is a best practice to right-click and toggle off the visibility of each work feature you create once you have finished using it. Leaving the visibility on or using the Object Visibility display override at the part level can make managing work features difficult at the assembly level.

Certification Objective

Creating Lip and Groove Features

Lip and groove features are used to mate two parts together so that they fit together precisely. You can use the Lip tool in Inventor to create either the lip or the groove of the part by specifying a path consisting of a set of tangent, continuous boundary edges. You can also use work planes to establish path extents where a lip is not needed around an entire edge. Open the file `mi_19a_036.ipt` from the `Chapter 19` directory of your `Mastering Inventor 2016` folder and then follow these steps to create lip features:

1. Expand the `Solid Bodies` folder in the browser, right-click the solid named Base, and choose Hide Others.

2. Select the Lip tool on the Plastic Part panel and set the type to Lip by clicking the Lip button on the left side of the dialog box.

3. Select the inside edge along the top of the part for the Path Edges selection and then select the top face for the Guide Face setting.

4. Next click the Lip tab, set the outside angle to **10 degrees** and the clearance to **0.5 mm** and then click the OK button. Figure 19.16 shows the Lip selections.

FIGURE 19.16
Creating a lip feature

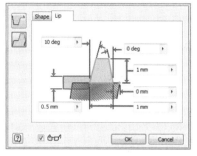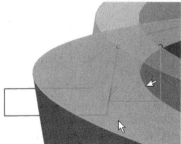

5. Next, you'll create the groove on the Cover solid. Expand the `Solid Bodies` folder in the browser, right-click the solid named Cover, and choose Hide Others.

6. Select the Lip tool and set the type to Groove by clicking the Groove button on the left side of the dialog box.

7. Select the inside edge of the part for the Path Edges selection and then select the Pull Direction check box in the dialog box. Next, select the top face of one of the bosses to establish a pull direction.

8. Click the Groove tab, set the outside angle to **10 degrees** and the clearance to **0.5 mm**, and then click the OK button.

Note that if you have not set a clearance value, you would likely get an error. The clearance value is useful for creating a planar surface along the path where needed. You can experiment with different settings and values by editing the lip features if you would like, and then you can close the file without saving changes.

Certification Objective

Creating Snap-Fit Features

Snap-fit features are used to secure a plastic part to another part. Although you can model any number of snap-fit connections using the standard modeling tools, Inventor includes a tool to create the common hook-and-loop cantilever snap fit. Figure 19.17 shows a few common snap fits you might create with the Snap Fit tool and standard modeling tools.

FIGURE 19.17
From left to right: a permanent locking snap, nonlocking snap, and U-shaped removable locking snap

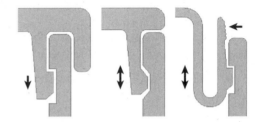

To insert a snap fit, select an insert point made of either a sketch point or a work point. Open the file mi_19a_038.ipt in the Chapter 19 directory of your Mastering Inventor 2016 folder and then follow these steps to create snap-fit features:

1. Bring an existing part into the design using the Derive tool. On the Manage tab, click the Derive button.

2. Locate and select the file mi_19a_099.ipt in the Chapter 19 folder and then click Open.

3. In the Derived Part dialog box, select the first button for the Derive Style to create a single solid-body part with merged seams between planar faces.

4. Next expand the Solid Bodies folder and make sure Solid1 is colored yellow, denoting that it is set to be derived into your current design. Expand the Work Geometry folder, set Work Axis1 to be derived as well, and then click the OK button. You can use the ViewCube to return to the home view.

5. You'll now use the derived part to subtract material from the Cover part so that it will fit into the opening. Click the 3D Model tab and then select the Combine tool on the Modify panel.

6. For the Base selection, select Cover. For tool body, select the derived part. Set the solution to Cut, click the Keep Toolbody check box, and click the OK button.

7. When the tool body component (in this case the derived part) is combined with the base part, its visibility is automatically toggled off. Expand the `Solid Bodies` folder, and you'll see the derived part listed as a solid with its visibility turned off.

8. Next, you'll create a work point to set the location of the snap-fit feature. Select the Point tool on the Work Features panel and zoom into the yellow face located on the cutout of the cover. Select the midpoint along the top edge of the yellow face to set the work point.

9. Now you're ready to create the snap fit. Select the Snap Fit tool on the Plastic Part panel.

10. Ensure that the Placement drop-down is set to On Point and the Cantilever Snap Fit Hook button is selected (on the left of the dialog box).

11. For the Centers selection, click the work point you created.

12. For the Direction selection, click the visible y-axis.

13. For the Hook Direction selection, click the derived work axis running through the yellow face.

14. Use the Flip button to set the direction correctly if the preview shows it facing down.

15. Ensure that the Extend check box is selected so that the snap will match the contour of the curved face on which it is being created. The Extend check box might make the pre-view of the snap-fit feature look as if the feature is going to build to the wrong side of the yellow face, but it should be correct if you've followed the previous steps.

16. Click the Beam tab, set the Beam Length setting to **7 mm**, set the Beam Width At Hook setting to **9 mm**, and set the Beam Width At Wall setting to **10 mm**.

17. Click the Hook tab, and take a look at the settings; leave these settings at the defaults and then click the OK button.

18. Use the Circular Pattern tool to pattern the hook around the opening for a total of three.

19. On the Solid bodies tab, right-click all the solids and choose Show All. Investigate the snap fit, and note that the derived part has the mating half of the hook built in. Figure 19.18 shows the completed snap-fit feature.

FIGURE 19.18
A snap-fit feature

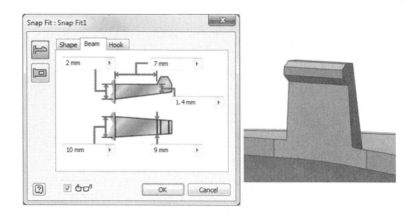

You can turn on the derived solid from the Solid Bodies folder to check to see how the snap feature fits with the derived part. Once you're done, you can close the file without saving changes.

For more on snap-fit features, you can open the file named mi_19a_040.ipt in the Chapter 19 folder to experiment with the various snap-fit settings. Use the work points to place hook and loop features to your liking. You can also open mi_19a_042.ipt for comparison. This file contains two halves of a simple plastic box. Examine the model features to see how the hook and loops were created in combination with extrude features to get a precise placement.

WORKING WITH MULTI-BODIES

At any point during your design, you can save the solids within a multi-body part as individual parts and even have them automatically placed into an assembly by using the Make Components tool. Creating multiple solid bodies in a single-part file offers some unique advantages compared to the traditional methods of creating parts in the context of an assembly file. You explored the steps for doing this in Chapter 5, "Advanced Modeling Techniques."

Certification
Objective

Creating Rib and Web Features

Ribs and webs are often used in plastic parts to prevent warping and to add stiffness to thin wall parts. To create a rib feature, first create an open profile sketch to define the cross section. Then define the direction and thickness. If the rib feature runs perpendicular to the sketch plane, you can add a draft taper. By default, the profile extends to intersect the next face. To create a rib network, you can select multiple sketch profiles at once. Alternatively, you can create a single rib feature and then pattern or mirror it.

Open the file mi_19a_044.ipt in the Chapter 19 directory of your Mastering Inventor 2016 folder and then follow these steps to create rib features:

1. You'll notice there is a small diagonal line sketched in the corner of the part. This will be the sketch profile of the first rib feature. Select the Rib tool on the Create panel, and the sketch profile will be selected automatically.

2. Select Rib Type from the two buttons on the left side of the dialog box to switch the type of rib being created.

   Normal To Sketch Plane   Extrudes geometry normal to the sketch plane. The thickness is parallel to the sketch plane.

   Parallel To Sketch Plane   Extrudes geometry parallel to the sketch plane. The thickness is normal to the sketch plane.

3. Use the direction buttons if needed to ensure that the rib is going from the sketch toward the bottom corner of the part.

4. Set the thickness to **1 mm** and use the arrows to adjust the direction in which the thickness is applied. In this case, you want to use the Midplane option.

5. Click the OK button, and notice how the rib extends to the profile.

6. Next, right-click Sketch3 in the browser and choose Visibility to make it available for use.

7. Select the Rib tool again, make sure the Normal To Sketch Plane option button on the left of the dialog box is selected, and select the four lines and the ellipse as profiles.

8. Toggle the Extend Profile check box off and on to notice the difference in the preview. Ensure that this check box is selected so that the profiles do extend.

9. Set the thickness to **1 mm** and use the arrows to adjust the direction in which the thickness is applied. In this case, you want to use the Midplane option.

10. To explore the Finite option, click the Finite button and type **3 mm**. This holds the depth of the ribs to 3 mm rather than allowing them to automatically terminate at the base. Set this option back to use the To Next option.

11. Click the Draft tab and enter **5 deg** in the Taper input. Ensure that the Hold Thickness option is set to At Root.

   At Top   Holds the specified thickness at the sketch plane

   At Root   Holds the specified thickness at the intersection of the rib feature and the terminating face

12. Click the Boss tab and make sure the Select All check box is selected. You will see bosses added at the locations of the four center points found in the sketch. You can use the Centers button to add or remove bosses as needed.

13. Set Diameter to **4**.

14. Set Offset to **3**.

15. Enter **12** for Draft Angle and then click the OK button to create the webbed rib and bosses feature.

To complete the part, you can use the Mirror tool and the XZ origin plane to copy the first rib to the opposite side of the part. Once it's mirrored, you can use the Rectangular Pattern tool to pattern the mirror feature 10 mm toward the end of the part. Finally, use the Mirror tool and the YZ origin plane to add four identical ribs to the opposite end of the part. Now if you make a change to the original rib feature, the copies will update as well. Figure 19.19 shows the finished example.

FIGURE 19.19
Complete rib features

Creating Draft Features

Taper or draft often needs to be applied to part faces so the part can be extracted from the mold in which it is manufactured. You can create draft features in three ways.

Fixed Edge   This method works by selecting a pull direction and then selecting the faces/edges on which to apply the draft.

Fixed Plane   This method works by selecting a fixed face and applying drafts to the faces intersecting it.

Parting Line   This method works by selecting a sketch to define the parting line where the top and bottom halves of a mold form would meet.

To explore the Fixed Edge and Fixed Plane methods, open the file mi_19a_046.ipt in the Chapter 19 directory of your Mastering Inventor 2016 folder and then follow these steps to create draft features:

1. Select the Draft tool on the Modify tab.

2. For the Pull Direction selection, click the yellow base face.

3. To select the faces, you will click the green faces near the edge that contacts the yellow base face. If you move your mouse pointer over the faces before selecting them, you will see that the edge closest to your mouse pointer will be selected. If you accidentally select an extra or errant edge, you can press the **Ctrl** key and deselect it.

4. Enter **5 deg** for the Draft Angle and then click the OK button. You'll notice the top faces of the thin walls have been reduced because of the draft taper. To remedy this, you'll place a draft on the outside faces also.

5. Rotate the part around so you can see the red and blue faces and then click the Draft tool again.

6. This time, click the Fixed Plane button on the left of the dialog box.

7. Select the red face for the Fixed Plane selection and ensure that the arrow is pointing out.

8. Select the blue faces for the Faces selection, enter **5 deg** for the Draft Angle, and then click the OK button.

You can close this file without saving changes and then open the file mi_19a_048.ipt in the Chapter 19 folder to compare how creating the same tapers is made easier by the inclusion of the corner fillet.

DRAFT ANALYSIS

You can analyze your part for proper draft using the Draft Analysis tool on the Inspect tab. This tool allows you to specify a pull direction and a draft taper to check against. If faces are found to be insufficient, they are shown by color variations correlating to departure from the specified draft. This can be particularly helpful for complex corners and areas of a part where drafted faces are blended together.

Once they are created, draft analyses are saved in the browser in a folder called `Analysis`. You can create multiple analyses and turn them on by double-clicking them. To turn existing analyses off, simply right-click the `Analysis` folder and choose Analysis Visibility.

To explore the final method of creating draft features, open the file `mi_19a_050.ipt` from the `Chapter 19` directory of your `Mastering Inventor 2016` folder; then follow these steps:

1. Select the Draft tool on the Modify panel.

2. Click the Parting Line button on the left of the dialog box.

3. For the Pull Direction selection, click the yellow face of the part.

4. For the Parting Tool selection, click the projected loop that encircles the part.

5. For the Faces selection, choose an outer face of the part.

6. Click the Asymmetric button so that you have two separate draft angle inputs.

7. Enter **3** for the first angle and **6** for the second angle and then click the OK button to create the draft feature.

As you can see, creating a draft using the parting line option is quite simple. Creating the sketch to use as a parting line is generally done by using the Project Cut Edges option when working with a 2D sketch or by using the Include Geometry tool or the Intersection Curve tool when working with a 3D sketch. You can open the file `mi_19a_052.ipt` from the `Chapter 19` folder to explore an example of the parting line created from an extruded surface and a 3D intersection curve created in a 3D sketch. Figure 19.20 shows a parting line used to create a draft feature.

FIGURE 19.20
Draft using a parting line

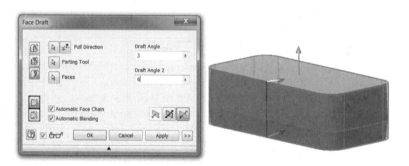

 Real World Scenario

PLASTIC PARTS AND COOLING SHRINKAGE

Designing plastic parts of uniform wall thickness is typically a fairly easy task when the part consists of a simple shell. However, when bosses and ribs are introduced, the resulting tees and feature intersections can create cross-section thicknesses that are significantly thicker than the

continues

continued

wall thickness average. As is often the case when modeling 3D parts, there is nothing to tell you that the model will not work in the real world other than knowledge and experience. For Autodesk® Inventor® Professional users, the Tooling functions that allow mold design include calculations for material shrinkage based on the material properties.

The issue with adding bosses and ribs arises when the part is cooling after the molding process. Uneven part thickness will often result in sinking and deformation where the thicker walls cool more slowly than the rest of the part. The result can bear a very disappointing resemblance to the eye-catching design you intended to create.

To deal with these problem areas, you can do one or more of the following:

◆ You can use a textured surface to disguise uneven cooling.

◆ You can create cores, corner reliefs, and tee inset features to eliminate thick areas.

◆ You can use foam- or gas-assisted molding processes.

◆ You can redesign the problem areas to avoid thickened walls.

Although it will certainly vary depending on the materials and process, a rule of thumb is to keep tee walls at 60 percent of the standard part wall thickness. As shown here, the feature on the left has some obvious problems with areas that exceed a consistent thickness. The feature on the right has been designed to perform the same function and yet maintain a desirable wall thickness throughout.

Mold Design Overview

The process of mold design is a complex combination of advanced science and knowledge of an individual producer's equipment and processes, and for the highest quality, it often requires a great deal of experience. Too often it isn't possible to access that experience, and with many companies having their plastic parts injection-molded outside of their own walls, it isn't reasonable to expect to have the thorough understanding of the equipment available. Securing the time and expertise of a plastics engineer helps to overcome these issues, but their time is expensive and in very high demand. As with the stress analysis tools, Inventor includes tools to help an engineer with a lower degree of expertise do a lot of the fundamental analysis to make the best use of an expert's time.

Inventor Tooling

Inventor Professional is an upgrade to the standard Inventor package and includes the Inventor Tooling functions used for plastic part analysis and injection mold design. This environment allows you to predict how a mold will fill and what defects might occur in the part. You can review defects such as weld lines and air pockets to decide whether you want to change gate placement or modify the part being manufactured.

The software includes data for more than 7,000 types of resin so you can select the appropriate material for the part. This material information affects the quality and fill analysis settings. The process is fairly straightforward, and the interface allows you to move from step to step easily and walks you through most of the tools in order.

The process of creating the mold guides you toward a standard component that will accomplish your unique design requirement. This is done in a specialized tooling environment. Each type of component is listed in the browser as an element of the design rather than just a component in the assembly; placing an element may affect several others. The power is in the fact that the user doesn't have to specify these interactions.

If you are using Inventor Professional, you can take a look at some of the tools used in the workflow to create a mold using the Tooling features. These will be the first tools you will use in the exercises to explore designing a mold. These exercises are just an introduction to the Tooling toolset. Inventor has several great built-in tutorials to augment this chapter if you want to look at some of the advanced features. The intent here is to get you started and introduce the possibilities. Here is a list of the major steps in working with the Inventor Tooling toolset:

Plastic Part   To create a new mold, this is the starting point. This tool will convert an existing part into a mold design element. Everything else will be built around this part.

Place Core And Cavity   If you have an existing Core and Cavity set, you can import it and use it as the basis for the mold design.

Adjust Orientation   To properly align the mold components, an opening direction must be established. This orientation can be altered by setting axis directions or rotating the part.

Select Material   To properly adjust for shrinkage and to load temperature properties for simulation, you must select the material the component will be made of.

There are a few tools that you can select in different stages depending on your preference. For example, you can place a sketch to define your runner before or after the core and cavity have been calculated. These tools are as follows:

Manual Sketch   This tool is a flyout option under the Auto Runner Sketch tool. It can also be used to create a runner sketch, but it is used to sketch complex cooling line routes as well.

Runner   Many of the standard runner shapes can be applied to the core, cavity, or both sides of the mold. These shapes have additional options such as applying a cold slug to the end of the runner.

Gate   Like the Runner, the Gate has a selection of the common gate types. You can enter values to modify their size to suit.

Importing a Plastic Part

You will now start the process of defining the plastic part and the material that will drop out of the mold in the context of the mold design:

1. In the New File dialog box, click the Metric node in the left pane and then select the Mold Design (mm).iam template.

2. Give the new design the name **Mastering Inventor Tooling**.

3. Click the Browse button to specify the save location for the files that will be generated for this mold design.

4. Select the Chapter 19 directory and then create a new folder called MI_Tooling_054.

5. Select this folder and click Save to return to the previous dialog box.

6. Check the filename and file location path and click the OK button to create the mold assembly file.

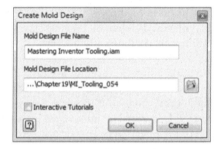

Two new tabs have been added to the ribbon: Mold Layout and Mold Assembly. Keep in mind that you may need to manually switch tabs to access certain tools at different times, depending on the tasks and the order in which you work. Other tabs will be created during the mold design process as well. Next, you'll import a plastic part to work with.

7. Click the Plastic Part button in the Mold Layout tab and select the file mi_19a_054 .ipt. Then click Open to import the file, right-click and make sure the Align With Part Centroid option is selected, and then select Finish.

8. Select the Adjust Orientation tool from the Mold Layout panel. The preview of the Opening Direction will appear. Using the Flip button in the dialog box, flip the Z direction of the part so your preview looks like Figure 19.21.

FIGURE 19.21
Setting the opening direction

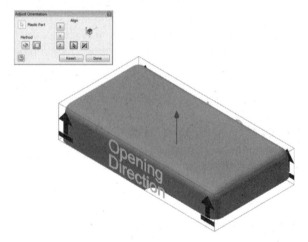

9. Click the OK button when the direction has been properly set.

10. Click the Select Material button from the Mold Layout panel and change the manufacturer to BASF and the Trade Name to Terluran GP-22; then click the OK button.

11. Rotate the model so you can see the bottom of the part.

12. On the Runners And Channels panel, click the flyout under the Auto Runner Sketch button and select the Manual Sketch button.

13. In the resulting dialog box, ensure that the Runner Sketch option is selected and select the bottom-most face on the part, as shown in Figure 19.22. Click the OK button to create the sketch.

FIGURE 19.22
Creating a runner sketch

14. Use the Project Geometry tool to project the x-axis (in the Origin folder) and the leftmost edge of the part into your sketch; then draw a line segment along the x-axis 13 mm long and 6 mm from the left edge of the part, as shown in Figure 19.23. Change the x-axis projection line to construction.

FIGURE 19.23
Dimensioning the runner

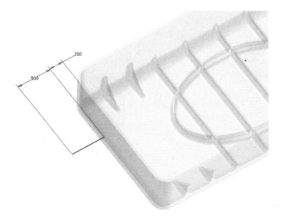

15. When the line is complete, right-click and choose Finish Edit to return to the Mold Layout tools.

16. Save your work, and you will notice that a number of components are being created. Note too that these files are being saved in the mold design directory you created.

In this case, you've created the runner sketch before creating and calculating the core and cavity. Although you are not required to work in this order, it can help to visualize how the runner and gate material will appear attached to the part when it drops from the mold. This is the approach you will take for the next exercises. You can close the file you have open and continue on to explore the creation of runners and gates.

Creating Runners and Gates

Now you will place the runner and gate. To continue, open the file mi_19a_056.iam from the Chapter 19 directory of your Mastering Inventor 2016 folder. This file picks up where you left off in the previous exercise:

1. On the Runners And Channels panel, click the Runner button to open the Create Runner dialog box.

2. Set Section Type to U Shape.

3. Use the radio button to set the runner to be created on the cavity side.

4. Set the radius to **3 mm**.

5. Move your mouse along the 13 mm sketched line and notice the runner changing directions at the ends. Select the 13 mm sketched line for the path selection. Be sure to select it on the end farthest from the part. Selecting the line toward the other end creates the runner turned in the opposite direction. If you select the wrong end, just hold the Ctrl key and click it again to deselect it; then try again.

6. For Segment1, set the Cold Slug Length to **4 mm**.

7. Check your settings against Figure 19.24 and then click the OK button to create the runner.

FIGURE 19.24
Placing the runner

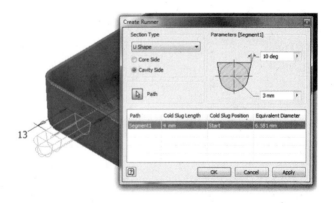

If you expand the Runner node in the browser, you will see your runner and runner sketch listed. You can double-click or right-click them to edit if changes are required. Next, you'll get ready to add a gate.

8. In the Runners And Channels panel, click the Gate Location button.

9. Select the top-left edge of the part. This is the edge with a sketch line running along it from the runner sketch. You can also use the ViewCube to verify the edge location where the left and bottom views intersect.

10. A ratio will appear in the dialog box. Set this to **0.5**, meaning the gate will be placed half-way along the length of the edge. The preview should show an X at the intersection of the runner sketch lines.

11. Click Apply to create the gate location and then click Done to close the dialog box.

Now you will add the gate. There are a lot of options, so this will take several steps.

12. Click the Gate button to open the Create Gate dialog box.

13. Set Placement to Two Points. Inventor will start looking for the gate location.

14. Ensure that Type is set to Edge and then set the Up/Down radio button to Up.

15. Select the work point that displays the gate location you previously defined.

16. Once the work point is selected, Inventor will want the endpoint. Select the end of the runner sketch nearest to the part (this correlates to the 6 mm offset dimension).

17. In the dialog box, set the value of W1 to **22**.

18. Set H1 to **12**.

19. Set W2 to **15**.

20. Set H2 to **6** and compare your inputs to Figure 19.25.

FIGURE 19.25
Placing the gate between the part and runner

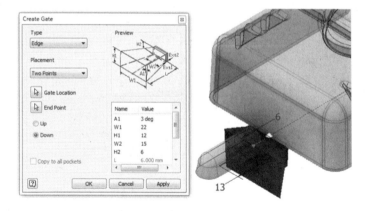

21. Click the OK button to create the gate when everything appears correct.

In the previous steps, you explored the creation of runner and gate features. Although these features have many variations, the basic selections and steps to create them are the same. You can close the current file without saving changes and continue to the next section, where you will explore core and cavity design.

Analyzing and Creating Cores and Cavities

Now that you have defined your part's material and how you want the plastic to flow into the mold, the next step is to begin defining the mold itself. Keep in mind that all the geometry you've been working on so far will become a void in the components you are about to create.

The tools needed to determine whether the part will fill properly and to establish the geometry of the core and cavity are more automated than other tools in Inventor. These tools will also inform you if you have missed a step in the process. Here is a brief overview of some of them:

Part Process Settings   Optimal values for the mold temperature and pressures are loaded from the material information. This dialog box allows you to make modifications to accommodate your equipment if need be.

Part Fill Analysis   Inventor Tooling has the ability to analyze the fill time, quality, and other important considerations regarding where weld lines may appear or air traps may occur.

Define Workpiece Setting   Establishing the size of the tool from which your core and cavity will be cut is an important step. You must accommodate the runner and eventually the components of the assembly that move the material to the cavity.

Create Runoff Surface   A runoff surface can be seen as an extension of the parting line. It is the surface that will be used to divide the workpiece so the parts of the mold can separate.

Generate Core And Cavity   This tool launches you into another environment that is focused on how the workpiece will be modified to create the void for the plastic to fill.

To continue, open the file mi_19a_057.iam from the Chapter 19 directory of your Mastering Inventor 2016 folder. This file picks up where you left off in the previous exercise. To create the core, cavity, and other components, you will first need to change the environment in which you are working:

1. On the Mold Layout panel, click the Core And Cavity button. This brings up the Core/Cavity tab, which gives you access to the tools needed to create the workpiece that will be added to the mold base to complete the design.

2. Select the Gate Location button on the Plastic Part panel to place the gate in the workpiece. Note that these steps will be the same as those you followed in the previous exercise.

3. Select the bottom-left edge of the part near the visible work point.

4. Set the ratio to **0.5** to place the gate halfway along the length of the edge.

5. Click the Apply button to create the gate location and then click Yes when warned about the existing analysis results. Then click Done to close the dialog box.

6. Select the Part Process Settings button from the Plastic Part panel. Review the settings and then click the OK button to accept the default and close the dialog box.

7. Select the Part Fill Analysis button from the Plastic Part panel. Understand that this analysis may take some time to run, so if you prefer, you can just click Close and skip this step. If you'd like to run an analysis yourself, click Start, click Yes when warned about existing analysis requests, and then click the OK button in the message box letting you know that the analysis is running.

8. When the analysis is complete, a summary showing the results will appear. If you skipped the previous step, you can view a previously prepared results summary. To do so, expand the node for mi_19a_054 in the browser and then expand the Results node and then the Fill node. Click the Summary node to bring up the results summary.

In Figure 19.26, you can see that the part can be filled, but there is concern about the quality obtained from the current setup.

FIGURE 19.26
Part fill analysis summary

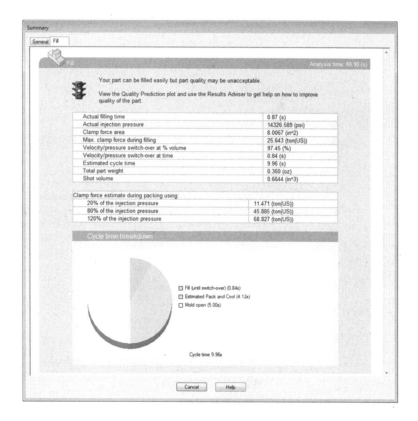

9. Click Cancel to close the summary.

10. Double-click Fill Time in the browser to display the graphic in the design window (Figure 19.27).

FIGURE 19.27
Fill time analysis results

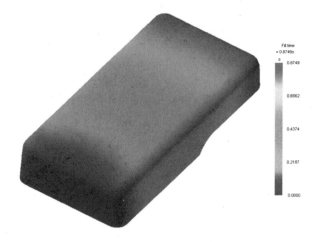

11. Select the Define Workpiece Setting button on the Parting Design panel and set the following values, as shown in the lower right of Figure 19.28:

◆ X_Total value to **150**

◆ Y_Total value to **75**

◆ Z_Total value to **30**

FIGURE 19.28
Generating the runoff
surface for splitting the
mold

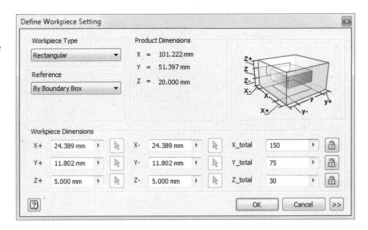

12. Click the OK button to preview the workpiece in the design window.

13. Select the Create Runoff Surface button on the Parting Design panel.

14. In the upper-left corner of the Create Runoff Surface dialog box, select the Auto Detect button to allow Inventor to search for the best parting line and create the runoff surface. The result should appear similar to Figure 19.29.

FIGURE 19.29
Setting the workpiece
size values

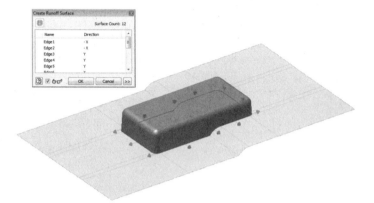

15. Click the OK button to create the parting surface that will divide the core and cavity.

16. Click the Generate Core And Cavity button on the Parting Design panel.

17. In the resulting dialog box, click the Preview/Diagnose button. This will preview the core in blue and the cavity in green.

18. Drag the Body Separation slider to the right and back to show how the parts will separate.

19. Click the OK button to generate the two parts.

On occasion, the runner and gate information created beforehand does not update with the generation of the core and cavity. Select the Mold Update tool from the Quick Access bar to bring this data up into the cavity side of the workpiece.

20. Click the Finish Core/Cavity button at the end of the ribbon to return to the Mold Layout tools and compare your work to Figure 19.30. You can close this file without saving changes and continue to the next section.

FIGURE 19.30
The completed workpiece

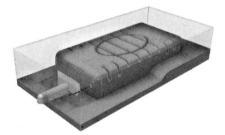

Working with Mold Bases

Now that the workpiece is complete, you can focus on generating the rest of the mold. These tools are located on the Mold Assembly tab. The tools in this tab are focused on the tools needed by manufacturing to generate the part efficiently. Inventor Tooling contains tens of thousands of parts for mold bases, as defined by the manufacturers. This works like a design accelerator to keep you from specifying something that will be a custom order or an inaccurate component. In the following exercise, you will focus on creating a mold base.

You will now build the entire mold base in just a few steps with minimal input and effort. This is a great example of how the functional design approach can work for you. To get started, open the file mi_19a_059.iam from the Chapter 19 directory of your Mastering Inventor 2016 folder and then follow these steps:

1. Switch to the Mold Assembly tab on the ribbon.

2. Click the Mold Base button in the Mold Assembly panel to open the Mold Base dialog box.

3. The Mold Base dialog box allows you to select from a huge library of standard mold base designs and to select options within those base designs. The following steps use items from the Content Center Mold database. To ensure that you can access these files, check your project and make sure the libraries are loaded. You can do so by selecting the Projects button on the Get Started tab, clicking the Configure Content Center Libraries button (in the lower-right corner), and selecting the Inventor Mold libraries.

4. From the Vendor And Type drop-down, select the DME; then click the Query button and select the type E base. Note that if you have previously selected the Immediately Query check box, you will not need to click the Query button.

5. Set the size to **346 mm × 346 mm**.

6. Expand the dialog box by clicking the double-arrow icons on the top- or bottom-right edge of the dialog box.

7. Expanding the dialog box will show the list of components included in the mold base.

8. Select the part labeled E 400 346X346X76.

9. Once the part is selected, several buttons appear for that row. Select the button with the ellipsis (three dots; the tool tip will say Property Settings). This will launch a dialog box for changing options (if any exist).

10. Click the H_value and change it in the drop-down list from 76 mm to **56 mm**, as shown in Figure 19.31.

11. Click the OK button to close the dialog box. Inventor will update the E400 plate's description and the preview in the dialog box.

12. Click the Placement Reference button and select the bottom point in the front-left corner of the workpiece (use the ViewCube for reference to find the left and front sides).

13. You will see a preview outline of where the mold base will be positioned around the workpiece. Make sure the workpiece appears inside the rectangle.

14. Once you've verified that the workpiece appears inside the rectangle, click the OK button in the dialog box to generate the mold base.

FIGURE 19.31
Changing the mold-base
components

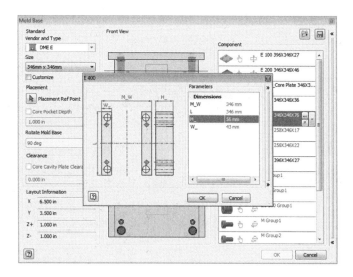

15. If the Mold Update button becomes visible in the Quick Access bar, click it and compare your work to Figure 19.32.

FIGURE 19.32
The mold base after
placement

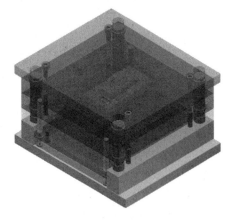

You may not have been expecting the entire mold base to be generated, but since the components are purchased, it makes sense to place them as a unit as they would be assembled. You can close this file without saving changes and continue to the next section.

Working with Ejectors and Sprue Bushings

You will now complete one last series of steps to see the final critical details of placing ejectors and the sprue bushing:

Ejector   Accessing the library of standard ejector pins is only part of this tool. It will make it easy for you to properly align the pins based on the center of the component, using a coordinate system that is used by the toolmakers.

Sprue Bushing   This tool places the standard sprue bushing based on the location of the runner, simplifying the process of placement and improving the quality.

To get started, open the file `mi_19a_060.iam` from the `Chapter 19` directory of your `Mastering Inventor 2016` folder. Then follow these steps:

1. On the Mold Assembly tab, click the Ejector button.

Doing so clears the screen of everything but the original part and runoff surface. It also opens the Ejector dialog box, which contains standard ejector pins and their optional sizes.

2. Leaving the options at the default, click the plastic part to place four ejectors. You can choose four approximate locations between the pairs of ribs, as shown in Figure 19.33.

FIGURE 19.33

Placing the ejectors

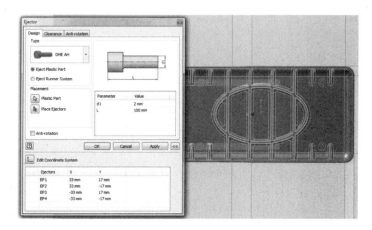

3. Click the >> button in the dialog box and set the values to **33 mm** or **−33 mm** for the X column and **17 mm** or **−17 mm** for the Y column.

The order in which you placed your ejectors might cause your positive or negative values to differ, but entering the inputs as shown will give you the correct result.

4. Set the diameter (d1 value) to **2 mm** and the length (L value) to **100 mm** and then click the OK button to place the ejectors in the mold.

Placing the ejector will cause Inventor to make clearance cuts in other plates and cut the length or even the contour of the ejector to prepare all the components in the mold base. Select any of the pins in the browser to show how they terminate at the core face of the mold.

Next, you'll place a sprue bushing and a locking ring.

5. On the Mold Assembly tab, click the Sprue Bushing button. It will be looking for a point from which to locate.

6. Select the visible sketch center point at the end of the runner sketch farthest from the part.

7. Set Type to **DME AGN**.

8. Set the length (L value) in the dialog box to 76 mm using the drop-down.

9. For an offset value, enter **−14 mm**.

10. Click the OK button to place the bushing and cut the clearance geometry in the relevant parts.

11. Select Sprue Bushing in the Design window.

12. Right-click and select Open from the context menu.

13. Rotate the part to see how the runner geometry has been cut from the bushing, as shown in Figure 19.34.

FIGURE 19.34
The runner geometry is cut into the sprue bushing.

14. To return to the assembly, close the Sprue Bushing part and do not save changes.

15. Click the Locating Ring button on the Mold Assembly panel.

16. Set the type to Rabourdin 646-Type B and choose the top of the base face (green plate).

17. Set the D2 value to **32 mm** and the A_ value to **22.5 mm** and then set the offset value to **−22.5 mm**.

18. Click the OK button to place the ring into the assembly.

The finished base should look like Figure 19.35.

FIGURE 19.35
The finished base

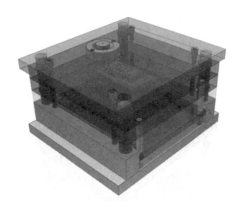

Through use of functional design techniques, the most tedious steps of designing a mold are eliminated or greatly simplified. You can close this file without saving changes, explore the Inventor Tooling tools with your own design, and take advantage of just how easy it is to create a complex mold design.

You can also find additional mold and tooling tutorials built right into Inventor by clicking the Tutorials button.

The Bottom Line

Create thicken/offset features.   When creating plastic parts, you will often find that working with surfaces allows you to achieve more free-form shapes than working with solids. Once the surfaces are created, you'll need to give them a thin wall thickness.

Master It   How would you create a plastic part file with many curved, free-form elements?

Create shell features.   Shelling solids parts and features is a common way to create base features for plastic parts. Once the shell feature is created, other features can be added to it.

Master It   You want to create a shell feature but need to have some faces be thicker than the rest. How would you accomplish this?

Create split features.   Many times you may want to establish the overall shape of a feature and then divide the shape into separate parts of the overall design. You can use the Split tool to do just that and more.

Master It   You have a plastic part that needs to have a raised face for a rubber grip applied during the manufacturing process. How would this be done?

Create grill features.   Grill features allow the inflow or outflow of air through a plastic thin-wall part. Grills can be created with a number of subfeatures such as islands, ribs, and spars, but only the outer profile of the grill is required.

Master It   How would you determine the area of a grill opening based on the airflow it needs to handle?

Create rule fillet features.   Rule fillets can be an extremely efficient way to apply fillets throughout the design to many edges that meet the same rule criteria.

Master It   How would you apply fillets to all of the edges that are generated by extruding a shape down to an existing set of base features?

Create rest features.   Rest features can be used to create level platform faces for mounting other parts to an irregular plastic part face.

Master It   You want to create a rectangular pocket on the inside of a plastic housing to hold an electronic component. How would you do this?

Create boss features.   Boss features are ideal for creating fastener-mounting standoffs for thin-wall plastic parts. You can use the Boss tool to create both halves of the fastener boss.

Master It   You want to create multiple boss features around the perimeter of a flat, pan-type base part, but you know this base part is likely to change size. How would you set up the boss features to adjust to the anticipated edits?

Create lip and groove features.   When designing plastic parts, you may need one half of a design to fit into the other half. The Lip tool allows you to create both lip and groove features for these situations.

> **Master It**   You want to create a groove around the edge of an irregular, curved edge. How can you ensure that the lip on the corresponding part will match?

Create snap-fit features.   Snap features are a common way to join plastic parts together so that they can be disassembled as needed. You can use the Snap Fit tool in Inventor to quickly create these features.

> **Master It**   How would you create a U-shaped snap fit with the Snap Fit tool?

Create rib and web features.   Ribs and webs are often used to add rigidity and prevent warping during the design of plastic parts. You can add ribs based on open profile sketches in Inventor.

> **Master It**   How would you create a network of ribs that are evenly spaced, with some of them containing different cutouts than others?

Create draft features.   Because plastic parts must be extracted from a mold during the manufacturing process, drafted faces must be included to ensure that the parts can indeed be extracted from the mold.

> **Master It**   You want to create drafted faces on a complex part containing various shapes within it. How would you do this?

Create an injection mold.   To generate the components you have designed with the plastic part features, you need to properly define the cavity to create the part and define how the material will flow into the cavity.

> **Master It**   You want to create a mold base design in an efficient manner using parts that can be purchased.

Chapter 20

iLogic

In this chapter, you will explore the use of iLogic to configure your models with intelligence and automation. iLogic is often used to speed up tedious design tasks, to enforce consistency across designs, and to allow the logic of programming to make design decisions based on predetermined design rules. Although this chapter focuses primarily on using iLogic in the parts environments, the fundamentals you'll learn will apply to the assembly and drawing environments as well.

In this chapter, you'll learn to

- ◆ Create iLogic rules
- ◆ Edit iLogic rules
- ◆ Use multi-value list parameters
- ◆ Work with multiple rules in the same file
- ◆ Use conditional statements
- ◆ Suppress features
- ◆ Work with iProperties
- ◆ Create iLogic forms
- ◆ Build a part configuration form

What Is iLogic?

iLogic is a programming add-in that is included with the Autodesk® Inventor® software. It extends and enhances the design capabilities and allows you to automate tedious design tasks. By creating custom iLogic code, you can add higher levels of design intelligence to your models. Using the iLogic tools, you can create simple, rule-based logic to set and drive parameters and properties in your designs. iLogic rules can be embedded directly into individual Inventor files, or they can be saved externally where they can be accessed by all your Inventor files. iLogic uses custom parameter types to allow you to customize more than just the numeric data available with standard Inventor model parameters. These types include Text parameters, True/False parameters, and multi-value list parameters.

To understand how iLogic works, you need to think in terms of design rules. Most design departments already have certain design rules they follow when creating parts and assemblies.

For instance, suppose a design requires a minimum hole spacing to ensure a strong connection. If a part length causes the spacing to exceed the minimum hole spacing, then another hole is added.

Currently, you might follow these rules manually as you design, but with the use of iLogic, you can add the rules to the model file so that the design rules are implemented automatically. You can even have rules trigger other rules so that a cascade of decisions is made based on initial input from the user.

Understanding iLogic Rules

An iLogic rule can be thought of as a small Visual Basic .NET "program" created and used to monitor and control Inventor objects such as parameters, features, and components. A rule can determine and/or set design parameters within your model. This allows you to control the values of the model automatically, based on conditions and inputs.

For example, you might have a product line offered to your customer in standard cataloged sizes, with standard features included or excluded based on the size and application. But you also offer this same design in custom sizes when needed. With traditional Inventor tools, you would determine whether the requested size is standard, and if it is not, you would create a new custom-size component to fit the need. Once the size is determined, you would decide to include or exclude features per your design guidelines and then include other features based on the specific application of this custom design.

Because the process of configuring your product line relies on your experience and memory, it might be time-consuming and error-prone, particularly if you need to have another Inventor user, with less experience with your product, create the design. You can use iLogic to set up a collection of rules in a template file. The first rule might allow you to input the requested size using a customized dialog form. Another rule would determine whether the requested size is an existing standard size or a new custom one. If it is a custom size, a part number and description are automatically generated to honor your standard nomenclature. Yet another rule would then determine whether standard features are included or excluded based on the size (for example, if the hole spacing exceeds X, add another hole). And finally, another rule might be invoked to add application-specific features (for example, add left-hand switch mounting holes, if the custom design is for a left-hand application).

What Are Functions?

A *function* is an instruction created and used within a rule to modify the Inventor model or read some data from the file. When a rule is run, the functions within it are executed. The predefined iLogic functions follow VB.NET syntax and require the coding to follow the syntax to work. This syntax consists of the function category, function name, and function arguments.

In the previous example, where the goal was to create a collection of rules to determine a standard or custom size, the first rule would control the dialog box to collect the input from the user. So, a function would be added to call an input box function and then assign the collected input to an Inventor parameter. Here is an example of an input box function used to prompt the user for a width value:

```
myWidth = InputBox("Please Enter A Width", "Width Input", "750")
```

The resulting input box displays as shown in Figure 20.1 and creates a return value called myWidth, which is set to the value the user enters into the input box. In this case, the default value has been set to 750. So if the user were to accept the default value by clicking the OK button, myWidth would be set to 750.

FIGURE 20.1
A basic iLogic
input box

You might include multiple functions in the same rule, depending on its complexity. When doing so, you will typically place functions in order so that information is created or gathered from one function and then used later by another function. Typically, each function is independent of the remaining code in the rule.

To use the myWidth value from the previous example, you could create a second function to set the Inventor parameter controlling the width of the part equal to myWidth. Here, the Inventor parameter is a dimension in a sketch that has been named Wid1:

```
myWidth = InputBox("Please Enter A Width", "Width Input", "750")
Parameter("Wid1") = myWidth
```

There are several categories of functions provided in iLogic. You can find all the available functions when creating rules by expanding the Snippets List in the rule editing interface. Here is the list of iLogic categories:

Parameter functions	Variables functions
Document functions	iFeature functions
Feature functions	Material Properties functions
Run Other functions	Assembly Constraint functions
Component functions	Sheet Metal functions
BOM functions	Measure functions
iProperties functions	Drawing functions
Math functions	Work Feature functions
Excel Data Links functions	Advanced Drawing API functions
String functions	Message Box functions
iPart and iAssembly functions	Advanced API functions

WORKING WITH FUNCTION ARGUMENTS AND DATA TYPES

Within functions, you can also have arguments. An *argument* is a value that is sent to the function when it is called. Passing an argument to a function gives the function information to work with. An argument can be one of the following data types:

Text Any value specified inside double quotes

Boolean A value of True or False

Numeric Any numeric value

SET VALUES WITH FUNCTIONS

Take a look at this example to see the text string and Boolean data types in use:

```
Feature.IsActive("Hole1") = False
```

Here, the function category Feature is being used. The Feature function IsActive is instructed to look for the feature called Hole1, and then the False argument tells the function to suppress Hole1. If the Boolean were set to True, then the hole would be set active or not suppressed. You'll notice Hole1 is set inside double quotes, thereby specifying it as a text string.

Next, look at this example to see numeric data in use:

```
Parameter("Diameter1") = 4.4
```

Here, the Parameter function is being told to look for the feature called Diameter1 and then use 4.4 as the value. In both of these examples, the function is setting a value. In addition to setting values, you can retrieve or get values using functions.

GET VALUES WITH FUNCTIONS

In the following examples, you'll look at how to get a value from a function. You'll start off with the reciprocal function for the previous function involving Diameter1.

```
Current_Dia = Parameter("Diameter1")
```

Here, the Parameter function is being told to create a return value placeholder called Current_Dia and then set it to the parameter called Diameter1. Next, look at an input box function:

```
Wid1 = InputBox("Please Enter A Width", "Width Input", Wid1)
```

In this function, the return value happens to be an Inventor dimension parameter named Wid1, which is a sketch dimension defining the width of the part. The input box reads the Wid1 parameter into the default value (on the far right) so that the user is presented with the current width and at the same time is prompted to enter a new value. When the user clicks the OK button, the input box value is written to the Inventor dimension parameter named Wid1.

Here is an example comparing the use of functions to get and set information:

```
iProperties.Value("Project", "Revision Number") = 2
RevNumber = iProperties.Value("Project", "Revision Number")
```

In the first line, the function is being given the arguments Project and Revision Number to specify that iProperty be set to 2. In the second line, the return value called RevNumber is being set to the current Revision Number iProperty for the file. Again, it uses the arguments Project and Revision Number to tell the iProperty collection which iProperty to read.

Conditional Statements

You use conditional statements to put the logic in iLogic. The conditional statements evaluate the present state of the model and execute logic depending upon that state. For example, if the hole spacing in a part exceeds a minimum value because of a change in length, then another set of holes is required.

```
Space1 = Parameter("Hole_Space")
If Space1 >= 45 Then
Feature.IsActive("Hole2") = True
Else
Feature.IsActive("Hole2") = False
End If
```

In the first line, a return value parameter named Space1 is set to the model parameter called Hole_Space. Then, Space1 is evaluated to determine whether it is less than or equal to 45. If so, it is set to be active (not suppressed). Otherwise, it is suppressed. The following sections include examples of each of the available conditional statements.

IF, THEN, ELSE STATEMENT

If, Then, Else is probably the most common of the conditional statements. It tests for a condition and then applies one or more actions if the condition is found to be true; otherwise, it applies one or more other actions.

```
If <condition> Then
<action if true>
Else
<action if false>
End If
```

IF, THEN STATEMENT

If, Then tests for a condition and then applies one or more actions if the condition is found to be true. If the condition is not true, then nothing happens.

```
If <condition> Then
<action if true>
End If
```

WHAT ARE COMMENTS?

Text preceded by an apostrophe in iLogic is interpreted as a comment and not as code. You can use this to your advantage by adding notes to your iLogic code to make it easier to understand.

NULL STATEMENT

A null If, Then tests for a condition and then applies no action if the condition is found to be true (the 'do nothing in the following statement is simply a comment and could be omitted). If the condition is not true, one or more actions are applied.

```
If <condition> Then 'do nothing
Else <action if false>
End If
```

SINGLE-LINE IF STATEMENT

You can use a single-line If statement when testing a simple, short condition with short true and false statements. Single-line If, Then tests for a condition and then applies one or more actions if the condition is found to be true. If the condition is not true, then nothing happens.

```
If <condition> Then <action if true> Else <action if false>
```

IF, THEN, ELSEIF STATEMENT

Using the If, Then, ElseIf format, you can add as many conditions as you want. Here is the format when three conditions are being tested. If, Then, ElseIf tests for a condition and then applies one or more actions if the condition is found to be true. If not true, it tests another condition, and so on. If none of the tested conditions is found to be true, it applies one or more other actions. If no final action is specified, nothing happens unless one of the conditions is found to be true.

```
If <condition 1> Then
<action if condition 1 is true>
ElseIf <condition 2> Then
<action if condition 2 is true>
ElseIf <condition 3> Then
<action if condition 3 is true>
Else
<action if none of the above conditions is true>
End If
```

SELECT CASE STATEMENT

The Select Case statement is another way to test what is inside a variable. You can use it when you know there are only a limited number of values that the variable could hold.

```
Select Case <test expression>
Case <expression list 1>
<statement list 1>
Case <expression list 2>
<statement list 2>
Case Else
<statement list n>
End Select
```

For instance, if a multi-value list parameter named Part_Size consisted of a list containing Small, Medium, and Large, you could set the test expression to Part_Size and set up three cases called Small, Medium, and Large, as shown here:

```
Select Case Part_Size
Case "Small"
Len = 50
Wid = 40
Case "Medium"
Len = 75
Wid = 65
Case "Large"
Len = 100
Wid = 90
End Select
```

When the `Part_Size` parameter is set to `Small`, the case named `Small` is selected, and the `Len` and `Wid` parameters are set to the values corresponding to the small size.

Understanding the iLogic Elements and Interface

There are two primary areas within Inventor used to create and manage iLogic rules: the Parameters editing dialog box and the iLogic browser. The Parameters dialog box is used to create and edit parameters to be used in iLogic, and the iLogic browser allows you to create and manage rules. Figure 20.2 shows the Parameters button, accessed from the Manage tab, and Figure 20.3 shows the iLogic Browser button, also accessed from the Manage tab.

FIGURE 20.2
The Parameters button

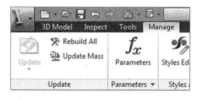

FIGURE 20.3
The iLogic Browser button

Exploring iLogic Parameter Types

Recall that Inventor has three types of parameters:

- ◆ Model parameters are created by dimensions and feature inputs.

- ◆ Reference parameters are created from driven dimensions.

- ◆ User parameters are created by you, the user.

Within the user parameter category, you can create three parameter types: the *Text parameter*, the *True/False parameter*, and the *Numeric parameter*. The Numeric parameter can be referenced into your Inventor model using the standard Inventor tools, but the Text and Boolean parameters can be used only with the iLogic tools.

To create user parameters and specify the type, you use the drop-down list in the Parameters dialog box, as shown in Figure 20.4.

FIGURE 20.4

User parameter types

TEXT PARAMETERS

A Text parameter is any value specified within double quotes. For instance, if you wanted to use product names in an iLogic rule to fill out iProperty information, you could create a Text parameter to contain that information. Keep in mind that you can create a Text parameter using numeric data by enclosing it in double quotes. For instance, Inventor will read "22 mm" as a text string but 22 mm as numeric data. Text parameters can be set to be multi-value list parameters or used as static, single-value parameters.

TRUE/FALSE PARAMETERS

True/False parameters fall within the Boolean data type. They have only two states: True and False. A True/False parameter would be used, for example, when asking a user a question. Figure 20.5 shows an input box with two radio buttons. Depending on which the user chooses, a True/False parameter named Part_Type is toggled.

FIGURE 20.5

An input box used to toggle a True/False parameter

Here is the iLogic rule that produces the input box and then sets the True/False parameter named `Part_Type`. The `Part_Type` parameter is then used to set the material iProperty of the part file.

```
Part_Type = InputRadioBox("Choose Manufacturing Type", "Machined", "Cast", _
Part_Type, Title:= "Select Part Type")

If Part_Type = True Then
iProperties.Material = "Aluminum-6061"
ElseIf Part_Type = False Then
iProperties.Material = "Cast Steel"
End If
```

NUMERIC PARAMETERS

Numeric parameters are the parameters used by Inventor sketch dimensions and feature dialog box inputs. When you create a sketch dimension and input value, you are creating a Numeric parameter. You can create Numeric user parameters to hold formulas, which are then called into sketch dimensions, and so on. In addition to using Numeric parameters with the standard Inventor modeling tools, you can use them with iLogic. Numeric parameters can be set to be multi-value list parameters or used as static, single-value parameters.

Note that you can add unit strings to Numeric parameters and Inventor will still read them as numeric. For instance, Inventor will read 45 mm as numeric data. If the model length unit is set to millimeters, Inventor will read 45 as numeric data and assume millimeters. Recall that you can set the default units for any model file by selecting the Tools tab, clicking the Document Settings button, and then selecting the Units tab.

MULTIVALUE LISTS

Text and Numeric parameters can consist of a single, static value or can be made into a multi-value list. To create a multi-value list, follow these general steps:

1. On the Manage tab, click the Parameters button.

2. In the Parameters dialog box, choose Add Text from the drop-down at the bottom left.

3. Name the Text parameter as you see fit (recall that spaces are not allowed in parameter names, but you can use an underscore).

4. Right-click the new parameter and choose Make Multi-Value.

5. Enter values into the list editor to populate your list.

Figure 20.6 shows a multi-value list for product names being populated. The values on the bottom have already been added; the ones on the top are being entered.

Once the multi-value list is populated, you can add or remove entries by right-clicking the parameter and choosing Edit Multi-Value List, as shown in Figure 20.7.

FIGURE 20.6
Populating a multi-value
list

FIGURE 20.7
Editing a multi-value list

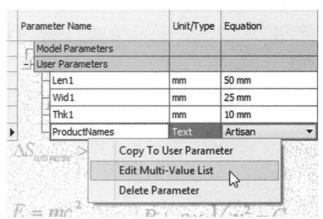

KEY PARAMETERS

You can designate some parameters as Key parameters to aid in the placement of iLogic components into an assembly later. For instance, if you had a part file with 50 parameters in it, you'd likely want to designate only a small number of those as key parameters. This allows you to choose which parameters the user can adjust during the file placement, and it streamlines the process as well. To set a parameter to be a key, check the box next to the parameter in the Key column. Once you have Key parameters, you can click the Filter button at the lower left of the Parameters dialog box to show All, Key, Non-Key, Renamed, or Equation only.

Using the iLogic Browser

The iLogic browser is the interface item used to create, edit, and manage rules and forms within Inventor. You can access the iLogic browser from the Manage tab by clicking the iLogic Browser button on the iLogic panel, as shown previously in Figure 20.3. Once it's displayed, you will find four tabs in the iLogic browser.

- Rules
- Forms

> ◆ Global Forms
>
> ◆ External Rules

THE RULES TAB

The Rules tab allows you to add, edit, run, regenerate, suppress, and delete rules. When rules are created, they are automatically listed in the Rules tab; therefore, the Rules tab will always list all rules embedded in the current document.

Adding Rules

To add a new rule to an Inventor file, right-click anywhere in the Rules tab of the iLogic browser and choose Add Rule (Figure 20.8).

FIGURE 20.8
Choose Add Rule from the browser to begin creating an iLogic rule.

Alternatively, you can use the Add Rule button on the iLogic panel of the Manage tab. The first step to adding a rule is entering a name for the rule in the Rule Name input box. Once the name is entered, you are presented with the Edit Rule dialog box, where you can build the rule. You'll explore the creation of rules in the coming pages.

Editing Rules

To edit an existing rule in an Inventor file, right-click the rule in the Rules tab of the iLogic browser and choose Edit Rule (Figure 20.9). You will be presented with the Edit Rule dialog box, where you can make changes to the rule. The section "Creating iLogic Rules" later in the chapter shows how to build rules in this dialog box.

FIGURE 20.9
Choosing to edit an iLogic rule from the browser

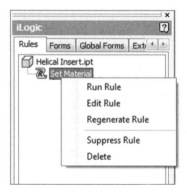

THE FORMS TAB

The Forms tab allows you to add iLogic user input forms. These forms are built using the iLogic Form Editor, which makes creating customized user input forms remarkably easy. You'll work with the Form Editor in "Creating iLogic Forms."

Adding Forms

To add a new form to an Inventor file, select the Forms tab in the iLogic browser, right-click in the tab, and choose Add Form (Figure 20.10).

FIGURE 20.10
Choosing to add an iLogic form from the browser

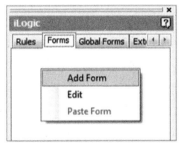

You can also add forms by selecting the Manage tab, clicking the drop-down on the iLogic panel, and then clicking the Add Form button. When using this method, you'll have an option to choose whether the form is intended to be embedded in the current document or to be a global form used by all documents.

Editing Forms

To edit an existing form in an Inventor file, right-click the Form button in the Form tab and choose Edit (Figure 20.11).

FIGURE 20.11
Choosing to edit an iLogic form from the browser

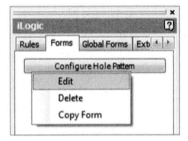

THE GLOBAL FORMS TAB

The Global Forms tab lists all the rules stored outside of Inventor, independent of the actual Inventor file you are working on. Global forms can be used when you want to use the same form across multiple rules so that you don't need to create the form over and over again. They also help promote consistency, and you can make edits to forms in multiple rules quickly and in one global location. To add a global form, you set the Global Forms tab to active, right-click in the tab, and choose Add Form (Figure 20.12).

FIGURE 20.12
Choosing to add a global iLogic form from the browser

You can also add global forms by selecting the Manage tab, clicking the drop-down on the iLogic panel, and then clicking the Add Form button. When using this method, you have an option to embed the form in the current document or use it as a global form in all documents.

Global forms are stored within the Design Data folder. You can find the location by clicking the Global Forms tab and choosing Open Containing Folder (shown in Figure 20.12). Recall from Chapter 1, "Getting Started," that the location of the Design Data folder can be specified in two ways.

Application Options On the Tools tab, click the Application Options button and then click the File tab. Set the Design Data path to the location of your choice. Be aware that this sets the location on the installation of Inventor being used to set the path. Therefore, if you work with other Inventor users and want to have all the installs looking at the same Design Data folder, you would need to walk around to each machine and set this path or use the Project Settings method.

Project Settings Close all open Inventor files. Ensure that no other users are accessing the project file (*.ipj) that you intend to edit. On the Get Started tab, click the Projects button. In the Projects editor dialog, locate the Folder Options node in the bottom pane and expand it. Set the Design Data path to the location of your choice. This method sets the path per the project file and therefore overrides the Application Options setting if the two do not match. If multiple users are using the same project, then all of them will now be using the new Design Data folder.

THE EXTERNAL RULES TAB

The External Rules tab lists all the rules stored outside of Inventor, independent of the actual Inventor file you are working on. External rules can be used as iLogic rules or as small programs that are run manually (like VBA macros). To add an existing external rule, set the External Rules tab active, right-click in the tab, and choose Create New External Rule, as shown in Figure 20.13.

FIGURE 20.13
Adding an external rule from the browser

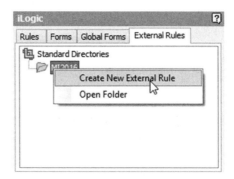

INVENTOR 2016 EXTERNAL iLOGIC CREATE RULE IS MISSING

At the time of writing, there is a bug that means Create New Rule is missing. You can find the latest on this by searching the Autodesk Inventor 2016 Help for incident ID 65889.

The workaround is to add a directory in the Advanced iLogic Configuration dialog box. You can open this by clicking Tools ➤ Options ➤ iLogic Configuration (see Figure 20.14).

FIGURE 20.14
Adding a new directory for external iLogic rules

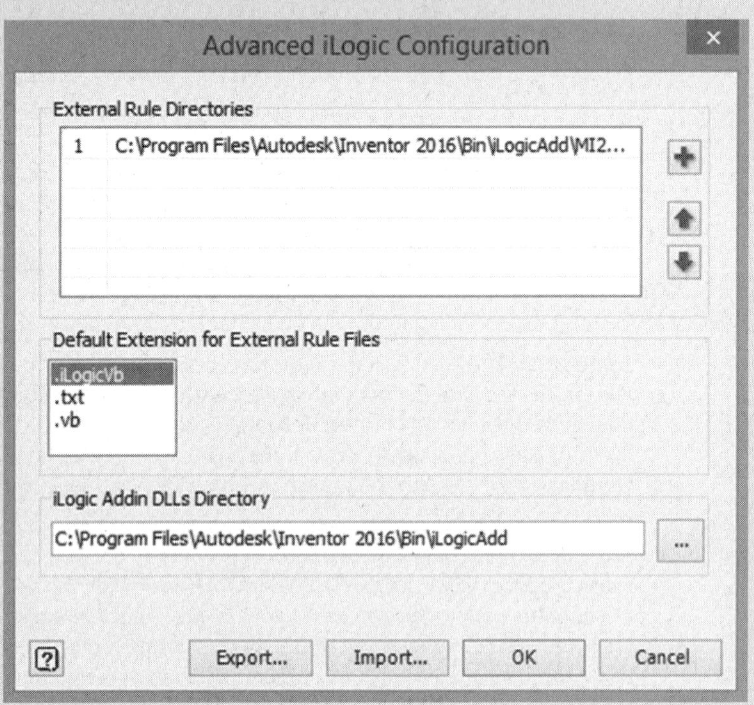

When you choose Create New External Rule, you will be prompted with the Create Rule File dialog box, where you can browse to a location and save the rule as one of the three available file formats: plain text (*.txt), iLogic VB (*.ilogicVb), or Visual Basic (*.vb). Generally, this location is on a shared network where all users can access the files. Figure 20.15 shows a new external rule being created and saved in a location called iLogic Rules in the Mastering Inventor project path. Once the rule file is created, you are presented with the Edit Rule dialog box, where you can build the rule. External rules are often used with event triggers, such as Before Save, which will run the rule when the file is saved.

FIGURE 20.15
Creating an external
rule

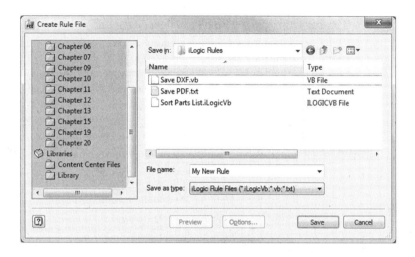

EXTERNAL RULE FILE SAVE LOCATION

You can set up default external rule file save locations and the default filename extension by selecting the Tools tab, clicking the drop-down on the Options panel, and then clicking the iLogic Configuration button, as shown here.

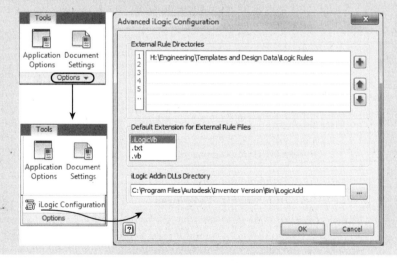

Understanding the iTrigger

An iTrigger is an Inventor user parameter that you can include in the current file to trigger rules manually. This parameter is often used to test a rule while you are creating it.

The iTrigger button on the iLogic panel of the Manage tab initially creates a user parameter named iTrigger0. If the parameter already exists, the value of the iTrigger parameter is incremented by 1 and triggers any rule containing the iTrigger0 parameter. If multiple rules contain the iTrigger, they are all triggered. Here is a rule to save the current file as a PDF that contains the iTrigger:

```
'set the trigger
trigger = iTrigger0
'path and file name without extension
path_and_name = ThisDoc.PathAndFileName(False)
'call the PDF addin
PDFAddIn = ThisApplication.ApplicationAddIns.ItemById_
("{0AC6FD96-2F4D-42CE-8BE0-8AEA580399E4}")
oDocument = ThisApplication.ActiveDocument
oContext = ThisApplication.TransientObjects.CreateTranslationContext
oContext.Type = IOMechanismEnum.kFileBrowseIOMechanism
oOptions = ThisApplication.TransientObjects.CreateNameValueMap
oDataMedium = ThisApplication.TransientObjects.CreateDataMedium

'set the PDF publish options
If PDFAddIn.HasSaveCopyAsOptions(oDataMedium, oContext, oOptions) Then
'oOptions.Value("All_Color_AS_Black") = 0
oOptions.Value("Remove_Line_Weights") = 1
oOptions.Value("Vector_Resolution") = 400
oOptions.Value("Sheet_Range") = Inventor.PrintRangeEnum.kPrintAllSheets
'oOptions.Value("Custom_Begin_Sheet") = 2
'oOptions.Value("Custom_End_Sheet") = 4
End If

'Set the destination file name
oDataMedium.FileName = path_and_name & ".pdf"
'Publish PDF
.Call PDFAddIn.SaveCopyAs(oDocument, oContext, oOptions, oDataMedium)
```

Working with Event Triggers

An event trigger is used to set up a rule to trigger automatically. For instance, you might want to create a rule to prompt you to fill out the file properties when you save the file. To do so, you simply add the rule to the Before Save event. The rule is triggered when you save a file, allowing you to enter or confirm the iProperties, and then the file is saved. Here is a list of the available event triggers:

◆ When a new file is created

◆ After a file is opened

- Before a file is saved

- After a file is saved

- Before a file is closed

- When any model parameter is changed

- When an iProperty is changed

- When a feature of a part is suppressed or unsuppressed

- When the geometry of a part is changed

- When the material of a part is changed

- When a component of an assembly is suppressed or unsuppressed

- When a component of an iPart or iAssembly is changed

- When a drawing view is changed

To add a rule to an event trigger, select the Manage tab and click the Event Trigger button on the iLogic panel. Then select the event you want to use and click the Select Rules button. You can then select from the available rules. Keep in mind that you will see only applicable event triggers in the list when setting a trigger for an event. For instance, if the current file you are working in is an IDW file, you will not see event triggers such as Material Change (changing the material of a part) in the list.

Creating iLogic Parameters, Rules, and Forms

Now that you've had an overview of the iLogic tools and components, you are ready to create iLogic parameters, rules, and forms. You'll start by focusing on rules using input and message boxes and then look at creating and using iLogic forms.

Creating iLogic Rules

In the following pages, you'll explore the methods and options of creating iLogic rules. To add a new rule to an Inventor file, you right-click the file node in the Rules tab of the iLogic browser and choose Add Rule.

Creating Your First Rule

Once a rule is created using Add Rule, you are presented with the Edit Rule dialog box. This dialog has four main interface panes, as shown in Figure 20.16.

Snippets List (#1)   Contains snippets (short sections of code that you can copy and paste) categorized by function for easy reference.

Rule Authoring Pane (#2)   The area where you input and edit your rule code.

Tabs Area (#3)   Provides access to the Model, Options, Search And Replace, and Wizards tools. In Figure 20.16, the Model tab is selected. You can see that it gives you access to the model parameters and features for inclusion in the rule.

Subtabs (#4)   A subset of the Model tab. As displayed in Figure 20.16, the Parameters tab lists the model parameters because Model Parameters is selected on the left.

FIGURE 20.16

The Edit Rule dialog box

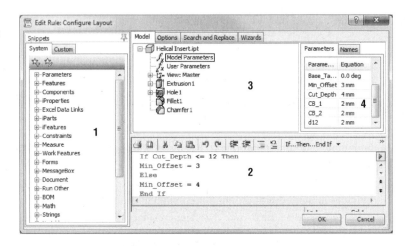

To see how all of this works, you can use the following steps to create a simple rule. If you have not already downloaded the Chapter 20 files from www.sybex.com/go/masteringinventor2016, please refer to the "What You Will Need" section of the introduction for the download and setup instructions. The goal of the rule you will create in this example is to create user inputs to control the width and length of the plate.

1. Click the Open button on the Get Started tab, browse for mi_20a_001.ipt in the Chapter 20 directory of your Mastering Inventor 2016 folder, and open it.

2. Click the Manage tab and select the iLogic Browser button on the iLogic panel to ensure your iLogic browser is displayed.

3. In the iLogic browser, ensure that the Rules tab is selected, right-click anywhere in the Rules tab, and choose Add Rule.

4. Enter **Size Input** into the Rule Name dialog box and then click the OK button.

5. In the Edit Rule dialog box, make sure the Model tab along the top is set active and then expand the model node (if needed) and select Model Parameters. All the model parameters for this part file are now listed in the Parameters subtab on the right.

6. In the Model tab, click Extrusion1 and notice the Parameters tab now shows only the parameters used in Extrusion1.

7. In the Snippets Category list (on the left), locate the MessageBox node and expand it by clicking the plus sign.

8. Locate the InputBox item toward the bottom of the list and double-click it. This will place the generic InputBox function into your rule, thereby providing the template syntax you need to follow. This function should read as follows:

```
myparam = InputBox("Prompt", "Title", "Default Entry")
```

◆ myparam is the placeholder for the return value (the value retrieved from the input box).

◆ InputBox is the name of the function.

◆ "Prompt" is the placeholder for the message to appear in the box.

◆ "Title" is the placeholder for the text to appear in the title bar of the box.

◆ "Default Entry" is the placeholder for the text to display in the input field of the box when it is first opened.

FUNCTION SYNTAX GUIDE

If you look in the help files under (Local) Help ➤ Inventor Help Topics ➤ iLogic ➤ About Functions For Rules In iLogic, you can find examples of all the functions.

---

9. Highlight myparam in the Rule Authoring pane and then double-click Width in the Parameters subtab. This will replace myparam with the word Width.

Note that the color coding indicates that Width is a recognized parameter. You could have just deleted the word myparam and then typed in the word **Width** as well. If you had done so and accidentally typed **width** with no uppercase *W*, the word would not have turned blue to indicate a recognized parameter.

10. Replace "Prompt" with **"Enter Width."**

11. Replace "Title" with **"Width Input"**.

12. Replace "Default Entry" with **100 mm** (no quotation marks).

Your result should read as follows:

```
Width = InputBox("Enter Width", "Width Input", 100 mm)
```

13. Click the OK button to close the Edit Rule dialog and test the rule. You should be prompted with an input box that looks like the one in Figure 20.17.

FIGURE 20.17
The width input box

14. Enter **150** in the input box and then click the OK button.

You'll notice that the model width did not change as you might have expected. This is because the input box has changed only the Width parameter, and now the file needs to be updated. You should see that the Update button is active, indicating the model needs to be updated. You can click the Update button to see the model width change to 150 mm. In the next section, you'll edit a rule to make the model automatically update when the rule is run.

You can right-click the rule and choose Run Rule to test it and change the width value again. When you have finished, you can close the file without saving changes.

EDITING YOUR RULE

In this exercise, you'll pick up where you left off and edit the Size Input rule you created in the previous exercise:

1. Click the Open button on the Get Started tab, browse for mi_20a_002.ipt in the Chapter 20 directory of your Mastering Inventor 2016 folder, and open it.

2. From the iLogic browser, locate the Size Input rule on the Rules tab and then right-click it and choose Edit Rule.

3. Place your cursor at the end of the existing function and press the **Enter** key on the keyboard a couple of times to provide some space in the rule.

4. In the Snippets list (on the left), locate the Document node and expand it by clicking the plus sign.

5. Locate the UpdateWhenDone item toward the middle of the list and double-click it. This will place the UpdateWhenDone function into your rule so that it looks like this:

```
Width = InputBox("Enter Width", "Width Input", 100 mm)

iLogicVb.UpdateWhenDone = True
```

6. Click the OK button to test the rule.

7. Enter **190** in the input box and click the OK button. Your part width should automatically change to 190 mm.

8. From the iLogic browser, right-click the Size Input rule and choose Edit Rule again.

Currently, your rule is coded to set the default entry of the input box to 100 mm. If you built this plate with a standard size of 100 mm for the width most of the time, then hard-coding that value might be the way to go. But often, it's more useful to retrieve the current parameter value and have it display in the input so the user knows the value before changing it.

9. Replace the 100 mm with **Width**. You can do this by typing over the value or by selecting it and then clicking Extrusion1 in the Model tab along the top. Then double-click the Width parameter to "push" it into the Rule Authoring pane. In either case, your function should look like this:

```
Width = InputBox("Enter Width", "Width Input", Width)
```

10. Click the OK button to test the rule and notice that the current width value of the model is listed in the input box. Replace this with **165** and click the OK button.

To finish this rule, you will add another function to change the length of the part. Follow the steps you used to create the width function so that your rule reads as follows and then test the part to see how it works:

```
Width = InputBox("Enter Width", "Width Input", Width)
Length = InputBox("Enter Length", "Length Input", Length)
iLogicVb.UpdateWhenDone = True
```

You can right-click the rule and choose Run Rule to test it and see how it functions. When you have finished, you can close the file without saving changes.

CREATING A RULE USING A MULTI-VALUE PARAMETER

In the previous exercises, you used an input box to change parameter values so that you could adjust the dimensions of the plate part. In this exercise, you'll create a multi-value parameter and then create a rule to get the user to select from the list. Follow these steps:

1. Click the Open button on the Get Started tab, browse for `mi_20a_003.ipt` in the Chapter 20 directory of your `Mastering Inventor 2016` folder, and open it.

2. From the Manage tab, click the Parameters button.

3. Right-click the `Length` parameter and choose Make Multi-Value.

4. In the Value List Editor dialog box, enter the following values into the top pane and then click Add. If 175 mm is listed in the bottom pane, select it and click Delete to remove it.

   ◆ **150**

   ◆ **160**

   ◆ **170**

   ◆ **180**

   ◆ **190**

5. Click the OK button to close the Value List Editor dialog box and then click Done to close the Parameters dialog box.

6. From the iLogic browser, ensure that the Rules tab is selected; then right-click anywhere in the Rules tab and choose Add Rule.

7. Enter **Size List Input** into the Rule Name dialog box and click the OK button.

8. In the Edit Rule dialog box, make sure the Model tab along the top is set active and then expand the model node (if needed) and select Model Parameters. All the model parameters for this part file are now listed in the Parameters subtab on the right.

9. In the Model tab, click Extrusion1 to show the parameters used in Extrusion1.

10. In the Snippets list (on the left), locate the MessageBox node and expand it by clicking the plus sign.

11. Locate the InputListBox item toward the bottom of the list and double-click it. This will place the generic `InputListBox` function into your rule, thereby providing the template syntax you need to follow. This function should look similar to this:

```
d0 = InputListBox("Prompt", MultiValue.List("d0"), d0,
 Title:= "Title", ListName:= "List")
```

- ◆ `d0` is the placeholder for the return value (the value retrieved from the input box).
- ◆ `InputListBox` is the name of the function.
- ◆ `"Prompt"` is the placeholder for the message to appear in the box.
- ◆ `MultiValue.List("d0")` is the subfunction and the name of the multi-value list to use.
- ◆ `d0` is the placeholder for the default list value to select in the input list of the box when it is first opened. `"Title"` is the placeholder for the text to appear in the title bar of the box.
- ◆ `"List"` is the placeholder for the text to appear above the list in the box.

12. Select `d0` in the Rule Authoring pane and then double-click Length in the Parameters subtab. This will replace `d0` with the word `Length` (no quotation marks).

WHEN TO USE QUOTATION MARKS

Quotation marks indicate a text string. When you want the function to see your entry as a text string, use quotation marks. When you want the function to read a parameter (either from the model or from the rule), don't use quotation marks.

---

13. Replace `"Prompt"` and replace it with `"Select Length"` (keeping the quotation marks).

14. Replace `"d0"` in `MultiValue.List("d0")` with `"Length"` (keeping the quotation marks).

15. Replace the next instance of `"d0"` with **150** (no quotation marks). In this case, you want the input box to have a hard-coded default of 150.

16. Delete the word `"Title"` and replace it with `"Length Selector"` (keeping the quotation marks).

17. Replace `"List"` with `"Available Standard Lengths"` (with the quotation marks).

Once the edits are made, your result should read as follows:

```
Length = InputListBox("Select Length", MultiValue.List("Length"),
 150, Title:= "Length Selector", ListName:= "Available Standard Lengths")
```

18. Click the OK button to exit the Edit Rule dialog and run the rule.

19. Select a value, press OK, and then click the Update button to see the model update.

To finish this rule, you will edit the `Width` parameter and make it a multi-value parameter with the same values you used for the length. Then, edit the rule and add another input list box function to change the width of the part. Follow the steps you used to create the length function. Then, add the function to make the part update when the rule is finished running (recall that you'll find this in the Document function category list) so that your rule reads as follows:

```
Length = InputListBox("Select Length", MultiValue.List("Length"),
150, Title:= "Length Selector", ListName:= "Available Standard Lengths")

Width = InputListBox("Select Width", MultiValue.List("Width"),
150, Title:= "Width Selector", ListName:= "Available Standard Widths")

iLogicVb.UpdateWhenDone = True
```

Finally, test the part to see how it works. When you have finished, you can close the file without saving changes.

WORKING WITH MULTIPLE RULES IN THE SAME FILE

In the next exercises, you'll work with both of the rules you created in the previous exercises and then create a third rule to choose which of the other two to run. Follow these steps to work with multiple rules in the same file:

1. Click the Open button on the Get Started tab, browse for `mi_20a_004.ipt` in the Chapter 20 directory of your `Mastering Inventor 2016` folder, and open it.

2. From the iLogic browser, locate the Size Input rule on the Rules tab; then right-click it and choose Run Rule.

3. Enter **150** for Length and click the OK button.

4. Enter **150** for Width and click the OK button.

You'll notice that the Size List Input rule is run automatically when you click the OK button, presenting you with the Length Selector list input box.

5. Click the OK button in both the Length Selector and Width Selector input boxes.

The issue here is caused by both rules handling the same parameters. Currently, any change to those parameters causes the rules to run automatically. Although this might be the desired result in some cases, in this instance it is causing a problem. To resolve this, you will edit both rules and change their options.

6. From the iLogic browser, locate the Size Input rule on the Rules tab; then right-click it and choose Edit Rule.

7. Along the top, select the Options tab and select the Don't Run Automatically option, as shown in Figure 20.18; then click the OK button to exit the Edit Rule dialog box.

8. Click the OK button in the Length Input and Width Input boxes to accept the default values.

Next, you'll do the same thing for the Size List Input box.

FIGURE 20.18
Rule options

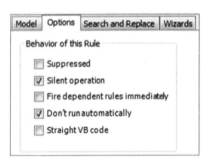

9. From the iLogic browser, locate the Size List Input rule on the Rules tab; then right-click it and choose Edit Rule.

10. Along the top, select the Options tab, select the Don't Run Automatically option, and then click the OK button to exit the Edit Rule dialog box.

11. Click the OK button in the Length Selector and Width Selector boxes to accept the default values.

As a test to see that the issue is resolved, you can run the rules and change the width and length values to ensure that neither rule runs when the other makes a change. Once you've tested this, you can close the file without saving and continue.

 Real World Scenario

HANDLING ERRORS

Often, your rules will work fine when you test them because you enter expected results. But you can rest assured that as soon as you have other people test your rules, they'll encounter errors when they provide invalid input, for example.

Depending on the complexity of your code, you can often add a simple error handler to manage null inputs and other issues created when the user doesn't provide predictable or desired input.

You can use a simple On Error Resume Next line to skip or ignore an error. Although this is not considered a good practice for programming, it will often suffice for simple errors. For example, you can open the file mi_20a_022.ipt and run Rule0. If you click the Cancel button in the input box, you'll receive an error because the rule returns an empty string value. If you do the same for Rule1, the error is skipped because Rule1 includes an On Error Resume Next line.

Rule2 includes an On Error Goto ErrorHandler line that instructs Inventor to skip to the ErrorHandler line and display a message if an error is encountered. You can run Rule2 and click the Cancel button in the input box to see how this works. Rule3 checks for the specific problem of an empty text string and provides the user with a message. Rule4 does the same but just uses the existing value rather than the null input.

You can search online for *VB error checking* to find many more error-checking strategies.

USE A CONDITIONAL STATEMENT TO RUN ANOTHER RULE

Next, your goal is to create a new rule to choose between two existing rules. But before doing so, you'll add a True/False user parameter and then edit the existing rule names to make them a bit more meaningful for your next task.

1. Click the Open button on the Get Started tab, browse for mi_20a_005.ipt in the Chapter 20 directory of your Mastering Inventor 2016 folder, and open it.

2. From the Manage tab, click the Parameters button.

3. From the lower-left corner, select the user parameter drop-down list (it shows Add Numeric by default).

4. Set it to Add True/False and then Enter **Standard_Size** for the parameter name.

5. Click Done to exit the Parameters dialog box.

Next, you'll rename the existing rules.

6. From the iLogic browser, locate the Size Input rule on the Rules tab, click it once to select it, and then slowly click it again to set the name active for renaming.

7. Enter **Custom Size Input** for the new name.

8. Repeat this for the Size List Input rule and rename it **Standard Size List Input**.

9. In the iLogic browser, right-click anywhere in the Rules tab and choose Add Rule.

10. Enter **Size Type Input** into the Rule Name dialog box and then click the OK button.

11. In the Snippets list (on the left), locate the MessageBox node and expand it by clicking the plus sign.

12. Locate the InputRadioBox item toward the bottom of the list and double-click it. This will place the generic InputRadioBox function into your rule, thereby providing the template syntax you need to follow. This function should read as follows:

```
booleanParam = InputRadioBox("Prompt", "Button1 Label", "Button2 Label",
booleanParam, Title:= "Title")
```

- booleanParam is the placeholder for the return value (the value retrieved from the input box).

- InputRadioBox is the name of the function.

- "Prompt" is the placeholder for the message to appear in the box.

- "Button1 Label" and "Button2 Label" are the labels for the radio buttons.

- booleanParam is the placeholder for the default radio button to select when the input box is first opened.

- "Title" is the placeholder for the text to appear in the title bar of the box.

13. Make sure the Model tab along the top is set active and then expand the model node (if needed) and select User Parameters. All the user parameters for this part file are now listed in the Parameters subtab on the right. In this case, there is just the one you created.

14. Select booleanParam in the Rule Authoring pane and then double-click Standard_Size in the Parameters subtab. This will replace booleanParam with Standard_Size (no quotation marks).

15. Delete the word "Prompt" and replace it with **"Select Size Type"** (keeping the quotation mark).

16. Replace "Button1Label" with **"Standard Sizes"** (keeping the quotation marks).

17. Replace "Button2Label" with **"Custom Size"** (keeping the quotation marks).

18. Replace booleanParam with **True** (no quotation marks). This sets the default to be true, which will be the first button, or the standard size option.

19. Delete the second instance of the word "Title" and replace it with **"Standard or Custom"** (keeping the the quotation marks). Once the edits are made, your result should read as follows:

```
Standard_Size = InputRadioBox("Select Size Type",
"Standard Sizes", "Custom Size", True, Title:= "Standard or Custom")
```

Currently, this rule doesn't do anything other than display an input box to let you choose between two buttons. To make those buttons do something meaningful, you will add a conditional statement to run one of the other existing rules.

20. From the toolbar along the top of the Rule Authoring pane, select the If…Then…End If button to place the syntax snippet in your rule.

21. Delete the My_Expression placeholder and leave your cursor between If and Then.

22. Right-click Standard_Size in the Parameters subtab and choose Capture Current State. This should result in Standard_Size = True unless you made changes to the True/False parameter when creating it. If so, just edit it to read **Standard_Size = True**.

23. In the Function Category list (on the left), locate the Run Other node and expand it by clicking the plus sign. Locate the RunRule item in the list.

24. In the Rule Authoring pane, place your cursor on the line after Then and above End If and double-click the RunRule node in the Function Category list. This will place the iLogicVb.RunRule("ruleName") function into your rule.

25. Replace "ruleName" with **"Standard Size List Input"** (keeping the quotation marks).

26. Add an empty line above End If and enter **Else**, hit **Enter** on the keyboard, add another RunRule function, and replace "Replace ruleName" with **"Custom Size Input"** (keeping the quotation marks).

Your resulting rule should read as follows:

```
Standard_Size = InputRadioBox("Select Size Type",
"Standard Sizes", "Custom Size", True, Title:= "Standard or Custom")
```

```
If Standard_Size = True Then
iLogicVb.RunRule("Standard Size List Input")
Else
iLogicVb.RunRule("Custom Size Input")
End If
```

Figure 20.19 shows the input radio dialog box.

FIGURE 20.19
The radio buttons allow
you to run one rule or
the other.

You can test this rule and notice that you can now choose between the two input types, Custom and Standard. If you choose Custom, you can add anything, and you can choose from only the approved standards for the standard inputs.

But what if you enter a value such as 300 for the length? You'll notice that the hole spacing becomes quite large. It would be nice to have a rule to add holes for large custom lengths and widths. In the next exercise, you'll investigate how to do just that. You can close the file without saving.

USE A MESSAGE BOX TO TROUBLESHOOT

Oftentimes, it is helpful to add a message box to return a value to you so you can see what the code is returning. This is particularly helpful when your code is throwing an error. For example, if, when working with a parameter named Shell_OD, you receive an error concerning that parameter, you might temporarily add the following line to visually confirm the value returned for Shell_OD:

```
MessageBox.Show(Shell_OD, "Test")
```

SUPPRESSING FEATURES

In this next exercise, two hole features have been added to the part for you. The goal is to create a rule to suppress a hole feature if the spacing is under a specified distance and activate it if the spacing exceeds the specified distance. You'll explore a couple of other tips and tricks along the way. Follow these steps:

1. Click the Open button on the Get Started tab, browse for mi_20a_006.ipt in the Chapter 20 directory of your Mastering Inventor 2016 folder, and open it.

2. From the Manage tab, click the Parameters button.

3. Notice that there are two reference parameters present.

These reference parameters were created in Sketch3, which controls the locations of Hole2 and Hole3. Recall that a reference parameter is created by adding a driven dimension to a sketch. In this case, the distance between the center holes and end holes along the horizontal and vertical edges was dimensioned after the sketch was fully constrained, resulting in the driven dimension/reference parameter. Then, those parameters were renamed.

4. On the Rules tab of the iLogic browser, click and drag the rule named Size Type Input to the top of the list. Since this is the rule that is utilized to choose between the others, it might be best to place it at the top.

5. Add a new rule and call it **Suppress Center Holes**.

6. From the toolbar along the top of the Rule Authoring pane, select the If...Then...End If button to place the syntax snippet in your rule.

7. Use the drop-down and add Else to the snippet so that you have the following:

```
If My_Expression Then

Else

End If
```

8. Highlight My_Expression in the function code and then look in the Model tab along the top and select Reference Parameters.

9. Select Center_Hole_Space_H from the Parameters subtab on the right and double-click it to replace My_Expression.

10. From the toolbar along the top of the Rule Authoring pane, select the Operators drop-down and notice that it contains a list of all the logic operators. Click >= to include it in your rule after Center_Hole_Space_H and then enter **45** so that the result is as follows:

```
If Center_Hole_Space_H >= 45 Then
```

On the next line, you will add the function to make the hole feature active.

11. Select Hole2 from the feature tree in the Model tab area and then right-click it and choose Capture Current State.

CAPTURE CURRENT STATE

You can use the Capture Current State option on any Inventor feature or parameter. You can just delete the unneeded information and keep what is pertinent.

12. Delete all the extra information and keep only the Feature.IsActive line. IsActive can be used to suppress or not suppress any Inventor feature that can be suppressed.

13. Copy that line below the Else and change True to **False** so the result reads as follows:

```
If Center_Hole_Space_H >= 45 Then
Feature.IsActive("Hole2") = True
Else
Feature.IsActive("Hole2") = False
End If
```

14. Copy your entire block of code and paste it under the original.

15. Change the reference parameter to **Center_Hole_Space_V** and the hole feature references to **Hole3** so your entire rule reads as follows:

```
If Center_Hole_Space_H >= 45 Then
Feature.IsActive("Hole2") = True
Else
Feature.IsActive("Hole2") = False
End If


If Center_Hole_Space_V  >= 45 Then
Feature.IsActive("Hole3") = True
Else
Feature.IsActive("Hole3") = False
End If
```

16. Click the OK button to test the rule.

Because the current hole spacing is less than 45 for both of the reference parameters, the hole is suppressed. Next, you'll modify the existing rules to call the Suppress Center Holes rule and format the Custom Size Input rule to include a "soft" warning in the form of a second line in the input boxes.

17. Edit the Standard Size List Input rule and add the following line to the end (after the UpdateWhenDone function):

```
iLogicVb.RunRule("Suppress Center Holes")
```

Of course, you can just type the line in as you are reading it, but for the sake of practice, use the Snippets list to find the RunRule function and double-click it to enter it.

18. Edit the Custom Size Input rule and add the same RunRule line to the end.

19. Change the top two lines of code to read as follows:

```
Length = InputBox("Enter Length " & vbCrLf & _
"(max length not to exceed 350)", " Length Input", Length)

Width = InputBox("Enter Width " & vbCrLf & _
"(max width not to exceed 300)", " Width Input", Width)
```

Inserting **& vbCrLf &** creates a second line in the input line. The underscore preceded by a space (**_)** provides a carriage return without disrupting the code. This makes it easier to read in the Edit Rule dialog box. When you test the rule, you'll see that that the second line contains a parenthetical statement advising the user of the maximum width. This is a "soft" warning because there is nothing in the rule to prevent the user from inputting values larger than the stated maximums.

Because your rules are changing the size of your part, it would be nice to add a bit of code to adjust the zoom level to match the size of the new part. To do so, you can call an application programming interface (API) object to make this happen with this line:

```
ThisApplication.ActiveView.Fit
```

20. Edit the rule named Size Type Input and add the previous line to the end.

21. Add a comment line above it by typing **This line Zooms All**.

22. To make that line be seen as a comment and not a line of code, simply add an apostrophe to the beginning. The result should be as follows:

```
'This Line Zooms All
ThisApplication.ActiveView.Fit
```

COMMENTING CODE

Any text preceded by an apostrophe is read by iLogic as a comment and not interpreted as code. Use this to your advantage by adding notes and documentation to your iLogic code to make editing it in the future easier.

You can also use the Comment and Uncomment buttons found on the toolbar above the top of the Rule Authoring pane to comment out entire blocks of code and then uncomment them later. This is particularly helpful when troubleshooting and working out "what if" strategies while creating rules.

If you anticipate using a particular snippet a lot, you might want to save it to the Custom Snippets tab. To see how this is done, you'll save the Zoom All snippet.

23. Highlight both the comment line and the code line and then right-click and choose Capture Snippet.

24. For the Title, type **Zoom All**.

25. Click the Use Code As Tooltip button and then click the OK button.

26. Click the Save Custom Snippets button on the toolbar of the Custom Snippets tab and choose a name and location for your custom snippet file.

You're likely beginning to see the power of iLogic and the use of simple rules to create configurations of your model templates. Feel free to experiment with this file to tweak the code as you like, or you can close the file without saving changes and move on to the next section.

OPERATORS

You'll find the use of operators to be a common method of building logic in your iLogic rules. An operator performs a function on one or more objects. Table 20.1 lists some common operators and examples of their uses for quick reference.

TABLE 20.1:   Common function operators

OPERATORS	DESCRIPTION	EXAMPLE	RESULTS
+	Adds two values	`12 + 5`	Returns `17`
−	Subtracts one value from another value	`12 - 5`	Returns `7`
*	Multiplies two values	`12 * 5`	Returns `60`
/	Divides two numbers and returns a floating-point result	`12 / 5`	Returns `2.4`
\	Divides two numbers and returns an integer result	`12 \ 5`	Returns `2`
^	Raises a value to a power	`2 ^ 2`	Returns `4`
&	Concatenates two strings	`"Autodesk" & "Inventor"`	Returns `"Autodesk Inventor"`
>	Greater than	`12 > 5`	Returns `True`
<	Less than	`12 < 5`	Returns `False`
=	Equal to	`12 = 5`	Returns `False`
>=	Greater than or equal to	`12 >= 5`	Returns `True`
<=	Less than or equal to	`12 <= 5`	Returns `False`
<>	Not equal to	`12 <> 5`	Returns `True`
Mod	Divides two numbers and returns only the remainder	`12 Mod 5`	Returns `2`
And	Performs a conjunction on two expressions and checks both even if the first is found to be false	`If 12 > 5 And 5 > 7 Then both are True Else at least one is False`	Returns the following: `At least one is False`
Or	Performs a disjunction on two expressions	`If 12 > 5 Or 5 > 7 Then at least one is True Else both are False`	Returns the following: `At least one is True`

continues

TABLE 20.1: Common function operators *(CONTINUED)*

OPERATORS	DESCRIPTION	EXAMPLE	RESULTS
AndAlso	Performs a conjunction on two expressions, but evaluates the second if and only if the first is true	If 12 = 5 AndAlso 5 < 7 Then both are True Else at least one is False	Returns At least one is False but doesn't evaluate 5 < 7
OrElse	Performs a disjunction on two expressions, but evaluates the second if and only if the first is true	If 12 = 5 OrElse 5 < 7 Then at least one is True Else at least one is False	Returns At least one is False but doesn't evaluate 5 < 7

Creating iLogic Forms

iLogic forms are used to create a custom user input and control form to work with iLogic rules or to handle parameter and iProperty changes directly. iLogic forms are created with an intuitive drag-and-drop interface that is easy to master.

WORKING WITH IPROPERTIES AND FORMS

In this next exercise, you'll explore the use of iProperties in iLogic rules and then create a basic iLogic form to manipulate them. The objective here is to create a rule to do the following:

◆ Read the available materials from the part file and populate a multi-value parameter list with those values.

◆ Set the material iProperty using the list box selection.

◆ Ask the user a question: Is this part to be painted?

◆ Set the part color iProperty based on the user input.

Follow these steps to explore the use of iProperties and forms:

1. Click the Open button on the Get Started tab, browse for mi_20a_007.ipt in the Chapter 20 directory of your Mastering Inventor 2016 folder, and open it.

2. From the Manage tab, select the Parameters button.

3. Add a new Text user parameter (use the drop-down in the lower-left corner) and call it **Materials_List**.

4. Right-click the new parameter and choose Make Multi-Value.

5. Add a new value called **Generic** to the list.

6. Create another new Text user parameter and call it **Colors_List**.

7. Make it a multi-value parameter also and add the following values (make sure your spelling and capitalization match exactly):

◆ **As Material**

◆ **Gunmetal**

◆ **Slate**

◆ **Tan**

◆ **White**

8. Close the Parameter dialog and open the iLogic browser. Add a rule named **Material and Color Input**.

9. Locate and expand the iProperties node in the Snippets list on the left.

10. Find the List Of Materials entry and double-click it to add it to your rule.

11. Clear *param* from between the parentheses and then select User Parameter from the model tree list at the top.

12. Double-click `Materials_List` in the Parameters subtab on the right to place it in the quotation marks. Your rule should read as follows so far:

```
MultiValue.List("Materials_List") = iProperties.Materials
```

This line retrieves the current list of materials from the part file and uses it to populate the `Materials_List` parameter you created. Next, you'll add a line to set the material iProperty to be whatever the value of the `Materials_List` parameter is. And then, you'll do the same for the `Colors_List` parameter.

13. From the iProperties node in the Function Category list on the left, select Material and double-click it to add it to your rule.

14. Add an equal sign to the end of the line and then ensure that User Parameter is still selected in the model tree list at the top. Double-click `Materials_List` in the Parameters subtab to add it to the code.

15. Do the same thing for the iProperty function called `PartColor` and the user parameter called `Colors_List` so that your final rule code reads as follows:

```
MultiValue.List("Materials_List") = iProperties.Materials
iProperties.Material = Materials_List
iProperties.PartColor = Colors_List
```

16. Click the OK button to exit the Edit Rule dialog box.

Next, you'll build an iLogic form to allow you to easily select a material and a color from a list.

17. In the iLogic browser, switch to the Forms tab and then right-click in the browser space and choose Add Form.

The Form Editor opens and shows the form building tools, as illustrated in Figure 20.20.

Here are the Form Editor tools:

Filter Tool (A) Allows you to filter the list on the Parameters, Rules, and iProperties tabs for All, Key, and Renamed

FIGURE 20.20
The iLogic Form Editor

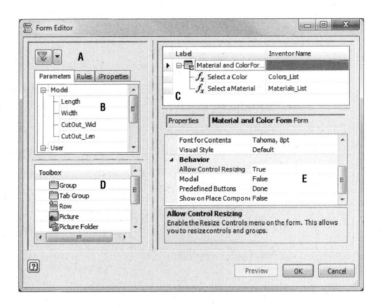

FIGURE 20.20
The iLogic Form Editor

Tabs Area (B)   Allows you to drag and drop items from the list to the Form Design pane to add controls for your custom interface

Form Design Pane (C)   Allows you to design a custom interface by doing the following:

- Dragging and dropping parameters, rules, iProperties, and Toolbox items onto the form

- Dragging and dropping items on the tree to organize the controls

- Editing label text

- Selecting an item to edit its properties in the Properties area

Toolbox (D)   Allows you to drag and drop controls onto your form

Properties Area (E)   Allows you to edit the properties for the items selected in the Form Design pane

18. In the Form Design pane (see area C in Figure 20.19), you will see the name of the form listed as Form 1. Change this to read **Material and Color Form**.

19. Use the Parameters tab in the top-left pane and select the Materials_List parameter. Then, click and drag it up to the top-right pane and drop it under the form name.

20. Notice that an input box is added to the preview form on the right.

21. In the Form Design pane, edit the Materials_List entry to read **Select a Material**, and then adjust the size of the preview form as needed.

22. Drag the Colors_List parameter to the Form Design pane. Add it above the material control by dragging either item to reorder them.

23. Rename Colors_List to read **Select a Color**.

24. Click the Colors_List control in the Form Design pane and then locate and expand the Behavior item in the Properties area at the bottom of the dialog box.

25. Set Edit Control Type to Radio Group, as shown in Figure 20.21.

FIGURE 20.21
Changing the control type

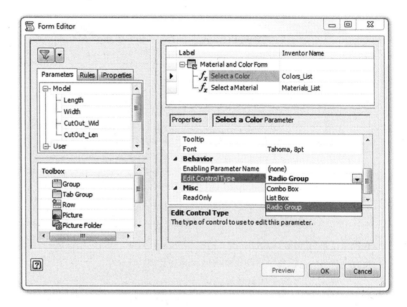

26. Click the OK button to close the Form Editor and then click the Material And Color Form button to bring up the form. Figure 20.22 shows the finished form.

FIGURE 20.22
The finished Material And Color Form

Play around with the controls, adjusting the material and color to your liking. Recall that setting a color overrides the material color, and therefore, you'll need to set the color to As Material to see the change of material have any effect on-screen. When you've finished, you can close this file without saving changes and continue to the next section.

> **FORM PROPERTIES**
>
> You can set various options for the form such as the font and color by selecting the node for the form itself in the Form Design pane and then using the Properties area options. The Visual Style property provides a list of color schemes for the form.
>
> By default, the form includes a Done button, but you can select from the Predefined Buttons list. If you're using the 'OK Cancel' or 'OK Cancel Apply' button options, the changes to the model do not take place until a button is clicked. If you're using the default 'Done' button, changes are applied automatically.

BUILDING A PART CONFIGURATION FORM

In the next exercise, you'll build an iLogic Form for use in configuring a small plate part. This part is a cast part that needs to be machined to include several features. The specifications of those features vary depending on the application, so it would be ideal to set up a template part with an iLogic form to allow quick and consistent configuration of the plate as needed. Follow these steps:

1. Click the Open button on the Get Started tab, browse for `mi_20a_008.ipt` in the Chapter 20 directory of your `Mastering Inventor 2016` folder, and open it.

2. Click the Manage tab and select the iLogic Browser button from the iLogic panel to make sure your iLogic browser is displayed.

On the Rules tab, you'll see three existing rules. Each rule checks a reference parameter found in Sketch6 used to create the sweep feature called Gasket Groove. If a specified reference parameter falls below a set minimum, a warning message is displayed.

3. Set the Forms tab of the iLogic browser active and then right-click the iLogic browser and choose Add Form.

4. Change the Form label from Form 1 to **Configure Plate**.

5. Locate the Parameters tab on the left. Notice that the list of parameters includes model, reference, and user parameters.

6. Find the parameter named `Mount_Dia` and then click and drag it into the Form Design pane on the right. Drop it under the form name in the tree and then change the label to **Mount Diameter (A)**.

7. Add the following parameters to the tree in the same manner and edit their labels to these values (note that `Gasket_ID` is a user parameter and therefore is found toward the bottom of the Parameters tab):

   ◆ Change `Hole_Dia` to **Hole Diameter (B)**.

   ◆ Change `Cen_Cen` to **Center to Center Hole Space (C)**.

   ◆ Change `Gasket_ID` to **Gasket Size (D)**.

Figure 20.23 shows the results you should have once all four parameters are added and renamed.

FIGURE 20.23
Parameters added and
renamed

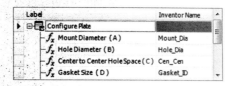

Label	Inventor Name
▶ ⊟ 🗔 Configure Plate	
𝑓ₓ Mount Diameter (A)	Mount_Dia
𝑓ₓ Hole Diameter (B)	Hole_Dia
𝑓ₓ Center to Center Hole Space (C)	Cen_Cen
𝑓ₓ Gasket Size (D)	Gasket_ID

8. Select the Group control from the Toolbox, drag it into the tree, and then drop it below Gasket Size (D).

9. Change the name of the label from Group 1 to **Minimum Dimension Values**.

10. Locate the Reference node in the list on the Parameters tab and click and drag the following parameters to the tree. Then edit their labels to these values:

◆ Change `Gasket_Space_Hold` to **Minimum Space = 2 mm (E)**.

◆ Change `Gasket_Space_Hold2` to **Minimum Space = 2 mm (F)**.

◆ Change `HoleChecks` to **Minimum Space = 2.5 mm (G)**.

Drop the parameters right on the Minimum Dimension Values group so they will land in the group. If you miss, you can just drag and drop them into the group afterward. It's worth mentioning that the values of 2 mm and 2.5 mm come from the existing check rules. The letters listed in parentheses correspond to a legend image to be embedded in the form in the next steps. Figure 20.24 shows the Configure Plate form at this stage.

FIGURE 20.24
The Configure Plate form
so far

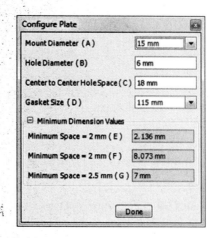

Configure Plate

Mount Diameter (A)	15 mm
Hole Diameter (B)	6 mm
Center to Center Hole Space (C)	18 mm
Gasket Size (D)	115 mm
⊟ Minimum Dimension Values	
Minimum Space = 2 mm (E)	2.136 mm
Minimum Space = 2 mm (F)	8.073 mm
Minimum Space = 2.5 mm (G)	7 mm

Done

11. Select the Picture control from the Toolbox and drag to the bottom of the tree.

12. Select the Picture node and then choose the Image property in the Properties pane at the bottom. Click in the cell that reads (none) and click the ellipses button to browse and select an image to use. Figure 20.25 shows the Image browse button.

FIGURE 20.25
Adding an image file

13. Click the browse button and locate and select the file `mi_20a_008_form_pic.png` from the `Chapter 20` folder.

The image file will be placed in your form automatically. This image was created by taking a screen capture of an IDW file, detailing the plate.

Next, you will change the properties of the Center To Center Hole Space controls to limit the inputs to an approved range. Doing so ensures that the user doesn't specify a value that exceeds the size of the plate or would create a need for custom tooling or a special-order gasket.

14. Select the Center To Center Hole Space (C) control from the tree at the top and then locate Edit Control Type in the Properties pane.

15. Change the control type from Text Box to Slider.

16. Expand the Slider Properties and set them as follows:

- Minimum Value set to **4**

- Maximum Value set to **25**

- Step Size set to **1**

17. Click the OK button to create the form and close the Form Editor.

18. Click the Configure Plate button on the Forms tab of the iLogic browser to bring up the new form. It should look like Figure 20.26.

FIGURE 20.26

The finished plate configuration form

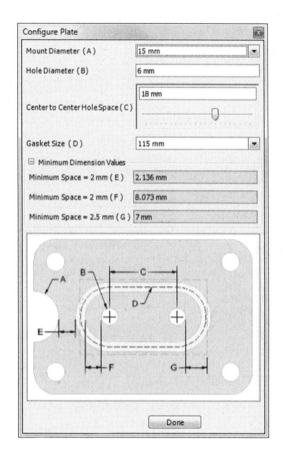

19. Test the functionality of the form as follows:

a. Set Mount Diameter to **20 mm** and notice that a warning message is thrown. Click the OK button in the warning and then set Mount Diameter back to **15 mm.**

b. Use the Center To Center Hole Space slider and drag it to the left. You'll notice at 11 mm, the hole becomes a slot. This is because of the Conditional Suppress option on the Slot Cut feature. You can right-click Slot Cut in the browser and choose Properties to see how this is done.

c. Set Mount Diameter back to **20 mm**, and click the OK button in the warning box.

d. Use the Gasket Size drop-down to select a smaller size of 100 mm.

SETTING THE FORM SIZE

You can set up the controls on your forms to maintain a specific size by following these simple steps:

1. Right-click the button in the iLogic Browser on the Forms tab to edit the form.

2. In the lower pane of the Form Editor, locate the Behavior section in the Properties list.

3. Set Allow Control Resizing to True.

4. Click the OK button to exit the Form Editor.

5. Run the form.

6. Right-click the form and choose Resize Controls; then resize as needed.

7. Then right-click the form again and choose Exit Resize Mode.

8. Close the form and then edit it again.

9. Now set Allow Control Resizing to False to prevent the controls from being accidentally resized in the future.

You can continue adjusting the inputs as you like to test the form. Be aware that if you choose a combination of values resulting in violations of all three minimum space rules, it can be a bit difficult to get the form back to usable values. In the next exercise, you'll add a reset button and more functions to the form to make it a bit more robust. You can close the file without saving.

USING ADVANCED API OBJECTS

One of the things that makes iLogic so powerful is the ability to use functions from the Inventor API from within an iLogic rule. If you're not familiar with the API, you can find several resources to help you get started by searching the Web for *Autodesk Inventor Developer Network*.

ADDING RULES, TABS, AND EVENT TRIGGERS

In the next exercise, you'll add a reset button to the form created in the previous exercise. You'll also create a second tab on the form to set standard iProperties. Then, you'll add event triggers to bring the form up automatically when a new part is created from this template and another to prompt for iProperty values when the file is closed. Follow these steps:

1. Click the Open button on the Get Started tab, browse for `mi_20a_009.ipt` in the Chapter 20 directory of your `Mastering Inventor 2016` folder, and open it.

2. Create a new rule named **Reset Form** and add the following code:

```
'resets parameters to default values
Mount_Dia = 15 mm
Hole_Dia = 6 mm
Cen_Cen = 18 mm
Gasket_ID = 115 mm
iLogicVb.UpdateWhenDone = True
```

3. To keep this rule from setting those parameter values automatically, you need to click the Options tab and select the Don't Run Automatically check box. Once this is done, you can click the OK button to exit the Edit Rule dialog box.

4. From the Forms tab of the iLogic browser, right-click the Configure Plate button and choose Edit.

5. Set the Rules tab active in the Tabs pane on the left.

6. Click and drag the Reset Form rule into Form Design pane and drop it under the picture at the bottom of the list. This automatically adds a button to run the reset rule, allowing you to quickly reset the form to the original values.

7. Select the Tab Group control from the Toolbox and drag and drop it into the Form Design pane to create a new tab.

8. Rename the tab **Size Entry**.

9. Drag the tab to the top of the tree and then drag and drop the following items onto Size Entry:

- Mount Diameter (A)
- Hole Diameter (B)
- Center To Center Hole Space (C)
- Gasket Size (D)

10. Drag and drop another Tab Group control into the Form Design pane and rename it **Property Entry**.

11. Set the iProperties tab on the left active and then drag the following iProperties into the Form Design pane so they reside in the Property Entry tab:

- Part Number
- Description
- Revision Number

Your Form Design pane and the top of your form should look like Figure 20.27.

FIGURE 20.27
The improved form

Next, you'll create a rule to call the Configure Plate form and set it to automatically trigger when the file is initially created (when this part file is used as a template) or opened (when an existing version of this part file is opened for modifications).

12. Create a new rule named **Call Form** and add the following code:

```
'displays the specified form
iLogicForm.Show("Configure Plate")
```

13. Once the rule is created, select the Manage tab and click the Event Triggers button on the iLogic panel.

14. Select the New Document event in the Rules Triggered By Events dialog box, click the Select Rules button, and then select the Call Form rule. Click the OK button to return to the list of events.

15. Add the Call Form rule to the After Open event using the same steps.

16. Click the Inventor button in the top-left portion of the application screen and then choose Save As and then Save Copy As Template.

17. The template directory opens as specified in the Application Options settings. Save the file as **Plate 4792**.

18. From the Get Started tab, select New and then make sure you are looking at the main Templates directory folder using the pane on the right. Then select the Plate 4792 template.

19. Once the template is loaded, the Configure Plate form displays, allowing you to configure the plate for the new variation. Use the controls to create a variation and then click Done.

20. Save the file to the Chapter 20 directory of your Mastering Inventor 2016 folder and name it **A-4792.ipt**.

21. Close the file and reopen it to make sure the Call Form rule is triggered by the After Open event.

Working with iLogic forms is quite simple because of the intuitive drag-and-drop interface. You can likely see the power and benefit to using iLogic rules and forms to configure repetitive tasks and to enforce consistency as demonstrated here. Feel free to experiment with this file to add more controls and functionality if you'd like. Or you can close the files used in the previous steps and continue to the next section without saving changes.

SET GLOBAL FORMS TO READ-ONLY

If you create your forms as global forms, they are saved outside of the Inventor file. Once your global forms are created and tested, you might want to prevent them from accidentally being changed by other users (or yourself). To do so, follow these steps:

1. Right-click any empty area of the Global forms panel in the browser.

2. Choose Open Containing Folder.

3. In this folder, locate the XML file with the same name as your form.

4. Right-click and choose Properties.

5. On the General tab, select the Read Only check box.

Working with iLogic Components

Because parts and subassemblies with iLogic rules are often configured to different sizes and with different components, placing them directly into an assembly is generally not the correct method. Changes to the iLogic component will impact every assembly it is placed in. Instead, you will typically use the Place iLogic Component tool to place a copy of an iLogic component into an assembly.

The copy is automatically created in the directory of the assembly you are working in, so it is important to save the assembly before using the Place iLogic Component tool. For example, you have an assembly called 45-1000.iam in a folder named 45-0000. When you attempt to place 45-6799.ipt using the Place iLogic Component tool, it's actually a copy that is placed in the assembly file, and the copy will be named 45-6799-01.ipt. This file will be created in the 45-0000 folder. If you placed another version of 45-6799.ipt into the same assembly using the Place iLogic Component tool, it would be named 45-6799-02.ipt and placed in the 45-0000 folder.

You can follow these steps to use the Place iLogic Component tool:

1. From the Component panel of the Assembly tab, click the Place drop-down arrow and select the Place iLogic Component button.

2. Browse for and select the component to be placed. Then click Open.

PLACING ILOGIC SUBASSEMBLIES

When you place an iLogic subassembly, all components in the same directory or subdirectories of that subassembly are copied to the directory of the main assembly and assigned unique names.

Therefore, it's recommended that you organize your iLogic subassembly files with standard models outside of the directory of the subassembly that will be placed as an iLogic component. This can be done by saving them in a Content Center directory or another library directory. When you place the assembly as an iLogic component, these files are not copied to the directory of the main assembly and the iLogic component in the assembly maintains its links to the original files, in their original locations.

The component parameters are listed in a small dialog box. If the component contains Key parameters, only those parameters are included in the list; otherwise, all parameters are included. Initially, all parameters are designated as <Free> in the From Assembly column. This indicates that they are not driven by assembly parameters. Changing a free parameter value during placement allows you to configure the component upon placement, and the preview updates to show the changes made.

3. Click the drop-down arrow in the From Assembly column to see the list of assembly parameters available to drive the corresponding parameter. (Driving parameters must

exist in the assembly and therefore should be created before placing the iLogic component.) If the iPart has a form with Show On Place Component marked as true, then the form will show up to help you configure the part before placing. The form will also appear if Event Trigger After Open is marked.

4. Click the OK button after making your changes.

5. iLogic starts the Place Component tool, allowing you to place a copy of the original iLogic component in the assembly.

iLogic Design Copy

You can use the iLogic Design Copy tool to create copies of assemblies and their documentation. To use the iLogic Design Copy tool, you must first close all your open Inventor files. Then, in the iLogic panel on the Tools tab, click the iLogic Design Copy button. In the resulting dialog box, you can select the iLogic files to copy. When a file is selected, the referenced files are selected as well. You can also choose to copy unlinked Inventor or non-Inventor files related to the job you are copying.

Once files are selected, you specify the destination folder to which the files will be copied, and you can set file prefixing or suffixing to be appended to the original filenames. Another important option is the ability to maintain or delete the existing rules in the new copy. This allows you to start over with a clean project when needed or use the existing iLogic rules in the new design when that is preferred.

 Real World Scenario

USE ILOGIC TO FILL OUT TITLE BLOCKS

If you have a Drawn By field and a Date field in your title block, you might find it difficult to remember to edit the iProperties when saving the file or rolling the revision to a new drawing. You can use iLogic to assist with this.

Create an iLogic rule to write the username (pulled from the General tab in the Application Options dialog) and the current date (pulled from your system setting) to the drawing file's iProperties. You can then set your title block fields to read those iProperties. And you can set the rule to be triggered using the Before Save Document event trigger so that the title block is always updated at the time of the file save.

Here is a bit of sample code to do this:

```
myName= ThisApplication.GeneralOptions.UserName
If iProperties.Value("Summary", "Author") <> myName Then
iProperties.Value("Summary", "Author") = myName
MessageBox.Show("The Title block has been updated", _
"an iLogic message for: " & myName)
End If
```

```
        iProperties.Value("Project", "Creation Date") = Now
        InventorVb.DocumentUpdate()
```

You can find this and more iLogic samples online at the "From the Trenches with Autodesk Inventor" blog: `http://inventortrenches.blogspot.com`.

The Bottom Line

Create iLogic rules.   Use iLogic rules to document and embed into your models the common design rules that you use every day to determine the decisions required in your design process.

> **Master It**   How can you add a rule to your part to change the size of it?

Edit iLogic rules.   A large part of working with iLogic is testing and editing the rules you create. Often, it's best to add a function at a time to the rule and test it along the way.

> **Master It**   Your rule works, but you have to manually update the model. Do you need to create a new rule to handle the update?

Use multi-value list parameters.   A common part of any design rule process is selecting from a list of standard entities. You can create multi-value list parameters from Numeric or Text parameters to add lists.

> **Master It**   How would you create a rule that prompts you to select from a list of approved sizes?

Work with multiple rules in the same file.   It is often best to create several small rules rather than try to create one large rule that does it all. This helps you maintain and troubleshoot the code later, and it also allows you to use rules in multiple applications without the need to remove or edit existing code. This is particularly true when working with external rules, which might be used in varying applications later.

> **Master It**   You've created two smaller rules because it makes sense to do so, but when you try to run one, the other is triggered also. Do you need to combine them into one rule?

Use conditional statements.   Conditional statements are the foundation of any programmed logic. Learning how to use `If`, `Then`, and `Select Case` statements will go a long way in helping you solve logical problems when creating rules.

> **Master It**   How can you check the value of a parameter or its state with an iLogic rule?

Suppress features.   Configuring a part file to include and exclude features is often based on engineering decisions you make every day. Setting up your iLogic rules to do this is straightforward, provided the model is well constructed to start with.

> **Master It**   When you use the `Feature.IsActive` function on one feature, it causes an error in the part. How can a feature be suppressed without suppressing a dependent feature?

Work with iProperties.   iProperties are a powerful part of working with Inventor. Being able to retrieve and use metadata helps with all parts of the engineering process. Automating the process of filling out iProperty data with iLogic is a big step forward.

  Master It   Can iLogic be used to update the title block of a drawing?

Create iLogic forms.   iLogic forms make creating a user interface for your iLogic pursuits quite easy. The drag-and-drop tools provide professional-looking forms with minimal effort.

  Master It   You have existing part files with no iLogic in them, and it would be nice to use the form you created in the most recent design to update those old designs as revisions require it. Can forms be created and shared across part files?

Build a part configuration form.   Configuring Inventor components saves time, reduces human error, and promotes consistency. Using iLogic forms to configure common designs is a good way to go.

  Master It   Can an iLogic form help with parts that are basically the same but have a lot of variation in the features they include?

The Bottom Line

Each of "The Bottom Line" sections in the chapters suggest exercises to deepen skills and understanding. Sometimes there is only one possible solution, but often you are encouraged to use your skills and creativity to create something that builds on what you know and lets you explore one of many possible solutions.

Chapter 1: Getting Started

Create parametric designs. The power of parameter-based design comes from the quick and easy edits, when changing a parameter value drives a change through the design.

To make changes easily, though, you need to follow certain general rules so that the changes update predictably.

Master It You want to create a model of a base plate, a rectangular-shaped part with a series of holes and rectangular cutouts. What would your initial sketch look like in the Autodesk® Inventor® software?

Solution To start a model for the base plate, your initial sketch would most likely be just a rectangle defining the width and length of the part. This rectangle would be extruded to give it a thickness, and then you would create secondary sketches for the other features and cut them from the plate.

This approach follows the best practice of creating simple sketches to create simple features to build a complex part.

Get the "feel" of Inventor. The interface contains many elements that change and update to give you the tools you need to perform the task at hand. Getting comfortable with these automatic changes and learning to anticipate them will help you get the "feel" of Inventor.

Master It You create an extrude feature using the Extrude button, but you cannot seem to find an Edit Extrude button. How can you edit the extruded feature to change the height?

Solution To edit an extruded feature (or any feature), you can simply right-click it in the browser and choose Edit Feature. This makes feature edits universal, so a separate edit tool is not required for each feature type.

Keep in mind that for most features, you can double-click the feature button in the browser to edit it as well.

Use the Inventor graphical interface.   Inventor 2016 uses the ribbon menu interface introduced in Inventor 2010. Tools are grouped, which makes finding them intuitive once you become familiar with the basic layout.

> **Master It**   You are trying to draw a line on the face of a part, but you seem to have lost the Sketch tab in the ribbon. How do you get it back?
>
> **Solution**   The Sketch tab is present only when you have created a new sketch or are editing an existing sketch. To draw a line, you need to access the Line tool.
>
> You must first use the New Sketch tool to create a sketch, and then you will see the Sketch tab and on it the Line tool.

Work with Inventor file types.   Inventor supports many different file types in its native environment, separating tasks and files to improve performance and increase stability.

> **Master It**   You have trouble keeping the various file types straight because all the file icons look rather similar to you. Is there a way you can see which file is what type?
>
> **Solution**   You may want to turn on the view of filename extensions on your system so that you can read them (.ipt, .iam, .idw, and so on) as you open and save files. See the sidebar "Turning on Filename Extensions" in Chapter 1, "Getting Started," for instructions on how to do so.

Understand how project search paths work.   Knowing how Inventor resolves file paths when it opens linked files, such as assembly files and drawings, goes a long way toward helping prevent broken links and repairing links that do get broken.

> **Master It**   What type of file does Inventor use to point the assembly file to the parts that it contains?
>
> **Solution**   Inventor uses the project file (*.ipj) to hold workspace and library search paths. If files are outside of these search paths, Inventor will not find the files, and you will be required to point the assembly to them every time.

Set up library and Content Center paths.   Library and Content Center paths are read-only library configurations set up in the project file.

> **Master It**   When you set up a library or Content Center path to a folder that does not exist, what happens?
>
> **Solution**   When you create a path to a nonexistent folder, Inventor will create that folder for you.
>
> Keep this in mind when you create paths in the project file, and watch out for spelling and syntax errors because Inventor will create a new folder with an incorrectly spelled name as well.

Create and configure a project file.   Project files are a key component of working successfully in Inventor, but for many people, this is a one-time setup. Once the project is created, for the most part you just use it as is.

> **Master It**   After creating a project file initially, you want to make one or more changes to the configuration, but you can't seem to do so. What could be the problem?
>
> **Solution**   Keep in mind that while you are working with a project file, it is held in a read-only status by Inventor.

To make changes, you need to first close all the files you have open that are included in the project path. If you close all the files and the project is still held in the read-only state, switch to a different project in Inventor, browse for the IPJ file in Windows Explorer, and then right-click and check the Read-Only attribute of the IPJ file.

Windows often seems to leave the Read-Only attribute set on IPJ files, and then it needs to be manually taken off. Once it is off, you can switch back to that project in Inventor and make changes.

Determine the best project type for you.   Although the Autodesk solution to a multiuser environment is Autodesk® Vault data management software, many people may not be able to use Vault. For instance, if you use another CAD application that links files like Inventor, Vault will likely not know how to manage the internal links for those files.

Master It   Because you generally do not work concurrently on the same files as your co-workers, you think it might be best to set up a single-user project for now while you continue to investigate the Vault solution, but you are not sure if that will work.

Can single-user projects be used in this manner?

Solution   Set up a single-user project and then point everyone's computer to that file.

Keep a close eye on how well it works in the first several days, and watch for signs that people are making changes to the file at the same time. If your workflow is fairly linear, with one department handing files off to the next, this may not be an issue.

If you see that people are reaching for the same files at the same time, you probably need to make Vault a priority.

Chapter 2: A Hands-on Test-Drive of the Workflow

Create a part model.   The process of creating a part model starts with an `*.ipt` template file. Once you've started a part model from a template, you create sketches to define feature profiles, and then you turn those profiles into 3D features using one of the 3D modeling feature tools.

Master It   You created a base 3D feature for your parts by extruding a sketch profile at a distance of 15 mm. Then you created other sketches on the top face of the base feature.

You now realize that the base feature should have been 25 mm thick. Can the base feature be changed after you've created other features on it?

Solution   To modify part features, you can right-click them in the browser and choose Edit Feature. Inventor employs the same dialog box used to create a feature originally to edit that feature.

Create and detail drawings of part models.   The process of creating a drawing file starts with an `*.idw` (or `*.DWG`) template file.

Once you've started a drawing from a template, you create views of a referenced part model file. After the views are created, you can add dimensions and other annotations to the view.

Master It You've created a drawing of a part model and then realize that you need to make a change to that model. How will the change to the part model be handled by the drawing file?

Solution When you edit a part model that is referenced in a drawing view, the view will automatically update.

If you change the length of a part model and you have created a dimension for this length in the drawing, that dimension will update as well.

If you dimensioned from the edge of the part to the center of a hole feature in the drawing and then edited the part model file and deleted the hole, Inventor will either remove the drawing dimension or reserve the dimension and highlight it in a different color to call attention to the removed feature.

Put part models together in assembly files. The process of creating an assembly model starts with an *.iam template file. Once you've started an assembly model from a template, you place part model files into the assembly and then use Assembly constraints to arrange and assemble the part models.

Master It You've assembled your part models in an assembly file and then need to make a change to a part-model file. How will the change to the part model be handled by the assembly file?

Solution Changes made to a part-model file will be reflected in all the assemblies in which that part-model file was used.

If the edit to the part model involved changing the length of the part, most likely the Assembly constraints will update properly, because the faces and edges of the part model used in the Assembly constraint are still present but have just been adjusted in size.

If a part feature such as a hole was deleted from the part, any Assembly constraints that used that hole feature geometry would need to be edited or deleted.

Create and detail drawings of assembly models. The process of creating an assembly drawing starts with an *.idw (or *.DWG) template file, just as it did with creating part drawings.

Once you've started a drawing from a template, you can create views of a referenced assembly model file. After the views are created, you can add annotations such as parts lists and callout balloons, as well as dimensions, text notes, and so on.

Master It You've created a drawing of an assembly model and then realize that you need to make a change to one of the part files within that the assembly model. How will the change to the part model be handled by the drawing of the assembly?

Solution When you edit a part model that is referenced in an assembly model, the assembly is updated.

If edits to the Assembly constraints are needed, it's best to open the assembly file and take care of those things first. Then the views in the assembly drawing will automatically update as expected.

Chapter 3: Sketch Techniques

Set up options and settings for the sketch environment. Understanding the settings and options that apply to the sketch environment is an essential first step in working with Inventor.

Master It   You want to configure your own set of options and settings for your sketch environment and then back them up and/or distribute them to other workstations. How would you do this?

Solution   There are primarily two sets of options you can configure in Inventor. The application options configure Inventor itself, and the document settings configure the settings on a per-file basis.

You access both options and settings by clicking either the Application Options or the Document Settings button on the Tools tab.

In the Application Options dialog box, select the Sketch tab to configure the sketch environment.

Once the changes are made, you can click the Export button to save the settings as an XML file for redistribution.

Create a sketch from a part file template.   Creating a sketch in a blank template file is the fundamental step in creating 3D parametric models. You will use this basic step to start most of your part designs.

Master It   How would you capture the intent of your design when creating a base sketch for a new part?

Solution   Use a combination of lines, arcs, and geometry as well as sketch constraints and dimensions to properly constrain your sketch. You can then use this sketch to create a base feature for your part.

Keep in mind the importance of keeping sketches simple and fully constrained.

Use sketch constraints to control sketch geometry.   Understanding what each sketch constraint does when applied will allow you to determine when to use each type. Recall that often more than one constraint will work in any given situation.

Master It   How would you create a sketch that allows you to test "what if?" scenarios concerning the general shape and size of your part?

Solution   First ensure that your sketches are properly constrained. Sketches that are properly constrained are needed to allow you to experiment with your dimensional parameters by changing values and testing "what if?" scenarios.

If the sketch geometry is not properly constrained, changes to dimensions may create unpredictable results.

Master general sketch tools.   Learning the features and tricks of the sketch tools will allow you to master Inventor sketching.

Master It   You are given a print of mixed units to work from, and you need to enter dimensions exactly as they are on the print.

You understand that you can enter any dimensions in any unit simply by adding the correct suffix. But how would you create a radius dimension on a circle or a dimension from the tangents of a slot?

Solution   Recall that you switch between variant dimension solutions such as diameter to radius simply by right-clicking after having selected the geometry.

You can also get alternate dimension solutions by selecting different parts of the same geometry. For instance, selecting a line and then almost anywhere on a circle will give you a dimension from the center point of the circle to the line, whereas selecting a line and the tangent quadrant point of the circle will give you a dimension from the tangent point of the circle and the line.

Create sketches from AutoCAD geometry. You can use existing AutoCAD files to create a base sketch for an Inventor model of the same part.

Master It You have many existing 2D AutoCAD drawings detailing legacy parts. You want to reuse these designs as you convert to 3D modeling. How would you proceed?

Solution You can copy and paste selected geometry from AutoCAD directly into an Inventor sketch and then turn it into a solid model.

Keep in mind that the results are dependent on the accuracy of the original AutoCAD data. Once you become proficient with Inventor, it is often just as quick to model a part from scratch rather than by copying it.

Use 3D sketch tools. Much of working with a 3D parametric modeler can be done by sketching in a two-dimensional plane and then giving depth to the sketch to create 3D features.

However, sometimes you need to create paths or curves that are not planar. In those cases, you use the 3D sketch tools.

Master It You know the profile of a complex curve as viewed from the top and side. How would you create a 3D sketch from this data?

Solution Start by creating a separate 2D sketch for both the top and side views of the curve. Then create a 3D sketch and use the 3D Intersection Curve tool to find the intersecting curve.

Chapter 4: Basic Modeling Techniques

Configure options and settings for part modeling. Understanding the settings and options that apply to the modeling environment is essential for getting the results you want from Inventor.

Master It You want to configure your options and settings for your part environment and then back them up and distribute them to other workstations. How would you go about doing this?

Solution You would first configure the options and settings by clicking Application Options on the Get Started tab and then selecting the Part tab in the Application Options dialog box. Then you would use the Export button to save the settings as an XML file.

Create basic part features. In this chapter, you learned how to plan a workflow that allows you to create stable, editable parts that preserve the design intent.

Master It You need to create a fairly complex part consisting of many extrusions, revolves, sweeps, and lofts. In addition, you will need to create holes, fillets, chamfers, and other part modifiers.

This part may need significant modification in the future by you or by other designers. What considerations will guide your part creation?

Solution Determine how this part will be manufactured.

Think about how the part might be designed to minimize production costs while still fulfilling the intent of the design by determining how many machining operations will be required.

Determine the design intent of this part and how your approach will affect stability and any future edits or modifications.

Use the Extrude tool. The Extrude tool is one of the most commonly used feature tools in the Inventor modeling toolset.

Understanding the options and solutions available in this tool will prove useful throughout your designs.

Master It Imagine that you need to create an extruded feature but don't know the exact length; instead, you know the extrude will always terminate based on another feature.

The location of that feature has not been fully determined just yet. How do you get started on the feature?

Solution Use the Extrude To option and extrude the feature profile to a face or work plane of the other feature. Then, as you determine the location of the other feature and make adjustments, your extrusion will update as well.

Create revolved parts and thread features. Creating revolved features and parts in Inventor can often resemble the creation of turned parts and features in the real world.

Applying thread features to a cylindrical face allows you to specify threads without having to actually model them.

Master It Let's say you have a part that you intend to fabricate on a lathe.

Although you could create the part with a series of stepped circular extrusions, it occurs to you that the Revolve tool might work also. How do you decide which method to use?

Solution Oftentimes it may make sense to create a base extrusion from an extruded circle and then use the Revolve tool to create revolved cuts.

This allows you to design both the stock material and the cut features with the intent of the design in mind, anticipating changes that might occur.

You can then use the Thread tool to apply threads to any features requiring them.

Create work features. Using work features, work planes, work axes, and work points enable you to create virtually any part or feature.

Work features are the building blocks for sketch creation and use.

Master It Your design will require creating features on spherical and cylindrical faces.

You need to precisely control the location and angle of these features. How do you do that?

Solution Using existing origin features, created model features and edges, sketch objects, and other existing geometry within the file will permit you to create parametric work features as the basis for additional geometry creation.

Use the Fillet tool. The Fillet tool has a great deal of functionality packed into it. Taking the time to explore all the options on a simple test model may be the best way to understand them all.

Master It You are trying to create a series of fillets on a part. You create four sets of edge selections to have four different fillet sizes, but when you attempt to apply them, you receive an error stating that the feature cannot be built. What went wrong?

Solution Sometimes the creation of multiple fillet sizes combined into one feature is not the way to go.

Instead, identify the edges that will "compete" for a common corner, particularly where they differ in radius size, and create these fillets as individual fillet features.

This allows Inventor to solve the corner in steps and makes the results more robust and less ambiguous.

Create intelligent hole features. Although you can create a hole in a part by sketching a circle and extrude-cutting it, this is typically not the recommended approach.

Master It You need to create a part with a series of various-sized holes on a plate.

You would like to lay out the hole pattern in a single sketch and then use the Hole tool to cut the holes to the sizes required.

When you select the From Sketch option in the Hole tool, it selects all the holes, so you think you must need to sketch out the hole pattern as circles and then use the Extrude tool to cut them out.

Is this really the way to proceed?

Solution Using the Extrude tool is not the way to go. Instead, create a sketch on the face of the plate and use center points to mark the hole centers.

Dimension each center point in place and then start the Hole tool. Hold down **Ctrl** to deselect the center points for holes of a different size and then create the hole feature for the first set of holes.

Locate your sketch in the browser, right-click it, and choose Share Sketch. Then use the Hole tool to place the next size holes.

Bend parts. You can bend a portion of a part after you define a bend line using a 2D sketch line. You can specify the side of the part to bend; the direction of the bend; and its angle, radius, or arc length.

Master It You need to create a model of a piece of rolled tube and would like to specify the bend direction, but when you use the direction arrow, you get a preview in only one direction.

How can you get a preview in either direction?

Solution Use a work plane to create a sketch in the middle of the part and then sketch the bend line on that work plane.

This will allow you to specify either direction for the bend.

Chapter 5: Advanced Modeling Techniques

Create complex sweeps and lofts. Complex geometry is created by using multiple work planes, sketches, and 3D sketch geometry.

Honing your experience in creating work planes and 3D sketches is paramount to success in creating complex models.

Master It   How would you create a piece of twisted, flat bar in Inventor?

Solution   Create the flat bar profile in a base sketch. Then create a work plane offset from the original sketch and make it the length of the bar.

Create the profile sketch on this work plane at a rotated orientation to match the degree of twist needed. Create a 3D sketch and connect the corners of the first profile to the appropriate corners of the second profile.

Using the 3D sketch lines as rails, use the Loft tool to loft from one profile to the other to produce the twisted part.

Work with multi-body and derived parts.   Multi-body parts can be used to create part files with features that require precise matching between two or more parts.

Once the solid bodies are created, you can create a separate part file for each component.

Master It   What would be the best way to create an assembly of four parts that require features to mate together in different positions?

Solution   Create the parts in a multi-body part file and subtract material from one part based on the profile of the other.

Consider creating the first two parts in one multi-body part file and the other two in another multi-body part file to keep the files as simple as possible.

You can also derive the first multi-body part into the second for better control.

Utilize part tolerances.   Dimensional tolerancing of sketches allows you to check stack-up variations within assemblies.

When you add tolerances to critical dimensions within sketches, you can adjust parts to maximum, minimum, and nominal conditions.

Master It   You want to create a model feature with a deviation so you can test the assembly fit at the extreme ends of the tolerances. How would this be done?

Solution   Use the Parameters dialog box to set up and adjust tolerances for individual dimensions.

In the Parameters dialog box, set the tolerance to the upper or lower limits for the part and then update the model using the Update button.

Check the fit of the feature against its mating part or parts in the assembly environment and then edit the part to set it back to the nominal once done.

Understand and use parameters and iProperties.   Using iProperties within files assists in the creation of title blocks, parts lists, and annotation within 2D drawings.

Using parameters in an assembly file allows the control of constraints and objects within the assembly.

Exporting parameters allows the creation of custom iProperties.

Proper use of iProperties facilitates the creation of accurate 2D drawings that always reflect the current state of included parts and assemblies.

Master It   You want to create a formula to determine the spacing of a hole pattern based on the length of the part. What tools would you use?

Solution   Set up a user parameter that calls the part length and divides by the number of holes or the spacing and then reference this user parameter in the hole pattern feature.

Troubleshoot modeling failures.   Modeling failures are often caused by poor design practices. Poor sketching techniques, bad design workflow, and other factors can lead to the elimination of design intent within a model.

Master It   You want to modify a rather complex existing part file, but when you change the feature, errors cascade down through the entire part.

How can you change the feature without this happening?

Solution   Position the end-of-part marker just under the feature you intend to modify and make the change.

Then move the end-of-part marker back down the feature tree one feature at a time, addressing each error as it occurs.

Use the Rebuild All tool from time to time to see whether recomputing the tree will force a "fix" to cascade down the tree.

Continue until all features have been fixed.

Chapter 6: Sheet Metal

Take advantage of the specific sheet-metal features available in Inventor.   Knowing what features are available to help realize your design can make more efficient and productive use of your time.

Master It   Of the sheet-metal features discussed, how many require a sketch to produce their result?

Solution   Five sheet-metal features consume a sketch: Contour Flange, Face, Cut, Punch, and Fold.

Since Inventor has well-established paradigms for how sketches can be manipulated, knowing which features consume sketches may allow you to develop designs that are flexible and parametrically configurable.

Understand sheet-metal templates and rules.   Templates can help get your design started on the right path, and sheet-metal rules and associated styles allow you to drive powerful and intelligent manufacturing variations into your design.

Combining the two can be productive as long as you understand some basic principles.

Master It   Name two methods that can be used to publish a sheet-metal rule from a sheet-metal part file to the style library.

Solution   Rules and styles can be published or written to the style library either from Inventor or by using the Style Management Wizard (the harvester).

Using the native Inventor method, right-clicking a given rule/style produces an option called Save To Style Library.

Using the harvester, you can select a specific file and add its style information to your existing style library, or you can create a new one.

Author and insert punch tooling.   Creating and managing Punch tools can streamline your design process and standardize tooling in your manufacturing environment.

Master It   Name two methods that can be utilized to produce irregular (nonsymmetrical) patterns of punch features.

Solution   Sketch center marks can be patterned within the insertion sketch as a symmetric array.

During Punch tool insertion, the Centers control on the Geometry tab can be used to deselect center marks where you want a tool to be placed.

The feature-patterning tools can also be used to create irregular patterns after a punch feature has been created. You can do this by first creating a symmetric pattern of punch features, then expanding the child pattern occurrences in the feature browser, and finally individually suppressing them.

Both methods prevent the feature from being displayed in the folded and flat pattern as well as omit the Punch tool information in the flat-pattern punch metadata.

Utilize the flat pattern information and options.   The sheet-metal folded model captures your manufacturing intent during the design process; understanding how to leverage this information and customize it for your needs can make you extremely productive.

Master It   How can you change the reported angle of all your Punch features by 90 degrees?

Solution   The flat pattern's orientation infers a virtual x-axis for punch angle calculation, so rotating the flat pattern by 90 degrees will change all the punch angles by the same amount.

The flat pattern can also affect the bend and punch direction (up or down) by flipping the base face, and reported bend angles can be changed from Bending Angle to Open Angle by changing options in the Bend Angle tab of the Flat Pattern Definition dialog box.

Understand the nuances of sheet-metal iPart factories.   Sheet-metal iPart factories enable you to create true manufacturing configurations with the inclusion of folded and flat pattern models in each member file.

Master It   If you created sheet-metal iPart factories prior to Inventor 2009, any instantiated files contain only a folded model. Name two methods that you could use to drive the flat pattern model into the instantiated file.

Solution   Once you have opened, migrated, and saved a legacy sheet-metal iPart factory, you can decide between two methodologies for obtaining the flat pattern model within your instantiated files: push or pull.

The *push method* is accomplished from within the iPart factory by using the context menu option Generate Files, which is associated with the member filename. This method pushes out a new definition of the member file including the flat pattern model.

The *pull method* requires you to be using the Inventor Rebuild All tool, followed by saving the factory file. Now that the factory has been rebuilt, any time you open one of the instantiated files associated with the factory, it will see that it's out-of-date and will trip the update flag.

Selecting Update will pull the flat pattern model into the instantiated member file.

Model sheet-metal components with non-sheet-metal features. Inventor doesn't always allow you to restrict yourself to sheet metal–specific design tools.

Understanding how to utilize non-sheet-metal features will ensure that your creativity is limitless.

Master It Name two non-sheet-metal features that can lead to unfolding problems if used to create your design.

Solution As discussed in the chapter, Loft and Shell can lead to numerous problems during unfolding because of nondevelopable curvature introduced by Loft and nonuniform thickness introduced by Shell.

Work with imported sheet-metal parts. Understanding the way in which Inventor accomplishes unfolding as well as how to associate an appropriate sheet-metal rule are keys to successfully working with imported parts.

Master It Name the one measured value that is critical if you want to unfold an imported part.

Solution The measured sheet thickness is the most important geometric measurement in an imported sheet-metal part.

Ensuring that the thickness of your imported part matches the active Thickness parameter means the difference between success and frustration.

Although you can change the active rule (or create a new one) to match all the geometric conditions of your imported part, these will affect only new features or topology that you introduce.

Thickness is the key.

Understand the tools available to annotate your sheet-metal design. Designing your component is essential, but it's equally important to understand the tools that are available to efficiently document your design and extract your embedded manufacturing intent.

Master It What process is required to recover flat pattern width and height extents within your Drawing Manager parts list?

Solution By creating custom iProperties within your sheet-metal part file set equal to *<FLAT PATTERN LENGTH>* cm and *<FLAT PATTERN WIDTH>* cm, you can reference flat pattern extents by your parts list by adding these new properties using the Column Chooser tool.

To make this process more efficient, you can predefine the custom iProperties in your sheet-metal template file, and the custom properties can be authored into a custom Drawing Manager parts list template for quick application.

Chapter 7: Reusing Parts and Features

Create and modify iParts.   iParts are the solution to creating parts that allow for an infinite number of variations without affecting other members of the same part family already used within your designs.

> **Master It**   You use a purchased specialty part in your designs and would like to create the many size configurations that this part comes in ahead of time for use within assembly design.
>
> How would this be done?
>
> **Solution**   Create or use an existing model and edit the parameter list to use logical names for specific parameters.
>
> Add the configuration table by creating an iPart from this model. Configure the parameters in the table and add rows according to variations needed.
>
> Finally, test the newly created iPart by inserting all variations of the part into a blank assembly.

Create and use iFeatures and punches.   Creating a library of often-used features is essential to standardization and improved productivity within your design workflow.

> **Master It**   You want to be able to place common punches, slots, and milled features quickly rather than having to generate the feature every time.
>
> What is the best way to approach this?
>
> **Solution**   Extract iFeatures from existing standard and sheet-metal part features and place them in user-defined folders within the `Catalog` subfolder.
>
> Using your custom-created iFeatures as well as standard iFeatures, practice placing them into your designs to see how they behave and how they can be modified.
>
> Finally, once the iFeatures or punches have been proven to work as expected, use them to quickly place common features in your production designs.

Copy and clone features.   You do not have to create iFeatures to reuse various part features in your designs. If a part feature will have limited use in other designs, it is often better to simply copy it from part to part or from face to face on the same part.

> **Master It**   You need to reuse features within a part or among parts. You consider iFeatures but realize that this feature is not used often enough to justify setting up an iFeature.
>
> How would you proceed?
>
> **Solution**   Right-click the existing feature and choose Copy. Determine whether dependent and independent features such as fillets and chamfers need to be copied as well and then paste the feature onto another face in the same part.
>
> Or open a different part file and paste onto a selected face. Copying between two parts is called *cloning*.

Link parameters between two files.   Linking design parameters between two or more files allows you to control design changes from a single source, making it easy to update an entire design from one file.

Master It You want to specify the overall length and width of a layout design in a base part and then have other components update as changes are made to this part.

What are the methods to do this?

Solution From the other component files, open the parameter editor, use the Link button to specify the source file, and then choose which parameters to link.

You can then call those linked parameters into the sketch and feature dimensions of the other components in your design.

Configure, create, and access Content Center parts. Content Center provides a great opportunity to reuse database-created geometry within assemblies and within functional-design modules.

The Content Center Editor provides the means to add custom content into Content Center. You can create and add custom libraries to your current project file.

Master It You would like to change the part numbers in some Content Center components to match the part numbers your company uses. You would also like to add proprietary components to Content Center.

How do you customize Content Center?

Solution Create a custom Content Center library. Configure your project file to include your newly created read/write Content Center library.

Utilize the Content Center Editor to create new categories within your custom Content Center library. Convert a part or an iPart to a Content Center component using the Publish option.

Chapter 8: Assembly Design Workflows

Create assembly relationships using the Constraint and Joint tools. Assembly relationships are an important part of working with Inventor assembly files. Assembly constraints determine how assembly components fit together. As relationships are applied between components, degrees of freedom are removed.

Master It You are new to 3D and find the concept of assembly relationships a bit challenging. Where can you find a simple overview of constraints?

Solution You can find a good overview of constraints by selecting the Get Started tab and clicking the Place And Connect Parts button in the Tutorials section.

From there, you can follow the interactive tutorial using the panel on the right.

Organize designs using structured subassemblies. Subassemblies add organization, facilitate the bill of materials, and reduce assembly relationships; all this results in better performance and easier edits.

One of the habits of all Inventor experts is their effective use and understanding of subassemblies.

Master It You need to hand off an accurate BOM for finished designs to the purchasing department at the end of each design project.

How can the BOM be extracted from Inventor?

Solution   Organize parts in subassemblies in a real-world manner matching the way components are assembled on the shop floor.

Use Phantom assemblies when structuring parts merely for the purpose of reducing assembly relationships.

Set assemblies as Purchased or Inseparable when you want multiple components to appear as a single item in the BOM.

Export the BOM from the assembly to an Excel spreadsheet or other intermediate format to give to purchasing.

Work with adaptive components.   Geometry can be set to be adaptive so that it can be sized and positioned in the context of where it is used in the assembly.

You can set underconstrained geometry to be adaptive by specifying the elements allowed to adapt.

Master It   You want to set a feature of a part to be adaptive so that it can adapt to another part in an assembly. However, the feature is based on a fully constrained sketch. How would this be done?

Solution   To set a fully constrained sketch to be adaptive, you would edit the sketch and then set the dimensions that are intended to adapt to be driven dimensions.

Doing so leaves the sketch in an underconstrained state, opening it up for adaptivity.

Create assembly-level features.   An assembly feature is a feature created and utilized within the active assembly file.

Because the feature is created within the assembly file, it does not exist at the single-part or subassembly level.

Master It   You want to make a notch in a standard part that will not affect its use in every other assembly it is used in.

Can this be done?

Solution   Create the notch in the assembly that it is used in rather than the part file itself, and then the notch will exist only for that instance of the part and not in other instances of it.

Manage bills of materials.   Managing a bill of materials can be a large part of any assembly design task. Understanding the BOM structure goes a long way toward successfully configuring your bill of materials.

Master It   You need to mark a component as a reference component in just one assembly file. However, when you attempt to do so using the BOM Editor, it is designated as a reference in every assembly.

How can you set just a single instance of a component to be a reference component?

Solution   When components are set to reference in the BOM Editor, the BOM structure for the file is being changed globally.

To override a component's BOM structure per instance, right-click it in the browser and choose BOM Structure; then select Reference.

Use positional reps and flexible assemblies together. Often, you may need to show a design in various stages of motion to test interference or proof of concept.

Copying assemblies so that you can change the assembly relationships to show different assembly positions can become a file management nightmare.

Instead, use flexible subassemblies and positional representations.

Master It You need to show your assembly in variations dependent on the position of the moving parts and the task the machine is accomplishing at given stages of its operation.

How do you do this?

Solution Leave subassemblies underconstrained if they have parts that determine their position based on the relationships with parts within another subassembly.

Set them to Flexible to allow them to be mated to other parts and used in different positions within the same top-level assembly.

Create positional representations to show the design in known kinematic states, such as fully opened, closed, opened at a given angle, and so on.

As an added benefit, animating assemblies in Inventor Studio is simple when positional representations have been set up in the model.

Copy assembly designs for reuse and configuration. Because of the live linked data that exists in Inventor assemblies, using Windows Explorer to copy designs and rename parts is difficult and often delivers poor results.

Using the tool provided in Inventor will allow you to copy designs and maintain the links between files.

Master It How do you duplicate an existing design to create a similar design?

Solution Use the Copy Components feature in the assembly environment to copy designs and choose which parts to copy and rename, reuse, or omit from the new design.

Use Autodesk Vault to take it to the next level and include all the 2D drawings in the copied design.

Substitute a single part for entire subassemblies. Working with large assemblies, particularly where large, complex assemblies are used over and over as subassemblies within a top-level design, can tax almost any workstation if not approached in the correct manner.

Master It You would like to swap out a complex assembly for a simplified version for use in layout designs or to use in large assemblies in an attempt to improve performance. What is the best way to do that?

Solution Create LOD representations to suppress components when not in use during the design cycle.

Create single substitute parts from large complex assemblies to be used as subassemblies within the design.

Enjoy the benefits of referencing fewer files while maintaining an accurate bill of materials.

Work with assembly design accelerators and generators. Design accelerators and generators allow you to rapidly create complex geometry and the associated calculations that verify the viability of your design.

Master It   Your design needs a bolted connection, but you are not certain about the number of bolts to use to ensure a proper connection. How do you determine this?

Solution   Use the Bolted Connections tool to determine the optimum number of bolts for a given material and loading conditions.

Use design calculators.   Design calculators do not create any geometry, but they permit you to store the calculations in the assembly and repeat the calculation with different input values at a later time.

Master It   You need to calculate the size of a weld between two plates to withstand a certain lateral force. What tool do you use?

Solution   Use the Fillet Weld calculator to determine the size, type, and material of the weld bead.

Chapter 9: Large Assembly Strategies

Select a workstation.   Having the right tool for the job is the key to success in anything you do. This is true of selecting a large assembly workstation.

You have learned that for optimal performance you should strive to keep your system working in physical memory (RAM).

Master It   You notice that your computer runs slowly when working with large assemblies, and you want to know whether you should consider a 64-bit system.

How do you determine whether your system is adequate or whether it's time to upgrade?

Solution   To decide whether your system is adequate, evaluate the amount of time you spend working on large assemblies and the percentage of that time you spend waiting on your workstation.

Monitor your RAM usage, and decide whether upgrading to a 64-bit system is a good solution for your needs. You should plan for hardware upgrades in your budget to make them more manageable.

Remember that your hardware may already be capable of running a 64-bit operating system, so you may need to upgrade only the OS rather than replace the hardware.

Adjust your performance settings.   You have learned that there are many settings in Inventor and in Windows that you can use to configure the application to work more efficiently with large assemblies.

Master It   You want to make your current workstation run as efficiently as possible for large assembly design. What are some ways to do that?

Solution   Disable the unneeded Windows visual effects and discontinue the use of screen savers, large-resolution screen sizes, and desktop wallpapers.

Learn the location of the Application Options settings within Inventor that will provide performance gains.

Use best practices for large assemblies.   Knowing the tools for general assembly design is only half of the battle when it comes to conquering large assemblies.

Understanding the methods of large assembly design and how they differ from those for general assembly design is a key to success.

Master It You want to create adaptive parts so that you can make changes during the initial design stage and have several parts update automatically as you work through the details. But you are concerned about how this will adversely affect your assembly performance.

How do you keep your performance level high in this situation?

Solution Create adaptive relationships between parts as you normally would, but ensure that the adaptivity is turned off once the initial design is done.

If the parts require an update, turn Adaptivity back on, make the edits, and then turn Adaptivity back off.

Manage assembly detail. Inventor includes several tools to help manage assembly detail so that you can accomplish your large assembly design goals.

Master It You want to reduce the number of files your large assembly is required to reference while you are working on it and yet maintain an accurate bill of materials. How do you do that?

Solution Use substitute level of detail (LOD) representations to derive a subassembly into a single part file. Place multiple instances of the subassembly into the top-level assembly at the substitute level of detail.

Simplify parts. Creating highly detailed parts may be required for generating production drawings or Inventor Studio renderings, but using those high-detail parts in large assemblies may have an adverse effect on performance.

Master It You want to create a lower-level-of-detail part file for common parts to be reused many times over in your large assemblies but are concerned about managing two versions of a part. How do you avoid versioning problems?

Solution Create an embedded link between the two versions so that you can easily locate and access the other version if the first version requires an edit.

Chapter 10: Weldment Design

Select and use the right weldment design methodology. You've been shown three weldment design methodologies. Before you start on any weldment design, it is imperative to keep the documentation, interference analysis, mass properties, and other design criteria in perspective and select the right design methodology.

Master It How do you choose the right weldment strategy for you?

Solution If you don't need to document the weldment design stages, you could consider the part files and part features methodology or the weldment assembly and derived methodology.

With the weldment assembly methodology, you get to document the different stages of weldment design and reap the benefits of any new enhancements.

Talk to your machine shop and then choose the one that best suits you. Use the weldment assembly design methodology if you can't decide.

Create and edit weld preparations and machining features.   Following the weldment methodology, you need to plan on creating the gaps needed (weld preparations) to deposit the weld beads. You need to create post-weldment machining features that go through the weld beads.

Master It   Weld preparations and machining features are similar to part modeling features.

Based on the weld-bead shape needed, you should plan on creating the preparations in advance. Once the welds are done, you must create the features for the machining processes.

Where can you find preparation and machining features, and when do you use them?

Solution   Double-click the Preparations or Machining tool in the assembly browser to go into those environments. Chamfer and Move Face are most commonly used. Most groove welds require some kind of weld preparations.

Create and edit different kinds of weld beads, such as cosmetic, fillet, and groove.   Weldment design involves the optimal mix of cosmetic and solid weld beads based on the requirements of your design goals and model verification needs.

Master It   You should create the weld annotations only in drawings, without any need to create them in the model.

You have weld subassemblies that need only lightweight representation in both the model and drawings.

In situations involving accurate interference and mass properties, you require accurate weld beads.

The question is, what type of weld beads should you use?

Solution   Double-click Welds in the assembly browser and choose the desired weld bead type.

For a lightweight representation with no interference and accurate mass properties, use cosmetic welds.

For interference and accurate mass properties, use the solid representation. Use a combination of fillet and groove welds as needed to generate the desired weld-bead shape.

Use the split technique in cases where you want precise control.

Observe that you can use a single weld symbol to call out multiple weld beads.

Document weldment stages in drawings.   Welds need to be documented in assemblies or drawings. It is important to show the different stages of weldment design in drawings to get a good idea of how to manufacture the weldment.

You can use the drawing tools effectively to annotate the welds in drawings. This will help the welder understand the design intent better.

Master It   Several tools are used for weld documentation. You can annotate the welds in assemblies.

If you prefer to document the welds in drawings, you could document the four stages of weldment design: the as-assembled, as-prepped, as-welded, and as-machined stages in drawings.

Name two other drawing tools that customize weld documentation.

Solution   While creating a drawing view on the Model State tab of the Drawing View dialog box, select Assembly, Machining, Welds, or Preparation. Use the End Fill tool to customize the weld-bead process shape. Weld Caterpillars is another useful tool to show welds in a drawing.

Generate and maintain a consistent BOM across welded assemblies, drawings, and presentations.   You have been shown how to generate and maintain a consistent bill of materials for weldment assemblies and a parts list in drawings. Mark parts or assemblies as inseparable to designate them as weldments.

Master It   How do you generate the BOM and parts list for your weldment?

Solution   You can generate the bill of materials and mark the components as inseparable.

In the drawing, you generate the parts list for the weldment assembly. Click the BOM tool in a weldment assembly. In the Structure column, you can set each part to be inseparable.

Use the Parts List tool and appropriate table-wrapping options to generate the parts list.

Chapter 11: Presentations and Exploded Views

Create an exploded assembly view by creating a presentation.   Presentation files are used to virtually disassemble an assembly so downstream consumers can better visualize the design.

The explosion created in the presentation file can be referenced in an assembly drawing to complement non-exploded assembly views.

Master It   Your assembly design is complex and contains many internal components that can't be visualized in traditional assembly drawing views.

What is a good approach to showing those components?

Solution   Create a new presentation file, reference an assembly, and tweak parts and subassemblies away from their constrained positions.

Add as many tweaks as necessary to communicate the design effectively. You may choose to create several explosions in one presentation file to achieve this goal.

Create basic linear tweaks.   Tweaks are used to move (or translate) components along a specified axis. This allows you to pull your assembly apart in order to show how it goes together.

Master It   Your assembly design includes a number of hardware connections, and you'd like to show how they go together in a clear and concise way. How should you do this?

Solution   Creating linear tweaks in a presentation view can often show screw, washer, and nut stack-ups more clearly than they can be shown in an assembled view on a drawing.

Create rotational tweaks.   Rotational tweaks allow you to move components in an orientation that is not along the standard x-, y-, and z-axes and that can be used to show rotation of parts for animations.

Master It   Your assembly has a housing that you'd like to tip out of the way to show both the parts within and the connection features of the housing. When you apply a linear tweak, you can move the housing up and off the assembly to show the parts, but you cannot see the connection features. What do you need to do to see the connection features?

Solution You can use a rotational tweak to tip over the housing part and expose the underside to the view. Using linear and rotational tweaks together is often the best way to add clarity to your assembly presentation views.

Group, reorder, and animate tweaks. Once tweaks are created, you may want to group several of them together into the same sequence of steps and reorder them to show a specific assembly step in an animation.

Master It You want to create an animated assembly presentation of your assembly going together, but when creating the tweaks, you did so by going from top to bottom of the assembly rather than following the order in which the assembly would actually take place.

Can this be resolved?

Solution You can use the Group and Reorder tools to refine your presentation after it's initially created.

This is often helpful when you've created a presentation for the purposes of a 2D drawing view and didn't consider the order in which tweaks were created but then decide later to animate it.

Publish presentation files. Although you can place views of your presentation file on a 2D drawing, it can be helpful to include the 3D animation for customers and colleagues in the form of a DWF or DWFx file.

Master It You want to supply the shop floor with assembly instructions of your assembly going together. What is a good way to do this?

Solution You can output your presentation sequences as a lightweight DWF or DWFx file and then allow the people on the shop floor to use Autodesk Design Review or Internet Explorer to view the files.

Using presentation files in this way can add a great deal of clarity to build procedures and assembly instructions.

Chapter 12: Documentation

Create templates and styles. Inventor provides numerous methods to create, store, and use drawing templates and styles.

Careful planning as to how and where to manage these resources is important. Consideration must be given to how templates are deployed on your network and how to use the style library.

Master It Rather than using one of the out-of-the-box drawing settings, you need to set up a drawing template, a drafting standard, and annotation styles to conform to a particular international, industry, or company drafting standard.

How do you get started?

Solution Use one of the drawing templates that are installed with Inventor, and reconfigure it to meet your or your company's requirements.

Edit the drawing resources to customize your title block, border, and sketched symbols. Define annotation styles such as dimension and parts list styles, and determine how best to share them across your workgroup.

Utilize drawing resources.   Each Inventor drawing file contains a number of commonly used drawing-resource definitions, such as title blocks, borders, symbols, and so on.

These resource definitions allow you to store preconfigured items for quick and easy reuse.

Master It   You have blocks of general notes that you place on every drawing file. However, some drawings get one set of notes, and others get another, so making these notes part of the title block seems to be the wrong approach.

Is there a way to handle this in Inventor?

Solution   You can create a sketched symbol for each of the note blocks and type out the notes using the Text tool. Then when you create a new drawing file, you can choose which block of notes to place on the drawing and insert it from the `Sketched Symbols` folder in the `Drawing Resources` folder.

Edit styles and standards.   Inventor's drawing styles and standards allow you to set up your dimension styles, layer styles, and so on, in advance so that you can maintain consistency across all your drawings.

Master It   You have set up your object defaults to use an inch-based dimension style, but occasionally you want to place a millimeter-based dimension.

Can this be done easily, or do you have to override the dimension style?

Solution   Typically, you will set up several dimension styles in your template file. In this case, you might have one for Imperial and another for metric dimensions.

Although only one dimension style can be the default style that is selected when you start the Dimension tool, you can set the Dimension tool to use another style.

To do this, first start the Dimension tool, then go to the Format panel and select the styles pull-down, and choose a different dimension style from list.

You can also select previously placed dimensions and change them to use a different style using the same pull-down.

Create drawing views.   Drawing views allow you to make 2D views of your 3D models. The hidden line generation and alignment of your projected views are automatic, as are updates to the 2D views when your 3D models change.

Master It   When placing a drawing view, the lines on curved edges don't show up. Is there an option to turn these on?

Solution   When placing a view or editing a view, you can click the Display Options tab.

Here, you'll find several options to control the visibility of tangent edges, interference edges, thread lines, and many other optional display items.

Annotate part drawings.   Adding annotation to your part drawings is accomplished primarily using the tools on the Annotate tab. Many of these tools automate traditional drafting annotation, but you might still find the need to add annotation in a more manual way.

Master It   You need to create sheet-metal flat patterns for your parts with laser etching on them. Often this is text, but you've noticed that if you attempt to create text as an extrusion on the part, you end up with a stencil effect, rather than single-line characters used for etching.

Is there a way to do this?

Solution   There are a couple of methods for doing this, but the most common is accomplished by creating a sketch in the drawing environment.

First you select the flat pattern view, and then you click the Create Sketch button from the Annotate tab. By selecting the view first, the sketch is associated to the view, and if the view is moved, the sketch will move also.

To add the laser etching information, you can use the Text tool and select a font such as Simplex. You can also sketch lines and other geometry if needed.

Using the Project Geometry tool lets you anchor and dimension your text and lines to the part edges for precise placement.

Annotate assembly drawings.   Often, much of the annotation created for assembly drawings concerns bill of materials information, but you can use most of the same annotation tools used for part drawings in an assembly drawing.

Master It   You created a section view of your assembly model and then noticed that you could hide the hatch pattern by right-clicking it and choosing Hide.

But now when you right-click the drawing view, you can't find an option to bring back the hatch pattern. Is it gone for good?

Solution   To bring back a hidden hatch pattern, edit the view and click the Display Options tab.

On this tab you'll find a Hatching check box. Select it and then your hatch pattern will be displayed again.

Work with sheet-metal drawings.   Inventor sheet-metal drawings give you access to the folded model and the flat pattern, provided that a flat pattern has been created in the 3D model.

Master It   When you place a bend note on a flat pattern drawing, it places the direction, angle, and bend radius. Your shop is accustomed to seeing only the direction and angle.

Is there a way to remove the bend radius?

Solution   If you right-click a bend note and choose Edit Bend Note, you can remove the radius notation for that note.

To do this for all of the bend notes on the sheet, right-click a bend note and choose Edit Dimension Style. This will take you to the Notes And Leaders tab of the edit dialog for the dimension style containing the bend note.

Use the radio button near the top to select the Bend Note option, and then you can make changes that will update all the bend notes.

Work with weldment views.   Weldment views offer some extra functionality over standard assembly views in that they allow you to document your assembly in each weldment stage.

Master It   You want to create a drawing package that shows all the weldment pieces in the prepped stage and then show the weldment assembly in the completed form.

What's the best way to do this?

Solution   When you place a view of the weldment assembly, you can use the Model State tab of the view creation dialog box to choose each component of the weldment in the Preparation stage.

Work with iParts and iAssembly drawings.   One of the benefits of creating part and assembly families as iParts and iAssemblies is the ability to create tabulated drawings that show each member and its key dimensions in a table.

> **Master It**   You've created an iPart table and want to set the dimension on the sheet to match the table heading.
>
> Is this possible?
>
> **Solution**   You can do this by simply overriding the dimension value. First, edit the dimension and then select the Hide Dimension Value check box. Then, type in the table heading name.

Share your drawings outside your workgroup.   You can save your drawings in DWF, DWFx, and PDF formats in order to share them with people who do not have Inventor.

You can use Autodesk Design Review to access DWF files and Adobe Acrobat Reader to access PDF files; both are free viewer applications.

> **Master It**   You have a multipage Inventor drawing, but when you export it as a PDF file, you get only the first page. Is this a bug, or is it just the way it is?
>
> **Solution**   When you export a drawing as a PDF, you will be presented with the Save Copy As dialog box.
>
> In this dialog box, there is an Options button; if you click this button, you'll find an option to include all drawing sheets.

Chapter 13: Tools Overview

Take your models from Inventor to the Autodesk Building Systems (ABS) program.   If you frequently need to take your Inventor models to ABS, BIM Exchange can help you in this process with three simple steps.

Inventor provides a variety of ways to simplify the model and author it. Such models can be published in ABS.

> **Master It**   Describe the basic steps involved in moving Inventor models to Autodesk Building Systems.
>
> **Solution**   You can do this with the following three steps: model simplifying, authoring, and publishing. Author the model with cables, conduit, ducts, or pipe. Create part families and catalogs.

Create AutoLimits (design sensors).   You use AutoLimits to monitor design parameters in which you are interested.

> **Master It**   You want to use AutoLimits for every dimension in your model. How many AutoLimits can you use at once?
>
> **Solution**   Create the AutoLimits and set up their boundaries.
>
> Although technically the number of AutoLimits you can use in your model is unlimited, you should consider limiting the number of AutoLimits to around 10 to avoid impacting the performance of your model.

Manage design data efficiently using Inventor tools.   There are different tools for managing design data, which is typically distributed across part, assembly, and drawing files.

You can associate Excel spreadsheets, text files, Word documents, and so on, with these tools.

Master It   Name some of the Inventor tools for managing design data. Describe what each one does and how to initiate it.

Solution   The Design Assistant keeps the file relationships while copying, renaming, and moving files.

Whenever you are sending Inventor files to others, use Pack And Go, which hunts down the file relationship for you, and then you can package them into a single zip file.

You can delegate many of the tasks in Inventor to the Task Scheduler.

You can propagate source drawing template information to several destination drawings using the Drawing Resource Transfer Wizard.

In the Design Assistant, click the Manage button. Right-click the file in the Action column and select Action. Right-click the file in the Name column and select Change Name. Click Save Changes.

Right-click the file in Windows Explorer to use Pack And Go.

In the Task Scheduler, use the Create Task menu to create your task.

In the Drawing Resource Transfer Wizard, select source resources, deselect any unwanted resources, and propagate the template information to destination drawings.

Manage styles.   You can use the Style Library Manager to organize your styles to keep them simple and clean.

Master It   Styles normally need to be copied, edited, and deleted.

How do you manage your styles?

How can you create a central repository of styles?

Solution   You can create a new style library using the Create New Style Library button in the Style Library Manager.

You can copy styles by clicking Style Library 1 and then clicking Style Library 2.

To delete styles, right-click the style in the Style Library Manager and then rename or delete the style.

Create expressions with iProperties.   Property fields can be concatenated to produce desired customized information in BOM and parts lists. For example, you can break down your parts by stock size to be used in your BOM with associativity to model parameters.

Master It   How do you create and manage expressions for iProperties?

Solution   You can create expressions on the Summary, Project, Status, or Custom tab. Start with the = sign and type in the text.

To include parameters or iProperty names, include them in brackets. A detected expression is denoted by *fx*.

You can create a template file with predefined expressions for iProperties to unify your parts list and other documentation.

Give feedback to Autodesk.   You can participate in the Customer Involvement Program (CIP). Customer error reporting (CER) helps Autodesk know about any issue you might experience.

Master It You have a repeatable crash that you suspect is related to a specific file or a specific machine and want to know whether Autodesk can help you determine this.

Solution You can use the CER form to supply contact information and step-by-step information about repeatable issues and then call reseller support or log a case with Autodesk through the subscription website.

Autodesk can look up your CER based on the submittal time and contact information you entered.

Chapter 14: Exchanging Data with Other Systems

Import and export geometry. In the design world today, you most likely need to transfer files to or from a customer or vendor from time to time. Chances are, the files will need to be translated to or from a neutral file format to be read by different CAD packages.

Master It You are collaborating with another design office that does not use Inventor. You are asked which you would prefer, IGES or STEP files. Which one should you request?

Solution Request a STEP file over IGES when you have the choice. Take advantage of the extra intelligence related to assembly structure and filenames that can be retained in the STEP file format.

Use Inventor file translators. Inventor offers native file translators for CATIA, Pro/ENGINEER, SolidWorks, Unigraphics, and other CAD file types. This allows you to access these file formats with Inventor and translate the files into Inventor files directly.

Master It You are a "job shop" and in the past have been required to maintain a copy of SolidWorks in addition to your copy of Inventor to work with customers who send you SolidWorks files. You would like to eliminate the cost of maintaining two software packages.

What is a good strategy for doing that?

Solution Use Inventor to access the customer's files directly and convert them to Inventor files for your in-house use. Use Save Copy As to export the file back out as a SolidWorks file to send to the client for review.

In this way, you may be able to eliminate the need to maintain two software packages.

Work with imported data. Using the construction environment in Inventor, you can repair poorly translated surface files.

Often, a file fails to translate into a solid because of just a few translation errors in the part. Repairing or patching the surfaces and promoting the file to a solid allows you to use the file more effectively.

Master It You download an IGES file from a vendor website, but when you attempt to use the component in your design, the surface data is found to have issues. How should you proceed?

Solution Open the file and copy the surfaces to the construction environment.

Use Stitch Surface to create composite surfaces, and identify the gaps in the surface data.

Use the construction tools to delete, patch, and extend surfaces in order to close the gaps and promote the data to a solid.

Before getting started on this, evaluate the amount of time required to repair the surface data. You may find that you can model the vendor component—by using catalog specs or by measuring an actual part—faster than you can repair some surface models.

Work with Design Review markups.   Design Review offers you and the people who collaborate with you an easy-to-use electronic markup tool that can be round-tripped from Inventor. Design Review markups can be made on both 2D and 3D files.

Master It   You want to use Design Review to communicate with vendors and clients to save time and resources, but you have found that others are unsure of what Design Review is and how to get it.

What are some good ways to help others begin to use this handy application?

Solution   Suggest using Design Review to the people you collaborate with and mention to them that this application is a free download.

Send them the link to download the application and the online demonstration found in Design Review's Help menu. Continue to offer your collaborators the review material in PDF, DWG, or any other traditional file type in case they end up in a time crunch, but send them DWF files as well.

If they use Internet Explorer 7, consider sending them DWFx files, and mention to them that they can open those files directly in their web browser.

Chapter 15: Frame Generator

Work with frame files.   Frame Generator puts all the members at the same level in the assembly.

Master It   You have a frame that is built up in sections that are welded together. How do you document the manufacturing process?

Solution   Use Demote to create subassemblies of frame members. Select the frame members in the browser.

From the context menu, select Component and then Demote Frame Generator Components.

This preserves the Frame Generator relationships.

Insert frame members onto a skeleton model.   Frame Generator builds a skeleton model for the frame from the selected lines and edges.

Master It   Since Frame Generator builds its own skeleton model, you don't have to build a master model before you start creating the frame.

What would you reference in your assembly to use as a frame skeleton?

Solution   Use layout sketches and surfaces to design the basic frame shape.

Position the components that will be mounted to the frame in the assembly and reference edges on the parts.

As you make changes to the assembly, such as the overall size or the position of components, the frame will automatically update.

Add end treatments to frame members.   Frame Generator does not support end treatments on merged members.

Master It   Let's assume you are building a stairway and the handrail has curved sections. How would you approach the curved handrail so that its ends can be treated?

Solution   You can handle this situation in several ways.

◆ When you create the frame member, don't select the Merge option. This creates individual files for each segment. You can add end treatments to the end segments and document the details in the assembly drawing.

◆ Create the sketches so the ends of the curved member terminate at the face of another member. If the mating member has a flat face, you don't need an end treatment.

◆ Add short linear segments that aren't merged with the rest of the curved member. You can document that the length of the curved member does not include end treatments.

◆ Manually create end treatments using part-modeling commands. Frame members are created as custom parts that can be edited.

Make changes to frames.   Inventor provides detailed frame-member information.

Master It   You need to determine the size and wall thickness of the tubing and make it either thicker or larger. How do you do that?

Solution   Use the Frame Member Info tool to get the properties for the frame members. Then, you can use the Change tool to increase the wall thickness, increase the size, or select a different structural profile.

Author and publish structural profiles.   Frame Generator uses structural shapes from Content Center.

Master It   How would you add custom aluminum extrusions to Content Center so Frame Generator can access them?

Solution   Use the Structural Shape Authoring tool to prepare the parts for publishing. Use the Publish Part tool to add the parts to Content Center.

Create BOMs for Frame Generator assemblies.   Frame Generator has special parameters for frame members.

Master It   How do you add the profile dimensions and the length of your frame members to the Description field?

Solution   Use the BOM expression builder to add the Stock Number and G_L parameters to the Description field.

Chapter 16: Inventor Studio

Create and edit appearances.   Help your models to look more lifelike by editing your model's appearance (color and texture).

Master It   How would you make your own library of appearances to reuse in future projects?

How would you define color options in a model so that you can review them with your internal or external customers?

Solutions   To Make your own library of Appearances use the Create New Library control found in the bottom left of the Appearances dialog in the Libraries drop-down (looks like a folder with a wrench on it).

Use part and assembly views to save color options so that you can easily toggle between them.   Create and edit visual styles.

Help your models to look more lifelike by placing them in a realistic setting.

Master It   How would you save your favorite lighting styles for reuse on future projects?

There are three ways of adjusting the background image, including using the application options to change the background color and picking a visual style that includes an IBL environment. What's the third way?

Solutions   Save your favorite lighting styles by clicking Manage Tab ➤ Styles and Standards ➤ Save, to save your styles to your styles library. (Make sure that your styles library is set to Read/Write in your project.) Alternatively, open the styles manager and right-click on a style to export.

The third way of including a back ground image is to build a Wrapper assembly with a part in it which will become the background of your render.

Create and animate cameras.   Adding a camera with lifelike focus and depth of field helps to make your rendering believable. Animating cameras positions adds power to your rendering. It becomes much more dynamic.

Master It   Real movie cameras track (move side to side), dolly (move up and down), tilt (angle up and down), pan (angle side to side), and Dutch (rotate). How would you mimic this in Inventor Studio?

Solutions   Remember that you can animate your cameras by using the Animate Camera tool, and then clicking on the Definition button to edit the camera's movements.

Animate components, constraint, and parameters.   Animating your assemblies so that the function of the mechanism is showcased is often the purpose of an assembly animation.

Master It   You have an existing animation but want to do a variation on it. How do you copy and edit an existing animation?

Solutions   Right-click on your Animation in the Animation Environment feature tree and choose Copy Animation, then right-click again and choose Paste Animation.

Use multiple cameras to create a video production of your animation.   Video Producer provides the means to combine camera shots into a single video output.

Master It   You have created several cameras, animated and static, and want to make a composite animation. What are the general steps you will follow?

Solution   Do the following:

1. In the Scene browser, expand the Productions node.

2. If no production exists, right-click the Productions node and click New Production.

3. The cameras are loaded into the Video Producer window and are ready for use.

4. Drag and drop shots into the timeline and set their parameters.

5. Drag and drop the desired transitions between the shots.

Use props to enhance your scene. Inventor assemblies can be combined with other components to create a more realistic scene for rendering.

Master It You have completed a design and want to render a realistic image of it in its working environment. How do you do this?

Solution Do the following:

1. Create a new assembly that will be used as a wrapper assembly.

2. Place your product assembly in the new assembly.

3. Add any props, other parts, and other assemblies that make the scene more realistic.

Render animations and video productions. Inventor provides the means to render animations and video productions.

Master It You've created a wrapper assembly and set up the scene with cameras, lighting, and a scene style. Now you want to render an animation for design review and render a video production for a multidisciplinary review or marketing. What are the basic steps in each process?

Solution To render the animation, do the following:

1. In the Scene browser, select and activate the animation you want to render.

2. Deactivate any active production. Remember, when a production is active, it is the render target. To render a single animation, you must deactivate any active production.

3. In the Inventor Studio tool panel, click Render Animation.

4. Specify the various styles to use and the render type.

5. Specify the output file type and other parameters.

6. Render the animation.

To render a production, do the following:

1. In the Scene browser, select and activate the production you want to render.

2. If you have not completed composing the production, you should do so.

3. In the Inventor Studio tool panel, click Render Animation.

4. Specify the various styles to use and the render type.

5. Specify the output file type and other parameters.

6. Render the animation.

Chapter 17: Stress Analysis and Dynamic Simulation

Set up and run Stress Analysis simulations.   Oftentimes you may find yourself guessing at what impact a change to your design might have on the strength and overall integrity of your part.

Questions such as "Can I make this part a bit lighter?" or "Can I move this cutout closer to the edge?" become important to the success of your design.

Master It   Set up a parameter study in your model to explore the consequences of editing features and their locations. Nominate all the crucial parameters to the table and then create the configuration simulations for all of the combinations.

Solution   Interpret the results of the parameter study, looking for the configuration that promises to exhibit the results that come closest to your goals, such as a target safety factor.

Examine the various configurations to see which ones would be considered underbuilt and overbuilt and then determine why.

Understanding what works and doesn't work will allow you to get closer to the target from the beginning of the design process next time.

Set up and run Dynamic Simulations.   When you find yourself working out the details of a design with many moving parts, consider using the Dynamic Simulation tools early in the process to prove what will or will not work before going forward.

Master It   Even before the assembly is complete, switch to the Dynamic Simulation environment and create assembly relationships in the simulation.

Test the motion as you build the parts, and attempt to understand how contact will occur from the beginning.

Solution   Enable the automatic assembly constraint option so that as you create relationships, standard joints are automatically created. Use the Input Grapher to design in the fourth dimension (time), understanding how a mechanism will or will not work as you go through the stages of its operation.

Export results from the Dynamic Simulation environment to the Stress Analysis environment.   Often when setting up a stress analysis simulation, you are guessing at what the loads might be, based on rough calculations.

As you make changes to the design, those calculations become out-of-date and therefore invalid.

Master It   How do you use the Dynamic Simulation tools to determine the force exerted on one part by another?

Solution   Export the FEA information for the crucial time steps from the Dynamic Simulation environment into the Stress Analysis environment, and run the simulation.

This helps keep your calculations both accurate and up-to-date. When the parts are modified, the load calculations will automatically update based on the mass properties.

Chapter 18: Routed Systems

Create routes and runs.   Using routed systems tools allows you to quickly define many different route types in order to check for clearance and fits within a design, all while creating a bill of materials that can be used downstream in the manufacturing process.

Master It You have a model containing equipment and structural components defining the space requirements for a new route. Can you create a route using this geometry, or are you required to create a sketch first?

Solution When you have geometry that needs to be referenced and routed around, you can create a sketch first, but it isn't required. Instead, you could use the orthogonal route tool to define the route.

Author a tube and pipe component. To create your own fittings, couplings, and so on to be used within tube and pipe design, you need to first author them for use with the tube and pipe tools.

Master It How can you set the depth at which pipe, tube, or hose segments are inserted into a fitting?

Solution The pipe engagement is set during the tube and pipe component authoring process to determine how deep the segment will fit into the fitting.

For butt weld–style components, the engagement is set to 0 since there is no insertion.

Content Center components have the engagement positioning already set.

Author an electrical component. To create your own electrical connector components to be used within cable and harness designs, you need to first define pins within the parts.

Master It How can you create a family of electrical connectors with varying numbers of pins?

Solution First, use the Place Pin or Place Pin Group tool to add the maximum number of pins to the connector part. Then convert the part to an iPart.

In the iPart Author dialog box, use the Work Features tab to include only the pins required for each pin variation.

Create and document cable and harness assemblies. Cable and harness assemblies are created using a specific subassembly and part structure. Each harness is contained in a harness subassembly, and the parts such as wires, cables, and segments are created within a harness part file.

Master It You have a complex design that includes many harness assemblies and would like to turn some of them off while you work on others and/or create new ones. What is the best way to do this?

Solution You can create level-of-detail representations in cable and harness assemblies in much the same way that you would in a standard assembly. You can suppress an entire harness assembly and the harness part. But you cannot suppress other harness objects within the harness. Harness objects do not include connectors that are within the harness assembly. These can be suppressed.

Chapter 19: Plastics Design Features

Create thicken/offset features. When creating plastic parts, you will often find that working with surfaces allows you to achieve more free-form shapes than working with solids. Once the surfaces are created, you'll need to give them a thin wall thickness.

Master It   How would you create a plastic part file with many curved, free-form elements?

Solution   You can use the extrude and revolve features, among others, to create surface shapes that are much more free-form than what you can generally create with solid features.

Once the surfaces are created, use the Thicken/Offset tool to give them a wall thickness.

Create shell features.   Shelling solids parts and features is a common way to create base features for plastic parts. Once the shell feature is created, other features can be added to it.

Master It   You want to create a shell feature but need to have some faces be thicker than the rest. How would you accomplish this?

Solution   You can use the >> button to expand the Unique Thickness option in the Shell tool dialog box to specify faces that require unique face thicknesses.

Or you can use the Thicken/Offset tool to change the thickness of faces after a shell is created.

Create split features.   Many times you may want to establish the overall shape of a feature and then divide the shape into separate parts of the overall design. You can use the Split tool to do just that and more.

Master It   You have a plastic part that needs to have a raised face for a rubber grip applied during the manufacturing process. How would this be done?

Solution   Use the Split tool to create a surface that is unique to the rubber grip area and then use the Thicken/Offset tool to build up the rubber face.

Create grill features.   Grill features allow the inflow or outflow of air through a plastic thin-wall part.

Grills can be created with a number of sub-features such as islands, ribs, and spars, but only the outer profile of the grill is required.

Master It   How would you determine the area of a grill opening based on the airflow it needs to handle?

Solution   Edit the sketch from which the grill feature was created and then use the Measure Region tool to determine the general area of the opening.

Or create a sketch on the grill; project all the islands, ribs, and spars into the sketch; and then use the Measure Region tool on it to determine the exact area of the opening.

Create rule fillet features.   Rule fillets can be an extremely efficient way to apply fillets throughout the design to many edges that meet the same rule criteria.

Master It   How would you apply fillets to all of the edges that are generated by extruding a shape down to an existing set of base features?

Solution   Use the Rule Fillet tool with the source set to the new extruded shape, the rule set to Against Features, and the scope set to include all the base features to create intersecting fillets.

If this feature changes to create new edges or remove existing edges that fit the rule, the fillets are added or removed automatically.

Create rest features. Rest features can be used to create level platform faces for mounting other parts to an irregular plastic part face.

Master It You want to create a rectangular pocket on the inside of a plastic housing to hold an electronic component. How would you do this?

Solution On a work plane, create a sketch that defines the shape of the pocket. The work plane location will define the orientation.

Use the Rest tool to create the pocket, using the options in the Rest tool to achieve the exact result you require.

Create boss features. Boss features are ideal for creating fastener-mounting standoffs for thin-wall plastic parts.

You can use the Boss tool to create both halves of the fastener boss.

Master It You want to create multiple boss features around the perimeter of a flat, pan-type base part, but you know this base part is likely to change size.

How would you set up the boss features to adjust to the anticipated edits?

Solution On a work plane, create a 2D sketch that defines the height of the bosses. Use the Offset tool in the sketch environment to create an offset loop based on the perimeter of the part. Add sketch center points at all the required locations. Ensure that the offset loop and the sketch center points are fully constrained and dimensioned and then use these points when creating the boss feature.

Create lip and groove features. When designing plastic parts, you may need one half of a design to fit into the other half. The Lip tool allows you to create both lip and groove features for these situations.

Master It You want to create a groove around the edge of an irregular, curved edge. How can you ensure that the lip on the corresponding part will match?

Solution Use the clearance height to remove uneven mating surfaces during the lip and groove creation, ensuring a proper fit.

Create snap-fit features. Snap features are a common way to join plastic parts together so that they can be disassembled as needed. You can use the Snap Fit tool in Inventor to quickly create these features.

Master It How would you create a U-shaped snap fit with the Snap Fit tool?

Solution Use the standard sketch and extrude methods to create the base of the U-shape. Then use the Snap Fit tool to add the snap and loop as needed.

Create rib and web features. Ribs and webs are often used to add rigidity and prevent warping during the design of plastic parts. You can add ribs based on open profile sketches in Inventor.

Master It How would you create a network of ribs that are evenly spaced, with some of them containing different cutouts than others?

Solution Create an open profile sketch for the first single rib. Then use the Rib tool to create it. Use the Rectangular Pattern tool to pattern the rib as needed and then create the cutout profile and use the Extrude tool to cut the shape from the first rib. Then pattern the cutout to match the rib pattern. Finally, suppress the cutouts you do not need.

Create draft features. Because plastic parts must be extracted from a mold during the manufacturing process, drafted faces must be included to ensure that the parts can indeed be extracted from the mold.

> **Master It** You want to create drafted faces on a complex part containing various shapes within it. How would you do this?

> **Solution** Start the Draft tool and then click the Help button in the lower-left corner, or just press **F1** on the keyboard. This will open the help page specifically for the Draft tool.

> Expand the nodes on the Concept tab to explore the examples of the various results achieved by different settings. Use the various methods throughout the part where they will provide the correct result.

> Set up work planes to help establish fixed-plane faces.

Create an injection mold. To generate the components you have designed with the plastic part features, you need to properly define the cavity to create the part and define how the material will flow into the cavity.

> **Master It** You want to create a mold base design in an efficient manner using parts that can be purchased.

> **Solution** Use the many steps of the Inventor Tooling package to properly define the core and cavity.

> Then use the analysis tools to ensure that the part will be made correctly.

> Finally, use the library of features included with Inventor to construct the mold base assembly.

Chapter 20: iLogic

Create iLogic rules. Use iLogic rules to document and embed into your models the common design rules that you use every day to determine the decisions required in your design process.

> **Master It** How can you add a rule to your part to change the size of it?

> **Solution** Create a rule and use a parameter function to get and set the model parameters.

Edit iLogic rules. A large part of working with iLogic is testing and editing the rules you create. Often, it's best to add a function at a time to the rule and test it along the way.

> **Master It** Your rule works, but you have to manually update the model. Do you need to create a new rule to handle the update?

> **Solution** You can edit your existing rule and add the `UpdateWhenDone` document function to run at the end of the rule.

Use multi-value list parameters. A common part of any design rule process is selecting from a list of standard entities.

You can create multi-value list parameters from Numeric or Text parameters to add lists.

> **Master It** How would you create a rule that prompts you to select from a list of approved sizes?

Solution To start, you will create a user parameter and then make it a multi-value list parameter. Then you can use the `InputListBox` function or create an iLogic form to reference that list.

Work with multiple rules in the same file. It is often best to create several small rules rather than try to create one large rule that does it all. This helps you maintain and troubleshoot the code later, and it also allows you to use rules in multiple applications without the need to remove or edit existing code.

This is particularly true when working with external rules, which might be used in varying applications later.

Master It You've created two smaller rules because it makes sense to do so, but when you try to run one, the other is triggered also. Do you need to combine them into one rule?

Solution When one rule updates the parameters another rule is referencing, the other rule is triggered by that update by default. To resolve this, you can choose to edit the rule.

Select the Options tab and then select the Don't Run Automatically option. This prevents the rule from running automatically when the parameters are updated.

Use conditional statements. Conditional statements are the foundation of any programmed logic. Learning how to use If, Then, and `Select Case` statements will go a long way in helping you solve logical problems when creating rules.

Master It How can you check the value of a parameter or its state with an iLogic rule?

Solution You can do this with an `If`, Then statement. For instance, if you want to check a parameter to ensure that it is not too small, you would use function operator such as < (less than) or <= (less than or equal to).

Suppress features. Configuring a part file to include and exclude features is often based on engineering decisions you make every day.

Setting up your iLogic rules to do this is straightforward, provided the model is well constructed to start with.

Master It When you use the `Feature.IsActive` function on one feature, it causes an error in the part. How can a feature be suppressed without suppressing a dependent feature?

Solution Oftentimes, the issue is the use of projected geometry in the sketch of the dependent feature. Other times, the part was simply modeled in a manner that prevents suppressing a base feature. In these cases, it's best just to edit the part and redefine the base feature so that it is based on the origin geometry and not on unrelated features.

Work with iProperties. iProperties are a powerful part of working with Inventor. Being able to retrieve and use metadata helps with all parts of the engineering process.

Automating the process of filling out iProperty data with iLogic is a big step forward.

Master It Can iLogic be used to update the title block of a drawing?

Solution If you set the title block up to read the iProperties of the model and/or the drawing, then an iLogic rule created to write to those properties will automatically update the title block.

Create iLogic forms.   iLogic forms make creating a user interface for your iLogic pursuits quite easy. The drag-and-drop tools provide professional-looking forms with minimal effort.

> **Master It**   You have existing part files with no iLogic in them, and it would be nice to use the form you created in the most recent design to update those old designs as revisions require it.
>
> Can forms be created and shared across part files?
>
> **Solution**   You can create an external global form and then use it in the future when you need to revise old designs of the same type.

Build a part configuration form.   Configuring Inventor components saves time, reduces human error, and promotes consistency. Using iLogic forms to configure common designs is a good way to go.

> **Master It**   Can an iLogic form help with parts that are basically the same but have a lot of variation in the features they include?
>
> **Solution**   Although you can't access the active status of the features directly, you can use rules to determine when a feature should be included or excluded and then use the rules in the form.

Appendix B

Autodesk Inventor 2016 Certification

Autodesk certifications are industry-recognized credentials that can help you succeed in your design career, providing benefits to both you and your employer. Getting certified is a reliable validation of skills and knowledge, and it can lead to accelerated professional development, improved productivity, and enhanced credibility.

This Autodesk Official Press guide can be an effective component of your exam preparation. Autodesk highly recommends (and we agree!) that you schedule regular time to prepare, review the most current exam preparation roadmap available at www.autodesk.com/certification, use Autodesk Official Press guides, take a class at an Authorized Training Center (find one near you: www.autodesk.com/atc), and use a variety of resources to prepare for your certification, including plenty of actual hands-on experience.

Certification Objective To help you focus your studies on the skills you'll need for these exams, the following tables show the objectives that could appear on an exam and in what chapter you can find information on that topic—and when you go to that chapter, you'll find certification icons like the one in the margin here.

Table B.1 is for the Autodesk Inventor 2016 Certified Associate Exam and lists the section, exam objectives, and chapter where the information is found. Table B.2 is for the Autodesk Inventor 2016 Certified Professional Exam.

These Autodesk certification exam objectives were accurate at press time; to find the latest information about the exam and what is covered, go to www.autodesk.com/certification. Good luck preparing for your certification!

TABLE B.1:   Autodesk Inventor 2016 Certified Associate Exam

TOPIC	LEARNING OBJECTIVE	CHAPTER
User Interface: Primary Environments	Name the four primary environments: Parts, Assemblies, Presentations, and Drawings.	Chapters 1, 2
User Interface: UI Navigation/Interaction	Name the key features of the user interface (ribbon ➤ panels ➤ tabs).	Chapter 1
	Describe the listing in the browser for an assembly file.	Chapter 8

continues

TABLE B.1:   Autodesk Inventor 2016 Certified Associate Exam   *(CONTINUED)*

TOPIC	LEARNING OBJECTIVE	CHAPTER
	Demonstrate how to use the context (right-click) menus.	Chapter 1
	Demonstrate how to use the menus.	Chapter 1
	Demonstrate how to add Redo to the Quick Access Toolbar.	Chapter 1
User Interface: Graphics Window Display	Describe the steps required to change the background color of the graphics window.	N/A (Tools tab ➤ Application Options ➤ Colors tab)
	Use Application Options ➤ Display.	N/A (Tools tab ➤ Application Options ➤ Display tab)
	Demonstrate how to turn on/off the 3D Indicator.	N/A (Tools tab ➤ Application Options ➤ Display Tab
	Name the key elements of the ribbon.	Chapter 1
User Interface: Navigation Control	Describe the functionality of the ViewCube.	Chapter 1
	Describe the Navigation bar.	Chapter 1
	Name the navigation tools started by the F2 to F6 shortcut keys.	N/A Pan (F2) Zoom (F3) Orbit (F4) Previous View (F5) Home View (F6)
File Management: Project Files	Name the file extension of a project file (.ipj).	Chapter 1
	List the types of project files that can be created.	Chapter 1
	Define the term workspace.	Chapter 1
	List the types of files stored in a library.	Chapter 1
	List the three categories in Folder Options.	Chapter 1
	Describe how to set the active project.	Chapter 1
Sketches: Creating 2D Sketches	Name the file extension of a part file (.ipt).	Chapter 1

TOPIC	LEARNING OBJECTIVE	CHAPTER
	Describe the purpose of a template file in the sketch environment.	Chapter 3
	Describe the function of the 3D Coordinate System icon.	N/A (Use the 3D Coordinate System to realign the sketch coordinate system.)
	Define a sketch plane.	Chapter 3
	Label the entries on the browser.	Chapter 3
Sketches: Draw Tools	Complete a 2D sketch using the appropriate draw tools: Line, Arc, Circle, Rectangle, Point, Fillet, Polygon.	Chapter 3 (The Fillet tool is used to round corners between sketch lines.)
Sketches: Sketch Constraints	List the available geometric constraints: coincident, colinear, concentric, fixed, parallel, perpendicular, horizontal, vertical, tangent, symmetric, smooth (G2), and equal.	Chapter 3
	Describe parametric dimensions (general and automatic).	Chapter 3
	Describe how to control the visibility of constraints.	Chapter 3
	Describe the degrees of freedom on a sketch and how they can be displayed.	Chapter 3
Sketches: Pattern Sketches	Demonstrate how to pattern a sketch (rectangular and circular).	N/A (Generally speaking, it is best to create a model feature and then pattern it at the feature level rather than to create a sketch entity and pattern it in the sketch. However, you can use the pattern tools found in the sketch environment if needed.)
Sketches: Modify Sketches	Demonstrate how to move a sketch.	Chapter 3
	Demonstrate how to copy a sketch.	Chapter 3
	Demonstrate how to rotate a sketch.	N/A (The sketch Rotate tool rotates sketch geometry relative to a specified center point. Results are impacted by constraints and dimensions.)

continues

TABLE B.1: Autodesk Inventor 2016 Certified Associate Exam *(CONTINUED)*

TOPIC	LEARNING OBJECTIVE	CHAPTER
	Demonstrate how to trim a sketch.	Chapter 3
	Demonstrate how to extend a sketch.	N/A (Use the Extend tool to extend curves to other curves. In a 3D sketch, extend curves to intersections with a face, work plane, or surface.)
	Demonstrate how to offset a sketch.	Chapter 3
Sketches: Format Sketches	Describe how to format sketch line types.	Chapter 3
Sketches: Sketch Doctor	Examine a sketch for errors.	Chapter 4
Sketches: Shared Sketches	Describe the function of a shared sketch.	N/A (Shared sketches can be used by more than one feature. To share a sketch, make it visible or right-click it in the browser and choose Share Sketch.)
Sketches: Sketch Parameters	Describe how parameters define the size and shape of features.	Chapter 3
Parts: Creating Parts	Name the file extension of a part file (.ipt).	Chapter 4
	Label the entries on the browser.	Chapter 4
	Define a base feature.	Chapter 4
	Define an unconsumed sketch.	Chapter 4 (An unconsumed sketch is any sketch that is not used by a feature, such as an extrusion.)
	Demonstrate how to create an extruded part.	Chapter 4
	Demonstrate how to create a revolved part.	Chapter 4
	Demonstrate how to create a lofted part.	Chapter 5
	Describe the termination options for a feature.	Chapter 4

TOPIC	LEARNING OBJECTIVE	CHAPTER
	Demonstrate how to create a hole feature.	Chapter 4
	Demonstrate how to create a fillet feature.	Chapter 4
	Demonstrate how to create a chamfer feature.	Chapter 4
	Demonstrate how to create a shell feature.	Chapter 5
	Demonstrate how to create a thread feature.	Chapter 4
Parts: Work Features	Describe the use of work features (plane, point, axis) in the part-creation workflow.	Chapter 4
Parts: Pattern Features	Demonstrate how to create a rectangular pattern.	Chapter 5
	Demonstrate how to create a circular pattern.	Chapter 5
	Demonstrate how to mirror features.	Chapter 5
Parts: Part Properties	Describe part properties and how they are applied.	Chapter 5
Assemblies: Creating Assemblies	Name the file extension of an assembly file (.iam).	Chapter 8
	Label the entries on the browser.	Chapter 8
	Name the six degrees of freedom on a component.	Chapter 8
	Demonstrate how to place a part in an assembly.	Chapter 8
	Discuss degrees of freedom and a grounded part.	Chapter 8
	Demonstrate how to apply various Assembly constraints.	Chapter 8
	Describe the various assembly environment techniques (top-down, bottom-up, and middle-out).	Chapter 8
	Demonstrate how to create a new part in the assembly environment.	Chapter 8
	Demonstrate how to place a Content Center part in an assembly.	Chapter 8

continues

TABLE B.1: Autodesk Inventor 2016 Certified Associate Exam *(CONTINUED)*

TOPIC	LEARNING OBJECTIVE	CHAPTER
Assemblies: Viewing Assemblies	Label the entries on the browser.	Chapter 8
Assemblies: Animation Assemblies	Demonstrate how to animate an assembly using drive constraints.	Chapter 8
Assemblies: Adaptive Features, Parts, and Subassemblies	Demonstrate how to make and use an adaptive part.	Chapter 8
Presentations: Creating Presentations	Name the file extension of a presentation file (.ipn).	Chapter 11
	Label the entries on the browser.	Chapter 11
	Discuss the various uses of Presentation files.	Chapter 11
	Demonstrate how to apply tweaks to a part.	Chapter 11
	Demonstrate how to apply trails to a part.	Chapter 11
	Demonstrate how to animate an assembly.	Chapter 11
Drawings: Creating Drawings	Name the file extension of a drawing file (.idw).	Chapter 12
	Describe the use of template files.	Chapter 12
	Label the entries on the browser.	Chapter 12
	Describe the content within Drawing Resources.	Chapter 12
	Demonstrate how to create a part drawing.	Chapter 12
	Demonstrate how to create an assembly drawing.	Chapter 12
	Describe the various annotation options.	Chapter 12
	Demonstrate how to add balloons to an assembly.	Chapter 12
Sheet Metal: Creating Sheet Metal Parts	Name the file extension of a sheet-metal part file (.ipt).	Chapter 6
	Discuss the use of sheet metal defaults.	Chapter 6

TOPIC	LEARNING OBJECTIVE	CHAPTER
	Demonstrate the creation of a sheet metal bend.	Chapter 6
Sheet Metal: Modify Sheet Metal Parts	Demonstrate the creation of a corner seam.	Chapter 6
	Demonstrate the creation of a punch tool.	Chapter 6
	Demonstrate the creation of a cut across a bend.	Chapter 6
Sheet Metal: Flat Pattern	Demonstrate how to create a flat pattern.	Chapter 6
	Demonstrate how to insert a flat pattern in a drawing.	Chapter 6
	Demonstrate how to export a flat pattern.	Chapter 6
Visualization: Create Rendered Images	Describe the process to activate Inventor Studio.	Chapter 16
	Demonstrate how to create a new camera.	Chapter 16
	Demonstrate how to create a rendered image.	Chapter 16
Visualization: Animate an Assembly	Demonstrate how to create a new animation.	Chapter 16
	Demonstrate how to create an animation by animating a camera.	Chapter 16
	Demonstrate how to create an animation by animating a constraint.	Chapter 16

TABLE B.2:   Autodesk Inventor 2016 Certified Professional Exam

TOPIC	LEARNING OBJECTIVE	CHAPTER
Advanced Modeling	Create a 3D path using the Intersection Curve and the Project to Surface commands.	Chapter 3
	Create a loft feature.	Chapter 5
	Create a multi-body part.	Chapter 5
	Create a part using surfaces.	Chapters 4, 5, 19

continues

TABLE B.2:   Autodesk Inventor 2016 Certified Professional Exam *(CONTINUED)*

TOPIC	LEARNING OBJECTIVE	CHAPTER
	Create a sweep feature.	Chapter 5
	Create an iPart.	Chapter 7
	Create and constrain sketch blocks.	Chapter 8
	Use iLogic.	Chapter 20
	Emboss text and a profile.	N/A (Create a sketch with text and then go to the 3D Model tab ➤ Create panel ➤ Emboss button.)
Assembly Modeling	Apply and use assembly constraints.	Chapter 8
	Apply and use assembly joints.	Chapter 8
	Create a level of detail.	Chapter 9
	Create a part in the context of an assembly.	Chapter 8
	Describe and use Shrinkwrap.	Chapter 9
	Create a positional representation.	Chapter 8
	Create components using the Design Accelerator commands.	Chapter 8
	Modify a bill of materials.	Chapter 8
	Find minimum distance between parts and components.	Chapter 8
	Use the Frame Generator commands.	Chapter 15
Drawing	Edit a section view.	Chapter 12
	Modify a style in a drawing.	Chapter 12
	Edit a hole table.	Chapter 12

Topic	Learning Objective	Chapter
Part Modeling	Create a pattern of features.	Chapter 5
	Create a shell feature.	Chapter 5
	Create extrude features.	Chapter 4
	Create hole features.	Chapter 4
	Create revolve features.	Chapter 4
	Create work features.	Chapter 4
	Use the Project Geometry and Project Cut Edges commands.	Chapter 3
	Edit existing parts using Direct Manipulation.	Chapter 4
Presentation Files	Animate a presentation file.	Chapter 11
Project Files	Control a project file.	Chapter 1
Sheet Metal	Create sheet metal features.	Chapter 6
Sketching	Create dynamic input dimensions.	Chapter 3
	Use sketch constraints.	Chapter 3
	Sketch using Relax Mode.	Chapter 3
Weldments	Create a weldment.	Chapter 10

Index

Note to the Reader: Throughout this index **boldfaced** page numbers indicate primary discussions of a topic. *Italicized* page numbers indicate illustrations.